Focus on Social Problems:

A Contemporary Reader

Mindy Stombler
Georgia State University

Amanda M. Jungels
Georgia State University

New York   Oxford
OXFORD UNIVERSITY PRESS

Oxford University Press is a department of the University of Oxford.
It furthers the University's objective of excellence in research,
scholarship, and education by publishing worldwide.

Oxford New York
Auckland   Cape Town   Dar es Salaam   Hong Kong   Karachi
Kuala Lumpur   Madrid   Melbourne   Mexico City   Nairobi
New Delhi   Shanghai   Taipei   Toronto

With offices in
Argentina   Austria   Brazil   Chile   Czech Republic   France   Greece
Guatemala   Hungary   Italy   Japan   Poland   Portugal   Singapore
South Korea   Switzerland   Thailand   Turkey   Ukraine   Vietnam

For titles covered by Section 112 of the US Higher Education
Opportunity Act, please visit www.oup.com/us/he for the
latest information about pricing and alternate formats.

Published by Oxford University Press
198 Madison Avenue, New York, New York 10016
http://www.oup.com

Library of Congress Cataloging-in-Publication Data
Focus on social problems : a contemporary reader / Mindy Stombler,
Amanda M. Jungels
    pages cm
  Includes bibliographical references.
  ISBN 978-0-19-932135-3
  1. Social problems--United States. 2. Sociology--United States. I. Stombler, Mindy,
editor. II. Jungels, Amanda M., editor.
  HN59.2.F63 2017
  301.0973--dc23

                                                            2015027016

Printing number: 9 8 7 6 5 4 3 2 1

Printed in the United States of America
on acid-free paper

CONTENTS

Colleges and universities around the country routinely offer courses studying social problems. To get students discussing and thinking critically about how social problems are created, perpetuated, interrelated, and cumulative, faculty often seek engaging readings to spark critical discussion and evoke a sense of moral outrage. These readings, ideally, will show students how to think systemically and critically about the social problems we face today.

We approached the construction of this reader from a unique position. Combined, we've taught Social Problems to thousands of students for more than fifteen years. We have worked with new graduate students who are entering the Social Problems classroom as instructors for the first time—Stombler as the director of instruction and Jungels as the former teaching associate at Georgia State University. We have spent years listening to new instructors evaluate and ultimately lament the dearth of quality Social Problems readers. This reader comes from our own frustration with the current offerings, as well as those of our graduate student instructors who are teaching Social Problems for the first time. We share the following goals: to expose our students to a variety of social problems; to help students understand how social problems are defined, constructed, and controlled; to increase students' empirical knowledge about the causes and consequences of social problems; to develop student empathy; and to encourage students to become agents of social change.

We endeavored to compile a collection of readings that is comprehensive, so that any instructor can find readings to supplement the topics they wish to cover in their course. The reader has a strong critical constructionist foundation, so that instructors can use it as a stand-alone text or as a companion to a traditional textbook. We include articles from a wide variety of sources to illustrate how sociologists, other academics, and claims makers recognize and define social problems, conduct relevant research, illustrate the lived experience of social problems, and actively drive social change.

In the introduction to this book, we discuss the sociological imagination, and we develop our constructivist approach to contemporary social problems. We highlight the way that social problems are interrelated and have a cumulative effect on individual actors. We want students to focus their attention on the systems and structures that are at the core of society's issues. Our readings provide depth, but are appropriately leveled for the average undergraduate taking an introductory course. We have edited our selections judiciously, so that students are not reading an excessive amount, nor are they losing important elements or the "heart" of the selection. Whereas traditional textbooks are able to offer incredible breadth, our readings provide additional depth on each featured social problem. Although our reader focuses predominantly on the social problems plaguing the United States, information on global social problems is woven in, especially as it relates to the United States.

ACKNOWLEDGMENTS

Soliciting, curating, and editing a reader that is so broad in scope is a challenging task. We thank our editor, Sherith Pankratz, for her guidance, trust, and support throughout the process. Katy Albis, our assistant editor, maintained impeccable organization and offered valuable technical assistance as we waded through the complex licensing process for the 125 or so pieces; we don't recall her ever saying "no" to a request for help. Thanks as well to Michael Kopf and the folks at S4Carlisle Publishing Services for their patience and attention to detail during the editing process. We also extend our thanks to the following reviewers, whose detailed feedback shaped the book's format and trajectory:

Steve Buban, Monmouth College
Susan Clampet-Lundquist, Saint Joseph's University
Kenneth Colburn, Butler University
Meredith Huey Dye, Middle Tennessee State University
Lisa Handler, Community College of Philadelphia
Jessica Hausauer, Syracuse University
Pamela Leong, Salem State University
Shoon Lio, University of Illinois at Springfield
Josh Packard, University of Northern Colorado
Gregory D. Squires, George Washington University
Robert Wonser, College of the Canyons

We are grateful to the activists (and their assistants—especially Raylene Hayes!) for taking time out of their incredibly busy schedules to allow us to interview them for the Activist Interview feature of this book. They offered thoughtful responses to our questions, shared heartfelt stories of their motivations, and provided concrete

social change strategies for our students. We also thank the authors who wrote original pieces for this book. We know that we were demanding and that you had to endure last-minute requests to incorporate new data, provide multitudes of drafts and revisions, and meet sometimes short deadlines. We appreciate your patience and hard work to make this book the best it could be.

Focus on Social Problems was built in a supportive environment. Our colleagues at Georgia State University provided assistance at every turn. Thanks to Matt Gayman for reading a draft of an original piece we struggled to perfect; to Natalie Deckard for helping us frame a chapter; to Beth Cavalier, Stacy Gorman Harmon, Megan Tesene, and Katie Acosta for their willingness to read last-minute drafts; to Kirstin Ralston-Coley and Nia Reed for suggesting readings; and to Brittany Michelle Garner, Deirdre Oakley, and Ashley Rockwell for their research on potential activist interviewees. We thank our Social Problems students (we've had thousands, combined) for providing valuable feedback on readings and for their excitement and passion for the material we present and discuss. Thanks to Mona Saraiya, Roshana Saraiya, and David Espey, who helped us in a targeted search for activists to interview in their fields. Finally, thanks to our wonderful subject librarian, Mandy Swygart-Hobaugh, who was always a source of immediate assistance. There are also innumerable colleagues, friends, and coworkers—too many to name here—who read drafts, acted as sounding boards, suggested content, and were generally supportive when we needed it.

We also thank our family and friends. In particular, Mindy thanks her husband, Nate Steiner, who was his usual sweet and supportive self, maintaining his own paid work and housework while taking over her share as well. This book was built on a foundation of his encouragement and patience (and even editing) during stressful times. She also thanks her son, Moey Rojas, for his independence (allowing her to work crazy hours) and his contributions to dinnertime discussions on the social problems in the book. She thanks her parents, Lynne and Milton Stombler, for their constant support of her endeavors. Finally, she thanks canine Rue (and her friends, Cooper and Tommy) for lovingly flanking her with warm, soft bodies throughout the entire process.

Amanda's parents, Robin and Betty Jungels, and her sister Rebecca, were constant sources of encouragement over the many months (years!) it took to create this book. Her friends and colleagues in Minnesota, Georgia, and Maryland (and everywhere else!) were also a huge source of support, always offering help when it was needed: a sympathetic ear, a spare bedroom or much-needed break during the final days of compiling the book, or words of encouragement.

She is forever grateful for your support. And, of course, she would be remiss if she failed to mention her adorable canine companion, Max Weber, who keeps things exciting, makes sure sociology is a constant presence in her life, and keeps the couch warm.

This project began several years ago, and although it wasn't the original plan, it was completed remotely because our careers took us to different states. Thankfully, through the wonders of Internet technology and file sharing, this project was collaborative in a way that neither of us anticipated at the outset. Working on this book was a true labor of love, and we hope you enjoy the result as much as we enjoyed compiling it.

Dedication

We dedicate this book to the tireless work of the activists we interviewed and their colleagues. We hope their stories and the readings in this collection inspire our students to enact sociologically grounded social change.

THE EDITORS

Mindy Stombler, Ph.D., is a senior lecturer of sociology at Georgia State University. She is co-editor of *Sex Matters: The Sexuality and Society Reader*, 4th edition (Norton). Her past research has focused on the production of sexual collective identities as well as pedagogical issues. She has been teaching Social Problems courses consistently over the past twenty-five years. She is also the 2016 winner of the Southern Sociological Society's Distinguished Contributions to Teaching Award, an award honoring outstanding teaching contributions beyond one's institution, benefiting the discipline as a whole.

Amanda M. Jungels, Ph.D., is an ORISE Fellow studying social and behavioral health among U.S. Army soldiers. She is a past recipient of the Jacqueline Boles Teaching Fellowship and Teaching Associate Award at Georgia State University. Her past research has focused on the social construction of privacy and sexuality, cognitive sociology, sex work, and pedagogical issues.

THE AUTHORS

Michelle Alexander is an associate professor of law with a joint appointment in the Moritz College of Law and the Kirwan Institute for the Study of Race and Ethnicity at the Ohio State University.

Natalie Angier is a nonfiction writer and a science journalist for *The New York Times*.

Dan Ariely is the James B. Duke professor in the Fuqua School of Business at Duke University.

Elizabeth A. Armstrong is an associate professor of sociology and public affairs at Princeton University.

Amanda Atwell is a doctoral student in the Department of Sociology at Georgia State University.

Allison Aubrey is a correspondent for National Public Radio News.

David Barboza is a correspondent for *The New York Times*.

Lanier Basenberg is a doctoral candidate in the Department of Sociology at Georgia State University.

Sutapa Basu is the executive director of the University of Washington Women's Center and co-chair of its Task Force against Human Trafficking.

Emily Bazelon is a journalist and staff writer for *The New York Times Magazine* and a senior research scholar in law and Truman Capote Fellow for creative writing and law at the Yale Law School.

Joel Best is a professor of sociology and criminal justice at University of Delaware.

Fred Block is a research professor in the Department of Sociology at University of California, Davis.

Ann Bookman is a senior research scientist in the Heller School for Social Policy and Management at Brandeis University.

Otis Webb Brawley, M.D., is the chief medical and scientific officer and executive vice president of the American Cancer Society.

Tristan Bridges is an assistant professor in the Department of Sociology at the College at Brockport, State University of New York.

Robert Brulle is a professor of sociology and environmental science in the Department of Sociology at Drexel University.

Frank Bruni is a journalist and op-ed columnist for *The New York Times*.

Elizabeth S. Cavalier is an assistant professor of sociology at Georgia Gwinnett College.

Ron Claiborne is a journalist and correspondent for ABC News.

Linda Darling-Hammond is a Charles E. Ducommun professor of education, emeritus, and faculty director of the Stanford Center for Opportunity Policy in Education.

Arthur Delaney is a reporter at *The Huffington Post*.

Jason DeParle is a senior writer at *The New York Times*.

Lisa Desai is a journalist, reporter, and producer.

Lisa Dodson is a research professor in the Department of Sociology at Boston College.

Douglas B. Downey is a professor of sociology at the Ohio State University.

Lee Drutman is a senior fellow in the program on political reform at New America.

Charles Duhigg is a reporter for *The New York Times*.

Erin Thomas Echols is a doctoral candidate in the Department of Sociology at Georgia State University and a health scientist at the Centers for Disease Control and Prevention.

Kathryn Edin is the Bloomberg distinguished professor in the Department of Sociology.

Sabrina Rubin Erdely is a feature writer, an investigative journalist, and a contributing editor at *Rolling Stone*.

John E. Farley is a professor emeritus of sociology at Southern Illinois University at Edwardsville.

Jessica Fields is an associate professor in the Department of Sociology at San Francisco State University.

Mark Follman is a senior editor at *Mother Jones*.

Food Chain Workers Alliance is a coalition of worker-based organizations whose members plant, harvest, process, pack, transport, prepare, serve, and sell food, organizing to improve wages and working conditions for all workers along the food chain.

Louis Fox is a director and writer.

Robert Gebeloff is a database projects editor at *The New York Times*.

Amanda M. Gengler is an assistant professor in the Department of Sociology at Wake Forest University.

Benjamin G. Gibbs is an assistant professor in the Department of Sociology at Brigham Young University.

Malcolm Gladwell is a staff writer for *The New Yorker*.

Paul Goldberg is an investigative reporter and is the editor and publisher of *The Cancer Letter*.

Roberto G. Gonzales is an assistant professor of education at Harvard University.

Desmond Goss is a doctoral student in the Department of Sociology at Georgia State University.

Sarah Gross is a journalist based in New York City.

Laura Hamilton is an associate professor of sociology at the University of California, Merced.

Stacy Gorman Harmon is a guest researcher at the Centers for Disease Control and Prevention.

Erin Hatton is an assistant professor in the Department of Sociology at the State University of New York at Buffalo.

Elis Herman is an environmental education intern at Hidden Villa, a nonprofit educational organization and organic farm in Los Altos, California, educating teenagers on social and environmental justice.

Jennifer Ann Hill is co-founder of Who Minds the Child?, a nonprofit dedicated to the protection and enhancement of children's development and childhood culture.

Kaitlin A. Hippen is a doctoral student in the Department of Family Science, Center on Young Adult Health and Development at University of Maryland.

Heather R. Hlavka is an assistant professor of sociology in the Department of Social and Cultural Studies at Marquette University.

Linda Holmes is a writer and editor for National Public Radio.

Kathleen E. Hull is an associate professor of sociology at the University of Minnesota.

Wil S. Hylton is a contributing writer at *New York Times Magazine* and contributing editor at *New York Magazine*.

J. Craig Jenkins is a professor of sociology at the Ohio State University.

Alexis Jetter is a journalist and adjunct professor/lecturer in the English Department and in Women & Gender Studies at Dartmouth College.

Allan G. Johnson is a writer, sociologist, public speaker, and trainer around issues of race and gender.

Emily Stutzman Jones is the academic director for the Institute of Sustainable Practice at Lipscomb University.

David Kamp is a contributing editor to *Vanity Fair*.

Victor E. Kappeler is a foundation professor and associate dean of the School of Justice Studies.

Jana Kasperkevic is a reporter for *The Guardian* (U.S. edition).

Maria Kefalas is a professor of sociology, director of the Richard Johnson Center for Anti-Violence, and co-founder of the Philadelphia Youth Solutions Project.

Delia Kimbrel is a research associate in the Institute on Assets and Social Policy in the Heller School for Social Policy and Management at Brandeis University.

Perri Klass, M.D., is a professor of journalism and pediatrics at New York University.

Miriam Konrad is a senior lecturer in the Department of Sociology at Georgia State University.

Anna C. Korteweg is an associate professor of sociology at the University of Toronto, Mississauga.

Kiersten Kummerow is a doctoral student in the Department of Sociology at Georgia State University.

Annie Leonard is an environmental advocate and founder of the Story of Stuff Project.

Wendy Luttrell is a professor at the CUNY Graduate Center in the urban education, sociology, and critical social/personality psychology programs.

Imrul Mazid is a teacher at the Athenian School.

Elaine McArdle is a journalist and writer based in Cambridge, Massachusetts.

Edward McClelland is an author and writer.

Chris McGreal is a senior writer for *The Guardian* (U.S. edition).

Stephanie Medley-Rath is an assistant professor of sociology in the Department of Sociology, History, and Political Science at Indiana University Kokomo.

Tatjana Meschede is the research director in the Institute on Assets and Social Policy in the Heller School for Social Policy and Management at Brandeis University.

Cindy L. Miller-Perrin is a distinguished professor of psychology at Pepperdine University.

Stefanie Mollborn is an associate professor in the Department of Sociology and a faculty associate in the Health and Science Program, Institute of Behavioral Science, at University of Colorado Boulder.

J. Jennings Moss is the editor of the *Upstart Business Journal*.

Michael Moss is an author and investigative reporter.

Ziad Munson is an associate professor of sociology in the Department of Sociology and Anthropology at Lehigh University.

Carmen Nobel is a senior editor at Harvard Business School.

Michael I. Norton is a professor of business administration in the marketing unit at the Harvard Business School.

NPR Staff are writers at National Public Radio.

Hollie Nyseth Brehm is an assistant professor of sociology at the Ohio State University and an affiliate member of the Mershon Center for International Security Studies and the Criminal Justice Research Center.

Sam Osoro is a senior financial analyst at Health Connector, in Boston, Massachusetts.

David Pellow is a professor and Don A. Martindale endowed chair of sociology at the University of Minnesota.

Robin D. Perrin is a professor in the Department of Sociology at Pepperdine University.

Pew Research Center is a nonpartisan fact tank.

Gary W. Potter is a professor in the Department of Criminal Justice and Police Studies at Eastern Kentucky University.

Monica Potts is a freelance writer.

Mary A. Prenovost [now Mary Gray] is a research associate at Harder+Company Community Research.

Deena Prichep is a freelance print and radio journalist based in Portland, Oregon.

Anastasia Prokos is an associate professor, Sociology and Women's & Gender Studies, at Iowa State University.

Yasmeen Qureshi is a broadcast reporter, producer, and shooter based in New York City.

Kirstin Ralston-Coley is a doctoral student in the Department of Sociology at Georgia State University.

Catherine Rampell is an opinion columnist at *The Washington Post*.

Mark R. Rank is the Herbert S. Hadley professor of social welfare at Washington University in St. Louis.

Emily Alpert Reyes is a reporter with the *Los Angeles Times*.

Elisabeth Rosenthal is a nonpracticing medical doctor and reporter for *The New York Times*.

Jonah Sachs is an author and co-founder and CEO of Free Range, a bicoastal messaging firm.

Zach Schiller is the research director for Policy Matters Ohio, a nonprofit research institute based in Cleveland.

Thomas Shapiro is the director of the Institute on Assets and Social Policy in the Heller School for Social Policy and Management at Brandeis University.

Gwen Sharp is the associate dean of liberal arts and sciences and an associate professor of sociology at Nevada State College and is co-founder of Sociological Images.

Renee M. Shelby is a doctoral student in the School of History, Technology, and Society at Georgia Institute of Technology.

Jennifer Sherman is an associate professor of sociology at Washington State University.

Rebecca Solnit is a writer, historian, and activist.

Alix Spiegel is a correspondent for National Public Radio.

Gregory D. Squires is a professor of sociology and public policy and public administration at George Washington University.

Nate Steiner is the director of technology at Armchair Media.

Tim Stelloh is a freelance journalist.

Joseph E. Stiglitz is a university professor at Columbia University.

Bruce Stokes is director of Global Economic Attitudes in the Pew Research Center's Global Attitudes Project.

Pamela Stone is a professor of sociology at Hunter College and the Graduate Center of the City University of New York.

Claire Suddath is a staff writer for *Bloomberg Businessweek*.

Melanie Tannenbaum is a doctoral candidate in social psychology at the University of Illinois at Urbana–Champaign.

Sabrina Tavernise is a journalist who writes for *The New York Times*.

Megan M. Tesene is a doctoral candidate in the Department of Sociology at Georgia State University.

Heather Ann Thompson is an associate professor in the Departments of African American Studies and History at Temple University.

András Tilcsik is an assistant professor of strategic management at the Rotman School and a Fellow at the Michael Lee-Chin Family Institute for Corporate Citizenship.

Tara Leigh Tober is an assistant professor in the Department of Sociology at the College at Brockport, State University of New York.

Donald Tomaskovic-Devey is a professor in the Department of Sociology at University of Massachusetts–Amherst.

Mary Nell Trautner is an associate professor in the Department of Sociology at University at Buffalo, SUNY.

Patricia Warren is an associate professor in the College of Criminology and Criminal Justice.

Rose Weitz is a professor of sociology and women and gender studies at Arizona State University.

Ronald Weitzer is a professor of sociology at the George Washington University.

Elroi J. Windsor is an assistant professor of sociology at Salem College.

Kerry Woodward is an assistant professor at California State University, Long Beach.

Deborah C. Youngblood is the vice president of research and innovation at Crittenton Women's Union, a nonprofit committed to breaking the cycle of poverty.

WHAT IS SOCIOLOGY?

If you're opening this book or enrolled in a sociology class for the first time, you might be wondering: what is sociology, and why would a sociologist study social problems? Even if you have no preexisting training in sociology or have never studied sociology before, don't worry—you are already immersed in the content of sociology on a daily basis, simply because you live in a society.

Sociology is the systematic study of human relationships (formal and informal), social interaction (between groups as small as two people or as large as many millions), and social institutions (like the educational system, political system, economic system, families, health-care systems, and more). The scope of what sociologists study varies from small group dynamics like speech interruption patterns in conversations between women and men, or doctors and patients, to large-scale comparisons of the efficacy of social welfare policies and programs. According to the American Sociological Association, sociologists study "social life, social change, and the causes and consequences of human behavior."[1] Sociologists want to know how and why people behave the way they do, as well as the result of those actions.

Sociologists often boast that they can study nearly anything. Subfields within sociology include political sociology; aging and the life course; children and youth; medical sociology; labor and labor movements; consumers and consumption; crime, law, and deviance; war, peace, and social conflict; race, gender, and class; sexuality; sociology of the family, of religion, of sport, and of the environment, just to name a few.[2] The number of research topics in the field is nearly limitless, as are the methods used in sociological research. Stombler (the first editor of this book), for example, has studied the social structure of and interactions in gay fraternities and also fraternity little sister/sweetheart programs at both predominantly black and predominantly white fraternities, whereas Jungels (the second editor) has studied men who solicit street prostitutes, privacy disclosures among sex toy party participants, and behavioral health among United States Army soldiers. Sociologists may conduct large-scale studies where thousands of people are surveyed, in-depth studies using interviews or observations, analyses of content (such as books or films), or some combination of methods. Just a quick glance through the table of contents of this book—or any course listing at a university that offers sociology classes—will give you a good idea of the areas and types of inquiry in which sociologists participate. The uniqueness of sociology not only is reflected in the endless available topics of study, but also is present in the perspective we use to guide our analyses: the sociological imagination.

THE SOCIOLOGICAL IMAGINATION

Most sociology classes, especially at the introductory level, begin with a discussion of C. Wright Mills' concept of the *sociological imagination*. The sociological imagination is a particular lens we use to view the world, one that encourages us to think like sociologists—to focus on the role social institutions and social structure have on our everyday lives. In fact, the idea of a lens used to view the world is why we decided to name this book *Focus on Social Problems: A Contemporary Reader*. We want readers to be reminded to use the appropriate lens—just as a photographer would—to see the world around them sharply: sometimes focusing closely on a subject, other times zooming out to get a sense of the bigger picture or context.

Mills argued that individuals often have trouble connecting the events of their lives to the larger society in which they live, for instance, how an individual's inability to find a job is connected to our capitalist economic system, where a financial downturn can result in downsizing and a reduction in available jobs. Understanding the history of a society can help explain the current structure of that society, which in turn can help explain how larger social forces affect the individual circumstances of members of the society. According to Mills, understanding the interplay between the individual and this history is critical.

The sociological imagination can be a difficult concept to grasp at first. Applying a sociological lens requires looking beyond individual circumstances and instead focusing on the social patterns that contribute to those circumstances, including historical, economic, political, familial, and global forces. Many of us have not been taught to think critically about the social structure (and social institutions) of which we are a part, to question why institutions exist the way they do, or to wonder who benefits from their continued existence or the maintenance of the status quo.

Distinguishing between two concepts, personal troubles and public issues, may help to clarify the sociological imagination. A *personal trouble* refers to an incident or challenge that takes place in a person's life; it "occurs within the characters of an individual and within the range of his immediate relationship with others . . . a trouble is a private matter."[3] *Public issues*, on the other hand, refer to the seemingly impersonal problems that are a result of larger social forces. They "have to do with matters that transcend these local environments of the individual . . . some value cherished by publics is felt to be threatened . . . [and] often involves a crisis in institutional arrangements."[4] A classic example, as mentioned above, is unemployment. If only one person in a large city is unemployed, then their unemployment may be a personal trouble, and we may ask questions about that individual's skills, education level, or work ethic to understand why they are unemployed. But in a society like the United States—with nearly 157 million people in the labor force[5] and an additional 8.6 million unemployed[6]—we must look at the structure of the economy to understand why so many people are unemployed. Is there something about capitalist economies that makes it impossible for all people to be gainfully employed at all times? Employing a sociological imagination means looking beyond personal explanations ("s/he is lazy, has a poor work ethic, or didn't study hard enough in school and that's why s/he doesn't have a job") to social and institutional forces. A sociological approach may argue that capitalism requires some employable, yet currently unemployed, people to be ready to step in and take over the jobs of the currently employed (what Karl Marx called "the reserve army of the poor"). This helps keep wage demands down (and thus the profits high) and keeps the workers from protesting or forming unions, because there is always the threat that they will be replaced by a member of the "reserve army." Or, rather than blaming the individual, we might look at the environment within which the person was educated and ask a series of questions about their educational experience. Were the schools s/he attended well-funded, with caring and well-trained teachers, proper learning tools (including textbooks and technology), and in buildings that were properly maintained? Was their home life peaceful; their neighborhood safe and free of environmental contamination that can cause long-term health impacts; and did they have access to the resources that lead to successful educational outcomes, like trips to museums, zoos, libraries, after-school activities, or private tutors—the things that many middle- and upper-class children, for example, find easily accessible? Did they have the assistance many young people and their parents need filling out financial aid forms for college, the funds for college testing preparation to raise their chances of acceptance and scholarships, the guidance necessary to complete the college application and interview process, or the economic resources to secure loans necessary to attend college? Sociologists might also focus on the gatekeepers to gainful employment, inquiring whether they hold any biases based on race, gender, class, sexuality, sex, or dis/ability. These are the questions that arise when we start to think critically about the social nature and structural causes of social problems.

The sociological imagination is relevant to the social problems discussed in this reader because it encourages us to look to the system (our social institutions) as the main sources of social problems (a *system-blame* approach) as opposed to those who are suffering from the problems (a *person-blame* approach). Most of us have been taught to take the person-blame approach: to look at those who are deviant in some way—the poor, those who have committed crimes, those who are marginalized for one reason or another—and to think of them as the source of the problem, rather than the society itself. We do this although those who experience social problems have neither constructed nor controlled the institutions or conditions under which they suffer.[7] Using a system-blame approach requires that we look beyond the individual to see how the institutions, structures, and systems of oppression that exist have contributed to these conditions' existence and perpetuation. A sociological lens asks us to be critical of a system from which many of us acquire our deeply held values, such as individuality and the ideas of meritocracy and freedom of choice; moreover, it asks us to question whether we benefit from these systems in any way. Questioning these deeply held assumptions can be uncomfortable and unfamiliar, but it is key to taking a critical approach to understanding social problems.

Of course, maintaining a strict adherence to either system-blame or person-blame approaches has its consequences. Focusing too much on person-blame can result in leaving the existing power structure and systems of inequality unchallenged and unchanged. Conversely, approaching every problem from a purely system-blame approach can oversimplify social problems wherein individuals are merely the products of their environment, with no free will or responsibility for their actions. Clearly, a balanced approach is needed, and the sociological imagination fosters the oft-ignored system-blame approach.

DEFINING A SOCIAL PROBLEM

So what are social problems? Many books and textbooks focus on the sociological study of social problems, and each seems to contain a slightly different definition. For example, Eitzen, Baca Zinn, and Smith[8] define social problems as "societally induced conditions that cause psychic and material suffering for any segment of the population, and acts and conditions that violate the norms and values found in a society." Similarly, Mooney, Knox, and Schacht[9] propose that a social problem is "a social condition that a segment of society views as harmful to members of society and in need of remedy." Treviño[10] offers a slightly different definition, wherein a social problem is "a social condition, event, or pattern of behavior that negatively affects the well-being of a significant number of people (or a number of significant people) who believe the condition, event, or pattern needs to be changed or ameliorated." As you can see, the definitions may vary, but there are some key similarities. At the very least, nearly all definitions include the idea that a social problem is a social condition (rather than a purely physical ailment, for example) that causes harm to many people.

Sociologists sometimes include additional elements within their definitions, for example, that social problems need to be recognized by people with power and influence or that people need to be actively trying to correct or ameliorate the condition for it to be defined as a social problem. These latter definitions stress the importance of power in defining conditions as worthy of change, which reflects the reality that much of our understanding of social problems supports the interests of those who have power in our society. This reader includes a reading by Miriam Konrad that questions why corporate crime is not considered as problematic as street crime, although it is arguably more costly and damaging to society (but more likely to be committed by those in power). Other readings ask why more attention is not paid to growing wealth inequality in America, to employment discrimination against minorities, to the expanding costs but declining quality of our health-care system, or to the exploding prison population—all issues that are more likely to affect those with less power in society.

Many definitions of social problems include a comparison between *subjective* and *objective* components of problems. Objective components focus on measurable amounts of harm or the number of people affected by an issue, reasoning that if a large number of people are harmed, then the condition is a social problem. Claims makers often take this approach, advocating for the amelioration of the problem. Claims makers can be individuals or groups and can hold a variety of positions in society including political leaders, members of the media, advocates and activists, community or religious leaders, researchers and academics, or individual people.[11] Claims makers will often use statistics to make the argument that the issue they want to bring attention to is serious and in need of change. The problem with this approach is that it relies on concepts on which there is little agreement. How many people is "a large number?" Is 10,000 enough? That might seem like a lot of people, but that is less than 0.003 percent of the population of the United States.[12] Do the conditions need to affect more than 10 percent of the U.S. population (more than 32 million people)? What counts as harm, and what is the threshold we should use to establish whether someone has been harmed? As you can see, even seemingly objective aspects can be difficult to define. Moreover, as is noted in Readings 1 (by Perrin and Miller-Perrin) and 3 (by Best) it is important for students to be able to critically assess the methods of research studies and statistics they may encounter. Understanding how researchers conduct research—how studies are designed, how samples are created, how variables are measured, and how findings are reported—is an essential way of assessing the claims that are presented to us every day.

An alternative approach is to focus on the *subjective* nature of social problems, which usually begins with a discussion about the social construction of social problems. This approach focuses on understanding how social conditions come to be seen or "discovered" as a problem. This process begins with claims makers identifying a problem in need of resolution and then attempting to bring attention to the problem. These claims makers enter an already crowded field; after all, as Best[13] argued, "there are many causes and a limited amount of space on the front page of the *New York Times*. Advocates must find ways to make their claims compelling." Claims makers attempt to garner public attention for their problem in the hopes that increased attention will translate to action on the part of citizens, lawmakers, or those in power who have the ability to help change the conditions that caused the problem, or to help alleviate the suffering of the victims. This process, called *claims-making*, essentially relies on "societal reaction and social definition. From this perspective, social problems come and go as societal reactions and responses to particular conditions change."[14]

A classic example of the subjective nature and process of the social construction and "discovery" of a social problem focuses on child abuse. Until the 1960s, there were no laws in the United States protecting children from abuse by their caretakers.[15] Although there were advances in the rights of children prior to this point, there was little attention to the issue of child abuse from those in the legal, political, or social welfare fields who had "little incentive for interfering with an established power set—the parent over the child."[16] Members of the general public were largely unconcerned with the issue as well, and studies at the time concluded that most people were tolerant of, and even empathetic toward, those who had been accused or convicted of abusing a child.[17] Attempts to deal with child abuse were framed as preventing future harm to society in the form of "future delinquents . . . it was the children, not their abusive guardians, who felt the weight of the moral crusade."[18]

So, although the condition of child abuse had existed for thousands of years, it wasn't until the 1940s and 1950s that pediatric radiologists—those who X-ray children admitted to the hospital with traumatic injuries—first "discovered" child abuse in the form of broken bones and skeletal traumas.[19] An article in the *Journal of the American Medical Association* entitled "The Battered Child Syndrome" labeled child abuse as an "illness" that children might be suffering from, making it more likely that doctors would be willing to "see" abuse, as well as seeing abusive parents as people who needed help. Various social welfare organizations joined in the call for more attention on the issue, arguing that children should be examined for child abuse symptoms; law enforcement advocates argued that child abuse should be criminalized and offenders prosecuted. Buttressed by the "objective" voices of doctors and law enforcement, the media coverage of this "new" condition of child abuse was prolific. In reaction to this increased attention and public outcry, over the course of four years (beginning in 1962), all fifty states had passed legislation to deal with the new problem of child abuse.[20]

A more contemporary example is the issue of using a cellphone while driving. Although today most people acknowledge that driving while talking on a cellphone is risky and many states have made using a cellphone while driving illegal, in the recent past this was not the case. As Parilla[21] demonstrates, concern about the distraction and possible fatal consequences that come from texting or talking while driving began to increase in the early 2000s, as cellphone use increased and more claims makers (including government officials, celebrities, and members of law enforcement) began to publicly warn about the dangers of distracted driving. Parilla argues that the key to the success of this movement was garnering media attention and support; after all, claims makers had to convince the public that something they did nearly every day was, in fact, dangerous. Garnering support meant relying on shifting definitions (e.g., initially focusing on handheld rather than hands-free devices; then on banning cellphone use for new drivers rather than more experienced ones; and, finally, an increased push against the broader problem of "distracted driving"). The media played an important role in guiding the public's understanding of the issue as a problem. From 1984 to 2010, the period of time that Parilla reviewed newspaper articles about cellphone use as the cause of traffic accidents, the vast majority of articles presented the claim that driving while on the phone caused accidents, but offered no *counterclaim* or alternative discussion of the issue (e.g., that driving and using the phone does not cause accidents or any more accidents than, say, eating and driving); less than 15 percent of the articles Parilla reviewed presented a counterclaim.[22] This highlights the importance of the media not only in disseminating claims, but also in framing how we understand a social problem.

THEORETICAL UNDERPINNINGS

Sociologists use different theoretical perspectives to help them explore the causes and consequences of social problems. As we selected readings to include in this book, one theoretical perspective primarily guided our choices. Although Mills emphasizes the importance of examining the social structure and social conditions to understand the lived experiences of one's self and others, he did not emphasize the process by which social problems come to be defined and recognized as such. When people interact, share ideas, and begin to create meaning and understandings of a particular situation (as the result of claims-making, for example), they are engaging in the social construction of a social problem. Social constructionism, or how we create ideas and define social problems through our interaction, helps us understand part of the "story" of social problems. But we believe that social constructionism, as a theoretical perspective, doesn't go far enough analytically.

Critical constructionism acknowledges that the process by which social problems come to be defined as such is a political process, where the desires of those who have the most power in society (political power, economic power, and so on) hold the most sway in the social problem construction process (see, for example, Reading 11 in this volume by Stiglitz and its accompanying "box" by Drutman). This power is defined as the ability to maintain or change the social structure in society. Critical constructionism assumes that those who have the most power will generally influence social structures in such a way as to maintain their power. Furthermore, those who have the most power to shape policy and control institutions (like education, media, or government) have the most resources at their disposal to influence the ideas of everyone in the society, thereby helping shore up their own positions and maintain the status quo. Critical constructionism encourages us to acknowledge that those with the fewest resources must work significantly harder to have their voices heard and that a main avenue to creating change may be by

convincing those in power that it is in their own interest to solve a social problem.[23] Although there are many ways to define social problems and theoretical lenses with which to view them, this book is designed to both illustrate how social problems come to be defined as such and, more importantly, to share the extent and causes of the social conditions of our society so that you, as changemakers, can approach them from a deep and broad base of sociological knowledge.

SOCIAL CHANGE

The readings in this book will highlight just how entrenched many social problems are in our society; we want you to understand the scope of the conditions (from microaggressions to systemic discrimination, for example) that create suffering in the lives of those affected directly by social problems.[24] As many of the readings and some of the examples mentioned in this introduction discuss, social problems are often interrelated and cumulative in nature. Indeed, social problems "exist in relation to other social problems . . . [and are] embedded within a complex institutional system of problem formulation and dissemination."[25] An individual born into poverty may be exposed to hazardous environmental conditions that impede his or her physical and mental development and then go on to attend a poorly funded public school that lacks the resources to teach the vast number of skills needed to succeed in college and on the job market, all of which may damage long-term economic prospects. An individual who lives in an impoverished area with few economic opportunities may turn to petty crime to survive, resulting in arrests or time spent in jail; a criminal record may subsequently affect their ability to get and keep a good job to provide for themselves and their families.

The realization that so many social problems are interrelated and that solutions are often hard to come by may cause students to feel powerless. Yet, it is important to remember that although our actions are certainly constrained by social institutions and the structure of our society, we retain individual and collective agency—the ability to act to create change for ourselves and others. Humans built the structures that reproduce our social problems, and thus they can also adapt, alter, or replace such structures.

FORMAT OF THE BOOK

Focus on Social Problems: A Contemporary Reader has several features that distinguish it from other textbooks and readers on social problems. The book is composed of fifteen chapters, each focusing on a different social problem (except for Chapter 1, which briefly covers the social construction of social problems). Each chapter consists of a selection of full-length readings and "boxes." Full-length readings cover what we consider important topics on a given social problem and address the breadth, depth, causes of, or solutions to that problem. Full-length readings and boxes may be read together or separately. Boxes are generally briefer than readings and are incorporated to delve into a narrower subject or simply generate reactions and discussion related to the chapter topic without overburdening the reader with additional full-length articles. We chose readings and boxes to engage students' sociological imaginations and provide access to recent data and analyses relevant to current social problems. Vetted by our students, our selections are designed to be accessible to undergraduates at an introductory level and to convey information about causes, consequences, and the scope of social problems.

Full-length readings and boxes come from a diverse group of sources: edited versions of academic, peer-reviewed articles and book chapters (for example, from the *American Sociological Review, Gender & Society, Social Problems*), articles from the popular press (*The New York Times, National Public Radio, Vanity Fair, Rolling Stone*), blogs (*The Society Pages, Sociological Images*), and reports from nonprofit organizations (Pew Research, the Sunlight Foundation, Food Chain Workers Alliance). When we were designing this book, we thought about the weight that each type of source should receive. Although we believe academic, peer-reviewed research is critical to a thorough understanding of social problems, popular press, investigative journalistic pieces, and research from the nonprofit sector offer important and accessible perspectives that both inform and have been informed by sociological research.

Previously published works are included alongside those written expressly for this book. We commissioned these pieces for several reasons. Sometimes we couldn't find articles on a given subject that contained all the information we wanted to share with students, so we invited academics to share knowledge they had about a subject. Other times there was a plethora of material from which to choose, and we asked an author to pull together the information that was the most salient and relevant to students.

The other feature of our book that sets it apart from others is the inclusion of Activist Interviews. Many of our social problems students complain that courses focusing on social problems, inequality, and injustice are depressing. It is hard for students to envision change; it is even harder for them to see how individuals or small groups could have any meaningful impact. The activists selected for this book represent social change work across the range of social problems covered in our book. We incorporate interviews with activists working within different types of organizations or collectives (from the small, local, grassroots organization to large national organizations) and who are doing a wide array of types of work (from field organizing to serving as directors). We hope that these interviews, as well as the variety of activist experiences contained within them, will demonstrate to students that they too can enact social change in their communities.

CONTENT OF THE BOOK

Chapter 1 focuses on the social construction of social problems. As discussed earlier, social problems only exist when key claims makers increase awareness of a particular issue. We focus on the process of claims-making and how social problems are brought to our attention as members of the public. A key element of this process—addressed in this chapter—is how statistics can be used to support or undermine claims-making arguments. An additional aspect of the claims-making process is claims makers' strategic use of language designed to persuade citizens to care about and act on a particular issue. This language may influence our opinions about whether a problem needs our attention, how empathetically we perceive victims of the problem, and what solutions may be best to solve or ameliorate the effects of the problem.

Chapter 2 focuses on a topic frequently neglected in social problems texts: the role American values and culture play in our understanding of social problems. Core American values such as individualism, meritocracy, and consumerism inform how we understand social problems and what we envision as possible solutions (and whether we believe they can be solved). As we have discussed in this introduction, taking a sociological approach to the study of social problems means focusing on the role social structure and institutions play in creating and maintaining the conditions by which social problems are created, as well as questioning the role that American norms and values have in the perpetuation of social problems. For example, if an individual believes that every American has an equal chance of achieving the American Dream if he or she works hard enough—that there is no discrimination based on race, gender, or sexual orientation impeding an individual's success—then that individual will likely have a different perspective on programs such as affirmative action, the social safety net, and legal protections for minorities compared to those who believe that the system itself produces unequal outcomes. This chapter also discusses the state of American democracy and democratic values in our culture. Have we really become more divided over politics as a nation? Do voters hold significant sway in policy decisions or is our democracy being bought and sold from under us?

One of the core American values addressed in Chapter 2 is the belief that Americans are upwardly mobile, that is, able to move themselves or their children from a lower economic class status to a higher one. But is this really true? Chapter 3 begins by examining the wealth and income distribution in the United States and whether Americans would prefer a more equal society. Other readings address how wealth and income inequality have increased over generations, leading to a society where few people are able to move up the income and wealth ladders. The chapter concludes by discussing the power of the superrich in our society, questioning whether this small group of people has too much power compared to the rest of society, and the potential consequences for our democracy.

Chapter 4 explores a social problem closely related to wealth and income inequality: poverty. The chapter begins by examining the problematic way that many people think about poverty; namely, that it is caused by individual pathology, weakness, or laziness. Readings in this chapter argue that, rather than being the fault of the individual, poverty is actually the result of a capitalist system wherein only a few people are truly allowed to "win." Readings also discuss the challenges facing those in poverty, especially regarding the benefits that are designed to assist them. These programs are not as generous as many people believe and often present individuals with challenging economic choices as they attempt to rise out of poverty. Finally, this chapter concludes with a reading that examines one group that is among the poorest in the United States—Native Americans—and how generations of government neglect and abandonment have resulted in poverty-stricken communities that are a stark cry from the common perception of communities shored up by vast casino wealth.

The United States is often touted as a "colorblind society," but what does that really mean? Chapter 5, which focuses on the social problem of racial and ethnic inequality, begins by answering this question, as well as discussing whether being colorblind is even a desirable or achievable goal. Other readings in this chapter discuss deeply entrenched issues contributing to racial and ethnic inequality in contemporary American society, including housing and residential segregation, where inequality is often hidden and hard to change; inequality in the criminal justice system, where generations of discrimination and racially biased policies have contributed to mass incarceration of racial minorities; and even the ubiquitous symbols used by sports teams that, although embedded in popular culture, have become contentious, as evidenced by protests over team mascot choices. Finally, the chapter concludes by discussing attempts to control immigration and the establishment of immigrant communities, including the challenges that undocumented young people face when transitioning from childhood to adulthood.

Chapter 6 examines gender inequality. Like racial discrimination, discrimination on the basis of gender can be both overt and covert. Readings in this chapter cover the difference between hostile and benevolent sexism—how seemingly inconsequential or even pleasant statements can perpetuate gender inequality—and how restrictive gender roles can be harmful to both women and men. Sexual violence against women is addressed in this chapter as well, in readings that examine why many young men and women perceive sexual violence as "normal" and what role gendered ideology and gender roles play in the perpetuation of this problem. Chapter 6 also includes a topic frequently neglected in social problems texts: how gender discrimination affects transgender individuals, especially in the workplace. Finally, this chapter concludes by discussing how improvements in gender equality are not only good for women, but also benefit the world as a whole.

Social problems related to sex and sexuality are the focus of Chapter 7. Although sexuality can seem like a deeply personal subject, our sexual practices and behaviors are informed by our culture and society, and our actions can similarly have a significant effect on the larger culture. Case in point: a reading on teen pregnancy opens this chapter, outlining some of the possible causes and consequences of an issue that affects individual lives, but also has ramifications for larger society. Closely related is the issue of sex education in the United States; how we choose to educate (or not educate) our children about sex and sexuality has lasting effects not only on their future reproductive and sexual knowledge and choices, but also on the public health of the country as a whole. Similarly, how we respond to the sexuality of our young people—especially those who identify as lesbian, gay, bisexual, transgender, or queer (LGBTQ), also has long-reaching implications. One reading in this chapter, about a community that has seen growing intolerance toward, and increasing suicides of, LGBT adolescents, probes how adult intolerance can have devastating consequences for young people, their families, and their communities. Finally, this chapter addresses commercial sexuality and sex work, questioning our assumptions about what sex work is and the ways in which it is damaging.

The media plays a unique role in our understanding of social problems. On the one hand, without the media, we would struggle to define the existence of social problems, as well as their size and scope. On the other hand, the media often perpetuates stereotypes and misinformation about those impacted by social problems (e.g., presenting biased depictions of those living in poverty, or perpetuating sexist or racist ideologies), and a number of aspects of the media can be considered social problems themselves. Chapter 8 begins by discussing one of these facets: the conglomeration and monopolization of media over time that limits consumer choice and the media messages available for consumption. Other articles discuss how the Internet—one of our largest media platforms—is not equally accessible to all people, and how media can be used to harm others (in the form of cyberbullying, for example). Finally, this chapter turns to the role the media plays in perpetuating social problems, beginning with how the media shapes our perception of crime and criminals and how sexualization in the media is increasing over time. These readings offer a roadmap to understanding the role media plays in our lives and how we understand social problems, as well as serving as examples of critiques of media that we can engage in on a regular basis.

Chapter 9 focuses on social problems in the institution of education. These problems can affect students at a variety of levels, from those entering preschool or elementary school to those attending college. This chapter includes readings that address educational inequality and unequal distribution of resources as well as the use of unequal and harsh punishments for minority children. It concludes by discussing topics that are likely near and dear to many of our readers: problems related to higher and postsecondary education. These readings focus on whether the college environment is designed to accommodate students from all economic backgrounds or whether it privileges students from higher socioeconomic statuses, as well as whether for-profit colleges prey on students who seek to improve their future economic prospects.

Families in the United States face a multitude of social problems, including many of the problems addressed in the preceding chapters. Chapter 10 focuses specifically on problems related to the family, including how parenthood can force single women and families into difficult economic and working situations such as deciding whether to keep or give up careers and jobs after having children. Other readings examine how employers discriminate against women with children, threatening the economic survival of some families. And, sadly, sometimes families can be a site of social problems, as evidenced by domestic violence; one reading in this chapter describes an innovative program designed to help victims escape violent relationships. Finally,

the issue of elder care is one that is receiving more attention as the Baby Boom generation ages, and this chapter addresses how families adjust to changing expectations and needs of the elderly.

We all interact with the health-care and medical system at some point in our lives. Like the media and the family, the medical system is an institution wherein problems can both be created and solved. With more and more medical intervention in our lives, it is important to develop a critical lens to view its role. In addition to questioning whether medical intervention is ideal in our individual lives, Chapter 11 addresses the social and economic costs of medical interventions (especially those that may be unnecessary) and addresses the question of why medical care in the United States is so much more expensive, but lower in quality, than medical care in other Western nations. Finally, this chapter concludes by examining the ways in which other systems of oppression can intersect with unequal access to medical care and treatment, looking specifically at the cases of low-income whites and African Americans.

Many social problems texts address crime by examining crime rates, victim and offender characteristics, and theories about why crime occurs. Although the selected readings in Chapter 12 touch on these issues, we focus more deeply on the ways in which the criminal justice system intersects with other systems of inequality, including wealth and poverty, racial inequality, and gender discrimination. We begin by examining an issue that is a matter of concern for many people—that of mass shootings—and the role that gender and culture play in this type of gun violence. Readings in this chapter also address wealth and income inequality in relation to the criminal justice system, including how the most powerful members of our society are able to use their resources to shape the legal system to focus on crimes of the poor rather than their own misdeeds. Readings also address how the criminal justice system perpetuates racial and class-based inequality through mass incarceration and its consequences; the death penalty; and the private prison industrial complex. Finally, we address ways to reform the criminal justice system to better serve citizens and law enforcement.

Many of the social problems featured in this book either are the result of problems in the economic system (for example, wealth and income inequality) or affect the economic system (for example, racial discrimination that results in stifled economic opportunities for minority group members). Chapter 13 focuses on work and economic problems specifically, beginning with examining the challenges that women—even wealthy, highly educated women—face when trying to balance family and work obligations. Readings in this chapter also address a variety of types of workplace discrimination by examining how sex segregation persists and damages women's advancement in the labor force and how and in what ways job discrimination against gay men continues. This chapter also includes readings on how the workplace and economic system continue to disadvantage those at the bottom rungs of the economic ladder, including those who work to supply us our food. We may not realize it, but low wages have long-term impacts not only on those workers, but also on the nation as a whole. Finally, we conclude by demonstrating how American consumers and corporations may affect the lives of workers overseas by contributing to dangerous and toxic work environments.

For us to survive and thrive in societies both locally and globally, our policies and actions will need to promote sustainability. Sustainability refers to "meeting the needs of the present without compromising the ability of future generations to meet their own needs."[26] Broadly understanding our environmental crises enables the necessary systemic and behavior changes. Whether we have healthy food and environments to support our population is a continuing question and one that impacts us all. We begin Chapter 14 by focusing on the environment, specifically, the environmental

inequalities that primarily affect low-income people and people of color. Environmental problems in these communities, including toxic waste and contamination of water, air, and soil, often go unaddressed because of the relative powerlessness of the populations that experience them. Readings also discuss the U.S. environmental movement, including how it changed from being characterized as a powerful movement with many successful campaigns to one that is languishing and becoming increasingly irrelevant to the average American. We also include readings that cover the American food system. Understanding how our food system is structured, who benefits from that structure, and how it affects our choices as consumers often goes unexamined in social problems courses. We address this topic by focusing both on policy and on consumer experiences. Other readings address how unhealthy food is designed to be addictive—physically and mentally—potentially increasing health problems for consumers. This chapter concludes with a reading focused on the food-protection system that ensures our meat and produce are free of harmful (and sometimes fatal) contaminants. This system has broken down, leaving consumers vulnerable and unprotected.

Finally, we address the topic of social change and activism in Chapter 15. The readings in this chapter demonstrate that social change can happen through a variety of mechanisms, with varying levels of success. Social change can happen relatively rapidly, as has been the case for LGBT rights in the United States, and it can happen in fits and starts and in ways that activists may not anticipate. Social change can happen in large, carefully orchestrated, risky movements, like the American civil rights movement of the 1960s, or it can happen in more fleeting ways, as has been evidenced with social media campaigns around the world. Finally, we address how students can become social activists in their own lives by challenging privilege and systems of oppression in their everyday lives.

NOTES

1. American Sociological Association. n.d. "What Is Sociology?" http://www.asanet.org/about/sociology.cfm/.

2. American Sociological Association. n.d. "Current Sections." http://www.asanet.org/sections/list.cfm/.

3. Mills, 1959:8.

4. Mills, 1959:8–9.

5. Bureau of Labor Statistics, U.S. Department of Labor. 2015. "United States Labor Force Statistics, Seasonally Adjusted, 1978–Present." http://www.dlt.ri.gov/lmi/laus/us/usadj.htm/.

6. As of March 2015, when the unemployment rate was 5.5 percent. Bureau of Labor Statistics, U.S. Department of Labor. 2015. "The Employment Situation, March 2015. http://www.bls.gov/news.release/pdf/empsit.pdf/.

7. Eitzen, Stanley D., Maxine Baca Zinn, and Kelly Eitzen Smith. 2014. *Social Problems*, 13th ed. New York: Pearson Higher Education.

8. Eitzen, Baca Zinn, and Smith, 2014:10.

9. Mooney, Linda A., David Knox, and Caroline Schacht. 2015. *Understanding Social Problems*, 9th ed. Stamford, CT: Cengage Learning, 3.

10. Treviño, Javier. 2015. *Investigating Social Problems*. Thousand Oaks, CA: Sage, 6.

11. Spector, Malcolm, and John I. Kitsuse. 1977. *Constructing Social Problems*. New Brunswick, NJ: Transaction.

12. Based on a U.S. population in May 2015 of 320 million people (U.S. Census Bureau. U.S. and World Population Clock. http://www.census.gov/popclock/).

13. Best, Joel. 2001. "Promoting Bad Statistics." *Society* 38(3):10–15.

14. Perrin, Robin D., and Cindy L. Miller-Perrin. 2011. "Interpersonal Violence as Social Construction: The Potentially Undermining Role of Claims Making and Advocacy Statistics." *Journal of Interpersonal Violence* 26(15): 3033–3049.

15. Pfohl, Stephen J. 1977. "The Discovery of Child Abuse." *Social Problems* 14(3):310–323.

16. Pfohl, 1977:314.

17. Pfohl, 1977.

18. Pfohl, 1977:311.

19. Pfohl, 1977.

20. Pfohl, 1977.

21. Parilla, Peter F. 2013. "Cell Phone Use while Driving: Defining a Problem as Worthy of Action." Pp. 27–46 in *Making Sense of Social Problems: New Images, New Issues*, Joel Best and Scott R. Harris, eds. Boulder, CO: Reiner.

22. Parilla, 2013.

23. Heiner, Robert. 2013. *Social Problems: An Introduction to Critical Constructionism*. New York: Oxford University Press.

24. Best, Joel. 2002. "Constructing the Sociology of Social Problems: Spector and Kitsuse Twenty-Five Years Later." *Sociological Forum* 17(4):699–706.

25. Hilgartner, Stephen, and Charles L. Bosk. 1988. "The Rise and Fall of Social Problems: A Public Arenas Model." *American Journal of Sociology* 94(1):55.

26. United Nations. 1987. "Report of the World Commission on Environment and Development, General Assembly Resolution 42/187." December 11, 1987. Retrieved May 20, 2015.

Social Construction of Social Problems

Sut Jhally

Sut Jhally is a professor of communication at the University of Massachusetts and the founder and executive director of the Media Education Foundation (MEF). MEF produces and distributes documentaries that encourage viewers to critically examine their social world. In particular, MEF focuses on the way mass media color our understanding of our culture and send powerful messages that affect our thoughts and behavior.

As a scholar, how did you first become interested in making documentaries that promote social change?

My documentary filmmaking actually started out preparing video material to use in my university classes as a teaching aid. My first film, *Dreamworlds*, was a classroom project about depictions of femininity in music videos, as that was the topic we were discussing. To this day I regard myself as a teacher first, and a filmmaker second, except that I try to use public pedagogy to widen the reach of our analyses beyond the classroom. The reason I was, and am, interested in video is that it has emerged as the medium and language of the modern world, and if you want to engage with people in that world you have to use a language that they understand.

What social problems do you highlight in your films?

One theme we find in our exploration of media is that those whose interests are served tend to be those with the most power in society. They have the power, for example, to reinforce ideologies that serve their interests and keep the current power structures intact. We also identify the role of the media in bringing social problems to our attention. The media play a role in defining whether an issue is problematic to begin with, and how those impacted by the problem are portrayed, making it important to pay attention to who is in charge of media messages and what those messages say. MEF deals with a whole range of issues (such as problematic representations of race, gender, and class; commercialization; and war) that people have to engage with as they answer two related questions. The first has to do with identity and subjectivity—*who am I and how do others understand me?* The second has to with consciousness and ideology—*how does the world work and in whose interests?*

As a scholar-activist, what are your goals?

Canadian media scholar, Marshall McLuhan, used to remark that we're not sure who discovered water, but we're pretty sure it wasn't the fish. I think we are in a similar situation with media these days in that it is so ubiquitous it disappears from our view. The *first* goal then is get the fish (us) to see the media. *Second*, once we see the media we then have to think critically about the messages they send, and understand why the media systems are structured the way they currently exist. Media systems do not come about naturally; they do not fall from heaven fully formed. They are social creations guided by particular interests. *Third*, because media systems are not natural, they can be changed, and it is the job of citizens in democratic societies to engage with and understand the processes that shape our social world.

What strategies do you use in your productions in order to promote social change?

We deal with many issues that impact people very directly. Our goal is to provide them with accessible ways to understand those issues in a deeper way. This deeper, critical understanding allows people to think of more productive and realistic ways to take action in the world. Before you do anything about social problems you have to be able to recognize them and understand how they are connected to multiple dimensions of the social world. Our films are designed to help people see these connections and make sure that people cannot think about the world the same way again. The media are an important part of how we understand the world and the social problems that exist in it, and addressing how a social problem is portrayed and represented in the media can be a first step to creating social change.

What is a major challenge that activists in your area face?

A major challenge is the prevailing sense that the media are controlled by a liberal agenda, rather than driven by the interests of the owners of the media (corporations), and its major customers (advertisers who provide the money to media). This failure to recognize that the media's prime role is to deliver audience eyeballs to be sold to advertisers makes it difficult to focus on the more important issues of power and representation. Consumers of media often think of ourselves as customers (the ones choosing the content) and because of that, we may believe we wield power over the owners of media. However we're enacting our power and choice from a very limited "menu" of media messages.

What would you consider to be your greatest successes as a scholar-activist?

We have produced many films on important subjects, but the recent public focus on violent masculinity as something that can potentially be changed is connected to our 2000 film *Tough Guise*. It certainly did not cause these changes, but it was part of the sea change that recognized that gender was not just about women and femininity. Feminist scholars and activists of course had been saying these things for years, but it required a visible male voice (Jackson Katz) to get people (men in particular) to listen with an open mind.

Why should students get involved in this type of activism?

Almost every social problem has a media component to it, in that *how* we think about issues is affected by how it is *represented* (whether it is the environment, undocumented immigration, violence, labor issues, gender issues, LGBT issues, etc.). In turn, how it is represented is a result of how the media are organized and who gets to speak and who doesn't. In other words, what stories are the media sharing with us, who has the power to create and share those stories, and whose interests do those stories serve?

If an individual has little money and time, are there other ways s/he can contribute to social change?

In whatever context you find yourself, speak out so that people can see there is another way in which the world can be organized, another set of values that exist. It is also important to engage critically with different forms of media; ask yourself who benefits from the depiction you are seeing or hearing, and how that depiction might reinforce the status quo rather than challenge it.

Interpersonal Violence as Social Construction: The Potentially Undermining Role of Claims Making and Advocacy Statistics

ROBIN D. PERRIN AND CINDY L. MILLER-PERRIN

Perrin and Miller-Perrin use a social constructionist approach to examine the social issue of interpersonal violence, discussing how claimsmakers can shape knowledge about social problems. They point out that although claimsmakers have an important role to play in defining problems and raising awareness, there can be negative consequences to advocacy as well, including undermining their own advocacy efforts and emboldening counterclaimsmakers.

I gather, young man, that you wish to be a Member of Parliament. The first lesson that you must learn is, when I call for statistics about the rate of infant mortality, what I want is proof that fewer babies died when I was Prime Minister than when anyone else was Prime Minister. That is a political statistic.

—Winston Churchill

The semester is only a week old and already the students are asking difficult questions. An introductory psychology student approaches the teacher after class and asks whether it is true that social scientists are often more motivated by political and moral agendas than by a commitment to empirical inquiry. Isn't it true, she wonders aloud, that there are no such things as "facts" in social science? The teacher acknowledges that sometimes moral agendas interfere, but ideally in a social *science*, this should not be the case. Another student who is taking an introductory statistics course asks if it is true that one can find statistics to support any claim one wants to make. The teacher responds that any such manipulation is not the fault of statistical procedures themselves, for indeed they are mathematically sound, but she also acknowledges that sometimes data are misused to further moral agendas.

One has to wonder how the social sciences—particularly psychology and sociology—got to this point. Surely, the physics teacher does not

Robin D. Perrin and Cindy L. Miller-Perrin, *Journal of Interpersonal Violence* (Volume 26 and Issue 15), pp. 3033–3049, Copyright © 2011. Reprinted by Permission of SAGE Publications.

have to answer these sorts of questions the first day of class. Part of the problem, of course, is the nature of the social scientist's subject matter. The empirical issues that social scientists address are often complex, and findings cannot be easily reduced to simple and straightforward statements of fact. In addition, many members of the public at large, it seems to us, do not believe that they need the findings of social science to understand the world. Their commonsense understanding will do just fine, thank you very much. And, of course, many of the topics social scientists study are politically charged. Empirical findings that question taken-for-granted "truths," or have political ramifications, will inevitably be met with some skepticism.

Yet it is probably too easy to blame this skepticism on the nature of our subject matter or a naïve and stubborn public. Indeed, one could reasonably argue that we social scientists brought some of the skepticism on ourselves. The conflict likely begins with the complex relationship between research evidence and advocacy efforts. What role, if any, should advocacy play in the study of social problems? When should research stop and advocacy begin? In this . . . [reading], we examine these important issues as they relate to the study of interpersonal violence. We focus specifically on interpersonal violence as viewed through a social constructionist lens, highlighting the important ways advocacy has influenced public perceptions of interpersonal violence as a social problem. We also identify potential consequences associated with advocacy efforts and claims that are not empirically grounded. Contrary to the goals of many advocates, some of these consequences may be detrimental to the very social problems they hope to alleviate.

Social Problems as Social Constructions

We begin where, arguably, all social science should begin; with a question . . . and with a theory. The question is this: How does a social condition come to be seen as a social problem? The answer, it seems to us, is found in social constructionist theory. Viewing a social problem as a social construction is to suggest that the social condition became a social problem because it was defined as such by claims makers. *Claims making* refers to the "activities of individuals or groups making assertions of grievances or claims with respect to some putative condition" (Spector & Kitsuse, 1977, p. 75). Generally speaking, the social construction of a social problem begins when a claims maker (whether an individual or a group) arouses concern among others about a particular condition that the claims maker deems unacceptable. Such claims-making reactions may come from many different sources, including individual citizens, religious organizations, advocacy organizations, political interest groups, academics, or the mass media. When society in general comes to accept the claims makers' assertions, the social conditions come to be perceived as social problems. Social problems, then, are essentially "discovered" through this process of societal reaction and social definition. From this perspective, social problems come and go as societal reactions and responses to particular conditions change.

Specific facts about the social problem are constructed in much the same way. As social problems compete for attention and resources, if one hopes to draw attention to a cause, the facts that one brings to the table must be compelling. "Advocates must find a way to make their claims compelling; they favor melodrama—terrible villains, sympathetic, vulnerable victims, and big numbers. Big numbers suggest that there is a big problem, and big problems demand attention, concern, action. They must not be ignored" (Best, 2001b, p. 11). For example, efforts during the 1980s to raise awareness about the "growing problem" of missing children were successful, in part, because advocates effectively paired tales of the most tragic and unusual atrocities committed against children (e.g., stranger abductions resulting in death) with statistical estimates drawn from very broad definitions (which included, for example, missing children who were with noncustodial parents for unauthorized visits). This strategy contributed to the perception among frightened citizens and concerned legislators that stranger abductions of children were more common than they actually are (Best, 1990).

The constructionist perspective directs our attention away from the objective conditions of a problem and toward claims made about the problem. Who has reacted? Why are they reacting? How have they defined the condition at issue? And what techniques are they employing to draw our attention to a particular condition? Recent research, primarily in the political science and communications literatures, addresses several of these questions through the lens of framing theory. Framing theory examines how individuals develop particular conceptualizations of various political and social issues and how certain communication frames might promote specific definitions and/or interpretations of particular issues (Shah, Watts, Domke, & Fan, 2002).

. . . This is not to say, of course, that the objective conditions of social problems are unimportant. Indeed, for those of us passionately concerned about various social problems, the emotional, social, and physical harm caused by them are *the most* important considerations. The social constructionist perspective merely acknowledges and examines some of the social processes relevant in the creation of all knowledge.

Interpersonal Violence as Social Construction

Social constructionist theory serves as an important beginning point in the study of intimate violence as a social problem because it encourages researchers to acknowledge that often the individuals and groups producing the facts about particular social problems have very strong feelings about those problems. This phenomenon is strikingly present in the area of intimate violence, where advocacy passions seem to run especially high. This passion is understandable given the historical indifference to the abuse of women and children. In fact, it was the heroic passions of the leaders of the "woman movement" (mid-1800s), the child-saving movement (late 1800s), and the modern feminist movement (1970s) that led to the discovery of family violence as a social problem in the first place. Such moral crusades, however, can and do lead to distortions of the facts, and such distortions, as we discuss below, may actually undermine attempts to alleviate the social problem.

To be clear, we believe that interpersonal violence is a very serious problem in the United States and around the world. This is a topic that we have written about ourselves and about which we have passionate feelings. . . . We believe, like most of our colleagues in this field, that Americans are more likely to be victimized in their own homes than elsewhere. We believe that the rates of child abuse and interpersonal violence between adults are unacceptably high, and we believe that we can be influential in reducing these rates through our research and writing. At the same time, however, we do not believe everything we read about the problem of interpersonal violence. The social constructionist perspective encourages one to question the context of research and the potential advocacy motives of claims makers. In the following sections, we focus on the many ways in which claims making has impacted public perceptions of interpersonal violence by influencing how it has come to be defined as a social problem both in terms of its nature and scope.

Definitional Problems

Terms such as *family violence, child abuse, sexual abuse, rape,* and *spouse abuse* are social constructs. Some may by troubled by this assertion, incorrectly assuming that we are suggesting interpersonal violence is "false," "made up," or "arbitrary." Yet to argue that *child sexual abuse*, for example, is a social construct is merely to draw our attention to the many human choices necessary in the definition and measurement of this phenomenon. Researchers can arrive at statistical estimates only after they have defined and operationalized the terms *child*, *sexual*, and *abuse*. The definitions of these terms must be negotiated.

It is informative to envision the many different claims-making groups and individuals engaged in this negotiation. One significant purpose of controversial groups such as the North American Man/Boy Love Association (NAMBLA, 2011), for example, is claims making. NAMBLA opposes "age-of-consent laws and all other restrictions which deny men and boys the full enjoyment of their bodies and control over their lives" (http://www.nambla.org/welcome.htm). Of course, it is easy to reject NAMBLA's extreme—and criminal—claims making on sexual behavior. It is important to remember, however, that when social scientists condemn NAMBLA, they too are engaged in claims making.

We see this illustrated in the history of academic debates about the definition and prevalence of child sexual abuse. Diana Russell (1984), working under the definitional assumption that unwanted hugs and kisses and exposure to exhibitionists constitute sexual abuse, has asserted that more than half of all females are victims of sexual abuse, an alarming fact to be sure. Finkelhor, Hotaling, Lewis, and Smith (1990) define abuse much more narrowly, asking adult respondents about experiences in their childhoods that they would now consider sexual abuse (e.g., activities involving "someone touching you or grabbing you, or kissing you, or rubbing up against your body either in a public place or private—anything like that?"). Finkelhor and his colleagues estimate the rate of child sexual abuse to be much lower.

Similar issues are at the center of the often heated debates concerning the definition and measurement of rape. The FBI has historically defined forcible rape very narrowly, as "carnal knowledge"—typically defined as a penis penetrating a vagina—of a female forcibly and against her will (U.S. Department of Justice, Federal Bureau of Investigation, 2008).[1] Koss (1992) has convincingly argued that all forced sexual acts should be condemned and that the notion of

"against her will" should be broadened to include situations in which a woman's ability to consent to sexual activity is compromised by alcohol or drugs, fear of losing a job, or "verbal coercion." Statistical estimates of the prevalence of rape based on these broader definitions have been alarmingly high (between 25% and 50% of college women), leading some critics to label them "advocacy statistics" (Gilbert, 1997).

Who has the right answer, the true statistics, the facts about sexual abuse and rape? Even asking these questions is to misunderstand the issue. The debate is not as much statistical as it is definitional. And the facts are *not* out there somewhere waiting for social scientific discovery.

Distorted Facts

Given the importance of facts in social problems debates, it should come as no surprise that they are often exaggerated or distorted. To be sure, exaggerated claims are not always the result of intentional crusading. A lack of understanding of statistics, shoddy scholarship, definitional ambiguity, and imprecise language are relevant as well (see Best, 2001a). However, it seems reasonable to conclude that some exaggerations and distortions are fueled, at least in part, by claims makers' convictions that they need to present dramatic information to illustrate the seriousness of the problem. Perhaps the most well-known illustration of this phenomenon is the claim, now discredited, that women are especially vulnerable to domestic attacks on Super Bowl Sunday. In this particular case, advocacy claims were so successful that NBC aired a public service announcement prior to the 1993 Super Bowl reminding viewers that domestic violence is a crime (Oths & Robertson, 2007).

A simple web search for domestic violence "facts" suggests that, while advocates are no longer making claims about the Super Bowl, statistical distortions and oversimplifications remain common. . . . One commonly repeated fact helps illustrate the point: one in four women is a *victim* of domestic *abuse*. The source of this original statistic is the Behavioral Risk Factor

Surveillance System, a telephone survey on health conditions and health risks conducted annually by the Centers for Disease Control and Prevention [CDC] (2008). Twenty-four percent of women report that an intimate has either threatened, attempted, or completed physical violence ("hit, slap, push, kick, otherwise hurt") or sexual violence ("unwanted sex"). Note, however, the subtle difference between what the CDC reports—one in four women *experience violence or attempted violence*—and the more dramatic statistical claim that one in four women is a *victim* of domestic *abuse*. . . .

A final example comes from our own writing. In the first edition of our text *Family Violence Across the Lifespan: An Introduction* (Barnett, Miller-Perrin, & Perrin, 1997), we mentioned the "rule of thumb" because we found it to be a dramatic illustration of historic indifference to the abuse of women. Citing the appropriate sources, we wrote that in English common law, "the 'rule-of-thumb' law gave the husband the right to hit his wife with a rod no thicker than his thumb" (Barnett, Miller-Perrin, & Perrin, 1997, p. 8). We reported this fact just as we had encountered it in numerous discussions. What we did not know when we were writing the book, however, was that there was literature questioning this statement of fact (Kelly, 1994; Sommers, 1994). Given the debate, stating the example as a historical fact was, at the very least, misleading. In the second edition of *Family Violence Across the Lifespan* (Barnett, Miller-Perrin, & Perrin, 2005), we removed reference to the rule of thumb.

Consequences of Claims Making

What, some might argue, is the downside of exaggerated claims making? If doing so brings more attention and resources to conditions that are indeed harmful to individuals and society, are the tactics not justified? After a recent class discussion of the "epidemic" of child abductions discussed above (Best, 1990), one of our students asked just that. "Isn't it a positive outcome," she asked, "if increased awareness about the problem of child abduction, however exaggerated,

led parents to watch their children more closely?" . . .

Her stance is not unreasonable. After all, children are sometimes randomly snatched from homes, supermarkets, and parks. If even one child is protected from harm, one could argue that the advocacy statistics are justified. We maintain, however, that advocacy driven research has the potential to bring about several negative consequences. In the paragraphs that follow, we hypothesize about some of the possible negative consequences of unabashed advocacy.

Damage to the Reputation/Integrity of the Field

When the public *perceives* that social scientists manipulate or misuse data to support certain causes, or that they make claims beyond what the data can justify, one might reasonably assume that public confidence in the social sciences is undermined. One can be deeply concerned about a problem and still wish to see that problem examined objectively and fairly. Indeed, it is the job of social scientists to do just that. Importantly, the passions of social scientists typically do *not* lead to the misuse of data. On those rare occasions, however, when social scientists let their passions interfere with their scholarship, they may unwittingly contribute to skepticism about findings.

Several years ago, our university invited a well-known local radio talk-show host to speak at graduation. Referring to his own distrust of research findings, and citing several examples from the social sciences, he advised the graduating class,

> When you hear the following words: "Studies show" . . . and you find that the studies that are reported show the opposite of what common sense suggests . . . may I tell you I am twice your age and I have been on radio 15 years. And I have debated these issues daily for 15 years. I have never once come across a study that contravenes common sense. Studies either substantiate common sense or they are wrong.

The faculty members in the audience—especially those of us in the social sciences—found his comments to be quite offensive. The fact that he was urging the graduates to do the opposite of what we had just spent 4 years encouraging our students to do in our classes—that is, to be open to empirical findings, especially those that challenge their preconceived notions—was beyond tolerable.

Yet as we suggested in the opening paragraphs of this . . . [reading], social scientists must recognize that we have sometimes brought this criticism on ourselves. "Scientific findings" indicating that 60% of female children are victims of sexual abuse (Russell, 1984) or that 50% of college women are victims of rape or attempted rape (Koss, 1992) may not ring true to people whose everyday interactions suggest otherwise.

Feeding the Backlash

It seems reasonable to argue that the public can more easily dismiss our claims about interpersonal violence if they perceive that the claims are ideologically motivated. Having dismissed the claims, it is easy to dismiss the issues themselves. Arguably, this is what we have seen in the "backlash" movements that have emerged in recent years. Often, backlash movements cite the very advocacy statistics misused by interpersonal violence organizations themselves. . . . For backlash movements, the "real problem" is not child abuse or battered women or date rape, but overly zealous child protectors, or "feminists" intent on pushing a particular social agenda. The people who need to be protected, furthermore, are those who are falsely accused. . . .

The "satanism scare" of the 1980s and 1990s provides an interesting illustration of how exaggerated claims can feed a backlash (Victor, 1993). During the "satanism scare" we heard that a new form of child sexual abuse, satanic ritual abuse (SRA), had been discovered. Numerous experts—including prominent clergy, mental health professionals, and social scientists—argued that thousands of adults had recovered repressed memories of childhood sexual abuse and torture at the hands of satanists. Given the severity of the abuse, they argued, it was likely that hundreds of thousands of victims of satanic ritual abuse had repressed their memories and needed therapy to recover the memories and deal with the trauma (see Victor, 1993, for a review).

Most mainstream social scientists and legal authorities, although acknowledging that the most severe forms of ritualistic abuse do sometimes occur, questioned the claims of a vast satanic conspiracy. Today, the satanism scare is primarily seen as a historically fascinating example of societal contagion. What is interesting in the context of the current discussion is the degree to which the satanism scare fueled a backlash against child sexual abuse. Advocate claims that hundreds of thousands of children were victims of satanic ritual abuse were met by competing advocacy claims that children are rarely if ever sexually abused. Claims that hundreds of thousands of victims of satanic ritualistic abuse had repressed their memories or created multiple personalities were met by counterclaims that one cannot repress memories and multiple personality disorder does not exist. Claims that the traumatic memories could only be recovered in therapy were met by counterclaims that all recovered memories are constructed memories. Most mainstream psychologists would question each of these backlash advocacy claims and provide evidence that sexual abuse is not rare, children do not tend to exaggerate their victimization, one can repress memories, and not all recovered memories are constructed memories (Miller-Perrin & Perrin, 2007).

Undermining Efforts to Identify the Inappropriateness of Normative Violence

The tendency in recent years has been for both academics and advocates to argue for "violence-free" families and to categorize more and more behaviors as inappropriate. Behavior such as corporal punishment and sibling aggression, which occur in most families, have been increasingly condemned as harmful, a trend most family violence researchers (including ourselves) applaud (Miller-Perrin & Perrin, 2007).

Sometimes, however, in our attempt to draw attention to the inappropriateness of normative violence, we may adopt alarmist language that may not serve our cause well. For example, surveys indicate that an overwhelming majority of children are at some time pushed, grabbed, or hit by their siblings. Such "sibling violence" was the subject of increasing concern among family violence scholars during the 1990s (Finkelhor & Dziuba-Leatherman, 1994). However, if one chooses to label sibling aggression as family abuse, then almost all children are victims (and/or perpetrators) of abuse. After all, how many siblings *do not* push, shove, or occasionally hit one another? If sibling pushing constitutes abuse, then most family members are either perpetrators or victims (or both). If nearly everyone is a "victim of abuse" then, arguably, the concept begins to lose its meaning and our claims are likely to be dismissed as unabashed advocacy.

Debates about corporal punishment are also illustrative of this point. . . . Corporal punishment is, in the words of Ian Hassall, "legally sanctioned *assaults*" (Hassall, 2010, p. 81, italics added). One can certainly understand the temptation to challenge convention with strong rhetoric. Indeed, a number of public opinion research studies have demonstrated that even small changes in the presentation of various political or social issues can sometimes produce large changes in opinion (Chong & Druckman, 2007). The problem is that the vast majority of corporal punishment is not assault, at least not from a legal perspective. . . . Calling all corporal punishment assault, while rhetorically powerful, is simply not accurate. And in a culture that overwhelmingly accepts spanking, claims that spanked children are victims of *assault* may fall on deaf ears (see Perrin & Miller-Perrin, 2010).

Conclusions

The notion of value-free inquiry can be traced to the very beginnings of many of the social sciences. Max Weber (1949), one of the founding fathers of sociology, reasoned that if values influence research, the findings will be rejected and the discipline discredited. In contrast, others have recognized that it may not be possible for human beings to conduct research that is completely value free (Kincaid, Dupre, & Wylie, 2007; Risman, 2001; Sheldon, Schmuck, & Kasser, 2000). The debate about whether value-free inquiry is possible is long standing and affects all of the diverse fields of science such as biology, political science, economics, environmental science, psychology, and sociology (Kincaid et al., 2007). Values likely affect many aspects of the scientific process, from the topic chosen, to the type of methodology employed, to the interpretation of the results. This may be especially true of social scientists, many of whom have been drawn to their discipline because they want to make a difference in society.

. . . Can a social scientist be both passionate and objective? If so, how? It is helpful to start with a solid theory of social problem construction, and that is in part what we have attempted to do in this . . . [reading]. The constructionist perspective has been controversial from the beginning, and it is easy to see why. The social constructionist is the "cynic" who asks the question, "says who?" Some may misunderstand the question, assuming that to label a social problem a "social construction" is to say that it is illegitimate and that the harm caused is not real. At the very least, the constructionist may appear to care less about the problem at hand. . . .

The social constructionist perspective encourages us to think of social problems as social products. Conceptualizing problems in this way need not make us cynical or uncaring, but it inevitably leads us to acknowledge that people often have an interest—whether moral or political—in specific issues. Constructionism leads us to ask certain questions and to think critically about the empirical claims we encounter. Who created particular facts or statistics? Why were the statistics or facts created?

The constructionist perspective also encourages social scientists to see themselves as advocates and claims makers.

It is tempting to assume that only "advocates" exaggerate claims and to think that social scientists are above doing so. Social scientists do sometimes hide behind the rhetoric of a commitment to science—to the data—and perceive themselves to be incapable of such distortions. They may even think that what they do as social scientists has nothing to do with what they believe. There is a growing body of recent evidence from philosophy and social studies of science, however, that suggests that this extreme view of the value-free inquiry debate must be tempered by findings suggesting that values affect numerous aspects of the scientific enterprise (Kincaid et al., 2007). As Loseke (2003) reminds us, any discussion of social problems involves moral evaluations: "To say that something is wrong is to take a moral stand. Issues of moral evaluation *always* and *necessarily* lie behind any claims—be they made on the basis of scientific research or not" (p. 35).

There is nothing inherently problematic with passion and advocacy. Indeed, most who study interpersonal violence feel passionately about the cause and are committed to alleviating the suffering of victims. Passions drive our research. Advocacy brings about change. Social scientists should be careful, however, not to let passions contaminate scholarship. When advocacy *replaces* science, claims making can have negative consequences, both for the field of social science and for the public's perceptions of the social problem of interpersonal violence.

NOTES

1. Editor's note: In December 2012, the FBI revised the definition of rape to include "penetration, no matter how slight, of the vagina or anus with any body part or object, or oral penetration by a sex organ of another person, without the consent of the victim." (United States Department of Justice Office of Public Affairs. 2012. "Attorney General Eric Holder Announces Revisions to the Uniform Crime Report's Definition of Rape." http://www.justice.gov/opa/pr/attorney-general-eric-holder-announces-revisions-uniform-crime-report-s-definition-rape)

REFERENCES

Barnett, O., Miller-Perrin, C. & Perrin, R.D. (1997). *Family violence across the lifespan: An introduction.* Newbury Park, CA: Sage Publications.

Barnett, O., Miller-Perrin, C. & Perrin, R.D. (2005). *Family violence across the lifespan: An introduction* (2nd Edition). Newbury Park, CA: Sage Publications

Barnett, O., Miller-Perrin, C. & Perrin, R.D. (2011). *Family violence across the lifespan: An introduction* (3rd Edition). Newbury Park, CA: Sage Publications.

Best, J. (1990). Threatened children: Rhetoric and concern about child-victims. Chicago, IL: University of Chicago Press.

Best, J. (2001a). *Damned lies and statistics: Untangling numbers from the media, politicians, and activists.* Berkeley: University of California Press.

Best, J. (2001b). Promoting bad statistics. *Society, 38*(3), 10–15.

Centers for Disease Control and Prevention. (2008). Adverse health conditions and health risk behaviors associated with intimate partner violence—United States, 2005. *Morbidity and Mortality Weekly Report.* Retrieved from www.cdc.gov/mmwr/preview/mmwrhtml/mm5705a1.htm.

Chong, D., & Druckman, J. N. (2007). Framing theory. *Annual Review of Political Science, 10,* 103–126.

Finkelhor, D., & Dziuba-Leatherman, J. (1994). Victimization of children. *American Psychologist, 49,* 173–183.

Finkelhor, D., Hotaling, G. T., Lewis, I. A., & Smith, C. (1990). Sexual abuse in a national survey of adult men and women: Prevalence, characteristics, and risk factors. *Child Abuse and Neglect, 14,* 19–28.

Gilbert, N. (1997). Advocacy research and social policy. In M. Tonry (Ed.), *Crime and justice: An annual review of research* (pp. 101–148). Chicago, IL: University of Chicago Press.

Hassall, I. (2010). Comment/reply. *International Journal of Child Abuse & Neglect, 34,* 81.

Kelly, H. A. (1994). Rule of thumb and the folklaw of the husband's stick. *Journal of Legal Education, 44*, 341–365.

Koss, M. P. (1992). The underdetection of rape: Methodological choices influence incidence estimates. *Journal of Social Issues, 48*, 61–75.

Kincaid, H., Dupre, J., & Wylie, A. (Eds.). (2007). *Value-free science? Ideals and illusions.* Oxford, UK: Oxford University Press.

Loseke, D. R. (2003). *Thinking about social problems: An introduction to constructionist perspectives* (2nd ed.). Hawthorne, NY: Aldine de Gruyter.

Miller-Perrin, C. & Perrin, R. D. (2007). *Child maltreatment: An introduction.* (2nd edition). Newbury Park, CA: Sage Publications.

North American Man/Boy Love Association. (2011). *Statement of purpose.* Retrieved from http://www.nambla.org/welcome.htm.

Oths, K. S., & Robertson, T. (2007). Give me shelter: Temporal patterns of women fleeing domestic abuse. *Human Organization, 66*(3), 249–260.

Perrin, R. D., & Miller-Perrin, C. (2010). Response to Dr. Hassell. *International Journal of Child Abuse and Neglect, 34*, 82–83.

Risman, B. J. (2001). Calling the bluff of value-free science. *American Sociological Review, 66*, 605–611.

Russell, D. (1984). *Sexual exploitation: Rape, child sexual abuse, and workplace harassment.* Beverly Hills, CA: Sage.

Shah, D. V., Watts, M. D., Domke, D., & Fan, D. P. (2002). News framing and cueing of issue regimes: Explaining Clinton's public approval in spite of scandal. *Public Opinion Quarterly, 66*, 339–370.

Sheldon, K., Schmuck, P., & Kasser, T. (2000). Is value-free science possible? *American Psychologist, 55*, 1152–1153.

Sommers, C. H. (1994). *Who stole feminism? How women have betrayed women.* New York, NY: Simon & Schuster.

Spector, M., & Kitsuse, J. I. (1977). *Constructing social problems.* Menlo Park, CA: Benjamin Cummings.

U.S. Department of Justice, Federal Bureau of Investigation. (2008). *Crime in the United States 2007: Uniform crime reports.* Washington, DC: U.S. Government Printing Office.

Victor, J. S. (1993). *Satanic panic.* Chicago, IL: Open Court.

Weber, M. (1949). *The methodology of the social sciences* (E. Shils & H. Finch, Eds. and Trans.). Glencoe, IL: Free Press.

Terrorism

ZIAD MUNSON

Munson discusses a contemporary social problem that many of us are concerned about, but that often goes unexamined from a critical perspective: terrorism. Munson examines how the term has changed over time, how claimsmakers such as members of the media, politicians, and law enforcement officials shape our understanding of the term, and how the term is understood and used today. By critically assessing our construction of the concept of terrorism and how it is used, Munson offers a roadmap for how we might do the same for other problems.

Terrorism may be the most influential buzzword of the decade. Beyond the obvious connection to national security and the war in Iraq, immigration, taxes, drug trafficking, and even corporate power today are inflected through the prism of terrorism. In many ways it has defined the collective lives of Americans since 2001.

The term "terrorism" originated during the French Revolution (1789–1799) and referred to attempts by the new regime to consolidate its power and intimidate opponents, many of whom were supporters of the old monarchy. The term had a much different connotation then— terrorism was associated with defending new notions of justice and democracy against an old order perceived as tyrannical and corrupt. For more than 100 years, terrorism was a method by which the weak and downtrodden might overcome the powerful and oppressive.

By the eve of World War II, though, terrorism had developed a much different meaning. The term referred to the actions of established government authorities to repress their own people. It was discussed in the context of Nazi Germany, fascist Italy, and Stalinist Russia. Terrorism regained its connection to revolutionary movements after the war, but any positive connotations it once possessed were lost. Today the word is used only in highly pejorative ways to describe actions seen as unjustified, destabilizing, and threatening to justice and democratic institutions.

Most social scientists would agree that terrorism can be defined as violence or the threat of violence directed at noncombatants for political purposes. But such a definition is seldom applied to the public discussion of terrorism. Politicians, the media, religious leaders, and even law enforcement and military officers help construct the meaning of the term by labeling some individuals and events with it, but not others. We find the brutality of terrorism horrifying, but often support the same violence when conducted by police or soldiers. Indeed, we call them heroes.

Our differing reactions result from how the meaning of terrorism has been socially constructed. The social construction of the term also makes it a shifting target in public discussions, subject to the political winds of the time.

Regardless of the definition, the central mechanism in all terrorism is the fear it evokes in a target population. The success of terrorism therefore depends critically not only on attacks themselves, but also on how the targets of terrorism react to attacks. Hysterical rhetoric from political leaders and alarmist, breathless coverage from journalists greatly contribute to the effectiveness of terrorism, and thus the likelihood of terrorist organizations pursuing further attacks. Research after the wave of terrorism in the mid-1980s showed the important role the media play in dramatizing terrorism and making it an effective means of communication. Newspaper and television coverage of attacks changed as a result, in order to minimize these impacts.

Most of what was learned during that time, however, was lost in the wake of the 9/11 attacks. The relentless focus on terrorism and security in public discourse in the United States since then has greatly exaggerated the threat it really poses—and concomitantly raised the level of fear terrorism can evoke. For example, more Americans have died in automobile accidents caused by deer in the last 40 years than all those killed by terrorists, including the attacks on 9/11. That such comparisons come as a surprise to many demonstrates just how effective the fear-mongering surrounding terrorism has been over the past . . . [decade]. Sparking this fear is precisely the goal terrorism seeks to achieve.

Organizations that can exploit such fear lie at the root of the vast majority of terrorist attacks. Individuals rarely decide on their own to bomb a shopping mall or hijack a plane. Terrorism doesn't result from disturbed personalities, psychopaths, or even individual rage or hatred; it's a specific strategy—the violent targeting of non-combatants—organizations choose because they believe it will help them gain recognition, highlight issues they perceive as being ignored,

force concessions from existing power holders, or solidify the allegiance of supporters. Thus, terrorism isn't a random act. It's part of a calculated, and often publicly declared, campaign of opposition to the status quo.

Sociologists, political scientists, and public policy analysts have paid a lot of attention to explaining when and where terrorism occurs. This research shows that organizations choose terrorism only when they or the populations they claim to represent have been previously subjected to significant violence by the state. Indeed this appears to be a prerequisite. Terrorism emerges only in the context of the state attempting to repress its opposition by force. The FARC in Columbia, the IRA in Ireland, the PLO in the Palestinian Territories, and the Tamil Tigers in Sri Lanka all represent populations that experienced significant state violence before an opposition group initiated any terrorist attacks.

If state violence is a necessary condition, however, it isn't on its own sufficient. State violence occurs all the time around the world without groups taking up terrorist campaigns. So what determines when government violence leads to terrorism? The availability of viable alternatives for political expression is an important factor. Terrorism is more likely to emerge in societies in which the population, or some subset of the population, is denied the ability to express political will or discontent. In practice, this means the lack of a democratic electoral process, the right to assembly, an independent media, and a robust civil society that can exert political pressure on behalf of citizens all make terrorism more likely. These factors reduce the available options opposition groups have to address their grievances.

A third important factor is international isolation. Groups well situated in a rich web of transnational connections are less likely to adopt terrorism because of its potential to alienate supporters in other parts of the globe. For example, in Turkey the Milli Görüs, an Islamic opposition group with deep connections to international organizations and European supporters, has never adopted terrorism to further its goals. In contrast

Ibda-C, also an Islamic opposition group in Turkey, but one relatively isolated from the outside world, has orchestrated a string of terrorist attacks. Similarly, the remarkable lack of terrorism by the African National Congress during South Africa's apartheid era can be traced in large part to its extensive ties around the world, including relationships with the Soviet Union and European governments. International allies have a moderating influence on opposition groups, opening up alternative options for accomplishing their goals and reducing the attractiveness of political violence.

Why would anyone join a terrorist group? The primary route into a terrorist organization is no different than the route into any other group—social network ties. People are drawn into violent groups because of who they know, particularly those they already know in the group. Families and friendships are the building blocks of any organization's recruitment of new members. The attraction of getting involved is thus a personal one.

No single "type" of person—with particular personality traits, economic circumstances, or even a certain set of beliefs and values—becomes involved in terrorism. What matters is the social context in which they're embedded. Indeed, very often group members learn the ideology (and hatred) that accompanies terrorism only after they get involved in the first place. Organized groups can shape benign discontent into focused anger and commitment. They offer an alternative narrative of how the world might be if those currently holding power, whether Americans or

Israelis or Colombians or Sri Lankans or anyone else, could just be overthrown through whatever tactics are possible and effective.

Current debates over terrorism have thus far incorporated few insights from existing research. Many liberal-minded people cling to the idea that poverty is the basis for global terrorism, but the reality is that economists have found no significant relationship between poverty and terrorism. More conservative-minded people focus on capturing or killing "evildoers" in order to eliminate terrorism. This view also finds little empirical support—rooting out all potential terrorists is impossible and attempts to stop terror campaigns through military force have been almost universally unsuccessful, even when large numbers of individuals tied to terror organizations are captured or killed. Not only do military strategies designed to punish terrorism or eliminate terrorists fail, they also create and reinforce exactly those conditions that raise the likelihood of terrorism in the future.

People today are well aware that we live in a world in which terrorism is an ever-present threat. But we are less aware that this world didn't begin on 9/11. The threat of terrorism has been with us for many decades and will continue into the future. Understanding the basic definition of terrorism and its social constructions can help us put the threat in proper perspective. Understanding the basic mechanisms responsible for its effectiveness as a strategy—the ability to evoke fear in a population disproportionate to its true threat—can help us better confront the threat and reduce its likelihood in the future.

Making Claims: The Role of Language in the Construction of Social Problems

Kiersten Kummerow

Original to *Focus on Social Problems: A Contemporary Reader.*

If I asked you whether you supported homosexuals serving in the military, what would you say? What if I asked you whether you supported gay men and

lesbians serving in the military? Would your answer change? Are you more concerned about the impact of global warming or climate change? Although on
continued

Continued

the surface it may seem like these terms are identical, people perceive and understand them in very different ways. Word choice is important for anyone trying to convince others of their position, but it is especially critical if you're trying to enact social change. Because language is a powerful tool capable of shaping people's attitudes and beliefs, choosing it strategically makes it easier to make claims about, draw attention to, and ultimately develop solutions for social problems.

Claimsmakers (people who are trying to shape the attitudes of others and convince them that they should be concerned about a particular problem) use language strategically to create a particular picture of what a social problem looks like and what, if anything, should be done about it. Claimsmakers choose language designed to highlight the aspects of a problem they believe are the most important or compelling (Best, 1987). In many cases, claimsmakers will choose words intended to elicit an emotional response. After all, they are trying to convince people to care about what they are saying (Best, 2013). The words we choose shape the way we interpret and feel about a social problem, whether we believe a solution is working, and even whether we believe a problem is real or deserving of our attention.

GAY MEN AND LESBIANS VERSUS HOMOSEXUALS

Words with the same meaning can have significantly different connotations in a particular culture. One example of the way similar words develop different undertones is the way the terms "homosexual" and "gay men and lesbians" are used in public discourse. A CBS/*New York Times* poll found that people responded differently when asked whether they favored or opposed permitting homosexuals to serve in the military than when asked whether they favored or opposed permitting gay men and lesbians to serve in the military. When the question used the terms gay men and lesbians, just over 50 percent of the respondents said they strongly favored it and only 12 percent said they strongly opposed.

When the question used the term homosexuals, only 34 percent of the respondents said they strongly favored it and 19 percent said they strongly opposed (Wade, 2010).[1]

This disparity resulting from language suggests that there are negative connotations to the term homosexual. At this moment in history, many people including academics, journalists, and many members of the lesbian, gay, bisexual, and transgender (LGBT) community tend to see the term homosexual as a more negative term than the terms gay men and lesbians. In 2006, the organization Gay and Lesbian Alliance against Defamation successfully lobbied the Associated Press to restrict use of the term homosexual because of the negative connotations of the term. Because the Associated Press style guide is used by many news organizations, the term is being used less and less frequently in the media (Peters, 2014).

There are several possible reasons that the term homosexual has come to be seen as negative. The first reason is that the term homosexual contains the word "sex," whereas neither the word gay nor lesbian does. This may draw attention to the sexualized aspects of the term, whereas the words gay and lesbian do not. Another possible explanation is that the term "homo" has a history as a derogatory term. The negative associations with this term may still exist because conservative pundits frequently use the term homosexual in disparaging ways. A final explanation for the negative associations with the term homosexual is the association of this word with the American Psychiatric Association's designation of same-sex attraction as a mental disorder until 1973. Members of the LGBT community prefer the terms gay and lesbian. The term gay, a synonym for joyful, was initially used as a code word for identifying same-sex desires to others who also knew the code. Because the alternate meaning of gay was positive, this term generally has more positive associations than the term homosexual (Peters, 2014).

Although the terms gay men and lesbians and homosexual have nearly identical definitions, they have different meanings and evoke different emotional responses. Determining the different responses words can elicit is critical for claimsmakers. In this instance there are strong emotional responses associated with the terms homosexual and gay men and lesbians, and claimsmakers interested in addressing issues concerning the LGBT community must be thoughtful about which words to use. A claimsmaker arguing in favor of legalizing marriage for gay men and lesbians would be better off choosing to use the term "gay marriage" or the more inclusive term "same-sex marriage," whereas someone opposed may wish to use the term "homosexual marriage."

GLOBAL WARMING VERSUS CLIMATE CHANGE

Word choice also makes a difference in how the public receives and assesses scientific information. The terms "global warming" and "climate change" are often used interchangeably in public discussions and in polls about the topic. However, just because they are used interchangeably does not mean people have the same associations with each term. People are more likely to report they think the phenomenon is "real" when they are asked about climate change than when they are asked about global warming (Schuldt et al., 2011). This discrepancy may exist because for many people the term global warming implies temperature increases; when regions are experiencing record low temperatures and record snowfalls it is much easier to believe the planet is not warming. The term climate change is more flexible and could potentially include both lower and upper extremes in temperature (Schuldt et al., 2011).

The different interpretations of these two terms are particularly interesting because there are strong political associations with each one. In one study, researchers found that conservative websites were more likely to use the term global warming (in an attempt to dismiss it) when discussing the phenomenon, whereas liberal websites were more likely to use the term climate change (in an effort to encourage others to recognize it) (Schuldt et al., 2011). These political connections

are important because people with different political affiliations differ in how they respond to the different terminology. People who identified as Democrats or as Independents reported believing the phenomenon was real at about the same rate regardless of whether it was called global warming or climate change. For example, nearly 87 percent of Democrats reported believing in the phenomenon regardless of whether the question was framed as either global warming or climate change. Independents differed slightly, with nearly 70 percent believing in global warming and 74 percent believing in climate change. The difference is much more dramatic, however, for self-identified Republicans, with 44 percent of Republicans believing in global warming and 60 percent believing in climate change (Schuldt et al., 2011). Claimsmakers should take note. Individuals and organizations that want to draw attention to and combat the phenomenon may make more headway by recognizing that the two terms have different interpretations and should consciously choose to use the term climate change instead of the term global warming. Note that even when claimsmakers have successfully garnered recognition and support for a social problem, word choice remains critical when advocating for specific solutions.

AFFORDABLE CARE ACT VERSUS OBAMACARE

Even if you recognize that our population's lack of health insurance coverage is a social problem, how claimsmakers frame solutions to such a problem will influence their acceptance. An example of this in action can be found in the discussion on the Patient Protection and Affordable Care Act, federal health care legislation passed in 2010. Two different terms for this legislation have become common in the public discourse: "the Affordable Care Act" (the ACA) and "Obamacare." These two terms refer to the same legislation, but people respond differently to each name. Obamacare has a lower level of support than the ACA does; a Gallup poll found that while 45 percent of Americans approved of the ACA, only 38 percent of people approved of
continued

■ Continued

Obamacare. The poll also found a higher disapproval rate for Obamacare than for the ACA (Newport, 2013).

This is a useful case because it illustrates how terms develop positive and negative associations over time as a result of claims-making. The negative associations with the term Obamacare were deliberately crafted. A Republican strategist argued that people want their health care to be personal and the term Obamacare was intentionally designed to link the president to the legislation and make the health care reform seem more political and less personal (Baker, 2012; Obernauer, 2013). In an effort to try to reclaim the term, Democrats started using it in 2012 (Baker, 2012). Even President Obama tried to put a positive spin on it. In 2012 he said "The Affordable Health Care Act—otherwise known as Obamacare—was the right thing to do. And you know what, they're right, I do care" (Obama, 2012). However, since then there has been a shift in the way Democrats have been using the term. Instead of trying to reclaim Obamacare, Democrats started using the term the ACA instead. In his 2014 State of the Union speech, President Obama referred to the health care reform as the ACA rather than as Obamacare (Obama, 2014a). However, at some point after the 2014 State of the Union address, President Obama made another effort to reclaim the term Obamacare and change the negative association with it (Obama, 2014b). Understanding the different associations is critical for claimsmakers interested in future developments in health-care reform. If the attempt to change the negative associations with Obamacare is successful, then claimsmakers trying to raise the levels of support for this legislation could use this term. If the attempt is not successful, these claimsmakers should consider using the term ACA instead.

CONCLUSION

Social problems do not exist in a vacuum. The ways in which we describe social problems influence the ways in which people respond to them. Even words that seem to mean the same thing can evoke different emotions and beliefs depending on who is reading or hearing them. Claimsmakers carefully and deliberately choose their words when taking a position on social problems. They select the words that will create the desired emotional response in people who listen to their claims (Best, 2013). By strategically choosing words to evoke particular responses, claimsmakers can shape the feelings people have about a certain topic and can even change whether people believe their claims are true. No matter which problems people are interested in solving, they must consider which words they will use to convince people that their claims are the best and that their solutions should be implemented.

NOTES

1. Results were obtained from a nationwide telephone poll of 1084 adults. Researchers asked 550 of those 1,084 respondents: "Do you favor or oppose permitting homosexuals to serve in the military? Do you favor/oppose that strongly or not so strongly?" Researchers asked 534 of those 1,084 respondents: "Do you favor or oppose permitting gay men and lesbians to serve in the military? Do you favor/oppose that strongly or not so strongly?" (*New York Times*, CBS News Poll, February 5–10, 2010). This suggests that the different results were a result of the language used in the question rather than a result of differences in the sample.

REFERENCES

Baker, Peter. 2012. "Democrats Embrace Once Pejorative 'Obamacare' Tag." *The New York Times*, p. A11.

Best, Joel. 1987. "Rhetoric in Claims-Making: Constructing the Missing Children Problem." *Social Problems* 34:101–121.

Best, Joel. 2013. *Social Problems*. New York: Norton.

Newport, Frank. 2013. "What's in a Name? Affordable Care Act vs. Obamacare." Vol. 2015: Gallup.

Obama, Barack. 2012. "Remarks by the President at Campaign Event in San Antonio, TX." The White House: Office of the Press Secretary.

Obama, Barack. 2014a. "President Barack Obama's State of the Union Address." The White House: Office of the Press Secretary.

Obama, Barack. 2014b. "Remarks by the President at Rally for Gary Peters and Mark Schauer—Detroit, Michigan." The White House: Office of the Press Secretary.

Obernauer, Charlene. 2013. "'Obamacare' vs. 'Affordable Care Act': Why Words Matter." Vol. 2015: Huffington Post.

Peters, Jeremy W. 2014. "The Decline and Fall of the 'H' Word: For Many Gays and Lesbians, the Term 'Homosexual' is Flinch-Worthy." *The New York Times*, p. ST10.

Schuldt, Jonathon P., Sara H. Konrath, and Norbert Schwarz. 2011. "'Global Warming' or 'Climate Change'?: Whether the Planet Is Warming Depends on Question Wording." *Public Opinion Quarterly* 75:115–124.

Wade, Lisa. 2010. "Survey Finds Different Levels of Acceptance for 'Gays' versus 'Homosexuals.'" in *Sociological Images: Inspiring Sociological Imaginations Everywhere*, Vol. 2014.

Telling the Truth about Damned Lies and Statistics

JOEL BEST

An essential part of the social construction of social problems involves quantifying the nature of the problem: the number and characteristics of people affected, the level of harm, and the cost of alleviating the problem. Statistics are often helpful in this process, as they are generally meant to objectively measure these concerns. But as Joel Best points out, these statistics can be poorly constructed, misinterpreted, and misunderstood. Best encourages us to be critical consumers of statistics by thoughtfully considering both the limits of and the uses for statistical claims.

The dissertation prospectus began by quoting a statistic—a "grabber" meant to capture the reader's attention. The graduate student who wrote this prospectus undoubtedly wanted to seem scholarly to the professors who would read it; they would be supervising the proposed research. And what could be more scholarly than a nice, authoritative statistic, quoted from a professional journal in the student's field?

So the prospectus began with this (carefully footnoted) quotation: "Every year since 1950, the number of American children gunned down has doubled." I had been invited to serve on the student's dissertation committee. When I read the quotation, I assumed the student had made an error in copying it. I went to the library and looked up the article the student had cited. There, in the journal's 1995 volume, was exactly the same sentence: "Every year since 1950, the number of American children gunned down has doubled."

This quotation is my nomination for a dubious distinction: I think it may be the worst—that is, the most inaccurate—social statistic ever.

What makes this statistic so bad? Just for the sake of argument, let's assume that "the number of American children gunned down" in 1950 was one. If the number doubled each year, there must have been two children gunned down in 1951, four in 1952, eight in 1953, and so on. By 1960, the number would have been 1,024. By 1965, it would have been 32,768 (in 1965, the F.B.I. identified only 9,960 criminal homicides in the entire country, including adult as well as child victims). By 1970, the number would have passed one million; by 1980, one billion (more than four times the total U.S. population in that year). Only three years later, in 1983, the number

Excerpted from Joel Best, "Introduction: The Worst Social Statistic Ever" in *Damned Lies and Statistics: Untangling Issues from the Media, Politicians, and Activists*, © 2012 by the Regents of the University of California, University of California Press.

of American children gunned down would have been 8.6 billion (nearly twice the earth's population at the time). Another milestone would have been passed in 1987, when the number of gunned-down American children (137 billion) would have surpassed the best estimates for the total human population throughout history (110 billion). By 1995, when the article was published, the annual number of victims would have been over 35 trillion—a really big number, of a magnitude you rarely encounter outside economics or astronomy.

Thus my nomination: estimating the number of American child gunshot victims in 1995 at 35 trillion must be as far off—as hilariously, wildly wrong—as a social statistic can be. (If anyone spots a more inaccurate social statistic, I'd love to hear about it.)

Where did the article's author get this statistic? I wrote the author, who responded that the statistic came from the Children's Defense Fund, a well-known advocacy group for children. The C.D.F.'s *The State of America's Children Yearbook 1994* does state: "The number of American children killed each year by guns has doubled since 1950." Note the difference in the wording—the C.D.F. claimed there were twice as many deaths in 1994 as in 1950; the article's author reworded that claim and created a very different meaning.

It is worth examining the history of this statistic. It began with the C.D.F. noting that child gunshot deaths had doubled from 1950 to 1994. This is not quite as dramatic an increase as it might seem. Remember that the U.S. population also rose throughout this period; in fact, it grew about 73 percent—or nearly double. Therefore, we might expect all sorts of things—including the number of child gunshot deaths—to increase, to nearly double, just because the population grew. Before we can decide whether twice as many deaths indicate that things are getting worse, we'd have to know more. The C.D.F. statistic raises other issues as well: Where did the statistic come from? Who counts child gunshot deaths, and how? What is meant by a "child"

(some C.D.F. statistics about violence include everyone under age 25)? What is meant by "killed by guns" (gunshot-death statistics often include suicides and accidents, as well as homicides)? But people rarely ask questions of this sort when they encounter statistics. Most of the time, most people simply accept statistics without question.

Certainly, the article's author didn't ask many probing, critical questions about the C.D.F.'s claim. Impressed by the statistic, the author repeated it—well, meant to repeat it. Instead, by rewording the C.D.F.'s claim, the author created a mutant statistic, one garbled almost beyond recognition.

But people treat mutant statistics just as they do other statistics—that is, they usually accept even the most implausible claims without question. For example, the journal editor who accepted the author's article for publication did not bother to consider the implications of child victims doubling each year. And people repeat bad statistics: The graduate student copied the garbled statistic and inserted it into the dissertation prospectus. Who knows whether still other readers were impressed by the author's statistic and remembered it or repeated it? The article remains on the shelf in hundreds of libraries, available to anyone who needs a dramatic quote. The lesson should be clear: Bad statistics live on; they take on lives of their own.

Some statistics are born bad—they aren't much good from the start, because they are based on nothing more than guesses or dubious data. Other statistics mutate; they become bad after being mangled (as in the case of the author's creative rewording). Either way, bad statistics are potentially important: They can be used to stir up public outrage or fear; they can distort our understanding of our world; and they can lead us to make poor policy choices.

The notion that we need to watch out for bad statistics isn't new. We've all heard people say, "You can prove anything with statistics." The title of my book, *Damned Lies and Statistics*, comes from a famous aphorism (usually attributed to Mark Twain or Benjamin Disraeli):

"There are three kinds of lies: lies, damned lies, and statistics." There is even a useful little book, still in print after more than 40 years, called *How to Lie with Statistics.*

Statistics, then, have a bad reputation. We suspect that statistics may be wrong, that people who use statistics may be "lying"—trying to manipulate us by using numbers to somehow distort the truth. Yet, at the same time, we need statistics; we depend upon them to summarize and clarify the nature of our complex society. This is particularly true when we talk about social problems. Debates about social problems routinely raise questions that demand statistical answers: Is the problem widespread? How many people—and which people—does it affect? Is it getting worse? What does it cost society? What will it cost to deal with it? Convincing answers to such questions demand evidence, and that usually means numbers, measurements, statistics.

But can't you prove anything with statistics? It depends on what "prove" means. If we want to know, say, how many children are "gunned down" each year, we can't simply guess—pluck a number from thin air: 100, 1,000, 10,000, 35 trillion, whatever. Obviously, there's no reason to consider an arbitrary guess "proof" of anything. However, it might be possible for someone—using records kept by police departments or hospital emergency rooms or coroners—to keep track of children who have been shot; compiling careful, complete records might give us a fairly accurate idea of the number of gunned-down children. If that number seems accurate enough, we might consider it very strong evidence—or proof.

The solution to the problem of bad statistics is not to ignore all statistics, or to assume that every number is false. Some statistics are bad, but others are pretty good, and we need statistics— good statistics—to talk sensibly about social problems. The solution, then, is not to give up on statistics, but to become better judges of the numbers we encounter. We need to think critically about statistics—at least critically enough to suspect that the number of children gunned down hasn't been doubling each year since 1950.

A few years ago, the mathematician John Allen Paulos wrote *Innumeracy*, a short, readable book about "mathematical illiteracy." Too few people, he argued, are comfortable with basic mathematical principles, and this makes them poor judges of the numbers they encounter. No doubt this is one reason we have so many bad statistics. But there are other reasons, as well.

Social statistics describe society, but they are also products of our social arrangements. The people who bring social statistics to our attention have reasons for doing so; they inevitably want something, just as reporters and the other media figures who repeat and publicize statistics have their own goals. Statistics are tools, used for particular purposes. Thinking critically about statistics requires understanding their place in society.

While we may be more suspicious of statistics presented by people with whom we disagree— people who favor different political parties or have different beliefs—bad statistics are used to promote all sorts of causes. Bad statistics come from conservatives on the political right and liberals on the left, from wealthy corporations and powerful government agencies, and from advocates of the poor and the powerless.

In order to interpret statistics, we need more than a checklist of common errors. We need a general approach, an orientation, a mind-set that we can use to think about new statistics that we encounter. We ought to approach statistics thoughtfully. This can be hard to do, precisely because so many people in our society treat statistics as fetishes. We might call this the mind-set of the awestruck—the people who don't think critically, who act as though statistics have magical powers. The awestruck know they don't always understand the statistics they hear, but this doesn't bother them. After all, who can expect to understand magical numbers? The reverential fatalism of the awestruck is not thoughtful—it is a way of avoiding thought. We need a different approach.

One choice is to approach statistics critically. Being critical does not mean being negative or hostile—it is not cynicism. The critical approach statistics thoughtfully; they avoid the extremes of both naive acceptance and cynical rejection of the numbers they encounter. Instead, the critical attempt to evaluate numbers, to distinguish between good statistics and bad statistics.

The critical understand that, while some social statistics may be pretty good, they are never perfect. Every statistic is a way of summarizing complex information into relatively simple numbers. Inevitably, some information, some of the complexity, is lost whenever we use statistics. The critical recognize that this is an inevitable limitation of statistics. Moreover, they realize that every statistic is the product of choices—the choice between defining a category broadly or narrowly, the choice of one measurement over another, the choice of a sample. People choose definitions, measurements, and samples for all sorts of reasons: Perhaps they want to emphasize some aspect of a problem; perhaps it is easier or cheaper to gather data in a particular way—many considerations can come into play. Every statistic is a compromise among choices. This means that every definition—and every measurement and every sample—probably has limitations and can be criticized.

Being critical means more than simply pointing to the flaws in a statistic. Again, every statistic has flaws. The issue is whether a particular statistic's flaws are severe enough to damage its usefulness. Is the definition so broad that it encompasses too many false positives (or so narrow that it excludes too many false negatives)? How would changing the definition alter the statistic? Similarly, how do the choices of measurements and samples affect the statistic? What would happen if different measures or samples were chosen? And how is the statistic used? Is it being interpreted appropriately, or has its meaning been mangled to create a mutant statistic? Are the comparisons that are being made appropriate, or are apples being confused with oranges? How do different choices produce the conflicting numbers found in stat wars? These are the sorts of questions the critical ask.

As a practical matter, it is virtually impossible for citizens in contemporary society to avoid statistics about social problems. Statistics arise in all sorts of ways, and in almost every case the people promoting statistics want to persuade us. Activists use statistics to convince us that social problems are serious and deserve our attention and concern. Charities use statistics to encourage donations. Politicians use statistics to persuade us that they understand society's problems and that they deserve our support. The media use statistics to make their reporting more dramatic, more convincing, more compelling. Corporations use statistics to promote and improve their products. Researchers use statistics to document their findings and support their conclusions. Those with whom we agree use statistics to reassure us that we're on the right side, while our opponents use statistics to try and convince us that we are wrong. Statistics are one of the standard types of evidence used by people in our society.

It is not possible simply to ignore statistics, to pretend they don't exist. That sort of head-in-the-sand approach would be too costly. Without statistics, we limit our ability to think thoughtfully about our society; without statistics, we have no accurate ways of judging how big a problem may be, whether it is getting worse, or how well the policies designed to address that problem actually work. And awestruck or naive attitudes toward statistics are no better than ignoring statistics; statistics have no magical properties, and it is foolish to assume that all statistics are equally valid. Nor is a cynical approach the answer; statistics are too widespread and too useful to be automatically discounted.

It would be nice to have a checklist, a set of items we could consider in evaluating any statistic. The list might detail potential problems with definitions, measurements, sampling, mutation, and so on. These are, in fact, common sorts of flaws found in many statistics, but they should not be considered a formal, complete checklist. It is probably impossible to produce a complete list of statistical flaws—no matter how long the list, there will be other possible problems that could affect statistics.

The goal is not to memorize a list, but to develop a thoughtful approach. Becoming critical about statistics requires being prepared to ask questions about numbers. When encountering a new statistic in, say, a news report, the critical try to assess it. What might be the sources for this number? How could one go about producing the figure? Who produced the number, and what interests might they have? What are the different ways key terms might have been defined, and which definitions have been chosen? How might the phenomena be measured, and which measurement choices have been made? What sort of sample was gathered, and how might that sample affect the result? Is the statistic being properly interpreted? Are comparisons being made, and if so, are the comparisons appropriate? Are there competing statistics? If so, what stakes do the opponents have in the issue, and how are those stakes likely to affect their use of statistics? And is it possible to figure out why the statistics seem to disagree, what the differences are in the ways the competing sides are using figures?

At first, this list of questions may seem overwhelming. How can an ordinary person—someone who reads a statistic in a magazine article or hears it on a news broadcast—determine the answers to such questions? Certainly news reports rarely give detailed information on the processes by which statistics are created. And few of us have time to drop everything and investigate the background of some new number we encounter. Being critical, it seems, involves an impossible amount of work.

In practice, however, the critical need not investigate the origin of every statistic. Rather, being critical means appreciating the inevitable limitations that affect all statistics, rather than being awestruck in the presence of numbers. It means not being too credulous, not accepting every statistic at face value. But it also means appreciating that statistics, while always imperfect, can be useful. Instead of automatically discounting every statistic, the critical reserve judgment. When confronted with an interesting number, they may try to learn more, to evaluate, to weigh the figure's strengths and weaknesses.

Of course, this critical approach need not—and should not—be limited to statistics. It ought to apply to all the evidence we encounter when we scan a news report, or listen to a speech—whenever we learn about social problems. Claims about social problems often feature dramatic, compelling examples; the critical might ask whether an example is likely to be a typical case or an extreme, exceptional instance. Claims about social problems often include quotations from different sources, and the critical might wonder why those sources have spoken and why they have been quoted: Do they have particular expertise? Do they stand to benefit if they influence others? Claims about social problems usually involve arguments about the problem's causes and potential solutions. The critical might ask whether these arguments are convincing. Are they logical? Does the proposed solution seem feasible and appropriate? And so on. Being critical—adopting a skeptical, analytical stance when confronted with claims—is an approach that goes far beyond simply dealing with statistics.

Statistics are not magical. Nor are they always true—or always false. Nor need they be incomprehensible. Adopting a critical approach offers an effective way of responding to the numbers we are sure to encounter. Being critical requires more thought, but failing to adopt a critical mind-set makes us powerless to evaluate what others tell us. When we fail to think critically, the statistics we hear might just as well be magical.

Core American Values

Stiv Wilson

Stiv Wilson is the director of campaigns for the Story of Stuff Project.

What is your organization and its mission?

The Story of Stuff Project is a community of 800,000 changemakers worldwide, working to build a more healthy and just planet. Together, we believe it's possible to create a society based on better, not more; sharing, not selfishness; and community, not division. We invite you to be inspired by and share our informational movies, participate in our study programs available on the Story of Stuff website, and take part in our campaigns on the issues you care about.

How did you first become interested in this type of activism?

I learned about the plastic pollution issue from being a surfer in the Pacific Northwest. At the time, I was a journalist, and I started researching and writing about the issue of plastic pollution. But writing wasn't enough. I started to act, as I realized just providing information on the issue wasn't leading to measurable conservation outcomes. I joined the Surfrider Foundation and started a plastic bag ban campaign in my then

hometown, Portland, Oregon. As the campaign grew wings, we ultimately were successful in banning plastic bags. But I wanted to see how plastic was affecting the oceans. I found a group of individuals setting out to sail around the world to study plastic in all the oceans. What I saw out there, the vast blue beyond, changed my life, and I went from journalist to activist. It blew my mind that so much human plastic garbage could be so far out in the ocean—two weeks from land. To me, plastic pollution was the canary in the coal mine—a visual representation of the human ability to corrupt nature profoundly, suggesting the role humans play in so many other sources of pollution, such as climate change.

As an activist in your organization, currently what are your top goals?

Banning plastic microbeads in personal care products designed to be washed down the drain. They escape sewage treatment and directly enter the environment. Once there, they concentrate toxins present in the water like pesticides, flame retardants, and oil from your car. Animals mistake the beads for food and after they ingest them, the toxins can transfer to their tissues and magnify up the food chain, to us!

Stopping plastic from being burned for energy. The Environmental Protection Agency (EPA) has created a loophole in the Clean Air Act for industry to burn plastic garbage in energy plants.

Working to get appliance manufacturers to design all future washing machines to filter fiber discharge from the wastewater stream, preventing microfibers from synthetic fabrics from entering the environment. This is the largest source, by count, of plastic pollution in the environment.

What strategies do you use to enact social change?

Our model is simple—we create award-winning films about difficult issues in a palpable, nonpartisan way, as an outreach mechanism to mobilize citizens to civic engagement to create change.

What are the major challenges activists in your field face?

There is a mantra all activists must live by—"constant pressure endlessly applied." I would say the biggest barrier to making positive change in the world is the fact that so much money is given by industry to elect sympathetic candidates. We work to get money out of politics. There is also a huge lack of understanding of the scientific evidence relating to many environmental issues.

What are major misconceptions the public has about activism?

I think the public tends to think of activists as extremist and anti-business. This may have been the case in the 1960s, but the new generation of activists understands our economic drivers, and we're looking to create a landscape for sustainable, triple bottom line business (businesses that account for the social, environmental, and financial "bottom lines") to replace the solely profit-driven, polluting type. We cannot have a

linear growth model on a finite planet, and there is certainly no business to be done on a dead planet.

With regard to plastic pollution, we have been trained to "throw away" our plastic garbage, but the reality is, there is no "away." Recycling is a small part of the solution. We simply use too much plastic and sometimes only for mere seconds (such as disposable water bottles). The products made from recycled plastic are often much longer-lasting and durable (e.g., decking material, park benches, or fleece jackets) than the single-use items from which they are made. Thus, the system of supply and demand doesn't work when the supply of plastic and other materials *to be* recycled outstrips the demand for products *made from* recyclable materials.

Why should students get involved in your line of activism?

Young people will inherit the sins against our planet from previous generations. You, as students, should be the change you want to see in the world because if you don't "do it" who will? We are a government by and for the people and students need to remember that they are the "we" in "we the people." Besides, elected officials listen to young people more than adults. The youth of today, engaged in change, have so much more power than they even understand.

What would you consider to be your greatest successes as an activist?

I have contributed to victories on plastic bag and styrofoam to-go container bans in dozens of cities. I also created a campaign to ban bottled water in national parks. My campaign to ban microbeads in personal care products is currently in 22 state legislatures.

If an individual has little money and time, are there other ways they can contribute?

Absolutely! Very few people have a lot of money and a lot of time. The first thing you need to do is figure out what to target to change the policy or issue that you care about. Then you organize amongst your friends to build a group. You can start petitions or create campaign videos and graphics to share on social media. A journey of a thousand miles begins with one step.

What ways can students enact social change in their daily lives?

Gandhi said, "be the change you want to see in the world." The first step is to model behavior on the issues you care about. If you don't like plastic pollution, you can make a big difference by using reusable bags, coffee cups, straws, cutlery and water bottles. The average per capita consumption of plastic in the United States is 326 pounds of plastic per year. Half of that is intended for single use. By taking reusables with you and promoting that behavior change in your network, you can dramatically reduce your plastic footprint and the footprints of others.

The Way We Were: Rethinking the American Dream

DAVID KAMP

Kamp discusses a uniquely American concept—the "American Dream"—and describes how it originated and has changed over time. From its origins with a focus on egalitarianism and prosperity for everyone to an ideal of consumerism, wealth, and fame, Kamp argues that the American Dream has become a "moving target" that drives us into debt, threatening the sustainability of the middle class for future generations. We need to consider, he says, what core values the American Dream should embody and how we can make the Dream accessible and achievable for all.

The year was 1930, a down one like this one. But for Moss Hart, it was the time for his particularly American moment of triumph. He had grown up poor in the outer boroughs of New York City—"the grim smell of actual want always at the end of my nose," he said—and he'd vowed that if he ever made it big he would never again ride the rattling trains of the city's dingy subway system. Now he was 25, and his first play, *Once in a Lifetime*, had just opened to raves on Broadway. And so, with three newspapers under his arm and a wee-hours celebration of a successful opening night behind him, he hailed a cab and took a long, leisurely sunrise ride back to the apartment in Brooklyn where he still lived with his parents and brother.

Crossing the Brooklyn Bridge into one of the several drab tenement neighborhoods that preceded his own, Hart later recalled, "I stared through the taxi window at a pinch-faced 10-year-old hurrying down the steps on some morning errand before school, and I thought of myself hurrying down the street on so many gray mornings out of a doorway and a house much the same as this one. . . . It was possible in this wonderful city for that nameless little boy—for any of its millions—to have a decent chance to scale the walls and achieve what they wished. Wealth, rank, or an imposing name counted for nothing. The only credential the city asked was the boldness to dream."

As the boy ducked into a tailor shop, Hart recognized that this narrative was not exclusive to his "wonderful city"—it was one that could happen anywhere in, and only in, America. "A surge of shamefaced patriotism overwhelmed me," Hart wrote in his memoir, *Act One*. "I might have been watching a victory parade on a flag-draped Fifth Avenue instead of the mean streets of a city slum. A feeling of patriotism, however, is not always limited to the feverish emotions called forth by war. It can sometimes be felt as profoundly and perhaps more truly at a moment such as this."

Hart, like so many before and after him, was overcome by the power of the American Dream. As a people, we Americans are unique in having such a thing, a more or less Official National Dream. (There is no correspondingly stirring Canadian Dream or Slovakian Dream.) It is part of our charter—as articulated in the second sentence of the Declaration of Independence, in the famous bit about "certain unalienable Rights" that include "Life, Liberty and the pursuit of Happiness"—and it is what makes our country and our way of life attractive and magnetic to people in other lands. But now fast-forward to the year 2009, the final Friday of January. The new president is surveying the dire economy he has been charged with righting—600,000 jobs lost in January alone, a gross domestic product that shrank 3.8 percent in the final quarter of 2008, the worst contraction in almost 30 years. Assessing these numbers, Barack Obama, a man who normally exudes hopefulness for a living, pronounces them a "continuing disaster for America's working families," a disaster that amounts to no less, he says, than "the American Dream in reverse."

In reverse. Imagine this in terms of Hart's life: out of the taxicab, back on the subway, back to the tenements, back to cramped cohabitation with Mom and Dad, back to gray mornings and the grim smell of actual want.

You probably don't even have to imagine, for chances are that of late you have experienced some degree of reversal yourself, or at the very least have had friends or loved ones get laid off, lose their homes, or just find themselves forced to give up certain perks and amenities (restaurant meals, cable TV, salon haircuts) that were taken for granted as recently as a year ago.

These are tough times for the American Dream. As the safe routines of our lives have come undone, so has our characteristic optimism—not only our belief that the future is full of limitless possibility, but our faith that things will eventually return to normal, whatever "normal" was

before the recession hit. There is even worry that the dream may be over—that we currently living Americans are the unfortunate ones who shall bear witness to that deflating moment in history when the promise of this country began to wither. This is the "sapping of confidence" that President Obama alluded to in his inaugural address, the "nagging fear that America's decline is inevitable, and that the next generation must lower its sights."

But let's face it: If Moss Hart, like so many others, was able to rally from the depths of the Great Depression, then surely the viability of the American Dream isn't in question. What needs to change is our expectation of what the dream promises—and our understanding of what that vague and promiscuously used term, "the American Dream," is really supposed to mean.

In recent years, the term has often been interpreted to mean "making it big" or "striking it rich." . . . Even when the phrase isn't being used to describe the accumulation of great wealth, it's frequently deployed to denote extreme success of some kind or other. Last year, I heard commentators say that Barack Obama achieved the American Dream by getting elected president, and that Philadelphia Phillies manager Charlie Manuel achieved the American Dream by leading his team to its first World Series title since 1980.

Yet there was never any promise or intimation of extreme success in the book that popularized the term, *The Epic of America*, by James Truslow Adams, published . . . in 1931. (Yes, "the American Dream" is a surprisingly recent coinage; you'd think that these words would appear in the writings of Thomas Jefferson or Benjamin Franklin, but they don't.) . . . Adams's goal wasn't so much to put together a proper history of the U.S. as to determine, by tracing his country's path to prominence, what makes this land so unlike other nations, so uniquely American. . . . What Adams came up with was a construct he called "that American dream of a better, richer, and happier life for all our citizens of every rank."

From the get-go, Adams emphasized the egalitarian nature of this dream. It started to take shape, he said, with the Puritans who fled religious persecution in England and settled New England in the 17th century. "[Their] migration was not like so many earlier ones in history, led by warrior lords with followers dependent on them," he wrote, "but was one in which the common man as well as the leader was hoping for greater freedom and happiness for himself and his children."

The Declaration of Independence took this concept even further, for it compelled the well-to-do upper classes to put the common man on an equal footing with them where human rights and self-governance were concerned. . . . America was truly a new world, a place where one could live one's life and pursue one's goals unburdened by older societies' prescribed ideas of class, caste, and social hierarchy. Adams was unreserved in his wonderment over this fact . . . noting a French guest's remark that his most striking impression of the United States was "the way that everyone of every sort looks you right in the eye, without a thought of inequality . . ."

Anecdotal as these examples are, they get to the crux of the American Dream as Adams saw it: that life in the United States offered personal liberties and opportunities to a degree unmatched by any other country in history—a circumstance that remains true today, some ill-considered clampdowns in the name of Homeland Security notwithstanding. This invigorating sense of possibility, though it is too often taken for granted, is the great gift of Americanness. Even Adams underestimated it. Not above the prejudices of his time, he certainly never saw Barack Obama's presidency coming. While he correctly anticipated the eventual assimilation of the millions of Eastern and Southern European immigrants who arrived in the early 20th century to work in America's factories, mines, and sweatshops, he entertained no such hopes for black people. Or, as he rather injudiciously put it, "After a generation or two, [the white-ethnic laborers] can be absorbed, whereas the negro cannot."

It's also worth noting that Adams did not deny that there is a material component to the

American Dream. *The Epic of America* offers several variations on Adams's definition of the dream (e.g., "the American dream that life should be made richer and fuller for everyone and opportunity remain open to all"), but the word "richer" appears in all of them, and he wasn't just talking about richness of experience. Yet Adams was careful not to overstate what the dream promises. In one of his final iterations of the "American Dream" trope, he described it as "that dream of a land in which life should be better and richer and fuller for every man, with opportunity for each according to his ability or achievement."

That last part—"according to his ability or achievement"—is the tempering phrase, a shrewd bit of expectations management. A "better and richer life" is promised, but for most people this won't be a rich person's life. "Opportunity for each" is promised, but within the bounds of each person's ability; the reality is, some people will realize the American Dream more stupendously and significantly than others. (For example, while President Obama is correct in saying, "Only in America is my story possible," this does not make it true that anyone in America can be the next Obama.) Nevertheless, the American Dream is within reach for all those who aspire to it and are willing to put in the hours; Adams was articulating it as an attainable outcome, not as a pipe dream. As the phrase "the American Dream" insinuated its way into the lexicon, its meaning continuously morphed and shifted, reflecting the hopes and wants of the day. Adams, in *The Epic of America*, noted that one such major shift had already occurred in the republic's history, before he'd given the dream its name. In 1890, the U.S. Census Bureau declared that there was no longer such a thing as the American frontier . . .

The tapering off of the frontier era put an end to the immature, individualistic, Wild West version of the American Dream, the one that had animated homesteaders, prospectors, wildcatters, and railroad men. . . . But by the time Woodrow Wilson became president, in 1913—after the first national election in which every voter in the continental U.S. cast his ballot as a citizen of an established state—that vision had become passé. In fact, to hear the new president speak, the frontiersman's version of the American Dream was borderline malevolent . . .

The American Dream was maturing into a shared dream, a societal compact that reached its apotheosis when Franklin Delano Roosevelt was sworn into office in 1933 and began implementing the New Deal. A "better and richer and fuller" life was no longer just what America promised its hardworking citizens individually; it was an ideal toward which these citizens were duty-bound to strive together. The Social Security Act of 1935 put this theory into practice. It mandated that workers and their employers contribute, via payroll taxes, to federally administered trust funds that paid out benefits to retirees—thereby introducing the idea of a "safe old age" with built-in protection from penury.

This was, arguably, the first time that a specific material component was ascribed to the American Dream, in the form of a guarantee that you could retire at the age of 65 and rest assured that your fellow citizens had your back. On January 31, 1940, a hardy Vermonter named Ida May Fuller, a former legal secretary, became the very first retiree to receive a monthly Social Security benefit check, which totaled $22.54. As if to prove both the best hopes of Social Security's proponents and the worst fears of its detractors, Fuller enjoyed a long retirement, collecting benefits all the way to her death in 1975, when she was 100 years old. Still, the American Dream, in F.D.R.'s day, remained largely a set of deeply held ideals rather than a checklist of goals or entitlements . . .

More soberly and less bombastically, Roosevelt, in his 1941 State of the Union address, prepared America for war by articulating the "four essential human freedoms" that the U.S. would be fighting for: "freedom of speech and expression"; "freedom of every person to worship God in his own way"; "freedom from want"; and "freedom from fear." Like Luce, Roosevelt was upholding the American way as a model for other nations to follow—he suffixed each of these freedoms with the phrase "everywhere in the world"—but he presented the four freedoms not as the lofty principles of a benevolent super race but as the homespun, bedrock values of a good, hardworking, unextravagant people. No one grasped this better than Norman Rockwell, who, stirred to action by Roosevelt's speech, set to work on his famous "Four Freedoms" paintings: the one with the rough-hewn workman speaking his piece at a town meeting (*Freedom of Speech*); the one with the old lady praying in the pew (*Freedom of Worship*); the one with the Thanksgiving dinner (*Freedom from Want*); and the one with the young parents looking in on their sleeping children (*Freedom from Fear*) . . .

The resonance of the "Four Freedoms" paintings with wartime Americans offers tremendous insight into how U.S. citizens viewed their idealized selves. *Freedom from Want*, the most popular of all, is especially telling, for the scene it depicts is joyous but defiantly unostentatious. There is a happily gathered family, there are plain white curtains, there is a large turkey, there are some celery stalks in a dish, and there is a bowl of fruit, but there is not a hint of overabundance, overindulgence, elaborate table settings, ambitious seasonal centerpieces, or any other conventions of modern-day shelter-mag porn.

It was freedom from want, not freedom to want—a world away from the idea that the patriotic thing to do in tough times is go shopping. Though the germ of that idea would form shortly, not long after the war ended.

William J. Levitt was a Seabee in the Pacific theater during the war. . . . One of his jobs was to build airfields at as fast a clip as possible, on the cheap. Levitt had already worked in his father's construction business back home, and he held an option on a thousand acres of potato fields in Hempstead, New York, out on Long Island. Coming back from the war with newly acquired speed-building skills and a vision of all those returning G.I.'s needing homes, he set to work on turning those potato fields into the first Levittown.

Levitt had the forces of history and demographics on his side. The G.I. Bill, enacted in 1944, at the tail end of the New Deal, offered returning veterans low-interest loans with no money down to purchase a house—an ideal scenario, coupled with a severe housing shortage and a boom in young families, for the rapid-fire development of suburbia.

The first Levitt houses, built in 1947, had two bedrooms, one bathroom, a living room, a kitchen, and an unfinished loft attic that could theoretically be converted into another bedroom. The houses had no basements or garages, but they sat on lots of 60 by 100 feet, and—McMansionistas, take note—took up only 12 percent of their lot's footprint. They cost about $8,000.

"Levittown" is today a byword for creepy suburban conformity, but Bill Levitt, with his Henry Ford–like acumen for mass production, played a crucial role in making home ownership a new tenet of the American Dream, especially as he expanded his operations to other states and inspired imitators. From 1900 to 1940, the percentage of families who lived in homes that they themselves owned held steady at around 45 percent. But by 1950 this figure had shot up to 55 percent, and by 1960 it was at 62 percent. Likewise, the homebuilding business, severely depressed during the war, revived abruptly at war's end, going from 114,000 new single-family houses started in 1944 to 937,000 in 1946—and to 1.7 million in 1950.

Levitt initially sold his houses only to vets, but this policy didn't hold for long; demand for a new home of one's own wasn't remotely limited to ex-G.I.'s . . .

Buttressed by postwar optimism and prosperity, the American Dream was undergoing another recalibration. Now it really did translate into specific goals rather than Adams's more broadly defined aspirations. Home ownership was the fundamental goal, but, depending on who was doing the dreaming, the package might also include car ownership, television ownership (which multiplied from 6 million to 60 million sets in the U.S. between 1950 and 1960), and the intent to send one's kids to college. The G.I. Bill was as crucial on that last count as it was to the housing boom. In providing tuition money for returning vets, it not only stocked the universities with new students—in 1947, roughly half of the nation's college enrollees were ex-G.I.'s—but put the very idea of college within reach of a generation that had previously considered higher education the exclusive province of the rich and the extraordinarily gifted. Between 1940 and 1965, the number of U.S. adults who had completed at least four years of college more than doubled.

Nothing reinforced the seductive pull of the new, suburbanized American Dream more than the burgeoning medium of television, especially as its production nexus shifted from New York, where the grubby, schlubby shows *The Honeymooners* and *The Phil Silvers Show* were shot, to Southern California, where the sprightly, twinkly shows *The Adventures of Ozzie and Harriet*, *Father Knows Best*, and *Leave It to Beaver* were made. While the former shows are actually more enduringly watchable and funny, the latter were the foremost "family" sitcoms of the 1950s—and, as such, the aspirational touchstones of real American families.

The Nelsons (*Ozzie and Harriet*), the Andersons (*Father Knows Best*), and the Cleavers (*Leave It to Beaver*) lived in airy houses even nicer than those that Bill Levitt built. . . . The Nelsons also offered, in David and especially the swoonsome, guitar-strumming Ricky, two attractive exemplars of that newly ascendant and clout-wielding American demographic, the teenager. "The postwar spread of American values would be spearheaded by the idea of the teenager," writes Jon Savage somewhat ominously in *Teenage*, his history of youth culture. "This new type was pleasure-seeking, product-hungry, embodying the new global society where social inclusion was to be granted through purchasing power."

Still, the American Dream was far from degenerating into the consumerist nightmare it would later become (or, more precisely, become mistaken for). What's striking about the *Ozzie and Harriet*–style 50s dream is its relative modesty of scale. Yes, the TV and advertising portrayals of family life were antiseptic and too-too-perfect, but the dream homes, real and fictional, seem downright dowdy to modern eyes, with none of the "great room" pretensions and tricked-out kitchen islands that were to come.

Nevertheless, some social critics, such as the economist John Kenneth Galbraith, were already fretful. In his 1958 book *The Affluent Society*, a best-seller, Galbraith posited that America had reached an almost unsurpassable and unsustainable degree of mass affluence because the average family owned a home, one car, and one TV. In pursuing these goals, Galbraith said, Americans had lost a sense of their priorities, focusing on consumerism at the expense of public-sector needs like parks, schools, and infrastructure maintenance. At the same time, they had lost their parents' Depression-era sense of thrift, blithely taking out personal loans or enrolling in installment plans to buy their cars and refrigerators.

While these concerns would prove prescient, Galbraith severely underestimated the potential for average U.S. household income and spending power to grow further. The very same year that *The Affluent Society* came out, Bank of America introduced the BankAmericard, the forerunner to Visa, today the most widely used credit card in the world.

What unfolded over the next generation was the greatest standard-of-living upgrade that this country had ever experienced: an economic sea change powered by the middle class's newly sophisticated engagement in personal finance via credit cards, mutual funds, and discount brokerage houses—and its willingness to take on debt.

Consumer credit, which had already rocketed upward from $2.6 billion to $45 billion in the postwar period (1945 to 1960), shot up to $105 billion by 1970. "It was as if the entire middle class was betting that tomorrow would be better than today," as the financial writer Joe Nocera put it in his 1994 book, *A Piece of the Action: How the Middle Class Joined the Money Class.* "Thus did Americans begin to spend money they didn't yet have; thus did the unaffordable become affordable. And thus, it must be said, did the economy grow."

Before it spiraled out of control, the "money revolution," to use Nocera's term for this great middle-class financial engagement, really did serve the American Dream. It helped make life "better and richer and fuller" for a broad swath of the populace in ways that our Depression-era forebears could only have imagined.

To be glib about it, the Brady family's way of life was even sweeter than the Nelson family's . . . the middle class's American Dream wish-fulfillment fantasy, again in a generically idyllic Southern California setting. But now there were two cars in the driveway. Now there were annual vacations at the Grand Canyon and an improbably caper-filled trip to Hawaii . . . and the house itself was snazzier—that openplan living area just inside the Brady home's entryway, with the "floating" staircase leading up to the bedrooms, was a major step forward in fake . . . family living.

By 1970, for the first time, more than half of all U.S. families held at least one credit card. But usage was still relatively conservative: only 22 percent of cardholders carried a balance from one month's bill to the next. Even in the so-called go-go 80s, this figure hovered in the 30s, compared to 56 percent today. But it was in the 80s that the American Dream began to take on hyperbolic connotations, to be conflated with extreme success: wealth, basically. The representative TV families, whether benignly genteel (the Huxtables on *The Cosby Show*) or soap-opera bonkers (the Carringtons on *Dynasty*), were undeniably rich. "Who says you can't have it all?" went the jingle in a ubiquitous beer commercial from the era, which only got more alarming as it went on to ask, "Who says you can't have the world without losing your soul?"

The deregulatory atmosphere of the Reagan years—the loosening of strictures on banks and energy companies, the reining in of the Justice Department's antitrust division, the removal of vast tracts of land from the Department of the Interior's protected list—was, in a sense, a calculated regression to the immature, individualistic American Dream of yore . . .

But this latest recalibration saw the American Dream get decoupled from any concept of the common good (the movement to privatize Social Security began to take on momentum) and, more portentously, from the concepts of working hard and managing one's expectations. You only had to walk as far as your mailbox to discover that you'd been "pre-approved" for six new credit cards, and that the credit limits on your existing cards had been raised without your even asking. Never before had money been freer, which is to say, never before had taking on debt become so guiltless and seemingly consequence-free—at both the personal and institutional levels. President Reagan added $1 trillion to the national debt, and in 1986, the United States, formerly the world's biggest creditor nation, became the world's biggest debtor nation. Perhaps debt was the new frontier.

A curious phenomenon took hold in the 1990s and 2000s. Even as the easy credit continued, and even as a sustained bull market cheered investors and papered over the coming mortgage and credit crises that we now face, Americans were losing faith in the American Dream—or whatever it was they believed the American Dream to be. A CNN poll taken in 2006 found that more than half of those surveyed, 54 percent, considered the American Dream unachievable—and CNN noted that the numbers were nearly the same in a 2003 poll it had conducted. Before that, in 1995, a *Business Week*/Harris poll found that two-thirds of those surveyed believed the American Dream had become harder to achieve in the past 10 years, and three-fourths believed that achieving the

dream would be harder still in the upcoming 10 years.

To the writer Gregg Easterbrook, who at the beginning of this decade was a visiting fellow in economics at the Brookings Institution, this was all rather puzzling, because, by the definition of any prior American generation, the American Dream had been more fully realized by more people than ever before. While acknowledging that an obscene amount of America's wealth was concentrated in the hands of a small group of ultra-rich, Easterbrook noted that "the bulk of the gains in living standards—the gains that really matter—have occurred below the plateau of wealth."

By nearly every measurable indicator, Easterbrook pointed out in 2003, life for the average American had gotten better than it used to be. Per capita income, adjusted for inflation, had more than doubled since 1960. Almost 70 percent of Americans owned the places they lived in, versus under 20 percent a century earlier. Furthermore, U.S. citizens averaged 12.3 years of education, tops in the world and a length of time in school once reserved solely for the upper class.

Yet when Easterbrook published these figures in a book, the book was called *The Progress Paradox: How Life Gets Better while People Feel Worse*. He was paying attention not only to the polls in which people complained that the American Dream was out of reach, but to academic studies by political scientists and mental-health experts that detected a marked uptick since the midcentury in the number of Americans who considered themselves unhappy.

The American Dream was now almost by definition unattainable, a moving target that eluded people's grasp; nothing was ever enough. It compelled Americans to set unmeetable goals for themselves and then consider themselves failures when these goals, inevitably, went unmet. In examining why people were thinking this way, Easterbrook raised an important point. "For at least a century," he wrote, "Western life has been dominated by a revolution of rising expectations: Each generation expected more than its antecedent. Now most Americans and Europeans already have what they need, in addition to considerable piles of stuff they don't need."

This might explain the existential ennui of the well-off, attractive, solipsistic kids on *Laguna Beach* (2004–6) and *The Hills* (2006–9), the MTV reality soaps that represent the curdling of the whole Southern California wish-fulfillment genre on television. Here were affluent beach-community teens enriching themselves further not even by acting or working in any real sense, but by allowing themselves to be filmed as they sat by campfires maundering on about, like, how much their lives suck.

. . . It says a lot about our buying habits and constant need for new, better stuff that Congress and the Federal Communications Commission were utterly comfortable with setting a hard 2009 date for the switchover from analog to digital television broadcasting—pretty much assuming that every American household owned or would soon own a flat-panel digital TV—even though such TVs had been widely available for only five years. (As recently as January 2006, just 20 percent of U.S. households owned a digital television, and the average price point for such a television was still above a thousand dollars.)

In hewing to the misbegotten notion that our standard of living must trend inexorably upward, we entered in the late 90s and early 00s into what might be called the Juiceball Era of the American Dream—a time of steroidally outsize purchasing and artificially inflated numbers. As Easterbrook saw it, it was no longer enough for people to keep up with the Joneses; no, now they had to "call and raise the Joneses."

"Bloated houses," he wrote, "arise from a desire to call-and-raise-the-Joneses—surely not from a belief that a seven-thousand-square-foot house that comes right up against the property setback line would be an ideal place in which to dwell." More ominously and to the point: "To call-and-raise-the-Joneses, Americans increasingly take on debt."

This personal debt, coupled with mounting institutional debt, is what has got us in the hole we're in now. While it remains a laudable proposition for a young couple to secure a low-interest loan for the purchase of their first home, the more recent practice of running up huge credit-card bills to pay for, well, whatever, has come back to haunt us. The amount of outstanding consumer debt in the U.S. has gone up every year since 1958, and up an astonishing 22 percent since 2000 alone. The financial historian . . . Niall Ferguson reckons that the over-leveraging of America has become especially acute in the last 10 years, with the U.S.'s debt burden, as a proportion of the gross domestic product, "in the region of 355 percent," he says. "So, debt is three and a half times the output of the economy. That's some kind of historic maximum."

James Truslow Adams's words remind us that we're still fortunate to live in a country that offers us such latitude in choosing how we go about our lives and work. . . . Still, we need to challenge some of the middle-class orthodoxies that have brought us to this point—not least the notion, widely promulgated throughout popular culture, that the middle class itself is a soul-suffocating dead end.

The middle class is a good place to be, and, optimally, where most Americans will spend their lives if they work hard and don't over-extend themselves financially. On *American Idol*, Simon Cowell has done many youngsters a great service by telling them that they're not going to Hollywood and that they should find some other line of work. The American Dream is not fundamentally about stardom or extreme success; in recalibrating our expectations of it, we need to appreciate that it is not an all-or-nothing deal—that it is not, as in hip-hop narratives and in Donald Trump's brain, a stark choice between the penthouse and the streets.

And what about the outmoded proposition that each successive generation in the United States must live better than the one that preceded it? While this idea is still crucial to families struggling in poverty and to immigrants who've arrived here in search of a better life than that they left behind, it's no longer applicable to an American middle class that lives more comfortably than any version that came before it. I'm no champion of downward mobility, but the time has come to consider the idea of simple continuity: the perpetuation of a contented, sustainable middle-class way of life, where the standard of living remains happily constant from one generation to the next.

This is not a matter of any generation's having to "lower its sights," to use President Obama's words, nor is it a denial that some children of lower- and middle-class parents will, through talent and/or good fortune, strike it rich and bound precipitously into the upper class. Nor is it a moony, nostalgic wish for a return to the scrappy 30s or the suburban 50s, because any sentient person recognizes that there's plenty about the good old days that wasn't so good: the original Social Security program

pointedly excluded farmworkers and domestics (i.e., poor rural laborers and minority women), and the original Levittown didn't allow black people in.

But those eras do offer lessons in scale and self-control. The American Dream should require hard work, but it should not require 80-hour workweeks and parents who never see their kids from across the dinner table. The American Dream should entail a first-rate education for every child, but not an education that leaves no extra time for the actual enjoyment of childhood. The American Dream should accommodate the goal of home ownership, but without imposing a lifelong burden of unmeetable debt. Above all, the American Dream should be embraced as the unique sense of possibility that this country gives its citizens—the decent chance, as Moss Hart would say, to scale the walls and achieve what you wish.

Endangered Childhoods: How Consumerism Is Impacting Child and Youth Identity

JENNIFER ANN HILL

Hill spotlights the core value of consumerism in our culture and its particularly problematic effect on children. Unlike in the past, children today are considered a lucrative niche market for advertisers to target "from cradle to grave." The media act as powerful agents of socialization, redefining childhood from a period where children were free to explore and play to one that is defined by them acting as consumers. While companies enjoy profits, the costs to children are high, essentially redefining children's identities as defined by their consumption, negatively affecting their physical and mental health, and limiting their creativity.

In today's world, we have engaged in a love–hate debate with media as far as children are concerned. On the one hand, media technology has been accused of interfering with and retarding children's physical and emotional development. Many of these technologies, it has been argued, are harmful at a physiological level. Technology is also said to induce anomie and anti-social behavior as well as to be responsible for reinforcing hegemonic patterns like racism and sexism. On the other hand, technology has been praised for its advancement of children's education. Computers and other electronics are heralded for enhancing learning at an unprecedented pace. Both of these arguments are based on the conception that childhood exists unaffected by cultural differences and social inequalities; this notion is in sharp contrast with the constructivist paradigm which suggests that context largely determines the nature of childhood for any given individual regardless of biological stages of growth. Yet, globalization of corporate operations and media has to a large extent infiltrated beyond differences of class, ethnicity and gender such that a discussion on endangered childhoods independent of these types of contexts is warranted. Indeed, it is the ubiquitous power of media and its concomitant consumerism that has spread across continents and cultures alike, infiltrating childhood with each pass. Consequently, many children are being deprived of a "full" childhood or series of experiences that distinctly differentiates them from that of the adult world and meets their needs as children.

Jennifer Ann Hill, *Media, Culture & Society* (Volume 33, Issue 3), pp. 347–362, Copyright © 2011. Reprinted by Permission of SAGE Publications.

Consumer Culture and Children

There is no disputing the fact that modern-day children live in cultures steeped in consumption driven by consumer behaviors and influenced by their outcomes. This is the case regardless of culture and geographical location though the extent of consumerism is particularly salient in the western world where the intensity remains relatively high. The drive towards materialism and consumption has never been so prevalent, affording such opportunity for expression and on some level satisfaction, as well as cause for concern (Kasser and Kanner, 2004). Consumption plays a major role in day-to-day living and leisure through the endless availability of technology in the form of television, computers, digital accessories and a wide array of goods. Children, especially in the past two decades, have experienced a barrage of media encouraging purchasing behavior and consumption in the same way that adults have. In particular, children from the ages of 4 to 12 are increasingly defined and viewed by their spending capacity. Childhood has essentially been co-opted by marketing conglomerates and now represents an enormously lucrative sector of consumer society to the tune of $130 [billion] dollars annually (Buckingham, 2000). . . . Now, media forces compete with adult caregivers in their ability to capture the attention of children and guide them accordingly. It is in this respect that childhood is endangered, pitted against the ubiquitous presence of media images and sound bites all of which persuade children to conform to a modality that is not necessarily in their best interests. At the heart of the struggle between childhood and consumerism, child identity formation is at stake; the relentless bombardment of media messages [arguing] that the self is predominantly defined by its capacity to consume, begins at such an early age . . . [that it] overtake[s] many competing thought processes.

One of the more significant outcomes of consumerism has thus been the steady and relentless erosion of childhood whether it is measured in terms of health trends, consumer behaviors or accessibility to adult culture. There are many academics (Jenks, 2005; Kline, 1995; Linn, 2004; Polakow, 1992; Postman, 1994; Schor, 2004; Steinberg and Kincheloe, 1997; Winn, 1983) who are concerned about the fact that childhood, at least as we know it in the West, is fading out altogether. Our cultural norms depend upon a belief system that verifies children and adults are intellectually, physically, emotionally and psychologically different, and children are incapable of making the same sorts of judgments that adults do. Close scrutiny of the media, particularly television, suggests that there is very little distinction made between adults and children. Kline (1995: 74) presented a compelling argument about how television is not only a significant socializing agent for children, it has become "the undisputed leader in the production of children's culture." The culture of childhood has an important play component that is impoverished and under-nourished by passive time associated with television, computers and other electronic media . . .

Postman (1994) opined that television, in particular, presents information in a form that is undifferentiated and that is easily accessible. In other words, television, computers and video games do not segregate their audience, not unlike the conditions that existed in the 14th and 15th centuries. Until the invention of the printing press there existed no means for adults to harbor exclusive information. With the advent of print, children were shielded from adult information such that the two cultures could develop side by side with next to no crossover. The new media environment fronted by television provided everyone, simultaneously, with the same information. Since there is virtually nothing left that television has not aired, Postman (1994) concluded that we are a culture without secrets and therefore cannot nurture a culture of childhood. Indeed, there is no aspect of adult life, whether it be perversity, promiscuity, dishonor or confusion, that seems outside the realm of today's children (Winn, 1983). Television is an open-admission technology to which there are no physical, economic, cognitive or imaginative restraints—it makes no difference as to whether the audience is a six-year-old or a sixty-year-old. Television has made use of every existing taboo in western culture, dissolving the shroud of adult secrets. And according to Postman (1994), when adults' secrets are easily accessed childhood dissolves. Television programming is for the most part not governed by theories on child development or mediated by a child's parental figure. Rather, it is driven by a profit-seeking conglomeration with few regulations . . .

Constructing the Tween

The social phenomenon of the "tween" is one of the more striking examples of how consumerism has led to the erosion of childhood. The tween category refers to children between seven or eight to 13 or 14 years. The tween has rapidly become a definable, knowable commercial persona and stage of youth since the 1990s (Cook and Kaiser, 2004). Nowhere is age compression (children getting "older" at younger ages) marketing more evident than in the 8 to 12 age range (Quart, 2003). Younger children are being enticed, encouraged and seduced into adopting an identity older than their developmental age. It is worth noting that in the US the income of the 36 million children in the 8 to 12 age bracket grew by 15 percent annually during the 1990s to $31.7 [billion] in 1999 (Rice, 2001). In addition, the 4 to 12 set annually influence $565 [billion] of their parents' purchases (Rice, 2001). It comes as no surprise, then, that marketers are clamoring for children's attention in a big way. In 1999, advertisers targeted more than $12 billion to marketing campaigns aimed at capturing children (Rice, 2001). Marketers are hiring child psychologists and other experts to maximize their understanding of the segments and nuances of the youth market. Natural or not, by 1998 mega marketing campaigns were being designed to cater to the tween phenomenon. For example, the somewhat conservative McDonald's Corporation launched its "Big Kids Meal," complete with its McWorld advertising campaign, aimed directly at tweens.

Gauging Children's Health

Trends in children's health, including their physical and psychological functioning, are indicators as to whether or not a culture is having a salubrious affect. Additionally, negative health indicators are intricately linked to issues of identity. Addictive behavior for example, reflects internalized aspects of the self that are harmful. It can be argued that children who engage in drug use, alcohol and/or smoking must construct an identity that includes and justifies this type of lifestyle (Kilbourne, 1999). . . . Disconnection and the insatiable desire to transform the self (the "cool" craze) are two of the more insidious outcomes of advertising and the corporate agenda that have paved the way toward negative self-esteem and health outcomes in children (Kilbourne, 1999; Linn, 2004; Quart, 2003; Schor, 2004).

Statistics on children's health point to a disturbing trend—children are being robbed of their childhoods not only at an emotional level, but physically as well. Their health concerns are similar to those of the adult population in many respects. In North America by 2004, almost 20 percent of youth are overweight or obese; since 1980, obesity rates for children have nearly tripled and those for teens have tripled. . . . By the time children are in the 8th grade, 3 percent of them are smokers and that number quadruples by the 12th grade (Wallman, 2008). As well, children are drinking alcohol and taking illegal drugs at significant rates; 10 percent of 12th graders drink alcohol and 7 percent report that they have used illegal drugs (Schor, 2004). Rates of emotional and behavior problems among children from ages 4 to 15 soared between 1979 and 1996 (Kelleher et al., 2000). Also, childhood and adolescent depression are prevalent, frequently recurrent and highly impairing; depressive disorders occur in approximately 2 percent of primary school–aged children and between 4 and 8 percent of adolescents (Olfson et al., 2003).

The average age for the onset of depression is now 14 and a half compared to 29 and a half in 1960 (Ben-Shahar, 2007). Finally, suicide rates for children aged 10 to 14 almost tripled between 1968 and 1985 (Goleman, 1995).

The Potency of Television and Advertising

As Jhally (cited in Kilbourne, 1999: 64) writes, "to not be influenced by advertising would be to live outside of culture. No human being lives outside of culture." Television is one of the more prominent media through which advertisers communicate to children. And children of practically all ages are being exposed. A recent study cited that 40 percent of three-month-olds are watching television (Zimmerman et al., 2007); on a typical day, almost 60 percent of children under two are also tuning in (Rideout et al., 2003). The exposure of American children and adolescents to television continues to exceed the time they spend in the classroom: 15,000 hours versus 12,000 hours by the time they graduate from school (Bar-on, 2000). In other words, almost three solid years will have been spent watching television. This figure does not include time spent watching videotapes or playing video games. To put it further in perspective, based on surveys of what type of television programming children watch, the average child sees about 12,000 violent acts, 14,000 sexual references and innuendos and 20,000 advertisements *annually* (Bar-on, 2000, emphasis added). Not surprisingly, the American Pediatrics Association recommends that children under two not watch television at all (Certain and Kahn, 2002). Research indicates that one-year-olds respond to positive and negative emotions on television (Mumme and Fernald, 2003); this makes them prime targets for manipulation, especially considering their cognitive capacity to mediate emotions is in its nascent state. Clearly, corporations, through advertising, aim to capture a child's attention by powerful messaging and shaping attitudes, motivation, behavior, and ultimately, one's identity. Essentially, brand loyalty is sought from the cradle . . .

Twenty-five years ago, advertising to young children was largely discouraged because children were thought to be unable to view adverts critically or with a discriminating eye. A comprehensive review of the literature over the past 25 years by John (1999), however, reveals that by age five most children are able to discriminate between advertising and programming. A deeper understanding of the persuasive intent of the ads occurs by about age eight and it is also at this age that children begin to recognize that ads do not always tell the truth. One might conclude therefore, that advertising to children by at least age eight is justifiable. And while children exhibit skepticism about the purpose of the advertisements, their desire for advertised products even at age nine or ten remains strong (Schor, 2004). . . . Despite decades of research, what is clear is that the *effects* of consumerism, in which advertising plays an important role, are psychologically and physically harmful (Dittmar, 2007; Kasser et al., 2007; Kramer, 2006; Linn, 2004; Schor, 2004).

Usurping Play

Children's play is not only about how they create their culture, but about how they learn. Play comes naturally to children, as a means of self-expression to gain a sense of control over their world (Weininger, 1979). When children are flooded with stimuli from television, computer or video games, they have fewer opportunities to learn to initiate action or to influence the world they inhabit, and less chance to exercise creativity. Indeed, the cost is high as play is the mode through which children develop and form a sense of identity (Polakow, 1992). Consumerism has led to a host of seemingly endless needs for sophisticated electronic media technology, making it increasingly difficult to provide children with an environment that allows for creativity or original thinking. As children are assaulted by a stream of media messages, accompanied by a flood of accessories including toys, books, videos and clothing the time and space available for their own ideas and images cannot compete (Winn, 1983). . . . The implicit, accompanying message is that children's creativity is simply not adequate—they are seen to "need" the toys to fully experience their environment and develop in an optimal way. Consequently, children learn at an early age that conformity, defining self-worth by what you own, and seeking happiness through the acquisition of material goods are traits towards which to aspire. These are antithetical to creativity, characterized by originality and the capacity for critical thinking. A sense of self is shaped in numerous ways by creativity that is expressed as play, and when that is squelched, identity suffers (Leach, 1994).

Erosion of Non-Commercial Space

In North America, few places remain for children devoid of corporate influence, even schools. Public schools have been venues for at least some corporate marketing since their inception. In the early 1990s, however, the scope of commercialization of schools began to sharply escalate (Molnar, 1996). Corporations began putting forth the message that they were "contributing" to education, like those that market their products on "Channel One" in the USA. Channel One is a daily in-school news and advertising program to which millions of children across the USA are exposed. In return for the use of video monitors and equipment, school officials promise marketers a captive student audience. Introduced in 1989, Channel One displays ads, camouflaged at times, to appear as public service announcements; among the advertised products are junk food, soft drinks, video games, movies, television programming and other products (Kilbourne, 1999). Defending arguments about the quality of Channel One's news distracts from the real issue—a corporate intrusion into the lives of children using school time to promote consumer products. And when products are advertised in school, there is the expectation that what is being advertised is good for the students' overall being (Schor, 2004).

Selling Cool

. . . There is considerable effort by marketers to expose children to violence and sex through toys, video games and television (Kilbourne, 1999; Linn, 2004; Schor, 2004). The sex and violence inundating children on various screens exists not because parents, teachers or caregivers think such content is good for children, but because sex and violence have proven to be profitable attention-grabbers. The monetary potential that children represent can be worth a lifetime of brand loyalty and marketers will use ruthless tactics to ensure this comes to fruition. Advertising and marketing work to create a continuous need for products by exploiting children's aspirations, whether for a certain body type, attitude or personality trait. Consequently, if media-created characters emulate the qualities children long for, the greater the likelihood that children will identify with them. Selling "cool" is one of the more pronounced media campaigns that have dominated over several decades. Cool is now revered as a quality every product tries to be and every child needs to have regardless of age. The selling of cool can lead to the exploitation of psychological vulnerabilities, most visible in the marketing of violence and sex . . .

More often than not, children are learning about sex through the media. Sex or sexuality has been exploited since the beginning of advertising to sell just about everything. Children are bombarded with messages about what it takes to be attractive, how men and women treat each other, and what is essential about being male or female. The groups most impacted in this regard are tweens. Like violence, visual images of sex and sexuality probably have more impact than content conveyed in language or the written word. . . . [Music], television shows, and movies are rife with implicit and explicit sexual references, all of which have the capacity to influence a child's self-image and invoke negative behaviors potentially harmful to self and others (Kilbourne, 1999; Linn, 2004; Schor, 2004) . . .

Ads for beer, alcohol, tobacco and drugs proliferate in venues that attract large numbers of children, and children are widely exposed to alcohol, tobacco and illegal drugs in television programs, films and music videos (Strasburger and Wilson, 2002). While there is significant public health concern about children's consumption of alcohol and tobacco, ads are designed to grab the interest of teens and tweens by exploiting the same vulnerabilities as ads for clothing—"you need this product to be cool." Research shows that children and adolescents are more likely to smoke, drink and use drugs when they are exposed to ads and programming depicting these products (Sargent et al., 2001). While it is difficult to identify the degree to which peers, parents or media influence negative health behaviors, there is clearly risk to children if food, tobacco and alcohol industries continue to be unregulated in their scope of advertising.

Consumerism and Identity

Hence, consumerism has attached itself to a novel identity politics in which business itself plays a role in forging identities conducive to buying and selling. Identity here becomes a reflection of "lifestyles" that are closely associated with commercial brands and the products they label, as well as with attitudes and behaviors linked to where we shop, how we buy, and what we eat, wear, and consume (Barber, 2007: 167).

At the start of the 21st century, young people are more about continuity than they are about change (Miles, 2000). Rebellion has given way to conformity by embracing the consumer culture ideology. Consumerism has increasingly come to affect mundane and everyday aspects of young people's lives. Children are constantly bombarded with messages to reproduce and uphold dominant power structures such as the corporation (Miles, 2000). Instead of empowering with freedom of choice, consumer culture represents an entrapment, an endless quest of acquisition tied to identity. Perhaps the most

pernicious aspect of consumerism lies in the fact that much of its message remains out of the conscious realm because it is so ubiquitous (Dittmar, 2007). . . . While consumer culture allows for the right of ownership to be exercised, it also perpetuates a number of myths particularly through advertising with the idealized references to the "good life" steeped in materialism and the endless quest for the "perfect body" as the second main target site. Many of us internalize these ideals and subsequently engage in negative comparison resulting in damage to both mental and physical health. . . . While not all media messages are taken at face value, it becomes difficult if not impossible, particularly for children, to remain untouched by the continuous exposure to these normative socio-cultural ideals portrayed by mass media as desirable and attainable. The quest for "body perfect" is a good example of how the media creates ideals that are unattainable for the majority, leading to potentially damaging effects for girls and boys as well. Likewise, the material "good life" in which affluence is associated with success, control, autonomy, and happiness is continuously promoted by the media as the desirable ideal. Media therefore plays a significant role in how individuals construct their own version of material and bodily norms, and hence identity (Miles, 2000).

Corporations accrue immense profits from children's misguided search for identity and happiness through consumption. . . . Materialism, epitomized by the unrealistic beliefs of money and material goods, can be labeled as *the* "risk" factor in contemporary society because it makes individuals vulnerable to excessive, dysfunctional consumer behavior such as compulsive buying. As to how all of this applies to children, the detrimental motive of pursuing a better identity through material goods is already evident in childhood within consumer cultures. Despite all of the evidence on the importance of meaningful relationships in achieving happiness, children are led to believe cool supersedes pro-social behaviors. Sadly, this is reflected in the number one aspiration of children in the USA and the UK—the acquisition of wealth (Dittmar, 2007).

In consumer cultures, to define oneself to others, even to one's self, requires an endless, ongoing stream of consumptive experiences. Regardless of individual context, in late modernity we are increasingly what we consume and measure most of our success on this level (Fromm, 1976). Within capitalist cultures, others judge and are judged along consumptive criteria. . . . To talk about socialization is to downplay the fact that choices related to consumption are not simply decisions about how to act, but also reflect one's identity. It is not difficult then to understand why many consumers would argue that they are fully aware of the omnipresence of consumption and despite this, are still in control, in charge (Kilbourne, 1999) . . .

Branding

Over the last decade, the exponential increase in the intensity of marketing directed at children has led to a phenomenon known as branding. The intimate entangling of brand and identity is nowhere more evident than in the experience of childhood over the last two decades. "The colonization of children's lives by the entertainment product cycle has woven Disney, Hasbro, Mattel and McDonald's into the fabric of everyday life for urban children across the globe" (Langer, 2004: 263). Children have been bombarded by brands defined by name products and intrusive and clever advertising strategies. As discussed previously, children as young as three can be avid consumers and devoted media watchers and by age five, many begin to show interest in brands and can recognize brand names in stores (Achenreiner and John, 2003; Kline, 2005). . . . As a child's identity goes through varying phases of change, it is unrealistic to assume that the child has the sophistication required to self-reflect on the true meaning and impact of brands on identity.

Branding goes much deeper than developing an affinity for particular brands, it also refers to the process in which children and youth consider their own characters and personae, brands onto themselves (Quart, 2003). Teen-oriented brands now register so strongly that an individual not only wears branded clothing, but strives to adopt the mask of the brand's aura in its entirety. . . . Children are now perceived as encompassing three markets: influencing parental spending, significant spending power, and a future market in which to build early brand loyalty. Remarkably, specific brand names are likely to be among a child's first words. Other studies have suggested that by six months, children are able to recognize brand logos (Preston and White, 2004). Establishing brand loyalty at such an early age has powerful implications—more than half of the brands used in childhood continue to be used in adulthood (Pecheux and Derbaix, 1999).

The branding trend infiltrates on many levels. For example, corporations are hiring teens to be "trend-spotters," insiders who advise on the current teen market (Quart, 2003). The outcome of such engagement leads "[teenagers to feel] that consumer goods are their friends—and that the companies selling products to them are trusted allies. [Tell] us how best to sell your products, they ask. If you do, we will always love you" (Quart, 2003: 35). . . . There are also "cool hunters"—adults who market to adolescents—who survey the latest trends to acquire product marketing strategies (Quart, 2003: 41). Such youth participation can largely be explained as a concerted effort or longing for popularity and acceptance. Corporations seek to ensure that identity is found in the brand and guaranteeing that those brand-associated products will be hard sought after.

. . . Hence, identity formation is closely aligned with branded images that infiltrate deep into the psyche of children and youth. More specifically, brands can essentially perform two main roles for consumers' identity: an emotional role through providing a means of identification, and a social role through shorthand communication of who we are (Dittmar and Howard, 2004).

According to Elliott and Wattanasuwan (1998), the consumer uses brands for both the construction and the maintenance of identity. Teenagers, in particular, may be highly motivated to use any material possessions available to create and communicate a sense of self . . .

Gender and Identity

Consumer cultures impact girls/women and boys/men in different ways though both of the sexes experience an onslaught of messages that uphold the ideals and body image very few can ever achieve. Children and indeed adults are all engaged in the continuous production of gendered identity via visual display. Appearance production is not an optional activity but is constituted of one's subjectivity or overall presentation of the self (Frost, 2005). . . . For many and perhaps even the majority of women and girls in consumer cultures, appearance is paramount to their self-definition. Socialization begins early as there is virtually no escaping the ubiquitous presence of thin, muscular, attractive role models marketers choose to use as advertising tools to promote their goods and lifestyles. Mass media is without a doubt the most powerful and vociferous purveyor of the ideal, slender beauty culminating in "perfection." Girls in particular, are swamped by ultra-thin ideals not only in the form of dolls but also in figures that appear in comics, cartoons, TV, movies and all forms of advertising along with all the associated merchandising. The synergistic effect of such exposure can have a profound impact on a child's developing identity. The young girls/women are bombarded by the images produced through consumer capitalism such that their internalized standard of normal is ultimately based on an illusion (Frost, 2005). Girls learn to see themselves as objects to be looked at and evaluated by appearance, as is characteristic of many women.

The world of a girl's/woman's senses, perspectives, and even future awareness is steeped in the context of consumerism (Little and Hoskins, 2004). Primarily, girls are told by advertisers that what is most important about them is their physical appearance (Kilbourne, 2004). This results in a preoccupation with how to improve the body and enhance attractiveness to become socially desirable. At the same time, while the cultural ideal is becoming progressively thinner, the body weight of women is increasing (Dittmar and Howard, 2004). Thus, it stands to reason that girls/women are likely to experience body dissatisfaction, low self-esteem and identities that reflect both of these phenomena. Dittmar et al. (2006) conducted a study to determine whether children as young as five to eight were impacted by the figure of the Barbie doll, historically the most popular doll of all time. "Barbie" is so extraordinarily thin that her weight and body proportions are not only unattainable but are also unhealthy . . . [to] put the matter in perspective, fewer than one in 100,000 women have "Barbie's" body proportions (Dittmar et al., 2006). The findings of the latter research project revealed that very young girls experience heightened body dissatisfaction after exposure to Barbie doll images. When exposed to a neutral control image, there was no effect. Dittmar et al. (2006) concluded that body image is highly salient for pre-adolescent children's self-concept. Barbie appears to have a strong and special role in girls' developing body image, so much so that exposure leads to detrimental effects when girls are young enough to identify with the Barbie doll (Dittmar et al., 2006).

Recent Research on Consumerism and Children

In her seminal study on media culture and children, Juliet Schor (2004), a recognized expert on consumerism, addressed the question: "How does children's involvement in consumer culture affect their well-being?" Four measures were used as indicators, those of: anxiety, depression, self-esteem, and psychosomatic symptoms. The results from Schor's study were significant in their importance and revelation; children who are more involved in consumer culture are more depressed, more anxious, have lower self-esteem and suffer from more psychosomatic complaints.

It is fair to conclude that psychologically healthy children will be made worse off if they engage in consumer culture. Likewise, children with emotional problems can expect improvements by disengaging in whatever manner is possible from consumer culture.

Schor (2004) also found that children who spend more time watching television and using other media are more likely to involve themselves in consumer culture. The latter finding may be a result of the fact that TV induces discontent with what one has, with its emphasis on materialism, and it causes children to place greater emphasis on brands and products and imbibe consumer values. Also, in this study, higher levels of consumer involvement resulted in worse relationships with parents. And as children's relations with their parents are compromised, there is an additional negative effect on well-being. Schor's 2004 findings suggest a strong causal relationship between consumerism and negative physical and psychological health. The significance of Schor's study cannot be overstated—children who suffer from anxiety, depression, low self-esteem and problematic physical symptoms are children whose childhoods are endangered.

Conclusion

As generations of children become socialized in consumer cultures their childhoods will have been so shortened that many will scarcely remember a time when they were not operating as a consumer. Children's identities have been inextricably linked to a corporate agenda that promotes and entices consumption. Children have been losing their grip on childhood as a result of the gradual but steady encroachment of media into every aspect of their lives. There is no doubt that childhood of the past was not so enmeshed with marketers' agendas. Though corporate interests in children had firmly commenced by the mid-20th century, more permissive regulations . . . resulted in a daily onslaught of advertisements that many adults, let alone children,

could not resist. As well, the revolution in technology added to the venues in which marketers could attract the child consumer including: DVD players, computers, iPods, cell phones, Game Boys, etc. Media involvement manifests most powerfully through consumer culture and eventually invades the ongoing sense of identity that children develop throughout their childhoods. This dramatic cultural shift has led to a fiercely competitive market to capture children's attention. Intent on attracting "cradle-to-grave" brand loyalty, marketers upped the ante, imposing their logos on the minds of pre-schoolers too young to even recite the alphabet. . . . Children's habits, attitudes and behaviors including the way they dress, the music they listen to . . . more and more resemble those of adults as they become acculturated to the same level of consumer involvement.

The depiction of the child consumer has been fashioned in a way that makes marketing and advertising toward children appear as a benign, even liberating undertaking. Ironically, since the 1990s marketers have touted the belief that children are better equipped to resist the power of advertising than their counterparts of several decades ago. They have argued that the "free" market inherently teaches children to become savvy, discerning consumers. The discourse of empowerment, not unlike that of socialization, renders marketing to children a morally defensible and ethically sound undertaking. . . . Corporations have thus successfully co-opted children's empowerment by equating "choice" with the consumption of heavily sponsored products.

Since consumer culture is so dominant in the West, resisting and rejecting those aspects that are less than desirable is challenging, particularly after being socialized and steeped in the culture as a child. . . . To be immersed in consumerism does not translate to awareness even if one protests to be in the know. It will, therefore, take concerted effort to muster a dissenting voice, one counter to the slow drip of implicit assumptions that keep the corporate market alive at a psychological level. Children are particularly vulnerable and generally unable to engage in self-reflection such that by the time they are adults the consumer ideology is well established as a foundation of identity.

REFERENCES

Achenreiner GB and John DR (2003) The meaning of brand names to children: a developmental investigation. *Journal of Consumer Psychology* 13(3): 205–219.

Barber BR (2007) *Consumed: How Markets Corrupt Children, Infantilize Adults, and Swallow Citizens Whole.* New York: Norton.

Bar-on ME (2000) The effects of television on child health: implications and recommendations. *Archives of Disease in Childhood* 83(4): 289–292.

Ben-Shahar T (2007) *Happier: Learn the Secrets to Daily Joy and Lasting Fulfillment.* New York: McGraw–Hill.

Buckingham D (2000) *After the Death of Childhood: Growing Up in the Age of Electronic Media.* Cambridge and Malden, MA: Polity.

Certain LK and Kahn RS (2002) Prevalence, correlates, and trajectory of television viewing among infants and toddlers. *Pediatrics* 109(4): 634–642.

Cook DT and Kaiser SB (2004) Betwixt and be tween: age ambiguity and the sexualization of the female consuming subject. *Journal of Consumer Culture* 4(2): 203–227.

Dittmar H (2007) The cost of consumers and the "cage within": the impact of the material "good life" and "body perfect" ideals on individuals' identity and well-being. *Psychological Inquiry* 18(1): 23–31.

Dittmar H and Howard S (2004) Professional hazards? The impact of models' body size on advertising effectiveness and women's body-focused anxiety in professions that do and do not emphasize the cultural ideal of thinness. *British Journal of Social Psychology* 43(4): 477–497.

Dittmar H, Halliwell E and Ive S (2006) Does Barbie make girls want to be thin? The effect of experimental exposure to images of dolls on the body image of 5- to 8-year-old girls. *Developmental Psychology* 42(2): 283–292.

Elliott R and Wattanasuwan K (1998) Brand as symbolic resources for the construction of identity. *International Journal of Advertising* 17(2): 131–144.

Fromm E (1976) *To Have or To Be.* New York: Harper and Row.

Frost L (2005) Theorizing the young woman in the body. *Body and Society* 11(1): 63–85.

Goleman D (1995) *Emotional Intelligence.* New York: Bantam.

Jenks C (2005) *Childhood.* London and New York: Routledge.

John DR (1999) Consumer socialization of children: a retrospective look at twenty-five years of research. *Journal of Consumer Research* 26(3): 183–213.

Kasser T and Kanner AD (2004) Where is the psychology of consumer culture? In: Kasser T and Kanner AD (eds) *Psychology and Consumer Culture: The Struggle for a Good Life in a Materialistic World.* Washington, DC: American Psychological Association, 3–7.

Kasser T, Cohn S, Kanner AD, et al. (2007) Some costs of American corporate capitalism: a psychological exploration of value and goal conflicts. *Psychological Inquiry* 18(1): 1–22.

Kelleher KJ, McInerny TK, Gardner WP, et al. (2000) Increasing identification of psychosocial problems: 1979–1996. *Pediatrics* 105(6): 1313–1321.

Kilbourne J (1999) *Deadly Persuasion: Why Women and Girls Must Fight the Addictive Power of Advertising.* New York: Free Press.

Kilbourne J (2004) "The more you subtract, the more you add": cutting girls down to size. In: Kasser T and Kanner AD (eds) *Psychology and Consumer Culture: The Struggle for a Good Life in a Materialistic World.* Washington, DC: American Psychological Association, 251–270.

Kline S (1995) *Out of the Garden: Toys, TV, and Children's Culture in the Age of Marketing.* London and New York: Verso.

Kline S (2005) Countering children's sedentary lifestyles: an evaluative study of a media-risk education approach. *Childhood* 12(2): 239–258.

Kramer JB (2006) Ethical analysis and recommended action in response to the dangers associated with youth consumerism. *Ethics and Behavior* 16(4): 291–303.

Langer B (2004) The business of branded enchantment: ambivalence and disjuncture in the global children's culture industry. *Journal of Consumer Culture* 4(2): 251–277.

Leach P (1994) *Children First: What Our Society Must Do—And Is Not Doing—For Our Children Today.* New York: Alfred Knopf.

Linn S (2004) *Consuming Kids: The Hostile Takeover of Childhood.* New York: New Press.

Little JN and Hoskins ML (2004) "It's an acceptable identity": constructing "girl" at the intersections of health, media and meaning-making. *Child and Youth Services* 26(2): 75–93.

Miles S (2000) *Youth Lifestyles in a Changing World.* Philadelphia, PA: Open University Press.

Molnar A (1996) *Giving Kids the Business: The Commercialization of America's Schools.* Boulder, CO: Westview Press.

Mumme DL and Fernald A (2003) The infant as onlooker: learning from emotional reactions observed in a television scenario. *Child Development* 74(1): 221–237.

Olfson M, Gameroff MJ, Marcus SC, et al. (2003) Outpatient treatment of child and adolescent depression in the United States. *Archives of General Psychiatry* 60(12): 1236–1242.

Pecheux C and Derbaix C (1999) Children and attitude toward the brand: a new measurement scale. *Journal of Advertising Research* 39(4): 19–27.

Polakow V (1992) *The Erosion of Childhood.* Chicago: University of Chicago Press.

Postman N (1994) *The Disappearance of Childhood.* New York: Vintage Books.

Preston A and White CL (2004) Commodifying kids: Branded identities and the selling of adspace on kids' networks. *Communication Quarterly* 53(2): 115–128.

Quart A (2003) *Branded: The Buying and Selling of Teenagers.* Cambridge, MA: Perseus.

Rice F (2001) "Superstars" of spending. *Advertising Age* 72(7): ps1–s1.

Rideout VJ, Vandewater EA and Wartella EA (2003) *Zero to Six: Electronic Media in the Lives of Infants, Toddlers and Preschoolers.* Henry J. Kaiser Family Foundation. Available (consulted 25 November 2010) at: http://www.kff.org/entmedia/loader.cfm?url=/commonspot/security/getfile.cfm&PageID=22754

Sargent JD, Beach ML, Dalton MA, et al. (2001) Effect of seeing tobacco use in films on trying smoking among adolescents: cross sectional study. *British Medical Journal* 323(7326): 1394–1397.

Schor J (2004) *Born to Buy: The Commercialized Child and the New Consumer Culture.* New York: Scribner.

Steinberg SR and Kincheloe JS (1997) No more secrets: Kinderculture, information saturation, and the postmodern childhood. In: Steinberg SR and Kincheloe JS (eds) *Kinderculture: The Corporate Construction of Childhood.* Boulder, CO: Westview, 1–30.

Strasburger VC and Wilson BJ (2002) *Children, Adolescents, and the Media.* Thousand Oaks, CA: Sage.

Wallman KK (2008) *America's Children in Brief: Key National Indicators of Well-Being,* 2008. Washington, DC: Federal Interagency Forum on Child and Family Statistics.

Weininger O (1979) *Play and Education: The Basic Tool for Early Childhood Learning.* Springfield, IL: Thomas.

Winn M (1983) *Children without Childhood.* New York: Pantheon.

Zimmerman FJ, Christakis DA and Meltzoff AN (2007) Television and DVD/video viewing in children younger than 2 years. *Archives of Pediatrics and Adolescent Medicine* 161(May): 473–479.

Public Attitudes toward the Next Social Contract

BRUCE STOKES

Acknowledging that compared to other Western countries Americans invest comparatively little money in their social safety net (old-age insurance, health insurance, programs to support the poor and the unemployed, and so on), Stokes explores the effect of our core values on our attitudes about the safety net. He focuses on the values of fairness, equality, individualism, and the role of the government and learns that our values often produce contradictory and ambivalent attitudes that affect how we feel about the U.S. social safety net (or particular parts of it) and how we should pay for it.

[There is] a national debate in the United States about the nature, extent and future sustainability of key elements of the U.S. social safety net: Social Security, Medicare, Medicaid, support for education, the unemployed and the poor. In the effort to tame the federal debt, cuts in spending on these social services have been a major part of the discussion—calling into question the social contract established with the American people during the Great Depression through the creation of public pensions and in the 1960s with the launching of limited government-provided health insurance.

America was a latecomer to the provision of many such social services. Germany put in place health and old age insurance in the 1880s. The United Kingdom instituted national health insurance after World War II. The benefits provided by the U.S. government cover a far smaller portion of the American population and are far less generous than those afforded to the citizens of other high-income nations. In 2012 the United States spent an estimated 19.4% of GDP on such social expenditures, according to the Organization for Economic Cooperation and Development, the Paris-based industrial country think tank. Denmark spent 30.5%, Sweden 28.2% and Germany 26.3%. All of these nations have a lower central government debt to GDP ratio than that of the United States.

Why the United States invests relatively less in its social safety net than many other countries and why those expenditures are even at risk in the current debate over debt reduction reflect Americans' conflicted, partisan and often contradictory views on fairness, inequality, the role and responsibility of government and individuals in society and the efficacy of government

This piece was originally published by Pew Research Center, special to New America Foundation, http://www .pewglobal.org/2013/01/15/public-attitudes-toward-the-next-social-contract/.

action. Rooted in value differences, not just policy differences, the debate over the U.S. social contract is likely . . . [to continue even as our economic situation improves].

A Question of Fairness

Recent years have not been good economically for most Americans. Thanks to the Great Recession, roughly 8.7 million lost their jobs. For those who lost employment, the average earnings loss two years later was 48%, according to a recent study by the Brookings Institution. And, even those who found new employment quickly earned 17% less, on average, in their new jobs than in their former employment. But such signs of trouble did not begin with the economy's downturn in 2008. The median earnings of all working-age men in the United States have declined by 19 percent since 1970. This means that the median man in 2010 earned as much as the median man did in 1964—nearly half a century earlier. Declining earnings have contributed to rising income and wealth inequality. Between 1983 and 2010, the richest 1% of households accounted for 38.3% of all growth in household wealth, according to the Economic Policy Institute. For the bottom 60% of households, their wealth actually declined during this time period.

It is little wonder then that most Americans think that the economy is stacked against them. Voters in the 2012 election told exit pollsters—by a margin of 55% to 39%—that the U.S. economic system generally favors the wealthy. Such sentiment was particularly prevalent among those who voted for president Barack Obama (79%) and voters age 29 and younger (61%). Only among those who voted for Republican presidential candidate Mitt Romney (63%) did people think that the system was fair to most Americans. And Americans strongly believe (76%) that the rich are getting richer and the poor are getting poorer. There is general agreement across socio-economic lines in this regard. Notably, such concerns are worsening. In 1986, 40% of Americans thought that the gap between living standards of the poor and the middle class had widened in

the previous decade. By 2012 61% of Americans said such inequality had risen in the previous ten years.

Yet the public is ambivalent about whether this unfairness affects them directly. In January 2012, 62% of Americans told Gallup that the economic system was fair to them personally. This distinction between personal experience and a broader judgment of the economy is not unique to fairness issues. People make the same distinctions between their personal finances and the health of the economy, generally judging their personal situation better than that of the nation. This dichotomy may help explain why the public often expresses disdain for the government in general while supporting particular government programs. And it may also help explain why inequality has not yet become a defining political issue in the United States despite demonstrable evidence of its rise.

Americans are actually less likely to say that income inequality is a problem than citizens of many other developed nations. This is, in part, because inequality is rising throughout most of the industrial world. Inequality is higher in the United States, but it is also rising in most of Europe and Japan. Overwhelming percentages of Europeans think the rich are getting richer and the poor poorer, including 91% of Italians, 89% of French and 87% of Germans, according to a Pew Global Attitudes survey. Moreover, 88% of European Union citizens think income differences in their country are far too large, according to a 2010 Eurobarometer poll. This includes 92% of Germans and Spanish, 90% of the French, 85% of the Italians and 82% of the British. Fewer Swedes (75%) and Danes (65%) share this concern, possibly reflecting the lower levels of inequality there and the stronger social safety net in their societies. But it is significant that even in these latter two nations strong concern for inequality remains.

Particularly Strong Support for Universal Entitlements

Americans are quite supportive of some of the major building blocks of the public social support network, such as the Medicare system. In an October 2012 Kaiser poll, 60% favored keeping Medicare as it is today, with the government guaranteeing all seniors the same set of health insurance benefits. . . . There is similar backing for Medicaid. Fully 78% of the public said they like knowing that the Medicaid program exists as a safety net to protect low-income people who can't afford needed care in a July 2012 Kaiser survey. Unemployment insurance has long been a pillar of the social contract. And the public has favored its recent extension. In January 2012 about half (52%) of the public thought it was a good idea to continue to provide unemployment benefits for up to 99 weeks, according to a NBC News/*Wall Street Journal* survey. Only 33% thought that it was a bad idea . . .

Greater Divisions in Support for Programs for the Poor

The Great Recession, the economy's slow recovery from it and the knock-on effect on incomes and income distribution have increased demand for a range of social services needed by society's most vulnerable. And that portion of the U.S. population that may need such services is growing. The percentage of Americans who say they are now in the lower middle or lower class has risen from a quarter of the adult population to about a third, according to a study by the Pew Research Center. Not only has the lower class grown, but its demographic profile also has shifted. People younger than 30 are disproportionately swelling the ranks of the self-defined lower classes. And the shares of Hispanics and whites who place themselves in the lower class are also growing. A majority of Americans have consistently agreed that it is the responsibility of government to help take care of such people.

Overall, however, the public majority in favor of the social safety net has slipped from 69% in 2007 to 63% in 2009 to 59% in 2012, according to the Pew Research Center. And Republicans and Democrats are far apart in their opinions about various aspects of the social safety net. There are

partisan differences of 35 percentage points or more in opinions about the government's responsibility to care for the poor, about whether the government should help more needy people if it means adding to the debt and if the government should guarantee all citizens enough to eat and a place to sleep.

The percentage of Republicans asserting a government responsibility to aid the poor has fallen sharply in recent years. Just 40% of Republicans say that "It is the responsibility of the government to take care of people who can't take care of themselves," down 18 points since 2007. By comparison, in three surveys during the George W. Bush administration, no fewer than half of Republicans said the government had a responsibility to care for those unable to care for themselves. And, in 1987, during Ronald Reagan's second term, 62% expressed this view. Majorities of Republicans now say they disagree that the government should guarantee every citizen enough to eat and a place to sleep (36% agree, 63% disagree) and take care of people who can't take care of themselves (40% agree, 54% disagree). As recently as 2009, Republican opinions on these questions were more evenly divided. Republicans also have consistently disputed the statement: "The government should help more needy people even if it means going deeper in debt." 76% now say they disagree, an increase of 15 points since 2007.

Democrats, however, continue to support government assistance to the poor and needy at the same level as they have over the last generation. Three-fourths (75%) of Democrats believe that the government should take care of those who can't take care of themselves. Similarly, 78% say basic food and shelter should be government guarantees and 65% think more support for the needy should be provided, even in the face of increased debt.

In addition to the partisan divide, there are gaps between demographic groups on views of the social safety net. But these gaps have been largely stable over the past 25 years and are now much smaller than the partisan gap. African

Americans have consistently been more supportive of a government safety net than whites. More than three-quarters (78%) of blacks support government guarantees of food and shelter, compared with 52% of whites. Support also is high among Hispanics: 78% now agree that the government should guarantee people food and shelter.

As might be expected, people with lower incomes are far more supportive of the social safety net than those with higher incomes. Women also have consistently been bigger backers of the social safety net than men: 64% of women and 54% of men support the government guaranteeing all citizens food and shelter. There are modest age and education differences, but these have changed little over the last quarter century.

In contrast, as might be expected of societies with a strong social contract, Europeans take a decidedly different view of the government's responsibility and role in providing a social safety net. Asked in 2007 by the Pew Global Attitudes survey whether it is the responsibility of the state to take care of very poor people who can't take care of themselves, 56% of the Swedes completely agreed, 53% of the British and Spanish similarly strongly assented and 52% of the Germans completely agreed, but only 28% of Americans held such firm views. And by 2012 that sentiment in the United States had fallen to 22% in a separate Pew Research Center survey.

The European social safety net is often held up as an example of a more generous and successful system of supplying health and welfare services. And many Europeans, especially northern Europeans, are particularly proud of their safety net: 81% of the French, 79% of the Danes, 75% of the Dutch, 69% of the Swedes and 62% of the Germans believe that their social welfare system could serve as a model for other countries, according to Eurobarometer . . .

Government's Role in Providing a Social Safety Net

One possible explanation for the lack of support for a robust social safety net in the United States

is that four in five Americans believe that the government does an ineffective job of helping poor and middle class Americans, according to a 2011 study by the Pew Economic Mobility Project. Americans also say that when government intervenes it is most likely to help the wrong people. And more than half (54%) believe government helps the rich a "great deal." Far fewer say it helps the poor (16%), the middle class (7%) and people like me (6%). This suggests that some Americans' antipathy toward the social safety net may stem from lack of faith in government efficacy and fairness rather than opposition to helping those in need.

But this wariness of government's side in the social contract may also have its roots in Americans' broader and conflicting views about the proper role for government in society. In March 2011, 58% of Americans said it was more important in the United States that everyone be free to pursue their life's goals without interference from the state. Just 35% thought that it was more important for the state to play an active role in society to guarantee that nobody was in need. Yet, Americans are conflicted about government's role. In April 2012, 59% of the public believed it is the responsibility of the government to take care of people who cannot take care of themselves (albeit down 10 points from 2007). And, more specifically, 59% said the government should guarantee every citizen enough to eat and a place to sleep.

In general, however, Americans favor a smaller government with fewer services (56%) than a bigger government that offers more services (38%), according to a *Washington Post/ABC News* survey in August 2012. And about half (51%) of voters in the 2012 presidential election told exit pollsters that they thought government was doing too many things better left to businesses and individuals. This may be, in part, because just 41% of the public believe that the government is really run for the benefit of all the people, according to the Pew Research Center. There is a strong partisan divide on the role of government. More than three-quarters (77%) of

Republicans say that when something is run by the government it is usually inefficient and wasteful. Just 41% of Democrats agree. . . . The relatively stronger European social safety net may, in part, reflect Europeans' belief that this is a governmental responsibility . . .

Attitudes a Reflection of Values

The interplay between economic conditions and fundamental values—such as faith in hard work—provides some insight into public attitudes toward the social safety net. It also helps to explain what would appear to be contradictory American sentiments about the role of the state and the responsibility of the individual in responding to economic challenges. Rugged individualism is a much prized and storied American value, at least in theory. Americans are among the most individualistic people in the world. In a view consonant with laissez-faire economic attitudes, roughly six in ten reject the notion that outside forces determine success in life. And Americans overwhelmingly agree that individuals, not society, are to blame for personal failures. But this broad individualistic self-image belies deep divisions among Americans. Half of lower-income Americans believe they are victims of fate, but only 22% of upper income Americans see their lives determined in that way. Democrats (41%) and Blacks (50%) are more likely than Republicans (29%) and Whites (31%) to believe that their destiny is beyond their control.

Americans largely stand alone in such an individualistic view of their personal fate. Unlike Americans, about seven in ten (72%) Germans, more than half (57%) of the French and nearly four in ten (41%) of the British see success determined by forces outside their influence. Moreover, Americans largely believe that personal effort is the key to success. Only 35% agree with the idea that "hard work offers little guarantee of success." . . . But such sentiment is clearly a class issue. Those with less education and lower incomes are more likely than those with more education and higher incomes to say that hard work does not ensure success.

Nevertheless, this broad American embrace of individualism as a matter of faith breaks down when people are asked to account for individual economic failures. When queried why unemployed people in the country are without jobs, Americans hesitate to place the blame on the jobless themselves. Less than one-in-five (18%) say those without work are responsible, according to a Pew Global Attitudes survey. . . . This seeming dichotomy between Americans' philosophical commitment to individual responsibility and yet an acknowledgment that individuals can be the victims of forces beyond their control plays itself out in attitudes toward the nature of the U.S. social contract and how to pay for it.

Paying the Price

Given declining incomes over time, the rise in inequality, the need for social services and yet Americans' wariness of government and traditional individualism, what are Americans willing to do to provide themselves with a social safety net, especially given current U.S. government indebtedness? When a price tag is attached to the provision of the social safety net, American backing for such aid declines. Since 1987, about half or less of the public has agreed with the statement that "government should help more needy people even if it means going deeper in debt" and in 2012 it was near the low point last seen in 1994. Just 43% agree that the government should help more needy people regardless of whether it means more debt, down from 48% in 2009 and 54% in 2007.

Partisan and other divides are particularly evident when cost is an issue. In 2012, only 20% of Republicans believed that government should help more needy people even if it means going deeper in debt, compared with 65% of Democrats. In 1992, 43% of Republicans were willing to pay such a price for a social safety net. In 2012, just 36% of whites were willing to see further public indebtedness to provide such government services; in 1992 50% were willing to bear that burden. Paying for the social safety net is intimately bound up with attitudes about the current U.S. budget deficit and what to do about it. This has been particularly true in the debate between Congress and the White House over a long-term deficit reduction deal. In any such agreement, the social safety net may be a major victim.

The public does not want to have to choose between deficit reduction and eroding the social safety net. If forced to choose, they prefer keeping programs rather than making cuts. In a Pew Research Center survey in August 2012, 51% of the public said that keeping Social Security and Medicare benefits as they are was more important than taking steps to reduce the budget deficit (33%). . . . There are no significant partisan differences on reducing Social Security and Medicare benefits for seniors with higher incomes. At the same time, people are willing to pay for major components of the social safety net. More than half (53%) favored raising Social Security taxes so that the benefits can be kept the same for everyone, according to a survey by the Associated Press in August 2012 . . .

In Europe, there is even greater support for paying for the social safety net. Despite their recent economic troubles, 61% of Europeans say that a higher level of health care, education and social spending must be guaranteed, even if it means that taxes may increase, according to a 2010 Eurobarometer survey. Such support is particularly strong in northern European countries with strong social safety nets: Sweden (84%), Finland (83%), and Denmark (80%). Nevertheless, there is some support in Europe for reducing the government's deficit through cutting spending rather than raising taxes. But there is also sympathy for the view that the rich should bear more of the tax burden . . .

Conclusion

The American social safety net is more porous than that afforded to citizens in many other high-income economies and the social contract is weaker. And in the effort to curtail the U.S. government debt, the support provided to average Americans who are unemployed, poor, or in need of health insurance and pensions may be further reduced. Americans oppose such cuts in social services. But they also oppose most other efforts to reduce the debt, while supporting debt reduction in principle. And they remain uncertain about the role government should play in the provision of health care, old age insurance and the like. Public ambivalence about the social safety net suggests the United States will never provide its citizens with support comparable to that provided to citizens of Germany or Scandinavia. At the same time, Americans value the social safety net that exists and do not want it changed. Americans do have a social contract with each other and with their government. But this bond is currently under great strain. Americans' conflicting values and goals and deep partisan divisions over the specifics of the social safety net, along with worries about how to pay for it, suggest that the tensions surrounding the social contract will continue for some time.

Hidden Beneficiaries of Federal Programs

Gwen Sharp

Reprinted by Permission of Gwen Sharp/*Sociological Images*, http://thesocietypages.org/socimages/.

[Editor's note: As the above article by Stokes illustrates, although many Americans rely on safety net programs such as Medicare, Social Security, and Medicaid, Americans' support for these programs is divided. In recent research, Suzanne Mettler (2010) examined one possible explanation for this varied support: Americans often do not recognize themselves as recipients of support]. Mettler, a professor in the Department of Government at Cornell, first asked survey participants whether they had ever used a federal U.S. government program. Then later in the survey she specifically asked respondents whether they had ever benefited from or participated in specific federal programs. As it turns out, large numbers of people who have benefited from various federal programs or policies do not recognize themselves as having done so. [For example, 60 percent of people who said they had not used a government social program participated in the home mortgage tax deduction program, and over 50 percent received tax credits from education, child care, or benefits from federally subsidized student loans. Only 30 percent of people who received benefits such as Medicaid, public assistance, subsidized housing, or food stamps stated that they had not participated in a government program].

Mettler argues that recipients are less likely to recognize themselves as benefiting from programs that are part of what she calls the "submerged state"—programs and policies that provide incentives and motivations for particular behaviors in the private sector, rather than overtly directing behavior. If you receive food stamps, you interact directly with a government agency, are required to periodically meet with a government worker and reapply to re-establish eligibility, and can point to a specific thing that links you to the program (these days usually a debit-type card rather than the old style coupons/stamps).

On the other hand, if you participate in the government's mortgage interest deduction program, which encourages home ownership by allowing people to deduct the cost of mortgage interest from their taxable income (which you can't do with rent costs, for instance), it's less noticeable that you are benefiting from a federal policy. You get a form from your mortgage company that provides the relevant number, and you transfer it over to the correct line when you're filling out taxes.

Notably, the programs recipients seem least likely to recognize as a government program are among those the middle (and higher) classes are most likely to use, while those more common among the poor are more clearly recognizable to those using them as government programs. Yet allowing you to write off mortgage interest (but not rent), or charitable donations, or the money you put aside for a child's education, are all forms of government programs, ones that benefit some more than others. But the "submerged" nature of these policies hides the degree to which the middle and upper classes use and benefit from federal programs.

REFERENCES

Mettler, Suzanne. 2010. "Reconstituting the submerged state: The challenges of social policy reform in the Obama era." *Perspectives on Politics* 8(3): 803–824.

Political Polarization in Contemporary American Society

MEGAN M. TESENE

The political system in America has become marked by polarization, ideological differences, and partisanship; it seems our political parties, leaders, and citizens have grown farther apart over time, leading to animosity and political gridlock. Tesene examines this trend, explaining how, in what ways, and why this shift has occurred, as well as its effects on our political system and on the average American. She also discusses major cultural and social trends predicted to occur within the next generation and their potential to change polarization in the political system (e.g., the growth of minority and immigrant populations, the decline of the working class, and the resolution of the "culture wars") and outlines strategies to begin to improve the current political climate.

Although partisanship and animosity between Republicans and Democrats have long contextualized the American sociopolitical landscape, the ideological distinction between the two parties has grown more prevalent since the 1970s (Cohn, 2014; DeSilver, 2014; Fiorina, 2014; Haidt and Hetherington, 2012; Levendusky, 2009). Prior to this shift, the Republican and Democratic parties both had strong liberal and conservative representation among their constituents and elected officials (Cohn, 2014; Haidt and Hetherington, 2012; Levendusky, 2009). Whereas liberal Republicans and conservative Democrats were once commonplace, the present-day political arena has become increasingly segregated on the basis of political ideology (Cohn, 2014; DeSilver, 2014; Fiorina, 2014; Haidt and Hetherington, 2012; Levendusky, 2009). Beginning in the 1960s, the Democratic Party began more closely associating with the Civil Rights Movement, whereas Republicans aligned themselves with the Religious Right (Haidt and Hetherington, 2012), creating distinct partisan homogeneity that previously did not exist (Fiorina, 2014). Issues that once divided the diverse membership of each political party—such as abortion, homosexuality, immigration, or gun ownership—now serve as points of unification and as a means to rally the base behind specific, common goals.

Original to *Focus on Social Problems: A Contemporary Reader*.

With each election cycle, political leaders take clearly defined "liberal" or "conservative" positions on social, cultural, and economic issues (Cohn, 2014; Fiorina, 2014; Levendusky, 2009). They distinguish themselves from the opposing party, delineating their own party's platform along clearly conservative or liberal lines. As political leaders define their parties as explicitly conservative or liberal, Americans are better able to sort themselves into the party that most represents their values (Cohn, 2014; Levendusky, 2009). These hard-and-fast ideological party lines have led liberals to the Democratic Party and conservatives to the Republican Party. Political analysts refer to this process as "political sorting" and in addition to dramatically shaping partisan affiliation, it occurs geographically and socially (Abdullah, 2013, 2014; Cohn, 2014; DeSilver, 2014; Fiorina, 2014; Levendusky, 2009; Tuschman, 2014). Compared to their counterparts from the mid- to late 20th century, present-day Americans are more likely to socialize with, marry, and live near those who are like themselves on a variety of social measures, including political affiliation (Abdullah, 2013, 2014; DeSilver, 2014; Pew, 2014; Tuschman, 2014); this is true for both conservatives and liberals, although self-segregating appears to be more common among conservatives than it is among liberals (Pew, 2014).

Such trends should not be misconstrued to imply that Americans are becoming more extreme or radical in their political views (Fiorina, 2014). Rather, they are using conservative and liberal ideology to gradually sort themselves into two distinct political "camps" (Abdullah, 2013, 2014; Fiorina, 2014; Levendusky, 2009). In this reading, I discuss how increasing political polarization is shaping the American public in a myriad of ways. In addition, I examine the effects of polarization on elected officials, governing bodies, and the broader sociopolitical landscape in general. I further describe the potential forms that political polarization may take in our country's future and highlight some of the bipartisan policy changes that may aid in creating a more efficient government and politically engaged electorate.

A Polarized Public: A Discussion of Pew's Research on Political Polarization

In 2014, the Pew Research Center carried out one of the largest nationally representative studies on American politics. The study sought to understand "the nature and scope of political polarization in the American public, and how it interrelates with government, society, and people's personal lives" (Pew, 2014). The study consists of data collected from two independent surveys. The first surveyed 10,013 American adults via telephone using 10 policy-oriented questions, which were dichotomously indexed as liberal or conservative positions (Doherty, 2014; Fiorina, 2014; Pew, 2014). Questions focused on issues such as health care, abortion, immigration, gun control, and other social, economic, and political issues (Pew, 2014). The second survey recruited a subset ($n = 3,308$) of the original respondents who identified themselves as active Internet users. These respondents form Pew's newly created American Trends Panel. For a small monetary incentive, respondents complete monthly surveys on various social, economic, and political issues (Goo, 2014). This format allows Pew to collect a breadth of data from the individual panelists that would not be possible through a single telephone survey (Goo, 2014).

The data discussed within this article highlight Pew's first and third reports on political polarization. The first report examines growing ideological uniformity and partisan antipathy among the American public (Pew, 2014). The third report focuses on American media habits within the context of increasing political polarization (Mitchell et al., 2014). Whereas the first uses data from both independent surveys, the third constitutes data solely from the American Trends Panel.

It is important to emphasize that this research does not focus on extremism or intensity of liberal–conservative ideology. Rather, it identifies and analyzes ideological consistency—that is, whether Americans' political views are consistently liberal, consistently conservative, or a mix of liberalism and conservatism (Fiorina, 2014; Pew, 2014). Consistent liberals and consistent conservatives are not necessarily on the far left or the far right ideologically. Rather, they are those who consistently supported liberal or conservative positions when presented with policy-related questions. Those that the study identifies as being in the center should not be understood to be centrist or moderate on the political spectrum (Fiorina, 2014; Pew, 2014). Instead, they are those who expressed mixed views that span the political ideology spectrum. For instance, someone may have conservative views on gun control but a liberal position on abortion. Such views may be extreme, moderate, or weak; however, the study does not measure the intensity of those views. Ultimately, the findings should be understood to reflect ideological consistency, not intensity.

Perhaps the most significant trend identified within the Pew Report (2014) is in regard to increased ideological consistency. According to the report, the proportion of Americans who are consistently liberal or conservative has doubled from 10 percent in 1994 to 21 percent in 2014. As highlighted above, an ideological sorting has been taking place since the 1970s with liberals identifying as Democrats and conservatives identifying as Republican (Cohn, 2014; DeSilver, 2014; Fiorina, 2014; Haidt and Hetherington, 2012; Levendusky, 2009). Ideological overlap is diminishing within each party and the data reflect these trends, showing that today's median Republican is 92 percent more conservative than the median Democrat and median Democrats are 94 percent more liberal than median Republicans (Doherty, 2014; Pew, 2014). This gap has been increasing over time; in 1994, those percentages were at 70 and 64, respectively (Doherty, 2014; Pew, 2014). Whereas liberals and conservatives

once constituted both parties, they are now segregated into distinct partisan camps (Abdullah, 2013, 2014).

As the two parties become more ideologically distinct from one another, their mutual feelings of distrust and antipathy have grown stronger toward those across the political aisle (Doherty, 2014; Pew, 2014). In fact, the number of Americans who view members of the "opposing" political party in a negative light has more than doubled in the past two decades, with partisan antipathy stronger among Republicans—a current difference that may be attributed to a sitting Democratic president in the White House (Pew, 2014). An earlier study confirms this trend, noting that since the Clinton administration, Republicans' and Democrats' dislike for one another has become more intense (Haidt and Hetherington, 2012). What's even more telling of the growing animosity and distrust between the two parties is that 27 percent of Democrats and 36 percent of Republicans view the other party and its policies as a "threat to the nation's well-being" (Doherty, 2014; Pew, 2014). Antipathy appears to be connected to ideological consistency because those who have the most partisan views are the ones most likely to express negativity toward the other party (Pew, 2014).

The report further notes that partisan antipathy, as well as ideological consistency, appears to drive the desire to be politically engaged and active. If one views the opposing party and its policies as inherently threatening, one may be more inclined to participate in the political process. Consequently, compromise and bipartisan politics are considered less desirable among consistent conservatives and liberals (Doherty, 2014; Pew, 2014). According to Pew (2014), these groups view the goal of compromise as getting what they want, while not giving in to the other party. For those who view the opposing party and its beliefs as inherently dangerous, bipartisanship itself appears to be a threat because it would enable those presumably harmful values to be implemented.

In addition to propelling a liberal–conservative segregation of the two parties, polarization also serves to sort liberals and conservatives both geographically and socially (Abdullah, 2013, 2014; Cohn, 2014; DeSilver, 2014; Fiorina, 2014; Levendusky, 2009; Pew, 2014; Tuschman, 2014). Both Republicans and Democrats prefer to live in communities where people share their ideological beliefs; however, this expressed desire is stronger among Republicans (Pew, 2014). Political ideology further shapes the type of neighborhoods and communities one hopes to live in. Whereas conservatives want to live in large homes that are far apart, liberals prefer smaller houses that are closer together in neighborhoods that are "walkable" (Doherty, 2014; Pew, 2014). Conservatives also have a stronger preference to live among people who share their religious faith. This difference was the most pronounced between consistent conservatives and liberals, with 57 percent of consistent conservatives and 17 percent of consistent liberals expressing such a desire (Pew, 2014). Liberals as a whole are more likely to desire living in neighborhoods that are racially and ethnically diverse; however, the contrast between consistent liberals and conservatives is once again stark. Whereas 76 percent of consistent liberals preferred racial and ethnic diversity in their communities, only 20 percent of consistent conservatives responded in kind (Pew, 2014).

Political polarization is also associated with media consumption habits as outlined in the third Pew report (Mitchell et al., 2014). Both conservatives and liberals tend to consume media that is consistent with their own ideological perspective and there is little overlap between the two in terms of their choices of news sources (Mitchell et al., 2014). One of the more marked differences is that whereas conservatives tend to rely on one primary media source (Fox News), liberals have more diverse media consumption patterns, relying on a handful of news media outlets such as CNN, MSNBC, NPR, and PBS (Mitchell et al., 2014). Another important difference is that conservatives were more likely than liberals to express distrust of the media sources identified in the study. Whereas conservatives are more likely to have social media communities that are ideologically similar, liberals are more likely to "defriend" someone for political reasons (Mitchell et al., 2014). This trend is not particularly surprising, considering conservatives are more likely than liberals to have friends who are ideologically similar on issues of politics and government (Mitchell et al., 2014).

These self-segregating patterns help to create what Pew regards as "ideological silos" or "echo chambers" where conservatives and liberals are isolated from one another and surrounded by friends, family, and communities that are ideologically homogenous. In consuming media and creating personal, political, and social media communities that are ideologically similar, they are less likely to interact with those who have differing values and beliefs (Doherty, 2014; Mitchell et al., 2014; Pew, 2014). Immersion in these ideological silos can further exacerbate ideological homogeneity and partisan antipathy (Pew, 2014).

As this political sorting takes place, the center—made up of those with mixed ideological views—continues to narrow (Doherty, 2014; Pew, 2014). Whereas almost half (49 percent) of the U.S. adult population expressed a combination of conservative and liberal ideology in 1994, that number has decreased to 39 percent today. However, they still constitute the majority of American adults. They also differ from those who have more partisan political perspectives. They tend to have more politically diverse friends and live in politically mixed communities; they express less negativity and antipathy toward either political party; they are less inclined to view partisan policies as a "threat to the nation;" and they are more likely to prefer congressional compromise and bipartisanship rather than "getting their way." Although they constitute the majority, they are often the least interested and least engaged at each stage of the political process (Doherty, 2014: Pew, 2014).

On the other hand, those who are the most consistent ideologically are the most active and engaged politically (Doherty, 2014; Pew, 2014)—they also make up just 21 percent of American adults. Despite their smaller numbers, their active engagement at every stage of the political process significantly shapes the broader sociopolitical landscape in America. They fund campaigns and candidates of their liking, help elect those candidates to positions of power, and actively work to ensure that the only candidates who remain in office are those who toe the party line (Abdullah, 2013, 2014). Their disproportionate representation during caucus, primary, and general elections ensures that their preferred candidates are the ones who are elected and reelected. Compounded with the inactive and somewhat apathetic position of those with mixed political ideologies, they have helped to create and sustain one of the most politically polarized Congresses since the Civil War and Reconstruction (DeSilver, 2014; Haidt and Hetherington, 2012; Hare et al., 2014).

Congressional Polarization: Trends and Outcomes

Although it is not clear whether Congressional polarization started before or after public polarization (DeSilver, 2014), there does appear to be a cyclical relationship between congressional and public polarization: (1) polarizing political leaders shape the ideological party platform—aligning with either conservative or liberal values (Cohn, 2014; Fiorina, 2014; Levendusky, 2009); (2) the public then sorts itself into the party that best fits their views—liberals become Democrats and conservatives become Republican (Abdullah, 2013, 2014; Cohn, 2014; DeSilver, 2014; Fiorina, 2014; Levendusky, 2009; Tuschman, 2014); (3) partisans support, elect, and reelect political leaders who strictly follow the party line (Abdullah, 2013, 2014); (4) those leaders continue to push their party's increasingly rigid ideological agenda—indeed, if they do not, they will lose their positions (Abdullah, 2013, 2014); and (5) the process continues.

A consequence of this cyclical process is that congressional polarization is currently at an all-time high. Using scores that identify and track congressional roll call votes on a liberal–conservative scale, Keith Poole and Howard Rosenthal (2015) mapped congressional polarization trends from 1879 to the present (DeSilver, 2014; Haidt and Hetherington, 2012; Hare et al., 2012; Matthews, 2013). Their analysis indicates that congressional leadership was significantly polarized just after the Civil War and Reconstruction; polarization dramatically decreased after World War I, remaining low through World War II and its postwar era; during the 1960s and 1970s, Congress started becoming polarized once more; and in the 1980s, the parties became more ideologically homogenous, leading to political sorting, and this trend has continued to the present day (Haidt and Hetherington, 2012).

The most recent Congresses have been described as the most polarized to date (Hare et al., 2014; Matthews, 2013). Not surprisingly, they've also been the least effective in congressional history (Bump, 2014), no doubt one of the causes for their "all-time low" ratings (Bipartisan Policy Center, 2014; Riffkin, 2014). As Democratic and Republican leaders grow apart ideologically, they become less capable of compromise and consequently, less capable of passing legislation and doing the jobs they were elected to do (DeSilver, 2014; Haidt and Hetherington, 2012; Hare et al., 2014; Matthews, 2013). Interestingly, congressional leaders' inability to push through legislation—often because of gridlock and a lack of bipartisanship—hasn't caused voters to push them out of office. In fact, although American voters "overwhelmingly disapprove of the job Congress" is currently doing, they continue to reelect most members back into office each election cycle (Mendes, 2013). Polls show that despite broader congressional approval ratings—or rather, a lack thereof—most Americans have a positive view of their own representatives (Mendes, 2013). Each election term, they reelect their local and regional representatives (Mendes,

2013) and thus contribute to the perpetuation of congressional discord.

Those voters who are consistently conservative or liberal actually prefer that their elected officials avoid bipartisan compromise (Doherty, 2014; Pew, 2014). As mentioned earlier, these individuals tend to view the goal of compromise as getting what they want, rather than giving in and working with those across the aisle (Doherty, 2014; Pew, 2014). However, as a whole, most Americans do not agree with this sentiment (Pew, 2014) and prefer that their elected leaders work together rather than against one another (Bipartisan Policy Center, 2014; Pew, 2014). But without substantial change, such as an increase in political engagement among the majority or a decrease in partisan political ideology, it is likely that these trends will persist (Haidt and Hetherington, 2012; Hare et al., 2014).

A Look to the Future

In their discussion of increasing political polarization and its effects, Hare et al. (2014) outline four distinct pathways polarization may take. The first, and most unlikely, is what they describe as a "hot decline in polarization." This would take place if our current two-party system simply broke down, much like it did just before the Civil War. Another possibility is that polarization could become even worse. If Democrats were to shift drastically to the left—embracing more European-style or social democratic principles— compromise and bipartisanship would become even less likely (Hare et al., 2014). The two more realistic options are that "polarization will stabilize at or near current levels for the foreseeable future" or we will instead witness what the researchers deem a "cooling-off period," where both parties shift back toward the ideological center (Hare et al., 2014). If such a shift took place, candidates with moderate or mixed conservative–liberal ideologies would become more commonplace (Hare et al., 2014).

In an analysis of demographic and geographic shifts taking place in the United States, Ruy Teixeira (2008) argues that the "cultural

wars" that currently shape the contemporary American politicosphere are nearing their end. As these social and cultural issues become less important to a changing American electorate, the political polarization we are currently accustomed to will gradually decline, taking its gridlocking and lack of congressional productivity along with it (Teixeira, 2008). According to Teixeira (2008), ongoing demographic and geographic changes will likely take us back to the ideological center, and that center will likely shift as well—causing both Democratic and Republican parties to reassess their platforms and goals to remain relevant to an ever-evolving American people.

Teixeira (2008) highlights several important trends that will significantly shape the face of the American electorate and, in doing so, will alter the American political landscape. As the population expands, we'll see emergent suburbs and exurbs grow on the "metropolitan fringes" of urban cities (Lang et al., 2008; Teixeira, 2008). Older suburbs will grow at a slower rate, urbanizing and becoming home to increasingly diverse communities (Lang et al., 2008; Teixeira, 2008). In doing so, they will likely become increasingly liberal (Lang et al., 2008; Teixeira, 2008). Traditionally, the farther out a community is from an urban core, the more likely it is to be both conservative and Republican (Teixeira, 2008). Although communities on the metropolitan fringe are expanding more rapidly, population densities of the urban core and urbanizing suburbs are significantly higher, thus retaining their political and electorate power.

Another important trend that will shape the political landscape is growing minority and immigrant populations who tend to lean more Democratic (Frey, 2008; Teixeira, 2008). Hispanic, Asian, and black communities are growing at much faster rates than are non-Hispanic whites. However, it must be noted that the electoral impact of Hispanics and Asians is weakened because many are either younger than 18 or currently not citizens (Frey, 2008; Teixeira, 2008). In addition, the current tendency of minority and immigrant communities to align themselves with the Democratic Party should not be taken for granted or assumed to be stable over the long haul (Frey, 2008; Teixeira, 2008). Region can play an important role in shaping voting patterns among minority communities. For instance, Hispanics living in the South vote more conservatively than their counterparts on the West Coast (Frey, 2008; Teixeira, 2008).

As communities of color expand, the white working class—a group that has long existed as a large and powerful voting bloc of the American electorate—is both transforming and declining in number (Abramowitz and Teixeira, 2008; Teixeira, 2008). Once characterized by blue-collar and manufacturing positions, today's white working class is seeing increases in level of education and in median income (Abramowitz and Teixeira, 2008; Teixeira, 2008). Changes in the economic structure have also led to a shift toward the service sector and low-level white-collar service positions (Abramowitz and Teixeira, 2008; Teixeira, 2008). In the past, white working-class communities tended to vote primarily Democratic; however, in recent decades they have more closely affiliated with the Republican Party. Although the working class is on the decline, the upper middle class—those households making $100,000 or more—is growing. These educated professionals tend to have mixed political ideologies—being socially liberal and economically moderate (Abramowitz and Teixeira, 2008; Teixeira, 2008). Thus, both political parties will need to vie for their support or shift their political ideology to be more palatable to this expanding voting bloc (Abramowitz and Teixeira, 2008; Teixeira, 2008).

Smith (2008) and Teixeira (2008) also identify the shifting American family structure as a potential source of the changing political landscape. The institution of marriage is no longer as dominant as it once was. Divorce, single-parent households, cohabitation, and never-married and same-sex families are all becoming more prevalent. In fact, those families who are described as "married with children" constitute less than 25 percent of American households (Smith, 2008; Teixeira, 2008). Whereas married voters are more likely to vote Republican, never-married persons are more likely to vote Democratic (Smith, 2008; Teixeira, 2008). Married couples with children are more likely to vote Republican, whereas single-parent households are significantly more likely to vote Democratic. As cultural mores change, we should expect an increase in the number of nontraditional families who will likely be more politically liberal (Smith, 2008; Teixeira, 2008).

Another change we are seeing is an increase in both secular and Evangelical populations (Green and Dionne, 2008; Teixeira, 2008). Secular voters are often liberal, whereas Evangelicals are overwhelmingly conservative. The researchers also note how Americans, as a whole, are becoming less religiously observant and that one's level of observance significantly shapes whether he or she votes Republican or Democrat (Green and Dionne, 2008; Teixeira, 2008). Those who are more religiously observant tend to vote Republican, whereas those who are less observant often vote for the Democratic Party (Green and Dionne, 2008; Teixeira, 2008). Noting the diverse range of issues facing Americans today, such as global warming, increasing economic inequality, and America's role in foreign policy, the researchers speculate that the cultural issues that often pit conservatives and liberals against one another are going to become less important over time (Green and Dionne, 2008; Teixeira, 2008). Along with other demographic changes, which will likely liberalize views on social and cultural issues, debate on such issues will become less heated and less polarized.

It is also possible that political polarization could decrease with generational changes (Haidt and Hetherington, 2012; Keeter, 2008; Teixeira, 2008). Indeed, each consecutive generational cohort becomes increasingly liberal, with Millennials being the most liberal of any age group (Kiley and Dimock, 2014; Lauter, 2014). As younger generations become older, start taking on political leadership positions, and begin constituting the majority of active voters, we could likely see a gradual decrease in polarization and, ultimately, an increase in legislative compromise (Haidt and Hetherington, 2012). Although each of these trends may help to lessen the current antagonisms between political parties, additional efforts will be needed to create substantive change.

Strategies for Change

In 2013, the Bipartisan Policy Center brought together engaged citizens, elected officials, and various "issue experts" from across the political spectrum to form a Commission on Political Reform (Bipartisan Policy Center, 2014). The commission worked toward identifying various strategies that might be implemented to help remedy some of the diverse social problems exacerbated by political polarization. According to the commission's report, there is a growing sense of distrust between Republicans and Democrats. Each party fears that the other is making extensive efforts to manipulate the electoral and legislative processes. In addition, many Americans are frustrated with legislators and their inability to do the job they were elected to do. The antagonism between parties and the distrust for the electoral process and, by extension, our government, has carried over into the American psyche—creating an apathetic and unengaged electorate (Bipartisan Policy Center, 2014).

Given these concerns, the commission identifies three key areas to focus on: electoral system reform, congressional reform, and encouraging Americans' civic engagement (Bipartisan Policy Center, 2014). Although they make several suggestions for how to address these key areas, I will highlight only a handful of their proposals. To improve the electoral system, they suggest making efforts to increase voter registration and participation and to develop new forms of candidate selection. In addition, they argue that trust for the electoral process can be improved if there is more transparency in political contributions. Americans have the right to know how

politicians, their campaigns, and their political action committees (PACs) are being funded.

In regard to congressional reform, the report identifies many strategies for ensuring the government becomes more functional than it is at present. Many suggestions address increasing communication and interaction between the two parties. They propose that the House and Senate synchronize their schedules and be required to have regular five-day workweeks. Since Newt Gingrich changed the legislative calendar in the mid-1990s, most legislators live in their home states rather than in Washington—thus preventing them from having face time and developing positive working relationships with other legislators (Haidt and Hetherington, 2012). Many fly in on Tuesday and out on Thursday, wasting time in transit instead of building relationships and networking with colleagues face-to-face (Haidt and Hetherington, 2012). Increasing expectations of fundraising further exacerbates this distance between congressional parties. Instead of performing their legislative responsibilities and connecting with their colleagues, congressional leaders spend a significant portion of their workdays fundraising and campaigning (Grim and Siddiqui, 2013; Kroll, 2013). They also propose that the president meet with congressional leaders at least once a month—a practical approach, but one not currently implemented. In addition, they argue it is important that congressional committees pay special attention to minority members because all members should have a voice and the opportunity to structure legislative bills (Bipartisan Policy Center, 2014).

Values that once defined a publicly engaged American electorate are falling by the wayside. Fewer and fewer Americans are volunteering. Charitable donations are decreasing and few see the appeal or benefit of pursuing office themselves. The commission contends that to have a strong democratic society, we must have an educated and engaged American citizenry. Some suggestions include efforts at the collegiate and university levels. By offering diverse resources, curricula, and developmental opportunities to their students, institutions of higher learning can cultivate a student body that is politically informed, impassioned, and engaged. They also suggest that all Americans aged 18 to 28 years give "one year of full service to their communities or nation" via civilian, military, volunteer, or other nonprofit organizations (Bipartisan Policy Center, 2014:9). Furthermore, they argue the federal government must increase opportunities and funding to organizations such as Ameri-Corps, Vista, and the Peace Corps. These efforts, in addition to those highlighted above, are just some of the ways that we can begin instituting change, making both our government and its citizenry better suited to address the diverse and challenging issues that our country faces today.

REFERENCES

Abdullah, Halimah. 2013. "It's Your Fault: How Our 'Tribes' Help Create Gridlock in Congress." *CNN News*. Retrieved March 21, 2015. http://www.cnn.com/2013/02/06/politics/congress-redistrict-fault/.

Abdullah, Halimah. 2014. "Partisan Politics in Congress the Product of a More Polarized Electorate." *CNN News*. Retrieved March 20, 2015. http://www.cnn.com/2014/06/12/politics/pew-survey-society-polarization/.

Abramowitz, Alan, and Ruy Teixeira. 2008. "The Decline of the White Working Class and the Rise of a Mass Upper-Middle Class." Pp. 109–143 in *Red, Blue & Purple America: The Future of Election Demographics,* edited by Ruy Teixeira. Washington, DC: Brookings Institution Press.

Bipartisan Policy Center. 2014. "Governing in a Polarized America: A Bipartisan Blueprint to Strengthen Our Democracy, Executive Summary." *Bipartisan Policy Center*. Retrieved March 20, 2015. http://bipartisanpolicy.org/wp-content/uploads/sites/default/files/files/BPC%20CPR%20Executive%20Summary.pdf/.

Bump, Philip. 2014. "The 113th Congress Is Historically Good at Not Passing Bills." *The Washington Post*. Retrieved March 23, 2015. http://www.washingtonpost.com/blogs/the-fix/wp/2014/07/09/the-113th-congress-is-historically-good-at-not-passing-bills/.

Cohn, Nate. 2014. "Polarization Is Dividing American Society, Not Just Politics." *The New York Times*. Retrieved March 20, 2015. http://www.nytimes.com/2014/06/12/upshot/polarization-is-dividing-american-society-not-just-politics.html?_r=0&abt=0002&abg=0/.

DeSilver, Drew. 2014. "The Polarized Congress of Today Has Its Roots in the 1970s." *Pew Research Center*. Retrieved March 20, 2015. http://www.pewresearch.org/fact-tank/2014/06/12/polarized-politics-in-congress-began-in-the-1970s-and-has-been-getting-worse-ever-since/.

Doherty, Carroll. 2014. "7 Things to Know about Polarization in America." *Pew Research Center*. Retrieved March 20, 2015. http://www.pewresearch.org/fact-tank/2014/06/12/7-things-to-know-about-polarization-in-america/.

Fiorina, Morris. 2014. "Americans Have Not Become More Politically Polarized." *The Washington Post*. Retrieved March 20, 2015. http://www.washingtonpost.com/blogs/monkey-cage/wp/2014/06/23/americans-have-not-become-more-politically-polarized/.

Frey, William. 2008. "Race, Immigration, and America's Changing Electorate." Pp. 79–108 in *Red, Blue & Purple America: The Future of Election Demographics,* edited by Ruy Teixeira. Washington, DC: Brookings Institution Press.

Goo, Sara. 2014. "How Pew Research Conducted the Polarization Survey and Launched a New Research Panel." *Pew Research Center*. Retrieved March 30, 2015. http://www.pewresearch.org/fact-tank/2014/06/12/how-pew-research-conducted-the-polarization-survey-and-launched-a-new-research-panel/.

Green, John, and E. J. Dionne Jr. 2008. "Religion and American Politics: More Secular, More Evangelical, or Both?" Pp. 194–224 in *Red, Blue & Purple America: The Future of Election Demographics,* edited by Ruy Teixeira. Washington, DC: Brookings Institution Press.

Grim, Ryan, and Sabrina Siddiqui. 2013. "Call Time for Congress Shows How Fundraising Dominates

Bleak Work Life." *Huffington Post*. Retrieved April 27, 2015. http://www.huffingtonpost.com/2013/01/08/call-time-congressional-fundraising_n_2427291.html/.

Haidt, Jonathan, and Marc Hetherington. 2012. "Look How Far We've Come Apart." *The New York Times*. Retrieved March 20, 2015. http://campaignstops.blogs.nytimes.com/2012/09/17/look-how-far-weve-come-apart/?_r=0&assetType=opinion/.

Hare, Christopher, Keith Poole, and Howard Rosenthal. 2014. "Polarization in Congress Has Risen Sharply. Where Is It Going Next?" *The Washington Post*. Retrieved March 20, 2015. http://www.washingtonpost.com/blogs/monkey-cage/wp/2014/02/13/polarization-in-congress-has-risen-sharply-where-is-it-going-next/.

Keeter, Scott. 2008. "The Aging of the Boomers and the Rise of the Millennials." Pp. 225–257 in *Red, Blue & Purple America: The Future of Election Demographics,* edited by Ruy Teixeira. Washington, DC: Brookings Institution Press.

Kiley, Jocelyn, and Michael Dimock. 2014. "The GOP's Millenial Problem Runs Deep." *Pew Research Center*. Retrieved March 21, 2015. http://www.pewresearch.org/fact-tank/2014/09/25/the-gops-millennial-problem-runs-deep/.

Kroll, Andy. 2013. "Retiring Senator: Congress Doesn't Work Because We Fundraise Way Too Much." *Mother Jones*. Retrieved April 27, 2015. http://www.motherjones.com/mojo/2013/01/tom-harkin-retire-senator-fundraise-money/.

Lang, Robert, Thomas Sanchez, and Alan Berube. 2008. "The New Suburban Politics: A County-Based Analysis of Metropolitan Voting Trends since 2000." Pp. 25–49 in *Red, Blue & Purple America: The Future of Election Demographics,* edited by Ruy Teixeira. Washington, DC: Brookings Institution Press.

Lauter, David. 2014. "Millennial Generation Less Religious, More Liberal Than Older Ones." *Los Angeles Times*. Retrieved March 21, 2015. http://articles.latimes.com/2014/mar/07/news/la-pn-millennials-liberal-views-pew-poll-20140306/.

Levendusky, Matthew. 2009. *The Partisan Sort: How Liberals Became Democrats and Conservatives Became Republicans*. Chicago, IL: University of Chicago Press.

Matthews, Dylan. 2013. "It's Official: The 112th Congress Was the Most Polarized Ever." *The Washington Post*. Retrieved March 20, 2015. http://www.washingtonpost.com/blogs/wonkblog/wp/2013/01/17/its-official-the-112th-congress-was-the-most-polarized-ever/.

Mendes, Elizabeth. 2013. "Americans Down on Congress, OK with Own Representatives." *Gallup*. Retrieved March 30, 2015. http://www.gallup.com/poll/162362/americans-down-congress-own-representative.aspx/.

Mitchell, Amy, Jeffrey Gottfried, Jocelyn Kiley, and Katerina Eva Matsa. 2014. "Political Polarization & Media Habits." *Pew Research Center*. Retrieved March 20, 2015. http://www.journalism.org/2014/10/21/political-polarization-media-habits/.

Pew Research Center. 2014. "Political Polarization in the American Public: How Increasing Ideological Uniformity and Partisan Antipathy Affect Politics, Compromise and Everyday Life." *Pew Research Center*. Retrieved March 20, 2015. http://www.people-press.org/2014/06/12/political-polarization-in-the-american-public/.

Poole, Keith, and Howard Rosenthal. 2015. "Polarized America." *The Voteview Website (1995–Present), University of Georgia, Department of Political Science*. Retrieved March 30, 2015. http://www.polarizedamerica.com/.

Riffkin, Rebecca. 2014. "2014 U.S. Approval of Congress Remains near All-Time Low." *Gallup*. Retrieved March 21, 2015. http://www.gallup.com/poll/180113/2014-approval-congress-remains-near-time-low.aspx/.

Smith, Tom. 2008. "Changes in Family Structure, Family Values, and Politics, 1972–2006." Pp. 147–193 in *Red, Blue & Purple America: The Future of Election Demographics,* edited by Ruy Teixeira. Washington, DC: Brookings Institution Press.

Teixeira, Ruy. 2008. "Beyond Polarization? The Future of Red, Blue, and Purple America."

Pp. 1–22 in *Red, Blue & Purple America: The Future of Election Demographics,* edited by Ruy Teixeira. Washington, DC: Brookings Institution Press.

Tuschman, Avi. 2014. "Why Americans Are So Polarized: Education and Evolution." *The Atlantic.* Retrieved March 20, 2015. http://www .theatlantic.com/politics/archive/2014/02/ why-americans-are-so-polarized-education- and-evolution/284098/.

 ## The Story of *Citizens United v. FEC:* Why Democracy Only Works When People Are in Charge

Annie Leonard, Jonah Sachs, and Louis Fox

Script written by Annie Leonard, Jonah Sachs, and Louis Fox. Reprinted with permission and provided by *The Story of Stuff.* To watch the movie, learn more, and get involved, visit storyofstuff.org/.

Why is it that every election season, it becomes impossible to hear the facts over all . . . [those] misleading [political] ads? And if it seems the problem is only getting worse, that's because it is.[1] We can thank the Supreme Court for that. In 2010, they decided that it'd be just fine for corporations to spend as much money as they want telling us who to vote for.[2]

Wait, why are corporations telling us who to vote for? . . . [Isn't] this is a democracy . . . [with] rule by the people? I'm a person. You're a person. And Chevron? Not a person. So shouldn't elections be all about what people want? Good jobs. Safe products. Healthcare. Responsible government. Clean air and water. It turns out that the vast majority of Americans want to see a lot more done on all of these . . . [issues].[3] But what people want will take a backseat as long as corporations can spend millions getting lawmakers elected. Oil companies[4] have gotten politicians to block laws protecting our climate. Manufacturers have pushed through trade agreements that gut product safety and help ship jobs overseas.[5] Insurance companies have been the first ones consulted on health care reform[6] and giant corporations have gotten bail-outs and subsidies.[7]

Maybe that's why all kinds of people—Republicans, Democrats, independents—are totally frustrated with our government. It's easy to get angry. But it's time we got smart and realized that the heart of our problem is not that we have bad lawmakers. We have a democracy in crisis. 85% of Americans feel that corporations have too much power in our democracy and people have too little.[8] 85 percent! . . . So let's get together and take our democracy back from corporations. It's the first and most important step in making real progress on all the issues people care most about.

So how did "we the people" lose control of our democracy to begin with? Let's go back a few centuries. Back then there were just people. Some of them owned businesses. Some of them worked for businesses. Still, there were just people. Then people invented something entirely new—the corporation.[9] These legal entities exist independently of the people who own them. If a corporation does something that gets it into trouble, the owners can say, "Don't blame me, blame the corporation. I'm just a shareholder!"[10] When the United States came into existence, corporations were easier to keep in check. Back then, the government would grant them charters for a specific short-term project, like building a bridge or a railroad.[11] Once they fulfilled their purpose, they were disbanded. But over time, the law changed and corporations no longer had to be "turned off" once their project was complete. They began to live on indefinitely, with a much more general purpose, *profit.*[12] And that's how the modern corporation was born. Today's corporations have evolved to have something very dangerous in their programming. Unlike people, who are driven by all kinds of motivations—doing the right thing, love for family, their country, the planet—publicly traded corporations are now required, by law and the markets, to pursue one single motivation above all others. Maximize value for shareholders—make as much money as possible.

That's it. No, really, that's what the law and the markets demand. Yet imagine a friend saying, "The only thing I really care about is money." Not someone you'd want to leave your kids with, or your democracy for that matter. Yes, it is people who run these corporations but their human motivations come second. If they prioritize anything at all over maximizing profits, they're . . . [fired]. Can corporate leaders do good things like give to charity or try to be more "green"? Sure. But not if it conflicts with maximum profits.[13]

And since their humble beginnings, corporations have grown huge. 53 of the 100 biggest economies on earth are now corporations.[14] So corporations have a single-minded profit motive. They're humongous. And their owners can easily dodge the blame for any harm they cause. That makes them tricky to share a country with. If we want them to serve us, and not the other way around, they need some basic ground rules. And that's where the government comes in, setting rules to keep things fair and safe and to protect society from corporations run amok.

Now if their main objective is to maximize profit, do you think corporations are content to follow rules[15] that keep them in check? No, of course not. They want to write those rules. But who is supposed to write the rules in a democracy? People. That's why one of the corporations' key strategies for sneaking into our democracy is saying they should have the same First Amendment rights as real, live people.[16] And that's exactly how they won that 2010 Supreme Court case known as *Citizens United v. FEC*.[17] In that case, five members of the Supreme Court decided that it [is] unconstitutional to put any limits on how much money corporations can spend influencing elections. Why? They said these limits violate the first amendment guaranteeing free speech.[18]

Obviously . . . [the] founding fathers who wrote the first amendment were trying to protect the free speech of people.[19] But this decision rides on the . . . argument that corporations should be treated the same as people and should get the same rights real people get![20] This means corporations can spend as much as they want, whenever they want, to intimidate or crush candidates running on a platform against their interests, and support candidates who will do what they ask. [The decision was] great news for corporations wanting to handpick the lawmakers whose job it is to keep them in check.

Now, I'm all for free speech! If every shareholder and employee at Exxon wants to personally support some oil lobbyist running for Senate, it's their right. There are millions more people who will support a different candidate. That's democracy in action! But . . . [after *Citizens United*], Exxon or any other corporation can decide to spend unlimited dollars from its huge corporate coffers to influence an election, without even consulting its shareholders. This is a big deal. If the top 100 corporations decided to throw in just 1% of their profits, they could outspend every candidate for President, House and Senate combined![21] Good luck having your free speech heard over that!

So did opening the floodgates on this money actually cause a flood? Sure did. In 2010, the kind of "independent" groups that corporations are now allowed to support spent $300 million.[22] That's more than every midterm election since 1990 combined![23] So corporations are drowning out our voices, getting what they want and our democracy is in trouble.

But we can totally save it! People are so outraged by the Supreme Court decision that a massive response is mobilizing. Such a huge problem requires a huge solution and we've got one: a new constitutional amendment. The amendment is smart and clear. It reverses this disaster to our democracy by clarifying that the first amendment isn't meant for for-profit corporations.[24] I get that amending the constitution is a big, ambitious goal. But it's not impossible. Every time huge positive change has been made in this country, it's because people dreamed big, aimed high, and set ambitious goals. It's time to do that now, because the life of our democracy is on the line. Public financing of campaigns

continues

■ Continued

would be another huge step forward.[25] Congress is working on a bill right now that would make it possible for candidates to get elected without corporate dollars.[26]

Remember, 85% of Americans think that corporations have too much influence in our democracy. That's enough to make change, if we can turn that sentiment into action. . . . [T]he corporations won't get out of our democracy until we, the people, get back in. So keep fighting for renewable energy, green jobs, health care, safe products and top-notch public education. But save some energy for the battle of our lifetimes . . . a battle that can open the door to solving all of these things. It's time to put corporations back in their place and to put people back in charge of our democracy.

NOTES

1. Bloomberg reported that spending on advertising in U.S. Senate races between January 1 and October 2, 2010 rose to $314 million from almost $157.5 million during the same period in 2008, and in House races to more than $210 million in 2010 from almost $142 million in 2008, according to an analysis by the Wesleyan Media Project of data from Kantar Media's Campaign Media Analysis Group (http://www .businessweek.com/ news/2010-10-27/election-spending-already-a-record-might-reach-4-billion .html). Those figures are based on a conservative methodology that likely underestimates total expenditures . . .

2. *Citizens United v. Federal Election Commission*, 558 U. S. (2010) (holding that "restrictions on corporate independent expenditures are therefore invalid.") http://www.supremecourt.gov/opinions/ 09pdf/08-205.pdf.

3. Americans list jobs as their top policy priority (http://www.politicsdaily.com/2011/01/20/ americans-say-economy-jobs-are-top-priorities-but-divide-on-ot/).

People are very angry about unemployment and poor functioning government (http://www .harrisinteractive.com/NewsRoom/HarrisPolls/ tabid/447/mid/1508/articleId/592/ctl/Read Custom%20Default/Default.aspx).

Voters strongly favor candidates who support clean energy (http://www.nrdcactionfund .org/updates/voters-overwhelmingly-support-clean-energy-candidates.html/).

4. The Center for Public Integrity found that more than 770 companies and interest groups hired an estimated 2,340 lobbyists to influence federal policy on climate change in 2008–2009, as the issue gathered momentum and came to a vote on Capitol Hill. That's an increase of more than 300 percent in the number of lobbyists on climate change in just five years, and means that Washington can now boast more than four climate lobbyists for every member of Congress. Opponents of climate change rules vastly outnumbered proponents, and even many of the proponents favored inadequate protections for the climate (http://www .publicintegrity.org/investigations/climate_ change/articles/entry/1171/).

After the 2010 election, most view federal climate change legislation as off the table.

. . . [F]ossil-fuel-friendly members of Congress are seeking to block the Environmental Protection Agency from implementing laws like the Clean Air Act and Clean Water Act to regulate carbon polluters.

5. For a detailed and devastating account of the deceptive Big Business campaign to win passage of NAFTA (the North American Free Trade Agreement), see John MacArthur, *The Selling of Free Trade: NAFTA, Washington, and the Subversion of American Democracy*, New York: Hill & Wang, 2000.

On the political campaign to win U.S. passage of World Trade Organization agreements, see Andrew Wheat, "A Year in the Life of the GATT Business Lobby," Multinational Monitor, October 1994 (http://www.multinationalmonitor.org/hyper/ issues/1994/10/mm1094_05.html).

To learn more and to track current issues related to trade agreements, see Public Citizen's

Global Trade Watch: http://www.citizen.org/trade/.

6. The Obama administration's health insurance reform was the culmination of a decades-long debate over healthcare policy. The administration included the health insurance lobby all along the process of developing its legislative proposal. By contrast, advocates of a Medicare-for-all, single payer policy were systematically excluded from negotiations. By way of example, the administration held a high-profile "summit" on health reform in March 2009. The CEO of America's Health Insurance Plans, the trade association for the health insurance industry, participated; but no advocates of single payer were invited (http://www.pbs.org/wgbh/pages/frontline/obamasdeal/etc/cron.html; http://www.pbs.org/newshour/updates/health/jan-june09/healthcare_03-05.html).

7. Most famously, of course, the banks obtained a giant $700 billion bailout, approved by Congress in 2008 and 2009 (formally known as the Troubled Assets Relief Program, TARP). Wall Street and the Big Banks actually received trillions of dollars in a wide array of much less well understood public supports. To be clear, many of these programs were so complicated they offered gigantic public subsidies without actually costing taxpayers; many created programs were not fully implemented; and Wall Street firms and the banks have paid back most of the loan-like subsidies they received through TARP. But the subsidies were of unfathomable size, and Wall Street would have collapsed but for the government intervention (http://www.sigtarp.gov/987egapograbme123654/J09-3-SIG-RTC.pdf). Many more subsidies are provided to a variety of other corporations, as Ralph Nader testified to Congress a few years ago (http://www.nader.org/releases/63099.html).

8. "Protecting Democracy from Unlimited Corporate Spending," a national survey conducted by Hart Research Associates for People for the American Way, June 6–7, 2010. (Survey report available at: http://www.pfaw.org/sites/default/files/CitUPoll-PFAW.pdf and more information

at: http://www.pfaw.org/press-releases/2010/06/new-pfaw-poll-shows-americans-want-action-to-correct-citizens-united). Results of the survey found:

- 85% of voters say that corporations have too much influence over the political system today while 93% say that average citizens have too little influence.
- 95% agree that "Corporations spend money on politics mainly to buy influence in government and elect people who are favorable to their financial interests . . ."
- 85% disagree that "Corporations should be able to spend as much as they want to influence the outcome of elections because the Constitution protects freedom of speech . . ."
- 93% agree that "There should be clear limits on how much money corporations can spend to influence the outcome of an election . . ."
- 77% think Congress should support an amendment to limit the amount U.S. corporations can spend to influence elections.
- 74% say that they would be more likely to vote for a candidate for Congress who pledged to support a Constitutional Amendment limiting corporate spending in elections.

9. For a brief history of the rise of the corporation, see Chapter One of Joel Bakan, *The Corporation: The Pathological Pursuit of Profit and Power*, New York: Free Press, 2004. The corporation traces back at least to the 1500s in the United Kingdom. (Think of the East Indian Company, for example.) In the United States, colonial legislatures had conferred charters on only seven business corporations by 1780, but roughly 300 by 1800. (Morton Horowitz, *The Transformation of American Law, 1780–1860*, Cambridge, Massachusetts: Harvard University Press, 1977, p. 112.) Many more corporations were created in the first half of the 1800s; and the modern corporation emerged in the United States in the second half of the nineteenth century.

10. Perhaps the key idea underlying the corporation is the notion of "limited liability." The corporation as an entity is responsible for what it does,

continues

■ Continued

and is obligated to pay for harm it causes and to pay its debts. But if it doesn't have enough money to compensate those it has injured, or to pay its debts, victims and creditors are out of luck. A victim of corporate wrongdoing or a creditor cannot seek to recover money from the company's shareholders, with very few exceptions. "Limited liability" means that shareholders' liability for a corporation's actions is limited to the amount of their investment in the company. Limited liability only became firmly embedded in U.S. law in the second half of the nineteenth century. Joel Bakan, *The Corporation*: op. cit., p. 13.

11. David Korten, *When Corporations Rule the World*, Kumarian Press, Inc. and Berrett-Koehler Publishers, Inc. 2001, pp. 60–68.; Lawrence Mitchell, 2007, op. cit.

12. U.S. corporate law shifted from requiring corporations to serve a specific purpose involving a particular line of business, to a more general purpose of rewarding shareholders with profit. (Lawrence Mitchell, *The Speculation Economy: How Finance Triumphed over Industry*, San Francisco: Berrett–Koehler, 2007.)

13. Corporate law is somewhat murky in this area, but existing practice for publicly traded corporations is not.

    In practice, the markets punish publicly traded corporations that fail to deliver strong short-term (typically quarterly) results. Companies that do not show strong short-term results see their stock prices fall. Top executives at companies with falling share prices will eventually be fired. As a result, executives pay attention to the daily ups-and-downs of their companies' share price . . .

    It is often stated that corporations have a legal duty to prioritize profits. This is not precisely accurate. By way of illustration, Delaware's corporate law establishes that companies may exist for the "purposes set forth in its certificate of incorporation." (Delaware Code, Title 8, Subchapter 121. http://delcode.delaware.gov/title8/

c001/sc02/index.shtml). That is a general grant of authority, with no requirement to maximize profit.

Corporations generally take advantage of this kind of language to establish that their purpose is to do anything that corporations are able to do—a circular reference that means they have general purpose with no restriction save adherence to the law . . .

Publicly traded corporations, however, have obligations to their shareholders, and if a corporation wastes assets, or pursues policies that recklessly cost the company, courts will hold the corporation and/or its directors liable to shareholders . . .

14. Medard Gabel, *Global Inc.: An Atlas of the Multinational Corporation*, 2003, p. 2, citing data from "The World's Largest Corporations: Fortune 2000 Global 500," *Fortune Magazine*, July 23, 2001, pp. F1–F10 (for corporate revenue data) and World Development Report, 2001, Washington D.C. World Bank, 2001 (for country GDP data).

    Note that other researchers place the number of corporations within the 100 largest economies at 52. (See: Sarah Anderson and John Cavanagh, *Field Guide to the Global Economy*, 2nd edition. (New Press, 2005). While we understand that comparing the economies of countries to corporations is an imperfect comparison, these figures do demonstrate the massive scale of corporate economic power today. When the economic clout of many companies is larger than entire countries, it is virtually impossible for State power to rein them in when necessary to ensure that their actions don't harm people and the planet. If you want to read more about this issue, we recommend IPS's *Field Guide to the Global Economy* (http://www.ips-dc.org/books/field_guide_to_the_global_economy_second_edition) . . .

15. There are roughly 13,000 registered lobbyists in Washington, D.C, with nearly $3.5 billion spent annually on lobbying. Lobbyists overwhelmingly

represent corporate interests, and their job is to influence the lawmaking process (http://www.opensecrets.org/lobby/index.php). In addition to officially defined lobbying, corporations spend huge amounts trying to influence public opinion and make election-related contributions to influence who gets elected.

16. Corporations did not have First Amendment speech rights until the 1970s. Then they won the right to spend money on political referenda (*First Nat'l Bank of Boston v. Bellotti*, 435 U.S. 765 (1978)). The Supreme Court also established a commercial speech right; while this was originally predicated on the right of consumers to get information, over time it morphed into an affirmative right for corporations to advertise, subject to minimal restrictions other than prohibition on misleading and deceptive advertising.

Using these newly established First Amendment speech rights, corporations have successfully challenged not only restrictions on their campaign spending, but rules restricting tobacco, alcohol and pharmaceutical advertising. An electric utility has used the First Amendment to defeat a requirement that it include in its billing envelope, at no cost to the utility, an invitation to join a consumer group. Milk producers have used the First Amendment to defeat requirements to label milk as containing hormones. For a compilation of cases, see Testimony of Jeffrey D. Clements, United States Senate Committee on the Judiciary March 10, 2010, footnote 13. (https://salsa.democracyinaction.org/o/476/images/Free%20Speech%20for%20People%20Testimony-United%20States%20Senate%20Committee%20on%20the%20Judiciary.pdf).

17. In this case, a 5–4 majority of the court held that corporations have a First Amendment right to spend whatever they like to influence election outcomes. (*Citizens United v. Federal Election Commission*, 558 U. S. (2010)). http://www.supremecourt.gov/opinions/09pdf/08-205.pdf.

The Court overruled two existing Supreme Court decisions. In *Austin v. Michigan Chamber of Commerce*, the Court held that the government can limit for-profit corporations to the use of PACs to fund express electoral advocacy. *McConnell v. FEC* applied that principle to uphold the constitutionality of the McCain–Feingold law's restrictions on "electioneering communications," that is, corporate funding of election-eve broadcasts that mention candidates and convey unmistakable electoral messages. Striking down these decisions unleashes unlimited corporate and union spending in candidate campaigns, and threatens the 1907 Tillman Act, which also prohibits corporate contributions to candidates.

18. Held the Court: "prohibition on corporate independent expenditures is thus a ban on speech" (ibid, page 22).

19. This point was made by Justice Stevens in his Dissent: There "is not a scintilla of evidence to support the notion that anyone believed it [the First Amendment] would preclude regulatory distinctions based on the corporate form. To the extent that the Framers' views are discernible and relevant to the disposition of this case, they would appear to cut strongly against the majority's position" (ibid., page 34–35). After surveying the early history of corporations, and emphasizing how they existed for limited purposes and under significant government limitations in early American history, Stevens continued, "The Framers thus took it as a given that corporations could be comprehensively regulated in the service of the public welfare. Unlike our colleagues, they had little trouble distinguishing corporations from human beings, and when they constitutionalized the right to free speech in the First Amendment, it was the free speech of individual Americans that they had in mind. While individuals might join together to exercise their speech rights, business corporations, at least, were plainly not seen as facilitating such associational or expressive ends. Even 'the notion that business corporations could invoke the First Amendment would probably have been quite a novelty,' given that 'at the time, the legitimacy of every corporate activity was thought to rest entirely in a concession of the sovereign'" (ibid., page 37).

continues

■ **Continued**

20. After holding that prohibition on corporate independent expenditures is a ban on speech, the majority on the Court went on to offer a ringing explication of the First Amendment: "Speech is an essential mechanism of democracy, for it is the means to hold officials accountable to the people" (ibid., page 23). Somehow, the Court missed the fact that corporations are not people, and that it undermines democracy if officials are held accountable to corporations rather than actual people!

21. According to the New York Times, those companies' 2008 profits were $605 billion, which "dwarfs the $1.5 billion that Federal Election Commission–registered political parties spent during the same election period, or the $1.2 billion spent by federal political action committees" (http://www.nytimes.com/2009/09/08/opinion/08tue1.html).

22. Few corporations are interested in taking out advertisements to support or oppose candidates on their own. Rather, to avoid accountability and to take advantage of the talents of political pros, they funnel their money through "independent" organizations. These are organized under different provisions of the tax code. So-called 527 groups (named after a provision of the tax code) at least must disclose their funders. However, organizations registered as 501(c)(4) charities and 501(c)(6) trade associations under the tax code are not required to disclose funders. About half of the money that flowed into outside organizations in the 2010 elections went into 501(c)(4) or 501(c)(6) organizations—meaning that the sources of the funding remain secret. Most corporate money—including the funding for the U.S. Chamber of Commerce, the single largest spending outside group in the 2010 elections—was funneled secretly. [The U.S. Chamber of Commerce spent over $31 million dollars in the 2010 elections; American Crossroads, which is required to disclose funders—spent over $21 million. In sum, the 10 groups that spent the most in the 2010 election spent over $138 million dollars, and only three of those groups, which spent approximately $36.5 million dollars combined, were required to disclose their funders] . . .

(Source: Public Citizen calculations, from data filed with the Federal Election Commission. http://www.citizen.org/documents/Citizens United-20110113.pdf.)

23. Data from opensecrets.org, http://www.opensecrets.org/outsidespending/index.php.

24. The *Citizens United v. Federal Election Commission* decision was a radical extension of corporate power in our democracy, but corporations had far too much influence before the decision. A constitutional amendment should not only directly overturn *Citizens United*, it should clarify that the First Amendment is designed to protect the speech of real persons, not corporations, and that We, the People have the authority to establish controls over corporations.

A constitutional amendment establishing that for-profit corporations do not have First Amendment speech rights would achieve this objective. It would overturn the *Citizens United* decision. More generally, it would mean that we, the People—through Congress, state legislatures or city councils—could prohibit various kinds of corporate expenditures or regulate different kinds of corporate speech.

With the amendment, we could stop corporate spending on elections. . . . We could prevent all independent expenditures and electioneering spending by corporations (not just . . . [those] shortly before an election). . . . We could eliminate or regulate corporate spending on lobbying, "grassroots" lobbying, and PR campaigns around political issues, and donations to think tanks and advocacy groups. We could regulate advertising.

A constitutional amendment establishing that for-profit corporations do not have First Amendment speech rights would not limit freedom of the press for corporations (or could be drafted to exclude media corporations carrying out broadcasting or publishing). Under the amendment, Rupert Murdoch's News Corp. would not have the right to make political donations, but Fox News would have the right to air whatever it chose . . .

25. A public financing system for elections would enable candidates to run for office without the backing of corporations and deep-pocketed donors.

In its simplest form, public financing of candidate campaigns consists of providing qualified candidates with public funds to conduct their campaigns. The idea is to provide candidates with the means necessary to pay for campaign activity while easing their fundraising frenzy and lessening the perception that politicians are granting private favors in exchange for their campaign funds.

Public financing would be a major step forward, even with the *Citizens United* decision still in place. It would give candidates a base of financial support, without forcing them to attract support from corporations and the ultra-wealthy.

It would not, however, be a cure for the *Citizens United* problem. A candidate receiving public financing might still face independent spending by corporations. Corporations could, if they choose, easily spend more in selected races than would be provided by a public financing system. And, even without such large expenditures, they would be able to tilt the playing field for their favored candidates.

26. The leading bill in Congress to advance public financing of elections is the Fair Elections Now Act (http://www.fairelectionsnow.org) that would permit participating candidates to raise a large number of small contributions ($100 or less) from their communities in order to qualify for Fair Elections funding (1500 contributions, totaling $50,000 for the House of Representatives). Qualified candidates for the House would receive $900,000 in public funds, 60 percent of which would be for the general election. Additionally, donations of $100 or less from in-state contributors would be matched by four dollars from the Fair Elections Fund for every dollar raised.

The Fair Elections Now Act made substantial advances in the last Congress. It was voted out of House Administration Committee, and obtaining 165 co-sponsors in the House, and 24 co-sponsors in the Senate.

Wealth and Income Inequality

Ann Larson

Ann Larson is an organizer with the Debt Collective, an organization that is related to Occupy Wall Street and Strike Debt.

What is the history of your organization and its mission?

In 2011, I participated in Occupy Wall Street, a movement that protested social and economic inequality. During the occupation, I joined a group of people who wanted to organize around the issue of ballooning student debt. Around that time, the total student debt in the U.S. topped one trillion dollars and has continued to climb since then.

Student debt was the first issue we focused on during Occupy, but we quickly expanded to other kinds of debt. In the absence of living wage jobs and a strong social safety net, people go into debt for things like medical care and to pay for other basic essentials like food and clothing.

To help turn the struggles of individuals into a political issue, we joined with others from Occupy and elsewhere and started the Rolling Jubilee, a project that buys and abolishes debt for pennies on the dollar on the secondary market. This initiative was incredibly successful. By the time the Rolling Jubilee had ended, we had bought and abolished more than $13 million in medical and student debt for individuals chosen at random for about $750,000, all of which came from small, individual donations.

We knew that we could never buy and abolish all the debt in the world. We wanted to use the attention that the Rolling Jubilee garnered to create a membership organization, a platform for people in debt to join together and fight back against creditors. In late 2014, we launched the Debt Collective, the first phase of what we hope will eventually become a kind of debtors union.

How did you first become interested in this type of activism?

As a student debtor myself and as a teacher who watched my students go into debt for education, I had been looking for an opportunity to organize around the issue. After Occupy Wall Street started, I found other people who were also passionate about changing the way we finance higher education in the U.S. and I've been collaborating with them ever since.

As an activist working to decrease economic inequality and help release people from debt, currently what are your top goals?

One of our goals is to change people's minds about debt. People in debt are often ashamed. They feel that what's happened to them is their fault. There's a myth that people go into debt for luxuries, but that's not true. Most people go into debt for basic needs.

Another goal is to reclaim a sense of collective power. We've gotten used to thinking of individuals and families as the most important units in society. We've come to think of politics as what happens when a person goes into a voting booth and chooses a candidate. At the same time, unions are in decline and there are fewer and fewer ways for people to act together in their own economic interests. A debtors union could help change that.

We also hope to encourage a broad conversation about public resources and how they should be distributed. Is it fair that people have to go into a lifetime of debt to attend college? Is it fair that a broken bone or unexpected illness can result in bankruptcy? Is this the world we want to live in, or are there other ways to organize society?

What strategies do you use to enact social change?

On the ground organizing, face-to-face meetings whenever possible, backed up by traditional media and social media.

What are the major challenges activists in your field face?

We're mostly volunteers. We do our organizing and activist work while trying to make a living in other ways. This is not a sustainable model for social change. People need material resources and support to commit to doing this kind of work. Burnout is a constant problem. We haven't been able to combat it. We've just worked around it, and we try to be respectful when someone expresses a need to take a break. Groups have to fundraise and earn money to support movement work.

What are major misconceptions the public has about activism in general and your issue specifically?

I think people underestimate how much work it is and how much commitment it takes to win even small victories. You have to be tenacious and maybe a little crazy.

What would you consider to be your greatest successes as an activist?

I'm proud to have supported the Corinthian 15, the group of 15 students who launched the first ever student debt strike in U.S. history. The Corinthian 15 are challenging the U.S. Education Department for their inability to supervise the Corinthian system of for-profit colleges, and they are demanding that the Department cancel their debt. The Corinthian 15 represent many students who were lured into taking out student loans with false information about educational quality, job placement success, and more. Their courage inspires me every day.

Why should students get involved in your line of activism?

There are really two choices: accept the world as it is or try to change it. Almost everyone is in some kind of debt, so there are a lot of different ways to bring people together around the issue.

If an individual has little money and time, are there other ways they can contribute?

Start having conversations with your friends and neighbors that challenge the conventional morality around debt. We can start by promoting the idea in our everyday conversations that some debts shouldn't be repaid.

Building a Better America— One Wealth Quintile at a Time

MICHAEL I. NORTON AND DAN ARIELY

If you had to join a society where you would be randomly placed in the class struc- ture, what kind of society would you like to live in: one with a very unequal wealth distribution, one with a less-unequal distribution, or one with a perfectly equal distri- bution of wealth? This is the question Norton and Ariely asked their survey respon- dents in an attempt to better understand Americans' knowledge of and beliefs about wealth inequality. Their results indicate that not only do Americans generally under- estimate the amount of wealth inequality in the United States, but also they desire greater equality than currently exists. Norton and Ariely question why this gap be- tween ideals and reality exists and whether it can be closed.

Most scholars agree that wealth inequality in the United States is at historic highs, with some estimates suggesting that the top 1% of Ameri- cans hold nearly 50% of the wealth, topping even the levels seen just before the Great Depression in the 1920s (Davies, Sandstrom, Shorrocks, & Wolff, 2009; Keister, 2000; Wolff, 2002). Al- though it is clear that wealth inequality is high, determining the ideal distribution of wealth in a society has proven to be an intractable question, in part because differing beliefs about the ideal distribution of wealth are the source of friction between policymakers who shape that distribu- tion: Proponents of the "estate tax," for example, argue that the wealth that parents bequeath to their children should be taxed more heavily than those who refer to this policy as a burden- some "death tax."

We took a different approach to determin- ing the ideal level of wealth inequality: Follow- ing the philosopher John Rawls (1971), we asked Americans to construct distributions of wealth they deem just. Of course, this approach may simply add to the confusion if Americans dis- agree about the ideal wealth distribution in the same way that policymakers do. Thus, we had two primary goals. First, we explored whether there is general consensus among Americans about the ideal level of wealth inequality, or whether differences—driven by factors such as political beliefs and income—outweigh any con- sensus (see McCarty, Poole, & Rosenthal, 2006). Second, assuming sufficient agreement, we hoped to insert the preferences of "regular Americans" regarding wealth inequality into policy debates.

Michael I. Norton and Dan Ariely, *Perspectives on Psychological Science* (Volume 6 and Issue 1), pp. 9–12, Copy- right © 2011. Reprinted by Permission of SAGE Publications.

A nationally representative online sample of respondents (N=5,522, 51% female, mean age=44.1), randomly drawn from a panel of more than 1 million Americans, completed the survey in December, 2005. . . . Respondents' household income (median=$45,000) was similar to that reported in the 2006 United States census (median=$48,000), and their voting pattern in the 2004 election (50.6% Bush, 46.0% Kerry) was also similar to the actual outcome (50.8% Bush, 48.3% Kerry). In addition, the sample contained respondents from 47 states.

We ensured that all respondents had the same working definition of wealth by requiring them to read the following before beginning the survey: "Wealth, also known as net worth, is defined as the total value of everything someone owns minus any debt that he or she owes. A person's net worth includes his or her bank account savings plus the value of other things such as property, stocks, bonds, art, collections, etc., minus the value of things like loans and mortgages."

Americans Prefer Sweden

For the first task, we created three unlabeled pie charts of wealth distributions, one of which depicted a perfectly equal distribution of wealth. Unbeknownst to respondents, a second distribution reflected the wealth distribution in the United States [wherein the top quintile owns 84 percent of the wealth; the second highest owns 11 percent; the third owns 4 percent, and the bottom two quintiles own .2 percent and .1 percent, respectively]; in order to create a distribution with a level of inequality that clearly fell in between these two charts, we constructed a third pie chart from the income distribution of Sweden . . . [where the top quintile owns 36 percent; the second highest owns 21 percent; the third highest owns 18 percent; and the bottom two quintiles own 15 and 11 percent, respectively].[1] We presented respondents with the three pairwise combinations of these pie charts (in random order) and asked them to choose

which nation they would rather join given a "Rawls constraint" for determining a just society (Rawls, 1971): "In considering this question, imagine that if you joined this nation, you would be randomly assigned to a place in the distribution, so you could end up anywhere in this distribution, from the very richest to the very poorest."

. . . The (unlabeled) United States distribution was far less desirable than both the (unlabeled) Sweden distribution and the equal distribution, with some 92% of Americans preferring the Sweden distribution to the United States. In addition, this overwhelming preference for the Sweden distribution over the United States distribution was robust across gender (females: 92.7%, males: 90.6%), preferred candidate in the 2004 election (Bush voters: 90.2%; Kerry voters: 93.5%) and income (less than $50,000: 92.1%; $50,001–$100,000: 91.7%; more than $100,000: 89.1%). In addition, there was a slight preference for the distribution that resembled Sweden relative to the equal distribution, suggesting that Americans prefer some inequality to perfect equality, but not to the degree currently present in the United States.

Building a Better America

Although the choices among the three distributions shed some light into preferences for distributions of wealth in the abstract, we wanted to explore respondents' specific beliefs about their own society. In the next task, we therefore removed Rawls' "veil of ignorance" and assessed both respondents' estimates of the actual distribution of wealth and their preferences for the ideal distribution of wealth in the United States. For their estimates of the actual distribution, we asked respondents to indicate what percent of wealth they thought was owned by each of the five quintiles in the United States, in order starting with the top 20% and ending with the bottom 20%. For their ideal distributions, we asked them to indicate what percent of wealth they thought each of the quintiles ideally should hold, again starting with the top 20% and ending with the bottom 20%.

To help them with this task, we provided them with the two most extreme examples, instructing them to assign 20% of the wealth to each quintile if they thought that each quintile should have the same level of wealth, or to assign 100% of the wealth to one quintile if they thought that one quintile should hold all of the wealth.

. . . First, respondents vastly underestimated the actual level of wealth inequality in the United States, believing that the wealthiest quintile held about 59% of the wealth when the actual number is closer to 84%. More interesting, respondents constructed ideal wealth distributions that were far more equitable than even their erroneously low estimates of the actual distribution, reporting a desire for the top quintile to own just 32% of the wealth. These desires for more equal distributions of wealth took the form of moving money from the top quintile to the bottom three quintiles, while leaving the second quintile unchanged, evincing a greater concern for the less fortunate than the more fortunate (Charness & Rabin, 2002).

We next explored how demographic characteristics of our respondents affected these estimates. . . . Males, Kerry voters, and wealthier individuals estimated that the distribution of wealth was relatively more unequal than did women, Bush voters, and poorer individuals. For estimates of the ideal distribution, women, Kerry voters, and the poor desired relatively more equal distributions than did their counterparts.

Despite these (somewhat predictable) differences, what is most striking . . . [is the] demonstration of much more consensus than disagreement among these different demographic groups. All groups—even the wealthiest respondents—desired a more equal distribution of wealth than what they estimated the current United States level to be, and all groups also desired some inequality—even the poorest respondents. In addition, all groups agreed that such

redistribution should take the form of moving wealth from the top quintile to the bottom three quintiles. In short, although Americans tend to be relatively more favorable toward economic inequality than members of other countries (Osberg & Smeeding, 2006), Americans' consensus about the ideal distribution of wealth within the United States appears to dwarf their disagreements across gender, political orientation, and income.

Overall, these results demonstrate two primary messages. First, a large nationally representative sample of Americans seems to prefer to live in a country more like Sweden than like the United States. Americans also construct ideal distributions that are far more equal than they estimated the United States to be—estimates which themselves were far more equal than the actual level of inequality. Second, there was much more consensus than disagreement across groups from different sides of the political spectrum about this desire for a more equal distribution of wealth, suggesting that Americans may possess a commonly held "normative" standard for the distribution of wealth despite the many disagreements about policies that affect that distribution, such as taxation and welfare (Kluegel & Smith, 1986). . . . Although some evidence suggests that economic inequality is associated with decreased well-being and health (Napier & Jost, 2008; Wilkinson & Pickett, 2009), creating a society with the precise level of inequality that our respondents report as ideal may not be optimal from an economic or public policy perspective (Krueger, 2004).

Given the consensus among disparate groups on the gap between an ideal distribution of wealth and the actual level of wealth inequality, why are more Americans, especially those with low income, not advocating for greater redistribution of wealth? First, our results demonstrate that Americans appear to drastically underestimate the current level of wealth inequality, suggesting they may simply be unaware of the gap. Second, just as people have erroneous beliefs about the actual level of wealth inequality, they may also hold overly optimistic beliefs about opportunities for social mobility in the United States (Benabou & Ok, 2001; Charles & Hurst, 2003; Keister, 2005), beliefs which in turn may drive support for unequal distributions of wealth. Third, despite the fact that conservatives and liberals in our sample agree that the current level of inequality is far from ideal, public disagreements about the causes of that inequality may drown out this consensus (Alesina & Angeletos, 2005; Piketty, 1995). Finally, and more broadly, Americans exhibit a general disconnect between their attitudes toward economic inequality and their self-interest and public policy preferences (Bartels, 2005; Fong, 2001), suggesting that even given increased awareness of the gap between ideal and actual wealth distributions, Americans may remain unlikely to advocate for policies that would narrow this gap.

NOTES

1. We used Sweden's income rather than wealth distribution because it provided a clearer contrast to the other two wealth distribution examples; although more equal than the United States' wealth distribution, Sweden's wealth distribution is still extremely top heavy.

REFERENCES

Alesina, A., & Angeletos, G. M. (2005). Fairness and redistribution. *American Economic Review*, 95, 960–980.

Bartels, L. M. (2005). Homer gets a tax cut: Inequality and public policy in the American mind. *Perspectives on Politics*, 3, 15–31.

Benabou, R., & Ok, E. A. (2001). Social mobility and the demand for redistribution: The POUM hypothesis. *Quarterly Journal of Economics*, 116, 447–487.

Charles, K. K., & Hurst, E. (2003). The correlation of wealth across generations. *Journal of Political Economy*, 111, 1155–1182.

Charness, G., & Rabin, M. (2002). Understanding social preferences with simple tests. *Quarterly Journal of Economics*, 117, 817–869.

Davies, J. B., Sandstrom, S., Shorrocks, A., & Wolff, E. N. (2009). The global pattern of household wealth. *Journal of International Development*, 21, 1111–1124.

Fong, C. (2001). Social preferences, self-interest, and the demand for redistribution. *Journal of Public Economics*, 82, 225–246.

Keister, L. A. (2000). *Wealth in America*. Cambridge, England: Cambridge University Press.

Keister, L. A. (2005). *Getting rich: America's new rich and how they got that way*. Cambridge, England: Cambridge University Press.

Kluegel, J. R., & Smith, E. R. (1986). *Beliefs about inequality: Americans' views of what is and what ought to be*. New York: Aldine de Gruyter.

Krueger, A. B. (2004). Inequality, too much of a good thing. In J. J. Heckman & A. B. Krueger (Eds.), *Inequality in America: What role for human capital policies* (pp. 1–75). Cambridge, MA: MIT Press.

McCarty, N., Poole, K. T., &Rosenthal, H. (2006). *Polarized America: The dance of ideology and unequal riches*. Cambridge, MA: MIT Press.

Napier, J. L., & Jost, J. T. (2008). Why are conservatives happier than liberals? *Psychological Science*, 19, 565–572.

Osberg, L., & Smeeding, T. (2006). "Fair" inequality? Attitudes to pay differentials: The United States in comparative perspective. *American Sociological Review*, 71, 450–473.

Piketty, T. (1995). Social mobility and redistributive politics. *Quarterly Journal of Economics*, 110, 551–584.

Rawls, J. (1971). *A theory of justice*. Cambridge, MA: Harvard University Press.

Wilkinson, R., & Pickett, K. (2009). *The spirit level: Why greater equality makes societies stronger*. New York: Bloomsbury.

Wolff, E. N. (2002). *Top heavy: The increasing inequality of wealth in America and what can be done about it*. New York: New Press.

For the Public, It's Not about Class Warfare, but Fairness

Pew Research Center

Reprinted by Permission of Pew Research Center. "For the Public, It's Not about Class Warfare, but Fairness," March 2, 2012, http://www.people-press.org/2012/03/02/for-the-public-its-not-about-class-warfare-but-fairness/.

A Pew Research Center poll . . . attracted wide attention when it found that as many as 66% of Americans believe there are "very strong" or "strong" conflicts between the rich and the poor, an increase of 19 percentage points since 2009. But while Americans are hearing more about class conflict, there is no sense that the American people are on the verge of class . . . [warfare]; they just want a better chance of achieving success themselves. They want government policies that give everyone a fair shot, reflecting bedrock American beliefs in the individual's ability to succeed through hard work.

A recent Gallup poll found 70% [of Americans said] . . . that it is extremely or very important that the federal government in Washington enact policies that increase the equality of opportunity for people to get ahead. By comparison, just 46% say it is extremely or very important for the government to reduce the income and wealth gap between the rich and poor; 54% say this is somewhat important or not important. Income inequality is an element of the economic system that is accepted by many Americans: 52% say the fact that some people in the U.S. are rich and others are poor is an acceptable part of our economic system.

A sense of economic inequality is hardly new. A broad majority [of the] public (77%) says that there is too much power in the hands of a few rich people and large corporations; and as far back as 1941, Gallup polling found a majority (60%) expressing this view. In addition, the public agrees with the statement that in general the rich just get richer while the poor get poorer—majorities have consistently said this since Pew Research first asked the question in 1987.

The public's desire for fairness in government policy is perhaps best seen in views of the tax system. A majority of Americans now say the federal tax system is unfair and there has been a seven-point rise in this view since 2003. The public's top complaint about taxes is not how much they themselves pay; rather, it is the belief that some wealthy people don't pay their fair share. Nearly six-in-ten (57%) say what bothers them most about taxes is the feeling that some wealthy [individuals] don't pay their fair share, just 11% say it is the amount they themselves pay [that bothers them]. The public supports overhauling the federal tax system, and this support stems primarily from concerns over the fairness of the system.

A desire for a level economic playing field is tied to American individualism. Belief in the individual's ability to achieve success through hard work is a bedrock American value. And there is a strong belief that the individual has the power to shape their own future. Three-quarters [of Americans] (75%) agree with the statement that everyone has it in their own power to succeed; just 19% say success is determined by outside forces. This view has been held by wide majorities ever since the question was first asked in 1994.

A majority of the public (58%) also agrees with the statement that most people who want to get ahead can make it if they're willing to work hard. However, public views of opportunity are not immune to hard economic times—agreement with this statement has slipped somewhat in recent years. But there is no less admiration for people who get rich by working hard: 90% agree with this sentiment; just 8% disagree. This near-unanimous opinion highlights that the public's fundamental complaint is not with the rich themselves.

Pew Global Attitudes surveys have consistently found that Americans' views of the individual and role of the state set them apart from the publics of many Western European nations. Nearly six-in-ten Americans (58%) say it is more important that everyone be free to pursue their life's goals without

continues

■ Continued

interference from the state; far fewer (35%) say it is more important that the state play an active role in society so as to guarantee that nobody is in need. The balance of opinion is reversed among Western European countries. In Spain, for example, 67% say the state guaranteeing that no one is in need is more important; just 30% say individual freedom to pursue goals should be prioritized. Similarly, [when] asked if they agree that "success in life is pretty much determined by forces outside our control," most Americans disagree. Opinion is much more mixed among Western European nations. For example, 57% of the French and 72% of Germans say that success in life is determined by outside forces.

Americans' more skeptical view of a strong social safety net has consequences. About a third of Americans (32%) say there have been times in the past year when they have been unable to afford health care, which is consistent with Pew Research Center surveys over the past decade. That is far higher than the percentages in four Western European countries who say this. People in the United States also are more likely to say they have been unable to afford food in the past year.

Rising Inequality
and the Fading American Dream

RENEE M. SHELBY

Shelby documents the rise in income and wealth inequality and how, despite our belief in the American Dream, the United States is more economically unequal than comparable nations. Increasing economic inequality clearly hurts individuals because their life chances are diminished, but Shelby demonstrates how the entire society suffers when rising inequality stunts economic growth, intensifies inflation, and even compromises democratic principles. The middle class, once economically strong, continues to face hardship and stagnation. The public is becoming increasingly aware of the costs of economic inequality, but it will be challenging to break the current patterns of accumulation.

The American Dream holds that if we work hard, each generation will enjoy a higher standard of living than the one before it. But will your generation enjoy a better life than your parents' generation? Perhaps not. Intergenerational gains have stalled among Americans. Although the nation has indeed prospered since the late 1970s,[1] only a few have reaped the economic rewards.

Income Inequality

When most people think of economic success, they think of income. *Income* is the money a person receives for work, transfers (e.g., gifts, inheritances, government assistance), or returns on investments. In the United States, income is highly concentrated among a small group of people. For example, in 2012, the highest earning 20 percent of Americans received nearly half of all available income—almost as much as the bottom 80 percent of Americans combined. Yet, the distribution of income is even more skewed than you may think. In 2012, the top 1 percent of earners alone took home nearly 20 percent of all available income. Even among the highest earners, income is densely concentrated; a huge share of the nation's income has gone not just to the top 1 percent, but to the top 0.01 percent of earners, who now earn, on average, over $10 million per year![2] When compared to the average income for the bottom 80 percent—a mere $40,197 by comparison—the level of inequality becomes even clearer.[3]

Despite increases in national productivity, since the 1970s, real wages have stagnated for the majority of Americans. *Real wages* are current wages adjusted for inflation. They provide a valuable measure for comparison because they

Original to *Focus on Social Problems: A Contemporary Reader*.

reflect the actual purchasing power of goods over time. This is important because the cost of living has steadily increased almost every year since 1960,[4] making it difficult for individuals to maintain their standard of living without the corresponding wage increase.[5] When we look at real wages over the past 40 years, earnings have actually decreased.[6] In 1973, the median income of a full-time male worker was $49,065. By 2010, the median dropped by $1,350 to $47,715.[7] Even during the wildly prosperous decade of the 1990s and before the Great Recession, the median value of real wages never surpassed that of 1973.[8] And as incomes have stalled, annual work hours have increased. In 1973, the average employee worked 1,679 hours. However, by 2007, annual work hours swelled to 1,868—an extra 189 hours per year.[9] Yet, despite these extra hours, workers, on average, have not received any additional economic benefits.

Although we see ourselves as a land of equal economic opportunity, globally, the United States ranks as one of the most economically unequal countries. Global income inequality is often measured and compared with the Gini Index—a statistic that represents a nation's income distribution. A Gini coefficient of zero represents perfect equality (everyone in the society earns the same amount), whereas a coefficient of 100 represents extreme inequality (one person earns all the money, and everyone else earns none).[10] In 2011, America's Gini Index was 45.0.[11] In fact, since the 1970s, our Gini index has steadily increased, making U.S. income concentration by far the highest of any other wealthy Western country. For example, compare America's score to the Gini indices of Australia (30.3), Germany (26.8), Canada (32.1), or Sweden (23.0).[12] Of 141 countries, America is ranked 41st in inequality, similar to countries such as Uruguay (45.3), Bulgaria (45.3), and Jamaica (45.5).[13]

Beyond our comparison to other nations, income inequality has many negative social and political consequences. Often these are direct, meaning that when a person experiences an economic gain, he or she is able to access more social and political resources. Conversely, when a person experiences an economic loss, social and political resources become more limited. As fewer individuals experience economic gain, their *life chances*—or the number of opportunities a person has to live a good life—shrink. Consequently, examining the broad effects of income inequality is an important site of investigation.

Wealth Inequality

Foremost, persistent income inequality drives *wealth inequality*. *Wealth* is the value of a person's assets (cash savings, house, car, etc.) minus their debts (outstanding loans). In 2011, the wealthiest 20 percent of Americans possessed 84 percent of all wealth, whereas the bottom 60 percent possessed less than 6 percent of all wealth.[14] Mirroring patterns of income inequality, wealth inequality is highly skewed toward the top.[15] For example, the top 400 Americans alone possess more wealth than half the population of the United States combined— approximately 150 million Americans.[16] This wealth gap has increased over the past 25 years,[17] particularly along racial and ethnic lines. In 2009, white households had a median wealth 22 times greater than that of African American households and 15 times greater than that of Latino households.[18] Because most wealth is transferred between generations through inheritances and cash transfers, many Americans are being financially left behind and the racial wealth gap persists.

Having the ability to accumulate wealth is beneficial in that it provides individuals with a cushion against income shocks (such as a job loss or serious injury/illness) and access to desirable neighborhoods and schools. Amassed wealth also increases a person's social status and political influence. Further, if an individual accrues enough wealth, they can live comfortably off dividends (income earned from investments) and no longer need to work. Fewer and fewer Americans are able to do this, and those who do are able to continue building their wealth.

Stunted Economy

On a broader scale, income and wealth inequality also hinder overall economic growth, are linked to rising interest rates, and create unstable and volatile economic conditions.[19, 20, 21] Since the 1960s, conservative economists and politicians have argued that inequality is unimportant and that it actually propels the economy forward, a theory colloquially called "trickle-down" or supply-side economics.[22, 23] This theory argues that economic growth is achieved by making it easier to produce goods and services and invest in capital. Essentially, when those at the top of the income ladder do well economically, the economic rewards trickle down to those at the bottom. Reducing taxes, particularly for the wealthy, has been a cornerstone of supply-side economics. However, new research using Census data has found the supposed benefits of trickle-down economics, such as job creation and the idea that "the rising tide floats all boats," are not supported by the data and that economic inequality actually benefits only the superrich.[24]

This can be seen in the recent case study of Kansas, where Governor Sam Brownback reduced the tax rate in 2012 for top earners from 6.45 percent to 4.9 percent, with another reduction scheduled to reduce the tax rate to 3.9 percent by 2018. As one of the largest cuts ever enacted by a state, the Kansas Department of Commerce promoted them nationally with print media ads stating, "Cut the taxes, cut the cost of doing business and you are left in a perfect state . . . Kansas" and "with one of the most pro-growth tax policies in the country, it's not hard to [become the best]."[25] A supply-side economist and member of Ronald Reagan's Economic Policy Advisory Board (1981–1989), Arthur Laffer, asserted Brownback's policies would benefit the Kansan economy, leading to immediate and long-term growth. In fact, Brownback hired Laffer to promote the new policies and referenced his work as justification for the tax cuts.[26]

Although Brownback asserted on MSNBC's *Morning Joe* (June 19, 2014) that he wanted Kansas to be a "real, live experiment" for supply-side economics, most Kansans have not benefited from this experiment, and the state is now lagging in its recovery from the Great Recession.[27] Foremost, the cuts have not boosted the Kansan economy; they have generated a $238 million budget deficit from a historic budget surplus.[28] In addition, fewer jobs have been added compared to the national trend, and the incomes and earnings of Kansans are now below national averages. Further, although tax cuts were aimed at high-income households, the taxes for low-income families were raised to compensate for the state's revenue loss. This loss—approximately 8 percent of revenues—has led to cuts in school, health care, and public service funding, services primarily used by lower- and middle-class citizens. Unfortunately, this trend is expected to continue as the official state revenue forecast projected that Kansan personal income would continue to lag behind national personal income in 2014 and 2015,[29] and state losses would double by 2019. The Kansas experiment shows that supply-side economics produces greater economic and social inequalities that may persist for years.

Intensifying Inflation and Debt

In addition to hampering economic growth, rising inequality is positively correlated with inflation,[30] meaning that as inequality rises, so does inflation, devaluing the money already in circulation and making it more difficult for the majority of Americans to buy the things they need. When incomes fail to keep pace with inflation and interest rates, families increasingly have to rely on credit, tap into savings and retirement accounts, or take out loans against their current assets to stay afloat. However, although most families own something, their overall amount of debt often cancels out the worth of their property, leaving around 25 percent of Americans with zero or negative net worth.[31] Consequently, many families are forced to live paycheck to paycheck, devoting most or all of their income to meeting regular household expenses.[32] In fact, a 2009 TNS Global Economic

Crisis Survey indicated that nearly half of all Americans are financially vulnerable, defined as unable to come up with $2,000 for an emergency within 30 days.[33] The survey found nearly 25 percent would definitely be unable to come up with the funds, whereas another 19 percent indicated they would have to take extreme measures, such as selling or pawning possessions, to get the money.[34] Consequently, many Americans are unable to accumulate the three-month savings cushion suggested by financial planners (to protect them in the event of job loss, medical emergency, or other financial challenges).

Increasingly, Americans have turned to "payday loans" as a strategy to survive. A payday loan is typically a small loan borrowed at a high interest rate with the expectation that it will be repaid with the borrower's next paycheck. Of the 12 million Americans with a payday loan, 69 percent reported borrowing to cover basic necessities, such as groceries or rent, and another 16 percent borrowed to cover an emergency.[35] Although payday loans are marketed as being short-term, the standard two-week payday loan has an interest rate between 391 percent and 521 percent. Given the extremely short repayment period, nearly all borrowers must take out subsequent loans just to pay off the initial loan. Consequently, 98 percent of borrowers get trapped in a cycle of payday debt, taking an average of seven or more loans per year.[36, 37]

Diminished Middle-Class Optimism and Rising Debt

Increasingly, the impact of persistent income inequality is affecting middle-class Americans—a group long considered the epitome of upward mobility and a hopeful economic future. Historically, joining the middle class meant owning a home and car, having comprehensive health care, retirement, and college savings, and earning enough surplus income to enjoy an annual vacation. However, rather than maintain this lifestyle, the middle class is increasingly anxious about falling further behind. According to the 2014 *Heartland Monitor Poll*, only 10 percent of

Americans said their current personal financial situation was "excellent," whereas an overwhelming 40 percent indicated their finances were "only in fair shape."[38] Further, nearly two-thirds of respondents felt their financial situation would either stay the same or become worse over the next year. This fear is not unwarranted; Pew Research[39] found that approximately one-third of those who identified as middle class in 2008 now classify as being in either the lower middle class or the lower classes.

This shift is remarkable because self-identification with an economic class is an identity people tend to consider permanent.[40] Further, identification with either the middle or lower classes is highly psychological, given, for example, the language usage and stereotypes common to each. A content analysis of common word associations with the terms middle and lower class reveals key distinctions. The *Corpus of Contemporary American English* is a database of speeches, media, and academic texts from 1990 to 2012, totaling more than 450 million words.[41] Notably, statements about the "middle class" are most likely to contain words of "emerging," "burgeoning," "burdened," and "squeezed." In contrast, statements about the "lower class" were likely to include the terms "judgment," "disapproval," and "help." The words associated with the middle class express challenges experienced by external influences, whereas the words associated with the lower class reflect negative views toward the group. Consequently, the cognitive shift required to change one's self-identify away from middle class, whose experience is seen as, at worst, burdened or squeezed, toward lower class, whose experience is commonly associated with judgment and disapproval, is extraordinary.

Although the middle class's waning optimism offers a bleak image of the state of the American Dream, the latest data from the Federal Reserve Bank indicate it is not unwarranted. For the majority of Americans, opportunities to grow earnings wane as workers grow older. Using data from U.S. Social Security Administration records, the Federal Reserve Bank found that by age 40, most individuals are within about $1000 of peak lifetime earnings, in which real wages tend to plateau, and the "average earnings growth from ages 35 to 55 is zero."[42] Only one group of Americans defies this trend: the top 20 percent, who show moderate growth beyond age 40, and the top 1 percent, who experience wage growth at every age bracket.[43]

Even for young Americans, economic prospects are dimming because employment for those aged 20 to 24 remains below 2007 levels. As wages continue to stagnate, this problem is exacerbated for college graduates who leave with student loan debt. In 2003, student loan debt totaled around $240 billion. A decade later, this figure swelled to $1.2 trillion, with more than 38 million Americans holding outstanding student loan debt.[44] Although this number is driven by the fact that there are more college students than ever before, the cost of a college education has also far outpaced the standard rate of inflation, particularly at four-year institutions. For example, in 1980 the average price of a year of college was $8,756, measured in real wages.[45] By 1990 this figure increased to $12,303; to $15,996 in 2000; and again to $21,657 in 2010.[46] Because more students rely on loans to attend college, outstanding student loan debt now exceeds that of credit card, auto loan, and home-equity debts.

For middle- and lower-income families who have access to fewer resources, paying for college is particularly difficult. In Sallie Mae's national survey, *How America Saves for College 2014*,[47] only 34 percent of low-income and 51 percent of middle-income families indicated they were able to save for college. Of the families that were saving, the amount they actually accrued equated only to $3,762 and $12,241, respectively— far below the cost of just a single year at the average four-year college. It is perhaps no wonder that the bottom 50 percent of the income distribution currently hold 75 percent of total student loan debt.

Although college is an important investment, the average borrower now leaves with $26,000 in debt, and 1 in 10 students graduate with more than $40,000 in debt. Consequently, beginning in 2012, student loan borrowers are now less likely than non–student loan borrowers to purchase a home by age 30.[48] Perhaps waning home purchases among those with student debt may be attributed to poor labor markets, whereby graduates expect to earn less and choose not to make large purchases. However, as creditors have tightened their lending restrictions, graduates with student loan debt may also fail to meet new debt-to-income ratio standards and are thus not credit qualified to make these purchases. According to the Federal Reserve, the credit scores of non–student loan borrowers are on average 15 points higher than that of student loan borrowers at age 25 and 24 points higher at age 30.[49] Although some members of Congress (such as Senator Elizabeth Warren of Massachusetts) have tried to reform student loan debt and ease the economic burden to student borrowers and their families, new measures have yet to be adopted. This is in part a result of polarized legislative processes that have stalled political solutions to economic inequality. As more and more Americans face economic hardship, those at the top of the income ladder continue to shape the political process in ways that prevent positive change for working- and middle-class families.

Upper-Class Political Gains

Although rising income inequality has limited many families' economic prospects, it also gives the upper class more influence over the political process via major contributions to think-tanks, political campaigns, and lobbying groups. Further, a growing portion of congressional representatives are superrich themselves, giving elite earners increased, direct control over economic policies. Nearly 50 percent of congressional members are millionaires, compared to only about 1 percent of Americans in general. Notably, the increase in the number of congressional millionaires has correlated with a decreasing tax burden for the wealthy. Since the 1940s, the tax rates for the superrich have plummeted. In 1945, a millionaire's tax rate was 66.4 percent. With Lyndon B. Johnson's tax cuts it dropped to 55.3 percent and further decreased to 47.7 percent with Ronald Reagan's cuts. Since 2010, with George W. Bush's cuts still in effect, a millionaire's tax rate was just 32.4 percent.[50, 51]

However, this tax rate is only for payroll wages and differs substantially from minimally taxed *capital gains* (income generated from long-term investments, such as homes, stocks, or bonds). When you sell an investment, the difference between the price you initially paid for the asset and the price you sold the asset for is your capital gain (if the change is positive) or capital loss (if the change is negative). Beginning in the early 1990s, earnings from capital gains began to concentrate toward the top of the income scale, whereby capital gains now comprise a significant portion of wealthier taxpayers' incomes.[52] As payroll wages have stagnated across the nation, earnings from capital gains have skyrocketed. Between 1992 and 2007 alone, the average earnings from capital gains increased by 1200 percent.[53] And with separate tax rates for income and capital gains, top earners can use this loophole to avoid paying their assigned income tax rates. In fact, most of the earnings from the *Forbes Richest 400* list[54] come from non–job creating capital gains, with the top tax rate for capital gains capped at a mere 15 percent.[55] Thus, when capital gains taxes are factored in, the tax rates for the rich and everyone else converge, so much so, in fact, that the effective tax rate for those earning between $43,000 and $69,000 is nearly the same as that for individuals earning more than $370,000 per year.[56]

The Fading American Dream

Given that our government is supposed to be of the people, by the people, and for the people, one would think there would be more public outrage over policies that benefit few at the expense of many. Although the Occupy Wall Street movement helped raise awareness of the growing inequality and the policies that support its growth,

it has not resulted in new economic policies and regulations that foster equality. However, Americans are beginning to take notice. In a 2011 survey, researchers found that many Americans—Democrats and Republicans, liberals and conservatives—support a more egalitarian model of income distribution, in which income is more fairly distributed among upper, middle, and lower classes.[57] This does not mean that every American wants a system in which everyone makes the same amount of money; it just means that Americans are not in favor of the current skewed system, in which for every dollar earned by the bottom 90 percent, taxpayers at the top take home $18,000.[58]

Similarly, in 2014 Princeton survey analysts found 65 percent of adults recognize there is a growing gap between rich Americans and everyone else,[59] and 60 percent feel the economic system unfairly favors the wealthy.[60] However, Americans are not only discouraged about the current economic outlook, but also believe the next generation's prospects are grim. According to a 2013 Pew Research Center survey, 65 percent of Americans now believe the next generation will be financially worse off than their parents.[61] Yet constituents continue to vote for politicians who do not share their economic interests—leaving few opportunities to change the economic state of affairs. The former labor secretary Robert Reich has argued that with sinking wages and growing economic insecurity, many people are so desperate for a job that they are unwilling to cause trouble, such as going on strike, protesting, or voting out politicians who do not support the middle and lower classes, leaving a substantial portion of the country without a political voice.[62] The consequence of this inactive approach has been 40 years of rising inequality.

NOTES

1. Morris, Martina, and Bruce Western. 1999. Inequality in Earnings at the Close of the 20th Century. *Annual Review of Sociology, 25*, 623–657.

2. Saez, Emmanuel. 2013. *Striking It Richer: The Evolution of Top Incomes in the United States (Updated with 2012 Preliminary Estimates).* Retrieved October 27, 2014, from http://eml.berkeley.edu/~saez/saez-UStopincomes-2012.pdf/.

3. Bureau of Labor Statistics. 2013. *Consumer Expenditure Survey, 2013.* Washington, DC: U.S. Department of Labor.

4. Bureau of Labor Statistics. 2014. *Consumer Price Indices.* Washington DC: U.S. Department of Labor.

5. Ashenfelter, Orley. 2012. Comparing Real Wage Rates. *American Economic Review, 102(2),* 617–642.

6. Pollin, Robert. 2009. Green Growth and Sustainable Development—The U.S. Case. *Paper Presented at the 64th Session of United Nations General Assembly,* October 26, 2009, New York, New York. Retrieved September 15, 2014 (http://www.un.org/en/ga/second/64/pollin.pdf/).

7. DeNavas-Walt, Carmen, Bernadette D. Proctor, and Jessica C. Smith. 2011. U.S. Census Bureau, Current Population Reports, P60-239, *Income, Poverty, and Health Insurance Coverage in the United States: 2010.* Washington, DC: U.S. Government Printing Office.

8. DeNavas-Walt, Carmen, Bernadette D. Proctor, and Jessica C. Smith. 2011. U.S. Census Bureau, Current Population Reports, P60-239, *Income, Poverty, and Health Insurance Coverage in the United States: 2010.* Washington, DC: U.S. Government Printing Office.

9. Mishel, Lawrence, Josh Bivens, Elise Gould, and Heidi Shierholz. 2012. *The State of Working America,* 12th ed. Ithaca, NY: Cornell University.

10. Bellu, Lorenzo Giovanni, and Paolo Liberati. 2006. *Inequality Analysis: The Gini Index.* Rome: Food and Agriculture Organization of the United Nations.

11. Central Intelligence Agency. 2013–2014. *The World Factbook.* Washington, DC: Central Intelligence Agency.

12. Central Intelligence Agency. 2013–2014. *The World Factbook.* Washington, DC: Central Intelligence Agency.

13. Central Intelligence Agency. 2013–2014. *The World Factbook.* Washington, DC: Central Intelligence Agency.

14. Norton, Michael I., and Dan Ariely. 2011. Building a Better America—One Wealth Quintile at a Time. *Perspectives on Psychological Science, 6(1),* 9–12.

15. Norton, Michael I., and Dan Ariely. 2011. Building a Better America—One Wealth Quintile at a Time. *Perspectives on Psychological Science, 6(1),* 9–12.

16. Wolff, Edward N. 2010. *Recent Trends in Household Wealth in the United States: Rising Debt and the Middle-Class Squeeze—An Update to 2007.* Annandale, NY: Levy Economics Institute.

17. Vornovitsky, Marina, Alfred Gottschalck, and Adam Smith. 2014. *Distribution of Household Wealth in the U.S.: 2000 to 2011.* Washington DC: U.S. Census.

18. Insight Center Community Economic Development. 2010. *Lifting as We Climb: Women of Color, Wealth, and America's Future.* Oakland, CA: Insight Center for Community and Economic Development.

19. Bagchi, Stritha, and Jan Svenjar. 2013. *Does Wealth Inequality Matter for Growth? The Effect of Billionaire Wealth, Income Distribution, and Poverty.* Institute for the Discussion of Labor. IZA Discussion Paper No. 7733, November 2013.

20. Ostry, Jonathan D., Andrew Berg, and Charalambos G. Tsangarides. 2014. *Redistribution, Inequality, and Growth.* Washington, DC: IMF.

21. Bruckner, Markus, Kerstin Gerling, and Hans Peter Gruner. 2010. Wealth Inequality and Credit Markets: Evidence from Three Industrialized Countries. *Journal of Economic Growth, 15,* 155–176.

22. The Laffer Center at the Pacific Research Institute. *Supply-Side Economics.* San Francisco: Laffer Center.

23. Galbraith, John Kenneth. 1982. Recession Economics. *New York Review of Books, 29(1)*. Online. Retrieved March 19, 2015, from http://www.nybooks.com/articles/archives/1982/feb/04/recession-economics/.

24. Van der Weide, Roy, and Branko Milanovic. 2014. *Inequality Is Bad for Growth of the Poor, but Not for That of the Rich*. Paper Number 6963. Washington, DC: Policy Research Working Paper Series.

25. Kansas Department of Commerce. 2014. *Tax Cut Ad in Small Business Resource*. Retrieved February 14, 2015, from http://www.motherjones.com/mojo/2014/09/sam-brownback-kansas-tax-cuts-marketing/.

26. Cooper, Brad. 2012, January 19. *Reaganomics Guru Arthur Laffer Touts Brownback Tax Plan at Capitol*. The Kansas City Star Online. Retrieved from http://www.kansascity.com/news/local/article300536/Reagonomics-guru-Arthur-Laffer-touts-Brownback-tax-plan-at-Capitol.html/.

27. Leachman, Michael, and Chris Mai. 2014. *Lessons for Other States from Kansas' Massive Tax Cuts*. Center on Budget and Policy Priorities: Washington, DC.

28. Kansas Legislative Research Department. 2013. *Consensus Revenue Estimate*. Retrieved February 14, 2015, from http://budget.ks.gov/files/FY2015/CRE_Long_Memo-Nov2013.pdf/.

29. Kansas Legislative Research Department. 2013. *Consensus Revenue Estimate*. Retrieved February 14, 2015, from http://budget.ks.gov/files/FY2015/CRE_Long_Memo-Nov2013.pdf/.

30. Albanesi, Stefania. 2006. Inflation and Inequality. *Journal of Monetary Economics*. doi:10.1016/j.jmoneco.2006.02.009.

31. Allegretto, Sylvia A. 2011. *The State of Working America's Wealth, 2011*. Briefing paper Number 292. Washington, DC: Economic Policy Institute.

32. Klawitter, Marieka, M., C. Leigh Anderson, and Mary Kay Gugerty. 2013. Savings and Personal Discount Rates in a Matched Savings Program for Low-Income Families. *Contemporary Economic Policy, 31(3)*, 468–485.

33. Lusardi, Annamaria, Daniel J. Scheider, and Peter Tufano. 2011. *Financially Fragile Households: Evidence and Implications*. Paper Number 17072. Cambridge, MA: National Bureau of Economic Research.

34. Lusardi, Annamaria, Daniel J. Scheider, and Peter Tufano. 2011. *Financially Fragile Households: Evidence and Implications*. Paper Number 17072. Cambridge, MA: National Bureau of Economic Research.

35. Kaufman, Alex. 2013. *PayDay Lending Regulation*. Finance and Economics Discussion Series. Divisions of Research and Statistics and Monetary Affairs. Washington, DC: Federal Reserve Board.

36. Kaufman, Alex. 2013. *PayDay Lending Regulation*. Finance and Economics Discussion Series. Divisions of Research and Statistics and Monetary Affairs. Washington, DC: Federal Reserve Board.

37. Kaufman, Alex. 2013. *PayDay Lending Regulation*. Finance and Economics Discussion Series. Divisions of Research and Statistics and Monetary Affairs. Washington, DC: Federal Reserve Board.

38. Allstate/National Journal. 2014. *Heartland Monitor Poll XXI*. Survey. October 22–26, 2014.

39. Pew Research Center. January 2014. *Most See Inequality Growing, but Partisans Differ over Solutions*. Survey. Retrieved from http://www.people-press.org/2014/01/23/most-see-inequality-growing-but-partisans-differ-over-solutions/.

40. Benson, Michaela. 2014. Trajectories of Middle-Class Belonging: The Dynamics of Place Attachment and Classed Identities. *Urban Studies, 51(14)*, 3097–3112.

41. Corpus of Contemporary American English. 2014. Website. http://corpus.byu.edu/coca/.

42. Guvenen, Fatih, Fatih Karahan, Serdar Ozkan, and Jae Song. 2015. *What Do Data on Millions of U.S. Workers Reveal about Life-Cycle*

Earnings Risk? Federal Reserve Bank of New York Staff Reports. Staff Report No. 710. Federal Reserve Bank of New York: New York.

43. Guvenen, Fatih, Fatih Karahan, Serdar Ozkan, and Jae Song. 2015. *What Do Data on Millions of U.S. Workers Reveal about Life-Cycle Earnings Risk?* Federal Reserve Bank of New York Staff Reports. Staff Report No. 710. Federal Reserve Bank of New York: New York.

44. Chopra, Rohit. 2013. *Student Debt Swells, Federal Loans Now Top a Trillion.* Consumer Financial Protection Bureau: Iowa City, IA.

45. Controlling for inflation, all estimates are in 2010 dollars.

46. U.S. Department of Education, National Center for Education Statistics. 2013. *Digest of Education Statistics, 2012* (NCES 2014–015), Chapter 3.

47. Sallie Mae's National Study of Parents with Children under Age 18. 2014. *How America Saves for College.* Conducted by Ipsos Public Affairs: Washington, DC.

48. Brown, Meta, and Sydnee Caldwell. 2013. *Young Student Loan Borrowers Retreat from Housing and Auto Markets.* Federal Reserve Bank of New York: New York.

49. Brown, Meta, and Sydnee Caldwell. 2013. *Young Student Loan Borrowers Retreat from Housing and Auto Markets.* Federal Reserve Bank of New York: New York.

50. Hungerford, Thomas, L. 2012. *Taxes and the Economy: An Economic Analysis of the Top Tax Rates since 1945. Congressional Research Service Report for Congress.* Washington, DC: Congressional Research Service.

51. Internal Revenue Service. 2013. *U.S. Individual Income Tax: Personal Exemptions and Lowest and Highest Bracket Tax Rates, and Tax Base for Regular Tax.* New Carrolton, MD: Department of the Treasury.

52. Congressional Budget Office. 2011. *Trends in the Distribution of Household Income between 1979 and 2007.* Washington, DC: Congress of the United States.

53. Hixson, Ronald R. 2013. *Endangered Private Practice.* Lanham, MD: Rowman & Littlefield.

54. Ali, Mazhar, Brian Miller, Shannon Moriarty, Jessica Mornealt, Tim Sullivan, and Michael Young. 2012. *Born on the Third Base: What the Forbes 400 Really Says about Economic Equality and Opportunity in America.* Boston: UFE.

55. Internal Revenue Service. 2014. *Topic 209—Capital Gains and Losses.* Retrieved September 15, 2014, from http://www.irs.gov/taxtopics/tc409.html/.

56. Internal Revenue Service. 2014. *Publication 505: Tax Withholding and Estimated Tax.* New Carrolton, MD: Department of the Treasury.

57. Norton, Michael I., and Dan Ariely. 2011. Building a Better America—One Quintile at a Time. *Perspectives on Psychological Science, 6*(1), 9–12.

58. Shapiro, Isaac. 2005. *New IRS Data Show Income Inequality Is Again on the Rise.* Washington, DC: Center on Budget and Policy.

59. Pew Research Center. January 2014. *Most See Inequality Growing, but Partisans Differ over Solutions.* Survey. Retrieved from http://www.people-press.org/2014/01/23/most-see-inequality-growing-but-partisans-differ-over-solutions/.

60. Pew Research Center. January 2014. *Most See Inequality Growing, but Partisans Differ over Solutions.* Survey. Retrieved from http://www.people-press.org/2014/01/23/most-see-inequality-growing-but-partisans-differ-over-solutions/.

61. Pew Research Center's Global Attitude Project. 2013. *39-Nation Survey* [Data file]. Retrieved from http://www.pewglobal.org/2013/05/01/spring-2013-survey-data/.

62. Reich, Robert. January 15, 2014. "Fear Is Why Workers in Red States Vote against Their Economic Self-Interest." Robert Reich Blog. Retrieved September 15, 2014, from http://robertreich.org/page/5/.

The "Middle Class" Myth: Here's Why Wages Are Really So Low Today

Edward McClelland

This article first appeared in Salon.com at http://www.Salon.com/. An online version remains in the Salon archives. Reprinted with Permission.

Let me tell you the story of an "unskilled" worker in America who lived better than most of today's college graduates. In the winter of 1965, Rob Stanley graduated from Chicago Vocational High School, on the city's Far South Side. Pay rent, his father told him, or get out of the house. So Stanley walked over to Interlake Steel, where he was immediately hired to shovel taconite into the blast furnace on the midnight shift. It was the crummiest job in the mill, mindless grunt work, but it paid $2.32 an hour—enough for an apartment and a car. That was enough for Stanley, whose main ambition was playing football with the local sandlot all-stars, the Bonivirs.

Stanley's wages would be the equivalent of $17.17 today—more than the "Fight For 15"[1] workers movement is demanding for fast-food workers. Stanley's job was more difficult, more dangerous and more unpleasant than working the fryer at KFC (the blast furnace could heat up to 2,000 degrees). According to the laws of the free market, though, none of that is supposed to matter. All that is supposed to matter is how many people are capable of doing your job. And anyone with two arms could shovel taconite. It required even less skill than preparing dozens of finger lickin' good menu items, or keeping straight the orders of 10 customers waiting at the counter. Shovelers didn't need to speak English. In the early days of the steel industry, the job was often assigned to immigrants off the boat from Poland or Bohemia. "You'd just sort of go on automatic pilot, shoveling ore balls all night," is how Stanley remembers the work.

Stanley's ore-shoveling gig was also considered an entry-level position. After a year in Vietnam, he came home to Chicago and enrolled in a pipefitters' apprenticeship program at Wisconsin Steel. So why did Rob Stanley, an unskilled high school graduate, live so much better than someone with similar qualifications could even dream of today? Because the workers at Interlake Steel were represented by the United Steelworkers of America, who demanded a decent salary for all jobs. The workers at KFC are represented by nobody but themselves, so they have to accept a wage a few cents above what Congress has decided is criminal.

The argument given against paying a living wage in fast-food restaurants is that workers are paid according to their skills, and if the teenager cleaning the grease trap wants more money, he should get an education. Like most conservative arguments, it makes sense logically, but has little connection to economic reality. Workers are not simply paid according to their skills, they're paid according to what they can negotiate with their employers. And in an era when only 6 percent of private-sector workers belong to a union,[2] and when going on strike is almost certain to result in losing your job, low-skill workers have no negotiating power whatsoever.

Granted, Interlake Steel produced a much more useful, much more profitable product than KFC. Steel built the Brooklyn Bridge, the U.S. Navy and the Saturn rocket program. KFC spares people the hassle of frying chicken at home. So let's look at how wages have declined from middle-class to minimum-wage in a single industry: meat processing. Slaughterhouses insist they hire immigrants because the work is so unpleasant Americans won't do it. They hired European immigrants when Upton Sinclair wrote "The Jungle," and they hire Latin American immigrants today. But it's a canard that Americans won't slaughter pigs, sheep and cows. How do we know this? Because immigration to the United States was more or less banned from 1925 to 1965, and millions of pigs, sheep and cows were slaughtered during those years. But they were slaughtered by American-born workers, earning middle-class wages. *Mother Jones* magazine explains what changed.[3]

[S]tarting in the early 1960s, a company called Iowa Beef Packers (IBP) began to revolutionize the industry, opening plants in rural areas far from union strongholds, recruiting immigrant workers from Mexico, introducing a new division of labor that eliminated the need for skilled butchers, and ruthlessly battling unions. By the late 1970s, meatpacking companies that wanted to compete with IBP had to adopt its business methods—or go out of business. Wages in the meatpacking industry soon fell by as much as 50 percent.

In Nick Reding's book "Methland,"[4] he interviews Roland Jarvis, who earned $18 an hour throwing hocks at Iowa Ham . . . until 1992, when the slaughterhouse was bought out by a company that broke the union, cut wages to $6.20 an hour, and eliminated all benefits. Jarvis began taking meth so he could work extra shifts, then dealing the drug to make up for his lost income.

Would Americans kill pigs for $18 an hour? Hell, yes, they would. There would be a line from Sioux City to Dubuque for those jobs. But Big Meat's defeat of Big Labor means it can now negotiate the lowest possible wages with the most desperate workers: usually Mexican immigrants who are willing to endure dangerous conditions for what would be considered a huge pile of money in their home country. Slaughterhouses hire immigrants not because they're the only workers willing to kill and cut apart pigs, but because they're the only workers willing to kill and cut apart pigs for low wages, in unsafe conditions.

In Rob Stanley's native South Side, there is more than one monument to the violence that resulted when the right of industry to bargain without the interference of labor unions was backed up by government force. In 1894, President Cleveland sent 2,500 troops to break a strike[5] at the Pullman Palace Car Factory. On Memorial Day, 1937, Chicago police killed 10 striking workers outside the Republic Steel plant. The names of those dead are cast on a brass plaque bolted to a flagpole outside a defunct steelworkers' hall. They were as polyglot as a platoon in a World War II movie:

Anderson, Causey, Francisco, Popovich, Handley, Jones, Reed, Tagliori, Tisdale, Rothmund.

I first saw those sites on a labor history tour led by "Oil Can Eddie" Sadlowski, a retired labor leader who lost a race for the presidency of the USW in 1977. Sadlowski was teaching a group of ironworkers' apprentices about their blue-collar heritage, and invited me to ride along on the bus. Oil Can Eddie had spent his life agitating for a labor movement that transcended class boundaries. He wanted laborers to think of themselves as poets, and poets to think of themselves as laborers. "How many Mozarts are working in steel mills?" he once asked an interviewer.

In the parking lot of the ironworkers' hall, I noticed that most of the apprentices were driving brand-new pickup trucks—Dodge Rams with swollen hoods and quarter panels, a young man's first purchase with jackpot union wages. Meanwhile, I knew college graduates who earned $9.50 an hour as editorial assistants, or worked in bookstores for even less. None seemed interested in forming a union. So I asked Sadlowski why white-collar workers had never embraced the labor movement as avidly as blue-collar workers. "The white-collar worker has kind of a Bob Cratchit attitude," he explained. "He feels he's a half-step below the boss. The boss says, 'Call me Harry.' He feels he's made it. You go to a shoe store, they got six managers. They call everybody a manager, but they pay 'em all shit."

The greatest victory of the anti-labor movement has not been in busting industries traditionally organized by unions. That's unnecessary. Those jobs have disappeared as a result of automation and outsourcing to foreign countries. In the U.S., steel industry employment has declined from 521,000 in 1974 to 150,000 today. "When I joined the company, it had 28,000 employees," said George Ranney, a former executive at Inland Steel, an Indiana mill that was bought out by ArcelorMittal in 1998. "When I left, it had between 5,000 and 6,000. We were making the same amount of steel, 5 million tons a year, with higher quality and lower cost."

continues

▪ Continued

The anti-labor movement's greatest victory has been in preventing the unionization of the jobs that have replaced well-paying industrial work. Stanley was lucky: After Wisconsin Steel shut down in 1980,[6] a casualty of obsolescence, he bounced through ill-paying gigs hanging sheetrock and tending bar before finally catching on as a plumber for the federal government. The public sector is the last bastion of the labor movement, with a 35.9 percent unionization rate. But I know other laid-off steelworkers who ended their working lives delivering soda pop or working as security guards.

Where would a high-school graduate go today if he were told to pay rent or get out of the house? He might go to KFC, where the average team member earns $7.62 an hour—57 percent less, in real dollars, than Stanley earned for shoveling taconite. (No hourly worker at KFC earns as much[7] as Stanley did.) The reasons given for the low pay—that fast-food work is an entry-level job that was never meant to support a family or lead to a career—are ex post facto justifications for the reality that KFC can get away with paying low wages because it doesn't fear unionization. It's a lot harder to organize workers spread across dozens of franchises than it is to organize a single steel mill.

As Oil Can Eddie pointed out, a class-consciousness discourages office workers from unionizing. There's a popular discounting company in Chicago called Groupon, where the account executives—who are all expected to have bachelor's degrees—earn $37,800 a year.[8] Adjusted for modern dollars, that's about Stanley's starting wage, without overtime. Because they're educated and sit safely at desks, they don't think of themselves as blue-collar mopes who need to strike for higher pay and better working conditions.

The fact that many of today's college graduates have the same standard of living as the lowest-skilled workers of the 1960s proves that attitude is wrong, wrong, wrong. If we want to restore what we've traditionally thought of as the middle class, we have to stop thinking of ourselves as middle class, no matter how much we earn, or what we do to earn it. "Working class" should be defined by your relationship to your employer, not whether you perform physical labor. Unless you own the business, you're working class. "The smartest people I ever met were guys who ran cranes in the mill," Oil Can Eddie once said. They were smart enough, at least, to get their fair share of the company's profits.

NOTES

1. Editor's Note: "Fight for 15" advocates for the right to unionize and for a $15 minimum wage for fast-food workers.
2. Bureau of Labor Statistics. 2013. "The Union Members Summary." http://www.bls.gov/news.release/union2.nr0.htm/.
3. Schlosser, Eric. 2001. "The Chain Never Stops." *Mother Jones.* http://www.motherjones.com/politics/2001/07/dangerous-meatpacking-jobs-eric-schlosser/.
4. Reding, Nick. 2009. *Methland: The Death and Life of an American Small Town.* Bloomsbury.
5. Smith, Carl. 2005. "Pullman Strike." http://www.encyclopedia.chicagohistory.org/pages/1029.html/.
6. Brown, Terry. "The Closing of Wisconsin Steel." *Chicago Tribune.* http://www.chicagotribune.com/news/nationworld/politics/chi-chicagodays-wisconsinsteel-story-story.html/.
7. http://www.glassdoor.com/Hourly-Pay/KFC-Hourly-Pay-E7860.htm/.
8. http://www.glassdoor.com/Salary/Groupon-Salaries-E301291.htm/.

The Roots of the Widening Racial Wealth Gap: Explaining the Black–White Economic Divide

THOMAS SHAPIRO, TATJANA MESCHEDE, AND SAM OSORO

As more people become concerned about the unequal distribution of wealth in the United States, increasing attention has been paid to the growing racial wealth gap—the large gap in wealth accumulation between white and minority families. This reading discusses the origins, growth, and consequences of the racial wealth gap on communities, families, and the nation as a whole.

All families need wealth to be economically secure and create opportunities for the next generation. Wealth—what we own minus what we owe—allows families to move forward by moving to better and safer neighborhoods, investing in businesses, saving for retirement, and supporting their children's college aspirations. Having a financial cushion also provides a measure of security when a job loss or other crisis strikes. The Great Recession of 2007–2009 devastated the wealth of all families except for those with the most. The unprecedented wealth destruction during that period, accompanied by long-term high unemployment, underscores the critical importance wealth plays in weathering emergencies and helping families move along a path toward long-term financial security and opportunity.

Extreme wealth inequality not only hurts family well-being, it hampers economic growth in our communities and in the nation as a whole. In the U.S. today, the richest 1 percent of households owns 37 percent of all wealth. This toxic inequality has historical underpinnings but is perpetuated by policies and tax preferences that continue to favor the affluent. Most strikingly, it has resulted in an enormous wealth gap between white households and households of color. In 2009, a representative survey of American households revealed that the median wealth of white families was $113,149 compared with $6,325 for Latino families and $5,677 for black families.[1]

Looking at the same set of families over a 25-year period (1984–2009), our research offers key insight into how policy and the real,

Shapiro, T., Meschede, T., & Osoro, S. (2013). *The Roots of the Widening Racial Wealth Gap: Explaining the Black–White Economic Divide*. Waltham, MA: Institute on Assets and Social Policy, Brandeis University. Full report can be found at www.iasp.brandeis.edu. Reprinted by permission of the Institute on Assets and Social Policy, Heller School for Social Policy and Management, Brandeis University.

lived-experience of families in schools, communities, and at work affect wealth accumulation. Tracing the same households during that period, the total wealth gap between white and African-American families nearly triples, increasing from $85,000 in 1984 to $236,500 in 2009. . . . To discover the major drivers behind this dramatic $152,000 increase, we tested a wide range of possible explanations, including family, labor market, and wealth characteristics. This allowed us, for the first time, to identify the primary forces behind the racial wealth gap. Our analysis found little evidence to support common perceptions about what underlies the ability to build wealth, including the notion that personal attributes and behavioral choices are key pieces of the equation. Instead, the evidence points to policy and the configuration of both opportunities and barriers in workplaces, schools, and communities that reinforce deeply entrenched racial dynamics in how wealth is accumulated and that continue to permeate the most important spheres of everyday life.

Data for this analysis derived from the Panel Study of Income Dynamics (PSID), a nationally representative longitudinal study that began in 1968. We followed nearly 1,700 working-age households from 1984 through 2009. Tracking these families provides a unique opportunity to understand what happened to the wealth gap over the course of a generation and the effect of policy and institutional decision-making on how average families accumulate wealth. Unfortunately, there were not enough data that tracked wealth information in a sufficient number of Latino, Asian American, or immigrant households to include in this report. As a result, the specific focus here is on black–white differences. Yet, while each group shares different histories and experiences, we believe this examination captures important dynamics that can be applied across communities of color.

[The wealth trends are troubling. In 1984, the median net worth for African-American families was $5,781 and $90,851 for white families (a gap of $85,070). But over the next 25 years,

white families saw steady growth, and by 2009 their median net worth grew to $265,000. During this same time frame African-American families saw stagnation and very slow growth, and by 2009 their median net worth only grew to $28,500 (a gap of $236,500)], reflecting a major increase in wealth disparities by race. [This] . . . beg[s] the question of what caused such dramatic racial wealth inequities.

With a gap of close to a quarter of a million dollars, virtually every possible explanation will have some degree of accuracy, no matter how miniscule a factor. The challenge is to identify the major evidence-based factors affecting the growing racial wealth gap. To discover the major drivers behind the $152,000 increase in the racial wealth gap, we tested a wide range of possible explanations that included family, labor market, demographic, and wealth characteristics, and we have determined how different factors affect the widening racial wealth gap over a generation. The compelling evidence-based story is that policy shaping opportunities and rewards where we live, where we learn, and where we work propels the large majority of the widening racial wealth gap.

The Foundations of Inequality

We started our analysis with an overriding question: Why has economic inequality become so entrenched in our post–Civil Rights era of supposed legal equality? The first step was to identify the critical aspects of contemporary society that are driving this inequality. . . . Next, we sought to determine whether equal accomplishments are producing equal wealth gains for whites and African Americans. . . . This approach allows for an evidence-based examination of whether the growing racial wealth gap is primarily the result of individual choices and cultural characteristics or policies and institutional practices that create different opportunities for increasing wealth in white and black families.

Among households with positive wealth growth . . . during the 25-year study period . . .

the number of years of homeownership accounts for 27 percent of the difference in relative wealth growth between white and African-American families, the largest portion of the growing wealth gap. The second largest share of the increase, accounting for 20 percent, is average family income. Highly educated households correlate strongly with larger wealth portfolios, but similar college degrees produce more wealth for whites, contributing 5 percent of the proportional increase in the racial wealth gap. Inheritance and financial support from family combine for another 5 percent of the increasing gap. How much wealth a family started out with in 1984 also predicts a portion (3 percent) of family wealth 25 years later.

Unemployment, the only significant factor that depleted wealth since it forced families to draw upon their nest eggs, explains an additional 9 percent of the growing racial wealth gap. In addition to continuing discrimination, labor market instability affects African Americans more negatively than whites.

The evidence we present to examine the racial wealth gap points to institutional and policy dynamics in important spheres of American life: homeownership, work and increased earnings, employment stability, college education, and family financial support and inheritance. Together, these fundamental factors account for nearly two-thirds (66 percent) of the proportional increase in the wealth gap. In the social sciences, this is a very high level of explanatory power and provides a firm foundation for policy and reform aimed at closing the gap.

The $152,000 Question: What Drove the Growing Gap?

Having identified the major drivers of the racial wealth gap, we now can dig deeper into each one—homeownership, income, college education, inheritance, and unemployment—to determine how similar accomplishments grow wealth differentially by race.... [Our data] provide a close look at how these factors, as well as marriage, which we will discuss later, translate into differences in wealth accumulation for black and white families. We know that wealth increases through accomplishments such as job promotions, pay increases, or the purchase of a home, as well as important life and family events including receiving an inheritance and getting married.... [Our data] highlight how similar accomplishments and life events lead to unequal wealth gains for white and African-American families. The result is that while wealth grew for African Americans as they achieve life advances, that growth is at a considerably lower rate than it is for whites experiencing the same accomplishments. This leads to an increase in the wealth gap.

Homeownership

The number of years families owned their homes was the largest predictor of the gap in wealth growth by race.... Residential segregation by government design has a long legacy in this country and underpins many of the challenges African-American families face in buying homes and increasing equity. There are several reasons why home equity rises so much more for whites than African Americans:

- Because residential segregation artificially lowers demand, placing a forced ceiling on home equity for African Americans who own homes in non-white neighborhoods;[2]
- Because whites are far more able to give inheritances or family assistance for down payments due to historical wealth accumulation, white families buy homes and start acquiring equity an average eight years earlier than black families;[3]
- Because whites are far more able to give family financial assistance, larger up-front payments by white homeowners lower interest rates and lending costs; and
- Due to historic differences in access to credit, typically lower incomes, and factors such as residential segregation, the homeownership rate for white families is 28.4 percent higher than the homeownership rate for black families.[4]

Homes are the largest investment that most American families make and by far the biggest item in their wealth portfolio. Homeownership is an even greater part of wealth composition for black families, amounting to 53 percent of wealth for blacks and 39 percent for whites. . . . Yet, for many years, redlining, discriminatory mortgage-lending practices, lack of access to credit, and lower incomes have blocked the homeownership path for African Americans while creating and reinforcing communities segregated by race. African Americans, therefore, are more recent homeowners and more likely to have high-risk mortgages, hence they are more vulnerable to foreclosure and volatile housing prices.

. . . Between 2007 and 2009, [households lost wealth] (12 percent for white families, 21 percent for African-American families), which reflects the destruction of housing wealth resulting from the foreclosure crisis and imploded housing market. Overall, half the collective wealth of African-American families was stripped away during the Great Recession due to the dominant role of home equity in their wealth portfolios and the prevalence of predatory high-risk loans in communities of color. The Latino community lost an astounding 67 percent of its total wealth during the housing collapse.[5]

Unfortunately the end to this story has yet to be written. Since 2007, 10.9 million homes went into foreclosure. While the majority of the affected families are white, borrowers of color are more than twice as likely to lose their homes. These higher foreclosure rates reflect a disturbing reality: borrowers of color were consistently more likely to receive high-interest risky loan products, even after accounting for income and credit scores.[6]

Foreclosures not only have a direct impact on families, they also result in severe collateral damage to surrounding neighborhoods. One report estimates that this collateral destruction led to nearly $2 trillion in lost property wealth for communities across the country. More than half of this loss is associated with communities

of color, reflecting concentrations of high-risk loans, subsequent higher foreclosure rates, and volatile housing prices.[7]

While homeownership has played a critical role in the development of wealth for communities of color in this country, the return on investment is far greater for white households, significantly contributing to the expanding racial wealth gap. . . . The paradox is that even as homeownership has been the main avenue to building wealth for African Americans, it has also increased the wealth disparity between whites and blacks.

Income and Employment

Not surprisingly, increases in income are a major source of wealth accumulation for many US families. However, income gains for whites and African Americans have a very different impact on wealth. At the respective wealth medians, every dollar increase in average income over the 25-year study period added $5.19 . . . wealth for white households . . . while the same income gain only added 69 cents of wealth for African-American households.

The dramatic difference in wealth accumulation from similar income gains has its roots in long-standing patterns of discrimination in hiring, training, promoting, and access to benefits that have made it much harder for African Americans to save and build assets. Due to discriminatory factors, black workers predominate in fields that are least likely to have employer-based retirement plans and other benefits, such as administration and support and food services. As a result, wealth in black families tends to be close to what is needed to cover emergency savings while wealth in white families is well beyond the emergency threshold and can be saved or invested more readily.

The statistics cited above compare change in wealth over the 25 years at the median wealth for typical white and black households. Yet we already know that the average white family starts out with abundantly more wealth and significantly higher incomes than the average black family. When whites and blacks start off on an equal playing field with a similar wealth portfolio, their wealth returns from similar income gains narrow considerably. . . . Black families under this scenario see a return of $4.03 for each dollar increase in income—a considerable closing of the wealth breach.

This analysis also captured the devastation of unemployment on wealth accumulation. Unemployment affects all workers but due to the discriminatory factors listed above, black workers are hit harder, more often, and for longer periods of time. With much lower beginning wealth levels and unequal returns on income, it is a greater challenge for African Americans to grow their family wealth holdings in the face of work instability.

Inheritance

Most Americans inherit very little or no money, but among the families followed for 25 years whites were five times more likely to inherit than African Americans (36 percent to 7 percent, respectively). Among those receiving an inheritance, whites received about ten times more wealth than African Americans. Our findings show that inheritances converted to wealth more readily for white than black families: each inherited dollar contributed to 91 cents of wealth for white families compared with 20 cents for African-American families. Inheritance is more likely to add wealth to the considerably larger portfolio whites start out with since blacks, as discussed above, typically need to reserve their wealth for emergency savings.

College Education

In the 21st century, obtaining a college degree is vital to economic success and translates into substantially greater lifetime income and wealth. Education is supposed to be the great equalizer, but current research tells a different story. The achievement and college completion gaps are growing, as family financial resources like income and wealth appear to be large predictors of educational success. While current research

identifies a narrowing black–white achievement gap, race and class intersect to widen the educational opportunity deficit at a time when workers without higher-level skills are increasingly likely to languish in the job market.

College readiness is greatly dependent on quality K–12 education. . . . Neighborhoods have grown more segregated, leaving lower-income students—especially students of color—isolated and concentrated in lower-quality schools, and less academically prepared both to enter and complete college. Further, costs at public universities have risen 60 percent in the past two decades, with many low-income and students of color forced to hold down jobs rather than attend college full time and graduating in deep debt. Average student debt for the class of 2011 was $26,600. Student debt is an issue that affects most graduates, but black graduates are far more vulnerable: 80 percent of black students graduate with debt compared with 64 percent of white students.[8] More blacks than whites do not finish their undergraduate studies because financial considerations force them to leave school and earn a steady income to support themselves and their families.[9]

The context of broad class and race educational inequity helps us better understand why a college education produces more wealth for white than black households, accounting for a 5 percent share of the widening racial wealth gap. . . . In the past 30 years, the gap between students from low- and high-income families who earn bachelor's degrees has grown from 31 percent to 45 percent.[10] Although both groups are completing college at higher rates today, affluent students (predominantly white) improved much more, widening their already sizable lead. In 1972, upper-income Americans spent five times as much per child on college as low-income families. By 2007, the difference in spending between the two groups had grown to nine to one; upper-income families more than doubled how much they spent on each child, while spending by low-income families grew by just 20 percent.[11]

Social and Cultural Factors

As part of this analysis we set out to test notions about the role social and cultural factors play in widening or closing the racial wealth gap. To determine how these factors might affect wealth, we zeroed in on the role of marriage in perpetuating the racial wealth gap. We find that getting married over the 25-year study period significantly increases the wealth holdings for white families by $75,635 but has no statistically significant impact on African Americans. Single whites are much more likely to possess positive net worth, most likely due to benefits from substantial family financial assistance, higher paying jobs, and homeownership. Hence, marriages that combine modest wealth profiles seem to move whites past emergency-level savings to opportunities to invest and build wealth.

By contrast, marriage among African Americans typically combines two comparatively low-level wealth portfolios and, unlike white households, does not significantly elevate the family's wealth. While the number of household wage earners bringing in resources does correlate to higher wealth, the impact of marriage is not statistically significant for blacks and the reality is that most do not marry out of the racial wealth gap.

Closing the Racial Wealth Gap

Public policy can play a critical role in creating a more equitable society and helping all Americans build wealth. College loans, preferential homeownership, and retirement tax policies helped build opportunities and wealth for America's middle class. Medicare and Social Security have protected that wealth. While the bold vision of policymakers, advocates, and others interested in social and racial justice is needed to develop a precise policy agenda, we believe the following broad public policy and institutional changes are critical to closing the gap:

- Homeownership—The data in this report clearly target homeownership as the biggest driver of the racial wealth gap. We need to ensure that mortgage and lending policies and fair housing policies are enforced and strengthened so that the legacy of residential segregation no longer confers greater wealth opportunities to white homeowners than it does to black homeowners. As our nation moves towards a majority people of color population, increasingly diverse neighborhoods must deliver equitable opportunities for growing home equity.

- Income—This report identifies the importance of stable, family-supporting jobs and increasing incomes as a prime avenue for building wealth. To address the gap caused by income disparity, proven tools should be fully implemented at the national, state, and local levels, including raising the minimum wage, enforcing equal pay provisions, and strengthening employer-based retirement plans and other benefits.

- Education—It is clear that differential educational opportunities and rewards are further widening the racial wealth gap. We need to invest in affordable high-quality childcare and early childhood development so every child is healthy and prepared for school. We need to support policies that help more students from low- and moderate-income families and families of color attend college and graduate. And we need to value education as a public good and invest in policies that do not leave students strapped with huge debt or a reason to drop out.

- Inheritance—Due to the unearned advantages it transmits across generations, inheritance widens inequality and is a key driver of the racial wealth gap. If we truly value merit and not unearned preferences, then we need to diminish the advantages passed along to a small number of families. Preferential tax treatment for large estates costs taxpayers and provides huge benefits to less than 1 percent of the population while diverting vital resources from schools, housing, infrastructure, and jobs. Preferential tax treatment for dividends and interests are weighted toward wealthy investors as is the home mortgage deduction and tax shielding benefits from retirement savings.

It is time for a portfolio shift in public investment to grow wealth for all, not just a tiny minority. Without that shift the wealth gap between white and black households has little prospect of significantly narrowing. A healthy, fair, and equitable society cannot continue to follow such an economically unsustainable trajectory.

NOTES

1. Rakesh, Kochhar, Richard Fry and Paul Taylor, *Wealth Gaps Rise to Record Highs between Whites, Blacks, Hispanics*. Pew Research Center, July 2011. Data is from the Survey on Income and Program Participation.
2. Shapiro, Thomas, *The Hidden Cost of Being African American*, Oxford University Press, 2004.
3. Joint Center for Housing Studies analysis of American Housing Survey, 2009, tabulations of 2009 AHS.
4. Joint Center for Housing Studies, State of the Nation's Housing 2012.
5. Rakesh, Kochhar, Richard Fry, and Paul Taylor, *Wealth Gaps Rise to Record Highs between Whites, Blacks, Hispanics*. Pew Research Center, July 2011.
6. Gruenstein Bocian, Debbie, Peter Smith, and Wei Li, *Collateral Damage: The Spillover Costs of Foreclosures*. Center for Responsible Lending, October 24, 2012.
7. Gruenstein Bocian, Debbie, Peter Smith, and Wei Li, ibid.
8. The Project on Student Debt, Student Debt and the Class of 2011, October 2012.
9. The Project on Student Debt, ibid.
10. Martha J. Bailey and Susan M. Dynarski, "Inequality in Postsecondary Education" in *Whither Opportunity?* Edited by Greg J. Duncan and Richard J. Murnane, 2011.
11. Kornrich, Sobino and Frank Furstenberg, *Investing in Children: Changes in Parental Spending on Children, 1972 to 2007*, Demography 2012 Sep 18.

Of the 1%, by the 1%, for the 1%

JOSEPH E. STIGLITZ

Stiglitz highlights the increasing power and privilege of the richest 1% and calls for change. He discusses how this economic inequality is bad for our country because increasing inequality contributes to decreasing equality of opportunity and a reluctance of the 1% to identify with and spend on the common needs of our society.

It's no use pretending that what has obviously happened has not in fact happened. The upper 1 percent of Americans are now taking in nearly a quarter of the nation's income every year. In terms of wealth rather than income, the top 1 percent control 40 percent. Their lot in life has improved considerably. Twenty-five years ago, the corresponding figures were 12 percent and 33 percent. One response might be to celebrate the ingenuity and drive that brought good fortune to these people, and to contend that a rising tide lifts all boats. That response would be misguided. While the top 1 percent have seen their incomes rise 18 percent over the past decade, those in the middle have actually seen their incomes fall. For men with only high-school degrees, the decline has been precipitous—12 percent in the last quarter-century alone. All the growth in recent decades—and more—has gone to those at the top. In terms of income equality, America lags behind any country in the old, ossified Europe. . . . Among our closest counterparts are Russia with its oligarchs and Iran. While many of the old centers of inequality in Latin America, such as Brazil, have been striving in recent years, rather successfully, to improve the plight of the poor and reduce gaps in income, America has allowed inequality to grow.

Economists long ago tried to justify the vast inequalities that seemed so troubling in the mid-19th century—inequalities that are but a pale shadow of what we are seeing in America today. The justification they came up with was called "marginal-productivity theory." In a nutshell, this theory associated higher incomes with higher productivity and a greater contribution to society. It is a theory that has always been cherished by the rich. Evidence for its validity, however, remains thin. The corporate executives who helped bring on the recession of the [mid-2000s] . . . whose contribution to our society, and to their own companies, has been massively negative—went on to receive large bonuses. In some cases, companies were so embarrassed about calling such rewards "performance bonuses" that they felt compelled to change the name to "retention bonuses" (even if the only thing being retained was bad performance). Those who have contributed great positive innovations to our society, from the pioneers of genetic understanding to the pioneers of the Information Age, have received a pittance compared with those responsible for the financial innovations that brought our global economy to the brink of ruin.

Some people look at income inequality and shrug their shoulders. So what if this person gains and that person loses? What matters, they argue, is not how the pie is divided but the size of the pie. That argument is fundamentally wrong. An economy in which *most* citizens are doing worse year after year—an economy like America's—is not likely to do well over the long haul. There are several reasons for this.

First, growing inequality is the flip side of something else: shrinking opportunity. Whenever we diminish equality of opportunity, it means that we are not using some of our most valuable assets—our people—in the most productive way possible. Second, many of the distortions that lead to inequality—such as those associated with monopoly power and preferential tax treatment for special interests—undermine the efficiency of the economy. This new inequality goes on to create new distortions, undermining efficiency even further. To give just one example, far too many of our most talented young people, seeing the astronomical rewards, have gone into finance rather than into fields that would lead to a more productive and healthy economy. Third, and perhaps most important, a modern economy requires "collective action"—it needs government to invest in infrastructure, education, and technology. The United States and the world have benefited greatly from government-sponsored research that led to the Internet, to advances in public health, and so on. But America has long suffered from an under-investment in infrastructure (look at the condition of our highways and bridges, our railroads and airports), in basic research, and in education at all levels. Further cutbacks in these areas lie ahead.

None of this should come as a surprise—it is simply what happens when a society's wealth distribution becomes lopsided. The more divided a society becomes in terms of wealth, the more reluctant the wealthy become to spend money on common needs. The rich don't need to rely on government for parks or education or medical care or personal security—they can buy all these things for themselves. In the process, they become more distant from ordinary people, losing whatever empathy they may once have had. They also worry about strong government—one that could use its powers to adjust the balance, take some of their wealth, and invest it for the common good. The top 1 percent may complain about the kind of government we have in America, but in truth they like it just fine: too gridlocked to re-distribute, too divided to do anything but lower taxes.

Economists are not sure how to fully explain the growing inequality in America. The ordinary dynamics of supply and demand have certainly played a role: labor-saving technologies have reduced the demand for many "good" middle-class, blue-collar jobs. Globalization has created a worldwide marketplace, pitting expensive unskilled workers in America against cheap unskilled workers overseas. Social changes have also played a role—for instance, the decline of unions, which once represented a third of American workers and now represent about 12 percent.

But one big part of the reason we have so much inequality is that the top 1 percent want it that way. The most obvious example involves tax policy. Lowering tax rates on capital gains, which is how the rich receive a large portion of their income, has given the wealthiest Americans close to a free ride. Monopolies and near monopolies have always been a source of economic power—from John D. Rockefeller at the beginning of the last century to Bill Gates at the end. Lax enforcement of anti-trust laws, especially during Republican administrations, has been a godsend to the top 1 percent. Much of today's inequality is due to manipulation of the financial system, enabled by changes in the rules that have been bought and paid for by the financial industry itself—one of its best investments ever. The government lent money to financial institutions at close to 0 percent interest and provided generous bailouts on favorable terms when all else failed. Regulators turned a blind eye to a lack of transparency and to conflicts of interest.

When you look at the sheer volume of wealth controlled by the top 1 percent in this country, it's tempting to see our growing inequality as a quintessentially American achievement—we started way behind the pack, but now we're doing inequality on a world-class level. And it looks as if we'll be building on this achievement for years to come, because what made it possible is self-reinforcing. Wealth begets power, which begets more wealth. During the savings-and-loan scandal of the 1980s—a scandal whose dimensions, by today's standards, seem almost quaint—the banker Charles Keating was asked by a congressional committee whether the $1.5 million he had spread among a few key elected officials could actually buy influence. "I certainly hope so," he replied. The Supreme Court, in its recent *Citizens United* case, has enshrined the right of corporations to buy government, by removing limitations on campaign spending. The personal and the political are today in perfect alignment. Virtually all U.S. senators, and most of the representatives in the House, are members of the top 1 percent when they arrive, are kept in office by money from the top 1 percent, and know that if they serve the top 1 percent well they will be rewarded by the top 1 percent when they leave office. By and large, the key executive-branch policymakers on trade and economic policy also come from the top 1 percent. When pharmaceutical companies receive a trillion-dollar gift—through legislation prohibiting the government, the largest buyer of drugs, from bargaining over price—it should not come

as cause for wonder. It should not make jaws drop that a tax bill cannot emerge from Congress unless big tax cuts are put in place for the wealthy. Given the power of the top 1 percent, this is the way you would *expect* the system to work.

America's inequality distorts our society in every conceivable way. There is, for one thing, a well-documented lifestyle effect—people outside the top 1 percent increasingly live beyond their means. Trickle-down economics may be a chimera, but trickle-down behaviorism is very real. Inequality massively distorts our foreign policy. The top 1 percent rarely serve in the military—the reality is that the "all-volunteer" army does not pay enough to attract their sons and daughters, and patriotism goes only so far. Plus, the wealthiest class feels no pinch from higher taxes when the nation goes to war: borrowed money will pay for all that. Foreign policy, by definition, is about the balancing of national interests and national resources. With the top 1 percent in charge, and paying no price, the notion of balance and restraint goes out the window. There is no limit to the adventures we can undertake; corporations and contractors stand only to gain. The rules of economic globalization are likewise designed to benefit the rich: they encourage competition among countries for *business*, which drives down taxes on corporations, weakens health and environmental protections, and undermines what used to be viewed as the "core" labor rights, which include the right to collective bargaining. Imagine what the world might look like if the rules were designed instead to encourage competition among countries for *workers*. Governments would compete in providing economic security, low taxes on ordinary wage earners, good education, and a clean environment—things workers care about. But the top 1 percent don't need to care.

Paying for Politics: How Elite Donors Purchase Political Power

Lee Drutman

Originally published as "The Political 1% of the 1%" in 2012. Reprinted by Permission of the Sunlight Foundation.

In the 2012 election, 28 percent of all disclosed political contributions came from just 31,385 people. In a nation of 313.85 million, these donors represent . . . 1% of the [richest] 1%, an elite class that increasingly serves as the gatekeepers of public office in the United States. More than a quarter of the nearly $6 billion in contributions from identifiable sources in the . . . [2012] campaign cycle came from just 31,385 individuals, a number equal to one ten-thousandth of the U.S. population. In the first presidential election cycle since the Supreme Court's decision in *Citizens United v. FEC*, candidates got more money from a smaller percentage of the population than any year for which we have data, a new analysis of 2012 campaign finance giving by the Sunlight Foundation shows. These donors contributed 28.1 percent of all individual contributions in the 2012 cycle, a record high.

One sign of the reach of this elite "1% of the 1%": Not a single member of the House or Senate elected last year won without financial assistance from this group. Money from the nation's 31,385 biggest givers found its way into the coffers of every successful congressional candidate. And 84 percent of those elected in 2012 took more money from these 1% of the 1% donors than they did from *all* of their small donors (individuals who gave $200 or less) combined. This elite 1% of the 1% dominated campaign giving even in a year when President Barack Obama reached new small donor frontiers. . . . In 2014, without a presidential race to attract small donors, all indicators are that the 1% of the 1% will occupy an even more central role in the money chase.

The nation's biggest campaign donors have little in common with average Americans. They hail predominantly from big cities, such as New York and Washington. They work for blue-chip corporations, such as Goldman Sachs and Microsoft. One in five works in the finance, insurance and real estate sector. One in 10 works in law or lobbying. The median contribution from this group of elite donors? $26,584. That's a little more than half the median family income in the United States.

VISUALIZING THE INEQUALITIES

What does 31,385 people look like? This elite group of donors would occupy a little more than a third of the seats in Fedex Field . . . [home of Washington, D.C.'s NFL team]. But they pay a much higher price of admission than ticket-holders there. The smallest contribution required to make it into the 1% of 1% of political donors last year? $12,950.

How unequal was political giving in 2012? If we let the Verizon Center (capacity of about 20,000 [and home of Washington D.C.'s NBA and NHL teams]) stand in for the entire U.S., it would be as if just two people bought out the best 5,610 seats. The price of entry to be in this elite group of donors has risen steadily over the years. . . . In 1990, a single $2,000 contribution (about $3,700 in 2012 dollars) could put you in the 1% of the 1%. By 2000, the minimum contribution had risen to $5,700. It crossed the $10,000 mark for the first time in 2008, reaching $11,000.

Why the increase? No doubt, the *Citizens United* and *SpeechNow* decisions, which paved the way for unlimited contributions to super PACs [political action committees], are a key factor. Of the 1% of the 1%'s $1.68 billion in the 2012 cycle, $500.4 million entered the campaign through a super PAC (including almost $100 million from just one couple, Sheldon and Miriam Adelson). However, more money ($670.5 million) went directly to parties. The vast majority of 1% of the 1% donors—87.5 percent—contributed absolutely nothing to super PACs, giving instead directly to candidates, parties and traditional PACs. Only 5.5 percent of the 1% of the 1% donors (1,635 individuals) contributed more than $10,000 to super PACs.

We should also note that this total does not include the at least $305 million in "dark money" in the 2012 election, since the donors behind that

continues

■ **Continued**

spending remain anonymous. But we can reasonably speculate that most of them are in the 1% of the 1%, and had we been able to include them, the share of 2012 money coming from the 1% of the 1% would almost certainly have been higher.

THE RISING TIDE OF THE 1% OF THE 1%
The 28.1 percent of total money from the 1% of the 1% marks a dubious new landmark in the history of modern elections—well above the previous high of 21.8 percent in 2006. . . . In 2010, 20.5 percent of the money going to federal candidates and campaign committees came from the most generous 0.01 percent of Americans. It's especially striking—and surprising—that the new record should have been set in a presidential election year. The race for the White House attracts more small donors than mid-term elections. In recent presidential election cycles (2000, 2004 and 2008), the slice of donations coming from the 1% of the 1% held solidly around 17 percent. This year's 28.1 percent share marks a significant break with the past. It is a new level in political contribution inequality.

WHY WE SHOULD CARE
The 1% of the 1% are the political gatekeepers of American politics. Through countless independent phone calls and fundraising events, they set the boundaries of acceptable political topics and positions (i.e., what *they care* about and believe). They determine who is an acceptable candidate (i.e., those individuals whom *they trust* to represent their interests). Their influence is very rarely found in simple favor trading. Rather, their influence arises from something subtler yet far more significant: shaping the limits of acceptable political discourse, one conversation at a time.

In the 2012 cycle, winning House members raised on average $1.64 million, or about $2,250 per day during the two-year cycle. The average winning senator raised even more: $10.3 million, or $14,125 per day. That money has to come from somewhere. And while it *could* come from small donors, it's much more time-efficient to host a $1,000-a-plate

fundraiser, or spend an afternoon calling corporate executives, hedge fund managers, lawyers, lobbyists, political action committee managers and others in a position to give a few thousand dollars. Rare is the candidate with enough small donor appeal to bring in the kind of money needed to run a successful campaign. This places limits on what is politically possible. As Sen. Chris Murphy, D-Conn., put it succinctly at a recent event at Yale University, recalling his time fundraising in his recent (2012) campaign: "I talked a lot more about carried interest inside of that call room than I did in the supermarket." ("Carried interest" refers to profits that private equity and hedge fund managers earn on investments.)

Murphy knows it is much easier to raise the kind of money he needs if he remains sympathetic to the concerns of private equity and hedge fund managers—and much harder if he supports increasing the tax rate on carried interest. Murphy is not alone. Every member of Congress faces the same concern. They don't want to upset the people most likely to fund their campaigns, and will try their best to avoid doing so. As costs of elections for office run higher and higher, candidates and parties have less freedom to cross a potential donor. It amounts to what Lawrence Lessig has called "dependence corruption"—the way in which political discourse must necessarily shift to reflect the demands and opinions of the most active donors.

These concerns are likely even more acute for the two parties. In 2012, the National Republican Senatorial Committee raised more than half (54.2 percent) of its $105.8 million from the 1% of the 1%, and the National Republican Congressional Committee raised one third (33.0 percent) of its $140.6 million from the 1% of the 1%. Democratic Party committees depend less on the 1% of the 1%. The Democratic Senatorial Campaign Committee raised 12.9 percent of its $128.9 million from these top donors, and the Democratic Congressional Committee raised 20.1 percent of its $143.9 million from 1% of the 1% donors.

Party aside, what all these donors have in common is the personal wealth that allows them to contribute tens of thousands of dollars in an election cycle. And as political scientists Benjamin Page, Larry Bartels and Jason Seawright explain in a recent paper, the rich are not like the rest of us—and not just because they have more money. They also have very different political priorities, particularly on issues of economics and government spending. And as political scientist Marty Gilens has shown, when rich people and poor people disagree on policy, elected officials almost always side with rich people. . . .[1]

WHERE THE MONEY GOES

[. . . We can also break] down all the sources of money in the 2012 election, comparing 1% of the 1% donors with other over-$200 donors, small donors and a few other sources of money. (PACs are not included separately in this total because they are conduits for individual donations). . . . In brief: $410 million went directly to candidates ($235 million to Republicans, $173 million to Democrats); $671 million went to party committees ($405 million to Republican committees, $265 to Democratic committees); $500 million went to super PACs; $89 million went to traditional PACs. Those in the top 10 percent of the 1% of the 1% (the top 3,139 givers in American politics) account for about half of the total spending by the 1% of the 1%. More than half of their contributions went to super PACs. . . .

PARTISANSHIP

Republicans are about 40 percent more common than Democrats among the 1% of the 1%. While almost half (49.8 percent) of the 1% of 1% gave at least 90 percent of their money to Republicans, just over one third (35.5 percent) of these donors gave at least 90 percent to Democrats. . . .

CONCLUSIONS

The U.S. now has a campaign finance system where a tiny slice of individuals—31,385 people, not even enough to fill half of a professional football stadium—collectively account for more than a quarter of all individual contributions (that we can trace), even though they represent just one in ten thousand Americans. Every single member of Congress elected in 2012 received a contribution from this group of individuals, and the vast majority of those elected (84 percent) received more money from the "1% of the 1%" than they did from all small donations (under $200).

A tiny sliver of Americans who can afford to give tens of thousands of dollars in a single election cycle have become the gatekeepers of public office in America. Through the growing congressional dependence on their contributions, they increasingly set the boundaries and limits of American political discourse—who can run for office, what their priorities should be and even what can be said in public. And in an era of unlimited campaign contributions, the power of the 1% of the 1% only stands to grow with each passing year.

NOTES

1. Editor's note: In 2014, scholars Gilens and Page found that both economic elites and the organized groups that represent business interests have significantly more independent impact on governmental policy in the United States than average citizens and mass-based interest groups, calling into question our core democratic values and the balance of power in the United States. Gilens and Page acknowledge that Americans "do enjoy many features central to democratic governance such as regular elections [and] freedom of speech and association . . . [but when] policymaking is dominated by powerful business organizations and a small number of affluent Americans . . . America's claims to being a democratic society are seriously threatened" (see page 577 of Giles, Martin, and Benjamin I. Page. 2014. "Testing Theories of American Politics: Elites, Interest Groups, and Average Citizens." *Perspectives on Politics* 12(3): 564–581).

Poverty

David Pirtle

David Pirtle is a homeless advocate who specializes in hate crimes and criminalization of homelessness issues. David works with the National Coalition for the Homeless (NCH) and is a member of their Homeless Speakers' Bureau.

Courtesy of the National Coalition for the Homeless.

What is the mission of the National Coalition for the Homeless (NCH)? How are you involved?

First and foremost, as a member of the Speakers' Bureau, I participate in a large number of presentations every year, primarily to college and high school students. I attempt to put a human face on the issue of homelessness in the United States, as well as inform students and others about the issues of criminalization and hate crimes that persons experiencing homelessness face every day. I think that public education is an important part of advocacy in and of itself.

Apart from that, the most important campaign I am involved in at the moment is an attempt to address the discrimination that homeless men and women face when seeking employment, housing, or simply utilizing public accommodations and businesses, due to the negative public perception of persons experiencing homelessness. Here in the District of Columbia, I am helping to organize an effort to amend the Human Rights Act of 1977 to include homelessness as a fully protected group in the same way that the law protects citizens from

discrimination based, for example, on their race, religion, or sexual orientation.

How did you first become interested in this type of activism?

I first became involved in activism around the issue of homelessness as a homeless person myself in 2006. I was residing in a men's shelter in Washington, D.C. slated to be closed the following year and converted into a boutique hotel for visiting tourists. A small number of the shelter's residents began to protest this move, and together we were able to forestall the closure for two years. During this campaign I came into contact with the National Coalition for the Homeless (NCH), and I've been working with them ever since.

My two inspirations in this work are the late Sister Mary Ann Luby and NCH's current director of community organizing, Michael Stoops. Sister Mary Ann was the woman who first showed me the impact that local advocates can have on the lives of people in need through her relentless efforts to help the homeless men and women of Washington to advocate on their own behalf. I've been working with Michael Stoops for over eight years now, and I have never met another person who is as dedicated and selfless in his or her efforts to battle the injustice of homelessness in America.

As an activist in your organization, currently what are your top goals?

My first goal is to educate as many people as possible about the reality of homelessness versus the myths that we as a society choose to believe in order to excuse ourselves from doing more to end the problem. My second goal is to help protect the civil rights of people who are homeless, both locally and around the country. Finally, my third goal would be to end the scourge of violence which homeless men and women experience all too regularly while living on the streets.

What strategies do you use to try to enact social change in your area of activism?

I think the three key strategies for enacting any change in our society are education, political lobbying, and public action. Educating both policy makers and the public about a problem that needs addressing should always come first. Once policy makers know what change needs to be made, it's important to work with them to make sure that the change is correctly accomplished. Failing that, public action in the form of petitions, ad campaigns, and protests can help get the public at large to put the pressure where it needs to be in order to make things right.

What are the major challenges activists in your field face?

While bureaucracy and other structural roadblocks can build frustration when attacking any social issue, I think what wears people down the fastest who work on this problem in particular is the general apathy that politicians and the public seem to have toward the issue. I think this apathy stems from two sources—our lack of empathy for those who are facing a situation most of us thankfully have a hard time relating to,

and an overall (false, in my opinion) sense of the "intractability" of the problem. However, every letter I get from a group of young people to whom I've spoken telling me what they are now doing to help in their community is a reason for me to keep doing what I do.

What would you consider to be your greatest successes as an activist?

On Christmas Eve of 2008 a homeless man I knew by the name of Yoshio Nakada was murdered while sleeping in downtown Washington, D.C. I think it helped to shock many in the District into action over an issue that had long been ignored, that of the violence being perpetrated upon our homeless community. Together we were able to get our local hate crimes law amended to protect our homeless neighbors in the same way it protects other vulnerable populations.

What are major misconceptions the public has about activism in general and your issue specifically?

I think one of the biggest misconceptions people have about activism is that it mostly involves protest marches and public rallies, when in actuality those are more likely to be the last resorts advocates turn to in an effort to bring attention to an issue. Another misconception that folks seem to have about activism, in general, and about my own issue, in particular, is that it requires testifying on Capitol Hill or phoning the President to make a significant impact. Most of the policies that cause the issue of homelessness in America are actually set and enforced at the local level.

Why should students get involved in your line of activism?

When most people think about helping the homeless, they picture volunteering at soup kitchens or something along those lines. The aforementioned Michael Stoops likes to say to young people that while those types of actions are important, if that's all they do, they'll still be doing it when they're his age (he's in his sixties).

If students want to actually work on ending the problem of homelessness instead of simply maintaining it, it is necessary for them to become activists.

If an individual has little money and time, are there other ways they can contribute? What ways can students enact social change in their daily lives?

Getting back to misconceptions, a lot of people seem to think activism is hard, and it can be, but there are a lot of easy ways to be an advocate.

Something as simple as a letter-writing campaign can cause a local politician to rethink an issue that he or she didn't realize was so important to his or her constituents. Attending local city council meetings and asking hard questions of their elected officials on the record can actually help a lot. And again, education is the first step when it comes to any activism, and not just getting educated, but sharing what they've learned with their friends and family, classmates and others. At its root, activism is simply being an involved member of your community.

Rethinking American Poverty

MARK R. RANK

When you think of someone living in poverty, how do you imagine they got there? Do they cause their own troubles or are there cultural and economic factors that contributed? Rank argues that the way we conceptualize poverty—as caused by individual failing or pathology—informs how we have worked (or in some cases, not worked) to solve the problem. Rank discusses three shifts in thought that are needed if we are to begin addressing the issue of poverty in America and notes that without this change, many Americans will continue to live in poverty in the wealthiest nation on earth.

It's a fundamental paradox: in America, the wealthiest country on earth, one also finds the highest rates of poverty in the developed world. Whether we examine children's rates of poverty, poverty among working adults, poverty within single parent families, or overall rates of poverty, the story is much the same—the United States has exceedingly high levels of impoverishment. As a result, half of U.S. children will reside in a household that uses food stamps at some point during childhood. Life expectancy in Harlem is shorter than in Bangladesh. The bottom 60 percent of the American population currently holds less than 1 percent of the financial wealth in the country. And two-thirds of the counties that black children are growing up in are considered high poverty with respect to impoverished neighborhoods. Although there are several possible explanations for why these conditions exist, the argument developed here is that a major reason has to do with how we as a society have tended to conceptualize the issue of poverty and, based upon this thinking, how we have acted (or better put, failed to act) toward the issue.

The traditional manner of thinking about poverty in the U.S. has viewed impoverishment as largely the result of individual inadequacies and failings. These shortcomings include not working hard enough, failure to acquire sufficient skills, or just making bad decisions. Consequently, the problem of poverty is often seen through a lens of individual pathology. Since individuals are perceived as having brought poverty onto themselves, our collective and societal obligations are seen as limited. The age-old distinction between the deserving versus the undeserving poor reflects this perspective—unless the working-age poor have very good grounds for their poverty, they're deemed largely undeserving of help. Poverty is therefore understood as primarily affecting those who choose

Mark R. Rank, *Contexts* (Volume 10 and Issue 2), pp. 16–21, Copyright © 2011. Reprinted by Permission of SAGE Publications.

not to play by the rules of the game. Ultimately, this perspective reflects and reinforces the myths and ideals of American society: there are economic opportunities for all, individualism and self-reliance are paramount, and hard work is rewarded.

This overall mindset has long influenced both the general public's attitudes toward the poor and much of the policy and academic work analyzing poverty. Nevertheless, it seriously misconstrues the true nature of poverty and fosters a lack of political and social will to address the problem itself. Three major changes are essential for realistically and proactively reframing American impoverishment.

Poverty Affects Us All

A first fundamental shift in thinking is the recognition that poverty affects us all. All too often we view poverty as someone else's problem, or think that poverty is confined to certain areas and neighborhoods (such as inner cities or remote rural areas), and that by avoiding such areas we can simply ignore the issue. The notion is "out of sight, out of mind."

Clearly, this perspective is incorrect and intellectually lazy. In one way or another, poverty affects us all. There are at least two ways of thinking about this. The first is that whether we realize it or not, we pay a steep price for our high rates of poverty. As mentioned earlier, the extent and depth of poverty and economic inequality in the U.S. are far greater than in any other Western industrialized country. As a result, we spend considerably more money than needed on social problems associated with poverty. These include greater health problems, family problems, a less able work force, and so on down a long list. When we speak about homeland security, these are the issues that undermine us and our security as a nation. We wind up paying a tremendous price for quietly allowing so many of our citizens and communities to remain mired in poverty.

As an example, a study by the economist Harry Holzer and colleagues attempted to quan-

tify the annual monetary cost of childhood poverty in the U.S. They calculated the economic costs that growing up in poverty had for future earnings, risk of engaging in crime, and health quality in later life. Their estimate was that the overall cost of childhood poverty was an eye opening $500 billion per year—nearly 4 percent of this country's GDP. The result is that we end up spending much of our tax dollars and resources on the by-products of poverty, assuredly a more expensive approach over the long term than preventing poverty in the first place. In short, each of us pays dearly in a number of ways for letting poverty exist at such levels, but we too often fail to see this connection.

However, there is also a second way of thinking about poverty as affecting us all. And that comes in considering the chances that an average American will directly encounter poverty at some point during his or her lifetime. As it turns out, the number of Americans who are touched by poverty during adulthood is exceedingly high. My co-author, sociologist Thomas Hirschl and I have estimated that between the ages of 20 and 75, nearly 60 percent of Americans will experience at least one year below the poverty line and three quarters will experience a year either in or near poverty. Perhaps more surprising is the fact that two thirds of Americans between the ages of 20 and 65 will wind up using a social welfare program such as Food Stamps or Medicaid; 40 percent will use such a program in at least five years scattered throughout their working age adulthood.

Consequently, although those in poverty and welfare recipients are routinely vilified and portrayed as members of "marginalized groups" on the fringes of society, most of us will find ourselves below the poverty line and using a social safety net program at some point. After all, during the course of a lifetime, any number of unexpected, detrimental things can happen—job loss, family break ups, or the development of a major health problem. In addition, recent research has shown that this life course risk of poverty and economic instability has been rising since the 1990s. More and more families, including middle class ones, are experiencing greater income volatility, greater instability in the labor market, and a lack of benefits such as health and unemployment insurance. Jobs are no longer as stable as they once were, health care benefits are harder to get, and the safety net has weakened over time. A first shift in thinking therefore asks the question, "Who is at risk of poverty and its consequences?" The answer is: virtually all of us. As a result, each of us has a vested interest in and an imperative for reducing poverty in the U.S.

Structural Failings

A second critical change in thinking is a recognition that American poverty is largely the result of failings at the economic and political levels, rather than at the individual level. In the past, we've emphasized individual inadequacies as the major reason for poverty; that is, people aren't motivated enough, aren't working hard enough, have failed to acquire enough skills and education, or have just made bad decisions. These behaviors and attributes are seen as leading people into poverty and keeping them there. And in fact, we tend to confront most social problems in this country as individual pathologies.

In contrast to this perspective, the basic problem lies in a shortage of viable opportunities for all Americans. Certainly, particular individual shortcomings, such as the lack of education or skills, help explain who is more likely to be left out in the competition to locate and secure good opportunities, but they cannot explain why there's a shortage of such opportunities in the first place. In order to answer that question, we must turn to the inability of the economic and political structures to provide the supports and opportunities necessary to lift all of us out of poverty.

The most obvious example is in the mismatch between the number of decent paying jobs and the pool of labor in search of those jobs. Over the past 30 years, the U.S. economy has been producing more and more low-paying jobs, part-time jobs, and jobs without benefits (it's es-

timated that approximately one third of all jobs are low-paying—less than $11.50 an hour). And of course, beyond those in low-paying jobs, there are millions of unemployed Americans at any point in time. During the recent economic downturn, six to seven people have been competing for every single job opening. Coupled with the country's lack of universal coverage for childcare, health care, and affordable housing, this situation leaves an increasing number of families economically vulnerable.

In class, I often use the analogy of musical chairs to help students recognize this disconnect. Picture a game with ten players, but only eight chairs. When the music stops, who's most likely to be left standing? It will be those who are at a disadvantage in terms of competing for the available chairs (less agility, reduced speed, a bad position when the music stops, and so on). However, given that the game is structured in a way such that two players are *bound* to lose, these individual attributes only explain who loses, not why there are losers in the first place. Ultimately, there are simply not enough chairs for those playing the game. . . . So while characteristics such as deficiencies in skills or education or being in a single parent family help to explain who's at a heightened risk of encountering poverty, the fact that poverty exists in the first place results not from these characteristics, but from a failure of the economic and political structures to provide enough decent opportunities and supports for the whole of society. By focusing solely upon individual characteristics, we can shuffle people up or down in terms of their likelihood to land a job with good earnings, but when there aren't enough of these jobs to go around, somebody will still end up in poverty. We're playing a large-scale version of musical chairs.

The recognition of this dynamic represents a fundamental shift in thinking from the past. It helps explain why the social policies of the last three decades have been largely ineffective in reducing poverty rates. We've spent our attention and resources on altering players' incentives and disincentives through various welfare reform measures, or, in a very limited way, upgrading their skills and ability to compete with various job-training programs, but we've left the structure of the game untouched. Overall rates of poverty do go up and down, but primarily as a result of changes on the structural level (that is, increases or decreases in the number of available opportunities—the "chairs"). In particular, the performance of the economy has been historically important, since, when the economy is expanding, more opportunities are available for the competing pool of labor and their families. The reverse occurs when the economy slows down, as we saw in the 2000s and the economic collapse that began in 2008. To attribute the rise of poverty over the past ten years to individual inadequacies or lowered motivation is absurd. Rather, the increase in poverty has everything to do with deteriorating economic conditions, particularly in the last few years.

Likewise, changes in various social supports and the social safety net affect how well families are able to avoid poverty. When such supports were increased by the War on Poverty initiatives of the 1960s and buoyed by a strong economy, poverty rates declined significantly. Likewise, when Social Security benefits were expanded during the 1960s and 1970s, poverty rates among the elderly dropped sharply. Conversely, when social supports have been eroded, as in the case of children's programs over the past 30 years, rates of poverty among those relying on such services have gone up.

The recognition of poverty as a structural failing also makes it clear why the U.S. has such high rates of poverty when compared to other Western countries. It's not that Americans are less motivated or less skilled than those in other countries, but that our economy has been producing millions of low-wage jobs and our social policies have done relatively little to economically support families compared to other industrialized countries. From this perspective, one key to addressing poverty is to increase the labor market opportunities and social supports available to American households. We must shift our thinking to recognize the fundamental distinction between who loses at the game and why the game produces losers in the first place.

The Moral Ground

Let's turn to the third shift in thinking that's needed to create a more realistic and proactive approach toward poverty. And that is the moral ground on which we view poverty in America must change. In the past, our moral perspective has been rooted in the ethos of individual blame, with a resulting general acceptance of the status quo. In other words, since people bring it upon themselves, poverty's their problem, not mine.

But poverty is a moral problem. It represents an injustice of a substantial magnitude. Severe deprivation and hardship have been documented in countless studies—not to mention millions of human lives. And, as argued earlier, a large portion of this poverty is the result of failings at the structural rather than the individual level, which places much of the responsibility for poverty beyond the poor. However, what makes this injustice particularly grievous is the stark contrast between the wealth, abundance, and resources of America and its levels of destitution. Something is seriously wrong when we find that, in a country with the most abundant resources in the world, there are children without enough to eat, families who cannot afford health care, and people sleeping on the streets for lack of shelter.

It should also be noted that the gap between extreme prosperity and vulnerability has never been wider. The venerable economist Paul Samuelson, writing in the first edition of his introductory economics textbook in 1948, observed that if we were to make an income pyramid out of a child's play blocks, with each layer representing $1,000 of income, the peak would be somewhat higher than the Eiffel Tower, but almost all of us would be within several yards of the ground. By the time of Samuelson's 2001 edition of the textbook, most of us would still be within several yards of the ground, but the Eiffel

Tower would now have to be replaced with Mount Everest to represent those at the top. Or consider the distance between the average worker's salary and the average CEO's salary. In 1980, the average CEO of a major corporation earned around 42 times the pay of the average worker. Today, it is well over 400 times. Adding insult to injury, during the past 30 years, an increasing number of companies have demanded concessions from their workers, including pay cuts and the elimination of health benefits in order to keep their labor costs down, while those at the top have prospered beyond any sense of decency. Patterns of wealth accumulation have become even more skewed. The top one percent of the U.S. population currently owns 42 percent of the country's entire financial wealth, while the bottom 60 percent of Americans are in possession of less than 1 percent. And while all of these trends have been emerging, our social policies have continued to give more to the well-to-do and less to the economically vulnerable, with the argument that these policies help all Americans through "trickle down economics."

A new way of thinking recognizes this as a moral outrage. Injustice, rather than blame, becomes the moral compass with which to view poverty amidst abundance. The magnitude of such injustice constitutes a strong impetus for change. It signals that a wrong is being committed and cries out for a remedy. A shift in thinking is premised upon the idea that social change

is essential for addressing the injustices of poverty. This is in sharp contrast with the old way of thinking, in which the moral focus is upon individual blame. Such thinking simply reinforces the status quo by letting us do little while poverty rates climb. The perspective of injustice exhorts us to actively engage and confront poverty, rather than comfortably settling for widespread impoverishment.

In his last book, *Where Do We Go from Here: Chaos or Community?*, the Rev. Dr. Martin Luther King, Jr. wrote, "A true revolution of value will soon cause us to question the fairness and justice of many of our past and present policies. We are called to play the Good Samaritan on life's roadside; but that will be only an initial act. One day the whole Jericho road must be transformed so that men and women will not be beaten and robbed as they make their journey through life. True compassion is more than flinging a coin to a beggar; it understands that an edifice that produces beggars needs restructuring. A true revolution of values will soon look uneasily on the glaring contrast of poverty and wealth." This revolution of values must begin with a fundamental shift in how American society understands, and ultimately acts toward, the poverty in which so many of our citizens live. These are the building blocks on which to challenge and confront the paradox of poverty amidst plenty.

Poverty as a Childhood Disease

Perri Klass, M.D.

Poverty is an exam room familiar. From Bellevue Hospital in New York to the neighborhood health center in Boston where I used to work, poverty has

filtered through many of my interactions with parents and their children. I ask about sleeping arrangements. Mother, father, older child and new baby live in one bedroom that they're renting in an apartment, worrying that if the baby cries too much, they'll be asked to leave. I encourage an overweight 9-year-old who loves karate, and his mother says, "We had to stop; too expensive." I talk to a new mother who is going back to work too soon, leaving her baby with the cheapest sitter she can find. Is your housing situation secure? Can you afford groceries? Do you go with the cheapest fast food? Can you get the prescription filled? Raising children in poverty means that everything is more complicated.

Me, I'm one generation out. My mother will tell you about her Depression childhood, the social worker who checked the family's pots to see whether they were secretly able to afford meat, the landlord who put the furniture out on the street. It wasn't character-building or noble, she says. It was soul-destroying, grinding and cruel. And it's even . . . [more cruel], now that social mobility has decreased and children who grow up poor are more likely to stay poor. . . .

At the annual meeting of the Pediatric Academic Societies . . . [in 2013], there was a new call for pediatricians to address childhood poverty as a national problem, rather than wrestling with its consequences case by case in the exam room. Poverty damages children's dispositions and blunts their brains. We've seen articles about the language deficit in poorer homes and the gaps in school achievement. These remind us that . . . poverty in this country is now likely to define many children's life trajectories in the harshest terms: poor academic achievement, high dropout rates, and health problems from obesity and diabetes to heart disease, substance abuse and mental illness. Recently, there has been a lot of focus on the idea of toxic stress, in which a young child's body and brain may be damaged by too much exposure to so-called stress hormones, like cortisol and norepinephrine. When this level of stress is experienced at an early age, and without sufficient protection, it may actually reset the neurological and hormonal systems, permanently affecting children's brains and even, we are learning, their genes. Toxic stress is the heavy hand of early poverty, scripting a child's life not in the

Horatio Alger scenario of determination and drive, but in the patterns of disappointment and deprivation that shape a life of limitations.

. . . Dr. Benard P. Dreyer, professor of pediatrics at New York University and a past president of the Academic Pediatric Association, [has] called on pediatricians to take on poverty as a serious underlying threat to children's health. He was prompted, he told me . . . by the widening disparities between rich and poor, and the gathering weight of evidence about the importance of early childhood, and the ways that deprivation and stress in the early years of life can reduce the chances of educational and life success.

"After the first three, four, five years of life, if you have neglected that child's brain development, you can't go back," he said. In the middle of the 20th century, our society made a decision to take care of the elderly, once the poorest demographic group in the United States. Now, with Medicare and Social Security, only 9 percent of older people live in poverty. Children are now our poorest group, with almost 25 percent of children under 5 living below the federal poverty level.

When Tony Blair became prime minister of Britain, amid growing socioeconomic disparities, he made it a national goal to cut child poverty in half in 10 years. It took a coalition of political support and a combination of measures that increased income, especially in families with young children (minimum wage, paid maternity and paternity leaves, tax credits), and better services—especially universal preschool programs. By 2010, reducing child poverty had become a goal across the British political spectrum, and child poverty had fallen to 10.6 percent of children below the absolute poverty line (similar to the measure used in the United States), down from 26.1 percent in 1999.

"Poor families who benefited from the reform were able to spend more money on items for children: books and toys, children's clothing and footwear, fresh fruits and vegetables," said Jane Waldfogel, a professor of social work at Columbia who has studied the British war on childhood poverty. Dr. Dreyer said: "Income matters. You get

continues

Continued

people above the poverty level, and they actually are better parents. It's critical to get people out of poverty, but in addition our focus has to be on also giving families supports for other aspects of their lives—parenting, interventions in primary care, universal preschool. . . ."

Think for a moment of poverty as a disease, thwarting growth and development, robbing children of the healthy, happy futures they might otherwise expect. In the exam room, we try to mitigate the pain and suffering that are its pernicious symptoms. But our patients' well-being depends on more, on public health measures and prevention that lift the darkness so all children can grow toward the light.

Surviving the Great Recession: Growing Need and the Stigmatized Safety Net

JENNIFER SHERMAN

What might encourage the recently unemployed, even those experiencing severe economic deprivation, to reject the programs designed to assist them? Sherman discusses the effects of the recession on low-income and poor individuals and families including the loss of identity caused by unemployment and decreased self-esteem. Even with their needs going unmet, shame and stigma push potential aid recipients away because they are unwilling to trade their identities as "workers" for that of "stigmatized dependents."

In Riverway,[1] Washington, the impacts of the economic downturn of 2007–2009 were not as obvious as in some parts of the nation. The region's sprawling nature diluted the visual evidence of widespread job loss and economic suffering. Nonetheless, the recession took its toll there, as revealed by empty storefronts and houses scattered throughout the area. It also heavily impacted the local labor market, particularly the low-wage service and construction jobs that were among its mainstays. The recession's human victims were dispersed throughout the region as well, sometimes seen panhandling at intersections or by the entrances to big-box stores, or congregating in larger numbers than ever at the few available shelters, food banks, and social service offices. Many struggled in even less visible settings, enduring unnoticed in crowded apartments and trailers, hoping to find

another job while trying to survive one more day without one, or trying to subsist on lowered wages and reduced work hours. Commonly the unemployed held themselves personally responsible for their labor market failures, and desperately wanted to avoid being among the lazy, dependent, or "entitled" poor.

Despite massive job loss and slow recovery throughout the nation during this time period, stigma and judgment of those in need did not abate. While the social stigma attached to programs like welfare is not new (Gans 1996; Hays 2003; Rogers-Dillon 1995; Seccombe 2010; Sherman 2006, 2009b), the recession has pushed increasing numbers of Americans into precarious situations, in which public and private forms of aid become necessary for survival (Grusky, Western, and Wimer 2011a). Yet for many American workers, including large numbers of

Jennifer Sherman, "Surviving the Great Recession: Growing Need and the Stigmatized Safety Net," *Social Problems*, 2013, Vol. 60 (4): 409–432, by permission of Oxford University Press on behalf of The Society for the Study of Social Problems.

those in the lowest paid positions, the ability to survive without means-tested aid has been an important source of pride and self-worth. Particularly for those at the bottom of the income ladder, the worker status provides a sense of distinction between themselves and the unemployed poor who are believed to lack moral values and work ethics. For recently downwardly mobile individuals and families, the decision to make use of "entitlements" and other sources of aid is often not an easy one, and its repercussions have impacts on their mental health and self-esteem, as well as on their abilities to survive the downturn. . . . This [reading] explores the impact of the economic downturn on low-income families, paying particular attention to the ways in which the stigma and shame associated with dependency in the American context contribute to the material and emotional suffering of vulnerable individuals and families as they weather the recession and its long, slow recovery.

Background: Economic Stress, Job Loss, and Social Stigma

The Great Recession: Increasing Insecurity for the Most Vulnerable

The recession of 2007–2009 has been longer and more severe than all recent economic downturns since the Great Depression (Grusky et al. 2011b; Hartmann and English 2010). Although it is now officially over, recovery has been almost imperceptible in many places, and its effects linger, including "high unemployment, a host of associated labor-market problems, and the ongoing threat of a double-dip recession" (Grusky et al. 2011a:3). By 2010 the national poverty rate was still rising and reached a 17-year high, at over 15 percent (DeNavas-Walt, Proctor, and Smith 2011). Food insecurity also reached record highs, with nearly 15 percent of households experiencing it in 2011 (Coleman-Jensen et al. 2012). Much of the distress associated with the recession has been caused by job loss and the

slow recovery in the labor market. While the unemployment rate doggedly remained over 8 percent even in 2012 (Bureau of Labor Statistics 2012b), of additional concern was the length of unemployment spells. In previous recessions unemployed workers experienced an average of 20 weeks of unemployment, but during the Great Recession the average spell was 35 weeks (Farber 2011). Among those who did find employment after a job loss, more than half were employed only part time, and thus experienced significant underemployment (Farber 2011). . . . The recession has also been unusual in its gendered nature, and has been called the "mancession" because men were highly concentrated in several of the hardest-hit industries, including construction, manufacturing, and finance (Hout, Levanon, and Cumberworth 2011). However, there were also substantial losses in feminized industries including retail, hospitality, and other service sectors, causing women's unemployment to rise as well, particularly for those at the bottom of the income ladder (Hartmann and English 2010).

The recession occurred during a larger time period characterized by widespread economic insecurity throughout the United States, which preceded the recession and accelerated during it. . . . As economic insecurity and repeated and persistent shocks have become the rule for many Americans, they have faced heightened anxiety and unmet needs. Although these trends have been felt at all income levels, for those at the lowest income quartile concerns were greater and levels of unmet need higher. Low-income individuals faced the greatest vulnerability in the labor market, and were the least likely to have resources to help them buffer shocks (Hacker, Rehm, and Schlesinger et al. 2010).

The impacts of the recession have been most severe for the most vulnerable workers, including minorities and immigrants (DeNavas-Walt et al. 2011; Hout et al. 2011), and those with less education (Farber 2011; Hout et al. 2011). For these groups, unemployment began significantly higher than for other groups, and continued to rise for longer (Hout et al. 2011). The industries in which these workers were concentrated, including service sector work, construction, and manufacturing, were among those most affected by the recession (Hout et al. 2011). Job losses in key sectors combined with historic labor market discrimination make minority workers among the first to be let go and the last to be rehired. However, the pattern was similar for less-educated workers in general, whose job loss rate was substantially higher than for more educated workers, and whose post-displacement reemployment rates were significantly lower (Farber 2011).

Two other vulnerable populations, the disabled (Bureau of Labor Statistics 2012a; Congressional Budget Office 2012; Fogg, Harrington, and McMahon 2010; Kaye 2010) and ex-convicts (Cox 2010; Nally, Lockwood, and Ho 2011), were also among the hardest hit by the recession. These groups tend to be placed at the very bottom of the job queue (Kaye 2010; Pager 2003; Western 2001), and experienced the impacts of the recession earlier than even minority workers (Kaye 2010:29). . . . For disabled workers, prior work experience was less of a protective factor, and many simply opted to leave the workforce rather than continuing to seek employment (Fogg et al. 2010; Kaye 2010). The experience was similar for job seekers with criminal records, who are considered to be less desirable workers (Pager 2003) and who also tend to be concentrated in those industries that were most negatively impacted by the recession. Incarceration is increasingly becoming a modal experience for young, less educated, minority men (Western 2001), and represents one more way in which the impacts of the recession have been both racialized and gendered. . . .

Interestingly, although the impacts of the recession were widespread, its impacts on public opinion have been small and inconsistent (Kenworthy and Owens 2011). While the recession was associated with a small rise in the number of Americans favoring government intervention into the economic arena, survey data suggest that "there is no indication of any increase in support for policies that enhance opportunity, support for the poor, or support for redistribution" (Kenworthy and Owens 2011:217). Media sources and politicians similarly have not backed away from blaming the poor and unemployed for their own misfortune and dependency (Johnson 2011, 2012; Shear 2012), despite the abundant evidence that structural conditions, not individual attributes, are responsible for the rise of job loss and poverty during this time period. This lack of movement in public opinion suggests that while more Americans than any time since the Great Depression may be experiencing unemployment and downward mobility, they do so without an increase in social sympathy or political support for their plight.

Negative Impacts of Downward Mobility

Job loss, underemployment, and downward mobility create numerous difficulties for families, the most obvious being a sudden loss of income and the strain this creates for maintaining existing lifestyles. Research suggests that job loss and reductions in hours and/or wages have substantial negative impacts on families, which stem from economic precariousness as well as numerous other related factors that increase conflict and undermine family stability (Kalil and Wightman 2010; McLanahan and Percheski 2008). Sudden loss of income exacerbates interpersonal conflicts, as well as creating multiple new stresses, "including increased food insecurity, residential instability due to the inability to afford one's mortgage or rent, loss of assets, and increasing debt" (Pedulla and Newman 2011:240). These material hardships, along with the insecurity and anxiety they cause, combine to undermine the health and stability of families.

The financial impact of job loss is generally the most significant and damaging for those living close to the edge already, particularly if they lack significant savings to help aid in survival until new work is found (Hacker et al. 2010; Oliver and Shapiro 2006). Although a sudden loss of income is difficult for most families, for those without savings a short time period without income can quickly create a devastating spiral downwards (Pedulla and Newman 2011). Thus in periods like the Great Recession, those families with the lowest paid jobs prior to the downturn are likely also facing the direst situations when they experience a layoff or cutback in pay, hours, or benefits. They also are the least likely to have social networks that include close friends or relatives with significant wealth and resources to contribute (Conley 1999; Lareau 2003). Unfortunately, they are also amongst those least likely to have job security (Collins and Mayer 2010), and thus are often particularly vulnerable during times of economic constriction. . . .

The negative impacts of job loss and underemployment go beyond simply the stresses caused by material and financial hardships, however. Economic difficulties are frequently compounded by emotional struggles caused by loss of prestige, power, and identity as a worker and/or provider. For many adults, work is more than simply a means to survival; it is frequently a core identity that is inextricably entwined with gender and moral identities (Cottle 2001; Dudley 1997; Elder, Robertson, and Ardelt 1994; Halle 1987; Lamont 2000; Newman 1988; Rubin 1977; Sherman 2006, 2009b). For those at the lowest wage levels it can be a powerful symbolic boundary . . . that separates them from the nonworking poor, who are often believed to lack moral values or mainstream work ethics (Hays 2003; Sherman 2006, 2009b; Woodward 2008). The loss of work as a moral identity and status marker can cause considerable emotional distress for many former workers (Newman 1988). These personal aspects of downward mobility have been shown to impact individuals and families in multiple ways that compound economic stress, including contributing to and exacerbating depression, substance abuse,

domestic violence, and relational instability (Cottle 2001; Dooley and Prause 2009; Howe, Levy, and Caplan 2004; Larson, Wilson, and Beley 1994; Liem and Liem 1990; McLoyd 1990).

Much attention has been paid to the ways in which men in particular are impacted by unemployment, underemployment, and even being out-earned by a female partner. American conceptions of manhood have for most of the nation's history "pivoted around the status of breadwinner" (Kimmel and Ferber 2006:132). Because of the enduring links between masculine identity and work and providing, job loss can be devastating for men, creating "crises in traditional patterns of male authority" (Segal 1990:97). . . . The anxiety and frustration caused by loss of income, status, and male privilege have been linked to both violence and substance abuse, as men externalize resentment and struggles over self-esteem (Connell 1995; Cottle 2001; Faludi 2000; Segal 1990). Even when status losses do not result in such destructive reactions, they can contribute to behaviors that undermine the health of families and relationships, including aggressive and controlling behaviors towards women (Nelson and Smith 1998; Sherman 2009a, 2009b), and refusals to share household chores and responsibilities (Brines 1994; Hochschild and Machung 1989). . . .

Identity, Stigma, and Boundary Work

In the American cultural context, with its focus on self-sufficiency and independence (Bellah et al. 1996), work is often more than simply a means to survival. It is a moral imperative for Americans of all income levels, whose fulfillment is necessary to most understandings of success (Hays 2003; Lamont 2000; Sherman 2009b), as well as to basic claims of full citizenship (Collins and Mayer 2010). Those who do not work are subject to scorn and judgment from the larger society (Lamont 2000; Sherman 2009b), and frequently viewed as immoral and undeserving of society's resources (Gans 1996; Hays 2003; Seccombe 2010). Work status is a focus of much boundary work for the poor, allowing individuals to construct collective identities in opposition to others deemed to be flawed (Small, Harding, and Lamont 2010). Research has found that amongst chronically poor and marginalized populations, there is a tendency for individuals to judge others in their same situation as immoral, often forming and making use of different types of symbolic boundaries (Bourdieu 1984; Lamont and Fournier 1992) to distance themselves from others who may be similarly disadvantaged (Bourgois 1995; Duneier 1999; Gowan 2010; Hays 2003; Kissane 2012; Purser 2009; Sherman 2009b). . . .

Researchers have documented the ways in which symbolic boundaries based in moral and gender discourses can help marginalized populations to justify their situations in order to create and maintain self-respect. Mitchell Duneier's (1999) study of homeless street vendors in New York City argued that the men who engage in these informal work activities portray them as morally superior to panhandling or illicit activities, allowing them to maintain self-respect and a sense of superiority. . . . Sharon Hays's (2003) study of welfare recipients described their use of moral boundaries to separate themselves as deserving recipients from "all those 'other' bad welfare mothers who fail to live up to social standards" (p. 219).

In addition to providing justifications for behaviors, symbolic boundaries can also provide the impetus for specific choices that individuals and families make, including income generation and survival strategies (Sayer 2011). Researchers in diverse settings have illustrated the various ways in which cultural ideals, moral norms, and gender ideologies influence the decisions that the poor make with regard to work and income generating activities in order to maintain positive self-images and avoid association with stigmatized groups. Kathryn Edin and Laura Lein's (1997) study of poor single mothers found a preference for work over welfare (and for legal over illegal income generation

activities), despite the fact that welfare-reliant women were closer to meeting their basic needs than were low-wage workers. The mothers cited self-respect and gendered notions of good motherhood as heavily influencing their economically irrational decisions (Edin and Lein 1997:144–46). Katherine Newman (1999) similarly found that fast food employees in Harlem chose this low-wage work over welfare because of its positive connections to mainstream work ethics and "family values. . . ."

Throughout the recession the popular press and political pundits continued to portray the unemployed as lazy and dependent on government aid (see, for example, Foster 2011; Johnson 2011, 2012; Shear 2012), without sufficient comprehension of the real strategies used by the newly unemployed to get by, or the rationales behind their choices. Nor is there an understanding of the ways in which this type of large-scale judgment is internalized by the affected populations, and the outcomes of this internalization. This [reading] addresses this gap in understanding by looking in depth at the experiences of individuals and families impacted by the Great Recession. I use in-depth interviews and ethnographic observations to explore the reactions of individuals who have recently experienced job loss, declining income, and/or inability to reenter the workforce after an exit. I illustrate the ways in which the desire to avoid the stigma and judgment associated with entitlements and dependency, as well as to adhere to specific moral and gender ideologies, constrains their survival strategies and adds emotional hardships to the economic suffering they incur.

Methods and Research

The research, conducted by the author, took place from August 2010 to August 2011 in multiple communities in Eastern Washington, the bulk of which are among the three adjoining small cities that make up the Riverway region, although several interviews also occurred in the surrounding county areas and unincorporated towns. Like most of the nation, Washington State experienced a dramatic rise in unemployment beginning in 2008. Although by 2011 the unemployment rate had begun to flatten, it remained above 9 percent, higher than the national average (Morgan et al. 2012). . . .

The research consisted of 55 recorded, open-ended, in-depth interviews and six months of ethnographic fieldwork, all focused on low-income populations. Interviews lasted from one to four hours, with the average interview length being about an hour and a half. . . . The bulk of interviews took place in the participants' residences, including many [Housing and Urban Development] HUD-subsidized apartments . . . low-cost apartments, trailers, and rental homes. . . .

. . . The sample was about 60 percent female and 40 percent male, and the average age was 44 years. About 70 percent of participants were white and 13 percent were Latino, while 9 percent reported a mix of white and Native American heritage, 7 percent were African American, and 2 percent were Asian. . . . About a third of the sample was currently married, including numerous participants who had been divorced once or more prior to the current marriage. About a quarter of respondents were cohabiting without being married to their current partners. . . . Despite this relatively low level of marriage, the majority of participants were parents, although not all had young children and not all parents of young children had either full- or part-time custody.

The modal educational attainment category was a high school degree or equivalent (31 percent), while 22 percent of the sample had not finished high school and 24 percent had taken some college classes but had not completed a degree. Fifteen percent had completed an associate's degree, and 6 percent had completed a bachelor's degree. . . . Forty-five percent of the sample was currently employed in some way, although many of the participants worked in low-wage, part-time, and contingent positions, and most had

experienced a loss of wages and/or working hours since 2008. Respondents were not asked to report their exact income, but were asked numerous questions about making ends meet and their qualification for and receipt of aid and subsidies from federal, state, local, and private sources. Using this information they were categorized into three income groups: middle class, low income, and poor. . . . According to these definitions, 16 percent of the sample was middle class (n = 9) . . . 31 percent was low income (n = 17), and 53 percent (n = 29) was poor. . . .

. . . In addition to the interviews, I also engaged in ethnographic fieldwork in the low-income community, including six months of participant observation as a regular volunteer in a local food bank, as well as extended observations in several low-income neighborhoods and public spaces. The volunteer work allowed me to engage in longer-term relationships with many members of the community and helped me to gain a deeper understanding of their perspectives and day-to-day challenges, thoughts, and struggles. It also provided a deeper understanding of how low-income and poor individuals interacted with and perceived one another, including the ability to observe social cleavages based on race, ethnicity, values, and behaviors. . . .

Results

The Great Recession and Employment Struggles

Despite the current low workforce participation rate of the sample, most of the respondents had long work histories, although as is common with low-wage workers (Collins and Mayer 2010; Edin and Lein 1997; Hays 2003; Wilson 1996), they were often interrupted by injuries and illness, layoffs, jail or prison time, and personal and/or family crises. In the past many participants had been able to reenter the workforce quickly after an interruption, but they found that the current conditions created challenges for them in finding new work. For those who still had jobs, the recession often meant that they had seen declines in their wages, hours, security, benefits, and choices of when and where to work. While the unemployed often expressed significant fear about their job prospects, even those who still had jobs were feeling a squeeze and generally experiencing either income, skills, or status underemployment (Pedulla and Newman 2011). For many staying in the workforce now meant making sacrifices in hours, benefits, and wages, while for others even the least desirable jobs were out of reach.

Many of Riverway's working families noticed the impact of the deepening recession, which made it harder to make ends meet even with full-time work. Katy Torres, a 25 year old part-time retail salesclerk and mother of one, relied heavily on her husband's construction job to support them, and viewed her own income as secondary. Recently, his typical seasonal layoff had turned into a permanent one, and he was currently working several hours away in order to support their middle-class lifestyle, coming home only on weekends. She explained:

> There's basically nothing we can really do about it right now. He wants to find something closer to home, but with everything going on right now, there's not really much options close, so. . . .

So it's hard to find other jobs here right now?

Uh-huh. Yeah. He has been looking. But they won't pay what he makes. Like, I think, one job was offering him $13 [an hour]. I think he'll make $19 to $30 where he's at.

Allison Foster, a cohabiting mother of three who worked at a big-box store, had also managed to keep a job through the recession. She had, however, been transferred by the company to several different stores, had her hours cut back, and been forced to take night shifts. She was grateful to have finally been switched back to a day shift, and described the struggles of trying to care for children while working nights:

> I was only getting 35 hours a week when I transferred from one [store] to the other. . . . For the first nine months, I worked graveyard. So my schedule consisted of: at night I went to work—I left the house at nine o'clock, after I put my kids in bed. Went to work. Came home at seven. Got home, got my kids up, got 'em fed, got 'em to day care. Came home. I went to sleep until five and I got up, went and got 'em, come home and just started my routine over again. It was just hard.

Despite these challenges, Katy and Allison were among the lucky ones in Riverway, who still had jobs and incomes that allowed them to survive, albeit on tighter budgets and with more constraints than before the recession began. For those who had lost their jobs or taken time out of the workforce, work was increasingly difficult to come by. Many participants expressed great amounts of frustration with their situations, and had lost faith in their abilities to find jobs in Riverway. For those with physical disabilities or criminal records, or who were somewhat older, jobs were especially difficult to find, regardless of their work histories, skills, and experience.

For those with a criminal record, the recession meant they were generally passed over even when their work records were exemplary,[2] and several participants described getting close to a job offer until the background check revealed their prior convictions. Doug Stark, a 42-year-old divorced, cohabiting father of two, had worked in blue-collar jobs for most of his life, and had been supporting his girlfriend Savannah and her children for several years. He was now out of work and struggling to find a new job, and worried that his unemployment benefits would soon run out. . . .

Despite his long work history and ability to find and keep jobs in the past, Doug and Savannah felt that his chances for finding work were now seriously diminished by his past mistakes, which included a conviction for marijuana possession in his early twenties.

> SAVANNAH: They don't want to give a chance. If you have a criminal record, there's somebody else that doesn't.
>
> DOUG: Yeah, especially with tons of people looking for work right now. Because when there was less, you know, qualified people looking for work, then they're like, well, I'm going to take a chance. He's got the qualifications.

Jill Carter, a 61-year-old divorced mother of three grown children, felt that her age presented a barrier to finding a job. Since being laid off from a clerical position in a large company she had struggled with depression and isolation, and relocated to Riverway to be near family for support. Despite a long employment history, she was unable to find work there. She explained:

> Now I'm on Social Security. I can only find $960-a-month jobs, part time, and a lot of them I'm overqualified. It's like, overqualified to file?! . . . The lady came out and said, "Well I really, you've got an impressive resume, but you're kind of overqualified." I said, "Overqualified or old?!"

While age, disability, and criminal records all hampered participants' chances of finding work, things were not always that much easier for the young and healthy with clean records. Nick Woods, a 28-year-old married stepfather of one, had been laid off from his security guard position when the company lost its contract with a local employer. In the following six months of job searching he had yet to find a new job, which surprised him:

> It used to be when I could, you know, when I get my foot in the door at an interview,

I'm 90 percent of the time used to—I've always been asked for the job. And now, it's like I can't even get my foot in the door. You know? I applied—I even went to—I applied to McDonald's last week and had two interviews, and they were like, "Oh, we'll give you a call back"—nothin'.

The recession's effects were evident for those at the bottom of Riverway's labor market. Many of the recently unemployed were less educated, less skilled workers who nonetheless had ample work experience. Those who were able to keep jobs were generally experiencing new constraints and struggles to make ends meet, while many others found themselves unable to find even low-paid or part-time work. For those whose age, health, or personal histories gave employers any reason to hesitate, chances of finding work were even smaller. Thus the recession dragged many previously low-income workers below the poverty line. Yet the commonality of their experience did not appear to diminish the sting of being out of work or underemployed, and finding oneself in need of aid from the state, charities, friends, and family. While some, particularly the elderly and disabled, turned to government-funded aid programs for income support, many others resisted these programs and their stigma, with deleterious impacts for them and their families. . . .

"I'd Like to Take Care of My Own": Growing Need and the Stigma of Aid

While many participants had grown up poor or low-income themselves, most had experienced some amount of upward mobility over their lifetimes, often rising into the ranks of the working class for some period of time before experiencing a downward trajectory. Almost all of the respondents had considerable work histories, and there were no respondents who had spent the bulk of their working age years receiving welfare, although several had turned to it for short spells in the past or present. For many, their work history was an important source of pride and identity, particularly since by and large they had few other positive sources of identity. As is common amongst low-income populations, many respondents had lived hard lives (Edin and Kefalas 2005; Rubin 1977; Western 2001; Wilson 1996) that included abuse (83 percent), addiction to drugs or alcohol (62 percent), and jail or prison time (40 percent). For parents, their relationships with children were often a source of pride and love, but for many they were also a cause of disappointment and regret, and they often spoke remorsefully of their past mistakes and the multiple ways in which they felt they had failed their children. Thus for many their ability to work and provide for themselves and their families was an important point of pride in a life that offered few other sources. Unfortunately, for those unwilling to let go of it, the recession turned this source of pride into a barrier to survival.

Many participants had limited experience with aid programs in the area prior to their exits from the labor market. While some chose to take advantage of available programs to assist them through difficult times, it was frequently a struggle to bring themselves to utilize certain types of aid. The receipt of welfare was often the most difficult for participants to accept, as they generally saw this as the most shameful and stigmatized type of assistance. Many respondents viewed the process of asking for any kind of help as humiliating, which further decreased their likelihood of utilizing all possible sources of assistance. While previous research has found that poor populations rely heavily on social and kin networks for support (Edin and Lein 1997; Nelson 2005; Sherman 2006, 2009b; Stack 1974), many participants in this research expressed a great deal of reluctance to ask for help from their family or friends, and several cut back on social interactions rather than admit their need and face potential shame or disapproval. Many others lacked strong social networks in the area, and thus had few people to whom they could turn for help. . . .

The Shame and Stigma of Aid

In the United States, most government forms of need-based aid are seen in a negative light, as the antithesis of work ethics and American values. This is particularly the case for feminized means-tested income supports such as TANF [Temporary Aid to Needy Families, commonly referred to as welfare] (Collins and Mayer 2010; Hays 2003; Piven and Cloward 1971; Rogers-Dillon 1995; Seccombe 2010; Sherman 2006, 2009b; Steensland 2006). Accepting income support programs was often very difficult for respondents, as it meant trading their identities as workers for that of stigmatized dependents. Seeking cash aid was often a last choice for the most desperate and isolated individuals, who frequently did so with substantial humiliation and shame that added to their struggles. . . .

Estela Lopez, a 60-year-old divorced mother and grandmother, had worked for most of her life in farm fields, warehouses, and factories, describing herself as "a workaholic." After a serious accident caused her to take time out of the workforce, she found herself incapable of doing these sorts of manual labor, but unable to find less physically demanding work. She described the transition from work as difficult, and she resisted leaving the labor force:

> I missed my jobs. I wanted to be out there. That's the way I grew up. That's the way I earned my money. I wanted to put in my day's work. I didn't want to have welfare support me or going on social security at a young age.

After months of unsuccessful searching, Estela eventually gave up the struggle to continue working. Unwilling to depend on her children, who were struggling financially themselves, she now relied on Social Security, subsidized housing, and the local food banks. She felt both shame and identity loss around the transition, commenting, "The day that I couldn't work anymore, I felt like that was the end of everything." For Estela, the symbolic boundary between work and aid was a clear one, and crossing over caused her a great deal of emotional distress. . . .

For 52-year-old cohabiter Christine Gorman, accepting aid was a lesson in the value of humility. She had done care work until her marriage to a man who supported her; however, the short marriage was troubled by alcoholism and violence, eventually ending after a particularly violent fight. On her own without resources, Christine was homeless and living in her van when she learned that she had cancer, for which she was still undergoing treatment. Although she accepted Medicaid at this point, she chose not to seek other forms of aid, and described sleeping in her van in the hospital parking lot after undergoing treatments. She eventually met her current boyfriend, but he was laid off soon afterwards, and the couple spent several months homeless and living in a tent while he searched for work. With winter coming and her health precarious, she finally had no choice but to trade stigma for survival; she sought assistance through several local charities, including both churches and nonprofit organizations, which helped them to find an apartment and pay for basic necessities. Christine described her current situation with both gratitude and frustration:

> I am goin' to the food bank. I have never experienced such humility in my life, you know? Because I have always had everything. I have always worked hard for everything. And now I am sick. I can't. And that is very frustrating.

Like for Estela and . . . for Christine, receiving aid was the antithesis of hard work, and she struggled to live with the shame she felt. Although things were beginning to look up for her, the experience had been difficult. Her reluctance to seek help had prolonged her material deprivation, but accepting aid had caused significant emotional distress:

> I am learnin' about how to ask for help. Because I used to help people. You know? And now to ask? It was very degrading for me. It really was, you know? And then it kept—it seemed like more and more [embarrassing] to get help, but then I slowly get poorer an' poorer, then getting sick. I can't even go out and get a job.

For participants like these, who were isolated, alone, and facing disabilities and other barriers to finding work, accepting aid was generally their only option for survival. Yet despite their intense need, many did so very reluctantly, and often at great personal cost in terms of their own self-esteem. While seeking aid allowed them to survive at a subsistence level, it also cost them dearly in terms of emotional health, frequently resulting in depression and tendencies to further curtail their social interactions. Contrary to the popular stereotypes of which they were all too aware (Gans 1996; Hays 2003; Seccombe 2010), these former workers took no pride in [using] the system, and were deeply impacted by society's judgment of those who seek aid.

. . . My fieldwork at the food bank provided a window into the ways in which low-income individuals managed the real and perceived stigma of dependency, often through boundary work that allowed them to place themselves above others in similar situations. The entire staff of the food bank was unpaid, and most of the permanent workers were reliant on both it and government forms of aid for survival, mainly Social Security, SSI [Supplemental Security Income], and GAU [General Assistance Unemployable]. Although most of these volunteers were in the same boat as their clients, social interactions between the two groups revealed an intricate web of boundary work that helped each to protect themselves from perceived judgment by the other. Among favored topics of conversation for the workers were the need to drug test welfare recipients; complaints about people stealing more than their allotments of food; the commonly voiced belief that many clients weren't truly needy; and racial stereotypes that portrayed specific groups, including Hispanics, Arabs, and Eastern European immigrants, as dishonest and undeserving. Some workers told stories of friends, family members, and regular clients who were cheating the welfare system because they had some sort of side income, shaking their heads and clucking their tongues at the dishonest, dependent poor. Although many workers discussed their own poverty in the context of the recession and struggles to find work, this same perspective was absent from their assessment of their clients' needs.

The discourse of the dishonest poor was a common way to separate oneself from others at the food bank, and thus manage the stigma associated with need. . . . Staff members constantly reminded me to watch and police people whom they suspected of stealing (I rarely saw this actually occur), and talked endlessly about people "caught in the act" on the rare occasions when it did happen. In one case, a large fuss was made over a Hispanic client who had seen other clients receive whole turkeys, and tried to help herself to one. While the staff talked at length about her thwarted attempt at thievery, my discussion with her suggested that the woman, whose English comprehension was poor, had failed to understand that the whole turkeys were only for larger families and that she had already been given her allotment of packaged meat for her family size. Yet for the staff, this woman was important evidence of those reviled "others"— separated from themselves by both race and moral character—who were constantly engaged in attempts to game the system. This discourse was not limited to the staff themselves; clients also sometimes complained about other people who weren't truly needy or who took more than their share.

Yet at the same time, the clients often resisted the judgment of staff and fellow recipients, complaining about the workers in particular being mean, stingy, condescending, and incompetent. While the staff members frequently pointed to nice clothes, expensive accessories, smartphones, or decent cars as signs of a client cheating the system, these same clients often offered unsolicited explanations to less judgmental distribution workers like myself, informing me about how recently they'd been laid off, or how seriously they were looking for work. Frequently these clients talked about how much harder finding work had become since the recession. These justifications for their positions as aid recipients suggested that they too were attempting to manage their images and make sure they were seen as workers rather than dependents. . . . Many who had been patronizing the food bank for longer simply avoided eye contact or conversation with even the friendliest workers. For those who had the option, sending another family member inside allowed them to avoid facing the scorn of the staff and other clients altogether. Frequently men would wait outside for their female partners, helping them to carry the bounty home, but refusing to enter the stigmatized space of the food bank.

Cutting Back and Avoiding Stigma

For individuals like the ones described above, the disgrace of aid was a difficult cross to bear. For many other participants, particularly men with families to support, some amount of deprivation was preferable to the humiliation they associated with assistance. Unwilling to completely let go of their moral and gender identities as good parents, partners, workers, and providers, they discussed making tough choices between shame and survival, often pursuing a middle strategy that avoided the most stigmatized programs but left their families struggling to meet basic needs. They described cutting back or living on the edge while refusing to ask friends, family, the state, or private organizations for available assistance. Within this sample, 85 percent of which was low-income or poor, the most commonly utilized forms of aid included SNAP [Supplemental Nutrition Assistance Program, formerly known as food stamps] (48 percent), food banks (42 percent) . . . and subsidized health care (35 percent). Although many participants discussed being eligible for TANF (more than half of the sample), less than 15 percent received it. . . . For many, the income that welfare might bring was simply not worth the stigma attached to it.

Doug Stark and Savannah Lewis, introduced earlier, exemplified this set of dilemmas and the choice to limit aid receipt. The family of five lived in a rented trailer and survived off of Doug's unemployment benefits, which were insufficient to meet their needs, and soon to expire. They had been struggling for some time, and eventually accepted some help, but had resisted pursuing more stigmatized forms of aid. Doug explained:

> I don't personally feel comfortable getting money from the state.

> *Yeah?*

> No. I mean, it just seems like—I don't know, it doesn't make me feel right. . . . [So] we just do whatever we can to avoid doing that.

For Doug and Savannah, the disgrace of TANF was too much to bear, even though they qualified for and needed it:

> SAVANNAH: We—technically, we could be going and getting welfare. You know, because we're so low income that we'd qualify. But we haven't. I mean, we get food stamps. We've had to. And we had to get medical for the kids, you know, through the state or whatever.
> DOUG: But we don't get any money.

These in-kind forms of aid helped the family survive, but they were still struggling to find enough cash to pay their bills. Although they did have some family in the area, reliance on social networks for financial help was also out of the question for Doug and Savannah:

> DOUG: I don't want to ask my family—I won't ask my family for money because—
> SAVANNAH: Me either.
> DOUG: I just don't like to. It's just, we'd just rather deal with it ourselves, however that may be. . . . I've gotten money from them before, and I even paid them back fast, and I still hear it. And I just don't want to hear it.

. . . Concerns about inability to reciprocate, as well as dread of judgment by others often act to prevent families in need from drawing on potential social network support (Nelson 2000; Smith 2010). For Doug and Savannah, asking for money from anyone, whether the state or family members, was a humiliating act that they wanted badly to avoid. Relying on only in-kind aid from institutional sources allowed them to manage and avoid this perceived shame and stigma to some degree, and to draw a symbolic boundary between themselves and the more dependent poor.

. . . Masculine pride made it difficult for many men in the sample to ask for or accept help, whether from family, public, or private sources. Nick Woods, the out-of-work security guard introduced earlier, discussed feeling less successful as a father and husband because of his acceptance of food stamps:

> I don't like it because I like working for my money. I don't like sittin' at home doin' nothing. So I have—I have to work. Like we get food, you know, we get that food assistance, whatever it's called and, um, and—I don't like it. Yeah, it gives us money for food, but I was like, no. I don't like it.

> *How come?*

> 'Cause I don't—it just makes me feel like I am not doing my job as a parent, nor as a husband, to supply for my family, so. It's like somebody else is doing it for me.

Because of this reluctance, Nick accepted food stamps for now, but insisted that he would find another job before he would be forced to apply for TANF. While he felt shame around this choice, he still believed himself to be better than those who accepted the most stigmatized form of aid. . . .

Many men made it clear that their refusal to accept aid was fueled in part by masculine pride and the belief that they should be able to provide for their families on their own, and that a man accepting help was worse than a woman doing so. Men were not the only ones who refused available services because of pride, however. Although single women were more likely to pursue public assistance than were married or cohabiting men, several also discussed refusing aid because of the stigma attached to it. Tracy Sheppard, a 31-year-old single mother of two, worked part time at a retail job. In the past she had received TANF for a period when her children were young. Now that she had managed to get back into the workforce, however, she eschewed the judgment and loss of self-respect that came with accepting public aid programs, even though she was struggling to make ends meet and care for her children on her own. When asked if she would ever consider going back on TANF in the future, she exclaimed, "God, no!" and explained,

> There's no way. I hate dealing with the [Department of Social and Health Services] DSHS. . . . I could get food stamps right now, I just can't stand it. If I never had to, I never would have. Turning in stuff and dealing with the people there—they've gotten nicer and it's easier to get to a representative on the phone. But I used to feel like they just treat you like crap. I guess I felt more, that's just how I felt about myself. But now that I pay taxes, I need food stamps. It just really helps.

Why does it matter, you think?

Because it's always been a self-esteem issue. I have a huge low self-esteem issue.

Although most of the low-income and poor participants relied on some form of help to survive, most refused at least some available options. . . . For these families, the American cultural and moral distinctions between work and dependency were extremely important, and colored the choices they made with regard to coping strategies to help them survive the economic downturn. Throughout their stories was the recurring theme of a desire to be as self-sufficient as possible, particularly when they had families to support. Despite their consistent difficulties in finding and keeping living-wage jobs in Riverway, the majority of participants wanted to think of themselves as workers and providers, an identity that was in direct conflict with reliance on the stigmatized social safety net. For some, need and lack of other options forced them into seeking aid, although in the process they often experienced shame, humiliation, and even self-hatred that exacerbated other problems. Frequently these were the most socially isolated individuals, who lacked social networks to whom they could turn. They also tended to be those without families or dependents to support, and thus few close connections to witness their slide from independence into the world of dependency and entitlements. . . .

Conclusion

In Riverway, as in most of the United States, the Great Recession has resulted in downward mobility for many people, and has been particularly hard for the less skilled and less educated workers who already held precarious positions within the dwindling working class. Regardless of prior experience, many workers experienced losses of jobs, wages, hours, and benefits, which for many created serious challenges to their basic survival. During this same period, use of government aid programs such as unemployment insurance and food stamps rose significantly . . . as did attacks by politicians and the popular press on these same programs and their recipients. [In 2012], Presidential hopefuls criticized Obama for being "the food stamp president" (Mosley 2012), while dismissing concerns about growing inequality and the plight of the poor (Johnson 2011, 2012), and disparagingly discussing the unemployed as lazy dependents who needed to go find jobs (Foster 2011; Shear 2012).

As this research suggests, such a simple solution was not available to many former workers who found themselves unemployed during this period. Particularly for those without advanced education or skills, or with disabilities or criminal records, the labor market constricted and wages fell to levels that made it very difficult to support themselves and their families. Yet the societal message that aid is shameful did not fall on deaf ears, even amongst this population. Many were very proud of their identities as workers, often a hard-won status in a life full of struggles, which allowed them some sense of self-respect and success. For these individuals, letting go of this identity in order to receive assistance from others was very difficult. For those who had no other options, the eventual acceptance of aid was often accompanied by self-hatred, shame, and depression. For those who could survive without turning to the most stigmatized forms of aid, it often meant going without basic necessities in order to salvage their pride and save face in front of family and friends. . . .

Of particular concern was the tendency for families with dependents to prefer cutting back and going without to acceptance of stigmatized forms of aid, particularly TANF. . . . Rather than providing the incentive to seek cash aid, children often seemed to act as a deterrent for parents, who felt that accepting it undermined their ability to be good parents and partners. In these cases cultural understandings of fathers—and increasingly mothers as well—as providers and breadwinners contributed to reluctance to accept aid that would have helped ensure that children were properly clothed and fed. Al-

though most parents prioritized their children's needs ahead of their own, their pride and desire to separate themselves from the undeserving poor nonetheless contributed to unnecessary material hardships for these families.

On the other hand, for those individuals without partners and children to support, there were fewer emotional barriers to acceptance of aid, and less fear of having to face loved ones in a newly diminished capacity. In these cases individuals were more likely to reluctantly pursue cash aid and other forms of assistance, but the stigma they encountered and the lowered self-esteem they often endured as a result was equally damaging. Those who accepted aid discussed depression, humiliation, and self-hatred as the common outcomes of their choices. Many felt so embarrassed by their status declines that they chose to avoid social contacts, including close family and friends, sinking deeper into isolation and emotional distress. . . . In choosing to isolate themselves from the better off in their own social networks, they unintentionally reinforced the symbolic boundaries and societal distinctions between working and nonworking poor, further entrenching their own stigma and moral pollution.

For the individuals and families described here, the cultural context of the United States impacts the unemployed and underemployed in ways that go beyond just those produced by job and income loss alone. The vilification of aid receipt and cultural understandings that create symbolic boundaries between work and dependency result in preferences for avoiding aid at all costs, and intense shame and stigma for those who fail to do so. In a setting like Riverway, where few options exist for surviving poverty through morally acceptable means, the sudden loss of income presents individuals with a harsh choice between deprivation and humiliation. For those whose status as workers and providers has been an important element of their identity and self-worth, deprivation can seem preferable to taking on the stigmatized identity of a dependent. As this research has illustrated, the results of the American cultural context and its focus on independence and self-sufficiency (Bellah et al. 1996; Hays 2003; Lamont 2000; Sherman 2009b), while creating strong incentives to work, can also contribute to increased material and emotional hardships for those who find themselves unable to find or keep jobs, whether due to structural or individual causes. . . .

These findings imply that a shift is needed both in the terms of debate and dialogue regarding unemployment and poverty, and in designing programs that address these issues. It is necessary to provide for the unemployed and underemployed in ways that preserve dignity and social standing, as well as material well-being. . . . Given the moral pollution that is attached to the welfare-poor in the U.S. context, social programs such as unemployment insurance and the Earned Income Tax Credit, which target workers and former workers, may be better able to address the needs of the recently unemployed and underemployed without damaging their dignity or social standing. Enhancing and extending the benefits of these less stigmatized programs might improve the fortunes of this population. However, a more inclusive program, like a guaranteed income floor coupled with universal health care, child care, and maternity benefits, could potentially replace TANF without its associations with feminized dependency and immorality. Just as the Great Depression made clear the need for a heretofore unprecedented social safety net in the United States, the Great Recession and its aftermath illuminate the necessity of making that safety net more inclusive and more effective at alleviating material and emotional suffering for both the working and the nonworking poor.

NOTES

1. All names, including those of people, places, organizations, and institutions, have been changed in order to preserve the confidentiality of participants.
2. The mark of a criminal record has been found to have a substantial effect in reducing one's likelihood of finding a job even in healthy economies. Pager's (2003) audit study found that for white applicants a criminal record reduced the chance of a job call-back by half, and the effect was even larger for black job seekers.

REFERENCES

Bellah, Robert N., Madsen Richard, M. Sullivan William, Swidler Ann, and M. Tipton Steven. 1996. *Habits of the Heart: Individualism and Commitment in American Life*. Berkeley: University of California Press.

Bourdieu, Pierre. 1984. *Distinction: A Social Critique of the Judgment of Taste*. Cambridge, MA: Harvard University Press.

Bourgois, Philippe. 1995. *In Search of Respect: Selling Crack in El Barrio*. Cambridge, UK: Cambridge University Press.

Brines, Julie. 1994. "Economic Dependency, Gender, and the Division of Labor at Home." *American Journal of Sociology* 100(3): 652–88.

Bureau of Labor Statistics. 2012a. "Persons with a Disability: Labor Force Characteristics—2011." Retrieved September 17, 2012 (www.bls.gov/news.release/pdf/disabl.pdf).

Bureau of Labor Statistics. 2012b. "The Employment Situation—August 2012." Retrieved September 17, 2012 (www.bls.gov/news.release/pdf/empsit.pdf).

Coleman-Jensen, Alisha, Mark Nord, Margaret Andrews, and Steven Carlson. 2012. *Household Food Security in the United States in 2011*. USDA Economic Research Service. Retrieved September 10, 2012 (www.ers.usda.gov/media/884525/err141.pdf).

Collins, Jane L. and Victoria Mayer. 2010. *Both Hands Tied: Welfare Reform and the Race to the Bottom in the Low-Wage Labor Market*. Chicago: University of Chicago Press.

Congressional Budget Office. 2012. *Policy Options for the Social Security Disability Insurance Program*. Congressional Budget Office. Retrieved August 23, 2012 (www.cbo.gov/sites/default/files/cbofiles/attachments/43421-DisabilityInsurance_screen.pdf).

Conley, Dalton. 1999. *Being Black, Living in the Red: Race, Wealth, and Social Policy in America.* 1st ed. Berkeley: University of California Press.

Connell, R. W. 1995. *Masculinities.* Berkeley: University of California Press.

Cottle, Thomas J. 2001. *Hardest Times: The Trauma of Long Term Unemployment.* Westport, CT: Praeger.

Cox, Robynn. 2010. "Crime, Incarceration, and Employment in Light of the Great Recession." *The Review of Black Political Economy* 37(3): 283–94.

DeNavas-Walt, Carmen, Bernadette D. Proctor, and Jessica C. Smith. 2011. *Income, Poverty, and Health Insurance Coverage in the United States: 2010.* U.S. Census Bureau. Retrieved February 9, 2012 (www.census.gov/prod/2011pubs/p60-239.pdf).

Dooley, David and JoAnn Prause. 2009. *The Social Costs of Underemployment: Inadequate Employment as Disguised Unemployment.* 1st ed. Cambridge UK: Cambridge University Press.

Dudley, Kathryn Marie. 1997. *The End of the Line: Lost Jobs, New Lives in Postindustrial America.* Chicago: University of Chicago Press.

Duneier, Mitchell. 1999. *Sidewalk.* New York: Farrar, Straus and Giroux.

Edin, Kathryn and Laura Lein. 1997. *Making Ends Meet: How Single Mothers Survive Welfare and Low-Wage Work.* New York: Russell Sage Foundation.

Edin, Kathryn and Maria Kefalas. 2005. *Promises I Can Keep: Why Poor Women Put Motherhood before Marriage.* Berkeley: University of California Press.

Elder, Glen H. Jr., Elizabeth B. Robertson, and Monika Ardelt. 1994. "Families under Economic Pressure." Pp. 79–103 in *Families in Troubled Times: Adapting to Change in Rural America,* edited by Rand D. Conger and Glen H. Elder, Jr. New York: Aldine de Gruyter.

Faludi, Susan. 2000. *Stiffed: The Betrayal of the American Man.* New York: Harper Perennial.

Farber, Henry S. 2011. *Job Loss in the Great Recession: Historical Perspective from the Displaced Workers Survey, 1984–2010.* NBER and IZA. Retrieved August 23, 2012 (ftp://ftp.iza.org/RePEc/Discussionpaper/dp5696.pdf).

Fogg, Neeta P., Paul E. Harrington, and Brian T. McMahon. 2010. "The Impact of the Great Recession upon the Unemployment of Americans with Disabilities." *Journal of Vocational Rehabilitation* 33(3):193–202.

Foster, Stephen D. 2011. "Herman Cain Blames the Unemployed for Being Unemployed." Addicting Info, October 5. Retrieved April 12, 2012 (www.addictinginfo.org/2011/10/05/herman-cain-blames-the-unemployed-for-being-unemployed/).

Gans, Herbert. 1996. *The War against the Poor: The Underclass and Antipoverty Policy.* New York: Basic Books.

Gowan, Teresa. 2010. *Hobos, Hustlers, and Backsliders: Homeless in San Francisco.* Minneapolis: University of Minnesota Press.

Grusky, David B., Bruce Western, and Christopher Wimer. 2011a. "The Consequences of the Great Recession." Pp. 3–20 in *The Great Recession,* edited by David B. Grusky, Bruce Western, and Christopher Wimer. New York: Russell Sage Foundation.

Grusky, David B., Bruce Western, and Christopher Wimer, eds. 2011b. *The Great Recession.* New York: Russell Sage Foundation.

Hacker, Jacob S., Philipp Rehm, and Mark Schlesinger. 2010. *Standing on Shaky Ground: Americans' Experiences with Economic Insecurity.* Rockefeller Foundation. Retrieved April 17, 2013 (www.rockefellerfoundation.org/news/publications/standing-shaky-ground-americans).

Halle, David. 1987. *America's Working Man: Work, Home, and Politics among Blue Collar Property Owners.* Chicago: University of Chicago Press.

Hartmann, Heidi and Ashley English. 2010. *Women and Men's Employment and Unemployment in the Great Recession.* Washington, DC: Institute for Women's Policy Research. Retrieved April 17, 2013 (www.iwpr.org/publications/pubs/women-and-men2019s-employment-and-unemployment-in-the-great-recession).

Hays, Sharon. 2003. *Flat Broke with Children: Women in the Age of Welfare Reform.* Oxford, UK: Oxford University Press.

Hochschild, Arlie and Anne Machung. 1989. *The Second Shift.* New York: Penguin Books.

Hout, Michael, Asaf Levanon, and Erin Cumberworth. 2011. "Job Loss and Unemployment." Pp. 59–81 in *The Great Recession*, edited by David B. Grusky, Bruce Western, and Christopher Wimer. New York: Russell Sage Foundation.

Howe, George W., Mindy Lockshin Levy, and Robert D. Caplan. 2004. "Job Loss and Depressive Symptoms in Couples: Common Stressors, Stress Transmission, or Relationship Disruption?" *Journal of Family Psychology* 18(4):639–50.

Johnson, Luke. 2011. "Rick Santorum: 'I Have No Problem with Income Inequality.'" *Huffington Post*. Retrieved February 15, 2012 (www.huffingtonpost.com/2011/12/20/rick-santorum-iowa-caucus-2012-income-inequality_n_1161061.html).

Johnson, Luke. 2012. "Mitt Romney: 'I'm Not Concerned about the Very Poor.'" *Huffington Post*. Retrieved February 15, 2012 (www.huffingtonpost.com/2012/02/01/mitt-romney-very-poor_n_1246557.html).

Kalil, Ariel and Patrick Wightman. 2010. *Parental Job Loss and Family Conflict*. National Center for Family & Marriage Research, Bowling Green State University, Bowling Green, OH. Retrieved March 30, 2012 (http://ncfmr.bgsu.edu/pdf/working_papers/file83645.pdf).

Kaye, H. Stephen. 2010. "The Impact of the 2007–09 Recession on Workers with Disabilities." *Monthly Labor Review* (October):19–30.

Kenworthy, Lane and Lindsay A. Owens. 2011. "The Surprisingly Weak Effect of Recessions on Public Opinion." Pp. 196–219 in *The Great Recession*, edited by David B. Grusky, Bruce Western, and Christopher Wimer. New York: Russell Sage Foundation Publications.

Kimmel, Michael and Abby L. Ferber. 2006. "White Men Are This Nation: Right-Wing Militias and the Restoration of Rural American Masculinity." Pp. 122–37 in *Country Boys: Masculinity and Rural Life*, edited by Hugh Campbell, Michael Mayerfeld Bell, and Margaret Finney. University Park: The Pennsylvania State University Press.

Kissane, Rebecca Joyce. 2012. "Poor Women's Moral Economies of Nonprofit Social Service Use: Conspicuous Constraint and Empowerment in the Hollow State." *Sociological Perspectives* 55(1):189–211.

Lamont, Michèle. 2000. *The Dignity of Working Men: Morality and the Boundaries of Race, Class, and Immigration*. New York: Russell Sage Foundation.

Lamont, Michèle and Marcel Fournier. 1992. *Cultivating Differences: Symbolic Boundaries and the Making of Inequality*. Chicago: The University of Chicago Press.

Lareau, Annette. 2003. *Unequal Childhoods: Class, Race, and Family Life*. 1st ed. Berkeley: University of California Press.

Larson, Jeffrey H., Stephan M. Wilson, and Rochelle Beley. 1994. "The Impact of Job Insecurity on Marital and Family Relationships." *Family Relations* 43(2):138–43.

Liem, Joan Huser and G. Ramsay Liem. 1990. "Understanding the Individual and Family Effects of Unemployment." Pp. 175–204 in *Stress between Work and Family*, edited by John Eckenrode and Susan Gore. New York: Plenum Press.

McLanahan, Sara and Christine Percheski. 2008. "Family Structure and the Reproduction of Inequalities." *Annual Review of Sociology* 34:257–76.

McLoyd, Vonnie C. 1990. "The Impact of Economic Hardship on Black Families and Children: Psychological Distress, Parenting, and Socioeconomic Development." *Child Development* 61(2):311–46.

Morgan, Greg, Dave Wallace, Keyi Lu, Chris Thomas, Alex Roubinchtein, Scott Bailey. 2012. *2011 Labor Market and Economic Report*. Washington State Employment Security Department. Retrieved August 27, 2012 (https://fortress.wa.gov/esd/employmentdata/docs/economic-reports/labor-market-and-economic-report2011.pdf).

Mosley, Walter. 2012. "'Food Stamp President': Gingrich's Poetry of Hate." CNN, January 26. Retrieved April 12, 2012 (www.cnn.com/2012/01/26/opinion/mosley-gingrich-food-stamp-president/index.html).

Nally, John M., Susan R. Lockwood, and Taiping Ho. 2011. "Employment of Ex-Offenders during the Recession." *Journal of Correctional Education* 62(2):117–31.

Nelson, Margaret K. 2000. "Single Mothers and Social Support: The Commitment to, and

Retreat from, Reciprocity." *Qualitative Sociology* 23(3):291–317.

Nelson, Margaret K. 2005. *The Social Economy of Single Motherhood: Raising Children in Rural America*. New York: Routledge.

Nelson, Margaret K. and Joan Smith. 1998. "Economic Restructuring, Household Strategies, and Gender: A Case Study of a Rural Community." *Feminist Studies* 24(1):79–114.

Newman, Katherine S. 1988. *Falling from Grace: The Experience of Downward Mobility in the American Middle Class*. New York: The Free Press.

Newman, Katherine S. 1999. *No Shame in My Game: The Working Poor in the Inner City*. New York: Vintage Books.

Oliver, Melvin and Thomas Shapiro. 2006. *Black Wealth/White Wealth: A New Perspective on Racial Inequality*. 2d ed. New York: Routledge.

Pager, Devah. 2003. "The Mark of a Criminal Record." *American Journal of Sociology* 108(5):937–75.

Pedulla, David S. and Katherine S. Newman. 2011. "The Family and Community Impacts of Underemployment." Pp. 233–52 in *Underemployment: Psychological, Economic, and Social Challenges*, edited by Douglas C. Maynard and Daniel C. Feldman. New York: Springer.

Piven, Frances Fox and Richard A. Cloward. 1971. *Regulating the Poor: The Functions of Public Welfare*. 1st ed. New York: Random House.

Purser, Gretchen. 2009. "The Dignity of Job-Seeking Men." *Journal of Contemporary Ethnography* 38(1):117–39.

Rogers-Dillon, Robin. 1995. "The Dynamics of Welfare Stigma." *Qualitative Sociology* 18(4):439–56.

Rubin, Lillian B. 1977. *Worlds of Pain: Life in the Working-Class Family*. New York: Basic Books.

Sayer, Andrew. 2011. *Why Things Matter to People: Social Science, Values and Ethical Life*. Cambridge, UK: Cambridge University Press.

Seccombe, Karen. 2010. *"So You Think I Drive a Cadillac?" Welfare Recipients' Perspectives on the System and Its Reform*. 3d ed. Upper Saddle River, NJ: Prentice Hall.

Segal, Lynne. 1990. *Slow Motion: Changing Masculinities, Changing Men*. New Brunswick, NJ: Rutgers University Press.

Shear, Michael D. 2012. "Romney Talks Bluntly of Those Dependent on Government." *The New York Times*, September 17. Retrieved September 18, 2012 (http://thecaucus.blogs.nytimes.com/2012/09/17/romney-faults-those-dependent-on-government/).

Sherman, Jennifer. 2006. "Coping with Rural Poverty: Economic Survival and Moral Capital in Rural America." *Social Forces* 85(2):891–913.

Sherman, Jennifer. 2009a. "Bend to Avoid Breaking: Job Loss, Gender Norms, and Family Stability in Rural America." *Social Problems* 56(4):599–620.

Sherman, Jennifer. 2009b. *Those Who Work, Those Who Don't: Poverty, Morality, and Family in Rural America*. Minneapolis: University of Minnesota Press.

Small, Mario Luis, David J. Harding, and Michèle Lamont. 2010. "Reconsidering Culture and Poverty." *The Annals of the American Academy of Political and Social Science* 629(1):6–27.

Smith, Sandra Susan. 2010. *Lone Pursuit: Distrust and Defensive Individualism among the Black Poor*. New York: Russell Sage Foundation.

Stack, Carol B. 1974. *All Our Kin: Strategies for Survival in a Black Community*. New York: Basic Books.

Steensland, Brian. 2006. "Cultural Categories and the American Welfare State: The Case of Guaranteed Income Policy." *American Journal of Sociology* 111(5):1273–1326.

Western, Bruce. 2001. "Incarceration, Unemployment, and Inequality." *Focus* 21(3):32–35.

Wilson, William Julius. 1996. *When Work Disappears: The World of the New Urban Poor*. New York: Knopf.

Woodward, Kerry. 2008. "The Multiple Meanings of Work for Welfare-Reliant Women." *Qualitative Sociology* 31(2):149–68.

Traps, Pitfalls, and Unexpected Cliffs on the Path out of Poverty

MARY A. PRENOVOST AND DEBORAH C. YOUNGBLOOD

Poor families receiving government benefits are encouraged to achieve economic independence as quickly as possible. But what are the challenges for families as they leave behind government support? Prenovost and Youngblood discuss some of the "cliffs" of poverty that exist when even small increases in household income (e.g., a raise at work or receiving irregular child support payments) can cause a loss of benefits; well-being declines because the additional income is not enough to compensate for the loss. This causes long-lasting impacts because it puts families in precarious financial positions and impedes their ability to become economically independent. Prenovost and Youngblood propose solutions to this problem, including gradual phasing-out of benefits as incomes increase, revised eligibility criteria, and improved access to higher education for low-income workers.

They designed [the government support system] in a way that you don't quite get over the hump. You get halfway up the hill and it's like driving a standard, you let go of the clutch and now you're rolling backwards.

> —Joanna,[1] a 30-year-old mother of two young children who lost both Food Stamps and ... [subsidized health care] because she began receiving child support payments.

Introduction

It is reasonable to assume that as a worker earns higher wages, he/she will have more money; however, this is not the case for many working poor families.... Although government supports (e.g., Food Stamps [also known as Supplemental Nutrition Assistance Program, or SNAP] ... child care assistance, Section 8 vouchers, etc.) help to sustain the needs of working poor families as they strive to attain economic independence, along the path rising wages and government supports come into conflict. As income increases, government supports are withdrawn and there is an overall decline in household resources—often referred to as the

Mary A. Prenovost and Deborah C. Youngblood, *Poverty & Public Policy* (Volume 2 and Issue 2). Reprinted by Permission of John Wiley and Sons. © 2010 Policy Studies Organization Published by Berkeley Electronic Press.

"cliff effect." In essence, the value of government supports often supersedes the value of the increased income that precipitates the loss. This is becoming a greater problem as more families transition from welfare to work, the number of working poor families is rising, the economy is floundering, and the cost of living is increasing.[2]

Crittenton Women's Union (CWU) in Boston, Massachusetts, conducted a qualitative study to explain the cliff effect phenomenon and depict how it is experienced by individual low-income mothers.... We ask: How do low-income women who are either on the verge of losing government support or who have recently experienced a loss of government support manage this circumstance and what does this mean for their family's well-being? Specifically, we explore ... [how] low-income female heads of household respond to opportunities to earn income at various wage rates along their journey to economic independence.... Through our qualitative interviews we aim to provide real-life context for the dramatic numbers shown by prior economic research indicating that families' net resources decrease alarmingly when their wages conflict with subsidy requirements.[3] Offering women's own words to illustrate the binds and contradictions of cliff effects, we hope to contribute a human perspective to a complex economic social issue.

Background

There are nearly 42 million adults and children in the United States who are struggling to make ends meet.[4] This means that one out of four working families with children is considered low income and this number is on the rise. Between 2002 and 2006 the number of working poor families increased by 350,000. It is misguided to assume that these families are not working hard. On the contrary, they work roughly one and one-quarter full-time jobs (or 2,552 hours per year).[5] Despite solid work efforts, low-income workers still find themselves trapped in poverty as low wages coupled with

increasing living costs continue to hinder their advancement to the middle class.

. . . The worker's wage path is unexpectedly potholed with large drops in net monthly resources as they progress from earning $8 per hour to $32 per hour. Illogically, the worker is financially better off making minimum wage than when she is making $18 per hour. To further illustrate this conundrum ... [consider the] story of a single mother who earns $11 per hour ($22,000 per year) and then decides to enroll in a medical assistant training program. Upon completion, she begins work at a job that pays $16 per hour ($32,000 per year). As a result of this $5 per hour raise, her childcare subsidy, housing voucher, and Earned Income Tax Credits are largely reduced, and [her benefits from] Food Stamps and the Women, Infants and Children (WIC) program are entirely terminated. Her $833 per month wage increase results in a monthly government support loss of $863 and she finds her net monthly resources drop from $547 (before the raise) to $391 (after the raise).... In this case, and in many others like this, wage increases may result in a family ending up worse off than they were before the income increase; thus, creating the feeling of never getting ahead regardless of increased work or earnings. The federal poverty level (FPL), which serves as the base measure for most of these eligibility requirements, is an antiquated gauge that does not vary according to family type or geographic location, and does not account for [a] state's high cost of living....

Government subsidies can help to close the gap between a family's needs and their earnings. However, many eligible individuals do not receive government supports due to a lack of funding and waiting lists that can take several years.[6] Furthermore, even when a family does receive government assistance, they are often cut off before they are able to independently meet their needs (i.e., the cliff effect) because the supports are contingent upon means-tested eligibility guidelines based on incomes that are too low to be family-supporting.

Not only do low-income individuals need to be aware of the existence of cliff effects as their income increases, but they also need to be able to anticipate and plan for exactly when and how cliff effects occur, and this requires intricate calculations and extensive policy knowledge. It is very difficult to map out all of the cliffs along the way because of changing eligibility requirements from program to program and shifting policies. . . . The conundrums of cliff effects have not been sufficiently explored and it is that terrain into which we ventured to better understand how low-income women themselves understand and navigate this dilemma and how social service providers serve and advise them.

Research Design

Participants and Recruitment

Women who self-reported their annual incomes between $15,000 and $40,000, who live in the Greater Boston area, and who are comfortable at reading and speaking in English were eligible to participate in the survey portion of the study. . . . Flyers were posted at Boston-based social service agencies and local businesses to recruit study participants.

Recipient research participants completed an initial survey that assessed their cliff effect experiences and measured their well-being in areas such as social support, economic well-being, physical health, and emotional health. The interview sample was drawn from survey participants who reported on the survey that they had experienced or had been close to experiencing a cliff effect. The interview guide for the recipient participants uses 13 questions to focus the conversation on the participants' cliff effect experience and decisions she made around employment and resource-use. . . .

Data Analysis

Interviews were transcribed verbatim and were analyzed . . . [to develop] key patterns of decision-making and well-being among low-income individuals faced with government support loss. . . .

Demographics

A total of 78 women participated in the "recipient participant survey" portion of the study and 18 women participated in the "recipient participant interview." The mean age is 31 years for the survey participants and 35 years for the interview participants. This sample population is a bit older compared to similar studies of this nature, which may explain why the average age of the children is 15 years (for the survey sample) and 14 years (for the interview sample). The survey sample consisted of 45% African Americans (50% for the interview), 18% Caucasians (17% for the interview), 27% Hispanics (33% for the interview), and 9% Others. The mean household incomes for both the survey (i.e., $21,250 per year) and interview (i.e., $28,500 per year) participants are above the FPL for 2008 and fall within critical cliff effect junctures. . . . In terms of educational attainment, 17% of both the survey and interview participants had completed a vocational degree or an Associate of Arts degree, whereas 16% of these same groups had earned a Bachelor of Arts (or Science) degree or higher. However, some of the remaining participants may be on their way to higher education, given that 42% of survey participants and 39% of interview participants had completed "some college." Only 12% of survey participants and 22% of interview participants were married, which may have important implications regarding their emotional or financial support systems. Additionally, 20% of the survey participants and 22% of the interview participants were divorced, which is significant because it allows for the greater possibility of receiving child support or alimony that may push them over the income limit and deem them ineligible for government supports.

Key Findings . . .

Working Your Way Up and Losing the Most

Contrary to expectations, but representative of the glitches in the current system, the participants with the highest average income ($34,000 per year) were doing worse in terms of their self-reported well-being than those with lower incomes. Consider Alicia, a 35-year-old mother of three children who works full-time as a case manager earning $32,000 per year. Alicia recently received a raise and lost all of her government supports. She said:

> Everyday there is a chokehold around me, you know, where sometimes it's really hard to breathe. . . . Because most days you feel this consistent choke because there is always a bill that needs to be paid. You can only pay a little on this bill, just to keep them off of your back about two weeks before you have to give them a little bit more money. And so it's this constant game of chess with these bills to just finagle the bills to keep everybody happy for the moment.

For Alicia to remain motivated or even for her to feel that she can handle her situation on a basic level, she needs to experience that working allows her to make ends meet. It is reasonable to expect that she will have to follow a careful budget that does not allow for luxuries. However, it is unreasonable that, despite her higher income, she still feels that there is a "chokehold" around her every day.

This finding—that those with higher incomes were doing the worst—is critical because it highlights the most pressing dilemma. The people who are having the most success at getting ahead in the workplace are having the least financial success. That is, if someone is earning $32,000 per year they are likely to have at least finished their high school diploma, they may have some postsecondary education or even a college degree, and they have developed some marketable work skills. Thus, they should be able to reap the benefits of these accomplishments. But the cliff effects conundrum means that their efforts leave them ineligible for work supports but still unable to afford to pay independently for basic necessities like shelter, health

care, food, and childcare. And so they are squeezed the tightest, and one might argue, the most unfairly. . . .

These families find themselves in a contradictory situation where they are not making enough to swim alone, but losing too much support to stay afloat. While our work support system cannot provide benefits at all income levels, recognizing that the current eligibility criterion creates a disincentive to success is crucial. Hard work has to pay off if people are going to be motivated to do it, and low-income families need to be able to cover their basic needs and see a promising future ahead if they are going to stay in the game.

Losing Government Supports

For the women we spoke with the issue of losing government supports was not about economics or statistics, it was about struggling to meet the basic needs of their families. They talked about these dilemmas in the most personal ways, sharing stories of losing their housing, struggling to obtain the medical care needed for children, and skipping meals so that their children would have enough food to eat. And all of these struggles were part of a life story in which the woman is trying to do the "right thing," trying to move ahead in her career, earn an independent income, and get off government subsidies. For the survey participants, housing was rated as the most troublesome government support to lose, MassHealth (i.e., the public health insurance program in Massachusetts) was the second, followed by Food Stamps, and child care assistance. . . .[7]

Although all forms of government assistance are vital in helping working families meet fundamental needs, housing is an essential need for every individual, and losing the ability to pay for this need creates substantial problems for families. For example, Emma recently lost her Section 8 voucher and her home. She lost her Section 8 because she was slightly over income, but did not earn enough to afford costly rents that are standard in Boston. Consequently, she has been shuffling between friends' couches and various shelters. She said, "Trying to go to college and be homeless is very difficult, so I had to quit the college." Emma is a discouraging example . . . a college education might be the most promising path out of poverty for her, but since she lost key supports while she was pursuing that education, she was derailed. Additionally, the social costs of remaining in poverty might be significantly higher than the cost of the Section 8 voucher. Emma went on to explain her frustration:

> I was honest with the Section 8 people, I told them that both of us were working, they calculated the rent, they said that you were over income by some ridiculous amount by twenty, thirty, forty dollars, so I was no longer on the Section 8 program, but yet not making enough money to pay market rent and having a four thousand dollar security deposit, so I fell in that gray area and there are so many people that have benefits that fall in that gray area.

The "gray area" that Emma refers to is the very cliff effect we are speaking about. It is the place where one cannot afford to pay for things independently but has become ineligible for supports. Reducing that "gray area" may be one of the key ways to promote economic independence for low-income people.

Another consequence of losing a benefit is the emotional toll that it takes on the family causing a great deal of distress and worry for all its members. Consider Joanna, a 30-year-old mother of two young children, who lost both Food Stamps and MassHealth around the same time because she began receiving child support payments for one of her sons. However, these payments were not consistent and were not an accurate reflection of her household income. She experienced great financial and emotional turmoil because she has a chronically ill son whose doctor visits and prescription costs are too expensive for her to cover herself. She discussed the debilitating, ". . . emotional effect of a lot of just not knowing and where's next month's food

gonna come from and how am I gonna pay for [her son's] prescriptions the following month."

The emotional toll hits both parents and children. Indeed, children are often hit the hardest by the stress of poverty.[8] Consider Alicia, who spoke about the effects that living in a homeless shelter had on her 2-year-old daughter:

> I had to sit down with the teacher and explain why she was acting certain ways because of the change from living in a house when she could do everything to living in a shelter by nine o'clock she had to be in bed and couldn't play around and do certain things so I guess she was acting up at the day care and I had to explain to them that she was acting that way because we went to living in a shelter and it changed. So, you know they can feel things and she was only 2 . . . not like I let her do whatever she wants, but living in a house to living in to like a structure where you go to bed by nine o'clock, so it impacted her.

As she describes it, her daughter went from living in a home to living in a "structure." The lack of personal warmth and autonomy connoted by the descriptor "structure" here is telling. And this challenge obviously affected both mother and daughter.

In addition to the emotional stress caused by losing supports, there are physical hardships that ensue. For example, Ellie, a 44-year-old mother of two young daughters making $30,000 per year as an administrative assistant, recently lost her Food Stamps because of an increase in her wages. She described how she would skip meals because she could not afford enough groceries to feed herself and her family. She said:

> If I eat with them I might eat a little tiny bit of what they have and I'll say, "Oh I had a big lunch," so that they can have the food, but then I can eat with them so they don't think I'm not eating and I'm starving myself.

A parent working full-time should not have to go without enough food—no family should. Should she have to pretend to her children that she is not hungry so they do not feel guilty eating? And when that is the case, what does that say about the cut-off for Food Stamps eligibility?

Finally, women who are mothers are unable to work if their children are not adequately cared for. The participants specifically emphasized that child care must be stable, reliable, and affordable in order to function as an effective support for parents who are working. Michelle is a 33-year-old mother of three children. She works full-time and currently receives child care assistance, Food Stamps, and MassHealth, but is anxious about losing these supports because of her impending annual raise. She maintains, ". . . if I didn't have [a child care voucher], I wouldn't be able to work, hold down a 9 to 5." Although . . . child care vouchers from the government help families cover the substantial cost of child care, getting through the waiting list may take years. . . . For all parents, but especially low-income parents, child care is remarkably expensive. It is estimated that about 65% of low-income single-earner households spend 40–50% of their income on childcare.[9] Thus, receiving a childcare voucher from the government is enormously valuable for those parents who are trying to succeed at work or school. Colleen, a 42-year-old mother of two young boys, cannot believe how expensive childcare is. She says, "How can you pay for that . . . if you worked full-time, you'd have to make so much money to be worth your while to put your kid in day care."

Given the long wait to obtain a childcare voucher and the huge expense of paying for childcare out of pocket, it is easy to imagine the impact of losing this benefit. Thus, when women are faced with a small earning increase that pushes them over the eligibility requirements line, the dilemma is huge. If they take the increase in earnings and lose the child care subsidy, they may not actually be able to maintain the job if they cannot realistically afford childcare. And if their childcare becomes unstable, it might cause them to lose their job because they will need to care for their children. If they lose their job, there is no guarantee they will be able to obtain another job at the same wage level. But even if their earnings were to decline to the point where they would be re-eligible for a childcare voucher, they would find themselves at the bottom of a very long waiting list. So it is never a simple case of moving up, it is more like a calculated risk with an enormous amount to lose.

. . . It is no wonder why the four most troublesome benefits to lose all cover the most fundamental needs. However, as previously emphasized, these benefits often get cut before the family can afford these expensive goods and services on their own, and often puts families in compromising positions such as homelessness (as in Emma's case), emotional distress (as in Alicia's case), and hunger (as in Ellie's case).

Applying for and Maintaining Benefits

Although the experience of losing supports is challenging, the process of acquiring and recertifying supports presents other obstacles. Many women deemed the application and recertification processes as problematic and expressed frustration because eligibility calculations fail to take into consideration irregular work schedules and inconsistent child support payments. They also talked about the process of applying and maintaining benefits as a degrading experience. Joanna, a 30-year-old mother of two young children, described it this way:

> You know and with all the rules that they have in place it's very degrading. I just feel like they need to reevaluate how they determine that. And if I'm coming in there asking you for Food Stamps, or for you know, welfare check I'm not a damn number . . . you literally walk in and you're standing in this little concrete wall, in—in a corridor, very small, with a toilet, like the bathroom is right there, and all you can smell is everybody that's come out of the

bathroom and you literally pull a number and you wait! And you wait, and you wait. Finally, they get to your number then you go over and they give you an application and another number! And you wait, and you wait, and you fill out your stuff, they come back and take it, they give you another number and then you wait some more. Even if you have a scheduled appointment, you wait for two hours. You have to clear a whole day just to go to the welfare office for something simple as like an ID.

When one is made to wait for hours, you are very clearly being told that your time is not worth much, when in fact every minute spent waiting may represent lost wages and other negative consequences of missed work. Moreover, when one is made to wait for hours in an ugly, small environment that smells like a toilet, you are getting an even more discouraging message about your worth.

Another common frustration was around the certification process. Numerous women had incomes that frequently shifted, either increasing or decreasing, for various reasons. Since income (even if it is unrepresentative) is central in determining eligibility for government work supports, many of the women we spoke with experienced great difficulty as a result of misconstrued income. Consider Darla, a 25-year-old expectant mother, who described a common situation of fluctuating pay:

A good month I can work thirty-eight to forty-five hours and it just happens to be that month they want my pay stubs for Food Stamps, ok, the next month comes around I've worked three hours one week, twelve hours another week, seven hours another week, ten hours another week, they don't want my pay stubs that week, they won't deal with 'em. Ok, next month comes and that's when they start picking up again, each month is different, it varies

and it is very very very hard to pinpoint really how much I making . . . when it comes down to dealing with people who are in my situation I don't have the same hours, I mean that goes for any job. Nobody really has the same set of hours unless you're guaranteed in writing a forty-hour a week position.

Darla points to the problem while offering a concrete solution. If someone has guaranteed hours, then his or her income should be counted differently than someone who does not. Other women suggested having longer time periods for calculating income, to better capture inconsistencies in it. As Tanya, a 30-year-old mother of one teenage son describes, those inconsistencies are not relevant in the eligibility criteria. She recently began receiving sporadic child support payments that pushed her over the income eligibility threshold for MassHealth. She said, "I voluntarily reported that I got child support, $65 a week, um, then I told them, 'Well it's not consistent.' It didn't matter." As a result of this loss, she now pays $218.53 dollars a week to cover health insurance for herself and her son. During the months when the child support payments are not paid, she has to try to make ends meet with insufficient resources.

And finally, women expressed frustration with the lack of sufficiency and efficiency in many of the benefit programs themselves. For example, Amanda, a mother of two, said this about the fuel assistance program:

$400 for a fuel assistance grant, that's not even one month's worth of a winter bill here in Massachusetts, that's a joke, it's a slap in the face when you're sitting there for 12 hours at a fuel assistance office, doing applications, and giving them your whole life, for them to come back and say we're gonna give you $400 and by the way we're not paying it until June, by the time that they get around to sending the check out to the gas company, your gas is already shut off, so it's useless, and now you can't get benefits for the following year because now your gas is shut off and you have to turn the bill on in your kids name, so now you're not gonna get the benefit.

It is a web of double binds that low-income workers find themselves in. And these double binds become challenges not just to the adult worker, but to their children as well.

Efforts to Plan for the Future

It is estimated that over three-quarters of low-income working families do not have enough assets to cover their family's basic living costs for three months should their source of income be altered or eliminated.[10] Given that the wages low-income individuals earn are so low, there is often very little (if anything) left at the end of the month to save after they pay all of their bills. Erin, who earns $37,500 per year, said:

> I have [a savings account], but I'm always taking out of it, like, because you end up needing it for something, so I really don't have it. . . . I'm trying to do it, but when the end of the check roll comes and like those two weeks, well I have to use the money. What was the point of me even having distributed it there?

Although Erin's motivation to save is apparent, she finds that it becomes recurrently unachievable to do so at the end of every month. This is largely because she needs to cover her basic living costs and has been cut off from government supports because her income has been deemed too high to need help. Most low-income families find themselves in a situation similar to Erin's as they try to use their insufficient wages to meet the high cost of living which often makes saving unfeasible.

Even in cases where families are able to spare some money to put aside, they are often hindered by asset limits. . . . Asset limits prevent these families from developing any sort of adequate safety net for crises or savings for future aspirations (e.g., saving for higher education, retirement, or even the ability to cover moving costs). One specific example that reflects the severity of the restrictions is illustrated by Joanna, a 30-year-old mother of two young children. She recalled:

> A $10 savings bond that you purchased for your child as a birthday present comes back to bite you in the butt when you go to collect Food Stamps. That's insane. . . . I had to cash in a $100 savings bond for my kid . . . they said, "It's worth $50, you need to cash it in, it's cash on hand, you need to get rid of it." That was my son's birthday present from his first birthday that he got from his grandmother . . . so now my son is not allowed to have a nest egg because I'm poor.

Erika, a 33-year-old mother of four young children, also expressed her frustrations by explaining how, "There's no way to save any money, and when they see you're saving, you can only save up to a certain amount before they cut you off of benefits because they feel that you have something. . . ."

All families, including those who receive government assistance, should have the freedom to develop their assets and realize their goals, including the goal of making ends meet without the help of government supports. As Erika puts it, they too need to feel they can "have something." The motivation to build a solid financial foundation for one's family needs to be supported and encouraged. Otherwise, we may inadvertently encourage families to live exclusively in the moment and discourage economic stability and mobility.

Hopes and Plans for the Future

The majority of women we spoke with aspired to achieve the traditional American notions of success—home ownership and education. When discussing her dreams for the future, Darla, a 25-year-old expectant mother said, "... having a home, a house, being a home-owner and saying that, you know, I'm paying my property tax, my water bill, my sewage bill, I'm paying for everything on my own." Cynthia, a 59-year-old mother taking care of nine children, spoke with a similar prideful tone; she said, "Hopefully I'll be paying on my house, I got a mortgage payment, I can sit on my front yard and say this is mine, I made it, I got this, it took a lot of sweat and pain, but I did it."

... [The economic crisis of the mid-2000s showed] us that providing home loans to individuals who are not positioned to make mortgage payments over the long term is not the appropriate response to support these goals. So what is it then? While the answer to this question lies beyond the scope of our study, providing access to and support for training and education that leads to jobs that pay family sustaining wages, supporting asset development for low-income households (i.e., removing asset limits, promoting savings, etc.), along with addressing the personal and family concerns that might create obstacles on this road is key to economic independence. ...

Many of the women in our study acknowledged the important role that education and training played in opening the doors to higher paying jobs or a "dream career," as one participant described it. Although many women discussed that they wanted to pursue higher education, most felt it was an impossible aspiration because of barriers in place that significantly impeded them.

For example, the inability to finance their education is one major barrier. Gina ... explains here that she cannot accomplish her goal of going back to school because of financial constraints. She said, "If it covers all my expenses, I would consider going to school, otherwise I cannot do it, I will not be able because, um, I need to pay my bills every month." Another

common fear expressed by the participants was that they would not receive a raise at their current jobs if they go back to school to get a higher degree. When weighing the pros and cons of going back to school, Erin, a 27-year-old mother of one young daughter, said:

> I'm gonna make the same amount of money. I mean, yeah, I could probably make a couple thousand more give or take, depending on what field, but not that much, it's not worth owing all that money.

As Gina points out, higher education is only feasible if she can support herself at the same time. Erin also astutely notes that college training needs to have a proven relationship to higher earnings at the other end if it is going to be a realistic choice for single parents. Accordingly, there needs to be clear, accessible information available to help prospective students make informed school decisions, as well as better financial and general support. ...

Policy Recommendations

The participants were asked to share any thoughts of possible solutions to the cliff effect situation. Based on their suggestions, CWU proposes three recommendations for policy and programmatic action. First, update eligibility criteria and increase support levels for all government work support programs. Second, develop "cliff effect trainings" and resources for social service providers. And third, improve accessibility for higher education for low-income working parents.

Work Support Programs

An important and long-awaited adjustment that must occur is updating the federal and state eligibility criteria for government supports while also increasing overall support levels. Individuals are being cut off before they are actually able to afford the goods and/or services that government supports cover. All government supports should gradually phase-out as wages rise (rather than drop-off suddenly . . .) to provide an incentive to workers to accept promotions or wage increases. In order to cover all families in need, there must be a corresponding increase in overall appropriations for these programs. Particular attention should be focused on childcare and housing vouchers, which are in high demand and short supply and are essential components of family stability.

In addition to the gradual phase-out of supports and overall increased appropriations, the way income eligibility is determined to approximate average earnings needs to be changed to take into account earnings over a longer period of time. For individuals who have fluctuating earnings (e.g., due to irregular hours or seasonal employment), recertification periods that occur frequently do not realistically capture one's overall income and may lead to inadequate assistance. In addition to improved evaluation of overall earnings, the application process may be made easier by moving to online applications and standardizing recertification periods to one year, as the Food Stamp program has recently done. Indeed, many of our participants discussed the "red-tape" or administrative barriers that prevented them from receiving much needed supports. We recommend streamlining the administrative process for application and recertification for work supports.

Social Service Provider Education

In order to better inform and prepare working poor families for subsidy cliffs, social service providers must be educated and knowledgeable about when and how work support cut-offs occur. Thus, "cliff effect trainings" for social service providers must be developed and highly encouraged by any organization that advises low-income individuals. The development of widely available calculators that allow providers and individuals to track eligibility requirements and plan for work support reductions would also be highly valuable.

Access to Higher Education for Low-Income Working Parents

By improving accessibility to financial aid for education to provide comprehensive coverage for working parents, it will give more low-income families an opportunity to progress toward economic independence that will position them in higher-paying jobs. One way to do this is to offer 2 years (or equivalent credit) of community college at no cost to low-income workers for degree or certificate programs.

Conclusion

Work should not be costing these low-wage earning individuals as they make solid efforts to increase their income. Rather, government work supports should *support* income advancement. The public assistance system should function in a way that allows individuals to make it all the way up the hill to economic independence without "rolling backwards" as Joanna attested to at the beginning of this . . . [reading]. There is an immediate need for more research and ample policy action concerning this vulnerable population as the strength of the economy falters, the cost of living is rising, and the numbers of working poor people are quickly escalating. We need to leverage government work supports so they effectively offer assistance to those who are forging a path to economic independence. The women who we spoke with plainly illustrated the double binds they are placed in, trying to live their lives in manners that adhere to two key social expectations—a good work ethic and a good motherhood model—within a government system that insists upon both but effectively supports neither. By and large, the women we spoke with offer the clearest and most profound conclusions:

> Even though you have a little, you're making a little bit more money, you're really not, you're still in the same category. . . . I don't see how they think that they're making it better . . . it's not beneficial,

actually . . . it feels like being punished for making more money . . . you contemplate whether you want to make more money or not, whether you want to work more hours because you could be at home with your kids and still be in the same situation. (Erika, a 33-year-old mother of four)

The system is not there to help people who are working, you have to be not working to get any help . . . it's not set up for single mothers who work. (Tanya, a 30-year-old mother of one)

NOTES

1. All names used are pseudonyms to ensure that the participants' identity remains confidential.
2. The Working Poor Families Project, Working Hard, Still Falling Short: New Findings on the Challenges Confronting America's Working Families, 2008, available from http://www.workingpoorfamilies.org.
3. Rebecca Loya, Ruthie Liberman, Randy Albelda, and Elisabeth Babcock, "Fits & Starts: The Difficult Path for Working Single Parents," for Crittenton Women's Union and The Center for Social Policy at McCormack Graduate School, University of Massachusetts Boston, 2008, available from http://www.liveworkthrive.org.
4. The Working Poor Families Project, available from http://workingpoorfamilies.org.
5. The Working Poor Families Project, available from http://workingpoorfamilies.org.
6. Albelda and Shea, available from http://www.umb.edu/bridgingthegaps/publications.html.
7. It is likely that the childcare subsidy was ranked lower primarily because the majority of study participants had children who were teenagers and thus they were no longer eligible for childcare vouchers. We know from other research and our work with families with young children in other contexts, that

childcare is consistently one of the most important factors in enabling women to be successful in the work place (e.g., Lowe and Weisner, 2004).

8. Jeanne Brooks-Gunn, Greg J. Duncan, and J. Lawrence Aber, eds., *Neighborhood Poverty: Vol. 1. Context and Consequences for Children* (New York: Russell Sage Foundation, 1997). See also Tama Leventhal and Jeanne Brooks-Gunn, "The Neighborhoods They Live In: The Effects of Neighborhood Residence on Child and Adolescent Outcomes," *Psychological Bulletin*, 126 (March): 309–337.
9. Richard Wertheimer, *Poor Families in 2001: Parents Working Less and Children Continue to Lag Behind* (Washington, DC: Child Trends, 2003).
10. Signe-Mary McKernan and Caroline Ratcliffe, *Enabling Families to Weather Emergencies and Develop: The Role of Assets*, for The Urban Institute, 2008, available from http://www.urban.org.

REFERENCES

Albelda, Randy, and Jennifer Shea. 2007. "Bridging the Gaps between Earnings and Basic Needs in Massachusetts," for The Center for Social Policy at McCormack Graduate School, University of Massachusetts Boston. http://www.umb.edu/bridgingthegaps/publications.html.

Brooks-Gunn, Jeanne, Greg J. Duncan, and J. Lawrence Aber, eds. 1997. *Neighborhood Poverty: Vol. 1. Context and Consequences for Children*. New York: Russell Sage Foundation.

Leventhal, Tama, and Jeanne Brooks-Gunn. 2000. "The Neighborhoods They Live In: The Effects of Neighborhood Residence on Child and Adolescent Outcomes." *Psychological Bulletin* 126 (March): 309–337.

Lowe, Edward D., and Thomas S. Weisner. 2004. "You Have to Push It—Who's Gonna Raise Your Kids?: Situating Child Care and Child Care Subsidy Use in the Daily Routines of Lower Income Families." *Children & Youth Services Review* 26 (February): 143–171.

Loya, Rebecca, Ruthie Liberman, Randy Albelda, and Elisabeth Babcock. 2008. "Fits & Starts: The Difficult Path for Working Single Parents," for Crittenton Women's Union and The Center for Social Policy at McCormack Graduate School, University of Massachusetts Boston. http://www.liveworkthrive.org.

McKernan, Signe-Mary, and Caroline Ratcliffe. 2008. "Enabling Families to Weather Emergencies and Develop: The Role of Assets," for The Urban Institute. http://www.urban.org.

The Working Poor Families Project. 2008. "Working Hard, Still Falling Short: New Findings on the Challenges Confronting America's Working Families," for the Working Poor Families Project. http://www.workingpoorfamilies.org.

Wertheimer, Richard. 2003. *Poor Families in 2001: Parents Working Less and Children Continue to Lag Behind*. Washington, D.C.: Child Trends.

Voices of the Near Poor

Sabrina Tavernise, Jason DeParle, and Robert Gebeloff

When the Census Bureau . . . released a new measure of poverty [in Fall 2011], meant to better count disposable income, it began altering the portrait of national need. The new method, called the Supplemental Poverty Measure, was designed to add in many of the things the old measure ignored, like the hundreds of billions the needy receive in food stamps and tax credits. At the same time, it subtracted the similarly large sums lost to taxes, medical care and work expenses.

One surprising difference with the new measure . . . was the 51 million people with incomes less than 50 percent above the poverty line. That category, sometimes called "near poor," was 76 percent higher than the official account, which was published in September [2011]. (The portion of people under the poverty line, meanwhile, increased by just 5 percent in the new measure.) About a fifth of the people who appear near poor in the new measure are lifted out of poverty by benefits the old measure ignores, like food stamps and tax credits. But more than half were pulled down into near poverty from higher income levels by taxes, medical costs and work expenses like childcare and gas. Taken together with people under the poverty line, a full third of

Americans—or about 100 million people—live in poverty or in the economically vulnerable area just above it.

In Washington and its suburbs, the near poor are people with incomes between $31,693 and $47,539 for a family of four with a mortgage. Reporters talked to people in the Washington area this week with incomes in this category. They spoke of the knife-edge quality of their lives, in which one unexpected bill could knock them off balance. Many owned the usual trappings of middle-class life—cars, houses, cellphones and air-conditioners. But payments on those possessions were juggled, often unsuccessfully, depending on the unpredictable tides of their incomes. None saw themselves as poor. Most saw themselves as part of the middle class. But they focused on how hard they had to struggle to remain there.

Here are some of their stories:

Debra Jeje earned about $31,000 last year as a secretary in an emergency room in a hospital in Washington. She struggles to pay her bills, which come to about $2,300 a month, including groceries. She sells Mary Kay makeup for extra income. Gas, health insurance premiums and taxes put Ms. Jeje just above poverty line. "What stresses me out most is payday," said Ms. Jeje, who is 50 and has one son living with her. "I don't have any extra money left over. My salary is less than my bills." Her job, she said, pays too little. "We're on the front lines," she said. "There's stress and headaches and ups and downs in the emergency room. You really feel that you're worth more."

Bille Allison, a health care worker with two children, earns $39,000 a year drawing blood at a doctor's office in Maryland. She qualified for the earned income tax credit last year, bringing her income to $42,000. But work expenses dragged her down. She pays $500 a month for day care for her 4-year-old daughter, $100 a month for bus and train fare to get to work, and $200 a month for health insurance—bringing her income down to about $32,000. Some months she is able to save enough for game tokens and a meal at Chuck E. Cheese for her daughter. Other months she can only afford to pay half her bills. She was turned away from the food stamps office because her income was too high. "I tried everything, and it's like, nope, you make too much," said Ms. Allison, who is 42 and divorced. "They tell you you have to work to get help, but then you work, and you still can't get help."

Jennifer Bangura works at Georgetown University Hospital as a cashier. Together with her husband, a driver for a catering company, their family income is just under $50,000, enough to pay a mortgage of $800 on a house she purchased in 1992. But after taxes, medical costs and the gas to get to work, they slip into the category of near poor. Their situation has been made worse by a second mortgage, taken out several years ago to raise money for their daughter's college tuition. The monthly payment shot up to $2,200, an amount she says is now untenable. "It's killing me," said Ms. Bangura, who is 50 and originally from Jamaica. She said she has been making payments for years and that "to lose it now would tear me apart."

Jessie Adams, a floor refinisher and his wife, a secretary, together earn about $49,000— too much to qualify for the earned income tax credit and food stamps, but too little to live without worrying about finances. Taxes and monthly subway commuting costs bring them down into the area of near poor. They own electronics—two flat-screen TVs and an Xbox game console for their 10-year-old— but cannot afford a car or a down payment on a house. Mr. Adams has not taken his family out on a weekend for five months. "It shouldn't be like this," he said. "Two people working full time in the house, we should be able to save, to take a vacation. But it ain't like that. It just ain't like that."

The Compassion Gap
in American Poverty Policy

FRED BLOCK, ANNA C. KORTEWEG, KERRY WOODWARD,
ZACH SCHILLER, AND IMRUL MAZID

Citing a "compassion gap" in poverty policy, the authors present evidence that Americans tend to blame poor people for their situations, resulting in limited governmental support and a war on individual poor people's "bad behavior." They explain that although poverty is at an all-time high, the government is providing less and less support, in part because of our tendency to victim-blame, while ignoring the economic and structural causes of poverty. Government policies have the ability to be truly helpful (e.g., Social Security), and the authors suggest we should look abroad to see effective governmental programs to reduce poverty.

Every 30 or 40 years, Americans seem to "discover" that millions of our citizens are living in horrible and degrading poverty. Jacob Riis shocked the nation in 1890 with a book entitled *How the Other Half Lives*, which helped to inspire a change in public opinion and the reforms of the Progressive Era. In the 1930s, the devastation of the Great Depression led FDR to place poverty at the top of the national agenda. In the early 1960s, Michael Harrington's *The Other America* made poverty visible and paved the way for Lyndon Johnson's brief War on Poverty. In 2005, an act of nature became the next muckraker—Hurricane Katrina, which shockingly revealed the human face of poverty among the displaced and helpless victims of the storm's devastation in New Orleans.

But what makes poverty so invisible between such episodes of discovery? The poor are always with us, but why do they repeatedly disappear from public view? Why do we stop seeing the pain that poverty causes?

Our society recognizes a moral obligation to provide a helping hand to those in need, but those in poverty have been getting only the back of the hand. They receive little or no public assistance. Instead, they are scolded and told that they have caused their own misfortunes. This is our "compassion gap"—a deep divide between our moral commitments and how we actually treat those in poverty.

The compassion gap does not just happen. It results from two key dynamics. First, powerful groups in American society insist that public help for the poor actually hurts them by making them weak and dependent. Every epoch in which poverty is rediscovered and generosity increases is followed by a backlash in which these arguments reemerge and lead to sharp reductions in public assistance. Second, the consequence of reduced help is that the assertions of welfare critics turn into self-fulfilling prophecies. They insist that immorality is the root cause of poverty. But when assistance becomes inadequate, the poor can no longer survive by obeying the rules; they are forced to break them. These infractions, in turn, become the necessary proof that "the poor" are truly intractable and that their desperate situations are rightly ignored.

The results are painfully clear in our official data. In 2004, 37 million people, including 13 million children, lived below the government's official poverty line of $15,219 for a family of three. The number of people in poverty increased every year . . . rising from 31.6 million in 2000. Moreover, our government's official poverty line is quite stingy by international standards. If we used the most common international measure, which counts people who live on less than half of a country's median income as poor, then almost 55 million people in the United States, or almost 20 percent of the population, would be counted as poor.

Most distressingly, the number of people living in catastrophic poverty—in households with incomes less than 50 percent of the official U.S. poverty line—has increased every year since 1999. . . . [In 2006, there were] 15.6 million people living in this kind of desperate poverty. This is close to the highest number ever, and it is twice the number of extremely poor people that we had in the mid-1970s, before the cuts in poverty programs of the Reagan administration.

Children, single mothers with children, and people of color—particularly African Americans and Latinos—make up a disproportionate segment of the nation's poorest groups, with women in each group consistently more likely to be poor than men in that group. But poverty is not unusual or rare—as many as 68 percent of

all Americans will spend a year or more living in poverty or near-poverty as adults. Nor is poverty always related to not working; there are still 9 million working-poor adults in the United States [in 2006].

Moreover, poverty has become more devastating over the past generation. Thirty years ago, a family living at the poverty line—earning a living at low-wage work—could still see the American Dream as an achievable goal. . . . With a bit more hard work and some luck, they too could afford a single-family home, comprehensive health insurance, and a college education for their children. Today, for many of the poor, including many of the faces we saw at the New Orleans Superdome and Convention Center [after Hurricane Katrina], that dream has become a distant and unattainable vision. Even a two-parent family working full-time at the minimum wage earns less than half of what is needed to realize the dream at today's prices. The old expectation that the poor would pull themselves up by their own bootstraps is increasingly unrealistic.

Despite the growing poor population and the increasing difficulty of escaping poverty into economic security through paid work, the government has been doing less and less to help. Aid to Families with Dependent Children (AFDC) used to be our biggest program to help poor people, but federal legislation passed in 1996 ended AFDC and replaced it with Temporary Aid to Needy Families (TANF). TANF's focus on moving recipients from "welfare to work" has led to a major decline in the number of households receiving benefits and a huge drop in cash assistance to the poor. The average monthly TANF benefit was $393 in 2003, compared to $490 in 1997.

Not only are our programs miserly, they reach too few people among those who are eligible, further reducing the chances that those in poverty can achieve the American Dream. Only 60 percent of eligible households receive food stamps. Despite a commitment to provide health insurance to all children under 18, nearly

12 percent of those children remained without such insurance in 2004, and only 27 percent of all poor families received TANF in 2000. Finally, subsidized housing is provided to only 25 percent of those who need it, and current budget proposals would cut this program dramatically.

Against this backdrop of decreasing spending on most antipoverty measures, the Earned Income Tax Credit (EITC) has become our biggest antipoverty program for the working-age population. EITC aids the working poor by providing an income-tax refund to lift the poorest workers above the poverty line. But for families to benefit significantly from the EITC, someone in the household must be earning at least several thousand dollars per year. Each year, millions of households do not have such an earner because of unemployment, illness, lack of childcare, or a mismatch between available skills and job demands. The consequence is a relentless increase in our rate of catastrophic poverty.

. . . [D]espite increases in EITC outlays, our total spending on the poor peaked in 1997 and has dropped almost 20 percent since then [even when adjusting for inflation and the shifting size of the poor population]. . . . Spending for each nonelderly poor person peaked at around $1,000 in 1997 and has dropped every year since, with a total decline of close to 30 percent. And if we added food stamps . . . the trend would be even stronger, since their real value has also fallen since 1997. There is no clearer evidence that our compassion gap has deepened poverty.

The compassion gap has been greatly increased by the revival in the 1980s and 1990s of the very old theory that the real source of poverty is bad behavior. Since African-American and Hispanic women and men, as well as single mothers of all ethnicities and races, are disproportionately represented among the poor, this theory defines these people as morally deficient. Its proponents assume that anyone with enough grit and determination can escape poverty. They claim that giving people cash assistance worsens poverty by taking away their drive to improve their circumstances through work. Arguing that poor people bear children irresponsibly and that they lack the work ethic necessary for economic success, they have launched a sustained war on bad behavior that targets those groups most at risk of poverty.

One of the key events in this war was the passage in 1996 of the Personal Responsibility and Work Opportunities Reconciliation Act (PRWORA), which replaced AFDC with TANF. TANF requires single mothers who receive welfare to find paid work, encourages them to marry, and limits their time on aid to a lifetime maximum of five years. Some states have even shorter time limits. Ultimately, this new program treats the inability to work as a personal, moral failing.

Can Governments Solve Poverty?

The flip side of the premise that poverty is the result of such moral failings is that government actions cannot solve poverty. Yet our own national experience points to the opposite conclusion. For generations, many of the elderly lived in extreme poverty because they were no longer able to work. But the creation of the Social Security system has sharply reduced poverty among seniors by recognizing that most people need government assistance as they age. Yet, rather than celebrating the compassion reflected in this program . . . [proposed] destructive changes in Social Security will make it less effective in preventing poverty among this group. And instead of recognizing that most young families also need assistance to survive and thrive, our major antipoverty program, the EITC, leaves out all those families who find themselves squeezed out of the labor market.

Looking abroad also shows that government policies can dramatically reduce poverty levels. The probability of living in poverty is more than twice as high for a child born in the United States than for children in Belgium, Germany, or the Netherlands. Children in single-mother households are four times more likely to be poor in the United States than in Norway. The fact that single-parent households are more common in the United States than in many of these countries where the poor receive greater assistance undermines the claim that more generous policies will encourage more single women to have children out of wedlock. These other countries all take a more comprehensive government approach to combating poverty, and they assume that it is caused by economic and structural factors rather than bad behavior.

Understanding the Compassion Gap: A Misguided Focus on Moral Poverty

The miserliness of our public assistance is justified by the claim that poverty is the consequence of personal moral failings. Most of our policies incorrectly assume that people can avoid or overcome poverty through hard work alone. Yet this assumption ignores the realities of our failing urban schools, increasing employment insecurities, and the lack of affordable housing, health care, and child care. It ignores the fact that the American Dream is rapidly becoming unattainable for an increasing number of Americans, whether employed or not.

The preoccupation with the moral failings of the poor disregards the structural problems underlying poverty. Instead, we see increasing numbers of policies that are obsessed with preventing "welfare fraud." This obsession creates barriers to help for those who need it. Welfare offices have always required recipients to "prove" their eligibility. Agency employees are in effect trained to begin with the presumption of guilt; every seemingly needy face they encounter is that of a cheater until the potential client can prove the contrary. With the passage of TANF, the rules have become so complex that even welfare caseworkers do not always understand them, let alone their clients. Some of those who need help choose to forego it rather than face this humiliating eligibility process.

But this system of suspicion also produces the very welfare cheaters that we fear. Adults in poor households are caught in a web of different programs, each with its own complex set of rules and requirements, that together provide less assistance than a family needs. Recipients have no choice but to break the rules—usually by not reporting all their income. A detailed study . . . conducted by Kathryn Edin and Laura Lein, showed that most welfare mothers worked off the books or took money under the table from relatives because they could not make ends meet with only their welfare checks. Since then we have reduced benefits and added more rules, undoubtedly increasing such "cheating."

Those who lack compassion have made their own predictions come true. They begin by claiming that the poor lack moral character. They use stories of welfare cheaters to increase public concerns about people getting something for nothing. Consequently, our patchwork of poorly funded programs reaches only a fraction of the poor and gives them less than they need. Those who depend on these programs must cut corners and break rules to keep their families together. This "proves" the original proposition that the poor lack moral character, and the "discovery" is used to justify ever more stringent policies. The result is a vicious spiral of diminishing compassion and greater preoccupation with the moral failings of the poor.

The War on Bad Behavior

The moral focus on poverty shifts our gaze from the social forces that create material poverty to the perceived moral failings of the poor. This shift has led to a war on bad behavior, exemplified by PRWORA, that is not achieving its goals. This war focuses on social problems like teenage pregnancy, high drop-out rates, and drug addiction. But research shows that it has been ineffective. Poverty has risen, and punitive measures have had little effect on the behaviors they were supposed to change.

The reduction of teen pregnancy through abstinence-only sex education was one of the main goals of the Personal Responsibility and Work Opportunity Act. Its drafters mistakenly believed that teen pregnancy is one of the root causes of poverty. In fact, if the teenagers who are having children were to wait until they were adults, their children would be just as likely to be born into poverty. But the drafters' other error was ignoring the fact that teen pregnancy rates had already been declining for years when the new law went into effect, primarily because teenagers were using more effective methods of birth-control. (These gains are now threatened by the dramatic expansion of "abstinence-only sex education," which provides no information on birth-control techniques.)

PRWORA also makes assistance to teen mothers contingent on "good behavior." Teen mothers must stay in school or be enrolled in a training program and live with their parents or under other adult supervision in order to receive aid. While it makes sense to help teens stay in school and learn skills, these coercive efforts are failing the children of teen parents. Teen mothers are just as likely today to drop out of school or live on their own as when the act was passed. The only change is that they are now much less likely to receive government assistance: ill-conceived reforms have ensured that children born to teen mothers experience deeper deprivation.

Neither have PRWORA's efforts to control the behavior of the poor had much impact on illicit drug use. Under TANF, states were required to deny benefits to anyone convicted of a drug crime. This was so obviously counterproductive that Congress amended the law in 1999 to allow states to opt out of this ban. Yet neither policy shift appears to have had much impact. According to Justice Department data, adult drug arrests have been increasing relentlessly, from 1 million per year in the early 1990s to 1.5 million in 2003.

But advocates of the war on bad behavior always have a convenient scapegoat for the failure of their punitive policies: they simply shift the blame to single mothers. TANF requires single mothers to work outside the home regardless of whether work gets them out of poverty. But long hours of work and inadequate child care mean that children are often left with inadequate supervision. When these children get into trouble, the mother gets the blame. Teen pregnancy, drug use, and delinquency are then attributed to the mother's lack of parenting skills. Poor single mothers cannot win; they are failures if they stay home with their kids— providing the full-time mothering that conservatives have long advocated for middle-class children. But they are also failures if they work and leave their children unsupervised. Viewing poverty as the result of bad behavior produces the conclusion that poor single mothers are bad by definition. Since a disproportionate number of these poor single mothers are African American or Hispanic, this rhetoric also hides the racial history that has excluded people of color from opportunities for generations and the systemic racism that persists today.

This war on bad behavior is a deeply mistaken approach to poverty. It ignores the lived reality of people who face crushing poverty every day. It ignores the fundamental wisdom that we should not judge people until we have walked a mile in their shoes. Most basically, it denies compassion to those who need it most.

What to Do?
Revitalize the American Dream

Reversing the compassion gap will not happen overnight. We have to persuade our fellow citizens that the war on bad behavior violates our society's fundamental values. We have to show them how far reality has departed from the American Dream, which holds that a child born in poverty in a ghetto or a barrio has the same chance for success and happiness as a child born in suburban affluence. We have to focus national debate on what policy measures would revitalize the American Dream for all of our citizens.

The reason the American Dream is now beyond reach for so many families is that the price of four critical services has risen much more sharply than wages and the rate of inflation: health care, higher education, high-quality child care, and housing. These are not luxuries, but indispensable ingredients of the dream.

Over the last three decades, our society has relied largely on market solutions to organize delivery of these indispensable services, but these solutions have not increased their supply. Instead, we use the price mechanism to ration their distribution; poor and working-class people are at the end of the line, and they find themselves priced out of the market.

We need new initiatives to expand the supply of these key services while assuring their quality. This requires accelerated movement toward universal health insurance and universal availability of quality childcare and preschool programs. We need to move toward universal access to higher education for all students who meet the admissions criteria. (We also need to ensure that all our public schools are preparing students for the higher education and training that most will need in order to succeed in the labor market.) And we need to create new public–private partnerships to expand the supply of affordable housing for poor and working-class families. These efforts would restore the American Dream for millions of working-class and lower middle-class families, while also putting the dream within the reach of the poor.

But we also need new policies that target the poor more directly. This requires restoring the value of the minimum wage. Between 1968 and 2002, the purchasing power of the federal minimum wage fell by a third. We need to reverse this trend and assure that in the future the minimum wage continues to rise with inflation. Most fundamentally, we must do what most other developed nations do—provide a stable income floor for all poor families so that no children grow up in horrible and degrading poverty. We could establish such a floor by transforming our present Earned Income Tax Credit into a program that provided all poor families with sufficient income to cover food and shelter. Households would be eligible for a monthly payment even if they had no earnings. Since such payments would target the poorest individuals and families, this would be a cost-effective way to immediately rescue millions of people from catastrophic poverty. Moreover, since payments would be coordinated through the tax system, a

household's income would definitely improve as its labor-force earnings rose.

The key to making these policy initiatives feasible is to remind our fellow citizens what true compassion requires. The war on bad behavior offers us an easy way out. It is easy to believe that those in poverty are responsible for their own problems and that ignoring their needs is the best thing for them. It absolves those of us who are better off from the responsibility of caring for others. However, if we want to live up to our national commitment to compassion, we need to recognize that we have a collective responsibility to ensure that in the wealthiest nation in the world there are not millions of people going hungry, millions without health insurance, and hundreds of thousands without homes. Sure, some of those in poverty have made bad choices, but who has not? It is deeply unfair that those who are not poor get second chances, while the poor do not. Rush Limbaugh pays no price for becoming addicted to painkillers, but millions of poor people go to jail and lose access to public housing and welfare benefits for the same offense.

True compassion requires that we build a society in which every person has a first chance, a second chance, and, if needed, a third and fourth chance, to achieve the American Dream. We are our brother's and our sister's keepers, and we need to use every instrument we have— faith groups, unions, community groups, and most of all government programs—to address the structural problems that reproduce poverty in our affluent society.

…A compassionate reauthorization of TANF requires four basic steps. First, we must increase assistance levels to rescue families from the deepest poverty and give them enough income to put them over the poverty line. Second, we must abandon the whole system of mandatory time limits on aid, so that families in poverty no longer find the doors to help closed in their faces. Eliminating time limits is particularly important in ensuring that programs serve the many poor women who are victims of domestic abuse. While TANF is supposed to protect such women, too often they are being forced back into the arms of their abusers. Third, we must recognize basic and postsecondary education and training as a "work activity," so that recipients can prepare for jobs that would get them out of poverty. Finally, we need to improve the child-care provisions in TANF. We must do more than provide child-care subsidies to only

one out of seven children who are federally eligible. Moreover, we must ensure that TANF children get a head start and are not relegated to the lowest-quality childcare.

By themselves, these reforms would not close the compassion gap, but they would mark an end to the futile and destructive war on bad behavior. They could represent an initial down payment on restoring the American Dream.

 ## "I Wish I Could Eat That Well": Misconceptions and Resentment about Food Stamps

Arthur Delaney

Janina Riley noticed a woman muttering behind her in the checkout line as she paid for food at a Giant Eagle grocery store in Pittsburgh last April. "I can't believe she's buying that big-ass cake with food stamps," the woman said, according to Riley. Riley, 19, had just used a government-issued debit card to pay for most of her groceries, which included a cake for her son that said "Happy First Birthday Xavier" in a theme from the movie "Cars." She glared at the women for a second, then decided to confront her. "I was just like, 'Shut . . . up,'" Riley said. "You don't know what I'm doing with these food stamps."

But many Americans do not want to let people on food stamps eat cake. This sentiment is particularly prevalent among conservatives in Congress. Cash register resentment of the sort directed at Riley feeds . . . animus toward the Supplemental Nutrition Assistance Program [SNAP]. . . . As SNAP enrollment has surged to nearly 50 million in the wake of the Great Recession, the program's annual cost has more than doubled to $80 billion. Republicans want to shrink those numbers, but they missed their best chance in June [2013], when a trillion-dollar farm bill failed in the House of Representatives, after the GOP sought deeper cuts than Democrats would accept. Following the vote, Rep.

Louie Gohmert (R-Texas) got to work telling a familiar story, one he said he'd heard many times from broken-hearted and angry constituents. Its protagonist is a hardworking Texan waiting in line at the grocery store. Someone's buying Alaskan king crab legs in front of him, and he's looking at them longingly, dreaming of the day he can afford such a luxury. Then the person buying them whips out his EBT—an Electronic Benefits Transfer card for food stamps. "He looks at the king crab legs and looks at his ground meat and realizes," Gohmert said, "because he does pay income tax . . . he is actually helping pay for the king crab legs when he can't pay for them for himself." And that's how cash register resentment becomes . . . the belief that your own struggles are tangled up in another person's safety net.

RIB-EYE STEAKS AND WINE

Janina Riley said the situation at Giant Eagle didn't escalate after she confronted the mumbling woman. She figured it wouldn't have started at all if the person had known that she was studying to become a nurse, and that she already worked more than 30 hours a week as an aide in a nursing home.

People have to be poor in order to receive nutrition assistance. The maximum gross monthly income for SNAP eligibility in Pennsylvania, for instance, is $2,018 for a household of two, and the family can't own assets worth more than $5,500 (though there are several exceptions, like a single car). Most recipients qualify based on their participation in another means-tested program like Medicaid. At $10 per hour, Riley's wages leave her poor enough to qualify for $124 a month in food stamps. At the Giant Eagle that day, she used her full monthly benefit to pay for part of her cart full of food and roughly $80 of her own money for the rest. "Most people do work. It's just we don't make enough money, that's the problem," Riley said. "The biggest misconception is that people on food stamps sit on their butts all day."

She's part of the 30 percent of SNAP recipients who earn money by working, and the 91 percent whose annual incomes are at or below the poverty line. Most recipients are . . . children, elderly or disabled. But in the public imagination, hard-working single moms rent a room with king crab welfare queens. It's a gripe going back at least 20 years. In 1993, the *Columbus Dispatch* ran a letter to the editor lamenting a food stamp recipient buying "two bottles of wine, steak and a large bag of king crab legs." The crab complaint has recurred more than a dozen times in newspapers around the country, including this 2007 missive from a reader in the *Myrtle Beach Sun-News*: "After working a typical 12-hour shift, I had to stop by the local grocery store. Standing in line behind an oversized woman with three kids, I noticed the items going through the checkout. She had two 10-pound packs of frozen crab legs and two large packs of rib-eye steaks among a couple of vegetable items totaling up to an excess of $60."

Nutrition assistance is a federal program administered by states at the ground level. State and federal lawmakers have long sought new restrictions on what nutrition assistance can buy. Fancy food stories are often the reason. For instance, Wisconsin state Rep. Dean Kaufert (R-Neenah) cited cash register situations as his rationale for a bill restricting food stamp purchases earlier this year. "Anecdotally, we've all heard the stories about people standing in line behind the person who is buying the tenderloin, the porterhouse and they're using their

EBT card to do it, while you and I who are getting by, we're buying ground beef," Kaufert told a local radio station. "That's a small share of those folks. But also I've been at the convenience store many times—the amount of nachos and soda that's being purchased by kids with their parents' EBT card, I think it's time to say no to that."

. . . Junk food and crab legs aren't even the worst of it. "Every day we hear of reports of food stamps being used to pay for beer, cigarettes, cell phone bills, and even cars," Sen. Dan Coats (R-Ind.) said on the U.S. Senate floor in February. "That hardly needs to be mentioned because it is something we have come to understand—there is a lot of misuse of tax dollars." Elizabeth Lower-Basch, an analyst for the Center for Law and Social Policy, noted the secondhand nature of many of the anecdotes. "It's definitely a meme. You hear it a lot," Lower-Basch said. "There's a lot of a-friend-told-me-she-saw type stories. I'm not going to tell you there aren't cases of people making lousy choices, but they are far more visible in the public imagination."

"PLAIN-OUT HATEFUL"

Federal law says food stamps can't be used to buy booze, cigarettes, vitamins, or household supplies. But they can buy almost anything else at a supermarket, so long as it isn't served hot for immediate consumption. So what *do* people buy with SNAP? A government survey from the late-'90s found that meats accounted for 34.9 percent of food stamp purchases, grains 19.7 percent, fruits and veggies 19.6 percent, and dairy products 12.5 percent. Soft drinks made up 5.6 percent and sweets 2.5 percent. If the government decides to restrict purchases to "wholesome" food, it won't be easy.

"No clear standards exist for defining individual foods as 'healthy' or 'unhealthy,' and federal dietary guidance focuses on an overall dietary pattern—that is, a total diet approach—that promotes moderation and consumption of a variety of foods without singling out individual foods as 'good' or 'bad,'" the Food Research and Action Center said in a January [2013] report. "Consider the following examples: some candy bars have fewer calories from fat than a serving of cheddar cheese, and soft drinks have less fat and sodium per serving than some granola bars," the report continued. "If the focus for restrictions was foods high in fat and sodium, would candy bars and soft drinks be eligible but cheddar cheese and some granola bars ineligible?" But not even avoiding the most obvious junk food or extravagances will spare an EBT card carrier from cash register resentment.

"You can't win," Lower-Basch said. "When someone's going to think you've got too much sugar, someone else is going to think you've got too much fat. Part of the reason we don't have restrictions is you could never get everyone to agree." While Janina Riley's birthday cake irked one fellow customer, Patrick McCallister's vegetables annoyed another. McCallister said that in 2003 and 2004, he had fallen on hard times after a divorce and used nutrition assistance to feed his three kids. "Especially because my family was on food stamps, I felt like that was a taxpayer-supported program aimed at helping my children do as well as they could in life," McCallister said. "I focused on buying fresh fruits, vegetables, whole-grain bread." McCallister, now 46 and living in Stuart, Fla., had been standing at the Publix supermarket register for several minutes as the cashier sorted through his month's worth of food and his coupons when the confrontation happened.

"This woman comes up behind me," he said. "The food is all tallied up, I pull out the food stamp card, which is very difficult to disguise. In Florida at the time it was a big American flag. The woman remarked, 'I wish I could eat so well. Maybe I should go on food stamps so I could eat that well.'" McCallister, who no longer receives assistance and now works as a reporter for a local newspaper, said he explained he'd taken care to buy good food since he was using taxpayer funds. The lady seemed annoyed by both the quality and perhaps also the quantity of McCallister's food. He said he turned his back as she insulted him. "I felt disappointed in the human race," McCallister said. "I was never happy using food stamps. I don't believe anybody who's shopping with food stamps takes any kind of thrill in standing at the register and pulling out that distinguishable card. . . ."

FEELING POOR

Actual food stamp fraud is a real thing. Since Carl Clark of Staten Island, N.Y., witnessed it firsthand, he thinks of it whenever he hears about nutrition assistance. Clark, 48, said that roughly 10 years ago, he and his ex-wife would habitually take their EBT cards to willing supermarkets and have the cashier ring up $100 worth of fake purchases in exchange for $70 in cash, a payday for customer and cashier both. It's a classic example of SNAP trafficking, a type of fraud the Agriculture Department has long tracked.

. . . The government says SNAP fraud has declined dramatically. The trafficking rate is down from 4 cents per dollar of benefits in 1993 to 1 cent from 2006 to 2008, according to the department's latest data.

Buying fancy stuff with food stamps isn't fraud—it's just something that seems unfair to people who think a government safety net should afford poor people modest food only. More broadly, the idea is that the poor should *feel* poor at all times until they're not poor anymore.

Not all poor people see things that way, though. Sara Woods of Knoxville, Tenn., is not ashamed to say she once bought crab legs with food stamps. In December, she and her husband asked their six kids what they wanted for Christmas dinner. Woods said her husband's good in the kitchen, since he works as a cook in one restaurant and as a sous-chef in another. It was one of the only times he didn't have to work on Christmas Day, and he wanted to cook for his family. Their 15-year-old daughter wanted crab legs. "Everybody could pick one thing, and that was the one thing she wanted," Woods said. She didn't get any guff at the store, but she's familiar with register resentment from when she worked as a cashier in 2004 and 2005. . . .

As for why people make questionable purchases, Woods has a theory from her own experience. "When you get that money, you feel like you can breathe," she said. "I can understand why people would buy things that people think are outrageous. When it comes, you feel like I can buy whatever food I want right now. You never can buy whatever you want. My clothes are hand-me-down, furniture second-hand. The food is new and mine."

The Myth of Prosperity: Poverty among Native Americans

CHRIS MCGREAL

Poverty is often a hidden social problem, but few groups experience poverty in as isolated circumstances as the Oglala Sioux of South Dakota. McGreal profiles a troubled community plagued by a history of abandonment by American policy makers, resulting in severe poverty, unemployment, overcrowding, substance abuse, and suicide. McGreal depicts a reality of life on Pine Ridge Indian reservation that is a stark cry from the common stereotype of wealth from casinos and gambling.

Indian country begins where the serene prairie of Custer County gives way to the formidable rock spires marking out South Dakota's rugged Badlands. The road runs straight until the indistinguishable, clapboard American homesteads fade from view and the path climbs into a landscape sharpened by an eternity of wind and water. At this time of year, the temperature slides to tens of degrees below freezing and a relentless gale sets the snow dancing on the road, a whirligig of white blotting out the black of the asphalt.

The first marker that this may be a part of the United States but is also apart from it, virtually invisible to most Americans, comes as the road descends on to the plains of the Pine Ridge Indian reservation. Here, an abandoned, half wrecked mobile home, daubed with the name of a Sioux rebel who led the last armed showdown between the tribe and US authorities nearly four decades ago, stands as a monument to defiance and despair.

The signal from South Dakota's Christian radio fades as an agitated caller elaborates on her belief that God created global warming as a taste of the fires of hell awaiting humanity. After a time the reservation's own station struggles through. The tribe's president, Theresa Two Bulls, is on air lamenting the death of a schoolboy, Joshua Kills Enemy, who hanged himself the day before. His funeral will be the second of the week, coming days after a 14-year-old girl took her own life in the same way. They are not the first. Two Bulls wonders how it can be that the Oglala Sioux tribe's children are killing themselves. "We must hug our children, we must tell them we love them. A lot of these youth do not get a hug a day. They are never told that they're loved. We need to start being parents and grandparents to them," she says.

Two days later, Two Bulls declares a "suicide state of emergency" in response to the deaths of the children and a spate of attempts by others to kill themselves, such as Delia Big Boy, who was

15 when she put a rope around her neck and came close to taking her own life. "It had a lot to do with my parents and alcohol abuse and what they say to you. The things they say make you think they don't love you," says the high school student, who is now 17. "I hear the same thing from my friends. There's a sense of hopelessness on the reservation. There's just not a sense of belonging. There's not a sense of a future. There's alcoholism. The parents drink. A lot of the children drink." In declaring the state of emergency, Two Bulls says that the deaths of the children are a symptom of a wider crisis that has taken hold of generations of Oglala Sioux, and this is certainly true. More than 100 people, mostly adults, tried or succeeded in taking their own lives on Pine Ridge reservation last year.

"This is about how defeated our people feel. There's hopelessness out there," Two Bulls tells me later. "People across the United States don't [realize] we could be identified as the third world. Our living conditions, what we have to live with, what we have to make do with. People think we are living high off the hog on welfare and casinos. I've asked them—US congressional people, US secretaries of these departments who deal with us—come out to our reservation, see firsthand how we live, why we live that way. Find out why our children are killing themselves. Learn who we are."

Pine Ridge is among the US's largest Indian reservations—much smaller than the vast plains of the [Midwest] that the Sioux once roamed . . . and also among its poorest. No one is sure how many people live on its 2.2 [million] acres, but the tribe estimates about 45,000. Conditions on the reservation are tough. More than 80% unemployment. A desperate shortage of housing—on average, more than 15 people live in each home and others get by in cars and trailers. More than one third of homes lacking running water or electricity. An infant mortality rate at three times the US national average. And a dependency on alcohol and a diet so poor that half the population over the age of 40 is diabetic.

The Oglala Sioux's per capita income is around $7,000 . . . a year, less than one sixth of

the national average and on a par with Bulgaria. The residents of Wounded Knee, scene of the notorious 1890 massacre of Sioux women and children and of the 1973 standoff with the FBI, are typically living on less than half of that. Young people have almost no hope of work unless they sign up to fight in Afghanistan. The few with jobs are almost all employed by the tribal authorities or the federal government. It is not uncommon to hear people quietly speak of the guilt they feel for having a job. Those who don't survive on pitifully small welfare [checks]. It all adds up to a life expectancy on Pine Ridge of about only 50 years.

The Myth of Prosperity

This is not how most Americans see the reservations. The Great Sioux Nation and the region it once ranged across are fixed in the popular imagination by the legends of Sitting Bull and Crazy Horse, of Custer's last stand at the Battle of Little Bighorn, and Wounded Knee. It's a history the Oglala Sioux constantly assert to remind themselves of past greatness and what they believe they are owed.

But the modern perception among many Americans is also of tribes growing rich on casinos and Native Americans living well from treaties that require the US government to provide [subsidized] housing, free healthcare and regular welfare [checks].

Close to a million people live on the US's 310 Native American reservations (exact figures are hard to pin down because the census is considered widely inaccurate on many of them). Some tribes have done well from a boom in casinos on the reservations, such as the Seminoles in Florida who made enough money from high-stakes bingo to pay close to $1 [billion] to buy the Hard Rock Cafe and hotel empire. Other tribes have made a more modest but comfortable income from gambling, but the key for almost all of them was to be close enough to major cities to keep the slot machines busy and the card tables full. Others pull in an income from tourism and minerals. Affirmative action [programs] have opened university doors and jobs in the cities to the Navajo, Cherokee and other tribes. But the leaders of many of the country's 564 [recognized] tribes speak of communities in crisis. . . .

The Sioux's treaties with the US government in the second half of the 19th century were similar to those of other tribes in that they were frequently broken as an expanding America sought more land for railways, mining and farming, and battered Native Americans into ceding ever more territory in return for promises of financial support. Defeated and dispossessed, the Sioux signed treaties that committed Washington to providing housing, education and health care. But the tribe's leaders today view the treaties as a trap—promising much but providing just enough to create a culture of dependency and despair. "The government wanted us to feel defeated and we played right in to their hands," says Two Bulls. "We were taught to feel defeated. Look how they brought welfare and our people lived on welfare and some of our people don't even know how to work. They're used to just staying at home all day, watching TV and drinking and taking drugs. That's the state the government wanted us to be in and we're in it."

Poverty and Overcrowding

It is a state Adelle Brown Bull has spent her life resisting, not always with success. The 69-year-old great-grandmother is still in the same tribal-owned house she raised her eight children in, and some of them never moved out. Today the [two bedroom] home is stuffed with grandchildren and great-grandchildren. She sits at her kitchen table, the green wall behind her dotted with photographs of the generations of babies. Some of the pictures are so old they are in black and white.

Among those living with Brown Bull are a daughter and her three children who are all in their 20s. Two of the granddaughters have several children of their own, one of them a baby. There's another grandchild, nine year old Michael, who Brown Bull is raising after his mother in effect abandoned him when he was 10

months old. The numbers fluctuate but there is anywhere between eight and 15 people sleeping in the house at any one time. None of the occupants has a job. Brown Bull gets a pension of $538 . . . a month, plus $323 . . . for caring for Michael. The other mothers in the house get welfare [checks] of a few hundred dollars a month. "We just manage," Brown Bull says, laughing.

The house shows its age and the wear and tear of so many residents. The tribal housing authority has just replaced the window frames because they were letting so much wind in. But it is almost impossible to heat the house, a common problem on the reservation where residents typically nail plastic over the outside of their windows in the winter as insulation. Brown Bull's house was built in the wake of President John F. Kennedy's pledge to include Native American reservations in the US public housing [program]. That led to a boom in construction through the 60s and 70s, when many of Pine Ridge's homes were put up. But in the 80s, Ronald Reagan shifted public housing policy dramatically away from new construction.

These days, Pine Ridge relies on a $10 [million] a year housing grant from Congress that is only enough to pay for the most basic maintenance—such as combating the poisonous black [mold] that infects many of the houses—and the construction of about 40 new homes each year. Which is far from enough. . . . Last year, the federal government offered to fulfill part of its treaty obligations by selling the tribe old houses from an Air Force base, no longer considered fit for service personnel, at a dollar each. The Pine Ridge authorities agreed but when the houses arrived they were charged $25,000 for the removal costs of each one—and then discovered the buildings were badly battered, with walls torn off and windows smashed in. The houses sit in a yard to this day, giving the impression of having been torn up by their roots.

Two Bulls regards overcrowded, bad housing as an important part of the explanation for the loss of self-worth. Brown Bull sees it in her own family. Among the baby pictures on the wall are photographs of two grandchildren serving in the military. "That one's signed on for a few more years," says Brown Bull, pointing to a young woman in a smart Army uniform. "She's in Afghanistan now. She says she might as well stay in the military because there's nothing for her here. No job. The only place she can live is with me. I have another grandson in the army in Afghanistan. He says the same thing."

Most of this goes unnoticed in the rest of America. "Some of them still think we live in teepees," says Alison Yellow Hair, a former shipyard worker wrapped up in a thick coat inside her freezing caravan. "Since we own the land they think we're rich and we shouldn't have to be working. We should be living high off the hog. I got a lot of that down there at the shipyards. You're Indian, aren't you? Yeah. Don't you get a [check] every week? Jeez, if I got a [check] every week I wouldn't be down here busting my ass for a [paycheck] or trying to keep up with my health insurance payments."

Now she is back in Pine Ridge, Yellow Hair and her husband, Walter, do get a [check] from the tribe's general assistance fund—$117 . . . between them each week. They live in a small caravan cocooned behind a pile of cardboard boxes and plastic trunks stuffed with clothes and furniture that cannot fit in to the cramped home, plastic sheeting protecting it all against the snow. Inside, there is little more than a few cooking utensils, a tiny heater that stays off most of the time and a large pile of blankets and duvets that they wrap themselves in to keep warm after the sun goes down and the temperature sinks to . . . –30F with the wind chill. . . .

There are jobs to be had but they are mostly working for the tribe in one form or another. One of the largest employers is the tribal-owned Prairie Wind Casino alongside the road between Pine Ridge town and the huge tourist draw of Mount Rushmore. The casino was built in an attempt to replicate the small fortunes made by other tribes but it is a sad affair, too isolated to make real money. On a cold winter night there is

no one at the card tables and most of those playing the slots come from the reservation.

The Curse of Alcohol

The streets of Pine Ridge, the town that carries the same name as the reservation, are dead at night. Aside from a Pizza Hut and a recently opened Subway sandwich bar, there is not much open as dusk falls. What street life there is occurs in Whiteclay, a few steps across the reservation's border with [neighboring] Nebraska. Whiteclay has a couple of dozen registered residents but no school, church or community [center]. There's only one street, the main road due south. And there is only one type of business along the [approximately 50 yards] that makes up the town: alcohol.

A bar and three liquor stores, all rotting, dilapidated buildings, sell more than 4 [million] cans and bottles of cheap beer and rough, powerful malt liquor each year. Almost all of it is to people from Pine Ridge, where alcohol has long been banned.

. . . Heading back across the state border, a large round sign greets arrivals: "Alcohol is not allowed on the Pine Ridge Indian Reservation." Possession is an arrestable office, as is intoxication. But the Pine Ridge police captain, Ron Duke, concedes the law has done little to deter the problem. "At one point we thought about putting up a border there, making people stop at that border to check 'em. But we have all these outlying roads and trails that people use and we'd probably be defeating our own purpose. We don't want to be like the Mexican border where we have to put a fence up all around," he says.

Duke is bitter at what he sees as the cynicism of the storeowners. "See how rundown that place is? But the people who own those bars are millionaires. We made them millionaires, the people here. Yet they treat us that way," he says. "I've been in law enforcement for 25 years. People I used to take to jail, their kids and now their grandkids, I'm dealing with them. I'd say a majority of the problems we're having right now, 90% of it is because of alcohol. We don't really have an economy where people have the opportunity to get a job. People have to live off a welfare grant or whatever's available for them. That really makes it tough on our people. Then they turn to alcohol, they turn to violence." . . . In theory, possession of alcohol is severely punished. The law allows prison sentences of six months to a year for keeping or selling beer. But it's more common for those arrested to be held overnight and fined $25 court costs—a fraction of the money they make from selling beer.

That might be about to change. Like much of the rest of America, the Oglala Sioux have decided that the way to deal with crime is to spend scarce resources on bigger prisons. The reservation authorities have built a new 280-cell jail to replace the old prison that crammed up to 200 inmates in to 25 cells. It's likely that many of the young will end up there. Rampant alcoholism has created a raft of problems, but none more serious than the alienation of the tribe's young people. Hundreds have retreated [into] gangs [modeled] on the black and Latino ones of Los Angeles and Chicago. . . .

Others, of course, find release by taking their own lives. Delia Big Boy only survived because she was discovered in time. "They found me and I got sent to the hospital," she says, her voice breaking. "When I did that, my Auntie, she came and talked to me and she invited me in to her home. I've been living with her since. That changed a lot." These days Big Boy counsels other young people as part of the Sweetgrass network, that encourages children in despair to call or send text messages. "I get calls all the time from friends and others. Usually it's because of the way their parents treat them. They don't feel loved. Our parents are not always good parents on this reservation," she says. "I tell them to focus on their big dreams about college and the military. I want to go to university to study chemistry."

Rash of Suicides

The 14 year old girl, Mariah Montileaux, who was buried—in her traditional dance dress—just days before 16-year-old Joshua Kills Enemy, had made no secret of her plans to kill herself. "The mother knew this girl was attempting to commit suicide," says Duke. "Everybody knew yet nobody knew what to do with her, how to help her. Whether or not anybody could have helped her, that's what she wanted to do. She made it known: I'm going to kill myself."

After Kills Enemy's death, the Pine Ridge high school principal, Robert Cook, surveyed students and concluded that one in five of the 370 pupils were at risk. Nine were immediately taken to the Indian Health Service because of what Cook described as "impending suicide." . . . In fact, Native Americans teenagers are more likely to kill themselves than any other minority group. Some statistics show the rate at three times the national average. But those figures shield the fact that self-harm is most likely to occur on poorer reservations, such as Pine Ridge and [neighboring] Rosebud; here rates are far higher.

The tribal government is attempting to entice businesses to the reservation, including a wind farm. . . . But Two Bulls and other Oglala Sioux leaders know that it will take the kind of money that only the federal government can provide to begin to turn the situation around. . . . Iron Cloud, the former reservation president, says . . . "what I feel is kinda like a light at the end of the tunnel where the Obama administration is looking at some new beginnings for the minorities and the poor people to have some jobs and give more money to education. Just taking care of our people in a better way than they have been. . . . If we can get enough of our tribal leaders—and I'm talking 500 tribes coming together and flooding the halls of Congress—and just say to them that it's time to take a good look at Indian tribes. We were the first Americans—and I know it'd have an impact."

Racial and Ethnic Inequality

Allegra Phox

Allegra Phox is the Campaigns Organizer for Million Hoodies Movement for Justice.

Your organization was founded relatively recently. What spurred the founding of the organization? What is its current mission?

Million Hoodies Movement for Justice was founded three years ago, in response to the murder of Trayvon Martin. Trayvon was a black teenager, a high school junior, who was unarmed and wearing a hoodie when he was fatally shot by a neighborhood watch volunteer, George Zimmerman, who had decided Martin looked suspicious. The Movement grew from the events leading up to and after his death, such as the failure by the mainstream media to accurately portray the story, and George Zimmerman's continuing freedom today[1].

We aim to empower young people of color and protect them from mass criminalization and gun violence, both by transforming the public narrative on criminalization within communities of color and by providing the necessary tools for communities to organize and protect themselves. In the past we have campaigned for George Zimmerman's arrest by collecting over two million signatures on a Change.org petition, fought to strike down the "Hoodie Ban Bill" in Oklahoma, and kicked off the national Demilitarize Police campaign.

As Campaigns Organizer, what do you do? What are your duties? What campaigns are you currently organizing?

At Million Hoodies the majority of our members are college students concentrated in various campus chapters around the country, as well as other activists interested in a variety of issues. We have a small main staff that coordinate the different groups and bring our members together in national action. As campaign organizer, I work in several different capacities, often

---

1 Editor's Note: In July 2013, George Zimmerman was found not guilty on charges of second-degree murder and manslaughter in the death of Trayvon Martin (Alvarez, Lizette and Cara Buckley. 2013. "Zimmerman Is Acquitted in Trayvon Martin Killing." *The New York Times*. Accessed from http://www.nytimes.com/2013/07/14/us/george-zimmerman-verdict-trayvon-martin.html).

with other members of Million Hoodies chapters to help support our national campaigns, putting pressure on campuses, local government, and fellow students to support relevant petitions, laws, and policies. One issue that many chapters are currently focusing on as part of our Campaign to Demilitarize Police is striking down the 1033 Program, a Pentagon program that provides military equipment at low cost to civilian police forces. Through this program even university police have gained access to modified grenade launchers, mine-resistant ambush protected armored vehicles, night-vision rifle scopes, and M-16 automatic rifles. I am also in the process of helping put together a chapter toolkit that will serve as a comprehensive source of information for those interested in getting involved with our work.

How did you first become interested in this type of activism? What/who was your inspiration?

I'm from Oakland, California, a traditionally black and socially aware city, and I grew up around activism of all different forms. I went to very diverse and progressive schools all my life; even in elementary school, my friends' parents were activists, artists and entrepreneurs. My first memory of traditional activism was in about 2008, when I was in fourth grade. Friends and I protested against Proposition 8 (a ballot proposition created by opponents of same-sex marriage, that sought to amend the California constitution to state that "only marriage between a man and a woman is valid or recognized in California"), holding signs on street corners, and asking pedestrians to sign our petition. Growing up with openly gay and lesbian, gender non-conforming, and non-gender binary friends, teachers, and couples around me, protesting Prop 8 was a no-brainer.

My parents were also heavily influential. As college educated black professionals they always encouraged me to read as much as possible and to interact with people from all walks of life. Growing up around their diverse group of friends definitely shaped me much more than I realized. I take a lot of pride in my family; my paternal grandfather was actually born on a plantation in Virginia, yet ended up in the movie business, working as a gaffer on movies like the original *Great Gatsby* and *Jaws*.

Because I was so immersed in social justice issues from such a young age, both in school and at home, and living in such an amazingly diverse area, I don't think I realized the extent of racism until I got to college. That realization has fueled a lot of my interest in activism, specifically in issues faced by the black community.

As an activist in your organization, currently what are your top three goals?

Personally, I aim to make activism more accessible to those who might not normally be involved. In many cases, the members of the population being exploited, taken advantage of, or mistreated by the government are not involved in their own empowerment, something that contributes to the savior complex commonly attributed to activists (particularly white activists). It's important that members of the community have a say in laws and social issues that affect them.

As an organization, we have several long-term goals, including protecting young people from state-sanctioned and vigilante violence, and empowering people with the tools and resources necessary to create transformational change in our communities (for example, we are developing an interactive online tool that can be used to gather and document relevant community stories for use both as a data source and as a way to uplift the stories of those most heavily impacted).

What strategies do you use to enact social change?

We tend to use three organizational strategies to help us accomplish our goals: we employ strategic communications (involving media and press relations, public awareness campaigns, national policy advocacy, and leadership training), grassroots organizing (such as our Action Network, campus chapters, and campaigns), and creative technology (such as our blog, toolkit, and the mapping project we have in the works).

What are the major challenges activists in your field face?

One of the biggest challenges faced by any activist is fatigue, or burning out. As an activist, change often comes in fits and starts, or slowly over years, and it can be really exhausting to be aware of all the injustice occurring in the world, and feel that you are powerless to make real and lasting change. That's why it is important to connect to other activists, and participate in issues outside of your immediate organization. Doing this allows you to gain strength from others and to get reinvigorated about doing your work. Everyone at Million Hoodies makes a point of attending other conferences, protests, and training sessions that are not directly related to our work; several activists with Million Hoodies recently attended the AFL-CIO's Next Up Labor Conference in Chicago, which was a joint convention with labor unions, activists for immigration reform, LGBTQ activists and black community organizers. Attending events like this allows us to see activism from a variety of different angles, as well as forge connections with those doing similar work.

It's also important to know when to take a step back from activism. Many, if not most of us, do this work in addition to other responsibilities like school, work, family, and more. At Million Hoodies, because many of us are students, we make sure to mark off weeks where we have finals or midterms as weeks that we will not be available to work, as well as setting aside personal time for ourselves.

What are major misconceptions the public has about activism in general and your issue specifically?

Particularly for those of us fighting police brutality and state violence, there is still a misconception that the state is there specifically to protect us, and that police and the criminal justice system are inherently just. A black person,

or an undocumented person, or a trans[gender] person may have had personal experiences that demonstrate that may be untrue, but for many white, middle class Americans who have not had negative experiences with law enforcement, it can be hard for them to see why their experiences are not universal. Getting people who have privilege to listen to and accept these experiences can be a major challenge.

A related misconception, particularly when discussing the large numbers of unarmed black men and women who have lost their lives to police violence, is the narrative that "if they weren't criminals, or doing anything wrong, they wouldn't have gotten shot," despite the fact that in some cases, there are videos showing otherwise. This is particularly harmful considering that this logic is not applied to armed white criminals who are taken into custody alive and given fair trials. It also assumes that the police or law enforcement acted correctly and the victim was in the wrong, which is often not the case. Getting past this bias is a challenge, but we believe every person is entitled to fair treatment at all levels of the criminal justice system.

Finally, another challenge is getting people to understand the importance of activism in general. Activism is often seen as unnecessary in a democratic society, but it is, in fact, essential to keeping our society a democratic one. The first amendment, which protects our right to free speech and freedom of the press, also demonstrates that it is our responsibility as citizens to keep our government accountable to the people, which is what many activists aim to accomplish. Being an activist doesn't necessarily mean you are interested in overthrowing the government, or even enacting radical change; it can just mean that you see something wrong or inefficient in our current government and you are fighting to right the wrong, or improve a policy.

Why should students get involved in your line of activism?

For black and brown students, I believe that getting involved is essential, because it's something that directly affects you. Mass criminalization is an epidemic, one that tears families apart, and that is disproportionately carried out in black and brown communities. The same can be said for police violence. For other students who may not be directly impacted, I believe involvement is equally important, because (I'm assuming) this is not how you believe your government and law enforcement agencies should operate.

If an individual has little money and time, are there other ways they can contribute?

I would highly encourage anyone interested to sign up for our campaign at www.mhoodies.org where they can receive a copy of our brand new toolkit, sign our petitions, and check to see if there is a local campus chapter near them (or to start one at their school). It's essential that our petitions get as many signatures as possible to show members of our government that the issues we raise affect people, and that we are demanding change and accountability. If you'd like to get more involved, attend a protest, community talk, conference, or event relevant to your issue. Not only will you meet other people that are more informed than you, you may witness first hand the mistreatment of peaceful protestors by police.

What ways can students enact social change in their daily lives?

Signing and sharing petitions is a great way to get started; it often doesn't feel like much, but it can make a huge difference, helping us get noticed by members of the government at the federal, state, and local levels. Another good first step is educating yourself on whatever topic interests you; as you become more educated, and more aware, you will more likely be able to educate others if the topic arises. If you are interested in learning more, downloading toolkits, reading articles, and signing up for newsletters can all be great first steps.

Previous generations have made a myriad of mistakes that are not necessarily our problem, but are up to us to fix. As students we have the opportunity to make our voices heard in a variety of issues, and the younger we get involved, the more change we can make. Also keep in mind that everything is connected; if you decide to participate in another form of activism, chances are it will improve life for everyone, not just those that immediately come to mind. Getting involved in environmental issues, animal rights, LGBTQ rights, can be equally rewarding and necessary. If everyone was involved in an issue they are passionate about, imagine how much positive change we could create as a generation!

Sociologists on the Colorblind Question

ELAINE MCARDLE

Americans often argue that they are "colorblind" and that racial discrimination against minority groups is a thing of the past, making America a true meritocracy. But sociological research has shown that discrimination does still exist—it is just hidden and less obvious than discrimination of the past. So why does the colorblind ideology still exist? McArdle discusses the origins and uses of the term and describes how it has been used by those arguing for policies that combat discrimination as well as by those who oppose such policies.

Each May, the city of Myrtle Beach, South Carolina, hosts two separate week-long motorcycle festivals, one at the start of the month, the other around Memorial Day. In most ways the festivals are identical: each attracts more than 200,000 bikers from around the country who gun their cycles down the city's main thoroughfare, proudly displaying their hardware to other cycle enthusiasts and admiring crowds. But there's one striking difference between the events: the bikers who flock to Myrtle Beach for Harley Week are white, those who come for Black Bike Week during Memorial Day are black.

For Georgia State University sociologist Charles A. "Chip" Gallagher, the twin festivals provided a rare and valuable real-life laboratory for examining racial disparities in modern American society. "For sociologists, it was a perfect natural experiment, which we don't get that often," says Gallagher. "It was, quite literally, two populations that are quite similar coming

into the same venue at almost the same time. We can look at the treatment of these two groups, see if it varies, and, if so, why."

Essentially, it provided the opportunity to test whether Myrtle Beach was as colorblind as it claimed to be. That is, whether it treated the bikers as individuals rather than members of the racial groups to which they belonged. The experiment was timely, as sociologists today are increasingly questioning the colorblind ideology and what effects it has on American culture and law. Their interest is due in no small part to the fact that colorblindness is used to support two very different social agendas that are in direct conflict. And there is no arena in which the struggle over the meaning of colorblindness is more consequential than in the nation's courts, where the fate of affirmative action programs and other racially based initiatives hang in the balance. The very different treatment each group received from Myrtle Beach and some

Elaine McArdle, *Contexts* (Volume 7 and Issue 1), pp. 35–37, Copyright © 2008. Reprinted by Permission of SAGE Publications.

local businesses wasn't difficult to measure. Gallagher's challenge was to demonstrate why it happened.

Myrtle Beach, which is about 85 percent white, is heavily dependent on tourism. Harley Week has been held each year since 1940. All week long, white bikers cruise up and down Pacific Boulevard and are enthusiastically embraced with welcome signs, special merchandising, and other displays of appreciation for the tourist dollars that flow in. But during Black Bike Week, the city shut down one lane of traffic on Pacific Boulevard, forcing bikers to wait in queue for their turn to cruise and causing long traffic jams. Myrtle Beach tripled the number of police on duty, ticketed bikers for minor infractions, and even (unsuccessfully) petitioned the governor to send in the National Guard. In contrast to the welcome mat laid out to white bikers by local businesses, 25 restaurants closed their doors over Memorial Day weekend.

In 2003, the National Association for the Advancement of Colored People (NAACP) sued the city of Myrtle Beach and the 25 restaurants, claiming they violated the civil rights of black bikers by treating them differently because of their race. When two prominent law firms in Washington, D.C., asked for his help as an expert witness in the case, Gallagher warned them what the defendants would claim: that their divergent treatment of the two groups was due to a variety of factors, but race wasn't among them.

Just as Gallagher predicted, the city claimed age differences and increased criminal activity, not race, were the reasons for ramped-up police numbers during Black Bike Week. It alleged the black bikers were younger, and younger men tend to be involved more in criminal activity. But this allegation weakened when the NAACP showed the average age of the black bikers was 34 versus 39 for the whites. Criminal activity peaks in men at age 18 and drops dramatically by age 30, so both groups of bikers had aged out of their peak years for misconduct.

The city also claimed more police were needed because the number of bikers was much higher during Black Bike Week. But it had no hard numbers to back this up, and Gallagher testified that research shows whites consistently overestimate the size of black populations by a factor of two to three times. Moreover, the NAACP claimed, the increase in criminal and traffic citations issued during Black Bike Week was the result of the extra police officers on duty, not excessive criminal activity by blacks. As for more traffic problems during Black Bike Week, this was a direct result of the city's own traffic restrictions, which caused traffic jams that didn't happen during Harley Week, the NAACP argued.

With each of the other factors debunked, the only difference between the two groups was race. "In effect, we were able to control for all the other variables typically used to dismiss charges of racism," Gallagher says. . . . [In 2007], the city settled the cases, agreeing to treat both groups of bikers the same.

The cases were a victory not only for black bikers but all people of color. And they also supported Gallagher's theories about the current state of race relations and attitudes in the United States. According to national polling, the vast majority of white Americans believe racial minorities no longer face discrimination in schools, housing, jobs, or other arenas, Gallagher notes. They believe the United States has achieved a state of colorblindness, in which a person's race has no meaning other than as a cultural symbol. "White Americans are very invested in the idea of colorblindness," says Gallagher, because it legitimizes their privileged position in society. If the United States has achieved a utopic state where people are no longer judged or disadvantaged by the color of their skin, then someone's fortunes or misfortunes are due entirely to the choices they make. If so, then life circumstances don't control one's fate, self-determination does, a notion deeply engrained in the American ethos, Gallagher notes. "The idea is, you get what you work for. Just like you can choose to be Donald Trump, you can choose to be Condoleezza Rice. And you can choose to be in a ghetto or a barrio. It's a choice, like a smorgasbord," explains Gallagher.

If whites get an advantage because of the color of their skin, then their dominant status isn't legitimate, an idea that's threatening to them. "Colorblindness lets them see the playing field as being level—because if it isn't level, it means [whites] have gotten privileges [they] didn't deserve," he says. By embracing the concept of colorblindness, "white America can truly imagine that we're a meritocracy and where you end up reflects individual hard work and bootstrapping." That's why the Myrtle Beach cases were so important, Gallagher says: despite the city's best efforts to prove it was colorblind and that the disparate treatment of blacks wasn't based on race, the facts proved otherwise.

"Advocates of colorblindness typically do not give the real reasons that they support colorblind social policies," says John Skrentny, a sociologist at the University of California, San Diego. "They will say that colorblindness is important because it preserves meritocracy and equal opportunity, but they also accept all sorts of exceptions to meritocracy—the law gives veterans preferences in civil service jobs, for example, and nepotism is legal."

In 2007 the U.S. Supreme Court struck down two school integration plans—one in Seattle, one in Louisville—that considered students' race during the admissions process in order to maintain diverse student bodies. The court based its decision on an interpretation of colorblindness that holds that racial classifications are unconstitutional except in very narrow circumstances—even when the intention is to redress racial inequities. Writing for the majority, Chief Justice John Roberts said, "The way to stop discrimination on the basis of race is to stop discriminating on the basis of race."

The school cases are the latest in a 20-year series in which the high court has relied on this new interpretation of colorblindness to dismantle programs and initiatives that assist minorities. This trend worries civil rights advocates and continues to garner the interest of social scientists. "What's most interesting about colorblindness is that it both has the ability to fight against inequality [and] can be used to fight against policies designed to reduce inequality. There aren't many ideologies that hold these opposing forces," says Brian Lowery, an associate professor of organizational behavior who studies perceptions of inequality at Stanford University.

In the school cases, both the majority and the dissent relied on *Brown v. the Board of Education*, the seminal case in the fight against racial discrimination, to support their opposing positions, with the majority relying on the notion of colorblindness to support its rejection of the school integration schemes. The majority's use of the term "colorblind" as a weapon against affirmative action is no small irony: it was coined in 1896 by Justice John Marshall Harlan to support civil rights for blacks. In his solo dissent to *Plessy v. Ferguson*, the landmark case that upheld the policy of "separate but equal" treatment for blacks and whites, Harlan—a former slave owner who became a champion of minorities—wrote, "Our Constitution is colorblind, and neither knows nor tolerates classes among citizens. In respect of civil rights, all citizens are equal before the law." Harlan's word became a rallying point for those supporting racial equality. During the civil rights movement, the term colorblind became essential to the argument that the U.S. Constitution requires all people, regardless of race, receive equal treatment, and overt racism was outlawed.

The civil rights movement focused on glaring examples of racial discrimination. But after that battle ostensibly was won, racism persisted, albeit in more subtle ways. "You still have a lot of racial inequalities but they aren't supported by overt racism. They're justified in more private or covert kinds of ways. Call it 'smiling discrimination,' where there are no names or bad words used, but practices are clear and consistent," says Eduardo Bonilla Silva, a sociologist at Duke University who studies race and ethnicity. Then, 20 years ago, an odd turn of events with enormous social and legal implications took place.

"Sometime in the 1980s, 'colorblind' was essentially hijacked by conservatives, whites and non-whites alike, and used for a very different purpose—to advocate for the rights and equal protection of white people," says Victoria Plaut, who studies models of diversity, including colorblindness, at the University of Georgia. If the U.S. Constitution requires the nation be colorblind, this argument goes, then it's illegal to use racial classifications for any purpose, even to address current instances of discrimination.

This interpretation took hold quickly. In the 1990s, the U.S. Supreme Court ruled against the use of racial classification to advance the rights of minorities in numerous cases in the areas of employment, redistricting for voting, and contracts, among others. In 2003, by a slim majority, the high court upheld the University of Michigan Law School's affirmative action program for admissions because race was only one of many factors taken into consideration. But at the same time, the court struck down the admissions scheme in the university's undergraduate program after finding it was more of a quota system where race was the primary factor. The 2007 school cases in Seattle and Louisville . . . seize[d] upon colorblindness to dismantle diversity plans. "That means on the one hand, affirmative action programs, school district plans, and other racially cognizant initiatives are illegal, but on the other, it's very difficult to prove discrimination exists because you don't have anyone owning up to it. So there's no intent to discriminate [unless you have] a smoking gun," says Bonilla Silva.

During the civil rights movement, the smoking guns for change were such things as signs that read: "No Jews, No Blacks." It was easy to use these as concrete evidence of discrimina-

tion, Bonilla Silva says. But with discrimination pushed underground today, and surfacing in far more subtle ways, it's much harder to prove. How does a person of color effectively argue to a court that he was discriminated against while shopping because clerks followed him around asking "Can I help you? Can I help you?"

The Supreme Court isn't out on an activist limb in its interpretation of the term colorblind, at least not a limb that's unpopular. Most white Americans share the same definition and believe the use of color or race for any purpose today is wrong, especially since—in their eyes— racial disparities no longer exist. At the same time, racial discrimination is thriving, as the Myrtle Beach cases and other sociologists' work demonstrate.

Devah Pager, a sociologist at Princeton University who studies race, conducted a series of classic audit studies that show just how prevalent discrimination is today. In these field experiments in 2001 and 2004, she had young men pose as job applicants at a variety of employers in Milwaukee and New York City. Their education and workplace qualifications were exactly the same, yet one set of men was white, the other black. She expected to find a disadvantage in hiring for black men, but the dramatic results surprised even her.

"The basic finding was that blacks were half as likely to get a call-back or job offer relative to an equally qualified white applicant," says Pager. But there was an even more disturbing result: Pager found black men with no criminal history fared no better than a white man just released from prison. "I expected race would be an issue but I didn't think it would rival the effect of a felony conviction," she says. Pager says that many employers believe themselves to be colorblind, looking only for the first person who is well-qualified for a job. But, especially with low-level, entry-level jobs that require few concrete skills or qualifications, employers tend to do a very cursory review of applicants. In those situations, race can unconsciously influence an employer's decision about who seems to be the best candidate. "Those are the ways in which the strength of continuing racial stereotypes undermine our conscious effort to achieve some sort of colorblindness," she says.

Sociologist Katherine Beckett of the University of Washington has studied racial disparities in the enforcement of drug laws in Seattle. She and her research colleagues have compared independent information on drug users against police arrest data and found blacks are dramatically overrepresented among arrestees. These disparities are impossible to explain by the race-neutral reasons police rely on, including that certain areas in their jurisdictions have higher crime rates or that they are merely responding to increased citizen complaints in a particular area. As Gallagher did in the Myrtle Beach cases, Beckett and her colleagues have demonstrated that these disparities are actually created by different policies and practices, including who's arrested, who's prosecuted, and even where police are patrolling. With regard to arrest rates, cities vary greatly in racial composition, geography, and the use of public space. "Some police departments are less aggressive on arrest, but the disparities are exacerbated at the prosecution or sentencing stage," she says.

"I try to assess the race-neutral explanations for racial disparities, either by looking at the literature or at what officials actually say," she continues. However, her research shows that these colorblind explanations usually fall short. And, for some crimes and in some areas of the law, as Beckett says, "it's nearly impossible to meet the evidentiary standards needed to establish discrimination." Making colorblind ideals and legal standards even more complicated, in Skrentny's view, are new values of diversity and multiculturalism. "Large institutions, including the government, universities, and corporations, want to be racially diverse. A value on diversity is overshadowing a value on colorblindness, in my view, at least in terms of what institutions promote about themselves," he says. But, "Americans don't universally value universalism, so to speak—we vary a lot in what kinds of differences we accept or find appropriate as criteria for preferences or exclusions," he continues. "We give preferences to veterans in civil service jobs and don't decry age categorizations, yet there is great controversy regarding race categorizations."

Meanwhile, the future of race in the legal arena will turn on which interpretation of colorblindness dominates. "If the idea that we can never take race into account is the one that wins, a slew of policies will go away," says Lowery. "On the other hand, if colorblindness means commitment to equality, then certain existing policies will be reinforced." [But] which will prevail?

"My guess is . . . that colorblindness as an aspiration for equality is losing ground," Lowery says. "I think right now colorblindness is a contested idea, in the sense that it's not obvious who's going to win the debate over what it means." Bonilla Silva goes even further. Colorblindness is "Martin Luther King's dream, but not our reality. . . . It's a language dream that provides an image of progress that allows Americans to think we've moved beyond race without really addressing our racial injustices and inequalities." His prediction? I'm afraid America is becoming meaner and more divided, holding on to colorblind ideas even as the situation of people of color continues to deteriorate. It'll be a schizophrenic America."

White Americans' Racial Attitudes and Their Effect on Antidiscrimination Policies in the "Age of Obama"

Amanda Atwell

Original to Focus on Social Problems: A Contemporary Reader.

The 2008 and 2012 presidential elections of Barack Obama seemed to signify that the United States was in the process of fulfilling its enduring commitment to ending white supremacy and beginning a new era of racial reconciliation. The fact that a black man could become president served to support the narrative of a postracial America, where black people can achieve the highest levels of success through their own merit and determination (Welch and Sigelman, 2011). Throughout his first presidential campaign Obama remarked that the amount of support he received was indicative that American race relations, especially between white and black Americans, had finally changed for the better. However, recent attitudinal research suggests that black and white Americans actually hold competing understandings of how contemporary racial discrimination functions in U.S. society. Considerable portions of white Americans believe that black Americans do not face a significant amount of discrimination (Norton and Sommers, 2011) and that the remnants of racial inequality in society are generated by black Americans' inherent inferiority and laziness (Tuch and Hughes, 2011). These attitudes have remained relatively stable over the past few decades.

In fact, just over forty-five years ago, Martin Luther King Jr. drew attention to the evolution of this phenomenon (referred to by Tuch and Hughes [2011] as "racial resentment" among whites) and argued that when it comes to white and black Americans, "There is not even a common language when the term 'equality' is used. Negro and white have a fundamentally different definition" (King, 1968:8). Although white Americans, when surveyed, generally support racial equality as a theoretical concept, they have been especially resistant to support the implementation of polices designed to redress centuries of racial oppression against black Americans. This discrepancy is referred to as the "principle–policy gap" (Tuch and Hughes, 2011).

Norton and Sommers (2011) demonstrate that whites now see racism as a "zero-sum" game where they associate decreases in perceived bias against black Americans as necessarily increasing bias against white Americans. It is noteworthy that black respondents did not share these perceptions. Despite an abundance of contradictory empirical evidence, white Americans now believe that they are victims of racism more often than black Americans (Norton and Sommers, 2011), which suggests that there are stark disparities between documented discrimination and white Americans' individual perceptions of race relations.

In effect, white attitudes and "racial resentment," specifically, decrease the likelihood that they will support antidiscrimination policies, such as affirmative action in education and employment. Although affirmative action was originally designed to atone for centuries of enslavement and Jim Crow laws that have historically disadvantaged black Americans, white Americans now view antidiscrimination policies as a form of "reverse racism" (Norton and Sommers, 2011). These attitudes have trickled all the way up to the Supreme Court, which has increasingly ruled affirmative action policies as injurious to white Americans' right to equal opportunity (Plaut, 2011). It should be no surprise, then, that 82.8 percent of white Americans strongly opposed or opposed hiring and promotion preferences for black Americans (Tuch and Hughes, 2011).

Plaut (2011:220) succinctly explains how white Americans' view of racism as a zero-sum game impacts public policy decisions: "We are witnessing a shift from the presumption of explicit discrimination against minorities—and the need to legally address that discrimination—to a presumption of discrimination against whites, intentionally, by the State through unfair preference schemes that advantage racial minorities." Therefore, white Americans have come to associate general, societal-wide affirmative action policies with purposeful discrimination against individual white Americans. In essence, white Americans think that substantial gains have been made toward racial equality for black Americans and that this progress has led to an inverse discrimination against white Americans, making it less likely that white Americans will support antidiscrimination policies in the future (Norton and Sommers, 2011). These issues are further complicated by the fact that the United States has elected a black man to the office of presidency, twice, although without the majority of the white vote (Harvey-Wingfield and Feagin, 2010). In the coming years, policy makers, educators, and activists will likely face nuanced challenges in creating a more equitable society.

REFERENCES

Harvey-Wingfield, Adia, and Joe Feagin. 2010. *Yes We Can? White Racial Framing and the 2008 Presidential Campaign*. New York: Routledge.

King, Martin Luther, Jr. 1968. *Where Do We Go from Here?: Chaos or Community*. New York: Harper & Row.

Norton, Michael I., and Samuel R. Sommers. 2011. "Whites See Racism as a Zero-Sum Game That They Are Now Losing." *Perspectives on Psychological Science* 6(3):215–218.

Plaut, Victoria C. 2011. "Law and the Zero-Sum Game of Discrimination: Commentary on Norton and Sommers (2011)." *Perspectives on Psychological Science* 6(3):219–221.

Tuch, Steven A., and Michael Hughes. 2011. "Whites' Racial Policy Attitudes in the Twenty-First Century: The Continuing Significance of Racial Resentment." *The Annals of the American Academy of Political and Social Science* 634(1):134–152.

Welch, Susan, and Lee Sigelman. 2011. "The 'Obama Effect' and White Racial Attitudes." *The Annals of the American Academy of Political and Social Science* 634(1):207–220.

Fences and Neighbors: Segregation in 21st-Century America

JOHN E. FARLEY AND GREGORY D. SQUIRES

Farley and Squires examine housing segregation in the United States, describing and offering several possible explanations for continued residential segregation, including groups' preferences for varied levels of racial integration in their neighborhoods and discriminatory practices by housing lenders and realtors. The authors discuss the short- and long-term consequences of residential discrimination (e.g., including the ability to accumulate wealth and access to high-quality employment and schools) and whether attempts to address racial discrimination in housing have been successful.

"Do the kids in the neighborhood play hockey or basketball?"

—Anonymous home insurance agent, 2000

America became less racially segregated during the last three decades of the 20th century, according to the 2000 census. Yet, despite this progress, despite the Fair Housing Act, signed [45] . . . years ago, and despite popular impressions to the contrary, racial minorities still routinely encounter discrimination in their efforts to rent, buy, finance, or insure a home. In 2005, the U.S. Department of Housing and Urban Development (HUD) estimate[d] that more than 2 million incidents of unlawful discrimination occur[ed] each year. Research indicates that blacks and Hispanics encounter discrimination in one out of every five contacts with a real estate or rental agent. African Americans, in particular, continue to live in segregated neighborhoods in exceptionally high numbers.

What is new is that fair-housing and community-development groups are successfully using antidiscrimination laws to mount a movement for fair and equal access to housing. Discrimination is less common than just ten years ago; minorities are moving into the suburbs, and overall levels of segregation have gone down. Yet resistance to fair housing and racial integration persists and occurs today in forms that are more subtle and harder to detect. Still, emerging coalitions using new tools are shattering many traditional barriers to equal opportunity in urban housing markets.

Segregation:
Declining but Not Disappearing

Although segregation has declined in recent years, it persists at high levels, and for some minority groups it has actually increased. Social scientists use a variety of measures to indicate how segregated two groups are from each other. The most widely used measure is the index of dissimilarity [D] ... which varies from 0 for a perfectly integrated city to 100 for total segregation. [A D of 100 would indicate that every neighborhood in the metropolitan area was either 100 percent white or 100 percent black. In real metropolitan areas, D always falls somewhere between those extremes. For example, the Chicago metropolitan area is 58 percent non-Hispanic white and 19 percent non-Hispanic black. Chicago's D was 80.8 in 2000. This means that 81 percent of the white or black population would have to move to another census tract in order to have a D of 0, or complete integration]. ... Values of D in the 60s or higher generally represent high levels of segregation.

Although African Americans have long been and continue to be the most segregated group, they are notably more likely to live in integrated neighborhoods than they were a generation ago. For the past three decades, the average level of segregation between African Americans and whites has been falling, declining by about ten points on the D scale between 1970 and 1980 and another ten between 1980 and 2000. But these figures overstate the extent to which blacks have been integrated into white or racially mixed neighborhoods. Part of the statistical trend simply has to do with how the census counts "metropolitan areas." Between 1970 and 2000, many small—and typically integrated—areas "graduated" into the metropolitan category, which helped to bring down the national statistics on segregation. More significantly, segregation has declined most rapidly in the southern and western parts of the United States, but cities in these areas, especially the West, also tend to have fewer African Americans. At the same time, in large northern areas with many

African American residents, integration has progressed slowly. For example, metropolitan areas like New York, Chicago, Detroit, Milwaukee, Newark, and Gary all had segregation scores in the 80s as late as 2000. Where African Americans are concentrated most heavily, segregation scores have declined the least. ... In places with the highest proportions of black population, segregation decreased least between 1980 and 2000. Desegregation has been slowest precisely in the places African Americans are most likely to live. There, racial isolation can be extreme. For example, in the Chicago, Detroit, and Cleveland metropolitan areas, most African Americans live in census tracts (roughly, neighborhoods) where more than 90 percent of the residents are black and fewer than 6 percent are white.

Other minority groups, notably Hispanics and Asian Americans, generally live in less segregated neighborhoods. Segregation scores for Hispanics have generally been in the low 50s over the past three decades, and for Asian Americans and Pacific Islanders, scores have been in the low 40s. Native Americans who live in urban areas also are not very segregated from whites (scores in the 30s), but two-thirds of the Native Americans who live in rural areas (about 40 percent of their total population) live on segregated reservations. Although no other minority group faces the extreme segregation in housing that African Americans do, other groups face segregation of varying levels and have not seen a significant downward trend.

Causes of Continuing Segregation

Popular explanations for segregation point to income differences and to people's preferences for living among their "own kind." These are, at best, limited explanations. Black–white segregation clearly cannot be explained by differences in income, education, or employment alone. Researchers have found that white and black households at all levels of income, education, and occupational status are nearly as segregated as are whites and blacks overall. However, this is not the case for other minority groups. Hispanics with higher incomes live in more integrated communities than Hispanics with lower incomes. Middle-class Asian Americans are more suburbanized and less segregated than middle-class African Americans. For example, as Chinese Americans became more upwardly mobile, they moved away from the Chinatowns where so many had once lived. But middle-class blacks, who have made similar gains in income and prestige, find it much more difficult to buy homes in integrated neighborhoods. For example, in 2000 in the New York metropolitan area, African Americans with incomes averaging above $60,000 lived in neighborhoods that were about 57 percent black and less than 15 percent non-Hispanic white—a difference of only about 6 percentage points from the average for low-income blacks.

Preferences, especially those of whites, provide some explanation for these patterns. Several surveys have asked whites, African Americans, and in some cases Hispanics and Asian Americans about their preferences concerning the racial mix of their neighborhoods. A common technique is to show survey respondents cards displaying sketches of houses that are colored-in to represent neighborhoods of varying degrees of integration. Interviewers then ask the respondents how willing they would be to live in the different sorts of neighborhoods. These surveys show, quite consistently, that the first choice of most African Americans is a neighborhood with about an equal mix of black and white households. The first choice of whites, on the other hand, is a neighborhood with a large white majority. Among all racial and ethnic groups, African Americans are the most disfavored "other" with regard to preferences for neighborhood racial and ethnic composition. Survey research also shows that whites are more hesitant to move into hypothetical neighborhoods with large African-American populations, even if those communities are described as having good schools, low crime rates, and other amenities. However, they

are much less hesitant about moving into areas with significant Latino, Asian, or other minority populations.

Why whites prefer homogeneous neighborhoods is the subject of some debate. According to some research, many whites automatically assume that neighborhoods with many blacks have poor schools, much crime, and few stores; these whites are not necessarily responding to the presence of blacks per se. Black neighborhoods are simply assumed to be "bad neighborhoods" and are avoided as a result. Other research indicates that "poor schools" and "crime" are sometimes code words for racial prejudice and excuses that whites use to avoid African Americans.

These preferences promote segregation. Recent research in several cities, including Atlanta, Detroit, and Los Angeles, shows that whites who prefer predominantly white neighborhoods tend to live in such neighborhoods, clearly implying that if white preferences would change, integration would increase. Such attitudes also imply tolerance, if not encouragement, of discriminatory practices on the part of real estate agents, mortgage lenders, property insurers, and other providers of housing services.

Housing Discrimination: How Common Is It Today?

When the insurance agent quoted at the beginning of this article was asked by one of his supervisors whether the kids in the neighborhood played hockey or basketball, he was not denying a home insurance policy to a particular black family because of race. However, he was trying to learn about the racial composition of the neighborhood in order to help market his policies. The mental map he was drawing is just as effective in discriminating as the maps commonly used in the past that literally had red lines marking neighborhoods—typically minority or poor—considered ineligible for home insurance or mortgage loans.

Researchers with HUD, the Urban Institute, and dozens of nonprofit fair housing organizations have long used "paired testing" to measure the pervasiveness of housing discrimination— and more recently in mortgage lending and home insurance. In a paired test, two people visit or contact a real estate, rental, home-finance, or insurance office. Testers provide agents with identical housing preferences and relevant financial data (income, savings, credit history). The only difference between the testers is their race or ethnicity. The testers make identical applications and report back on the responses they get. . . . Discrimination can take several forms: having to wait longer than whites for a meeting; being told about fewer units or otherwise being given less information; being steered to neighborhoods where residents are disproportionately of the applicant's race or ethnicity; facing higher deposit or down-payment requirements and other costs; or simply being told that a unit, loan, or policy is not available, when it is available to the white tester.

In 1989 and 2000, HUD and the Urban Institute, a research organization, conducted nationwide paired testing of discrimination in housing. They found generally less discrimination against African Americans and Hispanics in 2000 than in 1989, except for Hispanic renters. . . . Nevertheless, discrimination still occurred during 17 to 26 percent of the occasions when African Americans and Hispanics visited a rental office or real-estate agent. (The researchers found similar levels of discrimination against Asians and Native Americans in 2000; these groups were not studied in 1989.)

In 2000, subtler forms of discrimination, such as invidious comments by real estate agents, remained widespread. Even when whites and nonwhites were shown houses in the same areas, agents often steered white homeseekers to segregated neighborhoods with remarks such as "Black people do live around here, but it has not gotten bad yet"; "That area is full of Hispanics and blacks that don't know how to keep clean"; or "(This area) is very mixed. You probably wouldn't like it because of the income you and your husband make. I don't want to sound prejudiced."

Given the potential sanctions available under current law, including six- and seven-figure compensatory and punitive damage awards for victims, it seems surprising that an agent would choose to make such comments. However, research shows that most Americans are unfamiliar with fair housing rules, and even those who are familiar and believe they have experienced racial discrimination rarely take legal action because they do not believe anything would come of it. Most real estate professionals do comply with fair housing laws, but those who work in small neighborhoods and rely on word of mouth to get clients often fear losing business if they allow minorities into a neighborhood where local residents would not welcome them. In a 2004 study of a St. Louis suburb, a rental agent pointed out that there were no "dark" people in the neighborhood to a white tester. She said that she had had to lie to a black homeseeker and say that a unit was unavailable because she would have been "run out of" the suburb had she rented to a black family.

Discrimination does not end with the housing search. Case studies of mortgage lending and property insurance practices have also revealed discriminatory treatment against minorities. White borrowers are offered more choice in loan products, higher loan amounts, and more advice than minority borrowers. The Boston Federal Reserve Bank found that even among equally qualified borrowers in its region applications from African Americans were 60 percent more likely to be rejected than those submitted by whites. Other paired-testing studies from around the country conclude that whites are more likely to be offered home insurance policies, offered lower prices and more coverage, and given more assistance than African Americans or Hispanics.

The Continuing Costs of Segregation

Beyond constricting their freedom of choice, segregation deprives minority families of access to quality schools, jobs, health care, public services, and private amenities such as restaurants, theatres, and quality retail stores. Residential segregation also undercuts families' efforts to accumulate wealth through the appreciation of real estate values by restricting their ability both to purchase their own homes and to sell their homes to the largest and wealthiest group in the population, non-Hispanic whites. Just 46 percent of African Americans owned their own homes in 2000, compared to 72 percent of non-Hispanic whites. In addition, recent research found that the average value of single-family homes in predominantly white neighborhoods in the 100 largest metropolitan areas with significant minority populations was $196,000 compared to $184,000 in integrated communities and $104,000 in predominantly minority communities. As a result of the differing home values and appreciation, the typical white homeowner has $58,000 in home equity compared to $18,000 for the typical black homeowner. Segregation has broader effects on the quality of neighborhoods to which minorities can gain access. In 2000, the average white household with an income above $60,000 had neighbors in that same income bracket. But black and Hispanic households with incomes above $60,000 had neighbors with an average income of under $50,000. In effect, they lived in poorer neighborhoods, and this gap has widened since 1990.

Segregation restricts access to jobs and to quality schools by concentrating African Americans and Hispanics in central cities, when job growth and better schools are found in the suburbs. Amy Stuart Wells and Robert Crain found, for example, that black children living in St. Louis who attend schools in the suburbs are more likely to graduate and to go on to college than those attending city schools. Yet only busing makes it possible for these students to attend suburban schools, and America has largely turned away from this remedy to segregation. According to research by Gary Orfield at the Harvard Civil Rights Project, our nation's schools are as segregated today as they were [45] ... years ago. Most job growth also occurs in

suburban areas, and difficulty in finding and commuting to those jobs contributes to high unemployment rates among African Americans and Latinos.

The risks of illness and injury from infectious diseases and environmental hazards are also greater in minority neighborhoods, while resources to deal with them are less available than in mostly white areas. For example, in Bethesda, Md., a wealthy and predominantly white suburb of Washington, D.C., there is one pediatrician for every 400 residents compared to one for every 3,700 residents in Washington's predominantly minority and poor southeast neighborhoods. As John Logan has argued, "The housing market and discrimination sort people into different neighborhoods, which in turn shape residents' lives—and deaths. Bluntly put, some neighborhoods are likely to kill you. . . ."

Finally, segregation helps perpetuate prejudice, stereotypes, and racial tension. Several recent studies show that neighborhood-level contact between whites and African Americans reduces prejudice and increases acceptance of diversity. Yet with today's levels of housing segregation, few whites and blacks get the opportunity for such contact. More diverse communities generally exhibit greater tolerance and a richer lifestyle—culturally and economically—for all residents.

A Growing Movement

In 1968, the U.S. Supreme Court ruled that racial discrimination in housing was illegal, characterizing it as "a relic of slavery." In the same year, Congress passed the Fair Housing Act, providing specific penalties for housing discrimination along with mechanisms for addressing individual complaints of discrimination. These legal developments laid the groundwork for a growing social movement against segregation that has brought limited but real gains. Members of the National Fair Housing Alliance, a consortium of 80 nonprofit fair housing organizations in 30 cities and the District of Columbia, have secured more than $190 million for victims of housing discrimination since 1990 by using the Federal Fair Housing Act and equivalent state and local laws. In addition, they have negotiated legal settlements that have transformed the marketing and underwriting activities of the nation's largest property insurance companies, including State Farm, Allstate, Nationwide, American Family, and Liberty. The key investigative technique members of the alliance have used to secure these victories is paired testing.

Community reinvestment groups have secured more than $1.7 trillion in new mortgage and small business loans for traditionally underserved low- and moderate-income neighborhoods and minority markets since the passage of the Community Reinvestment Act (CRA). The CRA was passed in order to prevent lenders from refusing to make loans, or making loans more difficult to get, in older urban communities, neighborhoods where racial minorities are often concentrated. Under the CRA, third parties (usually community-based organizations) can formally challenge lender applications or requests by lenders to make changes in their business operations. Regulators who are authorized to approve lender applications have, in some cases, required the lender to respond to the concerns raised by the challenging party prior to approving the request. In some cases, just the threat of making such challenges has provided leverage for community organizations in their efforts to negotiate reinvestment agreements with lenders. Community groups have used this process to generate billions of new dollars for lending in low-income and minority markets. Sometimes, in anticipation of such a challenge, lenders negotiate a reinvestment program in advance. For example, shortly after Bank One and JP Morgan Chase announced their intent to merge in 2004, the lenders entered into an agreement with the Chicago Reinvestment Alliance, a coalition of Chicago-area neighborhood organizations. The banks agreed to invest an average of $80 million in community development loans for each of the next six years. Research by the Joint Center for Housing Studies at Harvard University indicates that mortgage loans became far more accessible in low-income and minority neighborhoods during the 1990s and that the CRA directly contributed to this outcome.

Many housing researchers and fair-housing advocates have criticized fair-housing enforcement authorities for relying too heavily on individual complaints and lawsuits to attack what are deeper structural problems. Currently, most testing and enforcement occurs when individuals lodge a complaint against a business rather than as a strategic effort to target large companies that regularly practice discrimination. Reinvestment agreements recently negotiated by community groups and lenders illustrate one more systemic approach. More testing aimed at detecting what are referred to as "patterns and practices" of discrimination by large developers and rental management companies would also be helpful. Such an undertaking, however, would require more resources, which are currently unavailable. Despite the limits of current enforcement efforts, most observers credit these efforts with helping to reduce segregation and discrimination.

Resistance to fair housing and integration efforts persists. For example, lenders and their trade associations continually attempt to weaken the CRA and related fair-housing rules. Yet fair-housing and community-reinvestment groups like the National Fair Housing Alliance and the National Community Reinvestment Coalition have successfully blocked most such efforts in Congress and among bank regulators. As more groups refine their ability to employ legal tools like the CRA and to litigate complex cases under the jurisdiction of the Fair Housing Act, we can expect further progress. The struggle for fair housing is a difficult one, but with the available tools, the progress we have made since 1970 toward becoming a more integrated society should continue.

The New Jim Crow

MICHELLE ALEXANDER

Many people learn about Jim Crow laws in their American history classes, so they believe that the racial caste system that existed prior to the civil rights movement is long gone. But Alexander presents a convincing case that the current trend of mass incarceration of drug offenders—which was developed as part of the War on Drugs and has disproportionately impacted minority communities—is a modern and perhaps more insidious version of Jim Crow.

The subject that I intend to explore today[1] is one that most Americans seem content to ignore. Conversations and debates about race—much less racial caste—are frequently dismissed as yesterday's news, not relevant to the current era. Media pundits and more than a few politicians insist that we, as a nation, have finally "moved beyond race." We have entered into the era of "post-racialism," it is said, the promised land of colorblindness. . . .

This triumphant notion of post-racialism is, in my view, nothing more than fiction—a type of Orwellian doublespeak made no less sinister by virtue of the fact that the people saying it may actually believe it. Racial caste is not dead; it is alive and well in America. The mass incarceration of poor people of color in the United States amounts to a new caste system—one specifically tailored to the political, economic, and social challenges of our time. It is the moral equivalent of Jim Crow.

I am well aware that this kind of claim may be hard for many people to swallow. Particularly if you, yourself, have never spent time in prison or been labeled a felon, the claim may seem downright absurd. I, myself, rejected the notion that something akin to a racial caste system could be functioning in the United States more than a decade ago—something that I now deeply regret.

I first encountered the idea of a new racial caste system in the mid-1990s when I was rushing to catch the bus in Oakland, California and a bright orange poster caught my eye. It screamed in large bold print: THE DRUG WAR IS THE NEW JIM CROW. . . . I sighed and muttered to myself something like, "Yeah, the criminal justice system is racist in many ways, but it really doesn't help to make such absurd comparisons. People will just think you're crazy." I then crossed the street and hopped on the bus. I was headed to my new job, director of the Racial Justice Project for the [American Civil Liberties Union] (ACLU) in Northern California.

When I began my work at the ACLU, I assumed the criminal justice system had problems of racial bias, much in the same way that all major institutions in our society are plagued to

Reprinted from the Ohio State Law Journal, by Permission of Michelle Alexander.

some degree with problems associated with conscious and unconscious bias. . . . While at the ACLU, I shifted my focus from employment discrimination to criminal justice reform, and dedicated myself to the task of working with others to identify and eliminate racial bias whenever and wherever it reared its ugly head.

By the time I left the ACLU, I had come to suspect that I was wrong about the criminal justice system. It was not just another institution infected with racial bias, but rather a different beast entirely. The activists who posted the sign on the telephone [pole] . . . were not crazy; nor were the smattering of lawyers and advocates around the country who were beginning to connect the dots between our current system of mass incarceration and earlier forms of social control. Quite belatedly, I came to see that mass incarceration in the United States had, in fact, emerged as a stunningly comprehensive and well-disguised system of racialized social control that functions in a manner strikingly similar to Jim Crow. I state my basic thesis in the introduction to my book, *The New Jim Crow*:

What has changed since the collapse of Jim Crow has less to do with the basic structure of our society than the language we use to justify it. In the era of colorblindness, it is no longer socially permissible to use race, explicitly, as a justification for discrimination, exclusion, and social contempt. So we don't. Rather than rely on race, we use our criminal justice system to label people of color "criminals" and then engage in all the practices we supposedly left behind. Today it is perfectly legal to discriminate against criminals in nearly all the ways it was once legal to discriminate against African Americans. Once you're labeled a felon, the old forms of discrimination—employment discrimination, housing discrimination, denial of the right to vote, and exclusion from jury service—are suddenly legal. As a criminal, you have scarcely more rights, and

arguably less respect, than a black man living in Alabama at the height of Jim Crow. We have not ended racial caste in America; we have merely redesigned it.[2]

I reached this conclusion reluctantly. . . . But after years of working on issues of racial profiling, police brutality, drug law enforcement in poor communities of color, and attempting to assist people released from prison "re-enter" into a society that never seemed to have much use for them in the first place. . . . I began to awaken to a racial reality that is so obvious to me now that what seems odd in retrospect is that I was blind to it for so long. Here are some facts I uncovered in the course of my work and research that you probably have not heard on the evening news:

- More African American adults are under correctional control today—in prison or jail, on probation or parole—than were enslaved in 1850, a decade before the Civil War began.[3]
- In 2007 more black men were disenfranchised than in 1870, the year the Fifteenth Amendment was ratified prohibiting laws that explicitly deny the right to vote on the basis of race.[4] During the Jim Crow era, African Americans continued to be denied access to the ballot through poll taxes and literacy tests. Those laws have been struck down, but today felon disenfranchisement laws accomplish what poll taxes and literacy tests ultimately could not.
- In many large urban areas in the United States, the majority of working-age African American men have criminal records. In fact, it was reported in 2002 that, in the Chicago area, if you take into account prisoners, the figure is nearly 80%.[5]

Those bearing criminal records and cycling in and out of our prisons today are part of a growing undercaste—not class, caste—a group of people, defined largely by race, who are relegated to a permanent second-class status by law. They can be denied the right to vote, automatically excluded from juries, and legally discriminated against in employment, housing, access to education, and public benefits, much as their grandparents and great-grandparents were during the Jim Crow era.

I find that when I tell people that mass incarceration amounts to a New Jim Crow, I am frequently met with shocked disbelief. The standard reply is: "How can you say that a racial caste system exists? Just look at Barack Obama! Just look at Oprah Winfrey! Just look at the black middle class!" The reaction is understandable. But we ought to question our emotional reflexes. The mere fact that some African Americans have experienced great success in recent years does not mean that something akin to a caste system no longer exists. No caste system in the United States has ever governed all black people. There have always been "free blacks" and black success stories, even during slavery and Jim Crow. During slavery, there were some black slave owners—not many, but some. And during Jim Crow, there were some black lawyers and doctors—not many, but some. The unprecedented nature of black achievement in formerly white domains today certainly suggests that the old Jim Crow is dead, but it does not necessarily mean the end of racial caste. If history is any guide, it may have simply taken a different form.

Any honest observer of American racial history must acknowledge that racism is highly adaptable. The rules and reasons the legal system employs to enforce status relations of any kind evolve and change as they are challenged.[6] . . . For example, following the collapse of slavery, the system of convict leasing was instituted—a system many historians believe was worse than slavery.[7] After the Civil War, black men were arrested by the thousands for minor crimes, such as loitering and vagrancy, and sent to prison. They were then leased to plantations. It was our nation's first prison boom. The idea was that prisoners leased to plantations were supposed to earn their freedom. But the catch was they could never earn enough to pay back the plantation owner the cost of their food, clothing and shelter

to the owner's satisfaction, and thus they were effectively re-enslaved, sometimes for the rest of their lives. It was a system more brutal in many respects than slavery, because plantation owners had no economic incentive to keep convicts healthy or even alive. They could always get another one.[8]

Today, I believe the criminal justice system has been used once again in a manner that effectively re-creates caste in America. Our criminal justice system functions more like a caste system than a system of crime control. For those who find that claim difficult to swallow, consider the facts. Our prison system has quintupled for reasons that have stunningly little do with crime. In less than 30 years, the U.S. penal population exploded from around 300,000 to more than 2 million.[9] The United States now has the highest rate of incarceration in the world, dwarfing the rates of nearly every developed country, including highly repressive regimes like China and Iran.[10] In fact, if our nation were to return to the incarceration rates of the 1970s—a time, by the way, when civil rights activists thought that imprisonment rates were egregiously high—we would have to release four out of five people who are in prison today.[11] More than a million people employed by the criminal justice system could lose their jobs.[12] That is how enormous and deeply entrenched the new system has become in a very short period of time.

As staggering as those figures are, they actually obscure the severity of the crisis in poor communities of color. . . . The overwhelming majority of the increase in imprisonment has been poor people of color, with the most astonishing rates of incarceration found among black men. It was estimated several years ago that, in Washington, D.C.—our nation's capital—three out of four young black men (and nearly all those in the poorest neighborhoods) could expect to serve time in prison.[13] Rates of incarceration nearly as shocking can be found in other communities of color across America.[14]

So what accounts for this vast new system of control? Crime rates? That is the common answer. But no, crime rates have remarkably little to do with skyrocketing incarceration rates. Crime rates have fluctuated over the past thirty years, and are currently at historical lows, but incarceration rates have consistently soared.[15] Most criminologists and sociologists today acknowledge that crime rates and incarceration rates have, for the most part, moved independently of one another.[16] Rates of imprisonment—especially black imprisonment—have soared regardless of whether crime has been rising or falling in any given community or the nation as a whole.[17]

So what does explain this vast new system of control, if not crime rates? Ironically, the activists who posted the sign on that telephone pole were right: The War on Drugs. The War on Drugs and the "get tough" movement explain the explosion in incarceration in the United States and the emergence of a vast, new racial undercaste. In fact, drug convictions alone accounted for about two-thirds of the increase in the federal system, and more than half of the increase in the state prison population between 1985 and 2000.[18] Drug convictions have increased more than 1000% since the drug war began, an increase that bears no relationship to patterns of drug use or sales.[19]

People of all races use and sell drugs at remarkably similar rates, but the enemy in this war has been racially defined.[20] The drug war has been waged almost exclusively in poor communities of color, despite the fact that studies consistently indicate that people of all races use and sell drugs at remarkably similar rates.[21] This evidence defies our basic stereotype of a drug dealer, as a black kid standing on a street corner, with his pants hanging down.[22] Drug dealing happens in the ghetto, to be sure, but it happens everywhere else in America as well. Illegal drug markets, it turns out—like American society generally—are relatively segregated by race.[23] Blacks tend to sell to blacks, whites to whites, Latinos sell to each other. University students sell to each other. People of all races use and sell drugs. A kid in rural Kansas does not drive to the 'hood to get his pot, or meth, or cocaine; he buys it from somebody down the road. In fact, the research suggests that where significant differences by race can be found, white youth are more likely to commit drug crimes than youth of color.[24] But that is not what you would guess when entering our nation's prisons and jails, overflowing as they are with black and brown drug offenders. In the United States, those who do time for drug crime are overwhelmingly black and brown.[25] In some states, African Americans constitute 80 to 90% of all drug offenders sent to prison.[26]

I find that many people are willing to concede these racial disparities once they see the data. Even so, they tend to insist that the drug war is motivated by concern over violent crime. They say: just look at our prisons. Nearly half of the people behind bars are violent offenders. . . . The problem with this abbreviated analysis is that violent crime is not responsible for the prison boom. Violent offenders tend to get longer sentences than nonviolent offenders, which is why they comprise such a large share of the prison population. One study suggests that the entire increase in imprisonment can be explained by sentence length, not increases in crime.[27] To get a sense of how large a contribution the drug war has made to mass incarceration, consider this: there are more people in prison today just for drug offenses than were incarcerated in 1980 for all reasons.[28] The reality is that the overwhelming majority of people who are swept into this system are non-violent offenders. In this regard, it is important to keep in mind that most people who are under correctional control are not in prison or jail. As of 2008, there were approximately 2.3 million people in prisons and jails, and a staggering 5.1 million people under "community correctional supervision"—i.e., on probation or parole. . . .[29]

How did this extraordinary system of control, unprecedented in world history, come to pass? Most people insist upon a benign motive. They seem to believe that the War on Drugs was launched in response to rising drug crime and the emergence of crack cocaine in inner city communities. For a long time, I believed that too. But that is not the case. Drug crime was actually declining, not rising, when President Ronald Reagan officially declared the drug war in 1982.[30] President Richard Nixon was the first to coin the term a "war on drugs," but President Reagan turned the rhetorical war into a literal one. From the outset, the war had little to do with drug crime and much to do with racial politics.

The drug war was part of a grand and highly successful Republican Party strategy—often known as the Southern Strategy—of using racially coded political appeals on issues of crime and welfare to attract poor and working class white voters who were resentful of, and threatened by, desegregation, busing, and affirmative action.[31] Poor and working class whites had their world rocked by the Civil Rights Movement. White elites could send their kids to private schools and give them all of the advantages wealth has to offer. But poor and working class whites were faced with a social demotion. It was their kids who might be bused across town, and forced to compete for the first time with a new group of people they had long believed to be inferior for decent jobs and educational opportunities.[32] Affirmative action, busing, and desegregation created an understandable feeling of vulnerability, fear, and anxiety among a group already struggling for survival. . . . H. R. Haldeman, President Richard Nixon's former Chief of Staff, reportedly summed up the strategy: "[T]he whole problem is really the blacks. The key is to devise a system that recognizes this while not appearing to."[33]

A couple years after the drug war was announced, crack cocaine hit the streets of inner-city communities.[34] The Reagan administration seized on this development with glee, hiring staff who were responsible for publicizing inner-city crack babies, crack mothers, the so-called "crack whores," and drug-related violence. The goal was to make inner-city crack abuse and violence a media sensation that, it was hoped,

would bolster public support for the drug war and would lead Congress to devote millions of dollars in additional funding to it.[35]

The plan worked like a charm. For more than a decade, black drug dealers and users became regulars in newspaper stories and saturated the evening TV news—forever changing our conception of who the drug users and dealers are.[36] Once the enemy in the war was racially defined, a wave of punitiveness took over. Congress and state legislatures nationwide devoted billions of dollars to the drug war and passed harsh mandatory minimum sentences for drug crimes—sentences longer than murderers receive in many countries. Many black politicians joined the "get tough" bandwagon, apparently oblivious to their complicity with the emergence of a system of social control that would, in less than two decades, become unprecedented in world history.[37]

Almost immediately, Democrats began competing with Republicans to prove that they could be even tougher on "them."[38] In President Bill Clinton's boastful words, "I can be nicked on a lot, but no one can say I'm soft on crime."[39] The facts bear him out. Clinton's "'tough on crime' policies resulted in the largest increases in federal and state prison inmates of any president in American history."[40] But Clinton was not satisfied with exploding prison populations. In an effort to appeal to the "white swing voters," he and the so-called "new Democrats" championed legislation banning drug felons from public housing (no matter how minor the offense) and denying them basic public benefits, including food stamps, for life.[41] Discrimination in virtually every aspect of political, economic, and social life is now perfectly legal, once you're labeled a felon.

All of this has been justified on the grounds that getting brutally tough on "them" is the only way to root out violent offenders or drug kingpins. The media images of violence in ghetto communities—particularly when crack first hit the street—led many to believe that the drug war was focused on the most serious offenders.

Yet nothing could be further from the truth. Federal funding has flowed to those state and local law enforcement agencies that increase dramatically the volume of drug arrests, not the agencies most successful in bringing down the bosses. What has been rewarded in this war is sheer numbers—the sheer volume of drug arrests.[42] To make matters worse, federal drug forfeiture laws allow state and local law enforcement agencies to keep for their own use 80% of the cash, cars, and homes seized from drug suspects, thus granting law enforcement a direct monetary interest in the profitability of the drug market itself.[43]

The results are predictable. People of color have been rounded up en masse for relatively minor, non-violent drug offenses. In 2005, for example, four out of five drug arrests were for possession, only one out of five for sales.[44] Most people in state prison for drug offenses have no history of violence or even of significant selling activity.[45] In fact, during the 1990s—the period of the most dramatic expansion of the drug war—nearly 80% of the increase in drug arrests was for marijuana possession, a drug generally considered less harmful than alcohol or tobacco and at least as prevalent in middle-class white communities as in the inner city.[46] In this way, a new racial undercaste has been created in an astonishingly short period of time. Millions of people of color are now saddled with criminal records and legally denied the very rights that were supposedly won in the Civil Rights Movement.

The U.S. Supreme Court, for its part, has mostly turned a blind eye to race discrimination in the criminal justice system. . . . Law enforcement officials are largely free to discriminate on the basis of race today, so long as no one admits it. That's the key. In *McCleskey v. Kemp* and *United States v. Armstrong*, the Supreme Court made clear that only evidence of conscious, intentional racial bias—the sort of bias that is nearly impossible to prove these days in the absence of an admission—is deemed sufficient.[47] . . . [The Supreme Court] has immunized the new caste system from judicial scrutiny for racial bias, much as it once rallied to legitimate and protect slavery and Jim Crow.

In my experience, those who have been incarcerated have little difficulty recognizing the parallels between mass incarceration and Jim Crow. Many former prisoners have told me, "It's slavery on the inside; Jim Crow when you get out." Prisoners are often forced to work for little or no pay. Once released, they are denied basic civil and human rights until they die. They are treated as though they possess an incurable defect, a shameful trait that can never be fully eradicated or redeemed. In the words of one woman who is currently incarcerated:

> When I leave here it will be very difficult for me in the sense that I'm a felon. That I will always be a felon . . . it will affect my job, it will affect my education . . . custody [of my children], it can affect child support, it can affect everywhere—family, friends, housing. . . . People that are convicted of drug crimes can't even get housing anymore. . . . Yes, I did my prison time. How long are you going to punish me as a result of it?[48]

Willie Johnson, a forty-three year old African American man recently released from prison in Ohio, explained it this way:

> My felony conviction has been like a mental punishment, because of all the obstacles. . . . I have had three companies hire me and tell me to come to work the next day. But then the day before they will call me and tell me don't come in—because you have a felony. And that is what is devastating because you think you are about to go to work and they call you and say because of your felony we can't hire [you]. I have run into this at least a dozen times. Two times I got very depressed and sad because I couldn't take care of myself as a man. It was like I wanted to give up—because in society nobody wants to give us a helping hand.[49]

Not surprisingly, for many trapped in the undercaste, the hurt and depression gives way to anger. A black minister in Waterloo, Mississippi put it this way: "'Felony' is the new N-word. They don't have to call you a nigger anymore. They just say you're a felon. In every ghetto you see alarming numbers of young men with felony convictions. Once you have that felony stamp, your hope of employment, for any kind of integration into society, it begins to fade out. Today's lynching is a felony charge."[50] What is painfully obvious to many trapped within the system, remains largely invisible to those of us who have decent jobs and zoom around on freeways, passing by the virtual and literal prisons in which members of the undercaste live.

None of this is to say, of course, that mass incarceration and Jim Crow are the "same." . . . Just as there were vast differences between slavery and Jim Crow, there are important differences between Jim Crow and mass incarceration. Yet all three (slavery, Jim Crow, and mass incarceration) have operated as tightly networked systems of laws, policies, customs, and institutions that operate collectively to ensure the subordinate status of a group defined largely by race. When we step back and view the system of mass incarceration as a whole, there is a profound sense of deja vu. There is a familiar stigma and shame. There is an elaborate system of control, complete with political disenfranchisement and legalized discrimination in every major realm of economic and social life. And there is the production of racial meaning and racial boundaries. Just consider a few of the rules, laws, and policies that apply to people branded felons today and ask yourself if they remind you of a bygone era:

- Denial of the right to vote. Forty-eight states and the District of Columbia deny prisoners the right to vote. . . .[51] Even after the term of punishment expires, states are free to deny people who have been labeled felons the right to vote for a period of years or their entire lives. In a few states, one in four black men have

been permanently disenfranchised.[52] Nationwide, nearly one in seven black men are either temporarily or permanently disenfranchised as a result of felon disenfranchisement laws.[53]

- Exclusion from jury service. One hallmark of Jim Crow was the systematic exclusion of blacks from juries. Today, those labeled felons are automatically excluded from juries, and to make matters worse, people are routinely excluded from juries if they "have had negative experiences with law enforcement."[54] Good luck finding a person of color in a ghetto community today who has not yet had a negative experience with law enforcement. The all-white jury is no longer a thing of the past in many regions of the country, in part, because so many African Americans have been labeled felons and excluded from juries.

- Employment discrimination. Employment discrimination against felons is deemed legal and absolutely routine.[55] Regardless of whether your felony occurred three months ago or thirty-five years ago, for the rest of your life you're required to check that box on employment applications asking the dreaded question: "Have you ever been convicted of a felony?" In one survey, about 70% of employers said they would not hire a drug felon convicted for sales or possession.[56] Most states also deny a wide range of professional licenses to people labeled felons.[57]

- Housing discrimination. Housing discrimination is perfectly legal. Public housing projects as well as private landlords are free to discriminate against criminals. In fact, those labeled felons may be barred from public housing for five years or more and legally discriminated against for the rest of their lives.[58] These laws make it difficult for former prisoners to find shelter, a basic human right.

- Public benefits. Discrimination is legal against those who have been labeled felons in public benefits. In fact, federal law renders drug offenders ineligible for food stamps for the rest of their lives.[59] Fortunately, some states have opted out of the federal ban, but it remains the case that thousands of people, including pregnant women and people with HIV/AIDS, are denied even food stamps, simply because they were once caught with drugs. . . .[60]

What, realistically, do we expect these folks to do? What is this system designed to do? It seems designed to send them right back to prison, which is what in fact happens most of the time. About 70% of released prisoners are rearrested within three years, and the majority of those who return to prison do so within a matter of months, because the barriers to mere survival on the outside are so immense.[61]

Remarkably, as bad as all the formal barriers to political and economic inclusion are, many formerly incarcerated people tell me that is not the worst of it. The worst is the stigma that follows you for the rest of your life. It is not just the denial of the job, but the look that crosses an employer's face when he sees the "box" has been checked. It is not just the denial of public housing, but the shame of being a grown man having to ask your grandma to sleep in her basement at night. The shame associated with criminality can be so intense that people routinely try to "pass." During the Jim Crow era, light-skinned blacks often tried to pass as white in order to avoid the stigma, shame, and discrimination associated with their race. Today, people labeled criminals lie not only to employers and housing officials, but also to their friends, acquaintances and family members. Children of prisoners lie to friends and relatives saying, "I don't know where my daddy is." Grown men who have been released from prison for years still glance down and look away when asked who they will vote for on election day, ashamed to admit they can't vote. They try to "pass" to avoid the stigma and discrimination associated with the new caste system.

An excellent ethnographic study conducted in Washington, D.C., found that even in neighborhoods hardest hit by mass incarceration—places where nearly every house has a family member behind bars or recently released from prison—people rarely "come out" fully about their own criminal history or that of their loved ones, even when speaking with relatives, friends and neighbors.[62] An eerie silence about this new system of control has befallen us, one rooted for some in shame, and for others in denial.

Yes, denial. There are two major reasons, I believe, that so many of us are in denial about the existence of racial caste in America. The first is traceable to a profound misunderstanding regarding how racial oppression actually works. If someone were to visit the United States from another country (or another planet) and ask: "Is the U.S. criminal justice system some kind of tool of racial control?," most Americans would swiftly deny it. Numerous reasons would leap to mind why that could not possibly be the case. The visitor would be told that crime rates, black culture, or bad schools were to blame. "The system is not run by a bunch of racists," the apologist would explain. They would say, "It is run by people who are trying to fight crime. . . ."

But more than forty-five years ago, Martin Luther King Jr. warned of the danger of precisely this kind of thinking. He insisted that blindness and indifference to racial groups is actually more important than racial hostility to the creation and maintenance of systems of racial control. Those who supported slavery and Jim Crow, he argued, typically were not bad or evil people; they were just blind.[63] Many segregationists were kind to their black shoe shiners and maids and genuinely wished them well. . . . But, he hastened to add, "They were victims of spiritual and intellectual blindness. They knew not what they did. The whole system of slavery was largely perpetuated by sincere though spiritually ignorant persons."[64] The same is true today. People of good will—and bad—have been unwilling to see black and brown men, in their humanness, as entitled to the same care, compassion, and concern that would be extended to one's friends, neighbors, or loved ones. After all, who among us would want a loved one struggling with drug abuse to be put in a cage, labeled a felon, and then subjected to a lifetime of discrimination, scorn and social exclusion? Most Americans would not wish that fate on anyone they cared about. But whom do we care about? In America, the answer to that question is still linked to race. Dr. King recognized that it was this indifference to the plight of African Americans that supported the institutions of slavery and Jim Crow. And this callous racial indifference supports mass incarceration today.

Another reason that we remain in deep denial is that we, as a nation, have a false picture of our racial reality. Prisoners are literally erased from the nation's economic picture. Unemployment and poverty statistics do not include people behind bars. In fact, standard reports underestimate the true jobless rates for less educated black men by as much as 24 percentage points.[65] During the much heralded economic boom of the 1990s—the Clinton years—African American men were the only group to experience a steep increase in real joblessness, a development directly traceable to the increase in the penal population.[66] During the 1990s—the best of times for the rest of America—the true jobless rates for non-college black men was a staggering 42%.[67]

Affirmative action, though, has put a happy face on this racial reality. Seeing black people graduate from Harvard and Yale and become CEOs or corporate lawyers—not to mention President of the United States—causes us all to marvel at what a long way we have come. As recent data shows, though, much of black progress is a myth.[68] In many respects, if you take into account prisoners, African Americans as a group are doing no better than they were when King was assassinated and uprisings swept inner cities across America. And that is with affirmative action! When we pull back the curtain and take a look at what our so-called colorblind society creates without affirmative action, we see a familiar social, political and economic structure—the structure of racial caste. And the entry into this new caste system can be found at the prison gate.

So where do we go from here? What can be done to dismantle this new system of control? . . . What is clear, I think, is that those of us in the civil rights community have allowed a human rights nightmare to occur on our watch. While many of us have been fighting for affirmative action or clinging to the perceived gains of the Civil Rights Movement, millions of people have been rounded up en masse, locked in cages, and then released into a parallel social universe in which they can be discriminated against for the rest of their lives—denied the very rights our parents and grandparents fought for and some died for. The clock has been turned back on racial progress in America, yet scarcely anyone seems to notice.

What is needed, I believe, is a broad based social movement, one that rivals in size, scope, depth, and courage the movement that was begun in the 1960s and left unfinished. It must be a multi-racial, multi-ethnic movement that includes poor and working class whites—a group that has consistently been pit against poor people of color, triggering the rise of successive new systems of control.

The drug war was born with black folks in mind, but it is a hungry beast; it has caused incalculable suffering in communities of all colors. . . . If we are going to succeed in bringing this brutal system to an end, we must map the linkages between the suffering of African Americans in the drug war to the experiences of other oppressed and marginalized groups. We must connect the dots. This movement must be multi-racial and multi-ethnic, and it must have a keen sense of the racial history and racial dynamics that brought us to this moment in time.

But before this movement can even get underway, a great awakening is required. We must awaken from our colorblind slumber to the realities of race in America. And we must be willing to embrace those labeled criminals—not necessarily their behavior, but them—their humanness. For it has been the refusal and failure to fully acknowledge the humanity and dignity of all persons that has formed the sturdy foundation of all caste systems. It is our task, I firmly believe, to end not just mass incarceration, but the history and cycle of caste in America.

NOTES

1. This article is adapted from two speeches delivered by Professor Michelle Alexander, one at the Zocolo Public Square in Los Angeles on March 17, 2010, and another at an authors symposium sponsored by the National Association of Criminal Defense Lawyers and the Open Society Institute on October 6, 2010.

2. MICHELLE ALEXANDER, THE NEW JIM CROW: MASS INCARCERATION IN THE AGE OF COLORBLINDNESS 2 (2010).

3. One in eleven black adults was under correctional supervision at year end 2007, or approximately 2.4 million people. PEW CTR. ON THE STATES, PEW CHARITABLE TRUSTS, ONE IN 31: THE LONG REACH OF AMERICAN CORRECTIONS 5 (Mar. 2009), available at http://www.pewcenteronthestates.org/uploadedFiles/PSPP_1in31_report_FINAL_WEB_3-26-09.pdf. According to the 1850 Census, approximately 1.7 million adults (ages 15 and older) were slaves. U.S. CENSUS BUREAU, THE SEVENTH CENSUS OF THE UNITED STATES: 1850 9 (1853), available at http://www2.census.gov/prod2/decennial/documents/1850a-01.pdf; see also University of Virginia Library, Historical Census Browser, UNIVERSITY OF VIRGINIA LIBRARY, http://mapserver.lib.virginia.edu/php/state.php (last visited July 17, 2011).

4. Contribution by Pamela S. Karlan, Forum: Pamela S. Karlan, in GLENN C. LOURY, RACE, INCARCERATION AND AMERICAN VALUES, 41, 42 (2008).

5. PAUL STREET, CHICAGO URBAN LEAGUE, THE VICIOUS CIRCLE: RACE, PRISON, JOBS, AND COMMUNITY IN CHICAGO, ILLINOIS, AND THE NATION 4 (2002).

6. See, e.g., Reva Siegel, Why Equal Protection No Longer Protects: The Evolving Forms of Status-Enforcing Action, 49 STAN. L. REV. 1111, 1113, 1146 (1997) (dubbing the process by which white privilege is maintained,

through the rules and rhetoric change, "preservation through transformation").

7. DOUGLAS A. BLACKMON, SLAVERY BY ANOTHER NAME: THE RE-ENSLAVEMENT OF BLACK AMERICANS FROM THE CIVIL WAR TO WORLD WAR II (2008); DAVID M. OSHINSKY, WORSE THAN SLAVERY: PARCHMAN FARM AND THE ORDEAL OF JIM CROW JUSTICE (1996).

8. See id.

9. Key Facts at a Glance: Correctional Populations, BUREAU OF JUSTICE STATISTICS (updated Dec. 16, 2010), available at http://bjs.ojp.usdoj.gov/content/glance/tables/corr2tab.cfm; JOHN IRWIN, ET AL., AMERICA'S ONE MILLION NONVIOLENT PRISONERS, THE JUSTICE POLICY INSTITUTE (1999), available at http://www.hawaii.edu/hivandaids/America_s_One_Million_Nonviolent_Prisoners.pdf; Robert Longley, U.S. Prison Population Tops 2 Million, U.S. GOVERNMENT INFORMATION, http://usgovinfo.about.com/cs/censusstatistic/a/aaprisonpop.htm.

10. PEW CTR. ON THE STATES, ONE IN 100: BEHIND BARS IN AMERICA 2008, at 5 (Feb. 2008), http://www.pewcenteronthestates.org/uploadedFiles/One%20in%20100.pdf.

11. According to data provided by the Sentencing Project, in 1972, the total rate of incarceration (prison and jail) was approximately 160 per 100,000. See MAUER, supra note 9, at 17. Today, it is about 750 per 100,000. LAUREN E. GLAZE, BUREAU OF JUSTICE STATISTICS, U.S. DEP'T OF JUSTICE, CORRECTIONAL POPULATIONS IN THE UNITED STATES, 2009, at 2 (2010), available at http://bjs.ojp.usdoj.gov/content/pub/pdf/cpus09.pdf. A reduction of 79% would be needed to get back to the 160 figure—itself a fairly high number when judged by international standards.

12. According to a report released by the U.S. Department of Justice's Bureau of Statistics

in 2006, the U.S. spent a record $185 billion for police protection, detention, judicial, and legal activities in 2003. Adjusting for inflation, these figures reflect a tripling of justice expenditures since 1982. The justice system employed almost 2.4 million people in 2003—58% of them at the local level and 31% at the state level. If four out of five people were released from prisons, far more than a million people could lose their jobs. KRISTEN A. HUGHES, BUREAU OF JUSTICE STATISTICS, U.S. DEP'T OF JUSTICE, JUSTICE EXPENDITURE AND EMPLOYMENT IN THE UNITED STATES, 2003, at 1 (2006), available at http://bjs.ojp.usdoj.gov/content/pub/pdf/jeeus03.pdf.

13. DONALD BRAMAN, DOING TIME ON THE OUTSIDE: INCARCERATION AND FAMILY LIFE IN URBAN AMERICA 3 (2004) (citing D.C. Department of Corrections 2000).

14. ERIC LOTKE & JASON ZIEDENBERG, JUSTICE POLICY INSTITUTE, TIPPING POINT: MARYLAND'S OVERUSE OF INCARCERATION AND THE IMPACT ON COMMUNITY SAFETY 3 (2005) (reporting that in Baltimore the majority of young African American men are currently under correctional supervision). Nationwide, one in three black men will go to prison during their lifetime. See THOMAS P. BONCSZAR, BUREAU OF JUSTICE STATISTICS, U.S. DEP'T OF JUSTICE, PREVALENCE OF IMPRISONMENT IN THE U.S. POPULATION, 1974–2001 (2003), available at http://bjs.ojp.usdoj.gov/content/pub/pdf/piusp01.pdf.

15. BRUCE WESTERN, PUNISHMENT AND INEQUALITY IN AMERICA 30 (2006) (Figure 2.1).

16. See, e.g., MARC MAUER, RACE TO INCARCERATE. 23–35, 92–112 (2d ed. 2006); MICHAEL TONRY, THINKING ABOUT CRIME: SENSE AND SENSIBILITY IN AMERICAN PENAL CULTURE 14 (2004).

17. See, e.g., WESTERN, supra note 16, at 35, 43.

18. MAUER, supra note 17, at 33.

19. MARC MAUER & RYAN S. KING, A 25-YEAR QUAGMIRE: THE WAR ON DRUGS AND ITS IMPACT ON AMERICAN SOCIETY 2, 4 (Sept. 2007), available at http://www.sentencingproject.org/doc/publications/dp_25yearquagmire.pdf.

20. The overwhelming majority of those arrested and incarcerated for drug crimes during the past few decades have been black and brown. When the War on Drugs gained full steam in the mid-1980s, prison admissions for African Americans "skyrocketed, nearly quadrupling in three years, then increasing steadily until it reached in 2000 a level more than twenty-six times the level in 1983." JEREMY TRAVIS, BUT THEY ALL COME BACK: FACING THE CHALLENGES OF PRISON REENTRY 28 (2002); see, e.g., U.S. DEP'T OF HEALTH & HUMAN SERVS., SUBSTANCE ABUSE & MENTAL HEALTH SERVICES ADMINISTRATION, SUMMARY OF FINDINGS FROM THE 2000 NATIONAL HOUSEHOLD SURVEY ON DRUG ABUSE 21 (2001), available at http://oas.samhsa.gov/NHSDA/2kNHSDA/chapter2.htm (reporting that 6.4 percent of whites, 6.4 percent of blacks, and 5.3 percent of Hispanics were current illegal drug users in 2000); U.S. DEP'T OF HEALTH AND HUMAN SERVS., SUBSTANCE ABUSE & MENTAL HEALTH SERVS. ADMIN., RESULTS FROM THE 2002 NATIONAL SURVEY ON DRUG USE AND HEALTH: NATIONAL FINDINGS 16 (2003), available at http://oas.samhsa.gov/nsduh/reports.htm#2k2 (revealing nearly identical rates of illegal drug use among whites and blacks, only a single percentage point between them); U.S. DEP'T OF HEALTH AND HUMAN SERVS., SUBSTANCE ABUSE & MENTAL HEALTH SERVS. ADMIN., RESULTS FROM THE 2007 NATIONAL SURVEY ON DRUG USE

AND HEALTH: NATIONAL FINDINGS 25 (2003), available at http://oas.samhsa.gov/nsduh/reports.htm#2k2 (showing essentially the same findings).

21. See generally supra, note 21.

22. A national survey conducted in 1995 illustrated the profound and pervasive racial stereotypes associated with drug crime. Survey respondents were asked: "Would you close your eyes for a second, envision a drug user, and describe that person to me?" 95% of respondents pictured a black drug user, while only 5% imagined all other racial groups combined. Betsy Watson Burston, Dionne Jones, and Pat Robinson-Saunders, Drug Use and African Americans: Myth versus Reality, 40 J. ALCOHOL & DRUG EDUC. 19, 20 (Winter 1995).

23. Researchers have found that drug users are most likely to report using as a main source of drugs someone who is of their own racial or ethnic background. See, e.g., K. JACK RILEY, OFFICE OF NAT'L DRUG CONTROL POLICY, NAT'L INST. OF JUSTICE, CRACK, POWDER COCAINE, AND HEROIN: DRUG PURCHASE AND USE PATTERNS IN SIX U.S. CITIES 1 (1997); Patricia Davis & Pierre Thomas, In Affluent Suburbs, Young Users and Sellers Abound, WASH. POST, Dec. 14, 1997, at A20.

24. The National Household Survey on Drug Abuse reported in 2000 that white youth aged 12–17 were more likely to have used and sold illegal drugs than African American youth. NEELUM ARYA & IAN AUGARTEN, CAMPAIGN FOR YOUTH JUSTICE, CRITICAL CONDITION: AFRICAN-AMERICAN YOUTH IN THE JUSTICE SYSTEM (2003), at table 5, p. 16 and p. 19, available at http://www.campaignforyouthjustice.org/documents/AfricanAmericanBrief.pdf. Another study published that year revealed that white students use cocaine and heroin at significantly higher rates than black students, while nearly identical percentages of black and white students report using marijuana. LLOYD D. JOHNSTON ET AL., NAT'L INST. ON DRUG ABUSE, MONITORING THE FUTURE, NATIONAL SURVEY RESULTS ON DRUG USE, 1975–1999, Vol. 1, SECONDARY SCHOOL UNITS 146, 197 (2000), available at http://monitoringthefuture.org/pubs/monographs/mtf-vol1_1999.pdf. More recent studies continue to suggest higher rates of illegal drug use and sales by white youth. See, e.g., HOWARD N. SNYDER & MELISSA SICKMUND, U.S. DEP'T OF JUSTICE, NAT'L CTR. FOR JUVENILE JUSTICE, JUVENILE OFFENDERS AND VICTIMS: 2006 NATIONAL REPORT 81 (2006), available at http://www.ojjdp.gov/ojstatbb/nr2006/downloads/NR2006.pdf (reporting that white youth are more likely than black youth to engage in illegal drug sales); LLOYD D. JOHNSTON ET AL., NAT'L INST. ON DRUG ABUSE, MONITORING THE FUTURE: NATIONAL SURVEY RESULTS ON DRUG USE, 1975–2006, VOLUME II: COLLEGE STUDENTS & ADULTS AGES 19–45, at 28 (2007), available at http://www.monitoringthefuture.org/pubs/monographs/vol2_2006.pdf (stating "African American 12th graders have consistently shown lower usage rates than White 12th graders for most drugs, both licit and illicit").

25. Although the majority of illegal drug users and dealers nationwide are white, roughly three-fourths of all people imprisoned for drug offenses since the War on Drugs began have been African American or Latino. MARC MAUER & RYAN S. KING, THE SENTENCING PROJECT, SCHOOLS AND PRISONS: FIFTY YEARS AFTER BROWN V. BOARD OF EDUCATION 3 (Apr. 2004). In recent years, rates of black imprisonment for drug offenses have dipped somewhat—declining approximately 22% from their zenith in the mid-1990s—but it remains the case that African Americans are incarcerated at grossly disproportionate rates

throughout the United States. MARC MAUER, THE SENTENCING PROJECT, THE CHANGING RACIAL DYNAMICS OF THE WAR ON DRUGS 5 (2009), available at http://www.sentencingproject.org/doc/dp_raceanddrugs.pdf.

26. HUMAN RIGHTS WATCH, PUNISHMENT AND PREJUDICE: RACIAL DISPARITIES IN THE WAR ON DRUGS, Vol. 12, No. 2, at 19 (May 2000).

27. According to this study, the entire increase in the prison population between 1980 and 2001 can be explained by sentencing policy changes, not increases in crime. MAUER, supra note 17, at 33, 36–38 (citing Warren Young & Mark Brown, Cross national Comparisons of Imprisonment, in CRIME AND JUSTICE: A REVIEW OF RESEARCH, Vol. 27, at 33, 1–49 (Michael Tonry, ed., 1993)).

28. "Unfairness in Federal Cocaine Sentencing: Is It Time to Crack the 100 to 1 Disparity?" Hearing on H.R. 1459, H.R. 1466, H.R. 265, H.R. 2178 and H.R. 18 before the H. Subcomm. on Crime, Terrorism, and Homeland Security of the H. Comm. on the Judiciary, 111th Cong. 2 (2009) (testimony of Marc Mauer, Executive Director, Sentencing Project)."

29. PEW CTR. ON THE STATES, supra note 3, at 4.

30. President Richard Nixon was the first to coin the term a "war on drugs," but the term proved largely rhetorical as he declared illegal drugs "public enemy number one" without proposing dramatic shifts in public policy. President Reagan converted the rhetorical war into a literal one, when he officially announced the War on Drugs in 1982. At the time, less than 2 percent of the American public viewed drugs as the most important issue facing the nation. See KATHERINE BECKETT, MAKING CRIME PAY: LAW AND ORDER IN CONTEMPORARY AMERICAN POLITICS 62, 163 (1997); see also Julian V. Roberts, Public Opinion, Crime, and Criminal Justice, in CRIME AND JUSTICE: A REVIEW OF RESEARCH, Vol. 16, at 99, 129–37 (Michael Tonry ed., 1992).

31. See, e.g., BECKETT, supra note 31, at 31; Vesla M. Weaver, Frontlash: Race and the Development of Punitive Crime Policy, 21 STUD. IN AM. POL. DEV. 230, 233, 237 (Fall 2007). See generally ROBERT PERKINSON, TEXAS TOUGH: THE RISE OF AMERICA'S PRISON EMPIRE (2010) (offering a compelling account of how the backlash against the Civil Rights Movement gave rise to mass incarceration in Texas, and, ultimately, the nation).

32. During the 1950s, the majority of Southern whites were better off than Southern blacks, but they were not affluent or well educated by any means; they were semiliterate (with less than twelve years of schooling) and typically quite poor. Only a tiny minority of whites was affluent and well educated. They stood far apart from the rest of whites and virtually all blacks. C. Arnold Anderson, Inequalities in Schooling in the South, 60 AM. J. ON SOCIOLOGY 547, 553, 557 (May 1955); Lani Guinier, From Racial Liberalism to Racial Literacy: Brown v. Board of Education and the Interest Divergence Dilemma, 91 J. AMER. HIST. 92, 103 (June 2004). What lower class whites did have was what W. E. B. Du Bois described as "the public and psychological wage" paid to white workers, who depended on their status and privileges as whites to compensate for their low pay and harsh working conditions. W. E. B. DUBOIS, BLACK RECONSTRUCTION IN AMERICA, AN ESSAY TOWARD A HISTORY OF THE PART WHICH BLACK FOLKS PLAYED IN THE ATTEMPT TO RECONSTRUCT DEMOCRACY IN AMERICA, 1860–1880, at 700 (1935). Because the Southern white elite had succeeded in persuading all whites to think

in racial rather than class terms, it is hardly surprising that poor and working class whites experienced desegregation as a net loss. Derrick A. Bell, Jr., Brown v. Board of Education and the Interest-Convergence Dilemma, 93 HARV. L. REV. 518, 525 (1980).

33. WILLARD M. OLIVER, THE LAW & ORDER PRESIDENCY 126–27 (2003).

34. See Craig Reinarman & Harry G. Levine, The Crack Attack: America's Latest Drug Scare, 1986–1992, in IMAGES OF ISSUES: TYPIFYING CONTEMPORARY SOCIAL PROBLEMS 152 (Joel Best ed., 1995).

35. Id. at 170–71 ("Crack was a godsend to the Right. . . . It could not have appeared at a more politically opportune moment").

36. Id.; DORIS MARIE PROVINE, UNEQUAL UNDER LAW: RACE IN THE WAR ON DRUGS 88 (2007).

37. PROVINE, supra note 38, at 117. Today the black community is divided in many respects about how best to understand and respond to mass incarceration, with some academics (and celebrities) arguing that poor education and cultural traits explain the millions of black men rotating in and out of correctional control, and others emphasizing the role of racial bias and structural inequality. See, e.g., DEMICO BOOTHE, WHY ARE SO MANY BLACK MEN IN PRISON? (2007) (emphasizing the discriminatory nature of the prison system); BILL COSBY & ALVIN F. POUSSAINT, COME ON PEOPLE: ON THE PATH FROM VICTIMS TO VICTORS (2007) (arguing that poor education, as well as lack of personal responsibility and discipline, largely explain the status of black men today). The fact that many African Americans endorse aspects of the current caste system, and insist that the problems of the urban poor can be best explained by their behavior, culture, lack of education, and attitude, does not, in any meaningful way, distinguish mass incarcer-

ation from its predecessors. To the contrary, these attitudes and arguments have their roots in the struggles to end slavery and Jim Crow. As numerous scholars have observed, many black advocates during the Jim Crow era embraced a "politics of respectability" and an "uplift ideology" that led them to distance themselves from the urban poor, and to blame the least educated members of the urban poor for their own condition. See, e.g., KAREN FERGUSON, BLACK POLITICS IN NEW DEAL ATLANTA 5–11 (2002). In fact, some of the most discriminatory federal programs of the New Deal era, including the slum clearance program, received strong support from African American bureaucrats and reformers. Id. At 13.

38. ALEXANDER, supra note 2, at 55–56; BECKETT, supra note 31, at 61.

39. Michael Kramer, The Political Interest Frying Them Isn't the Answer, TIME, Mar. 14, 1994, at 32, available at http://www.time.com/time/magazine/article/0,9171,980318,00.html.

40. Press Release, Justice Policy Institute, Clinton Crime Agenda Ignores Proven Methods for Reducing Crime (Apr. 14. 2008) (on file with the Ohio State Journal of Criminal Law).

41. See ALEXANDER, supra note 2, at 56.

42. See id. at 71–73; see RADLEY BALKO, CATO INST., OVERKILL: THE RISE OF PARAMILITARY POLICE RAIDS IN AMERICA 14–15 (2006).

43. See Eric Blumenson & Eva Nilsen, Policing for Profit: The Drug War's Hidden Economic Agenda, 65 U. CHI. L. REV. 35, 44–45, 51 (1998).

44. MAUER & KING, supra note 20, at 3.

45. Id. at 2.

46. ALEXANDER, supra note 2, at 59; RYAN S. KING & MARC MAUER, THE SENTENCING PROJECT, THE WAR ON MARIJUANA: THE TRANSFORMATION OF THE WAR ON DRUGS IN THE 1990S, at 1 (2005).

47. See United States v. Armstrong, 517 U.S. 456 (1996); McCleskey v. Kemp, 481 U.S. 279 (1987).

48. JEFF MANZA & CHRISTOPHER UGGEN, LOCKED OUT: FELON DISENFRANCHISEMENT AND AMERICAN DEMOCRACY 152 (2006).

49. Interview by Guylando A. M. Moreno with Willie Thompson, in Cincinnati, Ohio (Mar. 2005). See also ALEXANDER, supra note 2, at 158–59.

50. SASHA ABRAMSKY, CONNED: HOW MILLIONS WENT TO PRISON, LOST THE VOTE, AND HELPED SEND GEORGE W. BUSH TO THE WHITE HOUSE 140 (2006).

51. AMERICAN CIVIL LIBERTIES UNION, OUT OF STEP WITH THE WORLD: AN ANALYSIS OF FELONY DISENFRANCHISEMENT IN THE U.S. AND OTHER DEMOCRACIES 3 (2006); THE SENTENCING PROJECT, FELONY DISENFRANCHISEMENT LAWS IN THE UNITED STATES 1 (2011).

52. JAMIE FELLNER & MARC MAUER, THE SENTENCING PROJECT, LOSING THE VOTE: THE IMPACT OF FELONY DISENFRANCHISEMENT LAWS IN THE UNITED STATES 1 (1998), available at http://www.sentencingproject.org/doc/File/FVR/fd_losingthevote.pdf.

53. Id. These figures may understate the impact of felony disenfranchisement, because they do not take into account the millions of formerly incarcerated people who cannot vote in states that require people convicted of felonies to pay fines or fees before their voting rights can be restored. As legal scholar Pam Karlan has observed, "felony disenfranchisement has decimated the potential black electorate." LOURY, supra note 4, at 48.

54. See ALEXANDER, supra note 2, at 116–20 (discussing the discriminatory use of preemptory strikes against African American jurors).

55. See DEVAH PAGER, MARKED: RACE, CRIME AND FINDING WORK IN AN ERA OF MASS INCARCERATION 33 (2007); see also LEGAL ACTION CTR., AFTER PRISON: ROADBLOCKS TO REENTRY 10 (2004).

56. EMPLOYERS GRP. RESEARCH SERVS., EMPLOYMENT OF EX-OFFENDERS: A SURVEY OF EMPLOYERS' POLICIES AND PRACTICES 6 (2002); Harry J. Holzer, Steven Raphael & Michael A. Stoll, Will Employers Hire Former Offenders?: Employer Preferences, Background Checks, and Their Determinants, in IMPRISONING AMERICA: THE SOCIAL EFFECTS OF MASS INCARCERATION 205, 209 (Mary Pattillo et al., eds., 2004).

57. LEGAL ACTION CTR., supra note 58, at 10.

58. See HUMAN RIGHTS WATCH, NO SECOND CHANCE: PEOPLE WITH CRIMINAL RECORDS DENIED ACCESS TO PUBLIC HOUSING 33 (2004).

59. See Temporary Assistance for Needy Family Program (TANF), 21 U.S.C. § 862a(a)(2) (2006). See generally Legal Action Center, Opting out of Federal Ban on Food Stamps and TANF, at http://www.lac.org/toolkits/TANF/TANF.htm; Patricia Allard, The Sentencing Project, Life Sentences: Denying Welfare Benefits To Women Convicted Of Drug Offenses (2002), available at http://www.sentencingproject.org/doc/publications/women_lifesentences.pdf.

60. Black Men's Jail Time Hits Entire Communities, NPR TALK OF THE NATION (Aug. 23, 2010), http://www.npr.org/templates/story/story.php?storyId=129379700. 65 RACHEL L. MCLEAN & MICHAEL D. THOMPSON, COUNCIL OF STATE GOV'TS JUSTICE CTR., REPAYING DEBTS 7–8 (2007).

61. See JEREMY TRAVIS, BUT THEY ALL COME BACK: FACING THE CHALLENGES OF PRISONER REENTRY 94 (2005).

62. See BRAMAN, supra note 14, at 219–20.

63. MARTIN LUTHER KING, JR., STRENGTH TO LOVE 45 (Fortress Press 1981) (1963).
64. Id.
65. WESTERN, supra note 16, at 91–92.
66. See Robert W. Fairlie & William A. Sundstrom, The Emergence, Persistence, and Recent Widening of the Racial Unemployment Gap, 52 INDUS. & LAB. REL. REV. 252, 257 Tables 2-3; see also Bruce Western, Black–White Wage Inequality, Employment Rates, and Incarceration, 111 AM.J. SOC. 553, 557 Table 2.
67. WESTERN, supra note 16, at 97.
68. See THE EISENHOWER FOUNDATION, WHAT WE CAN DO TOGETHER: A FORTY YEAR UPDATE OF THE NATIONAL ADVISORY COMMISSION ON CIVIL DISORDERS: PRELIMINARY FINDINGS (2008), available athttp://www.eisenhowerfoundation.org/docs/Kerner%2040%20Year%20Update,%20Executive%20Summary.pdf.

Explaining and Eliminating Racial Profiling

DONALD TOMASKOVIC-DEVEY AND PATRICIA WARREN

The authors describe the history and efficacy of racial profiling, as well as legal challenges to the practice. They also consider how institutional policies (e.g., which neighborhoods are patrolled most intensely, practices like "out-of-place policing" where minorities who appear out of place are stopped, etc.) can contribute to racial bias and inequities in arrests, as well as how bias among individual officers (conscious and unconscious) contributes to the problem.

The emancipation of slaves is a century-and-a-half in America's past. Many would consider it ancient history. Even the 1964 Civil Rights Act and the 1965 Voting Rights Act, which challenged the de facto racial apartheid of the post–Civil War period, are now well over 40 years old. But even in the face of such well-established laws, racial inequalities in education, housing, employment, and law enforcement remain widespread in the United States.

Many Americans think these racial patterns stem primarily from individual prejudices or even racist attitudes. However, sociological research shows discrimination is more often the result of organizational practices that have unintentional racial effects or are based on cognitive biases linked to social stereotypes. Racial profiling—stopping or searching cars and drivers based primarily on race, rather than any suspicion or observed violation of the law—is particularly problematic because it's a form of discrimination enacted and organized by federal and local governments.

In our research we've found that sometimes formal, institutionalized rules within law enforcement agencies encourage racial profiling. Routine patrol patterns and responses to calls for service, too, can produce racially biased policing. And, unconscious biases among individual police officers can encourage them to perceive some drivers as more threatening than others (of course, overt racism, although not widespread, among some police officers also contributes to racial profiling).

Racially biased policing is particularly troubling for police–community relations, as it unintentionally contributes to the mistrust of police in minority neighborhoods. But, the same politics and organizational practices that produce racial profiling can be the tools communities use to confront and eliminate it.

Profiling and Its Problems

The modern story of racially biased policing begins with the Drug Enforcement Agency's (DEA) Operation Pipeline, which starting in

Donald Tomaskovic-Devey and Patricia Warren, *Contexts* (Volume 8 and Issue 2), pp. 34–39, Copyright © 2009. Reprinted by Permission of SAGE Publications.

1984 trained 25,000 state and local police officers in 48 states to recognize, stop, and search potential drug couriers. Part of that training included considering the suspects' race. Jurisdictions developed a variety of profiles in response to Operation Pipeline. For example, in Eagle County, Colo., the sheriff's office profiled drug couriers as those who had fast-food wrappers strewn in their cars, out-of-state license plates, and dark skin, according to the book *Good Cop, Bad Cop* by Milton Heuman and Lance Cassak. As well, those authors wrote, Delaware's drug courier profile commonly targeted young minority men carrying pagers or wearing gold jewelry. And according to the American Civil Liberties Union (ACLU), the Florida Highway Patrol's profile included rental cars, scrupulous obedience to traffic laws, drivers wearing lots of gold or who don't "fit" the vehicle, and ethnic groups associated with the drug trade (meaning African Americans and Latinos).

In the 1990s, civil rights organizations challenged the use of racial profiles during routine traffic stops, calling them a form of discrimination. In response, the U.S. Department of Justice argued that using race as an explicit profile produced more efficient crime control than random stops. Over the past decade, however, basic social science research has called this claim into question.

The key indicator of efficiency in police searches is the percent that result in the discovery of something illegal. Recent research has shown repeatedly that increasing the number of stops and searches among minorities doesn't lead to more drug seizures than are found in routine traffic stops and searches among white drivers. In fact, the rates of contraband found in profiling-based drug searches of minorities are typically lower, suggesting racial profiling decreases police efficiency.

In addition to it being an inefficient police practice, Operation Pipeline violated the assumption of equal protection under the law guaranteed through civil rights laws as well as the 14th Amendment to the U.S. Constitution. It meant, in other words, that just as police forces across the country were learning to curb the egregious civil rights violations of the 20th century, the federal government began training state and local police to target black and brown drivers for minor traffic violations in hopes of finding more severe criminal offending. The cruel irony is that it was exactly this type of flagrant, state-sanctioned racism the civil rights movement was so successful at outlawing barely a decade earlier.

Following notorious cases of violence against minorities perpetrated by police officers, such as the video-taped beating of Rodney King in Los Angeles in 1991[1] and the shooting of Amadou Diallo in New York in 1999[2], racially biased policing rose quickly on the national civil rights agenda. By the late 1990s, challenges to racial profiling became a key political goal in the more general movement for racial justice. The National Association for the Advancement of Colored People (NAACP) and the ACLU brought lawsuits against law enforcement agencies across the United States for targeting minority drivers. As a result, many states passed legislation that banned the use of racial profiles and then required officers to record the race of drivers stopped in order to monitor and sanction those who were violating citizens' civil rights.

Today, many jurisdictions continue to collect information on the race composition of vehicle stops and searches to monitor and discourage racially biased policing. In places like New Jersey and North Carolina, where the national politics challenging racial profiling were reinforced by local efforts to monitor and sanction police, racial disparities in highway patrol stops and searches declined.

Our analysis of searches by the North Carolina Highway Patrol shows that these civil rights–based challenges, both national and local, quickly changed police behavior. In 1997, before racial profiling had come under attack, black drivers were four times as likely as white drivers to be subjected to a search by the North Carolina Highway Patrol. Confirming that the high rate of searches represented racial profiling, black drivers were 33 percent less likely to be found with contraband compared to white drivers. The next year, as the national and local politics of racial profiling accelerated, searches of black drivers plummeted in North Carolina. By 2000, racial disparities in searches had been cut in half and the recovery of contraband no longer differed by race, suggesting officers were no longer racially biased in their decisions to search cars.

This isn't to suggest lawyers' and activists' complaints have stopped profiling everywhere. For example, Missouri, which has been collecting data since 2000, still has large race disparities in searching practices among its police officers. The most recent data (for 2007) shows blacks were 78 percent more likely than whites to be searched. Hispanics were 118 percent more likely than whites to be searched. Compared to searches of white drivers, contraband was found 25 percent less often among black drivers and 38 percent less often among Hispanic drivers.

How Bias Is Produced

Many police–citizen encounters aren't discretionary, therefore even if an officer harbors racial prejudice it won't influence the decision to stop a car. For example, highway patrol officers, concerned with traffic flow and public safety, spend a good deal of their time stopping speeders based on radar readings—they often don't even know the race of the driver until after they pull over the car. Still, a number of other factors can produce high rates of racially biased stops. The first has to do with police patrol patterns, which tend to vary widely by neighborhood.

Not unreasonably, communities suffering from higher rates of crime are often patrolled more aggressively than others. Because minorities more often live in these neighborhoods, the routine deployment of police in an effort to increase public safety will produce more police–citizen contacts and thus a higher rate of stops in those neighborhoods. A recent study in Charlotte, N.C., confirmed that much of the race disparity in vehicle stops there can be explained in terms of patrol patterns and calls for service. Another recent study of pedestrian stops in New York yielded similar conclusions—but further estimated that police patrol patterns alone lead to African American pedestrians being stopped at three times the rate of whites. (And, similar to the study of racial profiling of North Carolina motorists, contraband was recovered from white New Yorkers at twice the rate of African Americans.)

Police patrol patterns are, in fact, sometimes more obviously racially motivated. Targeting black bars, rather than white country clubs, for Saturday-night random alcohol checks has this character. This also happens when police stop minority drivers for being in white neighborhoods. This "out-of-place policing" is often a routine police practice, but can also arise from calls for service from white households suspicious of minorities in their otherwise segregated neighborhoods. In our conversations with African American drivers, many were quite conscious of the risk they took when walking or driving in white neighborhoods.

"My son ... was working at the country club. ... He missed the bus and he said he was walking out Queens Road. After a while all the lights came popping on in every house. He guessed they called and ... the police came and they questioned him, they wanted to know why was he walking through Queens Road [at] that time of day," one black respondent we talked to said.

The "wars" on drugs and crime of the 1980s and 1990s encouraged law enforcement to police minority neighborhoods aggressively and thus contributed significantly to these problematic patterns. In focus groups with African American drivers in North Carolina, we heard that many were well aware of these patterns and their sources. "I think sometimes they target ... depending on where you live. I think if you live in a side of town ... with maybe a lot of crime or maybe break-ins or drugs, ... I think you are a target there," one respondent noted.

These stories are mirrored in data on police stops in a midsize midwestern city. . . . Here, the fewer minorities there are in a neighborhood, the more often African Americans are stopped. In the whitest neighborhoods, African American drivers were stopped at three times the rate you'd expect given how many of them are on the road. In minority communities, minority drivers were still stopped disproportionally, but at rates much closer to their population as drivers in the neighborhood. This isn't to say all racial inequities in policing originate with the rules organizations follow. Racial attitudes and biases among police officers are still a source of racial disparity in police vehicle stops. But even this is a more complicated story than personal prejudice and old-fashioned bigotry.

Bias among Individual Officers

The two most common sources of individual bias are conscious prejudice and unconscious cognitive bias. Conscious prejudice is typically, but incorrectly, thought of as the most common source of individuals' racist behavior. While some individual police officers, just like some employers or real estate agents, may be old-fashioned bigots, this isn't a widespread source of racial bias in police stops. Not only is prejudice against African Americans on the decline in the United States, but most police forces prohibit this kind of racism and reprimand or punish such officers when it's discovered. In these cases, in fact, organizational mechanisms prevent, or at least reduce, bigoted behavior. Most social psychologists agree, however, that implicit biases against minorities are widespread in the population. While only about 10 percent of the white population will admit they have explicitly racist attitudes, more than three-quarters display implicit anti-black bias.

Studies of social cognition (or, how people think) show that people simplify and manage information by organizing it into social categories. By focusing on obvious status characteristics such as sex, race, or age, all of us tend to categorize ourselves and others into groups.

Once people are racially categorized, stereotypes automatically, and often unconsciously, become activated and influence behavior. Given pervasive media images of African American men as dangerous and threatening, it shouldn't be surprising that when officers make decisions about whom to pull over or whom to search, unconscious bias may encourage them to focus more often on minorities.

These kinds of biases come into play especially for local police who, in contrast to highway patrol officers, do much more low-speed, routine patrolling of neighborhoods and business districts and thus have more discretion in making decisions about whom to stop. In our research in North Carolina, for example, we found that while highway patrol officers weren't more likely to stop African American drivers than white drivers, local police stopped African Americans 70 percent more often than white drivers, even after statistically adjusting for driving behavior. Local officers were also more likely to stop men, younger drivers, and drivers in older cars, confirming this process was largely about unconscious bias rather than explicit racial profiles. Race, gender, age, class biases, and stereotypes about perceived dangerousness seem to explain this pattern of local police vehicle stops.

Strategies for Change

Unconscious biases are particularly difficult for an organization to address because offending individuals are typically unaware of them, and when confronted they may deny any racist intent. There is increasing evidence that even deep-seated stereotypes and unconscious biases can be eroded through both education and exposure to minorities who don't fit common stereotypes, and that they can be contained when people are held accountable for their decisions. Indeed, it appears that acts of racial discrimination (as opposed to just prejudicial attitudes or beliefs) can be stopped through managerial authority, and prejudice itself seems to be reduced through both education and exposure to minorities. For example, a 2006 study by sociologists Alexandra Kalev, Frank Dobbin, and Erin Kelly of race and gender employment bias in the private sector found that holding management accountable for equal employment opportunities is particularly efficient for reducing race and gender biases. Thus, the active monitoring and managing of police officers based on racial composition of their stops and searches holds much promise for mitigating this "invisible" prejudice.

Citizen and police review boards can play proactive and reactive roles in monitoring both individual police behavior as well as problematic organizational practices. Local police forces can use data they collect on racial disparity in police stops to identify problematic organizational behaviors such as intensively policing minority neighborhoods, targeting minorities in white neighborhoods, and racial profiling in searches.

Aggressive enforcement of civil rights laws will also play a key role in encouraging local police chiefs and employers to continue to monitor and address prejudice and discrimination inside their organizations. This is an area where the federal government has a clear role to play. Filing lawsuits against cities and states with persistent patterns of racially biased policing—whether based on the defense of segregated white neighborhoods or the routine patrolling of crime "hot spots"—would send a message to all police forces that the routine harassment of minority citizens is unacceptable in the United States.

NOTES

1. Editor's Note: Rodney King was beaten by Los Angeles police officers after a traffic stop, an assault that was video-taped by a witness and repeatedly aired on television. The acquittal of all four officers by an all-white jury is regarded as the trigger for the 1992 Los Angeles riots (Gray, Madison. 2007. "The L.A. Riots: 15 Years After Rodney King." Time Magazine. Accessed from http://content .time.com/time/specials/2007/la_riot/article/ 0,28804,1614117_1614084_1614831,00 .html).

2. Editor's Note: Amadou Diallo, a 22-year-old West African immigrant with no criminal record, was killed by New York City police officers who fired upon him 41 times, striking him 19 times. The four plain-clothes officers fired at Diallo because they believed he was drawing a weapon; in reality, he was unarmed, and was reaching for his wallet. The officers were charged with second-degree murder and reckless endangerment, but all four were acquitted (Susman, Tina. 2014. "Before Ferguson: Deaths of Other Black Men at the Hands of Police." Los Angeles Times. Accessed from http://www.latimes .com/nation/nationnow/la-na-nn-police -deaths-20140813-story.html).

Tomahawk Chops and "Red" Skin: Cultural Appropriation of Sport Symbols

ELIZABETH S. CAVALIER

Cavalier discusses the history and current controversy over the use of Native American mascots in sports. Whereas proponents of team names and mascots claim that these images and mascots are meant to honor Native Americans and represent team strength and pride, opponents argue that they are racially insensitive and damaging to members of Native American communities. Cavalier discusses the changes in public opinion regarding racialized mascots and why this issue should be relevant for us all.

In 1909, the University of Wisconsin–Lacrosse named their athletic team the "Indians" in the first known case of a college team using a Native American mascot (Davis, 1993). By the mid-1990s, Warriors and Indians ranked in the top ten most prevalent college sports team names (Williams, 2007). These team names, ostensibly meant to "honor" Native people, were often accompanied by caricatured imagery that reinforced stereotypes of Native Americans as "screaming savages" (Berg, 2013) and included halftime rituals that mocked sacred Native traditions. Facing a growing shift of public opinion on the issue of Native American mascots, several colleges voluntarily changed their Native American nicknames throughout the 1990s and early 2000s, including the Dartmouth Indians (Big Green), Stanford Indians (Cardinals), St. John's Redmen (Red Storm), and Marquette Warriors (Golden Eagles) (Cummings, 2008). In 2005, the National Collegiate Athletic Associa-

tion (NCAA) enacted a policy that prohibited NCAA teams from displaying "hostile and abusive" racial, ethnic, or national origin mascots, nicknames, or imagery at any of its championships. Although this policy led to nearly all college sports teams with Native American mascots changing their nicknames, the mascot issue remains a controversial one in the eyes of alumni, fans, and Native people themselves. Although the Native American mascot controversy is not new, there has been a considerable shift in public opinion and media attention in the past several years, resulting in significant developments around the use of racial and ethnic mascots in sport.

Resisting Efforts to Change

Although the tide of public opinion about Native American mascots in high school, collegiate, and professional sport has changed, resulting in critical op-eds, policy changes, and lawsuits,

Original to *Focus on Social Problems: A Contemporary Reader*.

sport stakeholders and alumni have often resisted efforts to change. In 2013, the Washington Redskins owner Dan Snyder told *USA Today*, "We will never change the name of the team. As a lifelong Redskins fan, and I think that the Redskins fans understand the great tradition and what it's all about and what it means. . . . We'll never change the name. It's that simple. NEVER—you can use caps" (Brady, 2013). In 1999, a hockey alumnus of the University of North Dakota donated $100 million to build a new hockey arena, with the stipulation that the university had to retain the "Fighting Sioux" moniker or he would withdraw his funding (Klugh, 2014).

The story at the high school level is mixed. Although there has been significant public attention and pressure aimed at changing mascot names for college and professional teams, nearly 92 percent of the current team names referencing Native Americans belong to high schools (Munguia, 2014). High schools have faced pressure at the local level to change names, but that pressure has rarely reached the national fervor that accompanies professional and collegiate mascot fights. In 2008 in Natick, Massachusetts, a group that was frustrated by a school board policy that dropped the nickname "Redmen" formed a grassroots protest group called the "Redmen Forever Committee." On their website, they declare the school board policy was "the tyrannical boot of political correctness run amok" and plan to never stop their quest to restore the team name back to the Natick Redmen (Munguia, 2014). In contrast to the approach in Massachusetts, in 2014 both the advisor and the editor-in-chief of the Neshaminy High School newspaper in Langhorne, Pennsylvania, were suspended for refusing to use the mascot name Redskin in the school paper (Mullin, 2014).

Making the Case against Native American Mascots

Proponents of Native mascots argue that the names, imagery, and logos are meant to honor Native Americans. They suggest that names like Braves and the imagery associated with Chiefs, Indians, and Warriors are complimentary, focusing on an idealized version of Native heritage. To these proponents, those who critique such imagery are being hypersensitive and are only against Native mascots because they are now seen as politically incorrect. They often argue that there are more significant issues to worry about than sports team names and strongly resist any attempts to change team nicknames. However, those who are against the use of Native imagery in sport argue that the rituals mimicked by sports fans (such as war paint and headdresses) are some of the most sacred, hallowed traditions, yet their use promotes caricatures of Native people and lumps disparate tribes into one homogenous group (Cummings, 2008). Logos rely on stereotypical, inaccurate reflections of Native culture, including the "decapitated heads of previously displaced, abused, conscripted, and eliminated people" (Williams, 2007), which have significant effects on contemporary understanding of Native lives. When sports logos and mascots serve as an unquestioned representation of Native people, and especially when it is packaged as "honoring" tribes, it perpetuates a continued misunderstood narrative about the realities of the historical experiences of Native Americans. Additionally, these names and the associated imagery help create and perpetuate a hostile climate on campuses for Native students and are connected to lowered self-esteem and negative self-image for Native people, especially children (Davis, 2002).

Students, fans, and stakeholders often rely on the assumption that Native mascots and imagery are traditional sources of pride for the school or team and that Native people are not offended by such imagery, despite repeated lawsuits, statements, opinion pieces, articles, and testimonies by Native people explicitly discussing how they feel about sport mascots. Some of these assumptions may be based on flawed data. A widely cited 2002 *Sports Illustrated* public opinion poll found that 81 percent of Native

American respondents did not feel that high school and college teams should cease the use of Native American mascots, and 83 percent of Native American respondents did not feel that professional teams should stop using such imagery; supporters of the problematic mascots and team names therefore concluded that generally speaking, Native Americans were not offended by Native sport mascots (Price, 2002). However, there has been considerable debate about the methodological accuracy of Price's findings, specifically critiquing the geographical sampling techniques and the false identification with "Indian" heritage claimed by many respondents in the sample (King et al., 2002). In contrast to Price's findings, Laveay et al. (2009) found significant evidence to suggest that American Indians find Indian sport team names, logos, and mascots offensive and were more adamant than the general population that teams that rely on Native American imagery should cease its use. The Oneida Indian Nation created an organization in 2013 called "Change the Mascot," which focuses specifically on ending the use of the name Redskins in the NFL. Along with the National Congress of American Indians, they created a powerful video called "Proud to Be" that aired during the 2013 National Basketball Association finals. The video focused on all of the words Native people use to describe themselves and highlighted the one word they do not—Redskin. Although there were major developments in the federal court system about the Washington Redskins in 2014, suggesting this was only recent "outrage," there have been organized protests and lawsuits about the nickname since 1972 (Steinberg, 2014).

College Sports and Native Mascots

When the NCAA enacted their mascot policy in 2005, they gave teams until 2008 to be in compliance. Prior to 2005, many of the remaining colleges and universities using Native imagery had begun the process to voluntarily change their names, but four schools appealed the NCAA ruling. Three of these teams—the University of Utah Utes, the Central Michigan University Chippewa, and the Florida State University Seminoles, were granted "special permission" to continue using the nicknames, as long as certain conditions were met. The University of Utah got permission from the local tribe to use the name and collaborated with tribal leaders on an appropriate mascot symbol. Central Michigan dropped their logo and some of their game-day traditions, but kept the name Chippewa in collaboration with the Saginaw Chippewa Tribal Council, while developing specific educational and cultural programs on campus to help foster the relationship between non-Native and Native students. Florida State (FSU) works closely with the Seminole Tribe, actively recruits Seminole students, and offers scholarships for them to attend FSU. However, considerable skepticism exists about the relationship between FSU and the local Seminole tribe—the "permission" by the Seminole tribal leadership happened to coincide with Florida State supporting casino-gambling legislation that would be beneficial to the Seminoles (Laveay et al., 2009). The only school that challenged the NCAA mascot policy and lost was the University of North Dakota Fighting Sioux, who could not gain permission from the local Sioux tribe to keep using the name. After years of legal battles, a two-thirds majority in a 2012 statewide referendum retired the name "Fighting Sioux" for good. They are currently operating as "University of North Dakota Athletics" until a three-year cooling-off period expires in 2015, enabling them to come up with a new nickname and mascot (Haga, 2012).

College sport has seen a tide of change regarding their use of Native American names, mascots, and imagery over the past few decades. Although the NCAA policy officially only prohibits the name, image, and mascot use in postseason play (because these games are more likely to be nationally televised), this policy has, in effect, forced schools into a change regardless. As Cummings and Harper (2009) argue, mascots that are "hostile and abusive" in the postseason should also be considered so in regular season play, and they lament the NCAA policy for not going far enough. However, with the exception of a few schools, most have eradicated the use of Native nicknames, mascots, and the associated imagery.

Professional Sports and Stalled Progress

The near eradication of the use of Native nicknames in college sports stands in contrast to the experience in professional sport. Whereas colleges and universities ostensibly have a mission to foster education and cultural competence and, thus, are under some obligation to ensure they do not perpetuate stereotypical and discriminatory practices, professional franchises are not under the same obligations and have, to this point, strongly resisted any pressure to change their names. Although a professional team has not adopted a Native American nickname since 1963 when the team relocating to Kansas City became the Chiefs (Hylton, 2010), there are still several professional franchises using Native nicknames, including the Cleveland Indians and Atlanta Braves in Major League Baseball, the Chicago Blackhawks in the National Hockey League, and the Kansas City Chiefs and Washington Redskins in the National Football League (NFL). Although some teams have reduced the most explicitly stereotypical imagery in response to public pressure, such as when the Atlanta Braves retired the mascot "Chief Noc-a-Homa" in 1986, practices such as the "Tomahawk Chop" at Braves games or the Warpaint Horse mascot at Kansas City Chiefs games, as well as usage of offensive logos on "throwback" jerseys, remain. The most significant public attention to team names in recent time has been on the Washington Redskins in the NFL. Despite the defiant pose struck by the owner, Dan Snyder, in 2014 the Trademark Trial and Appeals Board canceled the trademark registration of the name Redskins, deeming it "disparaging" and "offensive" (Vargas, 2014). Although this victory is largely symbolic, it is the first significant legal shift since a lawsuit was

first filed against the team in 1992. This case does not prevent the Redskins from using the team name, but it damages their ability to make money off of the name and imagery.

Why It Matters: Cultural Symbols, Native Lives

Why do Native American nicknames in sport matter? Nicknames are merely symbols, but cultural symbols matter. As Lindsay (2008) argues, in sport there is a preference for "animals (e.g. Bears, Tigers, Sharks), objects (Bullets, Socks, Maple Leaves), or non-living natural phenomena (Avalanche, Thunder, Lightning, Heat)" (p. 212). When human groups are used, they are most often groups whose "existence has long passed (Buccaneers, Patriots, 49ers, 76ers, Vikings, Packers, Steelers)" (p. 213). Lindsay notes that there is a "striking absence of religious, racial, and ethnic classifications [in sport], except, where the religious, racial, or ethnic group has provided the name to itself (as with Notre Dame's Fighting Irish)" (p. 213). The only group who we see caricaturized in sport against their will are Native Americans.

Native Americans have faced significant historical problems and continue to face considerable contemporary hurdles. As Williams (2007) notes, there was a 74 percent decrease in the population of Native Americans in North America between 1492 and 1800, and they now have the highest poverty, mortality, and unemployment rates and the lowest levels of educational attainment of all racial groups. Williams argues,

> In the case of Native mascots, the ability of Corporate America (or universities or other schools) to possess these symbols and cultural markers—and to legally trademark them—constitutes a theft from Native America. In stealing them, the dominant culture robs Native people of the ability to use their culture for themselves, whether for self-determination, profit, or mere survival. Native people

have had the whole of their heritage, customs, and imagery stolen, dominated, digested, and regurgitated back to them by the dominant culture; and thus they have no say in how their likeness, traditions, or history is used. Whites continue to "play Indian" without Native permission. (p. 41)

The use of Native mascots matters precisely because sport doesn't matter. When pundits, sports fans, and team owners suggest there are "bigger problems" than Native mascots, they are suggesting that sports are inconsequential and time would be better spent on "real problems." "Defenders of Native American team names who claim that 'it's no big deal' have it precisely correct: sports names and symbols are trivial—that's the point. The offense of Native American sports names lies precisely in the triviality of them" (Lindsay, 2008, p. 214). Finally, it matters because there is an absence of any other narrative about Native people. Native Americans are "underrepresented throughout the culture, in media, in schools, and in the U.S. political structure" (Laveay et al. 2009). Although they are underrepresented in contemporary social and political life, they very much still exist, unlike the Pirates, Buccaneers, 49ers, and Vikings of the past. As Lindsay (2008) concludes,

Like 49ers, Native Americans form a part of our past. But unlike 49ers, Native Americans are not only still with us, they are still with us as inheritors of a very different sort of past. Those two facts make their appropriateness for team symbols doubly incomparable. It is one thing to vanquish the historical losers, but it is quite another to strip them of their culture, tradition, history, land (and of course, a goodly number of them), and then in the aftermath, strip them of their dignity. (p. 220)

Imagine another ethnic group receiving the same treatment in sport as Native Americans have. Imagine team names with racial slurs, with negative, inaccurate stereotypical imagery and logo design. Imagine halftime rituals that take sacred, important rituals and mock them or have them mimicked by drunken college students who do not share the ethnic background of the group they are caricaturizing. Imagine opponents of that team creating t-shirts, signs, and chants that mock and disparage the team with ethnic slurs and violent imagery. Imagine this scenario for Hispanics, for African Americans, for Asians, for Germans, for Jews. Would that behavior be acceptable in those cases? Why, then, is it acceptable for Native Americans?

REFERENCES

Berg, 2013. "Braves Pull Back from 'Screaming Savage' Cap after Controversy." *USA Today*, February 11, 2013. Retrieved September 7, 2014. http://www.usatoday.com/story/gameon/2013/02/11/braves-ditch-racist-cap-for-spring-training/1910789/.

Brady, Erik. 2013. "Daniel Snyder Says Redskins Will Never Change Name." *USA Today*, May 10, 2013. Retrieved August 8, 2014. http://www.usatoday.com/story/sports/nfl/redskins/2013/05/09/washington-redskins-daniel-snyder/2148127/.

Cummings, Andre Douglas Pond. 2008. "Progress Realized? The Continuing American Indian Mascot Quandary." *Marquette Sports Law Review* 18(2):309–336.

Cummings, Andre Douglas Pond and Seth E. Harper. 2009. "Wide Right: Why the NCAA's Policy on the American Indian Mascot Issue Misses the Mark." University of Maryland Law Journal of Race, Religion, Class, and Gender 9:135.

Davis, Laurel R. 1993. "Protest against the Use of Native American Nicknames/Logos: A Challenge to Traditional American Identity." *Journal of Sport & Social Issues* 17(1):9–22.

Davis, Laurel R. 2002. "The Problems with Native American Mascots." Multicultural Education 9(4):11–14.

Haga, Chuck. 2012. "UND Ties Up Loose Ends as Nickname Is Retired." *Bakken Today*, June 16,

2012. Retrieved August 8, 2014. http://www
.bakkentoday.com/event/article/id/238935/
publisher_ID/40/.

Hylton, J. Gordon. 2010. "Before the Redskins Were
the Redskins: The Use of Native American Team
Names in the Formative Era of American Sports,
1857–1933." *North Dakota Law Review*
86(4):879–903.

King, C. Richard, Ellen J. Staurowsky, Lawrence
Baca, Laurel R. Davis, and Cornel Pewewardy.
2002. "Of Polls and Race Prejudice: *Sports Illustrated*'s Errant 'Indian Wars.'" *Journal of Sport
and Social Issues* 26(2):381–402.

Klugh, Justin. 2014. "'Fighting Sioux' Debate Leaves
University of North Dakota Nameless in Frozen
Four." Philly.com, April 10, 2014. Retrieved
August 8, 2014. http://www.philly.com/philly/
sports/colleges/University_of_North_Dakota_
goes_nameless_in_Frozen_Four_after_years_
of_Fighting_Sioux_debate.html/.

Laveay, Frahser, Coy Callison, and Ann Rodriguez.
2009. "Offensiveness of Native American
Names, Mascots, and Logos in Sports: A Survey
of Tribal Leaders and the General Population."
International Journal of Sport Communication
2:81–99.

Lindsay, Peter. 2008. "Representing Redskins: The
Ethics of Native American Team Names." *Journal of the Philosophy of Sport* 35:208–224.

Mullin, Benjamin. 2014. "High School Newspaper
Editor Suspended for Refusal to Use the
Term 'Redskin.'" http://www.poynter.org/news/
mediaware/270209/high-school-newspaper
-editor-suspended-for-refusal-to-use-the-term
-redskin/.

Munguia, Hayley. 2014. "The 2,218 Native American
Mascots People Aren't Talking About." Five
Thirty Eight. September 5, 2014. Retrieved
September 7, 2014. http://fivethirtyeight.com/
features/the-2128-Native-american-mascots
-people-arent-talking-about/.

Price, S. L. 2002. "The Indian Wars." *Sports Illustrated* 96(10):66.

Steinberg, Dan. 2014. "The Great Redskins Name
Debate of . . . 1972?" *The Washington Post*, June 3,
2014. Retrieved August 8, 2014. http://www
washingtonpost.com/blogs/dc-sports-bog/wp/
2014/06/03the-great-redskins-name-debate-of
-1972/.

Vargas, Theresa. 2014. "Federal Agency Cancels Redskins Trademark Registration, Says Name Is
Disparaging." *The Washington Post*, June 18,
2014. Retrieved August 8, 2014. http://www
washingtonpost.com/local/us-patent-office
-cancels-redskins-trademark-registration-says
-name-is-disparaging/2014/06/18/e7737bb8-f6ee
-8aa9-dad2ec039789_story.html/.

Williams, Dana M. 2007. "No Past, No Respect, and
No Power: An Anarchist Evaluation of Native
Americans as Sports Nicknames, Logos, and
Mascots." *Anarchist Studies* 15(1):31–54.

Learning to Be Illegal: Undocumented Youth and Shifting Legal Contexts in the Transition to Adulthood

ROBERTO G. GONZALES

Gonzales examines the transition to adulthood for young undocumented Latinos. These children transition from relatively protected to unprotected status when they leave the K–12 school system and enter adulthood. Means to adult status are often inaccessible because the youth face barriers to voting, driving, accessing work, and more. Drawing on more than 100 interviews, Gonzales examines the dramatic consequences of this change of status on the lives of young Latinos, as their life-course pathways are altered, affecting their identities, relationships, aspirations, and expectations, creating stumbling blocks in their successful transitions into adulthood.

During the past 25 years, the number of undocumented immigrants in the United States has grown substantially, from an estimated 2.5 million in 1987 to 11.1 million today (Passel 2006; Passel and Cohn 2010). . . . Scholars contend that this demographic trend is the unintended consequence of policies designed to curb undocumented migration and tighten the U.S.–Mexico border (Nevins 2010), transforming once-circular migratory flows into permanent settlement (Cornelius and Lewis 2006; Massey, Durand, and Malone 2002). Making multiple migratory trips back and forth became increasingly costly and dangerous throughout the 1990s and the first decade of the twenty-first century, so more unauthorized migrants began creating permanent homes in the United States. And they brought their children with them. According to recent estimates, there are more than 2.1 million undocumented young people in the United States who have been here since childhood. Of these, more than a million are now adults (Batalova and McHugh 2010). Relatively little is known about this vulnerable population of young people. . . .

. . . This . . . [reading] offers an up-close examination of the ways in which public schooling and U.S. immigration laws collide to produce a shift in the experiences and meanings of illegal status for undocumented youth at the onset of their transition to adulthood. I am interested in how these young people become aware of, and

Roberto G. Gonzales, *American Sociological Review* (Volume 76 and Issue 4), pp. 602–619, Copyright © 2011. Reprinted by Permission of SAGE Publications.

come to understand, their status under the law—that is, when they begin to notice their legal difference and its effects, and how they experience this shift as they move through late adolescence and young adulthood. The multiple transformations that undocumented youth experience have important implications for their identity formation, friendship patterns, aspirations and expectations, and social and economic mobility, and they also signal movement of a significant subset of the U.S. immigrant population into a new, disenfranchised underclass. . . .

Undocumented Youth and Shifting Contexts

Assimilation and Public Schooling

As today's children of immigrants come of age, contemporary immigration scholarship challenges the conventional expectation that they will follow a linear generational process of assimilation into mainstream U.S. life (Gans 1992; Portes and Rumbaut 2006; Portes and Zhou 1993). . . . Studies suggest that increasing fault lines of inequality along race and ethnicity, poor public schools, and differential access to today's labor market may cause recent immigrants' children to do less well than the children of previous waves (Gans 1992; Portes and Rumbaut 2001, 2006; Portes and Zhou 1993; Rumbaut 1997, 2005, 2008; Zhou 1997).

Given the changes in the U.S. economy and labor market, educational attainment has become critical to the social mobility of all children. . . . While some young people with modest levels of education manage to find skilled blue-collar jobs, most need a college degree to qualify for jobs that offer decent wages, benefits, job security, and the possibility of advancement. Children from poor and minority families, however, have historically experienced difficulty attaining significant levels of education (Alba and Nee 2003; Portes and Rumbaut 2001; Telles and Ortiz 2008) . . . although scholars have found that supplementary educational programs (Zhou 2008), extra-family mentors (Portes and Fernandez-

Kelly 2008; Smith 2008), and positive support networks (Stanton-Salazar 2001) can help overcome these disadvantages.

For generations, the public school system has been the principal institution that educates and integrates the children of immigrants into the fabric of U.S. society. This is especially true today, as more immigrant children spend more waking hours in school than ever before. . . . Certainly, the role of public schools is increasingly critical, as the returns on education have sharply increased over the past few decades. But public schools' socialization mechanisms are also powerful catalysts for promoting the acculturation processes of the children of immigrants. . . . This assimilating experience is profoundly different from what most adult immigrants encounter. While their parents may be absorbed into low-wage labor markets and often work with co-ethnics who speak their language and share their cultural practices, children are integrated into the school system, where they grow up side-by-side with the native-born (Gleeson and Gonzales forthcoming). Their "unity of experiences" with friends and classmates promotes feelings of togetherness and inclusion (Rumbaut 1997:944), and these feelings, in turn, shape immigrant youths' identification and experience of coming of age.

Today's Children of Immigrants Come of Age

Scholarly consensus on contemporary transitions to adulthood suggests that the process of coming of age is taking much longer today (Furstenberg et al. 2002). In particular, young people are spending more time in postsecondary schooling and are delaying exit from the parental household, entry into full-time work, and decisions about marriage and children (Settersten, Furstenberg, and Rumbaut 2005).

Life-course scholars traditionally define the transition to adulthood in terms of five milestones or markers: completing school, moving out of the parental home, establishing employment, getting married, and becoming a parent. . . .

Yet recent decades have brought significant shifts in the roles of social institutions as well as changes in the opportunities for entry into the labor market. By delaying entry into the workforce in favor of additional education, young adults build human capital that will make them more competitive in the high-skilled labor market. Some parents aid this process by assisting children over a longer period and using financial resources to help pay for college, providing down payments for their children's first homes, or defraying some of the costs associated with having children (Rumbaut and Komaie 2010). . . . Within the larger national context of coming of age, scholars have uncovered key differences by social class, country of origin, nativity, and immigrant generation (Mollenkopf et al. 2005; Rumbaut and Komaie 2010). Many youngsters from less-advantaged immigrant households put off postsecondary schooling because their parents are not able to provide financial assistance or because they carry considerable financial responsibilities in their households that make it impossible for them to make tuition payments (Fuligni and Pedersen 2002; Suárez-Orozco and Suárez-Orozco 1995). Many of the 1.5[1] and second generations of certain immigrant groups are in reciprocal financial relationships with their parents, often even supporting them (Rumbaut and Komaie 2010). As a result, they do not enjoy the same degree of freedom from the stresses and responsibilities of adult roles. These differences suggest that we should expect the children of immigrants—documented and undocumented alike—to experience coming of age differently from the native-born.

Conceptualizing the Transition to Illegality for Undocumented Youth

For undocumented youth, the transition into adulthood is accompanied by a transition into illegality that sets them apart from their peers. Undocumented youngsters share a confusing and contradictory status in terms of their legal rights and the opportunities available to them (Abrego 2008; Gonzales 2007). On the one hand

. . . they have the legal right to a K to 12 education. . . . Furthermore, the Family Educational Rights and Privacy Act [FERPA] prevents schools from releasing any information from students' records to immigration authorities, making school a protected space in which undocumented status has little to no negative effect. On the other hand, undocumented young adults cannot legally work, vote, receive financial aid, or drive in most states, and deportation remains a constant threat. Unauthorized residency status thus has little direct impact on most aspects of childhood but is a defining feature of late adolescence and adulthood and can prevent these youth from following normative pathways to adulthood. Therefore, coupled with family poverty, illegal status places undocumented youth in a developmental limbo. As family need requires them to make significant financial contributions and to assume considerable responsibility for their own care, they become less likely to linger in adolescence. At the same time, legal restrictions keep them from participating in many adult activities, leaving them unable to complete important transitions.

Researchers studying immigrant incorporation and the life course have not systematically considered the effects of the legal context on the children of immigrants, that is, the specific challenges facing undocumented immigrant youth and their complex and contradictory routes to adulthood. . . . K to 12 schooling certainly plays an important role in the development and integration of immigrant children, but significant questions remain about how undocumented status shapes educational trajectories and how, in turn, it affects the link between educational attainment and social and economic mobility. The scant existing research on undocumented youth notes that undocumented status depresses aspirations (Abrego 2006) and sensitizes them to the reality that they are barred from integrating legally, educationally, and economically into U.S. society (Abrego 2008).

For conceptual help, I turn to recent advances in the literature that move beyond the binary categories of documented and undocumented to explore the ways in which migrants move between different statuses and the mechanisms that allow them to be regular in one sense and irregular in another. . . . This deliberate shift in focus allows us to pay attention to the effects laws have on migrants' day-to-day lives, revealing the ways in which undocumented persons experience inclusion and exclusion and how these experiences can change over time, in interactions with different persons, and across various spaces. It also points to the two-sided nature of citizenship, which can allow the same person, citizen or not, to experience belonging in one context but not in another.

. . . While school contexts foster expectations and aspirations that root undocumented youngsters in the United States (Abrego 2006), they leave these young people grossly unprepared for what awaits them in adulthood. This [reading] focuses on the interactions between such favorable and unfavorable contexts during what I call the transition to illegality. I conceptualize this process as the set of experiences that result from shifting contexts along the life course, providing different meanings to undocumented status and animating the experience of illegality at late adolescence and into adulthood. The transition to illegality brings with it a period of disorientation, whereby undocumented youth confront legal limitations and their implications and engage in a process of retooling and reorienting themselves for new adult lives. . . . Because comparisons between differently achieving youth may help to more clearly identify mechanisms that mediate undocumented status during the transition to adulthood, I compare the experiences of college-going young adults (i.e., college-goers) with those who exit the education system after high school graduation or earlier (i.e., early-exiters).

Methods

While many recent immigrants have dispersed to new destination states in the South and the Midwest (Marrow 2009; Massey 2008; Singer 2004; Zúñiga and Hernández-León 2005), California remains home to the largest undocumented immigrant population in the country. The numbers of undocumented immigrants from countries outside of Latin America have risen slightly since 2000, but immigrants from Mexico continue to account for the majority. In fact, no other sending country constitutes even a double-digit share of the total (Passel and Cohn 2009). I thus focus on Mexican-origin immigrants in California, drawing on 150 individual semi-structured interviews with 1.5-generation young adults ages 20 to 34 years (who migrated before the age of 12). The interviews focused on respondents' experiences growing up in Southern California without legal status. Such close study of the 1.5 generation permits an examination of the unique ways in which undocumented status is experienced in childhood and adolescence (Rumbaut 2004; Smith 2006).

Until very recently, it has been difficult to study undocumented young adults like those interviewed for this study because their numbers have been prohibitively small. Researching hard-to-reach populations adds layers of difficulty, time, and cost to any study. While previous large-scale efforts have been successful at locating and interviewing undocumented Mexicans on both sides of the U.S.–Mexico border, and have provided useful direction for random sampling . . . today's anti-immigrant climate and localized immigration enforcement present challenges to finding respondents in the United States.

These conditions lead many unauthorized migrants to be more fearful in their everyday lives, thus posing significant challenges to random sampling efforts. Data collection for this study involved nearly four and a half years of field work in the periods 2003 to 2007 and 2008 to 2009, during which I conducted interviews and did additional ethnographic research in the Los Angeles Metropolitan Area.[2] I began conducting interviews after spending lengthy periods of time in the field gaining a rapport with respondents and community stakeholders. I recruited respondents from various settings, including continuation schools, community organizations, college campuses, and churches. After gaining trust, I accompanied respondents throughout their school and work days, volunteered at local schools and organizations, and sat in on numerous community meetings. I built on the initial group of respondents by using snowball sampling to identify subsequent respondents.

All 150 1.5-generation respondents interviewed spent much of their childhood, adolescence, and adulthood with undocumented status. With the exception of eight Central Americans (Guatemalan and Salvadoran), all were born in Mexico. . . . Most had parents who were undocumented (92 percent) and had fewer than six years of schooling (86 percent). Most respondents were also raised by two parents; one-quarter were raised by single parents and six were raised by other family members.

I designed the sampling process to include relatively equal numbers of males and females (71 males and 79 females) and equal numbers of individuals who dropped out of or completed high school (73) and those who attended some college (77). . . . Of the 77 college respondents, nine had advanced degrees at the time of the interview, 22 had earned bachelor's degrees, 26 were enrolled in four-year universities, and 20 were enrolled in or had attended community college. The majority attended a California public college or university. Of the 73 respondents who exited school at or before high school graduation, 31 had not earned a high school degree at the time of interview, and 42 had high school diplomas.

The life history interviews included questions regarding respondents' pasts and their present lives as well as future expectations and aspirations. Interviews ranged in length from 1 hour and 40 minutes to 3 hours and 20 minutes. . . .

The Transition to Illegality

To better conceptualize the ways in which legal status affects the transition to illegality, I focus on three transition periods—discovery (ages 16 to 18 years), learning to be illegal (ages 18 to 24 years), and coping (ages 25 to 29 years). . . . I add an earlier period to capture the awakening to newfound legal limitations, which elicits a range of emotional reactions and begins a process of altered life-course pathways and adult transitions. Next, as undocumented youth enter early adulthood, they engage in a parallel process of learning to be illegal. During this period, many find difficulty connecting with previous sources of support to navigate the new restrictions on their lives and to mitigate their newly stigmatized identities. At this stage, undocumented youth are forced to alter earlier plans and reshape their aspirations for the future. Finally, the coping period involves adjusting to lowered aspirations and coming to grips with the possibility that their precarious legal circumstances may never change.

Discovery: Ages 16 to 18

Most life-course scholars focus on age 18 as a time of dramatic change for young people. In the United States, 18 is the age of majority, the legal threshold of adulthood when a child ceases to be considered a minor and assumes control over his actions and decisions. This is traditionally the time when young people exit high school and enter college or full-time work. Yet young people adopt semi-adult roles, such as working and driving, while still in high school. Most respondents in this study began to experience dramatic shifts in their daily lives and future outlooks around age 16.

Because public schooling provided respondents with an experience of inclusion atypical of undocumented adult life in the United States (Bean, Telles, and Lowell 1987; Chavez 1991, 1998), respondents spent their childhood and early adolescence in a state of suspended illegality, a buffer stage wherein they were legally integrated and immigration status rarely limited activities. Through school, respondents developed aspirations rooted in the belief that they were part of the fabric of the nation and would have better opportunities than their parents (Gans 1992). They learned to speak English, developed tastes, joined clubs, dated, and socialized—all alongside their U.S.-born and legal resident peers. . . . As Marisol, a college-goer, explained, relationships with teachers and friends provided a comfortable space for many like her to learn and develop: "School was an escape from home. I felt happy, calm. . . . I could be myself. I could be recognized at school. My teachers encouraged me to keep going. And my friends, we believed in education and pushed each other. We helped each other with home-work and talked about college."

Such positive relationships, however, were not uniformly experienced by respondents. Many early-exiters (those who left the school system at or before completion of high school) recounted feeling disconnected from school and lacking significant relationships with teachers or counselors. They felt they were left to fall through the cracks and cut off from important services; they also reported having limited visits with counselors. . . . Nevertheless, even respondents who reported having trouble in school believed they would have more options than their parents. Eric, an early-exiter who grew up in River-side County, told me he had grown up thinking he was going to have a "better life": "I saw my older [U.S.-born] cousins get good jobs. I mean, they're not lawyers or anything like that, but they're not in restaurants or mowing lawns. I thought, yeah, when I graduate from school, I can make some good money, maybe even go to college."

Respondents uniformly noted a jolting shift at around age 16, when they attempted to move through rites of passage associated with their age. Life-course scholars refer to critical events in one's life as "turning points" that "knife off" past from present and restructure routine ac-tivities and life-course pathways (Elder 1987:452). . . . For undocumented youth, the pro-cess of coming of age is a critical turning point that has consequences for subsequent transi-tions. Finding a part-time job, applying for

college, and obtaining a driver's license—all markers of new roles and responsibilities—require legal status as a basis for participation.

As respondents tried to take these steps into adult life, they were blocked by their lack of a Social Security number. These incidents proved to be life changing and were often accompanied by the realization that they were excluded from a broad range of activities. Rodolfo, an early-exiter who is now 27 years old, spoke of his first experience of exclusion:

> I never actually felt like I wasn't born here. Because when I came I was like 10 and a half. I went to school. I learned the lan-guage. I first felt like I was really out of place when I tried to get a job. I didn't have a Social Security number. Well, I didn't even know what it meant. You know Social Security, legal, illegal. I didn't even know what that was.

Until this time, Rodolfo had never needed proof of legal residency. The process of looking for a job made the implications of his lack of legal status real to him for the first time. Like Rodolfo, many early-exiters (a little over 68 percent . . .) made such discoveries while applying for jobs or for driver's licenses.

On the other hand . . . most college-goers (almost 60 percent) reported finding out they were undocumented in the course of the college application process. Jose, for example, was on the academic decathlon and debate teams. He did well in school and was well-liked by teach-ers. During his junior year, he attempted to enroll in classes at the community college to earn college credits. But without a Social Secu-rity number, he could not move forward.

While most respondents did not know of their unauthorized status until their teenage years, some reported knowing in childhood. This was more true of early-exiters (almost 30 percent, compared with a little over 9 percent among college-goers), many of whom lived in households where older siblings had gone through the process of discovery before them. But even these respondents did not realize the full implications their illegal status would have for their futures until much later. Being undocumented only became salient when matched with experiences of exclusion. Early-exiter Lorena started cleaning houses with her mother and sisters at age 12. Even before she began working, reminders from her mother made her aware that she did not have "papers." But she explained to me that "it really hit home" when she tried to branch out to other work in high school and was asked for her Social Security number.

Discovery of illegal status prompted reactions of confusion, anger, frustration, and despair among respondents, followed by a period of paralyzing shock. Most respondents conveyed that they were not prepared for the dramatic limits of their rights. They struggled to make sense of what had happened to them, many feeling as though they had been lied to. "I always thought I would have a place when I grew up," David, an early-exiter, told me. "Teachers make you believe that. It's all a lie. A big lie." They often blamed teachers and parents for their feelings of anger and frustration. Cory, a college-goer, locked herself in her bedroom for an entire week. When she finally emerged, she moved out of her parents' house, blaming them for "keeping [her] in the dark during childhood." Cory said: "They thought that by the time I graduated I would have my green card. But they didn't stop to think that this is my life. . . . Everything I believed in was a big lie. Santa Claus was not coming down the chimney, and I wasn't going to just become legal. I really resented them."

Respondents reported that soon after these discoveries, they experienced a second shock as they came to realize that the changes they were experiencing would adversely affect their remaining adult lives. As they came to grips with the new meanings of unauthorized status, they began to view and define themselves differently. Miguel, a college-goer who has been caught in the part-time cycle of community college and work for six years, told me: "During most of

high school, I thought I had my next 10 years laid out. College and law school were definitely in my plans. But when my mom told me I wasn't legal, everything was turned upside down. I didn't know what to do. I couldn't see my future anymore." Miguel's entire identity was transformed, and the shift placed him, like many other respondents, in a state of limbo. Cory put it this way: "I feel as though I've experienced this weird psychological and legal-stunted growth. I'm stuck at 16, like a clock that has stopped ticking. My life has not changed at all since then. Although I'm 22, I feel like a kid. I can't do anything adults do."

Respondents' illegality was paired with a movement into stigmatized status that reinforced their legal exclusion. While laws limited their access to grown-up activities and responsibilities, fears of being found out curbed their interactions with teachers and peers. Ironically, while many respondents believed they had been lied to in childhood, they adopted lying themselves as a daily survival strategy that separated them from the very peer networks that had provided support and shaped a positive self-image. Many reported they were afraid of what their friends would think or how they would react if they learned of their illegal status. These fears were validated by observations of friends' behavior. Chuy, a college-goer who played sports throughout school, explained that after he saw a teammate on his high school soccer team berate players on an opposing team as "wetbacks" and "illegals," he was reticent to disclose his status even to good friends. "I grew up with this guy," he said. "We had classes together and played on the same team for like four years. But wow, I don't know what he would say if he knew I was one of those wetbacks."

Frustration with the present, uncertainty about the future, and the severing of support systems caused many respondents to withdraw, with detrimental effects on their progress during the last half of high school (see also Abrego 2006; Suárez-Orozco et al. 2008). In my interview with Sandra, an early-exiter, she recalled her struggles during junior year: "I felt the world caving in on me. What was I going to do? I couldn't ask my parents. They didn't know about college or anything. I was kind of quiet in school, so I didn't really know my teachers. Besides, I was scared. What would they do if they knew? I was scared and alone." Throughout high school, Luis, an early-exiter, hoped to attend college. During the latter part of his sophomore year, his grades fell considerably. As a result, he did not meet the requirements to gain entrance into the University of California system. His girlfriend convinced him to apply to the lower-tier California State University, but when he found out he was not eligible for financial aid, he gave up: "It took a while to get accepted. But I ended up not going (because of) financial aid. . . . It just kinda brought down my spirit, I guess." Like Sandra and Luis, many respondents had done moderately well in school before the cumulative disadvantages resulting from the transition to illegality caused them to lose motivation to continue. Lacking trusting relationships with teachers or counselors who could help them, they ended up exiting school much earlier than they had planned (Gonzales 2010).

Nationally, 40 percent of undocumented adults ages 18 to 24 do not complete high school, and only 49 percent of undocumented high school graduates go to college. Youths who arrive in the United States before the age of 14 fare slightly better: 72 percent finish high school, and of those, 61 percent go on to college. But these figures are still much lower than the numbers for U.S.-born residents (Passel and Cohn 2009). The combination of scarce family resources and exclusion from financial aid at the state . . . and federal levels makes the path to higher education very steep for undocumented high school students. . . . In several states, laws allowing undocumented students to pay in-state tuition have increased the number of high school graduates matriculating to college over the past decade (Flores 2010). Nonetheless, steep financial barriers prohibit many undocumented youth from enrolling in college.

While depressed motivation contributed to many respondents' early exit from the school system, limited financial resources within their families and a general lack of information about how to move forward also played a part in causing early departures. Karina, an early-exiter, maintained a B average in her general-track high school classes. When she applied to college, she had no guidance. Unaware of a California provision that should have made it possible for her to attend school at in-state tuition rates, Karina opted not to go to college: "I didn't know anything about [the provision]. . . . Maybe if I knew the information I could have gotten a scholarship or something. That's why I didn't go. I don't know if my counselors knew, but they never told me anything."

The experiences of successful college-goers, by contrast, unlock a key variable to success missing from the narratives of early-exiters: trusting relationships with teachers or other adults. Portes and Fernandez-Kelly (2008:26) find evidence linking school success to the presence of what they call "really significant others" who "possess the necessary knowledge and experience" and "take a keen interest in [their students], motivate [them] to graduate from high school and to attend college." When Marisol began to exhibit decreasing levels of motivation, for instance, her English teacher was there to intervene. Although Marisol felt embarrassed, she was able to talk frankly with her teacher because they had developed a trusting relationship. As a reward for her trust, Marisol's teacher helped her obtain information about college and also took up a collection among other teachers to pay for her first year of tuition at the community college.

Most college-goers reported they had formed trusting relationships with teachers, counselors, and other mentors in high school. These respondents were concentrated in the advanced curriculum tracks in high school; the smaller and more supportive learning environments gave them access to key school personnel. Compared to early-exiters, they disclosed their problems more easily and were able to draw on relationships of trust to seek out and receive help. At critical times when the students' motivations were low, these relationships meant the difference between their leaving school or going to college. When difficulties arose during the college admissions process for college-goer Jose, for instance, he went straight to his counselor, with positive results. The counselor called the college and found out about the availability of aid through . . . [the state provision allowing immigrants to pay in-state tuition], which neither he nor Jose had been aware of.

Learning to Be Illegal: Ages 18 to 24

For the children of unauthorized parents, success means improving on the quality of jobs and opportunities. Many youths end up only a small step ahead, however. Lacking legal status and a college degree, early-exiters confront some of the same limited and limiting employment options as their parents. Economic circumstances and family need force them to make choices about working and driving illegally. Nearly all respondents contributed money to their families, averaging nearly $300 per month. After high school, early-exiter Oscar, who at 27 still gives his parents $500 a month, moved through a string of short stints in the workforce, not staying in any one job more than six months at a time. He quit jobs because he was dissatisfied with the meager wages and generally uneasy about the ways in which employers treated him. Each new job proved no better than the previous one. Over time, Oscar realized he had few job choices outside of physical labor: "I wasn't prepared to do that kind of work. . . . It's tough. I come home from work tired every day. I don't have a life. . . . It's not like I can get an office job. I've tried to get something better, but I'm limited by my situation."

The effects of stress and difficult work took their toll on other respondents. Simon, who used to play piano, showed me calluses and cuts on his hands. "Can you believe this? I'm so far away from those days," he said. Janet, who has been employed by various maid services, told me she cried every day after work for the first two months: "I can't believe this is my life. When I was in school I never thought I'd be doing this. I mean, I was never an honors student, but I thought I would have a lot better job. It's really hard, you know. I make beds, I clean toilets. The sad thing is when I get paid. I work this hard, for nothing." Janet and others expressed difficulty coming to terms with the narrow range of bad options their illegal status forced on them.

While financial need forced respondents into the workforce, lack of experience put them at a disadvantage in the low-wage job sector, where they became part of the same job pool as their parents and other family members who have much less education but more work experience. . . . Respondents also recounted difficulty negotiating precarious situations because their undocumented status forced them to confront experiences for which K to 12 schooling did not prepare them. Pedro found himself in legal trouble when, after completing a day job, he tried to cash his check at the local currency exchange. A teller called Pedro's employer to verify its legitimacy, and he denied writing the check and called the police. When the police arrived, they found multiple sets of identification in Pedro's possession and took him to jail for identity fraud. This incident awoke Pedro to the reality that his inexperience with undocumented life could have grave consequences, including arrest and even deportation.

Given the limited employment options available to undocumented youth, moving on to college becomes critical. Making a successful transition to postsecondary schooling requires a number of favorable circumstances, however, including sufficient money to pay for school, family permission to delay or minimize work, reliable transportation, and external guidance and assistance. Respondents who enjoyed such conditions were able to devote their time to school and, equally important, avoid activities and situations that would place them in legal trouble. As a result, they suspended many of the negative consequences of unauthorized status.

When I met Rosalba, she had associate's, bachelor's, and master's degrees. Her parents had prohibited her from working, thus allowing her to concentrate fully on school. Throughout her time in school, she benefited from assistance from a number of caring individuals. "I've made it because I've had a support system," she said:

> At every step of my education, I have had a mentor holding my hand. It's a thousand times harder without someone helping you. Being undocumented, it's not about what you know, it's who you know. You might have all of the will in the world, but if you don't know the right people, then as much as you want to, you're gonna have trouble doing it.

... Many other respondents, however, found postsecondary education to be a discontinuous experience, with frequent stalls and detours. Several took leaves of absence, and others enrolled in only one school term per year. Faced with the need to work, few scholarships, debt, and long commutes, these respondents managed to attend college, but completing their schooling was an arduous task that required them to be creative, keep their costs low, and in many cases join early-exiters in the low-wage labor market. Several respondents' dreams of higher education did not materialize because financial burdens became too overwhelming. Margarita, for example, aspired to be a pharmacist, but after two years of community college, her mother started asking her to pay her share of the rent. She left school to clean houses, which she had been doing for almost four years when I met her.

Coping: Ages 25 to 29

The impact of not having legal residency status becomes particularly pronounced for respondents in their mid-20s, when prolonged experiences of illegality force them to begin viewing their legal circumstances as more permanent. By this time, most young adults in the United States have finished school, left the parental home, and are working full-time. They have also started to see the returns on their education in better jobs and have gained increased independence from their parents. Although sharp differences in educational returns persist among legal young adults, I found a high degree of convergence among college-goers and early-exiters as they finished the transition to illegality. By their mid-20s, both sets of respondents held similar occupations. While both groups were also starting to leave the parental home, early-exiters were already settled into work routines. Years on the job had provided them with experience and improved their human capital. Many had let go of hopes for career mobility long ago, opting instead for security and stability. While college-going respondents spent much of their late teens and early 20s in institutions of higher learning, by their mid-20s most were out of school and learning that they had few legal employment options, despite having attained advanced degrees.

... For my respondents, day-to-day struggles, stress, and the ever-present ceiling on opportunities ... forced them to acknowledge the distance between their prior aspirations and present realities. The realization was especially poignant for those who managed to complete degrees but ultimately recognized that the years of schooling did not offer much advantage in low-wage labor markets—the only labor markets to which they had access.

These are young people who grew up believing that because their English mastery and education surpassed those of their parents, they would achieve more. Instead, they came face-to-face with the limits on their opportunities—often a very unsettling experience. Early-exiter Margarita underscored this point:

> I graduated from high school and have taken some college credits. Neither of my parents made it past fourth grade, and they don't speak any English. But I'm right where they are. I mean, I work with my

mom. I have the same job. I can't find anything else. It's kinda ridiculous, you know. Why did I even go to school? It should mean something. I mean, that should count, right? You would think. I thought. Well, here I am, cleaning houses.

Others conveyed a tacit acceptance of their circumstances. When I interviewed Pedro, he had been out of school for nine years. He had held a string of jobs and was living with childhood friends in a mobile home. He was slowly making progress toward his high school diploma but was not hopeful that education would improve his opportunities or quality of life. I asked him what he wanted for himself. He replied:

> Right now, I want to take care of my legal status, clean up my record for the stupidity I committed and get a decent job. I'm thinking about five years from now. I don't want to extend it any longer. I wish it could be less, you know, but I don't want to rush it either, because when you rush things they don't go as they should. Maybe 10 years from now. I like where I live, and I wouldn't mind living in a mobile home.

Other respondents had similarly low expectations for the future, the cumulative result of years of severely restricted choices. When I first met Gabriel, he was 23 years old. He was making minimal progress at the community college. He had moved out of his mother's home because he felt like a financial burden, and he left his job after his employer received a letter from the Social Security Administration explaining that the number he was using did not match his name. He was frustrated and scared. When I ran into him four years later, near the end of my study, he seemed to be at ease with his life. He was working in a factory with immigrant co-workers and participating in a community dance group. He told me he was "not as uptight" about his situation as he had once been:

> I just stopped letting it [unauthorized status] define me. Work is only part of my life. I've got a girlfriend now. We have our own place. I'm part of a dance circle, and it's really cool. Obviously, my situation holds me back from doing a lot of things, but I've got to live my life. I just get sick of being controlled by the lack of nine digits.

Undoubtedly, Gabriel would rather be living under more stable circumstances. But he has reconciled himself to his limitations, focusing instead on relationships and activities that are tangible and accessible.

Such acceptance was most elusive for respondents who achieved the highest levels of school success. At the time of their interviews, 22 respondents had graduated from four-year universities, and an additional nine held advanced degrees. None were able to legally pursue their dream careers. Instead, many, like Esperanza, found themselves toiling in low-wage jobs. Esperanza had to let go of her long-held aspiration to become a journalist, in favor of the more immediate need to make ends meet each month. In high school, she was in band and AP classes. Her hopes for success were encouraged by high-achieving peers and teachers. Nothing leading up to graduation prepared her for the reality of her life afterward. Now three years out of college, she can find only restaurant jobs and factory work. While she feels out of place in the sphere of undocumented work, she has little choice:

> The people working at those places, like the cooks and the cashiers, they are really young, and I feel really old. Like what am I doing there if they are all like 16, 17 years old? The others are like senoras who are 35. They dropped out of school, but because they have little kids they are still working at the restaurant. Thinking about that makes me feel so stupid. And like the factories, too, because they ask me, "Que estas haciendo aqui? [What are you doing

here?] You can speak English. You graduated from high school. You can work anywhere."

Discussion and Conclusion

The experiences of unauthorized 1.5-generation young adults shed some important light on the powerful role played by immigration policy in shaping incorporation patterns and trajectories into adulthood. Contemporary immigration theory has made great strides in its ability to predict inter-generational progress. In doing so, however, it has paid less attention to the here-and-now experiences and outcomes of today's immigrants and their children. As Portes and Fernandez-Kelly (2008) point out, focusing exclusively on inter-generational mobility contributes to a failure to uncover key mechanisms that produce delayed, detoured, and derailed trajectories. Indeed, by focusing on individuals they call the "final survivors"—two to three generations out—we neglect the struggles of individuals today who end up disappearing from view. Many respondents in this study possess levels of human capital that surpass those of their parents, who tend to speak little English and have fewer than six years of schooling. We may be tempted to see this outcome as a sign of inter-generational progress. But these young men and women describe moving from an early adolescence in which they had important inclusionary access, to an adulthood in which they are denied daily participation in most institutions of mainstream life. They describe this process as waking up to a nightmare.

While life-course scholars note that most U.S. youngsters today face some difficulty managing adolescent and adult transitions, undocumented youth face added challenges. Their exclusion from important rites of passage in late adolescence, and their movement from protected to unprotected status, leave them in a state of developmental limbo, preventing subsequent and important adult transitions. Their entry into a stigmatized identity has negative and usually unanticipated consequences for

their educational and occupational trajectories, as well as for their friendships and social patterns. Unlike documented peers who linger in adolescence due to safety nets at home, many of these youngsters must start contributing to their families and taking care of themselves. These experiences affect adolescent and adult transitions that diverge significantly from those of their documented peers, placing undocumented youth in jeopardy of becoming a disenfranchised underclass.

Positive mediators at the early (discovery) and middle (learning to be illegal) transitions help cushion the blow, and a comparison of early-exiters and college-goers reveals a lot about the power, and the limitations, of these intermediaries. The keys to success for my respondents—extra-familial mentors, access to information about postsecondary options, financial support for college, and lower levels of family responsibility—are not very different from those required for the success of members of other student populations. For undocumented youth, however, they take on added significance. In adult mentors, they find trusting allies to confide in and from whom to receive guidance and resources. The presence of caring adults who intervene during the discovery period can aid in reducing anxiety and minimizing barriers, allowing undocumented youth to delay entry into legally restricted adult environments and to make successful transitions to postsecondary institutions. Eventually, however, all undocumented youth unable to regularize their immigration status complete the transition to illegality.

My findings move beyond simply affirming that immigrant incorporation is a segmented process. . . . As I demonstrate here, blocked mobility caused by a lack of legal status renders traditional measures of inter-generational mobility by educational progress irrelevant: the assumed link between educational attainment and material and psychological outcomes after school is broken. College-bound youths' trajectories ultimately converge with those who have minimal levels of schooling. These youngsters, who committed to the belief that hard work and educational achievement would garner rewards, experience a tremendous fall. They find themselves ill-prepared for the mismatch between their levels of education and the limited options that await them in the low-wage, clandestine labor market.

The young men and women interviewed for this study are part of a growing population of undocumented youth who have moved into adulthood. Today, the United States is home to more than 1.1 million undocumented children who, in the years to come, will be making the same sort of difficult transitions, under arguably more hostile contexts (Massey and Sanchez 2010). These demographic and legal realities ensure that a sizeable population of U.S.-raised adults will continue to be cut off from the futures they have been raised to expect. Efforts aimed at legalizing this particular group of young people have been in the works for more than 10 years without success. . . . In the meantime, proposals aimed at ending birthright citizenship for U.S.-born children of undocumented immigrants and barring their entry to postsecondary education threaten to deny rights to even greater numbers. These young people will very likely remain in the United States. Whether they become a disenfranchised underclass or contributing members to our society, their fate rests largely in the hands of the state. We must ask ourselves if it is good for the health and wealth of this country to keep such a large number of U.S.-raised young adults in the shadows. We must ask what is lost when they learn to be illegal.

NOTES

1. Editor's Note: the term "1.5 generation" refers to individuals who immigrated before they reached adolescence.
2. Given the respondents' immigration status, I went to great lengths to ensure confidentiality. . . . I gave pseudonyms to all respondents at the time of the initial meeting, and I never collected home addresses. Because of these precautions, personal information does not appear anywhere in this research. Respondents provided verbal consent rather than leaving a paper trail with a written consent form. I destroyed all audio tapes immediately after transcription. . . .

REFERENCES

Abrego, Leisy J. 2006. "I Can't Go to College Because I Don't Have Papers: Incorporation Patterns of Undocumented Latino Youth." *Latino Studies* 4: 212–31.

Abrego, Leisy J. 2008. "Legitimacy, Social Identity, and the Mobilization of Law: The Effects of Assembly Bill 540 on Undocumented Students in California." *Law & Social Inquiry* 33:709–34.

Alba, Richard and Victor Nee. 2003. *Remaking the American Mainstream: Assimilation and Contemporary Immigration*. Cambridge: Harvard University Press.

Batalova, Jeanne and Margie McHugh. 2010. "DREAM vs. Reality: An Analysis of Potential DREAM Act Beneficiaries." Washington, DC: Migration Policy Institute (http://www.migrationpolicy.org/pubs/DREAM-Insight-July2010.pdf).

Bean, Frank D., Edward Telles, and B. Lindsey Lowell. 1987. "Undocumented Migration to the United States: Perceptions and Evidence." *Population and Development Review* 13:671–90.

Chavez, Leo R. 1991. "Outside the Imagined Community: Undocumented Settlers and Experiences of Incorporation." *American Ethnologist* 18:257–78.

Chavez, Leo R. 1998. *Shadowed Lives: Undocumented Immigrants in American Society*. Fort Worth, TX: Harcourt Brace College Publishers.

Cornelius, Wayne A. and Jessa M. Lewis, eds. 2006. *Impacts of Border Enforcement on Mexican Migration: The View from Sending Communities*. Boulder, CO: Lynne Rienner Publishers and Center for Comparative Immigration Studies, UCSD.

Elder, Glen H., Jr. 1987. "War Mobilization and the Life Course: A Cohort of World War II Veterans." *Sociological Forum* 2:449–72.

Flores, Stella M. 2010. "State Dream Acts: The Effect of In-State Resident Tuition Policies and Undocumented Latino Students." *Review of Higher Education* 33:239–83.

Fuligni, Andrew J. and Sara Pedersen. 2002. "Family Obligation and the Transition to Young Adulthood." *Developmental Psychology* 38:856–68.

Furstenberg, Frank, Thomas Cook, Robert Sampson, and Gail Slap. 2002. "Early Adulthood in Cross National Perspective." *ANNALS of the American Academy of Political and Social Science* 580:6–15.

Gans, Herbert J. 1992. "Second Generation Decline: Scenarios for the Economic and Ethnic Futures of the Post-1965 American Immigrants." *Ethnic and Racial Studies* 15:173–92.

Gleeson, Shannon and Roberto G. Gonzales. Forthcoming. "When Do Papers Matter? An Institutional Analysis of Undocumented Life in the United States." *International Migration*.

Gonzales, Roberto G. 2007. "Wasted Talent and Broken Dreams: The Lost Potential of Undocumented Students." *Immigration Policy: In Focus* 5:13. Washington, DC: Immigration Policy Center of the American Immigration Law Foundation.

Gonzales, Roberto G. 2010. "On the Wrong Side of the Tracks: The Consequences of School Stratification Systems for Unauthorized Mexican Students." *Peabody Journal of Education* 85:469.

Marrow, Helen B. 2009. "Immigrant Bureaucratic Incorporation: The Dual Roles of Professional Missions and Government Policies." *American Sociological Review* 74:756–76.

Massey, Douglas S. 2008. *New Faces in New Places: The New Geography of American Immigration.* New York: Russell Sage Foundation.

Massey, Douglas S., Jorge Durand, and Nolan J. Malone. 2002. *Beyond Smoke and Mirrors: Mexican Immigration in an Era of Economic Integration.* New York: Russell Sage Foundation.

Massey, Douglas and Magaly Sánchez R. 2010. *Brokered Boundaries: Creating Immigrant Identity in Anti-Immigrant Times.* New York: Russell Sage Foundation.

Mollenkopf, John H., Mary Waters, Jennifer Holdaway, and Philip Kasinitz. 2005. "The Ever-Winding Path: Ethnic and Racial Diversity in the Transition to Adulthood." Pp. 454–97 in *On the Frontier of Adulthood: Theory, Research, and Public Policy*, edited by R. Settersten Jr., F. F. Furstenberg Jr., and R. G. Rumbaut. Chicago: University of Chicago Press.

Nevins, Joseph. 2010. *Operation Gatekeeper and Beyond: The War on "Illegals" and the Remaking of the U.S.–Mexico Boundary.* New York: Routledge.

Passel, Jeffrey S. 2006. "The Size and Characteristics of the Unauthorized Migrant Population in the U.S.: Estimates Based on the March 2005 Current Population Survey." Washington, DC: Pew Hispanic Center (http://pewhispanic.org/files/reports/61.pdf).

Passel, Jeffrey and D'Vera Cohn. 2009. "A Portrait of the Unauthorized Migrants in the United States." Washington, DC: Pew Hispanic Center (http://pewhispanic .org/files/reports/107.pdf).

Passel, Jeffrey and D'Vera Cohn. 2010. "U.S. Unauthorized Immigration Flows Are Down Sharply since Mid-Decade." Washington, DC: Pew Hispanic Center (http://pewhispanic.org/files/reports/126.pdf).

Portes, Alejandro and Patricia Fernandez-Kelly. 2008. "No Margin for Error: Educational and Occupational Achievement among Disadvantaged Children of Immigrants." *ANNALS of the American Academy of Political and Social Science* 620:12–36.

Portes, Alejandro and Rubén G. Rumbaut. 2001. *Legacies: The Story of the Immigrant Second Generation.* Berkeley: University of California Press.

Portes, Alejandro and Rubén G. Rumbaut. 2006. *Immigrant America: A Portrait*, 3rd ed. Berkeley: University of California Press.

Portes, Alejandro and Min Zhou. 1993. "The New Second Generation: Segmented Assimilation and its Variants." *ANNALS of the American Academy of Political and Social Science* 530:74–96.

Rumbaut, Rubén G. 1997. "Assimilation and Its Discontents: Between Rhetoric and Reality." *International Migration Review* 31:923–60.

Rumbaut, Rubén G. 2004. "Ages, Life Stages, and Generational Cohorts: Decomposing the

Immigrant First and Second Generations in the United States." *International Migration Review* 38:1160–1205.

Rumbaut, Rubén G. 2005. "Turning Points in the Transition to Adulthood: Determinants of Educational Attainment, Incarceration, and Early Childbearing among Children of Immigrants." *Ethnic and Racial Studies* 28:1041–86.

Rumbaut, Rubén G. 2008. "The Coming of the Second Generation: Immigration and Ethnic Mobility in Southern California." *ANNALS of the American Academy of Political and Social Science* 620:196–236.

Rumbaut, Rubén G. and Golnaz Komaie. 2010. "Immigration and Adult Transitions." *The Future of Children* 20.39–63.

Settersten, Jr., Richard A., Frank F. Furstenberg, and Rubén G. Rumbaut. 2005. *On the Frontier of Adulthood: Theory, Research, and Public Policy.* Chicago: University of Chicago Press.

Singer, Audrey. 2004. "The Rise of New Immigrant Gateways." Washington, DC: The Brookings Institution (http://www.brookings.edu/urban/pubs/20040301_gateways.pdf).

Smith, Robert Courtney. 2006. *Mexican New York: Transnational Lives of New Immigrants.* Berkeley: University of California Press.

Smith, Robert Courtney. 2008. "Horatio Alger Lives in Brooklyn: Extrafamily Support, Intrafamily Dynamics, and Socially Neutral Operating Identities in Exceptional Mobility among Children of Mexican Immigrants." *ANNALS of the American Academy of Political and Social Science* 620:270–90.

Stanton-Salazar, Ricardo. 2001. *Manufacturing Hope and Despair: The School and Kin Support Networks of U.S.–Mexican Youth.* New York: Teachers College Press.

Suárez-Orozco, Carola and Marcelo Suárez-Orozco. 1995. *Transformations: Migration, Family Life, and Achievement Motivation among Latino Adolescents.* Stanford, CA: Stanford University Press.

Suárez-Orozco, Carola, Marcelo M. Suárez-Orozco, and Irina Todorova. 2008. *Learning a New Land: Immigrant Students in American Society.* Cambridge: Harvard University Press.

Telles, Edward E. and Vilma Ortiz. 2008. *Generations of Exclusion: Mexican Americans, Assimilation, and Race.* New York: Russell Sage Foundation.

Zhou, Min. 1997. "Segmented Assimilation: Issues, Controversies, and Recent Research on the New Second Generation." *International Migration Review* 4:825–58.

Zhou, Min. 2008. "The Ethnic System of Supplementary Education: Non-profit and For-profit Institutions in Los Angeles' Chinese Immigrant Community." Pp. 229–51 in *Toward Positive Youth Development: Transforming Schools and Community Programs*, edited by B. Shinn and H. Yoshikawa. New York: Oxford University Press.

Zúñiga, Victor and Rubén Hernández-León, eds. 2005. *New Destinations: Mexican Immigration in the United States.* New York: Russell Sage Foundation.

6

Gender Inequality

Emily May

Courtesy of Carly Romero.

Emily May is the co-founder and executive director of Hollaback!

What is your organization and its mission?

Hollaback! is a movement to end sexual harassment that is powered by a network of local activists around the world. We work together to better understand street harassment, to ignite public conversations, and to develop innovative strategies to ensure equal access to public spaces.

How did you first become interested in this type of activism?

In 2005 a woman named Thao Nguyen was riding the train into work in New York City when she saw a man masturbating across from her. Thao took a picture and brought it to the police, but they didn't do anything. She posted the picture on Flickr, and it quickly went viral and landed on the front cover of the *New York Daily News*. All of a sudden, the whole city was talking about public masturbation, and women citywide were sharing their stories. It seemed like everyone had one.

After that, a group of friends and I (four woman and three men) were talking about street harassment, how pervasive it was, and how frus-

trating it is that we didn't have a response. Thao inspired us; we thought—what if we post pictures and stories of harassers on a blog? Hollaback! was born; New Yorkers from all five boroughs were snapping photos and swapping harassment stories.

But then something telling happened. We began to receive posts from outside New York—a lot of them. From outside the United States, even. That's when we knew we had hit a nerve. Now we are in 92 cities, 32 countries, and 18 different languages.

What are your current organizational goals?

We recently published *HOLLA 101: Guide to Street Harassment for Educators and Students* and distributed it to over 200 NYC schools. One of our goals is to train teachers, counselors, and administrators on how to respond to reports of street harassment. We will be working in the schools to provide extensive workshops, safety audits, and assemblies to talk in depth about how middle and high school students experience harassment, and what they want to do about it. We also want to launch and train 75 new leaders from 25 new sites. We currently have a wait-list of people in over 70 cities interested in bringing this movement to their community. We will also launch HeartMob, our new online harassment bystander platform. Recognizing that online harassment limits free speech, Hollaback! is creating a platform to encourage bystander intervention for online harassment.

What strategies do you use to enact social change?

We use a myriad of strategies to enact social change. We work to inspire international leadership by training over 500 activists from over 80 cities around the world to localize Hollaback! to their community using the Hollaback! digital storytelling platform and on-the-ground resources. We also use digital storytelling, by releasing free iPhone and Droid apps that provide a real time response to street harassment and illustrate the locations of the harassment on Hollaback!'s publicly available map (resulting in over 8,000 reports of harassment). Incidences are mapped and used to educate policymakers about the prevalence of harassment in their districts and inform research and community based solutions. We also work to engage elected officials. We meet with many legislators each year to discuss community-based solutions to street harassment, including safety audits, trainings, public art projects, and workshop series. We change minds through educational outreach. For example, globally, our site leaders have trained over 2,500 middle and high schools students in how to respond to and prevent street harassment. To engage the broad public, we use social media. For example, we've obtained over 1200 press hits, 40,000 Facebook fans and 17,000 Twitter followers. A final part of our strategy is performing research. Our site leaders have performed groundbreaking local research in over 38 cities. They use the research to demonstrate the prevalence of street harassment and to engage the community in solutions.

What are the major challenges activists in your field face?

The emerging field of street harassment struggles with a world that isn't ready to accept that street harassment isn't okay—and a funding community that thinks street harassment simply "isn't a big enough problem." I've had the door slammed in my face more times than I care to recount.

I find it helpful to remind myself that if you don't fail from time to time, you're not taking enough risks. That said, failure isn't easy for anyone—especially when the stakes are high, as they are for social entrepreneurs and movement builders.

When failure strikes, remember to take care of yourself: buy a mocha, take a walk, and let it hurt. The next day, you've got to ditch your ego and start learning. Make a list of what worked, what didn't, and figure out how to fix it. Remember that brilliant things often emerge out of failure.

What are major misconceptions the public has about activism in general and your issue specifically?

The one that makes me the craziest is the myth that it is mostly men of color who are doing the harassing. This problem isn't unique to the anti–street harassment movement. Initiatives combating various forms of sexual harassment and assault have continually struggled against the perpetuation of racist stereotypes, and in particular, the construction of men of color as sexual predators. There exist widespread fictions regarding who perpetrators are: the myth of racial minorities, particularly Latino and Black men, as prototypical rapists and as being more prone to violence is quite common. This stems in part from a tragic and violent history in which Black men in the U.S. were commonly and unjustly accused of assaulting White women and, as such, were "tried" in biased courts and lynched by mobs. Because of the complexity of institutional and socially ingrained prejudices, Hollaback! aims to highlight the interrelations between sexism, racism, and other forms of bias and violence.

Why should students get involved in your line of activism?

There are two reasons to hollaback: for you, and for the world.

For you: Hollaback! is all about your right to be you: A person who never has to take it and just keep walking, but one who has a "badass" response when they are messed with. Someone who knows they have the right to define themselves instead of being defined by some creep's point of view. We have a right to be who we are, not who we are told to be. We have a right to define ourselves on our own terms when we walk out the door, whatever that means that day. That hour. That minute.

Street harassment teaches us to be silent, but we aren't listening. We don't put up with harassment in the home, at work, or at school. And now we aren't putting up with it in the street,

either. By holla'ing back you are transforming an experience that is lonely and isolating into one that is sharable. You change the power dynamic by flipping the lens off of you and onto the harasser. And you enter a worldwide community of people who've got your back.

For the world: Stories change the world. Don't believe us? Think about Rodney King[1], Anita Hill[2], or Matthew Shepard[3]. These stories didn't just change the world; they shaped policy.

The Internet has given us a new campfire. Each time you hollaback, you are given a king-sized platform to tell your story. Thousands will read it and your story will shift their understanding of what harassment means. Some will walk away understanding what it feels like to be in your shoes, others will feel like they are not alone for the first time or that it's not their fault. Your story will redefine safety in your community—it

---

1. Rodney King, an African American man, was beaten by four white Los Angeles police officers after a traffic stop, an assault that was video-taped by a witness and repeatedly aired on television. The acquittal of the officers by an all-white jury is regarded as the trigger for the 1992 Los Angeles riots as well as the cause of significant reforms of the Los Angeles police department around the issues of excessive force and leadership oversight of officers (Gray, Madison. 2007. "The L.A. Riots: 15 Years After Rodney King." Time Magazine. Accessed from http://content.time.com/time/specials/2007/la_riot/article/0,28804,1614117_1614084_1614831,00.html. Bliss, Laura. 2015. "LAPD's Police Reforms and the Legacy of Rodney King." The Atlantic City Lab. Accessed from http://www.citylab.com/politics/2015/05/lapds-police-reforms-and-the-legacy-of-rodney-king/392000/).
2. In 1991, Anita Hill, a law professor at the University of Oklahoma, accused conservative Supreme Court Justice nominee Clarence Thomas of sexual harassment while they worked together at the Equal Employment Opportunity Commission. These accusations, Hill's treatment by the all-male Senate Judiciary Committee, and Thomas's confirmation by a narrow margin, created controversy and inspired abundant media coverage. The case had long-term impacts on American culture, including broader awareness of, and laws about, sexual harassment, as well as the increased representation of women holding elected office after the election cycle of 1992 ("The Year of the Woman"), which many attributed to women's reaction to the poor treatment of Hill (Siegel, Joel. 2011. "Clarence Thomas-Anita Hill Supreme Court Confirmation Hearing 'Empowered Women' and Panel Member Arlen Specter Still Amazed by Reactions." ABC NEWS. Accessed from http://abcnews.go.com/US/clarence-thomas-anita-hill-supreme-court-confirmation-hearing/story?id=14802217. O'Malley, Michael. N.d. "An Outline of the Anita Hill and Clarence Thomas Controversy." Accessed from https://chnm.gmu.edu/courses/122/hill/hillframe.htm).
3. In 1998, Matthew Shepard, a gay 21 year old college student, was attacked and later died after being left to die beside a road in Laramie, Wyoming. His murder, which was characterized as an anti-gay hate crime but could not be prosecuted as such because hate crime legislation did not exist in Wyoming at the time, increased attention regarding state and federal hate crime legislation, as well as the passage of 2009 federal legislation entitled "The Matthew Shepard and James Byrd, Jr. Hate Crimes Prevention Act," which increased federal law enforcement activities, funding, and tracking hate crimes (US Department of Justice. "The Matthew Shepard and James Byrd, Jr., Hate Crimes Prevention Act of 1999." Accessed from http://www.justice.gov/crt/matthew-shepard-and-james-byrd-jr-hate-crimes-prevention-act-2009-0).

will inspire legislators, the police, and other authorities to take this issue seriously—to approach it with sensitivity, and to create policies that make everyone feel safe. Your story will build an irrefutable case as to why street harassment is not okay—a case strong enough to change the world.

But it all starts with the simplest of gestures: Your hollaback.

What would you consider to be your greatest successes as an activist?

It's been an honor to watch the movement to end street harassment scale so large, include so many young activists globally—from the over 90 organizations that I've seen launch in the past ten years, to the site leaders we've trained in over 90 cities. It's a whole different landscape than the one we entered into in 2005, in the most beautiful way.

Our sites have collaborated with legislators to pass a resolution against street harassment in the Scottish Parliament, release mobile apps that will make NYC the first city in the world to document street harassment in real-time, and presented in front of the United Nations and European Union Parliament.

If an individual has little money and time, are there other ways they can contribute?

Yes, share your story. By doing so, you transform the lonely and isolating experience of street harassment into one that is sharable, and you enter a worldwide community of people who've got your back. Your story will build an irrefutable case as to why street harassment is not okay. Some will walk away understanding what it feels like to be in your shoes, others will feel like they are not alone for the first time or that it's not their fault. So far, we've collected over 8,000 stories of harassment from both victims and bystanders who tried to help. Join the conversation today. http://www.ihollaback.org/share/

You could also host a Chalk Walk. Grab some sidewalk chalk and a few friends and tell your stories on sidewalks in crowded public areas. It's a way to literally rewrite city streets. It's visceral and unapologetically public.

Finally, you could start a Hollaback site in your community. We'll train you, set you up with a website, and give you access to our supportive global community of over 400 site leaders around the world.

The Problem When Sexism Just Sounds So Darn Friendly

MELANIE TANNENBAUM

Tannenbaum discusses two different types of sexism: hostile sexism, characterized by negative attitudes toward women, and benevolent sexism, which seems more positive in tone but is perhaps more insidious and harmful because it undermines the perception of women's competence under the guise of seemingly positive or harmless statements. Tannenbaum illustrates that sexism exists in a variety of forms, but that benevolent sexism is particularly difficult to recognize and fight.

Something can't *actually* be sexist if it's really, really nice, right? I mean, if someone compliments me on my looks or my cooking, that's not sexist. That's awesome! I should be thrilled that I'm being noticed for something positive!

Yet there are many comments that, while seemingly complimentary, somehow still feel wrong. These comments may focus on an author's appearance rather than the content of her writing, or mention how surprising it is that she's a woman, being that her field is mostly filled with men. Even though these remarks can sometimes feel good to hear—and no one is denying that this type of comment *can* feel good, especially in the right context—they can also cause a feeling of unease, particularly when one is in the position of trying to draw attention towards her work rather than personal qualities like her gender or appearance.

In social psychology, these seemingly-positive-yet-still-somewhat-unsettling comments and behaviors have a name: *Benevolent Sexism*. Although it is tempting to brush this experience off as an overreaction to compliments or a misunderstanding of benign intent, benevolent sexism is both real and insidiously dangerous.

What Is Benevolent Sexism?

In 1996, Peter Glick and Susan Fiske wrote a paper on the concept of *ambivalent sexism*, noting that despite common beliefs, there are actually two different kinds of sexist attitudes and behavior. *Hostile sexism* is what most people think of when they picture "sexism"—angry, explicitly negative attitudes towards women. However, the authors note, there is also something called *benevolent sexism*:

We define *benevolent sexism* as a set of interrelated attitudes toward women that are sexist in terms of viewing women stereotypically and in restricted roles but that are subjectively positive in feeling tone (for the perceiver) and also tend to elicit behaviors typically categorized as prosocial (e.g., helping) or intimacy-seeking (e.g., self-disclosure). (Glick & Fiske, 1996, p. 491)

[Benevolent sexism is] a subjectively positive orientation of protection, idealization, and affection directed toward women that, like hostile sexism, serves to justify women's subordinate status to men. (Glick et al., 2000, p. 763)

Yes, there's actually an official name for all of those comments and stereotypes that can somehow feel both nice and wrong at the same time, like the belief that women are "delicate flowers" who need to be protected by men, or the notion that women have the special gift of being "more kind and caring" than their male counterparts. It might sound like a compliment, but it still counts as sexism.

For a very recent example of how benevolent sexism might play out in our everyday lives, take a look at this satirical piece,[1] which jokingly rewrites Albert Einstein's obituary. To quote:

He made sure he shopped for groceries every night on the way home from work, took the garbage out, and hand washed the antimacassars. But to his step-daughters he was just Dad. "He was always there for us," said his step-daughter and first cousin once removed Margo. Albert Einstein, who died on Tuesday, had another life at work, where he sometimes slipped away to peck at projects like showing that atoms really exist. His discovery of something called the photoelectric effect won him a coveted Nobel Prize.

Looks weird, right? Kind of like something you would never actually see in print? Yet the author of rocket scientist Yvonne Brill's obituary didn't hesitate before writing the following[2] about her . . . [in 2013]:

She made a mean beef stroganoff, followed her husband from job to job, and took eight years off from work to raise three children. "The world's best mom," her son Matthew said. But Yvonne Brill, who died on Wednesday at 88 in Princeton, N.J., was also a brilliant rocket scientist, who in the early 1970s invented a propulsion system to help keep communications satellites from slipping out of their orbits.

In fact, Obituaries editor William McDonald still sees nothing wrong with it. In his words, he's "surprised . . . [because] it never occurred to [him] that this would be read as sexist," and if he had to re-write it again, he still "wouldn't do anything differently."

I want to make one thing perfectly clear. There's not a problem with mentioning Brill's family, friends, and loved ones. It's not a problem to note how wonderfully Brill balanced her domestic and professional lives. Brill was a female scientist during a time when very few women could occupy that role in society, and that means something truly important.

But the problem here is really that if "Yvonne" were "Yvan," the obit would have looked fundamentally different. If we're talking up the importance of work–life balance and familial roles for women but we're not also mentioning those things about men, that's a problem. If a woman's accomplishments must be accompanied by a reassurance that she really was "a good Mom," but a man's accomplishments are allowed to stand on their own, that's a problem. And lest you think that I only care about women, let's not act like this doesn't have a real and dangerous impact on men, too. If a man spends years of his life as a doting father and caring husband, yet his strong devotion to his family is not considered an important fact for his obituary because he's male . . . then yes, that's also a big problem. The fact that so many people don't understand why it might be unnerving that the writer's idea for a good story arc in Brill's obituary was to lead with her role as a wife and mother, and then let the surprise that she was actually a really smart rocket scientist come in later as a shocking twist? That's benevolent sexism.

Why Is Benevolent Sexism a Problem?

Admittedly, this research begs an obvious question. If benevolently sexist comments seem like nothing more than compliments, why are they problematic? Is it really "sexism" if the content of the statements seems positive towards women? After all, the obituary noted nothing more than how beloved Brill was as a wife and a mother. Why should anyone be upset by that? Sure, men wouldn't be written about in the same way, but who cares? It's so nice!

Well, for one thing, benevolently sexist statements aren't *all* sunshine and butterflies. They often end up implying that women are weak, sensitive creatures that need to be "protected." While this may seem positive to some, for others—especially women in male-dominated fields—it creates a damaging stereotype. As Glick and Fiske themselves note in their seminal paper:

> We do not consider benevolent sexism a good thing, for despite the positive feelings it may indicate for the perceiver, its underpinnings lie in traditional stereotyping and masculine dominance (e.g., the man as the provider and woman as his dependent), and its consequences are often damaging. Benevolent sexism is not necessarily experienced as benevolent by the recipient. For example, a man's comment to a female coworker on how "cute" she looks, however well-intentioned, may undermine her feelings of being taken seriously as a professional. (Glick & Fiske, 1996, Pp. 491–492)

In a later paper, Glick and Fiske went on to determine the extent to which 15,000 men and women across 19 different countries endorse both hostile and benevolently sexist statements. First of all, they found that hostile and benevo-lent sexism tend to correlate highly across nations. So, it is *not* the case that people who endorse hostile sexism don't tend to endorse benevolent sexism, whereas those who endorse benevolent sexism look nothing like the "real" sexists. On the contrary, those who endorsed benevolent sexism were likely to admit that they *also* held explicit, hostile attitudes towards women (although one does not necessarily *have* to endorse these hostile attitudes in order to engage in benevolent sexism).

Secondly, they discovered that benevolent sexism was a significant predictor of nationwide gender inequality, independent of the effects of hostile sexism. In countries where the men were more likely to endorse benevolent sexism, *even when controlling for hostile sexism*, men also lived longer, were more educated, had higher literacy rates, made significantly more money, and actively participated in the political and economic spheres more than their female counterparts. The warm, fuzzy feelings surrounding benevolent sexism come at a cost, and that cost is often actual, objective gender equality.

The Insidious Nature of Benevolent Sexism

A recent paper by Julia Becker and Stephen Wright details even more of the insidious ways that benevolent sexism might be harmful for both women and social activism. In a series of experiments, women were exposed to statements that either illustrated hostile sexism (e.g., "Women are too easily offended") or benevolent sexism (e.g., "Women have a way of caring that men are not capable of in the same way.") The results are quite discouraging; when the women read statements illustrating benevolent sexism, they were less willing to engage in anti-sexist collective action, such as signing a petition, participating in a rally, or generally "acting against sexism." Not only that, but this effect was partially mediated by the fact that women who were exposed to benevolent sexism were more likely to think that there are many advantages to being a woman and were also more likely to engage in *system justification*, a process by which people justify the status quo and believe that there are no longer problems facing disadvantaged groups (such as women) in modern day society. Furthermore, women who were exposed to hostile sexism actually displayed the opposite effect—they were *more* likely to intend to engage in collective action, and *more* willing to fight against sexism in their everyday lives.

How might this play out in a day-to-day context? Imagine that there's an anti-female policy being brought to a vote, like a regulation that would make it easier for local businesses to fire pregnant women once they find out that they are expecting. If you are collecting signatures for a petition or trying to gather women to protest this policy and those women were recently exposed to a group of men making comments about the policy in question, it would be significantly easier to gain their support and vote down the policy if the men were commenting that pregnant women *should* be fired because they were dumb for getting pregnant in the first place. However, if they instead happened to mention that women are much more compassionate than men and make better stay-at-home parents as a result, these remarks might actually lead these women to be less likely to fight an objectively sexist policy.

"I Mean, Is Sexism Really Still a Problem [Today]?"

We often hear people claiming that sexism, racism, or other forms of discrimination that seem to be outdated are "no longer really a problem." Some people legitimately believe this to be true, while others (particularly women and racial minorities) find it ridiculous that others could be so blind to the problems that still exist. So why does this disparity exist? Why is it so difficult for so many people to see that sexism and racism are still alive and thriving?

Maybe the answer lies right here, on the benevolent side of prejudice. While "old fashioned" forms of discrimination may have died down quite a bit (after all, it really isn't quite as socially acceptable in most areas of the world to

be as explicitly sexist and/or racist as people have been in the past), more "benevolent" forms of discrimination still very much exist, and they have their own sneaky ways of suppressing equality. Unaffected bystanders (or perpetrators) may construe benevolently sexist sentiments as harmless or even beneficial; in fact, as demonstrated by Becker and Wright, targets may even feel better about themselves after exposure to benevolently sexist statements. This could be, in some ways, even worse than explicit, hostile discrimination; because it hides under the guise of compliments, it's easy to use benevolent sexism to demotivate people against collective action or convince people that there is no longer a need to fight for equality.

However, to those people who *still* may be tempted to argue that benevolent sexism is nothing more than an overreaction to well-intentioned compliments, let me pose this question: What happens when there is a predominant stereotype saying that women are better stay-at-home parents than men because they are inherently more caring, maternal, and compassionate? It seems nice enough, but how does this ideology affect the woman who wants to continue to work full time after having her first child and faces judgment from her colleagues who accuse her of neglecting her child? How does it affect the man who wants to stay at home with his newborn baby, only to discover that his company doesn't offer paternity leave because they assume that women are the better candidates to be staying at home?

At the end of the day, "good intent" is not a panacea. Benevolent sexism may very well seem like harmless flattery to many people, but that doesn't mean it isn't insidiously dangerous.

To conclude, I'll now ask you to think about recent events surrounding Elise Andrew, creator of the wildly popular I F–king Love Science Facebook page. When she shared her personal Twitter account with the page's 4.4 million fans, many commented on the link because they were absolutely SHOCKED . . . about what? Why, of course, about the fact that she is female.

"I had no idea that IFLS had such a beautiful face!"

"holy hell, youre a HOTTIE!"

"you mean you're a girl, AND you're beautiful? wow, i just liked science a lil bit more today ^^" . . .

"you're a girl!? I always imagined you as a guy; don't know why; well, nice to see to how you look like i guess"

"What?!!? Gurlz don't like science! LOL Totally thought you were a dude."

"It's not just being a girl that's the surprise, but being a fit girl! (For any non-Brits, fit, in this context, means hot/bangable/shagtastic/attractive)."

Right. See, that's the thing. Elise felt uncomfortable with this, as did many others out there who saw it—and rightfully so. Yet many people would call her (and others like her) oversensitive for feeling negatively about statements that appear to be compliments. Many thought that Elise should have been happy that others were calling her attractive, or pointing out that it's idiosyncratic for her to be a female who loves science. What Elise (and many others) felt was the benevolently sexist side of things—the side that perpetuates a stereotype that women (especially *attractive* women) don't "do" science, and that the most noteworthy thing to comment on about a female scientist is what she looks like.

Unfortunately, it's very likely that no one walked away from this experience having learned anything. People who could tell that this was offensive were obviously willing to recognize it as such, but people who endorsed those statements just thought they were being nice. Because they weren't calling her incompetent or

unworthy, none of them were willing to recognize it as sexism, even when explicitly told that that's what it was—even though, based on research, we know that this sort of behavior has actual, meaningful consequences for society and for gender equality. That right there? That's the *real* problem with benevolent sexism.

NOTES

1. http://www.lastwordonnothing.com/2013/04/01guest-post-physicist-dies-made-great-chili/.
2. http://www.newsdiffs.org/diff/192021/192137/www.nytimes.com/2013/03/31/science/space/yvonne-brill-rocket-scientist-dies-at-88.html/.

REFERENCES

Becker, J., & Wright, S. (2011). Yet another Dark Side of Chivalry: Benevolent Sexism Undermines and Hostile Sexism Motivates Collective Action for Social Change. *Journal of Personality and Social Psychology*, 101 (1), 62–77 DOI: 10.1037/a0022615

Glick, P., & Fiske, S. (1996). The Ambivalent Sexism Inventory: Differentiating Hostile and Benevolent Sexism. *Journal of Personality and Social Psychology*, 70 (3), 491–512 DOI:10.1037//0022-3514.70.3.491

Glick, P., Fiske, S., Mladinic, A., Saiz, J., Abrams, D., Masser, B., Adetoun, B., Osagie, J., Akande, A., Alao, A., Annetje, B., Willemsen, T., Chipeta, K., Dardenne, B., Dijksterhuis, A., Wigboldus, D., Eckes, T., Six-Materna, I., Expósito, F., Moya, M., Foddy, M., Kim, H., Lameiras, M., Sotelo, M., Mucchi-Faina, A., Romani, M., Sakalli, N., Udegbe, B., Yamamoto, M., Ui, M., Ferreira, M., & López, W. (2000). Beyond Prejudice as Simple Antipathy: Hostile and Benevolent Sexism across Cultures. *Journal of Personality and Social Psychology*, 79 (5), 763–775 DOI:10.1037//0022-3514.79.5.763

Selling Feminism, Consuming Femininity

Amanda M. Gengler

Amanda M. Gengler, Contexts *(Volume 10 and Issue 2), pp. 68–69. Copyright © 2011. Reprinted by Permission of SAGE* *Publications.*

Many women, even those of us now in our twenties, thirties, forties, and beyond, remember the thrill of coming home from school to the fresh, crisp pages of the latest issue of *Seventeen* (now in its 66th year), hoping for guidance as we struggled to navigate the perils of adolescence. Today's girls consume an even wider range of "teen 'zines," both in print and online, and at increasingly younger ages. Their pages are filled with how-to pieces—how to style your hair in the latest fashion, give your lips an enticing shine, even how to kiss correctly. But beyond beauty tips, teen magazines also teach girls, at a basic level, *what it means* to be a girl today.

While we might have hoped traditional ideas about femininity had been relegated to the past along with typewriters and Burma shave, teen magazines are still saturated with them. In their pages, girls should focus on being pretty, pleasing men, and decorating men's spaces. Without the colorful modern layouts and contemporary actresses splayed across their shiny covers, one might mistake the glossies for dusty relics left on the shelf since the 1950s.

Indeed, recent covers offer little more than provocative teases about boys and beauty, such as "Where will you meet your next boyfriend?" or "Is school secretly making you fat?" Pieces that focus on substantive issues—drunk driving, careers, or politics—are rare. The overall message a girl receives, journalist Kate Pierce found in her study of *Seventeen* over time, is that "how she looks is more important than what she thinks, that her main goal in life is to find a man who will take care of her . . . and that her place will be home with the kids and the cooking and the housework."

Sociologist Kelly Massoni also studied *Seventeen*, finding that men held 70 percent of the jobs represented in its pages. Women were disproportionately shown either not working or working in traditionally feminine jobs, with a particular

emphasis on modeling and acting careers. Advice on sexuality hasn't evolved much either. Sociologist Laura Carpenter explored the presentation of (almost exclusively hetero-) sexuality in *Seventeen* across the decades, and though she saw greater inclusion of sexual diversity and increased openness to women's sexual agency in recent years, these progressive messages were often presented alongside more traditional ones, with the author or editors emphasizing the latter. Girls might now learn they can "make the first move" or dress in clothing as risqué as fashion demands, but the subtext is clear: a hip young woman is more concerned with lipstick, boyfriends, and belly-button rings than books, politics, or careers.

So beside how-to features on hair styling, body shaping, and make-up application, there are explicit instructions for interacting with men and boys. While beauticians, personal trainers, actresses, or other women offer advice on beauty, fashion, and exercise, *men* (often adult men in their twenties) advise girls on how to support, entertain, and excite their boyfriends by cheering them on from the sidelines, doing personal favors, making them laugh, and "talking dirty." Despite a new millennium, much remains unchanged.

What *has* changed is the packaging: many of these messages are now couched in feminist language. Advertisers must convince young women that they are in need of constant improvement—largely to get and keep boys' attention—without threatening young women's views of themselves as intelligent, self-directed, and equal. Buzz words like "empowerment," "self-determination," and "independence" are sprinkled liberally across their pages. But this seemingly progressive rhetoric is used to sell products and ideas that keep girls doing gender in appropriately feminine ways, leading them to reproduce, rather than challenge, gender hierarchies. An ad for a depilatory cream, for instance, tells girls that they are "unique, determined, and unstoppable," so they should not "settle . . . for sandpaper skin." Feminist demands for political and economic equality—and the refusal to *settle* for low-wages, violence, and second-class citizenship—morph into a refusal to settle for less than silky skin. Pseudo-feminist language allows young women to believe that they can "empower" themselves at the checkout counter by buying the accoutrements of traditional femininity. Girls' potential choice to shun make-up or hair-removal disappears, replaced by their choice of an array of beauty products promising to moisturize, soften, and smooth their troubles away.

Everywhere, girls are flooded with messages urging them to see success, as achieved through beauty, just a purchase away. By some estimates, a ten-year-old is likely to spend $300,000 on her hair and face before she reaches fifty. In *Beauty and Misogyny*, Sheila Jeffreys catalogs the damage these beauty products, cosmetic treatments, and surgical procedures do to female bodies. Jeffreys argues that beauty practices normalized in Western culture—wearing high heels, for example—can injure women physically and socially. These practices are seductive, because we learn to take pleasure in them, but they also reinforce the underlying ideology that women's bodies are unattractive when unadorned and must be carefully groomed simply to be presentable.

On top of the advertising that accounts for around half of these texts' content, many articles that *appear* to be editorial—pieces comparing the merits of accessories, fingernail polishes, or facial cleansers, for example—are advertisements in disguise, conveniently including brand names, retail locations, and prices. In her ethnography of teen 'zine consumption in a junior high, Margaret Finders noted that girls often failed to recognize these as marketing, interpreting them as valuable, neutral information instead.

This is not to say that all girls consume teen 'zines uncritically. Interviews by sociologists have shown that girls are often critical of airbrushed models and claim to ignore advertisements. Melissa Milkie, for example, found that girls of color were especially skeptical, viewing teen magazines as oriented primarily to white girls and including girls and women of color only when they fit white beauty ideals. For the most part, however, girls' critiques stop at body image, failing to question these texts' nearly exclusive focus on beauty and heterosexual romance. Dawn Curie found that 70 percent of her interviewees were "avid" readers, for whom the reading and sharing of these texts was a significant pastime. These girls spent hours devouring their content, and admitted that they turned to the magazines' "real life" pieces for "practical advice," and used the girls in the magazines as yardsticks by which to measure their own lives and experiences.

Teen girl magazines breathe new life into some very old ideas. Today's successful woman, they proclaim, orients her life around looking beautiful and snagging a man. Seemingly esteem-boosting "grrl power" rhetoric makes this message seem fresh, and provides marketers an appealing way to sell even independent-minded girls old-fashioned deference and subordination as "empowerment." Those of us who grew up with these texts can't deny that consuming them, along with the products they push, was often a lot of fun, even a rite of passage. But if feminist goals of equality are to be realized, girls need better options.[1] We can also teach girls to question the basic assumptions embedded in popular media and to become critical consumers (or non-consumers) of these texts and the culture of beauty and romance they peddle. We might even offer girls the more radical message, learned and lived by earlier generations of feminists, that true empowerment comes not through consumption, but solidarity, critical-consciousness, and collective action.

NOTE

1. *New Moon*, newmoon.org, is one attempt to offer an alternative to traditional girls' magazines.

"Men Are Stuck" in Gender Roles . . .

EMILY ALPERT REYES

As the gender revolution has progressed, there has been increasing participation among women in areas that are traditionally viewed as masculine (e.g., business, law, etc.), but there has not been a similar increase among men in traditionally feminine fields (e.g., nursing, early childhood education, or as stay-at-home parents). Alpert Reyes discusses a number of explanations for this reluctance, including childhood socialization into gender roles as well as devaluation of feminine fields, and how this trend might be overcome.

Brent Kroeger pores over nasty online comments about stay-at-home dads, wondering if his friends think those things about him. The Rowland Heights father remembers high school classmates laughing when he said he wanted to be a "house husband." He avoids mentioning it on Facebook. "I don't want other men to look at me like less of a man," Kroeger said.

His fears are tied to a bigger phenomenon: The gender revolution has been lopsided. Even as American society has seen sweeping transformations—expanding roles for women, surging tolerance for homosexuality—popular ideas about masculinity seem to have stagnated.

While women have broken into fields once dominated by men, such as business, medicine and law, men have been slower to pursue nursing, teach preschool, or take jobs as administrative assistants. Census data and surveys show that men remain rare in stereotypically feminine positions. When it comes to gender progress, said Ronald F. Levant, editor of the journal *Psychology of Men and Masculinity*, "men are stuck."

The imbalance appears at work and at home: Working mothers have become ordinary, but stay-at-home fathers exist in only 1% of married couples with kids under age 15, according to U.S. Census Bureau data. In a recent survey, 51% of Americans told the Pew Research Center that children were better off if their mother was at home. Only 8% said the same about fathers. Even seeking time off can be troublesome for men: One University of South Florida study found that college students rated hypothetical employees wanting flexible schedules as less masculine.

Other research points to an enduring stigma for boys whose behavior is seen as feminine. "If girls call themselves tomboys, it's with a sense of pride," said University of Illinois at Chicago sociology professor Barbara Risman. "But boys make fun of other boys if they step just a little outside the rigid masculine stereotype." Two years ago, for instance, a Global Toy Experts survey found that more than half of mothers wouldn't give a doll to someone else's son, while only 32% said the same about giving cars or trucks to a girl. Several studies have found that bending gender stereotypes in childhood is tied to worse anxiety for men than women in adulthood.

In the southern end of Orange County, former friends have stopped talking to Lori Duron and her husband. Slurs and threats arrive by email. Their son calls himself a boy, but has gravitated toward Barbies, Disney princesses and pink since he was a toddler. In a blog and a book she wrote, Duron chronicles worries that would seem trivial if her child were a girl: Whether he would be teased for his . . . [rainbow] backpack. Whether a Santa would look askance at him for wanting a doll. "If a little girl is running around on the baseball team with her mitt, people think, 'That's a strong girl,'" said her husband, Matt Duron, who, like his wife, uses a pen name to shield the boy's identity. "When my 6-year-old is running around in a dress, people think there's something wrong with him."

Beyond childhood, the gender imbalance remains stark when students choose college majors: Between 1971 and 2011, a growing share of degrees in biology, business and other historically male majors went to women, an analysis by University of Maryland, College Park sociologist Philip N. Cohen shows. Yet fields like education and the arts remained heavily female, as few men moved the opposite way. Federal data show that last year less than 2% of preschool and kindergarten teachers were men. In the last 40 years, "women have said, 'Wait a minute, we are competent and assertive and ambitious,'" claiming a wider range of roles, said Michael Kimmel, executive director of the Center for the Study of Men and Masculinities at Stony Brook University. But "men have not said, 'We're kind, gentle, compassionate and nurturing.'"

As the Durons and other families have discovered, messages of gender norms trickle down early. In Oregon, Griffin Bates was stunned when the little boy she was raising with her lesbian partner at the time came back from a visit with Grandma and Grandpa without his beloved tutu and tiara. "They were perfectly OK with his mother being gay," Bates said. "But they weren't OK with their grandson playing dress-up in a tutu."

Boys stick with typically masculine toys and games much more consistently than girls adhere to feminine ones, Harvard School of Public Health research associate Andrea L. Roberts found. Biologically male children who defy those norms are referred to doctors much earlier than biologically female ones who disdain "girl things," said Johanna Olson of the Center for Transyouth Health and Development at Children's Hospital Los Angeles. Even the criteria for diagnosing gender dysphoria were historically much broader for effeminate boys than for masculine girls. Why? "Masculinity is valued more than femininity," University of Utah law professor Clifford Rosky said. "So there's less worry about girls than about boys."

Gender stereotypes do seem to have loosened: The Global Toy Experts survey found that most mothers would let their own sons play with dolls and dress-up sets, even if they shied from buying them for other boys. Parents in some parts of Los Angeles said their boys got barely any flak for choosing pink sneakers or toting dolls to school. And in a recent online survey by advertising agency DDB Worldwide, nearly three quarters of Americans surveyed said stay-at-home dads were just as good at parenting as stay-at-home moms. But while attitudes may have shifted, Rosky said, "nothing changes until men are willing to act."

Some experts say economic barriers have stopped men from moving further into feminized fields. Jobs held by women tend to pay less, an imbalance rooted in the historical assumption that women were not breadwinners. Women had an economic reason to take many of the jobs monopolized by men, particularly college-educated women trying to climb the economic ladder. "But if men made the switch, they'd lose money," New York University sociologist Paula England said.

Yet it isn't just economics that keeps men from typically female jobs. Men are still rare in nursing, for instance, despite respectable pay. England and other scholars see that dearth as another form of sexism, in which things historically associated with women are devalued.

Men who do enter heavily female fields are often prodded into other ones without even searching, as other people suggest new gigs that better fit the masculine stereotype, said Julie A. Kmec, associate professor of sociology at Washington State University. While women have "come out" to their families as people who want a life outside the home, men have not "come out" at work as involved fathers, Kimmel said. And that, in turn, holds many working mothers back, Risman argued.

Familiar measures of progress toward gender equality, such as women working in management or men picking up housework, began to plateau in the 1990s. Cohen found that in the first decade of the millennium jobs stayed similarly segregated by gender—the first time since 1960 that gender integration in the workplace had slowed to a virtual halt. "If men don't feel free to go into women's jobs," said Risman, a scholar at the Council on Contemporary Families, "women are not really free."

Normalizing Sexual Violence: Young Women Account for Harassment and Abuse

HEATHER R. HLAVKA

Despite the fact that rates of sexual harassment, coercion, and assault are high among young women and girls, most instances go unreported. Hlavka argues that the cultural ideology surrounding sexuality—that men are the aggressors and women the passive gate-keepers—reinforces and supports this type of violence.

Many regard harassment and violence to be a normal part of everyday life in middle and high schools (Fineran and Bennett 1999), yet most of these crimes go unreported. A 2011 American Association of University Women (AAUW 2011) study found that almost half (48 percent) of the 1,965 students surveyed experienced harassment, but only 9 percent reported the incident to an authority figure. Girls were sexually harassed more than boys (56 percent vs. 40 percent); they were more likely to be pressured for a date, pressured into sexual activity, and verbally harassed (AAUW 2001; Fineran and Bennett 1999).

...Data from the Youth Risk Behavior Survey (YRBS) show that almost 20 percent of girls experience physical and sexual violence from dating partners (Silverman et al. 2001), and sexual assault accounts for one-third of preteen victimization (Finkelhor and Ormrod 2000). It is tempting to ask: Why do so few young women formally report their victimization experiences? Assuming that peer sexual harassment and assault is an instrument that creates and maintains gendered and sexed hierarchies (e.g., MacKinnon 1979; Phillips 2000; Tolman et al. 2003), attention instead must turn toward understanding how and why these violent acts are produced, maintained, and normalized in the first place. Despite the considerable body of research that shows high rates of gendered violence among youth, there has been little discussion of its instruments and operations.

This study is concerned with girls' relational experiences of sexuality, harassment and assault, coercion, and consent. With few exceptions, girls' construction of violence has received little attention from victimization scholars and those interested in the gendered power dynamics of adolescent sexual development. The lack of research is clear and a shift in analytical focus

Heather R. Hlavka, *Gender & Society* (Volume 28 and Issue 3), pp. 337–358, Copyright © 2014. Reprinted by Permission of SAGE Publications.

toward appraisals of violence is critical. It cannot be assumed that legal definitions of sexual harassment and assault are socially agreed on, understood, or similarly enacted. Research from the vantage point of young women themselves is necessary. How do girls talk about experiences that researchers and the law would label as harassment and rape? In what ways do they account for these experiences? . . .

Feminist Perspectives and Hetero-Relational Discourses

Feminist scholarship on compulsory heterosexuality (Connell 1987; Rich 1980; Tolman et al. 2003), heteronormativity (Kitzinger 2005; Martin 2009; Thorne and Luria 1986), and heterogender (Ingraham 1994) consistently finds that traditional gender arrangements, beliefs, and behaviors reinforce women's sexual subordination to men. Heterosexuality is compulsory in that it is an *institution* (Rich 1980) that organizes the conventions by which women and men relate; it is assumed and expected (Jackson 2009) as it is understood as natural and unproblematic (Kitzinger 2005; Schippers 2007). Heteronormative discourses consistently link female sexuality with passivity, vulnerability, and submissiveness, and male sexuality with dominance, aggression, and desire (Butler 1999; Ingraham 1994).

Young people are socialized into a patriarchal culture that normalizes and often encourages male power and aggression, particularly within the context of heterosexual relationships (Fineran and Bennett 1999; Tolman et al. 2003). As men's heterosexual violence is viewed as customary, so too is women's endurance of it (Stanko 1985). For example, Messerschmidt (1986) has argued that "normative heterosexuality" involves a "presumption that men have a special and overwhelming 'urge' or 'drive' toward heterosexual intercourse" . . . normalizing the presumption that men's sexual aggression is simply "boys being boys" (Connell 1987; French 2003; Messerschmidt 2012). Stanko (1985, 73) argued that "women learn, often at a very early age, that their sexuality is not their own

and that maleness can at any point intrude into it." Girls are thus expected to endure aggression by men because that is *part* of man. Coupled with the presumption that women are the gatekeepers of male desire (Fine 1988; Tolman 1991), heteronormative discourses have allowed for men's limited accountability for aggressive, harassing, and criminal sexual conduct. . . .

Discourses of Children, Sexuality, and Sexual Abuse

. . . Children and youth have largely remained exempt from legal and policy discussions of consent to sexual activity, and little scholarly research has taken up the task, perhaps, in part, because Western cultures today often characterize children as innocent, asexual, ignorant, and in need of protection from adult sexual knowledge and practices (Angelides 2004; Best 1990). Adults have historically worked to police the sexual behavior of young people, particularly of girls (Fine 1988; Gilligan 1982). . . . Youth learn early that they should not talk about sex (Ryan 2000), often extending to sexual violence and harassment (Gilgun 1986; Phillips 2000; Thompson 1995).

. . . Further, feminist theorists argue that "real rape" (Estrich 1987)—or forcible stranger rape—is narrowly defined, largely enforced by law, and reinforced by popular media. Discursively, law and media draw absolutes between healthy heterosexual encounters and dangerous, abusive relationships, creating divisions between what is and what is not violence, between "real rape" and "everyday violence," or what Stanko (1985) termed "little rapes." What counts as sexual violence, then, are the extreme cases "which constrain[s] and construct[s] the framework through which women have to make sense of events" (Kelly and Radford 1990, 41). The struggle to negotiate these tensions has meaningful outcomes, and young people are not exempt. . . .

Methods

The data for this study include audio-videotaped interviews of youths seen by forensic interviewers for reported cases of sexual abuse between 1995 and 2004. The interviews come from the non-profit Children's Advocacy Center (CAC) located in an urban Midwest community. The CAC provides investigative interviews and medical examinations for youths who may have been sexually or physically assaulted or witnessed a violent crime. Interviews take place between one forensic interviewer and one child referred to the CAC by law enforcement or Child Protection Services (CPS). Youths were brought to the CAC for an interview because they reported sexual abuse to someone, someone else witnessed or reported the abuse to authorities, or the offender confessed to the abuse.

The forensic interview is based on a semi-structured interview protocol designed to maximize youth's ability to communicate their experiences and conforms to standards set by the American Professional Society on the Abuse of Children (APSAC 2002). Protocol components include first establishing rapport and, next, obtaining details about sexual abuse only if the child first verbally discloses victimization to the interviewer. The two then discuss the circumstances surrounding the abuse using non-suggestive, largely open-ended, questions. So, while the interview is set up to investigate whether or not abuse occurred, youths were consistently allowed to raise and discuss subjects important to them in response to questions such as "What happened? Did you tell anyone? How did they respond? How did you feel about that? Are you worried about anything?" . . .

The study sample included 100 interviews of youths between ages three and 17, stratified disproportionately by gender and age and proportionately by race. Descriptive data were gathered from case files, such as date of the interview, child and offender characteristics when available, pre-interview reports, family background, and CAC investigative assessments. Audiotaped interviews were transcribed verbatim by the author. . . .

The study subsample includes 23 racially diverse young women (13 white girls, six black girls,

and four Latina girls) between 11 and 16 years of age. The reported offenders were known to the girls, either as acquaintances or intimate others (intrafamilial abuse was more common in the larger study sample). Accounts were unpacked as everyday violence, instruments of coercion, and accounts of consent. These categories illuminate the heteronormative cultures within which girls accounted for sexual violence and negotiated what happened, how it happened, and why.

Findings

Everyday Violence

Objectification, sexual harassment, and abuse appear to be part of the fabric of young women's lives (Orenstein 1994). They had few available safe spaces; girls were harassed and assaulted at parties, in school, on the playground, on buses, and in cars. Young women overwhelmingly depicted boys and men as *natural* sexual aggressors, pointing to one of the main tenets of compulsory heterosexuality. Incorporating male sexual drive discourse (Phillips 2000), they described men as unable to control their sexual desires. Male power and privilege and female acquiescence were reified in descriptions of "routine" and "normal" sexualized interactions (Fineran and Bennett 1999; French 2003). Assaultive behaviors were often justified, especially when characterized as indiscriminate. For example, Patricia (age 13, white) told the interviewer: "They grab you, touch your butt and try to, like, touch you in the front, and run away, but it's okay, I mean . . . I never think it's a big thing because they do it to everyone." Referring to boys at school, Patricia described unwelcome touching and grabbing as normal, commonplace behaviors.

Compulsory heterosexuality highlights how conventional norms of heterosexual relations produce and often require male dominance and female subordination (Phillips 2000; Tolman et al. 2003). Young women like Patricia described sexually aggressive behaviors as customary: "It just happens," and "They're boys—

that's what they do." Similarly, Kelly (age 13, white) told the forensic interviewer about her experiences with 20-year-old Eric:

> [He] would follow me around all the time, tell me I was beautiful and stuff, that he could have me when he wanted to. He did that all the time, like, would touch me and say, "Am I making you wet, do you want me?" when he wanted. I think that's just . . . like, that's what he does, it's just, like, how it goes on and everyone knows it, no one says nothing.

Kelly trivializes her experiences of sexual harassment by a man seven years older, telling the interviewer of this ordinary and allowable "masculine" practice. Her description of ongoing harassment also confounds romance and aggression, because Eric's harassment was fused with courting, compliments, and sexual desire (Phillips 2000).

Girls' characterizations of everyday violence paralleled both their assessments that "boys will be boys" and their understanding of harassment as a normal adolescent rite of passage. Sexual harassment is an instrument that maintains a gendered hierarchy (MacKinnon 1979), and girls described the many ways they protected themselves against expected sexual aggression, at the expense of their own feelings. Carla (age 14, white), for example, cast assault and threats as expected because they were typical. In this passage, she described chronic harassment by a young man as they rode the school bus. He often threatened to "come over to [her] house and rape [her]":

> CARLA: Like, on the bus, like when I'll sit, he'll try and sit next to me and then slide his hand under my butt.
> INTERVIEWER: Okay, does he say anything?
> CARLA: No, he just kinda has this look on his face. And then I'll, like, shove him out of the seat and then he'll get mad.

> INTERVIEWER: What happens when he gets mad?
> CARLA: He just kinda doesn't talk. He gets, like, his face gets red and he doesn't talk. And he, I guess he feels rejected, but I don't care. He told me . . . he was like, "I'm gonna come over to your house and rape you." And then, I know he's just joking, but that can be a little weird to hear.
> INTERVIEWER: Yeah, so when did he tell you that?
> CARLA: He tells me it all the time, like the last time I talked to him. He just says that he's gonna come to my house and rape me since I won't do anything with him. And, I mean, I think . . . I'm . . . I know he's joking, it's just hard to, like, why would he say that?

Threats were used for compliance, becoming more persistent and coercive over time. Unsure of whether to take the threats seriously, Carla names her experience "weird" while normalizing the young man's behavior as understandable within a male sexual drive discourse ("I guess he feels rejected"), and trivializes his threats twice, saying, "I know he's just joking." Harassment was dangerously constructed as romance and flirting. These discourses often entitle young men to violate the bodies of young women (Connell 1995; Messerschmidt 2012). . . .

Given expectations of, and experiences with, male aggression, young women were charged with self-protection by reading and responding to potentially dangerous situations. While some girls attempted to "ignore" the behavior, others had to make additional maneuvers. In her interview, Lana (age 15, white) explained how 18-year-old Mike "tries to bring [girls] downstairs in the [school] basement and, like, try and force 'em to like make out with him and stuff." She said Mike tried to force her to go downstairs on numerous occasions and he would "get mad when [she'd] say no." In response, Lana altered her behavior by avoiding being alone in the school hallways, at her locker, or in the bathroom. Young women responded to harassment with a barrage of maneuvers, like avoidance and diverting attention. These tactics did not always work, however. In Lana's case, Mike was eventually "able to catch [her] off-guard":

> I was going to the bathroom and he wouldn't let me go in. He put his foot in front of [the door], and he's a really strong person, so I didn't really, like, I couldn't open the door. And he said, "I'll let you in if you give me a kiss," and I said, "No." And I was going back to the classroom and he pinned me against the wall and tried to, like, lift up my shirt. And, like, touched me, and then I . . . I got up . . . I started to scream, and I guess someone heard, 'cause then, um, someone started coming. So he got away from me, I just went back in the classroom and forgot about it. I just didn't think it was really anything.

Girls in this study said they did not want to make a "big deal" out of their experiences and rarely reported these incidents to persons in authority. Most questioned whether anyone would care about the behavior; if it was not "rape" it was not serious enough to warrant others' involvement. "Real" assault was narrowly defined and contingent on various conditions that were rarely met (Phillips 2000; Stanko 1985).

Young women constructed classic boundaries between "real rapes" and everyday violence or "little rapes." Terri (age 11, black) was interviewed at the CAC because she told a friend she was forced to perform oral sex on a 17-year-old neighbor boy: "He forced me, he, uh, he grabbed me tighter, and he said if I didn't do it he was gonna rape me." For Terri, rape was only intercourse, as she candidly explained: "They always say they gonna rape you, if you don't do what they want, they say they'll rape you." Terri's mother also cautioned her about male sexual drives, warning her to expect aggression and to

protect herself. Sitting in her apartment stairwell alone that day, Terri assumed responsibility for her own assault. Terri's experience demonstrates that if girls do not acquiesce to the pressure to have sex, they risk being raped. She did not tell her mother, because "I shouldn't have been there, my mom said I should've been home anyway, but I didn't want to get raped so I had to."

Instruments of Coercion

The normalization of violence was intensified in peer groups and assault was often perpetrated by one older man. Peers communicated a specialized sense of sexual acceptability largely based on the perception of women as sexual gatekeepers. Gatekeeping occurred in a variety of ways, including allocation of resources, such as food, alcohol, or a space away from adult others. Janice (age 14, white), for example, told the interviewer that 30-something-year-old Matt touched her and four girlfriends on a regular basis:

> He does, like, touch us, you know? Like, he like rubs my leg, the thigh, but none of us told him, told him to stop, you know? But I . . . I always moved away when he did it. He'd just rub my leg and touch my boobs. And one time when I was over at his house, I asked him for something to eat and he goes, "Not unless I can touch your boobs."

Via access to resources, Matt presented Janice with a "gatekeeping choice" that deflected responsibility. Janice later told the interviewer that Matt had also touched her vagina, commenting, "He does it to everyone, you know, it just happens sometimes," and justified Matt's behavior by placing responsibility on the group: "But none of us told him to stop." Matt's actions were minimized because they were customary and something they "just dealt with."

Sexualized bartering or exchange for in/tangible resources (Orenstein 1994; Thompson 1995; Van Roosmalen 2000) was common. Access or restriction to something was a tactic used by men to coerce young women like Natalie (age 16, Latina) into sexual contact. Natalie was sexually assaulted by Jim, a 37-year-old neighbor. She told the interviewer that Jim allowed Natalie and her friends to "hang out," play basketball in his backyard, and drink beer and vodka. During the interview, Natalie described Jim's sexual touching and kissing as typical male behavior:

> He'd just rub his hand across my butt, and then one time I was sitting there and he—I was, like, laying on the couch watching TV—and he came home. He was kinda drunk, then he, like, literally just, like, laid *on* me. That's what he . . . well, guys always try to get up on you, like just normal.

Because both were drinking alcohol, Natalie tolerated his actions: "He would be touching my butt, you know, with this hand, going under my butt, under the blanket. I was, like, oh well, but all this . . . nothing like totally big happened."

Overwhelmingly described as "normal stuff" that "guys do" or tolerating what "just happens," young women's sexual desire and consent are largely absent (Martin 1996; Tolman 1994). Sex was understood as something done to them and agency was discursively attributed only to gate-keeping. . . .

Accounts of Consent

The links between everyday harassment and violence were further reproduced through attributions of blame. Girls criticized each other for not successfully maneuvering men's normalized aggressive behavior. Even when maneuvers "failed," concessions were made. For example, Lily (age 14, Latina) was raped by a 17-year-old school acquaintance in a park as she walked home from school. The offender quickly spread rumors and she was labeled "sexually active" and a "slut" by her classmates: "There's rumors about me already, that aren't even true . . . that I want, that I want to, and I let him do that . . . and it wasn't even true." Cast as promiscuous, she

was deemed complicit in her rape. On the rare occasion that rape was reported to an adult or authority figure, young women described feeling suspect. Kiley (age 14, black) was raped by a 27-year-old family friend at his home. She provided details about the assault, including how he held her down and covered her mouth to muffle her cries:

> I didn't want to but he did, you know, and I don't know, [sex] just happened. I thought he was just a friend and that's it. . . . He was calling me names, he was calling me a "ho" and a "slut" and all this kind of stuff, and that I gave him a lap dance and everything. That I was, I can't . . . I took all my clothes off and that I was, like, asking him for it. That I wanted to be with him, and everyone believed him.

Sexual reputation mattered to girls (Van Roosmalen 2000) and the threat of being labeled a "ho" or a "slut" loomed large. The threat of sexualization and social derogation was often a barrier to rape reporting; it was connected with accusations of exaggeration through which peers decided whether and how to include, label, and ostracize. This finding is consistent with prior studies (Phillips 2000) that find young women are under pressure to manage their sexuality and sexual reputations. This is a confusing endeavor, of course, as girls may gain cultural capital among peers for being desired and pursued but not for sexual agency.

The precarious balancing act of attaining sexual status and avoiding the "slander of the slut" (Schalet 2010) proved powerful. Some girls belittled others' experiences, holding them responsible for their victimizations. Obligated to set limits for sexual behavior (Orenstein 1994), it was girls' duty to be prepared to say "no" (Tolman 1994) and to police each other. When asked about her friend who had reported sexual assault by a mutual acquaintance, Jacki (age 15, white) said, "I don't know why she's making such a big deal out of it anyway. He does it to everyone, so I say, well, 'Just back off,' I say 'No'—so she should if she don't want it, but she probably wants it anyway." Jacki worked to discursively separate herself from her friend as she spoke of sexual desire and exaggeration. . . .

Girls were also aware of double standards and traditional sexual scripts. They claimed "guys get away with everything" and "they can do anything and not get in trouble." This critique stopped short of attributions of sexual responsibility, however; girls self-framed as active subjects by labeling others as passive objects. In this way, the complexities of naming sexual aggression were premised on behavior comparisons. April (age 13, white) reported that her 13-year-old friend "had sex" with Sean, a 22-year-old man. During her interview, she described her friend as passive and naïve:

> I've heard rumors about that he's had sex with girls, and I know Sara has had sex with him, she came out and told me . . . she said that he came over and he was telling her that she was gorgeous and that he loved her and that he wanted to have her baby and all this stuff, and I guess it just happened, and that's what she said, it just happened, and I was like, "Oh, okay" [laughs], you know, which didn't surprise me, 'cause Sara, she'll be mad at him and then she'll go back to him, like, two days later.

April characterized sexual intercourse ("it") as something men do "to" women. She further interpreted Sean's manipulative tactics ("telling her that she was gorgeous and that he loved her and that he wanted to have her baby") as successful because "it [intercourse] just happened." April said similar ploys did not work on her: "First of all, he asked me, 'Would you . . . would you ever go out with me?' and I said, 'No' . . . and he's like, 'Well, would you ever have sex with me?' and I was like, 'No.'"

Despite April's resistance, Sean put his hands under her shirt, and tried to put her hands in his pants and her head on his penis. April told the interviewer: "I told him to stop and he didn't and he got to, like, right here, you know, he was tryin' to lift up my bra and I was like, 'No, stop!'" Further couched in rumors and reputation, April differentiated herself from Sara: "There's rumors going around saying that Sara had sex with him and so did I and that [she's] a slut and all this stuff." April insisted the rumors about her were untrue because, unlike Sara who let "it just happen," she "said no." As Nelson and Oliver (1998, 573) state, "Under these rules, any girl who permits herself to be persuaded into sexual activity is weak and to blame, as is a girl who voluntarily enters a situation where she can be raped."

Conclusion

Research on sexual violence has long asked why victims do not report these incidents. Studies with adults have examined how women account for and "name" their experiences, yet adolescents remain largely outside the scope of this work. Exploring sexual violence via the lens of compulsory heterosexuality highlights the relational dynamics at play in this naming process. . . .

Descriptions of assault here are concerning, having much to do with heteronormativity and compulsory heterosexuality. Sex was "something they [men and boys] do," or "something he wanted," and sexual assault was a "weird" threat, something "they just say," or "something she let happen." When resistance was voiced, as in April's case, it was couched in sexual refusal and used to establish boundaries. In their policing of each other, young women often held themselves and their peers responsible for acting as gatekeepers of men's behaviors; they were responsible for being coerced, for accepting gifts and other resources, for not fending off or resisting men's sexual advances, [or] for miscommunication. . . . The discourses offer insight into how some young women talked about their sexual selves and relationships as they navigated a world ordered by gendered binaries and heterosexual frame-works (Butler 1999).

Importantly, the violence described in this study must be situated both by context and as told within an institutionalized, forensic interview setting. Child crime victims are often positioned as passive in exploitative relationships, in reporting practices, and in criminal justice processes. . . . As the findings demonstrate, girls understand their position in a patriarchal sexual system and therefore might assume authority figures of all types will blame them or perceive them as bad girls who "let it happen." Revealing sexual desire or agency in this setting might be perceived risky in the same way involving law enforcement might be; girls may be viewed as blameworthy for putting themselves in a situation where one can be raped (Nelson and Oliver 1998). The fear of revealing one's use of drugs or alcohol could also influence what and how disclosure is made with interviewers. This might be especially true for minority and socioeconomically disadvantaged youths with little trust of criminal justice authorities (Hlavka 2013). Therefore, conclusions offered here must be tempered not only by class and neighborhood context, but also by how the forensic interview is perceived and interpreted differently by young women depending on race, class, and sexuality. In this study, age, type of offender, and peer groups seemed to affect girls' narratives in important ways, whereas race did not. Also, it is not assumed that all the girls in this study identified as heterosexual, but without a measure of sexual orientation, the question remains, "How might lesbian or bisexual girls interact with common heteronormative discourses?" . . .

. . . Alternative solutions for the education of young people on sexual relations and abuse are long overdue, and many have called for new sexual paradigms for some time (Fine 1988; Phillips 2000; Tolman 1994; Tolman et al. 2003). The sexual scripts culturally available to girls largely exclude sexual desire and pleasure, representing girls as victims in need of protection against boys' desires (Fine 1988). Placing responsibility on women and girls to "just say no" and excusing boys and men as they "work a 'yes' out" works to erase institutional and structural responsibilities. The lack of safe, supportive space for girls is palpable. We can thus better understand why young women in this study felt they were expected to protect themselves from everyday violence with little help from others, including those in authority positions. The lack of institutional support assumed by girls in this study should be deeply concerning for educators and policy makers. As Stein (1995) has argued, lack of adult interruption or response to sexual harassment and abuse functionally permits and encourages it. It is not enough to establish new policies and practices aimed at increasing reporting; there are larger underlying cultural practices and discourses acting as barriers. By drawing attention to youths' voices, structures of violence, power, and privilege become apparent in their gendered experiences that do not easily translate to law and policy reforms. Sexual education must be gender equity education (Stein et al. 2002), resistant to troubled, heteronormative binaries and cultural constraints that omit discourses of desire, gender, and sexuality. By treating young people as agents and decision makers, we could create spaces where they can work together with adults to appraise experiences of sex, assault, power, coercion, and consent prevalent in their lives.

REFERENCES

AAUW (American Association of University Women). 2001. *Hostile hallways II: Bullying, teasing and sexual harassment in school.* Washington, DC: AAUW.

AAUW (American Association of University Women). 2011. *Crossing the line: Sexual harassment at school.* Washington, DC: Catherine Hill and Holly Kearl.

Angelides, Steven. 2004. Feminism, child sexual abuse, and the erasure of child sexuality. *GLQ: A Journal of Lesbian and Gay Studies* 10:141–77.

APSAC (American Professional Society on the Abuse of Children). 2002. *Investigative interviewing in cases of alleged child abuse.* Chicago: APSAC.

Best, Joel. 1990. *Threatened children: Rhetoric and concern about child victims*. Chicago: University of Chicago Press.

Butler, Judith. 1999. *Gender trouble*. New York: Routledge.

Connell, Raewyn. 1987. *Gender and power*. Cambridge, UK: Polity Press.

Connell, Raewyn. 1995. *Masculinities*. Berkeley: University of California Press.

Estrich, Susan. 1987. *Real rape*. Cambridge, MA: Harvard University Press.

Fine, Michelle. 1988. Sexuality, schooling, and adolescent females: The missing discourse of desire. *Harvard Educational Review* 58:29–53.

Fineran, Susan, and Larry Bennett. 1999. Gender and power issues of peer sexual harassment among teenagers. *Journal of Interpersonal Violence* 14:626–41.

Finkelhor, David, and Richard Ormrod. 2000. *Characteristics of crimes against juveniles*. Washington, DC: U.S. Department of Justice, Office of Justice Programs.

French, Sandra L. 2003. Reflections on healing: Framing strategies utilized by acquaintance rape survivors. *Journal of Applied Communication Research* 31:298–319.

Gilgun, Jane. 1986. Sexually abused girls' knowledge about sexual abuse and sexuality. *Journal of Interpersonal Violence* 1:309–25.

Gilligan, Carol. 1982. *In a different voice*. Cambridge, MA: Harvard University Press.

Hlavka, Heather. 2013. Legal subjectivity among youth victims of sexual abuse. *Law & Social Inquiry*, 39:31–61.

Ingraham, Chrys. 1994. The heterosexual imaginary. *Sociological Theory* 12:203–19.

Jackson, Stevi. 2009. Sexuality, heterosexuality, and gender hierarchy. In *Sex, gender & sexuality*, edited by Abby Ferber, Kimberly Holcomb, and Tre Wentling. New York: Oxford University Press.

Kelly, Liz and Jill Radford. 1990. "Nothing really happened": The invalidation of women's experiences of sexual violence. *Critical Social Policy* 10:39–53.

Kitzinger, Celia. 2005. Heteronormativity in action: Reproducing the heterosexual nuclear family in after-hours medical calls. *Social Problems* 52:477–98.

MacKinnon, Catherine. 1979. *Sexual harassment of working women*. New Haven, CT: Yale University Press.

Martin, Karin. 1996. *Puberty, sexuality, and the self*. New York: Routledge.

Martin, Karin. 2009. Normalizing heterosexuality. *American Sociological Review* 74:190–207.

Messerschmidt, James. 1986. *Capitalism, patriarchy, and crime*. Totowa, NJ: Rowman & Littlefield.

Messerschmidt, James. 2012. *Gender, heterosexuality, and youth violence: The struggle for recognition*. New York: Rowman & Littlefield.

Nelson, Andrea, and Pamela Oliver. 1998. Gender and the construction of consent in child–adult sexual contact: Beyond gender neutrality and male monopoly. *Gender & Society* 12:554–77.

Orenstein, Peggy. 1994. *Schoolgirls: Young women, self-esteem, and the confidence gap*. New York: Doubleday.

Phillips, Lynn M. 2000. *Flirting with danger: Young women's reflections on sexuality and domination*. New York: New York University Press.

Rich, Adrienne. 1980. Compulsory heterosexuality and lesbian existence. *Signs: Journal of Women in Culture and Society* 5:631–60.

Ryan, Gail. 2000. Childhood sexuality: A decade of study. *Child Abuse & Neglect* 24:33–48.

Schalet, Amy. 2010. Sexual subjectivity revisited: The significance of relationships in Dutch and American girls' experiences of sexuality. *Gender & Society* 24:304–29.

Schippers, Mimi. 2007. Recovering the feminine other: Masculinity, femininity, and gender hegemony. *Theory & Society* 36:85–102.

Silverman, Jay, Anita Raj, Lorelei Mucci, and Jeanne Hathaway. 2001. Dating violence against adolescent girls and associated substance use, unhealthy weight control, sexual risk behavior, pregnancy, and suicidality. *Journal of the American Medical Association* 286:572–79.

Stanko, Elizabeth. 1985. *Intimate intrusions: Women's experience of male violence*. London: Routledge and Kegan Paul.

Stein, Nan. 1995. Sexual harassment in K–12 schools: The public performance of gendered violence. *Harvard Educational Review* 65:145–62.

Stein, Nan, Deborah Tolman, Michelle Porche, and Renée Spencer. 2002. Gender safety: A new concept for safer and more equitable schools. *Journal of School Violence* 1:35–50.

Thompson, Sharon. 1995. *Going all the way: Teenage girls' tales of sex, romance, and pregnancy.* New York: Hill and Wang.

Thorne, Barrie, and Zella Luria. 1986. Sexuality and gender in children's daily worlds. *Social Problems* 33:176–90.

Tolman, Deborah. 1991. Adolescent girls, women and sexuality: Discerning dilemmas of desire. In *Women, girls and psychotherapy: Reframing resistance,* edited by C. Gilligan, A. Rogers, and D. Tolman. New York: Haworth.

Tolman, Deborah. 1994. Doing desire: Adolescent girls' struggles for/with sexuality. *Gender & Society* 8:324–42.

Tolman, Deborah, Renée Spencer, Myra Rosen-Reynosa, and Michelle Porche. 2003. Sowing the seeds of violence in heterosexual relationships: Early adolescents narrate compulsory heterosexuality. *Journal of Social Issues* 59:159–78.

Van Roosmalen, Erica. 2000. Forces of patriarchy: Adolescent experiences of sexuality and conceptions of relationships. *Youth & Society* 32:202–27.

Tackling the Roots of Rape

Frank Bruni

Steubenville. The Naval Academy. Vanderbilt University. The stories of young men sexually assaulting young women seem never to stop, despite all the education we've had and all the progress we've supposedly made, and there are times when I find myself darkly wondering if there's some ineradicable predatory streak in the male subset of our species.

Wrong, Chris Kilmartin told me. It's not DNA we're up against; it's movies, manners and a set of mores, magnified in the worlds of the military and sports, that assign different roles and different worth to men and women. Fix that culture and we can keep women a whole lot safer. I reached out to Kilmartin, a psychology professor and the author of the textbook "The Masculine Self," after learning that the military is repeatedly reaching out to him. Right now he's in Colorado, at the Air Force Academy, which imported him for a year to teach in the behavioral sciences department and advise the school on preventing sexual violence. He previously worked on a Naval Academy curriculum with that aim, and helped to write a training film for the Army. At a time of heightened concern about rape and related crimes in the armed services, he's being welcomed as someone with insights into the problem.

Its deepest roots, he said, are the cult of hypermasculinity, which tells boys that aggression is natural and sexual conquest enviable, and a set of laws and language that cast women as inferior, pliable, even disposable. "We start boys off at a very early age," Kilmartin told me during a recent phone conversation. "When the worst thing we say to a boy in sports is that he throws 'like a girl,' we teach boys to disrespect the feminine and disrespect women. That's the cultural undercurrent of rape."

Boys see women objectified in popular entertainment and tossed around like rag dolls in pornography. They encounter fewer women than men in positions of leadership. They hear politicians advocate for legislation like the Virginia anti-abortion bill that would have required women who wanted to end pregnancies to submit to an invasive vaginal ultrasound. "Before you make a reproductive choice, you are going to be required to have somebody penetrate you with an object," he said. "That's very paternalistic: we know what's right. You're not in control of your own body." He noted that discussions of domestic violence more often included the question of why a battered woman stayed than the question of why a battering man struck, as if the striking was to be expected. Men will be brute men, just as boys will be lusty boys.

If Kilmartin's observations can read at times like humorless chunks of a politically correct tome, that's not how he actually comes across. He's loose, funny. In fact he's got a sideline hobby as a stand-up comic. No joke. And he's got a trove of less wonky riffs. He mentions the University of Iowa, which for decades has painted the locker room used by opponents pink to put them "in a passive mood" with a "sissy color," in the words of a former head football coach, Hayden Fry. He mentions the bizarre use of the term "sex scandals" for such incidents as Tailhook decades ago and the recent accusations that Bob Filner, the mayor of San Diego, groped women around him, among other offenses. "They're *violence* scandals," he said. "If I hit you over the head with a frying pan, I don't call that cooking."

The armed services are a special challenge, because they're all about aggression, summoning and cultivating Attila the Hun and then asking him to play Sir Walter Raleigh as well. But Kilmartin said that that's a resolvable tension, if men are conditioned to show the same self-control toward women that they do, successfully, in following myriad military regulations; if they're encouraged to call out sexist behavior; and if, above all, commanders monitor their own conduct, never signaling that women are second-class citizens. The integration of women into combat duties will help, bolstering women's standing and altering a climate of inequality, Kilmartin said.

But he and the rest of us are taking on fortified traditions and calcified mind-sets, and that's evident in the enrollment in the two classes of Interdisciplinary Perspectives on Men and Masculinity that he began teaching on Friday. Although female cadets are about 20 percent of the Air Force Academy, they're more than half of the students who signed up for Kilmartin's course, he said. He said that one of them, during the very first session, recounted that someone at flight school over the summer had told her that women shouldn't fly planes. "Oh, so do you fly a plane with your penis?" Kilmartin asked the class. One of the male cadets responded: "Sounds like you're issuing a challenge, sir."

Transgender Discrimination in the Workplace

ELIS HERMAN AND ELROI J. WINDSOR

When considering gender, sexism, and gender discrimination, the perspectives and experiences of those who do not fit easily into the existing gender categories are often disregarded or overlooked. Herman and Windsor discuss the experiences of transgender people, focusing on workplace experiences, legal protections, and advocacy organizations that seek equality on behalf of transgender or gender-nonconforming workers.

When studying social issues related to gender, the experiences of people whose genders do not fit into conventional categories—transgender people—are important to consider. In this reading, we define key terminology related to the transgender community and provide an overview of the transitions that some of these individuals undergo in their lives. Then, we consider one social institution that has a tremendous impact on the quality of life for this group: the workplace. For transgender people in the United States, job discrimination, bias, and mistreatment are common problems. Although legal protections exist that can help mitigate these circumstances, they are currently not widespread. However, organizations that advocate on behalf of transgender people are paving the way for improved opportunities and outcomes.

Terminology

Sex and gender terms are often used interchangeably, but it is important to note distinctions when discussing issues that affect gender-nonconforming people. The term "sex" describes internal and external physical characteristics including chromosomes, hormones, genitalia, reproductive organs, and secondary sex characteristics.[1] Although babies are typically assigned a sex of "male" or "female" at birth based on their genitals, variations in sex characteristics complicate these clear-cut categories.[2] Researchers estimate that around 1.7 percent of the world's population (approximately six babies born each day) have sex characteristics that vary from normative expectations of maleness and femaleness.[3] "Gender" is a more general term that describes cultural and social assumptions and expectations associated with women and men. For example, women are expected to be sensitive and nurturing, whereas men are expected be tough and provide for their families. "Gender identity" refers to a person's internal sense of gender. Gender identities include terms like woman, man, transgender man, and genderqueer.

Original to *Focus on Social Problems: A Contemporary Reader.*

"Gender expression" describes how an individual presents his or her gender to the world through style, behavior, mannerisms, name, and pronouns. Gender expression can range from masculine to feminine or it may be more blended or neutral. People may describe gender expression using words like "butch" (masculine gender expression), "femme" (feminine gender expression), or "androgynous" (characteristics of femininity and masculinity). Everyone has a sex, gender, gender identity, and gender expression.

"Cisgender" is used to describe individuals whose gender identities match the sex they were assigned at birth. In other words, cisgender simply means "not transgender."[4] An example would be a person who is assigned a female sex at birth, is raised as a girl, and feels comfortable identifying as a girl and, later in life, as a woman. The term "transgender" can be used as a broad, inclusive term to describe myriad gender identities and expressions that fall outside of the sex/gender binary or the expectation that there are only two sexes and two genders and that everyone's sex and gender align.[5]

Often when people think of transgender they assume "transsexual." The term transsexual is typically used to describe people who desire to transition from one binary sex to the other, often through the use of hormones and surgeries. Individuals who were assigned a female sex at birth, but identify and express as men, may call themselves transsexual men, trans men, or FTM (female-to-male). People who were assigned a male sex at birth but live as women may call themselves transsexual women, trans women, or MTF (male-to-female). Some people who go through this transition do not use the word transsexual at all and prefer to be called "people of transgender experience" or simply "women" and "men."[6]

But transsexuals are not the only people who may be included under the transgender umbrella term. Drag kings (typically women who perform masculine/men characters) and drag queens (typically men who perform feminine/women characters) can be considered part of the transgender community. Crossdressers, or people who wear the clothing of the "opposite" gender, also belong within this community. Even masculine women and feminine men may find that their gender-nonconforming experiences have much in common with others in this community.

The language of gender is changing, and many people use new words to describe experiences that fall outside of or between the gender binary. The word "genderqueer" is popular as a term for nonbinary gender expressions, which means having a gender that falls outside of the typical sex/gender binary. Like transgender, genderqueer can be used as both an umbrella term and a specific identity. Other nonbinary gender identities include agender (having no gender), neutrois (gender-neutral), bigender (having two gender identities or expressions), and third gender (identifying as a different gender entirely). Some gender-nonbinary people transition using hormones or surgeries to live as their genders; others do not. The range of identity terms and lived experiences within them indicate that there is no single "correct" way to be transgender.

Ultimately, gender is expressed in intricate and nuanced ways; thus, there is no single definition that describes either all transgender or all cisgender experiences. Transgender is also an identity in itself, and many people choose to identify with that word alone or in conjunction with others. Others refer to themselves simply as "trans."[7]

Transitioning Issues

Just as transgender encompasses numerous identities and expressions, there is also no universal transgender experience. However, because of the institutionalization of binary sex and gender, transgender people often interface with social, medical, and legal institutions in ways that cisgender people do not. These experiences can range from coming out as transgender, to seeking surgeries or hormones, to legally changing name and sex.[8] Although media typically portray transitioning as "getting a sex change," this phrasing is inaccurate and can be considered offensive.[9] For most transgender people, the reality of transitioning, if it is even desired, is a complex and extended process with social, medical, and legal implications.

First, gender is interactional and social. How we dress, style our hair, carry our bodies, and communicate are all pieces of how we convey our genders to the world around us. A trans person may take the first steps to living comfortably by changing the way he or she looks and dresses to better reflect his or her internal sense of gender. Often, trans people decide to go by names and pronouns different from the ones assigned to them as babies. Many trans people use hormones like estrogen and testosterone to feminize or masculinize their bodies. Some also seek various surgeries to further align their physical characteristics with their genders. Yet many trans people do not use hormones or surgeries for different reasons. Some face barriers to access, such as high costs of care, having preexisting health conditions, or lacking nearby doctors who are skilled in trans health. Others simply do not desire to change their bodies with hormones and surgeries.[10]

For transgender people who choose to medically transition, access to gender-affirming interventions is often heavily regulated. Many surgeons and hormone prescribers require a letter from a mental health professional confirming a diagnosis of "gender dysphoria" before they will approve a patient for gender-related surgeries and hormone therapy. Acquiring this letter can be difficult because therapy is expensive and often not covered by insurance. Many trans people resist the requirement of a diagnosis of gender dysphoria to make decisions regarding their bodies, arguing that gender nonconformity is not a mental illness.[11]

Because sex is so important to social categorization, many transgender people navigate legal and bureaucratic processes to make their lived genders "official." Birth certificates, driver's licenses, and passports are just a few legal documents that bear sex markers. To change sex designations on official documents, individuals must negotiate with different institutions on local, state, and federal levels. For example, to change the sex marker on a passport, an individual must submit a letter from a physician documenting "clinical treatment for gender transition" to the U.S. Department of State.[12] Requirements for changing legal sex on driver's licenses and birth certificates vary from state to state. To alter the sex designation on a driver's license, some states require proof of genital surgery, which most trans people in the United States have not had or do not seek.[13] Other states require a court order or letter from a medical professional affirming that the individual lives as his or her professed sex.[14] Forty-seven states and the District of Columbia will change the sex markers on birth certificates when presented with a court order, letter from medical professional, and/or proof of surgery. Many, however, mark new certificates with the word "amended" or leave other evidence that the sex has been altered. Ohio, Tennessee, and Idaho do not change the sex designation on birth certificates under any circumstance.[15] Outside of the United States, seven countries, including Nepal, India, Pakistan, Bangladesh, Germany, New Zealand, and Australia, provide a third option on legal documents.[16]

The processes that surround altering sex designations on official documents are fraught with complexity and ambiguity. Many trans people live as genders other than those assigned to them at birth, yet never undergo surgeries, so cannot change documentation. Additionally, each government agency requires a separate fee to alter paperwork, and the collective costs pose a barrier for many. The legal processes also fail to account for transgender people who do not identify as men or women. For individuals whose gender identities and expressions fall outside of the gender binary, it is impossible to obtain accurate and consistent identity documents. Almost half of trans people (if not more) do not possess official identity documentation that reflects their lived genders.[17] This lack of appropriate identification exposes transgender people to heightened discrimination and violence. For example, transgender women who do not possess legal documentation as "female" are often incarcerated in prisons for men, which puts them at an increased risk for sexual violence.

Trans at Work

The workplace can be a stressful environment for transgender people. In 2011, the National Center for Transgender Equality and the National Gay and Lesbian Task Force published a large-scale study of the United States and its territories that included more than 6,000 people. This groundbreaking study revealed that the workplace experiences of transgender and gender-nonconforming people were shaped by high rates of unemployment, underemployment, and poor working conditions. Still, workplace experiences were not entirely negative for trans people.[18]

At work, transgender people must make decisions about whether to disclose their trans status or remain "stealth" to their coworkers. If they are planning to take steps in their transitions, they must consider whether it is safe to do so openly. Overall, the 2011 study found that most transgender people were not out at work. In fact, 71 percent of the people in the study tried to hide their gender identity or gender transition to avoid negative reactions. Another 57 percent of trans people delayed their gender transitions because of fears of discrimination. For people who do not conform to expectations and assumptions of masculinity and femininity, coming out to coworkers is not a choice.

Presenting gender outside of the binary often makes being out unavoidable. People who do not "pass" as women or men may disrupt gendered expectations in the workplace and be subject to greater discomfort and discrimination, as extensive research and both authors of this reading can attest. But after trans people transitioned and were living in their desired gender, they mostly reported feeling more comfortable at work. Living in their genders also helped to improve their job performances, although half of these people still encountered harassment at work.[19]

Being out as trans can affect trans people's job security. Almost half of the people in the 2011 study reported being fired, not hired, or denied promotion for being trans. Another 44 percent reported being underemployed, working in positions where they were overqualified, or working in areas outside of their training and expertise. These numbers are startling, but when compared to the national rates, they become even more troubling. The study demonstrated that transgender people's unemployment rate was *twice as high* as the national unemployment rate. For trans people of color, the unemployment rate was *four times the national average*. These conditions translate into extremely compromised socioeconomic statuses for transgender people. Within the sample, 15 percent of people reported living in dire poverty, earning less than $10,000 annually, which is close to four times the rate of the general population of the United States.[20]

Transgender people also reported high rates of workplace mistreatment. Almost everyone in the study (90 percent) reported being harassed or mistreated on the job or took action to avoid these negative outcomes. As one trans man reported, "When one of my colleagues found out I was born female, I was forced to use the bathroom in another part of the building where I worked, because he said that I made the 'real' men uncomfortable with my presence. Now, I look like a [cisgender male], and the only reason they knew about my status is because a supervisor found out, and spread my business to the other supervisors and friends."[21] Mistreatment of trans workers included a wide variety of behaviors. More frequently occurring types of mistreatment included harassment and having coworkers share inappropriate information about trans workers.[22] Hostile workplaces may impose restrictive dress codes and bathroom policies. For example, people whose legal sex is "female" may be directed to wear feminine clothing and hairstyles, or they may be required to use the women's restroom, although these people may identify as male and look like men.[23] Other workplace hazards for trans people, although less common, included physical and sexual assault.[24]

Like other aspects of discrimination and bias, the workplace experiences of trans people vary by other demographic factors. Overall, trans women were more likely to experience anti-trans bias on the job than trans men, as were people of color, respondents who lived in the southern United States, undocumented immigrants, and those whose highest educational level was high school or lower. People who worked in lower-income jobs reported higher rates of harassment. Physical and sexual violence occurred more often among people with lower levels of educational attainment, with undocumented immigrant workers being three times more likely to experience violence at work compared to the rest of the sample.[25]

Given these stark realities, it is not surprising that poor working conditions push some transgender people into working in underground economies where they may sell sex and drugs to survive. Among workers who lost their jobs for being trans in the 2011 study, 28 percent of them turned to the underground economy. Although black and Latinx[26] workers were more likely to work in these trades compared to white workers, differences by gender were slight. In the study, 19 percent of trans women and 15 percent of trans men participated in underground economies, which suggests that both groups are at risk for additional problems.[27] The negative workplace experiences reported by transgender people have implications beyond employment. When people lose their jobs because of anti-transgender bias, they are at a greater risk for homelessness and incarceration. They are also more likely to experience negative health outcomes such as HIV infection, suicide, and tobacco, alcohol, and drug use.[28]

Despite these problems, transgender people exhibit resilience in the face of workplace discrimination. Among people who lost jobs because of being trans, 58 percent reported being employed at the time of the survey. After transitioning, almost 80 percent of both trans women and trans men said that their job situation improved. Of the people who did not lose their jobs because of bias, 86 percent were able to use their preferred bathrooms at work.[29] As one respondent stated, "When I started my transition, the place that I was working was very supportive. My boss had a family member who is transgender. I was treated with respect by everyone."[30]

The experience of Deirdre McCloskey, an economist at the University of Iowa, illustrates an example of a positive experience. When McCloskey announced her transition from male to female in 1995, she anticipated the worst: being denied compensation, being assigned to teach undesirable classes, or, most painfully, being shunned by the colleagues and friends with whom she had worked for decades. McCloskey feared she would be forced to take legal action, which would probably prove unsuccessful. Ultimately, however, McCloskey recalled her coming out to the dean of the College of Business as positive:

> Gary [Fethke, College of Business Dean,] sat stunned for a moment. He and I were both economists, conservatives by academic standards, free-market men. Then he spoke as a dean: "Thank God ... I thought for a moment you were going to confess to converting to socialism!" I laughed, relieved—the dean was going to react like a friend. "And this is great for our affirmative action program—one less man, one more woman!" More laughter, more relief. "And wait a minute—it's even better: as a woman I can cut your salary to 70 cents on the dollar!" Not quite so funny! And then seriously: "That's a strange thing to do." I agreed. And Gary continued: "How can I help?" ... Gary kept his word,

acting as an advocate for me and my strange choice in the administration and the faculty.[31]

McCloskey came out in 1995, before many of today's policies that protect trans people from discrimination at work were in place, but her supervisor's response was positive, nonetheless. But the dean's comments also reveal broader trends in workplace gender inequality. Dean Fethke's jibe about affirmative action exposes a seldom-acknowledged truth about the program. Although affirmative action was meant to increase racial minority representation in the workplace, in practice, the program is most beneficial for white women.[32] Thus, queers and people of color still lose out, despite government initiatives. Fethke's joke about cutting McCloskey's salary also hits a nerve about workplace inequality, given the gender pay gap where women earn about 82 cents for every dollar men make.[33] These realities throw transgender and gender inequalities into sharper focus.

(Trans)Gender Inequalities at Work

The experiences of trans people like Deirdre McCloskey help to expose broader gender inequalities. Ben Barres, a Stanford University neurobiologist and transgender man, is an outspoken critic of the claim that males are innately more capable in math and science fields than females. Barres believes, instead, that deeply rooted biases and social pressures prevent women from entering and remaining in the sciences. Barres discusses his own experiences working as both a man and a woman in the sciences as evidence that gender inequality persists. Barres recalls that, when working as a woman, his competence in math and science was often questioned; at one time, Barres was even passed over for a fellowship opportunity that was given instead to a less accomplished male peer:

> As a [female] undergrad at the Massachusetts Institute of Technology (MIT), I was the only person in a large class of nearly all

men to solve a hard [math] problem, only to be told by the professor that my boyfriend must have solved it for me. I was not given any credit. I am still disappointed about the prestigious fellowship competition I later lost to a male contemporary when I was a PhD student, even though the Harvard dean who had read both applications assured me that my application was much stronger (I had published six high-impact papers whereas my male competitor had published only one). Shortly after I changed sex, a faculty member was heard to say "Ben Barres gave a great seminar today, but then his work is much better than his sister's."[34]

Individuals like Barres and McCloskey who have lived on both sides of the gender binary can provide unique insight into the workings of gender privilege and inequality.

The experiences of transgender people like McCloskey and Barres lend evidence to the reality of workplace inequality for cisgender and transgender people alike. The sociologist Kristen Schilt has conducted some of the only large-scale ethnographic research on trans people's experiences in the workplace. Although this research focuses predominantly on transgender men, her findings shed light on the range of experiences trans people have at work.

Schilt's research, published in 2010, showed that many trans men experience pressure to conform to standards of hegemonic, or dominant, masculinity to be taken seriously in the workplace. Many trans men described feeling hypervigilant about passing as male, particularly early on in their transitions. They also worried that if their employers or coworkers perceived their genders as "in-between" or "ambiguous," they could be at greater risk for mistreatment. One gender-nonconforming respondent, Wayne, recalled being told by a potential employer: "I will hire you only on the condition that you don't ever come in the front [of the restaurant] because you make people uncomfortable."[35] Once Wayne transitioned and began passing as normatively male, his work experiences and opportunities dramatically improved.[36]

In general, transgender men reported that their lives at work got better following their transitions. Many reported that they were treated with more respect and taken more seriously after they transitioned. Some also believed that working as men was a direct reason for promotions, raises, and other economic advantages they would not have had access to prior to transitioning. One respondent, who worked in an office primarily with women, described how his masculine voice granted him undeserved competence at the expense of women: "[In meetings,] everyone will just get quiet and listen to me. But when this [woman expert] speaks, everyone talks over her. And I have no specialization in this area. I don't know anything, yet they are all listening to me."[37] Trans men's financial success and gains in status reflect trends in cisgender workplace inequality.[38]

Not all trans men, however, reported positive changes at work following their transitions. Because hegemonic masculinity is associated with whiteness, trans men of color often had different experiences than white trans men, which affected them both within and outside of the workplace. One Asian man in Schilt's study described feeling that "people have this impression that Asian guys aren't macho and therefore aren't really male."[39] This emasculated stereotype of Asian men may reduce or negate potential gains at work based on gender alone. Black and Latino men, too, suffered from white-centered ideals of masculinity. Several of Schilt's black respondents described being stereotyped as aggressive, threatening, and criminal once they moved through the world as men. This racialized hypermasculinity also tainted men's lives at work.[40] Given these factors, it is possible that the positive experiences described earlier by Deirdre McCloskey and Ben Barres were informed by their privileges as white, educated, and upper-middle-class academics.

Workplaces have different strategies for dealing with trans employees. Schilt found that employers' responses fit into four categories: neutralizing challenges to the male/female binary, policing the male/female binary, creating transgender tokens, and incorporating trans men as one of the guys. Some employers used methods of neutralizing trans workers by forcing them out of the workplace, either through overt means like firing or by creating environments that were so uncomfortable the trans employee chose to leave. Some workplaces, particularly those in conservative areas without nondiscrimination laws, were able to enforce the male/female binary by insisting that trans men work as women to keep their jobs. These employers often cited legal sex and workplace dress code policies to regulate trans employees' genders. Other trans men working in lesbian, gay, bisexual, and transgender (LGBT)-friendly jobs experienced being treated as the token trans person when they were out at work. These individuals described inhabiting an in-between category, where being trans was always or usually treated as their predominant identity. Some workplaces, mostly in the professional sector, chose to incorporate transgender men as "one of the guys." Supervisors in these environments often took steps to ensure that an employee's transition was smooth; some workplaces even held informative sessions about transgender issues. These employers helped make trans men one of the guys by assigning them to stereotypically masculine tasks, incorporating them into men's culture, or "forgetting" that an individual was trans.[41] Although workplaces' strategies for handling trans employees vary, legal recourse can help protect trans people from discriminatory employer reactions.

Legal Considerations

Although trans people experience many difficulties in the workplace, they can rely on some legal protections. In the United States, anti-transgender employment discrimination is prohibited on the federal level and in some states through additional legislation.

All workers in the United States are protected by Title VII of the Civil Rights Act, which prohibits discrimination in the workplace based on sex. In 2012, federal courts found that discrimination based on gender identity and expression qualifies as sex discrimination. So trans workers may file discrimination claims with the Equal Employment Opportunity Commission under Title VII.[42] This victory came after the Transgender Law Center filed a discrimination complaint on behalf of Mia Macy, a transgender woman who was denied a job as a ballistics technician. Macy, a veteran and former police detective, applied for the job as male. Her background expertise made her a highly qualified candidate. But when she disclosed that she was gender transitioning during the hiring process, she was told funding for the position had been cut. Later, the employer hired someone else for the position. Macy's landmark case set the stage for other trans workers to file suit under Title VII.[43]

In addition, eighteen states, plus the District of Columbia and Puerto Rico, offer explicit protection from discrimination in the workplace based on gender identity or expression. However, no statewide legal protections exist for trans people in the southern United States and most of the Midwest.[44] Some jurisdictions in these regions do provide limited protections to trans workers, such as the cities of Kansas City, Missouri, El Paso, Texas, and Nashville, Tennessee.[45] Ultimately, fewer than half of American workers reside in parts of the country that explicitly protect trans people through statewide nondiscrimination employment laws.[46] Despite the transgender-inclusive interpretation of Title VII, explicitly protecting gender identity and expression at the state level would provide trans people with a more secure foundation in filing discrimination claims.

Advocacy groups like the National Center for Transgender Equality and the Transgender Law Center recommend that Congress pass the Employment Non-Discrimination Act (ENDA), which would include protection from discrimination based on sexual orientation and gender identity.[47] This legislation has been jostled about in Congress since it was first introduced in 1994, when it addressed discrimination based on sexuality orientation only. It was not until 2007 that gender identity was added, albeit with reservation.[48]

Transgender Activism and Advocacy

On a broad, policy-based level, national LGBT organizations are working to ensure that transgender people at work are protected under actual legislation, as opposed to the interpretations of Title VII (discussed above). If passed, ENDA would be the only national law that protects LGBT people from employment discrimination.[49] It would expand existing laws that already forbid workplace discrimination based on race, color, religion, and national origin. In addition to lobbying, national organizations provide resources and support around the issue of employment inequality. The Transgender Law Center provides resources about employment discrimination and assistance filing Equal Employment Opportunity Commission claims.[50]

Smaller organizations and support centers are also critical to providing services for trans people regionally. The Transgender Economic Empowerment Initiative, based out of the Bay Area, California, is a community program that helps equip trans people with jobs that provide a living wage and benefits. The initiative reaches communities by partnering with other centers and organizations that serve transgender people.[51] In New York City, the Sylvia Rivera Law Project provides legal aid around trans issues, hosts informative trainings for community organizations and launches campaigns related to prisoners' rights, health-care issues, and policy reform.[52] These community organizations help meet the needs of individual people and work for legal reform and protections.

In recent years, advocacy work by well-known transgender people has become more visible. Laverne Cox, an African American trans woman and cast member of the popular television series *Orange Is the New Black*, has lobbied publicly for the acceptance of trans people. In May 2014, she appeared on the cover of *TIME* magazine.[53] Also in 2014, Jay Kelly came out publicly as trans and is now living as a boy.

As the teenage son of the famous R&B artist R. Kelly, he has gained much media attention and has begun educating people on his Ask.fm social media account.[54] Advocates like these help to raise awareness about the issues facing trans communities. With the work of national organizations, community partnerships, and vocal individuals, the issues facing trans people will continue to gain attention. As education of the public continues, the experiences of trans people at work will hopefully improve over time.

NOTES

1. GLAAD. 2014. "GLAAD Media Reference Guide–Transgender Issues." Retrieved December 19, 2014. http://www.glaad.org/reference/transgender/.

2. Intersex Society of North America. 2008. "How Common Is Intersex?" Retrieved January 11, 2015. http://www.isna.org/faq/frequency/.

3. Blackless, Melanie, Anthony Charuvastra, Amanda Derryck, Anne Fausto-Sterling, Karl Lauzanne, and Ellen Lee. 2000. "How Sexually Dimorphic Are We? Review and Synthesis." *American Journal of Human Biology* 12:151–166.

4. GLAAD, 2014.

5. Hill, Mel Reiff, and Jeff Mays. 2011. "The Transgender Umbrella." Pp. 38–39 in *The Gender Book*. Retrieved December 18, 2014. http://issuu.com/thegenderbook/docs/the_gender_book/.

6. GLAAD, 2014.

7. "Transgender" is an *adjective* that describes certain gender experiences. For example, one may identify as a transgender woman or man, as a "person of transgender experience," or as just transgender. Although some well-meaning people use it by mistake, the term "transgendered" is neither correct nor accurate. The term cannot be conjugated in the past tense, as in "transgendered," because it is not a verb. It is also inaccurate to use transgender as a noun, as in "John is a transgender." This may be likened to saying "John is a tall." John can be tall, or John can be a tall fellow, but John cannot just be "a tall."

8. Not all transgender people choose to transition; many simply choose to live as their genders without taking medical or legal steps.

9. "Getting a sex change" is often used more for sensationalism than accuracy. At the best, the phrase is inaccurate. Because sex encompasses a number of physical traits (hormones, reproductive organs, chromosomes, secondary sex characteristics), it is impossible to change it completely in one event. For example, an individual may have her ovaries removed (a hysterectomy), but she can never change her chromosomes. At the worst, describing transitioning as getting a sex change can be offensive. The phrase implies that an individual lives as one gender one moment and then gets a surgery that completely changes the way his or her sex is perceived the next moment. The vast majority of individuals who choose to pursue any sort of surgery already live as their chosen sex. Although transgender surgeries are often referred to as "sex reassignment surgeries," a more accurate description may be "gender-affirming surgeries," because surgical interventions simply help align people's bodies with the genders they feel and live.

10. Grant, Jaime M., Lisa A. Mottet, and Justin Tanis. 2010. *National Transgender Discrimination Survey Report on Health and Health Care.* Washington: National Center for Transgender Equality and the National Gay and Lesbian Task Force. Retrieved December 28, 2014. http://www.thetaskforce.org/downloads/reports/reports/ntds_summary.pdf/.

11. Dreger, Alice. 2013. "Why Gender Dysphoria Should No Longer Be Considered a Mental Disorder." *Pacific Standard*, October 18. Retrieved January 26, 2015. http://www.psmag.com/health-and-behavior/take-gender-identity-disorder-dsm-68308/.

12. U.S. Department of State. 2014. "Gender Reassignment Applicants." Retrieved December 28, 2014. http://travel.state.gov/content/passports/english/passports/information/gender.html#complete/.

13. Grant et al., 2010.

14. National Center for Transgender Equality. 2013. "Driver's License Policies by State." Retrieved December 28, 2014. http://transequality.org/Resources/DL/DL_policies_text.html/.

15. Lambda Legal. 2014. "Changing Birth Certificate Sex Designations: State-By-State Guidelines." Retrieved December 28, 2014. http://www.lambdalegal.org/publications/changing-birth-certificate-sex-designations-state-by-state-guidelines/.

16. Pasquesoone, Valentine. 2014. "Seven Countries Giving Transgender People Fundamental Rights the U.S. Still Won't." Retrieved February 23, 2015. http://mic.com/articles/87149/7-countries-giving-transgender-people-fundamental-rights-the-u-s-still-won-t/.

17. Grant, Jaime M., Lisa A. Mottet, Justin Tanis, Jack Harrison, Jody L. Herman, and Mara Keisling. 2011. *Injustice at Every Turn: A Report of the National Transgender Discrimination Survey.* Washington, DC: National Center for Transgender Equality and National Gay and Lesbian Task Force. Retrieved January 8, 2015. http://www.transequality.org/Resources/ntds_full.pdf/.

18. Ibid.

19. Ibid.

20. Ibid.

21. Grant et al., 2011, 60.

22. Ibid.

23. Bender-Baird, Kyla. 2011. *Transgender Employment Experiences: Gendered Perceptions and the Law.* Albany, NY: SUNY Press.

24. Grant et al., 2011.

25. Ibid.

26. The use of "Latinx" is an intentional way to describe Latinos and Latinas to reflect gender-neutral and nonsexist language. The letter "x" allows for a third option that resists language rooted in the gender binary, where the "o" in "Latino" is considered masculine and the "a" in "Latina" is feminine.

27. Grant et al., 2011.

28. Ibid.

29. Ibid.

30. Ibid, 64.

31. McCloskey, Deirdre. 1998. "Happy Endings: Law, Gender, and the University." *The Journal of Gender, Race and Justice* 2(1):78.

32. Goodwin, Michele. 2012. "The Death of Affirmative Action, Part 1." Retrieved January 20, 2015. http://chronicle.com/blogs/brainstorm/the-death-of-affirmative-action-part-i/44860/.

33. Bureau of Labor Statistics. 2013. *Labor Force Statistics from the Current Population Survey.* Retrieved January 26, 2015. http://www.bls.gov/cps/cpsaat39.htm/.

34. Barres, Ben A. 2006. "Does Gender Matter?" *Nature* 442:134.

35. Schilt, Kristen. 2010. *Just One of the Guys? Transgender Men and the Persistence of Gender Inequality.* Chicago: University of Chicago Press, 78.

36. Ibid.

37. Ibid, 71.

38. Ibid.

39. Ibid, 85.

40. Ibid.

41. Ibid.

42. National Center for Transgender Equality. 2014. "Employment Discrimination and Transgender People." Retrieved December 18, 2014. http://www.transequality.org/Resources/EmploymentKnowYourRights_July2014.pdf/.

43. Transgender Law Center. 2012. "Groundbreaking! Federal Agency Rules Transgender Employees Protected by Sex Discrimination Law." Retrieved December 12, 2014. http://transgenderlawcenter.org/archives/635/.

44. NCTE, 2014.

45. Transgender Law and Policy Institute. 2012. "Non-Discrimination Laws That Include

Gender Identity and Expression." Retrieved December 18, 2014. http://transgenderlaw.org/ndlaws/index.htm#maps/.

46. Ibid.

47. National Center for Transgender Equality. 2011. "Discrimination." Retrieved December 18, 2014. http://transequality.org/Issues/discrimination.html/. Transgender Law Center. 2014. "Advocacy." Retrieved December 18, 2014. http://transgenderlawcenter.org/issues/employment/.

48. Human Rights Campaign. 2014. "Employment Non-Discrimination Act: Legislative Timeline." Retrieved December 18, 2014. http://www.hrc.org/resources/entry/employment-non-discrimination-act-legislative-timeline/.

49. Human Rights Campaign. 2014. "Pass ENDA Now." Retrieved January 21, 2015. http://www.hrc.org/campaigns/employment-non-discrimination-act/.

50. Transgender Law Center. "Employment Discrimination." Retrieved January 21, 2015. http://transgenderlawcenter.org/issues/employment/.

51. Transgender Economic Empowerment Initiative. 2008. "About Us." Retrieved January 21, 2015. http://www.teeisf.org/about/.

52. Sylvia Rivera Law Project. 2015. Retrieved January 26, 2015. http://srlp.org/.

53. Steinmetz, Katy. 2014. "Laverne Cox Talks to TIME about the Transgender Movement." Retrieved January 27, 2015. http://time.com/132769/transgender-orange-is-the-new-black-laverne-cox-interview/).

54. Jay Kelly. 2015. "Jay_____ @MI_YLNO_NAMUH." Retrieved January 27, 2015. http://ask.fm/MI_YLNO_NAMUH/.

Why Gender Equality Is Good for the World

STACY GORMAN HARMON

When women and men are unequal, there are harmful consequences not only to individuals, but also to societies as a whole (e.g., decreased economic power, poverty, instability, and conflict). Gorman Harmon argues that closing the gap between men and women benefits everyone; therefore, it is in all our interests to work to eliminate gender inequality.

In 2000, the United Nations (UN) met to develop a set of goals for the millennium to improve health and welfare for people around the globe. The Millennium Development Goals (MDGs) address social problems like poverty, HIV/AIDS, and gender inequality through eight specific goals the UN set out to achieve by 2015. Since their creation, scholars and activists have monitored the world's progress of attaining these goals and suggested ways for increasing success. Research suggests that many social problems are connected and that gender equality, in particular, is necessary to reduce poverty, hunger, war, and disease (Hendra et al., 2013; United Nations Economic and Social Council, 2013). In other words, improving the condition of women is key to improving a variety of problematic conditions all over the world. Because it is not just women who will benefit from gender equality; it is everyone's responsibility and in everyone's best interest to work to close the gaps between men and women.

Measuring Gender Inequality

To understand how social problems intersect with gender inequality, one must first have a way to measure differences in women and men's lives around the world. The Global Gender Gap Index does this by measuring gender inequality and ranking countries based on their performance in four main areas: economic participation and opportunity, health and survival, educational attainment, and political empowerment. Economic participation measures gaps in women's and men's income and employment rates, as well as the type of employment that each is more likely to occupy. Health and survival outcomes are measured through life expectancy and sex ratio at birth, the latter of which assesses "missing women," or femicide, the killing of women and girls as a result of a society's preference for males. Educational attainment reflects both literacy rates and men and women's attendance in primary, secondary, and postsecondary schools. Last, to determine men and women's role in

Original to *Focus on Social Problems: A Contemporary Reader.*

decision making, political empowerment measures the ratio of women to men at the highest governmental positions. Through these four areas, the Global Gender Gap Index provides a picture of where countries are succeeding and where more effort is needed to decrease the gender gap.

The 2013 report of the Global Gender Gap Index ranked a total of 136 countries, with Iceland coming in first with the least amount of gender inequality. The United States was ranked twenty-third, falling behind many Western European nations like the United Kingdom, Sweden, and Denmark, as well as Cuba, South Africa, and the Philippines. The report also notes that no country had completely closed their gender gap. On a scale of 0 to 1, where 1 means complete equality and 0 means complete inequality, Iceland scored a 0.873. In comparison, the United States scored a 0.739, and Yemen, the lowest ranking country, received a 0.513. Although Nordic countries like Iceland, Finland, and Norway ranked highest for having the smallest gap between women and men, room for improvement remains, particularly in economic participation and political empowerment.

Because the Nordic countries have been most successful in decreasing gender inequality, they may offer important lessons to other countries. In these countries, the gap between men and women in education has closed, which impacts how successful women can be in the other measurable areas of the economy and politics. The report notes that these countries have the smallest salary gap between men and women, and "women have abundant opportunities to rise to positions of leadership" (World Economic Forum, 2013:20). For men and women in these countries, there is a greater balance between work and family, especially with the help of policies that provide workers with paid parental leave (World Economic Forum, 2013). In countries like Sweden and Norway where paid parental leave is guaranteed, there has been success with implementing policies that encourage men to also take time off by allotting a certain amount

of leave just for fathers (Rampell, 2013). Policies in Germany and Portugal grant families paid leave that must be shared between parents, and when fathers use their paid leave, mothers receive bonus weeks off (Rampell, 2013).

The United States is currently the only industrialized country that does not guarantee paid parental leave. Although more companies are starting to offer paid leave, including leave that fathers may take, men are still reluctant to use it (Weber, 2013). Men worry that by taking time off, they will be seen as less committed to their jobs, but this does not mean that fathers do not want to take time off to care for children. In fact, the majority of fathers in dual-income families report feeling conflicted between work and family responsibilities (Parker and Wang, 2013).

Paternity leave helps fathers to find better balance between work and home life and also has long-term benefits that promote gender equality. Fathers who take paternity leave are more likely to perform childcare tasks even after they have returned back to work (Mundy, 2013), reducing the gendered division of labor in the home and freeing women from some of the "second shift" of housework they experience after participating in the paid labor force (Hochschild, 1989). At a societal level, paternity leave reduces gender inequality. When more men choose to take paternity leave, employers have less of an incentive to discriminate against women when making hiring decisions (Mundy, 2013). Currently, employers may be more likely to hire men or to pay women less because women employees are more likely to take time off later to have children. However, if men are also choosing to take parental leave, then employers should be less likely to hire men over women or to pay women less based on the expectation that only women use parental leave.

Poverty, Economic Growth, and World Peace

The first MDG is to reduce poverty and hunger by half between 1990 and 2015 (Millennium Project, 2006). According to the 2013 MDG report, this first goal has been met and there are now 700 million fewer people living in extreme poverty, or living on less than $1.25 a day. However, even with the achievement of this goal, there are still about 1.2 billion people living in extreme poverty, and it is estimated that by 2015, 970 million people will still be relying on less than $1.25 a day (United Nations, 2013). Although achieving this goal is laudable, it is not enough.

Women make up the majority of the world's poorest adults while simultaneously playing a key role in agriculture and food production (Food and Agriculture Organisation, 2013). According to the Food and Agriculture Organisation (FAO) (2013), women are responsible for producing "a large portion of the world's food crops," and yet compared to men, women do not receive equal pay or have equal access to farming resources. Women working in agriculture typically own less land, are less able to hire labor, and are less likely to receive credit for farming expenditures than men (FAO, 2011). These disadvantages hurt women's economic potential and reduce the economy's productivity. The FAO predicts that decreasing the gender gap in farming would also significantly decrease global poverty and hunger. It is predicted that if women's access to agricultural resources were equal to men's, women's farming output could reduce the number of hungry people by 150 million (FAO, 2011).

Reducing gender inequality and increasing educational opportunities for women are essential for eliminating poverty. When a society's women are not educated, the consequences include higher fertility rates, lower-paying jobs, greater poverty, and higher mortality rates for women and children (Lawson, 2008). When families have higher incomes and better health, the country as a whole is more financially stable. Studies have consistently shown that women's participation in the labor market results in significant economic growth for both developed and developing countries (Loko and Diouf, 2009; Lawson, 2008; Daly, 2007; Dollar and Gatti, 1999). Educated women are more likely to work outside the home, which is linked to economic growth through higher productivity, greater agricultural yields, and higher investment returns (Lawson, 2008). If women's employment were equal to that of men, the gross domestic product would increase by 19 percent in Japan and 9 percent in Germany, France, and the United States (Daly, 2007). In developing countries, closing the education gap between men and women leads to better job opportunities with higher wages, which then increases productivity and gross domestic product growth (Lawson, 2008). In the United States, if women's earnings were equal to that of men's, women would make an additional $10,784 per year (Separa, 2012). Over one's lifetime, that translates to enough pay for seven college educations at a public university, a nest egg of $431,360 for retirement, or the ability to feed a family of four for 37 years (Separa, 2012).

Not only does gender equality translate into greater economic growth and a reduction in poverty, but also it means less conflict and, ultimately, a more peaceful world. A recent study found that "the larger the gender gap between the treatment of men and women in a society, the more likely a country is to be involved in intra- and interstate conflict, to be the first to resort to force in such conflicts, and to resort to higher levels of violence" (Hudson, 2012). According to Hudson (2012) and her colleagues, a society's treatment of women is connected to that society's stability, security, and overall peacefulness. When men use violence in their homes, they are also more likely to use it in other areas of society, including in government. Studies have shown that when groups composed entirely of men, compared to groups of men and women, make decisions, they are more likely to make aggressive and riskier choices, which can affect a country's level of conflict (Hudson, 2012).

When a country is in conflict, there is also a greater likelihood that women and children will be victims of violence. The UN estimates that the majority of casualties in war today are women and children. Women are also at increased risk for sexual violence during armed conflict, including rape, sexual slavery, forced pregnancy, and sterilization (United Nations, 2000). In a review of the world's progress in achieving MDGs for girls and women, the UN's Economic and Social Council (2013:15) wrote that "Countries experiencing conflict and fragility face the most significant challenges in achieving the Goals for women and girls." Without addressing gender inequality, it will be impossible to ever meet all of the UN's goals.

Everyone Wins with Gender Equality

Although there are clear benefits to gender equality, some may still be resistant. For instance, men in all societies may resist gender equality because it translates to a loss of benefits and potentially unsettling changes in the way we define masculinity (Connell, 2003). Many men benefit from the unpaid work that women do, including housework and childcare. Definitions of masculinity across the world situate men as providers, and so men may perceive women's entrance into paid professions as threatening to their role as the family breadwinner.

At the same time, men all over the world can benefit from changes in gender roles that will help to decrease gender inequality. Connell (2003) suggests that there are four main reasons that men and boys have to support gender equality. First, gender inequality promotes rigid gender roles that are damaging for women and men. In both developed and developing nations, definitions of masculinity that label men as providers also restrict men from participating in activities that are then labeled as feminine, including caring for children. For many men, this means added pressure to work more and spend less time with their families. Connell (2003) suggests that many employed men want more balance between work and home, but gender inequality is one major impediment to achieving that balance.

Second, gender equality also benefits families and communities through women's work in the paid labor market and as participants in society's decision-making process. As Connell (2003:13) explains, "In situations of mass poverty and underemployment, for instance in cities in developing countries, flexibility in the gender division of labour may be crucial to a household which requires women's earnings as well as men's." In developing countries especially, women's participation in the workforce usually means more spending to provide for the family's food needs, education for children, and health care (FAO, 2011). In rural areas of the United States where reliable and consistent work is difficult to find, families who have adopted more egalitarian roles are better able to navigate financial difficulty, particularly through women working outside of the home and men doing more in the home (Sherman, 2012). Additionally, women's role in their community's decision-making process can also mean less aggressive approaches to conflict resolution, which in turn is linked to less violence and conflict, making communities safer and more secure (Hudson, 2012; Connell, 2003).

Third, most men and boys have relationships with women and girls, and when women's lives are limited by gender inequality, so are men's. Because men care about the women in their lives, they also are harmed when women experience differential treatment based on gender. Studies around the world find that the majority of people support gender equality and that relationships, especially marriages, are more satisfying when partners share financial and household responsibilities (Pew Research, 2010). Couples living in countries with more gender equality even report having better sex lives than their counterparts living in countries that have more traditional gender roles in place (Laumann et al., 2006).

Last, Connell (2003) points out that many men agree with gender equality because of its connection to political or ethical principles. Put simply, supporting gender equality is the right thing to do. Going a step further, Hendra et al. (2013:109) discuss the concept of universalism in relation to gender equality and explain it as "a view of human rights whereby we all share not only rights, but also duties to one another." More specifically, we have a duty to protect the rights that we share by not discriminating against others.

Ultimately, everyone benefits from and is responsible for gender equality. To decrease gender disparity means that societies will benefit from less poverty and hunger, greater economic development, and more safety and security for all citizens. As the deadline for the 2000 MDGs approaches, researchers and activists remind us that the best way to reduce many of these global social problems is through focusing on gender equality and narrowing the gap between men and women.

WORKS CITED

Connell, R. W. 2003. "The Role of Men and Boys in Achieving Gender Equality." United Nations, Division for the Advancement of Women. http://www.un.org/womenwatch/daw/egm/men-boys2003/Connell-bp.pdf

Daly, Kevin. 2007. "Gender Inequality, Growth and Global Ageing." Global Economics Paper No. 154, Goldman Sachs. http://www.womenandtechnology.eu/digitalcity/servlet/PublishedFileServlet/AAAATKMI/Gender-inequality-Growth-and-Global-Aging.pdf/.

Dollar, David, and Roberta Gatti, 1999, "Gender Inequality, Income, and Growth. Are Good Times Good for Women?" World Bank Gender and Development Working Paper Series No. 1. http://siteresources.worldbank.org/INTGENDER/Resources/wp1.pdf/.

Food and Agriculture Organisation. 2011. "The State of Food and Agriculture." http://www.fao.org/docrep/013/i2050e/i2050e.pdf/.

Food and Agriculture Organization. 2013. http://www.fao.org/docrep/019/i3578e/i3578e.pdf/.

Hendra, John, Ingrid FitzGerald, and Dan Seymour. 2013. "Towards a New Transformative Development Agenda: The Role of Men and Boys in Achieving Gender Equality. Journal of International Affairs 67(1):105–122.

Hochschild, Arlie R. (1989) The Second Shift. New York: Avalon Books.

Hudson, Valerie M. 2012. "What Sex Means for World Peace." Foreign Policy. http://www.foreignpolicy.com/articles/2012/04/24/what_sex_means_for_world_peace/.

Laumann, Edward O., Anthony Paik, Dale B. Glasser, Jeong-Han Kang, Tianfu Wang, Bernard Levinson, Edson D. Moreira Jr., Alfredo Nicolosi, and Clive Gingell. 2006. "A Cross-National Study of Subjective Sexual Well-Being among Older Women and Men: Findings from the Global Study of Sexual Attitudes and Behaviors. Archives of Sexual Behavior 35(2):145–161.

Lawson, Sandra. 2008. "Women Hold up Half the Sky." Global Economics Paper No. 164, Goldman Sachs. http://www.goldmansachs.com/our-thinking/investing-in-women/bios-pdfs/women-half-sky-pdf.pdf/.

Loko, B., and Mame A. Diouf. 2009. "Revisiting the Determinants of Productivity Growth: What's New? http://www.imf.org/external/pubs/ft/wp/2009/wp09225.pdf/.

Millennium Project. 2006. "Goals, Targets, and Indicators." http://www.unmillenniumproject.org/goals/gti.htm#goal1/.

Mundy, Liza. 2013. "Daddy Track: The Case for Paternity Leave." The Atlantic. http://www.theatlantic.com/magazine/archive/2014/01/the-daddy-track/355746/.

Parker, Kim, and Wendy Wang. 2013. "Modern Parenthood: Roles of Moms and Dads Converge as They Balance Work and Family." Pew Research. http://www.pewsocialtrends.org/2013/03/14/modern-parenthood-roles-of-moms-and-dads-converge-as-they-balance-work-and-family/.

Pew Research. 2010. "Gender Equality Universally Embraced, But Inequalities Acknowledged." http://www.pewglobal.org/2010/07/01/gender-equality/.

Rampell, Catherine. 2013. "Lean in, Dad: How Shared Diaper Duty Could Stimulate the Economy." *The New York Times.* http://www.nytimes .com/2013/04/07/magazine/how-shared-diaper -duty-could-stimulate-the-economy.html?ref =itstheeconomy/.

Separa, Matt. 2012. "Infographic: The Gender Pay Gap. See What Equity in Earnings Costs Women and Their Families Each Year and over Their Lifetimes." Center for American Progress. http://www.americanprogress.org/issues/ women/news/2012/04/16/11435/infographic-the -gender-pay-gap/.

Sherman, Jennifer. 2012. "Bend to Avoid Breaking: Job Loss, Gender Norms, and Family Stability in Rural America." *Social Problems* 56(4):599–620.

United Nations. 2000. "Women and Armed Conflict." http://www.un.org/womenwatch/daw/followup/ session/presskit/fs5.htm/.

United Nations. 2013. "The Millennium Development Goals Report." http://www.un.org/ millenniumgoals/pdf/report-2013/mdg-report -2013-english.pdf/.

United Nations Economic and Social Council. 2013. "Challenges and Achievements in the Implementation of the Millennium Development Goals for Women and Girls." Commission on the Status of Women. http://www.un.org/ga/ search/view_doc.asp?symbol=E/CN.6/2014/3/.

Weber, Lauren. 2013. "Why Dads Don't Take Paternity Leave." The Wall Street Journal. http:// www.wsj.com/articles/SB1000142412788732404 95045785416337082836 70

World Economic Forum. "The Global Gender Gap Report 2013." 2013. http://www3.weforum.org/ docs/WEF_GenderGap_Report_2013.pdf/.

Social Problems Related to Sex and Sexuality

Heather Corinna

Heather Corinna is the founder and director of Scarleteen.

What is your organization and its mission?

I founded Scarleteen (http://www.scarleteen .com)—a sexuality, sexual health and relationships information, education, and support organization—in 1998. We were one of the very first sex education resources on the web. Most of our work is done online using static content, advice columns and several one-on-one direct services (using real people, not automated answers or templates). Our mission is to provide adolescents and emerging adults with comprehensive, inclusive and accessible sexuality information and support.

How did you first become interested in this type of activism?

I was teaching for years before I started teaching at Scarleteen, and to me, teaching well—truly doing what you can to educate and help people learn, not memorize or meet testing ideals—is, all by itself, a lot of what activism is. I also started doing some publishing in adult sexuality, but very quickly, young people began contacting me seeking help and support. It was clear their needs were not being met elsewhere. I wound up leaving my other teaching work within a year of starting Scarleteen, and it quickly became the bulk of what I do.

As an activist in your organization, currently what are your goals?

I want to give young people both the most in-depth, tailored-to-their-expressed-needs information I can and the support that they need to make informed and empowered choices about sex and sexuality. I also want to empower our young volunteers, almost all of whom are under 30 years old. A final goal is to change the cultural conversation about sex, relationships, and young people so that it becomes much more humane and focused on real people and real lives in all their diversity.

What strategies do you use to enact social change?

Talking about sex and sexuality honestly and positively—especially so widely and visibly—strikes me, all by itself, as something with the power for potentially sweeping social change. Treating teens and emerging adults as whole and capable people, and working with them respectfully is also extremely important to us.

What are the major challenges activists in your field face?

The stigma when working in the area of sex remains significant. Working with sex and young people adds another layer to that challenge, and doing so as anything but a white, cisgender, heterosexual, married parent creates additional challenges. So, those of us who are queer or gender nonconforming, of color, not parents, not in the kind of relationships considered to be a moral ideal, or who have been "too" sexual (which usually just means being sexual at all outside of heterosexual norms) have extra challenges. And the more marginalized we are, the more at risk we are doing the work that we do.

Additionally, being involved at a deep and daily level with young people and their struggles and questions about such complex things—and that includes working with abuse and assault—is so rewarding, but also very emotionally hard.

What are major misconceptions the public has about activism in general and your issue specifically?

Well, I do think the idea that activist = fanatic is still prevalent. And it would take volumes to talk about all the misconceptions the public has about sex, sexuality and sexuality education. But there's an interesting place where both activism in general and sex education activism meet regarding misconceptions, and that's the idea that we (the activists at hand) cannot be trusted, and that there must be some ulterior motive for what we do. But in my experience, it's not at all true of most activists; we're actually quite direct and we mean what we say.

Another misconception is the idea that young people are hurt by being provided sexual information. Of course, it is a total fallacy. In fact, we have so much evidence to the contrary, it's dizzying.

Why should students get involved in your line of activism?

Honestly, I think that peer sex education and peer sexual activism are the most powerful ways to go with this arena. Those of us—like myself— who are older adults, can do our part and have plenty to offer, but are not as powerful as young people speaking for themselves and working together with each other.

What would you consider to be your greatest successes as an activist?

When a young person says—and earnestly means—thank you to me, letting me know I served them well, it truly doesn't get any better than that. And of course, when it happens all the time, it is incredibly rewarding. The fact that there have been so, so many thank you's, from so many diverse youth all over the world tells me, better than anything else can, I'm succeeding in my goals. I've also heard many colleagues and organizations I respect over the years state that Scarleteen and my related work created a model for online education, sex education, and working with youth.

Despite the challenges of never receiving any foundational or institutional funding, staying financially independent has allowed us to truly be and stay radical, in the best meaning of the word, which is a big deal to me because the kind of change we need in the way we approach sexuality education is radical change.

If an individual has little money and time, are there other ways they can contribute?

Absolutely! For one, what we do actually does not cost very much. People are always amazed at how minimal our budget is for the level of service we can provide. So, the idea that this kind of activism has a big price tag is false.

And there are ways to contribute that ask so little. Even things like not getting on board for celebrity or youth shaming around sex (as in, don't retweet or chime in with a slut-shame, or hand-wring about the sexual irresponsibility of "these kids today") helps a lot, and that actually is just asking someone to do nothing rather than something, to *not* spend even a minute enabling that stuff, rather than spending time doing so. Being an askable, supportive person for youth around sex and sexuality is another major contribution.

"Children" Having Children

STEFANIE MOLLBORN

About one in three girls in the United States will become pregnant as teenagers, with most of them giving birth. These "children" having children have been the focus of media attention and public condemnation, and Mollborn discusses why they are viewed so negatively. Teen pregnancy hasn't always been recognized as a social problem, Mollborn argues, and she examines who these teens are, why rates of teen pregnancy are unequally distributed throughout the population, and the consequences of their pregnancies. Mollborn also offers ways to promote better outcomes for teen moms.

Adriana's Story

Meet Adriana. She's 17, lives with her parents, and, like about 1 in 6 teen girls in the U.S., she has a child. My research team got to know Adriana and 75 other teen parents through in-depth interviews in the Denver area in 2008–2009. A Latina high school student who looks and acts older than her age, Adriana has a two-year-old son, Marlon. Like the overwhelming majority of teen mothers, Adriana didn't intend to get pregnant: "I would always play with my little baby dolls and stuff, but I wasn't really thinking about, 'Oh, when am I gonna be a mom?' I didn't really care about that stuff. And then actually, to tell you the truth, when I got pregnant, I wasn't really thinking about being a mom yet, either. It just kind of happened."

Similarly, Adriana's boyfriend Michael was like many other young dads: "happy," even "over-excited," about becoming a father. But Adriana said, "Once I found out I was pregnant, I didn't want him to be my boyfriend." Still, he moved in with her family. Later, they lived with Michael's family. In contrast to stereotypes about uninvolved young fathers, it's very common for teen births to occur in the context of a long-term romantic relationship and for the child's father to live with the mom. However, these teen relationships frequently dissolve. Michael and Adriana were together for three years: ". . . after I had my son . . . I told him it was either my own place or I was leaving him. So he got me my own place. We lived there for about a year and a half, and then, like, we would fight all the time. We just realized that we were unhappy together. And last year we just broke up. It's been kind of hard on the baby." She says the breakup is "also a reason, kind of, why I feel awkward about getting pregnant so young, because I didn't really know what love was. I think it would be better if my son had his mom and his dad there together in a relationship, growing up with both parents involved daily. And I think that if I would have waited longer, I would have knew a little more, been a little wiser about who to have a baby with." Marlon saw his father infrequently right after the breakup, but now it's just on weekends at Michael's mother's house.

Marlon now lives with Adriana, her father and stepmother, grandmother, and several siblings. Adriana's father (a fast food worker) and grandmother pay for housing and other bills. Michael provides limited help, but as is typical for teen moms who don't live with their child's father, Adriana is responsible for keeping track of her son's needs and asking Michael for support. Michael's mother helps by providing childcare. Medicaid pays Adriana's medical bills, and the WIC program helped her with buying formula. This reliance on a network of extended family members for considerable support, supplemented by health care and nutritional support from the government (but not by welfare payments), is common. Despite this assistance, Adriana is still in a precarious financial situation. She doesn't often have spending money, because "as long as I don't need something really bad, I don't want to ask for it." Adriana worries about straining her family's resources.

While Adriana's story is certainly personal, it is far from unique. About 1 in 3 girls in the U.S. becomes pregnant before turning 20. About a third of these pregnancies end in abortion, but the majority of the rest become parents. (American girls ages 15–19 are about 3 times as likely as their Canadian peers to have a child, 7 times as likely as Swedes, and almost 9 times as likely as Japanese teens.) Adriana's experience exemplifies many of the larger social realities shaping teen parenthood today. These include historical changes in the typical American life course, shifting attitudes about the "problem" of teen pregnancy, social inequality and the polarized experience of teen parenthood in the U.S., and the many social consequences teen parents face for being "kids having kids."

Who Are the Kids Who Have Kids?

Parenting is not evenly distributed among American teenagers. In fact, we might say that teen parenthood is an extremely polarized experience—common in some segments of the population and rare in others.

Teen mothers and fathers overwhelmingly come from lower-income families and neighborhoods, and they are often struggling in school even before the pregnancy. A national study of babies born in 2001 revealed that about half of teen mothers' children live in poverty, and more than half of all children living in poverty have a mother who was once a teenage parent. Teen parenting also varies by race and ethnicity, with Latinos, African Americans, and Native Americans having the highest rates. . . . On the other hand, teen parenthood is relatively rare in high socioeconomic status, Asian American, and white families and neighborhoods.

There's little doubt that contraception (or lack thereof) is an important part of this package. While American teenagers start having sex at similar ages to their peers in many other Western countries, they are much more likely to get pregnant and have children, even though the vast majority of teen pregnancies are unintended. Many researchers attribute this difference to American teens' less consistent contraception patterns. Geography is another intriguing dimension of variation in teen parenthood. White teens in parts of the Southeast are more likely to get pregnant than elsewhere, as are Latina and African American teens in this region. Perhaps counterintuitively, [Southeastern and Southwestern] states with high levels of conservative religious affiliations have some of the highest teen birthrates, and many Evangelical young people are at risk of becoming teen parents.

My recent interviews with college students showed that particularly in low socioeconomic status, conservative religious communities, a negative view of teen parenting is balanced against a "pro-life" social norm that encourages teens not to have an abortion. Teens are told that having the child is the "lesser of two evils." This echoes the Palin family's reaction to daughter Bristol's unwed teen pregnancy, and some of our participants told us it was a recent opinion shift in their communities. In most of the study's higher socioeconomic status, less religious communities, there's no cautiously positive take on teen parenting. Parents actively encourage their children to delay sex, but believe that if they do have sex, they should contracept consistently. Teens who "mess up" by getting themselves or a partner pregnant are not judged as immoral, but as "stupid."

Problematic Perceptions

For many, teen parenthood symbolizes "what's wrong" with America today. Media outlets breathlessly report the details of celebrity pregnancies and create reality shows about teen mothers, then air call-in sessions about the irresponsibility of young people. This simultaneous attention and condemnation is shared by the general public. In a 2004 opinion poll, teen pregnancy was rated by 42 percent as a "very serious problem" in our society, and another 37 percent considered it to be an "important problem."

Why is such a commonplace event viewed so negatively? The fact that teenage pregnancy disproportionately impacts racial minorities and low-income communities is key. Such patterns play into mainstream fears about social disorder and excessive reliance on social services and the welfare state. There is a persistent, racialized public stereotype of the black or Latina "welfare queen" (even though the vast majority of teenage mothers do not receive welfare benefits).

This interpretation is somewhat confirmed by the fact that the general public's attitudes about teen childbearing are divided along racial lines, too. In a 2005 survey of American adults, for example, I asked people how embarrassed they would be by a hypothetical unwed teen pregnancy in their household. African Americans reported less embarrassment than other racial groups, and people who had attended college reported more embarrassment than those with less education.

Some historical perspective is important here as well. The U.S. has a long history of teen childbearing. . . . Since the start of the Second World War . . . the high point for teen births was in the mid-1950s. Yet teen parenthood did not fully emerge as an important "social problem" until the 1970s. The explanation probably lies in the marital context of teen births.

Back in the 1950s, it was common and socially acceptable for people to get married and immediately become parents in their late teens or early twenties. Technically, this made lots of young people teen parents, but it wasn't considered a problem because they were engaging in a "normal" life course. In contrast, nonmarital births were rare and stigmatized.

Since then, the experience of early adulthood has changed. Many young people now enjoy a longer period of independence before settling into adult roles, and most Americans delay marriage until at least their mid-twenties. At the same time, most have sex before their twentieth birthday, putting them at risk for unintended pregnancy. As it has for all births (4 in 10 births in the U.S. are now nonmarital, compared to 4 in 100 in 1950), the proportion of teen births that are nonmarital has risen dramatically over time: 87 percent of teen births were nonmarital in 2008. Sociologist Frank Furstenberg has pointed out that, as nonmarital teen births increased, so did the visibility of teen parenting as a social problem.

These social attitudes and community norms clearly impact young people. In my analysis of a national survey of teenagers in 1995, most teens said they would feel embarrassed if they got (or for boys, got a girl) pregnant. This contradicts the popular idea that teens today think pregnancy is "cool."

Adriana's story illustrates how family and community reactions can shape teen parents' lives. Some of her family members reacted fairly well to her pregnancy, but others did not. Adriana's intelligence and morality were questioned. "My mom was just like, she didn't get mad. She just kind of said that my boyfriend has to take responsibility, 'cause he's the one who got me pregnant. So she kind of was like, 'Oh, well, I guess you're moving in tomorrow and you're gonna pay this bill and this bill and this bill. . . . You're not taking my daughter out of the house.'" Adriana's brother called her "stupid" and wanted "to beat my boyfriend up." But "the only one who really made me feel bad was my grandma," who told her that it was "wrong" for her to get pregnant so young. Adriana said, "I was really close to her. So I took it kind of hard. . . . We really don't talk any more. She talks to my son more than to me."

Adriana also feels socially ostracized. She says, "I really don't have lots of friends." This social isolation is typical and differs sharply from the common stereotype of teen girls encouraging their friends to get pregnant or forming "pregnancy pacts." Out in public, she attracts negative attention: "Sometimes I would be on the bus and people would just stare at me. . . . [At] prenatal appointments, people were like, 'How old are you? What are you gonna do with a kid this young?' Stuff like that. It looks kind of bad to see a really young girl pregnant, but also, they don't know me, what I do." She's learning to cope, she says. "Now when I look at people, I'm like, 'Whatever. You don't even know me. I'm like, 'I still go to school.' I can throw that in their face. . . . I have something that would possibly hold me back, and I still do it." Like many other teen moms, Adriana has been forced to learn coping skills to negotiate public stigma. Proving skeptical people wrong is one reason why many teen parents told us they wanted to succeed in school.

Consequences

The consequences of teen parenthood, for young parents and their children alike, are complicated. For decades, researchers have documented negative outcomes for teen mothers in terms of education, income, mental health, marriage, and more. Teen fathers have lower levels of education and employment than their peers, and, compared to other kids, children of teen parents have compromised development and health starting in early childhood and continuing into adolescence.

In research explaining these consequences, two surprising findings have emerged. First, by comparing teen mothers to natural comparison groups such as their childless twins and sisters and pregnant teens who miscarried, scholars like public health researcher Arline Geronimus and economist V. Joseph Hotz have shown that most of the negative "consequences" of teen childbearing are actually due to experiences in teens' lives from before they got pregnant, such as socioeconomic background and educational achievement. In other words, the experience of teen childbearing itself only moderately worsens these teens' life outcomes.

Second, the negative consequences of teen parenthood are more severe in the short term. In the long term, many teen parents end up with better outcomes than it looked like they would have when they were teens. For example, developmental psychologist Julie Lounds Taylor found in a predominantly white, socioeconomically advantaged sample of 1957 Wisconsin high school graduates that at midlife, former teenage mothers and fathers lagged behind peers with similar characteristics in terms of education, occupational status, marital stability, and physical health. On the other hand, their work involvement, income levels, satisfaction with work and marriage, mental health, and social support were similar. Using more recent data from a national longitudinal study of eighth graders from 1988, I found that 75 percent of teen mothers and 62 percent of fathers finished a high school degree or GED by age 26. However, compared to the typical American, their outcomes were still problematic: both teen moms and dads ended up with two years less education than average by age 26.

Adriana's story is again illustrative. She wasn't on a traditional path to academic success before she got pregnant. As a Latina from a family with low socioeconomic status, she already belonged to a high-risk group, and her academic experiences reflected it. Adriana says, "Before I was a mom, I didn't really go to school. I didn't like school." But once she got pregnant, she thought, "'What am I gonna give my son?' . . . He's gonna have the same life that I had, and then he can follow in my footsteps, and I don't want that. I want him to do some things. . . ." She started attending a school for pregnant teen girls. "Ever since then . . . I've passed all my classes, and now I graduate in December." There are supportive teachers and understanding fellow students. Infant care and other forms of support are available. Adriana now plans to enroll in postsecondary education.

The support context of teen parenthood varies widely. For example, there are racial and ethnic differences in the key people helping teen mothers. My analysis of a national sample of babies born in 2001 found that about 60 percent of Latina and white teen moms were living with their child's father nine months after the birth, compared to just 16 percent of black teen moms. Instead, nearly 60 percent of black teen moms were living with other adults, such as a parent. It's not clear which of these situations is most beneficial for teen moms and their children: although as a society we often wish for fathers to be more involved, teen relationships often break up, and instability in mothers' relationships can compromise children's development.

Effective Social Supports

American teen parenthood is commonplace but polarizing. As our societal safety net shrinks, low-income families' prospects worsen, and education becomes increasingly important for financial success, teen parents face increasingly long odds. Adriana's story helps show how many teen parents are motivated to work hard and make a better life for themselves and their children. Our country has made an important commitment to reducing levels of teen pregnancy, but we also need to find better ways to support

teens who are already parents so their families can have a better future.

The federal government has now committed substantial funding for both prevention of teen pregnancies and support for teens who are already parents. Supporting parenting teens is a smart societal investment. First, because most mothers of children living in poverty today were teen moms, targeting these families for intervention would be an effective way to help some of the most marginalized members of our society. This is true regardless of whether the negative outcomes were caused by teen parenthood itself or by factors related to the teen's situation before the pregnancy.

Second, with less financial support available from the government, especially since welfare reform was passed in 1996, teen parents and their children are more dependent on their families for survival. Many low-income families have less money and time than they did in the past, making it harder for them to support teen parents and their children. Research finds that families still provide substantial support, but it often severely strains their budgets and their relationships with the young parents, and many teens' and children's basic needs such as for food and warm clothing are not being met. The current economic crisis has exacerbated this situation.

Finally, as many service providers have long known, the time after a teen birth is a magic moment when societal investments can help nudge young families onto a successful trajectory. Unlike many older parents who can take time out from the labor force and still have attractive options when they re-enter, teens are in a life stage when it is critical for them to invest in education and work. And almost all the teen parents we interviewed were willing to sacrifice to meet their goals. A strong motivation to achieve for their children's sake was common.

Without support from social programs, though, this motivation may not be enough. For example, though Adriana is fully committed to her education and has her family behind her, she has to surmount massive obstacles like transportation and childcare to stay in school. Talking to teen parents like her, it's easy to see how much some short-term support would pay off for her, her son, and our society in the long term.

Reducing Unintended Pregnancy: The Role of Long-Acting Reversible Contraceptives

Stacy Gorman Harmon

Original to Focus on Social Problems: A Contemporary Reader.

In the United States, about half of all pregnancies, or 3.4 million annually, are unintended, making the U.S. unintended pregnancy rate the highest among developed countries (Guttmacher Institute, 2013). Unintended and teen pregnancies are a problem because they are associated with greater risk of negative consequences for the families that experience them. For instance, women who have unintended pregnancies are more likely to delay prenatal care and are less likely to breastfeed (D'Angelo et al., 2004; Logan et al., 2007). Among teen parents, both mothers and fathers are more likely to have lower income and educational attainment than their counterparts who delay parenthood (Hoffman and Maynard, 2008; Logan et al., 2007). Children of teens may also be impacted; studies have shown they are more likely to have poorer physical and mental health (Hoffman and Maynard, 2008; Logan et al., 2007).

Low-income women, teens, and all women aged 20 to 24 are especially likely to experience unintended pregnancy, whereas women with higher levels of income and education have the lowest rates of unintended pregnancy (Guttmacher Institute, 2014a). There is also an association between age and planned pregnancy; as age increases, unplanned pregnancies decrease (Guttmacher Institute, 2013). Among teens who are sexually active, the rate of unintended pregnancy is twice that of all women (Guttmacher Institute, 2013). Although between 1990 and 2010 the teen pregnancy rate declined by 51 percent (Kost and Henshaw, 2014), in 2010, 615,000 teens still became pregnant in the United States, and 84 percent of these pregnancies were

unintended (Kost and Henshaw, 2014). Unlike the specific teen population, among all women of reproductive age (15–44) there has actually been a slight increase in unintended pregnancies since 2001 (Guttmacher Institute, 2013).

Even with the decline among teens, the unintended pregnancy rate is a serious problem for women of all ages. More teens and adult women are using contraceptives than in the past, and it is this behavior, not a decrease in sexual activity, that is largely credited with the most significant reduction in the teen pregnancy rate (Boonstra, 2014). In particular, the use of hormonal contraceptives has increased. Yet many girls and women do not have access to affordable birth control. Researchers and advocates argue that, for this reason, it is essential for publicly funded birth control to be made available to both teens and adult women who otherwise would not have affordable access to it. When birth control is accessible, unplanned pregnancies and abortion rates go down for women of all ages (Guttmacher Institute, 2014a; "Contraceptive Choice Project").

Throughout the United States, publicly funded family planning centers that provide women with contraceptives helped to prevent 2.2 million unintended pregnancies in 2010 (Guttmacher Institute, 2014b). Without these centers, the unintended pregnancy, unintended birth, and abortion rates would have been 66 percent higher (Guttmacher Institute, 2014b). The average woman has about three decades of fertility, so even the cost of less expensive (and often less reliable) methods like condoms can add up (Guttmacher Institute, 2014a). When

continues

▮ Continued

adult and teen women have education about and access to more reliable forms of contraceptives, they are much more likely to use these methods, ultimately resulting in lower rates of unintended pregnancy (Guttmacher Institute, 2014a; Secura et al. 2014).

Recent studies comparing the effectiveness of contraceptive methods have found that intrauterine devices (IUDs) and implants[1] are the most effective methods of birth control currently available (Hamblin 2014; "Contraceptive Choice Project"). In fact, one study found that they are even more effective than permanent options like tubal ligations or vasectomies (Hamblin, 2014). IUDs and implant birth control methods are known as "long-acting reversible contraceptives" (LARCs). That means they are methods that can be used for longer periods of time without having to be refilled and replaced, like birth control pills or the patch, but are not permanent or irreversible, like sterilization. A major benefit to these methods is that once they are inserted or implanted, no other action is necessary on the part of the user. In other words, a woman using an IUD or implant for birth control does not have to remember to take a pill every day, to change her birth control patch every week, to buy or carry condoms, or even to go to the doctor's office to get a shot every few months. Instead, for the three to ten years (depending on the IUD or implant), the user has continuous contraceptive coverage until she elects to have the device removed. If a woman using a LARC wants it removed before that time frame is complete, that is always an option.

Despite the ease of use and high effectiveness rates of IUDs and implants, the Guttmacher Institute (2014) reports that fewer than 5 percent of all women ages 15–44 use one of these methods. Instead, the most commonly used methods are the pill, sterilization, and condoms. With the exception of female sterilization,[2] the more commonly used methods also have higher failure rates than IUDs and implants, resulting in unintended pregnancies. So why aren't more women choosing the IUD or implant to prevent pregnancy? Part of the problem[3]

might be that these more reliable methods are not as familiar to women seeking birth control. But even for some women who know about IUDs and implants or who learn about them from their healthcare providers, choosing these methods can be cost prohibitive. Because LARCs are long-lasting methods, they are also more expensive up front than a pack of pills or the patch would be. For patients without insurance or insurance that does not cover LARCs, paying out of pocket would cost several hundred dollars. Although this is a greater expense at the time of purchase, compared to the pill or the patch, it actually works out to be much less expensive over time.

To better understand teens and adult women's contraceptive choices, researchers, doctors, and advocates in St. Louis started the Contraceptive Choice Project. The goals of this research project are "to remove the financial barriers to contraception, promote the most effective methods of birth control, and reduce unintended pregnancy in the St. Louis area" ("Contraceptive Choice Project"). Researchers report some significant findings. Of the 9,256 women who were counseled about all of their contraceptive options and provided their chosen method for free by the project, 75 percent of them chose a LARC ("Contraceptive Choice Project"). A year later, when researchers followed up with participants to see how they liked their chosen methods, a greater number of women who had chosen a LARC were still using their method and reported being satisfied with it than women who had chosen a non-LARC, like the pill. Not only did women using LARCs have the highest rates of continued use and satisfaction, but also they had the lowest rates of unintended pregnancies throughout the three years of the study. Participants who had chosen the pill, patch, or ring[4] were 20 times more likely to have an unintended pregnancy in the first year of the study compared to women using LARCs ("Contraceptive Choice Project"). Teens who participated in the study were also more likely to choose LARCs (72 percent), and because they did, the teen pregnancy rate for participants was 34 per 1,000 (Secura et al., 2014). This rate is significantly lower than the 2013 national teen pregnancy rate of 57 per 1,000 (Kost and Henshaw, 2014).[5]

The Contraceptive Choice Project is not the only recent example of women's preference for LARC's and their long-term effects. In Colorado, the Colorado Family Planning Initiative made LARCs available to 30,000 low-income women, funded by an anonymous donor (Sullivan, 2014). Since its implementation in 2009, researchers have made comparisons between the actual pregnancy rates of 15- to 24-year-old women and the expected rates for this age group of Colorado residents. As a result of the program, the number of teens and young women using LARCs has increased and, as a consequence, pregnancy, birth, and abortion rates have declined (Ricketts et al., 2014). In particular, abortion rates declined 34 percent for teens 15 to 19 years old and 18 percent for women 20 to 24 years old (Ricketts et al., 2014).

Making LARCs more affordable is essential to increasing access for many women and ultimately would have a substantial effect on the rate of unintended pregnancies. The Affordable Care Act mandates that health insurance plans cover contraceptives without requiring any copays, deductibles, or other out-of-pocket costs (Healthcare.gov). Although this mandate did not go into effect for most insurance plans until January 2013, researchers are already seeing the cost of birth control declining for many women (Sonfield et al., 2014). This is clearly a major improvement for women's reproductive health care, but despite its benefits, some opponents are challenging it. In June 2014, the Supreme Court struck down the birth control mandate, ruling in favor of a for-profit company's right to refuse birth control coverage when the refusal is based on religious beliefs (Totenberg, 2014). The craft store chain Hobby Lobby brought the suit because its owners objected to two types of birth control, emergency contraception and IUDs (Totenberg, 2014). This decision is important because it allows employers to opt out of covering any forms of birth control they may oppose on religious grounds. In the Hobby Lobby case, one of the types of birth control it now has the right to

refuse coverage of, the IUD, is the same method that many studies have shown to be one of the best ways to decrease unintended pregnancies (Hamblin, 2014; Guttmacher Institute, 2014a; "Contraceptive Choice Project").

When the rate of unintended pregnancy decreases, there are benefits to society at large. Fewer unplanned births mean less money spent on social programs like Women, Infants, and Children (WIC) and Medicaid. Ricketts et al. (2014) found a 23 percent decline in WIC enrollment between 2010 and 2013 in counties that participated in the Colorado Family Planning Initiative. *The Denver Post* (Draper, 2014) reported that for each dollar spent on birth control, there is a $5.68 savings in Medicaid costs. When teenagers are able to avoid unplanned pregnancies, they have a better chance of finishing high school, attending college, and obtaining a higher paying job, which translates to less money spent on public assistance (Griego, 2014). Reliable contraceptives like LARCs benefit not only individual women but also society as a whole; financial barriers to obtaining all methods should be removed. As the research shows, a majority of women want access to long-acting reversible contraceptives methods, and that access is essential to decreasing unplanned pregnancies and their associated social and financial costs in the United States.

NOTES

1. Implants are birth control devices implanted under the skin that release hormones to prevent pregnancy.
2. Tubal ligations (female sterilization) have a failure rate that is comparable to that of implants, but higher than that of some IUDs; male sterilization (vasectomy) has a higher failure rate than both IUDs and implants.
3. Some women may still avoid the IUD because they are familiar with the health risks associated with the first IUD, the Dalkon Shield. The Dalkon Shield was first introduced in the 1960s and then removed from the market in the 1970s after serious complications were reported. Today's IUDs are different from earlier versions

continues

■ Continued

and are not associated with the same health risks.

4. The ring is a small flexible ring that is placed in the vagina each month, remaining in place for three weeks to prevent pregnancy.

5. It is important to note that the sample in the Choice project is different from the national teenage population in several ways. More than half of the teens in the Choice sample were black; 97 percent were sexually active at the start of the study, and almost 75 percent reported having had sex in the past 30 days. These two measures of sexual activity are much higher among the Choice project sample than among the larger teen population.

REFERENCES

Boonstra, Heather D. 2014. "What Is Behind the Decline in Teen Pregnancy Rates?" Guttmacher Institute. http://www.guttmacher.org/pubs/gpr/17/3/gpr170315.html/.

"Contraceptive Choice Project." N.d. Washington University School of Medicine. http://www.choiceproject.wustl.edu/.

D'Angelo, Denise, Brenda Colley Gilbert, Roger W. Rochat, John S. Santelli, and Joan M. Herold. 2004. "Differences between Mistimed and Unwanted Pregnancies among Women Who Have Live Births," *Perspectives on Sexual and Reproductive Health* 36, 5. http://www.guttmacher.org/pubs/journals/3619204.html/.

Draper, Electa. 2014. "Colorado Claims Contraceptive Program Caused Big Drop in Teen Birth Rates." *Denver Post.* http://www.denverpost.com/news/ci_26085784/colorado-teen-birth-rates-drop-state-hands-out?ok/.

Griego, Tina. 2014. "The Simple Policy That Led America's Biggest Drop in Teen Birth Rates." *The Washington Post.* http://www.washingtonpost.com/news/storyline/wp/2014/08/20/the-simple-policy-that-led-americas-biggest-drop-in-teen-pregnancies/.

Guttmacher Institute. 2013. "Unintended Pregnancy in the United States." http://www.guttmacher.org/pubs/FB-Unintended-Pregnancy-US.html#14a/.

Guttmacher Institute. 2014a. "Contraceptive Use in the United States." http://www.guttmacher.org/pubs/fb_contr_use.html/.

Guttmacher Institute. 2014b. "Facts on Publicly Funded Contraceptive Services in the United States." http://www.guttmacher.org/pubs/fb_contraceptive_serv.html/.

Hamblin, James. 2014. "IUDs and Implants are the New Pill." *The Atlantic.* http://m.theatlantic.com/health/archive/2014/10/the-birth-control-shift/380952/.

Hoffman, Saul D., and Rebecca A. Maynard. 2008. *Kids Having Kids: Economic Costs and Social Consequences of Teen Pregnancy.* Washington, D.C.: Urban Institute Press.

Kost, Kathryn, and Stanley Henshaw. 2014. "U.S. Teenage Pregnancies, Births, and Abortions, 2010: National and State Trends by Age, Race and Ethnicity." Guttmacher Institute. http://www.guttmacher.org/pubs/USTPtrends10.pdf/.

Logan, Cassandra, Emily Holcombe, Jennifer Manlove, and Suzanne Ryan. 2007. "The Consequences of Unintended Childbearing." http://thenationalcampaign.org/sites/default/files/resource-primary-download/consequences.pdf/.

Ricketts, Sue, Greta Klingler, and Renee Schwalberg. 2014. "Game Change in Colorado: Widespread Use of Long-Acting Reversible Contraceptives and Rapid Decline in Births among Young, Low-Income Women." http://www.guttmacher.org/pubs/journals/46e1714.html/.

Secura, Gina M., Tessa Madden, Colleen McNicholas, Jennifer Mullersman, Christina M. Buckel, Quihong Zhao, and Jeffrey F. Peipert. 2014. "Provision of No-Cost, Long-Acting Contraception and Teenage Pregnancy." *The New England Journal of Medicine* 371:1316–1323.

Sonfield, Adam, Athena Tapales, Rachel K. Jones, & Lawrence B. Finer. 2014. "Impact of the Federal

Contraceptive Coverage Guarantee on Out-of-Pocket Payments for Contraceptives: 2014 Update." Guttmacher Institute. http://www.contraceptionjournal.org/article/S0010-7824(14)00687-8/pdf/.

Sullivan, Gail. 2014. "How Colorado's Teen Birth-rate Dropped 40% in Four Years." http://www.washingtonpost.com/news/morning-mix/wp/2014/08/12/how-colorados-teen-birthrate-dropped-40-in-four-years/.

Totenberg, Nina. 2014. "High Court Allows Some Companies to Opt Out of Contraceptive Mandate. http://www.npr.org/2014/06/30/327064710/high-court-allows-some-companies-to-opt-out-contraceptives-mandate/.

Sexuality Education in the United States: Shared Cultural Ideas across a Political Divide

JESSICA FIELDS

Debates over sex education today are usually framed as a fight between abstinence-only and comprehensive sex education. By tracing the history of sex education and examining its content, Fields argues that both types share similar flawed assumptions and messages (e.g., the often gender-, race-, and class-biased messages that frame some kids as sexual victims and others as likely victimizers). Both types ignore the ambiguity and ambivalence characterizing much sex, view sex among youth as inherently dangerous and risky, conflate sexual talk with sexual activity, and regulate youth and their sexuality. Fields calls to move beyond this polarized debate and to allow for a more inclusive and expansive approach to educate youth about sex and sexuality.

Introduction

In 2009, Barack Obama came through on a promise. His administration eliminated much direct funding for abstinence-only education and instead funded an Office of Adolescent Health (OAH) to administer over $100 million in new support for evidence-based teen pregnancy prevention approaches (Wagoner 2009). OAH funding effectively reversed the second Bush administration's consistent and increasing support for abstinence-only programming.[1] Ironically, the OAH commitment to teen pregnancy prevention also affirms a long-established and conventional approach to sexuality education as a grudging response to vexing social problems. OAH-sponsored teen pregnancy prevention programming might take the form of "comprehensive sexuality education," much to the dismay of those advocating abstinence-only education. Nevertheless, the OAH focus on sexual behaviors—and heterosexual intercourse in particular—threatens to come at the expense of discussing a range of sexual identities, desires, and institutions. The concern with teen pregnancy highlights harmful consequences of heterosexual behaviors for self and society and

Jessica Fields, *Sociology Compass* (Volume 6 and Issue 1). Reprinted by Permission of John Wiley and Sons. © 2012 Blackwell Publishing Ltd.

once again commits education to the conservative aim of promoting the personal and social regulation of young people's sexuality.

Prevailing health- and risk-oriented understandings of youth, sexuality, and education obscure an expansive portrait of youth, sexuality, and learning. Young people learn about sex and sexuality throughout their day-to-day lives, while watching television and movies, listening to music, texting, and surfing the web; at the family dinner table; during religious services; and in their sexual and romantic relationships (see, for example, Best 2000; Brown and Strasburger 2007; Clay 2003; Elliott (forthcoming); Luttrell 2003; Martin 1996; Pascoe 2007; Regnerus 2007; Shapiro 2010; Wilkins 2008). Nevertheless, as a host of researchers (see, for example, Fields 2008; Fine 1988; Fine and McClelland 2006; Irvine 2002; Levine 2002) have pointed out, much contemporary policy making, public debate, and research on sexuality education focuses on the lessons children and youth encounter about sexual danger: Will young people learn what they need to avert risk? Do the lessons themselves put them at risk? Invoking concerns with health and prevention, adults organize policy and instruction for young people around the conventional worry that the sexuality education youth encounter in these institutions and interactions does not help them navigate an increasingly sexualized and dangerous world. Policy and instruction is also motivated by another worry: that sexuality education's lessons are themselves damaging, exacerbating the sexual risks youth and children already face.

Few sites of young people's learning about sex and sexuality have proved more worrisome or contentious in the United States than the school (Fields 2008; Heins 2001; Irvine 2002; Levine 2002; Luker 2006). In school board meetings, state legislatures, and the US Congress, socially conservative advocates and policy makers have insisted that abstaining from sexual activity is the only reliable and safe way of preventing disease and pregnancy and, ultimately, that

abstinence is the best choice for all unmarried people. In this argument, "abstinence-only education" is a logical response to concerns over teen pregnancies, HIV and other sexually transmitted infections (STIs), and an overall assault on conventional understandings of gender, family, and sexual expression. Socially liberal educators, advocates, and policy makers have responded to this argument by promoting school-based comprehensive sexuality education, where teachers would emphasize abstinence as one strategy among others—condoms and other contraceptives, for example—that students could adopt to protect their health and well-being. Abstinence-only instruction would emphasize conventional gender and heterosexual expression and identity, including nuclear family structures; comprehensive sexuality education might also include lessons on masturbation, abortion, lesbian, gay, and bisexuality, and gender identity and norms.

Political actors and social movements may take up the cause of abstinence-only or comprehensive sexuality education in part out of concern for children and young people's immediate health and well-being. However, as I discuss below, no matter whether activists and movements advance abstinence-only or comprehensive curricula, the instruction they advocate promotes or defends against change in cultural ideas regarding gender, sexual expression and identity, and family (Duggan and Hunter 1995; Fields 2008; Irvine 2002; Levine 2002; Luker 2006; Moran 2000; Stein 2006; Zimmerman 2005). Of course, all education participates in, contributes to, and reflects broad cultural ideas (Bourdieu and Passeron 1990). These ideas include values (shared general ideas about what is good and desirable) and more stringent norms (rules and conventions that shape people's sense of what is appropriate and expected in social settings). However, sexuality education has a particular relationship to the broad conflicts over ideas, values, and norms that characterize contemporary US sexual politics. . . .

Lasting Struggles: Conservatives, Liberals, Abstinence-Only, and Comprehensive Sexuality Education

Sexuality education, the teaching and learning about puberty, sexuality, and relationships that happens in specially designated classrooms in primary and secondary schools, has long been linked to worry about the moral, psychological, and physical well-being of young people. In his history of sexuality education for US adolescents, Jeffrey Moran (2000) argues that public sexuality education emerged in the United States at the turn of the 20th century, as public officials grew concerned that the nation was ill prepared to contend with the sexual temptations associated with increasing urbanization. Over the course of the 20th century, many policy makers and educators came to believe that public health would be well served by what was called "social hygiene," "family life," and "puberty" education in the schools (Moran 2000). However, even as some schools and other public institutions took up the task of teaching children and youth about sexual health and well-being, sexuality education remained a primarily private concern in the early 20th century, with parents responsible for their children's upbringing (Kendall 2008).

From the late 1960s to early 1980s, feminism, youth culture, and the gay rights movement wrought significant changes in US sexual values. Though the sexual and gender revolution was neither uninterrupted nor uncontested, a shift was evident. The liberalization of divorce laws, increased funding for women's and girls' education, widespread availability of contraception, legalized abortion, and new sexual harassment laws allowed women and girls greater freedom and agency in private and public relationships. Same-sex desire and expression became increasingly visible, and lesbian, gay, bisexual, queer, and transgender people made new claims to a right to live free of discrimination. Young people with access to these broad cultural shifts increasingly imagined and pursued sexual and intimate lives that had previously seemed forbidden (Luker 1996).

According to Kristin Luker, the conflict over sexuality education at the turn of the 21st century reflects the ongoing contemporary "culture war" that arose in the wake of the sexual, youth, and civil rights revolutions of the 1960s, "when it seemed as if all of American society might implode" (2006, 68; see also Hunter 1992). In a two-decade study, Luker conducted more than one hundred interviews with adults living in US communities embroiled in sexuality education debates. She argues that sexuality education debates are ultimately "about how men and women relate to each other in all realms of their lives" (2006, 69). She finds also that, like other post-1960s battles, the conflict over sexuality education is caught in a clash between two poles—sexual conservativism and sexual liberalism.

Researchers have critiqued this two-camp account of the sexuality education debate (see, for example, Fields 2008; Fine and McClelland 2006; Irvine 2000, 2006). Abstinence-only and comprehensive sexuality education actually "rely on their opposition" to each other (Lesko 2010, 281), and their shared and interrelated ideas, values, and norms are obscured when educators and policy makers seem to have only two curricular options. In addition, the two-camp account obscures the insistent efforts of grassroots and community-based educators and activists to move beyond the boundaries set forth by a polarized sexuality education debate. Health Initiatives for Youth (http://www.hify.org/), a San Francisco–based multicultural organization that aims to improve the health and well-being of underserved young people, the Population Council's curriculum development guide, *It's All One Curriculum* (2009), and Scarleteen (http://www.scarleteen.com/), an independent website that provides sexuality education and support to young people, are all examples of sexuality education that breaches an apparently clear and unassailable divide between abstinence-only and comprehensive sexuality education.

Despite such efforts, to many onlookers, the contemporary "culture wars" continue to appear as Luker describes it—a contest between conservatives and liberals with two distinct and incompatible visions of gender, sexuality, and family. At one pole of this political spectrum, "sexual conservatives" consider sexuality sacrosanct and thus advocate abstinence-only instruction as part of a larger effort to confine sexual expression to marriage, protect parents' special right to determine the content of children's sexuality education, and preserve sexuality's sacred status in an increasingly secularized, disordered, and permissive world (Luker 2006). Conservative organizations like the John Birch Society lead efforts to challenge instruction they believe promotes promiscuity, immorality, and social degradation and—particularly when housed in public schools—constitutes an assault on the nuclear family and other valued social conventions and formations (Connell and Elliott 2009; Irvine 2002; Moran 2000). "Sexual liberals," the ostensible "other side" of this bifurcated debate, embrace comprehensive sexuality education that challenges social hierarchies and discrimination, affords all young people access to information necessary to responsible and healthy sexual decision making, and thus recognizes sexuality as a natural part of everyone's life. Liberal groups like the Sexuality Education and Information Council of the United States (SIECUS) are among the national leaders in this liberal effort to promote comprehensive sexuality education in the home, school, and community.

For many years, the conservative abstinence-only movement appeared to be winning this two-camp battle. Since the 1980s, the US government has supported educational programs that emphasize chastity, self-discipline, and abstinence as strategies for stemming the problems understood to arise from teen sexual activity. The 1996 Personal Responsibility and Work Opportunity Reconciliation Act, enacted by the Democratic administration of Bill Clinton, increased federal support (and required state grantees to provide matching funds) for "abstinence education." Qualified programs would instruct students in the "social, psychological, and health gains" that come with confining sexual expression to heterosexual marriage and the "harmful psychological and physical effects" of sexual activity and parenting outside marriage (U.S. Department of Health and Human Services 2008).

By 2008, US voters had witnessed an increase in federal funding for abstinence-only education to nearly $200 million, and abstinence-only sentiments increasingly dominated the messages of school-based instruction (Duberstein Lindberg et al. 2006). Despite a persistent failure to convince youth to remain abstinent or to stem disease and unwanted pregnancies among youth (Kirby 2008), abstinence-only education was "beginning to assert a kind of natural cultural authority, in schools and out" (Fine and McClelland 2006, 299). Comprehensive sexuality education advocates who might have otherwise promoted more liberal, progressive, or even radical curriculum and pedagogy were increasingly accountable to the cultural authority of abstinence. The Obama administration's decision to create an Office of Adolescent Health charged with supporting pregnancy prevention is only one example of this accountability.

Shared Commitments: The Regulation of Sexuality and Youth

The either/or rendering of a debate between a conservative abstinence-only and a liberal comprehensive sexuality education has not held with all policy makers and researchers. Instead, others have argued that the divisions in the battle over school-based abstinence-only and comprehensive sexuality education have not been as absolute as mainstream depictions suggest. . . . [T]hough policies and curricula may suggest discrete curricular options, both abstinence-only and comprehensive sexuality educators contribute to the regulation of young people and their sexuality.

This shared commitment rests on a number of cultural values, institutional and interpersonal practices, and social inequalities. As I discuss below, these cultural values are evident in discursive framings that cast children and youth as sexual victims or sexual victimizers; conflate sexual talk and sexual behavior; and assert teaching and learning as predictable and instrumental responses to social crises. These discursive practices contribute to school-based sexuality education remaining, as Laina Y. Bay-Cheng asserts, "a fundamental force in the very construction and definition of adolescent sexuality" as a site of danger risk, organized around normative heterosexual intercourse, and always entangled with entrenched social inequalities (2003, 62).

Corruptible, Corrupting, and Corrupted Children

Sexuality education debates and policy routinely posit young people as categorically less able, less intelligent, and less responsible than their adult counterparts. In the United States, young people's relationships are often denigrated as no more than puppy love, their sexual desires simply signs of raging hormones, and their sexual behaviors transgressions to control. Within this "adultist" framework, young people are at their best when sexually innocent. At their most vulnerable, they are on the verge of succumbing to sexual danger; and, at their most corrupting, they are the source of significant risks to others (Fields 2005; Lesko 2001; Levine 2002; Moran 2000). Consistently, images of the innocent, naïve child and the pubescent teenager undone by hormones point to that general practice that Irvine describes as "making up children" in debates over school-based sexuality education and in broader cultural conflicts over sexual and gender orders (2002, 108–11; see also Angelides 2004; Best 1993; Fields 2005; Kincaid 1997).

Though these adultist images of innocence and corruption are competing and conflicting, they also reflect a shared inclination that Amy

Schalet argues is particular to US adults—parents, educators, and policy makers—to "dramatize adolescent sexuality" by highlighting conflict between parents and children, antagonism between girls and boys, and the threat of youth being overwhelmed by new sexual feelings and experiences (2004). Together, these images reflect and buttress ideals of youth as free of sexual experience and knowledge and, in a necessary corollary, youth as reliant upon adults' guidance and protection.

Idealizing and dramatizing images have varying implications for children and youth in the United States. Like other social standards, childhood sexual innocence becomes not only an ideal to which youth are held but also a means of sorting young people into a range of categories: the innocent and the guilty, the vulnerable and the predatory, the pure and the corrupting, those who are "fully participating and valued members of their classrooms and broader communities" and those who are not (Fields and Hirschman 2007, 11). Schalet's sustained comparative analysis demonstrates that Dutch and US youth navigate distinctively normalizing and dramatizing models of youth, gender, and sexuality. Few US girls "are assumed capable of the feelings and relationships that legitimate sexual activity," leaving them vulnerable to charge of "slut" (Schalet 2010, 325). Dutch girls, on the other hand, living within a normalizing paradigm of sexuality, "are assumed to be able to fall in love and form steady sexual relationships"; this assumption defends against an equation of sexual activity with "sluttiness," though the assumption may also "obscure the challenges of negotiating differences" in sexual relationships (Schalet 2010, 325).

In the United States, the dramatizing discourse is a gendered and racialized discourse, and it consistently casts some young people's sexuality as particularly conflictual, antagonistic, and excessive. While white children and youth may find some shelter in the promise of innocence, African American youth cannot count on having access to even this problematic protection in sexuality education debates and classrooms. In an ethnographic study of community responses to abstinence-only legislation, Fields (2008) found that advocates deployed white girls in sexuality education debates as representations of the sexual innocence that sexuality education must protect, while African American girls and boys were routinely "adultified"—cast as "sinister, intentional, fully conscious [and] stripped of any element of childish naiveté" (Ferguson 2001, 83).

Class differences similarly inform sexuality education in insidious ways. Since its emergence at the turn of the 20th century, the category of adolescence has been the purview of White people in the upper and middle classes (Moran 2000; see also Fields 2005). 1996 federal funding for abstinence-only education emerged in the context of welfare reform, where lessons on sexual abstinence contributed to broader conservative efforts to discourage out-of-wedlock pregnancy and thereby, conservatives claimed, to address poverty (Fields 2005; Fineman et al. 2003, Luker 2006). Such policies shape not only formal classroom curriculum but also pedagogical practice: Fields (2008) found that public school teachers suffered greater scrutiny and less support than private school colleagues. In turn, the least advantaged students received the most restrictive instruction: only the relatively privileged private school students in her study heard in their sexuality education a call to sexual pleasure, agency, and knowledge. The public school students were consistently told that they should mute their desires and equip themselves for a violent sexual world.

Made-up and archetypal children afford both conservative and liberal advocates with foundations for compelling arguments for school-based sexuality education. Images of virgins, pregnant teens, promiscuous girls, predatory boys, suicidal gay students, doomed teens, and confused youth help to clarify and heighten the stakes in debates over curricular goals and social agendas (Connell and Elliott 2009; Fields 2008; Irvine 2002). . . . .

Conflating Sexual Talk and Sexual Activity

This sense of danger persists in another of the discursive conditions that sexuality education policy makers and advocates navigate—a diminished distinction between sexual speech and sexual activity. Talking with children and youth about sex becomes tantamount to engaging in sexual activity with children and youth: "Sexual speech, modern critics contend, provokes and stimulates. It transforms the so-called natural modesty of children into inflamed desires that may be outside the child's control and thus prompt sexual activity" (Irvine 2000, 62; see also Heins 2001; Irvine 2002). This framing threatens to render sexuality education an indefensible task: a violation of children and youth's sexual innocence and yet another assault on the embattled and idealized child-victim (Best 1993).

The depravity narratives that pervade US debates about sex and sexuality education—in which teachers seduce, corrupt, or otherwise sexually endanger their students—are one sign of this conflation of sexual speech and sexual activity. Through these narratives, classroom talk of even normative heterosexuality comes to constitute an assault that threatens to "persuade, incite, or otherwise arouse youth to later engage in the very acts spoken about" (Irvine 2000, 63); and talk about homosexuality becomes an inherently predatory act that initiates children or youth into a host of sexual perversions, including same-sex behaviors and desires (Irvine 2000, 2002; Levine 2002). Such narratives rest on a historically available discourse about the corruptible child; they also help to imagine and constitute a world in which the threat of sexual molestation looms everywhere, every teacher is potentially a pedophile, and learning happens when "the omnipotent, all-controlling adult" meets "the powerless, passive child" (Angelides 2004, 160). Sexuality education, resting as it does on talking with youth about sexuality, threatens to become a crime in which "any teacher is a suspect" (Irvine 2000, 70).

The panic fostered by fears of molestation has significant implications of sexuality education debates and practice. Some parents become mobilized to resist sexuality education in their children's schools; other parents, along with policy makers and educators, become reluctant to publicly endorse sexuality education that promotes anything other than sexual abstinence, normative family structures, and conventional gender expression (Irvine 2002). . . . In this climate, the conflation of sexual speech and sexual acts and the companion panic surrounding sexuality education and the threat of sexual molestation help to naturalize conventional sexual hierarchies in the name of protecting youth. Within this logic, protecting youth comes to mean protecting them from sexuality education.

Teaching, Learning, Knowing, and Doing

The conflation of sexual speech and acts shapes not only public debate but also teaching and learning in the classroom. Looming charges of depravity leave all sexuality education advocates, policy makers, and instructors in a nearly impossible situation: how can they convince parents and community members that their course of instruction does not put young people at risk, let alone that their instruction might ease the risks that young people face? In response, participants in sexuality education debates and policy-making acknowledge that the curriculum they advocate—whether abstinence-only, abstinence-based, or comprehensive—necessarily includes talk of sex; however, they argue, that speech is factually sound and medically accurate and thus the logical and rational choice for any adult committed to promoting the health of children and youth (Fields 2008; Fine 1988; Fine and McClelland 2006).

According to Lesko, comprehensive sexuality education and abstinence-only education build on each other and on a shared cultural moment and, as such, "touch in many ways" (Lesko 2010, 290). In prevailing comprehensive models of sexuality education, knowledge is presumed to be "positive and accurate," part of a broad definition of freedom as the product of scientific knowledge and empowerment.

Abstinence-only models similarly indulge in this "pan-optimism" (2010, 290), in which knowledge produces desired outcomes—discouraging sexual behavior and promoting compliance with gender and sexual norms. Such optimism is possible only with a notion of knowledge as stable and decontextualized—a notion that empirical research repeatedly indicates is at odds with meaningful sexuality education. . . . Even with such sensitivity to the context of teaching and learning, a well-designed, theoretically informed curriculum may improve the quality of young people's sexual and emotional lives but have little impact on sexual behaviors, included unprotected sex, contraceptive use, teen pregnancies, or abortions (Henderson, Wight, Raab, Abraham, Parkes, Scott, and Hart 2007; Wight, Raab, Henderson, Abraham, Buston, Hart, and Scott 2002). The path from knowledge to behavior is far from clear.

This determined pursuit of behavior change through sexuality education mirrors the confidence that the language of sexuality, especially when couched in scientific terms, is transparent and neutral. A stable, rational, and unambiguous relationship between knowledge and behavior is at the heart of sexuality education debates and practice and, in turn, sexuality education research. Both abstinence-only education and comprehensive sexuality education pursue knowledge as a route to desired behaviors. Mainstream curricular positions continue to try to recapture an imagined and predictable relationship between knowledge and behavior: teach young people to abstain, and they will; compromise young people with knowledge of sexual behaviors and desires, and they will be endangered; and present information about risk, prevention, and responsible behavior, and you will promote healthy decision-making in youth.

The consequences of dramatizing and idealizing ideas about youth continue inside the sexuality education classroom as sexuality education "socializes children into systems of inequality" (Connell and Elliott 2009, 84). Curriculum and pedagogy that pursue and claim rational and unambiguous knowledge routinely affirm oppressive values and norms about gender, race, and sexuality, even when presenting what appears to be rational, medically accurate information about bodies, diseases and pregnancy prevention, and puberty (Fields 2008; Trudell 1993; Trudell and Whatley 1991; Waxman 2004; Whatley and Trudell 1993). Lessons on menstruation and conception enact gendered norms regarding girls' and women's vulnerability and men's virility (Diorio and Munro 2000; Martin 1991). Youth and families of color appear in textbooks and other instructional material primarily in discussions of risk and disease prevention (Fields 2008; Whatley 1988). Overall, while abstinence-only education may more overtly discourage sexual expression among youth, both abstinence-only and comprehensive instruction persistently assign girls responsibility for managing boys' aggressive desires, maintain heterosexuality's normative status, and suggest that meaningful sexual expression and relationships among youth are unlikely, even rare (Fields 2008).

Much instruction and many curricular materials suggest that boys of all races are potential sexual predators. In a heteronormative sexuality education, this discourse prepares students for antagonistic sexual relationships between men and women. The messages girls receive are no better. Even in sexuality education classrooms formally designated "comprehensive," girls hear little talk from their teachers about female sexual desire. Instead they hear that, as girls and women, they bear the responsibility of deflecting the inevitable, aggressive sexual advances of their male peers (Fields 2008; Fine 1988; Fine and McClelland 2006; Tolman 2002).

Indeed, in practice, comprehensive sexuality education is rarely comprehensive: instructors often shy away from provocative stances on controversial topics, especially lesbian, gay, and bisexuality; and comprehensive educators routinely assert that sexual abstinence is the best choice for youth (Fields 2008; Gilbert 2010; Santelli 2006). Such heteronormative school-based sexuality education systematically denies sexually active young people access to educational resources and adult support that would promote their well-being and health. In addition, those youth who identify as lesbian, gay, bisexual, and queer (LGBQ) contend with sexuality education that emphasizes heterosexual behaviors, desires, and relationships and that, through its refusal to address LGBQ sexuality as anything other than a site of risk and deviance, denies non-conforming youth recognition as fully participating and valued members of their communities who are capable of creating and enjoying meaningful relationships with same-sex partners (Fields 2004; Fields 2008; Gilbert 2006; Russell 2002). . . .

Risking Ambiguity and Ambivalence

These shared ideas across a seemingly polarized public debate suggest that sexuality education policy and debates are sites of profound conflict and significant ambivalence and ambiguity. While national policy discussions and representations of those discussions often suggest a monolithic abstinence-only agenda, local providers of abstinence-only education are often quite resistant to and ambivalent about funding requirements and streams (Hess 2010). Feminists who strive for a sexuality education that fosters agency and subjectivity among girls and young women and recognizes the importance of intimacy and egalitarianism also grapple with the messiness and difficulty of the sexual relations in which youth and adults are similarly involved (Schalet 2009). And youth themselves navigate significant ambiguity: for example, conflicts between the instrumental lessons of the abstinence-only and abstinence-based sexuality education they encounter in schooling and the more ambiguous messages about sexuality they encounter in popular culture and their everyday lives appear to yield "highly personalized and often contradictory interpretations [of abstinence]" (Sawyer et al. 2007, 51).

Some researchers argue that this ambiguity threatens to undermine young people's well-being. Without a definition of what it means to abstain, adolescents appear to be at risk of stumbling into a world characterized by the dangers of pregnancy and sexual behavior (see, for example, Sawyer et al. 2007). According to this instrumental argument, if "misconceptions and ambiguities" about abstinence are allowed to stand (Goodson et al. 2003, 91), educators and researchers will be unable to offer effective sexuality education, evaluate sexuality education programs, and equip young people to recognize when they are being sexually active and when their behaviors constitute a sexual risk (Haglund, 2003). In response, many social science researchers, like policy makers, have sought an appropriate, clear definition that would help "provide adolescents with the information and decision-making skills to assess and maintain well-being" (Ott et al. 2006, 197).

An alternative lies in the work of researchers who, rather than positing these "highly personalized and often contradictory" definitions as problems to stamp out, approach terms like "abstinence" and their surrounding ambiguity as problems to engage, as conditions of learning and of sexual life. Young people's lack of clarity about abstinence and virginity reflects a broader lack of consensus in our society (Bersamin et al. 2007). Their resistance to clear-cut definitions suggests that young people's experiences of sexuality and of learning about sexuality exceed the normative cultural messages about risk, responsibility, and disease that characterize most abstinence-only and comprehensive sexuality education.

Articulating a vision of education that promotes well-being through a more expansive and less instrumentalist approach to risk, sexuality, and education involves both a rethinking of young people's sexuality as comprising more than risk and an acknowledgement that many of the risks young people face reflect adult-made social conditions (Schaffner 2005). . . .

While such understandings of risk, ambiguity, and ambivalence are not the norm in contemporary sexuality education, some educators and researchers have embraced the approach. . . .

In its "Genderpalooza! A Sex & Gender Primer," Scarleteen.com discusses gender not in the conventional binary terms of female and male but instead as

> a man-made set of concepts and ideas about how men and women are supposed to look, act, relate and interrelate, based on their sex. Gender isn't anatomical: it's intellectual, psychological and social (and even optional); about identity, roles and status based on ideas about sex and what it means to different people and groups. (http://www.scarleteen.com/article/body/genderpalooza_a_sex_gender_primer)

In its *Young Women's Survival Guide*, Health Initiatives for Youth (HIFY) offers readers a line drawing of "female external genitals" with the caption, "Everyone's vulva is different so don't judge yours by the pictures you see" (2003, 14). And the resource guide, *It's All One Curriculum*, ties values, beliefs, and norms to social contexts and power:

> We often tend to think of our own values and beliefs as "natural." However, . . . [s]ocieties enact laws that reflect norms and specify which behaviors are permitted and which are not. Those individuals or groups who have the most power often have the greatest influence in determining both social norms and laws. Some laws, norms, and individual values are concerned with sexuality. (International Sexuality and HIV Curriculum Working Group 2009, 23)

With these lessons, Scarleteen, HIFY, and It's All One Curriculum recognize the ambiguity and ambivalence that characterize young people's and adult's sexual lives, classroom efforts to address those lives, and policy debates about those classroom efforts. Rather than offering the false promise that all risk can be eliminated and avoided, these texts encourage young people to take risks responsibly, to recognize and challenge the ways that social conditions put them and their peers at risk, to think about what might make sexual choices more and less safe, and to contribute to a world that promotes the well-being of all.

Conclusions

Though abstinence-only and comprehensive sexuality education advocates may offer different responses to the problems routinely associated with teen sexual activity, much of what they offer shares assumptions about youth, sexuality, and learning: that teen sexuality is a site of danger and risk; that such danger and risk is a source of profound worry among adults; and that sexuality education is a necessary, rational, and corrective response to that danger, risk, and worry. Similarly, both abstinence-only and comprehensive sexuality education rest on a particular understanding of education: provide students the requisite knowledge, and they will adopt the behaviors—for example, sexual abstinence or contraceptive use—that teachers advocate.

Such an approach to knowledge casts sexual decision making as wholly rational and denies "affect as a central part of what knowledge does" (Lesko 2010, 282). The affective experiences of learning about sexuality exceed the bounds of rational and predictable knowledge. This excess animates young people's experiences of sexuality and persists in classroom practice. It also pervades local and national sexuality education debates. Consistently, sexuality education evokes a range of fraught social concerns about, for example, which family formations communities will accept and celebrate in their midst; how best to respond to increasing numbers of—and tolerance of—lesbian, gay, and bisexual youth; the relative responsibility of families and schools to provide for young people's sexual well-being and moral character; and how educators, families, service providers, and other community members will respond to the incidence and risk of teen pregnancies and STIs.

Ambiguity and ambivalence in sexuality education policy and practice represent a call to move beyond the polarized debate between abstinence-only and comprehensive sexuality education and allow instead for an expansive approach to learning and knowing that opens with and sustains questions. Indeed, Jen Gilbert has argued for teaching and learning in which "not knowing and feeling confused [might become] the basis of learning about sexuality" and not something to be corrected (2010, 5). In this vision of sexuality education, the ambivalence, pleasure, worry, and other sexual experiences and associations that are currently interpreted as intruding upon effective teaching, learning, and policy would be recognized and contended with as the cultural conditions in which communities debate sexuality education policy and practice and, ultimately, the stuff of sexuality education itself.

NOTES

1. Editor's Note: Despite President Obama's commitment to directing funding away from abstinence-only-until-marriage programs, since 2009, Congress has continued to fund these programs at $50 million a year through Title V Sec. 510 of the Social Security Act, reauthorized via the Affordable Care Act and extended through FY 2017, as well as $5 million per year through the Competitive Abstinence Education (CAE) grant program. (Personal correspondence between SIECUS and editor, 2015.)

REFERENCES

Angelides, Steven. 2004. "Feminism, Child Abuse, and the Erasure of Child Sexuality." *GLQ: A Journal of Lesbian and Gay Studies* 10(2): 141–77.

Bay-Cheng, Laina Y. 2003. "The Trouble of Teen Sex: The Construction of Adolescent Sexuality through School-Based Sexuality Education." *Sex Education: Sexuality, Society and Learning* 3(1): 61–74.

Bersamin, Melina A., Deborah A. Fisher, Samantha Walker, Douglas L. Hill and Joel W. Grube. 2007. "Defining Virginity and Abstinence: Adolescents' Interpretations of Sexual Behaviors." *Journal of Adolescent Health* 41: 182–8.

Best, Amy. 2000. *Prom Night: Youth, Schools and Popular Culture*. New York: Routledge.

Best, Joel. 1993. *Threatened Children: Rhetoric and Concern about Child-Victims*. Chicago: University of Chicago Press.

Bourdieu, Pierre and Jean Claude Passeron. 1990. *Reproduction in Education, Society and Culture*. Trans. Richard Nice. London: Sage Publications.

Brown, Jane D. and Victor C. Strasburger. 2007. "From Calvin Klein to Paris Hilton and MySpace: Adolescents, Sex, and the Media." *Adolescent Sexuality, Adolescent Medicine: State of the Art Reviews* 18(3): 484–507.

Clay, Andreana. 2003. "Keepin' It Real: Black Youth, Hip-Hop Culture, and Black Identity." *American Behavioral Scientist* 46(1): 1346–58.

Connell, Catherine and Sinikka Elliott. 2009. "Beyond the Birds and the Bees: Learning Inequality through Sexuality Education." *American Journal of Sexuality Education* 4: 83–102.

Diorio, Joseph A. and Jennifer A. Munro. 2000. "Doing Harm in the Name of Protection: Menstruation as a Topic for Sex Education." *Gender and Education* 12(3): 347–65.

Duberstein Lindberg, Laura, John S. Santelli and Susheela Singh. 2006. "Changes in Formal Sex Education: 1995–2002." *Perspectives on Sexual and Reproductive Health* 38(4): 182–9.

Duggan, Lisa and Nan D. Hunter. 1995. *Sex Wars: Sexual Dissent and Political Culture*. New York: Routledge.

Elliott, Sinikka. forthcoming. *Not My Kid: Parents and Teen Sexuality*. New York: New York University Press.

Ferguson, Ann Arnett. 2001. *Bad Boys: Public Schools in the Making of Black Masculinity*. Ann Arbor: University of Michigan Press.

Fields, Jessica. 2004. "Same-Sex Marriage, Sodomy Laws, and the Sexual Lives of Young People." *Sexuality Research and Social Policy: Journal of NSRC* 1(3): 11–23.

Fields, Jessica. 2005. "'Children Having Children': Race, Innocence, and Sexuality Education." *Social Problems* 52(4): 549–71.

Fields, Jessica. 2008. *Risky Lessons: Sex Education and Social Inequality*. New Brunswick, NJ: Rutgers University Press.

Fields, Jessica and Celeste Hirschman. 2007. "Citizenship Lessons in Abstinence-Only Sexuality Education." *American Journal of Sexuality Education* 2(2): 3–25.

Fine, Michelle. 1988. "Sexuality, Schooling, and Adolescent Females: The Missing Discourse of Desire." *Harvard Educational Review* 58(1): 29–53.

Fine, Michelle and Sara I. McClelland. 2006. "Sexuality Education and Desire: Still Missing after All These Years." *Harvard Educational Review* 76(3): 297–337.

Fineman, Martha A., Gwendolyn Mink and Anna Marie Smith. 2003. "No Promotion of Marriage in TANF!" *Social Justice* 30(4): 126–34.

Gilbert, Jen. 2006. "'Let Us Say Yes to What or Who Shows Up': Education as Hospitality." *Journal of the Canadian Association of Curriculum Studies* 4(1): 35–44.

Gilbert, Jen. 2010. "Ambivalence Only? Sex Education in the Age of Abstinence." *Sex Education: Sexuality, Society and Learning* 10(3): 233–7.

Goodson, Patricia, Sandy Suther, B. E. Pruitt and Kelly Wilson. 2003. "Defining Abstinence: Views of Directors, Instructors, and Participants in Abstinence-Only-Until-Marriage Programs in Texas." *The Journal of School Health* 73: 91–6.

Haglund, Kristin 2003. "'Sexually Abstinent African American Adolescent Females' Descriptions of Abstinence." *Journal of Nursing Scholarship* 25(3): 231–6.

Health Initiatives for Youth 2003. *Kickin' Back With the Girls: A Young Woman's Survival Guide*, 2nd ed. San Francisco, CA: Author.

Heins, Marjorie. 2001. *Not in Front of the Children: "Indecency," Censorship, and the Innocence of Youth*. New York: Hill and Wang.

Henderson, Marion, Daniel Wight, Gillian Raab, Charles Abraham, Alison Parkes, Sue Scott and Graham Hart. 2007. "Impact of a Theoretically Based Sex Education Programme (SHARE) Delivered by Teachers on NHS Registered Conceptions and Terminations: Final Results of a Cluster Randomised Trial." *British Medical Journal* 334: 133–36.

Hess, Amie. 2010. "Hold the Sex, Please: The Discursive Politics between National and Local

Abstinence Education Providers." *Sex Education: Sexuality, Society and Learning* 10(3): 251–66.

Hunter, James Davison. 1992. *Culture Wars: The Struggle to Define America*. New York: Basic Books.

International Sexuality and HIV Curriculum Working Group 2009. *It's All One Curriculum: Guidelines and Activities for a Unified Approach to Sexuality, Gender, HIV, and Human Rights Education*. New York: The Population Council.

Irvine, Janice M. 2000. "Doing It with Words: Discourse and the Sex Education Culture Wars." *Critical Inquiry* 27(1): 58–76.

Irvine, Janice M. 2002. *Talk about Sex: The Battles over Sex Education in the United States*. Berkeley: University of California Press.

Irvine, Janice M. 2006. "Emotional Scripts of Sex Panics." *Sexuality Research & Social Policy: Journal of NSRC* 3(3): 82–94.

Kendall, Nancy. 2008. "Sexuality Education in an Abstinence-Only Era: A Comparative Case Study of Two U.S. States." *Sexuality Research and Social Policy: Journal of NSRC* 5(2): 23–44.

Kincaid, James R. 1997. *Erotic Innocence: The Culture of Child Molesting*. Durham, NC: Duke University Press.

Kirby, Douglas. 2008. "The Impact of Abstinence and Comprehensive Sex and STD/HIV Education Programs on Adolescent Sexual Behavior." *Sexuality Research and Social Policy: Journal of NSRC* 5(3): 6–17.

Lesko, Nancy. 2001. *Act Your Age! A Cultural Construction of Adolescence*. New York: Routledge Falmer.

Lesko, Nancy. 2010. "Feeling Abstinent? Feeling Comprehensive? Touching the Affects of Sexuality Curricula." *Sex Education: Sexuality, Society and Learning* 10(3): 281–97.

Levine, Judith. 2002. *Harmful to Minors: The Perils of Protecting Children from Sex*. Minneapolis: University of Minnesota Press.

Luker, Kristin. 1996. *Dubious Conceptions: The Politics of Teen Pregnancy*. Cambridge, MA: Harvard University Press.

Luker, Kristin. 2006. *When Sex Goes to School: Warring Views on Sex—and Sex Education—Since the Sixties*. New York: W. W. Norton.

Luttrell, Wendy. 2003. *Pregnant Bodies, Fertile Minds: Gender, Race, and the Schooling of Pregnant Teens*. New York: Routledge.

Martin, Emily. 1991. "The Egg and the Sperm: How Science Has Constructed a Romance Based on Stereotypical Male–Female Roles." *Signs: Journal of Women in Culture and Society* 16(31): 485–501.

Martin, Karin A. 1996. *Puberty, Sexuality, and the Self: Boys and Girls at Adolescence*. New York: Routledge.

Moran, Jeffrey P. 2000. *Teaching Sex: The Shaping of Adolescence in the 20th Century*. Cambridge, MA: Harvard University Press.

Ott, Mary A., Elizabeth J. Pfeiffer and J. Dennis Fortenberry. 2006. "Perceptions of Sexual Abstinence among High-Risk Early and Middle Adolescents." *Journal of Adolescent Health* 39: 192–8.

Pascoe, C. J. 2007. *Dude, You're a Fag: Masculinity and Sexuality in High School*. Berkeley: University of California Press.

Regnerus, Mark D. 2007. *Forbidden Fruit: Sex & Religion in the Lives of American Teenagers*. New York: Oxford University Press.

Russell, Stephen T. 2002. "Queer in America: Citizenship for Sexual Minority Youth." *Applied Developmental Science* 6(4): 258–63.

Santelli, John S. 2006. "Abstinence-Only Education: Politics, Science, and Ethics." *Social Research* 73(3): 835–58.

Sawyer, Robin G., Donna E. Howard, Jessica Brewster-Gavin, Melissa Jordan and Marla Sherman. 2007. "'We Didn't Have Sex . . . Did We?' College Students' Perceptions of Abstinence." *American Journal of Health Studies* 22(1): 46–55.

Scarleteen.com. 2011. "Genderpalooza! A Sex & Gender Primer." [Online]. Retrieved on 11 October 2011 from: http://www.scarleteen.com/article/body/genderpalooza_a_sex_gender_primer

Schaffner, Laurie. 2005. *So Called Girl-on-Girl Violence is Actually Adult-on-Girl Violence* (Great Cities Institute Working Paper No. GCP-05-03). Chicago, IL: Author.

Schalet, Amy T. 2004. "Must We Fear Adolescent Sexuality?" *Medscape General Medicine* 6(4): 1–16.

Schalet, Amy T. 2009. "Subjectivity, Intimacy, and the Empowerment Paradigm of Adolescent

Sexuality: The Unexplored Room." *Feminist Studies* 35(1): 133–60.

Schalet, Amy T. 2010. "Sexual Subjectivity Revisited: The Significance of Relationships in Dutch and American Girls' Experiences of Sexuality." *Gender & Society* 24: 304.

Shapiro, Eve. 2010. *Gender Circuits: Bodies and Identities in a Technological Age.* New York: Routledge.

Stein, Arlene. 2006. *Shameless: Sexual Dissidence in American Culture.* New York: New York University Press.

Tolman, Deborah L. 2002. *Dilemmas of Desire: Teenage Girls Talk about Sexuality.* Cambridge, MA: Harvard University Press.

Trudell, Bonnie Nelson. 1993. *Doing Sex Education: Gender Politics and Schooling.* New York: Routledge.

Trudell, Bonnie Nelson and Mariamne H. Whatley. 1991. "Sex Respect: A Problematic Public School Sexuality Curriculum." *Journal of Sex Education and Therapy* 17(2): 122–40.

U.S. Department of Health and Human Services. 2008. *Health and Human Services Funding for Abstinence Education, Education for Teen Pregnancy and HIV/STD Prevention, and Other Programs that Address Adolescent Sexual Activity.* [Online]. Retrieved on 11 October 2011 from: http://aspe .hhs.gov/hsp/08/AbstinenceEducation/report .shtml

Wagoner, James. 2009. "Appropriations Bill Marks Victory for Sexual Health: Advocates Need to Remain Vigilant." Advocates for Youth Blog. [Online]. Retrieved on 11 October 2011 from: http://www.advocatesforyouth.org/blogs-main/ advocates-blog/1544-appropriations-bill-marks- victory-for-sexual-health-advocates-need-to- remain-vigilant

Waxman, Henry A. 2004. *The Content of Federally Funded Abstinence-Only Education Programs.* Washington, D.C.: U.S. House of Representatives, Special Investigation Division.

Whatley, Mariamne H. 1988. "Photographic Images of Blacks in Sexuality Texts." *Curriculum Inquiry* 18(2): 83–106.

Whatley, Mariamne H. and Bonnie Nelson Trudell. 1993. "Teen-Aid: Another Problematic School Sexuality Curriculum." *Journal of Sex Education and Therapy* 19(4): 251–71.

Wight, Daniel, Gillian Raab, Marion Henderson, Charles Abraham, Katie Buston, Graham Hart and Sue Scott. 2002. "The Limits of Teacher-Delivered Sex Education: Interim Behavioural Outcomes from a Randomised Trial." *British Medical Journal* 324: 1430–33.

Wilkins, Amy C. 2008. *Wannabes, Goths, and Christians: The Boundaries of Sex, Style, and Status.* Chicago: University of Chicago Press.

Zimmerman, Jonathan. 2005. *Whose America? Culture Wars in the Public Schools.* Cambridge, MA: Harvard University Press.

The Social Consequences of Abstinence-Only Sex Education

Lanier Basenberg

Original to Focus on Social Problems: A Contemporary Reader.

Issues related to sex often receive a lot of attention from social problems claimsmakers, especially when they relate to teen and young adult sexuality. Teen pregnancy, abortion, and rates of sexually transmitted infections (STIs) among teens garner frequent attention from lawmakers, members of the news media, and activists. One possible solution to these problems has been sex education. Unfortunately, the sex education available to many American teens has proven to be so ineffective that it might be considered a social problem itself.

Some type of sex education for children is required in all 50 states, and 39 of those require abstinence-only sex education (Guttmacher, 2015). Up to 87 percent of American students in public schools are getting abstinence-only sex education each year (Guttmacher, 2012). Abstinence-only sex education emphasizes the idea that young people should abstain from any sexual activity before marriage because it is morally wrong and unsafe. Courses on abstinence-only sex education are required by law to teach that abstinence before marriage is the "expected standard of human sexual activity" and that any sexual contact outside of marriage will have negative physical and psychological effects (Social Security Act, Section 510, 1996).

Although abstinence-only is the most common type of sex education, there are other types, most notably comprehensive sex education. Comprehensive sex education covers sex and sexuality in a factual, thorough way. Typically students are taught biological information about their genitals and sex organs; the possible negative consequences of sexual activity; and the ways to protect themselves from such consequences, including barrier methods (e.g., condoms and dental dams), hormonal birth control, and regular screenings for STIs.

Both types of sex education have avid supporters, although more Americans support comprehensive sex education than abstinence-only sex education (Bleakley et al., 2009; Kirby, 2006). In fact, about 80 percent of Americans support comprehensive sex education (Bleakley et al., 2006). Yet those who support abstinence-only tend to be more powerful politically (Perrin and DeJoy, 2003; SIECUS 2010). The result of the promotion of abstinence-only sex education by a powerful minority is that the majority of American students in public schools are getting abstinence-only sex education, with multiple, measurable negative effects. Some of these effects are widely recognized as social problems, including an earlier introduction to sexual activity, an increase in the number of sex partners when young people eventually become sexually active, a high rate of contraction of STIs, higher rates of unintended teen pregnancy, and the reinforcement of a negative view of women. Although abstinence-only sex education is meant to protect young people from the possible negative consequences of sexual activity, in this reading I show how it actually achieves the reverse. I also demonstrate how comprehensive sex education can mitigate those same effects.

INTRODUCTION TO SEXUAL ACTIVITY

One of the primary goals of abstinence-only sex education is to convince young people not to have sex until marriage, yet data show us that comprehensive sex education is more effective at delaying the onset of coitus (penile–vaginal intercourse) (Erkut et al., 2012; Kirby, 2007; Lindbergh and Maddow-Zimet, 2012). Although it may seem counterintuitive, repeated studies have shown that young people who are given comprehensive sex education actually tend to have sex *later* than their peers who receive abstinence-only sex education (Erkut et al., 2012; Kirby, 2007; Lindbergh and Maddow-Zimet, 2012). Talking with young people about sex seems to make them more comfortable when considering sex and less likely to jump into sexual activity without planning. Not only do young people who receive comprehensive sex education wait longer before having sex for the first time, but also they are more likely to use condoms and other forms of birth control when they do become sexually active (Lindbergh and Maddow-Zimet, 2012). Using birth control and condoms leads to fewer cases of STIs and fewer unintended pregnancies, outcomes valued by both comprehensive and abstinence-only sex education proponents. Parental involvement, such as talking about sex with children, providing educational materials, and simply spending time with children, has also been shown to delay sexual debut (Grossman et al., 2013; Meschke et al., 2002; Sieving et al., 2000).

NUMBER OF SEXUAL PARTNERS

In traditional abstinence-only curricula, teachers make clear that each person should have one partner and that the partner should be your spouse. However, once again, we find that abstinence-only education is less effective than comprehensive sex education in achieving its goals. Longitudinal studies of young people show that those who receive comprehensive sex education accumulate fewer partners before marriage than those who receive abstinence-only sex education (Chin et al., 2012; Kirby, 2007; Schalet et al., 2014; Trenholm et al., 2008). These lower numbers may be the result of young people being encouraged to think critically about sex and its possible consequences, making

continues

■ Continued

them less likely to enter into sexual relationships casually. In addition, students who receive abstinence-only education may actually be putting themselves at greater risk because not only do they have more partners, but also, as previously mentioned, they are less likely to use contraceptives compared to students who receive comprehensive sex education (Lindberg and Maddow-Zimet, 2012).

CONTRACTION OF STIs

One possible negative consequence of sexual activity, for individuals and society as a whole, is infection. Although a goal of abstinence-only sex education is to prevent the spread of STIs, it is ineffective. When measured against young people who receive comprehensive sex education, those who receive abstinence-only sex education actually contract STIs at higher rates. Studies have shown that when young people are not given access to information regarding how to protect themselves from STIs, they are more likely to contract them (Brückner and Bearman, 2005; Fortenbery, 2005; Santelli et al., 2006). It might not shock you to learn that abstinence-only educators occasionally exaggerate condom failure rates (Santelli et al., 2006), a practice designed to scare young people away from having sex at all. If teens have been told that condoms are ineffective, they may decide that using them is pointless, further increasing their risk of exposure to STIs when they do have sex.

There are other reasons teens (and people of all ages) might not use condoms. First, some people might feel embarrassed about buying them. In fact, some young people are so ashamed to be seen buying condoms that they refuse to do it (Brackett, 2004; Moore et al., 2006; Scott-Sheldon et al., 2006), even if they are sexually active. Condoms are also quite expensive. The combination of expense and embarrassment combine to create a situation where stores often feel compelled to keep condoms locked behind glass doors because they are frequently stolen. When condoms are provided free of charge and are easily accessible, people are more

likely to use them and are less likely to contract STIs (Cohen et al., 1999; Dodge et al., 2009; Tolosa, 2012). Additionally, some young people (especially young women) feel that carrying condoms and/or asking a partner to use a condom will make them look "slutty" or "easy" to their partners and that their partners would judge them negatively (Dahl et al., 2005; East et al., 2011). Finally, many young men attempt to avoid or outright refuse to wear condoms. Some do this because they say the sensations are not as pleasurable,[1] but scholarly research suggests they might be avoiding condoms because they see refusal to use condoms as reinforcing their masculinity (Davis et al., 2013; Davis and Logan-Greene, 2012; Measor, 2006).

RATES OF UNINTENDED TEEN PREGNANCY

One of the most easily measured effects of sex education is the rate at which young women who receive specific kinds of sex education become pregnant. Although teen pregnancy rates are declining, the United States leads the developed world in teen pregnancy rates (Guttmacher, 2014; U.S. Department of Health and Human Services, 2015). Although pregnancy in teenage women is not always unintentional, around 80 percent of young women who became pregnant report that it was not their intention to conceive (Finer and Zolna, 2011; Kost and Henshaw, 2014; Peipert et al., 2012). Abstinence-only sex education aims to prevent unintended pregnancy by teaching young people not to engage in sexual activity, but the high rates of unintended pregnancy among teenagers are some of the most damning evidence against the effectiveness of these abstinence-only programs. If abstinence-only sex education were working, students would not be having any sexual intercourse at all, much less becoming pregnant. Teaching young people about contraception, on the other hand, appears to help prevent unintended pregnancy. Students who learn about contraceptives through comprehensive sex education are less likely to experience accidental pregnancy as teenagers compared to those who receive abstinence-only sex education (Kohler et al., 2008; Stanger-Hall and Hall, 2011). Although we cannot say the relationship is a causal one, states that require abstinence-only sex education typically have the highest rates of teen pregnancy (Beadle, 2012; Cavazos-Rehg et al., 2012), and these rates are likely no coincidence.

ASSUMPTIONS OF HETEROSEXUALITY AND THE TREATMENT OF WOMEN

Finally, I would like to address one of the less easily measured but still important effects of abstinence-only sex education. Abstinence-only sex education assumes heterosexuality and a desire or ability to get married. By this I mean that abstinence-only sex education is directed at heterosexual young people, and when sex educators warn against sex before marriage, they imply that sex is only penile–vaginal penetration. Such assumptions ignore the entire nonheterosexual population, same-sex marriage, and the possibility for alternative, nonpenetrative forms of sexuality.

In addition, abstinence-only education focuses, in large part, on controlling the sexual behavior of young women, rather than young men (Ehrlich, 2013; Lamb, 2013). In modern American culture it is still considered more shameful for a young woman to be sexually active than for a young man (Attwood, 2007; Bay-Cheng, 2003), and abstinence-only sex education often reinforces this idea. Much of abstinence-only sex education is aimed at retaining the "purity" of young women who are taught to be "gate keepers," essentially placing the burden of refraining from or stopping sexual activity on their shoulders (Chittenden, 2010; Tolman, 2009; Wiederman, 2005). Young women have the responsibility of saying no and are not easily granted the agency to say yes. Young men, on the other hand, are depicted as unable to control their own urges, ignoring their autonomy and agency. Such thinking might excuse their behavior when they are sexually aggressive or act without the consent of their partner. This kind of gender essentialism is harmful for both

young women and men, and its consequences can reach into adulthood (Bay-Cheng, 2015; Fortenbery, 2014).

Addressing this gender imbalance is not only important for healthy gender relations among students; it can also increase the efficacy of sexuality education programs. Recent research has indicated that sexuality education programs that address gender (e.g., by specifically addressing power imbalances between young men and women, by encouraging students to think critically about how gender norms and power differences are created and are reproduced, and by urging personal reflection among students) were significantly more likely to see decreases in teen pregnancy, childbearing, and STIs compared to programs that did not address gender power imbalances (Haberland, 2015). Including this type of information in sexuality education programs is critical because it presents sexuality in the context of real-life relationships and social norms and helps young people understand how power dynamics affect relationships and sexual choices (Beck, 2015).

CONCLUSION

Rather than protecting students, abstinence-only sex education is actively harming them and perpetuating a variety of social problems. These social problems can be alleviated with more comprehensive sex education programs, and your actions can help encourage the implementation of those programs. First, you can empower yourself with knowledge about sex via websites like scarletteen.com, www.plannedparenthood.org, and http://goodmenproject.com and encourage your friends to do the same. You can follow groups that promote safe sex and comprehensive sex education on social media, which will educate you and give these groups a wider reach. Second, you can advocate for change. You can vote, you can email or call your government representatives, you can give money to organizations that help promote comprehensive sex education, and you can create change for yourself and the generations who are following behind you.

continues

■ Continued

NOTES

1. Research on condom usage has contradicted this reasoning, finding that a nationally representative sample of young adults who used condoms for sexual intercourse reported similar arousal, pleasure, and rates of orgasm compared to adults not using them (Fortenberry et al., 2010).

REFERENCES

Attwood, F. 2007. "Sluts and Riot Grrrls: Female Identity and Sexual Agency." *Journal of Gender Studies* 16(3):233–247. http://doi.org/10.1080/09589230701562921/.

Bay-Cheng, L. Y. 2003. "The Trouble of Teen Sex: The Construction of Adolescent Sexuality through School-based Sexuality Education." *Sex Education* 3(1):61–74. http://doi.org/10.1080/1468181032000052162/.

Bay-Cheng, L. Y. 2015. "The Agency Line: A Neoliberal Metric for Appraising Young Women's Sexuality." *Sex Roles* 1–13. http://doi.org/10.1007s11199-015-0452-6/.

Beadle, A. P. 2012. "Teen Pregnancies Highest in States With Abstinence-Only Policies." Retrieved from http://thinkprogress.org/health/2012/04/10/461402/teen-pregnancy-sex-education/.

Beck, J. 2015, April 27. *When Sex Ed Discusses Gender Inequality, Sex Gets Safer.* Retrieved April 28, 2015, from http://www.theatlantic.com/health/archive/2015/04/when-sex-ed-teaches-gender-inequality-sex-gets-safer/391460/.

Bleakley, A., M. Hennessy, and M. Fishbein. 2006. "Public Opinion on Sex Education in US Schools." *Archives of Pediatrics & Adolescent Medicine* 160(11):1151–1156. http://doi.org/10.1001/archpedi.160.11.1151/.

Bleakley, A., M. Hennessy, M. Fishbein, and A. Jordan. 2009. "How Sources of Sexual Information Relate to Adolescents' Beliefs about Sex." *American Journal of Health Behavior* 33(1):37–48.

Brackett, K. P. 2004. "College Students' Condom Purchase Strategies." *The Social Science Journal* 41(3):459–464. http://doi.org/10.1016/j.soscij.2004.04.006/.

Brückner, H., and P. Bearman. 2005. "After the Promise: The STD Consequences of Adolescent Virginity Pledges." *Journal of Adolescent Health* 36(4):271–278. http://doi.org/10.1016/j.jadohealth.2005.01.005/.

Cavazos-Rehg, P. A., M. J. Krauss, E. L. Spitznagel, M. Iguchi, M. Schootman, L. Cottler, R. A. Grucza, and L. J. Beirut. 2012. "Associations between Sexuality Education in Schools and Adolescent Birthrates: A State-level Longitudinal Model." *Archives of Pediatrics & Adolescent Medicine* 166(2):134–140. http://doi.org/10.1001/archpediatrics.2011.657/.

Chin, H. B., T. A. Sipe, R. Elder, S. L. Mercer, S. K. Chattopadhyay, V. Jacob, V., H. R. Wethington, D. Kirby, D. B. Elliston, M. Griffith, S. O. Chuke, S. C. Briss, I. Ericksen, J. S. Galbraith, J. H. Herbst, R. L. Johnson, J. M. Kraft, S. M. Noar, L. M. Romero, and Santelli, J. 2012. "The Effectiveness of Group-Based Comprehensive Risk-Reduction and Abstinence Education Interventions to Prevent or Reduce the Risk of Adolescent Pregnancy, Human Immunodeficiency Virus, and Sexually Transmitted Infections: Two Systematic Reviews for the Guide to Community Preventive Services." *American Journal of Preventive Medicine* 42(3):272–294. http://doi.org/10.1016/j.amepre.2011.11.006/.

Chittenden, T. 2010. "For Whose Eyes Only? The Gatekeeping of Sexual Images in the Field of Teen Sexuality." *Sex Education* 10(1):79–90. http://doi.org/10.1080/14681810903491404/.

Cohen, D., R. Scribner, R. Bedimo, and T. A. Farley. 1999. "Cost as a Barrier to Condom Use: The Evidence for Condom Subsidies in the United States." *American Journal of Public Health* 89(4):567–568. http://doi.org/10.2105/AJPH.89.4.567/.

Dahl, D. W., P. R. Darke, G. J. Gorn, and C. B. Weinberg. 2005. "Promiscuous or Confident? Attitudinal Ambivalence toward Condom Purchase." *Journal of Applied Social Psychology* 35(4):869–887. http://doi.org/10.1111/j.1559-1816.2005.tb02150.x/.

Davis, K. C., and P. Logan-Greene. 2012. "Young Men's Aggressive Tactics to Avoid Condom Use: A Test of a Theoretical Model." *Social Work Research* 36(3):223–231. http://doi.org/10.1093/swr/svs027/.

Davis, K. C., T. J. Schraufnagel, K. F. Kajumulo, A. K. Gilmore, J. Norris, and W. H. George. 2013. "A Qualitative Examination of Men's Condom Use Attitudes and Resistance: 'It's Just Part of the Game.'" *Archives of Sexual Behavior* 43(3):631–643. http://doi.org/10.1007/s10508-013-0150-9/.

Dodge, B., M. Reece, and D. Herbenick. 2009. "School-Based Condom Education and Its Relations with Diagnoses of and Testing for Sexually Transmitted Infections among Men in the United States." *American Journal of Public Health* 99(12):2180–2182. http://doi.org/10.2105/AJPH.2008.159038/.

East, L., D. Jackson, L. O'Brien, and K. Peters. 2011. "Condom Negotiation: Experiences of Sexually Active Young Women." *Journal of Advanced Nursing* 67(1):77–85. http://doi.org/10.1111/j.1365-2648.2010.05451.x/.

Ehrlich, S. (2013). "From Birth Control to Sex Control: Unruly Young Women and the Origins of the National Abstinence-Only Mandate." *Canadian Bulletin of Medical History/Bulletin Canadien D'histoire de La Médecine* 30(1):77–99.

Erkut, S., J. M. Grossman, A. A. Frye, I. Ceder, L. Charmaraman, and A. J. Tracy. 2012. "Can Sex Education Delay Early Sexual Debut?" *The Journal of Early Adolescence* 0272431612449386. http://doi.org/10.1177/0272431612449386/.

Finer, L. B., and M. R. Zolna. 2011. "Unintended Pregnancy in the United States: Incidence and Disparities, 2006." *Contraception* 84(5):478–485. http://doi.org/10.1016/j.contraception.2011.07.013/.

Fortenberry, J. D. 2005. "The Limits of Abstinence-Only in Preventing Sexually Transmitted Infections." *Journal of Adolescent Health* 36(4):269–270. http://doi.org/10.1016/j.jadohealth.2005.02.001/.

Fortenberry, J. D. 2014. "Sexual Learning, Sexual Experience, and Healthy Adolescent Sex." *New Directions for Child and Adolescent Development* 2014(144):71–86. http://doi.org/10.1002/cad.20061/.

Fortenberry, J. D., V. Schick, D. Herbenick, S. A. Sanders, B. Dodge, and M. Reece. 2010. "Sexual Behaviors and Condom Use at Last Vaginal Intercourse: A National Sample of Adolescents Ages 14 to 17 Years." *The Journal of Sexual Medicine* 7:305–314. http://doi.org/10.1111/j.1743-6109.2010.02018.x/.

Grossman, J. M., A. Frye, L. Charmaraman, and S. Erkut. 2013. "Family Homework and School-Based Sex Education: Delaying Early Adolescents' Sexual Behavior." *Journal of School Health* 83(11):810–817. http://doi.org/10.1111/josh.12098/.

Guttmacher Institute. 2012. "Facts on American Teens' Sources of Information about Sex." Retrieved from https://www.guttmacher.org/pubs/FB-Teen-Sex-Ed.html.

———. 2014. "U.S. Teen Pregnancy, Birth, and Abortion Rates Reach Historical Lows." Retrieved from http://www.guttmacher.org/media/nr/2014/05/05/

———. 2015. "State Policies in Brief: Sex and HIV Education." Retrieved from http://www.guttmacher.org/statecenter/spibs/spib_SE.pdf.

Haberland, N. A. 2015. "The Case for Addressing Gender and Power in Sexuality and HIV Education: A Comprehensive Review of Evaluation Studies." *International Perspectives on Sexual and Reproductive Health* 41(1):31–42. http://doi.org/10.1363/4103155/.

Kirby D. 2006. "Comprehensive Sex Education: Strong Public Support and Persuasive Evidence of Impact, but Little Funding." *Archives of Pediatrics & Adolescent Medicine* 160(11):1182–1184. http://doi.org/10.1001/archpedi.160.11.1182/.

Kirby, D. B., B. A. Laris, and L. A. Rolleri. 2007. "Sex and HIV Education Programs: Their Impact on Sexual Behaviors of Young People throughout the World." *Journal of Adolescent Health* 40(3):206–217. http://doi.org/10.1016/j.jadohealth.2006.11.143/.

Kohler, P. K., L. E. Manhart, and W. E. Lafferty. 2008. "Abstinence-Only and Comprehensive Sex Education and the Initiation of Sexual Activity and Teen Pregnancy." *Journal of Adolescent Health* 42(4):344–351. http://doi.org/10.1016/j.jadohealth.2007.08.026/.

Kost, K., and S. Henshaw. 2014. *US Teenage Pregnancies, Births and Abortions, 2010: National and State Trends by Age, Race and Ethnicity*. Retrieved from http://www.guttmacher.org/pubs/USTPtrendsstate10.Pdf/.

Lamb, S. 2013. "Just the Facts? The Separation of Sex Education from Moral Education." *Educational Theory* 63(5):443–460. http://doi.org/10.1111/edth.12034/.

Lindberg, L. D., and I. Maddow-Zimet. 2012. "Consequences of Sex Education on Teen and Young

continues

Continued

Adult Sexual Behaviors and Outcomes." *Journal of Adolescent Health* 51(4):332–338. http://doi.org/10.1016/j.jadohealth.2011.12.028/.

Measor, L. 2006. "Condom Use: A Culture of Resistance." *Sex Education* 6(4):393–402. http://doi.org/10.1080/14681810600982093/.

Meschke, L. L., S. Bartholomae, and S. R. Zentall. 2002. "Adolescent Sexuality and Parent–Adolescent Processes: Promoting Healthy Teen Choices." *Journal of Adolescent Health* 31(6, Supplement):264–279. http://doi.org/10.1016/S1054-139X(02)00499-8/.

Moore, S. G., A. P. D. W. Dahl, G. J. Gorn, and C. B. Weinberg. 2006. "Coping with Condom Embarrassment." *Psychology, Health & Medicine* 11(1):70–79. http://doi.org/10.1080/13548500500093696/.

Peipert, J. F., T. Madden, J. E. Allsworth, and G. M. Secura. 2012. "Preventing Unintended Pregnancies by Providing No-Cost Contraception." *Obstetrics and Gynecology* 120(6):1291–1297.

Perrin, K. (Kay), and S. B. DeJoy. 2003. "Abstinence-Only Education: How We Got Here and Where We're Going." *Journal of Public Health Policy* 24(3):445–459. http://doi.org/10.2307/3343387/.

Santelli, J., M. A. Ott, M. Lyon, J. Rogers, D. Summers, and R. Schleifer. 2006. "Abstinence and Abstinence-Only Education: A Review of U.S. Policies and Programs." *Journal of Adolescent Health* 38(1):72–81. http://doi.org/10.1016/j.jadohealth.2005.10.006/.

Schalet, A. T., J. S. Santelli, S. T. Russell, C. T. Halpern, S. A. Miller, S. S. Pickering, S. K. Goldberg, and J. M. Hoenig. 2014. "Invited Commentary: Broadening the Evidence for Adolescent Sexual and Reproductive Health and Education in the United States." *Journal of Youth and Adolescence* 43(10):1595–1610. http://doi.org/10.1007/s10964-014-0178-8/.

Scott-Sheldon, L. A. J., D. E. Glasford, K. L. Marsh, and S. A. Lust. 2006. "Barriers to Condom Purchasing: Effects of Product Positioning on Reactions to Condoms." *Social Science & Medicine* 63(11):2755–2769. http://doi.org/10.1016/j.socscimed.2006.07.007/.

Sexuality Information and Education Council of the United States (SIECUS). 2010. "A History of Federal Abstinence-Only-Until-Marriage Funding FY10." Retrieved from http://www.siecus.org/index.cfm?fuseaction=page.viewpage&pageid=1340&nodeid=1

Sieving, R. E., C. S. McNeely, and R. M. Blum. 2000. "Maternal Expectations, Mother–Child Connectedness, and Adolescent Sexual Debut." *Archives of Pediatrics & Adolescent Medicine* 154(8):809–816. http://doi.org/10.1001/archpedi.154.8.809/.

Social Security Act, Section 510 [42 U.S.C. 710], 1996. "Separate Program for Abstinence Education." Retrieved April 28, 2015, from http://www.ssa.gov/OP_Home/ssact/title05/0510.htm/.

Stanger-Hall, K. F., and D. W. Hall. 2011. "Abstinence-Only Education and Teen Pregnancy Rates: Why We Need Comprehensive Sex Education in the U.S." *PLoS ONE* 6(10):e24658. http://doi.org/10.1371/journal.pone.0024658/.

Tolman, D. L. 2009. *Dilemmas of Desire: Teenage Girls Talk about Sexuality*. Cambridge, MA: Harvard University Press.

Tolosa, A. 2012. *Using Targeted Facebook Ads to Link Youth to Take Action in Their Health*. Presented at the 2012 National Conference on Health Communication, Marketing, and Media, CDC. Retrieved from https://cdc.confex.com/cdc/nphic12/webprogram/Paper31401.html/.

Trenholm, C., B. Devaney, K. Fortson, M. Clark, L. Quay, and J. Wheeler. 2008. "Impacts of Abstinence Education on Teen Sexual Activity, Risk of Pregnancy, and Risk of Sexually Transmitted Diseases." *Journal of Policy Analysis and Management* 27(2):255–276. http://doi.org/10.1002/pam.20324/.

U.S. Department of Health and Human Services Office of Adolescent Health. 2015. "Trends in Teen Pregnancy and Childbearing." Retrieved from http://www.hhs.gov/ash/oah/adolescent-health-topics/reproductive-health/teen-pregnancy/trends.html.

Wiederman, M. W. 2005. "The Gendered Nature of Sexual Scripts." *The Family Journal* 13(4):496–502. http://doi.org/10.1177/1066480705278729/.

One Town's War on Gay Teens

SABRINA RUBIN ERDELY

Erdely discusses how anti-gay education policies (sponsored by conservative religious groups), coupled with homophobia in the community and among students, led to rampant bullying and subsequent suicides of LGBT students in one school district in Minnesota.

Every morning, Brittany Geldert stepped off the bus and bolted through the double doors of Fred Moore Middle School, her nerves already on high alert, bracing for the inevitable.

"Dyke."

Pretending not to hear, Brittany would walk briskly to her locker, past the sixth-, seventh- and eighth-graders who loitered in menacing packs.

"Whore."

Like many 13-year-olds, Brittany knew seventh grade was a living hell. But what she didn't know was that she was caught in the crossfire of a culture war being waged by local evangelicals inspired by their high-profile congressional representative Michele Bachmann, who graduated from Anoka High School and, until recently, was a member of one of the most conservative churches in the area. When Christian activists who considered gays an abomination forced a measure through the school board forbidding the discussion of homosexuality in the district's public schools, kids like Brittany were unknowingly thrust into the heart of a clash that was about to become intertwined with tragedy.

Brittany didn't look like most girls in blue-collar Anoka, Minnesota, a former logging town on the Rum River, a conventional place that takes pride in its annual Halloween parade—it bills itself the "Halloween Capital of the World." Brittany was a low-voiced, stocky girl who dressed in baggy jeans and her dad's Marine Corps sweatshirts. By age 13, she'd been taunted as a "cunt" and "cock muncher" long before such words had made much sense. When she told administrators about the abuse, they were strangely unresponsive, even though bullying was a subject often discussed in school-board meetings. The district maintained a comprehensive five-page anti-bullying policy, and held diversity trainings on racial and gender sensitivity. Yet when it came to Brittany's harassment, school officials usually told her to ignore it, always glossing over the sexually charged insults. Like the time Brittany had complained about being called a "fat dyke": The school's principal, looking pained, had suggested Brittany prepare herself for the next round of teasing with snappy comebacks—"I can lose the weight, but you're stuck with your

Reprinted by Permission of Sabrina Rubin Erdely from *Rolling Stone*, originally published in print on February 16, 2012 (Issue 1150) as "School of Hate."

ugly face"—never acknowledging she had been called a "dyke." As though that part was OK. As though the fact that Brittany was bisexual made her fair game.

So maybe she *was* a fat dyke, Brittany thought morosely; maybe she deserved the teasing. She would have been shocked to know the truth behind the adults' inaction: No one would come to her aid for fear of violating the districtwide policy requiring school personnel to stay "neutral" on issues of homosexuality. All Brittany knew was that she was on her own, vulnerable and ashamed, and needed to find her best friend, Samantha, fast.

Like Brittany, eighth-grader Samantha Johnson was a husky tomboy too, outgoing with a big smile and a silly streak to match Brittany's own. Sam was also bullied for her look—short hair, dark clothing, lack of girly affect—but she merrily shrugged off the abuse. When Sam's volleyball teammates' taunting got rough—barring her from the girls' locker room, yelling, "You're a guy!"—she simply stopped going to practice. After school, Sam would encourage Brittany to join her in privately mocking their tormentors, and the girls would parade around Brittany's house speaking in Valley Girl squeals, wearing bras over their shirts, collapsing in laughter. They'd become as close as sisters in the year since Sam had moved from North Dakota following her parents' divorce, and Sam had quickly become Brittany's beacon. Sam was even helping to start a Gay Straight Alliance [GSA] club, as a safe haven for misfits like them, although the club's progress was stalled by the school district that, among other things, was queasy about the club's flagrant use of the word "gay." Religious conservatives have called GSAs "sex clubs," and sure enough, the local religious right loudly objected to them. "This is an assault on moral standards," read one recent letter to the community paper. "Let's stop this dangerous nonsense before it's too late and more young boys and girls are encouraged to 'come out' and practice their 'gayness' right in their own school's homosexual club."

Brittany admired Sam's courage, and tried to mimic her insouciance and stoicism. So Brittany was bewildered when one day in November 2009, on the school bus home, a sixth-grade boy slid in next to her and asked quaveringly, "Did you hear Sam said she's going to kill herself?"

Brittany considered the question. No way. How many times had she seen Sam roll her eyes and announce, "Ugh, I'm gonna kill myself" over some insignificant thing? "Don't worry, you'll see Sam tomorrow," Brittany reassured her friend as they got off the bus. But as she trudged toward her house, she couldn't stop turning it over in her mind. A boy in the district had already committed suicide just days into the school year—TJ Hayes, a 16-year-old at Blaine High School—so she knew such things were possible. But *Sam Johnson*? Brittany tried to keep the thought at bay. Finally, she confided in her mother.

"This isn't something you kid about, Brittany," her mom scolded, snatching the kitchen cordless and taking it down the hall to call the Johnsons. A minute later she returned, her face a mask of shock and terror. "Honey, I'm so sorry. We're too late," she said tonelessly as Brittany's knees buckled; 13-year-old Sam had climbed into the bathtub after school and shot herself in the mouth with her own hunting rifle. No one at school had seen her suicide coming.

No one saw the rest of them coming, either.

Sam's death lit the fuse of a suicide epidemic that would take the lives of nine local students in under two years, a rate so high that child psychologist Dan Reidenberg, executive director of the Minnesota-based Suicide Awareness Voices of Education, declared the Anoka–Hennepin school district the site of a "suicide cluster," adding that the crisis might hold an element of contagion; suicidal thoughts had become catchy, like a lethal virus. "Here you had a large number of suicides that are really closely connected, all within one school district, in a small amount of time," explains Reidenberg. "Kids started to feel that the normal response to stress was to take your life."

There was another common thread: Four of the nine dead were either gay or perceived as such by other kids, and were reportedly bullied. The tragedies come at a national moment when bullying is on everyone's lips, and a devastating number of gay teens across the country are in the news for killing themselves. Suicide rates among gay and lesbian kids are frighteningly high, with attempt rates four times that of their straight counterparts; studies show that one-third of all gay youth have attempted suicide at some point (versus 13 percent of hetero kids), and that internalized homophobia contributes to suicide risk.

Against this supercharged backdrop, the Anoka–Hennepin school district finds itself in the spotlight not only for the sheer number of suicides but because it is accused of having contributed to the death toll by cultivating an extreme anti-gay climate. "LGBTQ students don't feel safe at school," says Anoka Middle School for the Arts teacher Jefferson Fietek, using the acronym for Lesbian, Gay, Bisexual, Transgender and Questioning. "They're made to feel ashamed of who they are. They're bullied. And there's no one to stand up for them, because teachers are afraid of being fired."

The Southern Poverty Law Center and the National Center for Lesbian Rights have filed a lawsuit on behalf of five students, alleging the school district's policies on gays are not only discriminatory, but also foster an environment of unchecked anti-gay bullying. The Department of Justice has begun a civil rights investigation as well. The Anoka–Hennepin school district declined to comment on any specific incidences but denies any discrimination, maintaining that its broad anti-bullying policy is meant to protect all students. "We are not a homophobic district, and to be vilified for this is very frustrating," says superintendent Dennis Carlson, who blames right-wingers and gay activists for choosing the area as a battleground, describing the district as the victim in this fracas. "People are using kids as pawns in this political debate," he says. "I find that abhorrent."

Ironically, that's exactly the charge that students, teachers and grieving parents are hurling at the school district. "Samantha got caught up in a political battle that I didn't know about," says Sam Johnson's mother, Michele. "And you know whose fault it is? The people who make their living off of saying they're going to take care of our kids."

Located a half-hour north of Minneapolis, the 13 sprawling towns that make up the Anoka–Hennepin school district—Minnesota's largest, with 39,000 kids—seems an unlikely place for such a battle. It's a soothingly flat, 172-square-mile expanse sliced by the Mississippi River, where woodlands abruptly give way to strip malls and then fall back to placid woodlands again, and the landscape is dotted with churches. The district, which spans two counties, is so geographically huge as to be a sort of cross section of America itself, with its small minority population clustered at its southern tip, white suburban sprawl in its center and sparsely populated farmland in the north. It also offers a snapshot of America in economic crisis: In an area where just 20 percent of adults have college educations, the recession hit hard, and foreclosures and unemployment have become the norm.

For years, the area has also bred a deep strain of religious conservatism. At churches like First Baptist Church of Anoka, parishioners believe that homosexuality is a form of mental illness caused by family dysfunction, childhood trauma and exposure to pornography—a perversion curable through intensive therapy. It's a point of view shared by their congresswoman Michele Bachmann, who has called homosexuality a form of "sexual dysfunction" that amounts to "personal enslavement." In 1993, Bachmann, a proponent of school prayer and creationism, co-founded the New Heights charter school in the town of Stillwater, only to flee the board amid an outcry that the school was promoting a religious curriculum. Bachmann also is affiliated with the ultraright Minnesota Family Council [MFC], headlining a fundraiser for them . . . alongside Newt Gingrich.

Though Bachmann doesn't live within Anoka–Hennepin's boundaries anymore, she has a dowdier doppelgänger there in the form of anti-gay crusader Barb Anderson. A bespectacled grandmother with lemony-blond hair she curls in severely toward her face, Anderson is a former district Spanish teacher and a longtime researcher for the MFC who's been fighting gay influence in local schools for two decades, ever since she discovered that her nephew's health class was teaching homosexuality as normal. "That really got me on a journey," she said in a radio interview. When the Anoka–Hennepin district's sex-ed curriculum came up for re-evaluation in 1994, Anderson and four like-minded parents managed to get on the review committee. They argued that any form of gay tolerance in school is actually an insidious means of promoting homosexuality—that openly discussing the matter would encourage kids to try it, turning straight kids gay.

"Open your eyes, people," Anderson recently wrote to the local newspaper. "What if a 15-year-old is seduced into homosexual behavior and then contracts AIDS?" Her agenda mimics that of Focus on the Family, the national evangelical Christian organization founded by James Dobson; Family Councils, though technically independent of Focus on the Family, work on the state level to accomplish Focus' core goals, including promoting prayer in public spaces, "defending marriage" by lobbying for anti-gay legislation, and fighting gay tolerance in public schools under the guise of preserving parental authority—reasoning that government-mandated acceptance of gays undermines the traditional values taught in Christian homes.

At the close of the seven-month-long sex-ed review, Anderson and her colleagues wrote a memo to the Anoka–Hennepin school board, concluding, "The majority of parents do not wish to have there [sic] children taught that the gay lifestyle is a normal acceptable alternative." Surprisingly, the six-member board voted to adopt the measure by a four-to-two majority, even borrowing the memo's language to fashion the resulting districtwide policy, which pronounced that within the health curriculum, "homosexuality not be taught/addressed as a normal, valid lifestyle."

The policy became unofficially known as "No Homo Promo" and passed unannounced to parents and unpublished in the policy handbooks; most teachers were told about it by their principals. Teachers say it had a chilling effect and they became concerned about mentioning gays in any context. Discussion of homosexuality gradually disappeared from classes. "If you can't talk about it in any context, which is how teachers interpret district policies, kids internalize that to mean that being gay must be so shameful and wrong," says Anoka High School teacher Mary Jo Merrick-Lockett. "And that has created a climate of fear and repression and harassment."

Suicide is a complex phenomenon; there's never any one pat reason to explain why anyone kills themselves. Michele Johnson acknowledges that her daughter, Sam, likely had many issues that combined to push her over the edge, but feels strongly that bullying was one of those factors. "I'm sure that Samantha's decision to take her life had a lot to do with what was going on in school," Johnson says tearfully. "I'm sure things weren't perfect in other areas, but nothing was as bad as what was going on in that school."

The summer before Justin Aaberg started at Anoka High School, his mother asked, "So, are you sure you're gay?"

Justin, a slim, shy 14-year-old who carefully swept his blond bangs to the side . . . studied his mom's face. "I'm pretty sure I'm gay," he answered softly, then abruptly changed his mind. "*Whoa, whoa, whoa, wait!*" he shouted—out of character for the quiet boy—"I'm positive. I am gay," Justin proclaimed.

"OK." Tammy Aaberg nodded. "So. Just because you can't get him pregnant doesn't mean you don't use protection." She proceeded to lecture her son about safe sex while Justin turned bright red and beamed. Embarrassing as it was to get a sex talk from his mom, her easy affirmation of Justin's orientation seemed like a promising sign as he stood on the brink of high school. Justin was more than ready to turn the corner on the horrors of middle school—especially on his just-finished eighth-grade year, when Justin had come out as gay to a few friends, yet word had instantly spread, making him a pariah. In the hall one day, a popular jock had grabbed Justin by the balls and squeezed, sneering, "You like that, don't you?" That assault had so humiliated and frightened Justin that he'd burst out crying, but he never reported any of his harassment. The last thing he wanted to do was draw more attention to his sexuality. Plus, he didn't want his parents worrying. Justin's folks were already overwhelmed with stresses of their own: Swamped with debt, they'd declared bankruptcy and lost their home to foreclosure. So Justin had kept his problems to himself; he felt hopeful things would get better in high school, where kids were bound to be more mature.

"There'll always be bullies," he reasoned to a friend. "But we'll be older, so maybe they'll be better about it."

But Justin's start of ninth grade in 2009 began as a disappointment. In the halls of Anoka High School, he was bullied, called a "faggot" and shoved into lockers. Then, a couple of months into the school year, he was stunned to hear about Sam Johnson's suicide. Though Justin hadn't known her personally, he'd known of her, and of the way she'd been taunted for being butch. Justin tried to keep smiling. In his room at home, Justin made a brightly colored paper banner and taped it to his wall: "Love the life you live, live the life you love."

Brittany couldn't stop thinking about Sam, a reel that looped endlessly in her head. Sam dancing to one of their favorite metal bands, Drowning Pool. Sam dead in the tub with the back of her head blown off. Sam's ashes in an urn, her coffin empty at her wake.

She couldn't sleep. Her grades fell. Her daily harassment at school continued, but now without her best friend to help her cope. At home, Brittany played the good daughter, cleaning the house and performing her brother's chores unasked, all in a valiant attempt to maintain some family peace after the bank took their house, and both parents lost their jobs in quick succession. Then Brittany started cutting herself.

Just 11 days after Sam's death, on November 22nd, 2009, came yet another suicide: a Blaine High School student, 15-year-old Aaron Jurek—the district's third suicide in just three months. After Christmas break, an Andover High School senior, Nick Lockwood, became the district's fourth casualty: a boy who had never publicly identified as gay, but had nonetheless been teased as such. Suicide number five followed, that of recent Blaine High School grad Kevin Buchman, who had no apparent LGBT connection. Before the end of the school year there would be a sixth suicide, 15-year-old July Barrick of Champlin Park High School, who was also bullied for being perceived as gay, and who'd complained to her mother that classmates had started an "I Hate July Barrick" Facebook page. As mental-health counselors were hurriedly dispatched to each affected school, the district was blanketed by a sense of mourning and frightened shock.

"It has taken a collective toll," says Northdale Middle School psychologist Colleen Cashen. "Everyone has just been reeling—students, teachers. There's been just a profound sadness."

In the wake of Sam's suicide, Brittany couldn't seem to stop crying. She'd disappear for hours with her cellphone turned off, taking long walks by Elk Creek or hiding in a nearby cemetery. "Promise me you won't take your life," her father begged. "Promise you'll come to me before anything." Brittany couldn't promise. In March 2010, she was hospitalized for a week.

In April, Justin came home from school and found his mother at the top of the stairs, tending to the saltwater fish tank. "Mom," he said tentatively, "a kid told me at school today I'm gonna go to hell because I'm gay."

"That's not true. God loves everybody," his mom replied. "That kid needs to go home and read his Bible."

Justin shrugged and smiled, then retreated to his room. It had been a hard day: the annual "Day of Truth" had been held at school, an evangelical event then-sponsored by the anti-gay ministry Exodus International, whose mission is to usher gays back to wholeness and "victory in Christ" by converting them to heterosexuality. Day of Truth has been a font of controversy that has bounced in and out of the courts; its legality was affirmed last March, when a federal appeals court ruled that two Naperville, Illinois, high school students' Day of Truth T-shirts reading BE HAPPY, NOT GAY were protected by their First Amendment rights. (However, the event, now sponsored by Focus on the Family, has been renamed "Day of Dialogue.") Local churches had been touting the program, and students had obediently shown up at Anoka High School wearing Day of Truth T-shirts, preaching in the halls about the sin of homosexuality. Justin wanted to brush them off, but was troubled by their proselytizing. Secretly, he had begun to worry that maybe he was an abomination, like the Bible said.

Justin was trying not to care what anyone else thought and be true to himself. He surrounded himself with a bevy of girlfriends who cherished him for his sweet, sunny disposition. He played cello in the orchestra, practicing for hours up in his room, where he'd covered one wall with mementos of good times: taped-up movie-ticket stubs, gum wrappers, Christmas cards. Justin had even briefly dated a boy, a 17-year-old he'd met online who attended a nearby high school. The relationship didn't end well: The boyfriend had cheated on him, and compounding Justin's hurt, his coming out had earned Justin hateful Facebook messages from other teens—some from those he didn't even know—telling him he was a fag who didn't deserve to live. At least his freshman year of high school was nearly done. Only three more years to go. He wondered how he would ever make it.

Though some members of the Anoka–Hennepin school board had been appalled by "No Homo Promo" since its passage 14 years earlier, it wasn't until 2009 that the board brought the policy up for review, after a student named Alex Merritt filed a complaint with the state Department of Human Rights claiming he'd been gay-bashed by two of his teachers during high school; according to the complaint, the teachers had announced in front of students that Merritt, who is straight, "swings both ways," speculated that he wore women's clothing, and compared him to a Wisconsin man who had sex with a dead deer. The teachers denied the charges, but the school district paid $25,000 to settle the complaint. Soon representatives from the gay-rights group Outfront Minnesota began making inquiries at board meetings. "No Homo Promo" was starting to look like a risky policy.

"The lawyers said, 'You'd have a hard time defending it,'" remembers Scott Wenzel, a board member who for years had pushed colleagues to abolish the policy. "It was clear that it might risk a lawsuit." But while board members agreed that such an overtly anti-gay policy needed to be scrapped, they also agreed that some guideline was needed to not only help teachers navigate a topic as inflammatory as homosexuality but to appease the area's evangelical activists. So the legal department wrote a broad new course of action with language intended to give a respect-ful nod to the topic—but also an equal measure of respect to the anti-gay contingent. The new policy was circulated to staff without a word of introduction. (Parents were not alerted at all, unless they happened to be diligent online read-ers of board-meeting minutes.) And while "No Homo Promo" had at least been clear, the new Sexual Orientation Curriculum Policy mostly just puzzled the teachers who'd be responsible for enforcing it. It read:

> *Anoka–Hennepin staff, in the course of their professional duties, shall remain neu-tral on matters regarding sexual orienta-tion including but not limited to student-led discussions.*

It quickly became known as the "neutrality" policy. No one could figure out what it meant. "What is 'neutral'?" asks instructor Merrick-Lockett. "Teachers are constantly asking, 'Do you think I could get in trouble for this? Could I get fired for that?' So a lot of teachers sidestep it. They don't want to deal with district backlash."

English teachers worried they'd get in trouble for teaching books by gay authors, or books with gay characters. Social-studies teachers wondered what to do if a student wrote a term paper on gay rights, or how to address current events like "don't ask, don't tell"[1]. Health teachers were faced with the impossible task of teaching about AIDS awareness and safe sex without mentioning homosexuality. Many teachers decided once again to keep gay issues from the curriculum altogether, rather than chance saying something that could be interpreted as anything other than neutral.

"There has been widespread confusion," says Anoka–Hennepin teachers' union president Julie Blaha. "You ask five people how to interpret the policy and you get five different answers." Silenced by fear, gay teachers became more vigilant than ever to avoid mention of their personal lives, and in closeting themselves, they inadvertently ensured that many students had no real-life gay role models. "I was told by teachers, 'You have to be careful, it's really not safe for you to come out,'" says the psychologist Cashen, who is a lesbian. "I felt like I couldn't have a picture of my family on my desk." When teacher Jefferson Fietek was outed in the community paper, which referred to him as an "open homosexual," he didn't feel he could address the situation with his students even as they passed the newspaper around, tittering. When one finally asked, "Are you gay?" he panicked. "I was terrified to answer that question," Fietek says. "I thought, 'If I violate the policy, what's going to happen to me?'"

The silence of adults was deafening. At Blaine High School, says alum Justin Anderson, "I would hear people calling people 'fags' all the time without it being addressed. Teachers just didn't respond." In Andover High School, when 10th-grader Sam Pinilla was pushed to the ground by three kids calling him a "faggot," he saw a teacher nearby who did nothing to stop the assault. At Anoka High School, a 10th-grade girl became so upset at being mocked as a "lesbo" and a "sinner"—in earshot of teachers—that she complained to an associate principal, who counseled her to "lay low"; the girl would later attempt suicide. At Anoka Middle School for the Arts, after Kyle Rooker was urinated upon from above in a boys' bathroom stall, an associate principal told him, "It was probably water." Jackson Middle School seventh-grader Dylon Frei was passed notes saying, "Get out of this town, fag"; when a teacher intercepted one such note, she simply threw it away.

"You feel horrible about yourself," remembers Dylon. "Like, why do these kids hate me so much? And why won't anybody help me?" The following year, after Dylon was hit in the head with a binder and called "fag," the associate principal told Dylon that since there was no proof of the incident she could take no action. By contrast, Dylon and others saw how the same teachers who ignored anti-gay insults were quick to reprimand kids who uttered racial slurs. It further reinforced the message resonating throughout the district: Gay kids simply didn't deserve protection.

"Justin?" Tammy Aaberg rapped on her son's locked bedroom door again. It was past noon, and not a peep from inside, unusual for Justin.

"Justin?" She could hear her own voice rising as she pounded harder, suddenly overtaken by a wild terror she couldn't name. "Justin!" she yelled. Tammy grabbed a screwdriver and loosened the doorknob. She pushed open the door. He was wearing his Anoka High School sweatpants and an old soccer shirt. His feet were dangling off the ground. Justin was hanging from the frame of his futon, which he'd taken out from under his mattress and stood upright in the corner of his room. Screaming, Tammy ran to hold him and recoiled at his cold skin. His limp body was grotesquely bloated—her baby—eyes closed, head lolling to the right, a dried smear of saliva trailing from the corner of his mouth. His cheeks were strafed with scratch marks, as though in his final moments he'd tried to claw his noose loose. He'd cinched the woven belt so tight that the mortician would have a hard time masking the imprint it left in the flesh above Justin's collar.

Still screaming, Tammy ran to call 911. She didn't notice the cellphone on the floor below Justin's feet, containing his last words, a text he had typed to a girlfriend in the wee hours:

:-(
What's wrong
Nothing
I can come over
No i'm fine
Are you sure you'll be ok
No it's ok i'll be fine, i promise

Seeking relief from bullying, Brittany transferred to Jackson Middle School. Her very first day of eighth grade, eight boys crowded around her on the bus home. "Hey, Brittany, I heard your friend Sam shot herself," one began.

"Did you see her blow her brains out?"

"Did you pull the trigger for her?"

"What did it look like?"

"Was there brain all over the wall?"

"You should do it too. You should go blow your head off."

Sobbing, Brittany ran from the bus stop and into her mother's arms. Her mom called Jackson's guidance office to report the incident, but as before, nothing ever seemed to come of their complaints. Not after the Gelderts' Halloween lawn decorations were destroyed, and the boys on the bus asked, "How was the mess last night?" Not after Brittany told the associate principal about the mob of kids who pushed her down the hall and nearly into a trash can. Her name became Dyke, Queer, Faggot, Guy, Freak, Transvestite, Bitch, Cunt, Slut,

Whore, Skank, Prostitute, Hooker. Brittany felt worn to a nub, exhausted from scanning for threat, stripped of emotional armor. In her journal, she wrote, "Brittany is dead."

As Brittany vainly cried out for help, the school board was busy trying to figure out how to continue tactfully ignoring the existence of LGBT kids like her. Justin Aaberg's suicide, Anoka–Hennepin's seventh, had sent the district into damage-control mode. "Everything changed after Justin," remembers teacher Fietek. "The rage at his funeral, students were storming up to me saying, 'Why the hell did the school let this happen? They let it happen to Sam and they let it happen to Justin!'" Individual teachers quietly began taking small risks, overstepping the bounds of neutrality to offer solace to gay students in crisis. "My job is just a job; these children are losing their lives," says Fietek. "The story I hear repeatedly is 'Nobody else is like me, nobody else is going through what I'm going through.' That's the lie they've been fed, but they're buying into it based on the fear we have about open and honest conversations about sexual orientation."

LGBT students were stunned to be told for the first time about the existence of the neutrality policy that had been responsible for their teachers' behavior. But no one was more outraged to hear of it than Tammy Aaberg. Six weeks after her son's death, Aaberg became the first to publicly confront the Anoka–Hennepin school board about the link between the policy, anti-gay bullying and suicide. She demanded the policy be revoked. "What about my parental rights to have my gay son go to school and learn without being bullied?" Aaberg asked, weeping, as the board stared back impassively from behind a raised dais.

Anti-gay backlash was instant. Minnesota Family Council president Tom Prichard blogged that Justin's suicide could only be blamed upon one thing: his gayness. "Youth who embrace homosexuality are at greater risk [of suicide], because they've embraced an unhealthy sexual identity and lifestyle," Prichard wrote. Anoka–

Hennepin conservatives formally organized into the Parents Action League [PAL], declaring opposition to the "radical homosexual" agenda in schools. Its stated goals, advertised on its website, included promoting Day of Truth, providing resources for students "seeking to leave the homosexual lifestyle," supporting the neutrality policy and targeting "pro-gay activist teachers who fail to abide by district policies."

Asked on a radio program whether the anti-gay agenda of her ilk bore any responsibility for the bullying and suicides, Barb Anderson, co-author of the original "No Homo Promo," held fast to her principles, blaming *pro-gay* groups for the tragedies. She explained that such "child corruption" agencies allow "quote-unquote gay kids" to wrongly feel legitimized. "And then these kids are locked into a lifestyle with their choices limited, and many times this can be disastrous to them as they get into the behavior which leads to disease and death," Anderson said. She added that if LGBT kids weren't encouraged to come out of the closet in the first place, they wouldn't be in a position to be bullied.

Yet while everyone in the district was buzzing about the neutrality policy, the board simply refused to discuss it, not even when students began appearing before them to detail their experiences with LGBT harassment. "The board stated quite clearly that they were standing behind that policy and were not willing to take another look," recalls board member Wenzel. Further insulating itself from reality, the district launched an investigation into the suicides and unsurprisingly, absolved itself of any responsibility. "Based on all the information we've been able to gather," read a statement from the superintendent's office, "none of the suicides were connected to incidents of bullying or harassment."

Just to be on the safe side, however, the district held PowerPoint presentations in a handful of schools to train teachers how to defend gay students from harassment while also remaining neutral on homosexuality. One slide instructed teachers that if they hear gay slurs—say, the word "fag"—the best response is a tepid "That language is unacceptable in this school." ("If a more authoritative response is needed," the slide added, the teacher could continue with the stilted, almost apologetic explanation, "In this school we are required to welcome all people and to make them feel safe.") But teachers were, of course, reminded to never show "personal support for GLBT people" in the classroom.

Teachers left the training sessions more confused than ever about how to interpret the rules. And the board, it turned out, was equally confused. When a local advocacy group, Gay Equity Team [GET], met with the school board, the vice-chair thought the policy applied only to health classes, while the chair asserted it applied to all curricula; and when the district legal counsel commented that some discussions about homosexuality were allowed, yet another board member expressed surprise, saying he thought any discussion on the topic was forbidden. "How can the district ever train on a policy they do not understand themselves?" GET officials asked in a follow-up letter. "Is there any doubt that teachers and staff are confused? The board is confused!"

With the adults thus distracted by endless policy discussions, the entire district became a place of dread for students. Every time a loudspeaker crackled in class, kids braced themselves for the feared preamble, "We've had a tragic loss." Students spoke in hushed tones; some wept openly in the halls. "It had that feeling of a horror movie—everyone was talking about death," says one 16-year-old student who broke down at Anoka High School one day and was carted off to a psychiatric hospital for suicidal ideation. Over the course of the 2010–2011 school year, 700 students were evaluated for serious mental-health issues, including hospitalizations for depression and suicide attempts. Kids flooded school counselors' offices, which reported an explosion of children engaging in dangerous behaviors like cutting or asphyxiating each other in the "choking game."

Amid the pandemonium, the district's eighth suicide landed like a bomb: Cole Wilson, an Anoka High School senior with no apparent LGBT connection. The news was frightening, but also horrifyingly familiar. "People were dying one after another," remembers former district student Katie MacDonald, 16, who struggled with suicidal thoughts. "Every time you said goodbye to a friend, you felt like, 'Is this the last time I'm going to see you?'"

As a late-afternoon storm beats against the windows, 15-year-old Brittany Geldert sits in her living room. Her layered auburn hair falls into her face. Her ears are lined with piercings; her nail polish is black. "They said I had anger, depression, suicidal ideation, anxiety, an eating disorder," she recites, speaking of the month she spent at a psychiatric hospital last year, at the end of eighth grade. "Mentally being degraded like that, I translated that to 'I don't deserve to be happy,'" she says, barely holding back tears, as both parents look on with wet eyes. "Like I deserved the punishment—I've been earning the punishment I've been getting."

She's fighting hard to rebuild her decimated sense of self. It's a far darker self than before, a guarded, distant teenager who bears little resemblance to the openhearted young girl she was not long ago. But Brittany is also finding a reserve of strength she never realized she had, having stepped up as one of five plaintiffs in the civil rights lawsuit against her school district. The road to the federal lawsuit was paved shortly after Justin Aaberg's suicide, when a district teacher contacted the Southern Poverty Law Center to report the anti-gay climate, and the startling proportion of LGBT-related suicide victims. After months of fact-finding, lawyers built a case based on the harrowing stories of anti-gay harassment in order to legally dispute Anoka–Hennepin's neutrality policy. The lawsuit accuses the district of violating the kids' constitutional rights to equal access to education. In addition to making financial demands, the lawsuit seeks to repeal the neutrality policy, implement LGBT-sensitivity training for students and staff, and

provide guidance for teachers on how to respond to anti-gay bullying.

The school district hasn't been anxious for a legal brawl, and the two parties have been in settlement talks practically since the papers were filed. Yet the district still stubbornly clung to the neutrality policy until, at a mid-December school-board meeting, it proposed finally eliminating the policy—claiming the move has nothing to do with the discrimination lawsuit—and, bizarrely, replacing it with the Controversial Topics Curriculum Policy, which requires teachers to not reveal their personal opinions when discussing "controversial topics." The proposal was loudly rejected both by conservatives, who blasted the board for retreating ("The gay activists now have it all," proclaimed one Parents Action League member) and by LGBT advocates, who understood "controversial topics" to mean gays. Faced with such overwhelming disapproval, the board withdrew its proposed policy in January—and suggested a new policy in its place: the Respectful Learning Environment Curriculum Policy, which the board is expected to swiftly approve.

The school district insists it has been portrayed unfairly. Superintendent Carlson points out it has been working hard to address the mental-health needs of its students by hiring more counselors and staff—everything, it seems, but admit that its policy has created problems for its LGBT community. "We understand that gay kids are bullied and harassed on a daily basis," and that that can lead to suicide, Carlson says. "But that was not the case here. If you're looking for a cause, look in the area of mental health." In that sense, the district is in step with PAL. "How could not discussing homosexuality in the public-school classrooms cause a teen to take his or her own life?" PAL asked *Rolling Stone* in an e-mail, calling the idea "absurd," going on to say, "Because homosexual activists have hijacked and exploited teen suicides for their moral and political utility, much of society seems not to be looking closely and openly at all the possible causes of the tragedies," including mental illness. Arguably, however, it is members of PAL who have hijacked this entire discussion from the very start: Though they've claimed to represent the "majority" opinion on gay issues, and say they have 1,200 supporters, one PAL parent reported that they have less than two dozen members.

Teachers' union president Blaha, who calls the district's behavior throughout this ordeal "irrational," speculates that the district's stupefying denial is a reaction to the terrible notion that they might have played a part in children's suffering, or even their deaths: "I think your mind just reels in the face of that stress and that horror. They just lost their way."

That denial reaches right up to the pinnacle of the local political food chain: Michele Bachmann, who stayed silent on the suicide cluster in her congressional district for months—until Justin's mom, Tammy Aaberg, forced her to comment. In September, while Bachmann was running for the GOP presidential nomination, Aaberg delivered a petition of 141,000 signatures to Bachmann's office, asking her to address the Anoka–Hennepin suicides and publicly denounce anti-gay bullying. Bachmann has publicly stated her opposition to anti-bullying legislation, asking in a 2006 state Senate committee hearing, "What will be our definition of bullying? Will it get to the point where we are completely stifling free speech and expression? . . . Will we be expecting boys to be girls?" Bachmann responded to the petition with a generic letter to constituents telling them that "bullying is wrong," and "all human lives have undeniable value." Tammy Aaberg found out about the letter secondhand. "I never got a letter," says Tammy, seated in the finished basement of the Aabergs' new home in Champlin; the family couldn't bear to remain in the old house where Justin hanged himself. "My kid died in her district. And I'm the one that presented the dang petition!" In a closed room a few feet away are Justin's remaining possessions: his cello, in a closet; his soccer equipment, still packed in his Adidas bag. Tammy's suffering

hasn't ended. In mid-December, her nine-year-old son was hospitalized for suicidal tendencies; he'd tried to drown himself in the bathtub, wanting to see his big brother again.

Justin's suicide has left Tammy on a mission, transforming her into an LGBT activist and a den mother for gay teens, intent upon turning her own tragedy into others' salvation. She knows too well the price of indifference, or hostility, or denial. Because there's one group of kids who can't afford to live in denial, a group for whom the usual raw teenage struggles over identity, peer acceptance and controlling one's own impulsivity are matters of extreme urgency—quite possibly matters of life or death.

Which brings us to Anoka Middle School for the Arts' first Gay Straight Alliance [GSA] meeting of the school year, where 19 kids seated on the linoleum floor try to explain to me what the GSA has meant to them. "It's a place of freedom, where I can just be myself," a preppy boy in basketball shorts says. This GSA, Sam Johnson's legacy, held its first meeting shortly after her death under the tutelage of teacher Fietek, and has been a crucial place for LGBT kids and their friends to find support and learn coping skills. Though still a source of local controversy, there is now a student-initiated GSA in every Anoka–Hennepin middle and high school. As three advisers look on, the kids gush about how affirming the club is—and how necessary, in light of how unsafe they continue to feel at school. "I'll still get bullied to the point where—" begins a skinny eighth-grade girl, then takes a breath. "I actually had to go to the hospital for suicide," she continues, looking at the floor. "I just recently stopped cutting because of bullying."

I ask for a show of hands: How many of you feel safe at school? Of the 19 kids assembled, two raise their hands. The feeling of insecurity continues to reverberate particularly through the Anoka–Hennepin middle schools these days, in the wake of the district's ninth suicide. In May, Northdale Middle School's Jordan Yenor, a 14-year-old with no evident LGBT connection, took his life. Psychologist Cashen says that at

Northdale Middle alone this school year, several students have been hospitalized for mental-health issues, and at least 14 more assessed for suicidal ideation; for a quarter of them, she says, "Sexual orientation was in the mix."

A slight boy with an asymmetrical haircut speaks in a soft voice. "What this GSA means to me, is: In sixth grade my, my only friend here, committed suicide." The room goes still. He's talking about Samantha. The boy starts to cry. "She was the one who reached out to me." He doubles over in tears, and everyone collapses on top of him in a group hug. From somewhere in the pile, he continues to speak in a trembling voice: "I joined the GSA 'cause I wanted to be just like her. I wanted to be nice and—loved."

NOTES

1. Editor's note: "Don't ask, don't tell" was an official U.S. military policy, repealed in 2011, that prohibited harassment and discrimination on the basis of sexual orientation yet did not allow gay, lesbian, or bisexual military personnel to be open about or share their sexual orientation.

Prostitution: Facts and Fictions

RONALD WEITZER

A re all sex workers victims of trafficking or sexual abuse? Weitzer describes the state of prostitution in the United States, arguing that instead of being a monolithically oppressive form of work, the conditions of prostitution vary significantly depending on the setting (e.g., indoor versus outdoor). Sex workers in different settings often differ in terms of age of entry into prostitution, reason for entry, job satisfaction, levels of autonomy, exposure to risk, and more, leading Weitzer to conclude that a one-dimensional approach to the issue—especially when considering solutions—is misguided.

When I mentioned the topic of prostitution to a friend recently, he said, "How disgusting! How could anybody sell themselves?" A few weeks later an acquaintance told me she thought prostitution was a "woman's choice, and can be empowering." These opposing views reflect larger cultural perceptions of prostitution, as well as much academic writing on the topic.

A growing number of scholars regard prostitution, pornography, and stripping as "sex work" and study it as an occupation. Exploring all dimensions of the work, in different contexts, these studies document substantial variation in the way prostitution is organized and experienced by workers, clients, and managers. These studies undermine some deep-rooted myths about prostitution and challenge writers and activists who depict prostitution monolithically.

The most popular monolithic perspective is that prostitution is an unqualified evil. According to this *oppression model*, exploitation, abuse, and misery are intrinsic to the sex trade. In this view, most prostitutes were physically or sexually abused as children, which helps to explain their entry into prostitution; most enter the trade as adolescents, around 13–14 years of age; most are tricked or forced into the trade by pimps or sex traffickers; drug addiction is rampant; customer violence against workers is routine and pervasive; working conditions are abysmal; and legalization would only worsen the situation.

Some writers go further, characterizing the "essential" nature of prostitution. Because prostitution is defined as an institution of extreme male domination over women, these writers say that violence and exploitation are inherent and omnipresent—transcending historical time period, national context, and type of prostitution. As Sheila Jeffreys writes, "Prostitution constitutes sexual violence against women in and of itself"; and according to Melissa Farley,

Ronald Weitzer, *Contexts* (Volume 6 and Issue 4), pp. 28–33, Copyright © 2007. Reprinted by Permission of SAGE Publications.

prostitution is a "vicious institution" that is "intrinsically traumatizing to the person being prostituted." Many writers who subscribe to the oppression model use dramatic language ("sexual slavery," "paid rape," "survivors," and so on) and describe only the most disturbing cases, which they present as typical—rhetorical tricks designed to fuel public indignation.

The oppression model's images of victimhood erase workers' autonomy and agency, and preclude any possibility of organizing sex work in order to minimize harm and empower workers. This model holds that prostitution should be eradicated, not ameliorated. But much research challenges the oppression model as well as some other popular fictions.

The Street vs. Indoors

Street prostitution differs sharply from *indoor prostitution*. Many of the problems associated with "prostitution" are actually concentrated in street prostitution and much less evident in the indoor sector. Certainly many street prostitutes work under abysmal conditions and are involved in "survival sex," selling sex out of dire necessity or to support a drug habit. Some are runaway youths with no other options. Many use addictive drugs; risk contracting and transmitting sexual diseases; are exploited and abused by pimps; are vulnerable to being assaulted, robbed, raped, or killed; and are socially isolated and disconnected from support services. This is the population best characterized by the oppression model.

Other street prostitutes are in less desperate straits. Some work independently, without pimps (a Miami study found that only 7 percent had pimps, but the percentage varies greatly by city). Regarding age of entry, the oppression model's claim of 13–14 years is clearly not the norm. A recent British study by Marianne Hester and Nicole Westmarland found that 20 percent of their sample had begun to sell sex before age 16 while almost half (48 percent) had begun after age 19. Childhood abuse (neglect, violence, incest) is indeed part of the biography of some prostitutes, but studies that compare matched samples of street prostitutes and non-prostitutes show mixed results; some find a statistically significant difference in experience of family abuse, while others find no difference. HIV infection rates are highest among street prostitutes who inject drugs and less common among others.

Different writers report very different rates of victimization. Scholar-activists and some "survivor organizations" (Breaking Free, Standing against Global Exploitation, Council for Prostitution Alternatives) cite high levels of violence against prostitutes (70–100 percent). Samples drawn from the clients of social service agencies or from anti-prostitution survivor groups yield a much higher level of victimization (their clients were desperate enough to seek help) than samples drawn from the wider population of street workers. A study by Stephanie Church and colleagues found that 27 percent of a sample of street prostitutes had been assaulted, 37 percent robbed, and 22 percent raped. Criminologists John Lowman and Laura Fraser reported similar results: 39 percent assaulted, 37 percent robbed, and 37 percent sexually assaulted. Since random sampling of this population is impossible, we must approach all victimization figures cautiously, but victimization is apparently not nearly as prevalent, even among street prostitutes, as the oppression model asserts.

Unfortunately, much popular discourse and some academic writing extrapolate from (a caricature of) street prostitution to prostitution in general. What gets less attention is the hidden world of indoor prostitution in venues such as bars, brothels, massage parlors, tanning salons, or in services provided by escort agencies or independent call girls. An estimated 20 percent of all prostitutes work on the streets in the United States. Although this number is hard to substantiate at the national level, some city-level studies support it. Regardless of the exact numbers, indoor sex work clearly accounts for a large share of the market.

Less research has been conducted on indoor prostitution, but available studies indicate that, compared to streetwalkers, indoor workers have lower rates of childhood abuse, enter prostitution at an older age, and have more education. They are less drug-dependent and more likely to use softer drugs (marijuana instead of crack or heroin). Moreover, they use drugs for different reasons. Street workers consume drugs or alcohol to help them cope with the adversities of the job, whereas indoor workers use them both for coping and as part of their socializing with customers. Sexually transmitted diseases are fairly rare among call girls, escorts, and women who work in brothels where condom use is mandatory. Indoor workers tend to earn more money, are at lower risk of arrest, and are safer at work. They are in a better position to screen out dangerous customers (through a referral system for call girls and vetting by gatekeepers in brothels and massage parlors), and they have a higher proportion of low-risk, regular clients.

Studies conducted in a variety of countries have found that indoor sex workers are less likely to experience violence from customers than those who work on the streets. For example, Church found that few call girls and sauna workers had experienced violence (only 1 percent had ever been beaten, 2 percent raped, and 10 percent robbed). This and other studies support Lilly Plumridge and Gillian Abel's conclusion that "street workers are significantly more at risk of more violence and more serious violence than indoor workers." (Obviously, this does not apply to persons recruited by force or fraud and trafficked into brothels, who are at high risk for subsequent exploitation and abuse.)

Research finds that many indoor workers made conscious decisions to enter the trade; they do not see themselves as oppressed victims and do not feel that their work is degrading. Consequently, they express greater job satisfaction than their street-level counterparts. And they may differ little from non-prostitutes: A study by psychologist Sarah Romans and

colleagues comparing indoor workers and an age-matched sample of non-prostitute women found no differences between the two groups in physical health, self-esteem, mental health, or the quality of their social networks.

Some prostitutes feel validated and empowered by their work. In some studies, a large percentage of indoor workers report an increase in self-esteem after they began working in prostitution, state that they are very satisfied with their work, or feel that their lives improved after entering prostitution. Escorts interviewed by sociologist Tanice Foltz took pride in their work and viewed themselves as morally superior to others: "They consider women who are not 'in the life' to be throwing away woman's major source of power and control, while they as prostitutes are using it to their own advantage as well as for the benefit of society." A study by the Australian government reported that half of the 82 call girls and 101 brothel workers interviewed felt their work was a "major source of satisfaction" in their lives; two-thirds of the brothel workers and seven out of ten call girls said they would "definitely choose this work" if they had it to do over again; and 86 percent in the brothels and 79 percent of call girls said that "my daily work is always varied and interesting." Ann Lucas's interviews with escorts and call girls revealed that these women had the "financial, social, and emotional wherewithal to structure their work largely in ways that suited them and provided . . . the ability to maintain healthy self-images." Other studies indicate that such control over working conditions greatly enhances overall job satisfaction among these workers.

Indoor and street prostitutes also differ in whether they engage in "emotion work" (providing intimacy, emotional support) in addition to sexual services. Emotion work is rare among streetwalkers, whose encounters are limited to quick, mechanical sex. But call girls and escorts (and, to a lesser degree, brothel and massage parlor workers) are often expected to support and counsel clients, and their encounters may resemble dating experiences, including conversation, gifts, hugging, massage, and kissing. Janet Lever and Deanne Dolnick's comparative study of a large number of street and indoor workers in Los Angeles found striking differences between the two groups in the quantity and quality of their sexual and emotional interactions with clients. Emotion work is not necessarily easy; workers who feign intimacy or emotional support over an extended period of time may find the work quite draining.

Many customers are looking for more than sex from indoor workers. Reviews of several websites where customers discuss their preferences and experiences indicate that many seek women who are friendly, conversational, generous with time, and who engage in cuddling and foreplay. This has come to be known as a "girlfriend experience" (GFE), with elements of romance and intimacy in addition to sex. One client writing in the popular Punternet websites said that he had "a gentle GFE that was more lovemaking than sex," and another stated, "There was intimacy and sweat and grinding and laughter, and those moments that are sexy and funny and warm and leave you with a grin on your face the next day. Girlfriend sex." Escorts and call girls also contribute to these websites, and their comments make it clear that many do not believe the oppression model applies to them.

In sum, prostitution takes diverse forms and exists under varying conditions, a complexity that contradicts popular myths and sweeping generalizations. Plenty of evidence challenges the notion that prostitutes, across the board, are coerced into the sex trade, lead lives of misery, experience high levels of victimization, and want to be rescued. These patterns characterize one segment of the sex trade, *but they are not the defining features of prostitution.* Sex workers differ markedly in their autonomy, work experiences, job satisfaction, and self-esteem. It's time to replace the oppression model with a polymorphous model—a perspective that recognizes multiple structural and experiential realities.

Legalization?

According to the oppression model, legalization would only institutionalize exploitation and abuse. Anti-prostitution groups insist that legalization is a recipe for misery and has a "corrosive effect on society as a whole," according to the Coalition against Trafficking in Women. It is difficult to measure something as vague as a "corrosive effect," but it is possible to evaluate some other dimensions of legalization, including the effects on workers themselves. To address this question, we need to examine cases where prostitution is legal and regulated by the government. Brothels are legal in a number of places, including Nevada, the Netherlands, Australia, and New Zealand. Statutory regulations vary by country, but a common objective is harm reduction. New Zealand's 2003 law, for instance, gives workers a litany of rights, provides for the licensing and taxing of brothels, and empowers local governments to determine where they can operate, limit their size, vet the owners, ban offensive signage, and impose safe-sex and other health requirements.

Research suggests that, under the right conditions, legal prostitution can be organized in a way that increases workers' health, safety, and job satisfaction. Mandatory condom use and other safe-sex practices are typical in legal brothels, and the workers face much lower risk of abuse from customers. According to a 2004 report by the Ministry of Justice in the Netherlands, the "vast majority" of workers in Dutch brothels and window units report that they "often or always feel safe." Nevada's legal brothels "offer the safest environment available for women to sell consensual sex acts for money," according to a recent study by sociologists Barbara Brents and Kathryn Hausbeck. And a major evaluation of legal brothels in Queensland, Australia, by the government's Crime and Misconduct Commission concluded, "There is no doubt that licensed brothels provide the safest working environment for sex workers in Queensland. . . . Legal brothels now operating in Queensland provide a sustainable model for a healthy, crime-free, and safe legal licensed brothel industry." In each of these systems, elaborate safety measures (surveillance, panic buttons, listening devices) allow managers to respond to unruly customers quickly and effectively. These studies suggest that legal prostitution, while no panacea, is not inherently dangerous and can be structured to minimize risks and empower workers.

The question of whether legalization is preferable to criminalization—in terms of harm reduction—is one thing. The question of its feasibility in the United States is another. Today, it is legal only in Nevada, where about 30 brothels exist in rural counties; it is prohibited in Las Vegas and Reno. According to a 2002 poll, 31 percent of Nevadans are opposed to the state's legal brothels while 52 percent support them. And a 2004 ballot measure to ban brothels in one of Nevada's rural counties was defeated: 63 percent voted to retain legal prostitution in Churchill County. Rural support comes largely from the tax revenues that counties derive from the brothels.

And the rest of the country? Although many Americans consider prostitution immoral or distasteful, a large minority disagrees. In the 1996 General Social Survey, 47 percent (52 percent of men, 43 percent of women) agreed that, "There is nothing inherently wrong with prostitution, so long as the health risks can be minimized. If consenting adults agree to exchange money for sex, that is their business." Moreover, a sizeable number favor alternatives to criminalization. A 1991 Gallup poll found that 40 percent of the public thought that prostitution should be "legal and regulated by the government." Unfortunately, no American poll has specified the meaning of legalization, which could involve licensing, mandatory health exams, brothels, a designated zone of street prostitution, or other regulations.

A fair number of men have bought sex. According to the 2000 General Social Survey, 17 percent of American men have paid for sex at some time in their lives, and 3 percent have done so

in the past year. Recent surveys indicate that 9 percent of British men and 16 percent of Australian men report paying for sex. The actual numbers are likely higher, given the stigma involved.

Despite the significant support for legalization and sizeable customer base, there has been almost no serious debate among American policymakers on alternatives to prohibition. As a 1999 task force in Buffalo, New York, reasoned, "Since it is unlikely that city or state officials could ever be convinced to decriminalize or legalize prostitution in Buffalo, there is nothing to be gained by debating the merits of either." This logic seems to put the cart before the horse, but on those rare occasions when policy alternatives have been floated in other cities, they have met with the same status-quo outcome. When a San Francisco task force boldly recommended decriminalization in 1996, the city's political leaders promptly rejected the idea. And in 2004 a Berkeley, California, ballot measure that called on police to refrain from enforcing prostitution laws was defeated: 64 percent voted against it. Opposition was likely due to the measure's laissez-faire approach; people are more inclined to support some kind of regulation, just as they are with regard to some other vices. Still, despite the substantial minority of Americans who support legalization in principle, outside of Nevada the idea has attracted little public attention.

Increasing Criminalization

Although the issue of legalization is dormant in the contemporary United States, prostitution policy has recently become a hot issue. An anti-prostitution coalition has gathered steam, composed of the religious right and abolitionist feminists. Judging by their publications and pronouncements, the coalition not only accepts the myths I have described but actively perpetuates them.

During the Bush administration, this coalition ... played a major role in redefining the issue and influencing public policy. Coalition views have been incorporated in key legislation and in the official policies of several federal agencies. What began (in the 1990s) as a campaign focused on international trafficking has morphed into a frontal assault on the domestic sex industry in America.

In 2001, the State Department created a new unit, the Office to Monitor and Combat Trafficking in Persons. This office has endorsed the same extraordinary claims that are made by the anti-prostitution coalition. One example is the State Department's remarkable website, "The Link between Prostitution and Sex Trafficking," which contains these nuggets: "Prostitution is inherently harmful. Few activities are as brutal and damaging to people as prostitution"; it "leaves women and children physically, mentally, emotionally, and spiritually devastated"; and "Prostitution is not the oldest profession, but the oldest form of oppression."

Similar claims appear in the websites and publications of some other government agencies—the Justice Department, Health and Human Services, United States Agency for International Development—and have been recapitulated by some members of Congress and by [President George W. Bush]. In 2002, President Bush signed a Presidential Directive on trafficking that defines prostitution as "inherently harmful and dehumanizing," and in a 2003 speech at the United Nations he declared, "The victims of the sex trade see little of life before they see the very worst of life—an underground of brutality and lonely fear.... Those who patronize this industry debase themselves and deepen the misery of others."

The Bush administration . . . funneled more than $350 million into international and domestic organizations fighting prostitution, many of which are right-wing, faith-based, or abolitionist feminist in orientation. These groups have received funds to conduct "research," operate "rescue" missions, and engage in other interventions. Organizations that provide services to sex workers but do not formally condemn prostitution have been denied funding.

Criminalization of other sectors of the sex industry also appears to be on the American agenda. Activists have been pressing the government to criminalize the commercial sex trade as a whole, contending that the oppression model applies to all forms of sex work. For example, in a 2005 report funded by the State Department, scholar-activist Donna Hughes condemned both stripping and pornography. She claimed that women and girls are trafficked to perform at strip clubs (though she found only six cases of this in the United States during 1998–2005) and that the producers of pornography "often rely on trafficked victims," a charge made with no supporting evidence. Some government officials have echoed these claims.

In 2005, the Justice Department launched a new crackdown on adult pornography and obscenity. (Under the Clinton administration, child pornography was the main target.) The stated objective of the 2005 End Demand for Sex Trafficking bill was to "combat commercial sexual activities" in general. The rationale for this sweeping approach, according to the bill, is that "commercial sexual activities have a devastating impact on society. The sex trade has a dehumanizing effect on all involved." Commercial sex is defined remarkably broadly as "any sex act on account of which anything of value is given to, or received by, any person." The overall trend is clear: the Bush administration . . . embraced the oppression model as a rationale for its expanding, multifaceted crackdown on the sex industry.

Although the oppression framework dominates today, there is a diametrically opposed cultural representation that romanticizes prostitution. We see this in some rock and hip-hop songs, films like *Pretty Woman* and *The Best Little Whorehouse in Texas*, novels like Tracy Quan's *Diary of a Married Call Girl*, television shows like HBO's *Cathouse*, and a handful of academic writings. Such representations portray prostitution as enjoyable, empowering, and lucrative work. In my view, this celebratory model is just as one-dimensional and empirically limited as the oppression model. The alternative, superior perspective recognizes that prostitution varies enormously across time, place, and sector—with important consequences for workers' health, safety, and job satisfaction.

Selling People: Sex, Money, and Brutality

Sutapa Basu

Sutapa Basu, Contexts *(Volume 13 and Issue 1), pp. 17–18, Copyright © 2014.*

The sale of human beings for profit, for both sexual and nonsexual labor, is the second largest and fastest growing underground industry in the world, valued by the International Labour Organization (ILO) at $32 billion yearly. The U.S. State Department estimates there are as many as 27 million trafficking victims at any given time. According to the ILO, of those trafficked into sex work, 98 percent are women and girls. In the last decade or so, government and non-governmental organizations have poured resources into the eradication of human trafficking, particularly sex trafficking, yet the industry continues to thrive. This can be attributed to the intractable structural and social inequality between women and men, poor and rich nations, as well as the huge disparity between the poor and rich within nations.

Due in part to their cultural devaluation in many parts of the world, women and girls are especially vulnerable to a host of injustices and brutalities that are connected to human trafficking. They are often mentally and physically abused and denied basic human rights of food, shelter, education and health care. And unlike drugs, women and girls can be repeatedly sold. Often time victims are trafficked as preteens and used until they are deemed too old (approximately at 20–25 years-old) or are dying of HIV/AIDS.

Globalization has created wealth and opportunities for some, but has widened already huge economic disparities and led to much social displacement for the poor majority. It has also exasperated the human trafficking problem. Women and girls are especially vulnerable to trafficking as a result of economic hardship that forces them to seek opportunities beyond home and family in the desperate search for income. Traffickers take advantage of this desperation by promising lucrative employment. Once these women are lured out of their homes and into the city, they are commonly tortured, abused, and sold to brothel owners, and forced to engage in the sex trade.

In research trips to India I have collected the narratives of nearly 100 sex workers who averaged 20 clients per day. I've heard heart-wrenching stories about how abandonment by a husband or the need to feed their family led them to take up offers of travel to larger cities on tenuous promises of getting jobs as household workers. Each of these women ended up in the brothels of India's most notorious red light districts including Kochi and Thiruvananthapuram in Kerala, Delhi, and Kolkata. Once there, they have no means of escape and are often too ashamed, and afraid of traffickers' threats of violent reprisal, to let their families know of their plight.

The young women I interviewed shared horrific stories of being forced into sex work and brutalized by their pimps and clients. One woman spoke about her pimp stuffing hot cayenne pepper into her vagina until she agreed to service any client of his choice—she was an 11-year-old girl at the time. Another woman shared how she became a sex worker when her parents gave her aunt custody of her when she

continues

was 13-years-old, believing the aunt intended to find the daughter employment as a domestic servant. The hope was that their daughter would have the opportunity for some basic education, gainful employment, and the ability to secure enough money to pay off her family's debt to landowners and prevent them from dying of starvation. While her family was thankful for their daughter's newfound opportunity, this young woman's aunt forced her into sex work. Today, she is 26 years old and still works in the sex industry, where she also provides day care in the brothel during her spare time to protect children from witnessing the sex acts performed by their mothers.

The never-ending pipeline of issues that feed into poverty, especially for women, have resulted in hundreds of thousands of girls and women being sold in the sex trafficking industry annually. I have seen the results of human trafficking with my own eyes and witnessed the inhuman condition and despair in which these girls and women work. It is imperative that we do everything in our power to eradicate sex trafficking and the selling of human beings in any form.

Social Problems Related to Media

Josh Golin

Courtesy of Shara Drew.

Josh Golin is the associate director of the Campaign for a Commercial-Free Childhood.

What organization are you currently working with and how would you describe its mission?

The Campaign for a Commercial-Free Childhood's (CCFC) mission is to support parents' efforts to raise healthy families by limiting commercial access to children and ending the exploitive practice of child-targeted marketing. In working for the rights of children to grow up—and the freedom for parents to raise them—without being undermined by corporate interests, CCFC promotes a more democratic and sustainable world.

What are your general duties?

As associate director I organize CCFC's advocacy campaigns and plan and implement our communication strategy. My work includes developing talking points for our campaigns, drafting communications to our members and press releases, cultivating allies and partners, and doing outreach to reporters.

How did you first become interested in this type of activism? Who was your inspiration?

My previous work as a teacher made me realize that childhood was being transformed by corporate marketing—and that kids' self-image and habits were being shaped by people who cared nothing about their well-being. My inspiration was Ralph Nader who has been both fearless and tireless in fifty years of activism. Reading *No Logo* by Naomi Klein was also a transformative experience.

As an activist, what are your current goals?

First, stopping Mattel from releasing Hello Barbie, a doll that records, stores, and analyzes kids' conversations. Second, ending the exploitative practice of McTeachers' Nights, where teachers "work" at a local McDonald's and encourage their students to eat there in hopes of raising much-needed funds for their schools.

Third, helping parents and caregivers understand the importance of keeping babies screen-free for their first two years of their lives.

What strategies do you use to enact social change?

Because CCFC is a small organization, we depend on creating campaigns that are interesting to both traditional media and people on social media who can amplify our concerns. We try to generate pressure on corporations so they understand that while engaging in practices that are harmful to children may generate short-term profits, they risk doing long-term damage to their brand.

What are the major challenges activists in your field face?

The biggest challenge is that we're trying to influence the actions of huge multi–billion dollar corporations that have budgets that are hundreds or thousands of times bigger than ours, and the power and access that comes along with that money. I combat fatigue by savoring every small victory, by recognizing that things would be considerably worse if we weren't doing the work we were doing, and spending as much time as possible talking to people who appreciate our work and to other activists.

What are major misconceptions the public has about activism in general and your issue specifically?

I think people tend to think of "activism" as the tactics they are most familiar with, whether it's street demonstrations, social media, etc. . . . But there is no set playbook and one of the most important things is to think strategically about who you are and what your strengths are and how to best leverage those strengths to bring about change.

Why should students get involved in your line of activism?

Because if corporations completely take over childhood, we will have generations of children who are more concerned about their own material desires than about community or making change in the world. Giving children the time and space to grow up to be critical thinkers is important no matter what your cause or issue is.

What would you consider to be your greatest success as an activist (in your current area of activism)?

I led a multi-year successful campaign to shut down BusRadio, a company that wanted to advertise to kids on school buses. We monitored BusRadio's content and advertising and publicized our findings so that when schools that were interested in BusRadio did Internet searches, the first or second thing that showed up were our documented concerns. We also organized parents to go to school board meetings and prevent BusRadio from coming to their districts. As a result of our efforts, BusRadio was unable to gain a foothold in very many school districts and was therefore unable to turn a profit.

If an individual has little money and time, are there other ways they can contribute?

Yes, we always make our campaigns and resources easy to share with friends and family. Spreading the word to others is a no-cost way to get involved that doesn't take a lot of time.

A Modern Empire:
The Concentration of Media

DESMOND GOSS

Spend a day surfing the Internet, watching TV, or listening to the radio and it may feel like your sources of information and entertainment are limitless. But Goss illustrates that this is a ruse and that actually a minute number of companies control the vast amount of content for all types of media. Goss provides historical and structural reasons for increasing consolidation and describes some of the many costs to consumers and to the society. He concludes by pointing to opportunities for change that may already be within reach.

What are your favorite television shows? Do you frequently succumb to the guilty pleasure of reality TV programs like *Duck Dynasty* or *The Real Housewives of Atlanta*? Are you partial to the heartwarming storylines of sitcoms like *Modern Family* or *The Big Bang Theory*? Are you drawn to the exciting drama of series like *Scandal* or *The Walking Dead*? Whatever your preference, there seems to be a great diversity in the kinds of programs to which one can "tune in and check out." However, behind the small screen, another world exists. This world is not of artistry or comedy, nor drama or thrill. There are no spinning oversized red chairs or cannibalistic zombies. There are no waltzing C-list celebrities, awkward millennials on nude dates, or superheroes-in-wait. There is only the bottom line: the venerable cultural power of corporate media economy. Beyond the cornucopia of media images on your television, tablet, or computer screen, there are but a few corporations in control.

In the Age of Information, media is everywhere. Billboards, clothing, websites, film, radio, magazines, newspapers, video games, and television all offer mechanisms for the communication of cultural messages. In fact, on average, we spend 70 percent of our day consuming digital media.[1] Clearly, from the mundane to the monumental, media plays a pivotal role in shaping our lived experiences. As such, the power to control media is an immense power indeed. In theory, competition between media enterprises creates a virtual marketplace of ideas that reflect any manner of sociocultural concepts. But as fewer and fewer corporations own more and more media outlets in the United States (and increasingly around the world), the power to control media communication becomes concentrated into the hands of just a few media conglomerates. In 1983, fifty

Original to *Focus on Social Problems: A Contemporary Reader*.

companies owned 90 percent of North American media. Today, that same proportion is owned by just six companies: General Electric (including NBC and Universal Pictures), News-Corp (including Fox and the *Wall Street Journal*), Disney (including ABC and Pixar), Viacom (including MTV and Paramount Pictures), Time Warner/AOL (including CNN and HBO), and CBS (including NFL.com and Showtime).[2]

The Conglomeration Process: Integration and Mergers

Media monopolization is not an accident. Underlying this process is an increasing reliance on a consumerist model of media communication where audiences are conceptualized as consumers. This profit-driven model has pronounced enormous financial gain for corporate media owners. For example, advertising revenue reached an astonishing $309 billion in 2009 during the height of the recession.[3] And, as ownership continues to concentrate among fewer and fewer owners, media communication profits continue to climb. Media conglomeration means more money in fewer hands, as separate companies are consolidated through integration and mergers. Media companies "vertically" integrate by purchasing the companies who supply them goods or to whom they supply. Thus, a cable provider may also possess several television channels, as Time Warner Cable owns HBO, CNN, TBS, and Cartoon Network.[4] "Horizontal" integration, on the other hand, involves purchasing companies that produce similar goods but at lower prices or different qualities. For example, a large movie production enterprise may purchase an independent film company. When companies merge, two or more enterprises become one, and media control that was once dispersed between competitors is now centralized into a single entity, as in the recent AOL and Time Warner merger.

No matter the method, the process of corporate conglomeration always has the same result: more money (and power) into fewer hands. Although the deregulatory character of free-market economies may encourage these proceedings,

various consumer watchdogs have raised red flags in opposition, although relatively few have had some measure of success. In the landmark Hollywood Antitrust Case of 1948, for example, the U.S. Supreme Court ruled that the "Big Five" movie production studios (Paramount, Loew's/MGM, 20th Century Fox, Warner Bros., and RKO) violated the antitrust law by vertically integrating movie theaters. Prior to this ruling, film production companies were free to restrict access to the films they produced to only the theaters under their ownership. As the studios purchased more and more independent theaters, there was more interference from executive bodies into the filmmaking process, less film diversity, and less variety in price. Thus, movie studios had essentially monopolized the film industry. The court's decision effectively reversed this trend, thereby marking the beginning of a popular independent film movement and the end of the "Golden Age" of the Big Five's unfettered corporate dominance in the film industry.[5]

Despite limited attempts by the federal government to prevent monopolization, media conglomeration would not be possible without governmental scaffolding. The increasing consolidation of media money and power is a product of cooperative efforts of government and corporate entities concerned with building a society where the needs of free-market capitalism trump the protectionist functions of government intervention. Deregulating industries and privatizing traditionally public organizations are crucial aspects of such neoliberal construction. Incidents like the Hollywood Antitrust Case, which immediately followed the Great Depression, capitalized on the protectionist sentiment that was widespread at the height of the American welfare state. During this time period, U.S. citizens saw the advent of federally mandated minimum wages, the Social Security Administration, and dramatic expansion of labor unions. Similarly, other federal endeavors were undertaken to prevent corporate misconduct and monopolization of markets, such as the invention of the Securities and Exchange

Commission, the Federal Trade Commission (FTC), and the Sherman Antitrust Act, under which the above-mentioned film corporates were tried in Hollywood Antitrust Case.

However, as the conservative turn of the 1970s and 1980s dismantled the welfare state, the power of government regulatory bodies was dramatically diminished—a trend that continues today. For example, in 1980 there were approximately sixty-five FTC antitrust investigations, whereas in 2009, at the height of the global economic crisis, there were only seven.[6] The controversial *Citizens United* ruling exemplifies a culmination of neoliberal corporate ideology because the Supreme Court ruled that corporations can no longer be restricted by political campaign finance limits.[7] In essence, corporations, including media enterprises, now have a political incentive to monopolize the market. As long as corporate media continues to grow through integration and mergers, media monopolization could have serious implications for diversity in the media marketplace.

The Effects of Media Concentration by Industry

Books

In 1980, only eleven corporations received more than half the revenue from national book sales. By 2009, the number of corporations controlling half the $23.9 billion market had fallen to just five: Bertelsmann (owner of Random House), Pearson, Hachette, News Corp (HarperCollins), and CBS (Simon & Schuster). As a student, you are intimately involved in the corporate concentration of book publishers through the purchase of textbooks. In 2013, the textbook publisher Pearson, the top publisher by revenue, garnered $9.33 billion in sales, almost more than the next two largest publishers combined.[8] Clearly, the textbook industry is booming . . . but at whose expense? Publishers perpetuate high prices by serializing textbooks (adding editions) and bundling them with software packages. The average cost of textbooks for undergraduate students is approximately $1,200.00 per academic year. One comprehensive survey demonstrated that, with costs this high, some 65 percent of students forgo purchasing one or more required texts, sometimes at the expense of their academic performance.[9]

Moreover, textbooks are at the center of formal education in many contexts, so when so few textbook publishers control so much of the market, there are political implications for curriculum development. Such effects are particularly salient when publishers act as a conduit for state indoctrination. In Hong Kong, for example, government education institutions have implemented a curriculum of "moral and national education" that promotes patriotic and nationalist ideology while condemning the republican principles of democracy.[10] A major tool in this educational reconstruction is the utilization of textbooks "that promote blind nationalism."[11] (Some of these textbooks are published by Pearson Hong Kong.)[12] In the United States, Texas has frequently been at the center of similar controversies. Conservative politicians, citizens, and lobbies have repeatedly used their influence to encourage governmental education entities to support only those textbooks that espouse conservative ideologies.[13] In the past, these entities have bent to conservative will about topics like evolution, sex education, war history, the civil rights movement, gay and lesbian culture, gender equality, Islam, Christianity, capitalism, and communism. Importantly, Texan textbook controversy is not sequestered by state boundary. Texas is the largest purchaser of K–12 textbooks in the country. As such, publishers edit textbooks for Texas schools, which they then market elsewhere around the country. Thus, following the actions of a Texas school board, students in New York may read that the religious figure Moses is also a "founding father" of the United States of America.[14]

Film and Television

Despite the court's ruling on the Hollywood Antitrust Act of 1948, a few major film companies still produce a vast majority of American movies.

In 2013, just seven studios (Warner, Disney, Universal, 20th Century Fox, Sony, Lionsgate, and Paramount) accounted for 84.8 percent of the revenue from the domestic film market.[15] In the television industry, 3,762 companies control 30 percent of cable television, whereas the remaining 70 percent is controlled by just six corporations (General Electric, News Corp, Disney, Viacom, Time Warner, and CBS).[16] In 2009, four media corporations (CBS, News Corp [Fox], Disney [ABC], and Universal–NBC) acquired 70 percent of all revenue generated from network television advertising. That same year, three cable networks (Disney, Time Warner, and Viacom) received more than 50 percent of the multi–billion dollar profits of the television advertising industry. Here, again, corporate control of media markets has consequences for audiences. In 2014, as pricing negotiations between AMC and satellite provider DirecTV stalled, AMC turned to consumers to push DirecTV toward cooperation. During an episode of the popular AMC television series *The Walking Dead*, viewers were presented with an on-screen warning during commercial breaks: "You are at risk of losing AMC and *The Walking Dead*."[17] Losing your favorite television show may be a trite example of the effects of media conglomeration but the theoretical implications are significant. The control of film and television media in fewer hands means that the content to which we are allowed access is increasingly restricted.

The Internet

Even newer media are subjected to monopolization. The majority of social media we use is owned by just five corporations: Facebook (which owns Instagram, Light Box, and WhatsApp), Google (which owns YouTube, Blogger, and Android), Twitter (which owns Vine and Bluefin), LinkedIn (which owns Pulse and Bizo), and Yahoo (which owns Tumblr, Summly, and Blink!).[18] In 2009, two companies, Google and Yahoo, received more than half the $20.9 billion in Internet advertising revenue. As the two leading search engines, the commercially driven

algorithms these corporations use to drive Internet exploration have a potentially profound influence on public knowledge. Companies that manage popular search engines like Google Search and Bing control the flow of Internet information by acting as a filter between raw data and consumers. As such, these companies have an integral role in the process through which we come to know things via the Internet. Moreover, this process has become increasingly tainted by commercialism. Search for virtually anything in these search engines and the top results are almost always paid advertisements for products. Many Internet browsers will also store your search history so that you will be repeatedly reminded of products you are considering to purchase. Search for a pair of Nikes on Zappos but decide not to buy them and you will likely see an ad for those very same shoes tempting you the next time you visit Facebook.

Whatever the industry, reducing the number of companies involved in the production of content increases the potential for limiting diversity in media messages and material. For example, numerous sociologists and other cultural critics have chided the advertising industry for its incessant objectification and over-sexualization of women's bodies. Turn on the TV, flip through a magazine, or look over album covers and you're bound to see images where women are reduced to body parts, where their bodies become the product for sale, or where their sole purpose is to serve as background to a male counterpart.[19] Racialized images in the media work in similar ways to support white supremacy and privilege. Media content that features people of color frequently does so while reproducing racist stereotypes. In addition, like women in media, people of color in media often function solely as sidekicks to white characters. A telling example of racialized media is the so-called "white savior phenomenon" in the film industry. White savior movies typically feature casts made up largely of minorities in some sort of duress. It takes a (white) hero to save them from their dire fate (think Sandra Bullock in

The Blind Side, Sam Worthington in *Avatar*, Michelle Pfeiffer in *Dangerous Minds*, Clint Eastwood in *Gran Torino*, or Emma Stone in *The Help*).[20] Gender and race ideologies portrayed in media are important because they provide a social discourse–that is, they function as building blocks for social processes in our daily lives. In these cases, the lack of informed diversity that results from media concentration catalyzes the dehumanization and objectification of women and minorities that is necessary for the processes of structural sexism and racism.

Women and people of color are not only misrepresented in media imagery, but also vastly underrepresented in American media. For example, although women compose nearly half of the gaming community, 88 percent of game developers are men. Of the 250 top-grossing films of 2013, women directed only 9 percent of them. Additionally, a study by USC's Media, Diversity, and Social Change Initiative found that of the 500 top-grossing films between 2007 and 2012, only 10.8 percent of the speaking roles were for black actors, 5 percent for Asian actors, and 4.2 percent for Hispanic actors.[21] People of color and women are both too often marginalized in media representation. For example, a review of more than 150 newspapers and websites by the Institute for Diversity and Ethics in Sports found that the sports journalistic community is more than 90 percent male and more than 90 percent white. However, there is evidence to suggest that including women and people of color in the administrative process of media production increases the racial and gender representativeness of media images. For example, in films directed by African Americans, more than half of speaking roles featured black characters, compared to just 9.9 percent in films with white directors. In 2013, men comprised more than 75 percent of those interviewed for political talk shows,[22] whereas MSNBC's Sunday political news/talk show, the *Melissa Harris-Perry Show* (hosted by an African American woman), featured "a more evenly balanced distribution of solo interviews with white men and women and African American men and women" than any other major Sunday political news/talk show.[23] Clearly, media diversity in any form is good for the numerical representation of minority communities.

Media for the People: Alt Media, Net Neutrality, and Open Access

Like all social institutions, the institution of American media is socially constructed. Therefore, it is open to deconstruction and reconstruction. Although the conglomeration of media may seem a towering monolith, over the past few decades, several alternative models to corporatized media have emerged in various industries. Broadly, alternative media models work within a more community-oriented structure of ownership, production, and audience relations.[24] Thus, the resulting content is presumably more sociologically informed. Similarly, the issues of "net neutrality" and "open access" offer other possibilities for institutional resistance against media conglomeration. For example, many of us enjoy playing games on our smartphones. Imagine if Verizon decided that all data usage associated with Words with Friends, Angry Birds, and other cellphone games would now be charged double what data usage costs during other applications. Or, imagine that Comcast decides that corporations will enjoy faster Internet, whereas individual consumers will be stuck with sluggish access (unless, of course, we pay for the upgrade). Under the current paradigm such situations are entirely possible and wholly legal. However, proponents of net neutrality argue that service providers and governments should treat all Internet data as equal, such that service providers cannot overcharge certain data usage for profit and governments cannot block certain Internet platforms in the name of state censorship.[25]

As students, the notion of open access may be of particular interest to you. Subscriptions to academic journals can be costly, yet they contain information on the cutting edge of research and theory in the sciences, arts, and humanities. From the efficacy of vaccinations to the consequences of terrorism, academic journals largely inform "what we know" as a society. Proponents of open access argue that this information is too significant to be restricted by publishers concerned primarily with profit-making.[26] Alternative media, net neutrality, and open access each provide a new direction for media, less restricted by capitalistic efforts for industry control through concentration and conglomeration. As the next generation of media consumers and producers, it will be up to you to decide: what is the future of media?

NOTES

1. Heppner, Jake. 2015. "30 Surprising Facts about How We Actually Spend Our Time," *Distractify,* January 6. http://news.distractify.com/dark/trivial-facts/astounding-facts-about-how-we-actually-spend-our-time/.

2. Lutz, Ashley. "These 6 Corporations Control 90% of the Media in America," *Business Insider*, June 14. http://www.businessinsider.com/these-6-corporations-control-90-of-the-media-in-america-2012-6.

3. Johnson, Bradley. 2010. "100 Leading Media Companies," *Advertising Age*, September 27. http://adage.com/article/media/100-leading-media-companies-2010/146004/.

4. Time Warner. 2015. "Operating Divisions." Retrieved May 2, 2015. http://www.timewarner.com/company/operating-divisions/.

5. The Society of Independent Motion Picture Producers Research Database. 2005. "The Independent Producers and the Paramount Case, 1938–1949." Retrieved May 2, 2015. http://www.cobbles.com/simpp_archive/paramountcase_3consent1940.htm/.

6. Wright, Josh. 2010. "Monopolization Enforcement at the Antitrust Division by the Numbers," *Truth on the Market: Academic Commentary on Law, Business, Economics and More*, August 2. http://truthonthemarket.com/2010/08/02/monopolization-enforcement-at-the-antitrust-division-by-the-numbers/.

7. Cornell University Law School. n.d. "Supreme Court Bulletin: *Citizens United v. Federal Election Commission* (-8-205)." Retrieved May 2, 2015. http://www.law.cornell.edu/supct/cert/08-205/.

8. Publishers Weekly. 2014. "The World's 56 Largest Book Publishers, 2014." Retrieved May 2, 2015. http://www.publishersweekly.com/pw/by-topic/industry-news/financial-reporting/article/63004-the-world-s-56-largest-book-publishers-2014.html/.

9. The Daily Take Team. 2014. "Is the Koch Brothers' Curriculum Coming to Your Child's School?" *Truthout*, December 11. http://truth-out.org/opinion/item/27965-is-the-koch-brothers-curriculum-coming-to-your-child-s-school/.

10. The Economist. 2012. "Textbooks Round the World: It Ain't Necessarily So." Retrieved May 2, 2015. http://www.economist.com/node/21564554/.

11. Zhao, Shirley, and Johnny Tam. 2013. "Debate Continues in Hong Kong over Introduction of National Education," *South China Morning Post*, October 8. http://www.scmp.com/news/hong-kong/article/1326760/debate-continues-hong-kong-over-introduction-national-education/.

12. The Government of the Hong Kong Special Administrative Region of the People's Republic of China Education Bureau. 2015. "Recommended Textbook List." Retrieved May 2, 2015. https://cd.edb.gov.hk/rtl/publisherlist.asp/.

13. Associated Press. "Texas Approves Disputed History Texts for Schools," *The New York Times*, November 22. http://www.nytimes.com/2014/11/23/us/texas-approves-disputed-history-texts-for-schools.html/.

14. Dietz, Jason. 2014. "Metacritic's 5th Annual Movie Studio Report Card: Ranking the Performance of Film Studios in 2013," *Metacritic*, January 23. http://www.metacritic.com/feature/film-studio-rankings-2014/.

15. Littleton, Cynthia. 2014. "AMC Sounds Alarm about DirecTV Tussle during 'Walking Dead' Episode," *Variety*, November 2. http://variety.com/2014/tv/news/amc-sounds-alarm-about-directv-tussle-during-walking-dead-episode-1201345695/.

16. Bennet, Shea. 2014. "Who Owns Social Media? [Infographic]," *Social Times*, September 18.

http://www.mediabistro.com/alltwitter/who-owns-social-media_b60182/.

17. Littleton. 2014.

18. Bennett. 2014.

19. Kilbourne, Jean. 1999. *Killing Us Softly 3.* DVD. New York: Insight Media.

20. Hughey, Matthew W. 2014. *The White Savior Film: Content, Critics, and Consumption.* Philadelphia: Temple University Press.

21. Women's Media Center. 2015. "The Problem." Retrieved May 2, 2015. http://www.womensmediacenter.com/pages/the-problem/.

22. Klos, Diana Mitsu. 2014. "The Status of Women in the U.S. Media 2013." Women's Media Center. Retrieved May 2. 2015. http://wmc.3cdn.net/51113ed5df3e0d0b79_zzzm6go0b.pdf.

23. Media Matters. 2013. "Report: The Sunday Morning Shows Are Still White, Conservative, and Male." Retrieved May 2, 2015. http://mediamatters.org/research/2013/07/10/report-the-sunday-morning-shows-are-still-white/194820.

24. Leung, Dennis, and Lee Francis. 2014. "Cultivating an Active Online Counterpublic Examining Usage and Political Impact of Internet Alternative Media." *The International Journal of Press and Politics* 4(1):340–359.

25. American Civil Liberties Union. 2015. "What Is New Neutrality?" Retrieved May 2, 2015. https://www.aclu.org/net-neutrality/.

26. Curry, Stephen. 2012. "Science Must Be Liberated from the Paywalls of Publishers," *The Guardian*, April 10. http://www.theguardian.com/commentisfree/2012/apr/10/science-open-access-publishing/.

Connection Failed: Internet Still a Luxury for Many Americans

Jana Kasperkevic

Whenever homework was assigned in school, Destinyjoy Balgobin would be filled with anxiety. Not because she wasn't familiar with the material or that she had better things to do. Rather, it was that she had no way to do it. As with most homework assignments today, Balgobin's often required the use of a computer and Internet, whether it be to do light research, read material, or type up an essay. With no computer or Internet at home, Balgobin, who recently graduated high school, had to rely on publicly available resources to complete her homework. Often, she would end up doing it with the Internet on her cellphone.

Among households with incomes of $30,000 and less, only 54% have access to broadband at home, says Kathryn Zickuhr, a research associate with Pew Research Center's Internet Project. Members of these households are most likely to use Internet access outside home—at work, school or a public library. Similar to Balgobin, about 13% of these households report accessing the Internet on their cellphones.[1] A further look into poverty reveals more and more unconnected Americans. According to Pew Research,[2] one-third of those making less than $20,000 a year do not go online at all. Another third go online, but do not have Internet access at home. Of those making $30,000 or less, 45% of mobile Internet users go online mostly with their cellphones.

The lower-income population that lacks Internet access can be divided into two main groups: the elderly and the young, says Zickuhr. While the elderly deem Internet irrelevant or feel that it's too late and too difficult to adapt, those in the younger generation like Balgobin struggle to keep up with their peers. Just consider President Barack Obama's[3] goal to bring Internet to schools nationwide. "[I]n an age when the world's information is just a click away, it demands that we bring our schools and libraries into the 21st century. We can't be stuck in the 19th century when we're living in a 21st century economy."

Even as some schools forge ahead by incorporating computers, many students are left behind due to the lack of connection at home. In a February 2013 survey[4] conducted by Pew Research, College Board Advanced Placement program and National Reading project, 54% of teachers said that all or almost all of their students had access to digital tools such as computer and Internet connection at school. Only 18% said the students had similar access to such tools at home. More than half of the teachers of the lowest income students, at 56%, said that students' lack of resources presents a major challenge to incorporating computers into their teaching. For teachers of students from mostly lower-middle income, that number was 48%.

Despite understanding that students face limited access, 79% of teachers said they have their students access or download assignments from an online site and 76% have students submit those assignments the same way. Other ways teachers ask their students to use Internet include posting their work to a website or a blog (40%), participating in online discussions (39%), and editing their classmates' work through web-enabled sharing tools such as Google Docs (29%).

It's difficult to make people understand how important Internet access is when they aren't without it, says Balgobin. In order to complete her homework, she often used the computer lab at school or at the public library. Overall, two-thirds of those using Internet at public library said that they did research for school or work, revealed a survey conducted by Pew Research.[5] Out of all age groups surveyed, 16 to 17 year olds were the group to access the Internet the most. About 39% of them said that they had used a library computer or Wi-Fi in the last 12 months. For 18 to 29 year olds, that number was 38%. For 30 to 49, it was 31%. For parents of minors, that number was 34%.

There are, however, limitations when it comes to using computers and Internet at the library.

Oftentimes, the demand for computers in the library exceeds the number of devices available. As a result, public libraries require members to sign up for 30-minute windows in which they can use the computer. When it comes to completing certain homework assignments, 30-minute windows are hard to navigate and might not be enough time to actually complete the assignment, says Balgobin.

With some libraries closing as early as 6pm, parents and students have had to come up with alternate places to access Internet. For those who have access to a computer, but lack Internet connection at home, coffee shops like Starbucks and even fast-food restaurants like McDonald's[6] have become after-school haunts. Other parents use their cell-phones to create Wi-Fi hot-spots at home.

Unwilling to leave unconnected students behind, some schools have chosen to only assign homework that does not require use of computers and Internet. Yet such policies are challenging, says Danielle Kehl, a policy analyst in the Open Technology Institute at the New America Foundation. By cutting out these tools from part of their homework, kids are losing out on valuable education.

KEEPING UP WITH MOORESVILLE

So, how should the US handle this predicament? Are there proven policies that could be replicated nationwide? "I wish there was a simple answer," said Kehl. Local efforts on a municipal level might prove more effective than a nationwide campaign. "Some communities have decided to make [connectivity] a priority," said Kehl, pointing to Mooresville as a perfect example.

Mooresville came into national spotlight after it was highlighted by President Obama. Out of 115 school districts in North Carolina, Mooresville ranked in the bottom 10 when it came to spending but ranked second in student achievement. "You're spending less money getting better outcomes," said Obama,[7] noting that "there is no reason why we can't replicate the success you've found here."

Yet keeping up with Mooresville won't be easy. Thanks to a partnership with One-to-One institute,[8] a national non-profit dedicated to implementing

continues

◼ Continued

one-to-one technology in K–12 settings, the district began implementing a six-year digital conversion plan. By fall of 2009, all students in grades four through 12 received laptops for their use 24/7. By fall of 2010, the program was expanded to include third grade as well. In February of 2012, the *New York Times* declared Mooresville "a shining example"—a laptop success story.[9]

When speaking at Mooresville last year, President Obama laid out a lofty goal in the form of a ConnectED initiative,[10] promising that in five years' time, FCC will have connected 99% of US students to high-speed broadband Internet. According to Kehl, other lawmakers like West Virginia senator John D Rockefeller IV, California congresswoman Anna Eshoo and FCC commissioner Jessica Rosenworcel have previously called for providing schools nationwide with one gigabit connection, something that almost none of the school have right now.

. . . AND SOUTH KOREA

"Only around 20% of our students have access to true high-speed Internet in their classroom," said Obama. "By comparison, South Korea has 100% of its kids with high-speed Internet. We've got 20%; South Korea 100%. . . . In a country where we expect free Wi-Fi with our coffee, why shouldn't we have it in our schools?"

If catching up to Mooresville seems difficult, catching up to South Korea might be impossible. More densely populated than the US, South Korea faced much lower costs in setting up its Internet infrastructure, according to CNN.[11] Furthermore, the country made Internet connection its priority as early as 1990s. One of the main obstacles facing US in its effort to catch up to South Korea is the funding necessary to make ConnectED a reality. The low-end estimates for the cost of the program are $4 billion, according to *The Washington Post*.[12] The White House has suggested raising the funds through imposing higher cellphone service fees, a plan that does not sit well with Republicans.

It's not just South Korea that seems to have a leg up on the US. Compared to most cities around the world, US cities provide slower-speed Internet for higher prices, says Kehl. According to her research,[13] "the best deal for a 150 Mbps home broadband connection from cable and phone companies is $130/month, offered by Verizon FiOS. By contrast, the international cities we surveyed offer comparable speeds for less than $80/month, with most coming in at about $50/month." Same goes for mobile data plans, which cost twice as much in US as they do in UK. With prices like these, it's no surprise that many low-income families opt to go without Internet.

Ultimately, getting better Internet access in schools won't make things easier for students like Balgobin, who have no access to computers and Internet at home. In fact, putting emphasis on digital tools in classrooms makes it even more likely that we will see likes of her in our local library, coffee shop or McDonald's attempting to do the homework that many can and do at home.

NOTES

1. Pew Research Center. 2013. "How Americans Go Online." http://www.pewinternet.org/2013/09/25/how-americans-go-online/.
2. Smith, Aaron. 2013. "Technology Adoption by Lower Income Populations." *Pew Research Center.* http://pewinternet.org/Presentations/2013/Oct/Technology-Adoption-by-Lower-Income-Populations.aspx.
3. Office of the Press Secretary, The White House. Remarks by the President at Mooresville Middle School—Mooresville, NC. June 6, 2013. http://www.whitehouse.gov/the-press-office/2013/06/06/remarks-president-mooresville-middle-school-mooresville-nc.
4. Purcell, Kristen, Alan Heaps, Judy Buchanan and Linda Friedrich. 2013. "How Teachers Are Using Technology at Home and in Their Classrooms." *Pew Research Center.* http://www.pewinternet.org/Reports/2013/Teachers-and-technology.aspx.
5. Zickuhr, Kathryn, Lee Rainie, and Kristen Purcell. 2013. "Library Services in the Digital Age." *Pew*

Internet & American Life Project. http://libraries.pewinternet.org/2013/01/22/library-services/.

6. Trioanovski, Anton. 2013. "The Web-Deprived Study at McDonald's." *The Wall Street Journal.* http://online.wsj.com/news/articles/SB10001424127887324731304578189794161056954.

7. Office of the Press Secretary, The White House. Remarks by the President at Mooresville Middle School—Mooresville, NC. June 6, 2013. http://www.whitehouse.gov/the-press-office/2013/06/06/remarks-president-mooresville-middle-school-mooresville-nc.

8. One-to-One Institute. n.d. "About Us." http://www.one-to-oneinstitute.org/index.php?/who-we-are/.

9. Schwarz, Alan. 2012. "Mooresville's Shining Example (It's Not Just about the Laptops." *The New York Times.* http://www.nytimes.com/2012/02/13/education/mooresville-school-district-a-laptop-success-story.html?pagewanted=all.

10. The White House. n.d. "ConnectED: President Obama's Plan for Connecting All Schools to the Digital Age." http://www.whitehouse.gov/sites/default/files/docs/connected_fact_sheet.pdf.

11. Sutter, John D. 2010. "Why Internet Connections Are Fastest in South Korea." *CNN.com.* http://www.cnn.com/2010/TECH/03/31/broadband.south.korea/.

12. Goldfarb, Zachary A. 2013. "Obama Pushes Ambitious Internet Access Plan." *The Washington Post.* http://www.washingtonpost.com/politics/obama-pushes-ambitious-internet-access-plan/2013/08/13/646bf410-f321-11e2-bdae-0d1f78989e8a_story.html.

13. Hussain, Hibah, Danielle Kehl, Patrick Lucey, and Nick Russo. 2013. "The Cost of Connectivity 2013 Data Release: A Comparison of High-Speed Internet Prices in 24 Cities Around the World." *New America Foundation.* http://newamerica.net/sites/newamerica.net/files/policydocs/Cost_of_Connectivity_2013_Data_Release.pdf.

How to Stop the Bullies

EMILY BAZELON

Cyberbullying among children and teenagers is a relatively new social problem, one that has received increased attention as more social media platforms emerge and more young people use them. But how should we define cyberbullying and what can be done to end it? Bazelon discusses how social media companies such as Facebook and Twitter deal with reports of harassment and bullying, how new technology and artificial intelligence can help detect harassment online, and how the hacker group Anonymous has intervened on behalf of bullying victims.

In the annals of middle-school mischief, the Facebook page Let's Start Drama deserves an entry. The creator of the page—no one knew her name, but everyone was sure she was a girl—had a diabolical knack for sowing conflict among students at Woodrow Wilson Middle School in Middletown, Connecticut. "Drama Queen," as I came to think of her in the months I spent reporting at the school to write a book about bullying,[1] knew exactly how to use the Internet to rile her audience. She hovered over them in cyberspace like a bad fairy, with the power to needle kids into ending friendships and starting feuds and fistfights.

In contrast with some other social networks, like Twitter, Facebook requires its users to sign up with their real names. Drama Queen easily got around this rule, however, by setting up Let's Start Drama with a specially created e-mail address that didn't reveal her identity. Wrapped in her cloak of anonymity, she was free to pass along cruel gossip without personal consequences. She started by posting a few idle rumors, and when that gained her followers, she asked them to send her private messages relaying more gossip, promising not to disclose the source. Which girl had just lost her virginity? Which boy had asked a girl to sent him a nude photo? As Drama Queen posted the tantalizing tidbits she gathered, more kids signed up to follow her exploits—a real-life version of *Gossip Girl*. She soon had an audience of 500, many drawn from Woodrow Wilson's 750 students, plus a smattering from the local high school and a nearby Catholic school. Students didn't just message rumors to Drama Queen; they also commented in droves on her posts, from their own real Facebook accounts, or from other fake ones. As one kid wrote about Drama Queen on the Let's Start Drama page, "She just starts mad shit and most of the time so do the ppl who comment."

What can be done about this online cruelty and combat? As parents try, and sometimes fail, to keep track of their kids online, and turn to schools for help, youth advocates like Robinson and Carbonella have begun asking how much responsibility falls on social-networking sites to enforce their own rules against bullying and harassment. What *does* happen when you file a report with Facebook? And rather than asking the site to delete cruel posts or pages one by one, is there a better strategy, one that stops cyberbullying before it starts? Those questions led me to the Silicon Valley headquarters of Facebook, then to a lab at MIT, and finally (and improbably, I know) to the hacker group Anonymous.

The people at Facebook who decide how to wield the site's power when users complain about content belong to its User Operations teams. The summer after my trips to Woodrow Wilson, I traveled to the company's headquarters and found Dave Willner, the 27-year-old manager of content policy, waiting for me among a cluster of couches, ready to show me the Hate and Harassment Team in action. Its members, who favor sneakers and baseball caps, scroll through the never-ending stream of reports about bullying, harassment, and hate speech. (Other groups that handle reports include the Safety Team, which patrols for suicidal content, child exploitation, and underage users; and the Authenticity Team, which looks into complaints of fake accounts.) Willner was wearing flip-flops, and I liked his blunt, clipped way of speaking. "Bullying is hard," he told me. "It's slippery to define, and it's even harder when it's writing instead of speech. Tone of voice disappears." He gave me an example from a recent report complaining about a status update that said "He got her pregnant." Who was it about? What had the poster intended to communicate? Looking at the words on the screen, Willner had no way to tell.

Drama Queen was particularly ingenious at pitting kids against each other in contests of her own creation. She regularly posted photographs of two girls side by side, with the caption "WHOS PRETTIERRR?!" Below the pictures, commenters would heckle and vote. One such contest drew 109 comments over three days. When it became clear which contestant was losing, that girl wrote that she didn't care: "nt even tryinqq to b funny or smart." The rival who beat her answered, "juss mad you losss ok ppl voted me! If you really loooked better they wouldve said you but THEY DIDNT sooo sucks for you." This exchange nearly led to blows outside of school, other students told me. And they said a fight *did* break out between two boys who were featured on Let's Start Drama, in dueling photos, above the caption "Who would win in a fight?" They reportedly ended up pummeling each other off school grounds one day after classes.

Melissa Robinson, who was a social worker for the Middletown Youth Services Bureau,[2] quickly got wind of Let's Start Drama because, she says, "it was causing tons of conflict." Robinson worked out of an office at Woodrow Wilson with Justin Carbonella, the bureau's director, trying to fill gaps in city services to help students stay out of trouble. Their connecting suite of small rooms served as a kind of oasis at the school: the two adults didn't work for the principal, so they could arbitrate conflict without the threat of official discipline. I often saw kids stop by just to talk, and they had a lot to say about the aggression on Let's Start Drama and the way it was spilling over into real life. "We'd go on Facebook to look at the page, and it was pretty egregious," Carbonella told me. Surfing around on Facebook, they found more anonymous voting pages, with names like Middletown Hos, Middletown Trash Talk, and Middletown Too Real. Let's Start Drama had the largest audience, but it had spawned about two dozen imitators.

Carbonella figured that all of these pages had to be breaking Facebook's rules, and he was right. The site has built its brand by holding users to a relatively high standard of decency. "You will not bully, intimidate, or harass any user," Facebook requires people to pledge when they sign up. Users also agree not to fake their identities or to post content that is hateful or pornographic, or that contains nudity or graphic violence. In other words, Facebook does not style itself as the public square, where people can say anything they want, short of libel or slander. It's much more like a mall, where private security guards can throw you out.

Carbonella followed Facebook's procedure for filing a report, clicking through the screens that allow you to complain to the site about content that you think violates a rule. He clicked the bubbles to report bullying and fake identity. And then he waited. And waited. "It felt like putting a note in a bottle and throwing it into the ocean," Carbonella said. "There was no way to know if anyone was out there on the other end. For me, this wasn't a situation where I knew which student was involved and could easily give it to a school guidance counselor. It was completely anonymous, so we really needed Facebook to intervene." But, to Carbonella's frustration, Let's Start Drama stayed up. He filed another report. Like the first one, it seemed to sink to the bottom of the ocean.

Facebook, of course, is the giant among social networks, with more than 1 billion users worldwide. In 2011, *Consumer Reports* published the results of a survey showing that 20 million users were American kids under the age of 18; in an update the next year, it estimated that 5.6 million were under 13, the eligible age for an account. As a 2011 report from the Pew Internet and American Life Project put it, "Facebook dominates teen social media usage." Ninety-three percent of kids who use social-networking sites have a Facebook account. (Teens and pre-teens are also signing up in increasing numbers for Twitter—Pew found that 16 percent of 12- to 17-year-olds say they use the site, double the rate from two years earlier.)

Social networking has plenty of upside for kids: it allows them to pursue quirky interests and connect with people they'd have no way of finding otherwise. An online community can be a lifeline if, say, you're a gender-bending 15-year-old in rural Idaho or, for that matter, rural New York. But as Let's Start Drama illustrates, there's lots of ugliness, too. The 2011 Pew report found that 15 percent of social-media users between the ages of 12 and 17 said they'd been harassed online in the previous year. In 2012, *Consumer Reports* estimated[3] that 800,000 minors on Facebook had been bullied or harassed in the previous year. (Facebook questions the methodology of the magazine's survey; however, the company declined to provide specifics.) In the early days of the Internet, the primary danger to kids seemed to be from predatory adults. But it turns out that the perils adults pose, although they can be devastating, are rare. The far more common problem kids face when they go online comes from other kids: the hum of low-grade hostility, punctuated by truly damaging explosions, that is called cyberbullying.

In an attempt to impose order on a frustratingly subjective universe, User Operations has developed one rule of thumb: if you complain to Facebook that you are being harassed or bullied, the site takes your word for it. "If the content is about you, and you're not famous, we don't try to decide whether it's actually mean," Willner said. "We just take it down." All other complaints, however, are treated as "third-party reports" that the teams have to do their best to referee. These include reports from parents saying their children are being bullied, or from advocates like Justin Carbonella.

To demonstrate how the harassment team members do their jobs, Willner introduced me to an affable young guy named Nick Sullivan, who had on his desk a sword-carrying Grim Reaper figurine. Sullivan opened the program that he uses for sorting and resolving reports, which is known as the Common Review Tool (a precursor to the tool had a better name: the Wall of Shame). Sullivan cycled through the complaints with striking speed, deciding with very little deliberation which posts and pictures came down, which stayed up, and what other action, if any, to take. I asked him whether he would ever spend, say, 10 minutes on a particularly vexing report, and Willner raised his eyebrows. "We optimize for half a second," he said. "Your average decision time is a second or two, so 30 seconds would be a really long time." (A Facebook spokesperson said later that the User Operations teams use a process optimized for accuracy, not speed.) That reminded me of Let's Start Drama. Six months after Carbonella sent his reports, the page was still up. I asked why. It hadn't been set up with the user's real name, so wasn't it clearly in violation of Facebook's rules?

After a quick search by Sullivan, the blurry photos I'd seen many times at the top of the Let's Start Drama page appeared on the screen. Sullivan scrolled through some recent "Who's hotter?" comparisons and clicked on the behind-the-scenes history of the page, which the Common Review Tool allowed him to call up. A window opened on the right side of the screen, showing that multiple reports had been made. Sullivan checked to see whether the reports had failed to indicate that Let's Start Drama was administered by a fake user profile. But that wasn't the problem: the bubbles had been clicked correctly. Yet next to this history was a note indicating that future reports about the content would be ignored. We sat and stared at the screen. Willner broke the silence. "Someone made a mistake," he said. "This profile should have been disabled." He leaned in and peered at the screen. "Actually, two different reps made the same mistake, two different times." There was another long pause. Sullivan clicked on Let's Start Drama to delete it.

With millions of reports a week, most processed in seconds—and with 2.5 billion pieces of content posted daily—no wonder complaints like Carbonella's fall through the cracks. A Facebook spokesperson said that the site has been working on solutions to handle the volume of reports, while hiring "thousands of people" (though the company wouldn't discuss the specific roles of these employees) and building tools to address misbehavior in other ways. One idea is to improve the reporting process for users who spot content they don't like. During my visit, I met with the engineer Arturo Bejar, who'd designed new flows, or sets of responses users get as they file a report. The idea behind this "social reporting" tool was to lay out a path for users to find help in the real world, encouraging them to reach out to people they know and trust—people who might understand the context of a negative post. "Our goal should be to help people solve the underlying problem in the offline world," Bejar said. "Sure, we can take content down and warn the bully, but probably the most important thing is for the target to get the support they need."

After my visit, Bejar started working with social scientists at Berkeley and Yale to further refine these response flows, giving kids new ways to assess and communicate their emotions. The researchers, who include Marc Brackett and Robin Stern of Yale, talked to focus groups of 13- and 14-year-olds and created scripted responses that first push kids to identify the type and intensity of the emotion they're feeling, and then offer follow-up remedies depending on their answers. In January, during a presentation on the latest version of this tool, Stern explained that some of those follow-ups simply encourage reaching out to the person posting the objectionable material—who typically takes down the posts or photos if asked. Dave Willner told me that Facebook did not yet, however, have an algorithm that could determine at the outset whether a post was meant to harass and disturb—and could perhaps head it off. This is hard. As Willner pointed out, context is everything when it comes to bullying, and context is maddeningly tricky and subjective.

One man looking to create such a tool—one that catches troublesome material before it gets posted—is Henry Lieberman, a computer scientist whose background is in artificial intelligence. In November, I took a trip to Boston to meet him at his office in MIT's Media Lab. Lieberman looked like an older version of the Facebook employees: he was wearing sneakers and a baseball cap over longish gray curls. A couple years ago, a rash of news stories about bullying made him think back to his own misery in middle school, when he was a "fat kid with the nickname Hank the Tank." (This is hard to imagine now, given Lieberman's lean frame, but I took his word for it.) As a computer guy, he wondered whether cyberbullying would wreck social networking for teenagers in the way spam once threatened to kill e-mail—through sheer overwhelming volume. He looked at the frustrating, sometimes fruitless process for logging complaints, and he could see why even tech-savvy adults like Carbonella would feel at a loss. He was also not impressed by the generic advice often doled out to young victims of cyberbullying. "'Tell an adult. Don't let it get you down'— it's all too abstract and detached," he told me. "How could you intervene in a way that's more personal and specific, but on a large scale?"

To answer that question, Lieberman and his graduate students started analyzing thousands of YouTube comments on videos dealing with controversial topics, and about 1 million posts provided by the social-networking site Formspring that users or moderators had flagged for bullying. The MIT team's first insight was that bullies aren't particularly creative. Scrolling through the trove of insults, Lieberman and his students found that almost all of them fell under one (or more) of six categories: they were about appearance, intelligence, race, ethnicity, sexuality, or social acceptance and rejection. "People say there are an infinite number of ways to bully, but really, 95 percent of the posts were about those six topics," Lieberman told me.

Focusing accordingly, he and his graduate students built a "commonsense knowledge base" called BullySpace[4]—essentially a repository of words and phrases that could be paired with an algorithm to comb through text and spot bullying situations. Yes, BullySpace can be used to recognize words like *fat* and *slut* (and all their text-speak misspellings), but also to determine when the use of common words varies from the norm in a way that suggests they're meant to wound. Lieberman gave me an example of the potential ambiguity BullySpace could pick up on: "You ate six hamburgers!" On its own, *hamburger* doesn't flash cyberbullying—the word is neutral. "But the relationship between *hamburger* and *six* isn't neutral," Lieberman argued. BullySpace can

parse that relationship. To an overweight kid, the message "You ate six hamburgers!" could easily be cruel. In other situations, it could be said with an admiring tone. BullySpace might be able to tell the difference based on context (perhaps by evaluating personal information that social-media users share) and could flag the comment for a human to look at.

BullySpace also relies on stereotypes. For example, to code for anti-gay taunts, Lieberman included in his knowledge base the fact that "Put on a wig and lipstick and be who you really are" is more likely to be an insult if directed at a boy. BullySpace understands that lipstick is more often used by girls; it also recognizes more than 200 other assertions based on stereotypes about gender and sexuality. Lieberman isn't endorsing the stereotypes, of course: he's harnessing them to make BullySpace smarter. Running data sets from the YouTube and Formspring posts through his algorithm, he found that BullySpace caught most of the insults flagged by human testers—about 80 percent. It missed the most indirect taunting, but from Lieberman's point of view, that's okay. At the moment, there's nothing effective in place on the major social networks that screens for bullying before it occurs; a program that flags four out of five abusive posts would be a major advance.

Lieberman is most interested in catching the egregious instances of bullying and conflict that go destructively viral. So another of the tools he has created is a kind of air-traffic-control program for social-networking sites, with a dashboard that could show administrators where in the network an episode of bullying is turning into a pileup, with many users adding to a stream of comments—à la Let's Start Drama. "Sites like Facebook and Formspring aren't interested in every little incident, but they do care about the pileups," Lieberman told me. "For example, the week before prom, every year, you can see a spike in bullying against LGBT kids. With our tool, you can analyze how that spreads—you can make an epidemiological map. And then the social-network site can target its limited resources. They can also trace the outbreak back to its source."

Lieberman's dashboard could similarly track the escalation of an assault on one kid to the mounting threat of a gang war. That kind of data could be highly useful to schools and community groups as well as the sites themselves. (Lieberman is leery of seeing his program used in such a way that it would release the kids' names beyond the social networks to real-world authorities, though plenty of teenagers have social-media profiles that are public or semipublic—meaning their behavior is as well.)

I know some principals and guidance counselors who would pay for this kind of information. The question is what to do with it. Lieberman doesn't believe in being heavy-handed. "With spam, okay, you write the program to just automatically delete it," he said. "But with bullying, we're talking about free speech. We don't want to censor kids, or ban them from a site. More effective, Lieberman thinks, are what he calls "ladders of reflection. . . ." Think about the kid who posted "Because he's a fag! ROTFL [rolling on the floor laughing]!!!" What if, when he pushed the button to submit, a box popped up saying "Waiting 60 seconds to post," next to another box that read "I don't want to post" and offered a big X to click on? Or what if the message read "That sounds harsh! Are you sure you want to send that?" Or what if it simply reminded the poster that his comment was about to go to thousands of people?

Although Lieberman has had exploratory conversations about his idea with a few sites, none has yet deployed it. He has a separate project going with MTV, related to its web and phone app called Over the Line?, which hosts user-submitted stories about questionable behavior, like sexting, and responses to those stories. Lieberman's lab designed an algorithm that sorts the stories and then helps posters find others like them. The idea is that the kids posting will take comfort in having company, and in reading responses to other people's similar struggles.

Lieberman would like to test how his algorithm could connect kids caught up in cyberbullying with guidance targeted to their particular situation. Instead of generic "tell an adult" advice, he'd like the victims of online pummeling to see alerts from social-networking sites designed like the keyword-specific ads Google sells on Gmail—except they would say things like "Wow! That sounds nasty! Click here for help." Clicking would take the victims to a page that's tailored to the problem they're having—the more specific, the better. For example, a girl who is being taunted for posting a suggestive photo (or for refusing to) could read a synthesis of the research on sexual harassment, so she could better understand what it is, and learn about strategies for stopping it. Or a site could direct a kid who is being harassed about his sexuality to resources for starting a Gay–Straight Alliance at his school, since research suggests those groups act as a buffer against bullying and intimidation based on gender and sexuality. With the right support, a site could even use Lieberman's program to offer kids the option of an IM chat with an adult. (Facebook already provides this kind of specific response when a suicidal post is reported. In those instances, the site sends an e-mail to the poster offering the chance to call the National Suicide Prevention Lifeline or chat online with one of its experts.)

Lieberman would like to build this content and then determine its effectiveness by asking kids for their feedback. He isn't selling his algorithms or his services. As a university professor, he applies for grants, and then hopes companies like MTV will become sponsors. He's trying to work with companies rather than criticize them. "I don't think they're trying to reflexively avoid responsibility," he told me. "They are conscious of the scale. Anything that involves individual action on their part, multiplied by the number of complaints they get, just isn't feasible for them. And it *is* a challenging problem. That's where technology could help a little bit. My position is that technology can't solve bullying. This is a people problem. But technology can make a difference, either for the negative or the positive. And we're behind in paying attention to how to make the social-network universe a better place, from a technological standpoint."

Internal findings at Facebook suggest that Lieberman's light touch could indeed do some good. During my visit to Silicon Valley, I learned that the site had moved from wholesale banishment of rule-breakers toward a calibrated combination of warnings and "temporary crippling of the user experience," as one employee put it. After all, if you're banished, you can sign up again with a newly created e-mail address under an assumed name. And you might just get angry rather than absorb the message of deterrence. Instead, Facebook is experimenting with threats and temporary punishments. For example, the Hate and Harassment Team can punish a user for setting up a group to encourage bullying, by barring that person from setting up any other group pages for a month or two. (If the account associated with the offensive group uses a made-up name, then the site's only leverage is to remove the group.) According to an in-house study, 94 percent of users whose content prompted a report had never been reported to the site before. As Dave Willner, the content-policy manager, put it when he told me about the study: "The rate of recidivism is very low." He explained, in his appealingly blunt way, "What we have over you is that your Facebook profile is of value to you. It's a hostage situation." This didn't surprise me. In the course of my reporting, I'd been asking middle-school and high-school students whether they'd rather be suspended from school or from Facebook, and most of them picked school.

The hacker group Anonymous isn't the first place most parents would want their bullied kids to turn. Launched a decade ago, Anonymous is best known for its vigilante opposition to Internet censorship. The group has defaced or shut down the web sites of the Syrian Ministry of Defense, the Vatican, the FBI, and the CIA. Its slogan, to the extent a loosely affiliated bunch of hackers with no official leadership can be said to have one, is "When your government shuts down the Internet, shut down your government." Anonymous has also wreaked financial havoc by attacking MasterCard, Visa, and PayPal after they froze payments to the accounts of WikiLeaks, the site started by Julian Assange to publish government secrets.

Since Anonymous is anarchic, the people who answer its call (and use its trademark Guy Fawkes mask in their online photos) speak for themselves rather than represent the group, and protest in all kinds of ways. Some, reportedly, have not been kind to kids. There was the case, for example, of a 15-year-old named McKay Hatch, who started a No Cussing Club in South Pasadena, California. When the concept took off in other cities, a group referring to itself as Anonymous launched a counter campaign, No Cussing Sucks, and posted Hatch's name, photo, and contact information across the web; he got 22,000 e-mails over two weeks. But other people in Anonymous have a Robin Hood bent, and this fall, they rode to the rescue of a 12-year-old girl who'd come in for a torrent of hate on Twitter. Her error was to follow the feed of a 17-year-old boy she didn't know and then stop following him when he posted remarks she found rude. The boy took offense and, with three friends, went after her. The boys threatened to "gang bang" her, and one even told her to kill herself. "I'm gonna take today's anger and channel it into talking shit to this 12 year old girl," one wrote. "Blow up [her Twitter handle] till she deletes her twitter," another one added. The girl lived far from the boys, so she wasn't in physical danger, but she was disturbed enough to seek help online. "I have been told to kill myself alot its scary to think people in the world want you to die :(," she wrote to another Twitter user who asked me to call her Katherine. "He has deleted some of them he was saying things like do you have a rope? and didnt the bleach work?"

Her pleas reached Katherine in the wake of the suicide of a 15-year-old Canadian girl named Amanda Todd. Before Amanda died, she posted a video of herself on YouTube, in which she silently told her story using note cards she'd written on. Amanda said that a man she'd met online had persuaded her to send him a topless photo, then stalked her and released the photo, causing her misery at school. The video is raw and disturbing, and it moved Katherine and a member of Anonymous with the screen name Ash. "It made me choke up," Ash told me. When Katherine discovered that people were still sending the compromising photo of Amanda around online, she and Ash teamed up to help organize a drive to stop them and report offending users to Twitter, which removes pornographic content appearing on its site. As Katherine and Ash came across other examples of bullying, like rape jokes and suicide taunts, they found that "Twitter will suspend accounts even if they are not in violation of Twitter rules when simply 1000s of people mass report an account as spam," Katherine explained to me in an e-mail. A Twitter spokesperson said this was possible (though he added that if spam reports turn out to be false, most accounts soon go back online). Twitter bans direct and specific threats, and it can block IP addresses to prevent users whose accounts are deleted from easily starting new ones. But the site doesn't have an explicit rule against harassment and intimidation like Facebook does.

While monitoring Twitter for other bullying, Katherine found the 12-year-old girl. When Katherine told Ash, he uncovered the boys' real names and figured out that they were high-schoolers in Abilene, Texas. Then he pieced together screenshots of their nasty tweets, along with their names and information about the schools they attended, and released it all in a public outing (called a "dox"). "I am sick of seeing people who think they can get away with breaking someone's confidence and planting seeds of self-hate into someone's head," he wrote to them in the dox. "What gives you the fucking right to attack someone to such a breaking point? If you are vile enough to do so and stupid enough to do so on a public forum, such as a social website, then you should know this. . . . We will find you and we will highlight your despicable behaviour for all to see."

"I informed them that the damage had been done and there was no going back," he explained to me. "They understood this to be an act by

Anonymous when they were then messaged in the hundreds." At first the boys railed against Ash on Twitter, and one played down his involvement, denying that he had ever threatened to rape the girl. But after a while, two of the boys began sending remorseful messages. "For two solid days, every time we logged on, we had another apology from them," Ash said. "You hear a lot of lies and fake apologies, and these guys seemed quite sincere." Katherine thought the boys hadn't understood what impact their tweets would have on the girl receiving them—they hadn't thought of her as a real person. "They were actually shocked," she said. "I'm sure they didn't mean to actually rape a little girl. But she was *scared*. When they started to understand that, we started talking to them about anti-bullying initiatives they could bring to their schools."

I tried contacting the four boys to ask what they made of their encounter with Anonymous, and I heard back from one of them. He said that at first, he thought the girl's account was fake; then he assumed she wasn't upset, because she didn't block the messages he and the other boys were sending. Then Ash stepped in. "When i found out she was hurt by it i had felt horrible," wrote to me in an e-mail. "I honestly don't want to put anyone down. i just like to laugh and it was horrible to know just how hurt she was." He also wrote, "It was shocking to see how big [Anonymous was] and what they do."

Ash also e-mailed his catalog of the boys' tweets to their principals and superintendents. I called the school officials and reached Joey Light, the superintendent for one of the districts in Abilene. He said that when Anonymous contacted him, "to be truthful, I didn't know what it was. At first the whole thing seemed sketchy." Along with the e-mails from Ash, Light got an anonymous phone call from a local number urging him to take action against the boys. Light turned over the materials Ash had gathered to the police officer stationed at the district's high school, who established that one of the boys had been a student there. The officer investigated, and determined that the boy hadn't done anything to cause problems at school. That meant Light couldn't punish him, he said. "I realize bullying takes a lot of forms, but our student couldn't have harmed this girl physically in any way," he continued. "If you can't show a disruption at school, the courts tell us, that's none of our business." Still, Light told me he that he felt appreciative of Anonymous for intervening. "I don't have the technical expertise or the time to keep track of every kid on Facebook or Twitter or whatever," the superintendent said. "It was unusual, sure, but we would have never done anything if they hadn't notified us."

I talked with Ash and Katherine over Skype about a week after their Texas operation. I wanted to know how they'd conceived of the action they'd taken. Were they dispensing rough justice to one batch of heartless kids? Or were they trying to address cyberbullying more broadly, and if so, how? Ash and Katherine said they'd seen lots of abuse of teenagers on social-networking sites, and most of the time, no adult seemed to know about it or intervene. They didn't blame the kids' parents for being clueless, but once they spotted danger, as they thought they had in this case, they couldn't bear to just stand by. "It sounds harsh to say we're teaching people a lesson, but they need to realize there are consequences for their actions," Ash said.

He and Katherine don't have professional experience working with teenagers, and I'm sure there are educators and parents who'd see them as suspect rather than helpful. But reading through the hate-filled tweets, I couldn't help thinking that justice Anonymous-style is better than no justice at all. In their own way, Ash and Katherine were stepping into the same breach that Henry Lieberman is trying to fill. And while sites like Facebook and Twitter are still working out ways to address harassment comprehensively, I find myself agreeing with Ash that "someone needs to teach these kids to be mindful, and anyone doing that is a good thing."

For Ash and Katherine, this has been the beginning of #OpAntiBully, an operation that has a Twitter account providing resource lists and links to abuse-report forms. Depending on the case, Ash says, between 50 and 1,000 people—some of whom are part of Anonymous and some of whom are outside recruits—can come together to report an abusive user, or bombard him with angry tweets, or offer support to a target. "It's much more refined now," he told me over e-mail. "Certain people know the targets, and everyone contacts each other via DMs [direct messages]."

In a better online world, it wouldn't be up to Anonymous hackers to swoop in on behalf of vulnerable teenagers. But social networks still present tricky terrain for young people, with traps that other kids spring for them. My own view is that, as parents, we should demand more from these sites, by holding them accountable for enforcing their own rules. After all, collectively, we have consumer power here—along with our kids, we're the site's customers. And as Henry Lieberman's work at MIT demonstrates, it *is* feasible to take stronger action against cyberbullying. If Facebook and Twitter don't like his solution, surely they have the resources to come up with a few more of their own.

NOTES

1. Editor's note: Bazelon's book, published in 2014, is entitled *Sticks and Stones: Defeating the Culture of Bullying and Rediscovering the Power of Character and Empathy*.
2. City of Middletown, Connecticut. n.d. "Youth Services Bureau." http://www.cityofmiddletown.com/content/117/123/187/default.aspx.
3. 2012. "Facebook and Your Privacy: Who sees the data you share on the biggest social network?" *Consumer Reports Magazine*. http://www.consumerreports.org/cro/magazine/2012/06/facebook-your-privacy/index.htm.
4. Dinakar, Karthik, et al. 2012. "Common Sense Reasoning for Detection, Prevention, and Mitigation of Cyberbullying." *ACM Transactions on Interactive Intelligent Systems* 2(3).

Constructing Crime

GARY W. POTTER AND VICTOR E. KAPPELER

Potter and Kappeler argue that consumers of media develop an inaccurate picture of crime in the United States. Most Americans will never be victims of a crime, yet they fear they are in imminent danger of being victimized. According to Potter and Kappeler, media representations of crime focus on violent stranger crime and rare types of crimes (e.g., those where wealthy white women are victims). Potter and Kappeler demonstrate how media portrayals of crime flame racial tensions through selective coverage and that media consumption may actually contribute to decreased accuracy in knowledge about crime, deflecting our attention from serious crime issues in our culture.

There is probably no issue that invokes greater emotion and more consistently influences public opinion than crime. Whether the issue is drug-related crime, violent crime, juvenile crime, child abductions, serial killers, youth gangs, or crime against the elderly, a public consensus exists that crime is rampant, dangerous, and threatening to explode. The dangers of crime are seen as immediate, omnipresent, and almost inescapable. For more than three decades in the United States, the fear of crime has been so real that one can almost reach out and touch it. Politicians, law enforcement executives, the private crime industry, and the media cater to the public mood. Their increasingly draconian responses—in the form of more police, more arrests, longer sentences, more prisons, and more executions—affirm public fears, and that fear grows unabated. Each new crime story, each new crime movie, each new governmental pronouncement on crime increases the public thirst for more crime control, less personal freedom, and greater intervention by the state.

In contrast to seemingly tangible public fear, crime facts are far more difficult to assess. The emotional reaction to crime makes the public policy issue of control intensely sensitive. The issue responds to manipulation and pandering so predictably that advertisers and public relations experts would be envious of the responses elicited. Why are crime facts so difficult to determine but crime fear so easy to manipulate? Through what process do rumors, gossip, urban legends, and apocryphal stories become public "common sense"? Through what mechanisms do isolated and rare incidents weave a tapestry of fear, panic, and hysteria? More importantly, who benefits from the construction of this labyrinth . . . ? . . . A careful look at crime and crime-related issues can help us see beyond the web of public fear. Public opinion and crime facts demonstrate no congruence. The reality of crime in the United States has been blanketed by a constructed reality. The policies and programs emanating from that constructed reality do far more damage than good to public safety and crime control.

Crime Knowledge

What does the public really know about crime and how do they know it? The most reliable crime data available clearly demonstrate that the vast majority of people living in the United States will never be victims of crime. In fact, over 90 percent of the U.S. population has no direct experience with crime at all (Kappeler & Potter, 2005). Yet the public remains convinced of imminent danger—changing their personal habits and lives to accommodate fears and voting for politicians who promise solutions to the conjured problem. What is the basis for these opinions, fears, and impressions?

In addition to their own experiences, people interpret and internalize the experiences of others. They hear—often second-, third-, or fourth-hand—about crime incidents involving neighbors, relatives, friends, and friends of friends. This process of socialization carries crime "facts" and crime-related experiences from one person to many others like a virus. Crime is a topic of conversation, both public and private. Strong opinions and reactions amplify and extend the content of actual experiences. Lost in the retelling is the relatively isolated aspect of the incidents. . . .

For centuries, the only means of disseminating knowledge from one person to another was oral communication. Reaching larger audiences was a slow, repetitive process limited by time and place. The printing press and public education were important revolutions that allowed written messages from one person to reach many read-

ers. Newer technologies today have created a maelstrom of information. The mass media can disseminate messages literally with the speed of light and sound. Publishers produce thousands of books about crime—some fictional, some true, some simply crude "pot-boilers." Movies make crime a central theme. Producers know that movies like *The Clearing, Kill Bill, Memento, Pulp Fiction, Natural Born Killers*, and *The Usual Suspects* attract large audiences. Television programs also use crime and violence to attract attention. Police programs have been a staple of television programming from *Dragnet* to *CSI*. The creator of the *Law & Order* series, Dick Wolf, comments:

> Crime is a constantly renewable resource. Every day people continue to kill each other in bizarre and unfathomable ways. Even if murder goes down by double digits, there are still thousands of people killed in this country every year and killers who warrant prosecution. (Smith, 2006, p. 16)

Because of the public's fixation on crime, the television industry constructed a new type of programming in 1989—a hybrid between entertainment and crime news called reality TV. By the end of 1993, there were seven national programs fitting this profile. Two survived until the mid 2010s . . . and continued to attract viewers: *America's Most Wanted* and *Unsolved Mysteries*. In 2006 the web site for *America's Most Wanted* advertised its hotline (1-800-CRIME-TV) for tips from viewers and proclaimed, "You have helped catch 876 fugitives to date." There is also an AMW case tracker that tells viewers there are 1,185 open cases. You . . . could select the type of crime from a drop-down list, including terrorism, or you can click on an area on the map of the United States and look at crimes by region. Other features of the web site included: "In the Line of Duty," which claims more than 1,600 law enforcement officers—"an average of one death every 53 hours"—died on the job during the past 10 years and an advertisement for a "fun safety DVD for kids" (AMW, 2006). In 2006 the portal to the web site for *Unsolved Mysteries* flashed "missing," "lost love," "homicide," and "fugitive" before showing the title of the program and a button to click to enter the site, where the viewer is told this is one of television's first interactive series (*Unsolved*, 2006).

According to research, the mass media are the basic sources of information on crime, criminals, crime control policies, and the criminal justice system for most people (Barak, 1994; Ericson, Baranek, & Chan, 1989; Graber, 1980; Warr, 1995). Crime themes are a mother lode for the media; crime attracts viewers. More viewers mean greater newspaper and magazine circulations, larger television audiences, and consequently larger advertising fees (Barkan, 1997). The local news and reality crime shows focus on dramatic themes to attract viewers: police "hot pursuits"; violent crimes (particularly strange and heinous crimes with innocent and unsuspecting victims); and crime alleged to be committed by social deviants like drug addicts, pedophiles, prostitutes, and terrorists.

The Portrayal of Crime in the Mass Media

Crime rates have decreased every year since 1991, and victimization surveys indicate that serious crime has been on a perpetual decline since the early 1970s (Kappeler & Potter, 2005). The media, however, provide a distorted view of how much crime there is in society. The media create a wholly inaccurate image of a society in which violent crime is rampant and in which crime is constantly and immutably on the increase. In addition, media coverage of crime seriously distorts public perception of the types of crime being committed and the frequency with which violent crimes occur. The media have a preoccupation with violent crime. Researchers have demonstrated a consistent and strong bias in the news toward murder, sexual crimes, gangs and violence, and drug-related violence (Beirne & Messerschmidt, 1995; Livingston, 1996).

One study looked at local television news programs in 13 major cities and found that crime far outdistanced all other topics in local newscasts, even weather and sports. Commercial advertisements and crime stories dominated the average 30-minute newscast in the study. Crime made up 20 percent of all local TV stories, followed by weather at 11 percent and accidents and disasters at 9 percent (*Public Health Reports*, 1998). The media not only overreport crime, but they also focus on the least common crimes, crimes of violence (Lundman, 2003). Another focus is random violence committed by strangers, despite the fact that violence overwhelmingly occurs among friends and intimates (Feld, 2003).

The less common a crime is, the more coverage it will generate. For example, crimes against small children and wealthy white women are featured in most crime reporting despite the fact that these groups have the lowest victimization rates of any social groups in the United States (Feld, 2003). Sensational and rare crimes that dovetail conveniently into news themes with moralistic messages are particularly popular. Over the years the media have created crime scares by formulating news themes around issues of "white-slavery" in the prostitution industry; sexual psychopaths running rampant in major cities; satanists engaged in mass murder, child sacrifice, and ritualistic child abuse; serial killers roaming the countryside; and many others. As Philip Jenkins (1996) comments:

> If we relied solely on the evidence of the mass media, we might well believe that every few years, a particular form of immoral or criminal behavior becomes so dangerous as almost to threaten the foundations of society. . . . These panics are important in their own right for what they reveal about social concerns and prejudices—often based on xenophobia and anti-immigrant prejudice. (pp. 67–70)

Mass murders by satanic cults, the predations of roaming serial killers, and organized child abuse in day-care centers are so rare as to be total aberrations. The media choose to ignore common, everyday, typical crime. White-collar crimes such as price-fixing, illegal disposal of toxic waste, and unsafe work conditions get little coverage, so the public tends not to view these activities as "real crime."

Crime reports in the media inflame racial tensions and fears through biased and selective coverage. Crime stories on television news programs and in newspapers focus on crimes by African-American and Hispanic offenders, creating a wildly exaggerated view of their involvement in street crime and violent crime (Dorfman & Schiraldi, 2001; Lundman, 2003). The media also distort the race of victims in three important ways. First, newspapers carry a vastly inflated number of stories about white victims when compared to NCVS [National Crime Victimization Survey] statistics on victimization. Second, stories featuring white victims are longer and more detailed than stories about African-American victims. Finally, despite the fact that violent crime is overwhelmingly intra-racial, newspapers focus on stories involving white victims and African-American offenders (Lundman, 2003).

When a story deals with an African-American or Hispanic offender, the focus is usually on interracial crime as evidenced by accompanying photographs of the offender being taken into police custody or a mug shot of the offender (Chiricos & Eschholz, 2002; Feld, 2003). The impact of this racial profiling by the media is stunning. One study found that 60 percent of the people interviewed recalled an offender being shown in a television news story about crime when no offender images were included. Of those who saw the phantom offender, 70 percent were certain the offender was African American (Gilliam & Iyengar, 2000).

The media are also guilty of bias by age in the depiction of crime and violent crime. Both television and newspaper coverage of crime portrays young people as offenders in violent incidents (Dorfman & Schiraldi, 2001). In fact, the research shows that 68 percent of all television news stories on violent crime highlight youthful

offenders, and 55 percent of all stories about young people highlight violence. The reality is that less than 4 percent of all arrests of youths are for violent crime, and less than 16 percent of all crime is committed by young people (FBI, 2005).

The many distortions about crime, types of crime, race, and demographics found in media reporting help explain public ignorance about crime, the criminal justice system, and crime control policy in the United States (Cullen, Fisher, & Applegate, 2000). A study of 500 students taking introductory criminal justice classes found that they estimated the annual number of homicides in the United States at about 250,000 (Vandiver & Giacopassi, 1997, p. 141). In 1997, there were slightly more than 18,208 murders; in 2004 there were 16,137. Similarly a Gallup Poll in 2002 found that 62 percent of the U.S. public thought crime was higher than in 2001, despite a steady ten year drop in crime rates (Maguire & Pastore, 2004).[1]

Media Attention and Citizen Fear of Crime

With such heavy exposure to crime themes in both news and entertainment programming, it would appear to be common sense that more media exposure should be directly related to a greater fear of crime. However, unlike media analysts and news anchors, social scientists are constrained by their craft to be more circumspect in their claims. A correlation between media exposure and concerns about crime is easy to demonstrate, but correlation is a long way from causation. Direct relationships are not easy to prove. For example, it is difficult to demonstrate whether greater media exposure causes fear of crime or whether fear of crime causes greater media exposure because people are staying home watching crime on television. As we pointed out earlier, people are exposed to information other than that provided by the media that may influence their viewpoints (i.e., rumors, gossip, urban legends). In addition, media research is difficult, complex, and subject to many pitfalls. For example, how does one measure the impact of the media? Is viewing time a measure?

Do column inches constitute an index? Does the quality and the impact of language and content take precedence? (Miethe & Lee, 1984; Skogan & Maxfield, 1981; Surette, 1998).

Despite the need for caution and the constraints of science, much evidence indicates that the media do influence the level of fear of crime and contribute to the persistence of crime as a major national issue. George Gerbner, a leading media researcher at the Annenberg School of Communications at the University of Pennsylvania, developed cultivation theory—the "mean world" syndrome—to describe the impact of the media. Gerbner argues that research demonstrates that heavy viewers of television violence, whether in entertainment or news mediums, increasingly develop the feeling that they are living in a state of siege. Gerbner's research shows that heavy television viewers: (1) seriously overestimate the probability that they will be victims of violence; (2) believe their own neighborhoods to be unsafe; (3) rank fear of crime as one of their most compelling personal problems; (4) assume crime rates are going up regardless of whether they really are; (5) support punitive anti-crime measures; and (6) are more likely to buy guns and anti-crime safety devices (Gerbner, 1994). Other research demonstrates that "heavy viewers ... exhibit an exaggerated fear of victimization and a perception that people cannot be trusted" (Carlson, 1995, p. 190).

It is difficult to gauge the impact of the media on fear of crime. One thing, however, is clear from the research: the more you watch television news, the more fearful you are of crime. People who watch more television news and more television crime dramas express dramatically higher rates of fear about crime than those who watch fewer broadcasts (Eschholz, Chiricos, & Gertz, 2003). A study in Philadelphia found that people who watched the television news four times a week were 40 percent more likely to be very worried about crime than those who did not watch the news (Bunch, 1999).

In addition to increasing public fear, media crime coverage has other effects on public

perceptions and views of crime. Heavy coverage shapes perceptions and directs much public discourse on the crime issue. For example, the media regularly and falsely direct attention to crimes allegedly committed by young, poor, urban males, who are often members of minority groups (Reiman, 2004). Media coverage directs people's attention to specific crimes and helps to shape those crimes as social problems (i.e., drug use, gangs). Media coverage limits discourse on crime control options to present policies—suggesting that the only options are more laws, more police, longer sentences, and more prisons (Kappeler & Potter, 2005). The impact of media coverage is readily apparent in the creation of crime scares and moral panics.

Moral Panics

The concept of a moral panic was developed by Stanley Cohen (1980). A moral panic occurs when a group or type of activity is perceived as a threat to the stability and well-being of society. The media provide copious details and information (not necessarily accurate); this is followed by attention from law enforcement officials, politicians, and editorial writers who begin to comment on the panic. "Experts" then join the fray and try to explain the panic and offer policy options for dealing with it.

Moral panics direct public attention toward the activity or group and organize public fear for the well-being of society. The attention amplifies the behavior of the groups under scrutiny. . . .

. . . In 1922, future Supreme Court Justice Felix Frankfurter and legal scholar Roscoe Pound took the media to task for creating crime scares. Frankfurter and Pound noted that newspapers in Cleveland had dramatically increased their coverage of crime stories during 1919, even though crimes reported to the police had increased only slightly. They charged that the press was needlessly alarming the public and that the effect was a dangerous tendency for the public to pressure police to ignore due process rights and constitutional protections in their pursuit of criminals (Frankfurter & Pound, 1922).

The "sex fiend" panic of the 1930s and 1940s resulted in the passage of sexual psychopath laws in 28 states. One analysis of the development of these laws reveals a key role played by the media (McCaghy & Capron, 1997). Sex fiend panics typically began with the commission of a sex crime, particularly a crime against a child, accompanied by heavy mass media coverage. This panic included estimates, without any basis in fact, that thousands of sex fiends were at large in the community. These "sex crime waves" were not related to any increase in the actual numbers of reported sex crimes; the panic was artificially induced by media coverage of particularly salacious cases (see Sutherland, 1950). The media advocated such solutions as castration, the outlawing of pornography, and life imprisonment for sex offenders. Special sexual psychopath laws were passed that allowed indeterminate confinement for any offender, whether a child molester or an exhibitionist or a fornicator, until the state deemed them to be cured. In some states, the original offense didn't even have to be a sex offense—it could be robbery or arson, as long as a psychiatrist could identify sexual dysfunctions in the accused. . . .

In the 1980s the same kind of moral panic surfaced with regard to the use of crack (a smokable form of cocaine hydrochloride). Craig Reinarman and Harry Levine (1989) carefully researched the media's creation of a drug scare surrounding crack. Reinarman and Levine define a "drug scare" as a historical period in which all manner of social difficulties (such as crime, health problems, the failure of the education system) are blamed on a chemical substance. "Drug scares" are not new. Problems of opiate addiction at the turn of the century were blamed on Chinese immigrants; African Americans were portrayed as "cocaine fiends" during the 1920s; violent behavior resulting from marijuana consumption was linked to Mexican farm laborers in the 1920s and 1930s. The construction of the crack scare was similar in that it linked the use of crack-cocaine to inner-city blacks, Hispanics, and youths. In the 1970s,

when the use of expensive cocaine hydrochloride was concentrated among affluent whites, both the media and the state focused on heroin, seen as a drug of the inner-city poor. Only when cocaine became available in an inexpensive form, crack, did the scapegoating common to drug scares begin.

The media hype began in 1986, following the spread of crack into poor and working class neighborhoods. *Time* and *Newsweek* ran five cover stories each on crack during 1986. The three major television networks quickly joined the feeding frenzy. NBC did 400 news stories on crack between June and December 1986; in July 1986, all three networks ran 74 drug stories on their nightly newscasts. These stories contained highly inflated estimates of crack use and warnings about the dangers of the drug.

Those news stories were particularly troubling precisely because they were entirely incorrect. Research from the National Institute of Drug Abuse [NIDA] showed that the use of all forms of cocaine by youth and young adults had reached its peak four years earlier and had been declining ever since. Every indicator showed that at the height of the media frenzy crack use was relatively rare (Walker, 1998). Surveys of high school students demonstrated that experimentation with cocaine and cocaine products had been decreasing steadily since 1980. In fact, the government's own statistics showed that 96 percent of young people in the United States had never even tried crack. If there had been an epidemic, it was long over.

Officially produced data strongly refuted other claims about crack use. The media reports claimed that crack and cocaine were highly addictive and that crack, in particular, was so addictive that one experience with the drug could addict a user for life. However, NIDA estimates showed that of the 22 million people who had used cocaine and cocaine-products, very few of them ever became addicted. In fact, very few of them ever escalated to daily use. NIDA's own estimates indicated that fewer than 3 percent of cocaine users would ever become "problem" users

(Kappeler & Potter, 2005). The health dangers of cocaine and crack were also widely exaggerated; few users ever required medical treatment because of using the drug.

The impact of the crack scare was tangible and immediate. New laws were passed increasing mandatory sentences for crack use and sales. Ironically, these laws resulted in a situation where someone arrested for crack faced the prospect of a prison sentence three to eight times longer than a sentence for cocaine hydrochloride, the substance needed to produce crack. The drug laws for crack inverted the typical ratio—wholesalers receive less severe sanctions than retailers and users. . . .

Crime Mythology

False beliefs about crime abound in U.S. society and play a disproportionate role in the formulation of government and law enforcement policies. The crime that does exist is not predominantly violent, and violent crime is not as common or debilitating as the media would lead us to believe. The media, the state, and criminal justice officials create and perpetuate crime myths.

Crime myths focus on unpopular, minority, and deviant groups in society. Drug problems have consistently been laid squarely at the feet of immigrant groups, minority groups, and inner-city residents, wholly displacing the reality of drug use. Problems of opiate addiction in the late 1800s and early 1900s were blamed on immigrant Chinese workers, while the actual problem resulted from the overuse of over-the-counter elixirs by white, middle-aged, rural, Protestant women. The reputed cocaine epidemic of the 1980s was blamed on the irresponsible and hedonistic lifestyles of inner-city minorities, while the facts were that cocaine was primarily a drug of choice of affluent, suburban whites. Law enforcement agencies and the media have combined their efforts to tie serial murder, child abduction, ritualistic child abuse, and child sacrifice and murder to the activities of unpopular religious groups and sexual minorities.

Crime myths come in many forms. For example, in the mid-1970s the media reported that children had been murdered as the result of the poisoning of their Halloween candy. However, careful investigation revealed something quite different from a wave of poisoning by strangers. There had been only two incidents: one child died from ingesting heroin he found in his uncle's house; the other child was poisoned by his father, who put cyanide in the boy's candy. As with most crime myths, the truth was ignored while tales of mythical savagery circulated (Best & Horiuchi, 1985). To this day local television stations run cautionary stories before each Halloween.

In the early 1980s the media and the government helped create a panic over the issue of child abduction. It was estimated that somewhere between 1.5 and 2.5 million children were abducted from their homes every year; of that number, 50,000 would never be heard from again, presumably the victims of homicides. Pictures of "missing children" appeared on milk cartons, billboards, in newspapers, and on television. Children and parents were cautioned against contacts with strangers. The police in one town even wanted to etch identification numbers on school children's teeth so their bodies would be easier to identify (Dunn, 1994). The child abduction "epidemic" never existed. About 95 percent of those missing children were runaways (most of whom were home within 48 hours) or children abducted by a parent in a custody dispute. The fact is there are no more than 50 to 150 child abductions by strangers each year in the United States (Kappeler & Potter, 2005).

From 1983 to 1985 official estimates and media hype fueled a serial killer panic. Using FBI estimates of unsolved and motiveless homicides, media sources falsely reported that roughly 20 percent of all homicides, or about 4,000 murders a year, were the handiwork of serial killers. The media fed the myth with shocking and untrue confessions from Henry Lee Lucas, Ted Bundy, and others. Congress funded the Violent Criminal Apprehension Program and a behavioral sciences center for the FBI. When the data was subjected to careful analysis, scholars determined that at most there were 50 or 60 serial killer victims a year and that serial killers could account for no more than 2 percent of all homicides (Jenkins, 1996). Serial murder remains an extremely uncommon event.

The media play a vital role in the construction of crime mythology. Through selective interviewing the media can, and often do, fit isolated and rare incidents into what Fishman calls "news themes" (Fishman, 1978). For example, reporting the details of a crime involving an elderly victim and then interviewing a police official in charge of a special unit targeting crimes against the elderly creates a news theme—and can eventually create both a "crime wave" and a "crime myth." The use of value-laden language also contributes heavily to crime mythology. Youth gang members "prey" upon unsuspecting victims; serial killers "stalk"; child abductors "lurk" in the shadows; organized criminals are "mafiosi." Such language is common in crime news and substantially changes both the content and the context of crime stories. The media also frequently present misleading data. . . . Uncritical reproduction of officially produced statistics often organizes stories into news themes and deflects alternative interpretations of the data.

Crime myths are not just curiosities or examples of sloppy work by journalists. They have tangible and serious policy implications. Spurred by crime mythology, politicians clamor for ever tougher sanctions against criminals. Crime myths divert attention away from the social and cultural forces that cause crime and toward individual pathologies; they reinforce stereotypes of minorities, poor people, and people who are "different."

Diverting Attention from Serious Social Problems

There is a corollary harm to directing our attention to certain kinds of criminality. Exaggerating the incidence and importance of violent crime, for example, deflects our attention from other serious issues. . . .

The media pay little substantive attention to corporate crime and other forms of white-collar crime. Since the public is far more likely to be seriously harmed by corporate criminals than by violent criminals, this is a major disservice. In addition, ignoring such offenses encourages corporate crime by removing one of the primary modes of deterring that behavior—publicity. The media's neglect of white-collar crime stems from several sources, including: the risk of libel suits; social relationships between media executives and business executives; a pro-business orientation in the media; and the difficulty of adequately investigating and reporting on white-collar crime. In addition, corporations own the major newspapers, television networks, and television stations. Finally, media revenue comes primarily from advertising purchased by corporations.

The processes through which the media amplify and exaggerate crime and focus our attention on disadvantaged and relatively powerless groups in society are also used to deflect and diffuse concern over other types of crime. A case in point is the media's treatment of crimes against women, particularly rape and wife battering.

The media frequently distort rape coverage by referring to "careless" behavior by the victim or provocative actions or clothing. The fact is that rape is a crime of violence, and the behavior of the perpetrator should be the focus. The media further distort the rape issue by giving primary coverage to stranger rapes, failing to emphasize the far more common case in which rape is committed by acquaintances, relatives, and "friends." Stories about non-stranger rape frequently repeat and reflect police skepticism about such cases. Acquaintance rape stories often emphasize cases of false reporting, a very rare occurrence.

Similarly, the media distort the issue of battering in a variety of ways. First, battering is a relatively uncovered story in a crime-saturated news environment. When battering is reported, it is treated as a bizarre spectacle and news stories make use of euphemistic or evasive language (i.e., marital disputes, domestic disturbance, spouse abuse). Such language obscures the gendered nature of battering and implies the woman may be at fault. Stories on battering often raise the question of why the woman didn't leave her batterer, ignoring the fact that many do try to leave and that many have good reasons not to leave. Battering stories often project a clear implication that women are responsible for their own victimization. In addition, the media frequently overplay the extremely rare occurrences of women abusing their husbands. Rather than focusing on the common crime of spouse battering, media sources often focus on cases where governors have released women from prison who were convicted of murdering abusive husbands. The story often reports that the woman was not living with her husband when she killed him, implying that the danger to the woman had passed. The story usually fails to report that this is precisely the most dangerous time for battered women. News stories frequently imply that pardons and releases encourage battered women to commit acts of violence against their abusers (Barkan, 1997; Devitt, 1992; Devitt & Downey, 1992; Kamen & Rhodes, 1992).

In a particularly egregious example of gender bias, media coverage of school shootings in the 1990s failed to point out that all the offenders were males and a majority of the victims were females (Danner & Carmody, 2001).

Making Sense of Media Representations of Crime

Three fundamental questions for analyzing how the media approach crime issues are: What functions do the media serve?; How do they accomplish those tasks?; and Who benefits from media actions? As one of society's dominant institutions, the media share certain characteristics with other dominant institutions, like the state, corporations, the law enforcement community, and the military. . . .

The media operate in the same ideological arena as do the educational system, religious institutions, and the family. Ideology is a means of organizing impressions, thoughts, knowledge, and observations to interpret the world around us. The media most frequently voice and, because of their ability to reach such an extensive audience, amplify the views and interests of groups with the greatest political, economic, and social power. Journalists and other media professionals are trained, educated, and socialized to internalize the values and norms of the dominant, mainstream culture. As a result, the media interpret or mediate news, information, and complex issues in a way that is usually consistent with the dominant culture and with the interests of powerful groups. The audience is, of course, free to interpret reports and stories by subjecting them to rigorous analysis, but people generally lack the time, resources, and information to construct alternative definitions and frameworks—in addition to having been socialized in the very same environment that influenced the stories.

The mass media are part of the culture industry that produces tangible products. In general, but not exclusively, the products they produce will reflect the ideas, conceptions, theories, and views of those with power in society. There have been notable examples of investigative reporters whose efforts, for example, have focused attention on abuses in the juvenile justice system in Chicago, forced the San Francisco police department to change how it tracks officers who abuse force, or exonerated inmates on death row (Coen, 2005; Headden, 2006; Worden, 2006). The media more frequently, however, present viewpoints that are consistent with those held by powerful groups. They present those viewpoints as the "obvious" or "natural" perspectives; alternative views, if presented at all, are clearly labeled as deviant, different, or dangerous. The mass media tend to avoid unpopular and unconventional ideas. They repeat widely held views that do not offend audiences, advertisers, or owners.

We discussed media reliance on the portrayal of violence in both news and entertainment programming. These portrayals are not just attention grabbing; they serve other purposes as well. They provide legitimacy to the criminal justice system and the police. They build support for more draconian laws and for more state intervention into people's daily activities. They warn us about people who are different, outsiders, and the dangers of defying social conventions. In other words, they reinforce, they amplify, and they extend the existing state of affairs that makes up the dominant culture and the current distribution of power (Althusser, 1971; Alvarado & Boyd-Barrett, 1992; Hall, 1980; Hall, Critcher, Jefferson, Clarke, & Roberts, 1978; Stevenson, 1995).

Of course, the media are only one half of the equation. The audience is the other half. Are audiences passive individuals who absorb ideological propaganda from newspapers, television, movies, and magazines? Of course not. People rely on other experiences and interactions. Social identities are determined by interactions with all kinds of institutions: the family, the school, the state, language, and the media. However, people generally find their sense of identity and their understanding of the reality around them as a result of social identities molded by those institutions—all of which are "ideological state apparatuses" (Althusser, 1971; Lapley & Westlake, 1988). The media have the capacity to concentrate those definitions and interactions in a way that convinces people that the media are presenting an accurate reflection of everyday lives.

Can audiences resist the power of media representations and definitions? Yes. We have seen that some crime scares and moral panics never get off the ground. Ideological state apparatuses are not always successful in defining people's roles and consciousness. While the mass media relay certain ideological images, the audience—if it has the ability, the resources, and the inclination—can remold, adapt, and integrate those messages into an entirely different system of meaning (Althusser, 1971; Berger, 1991; Hall, 1980; Hall et al., 1978; McQuail, 1994),

Mass media (movies, television, news organizations) form a culture industry in modern capitalist societies. They sell their products. The shape and content of those products will be influenced by the economic interests of the organization producing the products. Businesses operating in the culture industry must cater to the needs of advertisers. News shows are set up in standardized formats that cater to the demands of advertising. News must be fitted into the air time and column inches left over after paid advertising is accounted for. As a result, a standard format with news, weather, and sports segments has evolved around the needs of advertisers. They are unlikely to sponsor programs that attack their interests.

Media businesses must maximize their audiences. They do this in several ways. First, they include heavy doses of sex and violence. Second, they appeal to noncontroversial, mainstream views—trying to achieve a nonoffensive middle-ground on most issues. Finally, they treat the news as light entertainment, something not requiring a great deal of thought or attention on the part of the reader or viewer. In the process, they reduce the danger of alternative interpretations of a story by the audience.

In general we can safely say that: (1) ownership and economic control of the media are important factors in determining the content of media messages and (2) the media are a powerful influence in shaping public consciousness. The media are something of an irresistible force in modern society. The media are instrumental but not the only players in defining the terms through which we think about the world around us (Marcuse, 1991; Strinati, 1995). Stuart Hall points out that there is a "preferred reading" of the media's message that buttresses the dominant political, economic, and social relations in society. However, it is not the only interpretation. Some audiences "negotiate" that message and transform it slightly. Others read that message from a very different perspective and create "oppositional" meanings that are in direct conflict with the views of the powerful.

That is how we should interpret crime news. We must ask questions: Where did that information come from? Who supplied it? Do they have a vested interest in how we react to that information? We must begin to deconstruct the taken-for-granted "common sense" messages of the media.

NOTES

1. This trend has continued, with homicide rates currently at levels not seen since the mid 1960s (Cooper and Smith, 2011).

REFERENCES

Althusser, L. (1971). Ideology and ideological state apparatuses. In L. Althusser (Ed.), *Lenin and philosophy and other essays.* London: New Left Books.

Alvarado, M., & Boyd-Barrett, O. (Eds.). (1992). *Media education: An introduction.* London: BFI/Open University.

America's Most Wanted. Accessed February 15, 2006 from http://www.amw.com/.

Barak, G. (1994). Media, society, and criminology. In G. Barak (Ed.), *Media, process, and the social construction of crime* (pp. 3–45). New York: Garland Publishing.

Barkan, S. F. (1997). *Criminology: A sociological understanding.* Englewood Cliffs, NJ: Prentice-Hall.

Beirne, P., & Messerschmidt, J. (1995). *Criminology* (2nd ed.). Ft. Worth: Harcourt Brace Jovanovich.

Berger, A. (1991). *Media analysts' techniques* (Rev. ed.). Newbury Park, CA: Sage.

Best, J., & Horiuchi, G. (1985). The razor and the apple: The social construction of urban legends. *Social Problems, 32,* 488–499.

Bunch, W. (1999). Survey: Crime fear is linked to TV news. *Philadelphia Daily News,* March 16, p. Al.

Carlson, J. (1995). *Prime time enforcement.* New York: Praeger.

Chiricos, T., & Eschholz, S. (2002). The racial and ethnic: Typification of crime and the criminal typification of race and ethnicity in local television news. *Journal of Research in Crime and Delinquency, 39,* 400–420.

Coen, J. (2005, September 5). Report leads to changes in defense for juveniles. *Chicago Tribune,* sec. 4, p. 1.

Cohen, S. (1980). Folk devils and moral panics: The creation of the mods and rockers. New York: St. Martin's Press.

Cooper, A., & Smith, E. 2011. *Homicide Trends in the United States, 1980–2008.* Bureau of Justice Statistics. NCJ 236018. Washington, DC: U.S. Department of Justice. http://www.bjs.gov/index.cfm?ty=pbdetail&iid=2221.

Cullen, F., Fisher, B., & Applegate, B. (2000). Public opinion about punishment and corrections. *Crime and Justice: A Review of Research, 27,* 1–79.

Danner, M., & Carmody, D. (2001). Missing gender in cases of infamous school violence: Investigating research and media explanation. *Justice Quarterly, 18,* 87–114.

Devitt, T. (1992). Media circus at Palm Beach rape trial. *Extra!* (Publication of FAIR, Fairness and Accuracy in Reporting). Special issue, 9–10, 24.

Devitt, T., & Downey, J. (1992). Battered women take a beating from the press. *Extra!* (Publication of FAIR, Fairness and Accuracy in Reporting). Special issue, 14–16.

Dorfman, L., & Schiraldi, V. (2001). *Off balance: Youth, race and crime in the news.* Washington, DC: Building Blocks for Youth.

Dunn, K. (1994, April 10). Crime and embellishment. *Los Angeles Times Magazine,* p. 24.

Ericson, R., Baranek, P., & Chan, J. (1989). *Negotiating control: A study of news sources.* Toronto: University of Toronto Press.

Eschholz, S., Chiricos, T., & Gertz, M. (2003). Television and fear of crime: Program types, audience traits, and the mediating effect of perceived neighborhood racial composition. *Social Problems, 50,* 395–415.

Federal Bureau of Investigation. (2005). *Crime in the United States, 2004: Uniform crime reports.* Washington, DC: U.S. Department of Justice.

Feld, B. (2003). The politics of race and juvenile justice: The "due process revolution" and the conservative reaction. *Justice Quarterly, 20,* 765–800.

Fishman, M. (1978). Crime waves as ideology. In G.W. Potter & V.E. Kappeler (Eds.) (2006). *Constructing Crime: Perspectives on Making News and Social Problems* (2nd ed., pp. 42--58). Long Grove, IL: Waveland Press, Inc.

Frankfurter, F., & Pound, R. (1922). *Criminal justice in Cleveland*. Cleveland: The Cleveland Foundation.

Gerbner, G. (1994, July). Television violence: The art of asking the wrong question. *Currents in Modern Thought,* 385–397.

Gilliam, F., & Iyengar, S. (2000). Prime suspects: The influence of local television news on the viewing public. *American Journal of Political Science, 44,* 560–573.

Graber, D. (1980). *Crime news and the public*. New York: Praeger.

Hall, S. (1980). Encoding/decoding. In Centre for Contemporary Cultural Studies (Ed.), *Culture, media, language*. London: Hutchinson.

Hall, S., Critcher, C., Jefferson, T., Clarke, J., & Roberts, B. (1978). *Policing the crisis*. London: Macmillan.

Headden, S. (2006, February 20). A tempest over police shootings. *U.S. News & World Report, 140,* 18.

Jenkins, P. (1988). Myth and murder: The serial killer panic of 1983–5. *Criminal Justice Research Bulletin, 3,* 11, 1–7.

———. (1996). *Moral panic: Changing concepts of the child molester in modern America*. New Haven, CT: Yale University Press.

Kamen, P., & Rhodes, S. (1992). Reporting on acquaintance rape. *Extra!* (Publication of FAIR, Fairness and Accuracy in Reporting). Special issue, 11.

Kappeler, V., & Potter, G. (2005). *The mythology of crime and criminal justice* (4th ed.). Long Grove, IL: Waveland Press.

Lapley, R., & Westlake, M. (1988). *Film theory: An introduction*. Manchester, England: Manchester University Press.

Livingston, J. (1996). *Crime & criminology* (2nd ed.). Englewood Cliffs, NJ: Prentice-Hall.

Lundman, R. (2003). The newsworthiness and selection bias in news about murder: Comparative and relative effects of novelty and race and gender typifications in newspaper coverage of homicide. *Sociological Forum, 18,* 257–286.

Maguire, K., & Pastore, A. (Eds.). (2004). *Sourcebook of criminal justice statistics*. [Online]. Available: http://www.albany.edu/sourcebook.

Marcuse, H. (1991). *One-dimensional man* (Rev. ed.). Boston: Beacon.

McCaghy, C., & Capron, T. (1997). *Deviant behavior: Crime, conflict and interest groups* (4th ed.). New York: Macmillan.

McQuail, D. (1994). *Mass communication theory* (3rd ed.). London: Sage.

Miethe, T., & Lee, G. (1984). Fear of crime among older people: A reassessment of the predictive power of crime-related factors, *Sociological Quarterly, 25,* 397–415.

Public Health Reports. (1998). Health ranks fifth on local TV news. *Public Health Reports, 113,* 296–297.

Reiman, J. (2004). *The rich get richer and the poor get prison* (7th ed.). Boston: Allyn and Bacon.

Reinarman, C., & Levine, H. (1989). Crack in context: Politics and media in the making of a drug scare. *Contemporary Drug Problems, 16,* 535–577.

Skogan, W., & Maxfield, M. (1981). *Coping with crime: Individual and neighborhood reactions*. Beverly Hills, CA: Sage.

Smith, S. (2006, February 12). Police TV shows are all the rage, and here's why. *Chicago Tribune*, sec. 7, pp. 1, 16.

Stevenson, N. (1995). *Understanding media cultures: Social theory and mass communication*. London: Sage.

Strinati, D. (1995). *An introduction to theories of popular culture*. London: Routledge.

Surette, R. (1998). *Media, crime, and criminal justice: Images and realities* (2nd ed.). Pacific Grove, CA: Brooks/Cole.

Sutherland, E. (1950). The diffusion of sexual psychopath laws. *American Journal of Sociology, 56,* 142–148.

Unsolved Mysteries. Accessed February 15, 2006 from http://www.unsolved.com/.

Vandiver, M., & Giacopassi, D. (1997). One million and counting: Students' estimates of the annual number of homicides occurring in the U.S. *Journal of Research in Crime and Delinquency, 18,* 91–131.

Walker, S. (1998). *Sense and nonsense about crime and drugs: A policy guide* (4th ed.). Belmont, CA: Wadsworth.

Warr, M. (1995). Public perceptions of crime and punishment. In J. Sheley (Ed.), *Criminology: A contemporary handbook* (pp. 15–31). Belmont, CA: Wadsworth.

Worden, R. (2006). *Wilkie Collins's "The dead alive": The novel, the case, and wrongful convictions*. Evanston: Northwestern University Press.

#IfTheyGunnedMeDown and the Power of Social Media to Change the Message

Mindy Stombler and Nate Steiner

Original to Focus on Social Problems: A Contemporary Reader.

In August 2014, when Michael Brown, an unarmed black teenager, was killed by a police officer in Ferguson, Missouri, media outlets chose a photo of Brown to accompany their reports. Early stories used a photo of Brown in his cap and gown at his high school graduation. Later, a seemingly less-than-wholesome photo of Brown was used in the mainstream press showing Brown in a sports tank top and making a hand gesture. Conservative blogs picked up the photo and labeled the hand gesture as a gang sign; social media sources quoted Brown's friends, who retorted that it was simply a peace sign.[1] In a similar case, black teenager Trayvon Martin was frequently depicted as a hoodie-wearing delinquent in the media following his killing in 2012 by neighborhood watch volunteer George Zimmerman. Few alternate photos were used to depict his normal family life and relations, contributing to an air of suspicion and criminalization although he had committed no offense and was not a threat to Zimmerman. The use of such disparate images prompted a critical examination of such patterned narratives—where unarmed black boys and men are presented as less deserving of our empathy.

Frustrated by what he saw as the media's contribution to shift blame away from the Ferguson police officer and onto Brown, C. J. Lawrence, a criminal defense attorney, posted two photos of himself on Twitter, tagged with #IfTheyGunnedMeDown, raising a question that resonated strongly among many in the African American community: "If they gunned me down, what picture would the media use to represent me?" According to the BBC, "in the first, [Lawrence] is seen making a speech at his university graduation alongside guest speaker Bill Clinton. In the second, he is dressed as a rapper in a costume he wore to a Halloween party. The hashtag poses a rhetorical question, he says, 'but in reality it's something we ask ourselves every day as African Americans.'"[2]

Following Lawrence's posting, a trend emerged where like-minded people responded via social media, decrying the stereotypical stories told by the news media through words and images. Like Lawrence, other social media users posted two or more competing photos of themselves, shown side by side—one less flattering or conventionally negative photo where they could be interpreted by an audience as troublemaking (photographed at a party, in a costume, drinking alcohol, mugging for the camera, making a variety of hand gestures) and another that depicted the user as innocent, wholesome, or generally positive (in a military uniform, reading to children, in graduation regalia, standing at an entrance to their university). Users posted these photos with the hashtag #IfTheyGunnedMeDown to argue to viewers that if they ever were shot by police, as in the case of Michael Brown, or by a vigilante, as in the case of Trayvon Martin, they believed the media would choose the less flattering photo, contributing to a narrative that would make them appear less deserving of empathy or a presumption of innocence, in fact criminalizing them, although they were dead.[3] The hashtag and discussion surrounding the campaign also raised the point that in the age of social media, many people have unflattering images of themselves on the Internet—some within their control, some not—and that the selective use of these images to represent African American victims of violence may represent racial bias. Djuan Trent, a Miss America contestant, posted a photo of herself dressed for Halloween as a version of Whiz Khalifia, in a hoodie with fake tattoos, next to a photo of herself at the Miss America pageant in a formal evening gown. On her blog, Trent explained what motivated her participation:

> I understand that the point of the pictures was to really get people thinking about the way black people are targeted and portrayed

continues

■ Continued

by the media. I get that. But what I don't get is how unfair it is that we have to feel that our jeans and hoodie are any less respectable than a graduation gown, suit, dress, or uniform. At the end of the day, underneath the clothes, and underneath our skin, we are human and THAT is why we should be respected and treated as such. . . . Society has taught us that regardless of who we are and what we know, the color of our skin is a threat, so to compensate for the innate threat that we are, we must dress and present ourselves in a certain way as a deflection of our blackness.[4]

Critics of media have been paying attention to the stories told through use of imagery. They wonder who gets the benefit of the doubt when these stories are told and how the story changes based on the representation of those involved. The media has a long history of reproducing negative stereotypes of black men and women, in particular, as criminal or dangerous, biasing the narratives they present.[5] Even recently, the *Iowa Gazette* was criticized for presenting arrested white burglary suspects from their yearbook photos and arrested black burglary suspects using their mug shots.[6] Discrimination and its effects occur, then, at multiple levels: when members of the media make patterned choices—even unconscious ones—to depict black men and women stereotypically; then again at the level of media consumption; and also in the way that black women and men feel compelled to develop a greater consciousness about what they post, even self-censorsing, knowing they may encounter additional scrutiny, even in tragedy.

The use of social media (new media) to contradict narratives being established by the press (old media) shows how the older top-down publishing model and its near monopoly on the distribution of news is being disrupted by newer and more collective Internet-driven models. In old media, a story gains visibility by newsroom editors, journalists, and

publishers determining it to be "news worthy;" they are in control of the gathering and presentation of facts and associated potential biases. In new media, social media platforms like Twitter and Facebook in particular, a story or point of view gets visibility by liking, sharing, retweeting and hashtagging. These new methods are collective and can form from a groundswell of agreement from the general populace of social media users. More specifically, activists can use hashtags to promote their calls for social change, sometimes called "hashtag activism."[7] Social media also offers the press a feedback loop that creates new threads for the older media sources to follow up on, becoming a story in and of themselves (as exemplified by the sources quoted in this writing).[8]

The #IfTheyGunnedMeDown hashtag has not only clarified how a single photo can be uninformed and even intentionally misleading, but also successfully raised awareness of the potential for the press to disproportionately use unflattering photos when portraying black victims. If the established press still holds enough sway to misinform, at least new forms of social media provide a platform that allows for the discourse to contest those messages.

NOTES

1. BBC Trending. 2014. "#BBCtrending: The Two Faces of Michael Brown." *BBC News.* August 11. Retrieved April 19, 2015. http://www.bbc.com/news/blogs-trending-28742301?ocid=socialflow_twitter/.

2. BBC Trending. 2014. "#BBCtrending: The Two Faces of Michael Brown." *BBC News.* August 11. Retrieved April 19, 2015. http://www.bbc.com/news/blogs-trending-28742301?ocid=socialflow_twitter/.

3. Chappell, Bill. 2014. "People Wonder: 'If They Gunned Me Down,' What Photo Would Media Use?" *NPR.* August 11. Retrieved April 19, 2015. http://www.npr.org/blogs/thetwo-way/2014/08/11/339592009/people-wonder-if-they-gunned-me-down-what-photo-would-media-use/.

4. Djuan Trent. 2014. "#ForThoseWhoHaveBeen GunnedDown." *Life in 27* Blog. Retrieved April 19, 2015. http://2life7.blogspot.com/2014/08/forthosewhohavebeengunneddown.html/.

5. See, for example, "African American Men as 'Criminal and Dangerous': Implications of Media Portrayals of Crime on the 'Criminalization' of African American Men" by Mary Beth Oliver. *Journal of African American Studies*. Fall 2003, 7(2):3–18 and also *Punished: Policing the Lives of Black and Latino Boys* by Victor M Rios. 2011. New York: New York University Press.

6. Ferguson, David. 2015. "Charged with Same Crime, Iowa Paper Shows Black Suspects' Mug Shots while Whites Get Yearbook Photos." *Alternet*. April 1. Retrieved April 19, 2015. http://www.alternet.org/media/charged-same-crime-iowa-paper-shows-black-suspects-mug-shots-while-whites-get-yearbook-photos/.

7. Friedman, Ann. 2014. "Hashtag Journalism: The Pros and Cons to Covering Twitter's Trending Topics." *Columbia Journalism Review*. May 29. Retrieved April 19, 2015. http://www.cjr.org/realtalk/hashtag_journalism.php/.

8. Friedman, Ann. 2014. "Hashtag Journalism: The Pros and Cons to Covering Twitter's Trending Topics." *Columbia Journalism Review*. May 29. Retrieved April 19, 2015. http://www.cjr.org/realtalk/hashtag_journalism.php/.

Equal Opportunity Objectification? The Sexualization of Men and Women on the Cover of *Rolling Stone*

ERIN HATTON AND MARY NELL TRAUTNER

Hatton and Trautner's research examines the depictions of men and women on the cover of *Rolling Stone* over a period of four decades. Although sexualized depictions have increased for both groups, women are more likely to be depicted in a sexualized fashion. The high intensity of women's sexualization, or "hypersexualization," is dramatic and has skyrocketed in recent years. Their results support scholars' arguments that our culture has become increasingly sexualized, if not "pornified," with women bearing the brunt of the change.

Introduction

In recent years, a number of scholars and journalists have argued that American culture has become "sexualized" (APA Task Force 2007; Attwood 2009; Olfman 2009) or even "pornified" (Paul 2005; see also Dines 2010; McRobbie 2004; Paasonen et al. 2007). . . . "Increasingly *all* representations of women," Gill (2007:81) argues, "are being refracted through sexually objectifying imagery" (emphasis in original). It is not only women who are sexualized in the popular media, scholars argue; men are sexualized as well (Bordo 1999; Pope et al. 2000; Rohlinger 2002). "The erotic male," Rohlinger (2002:70) contends, "is increasingly becoming *the* depic-

tion that dominates mainstream conceptions of masculinity" (emphasis in original).

Researchers find evidence for the increased sexualization of women and men in a spate of cultural artifacts, including the mainstream popularity of adult film actress Jenna Jameson and her memoir, *How to Make Love Like a Porn Star* (e.g., Dines 2010; Levy 2005; Paul 2005); the "skyrocketing" number of undressed men in advertisements (Pope et al. 2000:56); the prevalence of pole-dancing exercise classes for women (e.g., Farley 2009; Levy 2005); the "blatant sexual fetishization—even idolatry—of the male organ" in TV and movies (Bordo 1999:30); and the success of "Girls Gone Wild," the "reality"

Reprinted from Erin Hatton and Mary Nell Trautner, 2011. Equal Opportunity Objectification? The Sexualization of Men and Women on the Cover of Rolling Stone, *Sexuality & Culture*, 15, pp. 256–278, with kind permission from Springer Science and Business Media.

television program and website that feature young women being urged to take off their clothes by off-screen cameramen in exchange for a T-shirt with the show's logo (e.g., Dines 2010; Farley 2009; Levy 2005; Paul 2005).

Yet analyzing only sexualized cultural artifacts—and there are certainly many to choose from—does not provide conclusive evidence that American culture has become "pornified." Indeed, it is easy to dismiss such charges unless we know whether sexualized representations of women and men have become more common—or more intensely sexualized—over time. Moreover, although the existence of sexualized images of men might suggest that, today, the popular media is something of an "equal opportunity objectifier" as some observers suggest (e.g., Frette 2009; Taylor and Sharkey 2003), the simple presence of images of sexualized men does not signal equality in media representations of women and men.

In a longitudinal content analysis of more than four decades of *Rolling Stone* magazine covers (1967–2009), we begin to answer such questions.[1] Using a unique analytical framework that allows us to measure both the frequency and intensity of sexualization, we find that representations of women and men have indeed become more sexualized over time, though women continue to be more frequently sexualized than men. Yet our most striking finding is the change in *how* women—but not men—are sexualized. Women are increasingly likely to be "hypersexualized," while men are not. In our analysis, hypersexualization is the combination of a multitude of sexualized attributes—body position, extent of nudity, textual cues, and more—the cumulative effect of which is to narrow the possible interpretations of the image to just, as de Beauvoir (1949) wrote, "the sex." Our findings thus not only document changes in the sexualization of men and women in popular culture over time, they also point to a narrowing of the culturally acceptable ways for "doing" femininity (West and Fenstermaker 1995; West and Zimmerman 1987) as presented in popular media.

These findings are important because research has shown that sexualized images may legitimize or exacerbate violence against women and girls, sexual harassment, and anti-women attitudes among men (Farley 2009; Kalof 1999; Lanis and Covell 1995; Machia and Lamb 2009; MacKay and Covell 1997; Malamuth and Check 1981; Malamuth et al. 2000; Milburn et al. 2000; Ohbuchi et al. 1994; Ward 2002; Ward et al. 2005), increase rates of body dissatisfaction and/or eating disorders among men, women, and girls (Abramson and Valene 1991; Aubrey and Taylor 2009; Aubrey et al. 2009; Groesz et al. 2002; Hargreaves and Tiggemann 2004; Harrison 2000; Hofschire and Greenberg 2001; Holmstrom 2004; Lucas et al. 1991; Pope et al. 2000; Stice et al. 1994; Tiggeman and Slater 2001; Turner et al. 1997), increase teen sexual activity (Brown et al. 2005; Brown et al. 2006; Pardun et al. 2005; Villani 2001), and decrease women and men's sexual satisfaction (American Psychological Association 2007; Roberts and Gettman 2004; Weaver et al. 1984; Zillmann and Bryant 1988).

Before turning to our findings, we consider research on the sexualization of women and men within the broader literature on gender and the media. We then discuss our data and methods, outlining our analytical framework that measures both the incidence and extent of sexualization. We conclude with a discussion of the implications of our findings.

Sexualization, Gender, and the Media

In *Gender Advertisements*, Erving Goffman (1979) sought to uncover the covert ways that popular media constructs masculinity and femininity. In a detailed analysis of more than 500 advertisements, Goffman contrasted women's lowered heads with men's straight-on gazes, men's strong grasps versus women's light touches, women's over-the-top emotional displays with men's reserved semblances, and more. The relationship between men and women, Goffman argued, was portrayed as a parent–child relationship, one characterized by male power and female subordination.

Missing from Goffman's analysis, however, was an examination of the sexualization of women (and men) in these images. Yet this was likely a conscious strategy on Goffman's part. As Vivian Gornick explained in the book's introduction, he eschewed images of "clutched detergents and half-naked bodies" in order to reveal the "unnatural in the natural" (vii–ix). And there may have been good reason for this. At the time, the sexual objectification of women in the popular media was already the subject of intense political debate. It had become the central target of many "second wave" feminists, who had launched campaigns to cover such advertisements with graffiti and stickers that read "this ad exploits women" (Bradley 2004; Castro 1990). Perhaps Goffman did not examine the sexualization of women because it was already considered passé, something that would soon be remedied by feminists' efforts. Or perhaps he avoided it because it was too obvious—such flagrant objectification did not require a high-powered sociological lens.

. . . In an examination of advertisements in women's magazines in 1979 and 1991, Kang (1997) added two new variables to Goffman's coding categories: body display (degree of nudity) and independence (self-assertiveness). Using this expanded empirical framework, Kang finds that while some aspects of gender stereotyping—such as men shown as taller than women—had virtually disappeared by 1991, body displays of women had increased. Interpreting this combination of increases and decreases in gender stereotyping as a kind of balancing scale, Kang concludes that little changed in advertisements' portrayal of women over the 11-year time span. "Twelve years after the Goffman study," Kang writes, "magazine advertisements are still showing the same stereotyped images of women" (988–989). But a closer look at Kang's data, in fact, reveals substantial changes: nude or partially nude images of women increased nearly 30% from 1979 to 1991.

. . . Krassas et al. (2003) also built on Goffman's framework in a study of sexualized representations of women and men in two men's magazines, *Maxim* and *Stuff*, in 2001. In addition to Goffman's categories, the authors added measures of nudity (breast/chest and buttock exposure) and objectification (some concealment of face combined with some level of body exposure). Using these variables, the authors find that—in 2001 at least—women were much more likely than men to have exposed breasts and buttocks, and were three times more likely to be sexually objectified.

These studies have made important steps in empirically examining sexualized representations of women and men in popular media. But they tell only part of the story. For example, Krassas et al. (2003) analyze[d] images of both men and women, but only at a single point in time. Kang (1997) . . . examine[d] change over time, but look[ed] only at images of women. This raises the question of whether men too have been increasingly sexualized in popular culture, as some have suggested (e.g., Bordo 1999; Pope et al. 2000; Rohlinger 2002; Thompson 2000). . . .

Furthermore, although each of the studies described uses additional variables in order to measure sexualization, in our assessment they do not yet capture the full range of sexualized attributes. They do not include variables for genital accentuation (but see Krassas et al. 2001), open mouths and/or tongue exposure, sex acts or simulations (but see Reichert and Carpenter 2004; Reichert et al. 1999; Soley and Kurzbard 1986), and sexual referents in the textual description of the images (but see Johnson 2007; Soley and Kurzbard 1986). And, perhaps more importantly, all studies of sexualization measure only the presence or absence of aspects of sexualization in isolation. As a consequence, while they document the incidence of sexualized attributes, they do not measure whether the image as a whole—the woman rather than just her breasts—has become more frequently or more intensely sexualized over time. In the following section, we outline our empirical framework that builds on these studies to provide a more comprehensive measure of sexualization.

Data and Methods

We examine the covers of *Rolling Stone* for two key reasons. First and foremost, *Rolling Stone* is a well-known popular culture magazine in the U.S. Although in the early years the magazine focused almost exclusively on music and music culture, by the 1970s its covers regularly featured an array of pop culture icons not limited to the music world. Today the magazine is well known for its coverage of politics, film, television, current events and, of course, popular music. Its covers generally feature a wide range of celebrities, including comedians, actors, musicians, models, politicians, record producers, military analysts, civil rights activists, journalists, film directors, athletes, and more. As a result, representations of men and women on the cover of *Rolling Stone* resemble popular cultural images broadly, particularly more so than lifestyle magazines which are often explicitly about sex, relationships, or sexuality. Our second reason for choosing *Rolling Stone* is its longevity. Launched in 1967, *Rolling Stone* has published more than one thousand covers across its lifespan. This extensive dataset offers an ideal window into changes in the sexualization of women and men in popular culture over time.

Dataset

There are 1,046 covers of *Rolling Stone*, starting with its first issue in November of 1967 through the end of 2009 (including those issues that featured multiple covers). We downloaded all covers from the *Rolling Stone* website in January 2010. . . .

Of the full set of 1,046 covers, we excluded 115 from our analysis for a number of reasons: they did not portray people (e.g., just text or cartoon characters), they showed crowds with no discernable image to code, or they featured collages of covers that had previously been published. Of the remaining 931 covers, 651 featured only men and 205 featured only women (either alone or in groups). In those covers that showed groups of either men or women, we coded the central figure in the image (usually this was

literally the person at the center of the image, but at times it was the dominant person in terms of his/her size or action). Another 75 covers featured women and men together. In those cases, the central man and woman were each coded separately. We thus analyzed a total of 1,006 cover images (726 images of men and 280 images of women) across 42 years of *Rolling Stone* magazine.

Coding Scheme

We conceptualize representations of women and men as falling along a continuum of sexualization: images may be not at all sexualized, slightly sexualized, clearly sexualized, or highly sexualized. To capture these differences, we developed a 23-point additive scale consisting of 11 separate variables, the sum of which indicates the degree to which an image is sexualized. We briefly describe each of the variables below. . . .

Clothing/Nudity (0–5 Points)

A number of studies have found style of clothing and extent of nudity to be important markers of sexualization (e.g., Johnson 2007; Kang 1997; Krassas et al. 2003; Lambiase and Reichert 2006; Nitz et al. 2007; Paek and Nelson 2007; Reichert 2003; Reichert and Carpenter 2004; Reichert et al. 1999; Soley and Kurzbard 1986; Soley and Reid 1988). We developed a six-point scale for this variable, ranging from unrevealing clothing (0 points) to completely naked (5 points). Those images that featured models wearing slightly revealing clothing, such as women wearing shirts with modestly low necklines or exposed arms and shoulders, scored a "1" on this measure. Images that scored a "2" in this category featured models wearing clothing that was somewhat revealing; this included exposed midriffs on both women and men. Images that scored a "3" featured models wearing highly revealing and/or skin-tight clothing. Images that scored "4" in this category featured models wearing swimsuits and lingerie, that is, apparel that is not generally considered "clothing" at all. Images that scored a "5" in this category featured models wearing nothing at all (or only minimal clothing, such as socks and shoes but nothing else).

Touch (0–3 Points)

A number of researchers have examined the use of "touch" to suggest sexualization in media images (e.g., Reichert and Carpenter 2004; Reichert et al. 1999; Soley and Kurzbard 1986). We analyzed the nature of "touch" for each cover image on a 0–3 scale. Our measure included all forms of touch, including self-touch, touching others, and being touched. Cover models who were neither touching nor being touched scored "0" on this measure. "Casual touching," for example, a model clasping his hands together or resting her arm on someone else's shoulder, scored a "1." Those images that scored a "2" exhibited some kind of provocative touching. These included, for example, Cameron Diaz lifting her shirt and resting her hand on her bare stomach just under her breast (August 22, 1996). The highest score in this category—3 points—was given to those covers that featured explicitly sexual touching (by oneself or someone else). These included, for example, David Spade pinching a woman's nipple (September 16, 1999) and Janet Jackson's breasts being cupped by disembodied male hands (September 16, 1993).

Pose (0–2 Points)

Extending Goffman's (1979) analysis of body posture to studies of sexualization, researchers have analyzed an image's pose as a key element of its sexualization (e.g., Johnson 2007; Krassas et al. 2003; Lambiase and Reichert 2006). We created three codes to capture sexualized body postures. Images in which the cover model was not posed in any way related to sexual activity—standing upright, for example—scored "0" in this category. Images scored "1" for a variety of poses that were suggestive or inviting of sexual activity, including lifting one's arms overhead and any kind of leaning or sitting. Images that scored a "2" on this measure were overtly posed for sexual activity; this included lying down or, for women, sitting with their legs spread wide open.

Mouth (0–2 Points)

Goffman (1979) found that women were often shown in advertisements to be covering their mouths or sucking on their finger as part of what he called "licensed withdrawal"—a lack of presence and, therefore, power. Although a number of studies have analyzed images in terms of their licensed withdrawal (e.g., Binns 2006; Kang 1997; Lindner 2004), we are not aware of any study that has examined a model's mouth as an element of his or her sexualization. In our study of *Rolling Stone* covers, however, we found mouths to be an important characteristic of sexualization and we developed three scores to measure it. The lowest score (0 points) was for mouths that did not suggest any kind of sexual activity, including closed lips, broad toothy smiles, and active singing, talking, or yelling. One point was given to mouths that were somewhat suggestive of sex; this included images in which the model's lips were parted slightly but not smiling. Images that scored a "2" featured models whose mouths were explicitly suggestive of sexual activity: This included models whose mouths were wide open but passive (not actively singing or yelling but, perhaps, posed for penetration), whose tongue was showing, or who had something (such as a finger) in his or her mouth.

Breasts/Chest; Genitals; Buttocks (0–2 Points Each)

A small number of studies have examined whether a focal point of the image is the model's breasts/chest, genitals, and/or buttocks (e.g., Krassas et al. 2001, 2003; Rohlinger 2002). We used these as three separate variables, scoring each of them on a 0–2 scale. Those images in which these body parts were either not visible or not a focal point scored a "0" for each of the three variables. If one or more of these body parts were somewhat emphasized—if, for example, a woman's breasts were a centerpiece of the image but still mostly concealed by clothing—the image received a "1" in the appropriate category. If one of these body parts was a major focus of the image—if a model's pants were unbuttoned and pulled down, for example—the image received a "2" for that variable.

Text (0–2 Points)

Relatively few studies analyze an image's text as part of its sexualization (but see Johnson 2007; Soley and Kurzbard 1986). In our examination of *Rolling Stone* cover images, however, we found the text describing an image to be an important element of its sexualization. We coded only the text on the magazine cover that was directly related to the cover image. Most of these "coverlines" were not related to sex or sexuality and scored "0" on this measure. Text that contained some sexual innuendo, such as "Kid Rock Gets Lucky" (October 10, 2007), scored "1" in this category, and coverlines that made explicit references to sex or sexuality, such as "Asia Argento: She Puts the Sex in XXX" (September 5, 2002), scored "2."

Head vs. Body Shot (0–1 Point)

A number of studies in this field distinguish between those images which are primarily head-shots, featuring only the model's head and perhaps shoulders, and those which feature substantially more of their body (e.g., Baumann 2008; Goffman 1979; Lambiase and Reichert 2006; Johnson 2007; Schwarz and Kurz 1989). On our scale of sexualization, headshots scored "0" and body shots scored "1."

Sex Act (0–1 Point)

Perhaps because relatively few popular media images depict models engaging in (or simulating) sex acts, only a few studies measure this variable (e.g., Reichert and Carpenter 2004; Reichert et al. 1999; Soley and Kurzbard 1986). In our analysis of *Rolling Stone* magazine covers, however, a small but hard to ignore number of such images prompted the creation of this new variable. Images in which the cover model was engaged in a sex act (e.g., kissing or embracing someone while lying naked in bed) or simulating a sex act (e.g., affecting fellatio or masturbation) scored "1" in this category.

Sexual Role Play (0–1 Point)

Finally, although we found no studies that measured symbols of sexual role playing—such as infantilization (e.g., child-like clothes) or bondage/domination (e.g., leather bustier, leather straps, dog collars, studded bracelets)—in our analysis the infrequent yet conspicuous presence of such symbols led to the creation of this variable. Cover images that suggested sexual role playing scored "1" in this category.

Analytic Strategy

We coded the covers of *Rolling Stone* in several passes. The authors first worked together to establish coding rules for all variables, jointly coding three randomly selected years of covers. The second author then coded the remaining cover images, working closely with the first author to resolve any questions that arose. Upon the completion of coding, we randomly selected 10% of covers (n = 93) to code independently as a reliability check (these 93 covers did not include the years we had coded together or the images that had been in question). . . .

After coding was complete, the images' scores on the 23-point scale of sexualization clustered into three distinct groups: nonsexualized images (which scored 0–4 points), sexualized images (5–9 points), and hypersexualized images (10 or more points). We tested for reliability between coders for these three categories as well. In our 10% random sample of covers, there was near-perfect agreement between authors' categorization of images as nonsexualized, sexualized, and hypersexualized. . . .

Dividing the images into these three categories—nonsexualized, sexualized, and hypersexualized—captures important differences between them. . . . Both covers feature people who are naked and in a kneeling position, yet the impact of the images is quite different. The band members of Blind Melon[2] are clearly sexualized—they are naked and the text asserts that they are "ripe and ready"—but they are not hypersexualized. They are not posed to engage in sexual activity; they do not touch themselves or each other; they are not arching their backs to emphasize their chests, genitals, or buttocks (in fact, their backs are rather slumped); and they gaze somberly into the camera, with their mouths closed. In fact, their nudity and textual description seem at odds with their otherwise nonsexualized characteristics.

In contrast, the cover image of Laetitia Casta[3] is hypersexualized. Like the members of Blind Melon, she is both naked and kneeling, but her back is arched to emphasize her breasts and buttocks. Rather than posing on an unremarkable white background, Casta is kneeling on a bed of pink rose petals. Her body faces away from the camera, but her head is tilted back and is turned so that her eyes can meet the viewer's gaze. Her lips are slightly parted. Her arm is raised over her head and touches her hair, which falls down her back. Her skin glistens, as though it has just been oiled. Casta, the text tells us, is the star of *Rolling Stone*'s "hot list."

The difference between these two images is clear, yet measuring nudity alone would not capture it. Our scale of sexualization does. By our measure, the Blind Melon cover scored 9 points, placing it at the top of the sexualized category. The Casta image, by contrast, scored 15 points, placing it well into the hypersexualized category. . . .

Findings

Before looking at questions of intensity, we first examine changes in the frequency of sexualized images over time. In order to do so, we combine sexualized and hypersexualized images into one category and compare them to nonsexualized images. . . . Sexualized representations of women have increased significantly . . . and sexualized representations of men have also increased, but not significantly. . . . In the 1960s, 11% of men and 44% of women on the covers of *Rolling Stone* were sexualized. In the 2000s, 17% of men were sexualized (a 55% increase), and 83% of women were sexualized (an 89% increase). It is also telling to look at these figures another way: nonsexualized images of women dropped from 56% in the 1960s to 17% in the 2000s, while nonsexualized images

of men dropped only slightly from 89% in the 1960s to 83% in the 2000s. Notably, in the 2000s, the same proportion of women were sexualized as men were nonsexualized (83%). . . .

These findings speak clearly to debates about the sexualization of men in popular media. While sexualized images of men have increased, men are still dramatically less likely to be sexualized than women. This difference is further highlighted by looking at the numerical frequency of such images: In the 2000s, there were 28 sexualized images of men (17% of male images) but 57 sexualized images of women (83% of female images), and there were 136 nonsexualized images of men (83% of male images) but only 12 nonsexualized images of women (17% of female images). Perhaps even more telling is the difference between men and women at the low end of the scale. In the 2000s, there were 35 images of men which scored a "0" on our scale and another 39 images which scored just 1 point, indicating that these images displayed no (or almost no) sexualized attributes. Together they accounted for 45% of all images of men in the 2000s. By contrast, there was not a single image of a woman in the 2000s that scored 0 points, and only 2 images of women scored 1 point on the scale, accounting for less than 3% of images of women in the 2000s.

Intensity of Sexualization

The difference in the sexualization of men and women is even more striking when we examine the intensity of their sexualization. In our analysis, we find a broad range in the degree of sexualization—some images are only somewhat sexualized while others are so intensely sexualized that we have labeled them "hypersexualized." In order to capture such differences, we split the sexualized category into two groups: those that were simply sexualized (such as the Blind Melon image described above) and those that were hypersexualized (such as the Casta image). In this more nuanced analysis we divide *Rolling Stone* cover images into three categories: nonsexualized, sexualized, and hypersexualized. . . .

Looking first at images of men, we see that the vast majority of them—some 83% of men in the 2000s—fall in the nonsexualized category. This represents a noteworthy, though comparatively small, decrease from the 1960s when 89% of men were not sexualized. Many nonsexualized images of men are close-up headshots (36% across all years): they do not show the man's body nor do they indicate any level of nudity with bare shoulders or chest. Typically the man's mouth is closed and he is looking directly into the camera, though at times he might be smiling or looking to one side. The text in such images usually does not carry any sexual innuendo. On more than four decades of *Rolling Stone*'s covers, 162 images of men—or 22%—scored a zero on our scale, displaying no sexualized attributes.

Other images of men in the nonsexualized category are slightly more sexualized. One example of this is a 1997 image of actor Brad Pitt (April 3). On our scale, this image scored 4 points, placing it at the top of the nonsexualized category. The cover shows Pitt's face and part of his torso (1 point). He is wearing a plush white bathrobe (1 point), which is open to reveal part of his chest (1 point). He looks directly into the camera through tousled hair, his lips are very slightly parted (1 point). The text reads, "Leader of the Pack: Brad Pitt Talks Tough." Although the majority of men on the cover of *Rolling Stone* are not sexualized, a sizeable minority fall into the sexualized (but not hypersexualized) category. In the 1960s, 10.5% of men were sexualized, and in the 1970s their proportion increased slightly to 12%. In the 1980s, sexualized representations of men dropped to just 5%, but in the 1990s sexualized images of men increased to 13.3%. Their numbers continued to increase somewhat, so that in the 2000s 14.6% of images of men were sexualized.

A 2006 cover featuring singer Justin Timberlake (September 21) offers an example of this category of sexualized men. On our scale, Timberlake's image scored 8 points—double that of the Brad Pitt cover described above—and falls squarely within the sexualized category. The image shows Timberlake's body from the thighs up (1 point). He is wearing a white T-shirt and jeans; he is looking directly into the camera and smiling broadly. Timberlake is carrying a guitar over one shoulder as if he were off to a gig, but his white T-shirt is soaking wet (3 points), clinging to his body and revealing his chest (2 points). The text reads, "Justin Timberlake: Wet Dream, The New King of Sex Gets Loose" (2 points).

Although sexualized images of men such as this one have become more common over time, *Rolling Stone* rarely features hypersexualized images of men. In the 1960s, there were no such images and, in the 1970s, there was just one hypersexualized image of a man, representing 1% of male images in that decade. In the 1980s, 2% of men were hypersexualized and, in the 1990s, 3% were. But in the 2000s, hypersexualized images of men dropped again to just over 2%.

The most prominent example of this category is a 2009 cover featuring pop singer Adam Lambert (June 25). . . . On our scale, the image scored 13 points, the highest score among men on the cover of *Rolling Stone*. The cover shows Lambert's body from the thighs up (1 point). He is lying on a bed (2 points) with his arms lifted overhead, conveying a sense of sexual passivity or vulnerability. One of his hands touches his hair (2 points). His eyes, which are lined with make-up, gaze into the camera, and his lips are slightly parted (1 point). Lambert is wearing tight black jeans and an unbuttoned black shirt (3 points), revealing part of his chest (1 point). His legs are spread and a bright green snake crawls up his leg, its head remarkably near his genitals (2 points). The text reads, "The Liberation of Adam Lambert: Wild Idol" (1 point). Given that Lambert is openly gay, perhaps it is not surprising that he is the most intensely sexualized man on the cover of *Rolling Stone*, since popular media portrayals of gay men often overemphasize their sexuality (Gross 2001; Nardi and Bolton 1998). But what is perhaps surprising about this image is its comparison to the highest scoring image of women, described below.

Turning to images of women, we see different trends not only in the frequency but also in the intensity of their sexualization. Overall, nonsexualized representations of women have decreased since the start of *Rolling Stone*. In the 1960s, 56% of women on the magazine's cover were nonsexualized. In the 1970s, nonsexualized images of women increased slightly to 58% and then, in the 1980s, dropped to 49%. In the 1990s, nonsexualized images of women took a sharp downturn, falling to 22%. In the 2000s, just 17% of women were nonsexualized.

A 2009 cover featuring country singer Taylor Swift (March 15) offers an example of this nonsexualized category. On our scale, Swift's image scored 3 points, placing it in the nonsexualized category even though it contains minor elements of sexualization, much like the Brad Pitt cover described above. The image shows Swift's upper body (1 point). She is wearing a white halter top that reveals her shoulders and arms (1 point), though her body is largely covered by her long blonde hair. Swift stares directly into the camera; her lips are closed. She is holding a guitar as though she is just about to play it, her fingers poised over the guitar strings. The text reads, "Taylor Swift: Secrets of a Good Girl" (1 point).

Just as nonsexualized images of women such as this one have become less common, in recent years sexualized (but not hypersexualized) images of women have also become less prevalent, though to a much lesser extent. In the 1960s, 33% of women on the cover of *Rolling Stone* were sexualized. This rate increased somewhat over the next several decades, taking an upturn in the 1990s to 42%. In the 2000s, however, sexualized (but not hypersexualized) images of women decreased by nearly half to 22%. But, as we will see in a moment, an even greater increase in hypersexualized images of women more than made up the difference.

A 2008 portrait of pop star Britney Spears (December 11) is an example of this sexualized category. On our scale, this image scored 6 points, placing it near the bottom of the category's range. The cover shows Spears' body from the hips up (1 point). She is looking away from the camera and smiling widely, as though she

were laughing heartily. Her tousled blonde hair falls below her shoulders. She is wearing low-slung jeans and a gray T-shirt, which is rolled up to reveal much of her stomach (3 points). One hand holds her cheek (1 point), conveying a sense of youthful enthusiasm, and her other hand rests in her jeans' belt loop, pulling down her pants slightly (1 point) to reveal a glimpse of a tattoo below. The text reads, "Yes She Can! Britney Returns." Although sexualized images of women such as this one have become less common in recent years, hypersexualized images of women have increased significantly since the start of *Rolling Stone* magazine. In the 1960s, there was just one hypersexualized image of a woman, representing 11% of images of women at the time. In the 1970s, 6% of women on the magazine's cover were hypersexualized and, in the 1980s, that number more than doubled to 13%. Hypersexualized images of women increased even more in the 1990s and 2000s, reaching 36 and 61% in each decade, respectively. As these data show, in the 2000s women were three and a half times more likely to be hypersexualized than nonsexualized, and nearly five times more likely to be sexualized to any degree (sexualized or hypersexualized) than nonsexualized. . . .

In our analysis, it might seem that the hypersexualized category encompasses a wide range of sexualized images because its scale (10–23) is wider than the other categories. Yet even with such a wide range, the images in this category leave little room for interpretation as being about anything other than sex. To demonstrate this, it is instructive to look at two images of hypersexualized women, one at each end of the category's range. . . . An example of the lower end of this category is a 2009 image of Blake Lively and Leighton Meester (April 2), two leads of the television show "Gossip Girl." On our scale, this image scored 12 points, one point less than the Adam Lambert cover, the top scorer among men. The image shows the upper bodies of both women (1 point), though Lively's portrait dominates the cover. She is wearing a very low-cut black tank top (3 points) that reveals much of her breasts (2 points). Meester leans in towards Lively; her face is touching Lively's hair (1 point), suggesting that beyond the image their bodies are also pressed together. The focal point of the image is a dripping, double-scoop ice cream cone, a phallus-like object which Lively holds up for both women to lick (1 point). Their mouths are wide open and their protruding tongues (2 points) are covered in ice cream. The text reads, "The Nasty Thrill of 'Gossip Girl'" (2 points).

Compare this image to one at the top end of the hypersexualized category: a 2002 cover featuring pop singer Christina Aguilera (November 14). This image scored 20 points, earning the highest score in our dataset. The picture shows nearly all of Aguilera's body (1 point). She is naked (5 points), except for black fishnet stockings on her lower legs and black motorcycle boots (1 point). She is lying on a bed (2 points), which is covered with a rippling red satin sheet. Her head is tilted downwards, but she is looking into the camera. Her lips are parted (1 point), and her long hair is spread out around her shoulders. Aguilera's left hand holds a guitar, but only decoratively, not giving any indication that it is an instrument she might play. The guitar's neck is strategically placed so that it covers her left nipple. Her right hand clasps her other breast (3 points), not to cover it but to push it up provocatively. Her breasts are otherwise uncovered (2 points). Aguilera's body is contorted so that not only are her breasts exposed, but her buttocks (2 points) and, to a lesser degree, her genitals (1 point) are accentuated. The text reads, "Christina Aguilera: Inside the Dirty Mind of a Pop Princess" (2 points).

The new predominance of hypersexualized images of women such as these is illustrated further by examining the numerical frequency of such images. In the 2000s, there were 12 nonsexualized images of women, 15 sexualized images, and 42 hypersexualized images.[4] By contrast, there were 136 nonsexualized images of men, 24 sexualized images, and only 4 hypersexualized images of men in the 2000s. That there are more sexualized images of men than women should

not be too surprising. Images of men have long dominated the cover of *Rolling Stone*. (Recall that our dataset is comprised of 726 images of men compared to 280 images of women.) What is surprising, however, is the asymmetry in non-sexualized and hypersexualized representations of men and women. In the 2000s, there were more than 10 times the number of hypersexualized images of women than men, and there were more than 11 times the number of nonsexualized images of men than women.

Discussion and Conclusion

In *The Male Body: A New Look at Men in Public and Private*, Susan Bordo (1999) describes the different implications for men and women when they are sexualized in the same way. As evidence, she analyzes advertisements in which women and men are shown with their pants around their ankles. Bordo (1999:28) argues that women in such images seem "stripped or exposed," even more than if their pants were off altogether, because they resemble rape or murder victims shown in movies and television. By contrast, Bordo observes, men shown with their pants around their ankles convey "much the same confident, slightly challenging machismo" as they would otherwise.

If similarly sexualized images can suggest victimization for women but confidence for men, consider the implications when women are sexualized at the same rate as men are *not* sexualized, as they were on the covers of *Rolling Stone* in the 2000s. And the vast majority of those sexualized images of women—some 74%—were hypersexualized, meaning that they did not exhibit only one or two signals of sex, but a multitude of them. Often women in these images were shown naked (or nearly so); they were shown with their legs spread wide open or lying down on a bed—in both cases sexually accessible; they were shown pushing up their breasts or pulling down their pants; they were described as having "dirty minds" or giving "nasty thrills"; and, in some cases, they were even shown to be simulating fellatio or other sex acts.

Some researchers argue against using the phrase "sexual objectification" to describe such images because they often depict women as active, confident, and/or sexually desirous (e.g., Bordo 1999; Gill 2003, 2008, 2009). We argue, however, that the intensity of their sexualization suggests that "sexual object" may indeed be the only appropriate label. The accumulation of sexualized attributes in these images leaves little room for observers to interpret them in any way other than as instruments of sexual pleasure and visual possession for a heterosexual male audience. Such images do not show women as sexually agentic musicians and actors; rather, they show female actors and musicians as ready and available for sex.

Yet some scholars have criticized such statements as overly homogenizing because they render invisible differences in this process of sexualization (e.g., Gill 2009).[5] In our view, however, the very problem is one of homogenization. We argue that the dramatic increase in hypersexualized images of women—along with the corresponding decline in nonsexualized images of them—indicates a decisive narrowing or homogenization of media representations of women. In *Female Chauvinist Pigs: Women and the Rise of Raunch Culture*, journalist Ariel Levy (2005:5) describes this trend: "A tawdry, tarty, cartoonlike version of female sexuality has become so ubiquitous, it no longer seems particular. What we once regarded as a *kind* of sexual expression," Levy writes, "we now view *as* sexuality" (emphases in original). In this article we offer empirical evidence for this claim.

Of concern is that this narrowing down of media representations of women to what Levy calls a single "cartoonlike version of female sexuality"—or what we might call "hypersexualized femininity"—suggests a corresponding narrowing of culturally acceptable ways to "do" femininity (West and Fenstermaker 1995; West and Zimmerman 1987). This is not to say that there are no culturally available alternatives for women and girls as they make decisions about how to look and behave, but it does suggest that

there may increasingly be fewer competing cultural scripts for ways of doing femininity. Thus, at least in popular media outlets such as *Rolling Stone*, it seems that just one aspect of femininity—sexuality, and *hyper*sexuality at that—has overshadowed other aspects of "emphasized femininity" (Connell 1987), such as nurturance, fragility, and sociability. Although such characteristics are themselves problematic, the ascendancy of only one version of femininity (and, at the same time, one version of female sexuality) seems particularly troubling.

Although *Rolling Stone* is a leader among popular culture magazines, more studies need to be done. We hope that our measure will be useful in analyzing representations of men and women in a wide variety of popular media, especially those targeting nonwhites and children. Yet in this article we have taken important steps toward empirically documenting the prevalence and intensity of the sexualization of men and women in popular culture. And what we found is striking: sexualized representations of both women and men increased, and hypersexualized images of women (but not men) skyrocketed. "While there is nothing wrong with a *little* objectification," Sut Jhally (1989:10) writes, "there is a great deal wrong and dangerous with a lot of objectification—that is when one is viewed as *nothing other than an object*" (emphases in original). And, for women on the cover of *Rolling Stone*, there is increasingly "a lot" of objectification.

NOTES

1. Editor's note: All covers referenced in this article are able for viewing at http://www.rollingstone.com/coverwall.
2. Editor's note: Featured on the cover of *Rolling Stone* on November 11, 1993.
3. Editor's note: Featured on the cover of *Rolling Stone* on August 20, 1998.
4. Some might attribute the increase in the hypersexualization of women on the cover of *Rolling Stone* to a change in management: In 2002, *Rolling Stone* hired a new managing

editor, Ed Needham, who was the former editor of *FHM*—the rather notorious "lad mag" that regularly features scantily-clad women on its covers. A closer look at our data, however, reveals a strong increase in the hypersexualization of women on the cover of *Rolling Stone* since the 1980s. Moreover, the proportion of hypersexualized images of women actually peaked at 78% in 1999, well before Needham's tenure. Hypersexualized images of women reached their second highest point (75%) in 2002, the first year of Needham's appointment, and then again in 2006, after Needham's 2-year stint at the magazine had ended.

5. Although a number of researchers have found that nonwhites are often sexualized in print media (Collins 1990; Hansen and Hansen 2000; West 2009), our analyses show no discernable difference in the frequency or intensity of sexualization of whites and nonwhites. Overall, 12% of women and 12% of men on the cover of *Rolling Stone* were nonwhite. They were nonsexualized, sexualized, and hypersexualized at about the same rate as their white counterparts.

REFERENCES

Abramson, E., & Valene, P. (1991). Media use, dietary restraint, bulimia, and attitudes toward obesity: A preliminary study. *British Review of Bulimia and Anorexia Nervosa*, 5, 73–76.

American Psychological Association (APA) Task Force. (2007). Report of the APA task force on the sexualization of girls. Washington, DC: American Psychological Association. Retrieved 10 March 2010 from http://www.apa.org/pi/women/programs/girls/report-full.pdf.

Attwood, F. (2009). *Mainstreaming sex: The sexualisation of western culture*. London: I. B. Tauris.

Aubrey, J., Stevens, J., Henson, K., Hopper, M., & Smith, S. (2009). A picture is worth twenty words (about the self): Testing the priming influence of visual sexual objectification on women's self-objectification. *Communication Research Reports*, 26, 271–284.

Aubrey, J. S., & Taylor, L. (2009). The role of lad magazines in priming men's chronic and temporary appearance-related schemata: An investigation of longitudinal and experimental findings. *Human Communication Research*, 35, 28–58.

Baumann, S. (2008). The moral underpinnings of beauty: A meaning-based explanation for light and dark complexions in advertising. *Poetics*, 36, 2–23.

Binns, R. K. (2006) "On the cover of a Rolling Stone": A content analysis of gender representation in popular culture between 1967–2004. M.A. Thesis, Wichita State University, Wichita, KS.

Bordo, S. (1999). *The male body: A new look at men in public and in private*. New York: Farrar, Straus, and Giroux.

Bradley, P. (2004). *Mass media and the shaping of American feminism, 1963–1975*. Jackson, MS: University Press of Mississippi.

Brown, J., Halpern, C. T., & L'Engle, K. L. (2005). Mass media as a sexual super peer for early maturing girls. *Journal of Adolescent Health*, 36, 420–427.

Brown, J., L'Engle, K. L., Pardun, C., Guo, G., Kenneavy, K., & Jackson, C. (2006). Sexy media matter: Exposure to sexual content in music, movies, and magazines predicts black and white adolescents' sexual behavior. *Pediatrics*, 117, 1018–1027.

Castro, G. (1990). *American feminism: A contemporary history*. Paris, France: Presses de la Fondation Nationale des Sciences Politiques.

Collins, P. H. (1990). *Black feminist thought: Knowledge, consciousness, and the politics of empowerment*. New York: Routledge.

Connell, R. W. (1987). *Gender & power: Society, the person, and sexual politics*. Palo Alto, CA: Stanford University Press.

de Beauvoir, S. (1949, 1972). *The second sex*. New York: Penguin.

Dines, G. (2010). *Pornland: How porn has hijacked our sexuality*. Boston, MA: Beacon Press.

Farley, M. (2009). Prostitution and the sexualization of children. In S. Olfman (Ed.), *The sexualization of childhood*. Westport, CT: Praeger.

Frette, J. (2009). *Men are altered and objectified too: Ryan Reynolds graces the cover of Entertainment*

Weekly. Retrieved 20 December 2010. http://www.examiner.com/women-s-issues-international/men-are-altered-and-objectified-too-ryan-reynolds-graces-the-cover-of-entertainment-weekly.

Gill, R. (2003). From sexual objectification to sexual subjectification: The resexualisation of women's bodies in the media. *Feminist Media Studies, 3,* 100–106.

Gill, R. (2007). *Gender and the media.* Cambridge, UK: Polity Press.

Gill, R. (2008). Empowerment/sexism: Figuring female sexual agency in contemporary advertising. *Feminism & Psychology, 18,* 35–60.

Gill, R. (2009). Beyond the "sexualization of culture" thesis: An intersectional analysis of "sixpacks," "midriffs" and "hot lesbians" in advertising. *Sexualities, 12,* 137–160.

Goffman, E. (1979). *Gender advertisements.* Cambridge, MA: Harvard University Press.

Groesz, L., Levine, M., & Murnen, S. (2002). The effect of experimental presentation of thin media images on body satisfaction: A meta-analytic review. *International Journal of Eating Disorders, 31,* 1–16.

Gross, L. (2001). *Up from invisibility: Lesbians, gay men, and the media in America.* New York: Columbia University Press.

Hansen, C., & Hansen, R. (2000). Music and music videos. In D. Zillmann & P. Vorderer (Eds.), *Media entertainment: The psychology of its appeal.* Mahwah, NJ: Erlbaum.

Hargreaves, D., & Tiggemann, M. (2004). Idealized media images and adolescent body image: "Comparing" boys and girls. *Body Image, 1,* 351–361.

Harrison, K. (2000). The body electric: Thin-ideal media and eating disorders in adolescents. *Journal of Communication, 50,* 119–143.

Hofschire, L., & Greenberg, B. (2001). Media's impact on adolescents' body dissatisfaction. In J. D. Brown & J. R. Steele (Eds.), *Sexual teens, sexual media.* Mahwah, NJ: Erlbaum.

Holmstrom, A. (2004). The effects of the media on body image: A meta-analysis. *Journal of Broadcasting & Electronic Media, 48,* 196–217.

Jhally, S. (1989). Advertising, gender and sex: What's wrong with a little objectification? *Working papers and proceedings of the center for psychosocial studies.* R. Parmentier and G. Urban (Eds.).

Johnson, S. (2007). Promoting easy sex without genuine intimacy: *Maxim* and *Cosmopolitan* cover lines and cover images. In M.-L. Galician & D. L. Merskin (Eds.), *Critical thinking about sex, love, romance in the mass media: Media literacy applications.* Mahwah, NJ: Erlbaum.

Kalof, L. (1999). The effects of gender and music video imagery on sexual attitudes. *Journal of Social Psychology, 139,* 378–385.

Kang, M.-E. (1997). The portrayal of women's images in magazine advertisements: Goffman's gender analysis revisited. *Sex Roles, 37,* 979–996.

Krassas, N., Blauwkamp, J., & Wesselink, P. (2001). Boxing Helena and corseting Eunice: Sexual rhetoric in *Cosmopolitan* and *Playboy* magazines. *Sex Roles, 44,* 751–771.

Krassas, N., Blauwkamp, J., & Wesselink, P. (2003). "Master your johnson": Sexual rhetoric in *Maxim* and *Stuff* magazines. *Sexuality and Culture, 7,* 98–119.

Lambiase, J., & Reichert, T. (2006). Sex and the marketing of contemporary consumer magazines: How men's magazines sexualized their covers to compete with *Maxim.* In T. Reichert & J. Lambiase (Eds.), *Sex in consumer culture: The erotic content of media, marketing.* Mahwah, NJ: Erlbaum.

Lanis, K., & Covell, K. (1995). Images of women in advertisements: Effects on attitudes related to sexual aggression. *Sex Roles, 32,* 639–649.

Levy, A. (2005). *Female chauvinist pigs: Women and the rise of raunch culture.* New York: Free Press.

Lindner, K. (2004). Images of women in general interest and fashion magazine advertisements from 1955 to 2002. *Sex Roles, 51,* 409–421.

Lucas, A., Beard, C. M., O'Fallon, W. M., & Kurland, L. (1991). 50-year trends in the incidence of anorexia nervosa in Rochester, Minn.: A population-based study. *American Journal of Psychiatry, 148,* 917–922.

Machia, M., & Lamb, S. (2009). Sexualized innocence: Effects of magazine ads portraying adult women as sexy little girls. *Journal of Media Psychology, 21,* 15–24.

MacKay, N., & Covell, K. (1997). The impact of women in advertisements on attitudes toward women. *Sex Roles*, 36, 573–583.

Malamuth, N., Addison, T., & Koss, M. (2000). Pornography and sexual aggression: Are there reliable effects and can we understand them? *Annual Review of Sex Research*, 11, 26–91.

Malamuth, N., & Check, J. (1981). The effects of mass media exposure on acceptance of violence against women: A field experiment. *Journal of Research in Personality*, 15, 436–446.

McRobbie, A. (2004). The rise and rise of porn chic. *Times Higher Education Supplement*. Retrieved 1 June 2010. http://www.timeshighereducation.co.uk/story.asp?sectioncode=26&storycode=182087.

Milburn, M., Mather, R., & Conrad, S. (2000). The effects of viewing R-rated movie scenes that objectify women on perceptions of date rape. *Sex Roles*, 43, 645–664.

Nardi, P., & Bolton, R. (1998). Gay bashing: Violence and aggression against gay men and lesbians. In P. M. Nardi & B. E. Schneider (Eds.), *Social perspectives in lesbian, gay studies: A reader*. London: Routledge.

Nitz, M., Reichert, T., Aune, A. S., & Velde, A. V. (2007). All the news that's fit to see? The sexualization of television news journalists as a promotional strategy. In T. Reichert (Ed.), *Investigating the use of sex in media promotion, advertising*. Binghamton, NY: Best Business Books.

Ohbuchi, K.-I., Ikeda, T., & Takeuchi, G. (1994). Effects of violent pornography upon viewers' rape myth beliefs: A study of Japanese males. *Psychology, Crime, and the Law*, 1, 71–81.

Olfman, S. (Ed.). (2009). *The sexualization of childhood*. Westport, CT: Praeger.

Paasonen, S., Nikunen, K., & Saarenmaa, L. (Eds.). (2007). *Pornification: Sex and sexuality in media culture*. Oxford: Berg.

Paek, H.-J., & Nelson, M. (2007). A cross-cultural and cross-media comparison of female nudity in advertising. In T. Reichert (Ed.), *Investigating the use of sex in media promotion, advertising*. Binghamton, NY: Best Business Books.

Pardun, C., L'Engle, K. L., & Brown, J. (2005). Linking exposure to outcomes: Early adolescents' consumption of sexual content in six media. *Mass Communication and Society*, 8, 75–91.

Paul, P. (2005). *Pornified: How pornography is transforming our lives, our relationships, and families*. New York: Times Books.

Pope, H. Jr., Phillips, K., & Olivardia, R. (2000). *The Adonis complex: The secret crisis of male body obsession*. New York: Free Press.

Reichert, T. (2003). *The erotic history of advertising*. Amherst, NY: Prometheus.

Reichert, T., & Carpenter, C. (2004). An update on sex in magazine advertising: 1983 to 2003. *Journalism & Mass Communications Quarterly*, 81, 823–837.

Reichert, T., Lambiase, J., Morgan, S., Carstarphen, M., & Zavoina, S. (1999). Cheesecake and beefcake: No matter how you slice it, sexual explicitness in advertising continues to increase. *Journalism & Mass Communication Quarterly*, 76, 7–20.

Roberts, T.-A., & Gettman, J. (2004). Mere exposure: Gender differences in the negative effects of priming a state of self-objectification. *Sex Roles*, 51, 17–27.

Rohlinger, D. (2002). Eroticizing men: Cultural influences on advertising and male objectification. *Sex Roles*, 46, 61–74.

Rolling Stone. (2006). *1,000 covers: A history of the most influential magazine in pop culture*. New York: Abrams.

Schwarz, N., & Kurz, E. (1989). What's in a picture? The impact of face-ism on trait attribution. *European Journal of Social Psychology*, 19, 311–316.

Soley, L., & Kurzbard, G. (1986). Sex in advertising: A comparison of 1964 and 1984 magazine advertisements. *Journal of Advertising*, 15, 46–64.

Soley, L., & Reid, L. (1988). Taking it off: Are models in magazine ads wearing less? *Journalism Quarterly*, 65, 960–966.

Stice, E., Schupak-Neuberg, E., Shaw, H., & Stein, R. (1994). Relation of media exposure to eating disorder symptomatology: An examination of mediating mechanisms. *Journal of Abnormal Psychology*, 103, 836–840.

Taylor, E., & Sharkey, L. (2003). Em & Lo's sex myths: Women's bodies are sexier. *The Guardian* (22 March). Retrieved 20 December 2010. http://www.guardian.co.uk/lifeandstyle/2003/mar/22/weekend.emmataylor.

Thompson, M. (2000). Gender in magazine advertising: Skin sells best. *Clothing and Textiles Research Journal*, 18, 178–181.

Tiggeman, M., & Slater, A. (2001). A test of objectification theory in former dancers and non-dancers. *Psychology of Women Quarterly*, 2, 57–64.

Turner, S., Hamilton, H., Jacobs, M., Angood, L., & Dwyer, D. H. (1997). The influence of fashion magazines on the body image satisfaction of college women: An exploratory analysis. *Adolescence*, 32, 603–614.

Villani, S. (2001). Impact of media on children and adolescents: A 10-year review of the research. *Journal of the American Academy of Child and Adolescent Psychiatry*, 40, 392–401.

Ward, L., Monique, E., & Hansbrough, E. W. (2005). Contributions of music video exposure to black adolescents' gender and sexual schemas. *Journal of Adolescent Research*, 20, 143–166.

Ward, L. M. (2002). Does television exposure affect emerging adults' attitudes and assumptions about sexual relationships? Correlational and experimental confirmation. *Journal of Youth & Adolescence*, 31, 1–15.

Weaver, J., Masland, J., & Zillmann, D. (1984). Effect of erotica on young men's aesthetic perception of their female sexual partners. *Perceptual and Motor Skills*, 58, 929–930.

West, C. (2009). Still on the auction block: The sexploitation of black adolescent girls in rape music and hip-hop culture. In S. Olfman (Ed.), *The sexualization of childhood*. Westport, CT: Praeger.

West, C., & Fenstermaker, S. (1995). Doing difference. *Gender & Society*, 9, 8–37.

West, C., & Zimmerman, D. (1987). Doing gender. *Gender & Society*, 1, 125–151.

Zillmann, D., & Bryant, J. (1988). Pornography's impact on sexual satisfaction. *Journal of Applied Social Psychology*, 18, 438–453.

At the Movies, The Women are Gone

Linda Holmes

I live in the D.C. metro area, which is a very good place to find films. If you don't live in New York or Los Angeles, it's about the best you can do. I'm within 10 miles of a multiplicity of multiplexes, not to mention four theaters I would consider "art house" theaters or at least mixes of wider-appeal fare and smaller stuff. According to Fandango and some back-of-the-envelope math, excluding documentaries and animation, there are 617 movie showings today—that's just today, Friday—within 10 miles of my house.

Of those 617 showings, 561 of them—90 percent—are stories about men or groups of men, where women play supporting roles or fill out ensembles primarily focused on men. The movies

making up those 561 showings: *Man of Steel* (143), *This Is the End* (77), *The Internship* (52), *The Purge* (49), *After Earth* (29), *Now You See Me* (56), *Fast & Furious 6* (44), *The Hangover Part III* (16), *Star Trek into Darkness* (34), *The Great Gatsby* (16), *Iron Man 3* (18), *Mud* (9), *The Company You Keep* (4), *Kings of Summer* (9), and *42* (5).

Thirty-one are showings of movies about balanced pairings or ensembles of men and women: *Before Midnight* (26), *Shadow Dancer* (4), and *Wish You Were Here* (1).

Twenty-five are showings of movies about women or girls: *The East* (8), *Fill the Void* (4), *Frances Ha* (9), and *What Maisie Knew* (4). Of the seven movies about women or balanced groups, only one—the Israeli film *Fill the Void*—is directed by a woman, Rama Burshtein. That's also the only one that isn't about a well-off white American. (Well, Celine in *Before Midnight* is well-off, white and French, but she's been living in the U.S.)

There are nearly six times as many showings of *Man of Steel* alone as there are of all the films about women put together.

If I were limited to multiplexes, as people are in many parts of the country, the numbers would be worse. In many places, the number would be zero. *Frances Ha* is by far the most widely available of the four women-centered movies, and it's at 213 theaters this weekend in the entire country. *The East* is at 115. *What Maisie Knew* is at 51. *Fill the Void* looks like it's in about 20 locations, judging by its site.

The Internship is at 3,399. Note: I originally had understood these to be screen counts; they're actually theater counts. Not a huge difference with non-blockbusters less likely to play on multiple screens at the same place, and if anything, makes the possible disparity with something like *The Internship* greater, but it's different nonetheless. This doesn't affect the numbers for my own local theaters, though—those are just individual showtimes counted by hand.

I want to stress this again: In many, many parts of the country right now, if you want to go to see a movie in the theater and see a current movie about a woman—*any* story about *any* woman that isn't a documentary or a cartoon—you can't. You cannot. There are not *any*. You cannot take yourself to one, take your friend to one, take your daughter to one.

There are not any.

By far your best shot, numbers-wise, at finding one that's at least even-handedly featuring a man and a woman is *Before Midnight* (at 891 theaters) so I hope you like it. Because it's pretty much that or a solid, impenetrable wall of movies about dudes. Dudes in capes, dudes in cars, dudes in space, dudes drinking, dudes smoking, dudes doing magic tricks, dudes being funny, dudes being dramatic, dudes flying through the air, dudes blowing up, dudes getting killed, dudes saving and kissing women and children, and dudes glowering at each other.

Somebody asked me this morning what "the women" are going to do about this. I don't know. I honestly am at the point where I have no idea what to do about it. Stop going to the movies? Boycott everything?

They put up *Bridesmaids*, we went. They put up *Pitch Perfect*, we went. They put up *The Devil Wears Prada*, which was in two-thousand-Meryl-Streeping-oh-six, and we went (and by "we," I do not just mean women; I mean *we, the humans*), and all of it has led right here, right to this place. Right to the land of zippedy-doo-dah. You can apparently make an endless collection of high-priced action flops and everybody says "win some, lose some" and nobody decides that They Are Poison, but it feels like every "surprise success" about women is an anomaly and every failure is an abject lesson about how we really ought to just leave it all to The Rock. Nobody remembers, it seems, how many people said *Bridesmaids* would fail. And it didn't! But it didn't matter.

My answer is that I have no idea what the women are going to do about it. It helps when critics, including men, care about the way women artists are treated and make it their problem to share, as Sam Adams did yesterday in a terrific piece about Sofia Coppola. It helps when people go out of their way to see *any* kind of film that's about people other than themselves. It helps when we acknowledge that what we have right now is a Hollywood entertainment business that has pretty much entirely devoted itself to telling men's stories—and to the degree that's for business reasons, it's because they've gotten the impression we've devoted ourselves to listening to men's stories.

But for crying out loud, let's at least notice. When it's 90 percent here, it's much worse elsewhere.

Social Problems Related to Education

Jesse Hagopian

Jesse Hagopian teaches history and is the co-adviser to the Black Student Union at Garfield High School in Seattle, Washington. He is a founding member of Social Equality Educators.

Courtesy of Truman Buffett.

What is the mission of Social Equality Educators?

Social Equality Educators emerged in 2008 from the struggle to stop school closures in the Seattle area. When the Recession was in full swing, many public schools in our area were slated for closure. We knew we needed an organization to push our union to fight these sorts of issues. We organized a grassroots movement of students, parents, and teachers and were successful in keeping some of those schools off of the chopping block, though some were still closed. We grew from a handful of teachers at the beginning to a large formal organization that focuses on defending our school from corporate education reform. We want to strengthen our teachers' unions by partnering with the community and having our schools, parents, and the community fight together against a variety of injustices, not just related to education and education reform. We believe that unions should to go far beyond various contractual disputes and actually partner with various social justice movements.

What is your role?

I'm on the Steering Committee. Last year we worked on elections in the union—we captured six seats on the executive board of our union. We've organized conferences, participation at various rallies, and protests in Olympia, Washington supporting more funding for the public schools. We're best known for helping spread a boycott against a high-stakes standardized test called "the MAP test" from Garfield High School in Seattle to several other schools.

What motivated the MAP test boycott?

The boycott was motivated by the complete uselessness of the MAP test as a pedagogical tool. It was not properly aligned to our curriculum and yet it was taking over schools. It was wasting weeks of classroom and instructional time; it wasn't culturally or linguistically appropriate for our English language learners; and it just wasn't giving any useful feedback for teachers. And, because it was computer-administered, it was taking over our computer labs and libraries and taking those resources away from students.

My fellow educators and I actually know what quality assessment looks like and we were already using far superior assessments in our classrooms. This test and punish model really was demoralizing. We agreed that we needed to push back against a corporate education reform model that believes in reducing the process of teaching and learning down to a single test score, which they then use to label schools as "failing" and to bust up teachers' unions by tying employment to this model of testing. We felt we didn't need to pull kids out of class and waste instructional time anymore, so we took a unanimous vote not to administer the exam. The teachers were threatened with a ten-day suspension, without pay. But because of the unanimous vote of the Parent–Teacher–Student Association (PTSA) and Student Government, the teachers had the confidence not to back down and continue with their struggle. Letters of solidarity poured in from all over the country—literally thousands of signatures came flooding into Garfield High School. Ever since, we've been in an ongoing "Education Spring" with record numbers of people engaged in resisting high stakes testing in U.S. history.

At the end of that year, the Superintendent announced that the MAP test would no longer be mandatory for high schools in Seattle. We have not had the MAP test since, which really showed the power of solidarity.

What inspired you to become an education activist?

I began teaching in Washington DC, in a school that was 100 percent African American, and I would pass the White House on the way to my school. My classroom had a hole in the ceiling and when it rained, my classroom literally flooded. I got to school one morning and the first project I had ever assigned, one where students were to write about a figure in American history that they admired, was ruined. That was the same year No Child Left Behind was implemented. I saw the federal government blaming

teachers, shaming schools, and focusing on standardized test scores, while at the same time they were unwilling to provide the basic resources that our kids needed. They were leaving our schools racially segregated and isolated. I realized it was going to have to be those of us in the classroom that would have to have to fight back.

What are your future activism goals?

In the immediate future we are working to build the Opt Out movement among parents. The Opt Out movement encourages individual parents and students to choose to opt out of high-stakes testing (like the new Common Core tests). The next step is to go beyond the individual act of acting on behalf of yourself or your own child and connecting the Opt Out movement to broader social movements to fight the corporate education reformers (or "testocracy" as I call them).

What types of strategies do you use to enact social change?

Most important is building relationships amongst colleagues, parents, community members, and leaders of various organizations. Within those relationships we need to educate leaders, activists, and the general public about how high stakes testing is ruining public education. Corporate stakeholders are trying to reduce the intellectual process of teaching and learning to a number—this trains a whole generation of children that wisdom is the ability to eliminate wrong answer choices rather than to collaborate on a project or to be creative and imaginative. Finally you need to organize and plan actions, big and small. Whether it is a forum, or a public film showing, or a boycott, you have to take action. It's not enough just to educate. You need to agitate.

What are major challenges you face in your activist efforts?

One of the major challenges is threats from those in power. Those in power stand to make a lot of money from high stakes standardized testing, such as directly profiting from sales of the tests (like the multi–billion dollar corporation, Pearson). Others who stand to benefit are the privatizers who want to be able to label schools as "failing" so they can shut them down and open up private charter schools. There's a lot of money to be made off high-stakes testing, and that's why the threats against those of us engaged in this work are getting more and more severe. The superintendent of the Seattle school district threatened the teachers of Seattle with the revocation of their teaching certificates if they engaged in boycotts. But threats can be overcome with solidarity, which we saw in action during the MAP test boycott. The real challenge is how to build solidarity amongst diverse communities and get parents, students, and teachers to see they have the same interest in the struggle.

What would you consider to be your greatest success as an activist?

The MAP test boycott is the clearest example of the power of solidarity. It inspired people around the country and the world and it was a decisive victory. But I think even more special to me has been seeing the Black Student Union at Garfield High School take leadership roles in the Black Lives Matter movement in Seattle. My ability to help support these students and watch them act on their own behalf has been a great victory.

Why should students get involved in educational activism?

We cannot ignore education. We face immense challenges in our world from mass incarceration, to historic levels of income inequality, to climate change, that affect the future of humanity to survive on the planet in the not too distant future. If we're going to continue to survive as a human race on this planet we have to redefine education, assessment, and learning as being more than filling in a bubble on a test. Returning critical thinking and problem solving to education is actually the fight for us to survive on this planet, as those skills will help us to solve the other challenges we face as a nation and as global citizens. It is worth the sacrifices this work entails to be part of that struggle.

What can students do with limited time and money?

Students can stay connected with others doing this work around the country, whether it's following the work of other activists online or attending conferences. *Rethinking Schools* magazine, for example, is a resource that continually inspires me. Students should organize actions instead of simply bemoaning what's wrong. Fighting back is the best antidote to pessimism.

Inequality and School Resources: What It Will Take to Close the Opportunity Gap

LINDA DARLING-HAMMOND

Darling-Hammond discusses the major factors that contribute to inequalities in educational outcomes, including high levels of child poverty, the unequal allocation of school resources, the resegregation of schools, and the lack of high-quality teachers and curriculum in low-income and minority schools. These inequities create formidable barriers to students' academic success.

Enormous energy is devoted in the United States to discussions of the achievement gap.[1] Much less attention, however, is paid to the opportunity gap, the cumulative differences in access to key educational resources that support learning at home and at school: expert teachers, personalized attention, high-quality curriculum opportunities, good educational materials, and plentiful information resources. Systemic inequalities in all of these resources, compounded over generations, have created what Gloria Ladson-Billings has called an "educational debt" owed to those who have been denied access to quality education for hundreds of years.[2] . . .

Institutionally sanctioned discrimination in access to education is as old as the United States itself. From the time that southern states made it illegal to teach an enslaved person to read, through Emancipation and Jim Crow, and well into the twentieth century, African Americans faced de facto and de jure exclusion from public schools, as did Native Americans and, frequently, Mexican Americans.[3] Even in the North, problems of exclusion, segregation, and lack of resources were severe. In 1857, for example, a group of African American leaders protested to a New York State investigating committee that the New York City board of education spent sixteen dollars per White child and only one cent per Black child for school buildings. While Black students occupied schools described as "dark and cheerless" in neighborhoods "full of vice and filth," White students were taught in "splendid, almost palatial edifices, with manifold comforts, conveniences, and elegancies."[4]

The *Williams v. California* case, a class action lawsuit filed in 2000 on behalf of California's low-income students of color, demonstrated that wide disparities still exist almost 150 years later.

CLOSING THE OPPORTUNITY GAP edited by Carter and Welner (2013) 8000w from Chp. "Inequality and School Resources: What Will It Take to Close the Opportunity Gap" by Darling-Hammond pp. 77–91, 237–239, 257–300. By permission of Oxford University Press, USA.

The plaintiffs' complaint included many descriptions of schools like this middle school in San Francisco:

> At Luther Burbank, students cannot take textbooks home for homework in any core subject because their teachers have enough textbooks for use in class only. . . . For homework, students must take home photocopied pages, with no accompanying text for guidance or reference, when and if their teachers have enough paper to use to make homework copies. . . . Luther Burbank is infested with vermin and roaches, and students routinely see mice in their classrooms. One dead rodent has remained, decomposing, in a corner in the gymnasium since the beginning of the school year. The school library is rarely open, has no librarian, and has not recently been updated. The latest version of the encyclopedia in the library was published in approximately 1988. Luther Burbank classrooms do not have computers. Computer instruction and research skills are not, therefore, part of Luther Burbank students' regular instruction. The school no longer offers any art classes for budgetary reasons. . . . Two of the three bathrooms at Luther Burbank are locked all day, every day. . . . Students have urinated or defecated on themselves at school because they could not get into an unlocked bathroom. . . . When the bathrooms are not locked, they often lack toilet paper, soap, and paper towels, and the toilets frequently are clogged and overflowing. . . . Ceiling tiles are missing and cracked in the school gym, and school children are afraid to play games in the gym because they worry that more ceiling tiles will fall on them during their games. . . . The school has no air conditioning. On hot days classroom temperatures climb into the 90s. The school heating system does not work well. In winter, children often wear coats, hats, and gloves during class to keep warm. . . .

> Eleven of the 35 teachers at Luther Burbank have not yet obtained regular, nonemergency teaching credentials, and 17 of the 35 teachers only began teaching at Luther Burbank this school year.[5]

These inequities are in part a function of how public education in the United States is funded. In most states, education costs are supported primarily by local property taxes, along with state grants-in-aid that are somewhat equalizing but typically insufficient to close the gaps caused by differences in local property values. Rich districts can spend more even when poorer districts tax themselves at proportionally higher rates. In most states there is at least a three-to-one ratio between per pupil spending in the richest and poorest districts.[6]

Disparities also exist among states, with per pupil expenditures in 2008 ranging from nearly $18,000 in Vermont to just over $6,000 in Utah.[7] The federal government has no policies that compensate adequately for these disparities. In fact, the largest federal education program, Title I of the Elementary and Secondary Education Act, which is intended to redress the effects of poverty on children's learning, allocates funds in part based on levels of state per pupil spending, reinforcing rather than ameliorating these wealth-based inequalities.[8]

Funding disparities might not undermine equal educational opportunity if the differentials were due to pupils' needs (such as special education, acquisition of English, or other learning requirements), or if they reflected differences in the cost of living. But differentials do not tend to favor the districts serving the highest-need students, and they persist after differences in the cost of living and pupil needs are taken into account. In California, for example, high-poverty districts spent, on average, $259 less per pupil than low-poverty districts, and high-minority districts spent $499 less than low-minority districts. In higher-spending New York, these differentials were even greater: $2,927 and $2,636, respectively.[9]

Explaining Inequality

Many great schools in this country offer students opportunities to learn in empowering and engaging ways, and more of them are open to a wider range of children than was once the case. The fact that de jure segregation is no longer legal and that some students of color can now attend good schools leads many Americans to assume that inequality has been eliminated from public education. Yet, precisely because de facto segregation currently cordons off poor communities of color from the rest of society, most policy makers, reporters, editorial writers, and concerned citizens don't know how the "other half" experiences school. . . . School segregation remains pervasive throughout the United States. The assumption that equal educational opportunity now exists reinforces beliefs that the causes of continued low levels of achievement on the part of students of color must be intrinsic to them, their families, or their communities. Educational outcomes for students of color are, however, at least as much a function of their unequal access to key educational resources, both inside and outside of school, as they are a function of race, class, or culture.[10]

Four major resource-linked factors . . . account for unequal and inadequate educational outcomes in the United States:

- The high level of childhood poverty coupled with the low level of social supports for low-income children's health and welfare, including their early learning opportunities
- The unequal allocation of school resources, which is made politically easier by the increasing resegregation of schools
- Inadequate systems for providing high-quality teachers and teaching to all children in all communities
- Rationing of high-quality curriculum through tracking and interschool disparities.

Together, . . . all these factors generate opportunity-to-learn barriers that can sabotage success.

Poverty and Social Supports

The United States not only has the highest poverty rates for children among industrialized nations but also provides fewer social supports for their well-being and fewer resources for their education.[11] Today, about one out of four US children lives in poverty, more than twice the rate of most European nations. Child poverty in America has risen since the early 1970s, when the War on Poverty improved the lives of many children.[12] This country has a much weaker safety net for children than other industrialized countries have, where universal health care, housing subsidies, and high-quality child care are the norm. In other developed countries, schools can focus primarily on providing education, rather than also having to provide breakfasts and lunches, help families find housing and health care, or deal with constant mobility due to factors such as evictions. US schools must also often address the effects of untreated physical and mental illness and the large gaps in children's readiness that exist when they enter school.

The devastating effects of these conditions were brought home poignantly in a . . . Congressional briefing by John Deasy, then superintendent of the Prince Georges County Public Schools, an urban district bordering on Washington, DC, who described a nine-year-old child in his district, living within sight of the Capitol building, who had recently died of sepsis from an infected cavity that had gone untreated because the child lacked dental insurance.[13] Disparate access to health care, including maternal prenatal care, contributes to a child mortality rate that is far higher in the United States than in any other wealthy country.[14]

Another contributing factor is unequal access to learning opportunities before children enter school. Many children do not have the kinds of experiences at home or in a preschool that allow them to develop the communication and interaction skills, motor skills, social–emotional skills, and cognitive skills that are required for them to be independent learners when they start school, which undermines their academic success in both the short and the longer run. . . .

Nobel prize–winning economist James Heckman points out that "compared to 50 years ago, a greater fraction of American children is being born into disadvantaged families where investments in children are smaller than in advantaged families."[15] The inadequacy of early education and health care negatively affects school success and adult outcomes. Yet, he argues, there is convincing evidence that if interventions occur early enough, they can significantly improve children's health, welfare, and learning.

Although prekindergarten enrollment has been growing recently, low-income children continue to participate in early education at much lower rates than children from higher-income families. In 2000, although 65 percent of children ages three to five whose parents earned $50,000 or more were enrolled in prekindergarten, only 44 percent of children the same ages with family incomes below $15,000 were enrolled. Publicly funded programs, which are the primary source of child care for low-income families, can serve only a minority of those who are entitled to participate.[16] By contrast, in most European countries, publicly supported child care and early education are widely available. In high-achieving Finland, for example, all children have the right to government-subsidized day care until they go to school at the age of seven, and 75 percent are enrolled. Parents also receive subsidies to stay home with their children if they so choose. In addition, over 96 percent of children attend tuition-free preschool at the age of six.[17] These kinds of policies eliminate the achievement gap that otherwise is created before school even begins.

Resegregation and Unequal Schooling

Beyond the large and growing inequalities that exist among families, profound inequalities in resource allocations to schools have been reinforced by increasing resegregation. Although desegregation has enabled many students of color to attend schools they could never before have accessed, many others have been left behind. Progress was made steadily only for about a decade after the passage of the 1964 Civil Rights Act. Segregation began to increase again in the 1980s, when desegregation policies were largely abandoned by the federal government, and courts were asked to end judicial oversight of desegregating districts.[18]

By 2000, 72 percent of the nation's Black students attended predominantly minority schools, up significantly from the low point of 63 percent in 1980. More than one-third of African American and Latino students (37 and 38 percent, respectively) attended schools with a minority enrollment of 90 percent to 100 percent.[19] At the turn of the twenty-first century, the level of segregation in US schools stood almost exactly where it had been 30 years earlier, as the ground gained during the 1970s was lost in a giant ideological tug-of-war.

The situation threatens to become worse as a result of the US Supreme Court's 2007 decision in conjoined cases brought by parents from Jefferson County, Kentucky, and Seattle, Washington. Both districts had placed race-based constraints on their school choice plans, as a way to avoid additional segregation. The court ruled that local school authorities could no longer routinely use individuals' race as a basis for decision making in school assignments.[20] More than 550 scholars signed a social science amicus brief offered by the Civil Rights Project at Harvard.

The . . . Civil Rights Project briefs summarized an extensive body of research showing the educational and community benefits of integrated schools for both White and minority students, documenting the persisting inequalities of segregated minority schools, and examining evidence that schools will resegregate in the absence of race-conscious policies. The Civil Rights Project's statement concluded that

> more often than not, segregated minority schools offer profoundly unequal educational opportunities. This inequality is

manifested in many ways, including fewer qualified, experienced teachers, greater instability caused by rapid turnover of faculty, fewer educational resources, and limited exposure to peers who can positively influence academic learning. No doubt as a result of these disparities, measures of educational outcomes, such as scores on standardized achievement tests and high school graduation rates, are lower in schools with high percentages of nonwhite students.[21]

Part of the problem is that segregated minority schools are almost always schools with high concentrations of poverty.[22] A number of studies have found that concentrated poverty has an independent influence on student achievement beyond the individual student's own socioeconomic status, confirming the 1966 Coleman Report finding that "the social composition of [a school's] student body is more highly related to student achievement, independent of the student's own social background, than is any school factor."[23]

The phrase "concentrated poverty" is shorthand for a constellation of mutually reinforcing socioeconomic inequalities that affect schooling. These schools typically have less qualified and less experienced teachers and fewer learning resources, lower levels of peer group support and competition, more limited curricula taught at less challenging levels, more serious health and safety problems, much more student and family mobility, and many other factors that seriously affect academic achievement.[24]

High levels of segregation produce linguistic isolation in schools with many native Spanish speakers and few fluent native speakers of English. The lack of opportunity for ongoing conversation with native English speakers impedes students' acquisition of academic English required for success in high school and college.[25] Furthermore, economic segregation reinforces disparities in educational quality. The social capital and clout brought by higher-income parents typically result in higher levels of services from the central administration and greater accountability for performance from schools.

Deepening segregation is closely tied to dwindling resources. Black and Hispanic students are increasingly concentrated in central city public schools, many of which have become majority minority over the past decade while their funding has fallen further behind that of their suburbs. . . . In 2005, students of color made up 71 percent of those served by the 100 largest school districts in the country.[26] By the late 1990s, in cities across the nation, a group of schools had emerged that might be characterized as "apartheid schools," serving exclusively students of color in low-income communities. Whether in Compton, California, or Chicago, Illinois, these schools have crumbling, overcrowded buildings, poor libraries and few materials, old and dilapidated texts so scarce that students must share them in class and cannot take them home for homework, and a revolving-door teaching force with little professional expertise.

These conditions arose as taxpayer revolts pulled the bottom out from under state education funding, and the distribution of funds became more unequal.[27] The extent to which many urban and some rural schools serving high proportions of low-income students of color could be abandoned without major outcry was in part a function of their intense segregation. Indeed, this public indifference to deprivation was one of the reasons civil rights advocates sought desegregation in the first place. Their long struggle to end segregation was not motivated purely by a desire to have minority children sit next to White children. Instead, there was strong evidence that the "equal" part of the "separate but equal" principle enunciated by the Supreme Court in its 1896 *Plessy v. Ferguson* decision had never been honored and that predominantly White schools offered better opportunities on many levels—more resources, higher rates of graduation and college attendance, more demanding courses, and better facilities and equipment.

Furthermore, there was a belief that these schools, once integrated, would continue to be advantaged by the greater public commitment occasioned by the more affluent people they serve. This belief seems borne out by the rapid deterioration of resegregated schools in cities that were turning black and brown during the 1980s and 1990s, where the conditions of severe resource impoverishment came to resemble those in underdeveloped nations.[28]

The differences in resources that typically exist between city and suburban schools can strongly influence school outcomes. For example, an experimental study of African American high school youth randomly placed in public housing in the Chicago suburbs rather than in the city found that, compared to their urban peers who started with equivalent income and academic attainment, the students who attended better-funded, largely White suburban schools with higher quality teachers and curriculum had better educational outcomes. They were substantially more likely to have the opportunity to take challenging courses, receive additional academic help, graduate on time, attend college, and secure good jobs.[29]

Finally, not only do urban districts receive fewer resources than their suburban neighbors, but schools with high concentrations of low-income and minority students typically receive fewer resources than other schools within these districts.[30] This disparity occurs for at least two reasons: upper-income parents lobby more effectively for academic programs, computers, libraries, and other supports and tolerate less neglect when it comes to building maintenance and physical amenities. Also, more-affluent schools generally secure more experienced and better educated teachers as schools with better conditions can attract a wider array of applicants.

Unequal Access to Qualified Teachers

More important than the contrasts between up-to-date and dilapidated buildings or even between overflowing libraries and empty shelves are the differences in the teachers children encounter. In the United States, teachers are the most inequitably distributed school resource.... As discussed below, this inequity is strongly linked to resources; financially struggling schools have a very difficult time hiring and retaining experienced, well-trained teachers.

Although federal policies such as service scholarships ended the shortage of teachers by the late 1970s, the cancellation of these policies in the 1980s led to increasing numbers of under-qualified teachers being hired in many cities when teacher demand began to increase while resources were declining. In 1990, for example, the Los Angeles Unified School District settled a lawsuit brought by students in predominantly minority schools because their schools were not only more crowded and less well funded than other schools but also disproportionately staffed by inexperienced and unprepared teachers hired on emergency credentials.[31] The practice of lowering or waiving credentialing standards to fill classrooms in high-minority, low-income schools—a practice that is unheard of in high-achieving nations and in other professions—became commonplace in many US states during this period, especially those with large minority and immigrant populations such as California, Texas, Florida, and New York.

A decade later, the entire California system was subjected to legal challenge, as disparities in access to well-qualified teachers had grown even worse. In 2001, for example, students in California's most intensely minority schools were more than five times as likely to have uncertified teachers than those in predominantly White schools. As standards were lowered and nearly half of the state's new teachers entered without training, virtually all of them were assigned to teach in high-need schools. In the 20 percent of schools serving almost exclusively students of color, more than one-fifth of teachers were uncertified, and in some schools they comprised the majority of the teaching force.[32] ...

A 1999 episode of the Merrow Report[33] illustrates how debilitating these policies had become for a group of students in Oakland—although the segment could as easily have been about schools in Philadelphia, Los Angeles, Chicago, Newark, Atlanta, or New York City. Zooming into a portable classroom in a middle school comprising entirely of American and Latino students, Merrow interviewed students in an eighth-grade math class that had been without a regular math teacher for most of the year, asking: "How many math teachers have you had this year?" One young man with a good memory started to count: "Let's see, there is Mr. Berry, Miss Gaines, Mr. Lee, Mr. Dijon, Mr. Franklin. . . . Coach Brown was one of our substitutes one day." A studious-looking girl chimed in: "We had Miss Nakasako; we had Miss Gaines; we had Miss Elmore; we had this other man named . . . he had like curly hair. His name was Mr. umm. . . ." Merrow remarked: "So you've had so many teachers you can't remember all their names?" The children nodded in agreement.

A few miles away at Oakland High School, a ninth-grade science class had had nothing but substitutes and spent the entire year without a certified science teacher. Merrow asked what it was like having so many teachers. Students' frustration was evident as they answered. Said one boy: "It's just weird. It's like we have to get used to a new teacher every couple of weeks or so." Another added, "I'm feeling short-handed, because this is the third year . . . ever since I got into junior high school, I haven't had a science teacher. . . . [I've had] substitutes all three years." When Merrow asked: "Have you learned much science this year?" the students shook their heads no. One particular Black student, laying his hand on the book in front of him as though it were a life raft, shook his head sadly and answered: "Not really. We haven't had the chance to."

The reporter went on to interview several fully certified science teachers who had applied to teach in the district and had not gotten a call back from the personnel office. Here, as in some other underresourced urban districts, instead of teachers with preparation and experience, un-credentialed teachers and temporary staff were

hired to save money. In recent years, Oakland's new leadership has worked heroically to change these practices and to seek out and hire teachers who will become better prepared and stay in the district. Yet the district, like many others in the state, still struggles with the inadequate funding and low salaries that make staffing its schools an uphill climb.

Similar inequalities have been documented in lawsuits challenging school funding in other states, including Massachusetts, New Jersey, New York, South Carolina, and Texas. In Massachusetts in 2002, students in predominantly minority schools were five times more likely to have uncertified teachers than those in the quartile of schools serving the fewest students of color.[34] In South Carolina and Texas they were four times more likely.[35]

By every measure of qualifications—certification, subject matter background, pedagogical training, selectivity of college attended, test scores, or experience—less qualified teachers are found in schools serving greater numbers of low-income and minority students.[36] As noted by Kati Haycock, president of The Education Trust, these statistics on differentials in credentials and experience, as shocking as they are, actually *understate* the degree of the problem:

> For one thing, these effects are additive. The fact that only 25% of the teachers in a school are uncertified doesn't mean that the other 75% are fine. More often, they are either brand new, assigned to teach out of field, or low-performers on the licensure exam. . . . There are, in other words, significant numbers of schools that are essentially dumping grounds for unqualified teachers—just as they are dumping grounds for the children they serve.[37]

The Influence of Teacher Quality on Student Achievement

All of these aspects of teacher quality matter. Studies at the state, district, school, and individual level have found that teachers' academic background, preparation for teaching, and certification status as well as their experience, significantly affect their students' achievement.[38] Similar patterns appear around the world. For example, the most significant predictors of mathematics achievement across 46 nations include teacher certification, a major in mathematics or mathematics education, and at least three years of teaching experience.[39]

Teachers' qualifications can have very large effects. For example, a recent study of high school students in North Carolina found that students' achievement was significantly higher if they were taught by a teacher who was certified in the field he or she taught, was fully prepared upon entry, had higher scores on the teacher licensing test, graduated from a competitive college, had taught for more than two years, or was National Board Certified.[40] While each of these traits made teachers more effective, the combined influence of having a teacher with most of these qualifications was larger than the effects of race and parent education combined. That is, the difference between the effect of having a very well-qualified teacher rather than one who was poorly qualified was larger than the average difference in achievement between a typical White student with college-educated parents and a typical Black student with high-school-educated parents. The achievement gap would be significantly reduced if low-income minority students were routinely assigned highly qualified teachers rather than the poorly qualified teachers they most often encounter. . . .

The good news is that when New York City raised salaries as the result of a school finance lawsuit and adopted policies to distribute teachers more equitably, improvements in these qualifications reduced achievement disparities between the schools serving the poorest and most affluent student bodies by one-fourth within only a few years.[41] Persistence in solving this problem could make a major difference in the opportunities available to students. Indeed, because of public attention to these disparities

and to the importance of teacher quality,[42] Congress included a provision in the No Child Left Behind Act of 2002 that states should ensure that all students have access to "highly qualified teachers," defined as teachers with full certification and demonstrated competence in the subject matter fields they teach. This provision was historic, especially because the students targeted by federal legislation—those who are low-income, low-achieving, new English language learners, or identified with special education needs—have in many communities been the least likely to be served by experienced and well-prepared teachers.[43]

At the same time, reflecting a key Bush administration agenda, the law encouraged states to expand alternative certification programs, and regulations developed by the US Department of Education (DOE) allow candidates who have just begun, but not yet completed, such a program to be counted as "highly qualified" classroom teachers. These regulations led parents of low-income, minority students taught by such teachers in California to sue the DOE.[44] They claimed that the rule sanctioned inadequate teaching for their children and masked the fact that they were being underserved, reducing the pressure on policy makers to create incentives that would give their children access to fully prepared teachers. . . .

The problems created by underprepared teachers have effects on schools as a whole. A teacher in a California school with a revolving door of underprepared teachers explained the consequences for students and other teachers:

> Teachers who had not been through [preparation] programs had more concerns about classroom management and about effective methods for delivering instruction to the student population at our school than teachers who had been through credential programs. It was a topic that was discussed at the lunch table . . . the fact we had a class that had had so many substitutes and had had an

uncredentialed teacher who was not able to handle the situation and ended up not returning, and that the kids were going to struggle and the teachers who received them the next year would probably have a difficult time with those students because of what they had been through.[45]

Student achievement declines as the proportion of inexperienced, underprepared, or uncertified increases within a school.[46] The high turnover rates of underprepared, inexperienced teachers, which disproportionately affect low-income, high-minority schools, drain financial and human resources.[47] Most important, the constant staff churn consigns a large share of children in high-need schools to a parade of relatively ineffective teachers, leading to higher rates of remediation, grade retention, and dropping out. These longer-term costs are borne by society as well as by individual students. Without additional resources, schools serving the nation's most vulnerable students are ill-prepared to create the working environments and compensation packages needed to attract and retain experienced, well-trained teachers.

Lack of Access to High-Quality Curriculum

In addition to being taught by less expert teachers than their White counterparts, students of color face stark differences in courses, curriculum programs, materials and equipment, as well as in the human environment in which they attend school. High-quality instruction, which is shaped by all these factors and supported by tangible resources, matters greatly for student achievement. For example, when sociologist Robert Dreeben studied reading instruction for 300 Black and White first graders across seven schools in the Chicago area, he found that differences in reading achievement were almost entirely explained, not by socioeconomic status or race, but by the quality of curriculum and teaching the students received:

Our evidence shows that the level of learning responds strongly to the quality of instruction: having and using enough time, covering a substantial amount of rich curricular material, and matching instruction appropriately to the ability levels of groups. . . . When Black and White children of comparable ability experience the same instruction, they do about equally well, and this is true when the instruction is excellent in quality and when it is inadequate.[48]

Yet the quality of instruction received by African American students was, on average, much lower than that received by White students, creating a racial gap in aggregate achievement at the end of first grade. In fact, the highest ability group in Dreeben's sample at the start of the study was in a school in a low-income African American neighborhood. These students attended a school that was unable to provide the quality instruction they deserved, and they learned less during first grade than their White counterparts.

In a variety of subtle and not-so-subtle ways, US schools allocate different learning opportunities to different students. Sorting often begins as early as kindergarten or first grade, with decisions about which students are placed in remedial or "gifted and talented" programs. Affluent and poor schools differ sharply in what is offered. Wealthy districts often offer foreign languages early in elementary school, while poor districts offer few such courses even at the high school level; richer districts typically provide extensive music and art programs, project-based science, and elaborate technology supports, while poor districts often have none of these and often offer stripped down drill-and-practice approaches to reading and math rather than teaching for higher-order applications.[49]

For reasons of both resources and expectations, schools serving African American, Latino, and Native American students are "bottom heavy"—that is, they offer fewer academic and college preparatory courses and more remedial and vocational courses that train students for low-status occupations, such as cosmetology and sewing.[50] For example, in 2005 only 30 percent of highly segregated schools serving African American and Latino students in California had a sufficient number of the state-required college preparatory courses to accommodate all their students. These schools, serving more than 90 percent students of color, constitute a quarter of all schools in the state. Furthermore, in a large majority of these highly segregated schools more than one-fifth of the college-preparatory courses they did offer were taught by underqualified teachers.[51] As a result of these conditions, very few African American and Latino high school graduates had taken and passed both the courses and the tests required to be eligible for admission to the state university system.[52]

Tracking is another well-established mechanism used to differentiate access to knowledge. . . . In racially mixed schools, the tracks are generally color-coded: honors or advanced courses are reserved primarily for White students, while the lower tracks are disproportionately filled with students of color. Unequal access to high-level courses and challenging curriculum explains much of the difference in achievement between minority students and White students.

Little has changed since Jonathan Kozol eloquently described two decades ago how, within ostensibly integrated schools in New York City, minority children were disproportionately assigned to special education classes that occupy small, cramped corners and split classrooms, while gifted and talented classes, which were exclusively composed of White and Asian students, enjoyed spaces filled with books and computers and learned logical reasoning and problem solving.[53] School pathways locking in inequality can be found in most districts today, as high-quality education is rationed to the privileged few. Furthermore, race and eth-

nicity are associated with placement in higher or lower tracks independently of students' achievement levels.[54] In addition to inequitable access to knowledge, cross-school segregation and within-school tracking reduce the extent to which different kinds of students have the opportunity to interact with one another and gain access to multiple perspectives. . . .

Funding Equitable Education

Ultimately, the proof is in the pudding. A number of states that have raised and equalized funding as part of systemic reforms have raised student achievement and reduced the opportunity gap.[55] Consider Massachusetts. For the past decade, Massachusetts has led all states in student achievement on the National Assessment of Educational Progress. The meteoric rise began in 1992 with a court decision in *Hancock v. Driscoll* requiring an overhaul of school funding. The school finance formula adopted in 1993 as part of Massachusetts' Education Reform Act led to substantially greater investments in needier schools by equalizing funding and local effort simultaneously and adding funding increments based on the proportions of low-income students and English language learners in a district.

This progressive funding approach was accompanied by new statewide learning standards, curriculum frameworks, and assessments; expanded learning time in core content areas; technology investments; and stronger licensing requirements for teachers. The next year Massachusetts adopted a plan for professional development that provided dedicated funding to districts, led to intensive summer institutes in math and science, and set up continuing education requirements for certification, as well as a new set of standards and expectations for local educator evaluation. The Attracting Excellence to Teaching Program subsidized preparation for qualified entrants to the profession.

In addition, the state quintupled its funding for local early childhood programs, created a Commission on Early Childhood Education to develop a statewide plan, established model pre-school programs, and awarded hundreds of Community Partnerships for Children grants to expand access to early education for children in need. By the year 2000, Massachusetts had underwritten these reforms with more than $2 billion in new state dollars for its public schools, greatly expanding the state share of funding and enhancing equity.

Economist Jonathan Guryan found that increased educational funding for historically low-spending districts led to improved student achievement in all subject areas, especially for traditionally low-scoring students.[56] By 2002, the state had dramatically improved overall achievement and sharply reduced its achievement gap. Massachusetts demonstrates how investments, wisely spent in concert with a systemic approach to reform, can make a difference in educational outcomes.

New Jersey provides another, more recent, case. For many years, the state spent about half as much on the education of low-income, minority students in cities like Camden, Trenton, Newark, and Paterson as it did in wealthy districts. After 30 years of litigation and nine court decisions finding the New Jersey school finance system unconstitutional, the state finally agreed to make a major infusion of funding to the 28 highest-need districts to bring them into parity with the per-pupil expenditures in the state's successful suburban districts. The new funding, which began in 1998, was spent to implement a new state curriculum linked to the state standards; support whole school reform; ensure early childhood education for three- and four-year-olds as well as full-day kindergarten; educate preschool teachers; reduce class sizes; invest in technology; ensure adequate facilities; and support health, social services, alternative, and summer school programs to help students catch up. In addition, an early literacy program provided reading coaches and professional development for teachers in kindergarten through third grade.[57]

New Jersey launched a set of new teacher education programs focused on preparing teachers for effective teaching in high-need urban districts, using school–university partnerships to provide both intensive field experiences for teacher candidates and professional learning opportunities for veteran teachers. It developed extensive professional development supports for teaching content area standards and for supporting English language learners and other special needs students, with dedicated funding and assistance in high-needs schools to model effective practices.[58] Gradually, the districts that had become dysfunctional during the lean years began to gain ground.

By 2007, New Jersey had substantially increased its standing on national reading and math assessments, ranking among the top five states in all subject areas and grade levels on the NAEP and first in writing. It was also one of four states that made the most progress nationally in closing performance gaps between White, Black, and Hispanic students in fourth- and eighth-grade reading and math.[59] By 2007, although parity had not yet been achieved, Hispanic and Black students scored between 5 and 10 points above their peers nationwide, depending on the test.[60] The state also reduced the achievement gap for students with disabilities and for socioeconomically disadvantaged students.

Clearly, money well spent does make a difference. Equalizing access to resources creates the possibility that all students will receive what should be their birthright: a genuine opportunity to learn.

NOTES

1. This reading draws in part on Linda Darling-Hammond, *The Flat World and Education: How America's Commitment to Equity Will Determine Our Future* (New York: Teachers College Press, 2010), and Linda Darling-Hammond, "Inequality and the Right to Learn: Access to Qualified Teachers in California's Public Schools," *Teachers College Record*, 106(10) (October 2004), 1936–1966.
2. Ladson-Billings, 2006.

3. Tyack, 1974, 109–125; Kluger, 1976; Meier, Stewart, & England, 1989; Schofield, 1995.
4. Quoted in Tyack, 1974, 119.
5. *Williams et al. v. State of California*, Superior Court of the State of California for the County of San Francisco, 2001, Complaint, 569–66.
6. Darling-Hammond, 2010.
7. Baker, Sciarra, & Farrie, 2010.
8. Liu, 2008.
9. Education Trust, 2006.
10. See Rothstein, 2013, and Darling-Hammond, 2010.
11. Bell, Bernstein, & Greenberg, 2008.
12. DeNavas-Walt, Proctor, & Lee, 2005; U.S. Bureau of the Census, 2006.
13. Darling-Hammond, 2010.
14. UNICEF, 2001, 3.
15. Heckman 2008, 49.
16. Children's Defense Fund, 2001.
17. Sahlberg, 2011.
18. Rumberger & Palardy, 2005; see also Orfield, 2013.
19. Orfield, G., 2001.
20. *Parents Involved in Community Schools v. Seattle School District No. 1*, 551 U.S. 701 (2007).
21. Civil Rights Project (2006), amicus brief filed in *Parents Involved in Community Education v. Seattle School District No. 1*, pg. 3.
22. Orfield, 2001.
23. 1966 Coleman Report, p. 325. For a recent review of this evidence, see Kahlenberg, 2001.
24. Schofield, 1995; Anyon, 1997; Dawkins & Braddock, 1994; Natriello, McDill, & Pallas, 1990.
25. Lee, 2004; Horn, 2002; See also the discussion in Gándara, 2013.
26. Garofano, Sable, & Hoffman, 2008.
27. Resnick, 1995
28. Darling-Hammond, 2010.
29. Kaufman and Rosenbaum, 1992.
30. Education Trust, 2006.
31. Darling-Hammond, 2004.
32. Shields et al., 2001.
33. John Merrow Reports are available from Learning Matters at http://learningmatters.tv/.
34. Darling-Hammond, 2004.
35. Analyses of teacher distribution data were conducted by the author.
36. NCES, 1997; Lankford, Loeb, & Wyckoff, 2002.
37. Haycock, 2000, 11.
38. These findings are documented in Betts, Rueben, & Dannenberg, 2000; Boyd et al., 2006; Clotfelter, Ladd, & Vigdor, 2007; Darling-Hammond, 2000; Darling-Hammond, Holtzman, Gatlin, & Heilig, 2005; Ferguson, 1991; Fetler, 1999; Goldhaber & Brewer, 2000; Goe, 2002; Hawk, Coble, & Swanson, 1985; Monk, 1994; Strauss and Sawyer, 1986.
39. Akiba, LeTendre, & Scribner, 2007.
40. Clotfelter, Ladd, & Vigdor, 2007.
41. Boyd et al., 2006.
42. NCTAF, 1996.
43. Ibid.
44. *Renee v. Duncan,* 623 F. 3d 787 (2010). The court ruling favored the plaintiffs, but Congress subsequently wrote the department's regulations into law, for a time period that currently extends until June 2013. This means that, until that time, teachers-in-training will be considered "highly qualified."
45. Darling-Hammond, 2003, 128.
46. Betts, Rueben, & Dannenberg, 2000; Darling-Hammond, 2000; Fetler, 1999; Fuller, 2000; Goe, 2002; Strauss & Sawyer, 1986.
47. Shields, Humphrey, Wechsler, et al., 2001.
48. Dreeben, 1987, 34.
49. Kozol, 2005; Darling-Hammond, 2010.
50. College Board, 1985; Pelavin & Kane, 1990; Oakes, 2005.
51. Oakes et al., 2006.
52. California Postsecondary Education Commission, 2007.
53. Kozol, 1992.
54. Oakes, 1993, 2005; Welner, 2001.
55. Baker & Welner, 2011; Darling-Hammond, 2010.

56. Guryan, 2001.
57. Assistant Commissioner Jay Doolan and State Assessment Director, Timothy Peters, Presentation to the New Jersey State Board of Education, *NAEP 2007: Reading and Mathematics, Grades 4 and 8,* October 17, 2007.
58. See "New Jersey's Plan for Meeting the Highly Qualified Teacher Goals," submitted July 7, 2006, to the US Department of Education, http://liberty.state.nj.us/education/data/hqt/06/plan.pdf.
59. NCES, *Top Four States in Closing Achievement Gap.* Retrieved on August 2, 2008, from http://www.fldoe.org/asp/naep/pdf/Top-4-states.pdf.
60. NCES, 2007.

REFERENCES

Akiba, M., LeTendre, G. K., & Scribner, J. P. (2007). Teacher quality, opportunity gap, and national achievement in 46 countries. *Educational Researcher, 36*(7), 369–387.

Anyon, J. (1997). *Ghetto schooling: A political economy of urban educational reform.* New York: Teachers College Press.

Baker, B. D., Sciarra, D., & Farrie, D. (2010). *Is school funding fair? A national report card.* Newark, NJ: Education Law Center.

Bell, K., Bernstein, J., & Greenberg, M. (2008). Lessons for the United States from other advanced economies in tackling child poverty. In *Big ideas for children: Investing in our nation's future,* ed. First Focus, 81–92. Washington, DC: First Focus.

Betts, J. R., Rueben, K. S., Danenberg, A. (2000). *Equal resources, equal outcomes? The distribution of school resources and student achievement in California.* San Francisco: Public Policy Institute of California.

Boyd, D., Grossman, P., Lankford, H., Loeb, S., and Wyckoff, J. (2006). How changes in entry requirements alter the teacher workforce and affect student achievement. *Education Finance & Policy, 1,* 176–216.

California Postsecondary Education Commission. (2007). *College-going rates: A performance measure in California's higher education accountability framework* (Commission Report No. 07–04). Sacramento, CA: Author.

Children's Defense Fund. (2001). Children's Defense Fund calculations, based on data from U.S. Bureau of the Census. June.

Clotfelter, C. T., Ladd, H. F., & Vigdor, J. L. (2007). Teacher credentials and student achievement: Longitudinal analysis with student fixed effects. *Economics of Education Review, 26*(6), 673–682.

College Board. (1985). *Equality and excellence: The educational status of Black Americans.* New York: College Entrance Examination Board.

Darling-Hammond, L. (2000). Teacher quality and student achievement: A review of state policy evidence. *Educational Policy Analysis Archives, 8*(1). Retrieved from http://epaa.asu.edu/epaa/v8n1.

Darling-Hammond, L. (2003). Access to quality teaching: An analysis of inequality in California's public schools. *Santa Clara Law Review, 43,* 101–239.

Darling-Hammond, L. (2004). Inequality and the right to learn: Access to qualified teachers in California's public schools. *Teachers College Record, 106*(10), 1936–1966.

Darling-Hammond, L. (2007). A Marshall Plan for teaching: What it will really take to leave no child behind. *Education Week.* Retrieved from http://www.edweek.org/ew/articles/2007/01/10/18hammond.h26.html.

Darling-Hammond, L. (2010). *The flat world and education: How America's commitment to equity will determine our future.* New York: Teachers College Press.

Darling-Hammond, L., Holtzman, D., Gatlin, S. J., & Heilig, J. V. (2005). Does teacher preparation matter? Evidence about teacher certification, Teach for America, and teacher effectiveness. *Education Policy Analysis Archives, 13*(42). Retrieved from http://epaa.asu.edu/epaa/v13n42/.

Dawkins, M. P., & Braddock J. H. (1994). The continuing significance of desegregation: School racial composition and African American inclusion in American society. *Journal of Negro Education, 63*(3), 394–405.

DeNavas-Walt, C., Proctor, B. D., & Lee, C. H. (2005). Income, poverty, and health insurance coverage in the United States: 2005. In *Current Population Reports.* Washington, DC: US Department of Commerce.

Dreeben, R. (1987). Closing the divide: What teachers and administrators can do to help black students reach their reading potential. *American Educator, 11*(4), 28–35.

Education Trust. (2006). *Funding gaps 2006.* Retrieved from http://www.edtrust.org/sites/edtrust.civications.net/files/publications/files/FundingGap2006.pdf.

Fetler, M. (1999). High school staff characteristics and mathematics test results. *Education Policy Analysis Archives, 7* (March 24). Retrieved from http://epaa.asu.edu.

Fuller, B., ed. (2000). *Inside charter schools: The paradox of radical decentralization.* Cambridge, MA: Harvard University. Press.

Gándara, P. (2013). Meeting the needs of language minorities. In *Closing the opportunity gap: What America must do to give every child an even chance,* ed. P. Carter and K. Welner, 156–168. New York: Oxford University Press.

Garofano, A., Sable, J., & Hoffman, L. (2008). *Characteristics of the 100 largest public elementary and secondary school districts in the United States: 2004–05.* US Department of Education, National Center for Education Statistics. Washington, DC: US Government Printing Office.

Goe, L. (2002). Legislating equity: The distribution of emergency permit teachers in California. *Educational Policy Analysis Archives online, 10*(42). Retrieved from http://epaa.asu.edu/epaa/v10n42/.

Goldhaber, D. D. & Brewer, D. J. (2000). Does teacher certification matter? High school certification status and student achievement. *Educational Evaluation and Policy Analysis, 22,* 129–145.

Guryan, J. (2001). *Does money matter? Regression-discontinuity estimates from education finance reform in Massachusetts.* NBER Working Paper 8269. Cambridge, MA.

Hawk, P., Coble, C. R., and Swanson, M. (1985). Certification: It does matter. *Journal of Teacher Education, 36*(3), 13–15.

Haycock, K. (2000). No more settling for less. *Thinking K-16, 4*(1), 3–8, 10–12. Washington, DC: Education Trust.

Heckman, J. J. (2008). The case for investing in disadvantaged young children. In *Big ideas for children: Investing in our nation's future,* ed. First Focus, 49–66. Washington, DC: First Focus.

Horn, C. (2002). *The intersection of race, class and English learner status.* Working Paper. Prepared for National Research Council.

Kahlenberg, R. D. (2001). *All together now: Creating middle class schools through public school choice.* Washington, DC: Brookings Institution Press.

Kaufman, J. E., & Rosenbaum, J. E. (1992). Education and employment of low-income Black youth in White suburbs. *Educational Evaluation and Policy Analysis, 14*(3), 229–240.

Kozol, J. (1992). *Savage inequalities: Children in America's schools.* New York: Harper Perennial.

Kozol, J. (2005). *The shame of the nation: The restoration of apartheid schooling in America.* New York: Crown Books.

Kluger, R. (1976). *Simple justice.* NY: Vintage.

Ladson-Billings, G. (2006). From the achievement gap to the education debt: Understanding achievement in U.S. schools. *Educational Researcher 35*(7), 3–12.

Lankford, H., Loeb, S., & Wyckoff, J. (2002). Teacher sorting and the plight of urban schools: A descriptive analysis. *Education Evaluation and Policy Analysis, 24*(1), 37–62.

Lee, C. (2004). *Racial segregation and educational outcomes in metropolitan Boston.* Cambridge, MA: The Civil Rights Project at Harvard University.

Liu, G. (2008). Improving Title 1 funding equity across states, districts, and schools, *Iowa Law Review, 93,* 973–1013.

Meier, K. J., Stewart, J. Jr., & England, R. E. (1989). *Race, class and education: The politics of second-generation discrimination.* Madison: University of Wisconsin Press.

Monk, D. H. (1994). Subject matter preparation of secondary mathematics and science teachers and student achievement. *Economics of Education Review, 13*(2), 125–145.

National Center for Education Statistics (NCES) (1997). *America's teachers: Profile of a profession,*

1993–94. Washington, DC: US Department of Education.

National Commission on Teaching and America's Future (NCTAF). (1996). *What matters most: Teaching for America's future.* New York: Author.

Natriello, G., McDill, E. L., & Pallas, A. M. (1990). *Schooling disadvantaged children: Racing against catastrophe.* New York: Teachers College Press.

Oakes, J. (1993). *Ability grouping, tracking, and within-school segregation in the San Jose Unified School District.* Los Angeles: University of California, Los Angeles.

Oakes, J. (2005) *Keeping track: How schools structure inequality,* 2nd ed. New Haven, CT: Yale University Press.

Oakes, J., Rogers, J., Silver, D., Valladares, S., Terriquez, V., McDonough, P., Renée, M., & Lipton, M. (2006). *Removing the roadblocks: Fair college opportunities for all California students.* Los Angeles: University of California/All Campus Consortium for Research Diversity and UCLA Institute for Democracy, Education, and Access.

Orfield, G. (2001). *Schools more separate: Consequences of a decade of resegregation,* Cambridge, MA: Civil Rights Project. Harvard University.

Orfield, G. (2013). Housing segregation produces unequal schools: Causes and solutions. In *Closing the opportunity gap: What America must do to give every child an even chance,* ed. P. Carter and K. Welner, 40–60. New York: Oxford University Press.

Pelavin, S. H., & Kane, M. (1990). *Changing the odds: Factors increasing access to college.* New York: College Entrance Examination Board.

Resnick, L. (1995). From aptitude to effort: A new foundation for our schools. *Daedalus, 124*(4), 55–62.

Rothstein, R. (2013). Why children from lower socioeconomic classes, on average, have lower academic achievement than middle-class children. In *Closing the opportunity gap: What America must do to give every child an even chance,* ed. P. Carter and K. Welner, 61–76. New York: Oxford University Press.

Rumberger, R. W., & Palardy, G. J. (2005). Does resegregation matter? The impact of social composition on academic achievement in Southern high schools. In *School resegregation: Must the South turn back?* ed. John Charles Boger & Gary Orfield, 127–147. Chapel Hill: University of North Carolina Press.

Sahlberg, P. (2011). *Finnish lessons: What can the world learn from educational change in Finland?* New York: Teachers College Press.

Schofield, J. (1995). Review of research on school desegregation's impact on elementary and secondary school students. In *Handbook of research on multicultural education,* ed. J. A. Banks & C. A. M. Banks, 799–812. New York: Simon & Schuster/Macmillan.

Shields, P. M., Humphrey, D. C., Wechsler, M. E., Riel, L. M., Tiffany-Morales, J., Woodworth, K., Youg, V. M., & Price, T. (2001). *The status of the teaching profession 2001.* Santa Cruz, CA: Center for the Future of Teaching and Learning.

Strauss, R. P., & Sawyer, E. A. (1986). Some new evidence on teacher and student competencies. *Economics of Education Review, 5*(1), 41–48.

Tyack, D. (1974). *The one best system: A history of American urban education.* Cambridge, MA: Harvard University Press.

UNICEF (2001). *A league table of child deaths by injury in rich nations: Innocenti report card 2.* Florence: UNICEF, Innocenti Research Centre.

U.S. Bureau of the Census (2006). *Poverty status of people, by age, race, and Hispanic origin: 1959–2006.* Washington, DC: US Department of Commerce.

Welner, K. G. (2001). *Legal rights, local wrongs: When community control collides with educational equity.* Albany, New York: State University of New York Press.

Why Some Schools Want to Expel Suspensions

NPR Staff

[Editor's note: Increasing public attention has been paid to discipline in schools, often resulting in schools establishing punitive forms of discipline such as zero-tolerance policies, suspensions, expulsions, and strict security measures. In 2010, Welch and Payne conducted a systematic analysis and found that these punishments were more likely to be used against racial minority students and that schools with larger minority populations were more likely to use punitive (and in some cases, extremely punitive) disciplinary policies, even when the schools had lower levels of "deviant" behavior, thus increasing the likelihood of negative educational and criminal justice outcomes for students (see Welch, Kelly, and Allison Ann Payne. 2010. "Racial Threat and Punitive School Discipline." *Social Problems* 57(1):25–48).]

The effectiveness of school suspensions is up for debate. California is the most recent battleground, but a pattern of uneven application and negative outcomes is apparent across the country. California students were suspended more than 700,000 times over the 2011–2012 school year, according to state data. One school district decided it was getting ridiculous. In May, the board for the Los Angeles Unified School District passed a new resolution to ban the use of suspensions to punish students for "willful defiance." Those offenses include: bringing a cellphone to school, public displays of affection, truancy or repeated tardiness. They accounted for nearly half of all suspensions issued in California last year. But there's mounting research that says that out-of-school suspensions put students on the fast track to falling behind, dropping out, and going to jail. Moreover, some groups are disproportionately suspended more than others.

IN A SPIRAL

Damien Valentine, now 16, received his first out-of-school suspension for repeatedly talking to another student in class and talking back to his teacher. That was four years ago at John Muir Middle School in South Central Los Angeles. Subsequently, the suspensions kept coming. In eighth grade, Damien had a few "confrontations"—not fights, he says, just some heated words between students. But he got suspended again. Then, his freshman year of high school, he was suspended from campus for three weeks, accused of helping to start a gang. Damien says he believes teachers and principals have an unspoken way of seeing boys and girls of color. "As soon as you go inside the class and get in trouble, they say they already expected it," he says. "They already expected for this African-American male to act like that." In the 2008 school year at John Muir, black students received half of the total suspensions, though they made up 23 percent of the student body.

WHAT FOLLOWS SUSPENSION

That pattern extends beyond Los Angeles, says lawyer and educator Daniel Losen, who directs the Civil Rights Project at the University of California, Los Angeles. In April, Losen co-authored the report, "Out of School and Off Track," which found skewed suspension rates for certain demographics. [This report found that between 2009 and 2010, 24.3 percent of Black students, 12 percent of Latino students, 8.4 percent of American Indian students, 7.1 percent of White students, and 2.3 percent of Asian/Pacific Islander students were suspended]. "As we've gotten to this sort of zero-tolerance mentality, that kind of policy has been especially applied to poor kids and especially black kids; and also, kids with disabilities," he says. Losen notes that even being suspended once doubles the chance a student will drop out, raising the risk to 32 percent from 16 percent [which is the dropout rate for students who are not suspended]. Suspended two or more times?

continues

Continued

The dropout rate is 49 percent. "All the research says that [being suspended] contributes to their disengagement from school," he says. "So you can imagine that for poor students, students from single-parent households or kids who are homeless, they're much more likely to wind up on the streets unsupervised." In addition to being more likely to drop out, suspended students also have a higher likelihood of falling into the juvenile justice system. "That brings up another really important issue: The costs of suspending students are really sky high, but they're hidden costs," Losen says.

THE RIGHT TO REMOVE A DISRUPTION

But Los Angeles teacher Martha Infante says she does not believe eliminating suspensions is the right move for her school district. "If I see the classroom environment is suffering, that the students are getting scared, I will remove the problem student because my other students have rights, too," she says. She teaches at Los Angeles Academy Middle School. Infante, who has taught for 16 years, says she believes her ability to suspend disruptive students is an important tool to maintain control of her classroom. "The more time you spend on discipline issues, it affects the classroom environment," she says. "And sometimes, it doesn't matter how much time I take. It ends up not making a difference, and there's no change in behavior." Infante says she doesn't hand out suspensions willy-nilly, and often just the threat of a suspension can be effective. Otherwise, she says, "You offer counseling, you get services, whatever services are available." The problem is, in this era of budget cuts, counselors and psychiatric social workers are in short supply.

CREATING A CONNECTION

At Garfield High School, there's no more money for counselors and social workers—and there are few suspensions. Principal Jose Huerta says he has a found a third way. "It's simple. It doesn't cost money. It's just connecting with kids and having a strong instructional program," he says. The year before

Huerta took over as principal, there were 683 suspensions. Heurta says suspending students had become a reflex to poor behavior. But when he took over in 2010, he said, "No more." The results have been dramatic: just two suspensions in the past three years. "I didn't come into Garfield saying, 'OK, my mission in life is to lower suspensions.' It wasn't. It was to enhance and improve the instruction," he says. "And because we did, we were successful with a great teacher group, a great administrative staff, great parents." When a student does act out in class, Huerta says the teachers act quickly with counselors or the student support team to "find out what the real deal is." "Ninety percent of the time, we find out something happened the night before," he says. Issues at home could range from divorce, to a death or even a family member being deported. "But these are teenagers. They're not going to go and cry to anybody, they're [in] a tough neighborhood," he says. "So when that kid acts out, we get in his face immediately. . . . And we resolve it. And you know what? These kids respond well. Their needs were met." Since there's no money for additional professionals, Huerta has substituted with parents and nonprofit community groups. He says he believes everyone needs to be accountable: students, parents, teachers and the local community.

"STARTING FRESH"

Across town in South Central LA, Damien is about to finish his sophomore year of high school. That three-week suspension for alleged gang activities made him believe he didn't have a future at that school, so he took action and transferred. He says he told himself, "All right, this is a new start." It has been a new start. At Manual Arts High, he's been able to stay out of trouble. And at the LA Unified School Board Meeting where the decision to curtail suspensions was made, Damien testified about how suspensions almost pushed him out of the school system altogether. He's proud he was a part of the process of changing the district's suspension policy.

How Schools Really Matter

DOUGLAS B. DOWNEY AND BENJAMIN G. GIBBS

Although the authors acknowledge structural inequalities across schools and their role in reproducing educational inequality, Downey and Gibbs focus on factors outside of the school environment (such as home environment, access to educational resources, and parents' ability to assist children with homework) that contribute to inequality. Downey and Gibbs take a "contextual approach" to understanding education gaps and conclude by discussing policies that may help to close them.

There's an old joke about a man on a street corner, down on his hands and knees searching for his lost wallet. A passerby stops to help, asking, "So you lost it right around here?" "Oh no," the man replies, "I lost the wallet several blocks ago. I'm just looking on this street corner because this is where the lighting is good."

It's tempting to look for the source of a problem in places where the lighting is good even if we're not in the right place. When we hear about high dropout rates; persistent black/white gaps in test scores; low American reading, math, and science scores; dramatic differences in resources among schools; and even growing childhood obesity, it's sort of easy to ascribe these negative outcomes to schools. In fact, this is the "traditional" story we hear about American schools.

The Traditional Tale of Schools

The tendency to view schools as the source of so many problems is especially true when we consider equality of opportunity, an important American value. There are many good reasons to believe that schools are the primary engines of inequality. First, children attending schools with lots of high-income children tend to perform better on standardized tests than kids at schools with lots of low-income children. Second, there are clear resource differences between these schools, rooted in the fact that, in most states, local tax revenues constitute a significant portion of the school's budget. For example, Ohio's local taxes constitute about half of a school's budget (state taxes constitute 43% and federal taxes about 7%). As a result of the heavy emphasis on local taxes, some schools are able to spend substantially more money per student than others. This means schools located in areas with expensive houses and successful businesses can spend more on new textbooks, teacher pay, recreational facilities, extracurricular activities, and help for students with special needs. Third, in high-resource schools, teachers encounter fewer children with behavioral problems and more parents engaged in

Douglas B. Downey and Benjamin G. Gibbs, *Contexts* (Volume 9 and Issue 2), pp. 50–54. Copyright © 2010. Reprinted by Permission of SAGE Publications.

their children's education, factors that can attract and retain better teachers. Based on these patterns, it seems obvious that if we want to improve the quality of life for the disadvantaged in the U.S., the best place to start is schools.

But this traditional story has developed largely without understanding the way in which children's academic outcomes are shaped by many factors outside of schools. Simply look at the amount of time children spend outside of school. If we focus on the 9-month academic year only, the proportion of time children spend in school is about *one-third*. And if we include the non-school summer, children spend just one-quarter of their waking hours in school each year. Now if we also include the years before kindergarten—which certainly affect children—we find that the typical 18-year-old American has spent just 13% of his or her waking hours in school. For most of us, it's surprising to learn that such a large percentage of children's time is spent outside of school, but it's important to keep in mind if we're serious about understanding how schools really matter.

A contextual perspective reminds us to look at the rest of kids' lives. For instance, not every student comes to school with the same economic, social, or cultural resources. Even with the same educational opportunities, some students benefit from home environments that prepare them for school work and so they are better able to take advantage of education.

Moving away from the traditional, narrow view of schools that forgets the importance of children's time outside the classroom, we endorse adopting a contextualized (or impact) view of schools. This new emphasis can really change how we think about what schools can—and can't—do for our kids.

Pianos and Parents

Imagine that we want to compare the effectiveness of two piano instructors who will both teach 10-week piano classes for beginners. We flip a coin and assign one instructor to place A and the other to place B. Our goal is compli-cated, however, by the fact that in place B, due to cost, almost no students come from a home with a piano, whereas in place A, whose parents have more disposable income, most students have a piano at home. As a result, place A's students have already had some practice time on a piano, whereas place B's students have had little to none. In addition, while both instructors teach a session once a week, place A's students practice on their own several times a week, whereas in place B—where few have pianos at home—students have a much harder time finding a way to practice.

Obviously, if we just compared the piano students' skills at the end of the 10-week program we couldn't accurately assess the quality of the two instructors—the two groups' skills differed before the lessons began. And if we compared how much the students' skills improved during the instructional period, it would still be hard to know which instructor was more effective because place A's students practiced more often than place B's students did. Given that these two instructors face different challenges, is there a way to evaluate them fairly? Can we isolate how the piano teachers really mattered?

This is the quandary we have when trying to understand how schools (or teachers) matter for children's lives; the same kinds of complicating factors are at work. First, children begin schooling with very different levels of academic skills. For example, the black/white gap in math and reading skills is roughly a standard deviation at the end of high school, but half of this gap is evident at the beginning of kindergarten, before schools have had a chance to matter. And the differences in skills between high- and low-socioeconomic status (SES) students at the start of kindergarten are even larger. Obviously, these variations aren't a consequence of differences in school quality, but of the different kinds of students schools serve.

Thinking contextually, some home environments complement what occurs at school as parents help with homework, communicate with teachers, reinforce school concepts, provide a safe and stable environment for study, and attend to children's medical needs (by, for instance, providing consistent visits to doctors and dentists). In her book *Home Advantage*, sociologist Annette Lareau gives a poignant description of just how important parents can be, getting involved in their child's coursework and with their teachers in ways that promote academic success and instilling in their children a kind of academic entitlement. She wrote that these parents "made an effort to integrate educational goals into family life including teaching children new words when driving by billboards, having children practice penmanship and vocabulary by writing out shopping lists, practicing mathematics during baking projects, and practicing vocabulary during breakfast time." Interacting with instructors, the upper-middle class parents Lareau observed requested specific classroom teachers or asked that their child be placed in school programs for the gifted, for speech therapy, or with the learning resource center. In contrast, low-SES parents tended to have less time for involvement with their children's schoolwork, leaving educational experiences in the hands of the "experts." Much like having a piano at home, these contexts of advantage and disadvantage play a critical role in shaping how children gain academic skills during their school years.

Bringing in Context

By using a contextual perspective, sociologists have contributed considerably to our understanding of how schools matter. One of the most influential studies was the 1966 Coleman Report, a massive analysis of American schools that was commissioned by the Federal Department of Education. James Coleman, the lead author of the report, directed the collection of data from 4,000 schools and more than 645,000 American school children in the early 1960s. The researchers were interested in why some children had high math and reading skills and others did not. They measured many characteristics of schools (including school curriculum, facilities, teacher

qualities, and student body characteristics) and many characteristics of children's home lives (like parents' SES—education, income, and occupation level) to see which were more closely related to academic skills. Surprisingly, school characteristics were only weakly related to academic skills. It turned out that differences between schools in terms of quality played only a small role in understanding the variation in students' academic skills while home life (parents' SES showed the strongest relationship) mattered much more. Skeptics of this conclusion, such as sociologist Christopher Jencks, re-evaluated Coleman's conclusion with new data, but ended up finding similar patterns.

Of course, one limitation of this approach is that it depends heavily on whether Coleman and Jencks were measuring the right things about schools. Maybe they were missing what really mattered. While they were measuring per pupil expenditures, teacher/student ratios, and racial composition, they missed critical factors like teacher quality. If they failed to measure a lot of important things about schools, then their conclusions that schools play only a minor role in explaining inequality of skills might be wrong.

Seasonal Comparison Research

What researchers need is a way to untangle the role of school and non-school influences. Observing student learning during the school year tells us little about how schools matter because students are exposed to both school and non-school environments. When we compare annually-collected test scores, for example, it becomes very difficult to know why some students fall behind and some get ahead. Sociologist Barbara Heyns pointed out that during the summer children are influenced by non-school factors only. The best way to understand how schools matter, she reasoned, was to observe how things change between the non-school period (summer) and the school period. This strategy works like a natural experiment, separating the "treatment" from the treated. Knowing what happens to group-level differences in achievement by race, class, or gender when school is in session (the treatment) compared to when it is not (the control) is a good way to know if schools make educational gaps bigger or smaller.

This important insight led Heyns to collect a different kind of data. She evaluated fifth, sixth, and seventh grade students at the beginning and end of the academic years in Atlanta. By testing them both in the fall and spring, she was able to tell how much they learned during the summer, when school was out. This study design allowed her to uncover a provocative pattern—high- and low-SES students gained academic skills at about the same rate during the nine-month academic year. Gaps in skills developed during the summers. Although schools did not close achievement gaps between groups, these results bolstered Coleman and Jencks's initial conclusions that schools were not the primary reason for group-level inequalities. Heyns's provocative findings were replicated by sociologists Doris Entwisle and Karl Alexander in Baltimore and, more recently, by myself with colleagues at Ohio State. With nationally representative data, we found that low- and high-SES children learned math and reading at similar rates during the 9-month kindergarten and first grade periods, but that gaps in skills grew quickly during the summer in between, when school was out.

Taken together, the overall pattern from this seasonal research supports Coleman's conclusion: schools are not the source of inequality. The seasonal approach to understanding schools gives us a much more accurate understanding of how schools influence inequality. This research consistently produces an unconventional conclusion—if we lived in a world with no schools at all, inequality would be much worse. In other words, when it comes to inequality, schools are more part of the solution than the problem.

This contextual way of thinking about schools and inequality is difficult to reconcile, however, with the "traditional" story—that wide variations in school quality are the engine of inequality. By adopting a more contextual perspective on schools, we can understand this counterintuitive claim: despite the fact that some schools have more resources than others, schools end up being an equalizing force. The key is that the inequalities that exist outside of school are considerably larger than the ones students experience in school.

Schools, Context, and Policy

At the beginning of this article, we pointed out that it's natural to look to schools for the source of many of our kids' problems—they're the corner with the best "lighting." The often-unexplored terrain *outside* of schools, though, remains shadowy and seemingly inaccessible. This doesn't need to be the case. And, though extending the light beyond schools reveals that group-level inequality would be much worse if not for schools, it doesn't mean that schools are off the hook. In fact, using school impact as a guide, many "successful" schools in the traditional view are revealed as low-impact—good students don't always signal good instructors. In these schools, children pass proficiency exams, but since they started off in a better position, it's arguable that the schools didn't actually serve their students.

Clearly, when we employ a contextual perspective, we think about school policy, child development, and social problems in a new light. A contextual approach to schools promotes sensible policy, efficiently targeted resources, and reasonable assessment tools that recognize that some schools and teachers face very different challenges than others.

For example, a tremendous amount of energy and money is directed toward developing accountability systems for schools. But recall the analogy of the two piano instructors. It's difficult to determine which instructor is best, given that place A has students that start with more skills and practice more outside of instruction. Now suppose that we knew one more piece of information: how fast each group of piano players gained skills when not taking lessons. Suddenly, we could compare the rate of improvement outside of instruction with the rate observed during the instructional period. We could see how much instruction mattered.

This "impact" view has recently been applied to schools. In 2008, with fellow sociologists Paul T. von Hippel and Melanie Hughes, I constructed impact measures by taking a school's average difference between its students' first-grade learning rate and the learning rate observed in the summer prior to first grade. The key finding was that not all the schools deemed as "failing" under traditional criteria were really failing. Indeed, three out of four schools had been incorrectly evaluated. That's not to say that there were no variations in school quality, but many schools did much better than expected when we took a contextual approach to measurement. And some did much worse. If impact evaluations are more accurate, then teachers serving disadvantaged children are doing a better job than previously thought and current methods of school evaluation are producing substantial errors.

With its contextual orientation, seasonal research has also provided insights into other ways that schools matter. For example, researchers have considered whether "summer setback" can be avoided by modifying the school year so that there is no long gap in school exposure. Von Hippel has compared math and reading learning in schools with year-long calendars versus those with traditional school-year/summer break calendars. In both conditions, children attended school for about 180 days a year, but the timing of those days was spread more evenly in year-round schools. It turned out that, once a calendar year was up, both groups had learned about the same. The policy lesson is that increasing school exposure is probably more important than fiddling with how school days are distributed across the year.

Given that school exposure appears critical, many have viewed summer school (restricted to academically struggling children) as an attractive option for reducing inequality. It turns out, though, that children attending summer school gain fewer academic skills than we would expect. This may be because the academic programs in the summer are of lower quality, but it may also be because the kinds of students who typically attend summer school are also the kind who would typically suffer a "summer setback" without it. Viewed in this light, just treading water or maintaining the same academic skills during the summer could be viewed as a positive outcome.

And in other research employing seasonal comparisons, researchers have shown that children gain body mass index (BMI) three times faster during the summer than during the school year. Obviously, schools shouldn't abandon attempts to improve the quality of lunches or the schooling environment, but research suggests that attention should be paid to non-school factors as the primary sources of childhood obesity.

In the end, looking at schools through a contextual lens provides exciting insights. When we forget how other aspects of children's lives figure into their development, we create a distorted view of schools. The contextual perspective corrects this error and produces a more accurate understanding of how schools really matter. It suggests that if we are serious about improving American children's school performance, we will need to take a broader view of education policy. In addition to school reform, we must also aim to improve children's lives where they spend the vast majority of their time—with their families and in their neighborhoods.

The (Mis)Education of Monica and Karen

LAURA HAMILTON AND ELIZABETH A. ARMSTRONG

Although some research on college education focuses on the skills and abilities that students bring with them to college campuses, it is also important to consider how higher education is organized to help understand why some students succeed and others do not. The authors conducted ethnographic research on a cohort of college students at a large midwestern state college. Hamilton and Armstrong argue that four-year residential colleges and universities cater primarily to upper-income students, creating a "mismatch" between what they offer and what lower-income students need. As the campus demographics shift toward heavily recruited affluent college students, lower-income students find themselves pushed out of social and academic life on campus, while simultaneously incurring large amounts of debt.

Monica grew up in a small, struggling Midwestern community, population 3,000, that was once a booming factory town. She was from a working-class family, and paid for most of her education at Midwest U, a "moderately selective" residential university, herself. She worked two jobs, sometimes over 40 hours a week, to afford in-state tuition. Going out-of-state, or to a pricey private school, was simply out of the question without a large scholarship. Attending MU was even a stretch; one year there cost as much as four years at the regional campus near her hometown.

Karen grew up in the same small town as Monica, but in a solidly middle-class family. Her college-educated parents could afford to provide more financial assistance. But even though MU was only three hours away, her father "wasn't too thrilled" about her going so far from home. He had attended a small religious school that was only 10 minutes away.

Neither Karen nor Monica was academically well prepared for college. Both had good, but not stellar, grades and passable SAT scores, which made admission to a more selective school unlikely. Given the lower cost, ease of admission, and opportunity to commute from home, they might have started at the regional campus. However, MU offered, as Monica's mother put it, a chance to "go away and experience college life." Karen refused to look at any other school because she wanted to leave home. As she noted, "I really don't think I'm a small town girl." Monica's family was betting on MU as the best place for her to launch her dream career as a doctor. Karen and Monica's stories offer us a glimpse into the college experiences of average, in-state students at large, mid-tier public universities. Though they struggled to gain entrance to the flagship campus, they soon found that the structure of social and academic life there served them poorly—and had deleterious effects.

The Great Mismatch

Most four-year residential colleges and universities in the United States are designed to serve well-funded students, who have minimal (if any) caretaking responsibilities, and who attend college full-time after they graduate from high school. Yet only a minority of individuals who pursue postsecondary education in the United States fit this profile. There is a great gap between what the vast majority of Americans need and what four-year institutions offer them.

This mismatch is acutely visible at Midwest U, where Karen and Monica started their college careers. Almost half of those attending four-year colleges find themselves at schools like this one. Students from modest backgrounds who have above average, but not exceptional, academic profiles attend state flagship universities because they believe such schools offer a surefire route to economic security.

Public universities were founded to enable mobility, especially among in-state populations of students—which contributes to their legitimacy in the eyes of the public. In an era of declining state funding, schools like Midwest U have raised tuition and recruited more out-of-state students. They especially covet academically accomplished, ambitious children of affluent families.

As sociologist Mitchell Stevens describes in *Creating a Class*, elite institutions also pursue such students. While observing a small, private school, Stevens overhead an admissions officer describe an ideal applicant: "He's got great SATs [and] he's free [not requiring any financial aid]. . . . He helps us in every way that's quantifiable." Once private colleges skim off affluent, high-performing students, large, middle-tier, public universities are left to compete for the tuition dollars of less studious students from wealthy families.

How, we wondered, do in-state students fare in this context? To find out, for over five years we followed a dormitory floor of female students through their college careers and into the workforce, conducted an ethnography of the floor, and interviewed the women and their parents. What we found is that schools like MU only serve a segment of the student body well—affluent, socially-oriented, and out-of-state students—to the detriment of typical in-state students like Karen and Monica.

"I'm Supposed to Get Drunk"

Monica and Karen approached the housing application process with little information, and were unprepared for what they encountered when they were assigned to a room in a "party dorm." At MU, over a third of the freshman class is housed in such dorms. Though minimal partying actually took place in the heavily policed residence halls, many residents partied off-site, typically at fraternities, returning in the wee hours drunk and loud. Affluent students—both in and out-of-state—often requested rooms in party dorms, based on the recommendations of their similarly social siblings and friends.

Party dorms are a pipeline to the Greek system, which dominates campus life. Less than 20 percent of the student body at MU is involved in a fraternity or sorority, but these predominantly white organizations enjoy a great deal of power. They own space in central campus areas, across from academic buildings and sports arenas. They monopolize the social life of first-year students, offering underage drinkers massive, free supplies of alcohol, with virtual legal impunity. They even enjoy special ties to administrators, with officers sitting on a special advisory board to the dean of students.

Over 40 percent of Monica and Karen's floor joined sororities their first year. The pressure to rush was so intense that one roommate pair who opted out posted a disclaimer on their door, asking people to stop bugging them about it. The entire campus—including academic functions—often revolved around the schedule of Greek life. When a math test for a large, required class conflicted with women's rush, rather than excusing a group of women from a few rush events, the test itself was rescheduled.

Monica, like most economically disadvantaged students, chose not to rush a sorority, discouraged by the mandatory $60 t-shirt, as well as by the costly membership fees. Karen, who was middle class, had just enough funds to make rushing possible. However, she came to realize that Greek houses implicitly screened for social class. She pulled out her boots—practical rain boots that pegged her as a small town, in-state girl instead of an affluent, out-of-state student with money and the right taste in clothing. They were a "dead give-away," she said. She soon dropped out of rush.

Like all but a few students on the 53-person floor, Monica and Karen chose to participate in the party scene. Neither drank much in high school. Nor did they arrive armed with shot glasses or party-themed posters, as some students did. They partied because, as a woman from a similar background put it, "I'm supposed to get drunk every weekend. I'm supposed to go to parties every weekend." With little party experience, and few contacts in the Greek system, Monica and Karen were easy targets for fraternity men's sexual disrespect. Heavy alcohol consumption helped to put them at ease in otherwise uncomfortable situations. "I pretty much became an alcoholic," said Monica. "I was craving alcohol all the time."

Their forced attempts to participate in the party scene showed how poorly it suited their needs. "I tried so hard to fit in with what everybody else was doing here," Monica explained. "I think one morning I just woke up and realized that this isn't me at all; I don't like the way I am right now." She felt it forced her to become more immature. "Growing up to me isn't going out and getting smashed and sleeping around," she lamented. Partying is particularly costly for students of lesser means, who need to grow up sooner, cannot afford to be financially irresponsible, and need the credentials and skills that college offers.

Academic Struggles and "Exotic" Majors

Partying also takes its toll on academic performance, and Monica's poor grades quickly squelched her pre-med dreams. Karen, who hoped to become a teacher, also found it hard to keep up. "I did really bad in that math class, the first elementary ed math class," one of three that were required. Rather than retake the class, Karen changed her major to one that was popular among affluent, socially-oriented students on the floor: sports broadcasting.

She explained, "I'm from a really small town and it's just all I ever really knew was jobs that were around me, and most of those are teachers." A woman on her floor was majoring in sports broadcasting, which Karen had never considered. "I would have never thought about that. And so I saw hers, and I was like that's something that I really like. One of my interests is sports, watching them, playing them," she reasoned. "I could be a sportscaster on ESPN if I really wanted to."

Karen's experience shows the seductive appeal of certain "easy majors." These are occupational and professional programs that are often housed in their own schools and colleges. They are associated with a higher overall GPA and, as sociologists Richard Arum and Josipa Roksa report in *Academically Adrift*, lower levels of learning than majors in the more challenging sciences and humanities housed in colleges of arts and sciences.

In many easy majors, career success also depends on personal characteristics (such as appearance, personality, and aesthetic taste) that are developed outside of the classroom—often prior to entering college. Socially-oriented students flock to fields like communications, fashion, tourism, recreation, fitness, and numerous "business-lite" options, which are often linked to sports or the arts, rather than the competitive business school. About a third of the student body majored in business, management, marketing, communications, journalism, and related subfields.

Karen's switch to sports broadcasting gave her more time to socialize. But education is a more practical major that translates directly into a career; hiring rests largely on the credential. In contrast, success in sports broadcasting is dependent on class-based characteristics—such as family social ties to industry insiders. Several of Karen's wealthier peers secured plum internships in big cities because their parents made phone calls for them; Karen could not even land an unpaid internship with the Triple-A baseball team located 25 minutes from her house.

No one Karen encountered on campus helped her to assess the practicality of a career in this field. Her parents were frustrated that she had been persuaded not to graduate with a recognizable marketable skill. As her mother explained, "She gets down there and you start hearing all these exotic sounding majors.... I'm not sure quite what jobs they're going to end up with." Her mother was frustrated that Karen "went to see the advisor to make plans for her sophomore year, and they're going, 'Well, what's your passion?'" Her mother was not impressed. "How many people do their passion? To me, that's more what you do for a hobby.... I mean most people, that's not what their job is."

Halfway through college, when Karen realized she could not get an internship, much less a job, in sports broadcasting, her parents told her to switch back to education. The switch was costly: it was going to take her two more years to complete. As her mother complained, "When you're going through the orientation ... they're going, 'oh, most people change their major five times.' And they make it sound like it's no big deal. But yeah, they're making big bucks by kids changing."

Leaving Midwest U Behind

Monica left MU after her first year. "I was afraid if I continued down there that I would just go crazy and either not finish school, or get myself in trouble," she explained. "And I just didn't want to do that." She immediately enrolled in a beauty school near her home. Dissatisfied with the income she earned as a hairstylist, she later entered a community college to complete an associate degree in nursing. She paid for her nursing classes as she studied, but had 10,000 dollars in student loan debt from her time at MU. Still, her debt burden was substantially smaller than if she had stayed there; some of her MU peers had amassed over 50,000 dollars in loans by graduation.

Because her GPA was too low to return to elementary education at MU, Karen transferred to a regional college during her fourth year. Since the classes she took for sports broadcasting did not fulfill any requirements, it took her six years to graduate. Karen's parents, who reported that they spent the first 10 years of their married life paying off their own loans, took out loans to cover most of the cost, and anticipated spending even longer to finance their daughter's education. Monica and Karen were not the only ones on their dormitory floor to leave MU. Nine other in-state women, the majority of whom were from working-class or lower-middle-class backgrounds, did as well. The only out-of-state student who transferred left for a higher-ranked institution. While we were concerned that the in-state leavers, most of whom were moving down the ladder of prestige to regional campuses, would suffer, they actually did better than in-state women from less privileged families who stayed at MU. Their GPAs improved, they selected majors with a more direct payoff, and they were happier overall.

The institutions to which women moved played a large role in this transformation. As one leaver described the regional campus to which she transferred, it "doesn't have any fraternities or sororities. It only has, like, 10 buildings." But, she said, "I just really love it." One of the things she loved was that nobody cared about partying. "They're there just to graduate and get through."

It prioritized the needs of a different type of student: "Kids who have lower social economic status, who work for their school."

Without the social pressures of MU, it was possible to, as Karen put it, "get away from going out all the time, and refocus on what my goal was for this part of my life." Few majors like sports broadcasting and fashion merchandising were available, reducing the possible ways to go astray academically. Those who attended regional or community colleges trained to become accountants, teachers, social workers, nurses or other health professionals. At the conclusion of our study, they had better employment prospects than those from similar backgrounds who stayed at MU.

The Importance of Institutional Context

It is tempting to assume that academic success is determined, in large part, by what students bring with them—different ability levels, resources, and orientations to college life. But Monica and Karen's stories demonstrate that what students get out of college is also organizationally produced. Students who were far more academically gifted than Monica or Karen sometimes floundered at MU, while others who were considerably less motivated breezed through college. The best predictor of success was whether there was a good fit between a given student's resources and agendas, and the structure of the university.

Monica and Karen's struggles at MU can be attributed, in part, to the dominance of a "party pathway" at that institution. These organizational arrangements—a robust, university-supported Greek system, and an array of easy majors—are designed to attract and serve affluent, socially-oriented students. The party pathway is not a hard sell; the idea that college is about fun and partying is celebrated in popular culture and actively promoted by leisure and alcohol industries. The problem is that this pathway often appeals to students for whom it is ill suited.

Regardless of what they might want, students from different class backgrounds require different things. What Monica and Karen needed was a "mobility pathway." When resources are limited, mistakes—whether a semester of grades lost to partying, or courses that do not count toward a credential—can be very costly. Monica and Karen needed every course to move them toward a degree that would translate directly into a job.

They also needed more financial aid than they received—grants, not loans—and much better advising. A skilled advisor who understood Karen's background and her abilities might have helped her realize that changing majors was a bad idea. But while most public universities provide such advising support for disadvantaged students, these programs are often small, and admit only the best and brightest of the disadvantaged—not run-of-the-mill students like Monica and Karen. Monica, Karen, and others like them did not find a mobility pathway at MU. Since university resources are finite, catering to one population of students often comes at a cost to others, especially if their needs are at odds with one another. When a party pathway is the most accessible avenue through a university, it is easy to stumble upon, hard to avoid, and it crowds out other pathways.

As Monica and Karen's stories suggest, students are not necessarily better served by attending the most selective college they can get into. The structure of the pathways available at a given school greatly influences success. When selecting a college or university, families should consider much more than institutional selectivity. They should also assess whether the school fits the particular student's needs. Students and parents with limited financial resources should look for schools with high retention rates among minority and first-generation students, where there are large and accessible student services for these populations. Visible Greek systems and reputations as party schools, in contrast, should be red flags. Families should investigate what majors are available, whether they require prerequisites, and, to the extent it is possible, what additional investments are required to translate a particular major into a job. Are internships required? Will the school link the student to job opportunities, or are families expected to do so on their own? These are some questions they should ask.

Collectively, the priorities of public universities and other higher education institutions that support "party pathways" should be challenged. Reducing the number of easy majors, pulling university support from the Greek system, and expanding academic advising for less privileged students would help. At federal and state levels, greater commitment to the funding of higher education is necessary. If public universities are forced to rely on tuition and donations for funding, they will continue to appeal to those who can pay full freight. Without these changes, the mismatch between what universities offer and what most postsecondary students need is likely to continue.

A Campus More Colorful Than Reality: Beware That College Brochure

Deena Prichep

Reprinted by Permission of Deena Prichep/NPR.

Diallo Shabazz was a student at the University of Wisconsin in 2000 when he stopped by the admissions office. "One of the admissions counselors walked up to me, and said, 'Diallo, did you see yourself in the admissions booklet? Actually, you're on the cover this year,'" Shabazz says. The photo was a shot of students at a football game—but Shabazz had never been to a football game. "So I flipped back, and that's when I saw my head cut off and kind of pasted onto the front cover of the admissions booklet," he says. This Photoshopped image went viral and became a classic example of how colleges miss the mark on diversity. Wisconsin stressed that it was just one person's bad choice, but Shabazz sees it as part of a bigger problem. "The admissions department that we've been talking about, I believe, was on the fourth floor, and multicultural student center was on the second floor of that same building," he says. "So you didn't need to create false diversity in the picture—all you really needed to do was go downstairs."

SELLING AN IMAGE

Even without Photoshop, colleges try to shape the picture they present to prospective students, says Tim Pippert, a sociologist at Augsburg College in Minnesota. "Diversity is something that's being marketed," Pippert says. "They're trying to sell a campus climate, they're trying to sell a future. Campuses are trying to say, 'If you come here, you'll have a good time, and you'll fit in.'" Pippert and his researchers looked at more than 10,000 images from college brochures, comparing the racial breakdown of students in the pictures to the colleges' actual demographics. They found that, overall, the whiter the school, the more diversity depicted in the brochures, especially for certain groups. "When we looked at African-Americans in those schools that were predominantly white, the actual percentage in those campuses was only about 5 percent of the student body," he says. "They were photographed at 14.5 percent."

A PICTURE OF WHAT DIVERSITY COULD LOOK LIKE

Just where should colleges draw the line? There's no clear answer, says Jim Rawlins, admissions director at the University of Oregon and past president of the National Association for College Admissions Counseling. "If your campus is 20 percent racially and ethnically diverse, and I were to look at all your photos and you were 30 percent, is 30 unreasonable?" Rawlins says. "Is 30 OK, but 35 would be too far? I mean, where's that number?" Rawlins says that

continues

■ **Continued**

showing inflated diversity can actually be a step toward creating a more diverse campus. It helps students imagine themselves at those schools. But balancing representation and aspiration is difficult. "I also wouldn't want to suggest it's something we all feel we can easily quantify, and start counting faces in pictures and reach our answer as to whether we're doing this right or not," he says. "I think very much any campus that wants to do this right has to talk to the students they have, and see how they're doing."

THE STUDENTS' VIEW

NPR checked in with a group of 12th graders at Jefferson High School in Portland, Ore., who are awash in college brochures. None of them had any illusions. "I think it's best, if you are trying to go to a school, to visit it for yourself, so you can really see," senior Tobias Kelly says. "Because this can fool you sometimes." The students all stress that their highest priority is finding a school that will give them the best education. But many, like Brandon Williams, say that diversity is a part of the package. "When you go to college, it's not just about the classroom, but it's also about the stuff you learn from the people," he says. Even after his Photoshop experience, Shabazz thinks colleges can and should paint a picture of their student population with an eye toward the future. "I think that universities have a responsibility to portray diversity on campus, and to portray the type of diversity that they would like to create," he says. "It shows what their value systems are. At the same time, I think they have a responsibility to be actively engaged in creating that diversity on campus that goes deeper than just what's in the picture."

Screw U: How For-Profit Colleges Rip You Off

YASMEEN QURESHI, SARAH GROSS, AND LISA DESAI

As more and more people pursue college education, for-profit colleges and universities have become common, reaping huge profits from those seeking to better themselves and their economic well-being. But, as this reading discusses, for-profit institutions have come under fire as of late, accused of unscrupulous recruitment strategies that leave unsuspecting students saddled with large amounts of debt and worthless degrees, partly subsidized by American taxpayers.

The folks who walked through Tressie McMillan Cottom's door at an ITT Technical Institute campus in North Carolina were desperate. They had graduated from struggling high schools in low-income neighborhoods. They'd worked crappy jobs. Many were single mothers determined to make better lives for their children. "We blocked off a corner, and that's where we would put the car seats and the strollers," she recalls. "They would bring their babies with them and we'd encourage them to do so, because this is about building motivation and urgency."

McMillan Cottom now studies education issues at the University of California–Davis' Center for Poverty Research, but back then her job was to sign up people who'd stopped in for information, often after seeing one of the TV ads in which ITT graduates rave about recession-proof jobs. The idea was to prey on their anxieties—and to close the deal fast. Her title was "enrollment counselor," but she felt uncomfortable calling herself one, because she quickly realized she couldn't act in the best interest of the students. "I was told explicitly that we don't enroll and we don't admit: We are a sales force." After six months at ITT Tech, McMillan Cottom quit. That same day, she called up every one of the students she'd enrolled and gave them the phone number for the local community college.

With 147 campuses and more than 60,000 students nationwide, ITT Educational Services (which operates both ITT Tech and the smaller Daniel Webster College) is one of the largest companies in the burgeoning for-profit college industry, which now enrolls up to 13 percent of higher-education students. ITT is also the most profitable of the big industry players: Its revenue has nearly doubled [between 2007 and 2014], closing in on $1.3 billion [in 2013], when CEO Kevin Modany's compensation topped $8 million.

To achieve those returns, regulators suspect, ITT has been pushing students to take on financial commitments they can't afford. The Consumer Financial Protection Bureau is looking into ITT's student loan program, and the Securities and Exchange Commission is investigating how those loans were issued and sold to investors. (Neither agency would comment about the probes.) The attorneys general of some 30 states have banded together to investigate for-profit colleges; targets include ITT, Corinthian, Kaplan, and the University of Phoenix.

A 2012 investigation led by Sen. Tom Harkin (D-Iowa) singled out ITT for employing "some of the most disturbing recruiting tactics among the companies examined." A former ITT recruiter told the Senate education committee that she used and taught a process called the "pain funnel," in which admissions officers would ask students increasingly probing questions about where their lives were going wrong. Properly used, she said, it would "bring a prospect to their inner child, an emotional place intended to have the prospect say, 'Yes, I will enroll.'"

For-profit schools recruit heavily in low-income communities, and most students finance their education with a mix of federal Pell grants and federal student loans. But government-backed student loans max out at $12,500 per school year, and tuition at for-profits can go much higher; at ITT Tech it runs up to $25,000. What's more, for-profit colleges can only receive 90 percent of their revenue from government money. For the remaining 10 percent, they count on veterans—GI Bill money counts as outside funds—as well as scholarships and private loans. [96 percent of students at for-profit colleges take out student loans, compared to 13 percent of community college students, 48 percent of public college students, and 57 percent of students at nonprofit private colleges. Students at for-profit colleges are also more likely to default on student loans than students that graduate from college (one of five students at two-year for-profit colleges compared to one in 25 students who graduate from college), and students

who attended for-profit colleges constitute 47 percent of all student loan defaults. For-profit colleges receive a disproportionate amount of federal student aid; though they enroll only 13 percent of students, they receive 25 percent of federal student aid. This aid comprises a significant portion of the earnings of for-profit colleges; the 15 publicly-traded for-profit colleges receive more than 85 percent of their revenue from federal student loans and aid].[1]

Whatever the source of the funds, the schools' focus is on boosting enrollment. A former ITT financial-aid counselor named Jennifer (she asked us not to use her last name) recalls that prospects were "browbeaten and hassled into signing forms on their first visit to the school because it was all slam, bam, thank you ma'am." The moment students enrolled, Jennifer would check their federal loan and grant eligibility to see how much money they qualified for. After students maxed out their federal grants and loans, there was typically an outstanding tuition balance of several thousand dollars. Jennifer says she was given weekly reports detailing how much money students on her roster owed. She would pull them from class and present them with a stark choice: get kicked out of school or make a payment on the spot. For years, ITT even ran a (now discontinued) in-house private loan program, known as PEAKS, in partnership with Connecticut-based Liberty Bank, with interest rates reaching 14.75 percent. (Federal student loans top out at 6.8 percent.)

Jennifer, who had previously worked at the University of Alabama, says she felt like a collection agent. "My supervisors and my campus president were breathing down my neck, and I was threatened that I was going to be fired if I didn't do this," she says. Yet she knew that students would have little means to get out from under the debt they were signing up for. Roughly half of ITT Tech students dropped out during the period covered by the Harkin report, and the job prospects for those who did graduate were hardly stellar. Even though a for-profit degree "costs a lot more," Harkin told *Dan Rather*

Reports, "in the job market it's worth less than a degree from, say, a community college."

Jennifer says the career services office at her campus wasn't much help; students told her they were simply given a printout from Monster.com. (ITT says its career counselors connect students with a range of job services and also help them write résumés, find leads, and arrange interviews.) By the time she was laid off, Jennifer believed the college "left students in worse situations than they were to begin with."

It's not just whistleblowers who are complaining about ITT. There's an entire website, myittexperience.com, dedicated to stories from disappointed alumni. That's how we found Margie Donaldson, a 38-year-old who says her dream has always been to get a college degree and work in corporate America: "Especially being a little black girl in the city of Detroit, [a degree] was everything to me." Donaldson was making nearly $80,000 packing parts at Chrysler when the company, struggling to survive the recession, offered her a buyout. She decided to use it to get the college degree that she never finished 13 years before. Five years later, she is $75,000 in debt and can't find a full-time job despite her B.A. in criminal justice from ITT. She's applied for more than 200 positions but says 95 percent of the applications went nowhere because her degree is not regionally accredited, so employers don't see it as legitimate. Nor can she use her credits toward a degree at another school. Working part time as an anger management counselor, she brings in about $1,400 a month, but there are no health benefits, and with three kids ages 7, 14, and 18, she can barely make ends meet. She has been able to defer her federal student loans, but the more than $20,000 in private loans she took out via ITT can't be put off, so she's in default with 14.75 percent interest—a detail she says her ITT financial-aid adviser never explained to her—and $150 in late fees tacked on to her balance each month. Donaldson says she has tried to work out an affordable payment plan, but the PEAKS servicers won't agree until she pays an outstanding balance of more than $3,500—more than double her monthly income. "It puts me and my family, and other families, I'm sure, in a very tough situation financially," she says.

Donaldson says she didn't understand how different ITT was from a public college. If she had attended one of Michigan's 40-plus state and community colleges, her tuition would have been roughly one-third of what it was at ITT. Now, she says, all that time and money feels wasted: "It's almost like I'm like a paycheck away from going back to where I grew up."

NOTES

1. Sen. Harkin, Consumer Finance Protection Bureau, Education Sector.

Social Problems
Related to Families

Oscar Hernandez

Oscar Hernandez is the lead field organizer for United We Dream, Houston. United We Dream is a national immigrant youth-led organization composed of more than 100,000 immigrant youth and their allies. They currently operate fifty-five affiliate organizations in twenty-six states. United We Dream organizes and advocates for the dignity and fair treatment of immigrant youth and families, regardless of immigration status.

[Editor's note: Congress has not yet passed the DREAM Act, which proposes giving legal status to undocumented immigrants who were brought to the United States before they turned sixteen (and are currently no older than thirty years old) that meet a variety of other requirements related to years in residence, educational attainment, lack of criminal record, and possible military service. But in 2012, following the spirit of the proposed DREAM Act, President Obama issued a directive to the Department of Homeland Security to stop deporting and to allow work permits for immigrants in this group ("Dreamers").]

What campaign are you currently working on for United We Dream?

I lead the Own the Dream (OTD) campaign in Houston. OTD is a campaign led by undocumented people to ensure that "Dreamers" (undocumented minors who would have been covered under the DREAM Act that Congress has yet to pass) and their families receive the best support when applying for DACA (Deferred

Action for Childhood Arrivals) and DAPA (Deferred Action for Parents of Americans and Lawful Permanent Residents) in order to be able to stay in the country together. Deferred action grants certain undocumented immigrants a worker's permit and protection from deportation. It provides families some relief, allowing undocumented immigrants to get a driver's license and to push for fair wages at their jobs.

What are your duties as a lead field organizer in Houston?

I work with different schools, churches, community organizations, and attorneys to make sure we help as many members of our undocumented community as possible. My primary responsibility as lead field organizer in Houston is hosting DACA Clinics. My awesome team and I take care of all of the logistics, planning, and execution for each event. We also host community outreach events (presentations and information sessions) where I am the lead presenter and document workshops where we help our applicants get all their documents in order so they can attend our DACA Clinics. We recruit pro bono attorneys that we believe are ethical and have the immigrant community's best interest at heart. At the DACA Clinics we ensure that all the applicants finish with a packet ready to send to United States Citizenship and Immigration Services (USCIS) for review. After the DACA Clinics we follow up with our community members and ask them to get involved and help others in the immigrant rights movement.

In addition to the DACA Clinics, we focus on empowering our immigrant community by providing a safe space for undocumented immigrants. We want them to be empowered by meeting people with similar needs and interests. Our intention is to illustrate that we have been doing great things and that we will continue to make progress if we can work together as a community.

How did you first become interested in this type of activism? What was your inspiration?

I have been involved in immigrant rights issues for over five years. I have helped with the Dreamer movement and on issues of workers' rights, in general. I have an interest in helping people who think that they have no power, by showing them the enormous power that they actually possess. Being undocumented myself, I know what it is like to think and feel that you are disempowered.

As an activist in your organization, currently what are your top goals (or projects)?

As an organizer, I try to help as many people as I can with their DACA applications to give them the opportunity to live in the U.S. without immediate fear of deportation. I work to build a foundation where immigrants feel safe so we can talk about our issues, advocate for ourselves, and continuously build new leadership. The next generation will lead this movement.

What strategies do you use to enact social change?

First we need to define what change means to the community and understand where everyone fits in this change process, collectively. Only after that can we strategize and plan our goals.

What are the major challenges activists in your field face?

Funding is always an issue but I believe that our work speaks for itself and we will continue successfully for the long run.

What are major misconceptions the public has about activism in general and your issue specifically?

I think that most of the time the general public doesn't understand the concept of activism and organizing as a whole. It's more than just marching and protesting, it's what comes out of those actions and what can escalate and develop into a community power. That power of the community can be harnessed to help individuals navigate the complex system of immigration, but more importantly it can work to change the policies and legislation that affects our lives.

Why should students get involved in your line of activism?

I think that immigrant rights are a big part of civil rights. Generally at the core of every movement is the fight against oppression towards any minority. I am highly active with immigrant rights because it's critical to my life, but I also understand that this is a community issue that affects citizens and non-citizens alike.

What would you consider to be your greatest successes as an activist?

I'd like to share the story of a young man who came to visit us at our first DACA Clinic. He needed to apply for DACA but he wasn't happy about joining us and had a very negative attitude and an unwillingness to participate. I had a brief conversation with him and then I spoke with his mother. She told me that the boy's step dad had recently died crossing back into the U.S. and that he was taking it very hard. He had dropped out of school and didn't want to participate in anything. Realizing why he was so uncomfortable helped me relate to him and after our conversation he ended up coming back to our events and became one of our lead volunteers. He went back to school, earned his last credits, and enrolled in community college. This sort of impact is almost a daily occurrence when we offer our assistance and support. And this is how I measure if what we are doing is successful. It is more than numbers. I ask if we are truly making a difference and impacting the lives of those we assist.

If an individual has little money and time, are there other ways they can contribute?

Yes, we have all kinds of volunteers. At the very least they can share our information and invite people to our events. Word of mouth has been our most successful form of outreach.

What ways can students enact social change in their daily lives?

If they can vote, then VOTE! Voting is one of the most impactful actions anyone can take and more people need to participate in this process. In addition, students can have political conversations at home at the dinner table with their entire families, even when it is outside of their comfort zone.

Families Facing Untenable Choices

LISA DODSON AND WENDY LUTTRELL

Dodson and Luttrell discuss the strains on low-wage mothers and their children and how the norms of social institutions demand "untenable choices" from these families. The authors discuss how the emphasis on work as part of welfare reform has created additional problems for low-income women and their children and how middle-class ideologies about "good mothering" create stigma against low-income working mothers.

It is 9:00 a.m. and six-year-old Antonio stands in the doorway of his school's main office. He and his brother Cesar live in a public housing complex around the corner from the school in an urban district that serves working poor families of color, mostly immigrants. Miss Corey, the school secretary, greets him with a smile, asking, "Did you just get here?" Antonio nods his head yes. "Your mother didn't wake you up this morning?" Antonio rocks back and forth. "Did your brother already go to his classroom?" Antonio grins from ear to ear and nods his head yes. "Go ahead on, I won't write you up." Before Antonio's out the door, Miss Corey remarks, "He's covering for his mother. It is a tough home situation, so tough. His mom has two jobs and works double shifts every other weekend. His older brother is in third grade and has been getting himself to school since kindergarten, and now he's responsible for getting Antonio to school, too. They are late all the time."

Miss Corey is sympathetic to the boys' single mom who works tirelessly to provide for her children, and so she reluctantly stretches school rules to accommodate the situation. She feels it isn't fair to punish the boys because of their mother's work demands. A single mom herself, Miss Corey explains that, were it not for the fact that her own children are on an "early school schedule" that allows her to drop them off on her way to work, she doesn't know how she would manage. Miss Corey is grateful for her job; even though she "pinches pennies at the end of each month," she has health insurance, paid sick days, vacation days, and, if need be, she can always get someone to "cover" for her in the office if one of her children gets sick at school. In contrast, Antonio's mom couldn't be reached when he got a fever. "We called her employer (she works at a nursing home across town) but they didn't give her the message, and the poor child sat in the nurse's office all day. It breaks my heart."

Antonio's mom and Miss Corey are part of an important and expansive group within the labor force: working mothers. According to the

Bureau of Labor Statistics, in 2008, seven out of ten mothers were employed. Based on the growth of the service, retail, and carework job sectors, many mothers—disproportionately women of color, immigrants, and single women—are working in low paying, demanding jobs.

For decades, sociologists have studied women's increased labor force participation, focusing on women's lost career opportunity related to family care needs. Arlie Hochschild famously coined the term "second shift" for women's juggling of family care with work demands. The gendered division of household labor that Hochschild reported years ago continues largely unaltered, with women responsible for family care whether they provide it themselves or organize and schedule others to do so. In light of this second shift, sociologist Pam Stone describes how some professional women may feel compelled to "opt out" of high-powered professions to take care of family needs.

Our focus is the dynamic of the second—or more accurately, *multiple*—shifts faced by low wage mothers with few (if any) opting-out choices. Service, retail, and care work jobs pay $8-$12 per hour, so workers are hard-pressed to cover their basics: rent, food, transportation, heat, healthcare, and utilities. Further, these kinds of jobs are more likely to encroach on routine family time, before and after school, or in the evenings and on weekends. The work often involves irregular schedules and unpredictable hours, leaving little flexibility to take care of everyday family life, and employment in these sectors offers few benefits or career ladders that might mean sacrifice today, but bring better times tomorrow. Perhaps most startlingly, taking one of these jobs can also mean taking immediate losses. Economist Randy Albelda calls this the "cliff effect" of post-welfare policy: even the smallest wage increase can result in steep losses in essential public benefits such as housing, healthcare, and food stamps.

What are the particular conditions—material and social—that moms and children face in the real world of low wage work and family? Across the scholarship on low-income families, we find three themes that stand out. First, research points out how inflexible and often unpredictable work schedules undermine mothers' abilities to provide family care. While higher earnings could offset some of this dilemma, a "market solution" is out of reach for these families. The second theme is the stigma faced by low-income mothers and children when they don't meet the middle class norms of work and school in order to put family care first. Finally, we explore a theme infused throughout low-income work/family scholarship: how the norms of major social institutions (employment and education) operate according to rules that demand untenable choices from mothers and children. This angle on the work and family dilemma tends to be ignored or, if highlighted, used as evidence of personal irresponsibility and failed families. Recognizing the true conditions facing tens of millions of families is crucial for reformulating work, family, and educational policy.

Inflexibility at Work

In 2004, Norma described her job loss this way: "My company is a big corporation, and there are no exceptions.... I had attendance problems because of my son's illness ... but I went ahead.... I pushed it and made a choice for family. No matter what it took, I was going to be there sacrificing a risk of attendance problems. So I had no flexibility with work at my employment ..." For Norma, "pushing it" meant taking two extra days off until her son, who had been gravely ill, was in stable condition. She lost her job for "abusing" the company's sick day policy.

Research on work schedules in retail, service, and care work jobs reveals a wide spectrum of inflexibilities. Schedules may change with little notice, overtime work may suddenly become mandatory, and productivity (often involving direct contact with customers) may be constantly monitored. The face-to-face nature of much of the retail, personal care, and service labor markets makes small accommodations like breaks, adjustments to start and stop time, or phone calls all but impossible. Work and family scholars Julie Henly and Elaine Waxman, researching retail workers, reported that employees may learn of their work schedule with only a few days' notice. They wrote, for these workers, "Everything is open. Nothing is consistent." Just as Norma described, employees find almost no room for negotiation, regardless of the gravity of a family need.

In the past, the rigidity and unpredictability of these jobs led many mothers who had no savings, family money, or higher-earning spouse to turn to welfare if their children needed more intensive care. But by the late 1990s, the policy for low-income moms became "work first." Mothers had to negotiate family care based on the hard terms set by the low-wage labor market.

Deborah spoke of how she once used welfare to navigate family and job demands, believing children "should be with someone who's about raising them." By 2002, new welfare regulations meant Deborah saw no choice but to take a low-wage job, even though her childcare arrangements were "sub par."

This is a hidden layer of risk that arises when inflexible work is coupled with insufficient income to buy good childcare. According to the National Center for Children in Poverty, only 8 percent of infant/toddler care and 24 percent of preschool care is considered high quality. Thus, like many parents, Deborah could find no affordable and decent childcare so she left them in "self care," which is to say, on their own. But she says, "I'm always afraid. I'm afraid they will say something at school [about her absence] and I'm afraid that something will happen to them." Deborah isn't alone. Federal research reveals that [in 2011] only 17 percent of eligible children receive publicly subsidized childcare. Many parents, then, are living with twin fears: they're terrified by both the possibility of harm that could come to children left alone and the possibility that they'll face investigation by state children's services for child neglect.

Tayisha discovered something else that plagues other parents: childcare cheap enough for her budget can be substandard. Cleaning out her daughter Amy's bag she found ". . . all these notes in the bottom of her backpack. She hated it [the after school program]. These kids were picking on her, and the teacher told her she had to work it out. So she would write me notes about being shoved around, spat at . . ." Trying to handle the abuse on her own, Amy had apparently written down what was happening to her, but didn't pass along the notes in order to protect her mother. Coming upon these frequent, painful, but hidden moments in her daughter's life led Tayisha to quit her job. She had little else to fall back on and nothing in the bank. But Tayisha said, "I don't care what . . . I am not going to have her be in a situation like that." Tayisha knew that her job supervisor regarded the abrupt quit a confirmation of her poor work ethic.

Pointedly, the growing demand for all kinds of care work draws low wage mothers' caring labor out of the family and into the labor market. Antonio's mom and so many others like her face this paradox. One nurse's aide said the supervisors in her nursing home workplace "kind of make you feel like 'We're first and your family's second.'"

Inflexible, family-unfriendly, low-paid jobs create a minefield of bad options for millions of families. Yet, it gets worse because mothers and children find that the strategies they design to try to handle these tough conditions can lead to multiple layers of stigma. Studying workplace discrimination, legal scholar Joan Williams notes, "professional women who request a flexible schedule find themselves labeled as uncommitted. Low-wage mothers, for whom no flexibility is available, find themselves stigmatized as irresponsible workers when they need time off in order to be responsible mothers."

Stigma

"They (teachers) see it as we aren't being responsible if we don't attend [meetings] and all that."

Low-wage working mothers find that while they are . . . [faced with] inflexible work demands, they must also contend with the contemporary standards of "good mothering." Numerous sociological studies have documented class differences in the meaning of good mothering. Poverty researchers Kathryn Edin and Maria Kefalas have written, "Ask a middle-class woman if she's a good mother, and she'll likely reply, 'Ask me in twenty years,' for then she will know her daughter's score on the SAT, the list of college acceptances she has garnered, and where her career trajectory has led. . . . Ask a poor woman whether she's a good mother, and she'll likely point to how clean and well-fed her children are, or how she stands by them through whatever problems come their way."

Middle-class working moms are operating in the world of *hurried* childhood, aimed at creating early academic and social wins. The standard for them requires countless extracurricular activities and skill enhancement to give children a competitive edge throughout life. Family sociologist Annette Lareau describes the demands that this intense schedule places on both children and parents, primarily mothers. By contrast, low-income moms are operating in the world of *adultified* childhood, in which children join the "heavy lifting" in the service of family survival. In these conditions, "girls' family labor" has long been a critical, if largely ignored, alternative source of family work. Family and poverty scholar Linda Burton's work on youth in low income families explores how the *adultification* of children is a critical family coping strategy, yet is out of sync with contemporary expectations of intense and early achievement for future success.

This is the world that Antonio, Cesar, and their mother inhabit. They know their "out of sync" care strategies are stigmatized. Low-income school children, perhaps very involved in family care that pulls them out of school, can easily run into conflict with authorities, attitudes, and regulations in their schools. Indeed, a U.S. Department of Education survey of dropout rates indicates that shouldering family responsibilities plays a major role in kids' decisions to leave school. Importantly, low-income youth recognize the stigma that surrounds their families' ways of getting by; they're attuned to social judgment. Sociologist . . . Barrie Thorne has documented that children hear adult talk at home and at school, and they learn how to listen for and read signs of anxiety and stigma. Antonio heard the sympathetic Miss Corey describe how he was "covering for his mother." Her words were a kindness, but one tinged with implications of maternal deficiency. Very early in their lives, children sense the public scrutiny that their working poor mothers face and will attempt to protect them (as Amy did when she hid the notes that would upset her mother). Or children may actively duplicate the stigmatized family ethic, treating the immediate care needs of siblings, parents, even extended family as immediate priority. Yet, just as job supervisors regard mothers engaging in such behavior as "abusing" the system, teachers and school authorities may regard children as uncooperative with school rules and uninterested in getting an education.

Mothers may also find themselves regarded as uncommitted to their children's education by those pointing to their lack of parental participation in school activities. Focusing on the hidden work of mothers, researchers Alison Griffith and Dorothy Smith argue that unequal educational opportunities are built into the contemporary institution of schooling that expects "mothering for schooling," or maternal involvement, to be integral to children's progress. No-show mothers (and their kids) are known by school authorities. Studying urban schools, Michelle Fine quotes a mother who recognizes this attitude, "Society says you're supposed to know what your children are doing at all time. It's not so. I take 2 hours to travel to work, 2 hours to travel back and I'm on my feet 10 hours a day."

We heard the same story in our research. For example, Atlanta, a mother of three in Denver, described a 19-hour day. First she gets one child off to school, and then "I get back and get my older daughters off to their school. So then I can do . . . any extra jobs [under the table manicuring] and then pick her up and later her sisters can watch her and then I go to work at 5:00 p.m. I do cleaning office buildings at this point; it starts late so I can spend a little time before." She works until midnight. "I don't even think about ever getting sick."

Cultural critic Joan Morgan describes the "strong black-woman" image (which extends its cultural reach to ethnic minority, immigrant, and even working class white women) as one that celebrates a capacity to endure hardship and pain. It's true that, in the face of such challenges, Atlanta took pride in her child-rearing accomplishments and her older daughters took pride in their skills as substitutes when their mother needed them. Yet, these are hardly recognized as essential capabilities or remarkable achievements in most work and family and schooling discourse. In fact, these caring strategies may even be turned into their opposite, treated as signs of negligent parenting and inappropriately adultified children, stigmatizing both mothers and children.

Untenable Choices

"Don't expect 'them' to get it cause 'they' don't . . . and they don't matter . . . in the end you got to choose."

Mothers and children, trying to manage inflexible work and school demands, without sufficient income to purchase help, face untenable choices. Mothers are pulled to spend more time at work to meet supervisors' expectations and to bring in more sorely needed income. They may turn to children to manage daily household needs and younger children's care. But, in the intensified world of high stakes schooling and extracurricular engagement, siphoning off young people's time and attention to provide family care can cost them dearly. Youngsters are aware of the stakes; they hear talk about achievement and failure all the time and are constantly advised to focus on scoring and winning. In both work and school cultures, the focus on individual effort and personal gain is primary. Yet, in a context in which keeping a family intact may depend on practices that include consciously putting self aside for family needs, mothers and children who put care first may find themselves viewed as deficient, even deviant.

The sociologist Judith Hennessey describes a "moral hierarchy" that guides low-income mothers as they try to manage their choices; mothers commonly say, "children come first." In our research, this language of priority comes up often. We believe that this assertion of primacy of caring for others reflects extreme work, family, and education conditions. It is, ultimately, about survival. Social theorist Patricia Hill Collins, describing how women of color approach family care, asserts, "Without women's motherwork, communities would not survive." Choosing children (and in the children's case, sometimes choosing family care) "first" can be seen as an assertion of the family's right to continue to even be a family tomorrow.

The interplay of low pay, inflexible work, and school design, coupled with social stigma, create untold hardship for millions of low-income families. These forces also set the stage for the people who live in and care for these families to question the priorities of major social institutions. Reflecting this, in a low-income mothers' group discussion in 2005, we heard a woman offer advice: "It's yours to take care of, and that means your kids come first. That's it, there's no other way. Don't expect 'them' to get it cause 'they' don't . . . and they don't matter . . . in the end you got to choose." All the other mothers nodded as if they knew who "they" were.

Private Troubles, Collective Responsibilities

Echoes of the private troubles these difficult care choices create, the structural barriers that must be overcome, and a call for "them" to "get it" are heard from wage-poor, working mothers throughout sociological literature. If "they" are government entities, responsible for the good of the people, establishing a sustainable wage and also providing subsidies to reach it would make a significant difference. If "they" are employers, whose market success rests on the larger society, investing in families by providing work flexibility would go a long way to support that society. If "they" are public education leaders who oversee the route to social mobility, then integrating the real conditions of low-income youth into school policies and practices would help provide equity. But, for now, none of these powerful social institutions demonstrates a commitment to address the real conditions facing low-wage families.

Taking care of family remains a private enterprise in the U.S. Antonio's mother must rely on working multiple shifts, self-care by Antonio and his brother, and self-styled flexibilities, while other families can purchase services to take care of family needs. Yet, the focus on private strategies for untenable choices, some stigmatized and others affirmed, diverts us from the collective responsibility we share for the care of all families.

Challenges Faced by LGBT Families with Children

Kaitlin A. Hippen

Original to Focus on Social Problems: A Contemporary Reader.

An estimated 6 million people of all ages in the United States have a lesbian, gay, bisexual, or transgender (LGBT) parent, comprising about 2 percent of the population (Gates, 2013). Among the 650,000 same-sex couples living in the United States, 35 percent are currently raising children under the age of eighteen—220,000 children in total (Gates, 2013).[1] There are many different pathways to LGBT parenthood: one partner could have already had a biological child with a previous partner, they could adopt a child, or they could use assisted reproductive technologies that use donor insemination to impregnate one of the partners (if female) or a surrogate mother (Moore and Stambolis-Ruhstorfer, 2013). With about 9 million LGBT-identified adults (Gates, 2011), in addition to the millions of children and adults with an LGBT parent, it is safe to say that there is a significant proportion of the American population that is affected by the structural challenges LGBT families often face. These challenges are overwhelmingly caused by the lack of legal and social equality for LGBT families, although some of these inequities are being addressed, as evidenced by the U.S. Supreme Court's decision in *Obergefell vs. Hodges* to legalize same-sex marriage in June 2015.

The authors of the 2011 report *All Children Matter: How Legal and Social Inequalities Hurt LGBT Families* argued that laws governing marital and child relations have not evolved at the same pace as families over the past few decades. Various family types have become prevalent in recent history, such as same-sex couples (both married and nonmarried) and their children; nonmarried cohabiting heterosexual couples (with or without children); individuals having children with more than one partner (also called multiple-partner fertility) (Martin, 2011); single parents of all genders and sexual orientations; grandparents raising grandchildren; blended families with stepparents, stepchildren, and half-siblings; couples in relationships who, for whatever reason, don't live in the same household but who may share children; and many more. The various compositions of families will most likely continue to change and expand, yet the laws in place have historically only supported married heterosexual partners (or single parents) and their biologically or legally related children. Accompanying these increases in diverse family types is an increasingly inclusive American definition of "family," with more than half of Americans now including LGB couples with children as a type of family (Powell et al., 2010). Thus the laws are lagging behind, both in Americans' lived experiences and in their changing opinions of how family should be defined. With so many different types of families

continues

■ Continued

becoming common in our culture, the current state of the law contributes to unequal treatment of many nontraditional families by state and federal governments and by society.

BUSTING MYTHS ABOUT CHILDREN IN LGBT FAMILIES

Despite the 2015 Supreme Court ruling legalizing same-sex marriage, several arguments made by conservative advocacy organizations and antigay groups as to why LGBT individuals should not be allowed to parent or have their parent–child relationships legally recognized remain (Cooper and Cates, 2006). However, most of these arguments can be disputed by looking at research by sociologists, psychologists, and other social scientists.[2] One of the most common arguments is that children should have both a mother and a father. Yet the research supporting that argument is based on comparisons between single and coupled heterosexual parents. This research indicates more generally that it may be more beneficial to grow up in a two-parent household, largely because of the increased access to economic resources that comes from two working parents rather than that provided by only one parent; the research does not tell us anything about the effect of the parents' gender or sexual orientation on their parenting ability (Cooper and Cates, 2006; McLanahan, 1985). Research that does study the ability of same-sex parents to raise children overwhelmingly shows that their children have the same outcomes and well-being as children with heterosexual parents. A recent study even indicates that children of same-sex parents score 3 to 6 percent higher than children of heterosexual parents on three separate measures of well-being: general behavior, general health, and family cohesion (Crouch et al., 2014). Generally, children's well-being is determined by factors other than the parents' sexual orientation or gender, such as high levels of family conflict or an increased number of family disruptions—like divorce or remarriage—that may cause an environment of familial instability (American Sociological Association, 2013; Cooper and Cates, 2006; McLanahan, 1985).

The psychologists and child development scholars Rachel Farr and Charlotte Patterson (2013) conducted the first empirical study comparing coparenting among lesbian, gay, and heterosexual couples through an analysis of unstructured family play sessions with toys in the families' homes. Farr and Patterson found that all couple types seemed to be relatively similar in their parenting styles. Gay and lesbian couples in the study "demonstrated relatively high levels of supportive coparenting and low levels of undermining coparenting behaviors during family play," just as the heterosexual couples did (Farr and Patterson, 2013:1237). However, gay and lesbian couples actually exhibited fewer undermining behaviors than the heterosexual couples, perhaps because they were also "more likely than heterosexual couples to share parenting tasks evenly" (Farr and Patterson, 2013:1236). Similarly, in a study using a large national sample by Wainright et al., no difference in "personal, family, and school adjustments" was found between children raised in same-sex households and children raised in heterosexual households (2004:1895). Recent research by Prickett et al. (2015) comparing time parents spend in child-focused activities (reading to them, helping them with homework, or actively playing with them, all of which support healthy development) indicated that children with same-sex parents received an hour more of child-focused parent time a day (3.5 hours) than children in families with a mother and father (2.5 hours). Many other studies report comparable findings (Movement Advancement Project, 2011).

A related argument against LGB parental fitness is that children of LGB parents will be sexually abused. There is no evidence to support this allegation; furthermore, pedophiles are just as likely to be heterosexual as they are to be gay, and sexual victimization and abuse of children transpires in heterosexual families as well (Cooper and Cates, 2006). In fact, some studies show that "a child's risk of being molested by his or her relative's heterosexual partner is over 100 times greater than by someone who might be identifiable as being homosexual, lesbian, or bisexual" (Carole, 1994).

Last, some people suggest that children raised by LGB parents will become lesbian, gay, or bisexual as well. Although this suggestion fallaciously implies that there is something inherently wrong with being an LGB individual, empirical research shows parental sexual orientation does not affect the formation of children's sexual orientations and that the majority of children from LGB families are, in fact, heterosexual (Golombok and Tasker, 1996; Stacey and Biblarz, 2001). However, children of LGB parents may be more open to a variety of gender identities and sexual experiences, and LGB parents are more likely to be supportive of their children's sexual choices (American Civil Liberties Union [ACLU], 1999; Golombok and Tasker, 1996; Stacey and Biblarz, 2001). Dispelling myths about LGBT families is essential in the fight for equal rights and nondiscrimination in all areas of social life; empirical research in the social sciences supports these efforts. The fact is, these families already exist, and the historical denial of legal protection and a lingering atmosphere of social stigma harms American children.

RAMIFICATIONS OF SOCIAL STIGMA

However, extending legal protections and marriage rights to LGBT families has not immediately removed all forms of discrimination and bias. Many children of LGBT families must deal with bullying and negative social interactions in response to their family structure. In a study performed by the Gay, Lesbian, and Straight Education Network, Children of Lesbians and Gays Everywhere, and the Family Equality Council, 23 percent of children with LGBT parents reported feeling unsafe at school because of their family type and about 40 percent had been verbally harassed about their family type by other students, other students' parents, or their teachers (Kosciw and Diaz, 2008). Although there are communities that are welcoming of LGBT families, being a part of communities that do not welcome LGBT families means their "full participation in schools, community, and society" is limited (Movement Advancement Project, 2011:15). Inequitable laws mean inequitable social treatment of LGBT families.

It is important to realize that having LGBT parents is not the cause of these negative social interactions; the source of the problem is a society that does not accept all family types. The arguments made against LGBT families are similar to those in the 1967 *Loving v. Virginia* case, in which the prohibition against interracial marriage was lifted. Individuals who were against interracial marriage argued that it was harmful to children because "interracial marriages were uniquely prone to divorce and placed undue psychological stress on children" (Palmer, 2013). In opposition, Justice Potter Stewart suggested, "It could be argued that one reason that marriages of this kind are sometimes unsuccessful is the existence of the kind of laws that are in issue here and the attitudes the laws reflect" (U.S. Supreme Court, 1967). In this case, Justice Potter Stewart was asserting the idea that the type of relationship parents have—interracial, in this case, but his statement could also be applied to LGBT partnerships—is not inherently harmful to children; instead, it is the laws that are in place affecting their unions and families that cause harm. Despite the legalization of same-sex marriage, there is still much work to do, such as legally protecting LGBT families from discrimination and bias in all sectors of society (i.e., workplace, housing, school).

RAMIFICATIONS OF DISCRIMINATORY LAWS

The types of challenges faced by LGBT families with children are mostly a result of a lack of legal protections and social stigma (Movement Advancement Project, 2011). Even after the Supreme Court's ruling to legalize same-sex marriage, more than half of the states "still lack clear, fully-inclusive nondiscrimination protections for LGBT people" (Human Rights Campaign, 2015). Adoption is one common way that LGBT couples (and individuals) begin to form families, but many states have historically restricted LGBT individuals' and couples' access to adoption. Two types of adoption are generally recognized: second-parent adoption (when a child is biologically or legally related to one parent and is then adopted by the other parent, giving them joint custody of the child) and joint adoption (when the parents adopt the child at the same time and are both allowed to have joint custody of the child).

continues

■ Continued

Following the legalization of same-sex marriage, LGBT couples in legally recognized relationships are allowed to petition for second-parent adoption in states that do not explicitly ban second-parent adoption; however, only a handful of states and Washington, DC, have policies in place to protect the rights of LGBT couples to petition for second-parent adoption (Movement Advancement Project, 2015). Universal protections and guidelines do not currently exist, leaving LGBT families at the mercy of the judgment of social workers and private agency employees who set the policies. For example, state-licensed child welfare agencies can still "refuse to place and provide services to children and families . . . if doing so conflicts with their religious beliefs" (Movement Advancement Project, 2015). Being denied second-parent and/or joint adoption is one of the most significant problems for LGBT families. By preventing second-parent and/or joint adoptions, states restrict access to health care, medical decision making, and visitation; wrest children from noncustodial parents after the dissolution of a relationship; deny benefits and inheritance after the death of a noncustodial parent; and exclude children from safety net programs for impoverished families (Movement Advancement Project, 2012). All of these potential issues are harmful to children of LGBT families that lack joint custody in some form. LGBT families, in addition to many other family types not normally recognized by the state, may spend significant money drawing up legal agreements such as living wills, health-care directives, and financial powers of attorney to protect their families in case of unfortunate circumstances. Yet, these directives are not always understood or honored, especially during emergency situations.

Denying second-parent or joint adoption can affect a child's life, as evidenced in the number of past and active child custody court cases involving lesbian and gay parents. Recently, many of these child custody and visitation cases have ruled in favor of the child, granting the parents joint custody and visitation rights when it will benefit the child, which in most cases it will. One example is the *Burch v. Smarr* case that took place in West Virginia in 2005.

According to the ACLU (2005), Christina Smarr and Tina Burch had been in a committed relationship—although not allowed to legally marry—and had a son together, to whom Christina gave birth. When Christina died in a car accident in 2002, her parents tried to take custody of the child. However, the court ruled in favor of Tina being the child's custodial parent because she was his "psychological parent" (ACLU, 2005).

In another case in 2000, a couple named Christine and Janis decided to have two children through artificial insemination, to whom Christine gave birth. Like approximately half of all legally married couples in America, Christine and Janis eventually broke up, and Christine lobbied the court for sole custody of their children. Eventually, after several months of hearings, Janis won visitation rights to see her children (Campbell, 2014). Unfortunately, not all LGBT parents are recognized by family courts. Gay fathers Jason Hanna and Joe Riggs had two sons by surrogate mother after obtaining donor eggs and each providing their own sperm; they then planned to pursue second-parent adoption of each other's biological sons (Signorile, 2014). Because of the discrimination against LGBT couples in Texas, not only were the men not allowed to pursue second-parent adoption, but also the fathers were not allowed to put either of their names on either of their sons' birth certificates, although they were each a biological father of one of the sons; instead, the surrogate mother's name is the only name on the birth certificates, although she is not biologically related to the two sons (Signorile, 2014). After taking their case to court, the judge denied their petition (Signorile, 2014).

Situations like these happen far too often for LGBT families. They can be physically and emotionally scarring for children and are unacceptable consequences of the current legal system. The laws also vary by location, adding to the confusion and social control of families. Although all families must make long-term decisions about where they want to live, LGBT families must consider the stability and recognition of their families when making those choices. These legal decisions about second-parent and joint adoption—which, again, affect real families—are inappropriately determined by the parents' sexual orientations and gender identities, not their desire to raise children or their ability to be good parents (Cooper and Cates, 2006).

CONCLUSION

The estimated 6 million people with an LGBT parent (Gates, 2013), in addition to the 9 million LGBT-identified adults who live in this country, will benefit from the extension of laws and policies that protect heterosexual individuals and their families to all family types. There is no reason why 220,000 children under the age of eighteen (Gates, 2013) should be vulnerable because of an absence of legal protections for their families. The arguments by individuals who are against equitable rights for LGBT families have been, and will continue to be, dispelled by social science. The U.S. legal system must continue to evolve along with the families of this country to ensure the most positive outcomes for all its citizens. Until then, there will be inequality, not only for LGBT families, but also for all family types that fall into the changing definition of "the family."

NOTES

1. Compared to 70 percent of non-LGBT men and women who are raising children under the age of eighteen (Gates, 2013).
2. Unfortunately, little research on children of transgender parents exists, so most of these statements will be made based on research on same-sex parents.

REFERENCES

American Civil Liberties Union. 1999. *Overview of Lesbian and Gay Parenting, Adoption and Foster Care.* New York: American Civil Liberties Union. https://www.aclu.org/lgbt-rights_hiv-aids/overview-lesbian-and-gay-parenting-adoption-and-foster-care/.

American Civil Liberties Union. 2005. *Burch v. Smarr—Case Profile.* New York: American Civil Liberties Union. https://www.aclu.org/lgbt-rights_hiv-aids/burch-v-smarr-case-profile/.

American Sociological Association. 2013. Brief of Amicus Curiae Submitted in *Hollingsworth et al. v. Perry et al. and U.S. v. Windsor,* Nos. 12-144, 12-307.

Campbell, Julia. 2014. *Lesbian Partner Wins Visitation Rights.* New York: ABC News. http://abcnews.go.com/US/print?id=96539/.

Carole, Jenny. 1994. "Are Children at Risk for Sexual Abuse by Homosexuals?" *Pediatrics* 94(1):41–44.

Cooper, Leslie, and Paul Cates. 2006. *Too High a Price: The Case against Restricting Gay Parenting,* 2nd ed. New York: American Civil Liberties Union Foundation. https://www.aclu.org/files/images/asset_upload_file480_27496.pdf/.

Crouch, Simon R., Elizabeth Waters, Ruth McNair, Jennifer Power, and Elise Davis. 2014. "Parent-reported Measures of Child Health and Wellbeing in Same-sex Parent Families: A Cross-sectional Survey." *BMC Public Health* 14(1):1412–1434.

Farr, Rachel H., and Charlotte J. Patterson. 2013. "Coparenting among Lesbian, Gay, and Heterosexual Couples: Associations with Adopted Children's Outcomes." *Child Development* 84(4):1226–1240.

Gates, Gary J. 2011. *How Many People Are Lesbian, Gay, Bisexual, and Transgender?* Los Angeles: The Williams Institute. http://williamsinstitute.law.ucla.edu/wp-content/uploads/Gates-How-Many-People-LGBT-Apr-2011.pdf/.

Gates, Gary J. 2013. *LGBT Parenting in the United States.* Los Angeles: The Williams Institute. http://williamsinstitute.law.ucla.edu/wp-content/uploads/LGBT-Parenting.pdf/.

Golombok, Susan, and Fiona Tasker. 1996. "Do Parents Influence the Sexual Orientation of Their Children? Findings from a Longitudinal Study of Lesbian Families." *Developmental Psychology* 32(1):3–11.

Human Rights Campaign. 2015. "Why the Equality Act?" Retrieved from http://www.hrc.org//resources/entry/why-the-equality-act/.

Kosciw, Joseph G., and Elizabeth M. Diaz. 2008. *Involved, Invisible, Ignored: The Experience of Lesbian, Gay, Bisexual and Transgender Parents and Their Children in Our Nation's K–12 Schools.* New York: GLSEN. http://www.glsen.org/learn/research/national/report-iii/.

Martin, Michel. (Host). 2011. "Multiple Partner Families: More Common Than You Think." Radio

continues

Continued

Broadcast Episode. Washington, DC: National Public Radio. http://www.npr.org/templates/story/story.php?storyId=135541549/.

McLanahan, Sara S. 1985. "Family Structure and the Reproduction of Poverty." *American Journal of Sociology* 90(4):873–901.

Moore, Mignon R., and Michael Stambolis-Ruhstorfer. 2013. "LGBT Sexuality and Families at the Start of the Twenty-First Century." *Annual Review of Sociology* 39:491–507.

Movement Advancement Project, Family Equality Council, and Center for American Progress. 2011. *All Children Matter: How Legal and Social Inequalities Hurt LGBT Families.* Denver, Boston, and Washington, DC: Movement Advancement Project, Family Equality Council, and Center for American Progress. http://action.familyequality.org/site/DocServer/AllChildrenMatterFullFinal10212011.pdf?docID=2401/.

Movement Advancement Project, Family Equality Council, and Center for American Progress. 2012. *Securing Legal Ties for Children Living in LGBT Families.* Denver, Boston, and Washington, DC: Movement Advancement Project, Family Equality Council, and Center for American Progress. http://www.lgbtmap.org/file/securing-legal-ties.pdf/.

Movement Advancement Project. 2015. "Foster and Adoption Laws." Retrieved from http://www.lgbtmap.org/equality-maps/foster_and_adoption_laws/.

Palmer, Brian. 2013. "Won't Somebody Think of the Children?" *Slate.* http://www.slate.com/articles/news_and_politics/explainer/2013/03/gay_marriage_at_the_supreme_court_did_interracial_marriage_opponents_claim.html/.

Powell, Brian, Catherine Bolzendahl, Claudia Geist, and Lala Carr Steelman. 2010. *Counted Out: Same-sex Relations and Americans' Definition of Family.* New York: Russell Sage Foundation.

Prickett, Kate C., Alexa Martin-Storey, and Robert Crosnoe. 2015. "A Research Note on Time with Children in Different- and Same-Sex Two-Parent Families." *Demography* 52(3):905–918. doi:10.1016/j.jco.2008.01.001.

Signorile, Michelangelo. 2014. "Jason Hanna and Joe Riggs, Texas Gay Fathers, Denied Legal Parenthood of Twin Sons." *Huffington Post (HuffPost Gay Voices)*, June 18. http://www.huffingtonpost.com/2014/06/18/jason-hanna-and-joe-riggs_n_5506720.html?ncid=fcbklnkushpmg00000050/.

Stacey, Judith, and Timothy J. Biblarz. 2001. "(How) Does the Sexual Orientation of Parents Matter?" *American Sociological Review* 66:159–183.

U.S. Supreme Court. 1967. Oral arguments from *Loving v. Virginia*, 388 U.S. 1. http://www.encyclopediavirginia.org/Excerpts_from_a_Transcript_of_Oral_Arguments_in_Loving_v_Virginia_April_10_1967/.

U.S. Supreme Court. 2015. *Obergefell v. Hodges*, 576 U.S. 14-556.

Wainright, Jennifer L., Stephen T. Russell, and Charlotte J. Patterson. 2004. "Psychosocial Adjustment, School Outcomes, and Romantic Relationships of Adolescents with Same-sex Parents." *Child Development* 75(6):1886–1898.

Unmarried with Children

KATHRYN EDIN AND MARIA KEFALAS

Many Americans wonder why poor young women choose to have children outside of marriage, despite the potential economic and social consequences. Based on their interviews with poor single mothers, Edin and Kafalas argue that many impoverished young women who become single mothers choose to remain single not because marriage has declined in value, but because they revere it and believe that a failed marriage is a more significant stigma than an out-of-wedlock birth. The authors conclude that until poor young women have access to jobs that will allow them to be financially independent, they will continue to have children first, while waiting for potentially stable marital partners.

Jen Burke, a white tenth-grade dropout who is 17 years old, lives with her stepmother, her sister, and her 16-month old son in a cramped but tidy row home in Philadelphia's beleaguered Kensington neighborhood. She is broke, on welfare, and struggling to complete her GED. Wouldn't she and her son have been better off if she had finished high school, found a job, and married her son's father first?

In 1950, when Jen's grandmother came of age, only 1 in 20 American children was born to an unmarried mother. Today, that rate is 1 in 3— and they are usually born to those least likely to be able to support a child on their own. In our book, *Promises I Can Keep: Why Poor Women Put Motherhood before Marriage*, we discuss the lives of 162 white, African American, and Puerto Rican low-income single mothers living in eight destitute neighborhoods across Philadelphia and its poorest industrial suburb, Camden. We spent five years chatting over kitchen tables and on front stoops, giving mothers like Jen the opportunity to speak to the question so many affluent Americans ask about them: Why do they have children while still young and unmarried when they will face such an uphill struggle to support them?

Romance at Lightning Speed

Jen started having sex with her 20-year-old boyfriend Rick just before her 15th birthday. A month and a half later, she was pregnant. "I didn't want to get pregnant," she claims. "*He* wanted me to get pregnant." "As soon as he met me, he wanted to have a kid with me," she explains. Though Jen's college-bound suburban peers would be appalled by such a declaration, on the streets of Jen's neighborhood, it is something of a badge of honor. "All those other girls he was with, he didn't want to have a baby with

Kathryn Edin and Maria Kefalas, *Contexts* (Volume 4 and Issue 2), pp. 16–22, Copyright © 2005. Reprinted by Permission of SAGE Publications.

any of them," Jen boasts. "I asked him, 'Why did you choose me to have a kid when you could have a kid with any one of them?' He was like, 'I want to have a kid with *you*.'" Looking back, Jen says she now believes that the reason "he wanted me to have a kid that early is so that I didn't leave him."

In inner-city neighborhoods like Kensington, where childbearing within marriage has become rare, romantic relationships like Jen and Rick's proceed at lightning speed. A young man's avowal, "I want to have a baby by you," is often part of the courtship ritual from the beginning. This is more than idle talk, as their first child is typically conceived within a year from the time a couple begins "kicking it." Yet while poor couples' pillow talk often revolves around dreams of shared children, the news of a pregnancy—the first indelible sign of the huge changes to come—puts these still-new relationships into overdrive. Suddenly, the would-be mother begins to scrutinize her mate as never before, wondering whether he can "get himself together"—find a job, settle down, and become a family man—in time.

Jen began pestering Rick to get a real job instead of picking up day-labor jobs at nearby construction sites. She also wanted him to stop hanging out with his ne'er-do-well friends, who had been getting him into serious trouble for more than a decade. Most of all, she wanted Rick to shed what she calls his "kiddie mentality"—his habit of spending money on alcohol and drugs rather than recognizing his growing financial obligations at home.

Rick did not try to deny paternity, as many would-be fathers do. Nor did he abandon or mistreat Jen, at least intentionally. But Rick, who had been in and out of juvenile detention since he was 8 years old for everything from stealing cars to selling drugs, proved unable to stay away from his unsavory friends. At the beginning of her seventh month of pregnancy, an escapade that began as a drunken lark landed Rick in jail on a carjacking charge. Jen moved back home with her stepmother, applied for welfare, and

spent the last two-and-a-half months of her pregnancy without Rick.

Rick sent penitent letters from jail. "I thought he changed by the letters he wrote me. I thought he changed a lot," she says. "He used to tell me that he loved me when he was in jail. . . . It was always gonna be me and him and the baby when he got out." Thus, when Rick's alleged victim failed to appear to testify and he was released just days before Colin's birth, the couple's reunion was a happy one. Often, the magic moment of childbirth calms the troubled waters of such relationships. New parents typically make amends and resolve to stay together for the sake of their child. When surveyed just after a child's birth, eight in ten unmarried parents say they are still together, and most plan to stay together and raise the child.

Promoting marriage among the poor has become the new war on poverty. . . . And it is true that the correlation between marital status and child poverty is strong. But poor single mothers already believe in marriage. Jen insists that she will walk down the aisle one day, though she admits it might not be with Rick. And demographers still project that more than seven in ten women who had a child outside of marriage will eventually wed someone. First, though, Jen wants to get a good job, finish school, and get her son out of Kensington.

Most poor, unmarried mothers and fathers readily admit that bearing children while poor and unmarried is not the ideal way to do things. Jen believes the best time to become a mother is "after you're out of school and you got a job, at least, when you're like 21. . . . When you're ready to have kids, you should have everything ready, have your house, have a job, so when that baby comes, the baby can have its own room." Yet given their already limited economic prospects, the poor have little motivation to time their births as precisely as their middle-class counterparts do. The dreams of young people like Jen and Rick center on children at a time of life when their more affluent peers plan for college and careers. Poor girls coming of age in the inner city value children highly, anticipate them eagerly, and believe strongly that they are up to the job of mothering—even in difficult circumstances. Jen, for example, tells us, "People outside the neighborhood, they're like, 'You're 15! You're pregnant?' I'm like, it's not none of their business. I'm gonna be able to take care of my kid. They have nothing to worry about." Jen says she has concluded that "some people . . . are better at having kids at a younger age. . . . I think it's better for some people to have kids younger."

When I Become a Mom

When we asked mothers like Jen what their lives would be like if they had not had children, we expected them to express regret over foregone opportunities for school and careers. Instead, most believe their children "saved" them. They describe their lives as spinning out of control before becoming pregnant—struggles with parents and peers, "wild," risky behavior, depression, and school failure. Jen speaks to this poignantly. "I was just real bad. I hung with a real bad crowd. I was doing pills. I was really depressed. . . . I was drinking. That was before I was pregnant." "I think," she reflects, "if I never had a baby or anything . . . I would still be doing the things I was doing. I would probably still be doing drugs. I'd probably still be drinking." Jen admits that when she first became pregnant, she was angry that she "couldn't be out no more. Couldn't be out with my friends. Couldn't do nothing." Now, though, she says, "I'm glad I have a son . . . because I would still be doing all that stuff."

Children offer poor youth like Jen a compelling sense of purpose. Jen paints a before-and-after picture of her life that was common among the mothers we interviewed. "Before, I didn't have nobody to take care of. I didn't have nothing left to go home for. . . . Now I have my son to take care of. I have him to go home for. . . . I don't have to go buy weed or drugs with my money. I could buy my son stuff with my money! . . . I have something to look up to now." Children also are a crucial source of relational intimacy, a self-made community of care. After a nasty fight with Rick, Jen recalls, "I was crying. My son came in the room. He was hugging me. He's 16 months and he was hugging me with his little arms. He was really cute and happy, so I got happy. That's one of the good things. When you're sad, the baby's always gonna be there for you no matter what." Lately she has been thinking a lot about what her life was like back then, before the baby. "I thought about the stuff before I became a mom, what my life was like back then. I used to see pictures of me, and I would hide in every picture. This baby did so much for me. My son did a lot for me. He helped me a lot. I'm thankful that I had my baby."

Around the time of the birth, most unmarried parents claim they plan to get married eventually. Rick did not propose marriage when Jen's first child was born, but when she conceived a second time, at 17, Rick informed his dad, "It's time for me to get married. It's time for me to straighten up. This is the one I wanna be with. I had a baby with her, I'm gonna have another baby with her." Yet despite their intentions, few of these couples actually marry. Indeed, most break up well before their child enters preschool.

I'd Like to Get Married, But . . .

The sharp decline in marriage in impoverished urban areas has led some to charge that the poor have abandoned the marriage norm. Yet we found few who had given up on the idea of marriage. But like their elite counterparts, disadvantaged women set a high financial bar for marriage. For the poor, marriage has become an elusive goal—one they feel ought to be reserved for those who can support a "white picket fence" lifestyle: a mortgage on a modest row home, a car and some furniture, some savings in the bank, and enough money left over to pay for a "decent" wedding. Jen's views on marriage provide a perfect case in point. "If I was gonna get married, I would want to be married like my Aunt Nancy and my Uncle Pat. They live in the mountains. She has a job. My Uncle Pat is a state trooper; he has lots of money. They live in the [Poconos]. It's real nice out there. Her kids go to Catholic school.... That's the kind of life I would want to have. If I get married, I would have a life like [theirs]." She adds, "And I would wanna have a big wedding, a real nice wedding."

Unlike the women of their mothers' and grandmothers' generations, young women like Jen are not merely content to rely on a man's earnings. Instead, they insist on being economically "set" in their own right before taking marriage vows. This is partly because they want a partnership of equals, and they believe money buys say-so in a relationship. Jen explains, "I'm not gonna just get into marrying him and not have my own house! Not have a job! I still wanna do a lot of things before I get married. He [already] tells me I can't do nothing. I can't go out. What's gonna happen when I marry him? He's gonna say he owns me!"

Economic independence is also insurance against a marriage gone bad. Jen explains, "I want to have everything ready, in case something goes wrong.... If we got a divorce, that would be my house. I bought that house, he can't kick me out or he can't take my kids from me." "That's what I want in case that ever happens. I know a lot of people that happened to. I don't want it to happen to me." These statements reveal that despite her desire to marry, Rick's role in the family's future is provisional at best. "We get along, but we fight a lot. If he's there, he's there, but if he's not, that's why I want a job . . . a job with computers . . . so I could afford my kids, could afford the house.... I don't want to be living off him. I want my kids to be living off me."

Why is Jen, who describes Rick as "the love of my life," so insistent on planning an exit strategy before she is willing to take the vows she firmly believes ought to last "forever?" If love is so sure, why does mistrust seem so palpable and strong? In relationships among poor couples like Jen and Rick, mistrust is often spawned by chronic violence and infidelity, drug and alcohol abuse, criminal activity, and the threat of imprisonment. In these tarnished corners of urban America, the stigma of a failed marriage is far worse than an out-of-wedlock birth. New mothers like Jen feel they must test the relationship over three, four, even five years' time. This is the only way, they believe, to insure that their marriages will last.

Trust has been an enormous issue in Jen's relationship with Rick. "My son was born December 23rd, and [Rick] started cheating on me again . . . in March. He started cheating on me with some girl—Amanda. . . . Then it was another girl, another girl, another girl after. I didn't wanna believe it. My friends would come up to me and be like, 'Oh yeah, your boyfriend's cheating on you with this person.' I wouldn't believe it. . . . I would see him with them. He used to have hickies. He used to make up some excuse that he was drunk—that was always his excuse for everything." Things finally came to a head when Rick got another girl pregnant. "For a while, I forgave him for everything. Now, I don't forgive him for nothing." Now we begin to understand the source of Jen's hesitancy. "He wants me to marry him, [but] I'm not really sure.... If I can't trust him, I can't marry him, 'cause we would get a divorce. If you're gonna get married, you're supposed to be faithful!" she insists. To Jen and her peers, the worst thing that could happen is "to get married just to get divorced."

Given the economic challenges and often perilously low quality of the romantic relationships among unmarried parents, poor women may be right to be cautious about marriage. Five years after we first spoke with her, we met with Jen again. We learned that Jen's second pregnancy ended in a miscarriage. We also learned that Rick was out of the picture—apparently for good. "You know that bar [down the street?] It happened in that bar. . . . They were in the bar, and this guy was like badmouthing [Rick's friend] Mikey, talking stuff to him or whatever. So Rick had to go get involved in it and start with this guy. . . . Then he goes outside and fights the guy [and] the guy dies of head trauma. They were all on drugs, they were all drinking, and things just got out of control, and that's what happened. He got fourteen to thirty years."

These Are Cards I Dealt Myself

Jen stuck with Rick for the first two and a half years of his prison sentence, but when another girl's name replaced her own on the visitors' list, Jen decided she was finished with him once and for all. Readers might be asking what Jen ever saw in a man like Rick. But Jen and Rick operate in a partner market where the better-off men go to the better-off women. The only way for someone like Jen to forge a satisfying relationship with a man is to find a diamond in the rough or improve her own economic position so that she can realistically compete for more upwardly mobile partners, which is what Jen is trying to do now. "There's this kid, Donny, he works at my job. He works on C shift. He's a supervisor! He's funny, three years older, and he's not a geek or anything, but he's not a real preppy good boy either. But he's not [a player like Rick] and them. He has a job, you know, so that's good. He doesn't do drugs or anything. And he asked my dad if he could take me out!"

These days, there is a new air of determination, even pride, about Jen. The aimless high school dropout pulls ten-hour shifts entering data at a warehouse distribution center Monday through Thursday. She has held the job for three years, and her aptitude and hard work have earned her a series of raises. Her current salary is higher than anyone in her household commands—$10.25 per hour, and she now gets two weeks of paid vacation, four personal days, 60 hours of sick time, and medical benefits. She has saved up the necessary $400 in tuition for a high school completion program that offers evening and weekend classes. Now all that stands between her and a diploma is a passing grade in mathematics, her least favorite subject. "My plan is to start college in January. [This month] I take my math test . . . so I can get my diploma," she confides.

Jen clearly sees how her life has improved since Rick's dramatic exit from the scene. "That's when I really started [to get better] because I didn't have to worry about what *he* was doing, didn't have to worry about him cheating on me, all this stuff. [It was] then I realized that I had to do what I had to do to take care of my son. . . . When he was there, I think that my whole life revolved around him, you know, so I always messed up somehow because I was so busy worrying about what *he* was doing. Like I would leave the [GED] programs I was in just to go home and see what he was doing. My mind was never concentrating." Now, she says, "a lot of people in my family look up to me now, because all my sisters dropped out from school, you know, nobody went back to school. I went back to school, you know? . . . I went back to school, and I plan to go to college, and a lot of people look up to me for that, you know? So that makes me happy . . . because five years ago nobody looked up to me. I was just like everybody else."

Yet the journey has not been easy. "Being a young mom, being 15, it's hard, hard, hard, you know." She says, "I have no life. . . . I work from 6:30 in the morning until 5:00 at night. I leave here at 5:30 in the morning. I don't get home until about 6:00 at night." Yet she measures her worth as a mother by the fact that she has managed to provide for her son largely on her own. "I don't depend on nobody. I might live with my dad and them, but I don't depend on them, you know." She continues, "There [used to] be days when I'd be so stressed out, like, 'I can't do this!' And I would just cry and cry and cry. . . . Then I look at Colin, and he'll be sleeping, and I'll just look at him and think I don't have no [reason to feel sorry for myself]. The cards I have I've dealt myself so I have to deal with it now. I'm older. I can't change anything. He's my responsibility—he's nobody else's but mine—so I have to deal with that."

Becoming a mother transformed Jen's point of view on just about everything. She says, "I thought hanging on the corner drinking, getting high—I thought that was a good life, and I thought I could live that way for eternity, like sitting out with my friends. But it's not as fun once you have your own kid. . . . I think it changes [you]. I think, 'Would I want Colin to do that? Would I want my son to be like that . . . ?' It was fun to me but it's not fun anymore. Half the people I hung with are either. . . . Some have died from drug overdoses, some are in jail, and some people are just out there living the same life that they always lived, and they don't look really good. They look really bad." In the end, Jen believes, Colin's birth has brought far more good into her life than bad. "I know I could have waited [to have a child], but in a way I think Colin's the best thing that could have happened to me. . . . So I think I had my son for a purpose because I think Colin changed my life. He *saved* my life, really. My whole life revolves around Colin!"

Promises I Can Keep

There are unique themes in Jen's story—most fathers are only one or two, not five years older than the mothers of their children, and few fathers have as many glaring problems as Rick—but we heard most of these themes repeatedly in the stories of the 161 other poor, single mothers we came to know. Notably, poor women do not reject marriage; they revere it. Indeed, it is the conviction that marriage is forever that makes them think that divorce is worse than having a baby outside of marriage. Their children, far

from being liabilities, provide crucial social–psychological resources—a strong sense of purpose and a profound source of intimacy. Jen and the other mothers we came to know are coming of age in an America that is profoundly unequal—where the gap between rich and poor continues to grow. This economic reality has convinced them that they have little to lose and, perhaps, something to gain by a seemingly "ill-timed" birth.

The lesson one draws from stories like Jen's is quite simple: Until poor young women have more access to jobs that lead to financial independence—until there is reason to hope for the rewarding life pathways that their privileged peers pursue—the poor will continue to have children far sooner than most Americans think they should, while still deferring marriage. Marital standards have risen for all Americans, and the poor want the same things that everyone now wants out of marriage. The poor want to marry too, but they insist on marrying well. This, in their view, is the only way to avoid an almost certain divorce. Like Jen, they are simply not willing to make promises they are not sure they can keep.

The Changing American Family: Bonding from behind Bars

Natalie Angier

One variant of the modern American family—sadly characteristic, if often ignored—is the family struggling with the impact of an incarcerated parent. Largely as a result of harsh drug laws and mandatory minimum sentences, the nation's prison population has almost quadrupled over the past 30 years, according to a 2010 Pew Charitable Trusts study.

Today the United States is the world's leading jailer by far, housing more of its citizens behind bars than the top 35 European countries combined. And of the estimated 2.3 million inmates serving time,

more than half are parents of children under age 18. That translates into 2.7 million affected children nationwide, or one of every 28, up from one in 125 in 1990.

Some groups have been hit much harder than others. "African-American children living in lower-income, low-education neighborhoods are seven and a half times more likely than white kids to experience the incarceration of a parent," said Julie Poehlmann, professor of human development and family studies at the University of Wisconsin. "And by age 14, more than half of these kids with a low-education parent will have an imprisoned parent." Families are left to cope as best they can, not only with the deafening absence, the economic hardship, the grief and loneliness that separation from a loved one can bring, but also with the stigma that accompanies a criminal conviction, the feelings of humiliation, debasement and failure.

It's one thing if your father is taken away by disease or divorce; it's another if he's taken away in handcuffs. Studies have shown that even accounting for factors like poverty, the children of incarcerated parents are at heightened risk of serious behavioral problems, of doing poorly in school or dropping out, of substance misuse, of getting in trouble with the law and starting the cycle anew.

In a telling sign, "Sesame Street" recently introduced a Muppet named Alex, who looks as glum as Eeyore and is ashamed to admit why only his mother shows up at school events: Dad is in prison. The show offers an online tool kit for children and their caregivers, "Little Children, Big Challenges: Incarceration," with a coloring book, cutout mobile and "how am I feeling?" cards (angry, upset, sad). "We know a lot of kids who need help understanding what is happening with their parents, and caregivers who need to know how to talk about it," said Dr. Poehlmann, who helped develop the tool kit. Nearly half the caregivers never talk about the imprisoned parent, while another third simply lie, Dr. Poehlmann said. "They don't have the words, they don't know what the kids will understand," she said. "But kids have big ears, and if no one talks about it directly, the kids will feel they should keep it secret." Caregivers are also often hesitant to take children to visit incarcerated parents, either out of fear the visit will be traumatic, or because the prison is usually in a remote rural area hours from public transportation. Whatever the reason, a vast majority of prisoners get no visits, from their children or anybody else, Dr. Poehlmann said, "and they feel very sad about that."

During several recent visits to a men's low-security federal prison in rural New Jersey, the joy, pain and unsettling ordinariness of family time, peni-tentiary style, were on fluorescent-lit display. Women brought babies, children, teenagers and bags of quarters for the vending machines. Fathers wearing prison khakis and work boots were required to stay seated in their molded plastic chairs, but as family members filed in, the men's Humpty Dumpty grins threatened to split their faces. Older children settled into seats beside their fathers, while younger ones played at kiddie tables in the corner. Everybody ate chips, microwaved sandwiches, bags of M&Ms. The prison photographer snapped family portraits in front of fake backdrops of palm trees and sunsets. One day at the end of visiting hours, as family members lined up to await escorted passage through multiple locked doors, a 10-year-old boy in a striped polo shirt stood next to his mother, crying and crying. She pulled him close, but the boy didn't stop. He was weeping his quiet ocean of loss and would give no thought to the shore.

In interviews, conducted in person and through an intermediary, the prisoners, too, teared up when they talked about their children, and the great difficulty they had maintaining bonds through sentences long enough to turn those children into adults. All are nonviolent offenders, as are about two-thirds of prisoners overall. They spoke on condition that only their first names be used. Sing, a tall, slim man in his early 40s, has been in prison for 15 years on drug charges, with two years to go. His son and daughter are now 17 and 23, but he has been "adamant" about staying involved in their lives—through letters, phone calls and emails. "They are doing very well," he said. "They have no criminal problems." Yet because they live in Florida, 1,000 miles away, Sing hasn't seen them in five years. He and other inmates expressed frustration at how often the Bureau of Prisons flouted its official policy of trying to house inmates in facilities within 500 miles of their families. The authorities are supposed to do as much as possible to keep families together, Sing said bitterly, "but they do more to keep families apart."

Other inmates said that no matter where it was, prison had a way of corroding emotional ties to the outside world. Jon, who is 55 and three years into a

continues

■ Continued

five-year sentence, scoffed when he first arrived and a seasoned inmate told him he'd soon stop caring about the everyday concerns of the people he left behind, including those of his only child, a teenage girl. The veteran, Jon sighed, was right. "I have to make a special effort now to stay emotionally connected with my daughter and to keep up with her daily experiences," he said. "It's hard for me to do. She'll start talking about her friends and I'll have no idea who they are." Perseverance helps. "My top priority is to stay relevant in my kids' lives," said Rob, an athletic 46-year-old who has been in prison four years and has three teenage daughters. "I put them first as much as I can." He calls each girl once a week and prepares conversation notes ahead of time. He sends gifts he's drawn or crocheted. They have a family book club. His daughters seem to be doing well: One is at Bryn Mawr College, and another is at Tabor Academy, a highly competitive prep school. But with nine years of hard time yet to go, who knows if all the threads will hold?

Does It Pay to Have Kids?
Not for Working Moms

KIRSTIN RALSTON-COLEY

Much of the research about gender inequality in the workplace focuses on discrimination faced by women, but little focuses on the experiences of working women with children. The "motherhood penalty," or the fact that women with children earn less than child-free men and women as well as working fathers, is a major obstacle that working mothers face. Ralston-Coley discusses the factors that contribute to the existence of this penalty, including the gendered division of labor within families and the role of discrimination and bias against mothers in the workplace. Ralston-Coley argues that until attitudes about gendered expectations for mothers and fathers change and until there are more supportive workplace policies for parents, the motherhood penalty will likely persist.

Since the turn of the past century, women have made great strides in labor force participation. According to the Bureau of Labor Statistics (BLS), the percentage of women working in the paid labor force, full time, year round, has increased from just over 40 percent in 1970 to 58 percent in 2011. Although these statistics show a dramatic increase in the labor force participation of women in the past four decades, the numbers are even more impressive for working mothers. In 1975, just over 47 percent of mothers with children under eighteen years of age were working at least part-time. In 2011, this number had jumped to almost 71 percent (Bureau of Labor Statistics, 2011). Additionally, according to the Pew Research Center (2013), in 1960 just 4 percent of married women with children earned more than their husbands, and by 2011,

this number jumped to 23 percent. You've come a long way, Mom! Well, not quite.

Unfortunately, although mothers are increasing their labor force participation and their contribution to the family income, the wages for working mothers continue to be significantly less than the wages of child-free working women, child-free working men, and working fathers. In 2001, researchers Budig and England estimated full-time working mothers earned between 5 and 7 percent less *per child* than women without children. For a mother of two, this works out to roughly 10 to 14 percent less per paycheck than working women without children. When this wage gap is coupled with the significant gender wage gap (78 cents earned by a full-time, year-round working woman for every dollar earned by a man in 2013), it is no

Original to *Focus on Social Problems: A Contemporary Reader*.

surprise that mothers, in particular, are disproportionately represented at the bottom of the earnings distribution of workers. In fact, Glass (2004) argues the low wages earned by mothers are what account for the majority of the gender wage gap as a whole.

What's the reason for this significant wage gap for working mothers? The short answer: the motherhood penalty. The motherhood penalty is the negative impact on wages that is experienced by working women who are also mothers. It has been well documented in the United States and even, to a much smaller extent, in the family-friendly country of Sweden, with its sixteen months of paid parental leave that is shared between mothers and fathers (Budig and England, 2001; Harkness and Waldfogel, 2003; SCB, 2012). The motherhood penalty seems to persist across all earning levels but appears most significant for low-wage workers and workers toward the bottom of the earnings distribution (Budig and Hodges, 2010). Unfortunately, it seems the women who "can least afford it pay the largest proportionate penalty for motherhood" (Budig and Hodges, 2010:725). This motherhood penalty is explained, in large part, by two perspectives on parenting and work: (1) research that focuses on the gendered division of labor and how it negatively impacts a working mother's wages and (2) research that focuses on actual discrimination experienced by the working mother for simply being a mother.

Gendered Division of Labor Perspective

The body of research on the gendered division of labor and its negative impact on working mother's wages examines the effect of society's (and the workplace's) traditional notions of gender where mothers and fathers were believed to be experts in separate "spheres." This is an extension of gender roles expected of men and women (and boys and girls) in general. A mother's sphere of expertise was believed to be within a family's private life, such as with childcare and the management of the home. A father's sphere of expertise was within public life, such as the

workforce or politics. This belief in separate spheres starts with how children are socialized to fit into these roles and how their parents reinforce them. In 2007, a study from the University of Michigan's Institute of Social Research asked children to keep track of their time using time diaries and found that school-age girls do two more hours of chores at home per week than boys their own age, and boys spend even *less* time doing chores when they have a sister in the home. Yet, although school-age girls are doing more chores inside the home, they are actually being paid less allowance, on average, than boys for said chores, according to the same study. Thus, the gender wage gap starts early and continues, albeit in more complicated ways, in the sphere of paid work. Approaching the issue of the wage gap for working mothers from the division of labor perspective largely focuses on the work decisions of mothers and fathers when dealing with childcare.

Some researchers who focus on the gendered division of labor perspective have found that a portion of the motherhood penalty is explained by the actual loss of employment time resulting from pregnancy, childbirth, and childcare later in the home (Cohen and Bianchi, 1999). As a result, working mothers, especially hourly workers who may not be eligible for paid maternity leave, lose wages because they are not actually working for some length of time because of things like labor and recovery. Only 13 percent of full-time employees are eligible for paid leave and these employees are more likely to be highly educated, higher-earning males (U.S. Bureau of Labor Statistics, 2013). Over time, this loss of wages impacts lifetime earnings for mothers. Although it affects low-wage earners more significantly, research suggests that even high wage–earning mothers experience a loss in opportunities and seniority because of missed work (Budig and England, 2001; Budig and Hodges, 2010). It seems easy to say, "You miss work, therefore you miss opportunities." Unfortunately, the reality is far more unfair when we consider that historically women have been considered the go-to parent for child-care. According to researchers at the Kaiser Family Foundation (Ranji and Salganicoff, 2014), only 3 percent of fathers report being the parent who usually leaves work to take care of a sick child.

Other division-of-labor research focuses on the types of jobs working mothers take to maintain their primary caretaker status. For example, Budig and England (2001) found that working mothers may choose more flexible occupations or leave full-time work altogether, opting for part-time work, so their time away from home is minimized or is adaptable to the needs of the family. Unfortunately, most part-time or flexible jobs are more unstable, offer fewer work-related benefits (like retirement or health insurance), and pay less per hour than full-time jobs. As a result, working mothers in these types of jobs will have lower earnings over time as well. Some might argue this is a choice mothers make, but with skyrocketing childcare costs it might not be much of a choice. In most of the United States, monthly childcare for two children can be more expensive than a mortgage or rent (Child Care Aware, 2013). If a mother is the lower wage earner in a married household (often making less than the cost of childcare per month), many will choose to maximize the higher wage earner's income and opt out of working altogether. Of course, having a "choice" to take a part-time job or leave work altogether means there is most likely another paycheck coming into the household. For the nearly 29 percent of mothers in the full-time workforce who are also single, there is no choice, and reduced paychecks resulting from labor, delivery, parenting, and childcare are a stinging fact of life.

Discrimination in the Workplace

Research into the role of the gendered division of labor explains some portion of the motherhood penalty, especially as it relates to some of the decisions mothers and fathers make when it comes to having and taking care of their children. However, it doesn't account for the reality that women also experience outright discrimination for simply being mothers. One study suggests working mothers might face significant discrimination even in the job application process. Correll et al., 2007 conducted an experimental study and asked participants to evaluate two potential applicants who were equally qualified in education and experience for a mid-level marketing position. The only difference between the applicants was the inclusion of outside activities that might be relevant. The fictitious mother was listed as being a "Parent–Teacher Association Coordinator," whereas the other applicant was listed as being involved in "fundraising" for her neighborhood association. In this particular study, the mother was significantly less likely to be recommended for the position. In addition, if recommended for the position, the suggested starting salary for the mothers was $11,000 less than the starting salary for the applicants without children. In a similar follow-up study with actual employers, Correll et al. (2007) found employers, when presented with a fictional pair of equally qualified candidates, *never* chose to contact the mother for an interview over the applicant without children. Although directly asking about marital status in an interview is potentially illegal, employers can get around this by asking questions like "Can you travel?" or "Do you have other responsibilities that might prevent you from working overtime, if needed?"

Why would employers devalue working mothers? Since mothers are assumed to be experts in the family's private sphere, it is most likely presumed they will either be bad workers (because they will always be prioritizing their families) or they will be bad mothers (by not prioritizing their families). Thus, employers may be assuming that a working mother is going to fail somewhere and it will most likely be her job, given traditional gender expectations.

In addition, mothers who prioritize their family often lose a portion of their wages because of a lack of family-friendly work policies. As mentioned previously, the Kaiser Family

Foundation (2013) found that only 3 percent of working fathers are usually the parent who takes off work when a child is sick, compared to 39 percent of working mothers. When mothers do not have backup childcare options and/or when mothers are paid by the hour, this can have significant economic ramifications. According to data cited by Ranji and Salganicoff (2013), as many as one-fifth of school-age children miss a week or more of school during the school year for which mothers might be required to miss work. These most likely unpaid, missed days of work directly translate to lower paychecks.

Unfortunately, even working mothers who prioritize their careers over family cannot escape discrimination. Benard and Correll (2010) found that on the job, women with children face additional discrimination through lower performance evaluations and are viewed as less likeable or selfish compared to other workers. In terms of career advancement, these qualities impacted mothers negatively because they were less likely to be offered promotions. This type of discrimination is not based on job performance, but on the woman's violation of gender expectations, much like the violations of separate spheres discussed previously. The expectation is that mothers *should* prioritize family over work. Thus, even when a mother is seen as a competent and committed employee, she is still penalized for violating the gendered division of labor that necessitates putting family first.

What about Fathers?

It might be easy to assume this is merely a parenthood penalty and perhaps fathers, too, experience similar discrimination in the workplace. In April 2014, Daniel Murphy, second baseman for the New York Mets, was eviscerated by talk radio hosts for missing two games to be with his wife during and after the birth of their first child. Although this instance probably did not result in lost wages for Mr. Murphy, some research does suggest fathers who violate gender norms by taking employer-approved paternity leave experience negative evaluations. In an experimental study, Allen and Russell (1999) found that men who took employer-approved paternity leave were less likely to be considered for promotions than men who did not take paternity leave. Later, Wayne and Cordeiro (2003) asked undergraduate students to read a fictitious personnel file and rate the employees on compliance to work expectations. They found that fathers who took leave were rated lower in competence than mothers who took leave, especially by male students in the study.

Although these two studies suggest fathers might experience a fatherhood penalty, the bulk of research (and more recent research) on parental wage penalties suggests that most fathers actually experience "fatherhood benefits" in terms of positive evaluations and higher salaries. Correll et al. (2007) found that unlike mothers, who are seen as less committed employees than women without children, fathers were actually perceived as *more* committed than men without children. As a result, fathers were recommended for higher starting salaries than the men without children. Using data collected from 1979 to 2014, Budig (2014) found that women's earnings decreased 4 percent for each child and men's earnings increased by more than 6 percent for each child. The gap was consistent when controlling for education, income earned by a spouse, and number of hours worked. Some evidence suggests that even in academia, a seemingly egalitarian and progressive landscape, a father is far more likely to achieve the status of full professor than a mother with similar experience, work output, marital status, and background (Garmendia, 2011). One notable exception is sociology departments, where women with children are just as likely to have "ideal" careers (defined as being in a tenured position with high scholarly productivity) as the fathers and men without children (Spalter-Roth and Van Vooren, 2012). However, fathers, for the most part, have an advantage that mothers do not. The expectation of fathers to be the breadwinner is confirmed and *rewarded* in the workplace, whereas the expectation of mothers to be the primary caretaker is confirmed and *penalized*.

Future of the Motherhood Penalty

In August 2014, Ipshita Pal and Jane Waldfogel released a paper for Columbia University that suggests the motherhood penalty has remained consistent since at least 1977. Despite the significant gains working mothers have made in labor force participation in the past thirty-seven years, they continue to experience the most significant penalty for being in the labor force—more than three decades of persistent wage penalties for mothers compared to child-free women, child-free men, and fathers.

Not all the news is bad. Some recent research suggests attitudes are changing toward gender expectations of mothers (and fathers) in the workforce and other research suggests discrimination toward mothers in the workforce might become less prevalent in the future. In 2011, Coleman and Franuik found that undergraduates rated parents (both mothers and fathers) who took some form of parental leave more favorably in competence and overall impression than parents who stayed at home permanently or parents who took no leave. Although this study focused on attitudes toward parents and not just mothers or fathers, the results are in direct contrast to the previously mentioned findings of Wayne and Cordeiro from 2003. Although this may be a cohort effect, given that younger generations are more likely to hold more gender egalitarian attitudes, it is a sign of potential progress. This generation's attitudes have empirical support. A study from January 2014 suggests that working mothers (and fathers) with two or more children are actually slightly more productive than their peers with fewer or no children (Krapf et al., 2014). The authors speculate this may be because parents use their time more efficiently than their childless coworkers. Although this may not translate into less discrimination for working mothers at the moment, there may come a time when working mothers are seen as less of a liability simply because they are mothers.

Changing perceptions of gender roles in the workforce combined with decreasing discrimination toward working mothers may be the key to weakening (or even ending) the motherhood penalty. The evidence for this argument may already be seen in countries like Sweden, with its public policy push toward more egalitarian views and family-friendly policies. Swedes, it seems, have realized that mothers leaving the workforce (or even switching to part-time work) has not been beneficial to the country as a whole. In fact, Swedish fathers are encouraged to take some portion of parental leave and parents, combined, can take up to sixteen months of paid leave. Yes, *paid* leave, earning 90 percent of their wages! Additionally, tax breaks are in place to help with the cost of childcare for all working parents, regardless of marital status (SCB, 2012). Perhaps the recent Swedish baby boom is a testament to how well these policies are working for the Swedes! Research in the United States suggests these policies are actually beneficial to the economy and the businesses that choose to offer paid leave. California, for example, saved employers more than $85 million a year by implementing paid leave programs. Employees took the paid leave and ultimately returned to work. This saved their employers from the time-consuming and costly hiring and training process involved with finding replacements (Applebaum and Milkman, 2011).

The evidence reported here suggests maintaining the status quo in the United States will continue to perpetuate the motherhood penalty, as it has for approximately four decades. Changing gender attitudes alone are not enough, especially given that gender attitudes have already changed during those same four decades. Changing gender attitudes coupled with workplace policies that truly give all parents an alternative to opting out of work or settling for lower-wage jobs might be a good place to start. In February 2015, the Council of Economic Advisers at the Federal Reserve Bank reported that although women's labor force participation in the United States had been on track with that of women in Canada, the United Kingdom, Germany, France, and Japan for decades, it was now falling behind (Federal Reserve Bank, 2015). What is different about these other countries? They recognize the benefit of working mothers and have made it easier for them to continue working by offering workplace benefits like childcare and paid leave. In the United States, until we significantly change the way we see mothers and acknowledge the value (and growing necessity) of their careers, the motherhood penalty will most likely persist. President Barack Obama called for such action in his January 2015 State of the Union Address by stressing the necessity of women working in our economy today and arguing that programs like affordable childcare are not only a woman's issue, but also a "national economic priority" for us all.

REFERENCES

Allen, Tammy D., and Joyce E. A. Russell. 1999. "Parental Leave of Absence: Some Not So Family-Friendly Implications." *Journal of Applied Social Psychology* 29(1): 166-191.

Applebaum, Eileen, and Ruth Milkman. 2011. *Leaves That Pay: Employer and Worker Experiences with Paid Family Leave in California*. Washington, DC: Center for Economic and Policy Research.

Benard, Stephen, and Shelley J. Correll. 2010. "Normative Discrimination and the Motherhood Penalty." *Gender & Society* 24:616–646.

Budig, Michelle. 2014. *The Fatherhood Bonus and the Motherhood Penalty: Parenthood and the Gender Gap in Pay*. Washington, DC: Third Way.

Budig, Michelle, and Paula England. 2001. "The Wage Penalty for Motherhood." *American Sociological Review* 66:204–225.

Budig, Michelle, and Melissa Hodges. 2010. "Differences in Disadvantage: Variation in the Motherhood Penalty across White Women's Earnings Distribution." *American Sociological Review* 75:705–728.

Child Care Aware. 2013. *Cost of Care Survey Report 2013*. http://www.childcareaware.org/.

Cohen, Philip N., and Suzanne M. Bianchi. 1999. "Marriage, Children, and Women's Employment: What Do We Know?" *Monthly Labor Review* 122(12):22–31.

Coleman, Jill M., and Renae Franiuk. 2011. "Perceptions of Mothers and Fathers Who Take Temporary Work Leave." *Sex Roles* 64(5):311-323.

Correll, Shelley J., Stephen Benard, and In Paik. 2007. "Getting a Job: Is There a Motherhood Penalty?" *American Journal of Sociology* 112:1297–1338.

Federal Reserve Bank. 2015. *Activity Rate for Global Female Workers Aged 25–54*. http://research.stlouisfed.org/fred2/series/LRAC25FEJPM156S/.

Garmendia, Cristina. 2011. *White Paper on the Position of Women in Science in Spain*. http://www.idi.mineco.gob.es/stfls/MICINN/Ministerio/FICHEROS/UMYC/WhitePaper_Interactive.pdf/.

Glass, Jennifer. 2004. "Blessing or Curse? Work–Family Policies and Mothers' Wage Growth over Time." *Work and Occupations* 31:367–394.

Harkness, Susan, and Jane Waldfogel. 2003. "The Family Gap in Pay: Evidence from Seven Industrialized Countries." *Research in Labor Economics* 22:369–414.

Krapf, Matthias, Heinrich Urpsrung, and Christian Zimmerman. 2014. "Parenthood and Productivity of Highly Skilled Labor: Evidence from the Groves of Academe." Working Paper Series. St. Louis: Federal Reserve Bank.

Pal, Ipshita, and J. Waldfogel. 2014. "Re-Visiting the Family Gap in Pay in the United States." Paper presented for Columbia University, New York.

Pew Research Center. 2013. *Social and Demographic Trends*. http://www.pewsocialtrends.org/.

Ranji, Usha, and Alina Salganicoff. 2014. "Data Note: Balancing on Shaky Ground: Women, Work, and Family Health." Menlo Park, CA: Kaiser Family Foundation. http://kff.org/womens-health-policy/issue-brief/data-note-balancing-on-shaky-ground-women-work-and-family-health/

SCB. 2012. *Official Statistics of Sweden*. http://www.scb.se/en_/.

Spalter-Roth, Roberta, and Nicole Van Vooren. 2012. "Mothers in Pursuit of Ideal Careers." Washington DC: American Sociological Association.

University of Michigan, Institute for Social Research. 2007. "Time, Money, and Who Does the Laundry." Research Update. January 2007: Number 4.

U.S. Bureau of Labor Statistics. 2011. "Women in the Labor Force: A Databook." Washington, DC: U.S. Government Printing Office. http://www.bls.gov/cps/wlf-databook-2012.pdf/.

U.S. Bureau of Labor Statistics. 2013. "Paid Leave in Private Industry Over the Past 20 Years." *Beyond the Numbers* 2(18). http://www.bls.gov/opub/btn/volume-2/paid-leave-in-private-industry-over-the-past-20-years.htm

Wayne, Julie H., and Bryanne L. Cordeiro. 2003. "Who Is a Good Organizational Citizen? Social Perception of Male and Female Employees Who Use Family Leave." *Sex Roles* 49:233–246.

Lean in, Dad: How Shared Diaper Duty Could Stimulate the Economy

Catherine Rampell

I happen to be an educated young woman who loves her job, sometimes gushingly, occasionally annoyingly. And yet, even in this enlightened age, I've had two relationships end—at least in large part thanks to that clammy-palmed discussion in which couples plot hypothetical milestones and life goals. The gentlemen in question said that, somewhere in our semicharted future, they expected me to quit my job. At least for a couple of years, anyway, in order to be the kind of hypothetical mother they wanted to raise their hypothetical kids, if that hypothetical day ever came.

I don't pretend to know how common this situation is, and how many other young women have found themselves in it. But it clarified not only the choices that future mothers must make about their careers, but also how early in their careers they must begin to think about them. And while fairness and feminism may urge us to find better ways for women to balance work and life . . . the most convincing argument seems to be an economic one.

In the United States, women represent not only a majority of college graduates but also a majority of advanced-degree holders. But the lack of policies facilitating the work–life balance—like paid maternity leave and flexible work hours—has millions of them underemployed. It's hard to quantify exactly how much human capital is being wasted, but one clue lies in a study by economists at the University of Chicago and Stanford. It estimates that 15 to 20 percent of American productivity growth over the last five decades has come from more efficient allocation of underrepresented groups, like women, into occupations that were largely off-limits, like doctors or lawyers. Even more efficient allocation of women's talents would, presumably, drive further growth, which will become even more critical in the years ahead. By 2050, there are projected to be just 2.6 working-age Americans for every American of retirement age. (In 2008, it was 4.7.)

Other rich countries have figured out ways to keep women in the labor force. While companies like Yahoo and Best Buy bar employees from working from home, the European Union has issued a directive that all member countries must allow parents—men and women—to request part-time, flexible or home-based work arrangements in addition to paid leave. Other developed countries also

continues

■ Continued

have affordable, high-quality public childcare. In Sweden, some public nurseries are even available 24 hours a day.

Such policies contribute to these countries' swollen welfare states and higher tax burdens, but they do keep women at work. Back in 1990, in a ranking of 22 developed countries, the United States had the 6th-highest share of its prime-working-age women active in the work force. By 2010, it had tumbled to 17th place. A new study from Francine D. Blau and Lawrence M. Kahn, both economists at Cornell, estimates that if the United States had the average of other developed countries' work–life policies, 82 percent of America's prime-working-age women would be in the labor force, instead of the current 75 percent.

But what kind of employment would they have, exactly? New research suggests that, because it's primarily women who take advantage of leave and part-time entitlements, work–life accommodations often paradoxically limit career trajectories. Women in Sweden, Finland and Denmark—and other countries held up as paragons of gender parity—are much more likely to end up in traditional pink-collar positions than are their counterparts in the United States. They are certainly much less likely to end up as managers, or in traditionally male professional arenas like law or finance. "In a regime where anyone can go part time, where it's hard to get rid of people if they do, employers might sort on the front end and not hire people they think are likely to want to go part time, which usually means women," said Lawrence F. Katz, an economist at Harvard. "There may be no way a woman can credibly commit to sticking around and not going part time." The U.S., where these policies do not exist, has the smallest gap between women's representation in the labor force and their representation in senior management positions.

In order to prescribe policies that really allow female workers to "lean in" at work, social scientists

are trying to find ones that recast social norms and encourage male workers to "lean in" at home. One area where there seems to be a lot of potential is paternity leave, which still has a stigma in both the United States and Europe. To remedy this bad rap, countries like Sweden and Norway have recently introduced a quota of paid parental leave available *only* to fathers. If dads don't take it, they're leaving money on the table. In Germany and Portugal, moms get bonus weeks of maternity leave if their husbands take a minimum amount of paternity leave. All these countries have seen gigantic increases in the share of fathers who go on leave.

This might not sound like such a big deal, but social scientists are coming around to the notion that a man spending a few weeks at home with his newborn can help recast expectations and gender roles, at work and home, for a long time. A striking new study by a Cornell graduate student, Ankita Patnaik, based on a new paid paternity-leave quota in Quebec, found that parents' time use changed significantly. Several years after being exposed to the reform, fathers spent more time in child care and domestic work—particularly "time-inflexible" chores, like cooking, that cut into working hours than fathers who weren't exposed to the reform. More important, mothers spent considerably more time at work growing their careers and contributing more to the economy, all without any public mandates or shaming.

Paid paternity leave, like paid maternity leave, may sound like a pipe dream, but states (New Jersey, California) and big companies (Ernst & Young, Bank of America) are increasingly offering it and financing it out of their own pocket. They have a vested interest in lobbying Congress to federalize the costs of these accommodations. And that seems only fair. After all, unleashing the full potential of the second sex benefits not only this handful of players but the entire U.S. economy, too.

Fighting Back

TIM STELLOH

Despite the development of a successful movement to support victims of domestic violence, the number of domestic violence homicides remains high. Police officers often discount the risk that male partners and ex-partners pose to women, and many strategies used by law enforcement to intervene in domestic violence cases are inadequate. Stelloh examines Maryland's success reducing their domestic violence homicide rate by 40 percent, largely by training officers to use a particular set of screening questions called the "lethality screen." The screen allows officers to effectively assess the risk of homicide, allowing them to act more effectively and to communicate this increased risk to the victim.

Jo'Anna Bird arrived at her family's two-story, wood-frame house at about 11 p.m. on a winter night three years ago. The house sits on a quiet street in one of the poorer corners of one of America's richest counties: New Cassel, in Nassau, on Western Long Island. Bird, 24, was a mother of two who often wore her long brown hair in a ponytail. She had worked as a school bus monitor, a medical assistant, a Walmart cashier, a supervisor at BJ's Wholesale Club, and she now hoped to be a corrections officer. She had come to stay with her mother and stepfather because the possessiveness of her ex-boyfriend—the father of her young son—had evolved into something much more frightening, and she did not want to be alone.

Leonardo Valdez-Cruz, known to most as "Pito," waited for Bird that night behind a row of hedges in the front yard. After she parked, he appeared and said he wanted to talk. Bird refused, went into the house, and locked the front door. "We assumed he left. We all went to bed," says Sharon Dorsett, Bird's mother. "The next thing we heard was her screaming." Valdez-Cruz had broken in through the basement and tried to smother Bird, who was lying on a couch in the living room watching television, Dorsett told me. When he dashed to the kitchen and grabbed a steak knife, Bird ran to her nephew's room. Bird's stepfather told Valdez-Cruz to leave, which he did. A short time later, Valdez-Cruz tried climbing in through a bedroom window, but Bird's nephew threatened to stab the intruder with a fork. Next, Valdez-Cruz tried squeezing in the bathroom window, but he couldn't fit, although his baseball cap toppled into the tub. Bird's stepfather called the police.

The two officers arrived sometime after midnight. As the family crowded into the living room to explain what had happened, Valdez-Cruz returned to the house and casually knocked on the front door. One of the officers let him in. Bird had

Fighting Back by Tim Stelloh, *The New Republic,* May 10, 2012. Reprinted with Permission from the author.

two protection orders against Valdez-Cruz, but the police did not arrest him. "They said, 'Pito, get out of here, go take a walk somewhere,'" Dorsett says. It was a response that was by now familiar to Bird. "He's going to kill me," Dorsett recalls her daughter saying. "I'm going to die."

A couple of months later, on the afternoon of March 19, 2009, Jo'Anna Bird's body was in the back of a Nassau County Police ambulance. Her outstretched hand dangled off the side of a stretcher; her blood-streaked face tilted to the left. A gland ballooned from her neck, which had been sliced from ear to ear. As the investigator filming the area moved from the ambulance into Bird's spartan two-bedroom apartment, the evidence of a brutal struggle and its aftermath was everywhere: a clump of hair in the front yard; pools of blood in the stairwell; a knocked-out screen in the window. Bird had been tortured and left bleeding to death inside her apartment. According to the autopsy, she had suffered blunt force trauma to the torso and head, and her trachea, esophagus, and jugular had been perforated.

By the following year, Valdez-Cruz had been convicted of Bird's murder and given a life sentence. Dorsett believed her daughter's death had been preventable, so she sued Nassau County in federal court. Her case cast the police department and other government officials as completely ineffective. Even as Bird lay dying, Dorsett's lawsuit claimed, police officers who had been called to her apartment did nothing; one dismissed the call as "the Pito thing again." Eventually, Nassau County settled with Dorsett for $7.7 million. The police commissioner said that seven officers were found to have improperly handled Bird's calls. But, earlier this year, after reading a secret internal affairs report detailing Bird's death, a member of the legislature told a local TV station that 22 officers "ought to be ashamed to look at themselves in the mirror every morning when they get up to shave—much less be wearing the badge."

In recent decades, one of the great grass-roots movements of the twentieth century built a raft of protections designed to help abused women. These included a sprawling network of community shelters, gun restrictions for abusers, protection orders, and the nation's first federal anti-domestic violence legislation, the Violence against Women Act (VAWA). Yet, despite this sustained effort—and even as overall homicides have plummeted nationwide—victims of domestic violence like Jo'Anna Bird are today killed in basically the same numbers as they were about 15 years ago. Between 40 and 50 percent of female homicide victims are killed by their husbands, boyfriends, and exes. And, for about half of these victims, police had been alerted to previous incidents of abuse.

There is, however, one exception to this grim trend: Maryland. Since 2007, domestic violence homicides in the state have fallen by a stunning 40 percent. What is Maryland doing that other states are not? The answer appears to lie with a former high school nurse, an ex-Washington, D.C., police lieutenant, and their ground-breaking efforts to protect the most vulnerable victims of abuse.

In a recent afternoon, Jacquelyn Campbell, a professor of nursing at Johns Hopkins University, stood at the foot of a large, sloped lecture hall at Quinnipiac University's law school, just outside New Haven, Connecticut. Peering down at her were more than 150 police officers, advocates, lawyers, and social workers. Campbell, who is 65, and has wavy, reddish-brown hair, spends much of her time traveling the country, explaining tools to help predict domestic violence—tools which she has spent much of her career developing. In her personable, matter-of-fact manner, she moved through a PowerPoint presentation, illuminating numbers and graphs with harrowing anecdotes. At one point, she recalled the response of a man from Baltimore who admitted to police that he had strangled his wife to death. "You have to understand: I didn't mean to kill her," the man said, according to Campbell. "I've done this a bunch of times before and she never died."

Campbell has been researching domestic violence since the late 1970s, when she was pursuing a master's degree in nursing at Wright

State University in Dayton, Ohio. A former high school nurse, she had moved into community health work and wanted to know why so many young black women in the area were being murdered. For her thesis, Campbell spent a year digging through case files with the local homicide unit. She was shocked to find that most of the women had been killed by their husbands, boyfriends, and exes. In one case, police had been called to a home 54 times before the woman was killed. Then, her research took on a personal significance: The mother of Campbell's own goddaughter was stabbed to death by her boyfriend, a charming man whom Campbell had never suspected of abuse. "It was one of those incredibly horrible tragic things that made me all the more committed to doing something about it," she says.

Back then, there was little awareness of domestic violence. There was no such thing as a protection order or a mandatory arrest. It was the era of "The Burning Bed," the infamous case of Francine Hughes, a Michigan housewife who, after suffering years of abuse, waited until her husband was asleep one night, then doused him with gasoline and set him ablaze. At the time, nearly as many men died from domestic violence as women—about 2,100 women and 1,600 men in 1976, according to Campbell, who provided the statistics for this story. (Campbell uses Department of Justice and FBI statistics on domestic violence homicides, but includes women murdered by their ex-boyfriends, a category often left out of final reports.) About three-quarters of the men were, like Hughes's husband, both victim and abuser.

In 1980, Campbell moved to Detroit, where she began teaching at Wayne State University and volunteering at a shelter. When women would tell her their stories, she was reminded of the homicides she had studied in Dayton. These women had been choked and raped, punched while they were pregnant, threatened with murder. Campbell gave the women calendars so they could mark the days that they had been abused. And she developed a 15-item questionnaire, which she called a "danger assessment,"

that nurses, advocates, and others who dealt with abused women could use to determine if someone was high-risk.

A few years after moving to Johns Hopkins in 1993, Campbell and a team of researchers began studying domestic violence murders in Maryland. Their work, which was published in 2002, sought to identify the key indicators that predicted whether a case of domestic violence was likely to become a domestic homicide. The study produced some surprisingly precise findings. If a man had a history of hitting his partner, that in itself was a predictor of murder. But certain kinds of behavior came with even higher chances of death. For instance, if a man choked his partner, she was five times more likely to be killed by him at some point. If he was unemployed, he was four times more likely to kill her. The researchers also found that only 4 percent of homicide victims had ever sought help from a shelter; in a follow-up study, they found that a stay in a safehouse decreased the risk of violent re-assault by 60 percent. Their findings offered new ways to measure risk. "It also informed the system about which cases needed heightened scrutiny," says Campbell.

After Campbell's work was published, she was contacted by David Sargent, a former lieutenant in the Metropolitan Police Department in Washington, D.C. Sargent is the law enforcement coordinator with the Maryland Network against Domestic Violence, and, during the '90s, he had developed a training course for police officers to help them respond to domestic abuse calls. But that seemed to have little effect on intimate partner murders, and the "referral"—the standard police approach of giving victims a shelter hotline phone number—seemed too passive to do much good.

Indeed, it was clear that the prevailing methods of dealing with domestic violence were inadequate. There had been a slight dip in domestic violence murders in the '90s following the passage of VAWA (which funded anti-domestic violence training and services) and the Brady Law (which required gun dealers to run background checks). But, since then, the number of women killed each year by their partners and exes has hovered around 1,600—that is, only about 500 fewer deaths per year than in 1976. For men, however, domestic homicides have declined from about 1,600 to 600. In other words, all the increased protections for women, the infrastructure of shelters and hotlines, had done a better job of protecting abusers rather than their victims.

In 2003, Sargent, Campbell, and 15 other academics, lawyers, and law enforcement officials met at the Maryland Network's offices in Bowie. There, they began the first of two years of discussions on how to translate Campbell's danger assessment into an easy-to-use field tool for first-responders. At one point, Michael Cogan, a prosecutor from Anne Arundel County, told the group, "If we do this, this is going to represent a paradigm shift in the way we work with victims."

By the end of 2005, the group had developed a series of questions that they called "the screen." The first three questions concerned the most important predictors of future homicide: Has the abuser used a weapon against you? Has he threatened to kill you? Do you think he might kill you? If the woman answered yes to any of those questions, she "screened in." If she answered no, but yes to four of the remaining eight questions, again, she was in. Among these were other, less obvious indicators of fatal violence: Has he ever tried to kill himself? Does she have a child that he knows isn't his?

The officer would then present her with an assessment: Others in your circumstances have been killed; help is available if you want it. If the woman agreed, an officer would dial the local shelter from a police cell phone (to prevent the abuser from finding out about the call) and hand it over.

The screen's first taker was the Sheriff's Office in Kent County, a rural, lightly populated region on Maryland's Eastern Shore. "They don't have drug problems. They don't have gang problems," Sargent told me. "They do have domestic

violence. And, when they have homicides, they're domestic violence homicides."

Today, the screen is used by nearly all of the state's police departments. More than 3,000 women have sought help with everything from filing protection orders to counseling. Proponents are careful to say it is not the only solution to stopping domestic violence murders and that it is impossible to determine precisely why Maryland's domestic homicide rate has fallen. Still, Juley Fulcher, director of policy programs at Break the Cycle, an anti-domestic violence organization, told me that Maryland's 40 percent drop in intimate partner murders is "incredible." Scott Shepardson, a veteran officer in Frederick, Maryland, observed that, for years, he had watched victims of repeated abuse fill out incident forms seemingly out of routine, paying little attention to the injuries they were describing. "They're so used to it," Shepardson says. The process of answering the screening questions enabled them to see the seriousness of the violence in a new light. "It's changed to, 'Oh my God—he *did* try to kill me.'"

Christine considered herself a well-informed, responsible adult. She had a degree in psychology and had bought a house when she was 24. Two years later, she got married. The abuse wasn't that bad at first. But as it got worse, it became harder to leave. Christine and her husband had a son and a daughter. They lived in a nice home in a quiet neighborhood. "By that time, you're in it," says Christine, whose name I've changed to protect her identity.

Once, while she was eating at the dinner table, her husband jammed her bean burrito from Taco Bell into her mouth and up her nose, then held it there. "It was suffocation by burrito," she says. (Christine called the police; he disputed her claims and was not arrested.) In a petition to the court, she wrote, "He has stalked me, threatened to cap my ass, knock my teeth in, kill me, rape me, etc." After her husband moved out for a brief time, Christine told me that he called her and said he was going to slice her throat and watch her bleed. She called the police and sought a protection order. However, he was not arrested and the order was denied for insufficient evidence.

One Friday night two years ago, Christine was outside talking to a neighbor, enjoying a beer. This didn't sit right with her husband, who left for a bar, she told me. Later that night, after he stumbled into the house, Christine heard what sounded like a dresser drawer being emptied—the rustling of papers, the clinking of drill bits and coins. She panicked. "It clicked in my head what he was doing," she recalls. "He was searching for bullets."

Christine is about five and a half feet tall and 130 pounds. Her husband is over six feet and pushing 270. Though Christine didn't have much of a plan, she raced upstairs—all she knew was that she needed to "make it stop," she says. There, in the bedroom, they struggled for his loaded .357 revolver. Christine grabbed the gun, trying to jerk it free. "Somehow, I got between him and it," she says. "I got it in my hand and spun." She doubled over on the bed, with him on top of her, still hanging on. Christine eventually wrestled the revolver away and things calmed down for a few hours. But the next morning, as she was preparing to go to a softball match with their daughter, he threw her over the living room couch, then pushed her into the bathroom. Christine called the police.

After the officers arrived, they asked her questions that she doesn't remember. They put her on the phone with someone at the local shelter, but today, most of the details of that conversation escape her, too. By Monday, she had a lawyer and an advocate who had been provided by the shelter. She was at the courthouse seeking a protection order—something she thought she would never do again.

Over the next year and a half, her advocate was there if she had to go to the sheriff's office, if she had to go to court, or if she panicked about her husband. The protection order came through. Then came the next step: divorce. "There were

many times when she wanted to give up," her advocate told me. "I said, 'No.' I said, 'It's not worth it.'" By October of last year, it was over: Christine and her husband were legally divorced. "If that police officer hadn't handed me that phone," she told me, "I probably would have washed it under the best that I could."

The lethality screen has now been adopted by law enforcement agencies in 14 states, from Barre City, Vermont, to Kansas City, Missouri. Nurses use it in emergency rooms, as do case workers from children's services departments. Since the Washington D.C. police department introduced a variation of the screen in 2009, domestic violence homicides have been cut in half, according to Elisabeth Olds, co-executive director at SAFE, an advocacy group. As for other states, there has been no equivalent of the 40 percent decline in homicides that occurred in Maryland, Sargent told me, but it is too soon to expect such dramatic results. In 2008, a Harvard competition named the Lethality Assessment Program one of the country's 50 best innovations in government.

Yet, as simple as the screen is, it requires increased funding. Training police to use the questionnaire is financially negligible, Sargent told me—the process takes less than an hour. But, if the screen leads to more victims seeking legal help, counseling, or refuge, that means greater costs for the places that provide those services.

When the Kansas City Police Department introduced the screen in 2009, a local shelter, the Rose Brooks Center, had anticipated less than a half-dozen new calls every week to its hotline. "From day one, we were getting four to six [more] calls a day," says Susan Miller, the center's CEO. The number of people staying at the shelter rose from about 70 nightly to an average of 90; cots were added to conference rooms and offices. In the first year that the screen was in use, the center turned away 2,300 people seeking shelter. In 2011, it turned away 4,178. At the same time, the center has seen cutbacks in state and federal funding and has launched a $2 million emergency fund-raising drive to build a new wing containing 25 additional beds.

The future of the lethality assessment is now caught up, like so much else, in the ongoing ideological war over government spending. Every five years, VAWA—which acts, among other things, as a funding mechanism for domestic violence shelters and training programs—must be reauthorized, a process that allows lawmakers to refocus how the money is spent based on new developments in the field. Earlier this year, Vermont Democratic Senator Patrick Leahy offered a reauthorization bill that included funding for "evidence-based" anti-domestic violence programs, such as the lethality screen.

Though the previous two reauthorizations of VAWA enjoyed broad bipartisan support, this year was different. In anticipation of the reauthorization, conservative activist Phyllis Schlafly wrote on Townhall.com last summer that VAWA was "feminist pork"; Janice Shaw Crouse, a senior fellow at the conservative Beverly LaHaye Institute, has argued that VAWA's overly broad definitions of violence have sent men to jail for "unpleasant speech" and "emotional distress."

Senator Leahy's bill was voted out of a subcommittee along party lines in February [2012], with Iowa Senator Chuck Grassley leading the Republican opposition. In a *New York Times* op-ed, Grassley argued that the bill failed to recognize the country's "dire fiscal situation," and railed against "controversial" provisions that would allow increased numbers of immigrant victims of domestic violence into a temporary visa program. . . . For high-risk women, such a program could mean the difference between life and death—between ending up like Jo'Anna Bird or ending up like Christine. [Editor's Note: VAWA was reauthorized by the Senate in the spring of 2012 in a 68 to 31 vote, with only Republican lawmakers voting against reauthorization[1]].

These days, Christine is trying her best to create some semblance of normality. She has a few key rules that she follows to keep herself safe. She only answers phone calls from numbers she recognizes. She tries to avoid places her ex might be. But, in the six months since her divorce was finalized, she has found something she hasn't known in a long time: "Relief," she wrote to me in a text message. "With the ability to breathe."

NOTES

1. Weisman, Jonathan. 2012. "Senate Votes to Reauthorize Domestic Violence Act." *New York Times*. http://www.nytimes.com/2012/04/27/us/politics/senate-votes-to-renew-violence-against-women-act.html?_r=0/.

Families and Elder Care in the Twenty-First Century

ANN BOOKMAN AND DELIA KIMBREL

Women have provided the bulk of unpaid elder care for generations, but women's mass entry into the paid labor force has challenged this arrangement. Bookman and Kimbrel discuss the many ways elder care has changed over the past few generations, including the outsourcing of care to paid nonfamily caregivers and how employer and governmental policies must be modified to create an "aging-friendly" society.

For most of the nation's history, caring for the elderly was a family affair carried out largely by women in the home. As the twenty-first century unfolds, however, elder care in the United States is an increasingly complex enterprise, with much personal care "outsourced" to paid nonfamily caregivers. Today elder care is a multisector undertaking with six key stakeholder groups—health care providers, nongovernmental community-based service agencies, employers, government, families, and elders themselves. The six groups, however, often work separately, or even at cross-purposes. They must be better integrated and resourced to ensure that seniors can age with dignity, families can receive appropriate supports, and society can manage the costs associated with geriatric health care and elder economic security.

In this . . . [reading] we examine the changing demographics of elders and families; what it means to engage in care work of an elderly parent or relative; how caregiving varies by race, gender, and socioeconomic status; and institutional responses to the challenges of caregiving from employers and the government. We close with reflections on the need for a coordinated, cross-sector movement to create an "aging-friendly" society in the United States—a society that values well-being across the life course and seeks multi-generational solutions.

Changing Demographics

With the numbers of older Americans rapidly growing ever larger, the landscape of elder care in the United States is changing. During the past century, the population of Americans aged sixty-five and older increased eleven-fold.[1] According to the 2010 census, 13 percent of the population, or 40.3 million individuals, were sixty-five or older.[2] The population share of those aged eighty-five and older, sometimes called the "oldest old," was 1.1 percent. By 2030

From the *Future of Children*, a collaboration of the Woodrow Wilson School of Public and International Affairs at Princeton University and the Brookings Institution.

approximately 80 million Americans, or 20 percent of the population, are projected to be sixty-five or older, and 2.3 percent of the population will be eighty-five and older.[3]

In addition to its increasing numbers over the coming decades, the elderly population will change in a variety of ways—more people will live longer and healthier lives, the number of older males will grow, and the group's racial and ethnic diversity will increase.[4] But not all trends are positive. Although the poverty rate among the elderly fell from 25 percent in 1970 to 13 percent in 1992, as the real median income of both males and females increased,[5] in 2009, approximately 12.9 percent of people 65 and older still had incomes at the poverty level.[6] The Great Recession that began in 2007 eroded the economic status of moderate-income and middle-class elders, many of whom saw their pensions and 401(k)s decrease, the value of their homes decline, and their other financial investments lose value.[7]

Clearly these changes in the nation's elderly population will present challenges to family members who help provide elder care. And other national demographic shifts—delayed marriage and childbearing for young adults, decreased family size, and changes in family composition and structure—are complicating that challenge. Increased longevity among elders not only extends the years of caregiving by their adult children but may require their grandchildren to become caregivers as well. Married couples may have as many as four elderly parents living; in fact, they may have more parents or relatives in need of care than they have children living at home or on their own. In the past, research on elder care focused on the challenges facing working adults who were caring for both children and elderly parents—the so-called *sandwich generation*—a term coined by sociologist Dorothy Miller to refer to specific generational inequalities in the exchange of resources and support.[8] Miller's research highlighted the stress on the middle generation of employees who are caring for two groups of dependents

while receiving little support. The sandwich metaphor, however, is outmoded in several respects: it does not convey that more than one generation may provide elder care or that members of any generational cohort can be both caregivers and care receivers. Nor does the image of static layers do justice to the dynamic interaction between generations, such as transfers of financial aid, sharing residential space, or exchanging personal and emotional care.

Today researchers are increasingly finding that adults may spend more years caring for their parents than caring for their children.[9] And because families today tend to be small, middle-aged adults may have smaller sibling networks to share elder care responsibilities. In short, elder care in the United States is a demanding task, and caregivers, especially the almost 60 percent of family caregivers who are employed, are finding it harder to undertake that task alone.[10]

Care Work and the Dimensions of Elder Caregiving

There is an extensive body of research on family "care work" dating back to the 1960s with a study that challenged the "myth of the abandoned elderly" and showed that families were still caring for elders, but that changes in external conditions in the family, the workplace, and the community were making caregiving more challenging.[11]

One of the contributions of recent care work research is to draw attention to the "work" aspects of caregiving. This framing contradicts personal and cultural ideas about why families care for elders and makes two related arguments: the first is that because family caregiving is largely done by women and is unpaid, it is often devalued; the second is that despite this devaluing, unpaid care work adds huge value to U.S. society in providing much needed care and "services" to the most vulnerable in the nation's population. Some scholars have tried to calculate the monetary value of unpaid care work to strengthen the argument about its value. Estimates vary from $196 billion a year, calculated in 1997,[12] to $257 billion a year based on a subsequent study by the United Hospital Fund in 2004.[13] In either case, the numbers far exceed what the United States spends on home health care and nursing home care, underscoring the importance of family care.

To differentiate the work families provide from the work that professionals and paraprofessionals provide, many studies of caregiving use the terms "informal care" to refer to the care provided by families and "formal care" to refer to that provided by trained health and social service staff. The distinction creates a sharp line between the informal care that is unpaid and takes place in private homes and the formal care that is paid and takes place in institutional and community settings. The distinction, however, has been challenged by some elder care scholars who find that family caregivers of elders provide care in hospitals, rehabilitation facilities, outpatient clinics, and community agencies. Family caregivers are a "shadow workforce" in the geriatric health care system.[14]

Elder care entails a variety of supports and responsibilities, many of which can change in intensity and complexity over time. Cultural differences unique to elders and their families shape their views on what aging, health, and end of life mean and thus affect expectations about who provides care and what is provided.[15] The variations in elder care are numerous, as the following eight dimensions illustrate.

Time Dimension

Elder care takes three forms: short-term, intermittent, and long-term. Elderly parents may, for example, have surgery that immobilizes them temporarily, but restores them to a high level of daily functioning. In such cases the care needed may be fairly intense but of short duration, and so it disrupts the caregiver's job, family, and personal life, but only temporarily. In contrast, the seven in ten care recipients who have chronic health conditions[16] may require intermittent care. . . . In such cases, the caregiver is needed

frequently over a longer period and may be hard pressed to integrate caregiving demands with paid work. In other cases elder care may be long-term, lasting for months or years. Such caregiving may be required on a daily basis and can seriously complicate the caregiver's ability to maintain a job, provide care for other family members, and maintain personal and community involvement.

Since 1987 the American Association of Retired Persons (now called AARP) and the National Alliance for Caregiving (NAC) have conducted several national surveys tracking the time Americans invest in elder care.[17] The most recent survey, in 2009, found intermittent elder care to be the type most commonly provided. Caregivers surveyed in that poll report providing such care for an average of 4.6 years; 31 percent report giving such care for more than five years.[18] Half of all of caregivers spend eight hours or less a week, while 12 percent spend more than forty hours. Short-term or intermittent care may evolve into long-term care as an elder's physical or mental function, or both, deteriorates.

Geographic Dimension

The distance between an elder's place of residence and that of the caregiver has a major effect on the type and frequency of care. Because some American families are mobile—about 16 percent of families move each year[19]—adult children sometimes live in different cities, states, or even regions from their elderly parents. According to the most recent AARP–NAC survey data, 23 percent of caregivers live with the elder for whom they are caring (co-residence is particularly common among low-income caregivers) and 51 percent live twenty minutes away.[20]

Long-distance caregiving, however, has been on the rise over the past fifteen years.[21] One study by MetLife finds that at least 5 million caregivers live an hour or more away from the elder for whom they care.[22] Of this group, about 75 percent provide help with daily activities, such as shopping, transportation, and managing household finances. Most long-distance caregivers share responsibilities with siblings or paid caregivers, or both. Several studies document that adult children who live near an elderly relative are most likely to provide the majority of elder care,[23] underscoring the importance of geographic location. . . .

Financial Dimension

The economic resources available to caregiving families vary widely. Upper-middle-class and affluent families usually have adequate funds to pay for elder care services, while poor families are usually eligible for a variety of subsidized services, such as home health care. The hardest-hit families are the working poor and those with moderate incomes, who are too "rich" to qualify for subsidized services but unable to pay for care themselves. Many families caring for elderly relatives encounter this type of "middle-class squeeze."

Researchers who explore the financial dimension of elder care find that cross-generational transfers are fairly common. In a 2005 study, 29 percent of baby boomers provided financial assistance to a parent in the previous year, while about a fifth received financial support from a parent.[24] A recent nationally representative survey of elders over sixty-five offers a slightly different picture: half of these elders say they have given money to their adult children, while about a third say they help their adult children with child care, errands, housework, and home repairs. When asked what their adult children give them, more than 40 percent report receiving help with errands and rides to appointments; about a third, help with housework and home repairs; and about a fifth, help with bill paying and direct financial support.[25] What is striking is that care, time, and money are being exchanged between the generations, going both ways.

Health Dimension

Some caregivers provide help in a short-term acute health care crisis, others care for elders with one or more chronic diseases, and a third group cares for elders with long-term incurable or progressive diseases. Families are a critical resource for the nation's health care system when they care for a relative with a debilitating disease, such as dementia or Alzheimer's, for which paid care is very expensive. Giving such care, however, is a major burden on these families, who frequently find that caregiver training—both how to manage the behavior and symptoms of the elder *and* how to cope with their own feelings—is often not available.[26] . . .

One elderly cohort that is growing is "frail elders," defined as those sixty-five and older who do not live in nursing homes, but have difficulty with at least one aspect of independent living or are severely disabled, or both. This group numbered about 10.7 million people in 2002.[27] Analyses of a national data set showed that two-thirds of frail elders receive help—an average of 177 hours a month—with personal care from an unpaid family caregiver. More than half of that help comes from their daughters, most of whom are working.[28]

Legal and Ethical Dimension

When significant declines in physical and mental health compromise elders' ability to manage their own affairs, it is usually the family caregiver who assumes some level of control, decision-making power, and ultimately legal authority such as power of attorney. Studies on the legal issues of elders often focus, particularly when financial resources are involved, on the caregiver as a source of interfamilial conflict and even elder abuse. A recent study of financial elder abuse, however, found that only 16.9 percent of the perpetrators were family members.[29]

Legal issues may also require caregivers to take on complex health-related roles, such as acting as health care proxy or setting up an advance directive or DNR (do not resuscitate) order. These steps can involve complex ethical questions and decisions, such as when to discontinue life supports for a terminally ill parent. Studies on elders at the end of life show the critical role that family caregivers play once palliative care is chosen, including assisting elders with daily living, handling medications, and making medical decisions.[30] . . . Other studies emphasize the high degree of stress on families with terminally ill elders, showing the unresponsiveness of some health care systems, as well as the ways in which community services can ease stress.[31]

Outsourcing Elder Care and Care Coordination

When family members cannot provide care, particularly if they are full-time workers or long-distance caregivers, or both, their job is to find an agency close to where the elder lives that will provide services for a fee. It takes time and effort to find an appropriate multiservice or aging service agency,[32] to provide the agency with detailed personal and health information about the elder to ensure a good "client–provider fit," and to monitor services to be sure that needs are met and the elder is comfortable with the provider. Carrying out all these tasks to find just one type of service is difficult enough; if an elder needs multiple services, the work for the family can be significant.

Many studies have documented the fragmentation in the geriatric health care and social services system, and others have called for greater care coordination to support caregivers.[33] The handoffs between hospitals and families, or between rehabilitation facilities and families, can often be unsafe and unsatisfying, and the need for improved communication is widely documented.[34] . . .

Elder Caregiving and Diversity

Most studies on aging and elder care treat elders and their caregivers as monolithic groups. But as the nation has become more diverse, so too has the population of elders. Elder caregiving varies by gender, race, and socioeconomic status, and families from African American, Latino, Asian, Native American, and other groups bring their own strengths and needs to the caregiving

experience. Although gender, race, and socioeconomic status are treated separately below, it is important to note that these variables often intersect in powerful and important ways in the lives of caregivers. An "intersectionality" approach shows how unequal opportunity over the life course shapes trajectories of advantage and disadvantage for elders and the families who care for them. Future research must explore multiple aspects of diversity in order to develop new policies that address the interaction between socioeconomic inequality *and* differences based on gender, race, and culture.

Gender and Elder Care

Elderly women live longer than do elderly men, and despite a lifetime of providing care to others, they are more likely than men to live alone, live in poverty, and lack care themselves when they are elderly.[35] Research on gender and caregiving has two major themes. First, the majority (67 percent) of family caregivers are women,[36] with wives providing care to spouses and adult daughters providing the majority of care to elderly parents. Second, given the persistence of gender inequality in the workforce, including the gender gap in wages, women caregivers are more likely than men to cut back on work hours or quit their jobs because of their caregiving duties and are thus left with less income, small savings, and reduced pensions.

Although women in the general population have greater elder care responsibilities than do men, recent studies reveal that employed women and employed men provide care in roughly equal numbers.[37] But gender differences persist nonetheless: employed women are more likely than employed men to provide family care on a regular basis, they spend more hours providing care, and they spend more time providing direct care such as meal preparation, household work, physical care, and transportation.[38] This finding is consistent with other evidence on gender trends in elder care showing that women tend to perform household and personal care tasks that are physically draining and likely to interrupt daily activities, while men tend to give periodic assistance.[39] Both working and nonworking male caregivers receive more assistance with their caregiving efforts than do women; they also tend to delegate their tasks to others and to seek paid assistance to alleviate some of their caregiving responsibilities.[40]

Despite the growing number of men balancing work and elder care responsibilities, women are particularly vulnerable to negative work-related consequences.[41] Women who are caring for elders generally reduce their work hours, leave the workforce, or make other adjustments that have negative financial or career implications. Some refuse overtime and pass up promotions, training, assignments that are more lucrative, jobs requiring travel, and other challenging but time-consuming job opportunities.[42] Many low-income women and women of color who are employed do not have sufficient flexibility or autonomy in their jobs to be able to take an elderly parent to the doctor or attend to other needs.[43]

Despite feelings of satisfaction from their care, caregivers can sometimes feel burdened, socially isolated, strained, and hopeless. A recent MetLife study of working caregivers, based on a large corporate employer's health risk appraisal database of roughly 17,000 respondents, found that employed women are significantly more likely than employed men caregivers to self-report negative effects on personal well-being.[44] Caregivers in general report more physical and mental health problems than noncaregivers,[45] and more female caregivers (58 percent) report negative health effects than male caregivers (42 percent).[46] . . .

Race, Ethnicity, and Elder Care

The growing diversity of the United States makes it important for researchers to consider how race and ethnicity—both socially constructed categories—shape aging and the caregiving experience. The nation's legacy of racial oppression and structural inequality has created socioeconomic inequities in education, health, housing, income, and wealth. Many low-income men and women of color enter old age after a lifetime of cumulative disadvantage, during which limited access to economic opportunity has obstructed efforts to accumulate savings for retirement and limited access to health care has led to poorer health.

Few families from racial and ethnic minority groups use paid or outsourced care, and those who do can sometimes face structural barriers in accessing them. Although most Americans refrain from putting their elderly kin in nursing homes, Latinos, African Americans, and Asians are least likely to do so.[47] Even elders of color with greater care needs, such as those afflicted with dementia or chronic illnesses, are more likely than whites to receive care from their children and live in the community with them.[48]

Many studies show that families of color rely on extended kin networks and friends for financial assistance, material goods, domestic duties, and other supports.[49] African Americans, especially, rely on networks of neighbors, friends, and fellow congregants. Language and cultural barriers often lead Chinese American and Puerto Rican caregivers to use ethnically oriented organizations in their communities for support.[50]

Extensive social support may partially explain why racial and ethnic minority groups tend to have more favorable attitudes toward caregiving and higher caregiving satisfaction.[51] Studies suggest that many groups of color value mutual exchange, reciprocity, filial responsibility, and interdependence, whereas Western European and white ethnic groups value self-reliance and independence. . . .

Among some Latino groups, the extended family is expected to provide care to older relatives,[52] and Native Americans strongly value giving back to those who have provided for them, reinforcing the value of reciprocity in their culture.[53] White caregivers report greater depression and view caregiving as more stressful than do caregivers of color.[54] . . .

Socioeconomic Status and Elder Care

Although researchers do not often explore the implications of socioeconomic status—defined by education, occupational status, family income, net worth, and financial assets—for elder care, it can nevertheless have important effects on elders' quality of life and the kind of care their families can provide.

In the first place, many low-income elders have insufficient resources. More than half of all senior households (54 percent) cannot meet their expenses even using their combined financial net worth, Social Security benefits, and pension incomes.[55] Among older persons reporting income in 2008, 20.3 percent had less than $10,000.[56] Such economic challenges often increase the financial burden, hardship, and strain on their families. Many studies do show that families with higher socioeconomic status tend not to provide physical care themselves, and instead tend to purchase elder care services, provide financial gifts, buy alternative lodging, and remodel homes to accommodate an elder.[57]

A scarcity of resources makes working poor and working-class caregivers more likely to provide direct care themselves rather than to hire professional care managers. When low-income families do purchase formal services, they use them only for short periods. Middle-class and higher-income caregivers hire elder care assistance for longer periods or until their resources run out.[58]

Responses from Employers and Government

Researchers have also investigated how employers and government are responding to the challenges families face in providing elder care. Are employers, for example, providing working caregivers of elders with "family-friendly" benefits and policies? Are federal, state, and local governments meeting the needs of elders and caregivers with public policies? We explore the adequacy of their responses to the needs of both elders and family caregivers to gain insight into what policy changes may be needed in the future.

Responses from Employers

Given the aging of the population and the high rate of female labor force participation, the share of elder caregivers who are employed has been growing over the past thirty years and is expected to continue, nearing the percentage of employees with child care responsibilities. One 2010 study found that six in ten family caregivers are employed;[59] another found that considered as a group, 50 percent of employed caregivers of elders work full time, and 11 percent work part time. In the coming years, employers will need to respond to the elder care needs of their workforce lest they compromise the performance of their firms and the retention of some of their most valued employees.

Research on work and family conflict is extensive, and many studies focus on work and elder care for employees.[60] Beyond general feelings of role conflict, working caregivers in one study report using their own sick leave or vacation hours to accommodate elder care needs (48 percent), cutting back on hours or quitting their job (37 percent), taking an additional job or increasing their hours to get funds for elder care expenses (17 percent), taking unpaid leave (15 percent), and leaving their job for a different one (14 percent).[61] . . . If caregivers cut back work hours, take unpaid leaves, or leave their jobs, the negative effects can go beyond the individual caregivers themselves to include whole families. For example, a MetLife study documented negative financial repercussions for families from short-term income losses, long-term losses of retirement savings, and lost opportunities for career advancement.[62]

Researchers are also examining the policies and programs of employers to address their employees' elder care needs; rough estimates are that from 25 to 50 percent of employers offer these programs.[63] Large firms are more likely than small companies to have elder care programs. . . . Studies on how the recent recession affected elder care programs are just now becoming available; one, for example, shows that most employers are maintaining workplace flexibility, although reduction of hours may translate into reduction in pay, so increased flexibility entails both costs and benefits.[64]

Elder Care Assistance Programs, introduced by companies during the late 1980s, have grown in scope. The early programs—paralleling those developed to support workers with young children—included resource and referral services to locate elder care services in the elder's community, and flexible spending accounts for putting aside funds on a pre-tax basis to cover elder care expenses.[65] During the 1990s, some companies expanded elder care benefits through Employee Assistance Programs or new "work–life programs" to include flexible work arrangements (58 percent), personal or sick leaves (16 percent), and access to short-term emergency backup care when a paid caregiver was unexpectedly absent (4 percent).[66] . . .

To date, the needs of employed elder caregivers far exceed the employer response, and elder care assistance tends to be offered only by the largest employers. Some studies about "family-responsive" workplaces do not even mention elder care as a benefit needed by families,[67] and the findings of studies that do focus on elder care have less than encouraging findings. . . . Elder care programs are still less frequently offered than child care programs, and a 2006 study found that although almost three-quarters of employers offered some child care assistance, only one-third offered elder care assistance.[68]

What accounts for employers' lag in offering elder care assistance? And how can workplaces make elder care a key component of the work–family or work–life agenda? Elder care may have received less attention than child care because ageism and denial about aging is deeply entrenched in U.S. culture. . . . This denial can lead employers to ignore or minimize the elder care needs of their workforce, using arguments about high costs and low utilization to justify having few elder care programs.

Some work–family scholars argue that developing a family-friendly workplace is a long-term process with three distinct stages. In the first stage the goal is to promote the recognition of a particular work–family issue as a visible, legitimate need. In the second stage the goal is to implement and then refine specific programs, including effective communication and supervisor training. The third stage involves institutionalizing the new work–family programs into the culture of the workplace to heighten program reach and effectiveness.[69] . . . Only a minority of firms—mainly large companies—are in the third stage. Making the "family-friendly workplace" an "elder-care-friendly workplace" remains an unrealized project for many employers.

Responses from Government

During the nineteenth and twentieth centuries the United States gradually transferred responsibility for elder care from the family to the government, from the private sphere to the public sphere.[70] But despite landmark twentieth-century legislation, it can be argued that the United States lacks the full range of public policies needed to address the aging of the population, and that families still bear the primary responsibility.

. . . [Several] public policies . . . are key to the well-being of elders and their family caregivers. Some have enhanced health and income security for elders; others have enhanced the supports available to both employed and nonemployed family caregivers. We briefly address the strengths and weaknesses of some of these policies to suggest possible areas for policy expansion.

Social Security is critical to providing a basic level of financial support and security to elders. Several issues, however, weaken its effectiveness. Initially the system strengthened intergenerational ties because those who retired—only 5.2 percent of the population was sixty-five or older in 1930—were reaping benefits based on the productivity of younger workers. But in the decades ahead, more people will be needing retirement income, and fewer young workers will be available to replenish Social Security funds, thus putting pressure on the younger generation and creating tension between generations.[71] In addition, because Social Security is based on wages in the paid labor force, women who delayed work, interrupted work, or never entered the workforce because of family caregiving responsibilities have smaller benefits in old age than men (though at the death of her spouse, a woman is eligible to collect a "survivor" Social Security benefit).

Medicare, a second foundational piece of economic security for elders, ensures coverage of many health care costs. It, too, however, is problematic. Originally enacted to cover the costs of acute care and hospitalization, Medicare does not provide adequate insurance for chronic illnesses, those common to most elders. Medicare does not reimburse hospitals fully for the care they provide, so many hospitals have shortened patient stays, creating difficulties for caregivers when an elder is prematurely discharged to rehab or to home. Medicare will cover a stay in a skilled nursing facility only if daily nursing or rehab services are needed, and will cover ten hours a week of home care only if skilled nursing care is required. Finally, Medicare does not cover the cost of long-term care.

Medicaid, the third key government policy, is the largest source of payment for nursing home care, and it will become increasingly important as the nation's population ages. In 2008, nearly 41 percent of the nation's nursing facility care was paid by Medicaid, averaging nearly $30,000 for each beneficiary.[72] In most states, Medicaid also pays for some long-term care services at home and in the community. Although eligibility varies from state to state, those elders who are eligible for Medicaid assistance must have limited assets and incomes below the poverty line. . . .

The Family and Medical Leave Act (FMLA) is the only law that deals specifically with the challenges of working and providing elder care. A bipartisan commission that conducted two nationally representative random-sample surveys to study the impact of the FMLA on employers and employees reported to Congress in 1996 that the law was not the burden to business that some had anticipated.[73] . . . On the employee side, the FMLA was found to be a boon to families in their caregiving roles. Most leaves were

short, and concerns that employees would abuse the law and use it for recreational time off proved unwarranted. In fact, some "leave-needers" did not take advantage of the law because they could not afford an unpaid leave. . . . Between the 1995 and 2000 surveys there was a statistically significant increase in the use of FMLA for elder care.[74]

From a policy perspective, the FMLA is like a minimum labor standard. It provides valuable protections to workers, but has limitations that hamper its effectiveness. Access to FMLA, for example, is restricted to about 55 percent of the workforce because of eligibility requirements for firms and employees. The definition of "family" is limited to parent, child, and spouse, depriving many elderly relatives such as grandparents or aunts and uncles, as well as those who are members of the lesbian, gay, bisexual, and transgendered (LGBT) community or who are not legally married, of coverage. And because the leave provided is unpaid, it is difficult for low-income workers to use. Recently two states, California and New Jersey, passed laws to establish paid leave programs. . . .

Finally, the National Family Caregiver Support Program (NFCSP) is the first federal law to acknowledge fully the needs of caregivers regardless of their employment status. Preliminary studies have shown that the program is expanding caregivers' access to elder care information and providing needs assessments, support groups, and stress reduction programs.[75] Although NFCSP offers many excellent services, such as respite care, counseling, and training for family caregivers, the funds available to deliver them are limited, particularly in the area of respite care.[76] . . .

When government and employers cannot provide adequate support for elder care, family caregivers often rely on nongovernmental organizations, such as health care providers and community-based aging service agencies. Although NGOs are often created and funded by government, they are not direct policy-making organizations, and their role is beyond the scope of this [reading]. Caregivers do, however, receive significant support, information, and services from these groups, including faith-based organizations, neighborhood centers in communities of color, LGBT advocacy organizations, and educational organizations. Because so many elder caregivers are employed, NGOs that provide services for elders and their caregivers must take the needs of employees into account.

Creating an Aging-Friendly Society

The challenges faced today by elders and their family caregivers are enormous and will continue to increase during the twenty-first century as the population ages. Families alone cannot provide elder care, employers alone cannot provide all the supports employed caregivers need, and the government alone cannot provide or fund all the elder policies required. A large-scale, cross-sector initiative is needed to coordinate efforts at the national, state, and local level and to support all citizens from diverse cultures and income levels as they age.

Public policies must move in a universal direction, like Social Security and Medicare, to help transform U.S. communities and make housing, transportation, and open space accessible to all elders. There is a pressing need to better integrate nongovernmental organizations in the health care and social service sectors and to ensure they are culturally responsive. Employers must be encouraged to give employees in both professional and hourly jobs access to flexible work arrangements including part-time work, paid leave policies, paid sick days, and other "elder-friendly" workplace benefits. Overall, these groups must work together to create a culture in which aging is seen as a natural part of the life course and caregiving is seen as a multigenerational enterprise of great value to children, adults, elders, and society.

Elders themselves and their family caregivers, as well as the public and private sectors, must build support for social investment in the next generation. Today's children will be the workers, citizens, and family caregivers who will care for the growing U.S. elderly population

tomorrow. Focusing on children's healthy development and education will build their capacity to provide supportive care for the elders of future generations.

NOTES

1. Frank B. Hobbs, "Population Profile of the United States: The Elderly Population," U.S. Census Bureau (www.census.gov/population/www/pop-profile/elderpop.html).

2. Census 2000 Brief, C2KBR/01-12, U.S. Census Bureau (2001).

3. Jennifer Cheeseman Day, *Population Projections of the United States by Age, Sex, Race, and Hispanic Origin: 1993–2050*, Current Population Reports, P25-1104, U.S. Census Bureau (1993); Administration on Aging, Table 12, "Older Population as a Percentage of the Total Population, 1900–2050" (www.aoa.gov/aoaroot/aging_statistics/future_growth/future_growth.aspx#age).

4. U.S. Census Bureau, "Age: 2000," Census 2000 Brief, October 2001 (www.census.gov/prod/2001pubs/c2kbr01-12.pdf).

5. Wan He and others, "Sixty-Five Plus in the United States," *Current Population Reports, Special Studies,* Series P23-209 (Washington: December 2005).

6. U.S. Census Bureau, Current Population Survey, Annual Social and Economic Supplements (www.census.gov/hhes/www/poverty/histpov/hstpov5.xls); U.S. Census Bureau, Historical Poverty Tables, table C, "Poverty Rates for Elderly and Non-Elderly Adults, 1966–2009."

7. The percentage of homeless adults fifty and older appears to be increasing, particularly in cities. M. William Sermons and Meghan Henry, "Demographics of Homelessness Series: The Rising Elderly Population," National Alliance to End Homelessness (April 2010).

8. Dorothy A. Miller, "The 'Sandwich' Generation: Adult Children of the Aging," *Social Work* 26, no. 5 (September, 1981): 419–23.

9. Leslie Foster Stebbins, *Work and Family in America: A Reference Handbook* (Santa Barbara, Calif.: ABC-CLIO, 2001), p. 40.

10. National Alliance for Caregiving and AARP, *Caregiving in the United States* (Washington: 2009), p. 53.

11. E. Shanas and G. F. Streib, eds., *Social Structure and the Family: Generational Relations* (Englewood Cliffs, N.J.: Prentice-Hall, 1965).

12. Peter S. Arno, Carol Levine, and M. N. Memmott, "The Economic Value of Informal Caregiving," *Health Affairs* 18, no. 2 (1999): 182–88.

13. Carol Levine, ed. *Always on Call: When Illness Turns Families into Caregivers* (Vanderbilt University Press, 2004), p. 5.

14. Ann Bookman and Mona Harrington, "Family Caregivers: A Shadow Workforce in the Geriatric Health Care System?" *Journal of Health Policy, Politics and Law* 32, no. 6 (2007): 1026.

15. Carol Levine and Thomas H. Murray, eds., *The Cultures of Caregiving: Conflict and Common Ground among Families, Health Professionals and Policy Makers* (Johns Hopkins University Press, 2004).

16. *Family Caregiving in the U.S.: Findings from a National Survey* (Washington: National Alliance for Caregiving and the American Association of Retired Persons, 1997).

17. Donna Wagner, *Comparative Analysis of Caregiver Data for Caregivers to the Elderly, 1987 and 1997* (Bethesda, Md.: National Alliance for Caregiving, June 1997).

18. National Alliance for Caregiving, *Caregiving in the U.S.*, National Alliance for Caregiving in collaboration with the AARP (November 2009), p. 5.

19. "What Moves Americans to Move?" Census 2000, U.S. Census Bureau (http://usgovinfo.about.com/library/weekly/aa060401a.htm).

20. National Alliance for Caregiving, *Caregiving in the U.S.* (see note 18), p. 14.

21. Linda K. Bledsoe, Sharon E. Moore, and Lott Collins, "Long Distance Caregiving: An Evaluative Review of the Literature," *Ageing International* (New York: Springer Science, 2010); Beverly Koerin and Marcia Harrigan, "P.S. I Love You: Long Distance Caregiving," *Journal of Gerontological Social Work* 40, no. 1/2 (2003): 63–81.

22. MetLife, *Miles Away: The MetLife Study of Long-Distance Caregiving* (Westport, Conn.: MetLife Mature Market Institute, July 2004).

23. S. H. Matthews and T. T. Rosner, "Shared Filial Responsibility: The Family as the Primary Caregiver," *Journal of Marriage and the Family* 50, no. 1 (1998): 278–86; E. P. Stoller, L. E. Forster, and T. S. Duniho, "Systems of Parent Care within Sibling Networks," *Research on Aging* 14, no. 1 (1992): 472–92.

24. Pew Research Center, "From the Age of Aquarius to the Age of Responsibility: Baby Boomers Approach Age 60, A Social Trends Report" (2005), pp. 10–13.

25. Pew Research Center, *Growing Old in America: Expectations vs. Reality*, A Social and Demographic Trends Report (June 2009), p. 11.

26. E. Papastavrou and others, "Caring for a Relative with Dementia: Family Caregiver Burden" (JAN Original Research, Blackwell Publishing, Ltd., 2007).

27. R. Johnson and J. Wiener, *A Profile of Frail Older Americans and Their Caregivers,* The Retirement Project, Occasional Paper 8 (Washington: Urban Institute, 2006).

28. Ibid, p. 24.

29. MetLife, *Broken Trust: Elders, Family, and Finances* (Westport, Conn.: MetLife Mature Market Institute, 2009), p. 12.

30. Joshua Hauser and Betty Kramer, "Family Caregivers in Palliative Care," *Clinics in Geriatric Medicine* 20, no. 4 (November 2004): 671–88.

31. Kevin Brazil, Daryl Bainbridge, and Christine Rodriguez, "The Stress Process in Palliative Cancer Care: A Qualitative Study on Informal Caregiving and Its Implication for the Delivery of Care," *American Journal of*

Hospice and Palliative Medicine 27, no. 2 (2010): 111–16.

32. The Administration on Aging has a website to help families find an agency near where their elderly relative lives (www.eldercare .gov/Eldercare.NET/Public/Home.aspx).

33. T. Semla, "How to Improve Coordination of Care," *Annals of Internal Medicine* 148, no. 8 (April 15, 2008): 627–28.

34. Grif Alspach, "Handing off Critically Ill Patients to Family Caregivers: What Are Your Best Practices?" *Critical Care Nurse* 29, no. 3 (2009): 12–22.

35. Laura Katz Olsen, *The Not-So-Golden Years: Caregiving, the Frail Elderly, and the Long-Term Care Establishment* (Lanham, Md.: Rowman & Littlefield Publishers, Inc., 2003), p. 98; Nancy R. Hooyman, "Research on Older Women: Where Is Feminism?" *Gerontologist* 39, no. 1 (1999): 115–18.

36. National Alliance for Caregiving and AARP, *Caregiving in the U.S.: A Focused Look at Those Caring for Someone Age 50 or Older* (Washington, 2009), p. 22.

37. Kerstin Aumann and others, *Working Family Caregivers of the Elderly: Everyday Realities and Wishes for Change* (New York: Families and Work Institute, 2010), p. 2.

38. Ibid.

39. Lynn M. Martire and Mary Ann Parris Stephens, "Juggling Parent Care and Employment Responsibilities: The Dilemmas of Adult Daughter Caregivers in the Workforce," *Sex Roles* 48, no. 3/4 (2003): 167–73.

40. Olsen, *The Not-So-Golden Years*.

41. Margaret B. Neal and Donna L. Wagner, "Working Caregivers: Issues, Challenges, and Opportunities for the Aging Network," *National Family Caregiver Support Program Issue Brief* (2002): 1–31.

42. Susan C. Eaton, "Eldercare in the United States: Inadequate, Inequitable, but Not a Lost Cause," *Feminist Economics* 11, no. 2 (2005): 37–51; MetLife Mature Market Institute, *Employer Costs for Working Caregivers* (Washington: MetLife Mature Market Institute and National Alliance for Caregivers, 1997).

43. Karen Bullock, Sybil L. Crawford, and Sharon L. Tennstedt, "Employment and Caregiving: Exploration of African American Caregivers," *Social Work* 48, no. 2 (2003): 150–62.

44. MetLife, *MetLife Study of Working Caregivers and Employer Health Costs* (Westport, Conn.: National Alliance for Caregiving and MetLife Mature Market Institute, February 2010).

45. Peter P. Vitaliano, Jianping Zhang, and James M. Scanlan, "Is Caregiving Hazardous to One's Physical Health? A Meta-Analysis," *Psychological Bulletin* 129, no. 6 (2003): 946–72.

46. Martin Pinquart and Silvia Sörensen, "Gender Differences, Caregiver Stressors, Social Resources, and Health: An Updated Meta-Analysis," *Journals of Gerontology Series B: Psychological Sciences & Social Sciences* 61, no. 1 (2006): 33–45.

47. Sara Torres, "Barriers to Mental-Health Care Access Faced by Hispanic Elderly," in *Servicing Minority Elders in the Twenty-First Century*, edited by Mary L. Wykle and Amasa B. Ford (New York: Springer, 1999), pp. 200–18.

48. Sarah J. Yarry, Elizabeth K. Stevens, and T. J. McCallum, "Cultural Influences on Spousal Caregiving," *American Society on Aging* 31, no. 3 (2007): 24–30.

49. James Jackson, "African American Aged," in the *Encyclopedia of Aging*, 2nd ed., edited by George L. Maddox (New York: Springer, 1995), pp. 30–80; Sharon L. Tennstedt, Bei-Hung Chang, and Melvin Delgado, "Patterns of Long-Term Care: A Comparison of Puerto Rican, African-American, and Non-Latino White Elders," *Journal of Gerontological Social Work* 30, no. 1/2 (1998): 179–99.

50. Sue Levkoff, Becca Levy, and Patricia Flynn Weitzmann, "The Role of Religion and Ethnicity in the Help Seeking of Family

Caregivers of Elders with Alzheimer's Disease and Related Disorders," *Journal of Cross-Cultural Gerontology* 14, no. 4 (1999): 335.

51. Martin Pinquart and Silvia Sörensen, "Associations of Stressors and Uplifts of Caregiving with Caregiver Burden and Depressive Mood: A Meta-Analysis," *Journals of Gerontology Series B: Psychological Sciences & Social Sciences* 58B, no. 2 (2003): 112; D. W. Coon and others, "Well-Being, Appraisal, and Coping in Latina and Caucasian Female Dementia Caregivers: Findings from the REACH Study," *Aging & Mental Health* 8, no. 4 (2004): 330–45.

52. Tennstedt, Chang, and Delgado, "Patterns of Long-Term Care."

53. Catherine Hagan Hennessey and Robert John, "American Indian Family Caregivers' Perceptions of Burden and Needed Support Services," *Journal of Applied Gerontology* 15, no. 3 (1996): 275–93.

54. Martin Pinquart and Silvia Sörensen, "Ethnic Differences in Stressors, Resources, and Psychological Outcomes of Family Caregiving: A Meta-Analysis," *Gerontologist* 45, no. 1 (2005): 90–106; M. R. Janevic and M. C. Connell, "Racial, Ethnic, and Cultural Differences in the Dementia Caregiving Experience: Recent Finding," *Gerontologist* 41, no. 3 (2001): 334–47.

55. Tatjana Meschede, Thomas M. Shapiro, and Jennifer Wheary, *Living Longer on Less: The New Economic Insecurity of Seniors* (Institute on Assets and Social Policy and Demos, 2009).

56. Administration on Aging, *A Profile of Older Americans: 2009* (www.aoa.gov/AoAroot/Aging_Statistics/Profile/2009/docs/2009profile_508.pdf).

57. Deborah M. Merrill, *Caring for Elderly Parents: Juggling Work, Family, and Caregiving in Middle and Working Class Families* (Westport: Auburn House, 1997), pp. 13–15.

58. Ibid.

59. MetLife, *MetLife Study of Working Caregivers and Employer Health Costs*.

60. Margaret B. Neal and others, *Balancing Work and Caregiving for Children, Adults, and Elders* (Newbury Park, Calif.: Sage, 1993); Urie Bronfenbrenner and others, *The State of Americans: This Generation and the Next* (New York: Free Press, 1996); J. L. Gibeau, J. W. Anastas, and P. J. Larson, "Breadwinners, Caregivers, and Employers: New Alliances in an Aging America," *Employee Benefits Journal* 12, no. 3 (1987): 6–10; Andrew E. Scharlach, "Caregiving and Employment: Competing or Complementary Roles?" *Gerontologist* 34, no. 3 (1994): 378–85.

61. Evercare, *Family Caregivers—What They Spend, What They Sacrifice* (Minnetonka, Minn.: 2007), p. 21.

62. National Alliance for Caregiving and the National Center for Women and Aging at Brandeis University, *The MetLife Juggling Act Study: Balancing Caregiving with Work and the Costs Involved* (New York: The MetLife Mature Market Institute, 1999).

63. Society for Human Resource Management (SHRM), *2007 Employee Benefits Survey* (Alexandria, Va.: 2007).

64. Ellen Galinsky and James T. Bond, *The Impact of the Recession on Employers* (New York: Families and Work Institute, 2009), p. 7 (www.familiesandwork.org/site/research/reports/Recession2009.pdf).

65. Allarde Dembe and others, "Employer Perceptions of Elder Care Assistance Programs," *Journal of Workplace Behavioral Health* 23, no. 4 (2008): 360.

66. SHRM, *2007 Employee Benefits Survey* (see note 82).

67. J. L. Glass and A. Finley, "Coverage and Effectiveness of Family Responsive Workplace Policies," *Human Resources Management Review* 12, no. 3 (Autumn 2002): 313–37.

68. Bond, *The National Study of Employers*.

69. Ellen Galinsky, Dana Friedman, and C. Hernandez, *The Corporate Reference Guide to Work–Family Programs* (New York: Families and Work Institute, 1991).

70. Tamara Haraven, "The Changing Patterns of Family Life as They Affect the Aged," *Families and Older Persons: Policy Research and Practice,* edited by G. K. Maddox, I. C. Siegler, and D. G. Blazer (Durham, N.C.: Duke University Center for the Study of Aging and Human Development, 1980), pp. 31–41.

71. Nancy Folbre, *The Invisible Heart* (New York: The New Press, 2001), p. 102.

72. Centers for Medicare and Medicaid Services, "National Health Accounts" (http://cms.hhs.gov/statistics/nhe).

73. Centers for Medicare and Medicaid Services, "National Health Accounts" (http://cms.hhs.gov/statistics/nhe).

74. Commission on Leave, *A Workable Balance: A Report to Congress on Family and Medical Leave Policies* (Washington: U.S. Department of Labor, May 1996).

75. Jane Waldfogel, "Family and Medical Leave: Evidence from the 2000 Surveys," *Monthly Labor Review* 124, no. 9 (September 2001): 17–23.

76. Stephanie Whittier, Andrew Scharlach, and Teresa S. Dal Santo, "Availability of Caregiver Support Services: Implications for Implementation of the National Family Caregiver Support Program," *Journal of Aging and Social Policy* 17, no. 1 (2005): 45–62.

Social Problems Related to Health and the Health-Care System

Elba L. Saavedra

Courtesy of Shannon Kathleen
Jaramillo, University of New Mexico.

Elba L. Saavedra, PhD, is the director of the Comadre a Comadre program, University of New Mexico, College of Education, Department of Health, Exercise & Sports Sciences, Health Education program.

What are the history and mission of the Comadre a Comadre [Friend to Friend] program?

I co-created the Comadre a Comadre program along with six Hispanic/Latina breast cancer survivors in 2003. Our mission is to empower the lives of Hispanic/Latina women and their loved ones through advocacy, education, information, resources, and support about breast health and breast cancer. In the Hispanic/Latina community, a *comadre* is a close and supportive female friend; this bond can be as strong as family. The Comadre program integrates traditional Hispanic/Latino cultural values such as the importance of family and spirituality as part of a community-based culturally and linguistically competent intervention. We offer patient navigation, peer support and case management to assist Hispanic/Latina woman who have been diagnosed with breast cancer, need free or low-cost mammograms, or need assistance with medical appointments. We do this through a racially and ethnically diverse network of breast cancer survivors who are culturally and linguistically competent to provide support to women and their loved ones during a time of great stress. The

Comadre program is rooted in the principles of *community-based participatory research* methodology. We emphasize shared decision-making processes, seeking input from peer survivors, staff, and students alike.

What are your main duties as a program director?

My duties as director involve a variety of administrative functions overseeing the day-to-day activities of the Comadre program. This includes monitoring our program's implementation, goals, and objectives and ensuring that we are accomplishing them in a timely fashion. I also prepare grant applications and conduct analysis on data collected through the program. I use the analysis to write reports on program outcomes to our funding sponsors. I also oversee staff meetings and volunteer training and provide mentorship for student interns who conduct their practicum with our Comadre Program.

Why is there a need to reach out to Latinas, in particular?

As an ethnic group, Hispanic/Latina women have lower rates of mammography utilization.

When they receive abnormal screening results or discover breast abnormalities on their own, their follow-up care is more likely to be delayed, negatively affecting their health outcomes. Hispanic women are also more likely to be diagnosed with the types of tumors that are more difficult to treat. Yet even when their age, stage of cancer, and tumor characteristics are similar, Hispanic women are still more likely to die from breast cancer compared to non-Hispanic white women. What contributes to these disparities in outcomes? Researchers point to differences in access to health care (both prevention and treatment). Intervention programs, like ours, that follow patients throughout treatment in order to enhance communication between the surgeon, oncologist, and patient have been shown to reduce disparities in breast cancer care.[1]

How did you first become interested in advocating for underserved populations in the area of health?

I arrived from Puerto Rico when I was five years old, speaking only Spanish and later becoming the interpreter for my parents. Six years later, I experienced the devastating loss of my father to medical negligence at a local county hospital. Still etched in my mind is the horror I felt watching my mother grabbing the physician's necktie and shaking him, yelling, "You killed my husband!" in her broken English as he broke the news to her. The death of my father changed my life forever, as I came to realize the role that injustice would play in my life. I was awakened to the realities of our lives as Puerto Ricans in New York and in the United States.

Later, at 17 years old, I became involved in community activism, wanting to change the living conditions in my South Bronx, New York City, neighborhood. I took part in beautification projects (like cleaning up a dilapidated empty lot, where children played amidst broken glass, adorning a nearby wall with a freshly painted mural) and tenant and block organizing (helping push slumlords to make housing repairs). At 19 years old, I moved away from home and worked

at a shoe factory where I encountered poor safety practices. I led efforts to unionize workers at the factory. These experiences drove me to be an agent of change, seeking improvements especially in the area of health-care access to good patient care for Hispanic/Latinas with breast cancer.

I know first-hand what it feels like to be overwhelmed with decisions about treatment. I know first-hand the importance of advocacy. For this reason, Comadre a Comadre's mission is deeply personal. Not only did I experience the devastating loss of my father through medical negligence, perhaps due to lack of medical interpretation, but I would myself later become a caregiver and patient advocate to my mother, my brother, and my sister—all of whom were diagnosed with cancer.

Who was your inspiration?

My mother was a tremendous role model for self-advocacy. She supported our involvement for change though she often feared what was to become of us. Suddenly widowed at the age of 50, she continued to provide for my siblings and me through her hard work.

What strategies do you find are most successful in enacting social change?

Change needs to come from within the community, or in the case of the work I do, the change or program or intervention must truly be derived from the survivors themselves. I try to "make change *with*" and not "do change *to*." The specific strategies also need to be derived or flow from a collective process. Strategies include:

1. Pay attention to what has been done before to enact that change—what can be learned from what has come before? Do we reinvent the wheel or enhance?
2. Build partnerships and collaborate with others from the start.
3. Acknowledge that power imbalances exist and that in order to build trust, egos need to be left at the door. This involves establishing ground

rules so that everyone has an equal voice and feels safe using it. As members of communities of color who have been marginalized, this is absolutely critical. A place must be made at the table for *all* who are participating.

4. Strive to be inclusive of other issues. While efforts may require that you stay somewhat focused on one driving issue, people experience a host of related issues to which activists should be attentive.

Change is most gratifying and empowering when it is imbued with a collective voice. I grew up listening to my mother recite her favorite "*dicho*" [saying]: "*en la union esta la fuerza*"—"in unity there is strength." I live by that dicho!

What are the major challenges activists and advocates in your field face?

One of the challenges is the lack of experience among advocacy groups or community-based groups to commit to working together in a collaborative manner. This includes a willingness to share resources among groups and to be aware that we are stronger when we are united than when we stand alone.

What are major misconceptions the public has about activism in general and in your area of advocacy, specifically?

Misconceptions that exist have to do with relegating activism to the act of "one" individual instead of the strengths of a cohesive group or coalition. In my area of advocacy, health-care system change, a misconception that patients and families and health advocates may have is that they can't enact change from within. But health-care administrators can be open to change, and when patients and their families are given that place at the table, they are well positioned to enact change within the health-care system.

What would you consider to be your greatest successes as an activist (in your current area of activism)?

It has been most rewarding, as an activist, to witness the growth of our program over the past 10 years. Breast cancer survivors in our program have moved beyond the role of "passive patients" to both actively influencing their own health care and changing the realities of care for other women with breast cancer. Survivors in our program now serve as role models and supporters for the community of women experiencing the same health challenges. The peer survivors teach other women about breast health, they serve on advisory councils, they provide input on research and have become leaders in their community. For me, my personal success has been my commitment to assisting my own family, as the only college graduate, and despite all the financial hardships I faced. I became that "voice" for my own family members as they interfaced with the health-care system. Finally, I am most proud of my own "self-advocacy"—reaching the highest level of educational attainment by earning my doctorate. With that I kept my promise to my father—to become educated in this country.

Why should students get involved in the work that you do?

Students who intern and volunteer with our Comadre Program learn a lot about community engagement and especially advocacy in the health-care system. They learn about the challenges that people face and how structural barriers make change challenging to accomplish. Students become sensitized to the social determinants of health. They see how food and housing insecurity and inadequate transportation—even not having enough gasoline—become seemingly insurmountable barriers to treatment completion. When students work shoulder to shoulder with peer survivors or community health-care workers, observing factors such as low literacy, lack of health literacy, absence of language interpretation, and limited medical insurance for immigrant patients with cancer, they learn how to develop effective strategies for change.

NOTES

1. American Cancer Society. Cancer Facts & Figures for Hispanics/Latinos 2012–2014. Atlanta: American Cancer Society, 2012.

They've Got a Pill for That: The Medicalization of Society

STEPHANIE MEDLEY-RATH

If you watch TV, you know that there are more and more illnesses and accompanying medications being advertised to consumers. Although seemingly inconsequential, Medley-Rath argues that this is evidence of the medicalization of society, or the interpretation of behavior through the lens of medicine. Medicalization can lead to increased medical intervention into our daily lives (in the form of more doctors' visit, prescriptions, and unnecessary tests), with possible negative outcomes for the patient and larger society. Medley-Rath argues that although demedicalization can be challenging, there are routes that individuals and the society can take to reduce the medicalization of our culture.

Introduction

Medicalization refers to how we interpret social behavior through the lens of medicine, regardless of medical necessity. Medicalization has some benefits, such as promoting access to resources (e.g., insurance coverage, school accommodations), reducing stigma by implying a condition is out of a person's control (e.g., mental illness explained by a chemical imbalance of the brain), and promoting harm reduction (e.g., needle-exchange programs for heroin users). Moreover, medicalization provides an explanation and treatment options for people who are suffering—that is, providing relief by acknowledging their complaints. Yet, many people argue that medicalization is, instead, a social problem. Social problems are phenomena that at least some people (i.e., claims makers) argue are

harmful to the well-being of society. Opponents of medicalization argue that the boundaries of what is a medical matter are expanding, so that more challenges of everyday life are treated medically. Further, medicalization occurs through increasing levels of medical intervention regardless of increasing levels of medical need.

Medicalization achieves social problem status when medical intervention occurs regardless of medical need and causes harm to members of society. Critics of medicalization point out that there are several harmful consequences of medicalization, including narrowing the boundaries of what is considered "normal," increased medical interventions providing minimal benefits and occasional harms, and recommending individual rather than structural solutions for large-scale problems. In this reading, we will explore how

Original to *Focus on Social Problems: A Contemporary Reader.*

medicalization works using examples such as erectile dysfunction and attention deficit hyperactivity disorder (ADHD). Keep in mind that it is beyond the scope of this reading to assess the validity of a medical designation for any condition considered.

Claims-Making

For a social phenomenon or complaint to become medicalized, someone must make the claim that a medical solution exists or that more medical intervention is necessary—primarily through using medicalized language to describe the complaint. These claims makers (Best, 2013) or agents of medicalization (Conrad and Leiter, 2004) include doctors, patients, pharmaceutical companies, social movement organizations, and potential patients, among others.

Claims-making is used to promote conditions as legitimate medical problems. For instance, pharmaceutical companies advertise diseases and conditions directly to consumers. This advertising encourages potential patients to ask their doctor about the promoted drug to treat their problems and complaints (see Conrad, 2007). In 1997, the Food and Drug Administration weakened guidelines regarding direct-to-consumer advertising so that pharmaceutical companies could begin advertising directly to consumers. Direct-to-consumer advertising led to the runaway success of Viagra, which was approved to treat erectile dysfunction in 1998. Viagra was originally intended to treat angina (chest pains associated with heart disease), yet produced erections as an unintended side effect. The side effect's discovery led to Pfizer Pharmaceuticals redefining erectile dysfunction from an individual psychological issue or a symptom of aging to a medical condition that a pill (i.e., Viagra) would fix (Loe, 2004). Pfizer Pharmaceuticals began marketing this newly defined medical condition and its fix to Americans through direct-to-consumer advertising, targeting men who suffered from erectile dysfunction because of age, prostate cancer, or other medical conditions. The advertising (for Viagra and its competitors) has shifted to market the pill to younger

men who did not meet original diagnostic criteria (a concept called diagnostic expansion). For example, in the early 2000s, thirty-seven-year-old professional baseball player Raphael Palmeiro starred in an advertising campaign for Viagra. When asked about it, he indicated that he had used Viagra, but that he did not need the pill (for erectile dysfunction) (Moore, 2002). Viagra patients now include men who are not suffering from erectile dysfunction, but instead are seeking improved sexual performance more generally (Conrad and Leiter, 2004, 2008; Loe, 2004).

Medicalization rarely happens because of one claims maker's persistence. The medicalization of erectile dysfunction occurred through the collaboration of pharmaceutical companies marketing directly to consumers, potential patients asking their doctors about gaining access to the drugs, doctors writing prescriptions, and the willingness of insurance companies to pay for treatment (see Frances, 2013; Watters, 2010). In recent years, prescriptions for Viagra (and other erectile dysfunction drugs) have declined in the United States because of the limited coverage provided by insurance for these drugs. James (2011) reports that "many insurance companies don't cover these so-called 'lifestyle drugs,' and those that do only pay for four pills a month. Out of pocket, they cost $12 to $15 a tablet." Similarly, Medicare no longer covers their cost (Berenson, 2005). Insurance companies limiting coverage combined with consumer disenchantment of these products led to a decrease in the number of prescriptions written (James, 2011). Claims-making by one group (e.g., pharmaceutical companies) may be challenged by other groups (e.g., insurance companies). As the case of erectile dysfunction shows, diagnostic expansion may be pursued to maintain profit. Diagnostic expansion, however, comes at the cost of redefining normal.

Redefining Normal

Medicalization involves extending the boundaries regarding the types of behavior requiring medical treatment—a process known as "diagnostic expansion." When this occurs, a narrower range of behaviors and conditions are deemed "normal." According to Conrad (2007), the diagnostic criteria are expanded in such a way that more people (previously deemed "healthy" or "normal") are inevitably diagnosed with medical conditions. For example, attention deficit disorder expanded to include hyperactivity (i.e., ADHD)—both childhood disorders. The diagnosis broadened yet again to include adults (a disorder known as adult ADHD). Behavior that was once within the bounds of normality becomes medicalized and normal variation among humans begins to be erased with a pill (see Frances, 2013).

Consider the example of idiopathic short stature (ISS), which illustrates how normal changes. ISS diagnosis is based on a person's height deviating too far below the norm. Children who are part of the shortest 1.2 percent of children with ISS can be treated with synthetic human growth hormones (Conrad, 2007). As more children receive treatment for ISS, the entire population of children gets taller, on average, and the statistical cutoff point for diagnosis moves upward—meaning what counts as "too short" changes, and those kids previously considered normal become regarded as too short and offered treatment (some of which includes possible harmful side effects). In general, as the boundaries of normality further constrict, there is more pressure for people to conform to a narrower range of acceptability, thereby decreasing "diversity in society" (Conrad, 2007:95). Pharmaceutical companies have become successful at "turning difference into illness" (Frances, 2013:280) and then proposing possible treatments. But it's not just the fault of pharmaceutical companies. This vicious cycle is perpetuated by consumers as well, who then seek medical intervention to achieve normal.

Perhaps the most troubling aspect of the narrowing of normal is that American medical interpretations of mental disorders are being inappropriately applied cross-culturally (Watters, 2010). For example, Japan went from not having a word for depression to a doubling of the rates of depression diagnoses between 1999 and 2008 (Luhrmann, 2014) coinciding with GlaxoSmith-Kline's marketing push for antidepressant drugs in Japan (Watters, 2010). In the Middle East, signs of happiness and sadness differ and mental illness has long been addressed with traditional and religious healers along with broader family support (Sayar and Kose, 2012). Sayar and Kose (2012) caution against applying Western models of psychiatric care cross-culturally because both the meaning and the treatment of mental illness vary across cultures. Critics (see Watters, 2010) contend that pushing the same medical model globally runs the risk of decreasing the diversity among humanity, as well as exporting potentially harmful overreliance on medicine to solve problems.

What's the Harm?

The market for antidepressants has grown overseas and in the United States, with increasing numbers of youth diagnosed, for example, with bipolar disorder (Moreno et al., 2007). Zito and colleagues (2003:17) found that between 1987 and 1996, the use of psychotropic medications among youth "increased 2- to 3-fold." Although these prescriptions undoubtedly help some patients, they are not without consequences. Since 2004, selective serotonin reuptake inhibitors or SSRIs (i.e., antidepressants) include a "black box" warning when prescribed to patients twenty-five and younger because they produce a higher risk of suicidal thinking and behavior among this age group (National Institute of Mental Health, n.d.). Research suggests that the black box warning contributed to a decline in the number of SSRI prescriptions for children (Mitchell et al., 2014). Further, Sharpe (2012) points out that prescribing antidepressants during this time of life coincides with and may impact teens' developing sense of self and identity. As these teenagers reach adulthood, they may be less willing to try living without antidepressants, even if their symptoms have declined, because they have little idea what that might actually mean. The antidepressant becomes the safer bet even if it is not the cause of declining depressive symptoms (see Whitaker, 2010).

Medicalization has harmful side effects and is economically costly (Conrad et al., 2010; Hinshaw and Scheffler, 2014b). For example, annual cancer screenings treat people like potential patients, yet research indicates that the costs and risks of some of these screenings outweigh the benefits (Brawley, 2012a). High rates of false positives result in invasive follow-up testing and treatment, costing both time and money and putting healthy people at risk. This, in part, explains the rational for the U.S. Preventive Services Task Force's 2009 statement recommending fewer mammograms for women and basing their use on individual risk factors (see Pace and Keating, 2014). One in five breast cancers is overdiagnosed (i.e., will never cause disease or death) but is treated with surgery or radiation, with possible serious side effects (Jin, 2014). Perhaps most troubling is that a false positive can cause undue emotional distress because the person now comes to identify falsely as a cancer patient.

In addition to the emotional and physical costs of overdiagnosis and false positives, Kale and colleagues (2011) have found that approximately $6.8 billion is spent each year on unnecessary medical services. These services account for 2.7 percent of Medicare spending (Schwartz et al., 2014). Further, the side effects of one medical intervention can lead to more medical interventions. For instance, the pharmaceutical company Eli Lilly developed Zyprexa to treat manic episodes caused by SSRIs such as Prozac (another Eli Lilly product), which is used to treat depression (Whitaker, 2010).

Medicalization is big business. A majority of doctors (84 percent as of 2009) have financial ties with a drug or medical device company, and payments to doctors were valued at $1.4 billion in 2013 (Ornstein et al., 2014). The pharmaceutical industry has higher profit margins—ranging from 10 to 43 percent in 2013—than other industries (Anderson, 2014). A substantial amount of money stands to be made through the medicalization of more conditions, especially those with the best potential for profit. Pedrique and colleagues (2013) found that from 2000 to 2011 only 4 percent of new therapeutic products were intended to treat (low-profit) neglected diseases, such as malaria and Ebola. The medicalization of high-profit conditions and behaviors comes at the cost of neglecting research on treating, preventing, and curing deadly diseases around the world.

Proponents of medicalization claim that increased medical intervention reduces stigma among sufferers. Direct-to-consumer advertising is argued as having an educational benefit by emphasizing the causes and symptoms of a condition, which is theorized to reduce stigma and to educate the population. But research has shown that having an understanding of the biological underpinnings of a disease or condition does not reduce stigma. Payton and Thoits (2011) found that the introduction of direct-to-consumer advertising did not reduce the stigma of having a mental illness for which pharmaceutical treatments were heavily advertised (i.e., depression) compared to a mental illness that was not advertised (i.e., schizophrenia). In other words, exposure to a medical explanation of depression did nothing, comparatively, to reduce the stigma associated with the illness.

Medicalization, Social Control, and Individualized Solutions

In addition to the costs of medicalization, it is important to understand how medicalization expands the reach of medical social control as increasing amounts of authority are given to medical experts (Conrad, 1979, 1992, 2007). Conrad (1979:2) writes, "medical social control of deviant behavior is usually a variant of medical intervention that seeks to eliminate, modify, isolate or regulate behavior, socially defined as deviant, with medical means and in the name of health." Medicalizing a behavior or complaint suggests that it resides within the individual rather than in the social structure (Conrad, 2007). Critics of medicalization contend that ADHD is an example of medicalizing the problem behaviors of students rather than a medical condition with a known etiology (see Saul, 2014). In the case of ADHD, the problem of a child who does not behave as expected in the classroom now belongs to the physician rather than the teacher or parent. The child's problem behavior and a teacher's classroom management are then controlled by medical means (i.e., pharmaceutical drugs).

ADHD rates (4 percent of adults and 11 percent of children [Saul, 2014]) may have more to do with structural issues than an increase in true cases of ADHD because an ADHD diagnosis is both biologically and socially determined (Bowden, 2013). Even defining ADHD as a diagnosis is misleading because it is more accurately a constellation of symptoms (Saul, 2014) and parents and teachers do not consistently agree on the presence or absence of ADHD symptoms (Murray et al., 2007).

An ADHD diagnosis may be treating real biological symptoms or it may be making a student fit better into the expectations of school, making the medication use an enhancement rather than treatment of a medical condition (see Conrad, 2007). Some children are prescribed ADHD medications only during the school week and not at home (Hruska, 2012), suggesting that environment plays a major role. Doctors admit to prescribing ADHD drugs to "boost academic performance," rather than because of medical need (Schwartz, 2012). In particular, poorer children in underfunded schools are prescribed drugs to treat ADHD in lieu of adequately funding schools to help these students succeed academically (Schwartz, 2012; see also Hinshaw and Scheffler, 2014a).

Even more disturbing is that ADHD diagnosis rates correlate with the implementation of education policies that penalize schools for not meeting standardized testing goals (e.g., No Child Left Behind) (Hinshaw and Scheffler, 2014b). No Child Left Behind was signed into law in 2002. Since then, sales of stimulants used to treat ADHD have quintupled (Schwartz, 2013). This indicates that there is a belief that the social problem of "failing schools" is at least partially caused by children's medical conditions rather than problems within the institution. The problems of schools can then be resolved through medical intervention of individual students

rather than through adequate funding and support for educational institutions and the people they serve.

Is Demedicalization Possible?

It appears that an ever-growing number of medical solutions exist for complaints of everyday living (e.g., erectile dysfunction) and social problems (e.g., rising educational expectations while decreasing government funding for education). Medicalization, however, is not inevitable. Once a complaint is medicalized, it can be demedicalized; that is, it is "no longer defined in medical terms and the involvement of medical personnel is no longer deemed appropriate" (Conrad, 2007:97).

Physicians and their professional organizations (e.g., the American Medical Association), among other health-care workers, have long promoted preventative medicine via annual exams and screenings regardless of our own perception of illness (Frances, 2013). The increasing sophistication of technology has encouraged us to put a great deal of trust in its ability to prevent disease, and we rely on this technology to manage risk (Sulik, 2011). Most of us have long been trained to imagine ourselves as potential patients and are reminded of this during reoccurring physicals or screenings (e.g., Pap test, colonoscopies).

Few women look forward to their annual Pap test because of its invasiveness (cells are scraped from the cervix) and potentially alarming result of a cancer diagnosis. The Pap test screens for cervical cancer—a disease that was once the deadliest form of cancer for women (Brawley, 2012b). But is there such a thing as too much screening? In the case of cervical cancer screening, yes. Brawley (2012b) states that women under age twenty-one, for example, should not be screened:

> Many sexually active women under 21 will develop a human papillomavirus infection, or HPV, which can lead to pre-cancerous lesions. And when doctors see those lesions on a Pap test, they want to treat them. Yet nearly all of those lesions will disappear on

their own without residual effects. And those that do not are easily treated years later. Treating them as soon as they're spotted can lead to cervical incompetence and miscarriage down the road.

In other words, most lesions are nothing to worry about, but overtreatment can cause harm. Today, depending on a woman's age and whether she receives a human papillomavirus test, it is recommended that she receive a Pap test every three to five years (Brawley, 2012b). Although revised cancer screening recommendations do not eliminate medical social control, they do suggest the possibility of demedicalization.

The model case of demedicalization is homosexuality (Conrad, 2007). Homosexuality was initially medicalized in an effort to provide protection to gays and lesbians from punitive legal sanctions (Conrad and Angell, 2004). Medical treatment for homosexuality included electroshock aversion therapy, psychoanalysis, and hormone treatment (Smith et al., 2004). Medicalizing homosexuality reduced the harm directed to gays and lesbians by the legal system, but introduced new and reinforced existing harms by the mental health community. For example, mental health professionals have used conversion therapy under the premise that a person can change his or her sexual orientation. In 1973, homosexuality was declassified as a mental illness in the *DSM-II*. Today, the American Psychological Association condemns the practice of conversion or reparative therapy on the grounds that it causes harm and is not grounded in science (APA Task Force on Appropriate Therapeutic Responses to Sexual Orientation, 2009). Complete demedicalization may be possible and certainly desirable for some complaints, whereas partial demedicalization may be more appropriate for other features of our lives (e.g., cancer prevention).

Conclusion

Medicalization is both a positive and a negative force in our lives. Medicalization means that an individual can gain access to resources used to

treat or manage complaints, along with having socially acceptable language to explain the complaint. Moreover, medicalization promotes harm reduction caused by the complaint. Yet many people consider medicalization itself a social problem. A complaint that is medicalized may not really be a medical matter, thereby expanding medical social control. The medical solution may provide few, if any, benefits (e.g., reducing stigma), with high emotional and financial costs and even physical harm. Medicalization narrows what is accepted as normal human variation.

The tendency to medicalize social phenomena should be viewed with a critical eye. The costs of medicalizing a particular issue should be carefully weighed against any benefits of medicalization. In particular, we should ask the following questions: (1) is medicalization necessary, (2) does medicalization further narrow what it means to be normal, (3) do the benefits of the treatment outweigh any harms of the treatment, and (4) are there changes that could be made at the structural level that could replace the need of medicalizing at the individual level? As the quest for profit and quick fixes encourages more aspects of everyday life to become medicalized, it is important to remember that it is not inevitable and demedicalization is possible.

REFERENCES

Anderson, Richard. 2014. "Pharmaceutical Industry Gets High on Fat Profits." *BBC News*, November 6. Retrieved March 19, 2015. http://www.bbc.com/news/business-28212223/.

APA Task Force on Appropriate Therapeutic Responses to Sexual Orientation. 2009. Report of the Task Force on Appropriate Therapeutic Responses to Sexual Orientation. Washington, DC: American Psychological Association. Retrieved June 23, 2014. http://www.apa.org/pi/lgbt/resources/therapeutic-response.pdf/.

Berenson, Alex. 2005. "Sales of Impotence Drugs Fall, Defying Expectations." *The New York Times*, December 4. Retrieved February 11, 2015. http://www.nytimes.com/2005/12/04/business/yourmoney/04impotence.html/.

Best, Joel. 2013. *Social Problems*. 2nd ed. New York: Norton.

Bowden, Gregory. 2013. "The Merit of Sociological Accounts of Disorder: The Attention-Deficit Hyperactivity Disorder Case." *Health* 18(4):422–438.

Brawley, Otis. 2012a. "Value of Mass Prostate Cancer Screenings Questioned." *CNN*, March 14. Retrieved June 3, 2014. http://www.cnn.com/2012/03/14/health/brawley-prostate-cancer-screenings/.

Brawley, Otis. 2012b. "No More Annual Pap Smear: New Cervical Cancer Screening Guidelines." *CNN*, March 15. Retrieved April 25, 2014. http://www.cnn.com/2012/03/14/health/brawley-cervical-cancer-screenings/index.html/.

Conrad, Peter. 1979. "Types of Medical Social Control." *Sociology of Health and Illness* 1(1):1–11.

Conrad, Peter. 1992. "Medicalization and Social Control." *Annual Review of Sociology* 18:209–232.

Conrad, Peter. 2007. *The Medicalization of Society: On the Transformation of Human Conditions into Treatable Disorders*. Baltimore: Johns Hopkins University Press.

Conrad, Peter, and Alison Angell. 2004. "Homosexuality and Remedicalization." *Society* 41(5):32–39.

Conrad, Peter, and Valerie Leiter. 2004. "Medicalization, Markets and Consumers." *Journal of Health and Social Behavior* 45:158–176.

Conrad, Peter, and Valerie Leiter. 2008. "From Lydia Pinkham to Queen Levitra: Direct-to-Consumer Advertising and Medicalisation." *Sociology of Health & Illness* 30(6):825–838.

Conrad, Peter, Thomas Mackie, and Ateev Mehrotra. 2010. "Estimating the Costs of Medicalization." *Social Science & Medicine* 70(12):1943–1947.

Frances, Allen. 2013. *Saving Normal: An Insider's Revolt against Out-of-Control Psychiatric Diagnosis, DSM-5, Big Pharma, and the Medicalization of Ordinary Life*. New York: Morrow.

Hinshaw, Stephen P., and Richard M. Scheffler. 2014a. "Expand Pre-K, Not A.D.H.D." *New York Times*, February 23. Retrieved April 28, 2014. http://www.nytimes.com/2014/02/24/opinion/expand-pre-k-not-adhd.html/.

Hinshaw, Stephen P., and Richard M. Scheffler. 2014b. *The ADHD Explosion: Myths, Medication, Money, and Today's Push for Performance*. New York: Oxford University Press.

Hruska, Bronwen. 2012. "Raising the Ritalin Generation." *The New York Times*, August 18th. http://www.nytimes.com/2012/08/19/opinion/sunday/raising-the-ritalin-generation.html

James, Susan Donaldson. 2011. "Honeymoon with Viagra® Could Be Over, Say Doctors." *ABC News*, June 9. Retrieved February 11, 2015. http://abcnews.go.com/Health/Viagra®-prescription-sales-sexual-expectations/story?id=13794726/.

Jin, Jill. 2014. "Breast Cancer Screening: Benefits and Harms." *Journal of the American Medical Association* 312(23):2585.

Kale, Minal, Tara F. Bishop, Alex D. Federman, and Salomeh Keyhani. 2011. "'Top 5' Lists Top $5 Billion FREE." *Archives of Internal Medicine* 171(20):1858–1859.

Loe, Meika. 2004. *The Rise of Viagra®: How the Little Blue Pill Changed Sex in America*. New York: New York University Press.

Luhrmann, T. M. 2014. "Is the World More Depressed?" *New York Times*, March 24. Retrieved April 30, 2014. http://www.nytimes.com/2014/03/25/opinion/a-great-depression.html/.

Mitchell, Ann M., Marilyn A. Davies, Christine Cassesse, and Ryan Curran. 2014. "Antidepressant Use in Children, Adolescents, and Young Adults: 10 Years after the Food and Drug Administration Black Box Warning." *The Journal of Nurse Practitioners* 10(3):149–156.

Moore, Jim. 2002. "Hard Topic, Easy Money; Palmeiro Cashes in on Viagra." *Seattle Post-Intelligencer*, August 1. Retrieved March 19, 2015. http://www.seattlepi.com/news/article/Hard-topic-easy-money-Palmeiro-cashes-in-on-1092712.php/.

Moreno, Carmen, Gonzalo Laje, Carlos Blanco, Huiping Jiang, Andrew B. Schmidt, and Mark Olfson. 2007. "National Trends in the Outpatient Diagnosis and Treatment of Bipolar Disorder in Youth." *Archives of General Psychology* 64(9):1032–1039.

Murray, Desiree W., Scott H. Kollins, Kristina K. Hardy, Howard B. Abikoff, James M. Swanson, Charles Cunningham, Benedetto Vitiello, Mark A. Riddle, Mark Davies, Laurence L. Greenhill, James T. McCracken, James J. McGough, Kelly Posner, Anne M. Skrobala, Tim Wigal, Sharon Wigal, Jaswinder K.

Ghuman, and Shirley Z. Chuang. 2007. "Parent versus Teacher Ratings of Attention-Deficit/Hyperactivity Disorder Symptoms in the Preschoolers with Attention-Deficit/Hyperactivity Disorder Treatment Study (PATS)." *Journal of Child and Adolescent Psychopharmacology* 17(5):605–619.

National Institute of Mental Health. n.d. "Antidepressant Medications for Children and Adolescents: Information for Parents and Caregivers." Retrieved February 19, 2015. http://www.nimh.nih.gov/health/topics/child-and-adolescent-mental-health/antidepressant-medications-for-children-and-adolescents-information-for-parents-and-caregivers.shtml/.

Ornstein, Charles, Eric Sagara, and Ryann Grochowski Jones. 2014. "What We've Learned From Four Years of Diving into Dollars for Docs." *ProPublica*. http://www.propublica.org/article/what-weve-learned-from-four-years-of-diving-into-dollars-for-docs

Pace, Lydia E., and Nancy L. Keating. 2014. "A Systematic Assessment of Benefits and Risks to Guide Breast Cancer Screening Decisions." *JAMA: The Journal of the American Medical Association* 311(13):1327–1335.

Payton, Andrew R., and Peggy A. Thoits. 2011. "Medicalization, Direct-to-Consumer Advertising, and Mental Illness Stigma." *Society and Mental Health* 1(1):55–70.

Pedrique, Belen, Nathalie Strub-Wourgaft, Claudette Some, Piero Olliaro, Patrice Trouiller, Nathan Ford, Benard Pécoul, and Jean-Hervé Bradol. 2013. "The Drug and Vaccine Landscape for Neglected Diseases (2000–11): A Systematic Assessment." *The Lancet* 1:e371–379.

Saul, Richard. 2014. *ADHD Does Not Exist: The Truth about Attention Deficit and Hyperactivity Disorder*. New York: Harper Wave.

Sayar, Kemal, and Samet Kose. 2012. "Psychopathology and Depression in the Middle East." *Journal of Mood Disorders* 2(1):21–27.

Schwartz, Aaron L., Bruce E. Landon, Adam G. Elshaug, Michael E. Chernew, and Michael McWilliams. 2014. "Measuring Low-Value Care in Medicare." *JAMA Internal Medicine* 1101.

Schwartz, Alan. 2012. "Attention Disorder or Not, Pills to Help in School." *New York Times*, October 9. Retrieved April 28, 2014. http://www.nytimes.com/2012/10/09/health/attention-disorder-or-not-children-prescribed-pills-to-help-in-school.html?/.

Schwartz, Alan. 2013. "The Selling of Attention Deficit Disorder." *New York Times*, December 14. Retrieved March 19, 2015. http://www.nytimes.com/2013/12/15/health/the-selling-of-attention-deficit-disorder.html/.

Sharpe, Katherine. 2012. *Coming of Age on Zoloft: How Antidepressants Cheered Us Up, Let Us Down, and Changed Who We Are*. New York: Harper Perennial.

Smith, Glenn, Annie Bartlett, and Michael King. 2004. "Treatments of Homosexuality in Britain Since the 1950s—An Oral History: The Experience of Patients." *British Medical Journal* 328:429. Retrieved June 23, 2014. http://www.bmj.com/content/328/7437/427/.

Sulik, Gayle A. 2011. "'Our Diagnoses, Our Selves': The Rise of the Technoscientific Illness Identity." *Sociology Compass* 5(6):463–477.

Watters, Ethan. 2010. *Crazy Like Us: The Globalization of the American Psyche*. New York: Free Press.

Whitaker, Robert. 2010. *Anatomy of an Epidemic: Magic Bullets, Psychiatric Drugs, and the Astonishing Rise of Mental Illness in America*. New York: Broadway Books.

Zito, Julie Magno, Daniel J. Safer, Susan DosReis, James F. Gardner, Laurence Magder, Karen Soeken, Myde Boles, Frances Lynch, and Mark A. Riddle. 2003. "Psychotropic Practice Patterns for Youth: A 10-Year Perspective." *Archives of Pediatric Adolescent Medicine* 157(1):17–25.

Selling Sickness: How Drug Ads Changed Health Care

Alix Spiegel

David Couper went to his doctor after watching a small green creature jump up and down on the nail of an infected toe. For Anne Nissan, a 17-year-old in Prescott, Ariz., the image that stayed with her was of a party. Women were on a roof in a city, pimple-free and laughing, utterly unbothered by the cramps that immobilized her once a month. And then there is Samantha Saveri, a transportation planner in Baltimore. She remembers bunnies and the promise of digestive regularity.

Three different people in three different places were all driven to contact their doctors after watching an ad for a prescription medication on television. Each walked into a doctor's office with a specific request, and walked out with a prescription for exactly the medication he or she desired.

THE RISE OF PRESCRIPTION DRUGS IN AMERICA

Prescription drug spending is the third most expensive cost in our health care system. And spending seems to grow larger every year. Just last year, the average American got 12 prescriptions a year, as compared with 1992, when Americans got an average of seven prescriptions. In a decade and a half, the use of prescription medication went up 71 percent. This has added about $180 billion to our medical spending. While there are more medicines on the market today than in 1992, researchers estimate that around 20 percent of the $180 billion increase has absolutely nothing to do with the number of medications available, or increases in the cost of that medication.

To understand this change, one place to look is Wilder, [Vermont]. There, in a tasteful housing complex on the side of a mountain, is the home of Joe Davis.

Davis is retired now, but in his speech and manner it's easy to hear the breezy salesmanship that made him so successful. Davis was an adman: "I was trained—or I was toilet-trained as we like to say—in packaged goods," Davis says. "General Foods, Procter & Gamble—that kind of thing." Until the 1980s, the kind of people who sold stuff like packaged goods were completely different from the kind of people who sold stuff like prescription drugs. In those days, drugs ads were for doctors, not the public. They were designed by people who worked at these small, technically minded medical advertising companies and targeted this small, technically minded audience. "Nobody had ever thought that these drugs should be or could be advertised to the patients. It was just outside of people's brains," Davis says. "They thought that only doctors could understand the products. They're technical products. They're scientific products."

But it was more than that. There was a fear—shared by doctors and drug companies alike—that advertising drugs directly to consumers could be harmful. Both the drug companies and the doctors worried that even though consumers couldn't really evaluate whether or not a drug was appropriate, they might become convinced by an ad, and pressure their doctor to prescribe it. Not only might doctors end up passing out inappropriate medications, but also, drug ads could disrupt the doctor–patient relationship—a relationship that, at the time, was mostly a one-way street.

Davis tells this story about his own mother, a sophisticated woman whom he found fumbling with a bottle of pills one day. When he asked what she was taking: "'Well,' she said, 'I take a yellow pill, a green pill and a white pill.' I said, 'That's great. What are they for?'"

continues

◼ Continued

His mother had no idea what they were for, Davis says. All she knew was that her doctor had told her to take them. "It was very passive from the patient standpoint," Davis says. "The patient just took whatever orders were given by the doctor."

AN ADVERTISING REVOLUTION

It used to work like this: Doctors decided what to prescribe. Drug companies—through medical advertisers—tried to influence doctors. Patients did what they were told. The only problem, says Davis, was that the system wasn't working out for the drug companies. For them, the system was much too slow. Because doctors exclusively held the keys to the kingdom, drug companies spent enormous amounts of time and money trying to get their attention. To give you a sense, the average doctor got around 3,000 pieces of mail a year from the drug industry, and to break through this noise often took years.

And so Davis, who had previously only sold packaged goods, approached William Castagnoli, the then-president of a large medical advertising company. The two came up with a solution: They would advertise directly to the patient. They'd get the patient to go in and ask the doctor for the drug. "Pull the drug through the system," Davis says with a certain amount of glee. There was only one small problem with this solution: It was almost impossible to do.

In the early 1980s, FDA regulations required that drug ads include both the name of a drug and its purpose, as well as information about all the side effects. But side-effect information often took two or three magazine pages of . . . [fine] print to catalog, and this wouldn't do for a major television campaign. As Castagnoli says, "We couldn't scroll the whole disclosure information over the television screen—OK?"

But then, in 1986, while designing an ad for a new allergy medication called Seldane, Davis hit on a way around the fine print. He checked with the Food and Drug Administration to see if it would be OK. "We didn't give the drug's name, Seldane," he says. "All we said was: 'Your doctor now has treatment which won't make you drowsy. See your doctor.'"

This was one of the very first national direct-to-consumer television ad campaigns. The results were nothing short of astounding. Before the ads, Davis says, Seldane made about $34 million in sales a year, which at the time was considered pretty good. "Our goal was maybe to get this drug up to $100 million in sales. But we went through $100 million," Davis says. "And we said, 'Holy smokes.' And then it went through $300 million. Then $400 million. Then $500 million. $600 [million]! It was unbelievable. We were flabbergasted. And eventually it went to $800 million." Pharmaceutical companies took note.

Today, drug companies spend $4 billion a year on ads to consumers. In 1997, the FDA rules governing pharmaceutical advertising changed, and now companies can name both the drug and what it's for, while only naming the most significant potential side effects. Then, the number of ads really exploded. The Nielsen Co. estimates that there's an average of 80 drug ads every hour of every day on American television. And those ads clearly produce results: "Something like a third of consumers who've seen a drug ad have talked to their doctor about it," says Julie Donohue, a professor of public health at the University of Pittsburgh who is considered a leading expert on this subject." About two-thirds of those have asked for a prescription. And the majority of people who ask for a prescription have that request honored."

Whether the increase in the number of prescription drugs taken is good or bad for patient health is an open question. There's evidence on both sides. What's not up for debate is this: By taking their case to patients instead of doctors, drug companies increased the amount of money we spend on medicine in America.

Paying till It Hurts:
The $2.7 Trillion Medical Bill

ELISABETH ROSENTHAL

Why are medical costs so high in the United States? Using colonoscopies as a case study, Rosenthal explores how inflated price tags for regular procedures are a significant contributor to rising medical costs. The increasing medicalization of these procedures along with attempts from multiple parties to maximize revenue and obscure pricing policies, mask both procedural costs and whether procedures are even medically necessary. Despite what we spend, our health outcomes are no better (and are sometimes worse) than those in other countries where costs are lower.

Deirdre Yapalater's recent colonoscopy at a surgical center near her home here on Long Island went smoothly: she was whisked from pre-op to an operating room where a gastroenterologist, assisted by an anesthesiologist and a nurse, performed the routine cancer screening procedure in less than an hour. The test, which found nothing worrisome, racked up what is likely her most expensive medical bill of the year: $6,385.

That is fairly typical: in Keene, N.H., Matt Meyer's colonoscopy was billed at $7,563.56. Maggie Christ of Chappaqua, N.Y., received $9,142.84 in bills for the procedure. In Durham, N.C., the charges for Curtiss Devereux came to $19,438, which included a polyp removal. While their insurers negotiated down the price, the final tab for each test was more than $3,500.

"Could that be right?" said Ms. Yapalater, stunned by charges on the statement on her dining room table. Although her insurer covered the procedure and she paid nothing, her health care costs still bite: Her premium payments jumped 10 percent last year, and rising co-payments and deductibles are straining the finances of her middle-class family, with its mission-style house in the suburbs and two S.U.V.'s parked outside. "You keep thinking it's free," she said. "We call it free, but of course it's not."

In many other developed countries, a basic colonoscopy costs just a few hundred dollars and certainly well under $1,000. That chasm in price helps explain why the United States is far and away the world leader in medical spending, even though numerous studies have concluded that Americans do not get better care.

Whether directly from their wallets or through insurance policies, Americans pay more for almost every interaction with the medical system. They are typically prescribed more expensive procedures and tests than people in other countries, no matter if those nations operate a private or national health system. A list of drug, scan and procedure prices compiled by the International Federation of Health Plans, a global network of health insurers, found that the United States came out the most costly in all 21 categories—and often by a huge margin.

Americans pay, on average, about four times as much for a hip replacement as patients in Switzerland or France and more than three times as much for a Caesarean section as those in New Zealand or Britain. The average price for Nasonex, a common nasal spray for allergies, is $108 in the United States compared with $21 in Spain. The costs of hospital stays here are about triple those in other developed countries, even though they last no longer, according to a recent report by the Commonwealth Fund, a foundation that studies health policy.

While the United States medical system is famous for drugs costing hundreds of thousands of dollars and heroic care at the end of life, it turns out that a more significant factor in the nation's $2.7 trillion annual health care bill may not be the use of extraordinary services, but the high price tag of ordinary ones. "The U.S. just pays providers of health care much more for everything," said Tom Sackville, chief executive of the health plans federation and a former British health minister.

Colonoscopies offer a compelling case study. They are the most expensive screening test that healthy Americans routinely undergo—and often cost more than childbirth or an appendectomy in most other developed countries. Their numbers have increased many fold over the last 15 years, with data from the Centers for Disease Control and Prevention suggesting that more than 10 million people get them each year, adding up to more than $10 billion in annual costs.

Largely an office procedure when widespread screening was first recommended, colonoscopies have moved into surgery centers—which were created as a step down from costly hospital care but are now often a lucrative step up from doctors' examining rooms—where they are billed like a quasi operation. They are often prescribed and performed more frequently than medical guidelines recommend.

The high price paid for colonoscopies mostly results not from top-notch patient care, according to interviews with health care experts and economists, but from business plans seeking to maximize revenue; haggling between hospitals and insurers that have no relation to the actual costs of performing the procedure; and lobbying, marketing and turf battles among specialists that increase patient fees.

While several cheaper and less invasive tests to screen for colon cancer are recommended as equally effective by the federal government's expert panel on preventive care—and are commonly used in other countries—colonoscopy has become the go-to procedure in the United States. "We've defaulted to by far the most expensive option, without much if any data to support it," said Dr. H. Gilbert Welch, a professor of medicine at the Dartmouth Institute for Health Policy and Clinical Practice.

. . . Hospitals, drug companies, device makers, physicians and other providers can benefit by charging inflated prices, favoring the most costly treatment options and curbing competition that could give patients more, and cheaper, choices. And almost every interaction can be an opportunity to send multiple, often opaque bills with long lists of charges: $100 for the ice pack applied for 10 minutes after a physical therapy session, or $30,000 for the artificial joint implanted in surgery.

The United States spends about 18 percent of its gross domestic product on health care, nearly twice as much as most other developed countries. The Congressional Budget Office has said that if medical costs continue to grow unabated, "total spending on health care would eventually account for all of the country's economic output." And it identified federal spending on government health programs as a primary cause of long-term budget deficits.

While the rise in health care spending in the United States has slowed in the past four years—to about 4 percent annually from about 8 percent—it is still expected to rise faster than the gross domestic product. Aging baby boomers and tens of millions of patients newly insured under the Affordable Care Act are likely to add to the burden.

With health insurance premiums eating up ever more of her flat paycheck, Ms. Yapalater, a customer relations specialist for a small Long Island company, recently decided to forgo physical therapy for an injury sustained during Hurricane Sandy because of high out-of-pocket expenses. She refused a dermatology medication prescribed for her daughter when the pharmacist said the co-payment was $130. "I said, 'That's impossible, I have insurance,'" Ms. Yapalater recalled. "I called the dermatologist and asked for something cheaper, even if it's not as good."

The more than $35,000 annually that Ms. Yapalater and her employer collectively pay in premiums—her share is $15,000—for her family's Oxford Freedom Plan would be more than sufficient to cover their medical needs in most other countries. She and her husband, Jeff, 63, a sales and marketing consultant, have three children in their 20s with good jobs. Everyone in the family exercises, and none has had a serious illness.

Like the Yapalaters, many other Americans have habits or traits that arguably could put the nation at the low end of the medical cost spectrum. Patients in the United States make fewer doctors' visits and have fewer hospital stays than citizens of many other developed countries, according to the Commonwealth Fund report. People in Japan get more CT scans. People in Germany, Switzerland and Britain have more frequent hip replacements. The American population is younger and has fewer smokers than those in most other developed countries. Pushing costs in the other direction, though, is that the United States has relatively high rates of obesity and limited access to routine care for the poor.

A major factor behind the high costs is that the United States, unique among industrialized nations, does not generally regulate or intervene in medical pricing, aside from setting payment rates for Medicare and Medicaid, the government programs for older people and the poor. Many other countries deliver health care on a private fee-for-service basis, as does much of the American health care system, but they set rates as if health care were a public utility or negotiate fees with providers and insurers nationwide, for example.

"In the U.S., we like to consider health care a free market," said Dr. David Blumenthal, president of the Commonwealth Fund and a former adviser to President Obama. "But it is a very weird market, riddled with market failures."

Consider this:

Consumers, the patients, do not see prices until after a service is provided, if they see them at all. And there is little quality data on hospitals and doctors to help determine good value, aside from surveys conducted by popular Web sites and magazines. Patients with insurance pay a tiny fraction of the bill, providing scant disincentive for spending.

Even doctors often do not know the costs of the tests and procedures they prescribe. When Dr. Michael Collins, an internist in East Hartford, Conn., called the hospital that he is affiliated with to price lab tests and a colonoscopy, he could not get an answer. "It's impossible for me to think about cost," he said. "If you go to the supermarket and there are no prices, how can you make intelligent decisions?"

Instead, payments are often determined in countless negotiations between a doctor, hospital or pharmacy, and an insurer, with the result often depending on their relative negotiating power. Insurers have limited incentive to bargain forcefully, since they can raise premiums to cover costs.

"It all comes down to market share, and very rarely is anyone looking out for the patient," said Dr. Jeffrey Rice, the chief executive of Healthcare Blue Book, which tracks commercial insurance payments. "People think it's like other purchases: that if you pay more you get a better car. But in medicine, it's not like that."

A Market Is Born

As the cases of bottled water and energy drinks stacked in the corner of the Yapalaters' dining room attest, the family is cost conscious—especially since a photography business long owned by the family succumbed eight years ago in the shift to digital imaging. They moved out of Manhattan. They rent out their summer home on Fire Island. They have put off restoring the wallpaper in their dining room.

And yet, Ms. Yapalater recalled, she did not ask her doctors about the cost of her colonoscopy because it was covered by insurance and because "if a doctor says you need it, you don't ask." In many other countries, price lists of common procedures are publicly available in every clinic and office. Here, it can be nearly impossible to find out.

Until the last decade or so, colonoscopies were mostly performed in doctors' office suites and only on patients at high risk for colon cancer, or to seek a diagnosis for intestinal bleeding. But several highly publicized studies by gastroenterologists in 2000 and 2001 found that a colonoscopy detected early cancers and precancerous growths in healthy people.

They did not directly compare screening colonoscopies with far less invasive and cheaper screening methods, including annual tests for blood in the stool or a sigmoidoscopy, which looks at the lower colon where most cancers occur, every five years.

"The idea wasn't to say these growths would have been missed by the other methods, but people extrapolated to that," said Dr. Douglas Robertson, of the Department of Veterans Affairs, which is beginning a large trial to compare the tests.

Experts agree that screening for colon cancer is crucial, and a colonoscopy is intuitively appealing because it looks directly at the entire colon and doctors can remove potentially precancerous lesions that might not yet be prone to bleeding. But studies have not clearly shown that a colonoscopy prevents colon cancer or death better than the other screening methods. Indeed, some recent papers suggest that it does not, in part because early lesions may be hard to see in some parts of the colon.

But in 2000, the American College of Gastroenterology anointed colonoscopy as "the preferred strategy" for colon cancer prevention—and America followed.

Katie Couric, who lost her husband to colorectal cancer, had a colonoscopy on television that year, giving rise to what medical journals called the "Katie Couric effect": prompting patients to demand the test. Gastroenterology groups successfully lobbied Congress to have the procedure covered by Medicare for cancer screening every 10 years, effectively meaning that commercial insurance plans would also have to provide coverage.

Though Medicare negotiates for what are considered frugal prices, its database shows that it paid an average of $531 for a colonoscopy in 2011. But that does not include the payments to anesthesiologists, which could substantially increase the cost. "As long as it's deemed medically necessary," said Jonathan Blum, the deputy administrator at the Centers for Medicare and Medicaid Services, "we have to pay for it."

If the American health care system were a true market, the increased volume of colonoscopies—numbers rose 50 percent from 2003 to 2009 for those with commercial insurance—might have brought down the costs because of economies of scale and more competition. Instead, it became a new business opportunity.

Profits Climb

Just as with real estate, location matters in medicine. Although many procedures can be performed in either a doctor's office or a separate surgery center, prices generally skyrocket at the special centers, as do profits. That is because insurers will pay an additional "facility fee" to ambulatory surgery centers and hospitals that is intended to cover their higher costs. And anesthesia, more monitoring, a wristband and some-times preoperative testing, along with their extra costs, are more likely to be added on.

. . . Ms. Yapalater, a trim woman who looks far younger than her 64 years, had two prior colonoscopies in doctor's offices (one turned up a polyp that required a five-year follow-up in-stead of the usual 10 years). But for her routine colonoscopy this January, Ms. Yapalater was re-ferred to Dr. Felice Mirsky of Gastroenterology Associates, a group practice in Garden City, N.Y., that performs the procedures at an ambu-latory surgery center called the Long Island Center for Digestive Health. The doctors in the gastroenterology practice, which is just down the hall, are owners of the center.

"It was very fancy, with nurses and ORs," Ms. Yapalater said. "It felt like you were in a hospital."

That explains the fees. "If you work as a 'fa-cility,' you can charge a lot more for the same procedure," said Dr. Soeren Mattke, a senior sci-entist at the RAND Corporation. The bills to Ms. Yapalater's insurer reflected these charges: $1,075 for the gastroenterologist, $2,400 for the anesthesia—and $2,910 for the facility fee.

When popularized in the 1980s, outpatient surgical centers were hailed as a cost-saving in-novation because they cut down on expensive hospital stays for minor operations like knee ar-throscopy. But the cost savings have been offset as procedures once done in a doctor's office have filled up the centers, and bills have multiplied.

It is a lucrative migration. The Long Island center was set up with the help of a company based in Pennsylvania called Physicians Endos-copy. On its Web site, the business tells prospec-tive physician partners that they can look forward to "distributions averaging over $1.4 million a year to all owners," "typically 100 percent return on capital investment within 18 months" and "a return on investment of 500 percent to 2,000 per-cent over the initial seven years."

Dr. Leonard Stein, the senior partner in Gastroenterology Associates and medical direc-tor of the surgery center, declined to discuss pa-tient fees or the center's profits, citing privacy issues. But he said the center contracted with insurance companies in the area to minimize patients' out-of-pocket costs.

In 2009, the last year for which such statis-tics are available, gastroenterologists performed more procedures in ambulatory surgery centers than specialists in any other field. Once they bought into a center, studies show, the number of procedures they performed rose 27 percent. The specialists earn an average of $433,000 a year, among the highest paid doctors, according to Merritt Hawkins & Associates, a medical staffing firm.

Hospitals and doctors say that critics should not take the high "rack rates" in bills as reflective of the cost of health care because in-surers usually pay less. But those rates are the starting point for negotiations with Medicare and private insurers. Those without insurance or with high-deductible plans have little weight to reduce the charges and often face the highest bills. Nassau Anesthesia Associates—the group practice that handled Ms. Yapalater's sedation—has sued dozens of patients for nonpayment, including Larry Chin, a businessman from Hicksville, N.Y., who said in court that he was then unemployed and uninsured. He was billed $8,675 for anesthesia during cardiac surgery.

For the same service, the anesthesia group accepted $6,970 from United Healthcare, $5,208.01 from Blue Cross and Blue Shield, $1,605.29 from Medicare and $797.50 from Med-icaid. A judge ruled that Mr. Chin should pay $4,252.11.

Ms. Yapalater's insurer paid $1,568 of the $2,400 anesthesiologist's charge for her colonos-copy, but many medical experts question why anesthesiologists are involved at all. Colonosco-pies do not require general anesthesia—a deep sleep that suppresses breathing and often re-quires a breathing tube. Instead, they require only "moderate sedation," generally with a Valium-like drug or a low dose of propofol, an intravenous medicine that takes effect quickly and wears off within minutes. In other coun-tries, such sedative mixes are administered in offices and hospitals by a wide range of doctors and nurses for countless minor procedures, including colonoscopies.

Nonetheless, between 2003 and 2009, the use of an anesthesiologist for colonoscopies in the United States doubled, according to a RAND Corporation study published last year. Payments to anesthesiologists for colonoscopies per patient quadrupled during that period, the researchers found, estimating that ending the practice for healthy patients could save $1.1 billion a year because "studies have shown no benefit" for them, Dr. Mattke said.

But turf battles and lobbying have helped keep anesthesiologists in the room. When propofol won the approval of the Food and Drug Administration in 1989 as an anesthesia drug, it carried a label advising that it "should be administered only by those who are trained in the administration of general anesthesia" because of concerns that too high a dose could depress breathing and blood pressure to a point requiring resuscitation.

Since 2005, the American College of Gastroenterology has repeatedly pressed the F.D.A. to remove or amend the restriction, arguing that gastroenterologists and their nurses are able to safely administer the drug in lower doses as a sedative. But the American Society of Anesthesiologists has aggressively lobbied for keeping the advisory, which so far the F.D.A. has done.

A Food and Drug Administration spokeswoman said that the label did not necessarily require an anesthesiologist and that it was safe for the others to administer propofol if they had appropriate training. But many gastroenterologists fear lawsuits if something goes wrong. If anything, that concern has grown since Michael Jackson died in 2009 after being given propofol, along with at least two other sedatives, without close monitoring.

"Too Much for Too Little"

The Department of Veterans Affairs, which performs about a quarter-million colonoscopies annually, does not routinely use an anesthesiologist for screening colonoscopies. In Austria, where colonoscopies are also used widely for cancer screening, the procedure is performed, with sedation, in the office by a doctor and a nurse and "is very safe that way," said Dr. Monika Ferlitsch, a gastroenterologist and professor at the Medical University of Vienna, who directs the national program on quality assurance.

But she noted that gastroenterologists in Austria do have their financial concerns. They are complaining to the government and insurers that they cannot afford to do the 30-minute procedure, with prep time, maintenance of equipment and anesthesia, for the current approved rate—between $200 and $300, all included. "I think the cheapest colonoscopy in the U.S. is about $950," Dr. Ferlitsch said. "We'd love to get half of that."

Dr. Cesare Hassan, an Italian gastroenterologist who is the chairman of the Guidelines Committee of the European Society of Gastrointestinal Endoscopy, noted that studies in Europe had estimated that the procedure cost about $400 to $800 to perform, including biopsies and sedation. "The U.S. is paying way too much for too little—it leads to opportunistic colonoscopies," done for profit rather than health, he said.

. . . And some large employers have begun fighting back on costs. Three years ago, Safeway realized that it was paying between $848 and $5,984 for a colonoscopy in California and could find no link to the quality of service at those extremes. So the company established an all-inclusive "reference price" it was willing to pay, which it said was set at a level high enough to give employees access to a range of high-quality options. Above that price, employees would have to pay the difference. Safeway chose $1,250, one-third the amount paid for Ms. Yapalater's procedure—and found plenty of doctors willing to accept the price.

Still, the United States health care industry is nimble at protecting profits. When Aetna tried in 2007 to disallow payment for anesthesiologists delivering propofol during colonoscopies, the insurer backed down after a barrage of attacks from anesthesiologists and endoscopy groups. With Medicare contemplating lowering facility fees for ambulatory surgery centers, experts worry that physician-owners will sell the centers to hospitals, where fees remain higher.

And then there is aggressive marketing. People who do not have insurance or who are covered by Medicaid typically get far less colon cancer screening than they need. But those with insurance are appealing targets.

Nineteen months after Matt Meyer, who owns a saddle-fitting company near Keene, N.H., had his first colonoscopy, he received a certified letter from his gastroenterologist. It began, "Our records show that you are due for a repeat colonoscopy," and it advised him to schedule an appointment or "allow us to note your reason for not scheduling." Although his prior test had found a polyp, medical guidelines do not recommend such frequent screening.

"I have great doctors, but the economics is daunting," Mr. Meyer said in an interview. "A computer-generated letter telling me to come in for a procedure that costs more than $5,000? It was the weirdest thing."

Big Pharma Comes of Age

ROSE WEITZ

The pharmaceutical industry is the most profitable industry in the United States. Following major legal changes in the 1980s that were deemed "business-friendly," such as direct marketing to consumers and doctors, profits rose dramatically. Weitz demonstrates that this enhanced profitability is accompanied by significant expenses, usually borne by patients, whose prescription drugs may no longer be adequately researched or who may pay excessively high prices for their medicines. Compromises to safety and integrity are made in the name of profit, Weitz argues, and health-care consumers suffer as a result.

Big Pharma Comes of Age

The pharmaceutical industry is an enormous—and enormously profitable—enterprise. Indeed, it has been the most profitable industry in the United States since the early 1980s (Angell, 2004). Although the pharmaceutical industry routinely argues that their high profits merely reflect the high cost of researching and developing new drugs, such work accounts for only 14% of their budgets. In contrast, marketing accounts for about 50% (Angell, 2004). Largely because of this marketing, American citizens now spend a total of about $230 billion per year—10% of all U.S. health care expenses—on prescription drugs, *not* including drugs purchased by doctors, nursing homes, hospitals, and other institutions (Centers for Medicare & Medicaid Services, 2010). Americans are buying *more* drugs, buying more *expensive* drugs, and seeing the *prices* of popular drugs rise more often than ever before. (The price of the popular antihistamine Claritin, for example, rose 13 times in five years.)

The pharmaceutical industry has not always been this profitable. Profits only began soaring in the early 1980s after a series of legal changes reflecting both the increasingly "business-friendly" atmosphere in the federal government and the increased influence of the pharmaceutical industry lobby—now the biggest spending lobby in Washington. First, new laws allowed researchers funded by federal agencies (including university professors and researchers working for small biotech companies) to patent their discoveries and then license those patents to pharmaceutical companies. This change dramatically reduced pharmaceutical companies' research costs—while giving these researchers a vested interest in emphasizing the benefits of new drugs. Second, new laws almost doubled the life of drug patents. As long as a drug is under patent, the company owning that patent has the sole right to sell that drug. As a result, it can set the drug's price as high as the market will bear. In addition, companies can now extend their patents by developing "me-too" drugs, which differ only slightly from existing drugs; these drugs now account for about 75% of all new drugs (Angell, 2004). Third, the pharmaceutical industry won the right to market drugs direct to consumers. Direct-to-consumer advertising—a $4.3 billion business in 2009—has proven highly effective (Centers for Medicare & Medicaid Services, 2010b). According to a nationally representative survey conducted in 2008 for the nonprofit Kaiser Family Foundation, almost one-third of American adults have asked their doctors about drugs they've seen advertised, and 82% of those who asked for a prescription received one (Appleby, 2008).

Passage of the Medicare drug benefit program, which went into effect in 2008, has increased pharmaceutical profits even more. The pharmaceutical industry was heavily involved in the drafting and passage of this program, under which Medicare recipients can choose to buy supplemental insurance to cover some of their prescription drug costs (Abramson, 2004; Angell, 2004). However, most Medicare recipients who participate in the drug program now pay more in premiums and in *deductibles* (required minimum amounts individuals must pay out of pocket before their insurance coverage kicks in) than they save by enrolling in the program.

Developing New Drugs

Much of the recent rise in health care costs in the United States comes from the shift to new drugs. Whenever a new drug is developed, the crucial question for health care providers and patients is whether its benefits outweigh its dangers. For this reason, it is crucial that any new drug be extensively tested to determine whether it works better than already available drugs (which almost certainly are cheaper), whether it works differently in different populations (does

it help men as well as women? persons with both early- and late-stage disease?), what dosages are appropriate, and what side effects are likely. But because pharmaceutical companies earn their profits by selling drugs, they have a vested interest in overstating benefits and understating dangers. And increasingly, these companies are both willing and able to manipulate the data available to outside researchers, doctors, federal regulators, and consumers (Abramson, 2004; Angell, 2004). For example, because scientific testing is typically designed to be accurate 95% of the time, manufacturers know that if they test a drug enough times, they will eventually hit the other 5% and obtain data that inaccurately suggest a drug works in some population. . . .

In the past, university-based drug researchers provided at least a partial check on the drug research process by bringing a more objective eye to their research. Since 1980, however, pharmaceutical industry funding for research by university-based scientists has skyrocketed (Lemmens, 2004). That funding comes in many forms, from research grants, to stock options, to all-expenses-paid conferences in Hawaii. Moreover, as other federal funding for universities declined over the past quarter century, university administrators came to expect their faculty to seek pharmaceutical funding. Importantly, when the pharmaceutical industry funds university-based research, it often retains the rights to the research results and so can keep university researchers from publishing any data suggesting that a particular drug is ineffective or dangerous (Angell, 2004; Lemmens, 2004).

At the same time that the pharmaceutical industry has increased its funding to university-based researchers, it has even more dramatically increased funding to *commercial* research organizations (Lemmens, 2004). These organizations are paid not only to conduct research but also to promote it. To keep on the good side of the companies that fund them, these research organizations must make drugs look as effective and safe as possible by, for example, selecting research subjects who are least likely to experience side effects, studying drugs' effects only briefly before side effects can appear, underestimating the severity of any side effects that do appear, and choosing not to publish any studies suggesting that a drug harms or doesn't help.

Doctors, medical researchers, sociologists, and others have raised concerns about the impact of bias on research publications (Bodenheimer, 2000). Researchers have found that medical journal articles written by individuals who received pharmaceutical industry funding are four to five times more likely to recommend the tested drug than are articles written by those without such funding (Abramson, 2004:97). Similarly, researchers have found that research studies suggesting a drug is effective are several times more likely to be submitted and accepted for publication than are those that suggest it is ineffective (Hadler, 2008; Turner et al., 2008). Concern about such biases led the *New England Journal of Medicine* (one of the top two medical journals in the United States) to forbid authors from publishing articles on drugs in which they had financial interests. The policy, however, was dropped quickly because it proved virtually impossible to find authors who did *not* have financial conflicts (Lemmens, 2004).

Even more astonishing than pharmaceutical industry funding of university-based researchers is the growing practice of paying such researchers to sign their names to articles written by industry employees (Elliott, 2004). For example, between 1988 and 2000, 96 articles were published in medical journals on the popular antidepressant Zoloft. Just over half of these were written by pharmaceutical industry employees but published under the names of university-based researchers. Moreover, these ghost-written articles were *more* likely than other articles to be published in prestigious medical journals (Elliott, 2004).

Regulating Drugs

In the United States, ensuring the safety of pharmaceutical drugs falls to the Food and Drug Administration (FDA). But during the same time period that the profits and power of the pharmaceutical industry grew, the FDA's power and funding declined as part of a broader public and political movement away from "big government." These two changes are not unrelated: The pharmaceutical industry now routinely provides funding of various sorts to staff members at government advisory agencies, doctors who serve on FDA advisory panels, and legislators who support reducing the FDA's powers (Lemmens, 2004).

Under current regulations, the FDA must make its decisions based primarily on data reported to it by the pharmaceutical industry. Yet the industry is required to report only a small fraction of the research it conducts. For example, the company that produced the antidepressant Paxil had considerable data indicating that, among teenagers, Paxil did *not* reduce depression but *could* lead to suicide. To avoid making this information public, the company submitted to the FDA only its data from studies on adults (Lemmens, 2004). Similarly, drug companies need only demonstrate that new drugs work better than *placebos*, not that they work better than existing (cheaper) drugs. For example, because of intensive marketing campaigns, new antipsychotic drugs such as Zyprexa have largely replaced older, cheaper drugs even though the new drugs work little better than placebos and carry life-threatening risks (Wilson, 2010).

Marketing Drugs

Once the pharmaceutical industry develops a drug and gets FDA approval, the next step is to market the drug. One of the most important limitations to the FDA's power is that, once it approves a drug for a single use in a single population, doctors legally can prescribe it for *any* purpose to *any* population. For example, doctors increasingly are prescribing Botox injections to treat migraines even though the FDA has not approved its use for that purpose.

Drug marketing has two major audiences, doctors and the public. Marketing to doctors begins during medical school as students quickly learn that pharmaceutical companies provide a ready source not only of drug samples and information but also of pens, notepads, lunches, and all-expense-paid "educational" conferences at major resorts. After graduation, the pharmaceutical industry continues to serve as doctors' main source of information about drugs. The *Physicians' Desk Reference* (or *PDR*), the main reference doctors turn to for drug information, is solely composed of drug descriptions written by drug manufacturers. In addition, the pharmaceutical industry spends $6,000 to $11,000 (depending on medical specialty) per doctor per year to send salespeople to doctors' offices on top of the money it spends advertising drugs to doctors in other ways. Most doctors meet with pharmaceutical salespeople at least four times per month and believe their behavior is unaffected by these salespeople. Yet doctors who meet with drug salespeople prescribe promoted drugs more often than do other doctors, even when the promoted drugs are more costly and less effective than the alternatives (Angell, 2004; Shapiro, 2004). In addition, the pharmaceutical companies now surreptitiously provide much of the "continuing education courses" doctors must take each year by paying for-profit firms to teach the courses and to arrange with universities to accredit the courses (Angell, 2004).

In recent years, and as noted earlier, marketing directly to consumers has become as important as marketing to doctors. To the companies, such advertising is simply an extension of normal business practices, no different from any other form of advertising. Moreover, they argue, advertising to consumers is a public service because it can encourage consumers to seek medical care for problems they otherwise might have ignored. Finally, companies have argued that these advertisements pose no health risks because consumers still must get prescriptions before they can purchase drugs, thus leaving the final decisions in doctors' hands. Those who oppose such advertisements, on the other hand, argue that the advertisements are frequently misleading, encourage consumers to pressure their doctors into prescribing the drugs, and encourage both doctors and patients to treat normal human conditions (such as

baldness) with pharmaceutical drugs (Angell, 2004; Hadler, 2008).

Marketing Diseases

As this suggests, the pharmaceutical industry sells not only drugs but also diseases to doctors and the public alike. In some cases, drug companies have encouraged doctors and the public to define disease *risks* (such as high blood pressure) as *diseases* (such as hypertensive disease). In other cases . . . drug companies have defined symptoms into new diseases.

One example of this is the newly defined illness *pseudobulbar affect*, or PBA. PBA refers to uncontrollable laughing or crying unrelated to individuals' emotional state and can be caused by various disabling neurological conditions (such as head trauma, stroke, and Lou Gehrig's disease). The concept of PBA was developed by Avanir Pharmaceuticals, which markets the drug Neurodex as a treatment for it (Pollack, 2005). Although Neurodex seems to help some patients, its side effects are serious enough that at least one-quarter of users—all of whom already have serious health problems and must take numerous other medications—soon stop taking it.

To convince doctors that uncontrollable laughing and crying is a disease in itself, Avanir has advertised in medical journals and sponsored continuing education courses, conferences, and a PBA newsletter. Avanir also has marketed the concept of PBA directly to consumers through its PBA website and through educational grants it has given to advocacy groups for those living with stroke, multiple sclerosis, and other diseases (Pollack, 2005).

REFERENCES

Abramson, John. 2004. *Overdosed America: The Broken Promise of American Medicine*. New York: Harper Collins.

Angell, Marcia. 2004. *The Truth about the Drug Companies: How They Deceive Us and What to Do About It*. New York: Random House.

Appleby, Julie. 2008. "Survey: Many Request Drugs Advertised on TV." *Arizona Republic* March 4:A12.

Bodenheimer, Thomas. 2000. "Uneasy Alliance: Clinical Investigators and the Pharmaceutical Industry." *New England Journal of Medicine* 342:1539–1543.

Centers for Medicare & Medicaid Services. 2010. *National Health Expenditure Accounts, Historical.* http://www.cms.gov/NationalHealthExpend-Data/, accessed November 2010.

Elliott, Carl. 2004. "Pharma Goes to the Laundry: Public Relations and the Subject of Medical Education." *Hastings Center Review* 34:18–23.

Hadler, Nortin M. 2008. *Worried Sick.* Chapel Hill, NC: University of North Carolina Press.

Lemmens, Trudo. 2004. "Piercing the Veil of Corporate Secrecy about Clinical Trials." *Hastings Center Review* 34:14–18.

Pollack, Andrew. 2005. "Marketing a Disease, and also a Drug to Treat It." *New York Times* May 9:C1+.

Shapiro, Dan. 2004. "Drug Companies Get Too Close for Med School's Comfort." *New York Times* January 20:D7+.

Turner, Erick H., Annette M. Matthews, Eftihia Linardatos, Robert A. Tell, and Robert Rosenthal. 2008. "Selective Publication of Antidepressant Trials and Its Influence on Apparent Efficacy." *New England Journal of Medicine* 358:252–260.

Wilson, Duff. 2010. "Side Effects May Include Law Suits." *New York Times* October 3:BY 1+.

The Patient Protection and Affordable Care Act

Rose Weitz

From Weitz. The Sociology of Health, Illness, and Health Care, 6E. © 2013 South-Western, a part of Cengage Learning, Inc. Reproduced by permission. www.cengage.com/permissions.

Concern about the millions of Americans who lack health insurance or who face devastating medical bills even though they have insurance came to a head with passage in 2010 of the Patient Protection and Affordable Care Act [(ACA)]. The ACA constitutes the biggest move toward health care reform in several decades.

The central goal of the ACA was to increase access to health care through a variety of mechanisms that will be phased in between 2011 and 2018 (Kaiser Family Foundation, 2011). Rather than requiring the *government* to provide health insurance or care (as Canada does), the ACA establishes an *individual mandate*: that is, the requirement that each U.S. citizen and legal resident obtain health insurance or face fines. Several states have challenged the constitutionality of this individual mandate, and it is likely that the U.S. Supreme Court will eventually rule on its constitutionality.

One of the core pieces of the ACA is the requirement that each state establish nonprofit or state-run "health exchanges" through which individuals and small businesses can purchase coverage (helped by subsidies and tax credits for middle- and working-class individuals). The hope is to lower the costs of insurance by combining many individuals together in these exchanges, thus sharing (and, presumably, reducing) the health risks of the group as a whole.

In addition, the ACA establishes an *employer mandate*: a legal requirement that employers subsidize health insurance for their employees. Employers with more than 50 employees will be required to offer (for-profit) health insurance, and small businesses will receive tax credits to make it easier for them to do so. Also, Medicaid will be expanded to include all poor and near-poor Americans younger than age 65.

Finally, the ACA establishes various new restrictions on insurance companies. Among other things, companies will be prohibited from capping annual or lifetime benefits, refusing to cover those with preexisting health problems, or charging higher premiums to such individuals. In addition, companies must allow young people to remain on their parents' insurance policies until they turn 26. Insurers also will be forbidden from charging more than $6,000 per individual per year (or $12,000 per family per year) for out-of-pocket expenses such as deductibles and co-payments and must cover at least 60% of average medical costs.

Taken together, the provisions of the ACA are expected to reduce the uninsured population from an estimated 57 million in 2019 to 23 million (about one-third of whom will be undocumented immigrants). It will also increase funding for community health centers, reduce out-of-pocket costs for some services, provide new incentives for doctors to enter primary care, and establish some new mechanisms that may reduce future costs to the system overall.

On the other hand, the system will still leave millions without insurance because it will continue to be built around for-profit insurance companies that, to please their stockholders, must find ways to increase revenues while avoiding costs. For example, new ACA regulations require companies that sell individual health insurance policies for children to cover children with preexisting illnesses. In response, several of the largest insurance companies have stopped selling *any* individual policies for children. Those children and adults who do obtain coverage under the ACA may still find that they can't afford needed care because of co-payments, deductibles, and other costs not covered by their insurance. And although insurers will no longer be able to refuse insurance to those with preexisting health problems, insurers (other than in the state health exchanges) will be allowed to charge considerably more to entire groups that typically have worse health (including older people and individuals who work in female-dominated industries).

Moreover, in the long term, the costs to the government (and thus consumers) are likely to increase substantially. The ACA continues the nation's reliance on a vast web of insurers, thus guaranteeing huge administrative costs and inefficiencies. At the same time, most of those insurers will be for-profit corporations that will continue to seek out individuals likely to have *low* medical bills, whereas the states will be responsible for insuring those most likely to have *high* medical bills (via the state insurance exchanges). Finally, to appease health industry opponents, most proposals to incorporate well-established cost control mechanisms into the ACA were dropped from the bill before it was passed. For all these reasons, the Centers for Medicare & Medicaid Services (2010), a nonpartisan federal bureau that advises Congress and the president, estimates that the ACA will cost the federal government an additional $251 billion between 2010 and 2019. Costs to individuals can only climb if, as seems likely, the government finds itself unable to offer the insurance subsidies for poor and middle-class Americans that constitute the core of the ACA.

It will be some time, however, before the full impact of the ACA becomes known. Although the ACA was designed to work within the existing health care system rather than to stimulate any larger changes, opposition was and remains fierce, and court battles over the laws will likely continue for years. Similarly, Congress will need to approve budgets annually for various aspects of the ACA's provisions, and these battles will likely be bloody. Finally, hundreds of new regulations will need to be written to implement the highly complex ACA, and this process, too, is likely to become a battlefront (Jacobs and Skocpol, 2010).

REFERENCES

Centers for Medicare & Medicaid Services. 2010. *Estimated Financial Effects of the "Patient Protection and Affordable Care Act," as Amended.* https://www.cms.gov/ActuarialStudies/Downloads/PPACA_Medicare_2010-04-22.pdf, accessed January 2011.

Jacobs, Lawrence R. and Theda Skocpol. 2010. *Health Care Reform and American Politics: What Everyone Needs to Know.* New York: Oxford University Press.

Kaiser Family Foundation. 2011. *Summary of New Health Reform Law.* http://www.kff.org/healthreform/upload/8061.pdf, accessed January 2011.

What's Killing Poor White Women?

MONICA POTTS

Potts follows the life history of a poor rural woman, attempting to understand why life expectancy for poor, undereducated white women has dropped dramatically in the past two decades. Potts discusses cultural factors (e.g., traditional gender norms), structural issues (e.g., poverty and unemployment), and less tangible factors (e.g., feelings of desperation) that may be contributing to their early deaths.

On the night of May 23, 2012, which turned out to be the last of her life, Crystal Wilson baby-sat her infant granddaughter, Kelly. It was how she would have preferred to spend every night. Crystal had joined Facebook the previous year, and the picture of her daughter cradling the newborn in the hospital bed substituted for a picture of herself. Crystal's entire wall was a catalog of visits from her nieces, nephews, cousins' kids, and, more recently, the days she baby-sat Kelly. She was a mother hen, people said of Crystal. She'd wanted a house full of children, but she'd only had one.

The picture the family chose for her obituary shows Crystal and her husband holding the infant. Crystal leans in from the side, with dark, curly hair, an unsmiling round face, and black eyebrows knit together. She was 38 and bore an unhealthy heft, more than 200 pounds. Crystal had been to the doctor, who told her she was overweight and diabetic. She was waiting to get medicine, but few in her family knew it, and no one thought she was near death.

Crystal's 17-year-old daughter, Megan, split her time between her parents' house in Cave City, Arkansas, and that of her boyfriend, Corey, in nearby Evening Shade. Megan made sure that each set of grandparents could spend time with the baby. The night before Crystal's death, Megan and Corey were moving with his parents to a five-acre patch near Crystal. Megan and Corey were running late, so they didn't pick the baby up until 11 P.M. Crystal seemed fine. "You couldn't tell she was sick," Megan says. "She never felt sick." They went back home, and Megan got a text from her mom around midnight. "She said she loved me, give Kelly kisses, and give Corey hugs and tell him to take care of her girls and she'd see me in the morning. I was supposed to drop Kelly off at ten o'clock and finish moving."

Instead, at around 9:30 the next morning, when Megan was getting ready to leave, Corey's grandfather called and said Crystal was dead. Megan didn't believe him. If one of her parents passed, it had to be her dad. "I thought it was my dad that died because he was always the unhealthy one." Megan left Kelly with her mother-in-law and raced with Corey and his dad in the truck, hazards on, laying on the horn, and pulled into the dirt driveway outside her parents' tan-and-brown single-wide trailer. "Daddy was sitting there in the recliner crying," Megan says. "It was Momma gone, not him." Crystal had died in her bed early in the morning.

Just after 10 A.M., nearly every relative Crystal had was in the rutted driveway in front of the trailer. Crystal was the last of six children and considered the baby of the family. She was the third sibling to die. Her brother Terry, the "Big Man," who hosted all the holiday dinners and coached the family softball team, had died three months earlier at age 47, and her sister Laura, whom everybody called Pete, died at age 45 in 2004. The police—dozens, it seemed, from the county and from the town—had arrived and blocked off the bedroom where she lay and were interviewing people to figure out what had killed her.

The coroner arrived and pronounced Crystal dead at 11:40. Her body was rolled out on a gurney and shipped to the state lab in Little Rock. One of the officers, Gerald Traw, later told me an autopsy is routine when someone dies without a doctor present. "We like to know why somebody died," he says.

Everything about Crystal's life was ordinary, except for her death. She is one of a demographic—white women who don't graduate from high school—whose life expectancy has declined dramatically over the past 18 years. These women can now expect to die five years earlier than the generation before them. It is an unheard-of drop for a wealthy country in the age of modern medicine. Throughout history, technological and scientific innovation have put death off longer and longer, but the benefits of those advances have not been shared equally, especially across the race and class divides that characterize 21st century America. Lack of access to education, medical care, good wages, and healthy food isn't just leaving the worst-off Americans behind. It's killing them.

The journal *Health Affairs* reported the five-year drop last August. The article's lead author, Jay Olshansky, who studies human longevity at the University of Illinois at Chicago, with a team of researchers looked at death rates for different groups from 1990 to 2008. White men without high-school diplomas had lost three years of life expectancy, but it was the decline for women like Crystal that made the study news. Previous studies had shown that the least-educated whites began dying younger in the 2000s, but only by about a year. Olshansky and his colleagues did something the other studies hadn't: They isolated high-school dropouts and measured their outcomes instead of lumping them in with high-school graduates who did not go to college.

The last time researchers found a change of this magnitude, Russian men had lost seven years after the fall of the Soviet Union, when they began drinking more and taking on other risky behaviors. Although women generally outlive men in the U.S., such a large decline in the average age of death, from almost 79 to a little more than 73, suggests that an increasing number of women are dying in their twenties, thirties, and forties. "We actually don't know the exact reasons why it's happened," Olshansky says. "I wish we did."

Most Americans, including high-school dropouts of other races, are gaining life expectancy, just at different speeds. Absent a war, genocide, pandemic, or massive governmental collapse, drops in life expectancy are rare. "If you look at the history of longevity in the United States, there have been no dramatic negative or positive shocks," Olshansky says. "With the exception of the 1918 influenza pandemic, everything has been relatively steady, slow changes. This is a five-year drop in an 18-year time period. That's dramatic."

Researchers had known education was linked to longer life since the 1960s, but it was difficult to tell whether it was a proxy for other important factors—like coming from a wealthy family or earning a high income as an adult. In 1999, a Columbia economics graduate student named Adriana Lleras-Muney decided to figure out if education was the principal cause. She found that each additional year of schooling added about a year of life. Subsequent studies suggested the link was less direct. Education is strongly associated with a longer life, but that doesn't mean that every year of education is an elixir. "It is the biggest association, but it is also the thing that we measure about people the best," Lleras-Muney says. "It is one of those things that we can collect data on. There could be other things that matter a lot more, but they're just very difficult to measure."

As is often the case when researchers encounter something fuzzy, they start suggesting causes that sound decidedly unscientific. Their best guess is that staying in school teaches people to delay gratification. The more educated among us are better at forgoing pleasurable and possibly risky behavior because we've learned to look ahead to the future. That connection isn't new, however, and it wouldn't explain why the least-educated whites like Crystal are dying so much younger today than the same group was two decades ago.

Cave City gives itself the low-stakes title of "Home of the World's Sweetest Watermelons." Beneath the ground, the Crystal River carves out the caverns that lend the town its name. Above it, 1,900 people live in single-wides in neighborhoods dotted with fenced lawns or along spindly red-dirt trails off the main highway. In this part of Arkansas, the Ozark Plateau flattens to meet the Mississippi embayment, and the hills give way to rice paddies. About 17,000 people live in Sharp County, a long string of small towns with Cave City at the bottom and the Missouri border at the top. Most of the residents are white—96 percent—with a median household income of $29,590. Nearly a quarter live in poverty, and Crystal was among them; for most of her married life, she relied on income from her husband's disability checks.

For work, people drive to the college town of Batesville, about 20 minutes south, which has a chicken-processing plant that periodically threatens to close and an industrial bakery with

12-hour shifts that make it hard for a mother to raise children. Less than 13 percent of county residents have a bachelor's degree. Society is divided into opposites: Godly folk go to church and sinners chase the devil, students go to college and dropouts seek hard labor, and men call the shots and women cook for them.

Crystal's parents, Junior and Martha Justice, had moved to the area when her three oldest siblings were still toddlers. . . . Junior farmed, which fed his family and brought in a little money. He found a piece of land on a country road called Antioch and bought a prefabricated home from the Jim Walters company. It was on this land they had their next three children. Crystal, born July 6, 1973, was the sixth and youngest.

Their life was old-school country. They raised chickens and goats and grew their own vegetables. The house was small, with only three bedrooms. Crystal's closest sibling, Terry, was 7 years older. Linda was a full 15 years older than Crystal, which made her more like a second mom than a sister. When Crystal was two, Linda's twin sister, Pete, began having children and, fleeing a string of abusive relationships, turned over custody to her parents. Having four slightly younger nieces and nephews in the house gave Crystal playmates her own age.

It was Linda, the doting older sister and aunt, who would take all the kids to Dogpatch, a creaky little Ozarks amusement park based on the comic strip, with actors playing Daisy Mae and Li'l Abner. Linda keeps Polaroids of Crystal from that time. They show her with long, curly blond hair and often half-clothed, happy, covered in clay and mud. "Grandpa used to call her his little Shirley Temple," says Crystal's niece, Lori.

When Crystal was starting out in elementary school, the family moved to a trailer to be closer to town. . . . Crystal was well behaved in school, and teachers would ask Lori, only two years behind, "Why aren't you like her, she was so quiet and shy?" Crystal loved basketball and, especially, softball, which she played in summer clubs even as an adult. As she got older, her hair darkened and she became stocky and muscular.

She played ball like a bulldozer and was aggressive on the field and mouthy off. The whole family would play and bicker and joke. Crystal would smack people across the butt with the bat if they weren't moving fast enough.

"It wasn't until we got in high school that I realized she was struggling so bad in school," Lori says. "I was in the seventh grade, and she was in the ninth, and I wasn't really smart myself. But I could help her do some of her work." In 1988, Junior died from lung cancer at age 55. Both he and Martha were smokers. The next year Crystal met Carl Wilson, whom everybody called Possum. He was related to a cousin through marriage and, at 28, was 12 years her senior. They kept their relationship secret for a few months. "He came up to see her at the school," Lori says. "So I pretty much put two and two together. I was the one that told my grandmother." Lori thought that would put an end to it; instead, Martha let them marry. According to Linda, Martha had one admonition for Possum: "Momma said, 'As long as you take care of her and don't hit her, you have my permission.' He done what he could do for her. They was mates."

Possum moved in with the family in the trailer. He and Crystal had one room, Martha another, and the four nephews and nieces shared two bunk beds in the third. Crystal dropped out in the tenth grade because she had married. That was the way things were. None of Crystal's siblings finished high school. Instead, they became adults when they were teenagers. Crystal would spend the rest of her years as a housewife to a husband who soon became ill and as a mother to a daughter who would grow up as fast as she did.

Researchers have long known that high-school dropouts like Crystal are unlikely to live as long as people who have gone to college. But why would they be slipping behind the generation before them? James Jackson, a public-health researcher at the University of Michigan, believes it's because life became more difficult for the least-educated in the 1990s and 2000s. Broad-scale shifts in society increasingly isolate those who don't finish high school from good jobs, marriageable partners, and healthier communities. "Hope is lowered. If you drop out of school, say, in the last 20 years or so, you just had less hope for ever making it and being anything," Jackson says. "The opportunities available to you are very different than what they were 20 or 30 years ago. What kind of job are you going to get if you drop out at 16? No job."

In May, Jennifer Karas Montez of the Harvard University Center for Population and Development Studies co-authored the first paper investigating why white women without high-school diplomas might be dying. Most research has looked at which diseases are the cause of death, but Montez and her co-author wanted to tease out quality of life: economic indicators like employment and income, whether women were married and how educated their spouses were, and health behaviors like smoking and alcohol abuse. It is well known that smoking shortens life; in fact, smoking led to the early deaths of both of Crystal's parents and her sister and brother. Crystal, though, never smoked or drank. But the researchers discovered something else that was driving women like her to early graves: Whether the women had a job mattered, and it mattered more than income or other signs of financial stability, like homeownership. In fact, smoking and employment were the only two factors of any significance.

At first, Montez and her co-author suspected that women who are already unhealthy are less able to work and so are already more likely to die. When they investigated that hypothesis, however, it didn't hold up. Jobs themselves contributed something to health. But what? It could be, the authors suggested, that work connects women to friends and other social networks they otherwise wouldn't have. Even more squishy sounding, Montez wrote that jobs might give women a "sense of purpose."

Better-educated women are the most likely to work and to achieve parity with men: Seventy-two percent are in the workforce, compared with 81 percent of their male counterparts. Women without high-school diplomas are the least likely to work. Only about a third are in the workforce, compared to about half of their male counterparts. If they do find work, women are more likely than men to have minimum-wage jobs. They account for most workers in the largest low-paying occupations—child-care providers, housecleaners, food servers. Even if they do have minimum-wage jobs, this group of women is more likely to leave the labor force to take care of young children because child care is prohibitively expensive.

Montez's joblessness study, however, raised more questions. Would any job do? What does giving women a "sense of purpose" mean? And why would joblessness hit white women harder than other groups? Overall, men lost more jobs during the Great Recession. Why are women losing years at a faster rate?

. . . Crystal wanted to start a family as soon as she was married but couldn't. Her first three pregnancies, in the early '90s, ended in miscarriages. The first two occurred so late she gave the babies names, Justin and Crystal; the last was a set of twins. None of her relatives knew if she ever went to a doctor to find out why she miscarried. "I just thought maybe it was one of those things, you know, some people can have them and carry them and some can't," Lori says. Megan said her mother had had "female cancer," a catchall phrase for cervical cancer and the infections and dysplasia leading up to it.

When Lori's son was born, Crystal teased her about stealing him. She was always volunteering to baby-sit the kids in the family. When Crystal finally got pregnant with Megan, no one was sure she would make it, least of all Crystal and Possum. "They ended up just praying for me," Megan says. She was born July 20, 1994, and became the center of Crystal's world.

By the time Megan was born, Crystal and Possum were living in their own trailer but were struggling financially. Possum had worked the first four years of their marriage at the chicken-processing plant before quitting for good because of health problems. An accident on an oil rig when he was a teenager had left him with a plate in his skull. Chicken-processing plants are tough places to work, and besides, he qualified for disability. Crystal spent her life taking him to specialists—he was covered by Medicaid—but the problems piled up. He had a congenital heart condition and a bad back. A young-old man.

When Megan was 12, Crystal worked for a brief spell as a housekeeper at a nursing home in Cave City, where Linda and Lori worked. Mostly, though, she stayed home to take care of Possum and Megan. Baby-sitting brought in small amounts of cash, but she and Possum relied on disability, which was about $1,000 a month. Outside of a brief trip to Texas after Megan was born to show her off to Possum's family, and a trip to a small town near St. Louis to visit a niece after one of the trailers they lived in burned down, Crystal passed her entire life in Cave City.

Crystal spent what money she had on Megan. She gave her any new toy she wanted and, later, name-brand clothes, a four-wheeler, a laptop, and a phone. When Megan started playing softball, Crystal spent money on shoes, gloves, and club fees. "Crystal was a super mom," says Steve Green, the school superintendent and Megan's softball coach. "They didn't have a lot of revenue, but they put everything they had into Megan." Crystal and Possum made it to every practice and every game, even if it meant driving for an hour, deep into the mountains. They brought snacks and sports drinks for Megan's teammates. Crystal would watch her nieces, nephews, and cousins' kids play, and she still played for her family team in Batesville. Crystal went with Linda to a missionary Baptist church near the family road in Antioch, but she and Possum weren't every-Sunday Christians—it was the softball field her spring weekends revolved around. But when Terry was diagnosed with cancer in 2009, the family stopped playing, and Crystal lost her favorite activity.

When her relatives look back, they think Crystal was probably lonely. Her mother had died three years after Megan was born. Although she and Possum had a Ford Contour, Crystal seldom drove, relying on relatives to come by to take her to the grocery store. It was a chance to visit. When Linda's daughter took her truck-driver husband to pick up his 18-wheeler for his next haul, Crystal would always want to go with them. She would call her family members throughout the day, gossiping. She didn't stir up trouble, but she reveled in drama. Crystal would often go to Linda's for homemade biscuits and gravy for breakfast, and she'd ask Linda to buy her liter bottles of Dr Pepper whenever she ran out. She was addicted to Dr Pepper. Sometimes, relatives paid for Possum's medicine; Linda's daughter remembers paying as much as $64 in one visit. Crystal's nieces and nephews had gotten older and started their own families, and now she relied on them as much as she had her older siblings.

Another mystery emerged from the lifespan study: Black women without a high-school diploma are now outliving their white counterparts.

As a group, blacks are more likely to die young, because the factors that determine well-being—income, education, access to health care—tend to be worse for blacks. Yet blacks on the whole are closing the life-expectancy gap with whites. In a country where racism still plays a significant role in all that contributes to a healthier, longer life, what could be affecting whites more than blacks?

One theory is that low-income white women smoke and drink and abuse prescription drugs like OxyContin and street drugs like meth more than black women. Despite Crystal's weight and diabetes, those problems are more common among black women and usually kill more slowly. Meth and alcohol kill quickly. It could be that white women, as a group, are better at killing themselves.

Still, why would white women be more likely to engage in risky behaviors? Another theory is that the kind of place people live in, who is around them, and what those neighbors are doing play a central role. Health is also a matter of place and time.

In March, two researchers from the University of Wisconsin reported that women in nearly half of 3,140 counties in the United States saw their death rates rise during the same time period that Olshansky studied. The researchers colored the counties with an increase in female mortality a bright red, and the red splashed over Appalachia, down through Kentucky and Tennessee, north of the Cotton Belt, and across the Ozarks—the parts of the South where poor white people live. Location seemed to matter more than other indicators, like drug use, which has been waning. The Wisconsin researchers recommended more studies examining "cultural, political, or religious factors."

Something less tangible, it seems, is shaping the lives of white women in the South, beyond what science can measure. Surely these forces weigh on black women, too, but perhaps they are more likely to have stronger networks of other women. Perhaps after centuries of slavery and Jim Crow, black women are more likely to feel like they're on an upward trajectory. Perhaps they have more control relative to the men in their communities. In low-income white communities of the South, it is still women who are responsible for the home and for raising children, but increasingly they are also raising their husbands. A husband is a burden and an occasional heartache rather than a helpmate, but one women are told they cannot do without. More and more, data show that poor women are working the hardest and earning the most in their families but can't take the credit for being the breadwinners. Women do the emotional work for their families, while men reap the most benefits from marriage. The rural South is a place that often wants to remain unchanged from the 1950s and 1960s, and its women are now dying as if they lived in that era, too.

Crystal's world was getting smaller and smaller and more sedentary. Everyone was worried about Possum, but Crystal's own health was bad. She'd had a cystic ovary removed when Megan was 13, and about a year before her death she had a hysterectomy. The surgery was necessary after Crystal had started hemorrhaging, which was brought on by another miscarriage—something her family didn't know about until the autopsy. It's unclear when she learned she was a diabetic. Megan thinks her mom might have heard it for the first time when she was pregnant with her, but Crystal never had regular medical care because she didn't qualify for Medicaid as Possum did.

Megan started spending more time away from her mom in the tenth grade, when Corey and his family moved to town. Crystal consented to their high-school romance, though she warned Corey that if he ever hit her daughter, she'd put him in the ground herself. Within a year of going out with Corey, Megan was pregnant. She swears she didn't know it until she was seven and a half months along, when Corey's mother made her take a pregnancy test. They had a short time to prepare for Kelly's birth in February 2012, but Crystal was happy about the new baby. It was a way for her to have another child. But after Kelly's birth, Crystal and Megan argued; Megan was worried her mother would spoil Kelly. Because Corey's father worked, his family had a bit more money, and they bought more baby clothes than Crystal could, which only made her feel worse.

In the final months of her life, Crystal complained of chest aches, but when she went to the emergency room, the doctors assured her it wasn't a heart attack. She said that she felt like she had the flu or allergies. In hindsight, it was after Terry's death—he died a week after Kelly was born—when Crystal really began to suffer. He had been the linchpin of the family, and now they were breaking apart. After he died, Crystal would call Linda's daughter and say, "I wish God would have took me instead of Terry." Crystal posted regularly about Terry on her Facebook page. Crystal had stopped coming to Linda's for breakfast, too, because Possum was growing sicker and had started falling when he tried to walk on his own. He was diagnosed with cancer about a week before Crystal's death. "I couldn't help but wonder if maybe some of it might have been attributed to her system just being drug down from having to take care of Carl and Megan," says Steve Green, the school superintendent. "Just everyday stress."

The night before she died, Crystal made herself a peanut-butter-and-jelly sandwich for dinner. After Megan took Kelly home, she went to bed and fell asleep, but Possum said she woke up at 1 A.M., said she was thirsty, and went to the kitchen. She was a fitful sleeper, and she returned to bed. When Crystal wasn't up before him the next morning, it struck Possum as odd, but he let her sleep. Crystal usually called her relatives around 6 or 7 A.M. to see what their plans were for the day. They wondered if something was wrong when their phones didn't beep. Finally, Possum sent in his brother, who'd been staying with them, to wake Crystal up; they were always going after each other, and he thought the teasing would spur her out of bed.

Crystal's funeral was small, mostly attended by family, and held at the funeral home in Cave City. They buried her in a tiny graveyard next to a little white chapel on Antioch Road, near the land where Crystal was born. Megan went to stay with Corey's family, and they offered to buy Possum a prefabricated barn so he could come live near them, but there was no need. He spent most of the next four weeks in and out of the hospital, until he died of massive heart failure on June 22. Possum was buried right beside Crystal. Both graves are marked with temporary notices. Linda has promised Megan she will help buy tombstones.

The medical examiner's investigation into Crystal's death was closed because it was determined she died of natural causes. The police report lists no official cause. With untreated, unmanaged diabetes, her blood would have been thick and sticky—the damage would have been building for years—and it could have caused cardiac arrest or a stroke. Linda has her own explanation: "Her heart exploded." And, in a way, it had.

After her mom's death, Megan was 17, hitched, and living on the same land where Crystal had given birth to her. Was it going to be the same life over again?

At school, a number of administrators and teachers stepped in to make sure Megan felt supported; one of them was the technology coordinator for the Cave City schools, Julie Johnson. With big gray eyes and a neat gray bob, she seems younger than 46. When I visited the school this spring, Julie showed me a picture of Megan with Kelly, Corey, and his family that Megan copied and gave to her. They became close last winter when Julie walked into one of Megan's classrooms and the teacher asked, "Have you congratulated Megan?" Julie turned to her and said, "What have you done, sister?" Megan told her that she'd given birth only a week before but that she'd wanted to come back to school. Julie said, "Dang, you're tough!"

Julie has seen a lot of teen mothers. Arkansas ranks No. 1 in the country in teenage births. About a month before Megan gave birth to Kelly, another young woman from the school had gotten married and had a baby, then died mysteriously. Nobody knew what had caused it, and the girl, Bethany, was in the back of Julie's mind when she saw Megan. "I've been in education for 25 years. I kind of got a good eye and sensed where she was coming from. And I was troubled because, as I kept thinking, OK, if a teacher here at school has a baby, they have a big shower for her, and if somebody at church has a baby, they have a shower for her, but if you have a child as a child, we don't do anything."

She prayed on what to do, and prayed some more. It led her to start the Bethany Project, a donation program that would give Megan and other young mothers baby clothes, school supplies, and community support. Megan was only in the spring of her junior year when she had Kelly. Megan told Julie she'd promised her mother she'd stay in school—Megan told me Crystal wanted her to have a good job so she could take care of Kelly and spoil her rotten—and Julie thinks Megan's mother-in-law helped her uphold her promise. "Corey's mother, I think she would have fought the devil to make sure those two finished school." They did. Megan and Corey finished school on May 3 of this year, were married eight days later on May 11, and then graduated on May 18, just a few days shy of the anniversary of Crystal's death. Megan found a job at Wendy's and plans to enroll in the community college in Batesville. Finishing college would give her the best chance to escape her mother's fate.

Julie knows a lot of young women who will never break the cycle. She has her own thoughts about what might be dragging down their life expectancy. "Desperation," she says. "You look at the poverty level in this county—I love this place. It's where I'm from. I don't want you to think I'm being negative about it." But she gestures toward the highway and notes how little is there: a few convenience stores, a grocery, and a nursing home. You have to drive north to the county seat in Ash Flat for a Walmart, or you can negotiate traffic in Batesville, where you might get a job at the chicken plant or a fast-food restaurant. "If you are a woman, and you are a poorly educated woman, opportunities for you are next to nothing. You get married and you have kids. You can't necessarily provide as well as you'd like to for those kids. Oftentimes, the way things are, you're better off if you're not working. You get more help. You get better care for your kids if you're not working. It's a horrible cycle.

"You don't even hear about women's lib, because that's come and gone. But you hear about glass ceilings, and I think girls, most especially girls, have to be taught that just because they're girls doesn't mean they can't do something. That they are just as smart, that they are just as valuable as males. And we have to teach boys that girls can be that way, too. They all need the love, nurturing, and support from somebody from their family or who's not their family. Somebody who's willing to step up. There has to be something to inspire kids to want more, to want better. And they have to realize that they're going to have to work hard to get it. I don't know how you do that.

"It's just horrible, you know? I don't know if 'horrible' is the right word." Julie puts her face into her hands. "The desperation of the times. I don't know anything about anything, but that's what kills them."

How We Do Harm

OTIS WEBB BRAWLEY, M.D. AND PAUL GOLDBERG

With the tragic story of one of his patients framing his analysis, Brawley discusses racial and class disparities in the health-care system and how the current organization of the system harms patients.

She walks through the emergency-room doors sometime in the early morning. In a plastic bag, she carries an object wrapped in a moist towel. She is not bleeding. She is not in shock. Her vital signs are okay. There is no reason to think that she will collapse on the spot. Since she is not truly an emergency patient, she is triaged to the back of the line, and other folks, those in immediate distress, get in for treatment ahead of her. She waits on a gurney in a cavernous, green hallway. The "chief complaint" on her chart at Grady Memorial Hospital, in downtown Atlanta, might have set off a wave of nausea at a hospital in a white suburb or almost any place in the civilized world. It reads, "My breast has fallen off. Can you reattach it?" She waits for at least four hours—likely, five or six. The triage nurse doesn't seek to determine the whereabouts of the breast. Obviously, the breast is in the bag.

I am making rounds on the tenth floor when I get a page from Tammie Quest in the Emergency Department. At Grady, we take care of patients who can't pay, patients no one wants. They come to us with their bleeding wounds, their run-amok diabetes, their end-stage tumors, their drama. You deal with this wreck-age for a while and you develop a coping mechanism. You detach. That's why many doctors, nurses, and social workers here come off as if they have departed for a less turbulent planet. Tammie is not like that. She emotes, and I like having her as the queen of ER—an experienced black woman who gives a shit. When Dr. Quest pages me, I know it isn't because she needs a social interaction. It has to be something serious. "We are wanted in the ER," I tell my team. The cancer team today consists of a fellow, a resident, two medical students, and yours truly, in a flowing white coat, as the attending physician. I lead the way down the hall. Having grown up Catholic, I can't help thinking of the med students and young doctors as altar boys following a priest.

I am a medical oncologist, the kind of doctor who gives chemotherapy. My other interests are epidemiology and biostatistics. I am someone you might ask whether a drug works, whether you should get a cancer screening test, and whether a white man's cancer differs from a black man's cancer. You can also ask me if we are winning the "war" on the cluster of diseases we call cancer. As chief medical officer of the American Cancer Society [ACS]—a position I have held since 2007—I often end up quoted in the newspapers, and I am on television a lot. In addition to my academic, journalistic, and public-policy roles, I have been taking care of cancer patients at Grady for nearly a decade, first as the founding director of the cancer center, and now as chief doctor at the ACS.

My retinue behind me, I keep up a fast pace, this side of a jog. Bill Bernstein, the fellow, is the most senior of the group. Bill is a Newton, Massachusetts, suburbanite, still boyish. He is having trouble adjusting to the South, to Atlanta, to its inner city. He is trying, but it's hard to miss that black people and poor people perplex him. Contact with so much despair makes him awkward. But he has a good heart, a surfeit of common sense—and he is smart. Whatever we teach him at Grady will make him a better doctor wherever he ends up. Grady suffers from what the administration here calls a "vertical transportation problem." Our elevators are slow at best, broken at worst. We head for the stairs, rushing down to the first floor, then through long, green hallways into the ER.

Grady is a monument to racism. Racism is built into it, as is poverty, as is despair. Shaped like a capital letter *H*, Grady is essentially two hospitals with a hallway—a crossover—in the middle to keep things separate but equal for sixteen stories. In the 1950s and '60s, white patients were wheeled into the front section, which faces the city. Blacks went to the back of the *H*. This structure—built in 1953—was actually an improvement over the previous incarnation. The Big *H*—the current Grady—replaced two separate buildings—the whites got a brick building, the blacks a run-down wood-frame structure. Older Atlantans continue to refer to the place in a chilling plural, the Gradys.

You end up at Grady for four main reasons. It could happen because you have no insurance and are denied care at a private hospital, or because you are unconscious when you arrive by ambulance. When your lights are out, you are in no position to ask to be taken to a cleaner,

better-lit, suburban palace of medicine. A third, small contingent are older black folks with insurance, who could go anywhere but have retained a dim memory of Grady as the only Atlanta hospital that accepted us. The fourth category, injured cops and firemen, know that we see a lot of shock and trauma and are good at it. We are their ER of choice.

Today, our 950-bed behemoth stands for another form of segregation: poor versus rich, separate but with no pretense of equality. Grady is Atlanta's safety-net hospital. It is also the largest hospital in the United States. The ER, arguably the principal entry point to Grady, was built in the center of the hospital, filling in some of the *H* on the first floor. To build it, Grady administrators got some federal funds in time for the 1996 Summer Olympics. This fueled financial machinations, which led to criminal charges, which led to prison terms. (In retrospect, the bulk of the money was put to good use. Many of the victims of the Olympic Park bombing came through our ER.) The hallways here are incredibly crowded, even by the standards of inner-city hospitals. Patients are triaged into three color-coded lines—surgery, internal medicine, obstetrics—and placed on gurneys two-deep, leaving almost no room for staff to squeeze through.

You might see a homeless woman drifting in and out of consciousness next to a Georgia Tech student bloodied from being pistol-whipped in an armed robbery, next to a fifty-seven-year-old suburban secretary terrified by a sudden loss of vision, next to a twenty-eight-year-old hooker writhing in pain that shoots up from her lower abdomen, next to a conventioneer who blacked out briefly in a cylindrical tower of a downtown hotel, next to a fourteen-year-old slum dweller who struggles for breath as his asthma attack subsides. When I first arrived in Atlanta and all of this was new to me, I took my wife, Yolanda, through the Grady ER on a Friday night. "Oh, the humanity," she said. Yolanda, a lawyer with the U.S. Securities and Exchange Commission, feels happier above the Mason–Dixon Line.

. . . Elsewhere, patients might trust us doctors, admire us, even bow to our robes, our honorifics, and the all-caps abbreviations that follow our names. Here, not so much. A place called Tuskegee is about two hours away from here. It's where government doctors staged a medical experiment in the thirties: they watched black men die of syphilis, withholding treatment even after effective drugs were invented. Tuskegee is not an abstraction in these parts. It's a physical place, as palpable as a big, deep wound, and eighty-plus years don't mean a thing. Tuskegee is a huge, flashing CAUTION sign in the consciousness of Southern black folks. It explains why they don't trust doctors much and why good docs such as Tammie have to fight so hard to earn their elementary trust. Like me, Tammie is a member of the medical-school faculty at Emory University, and, like me, she has several academic interests. One of these interests is end-of-life care for cancer patients: controlling the symptoms when someone with advanced cancer shows up in your ER.

Seeing us approach, she walks toward us and hands me a wooden clipboard with the Grady forms. I look at her face, gauging the mixture of sadness, moral outrage, and fatigue. She says something like "This patient *needs* someone who cares," and disappears. I glance at the chief complaint. "Holy shit," I say to Bill Bernstein and, more so, to myself.

I introduce myself to a trim, middle-aged, black woman, not unattractive, wearing a blue examination gown conspicuously stamped GRADY. (At Grady, things such as gowns, infusion pumps, and money tend to vanish.) From the moment Tammie paged me, I knew that the situation had to be more than a run-of-the-mill emergency. This patient clearly is not about to die on the examination table. She doesn't need emergency treatment. Before anything, she needs somebody to talk to. She needs attention, both medical and human.

The patient, Edna Riggs, is fifty-three. She works for the phone company and lives on the southeast side of Atlanta. Sitting on an exam table, she looks placid. When she extends her hand, it feels limp. She makes fleeting eye contact. This is depression, maybe. Shame does the same thing, as does a sense of doom. *Fatalism* is the word doctors have repurposed to describe this last form of alienation.

In medicine, we speak a language of our own, and Edna's physical problem has a name in doctorese: automastectomy. It's a fancy way of saying that the patient's breast has fallen off by itself. An automastectomy can occur when a tumor grows so big and so deep that it cuts off the blood supply from the chest to the breast. Denied oxygen, breast tissue dies and the breast starts to detach from the chest wall. At places such as Grady, automastectomies are seen a couple of times a year, often enough to be taken in stride.

This case is different from others I have seen only because Edna Riggs has wrapped her detached breast in a moist, light-blue towel and brought it with her for reattachment. I can't help wondering why the towel is moist. Some deliberateness has gone into the breast's care. I cringe at the thought that Edna has kept that package next to her on the gurney in the ER for hours. In the exam gown, Edna's chest looks surprisingly normal. I ask how long she has had a "breast problem." She first felt something in her breast when her son was in second grade, she replies. It has grown over the years. She speaks correct English, not the language of the streets. She sounds like someone who has had schooling, a person who reads. Her hair is clean and combed, she is dressed neatly. What grade is her son in now? Eleventh. I don't react, not visibly. She has known she had a problem for nine years—why did she do nothing? I ask Edna's permission to examine her. She nods. I ask her to lie down, my entourage gathering around.

I help her remove her right arm from the gown, trying to respect her modesty and preserve as much dignity as possible. I undrape the right breast, or the place where the right breast had been. The chest wall is now rugged. I see yellowish, fibrous tissue and dry blood. There is the unforgettable smell of anaerobic bacteria. The wound is infected. I reach for examination gloves. I palpate her chest wall and feel under her armpit, looking for evidence of enlarged nodes. After examining the breast wall, I look in the towel. Her amputated breast could fit on her chest as if it were a puzzle piece.

I am not looking forward to Edna's repeating her request to reattach the breast. If she asks directly, I will have to say that this is not possible and explain why not. My preference is to move slowly, to let her adjust, to make her comfortable with me, with receiving medical care for her condition. I fear that she will get up, leave, and never return. Fortunately, Edna doesn't repeat her request. Perhaps the magnitude of the problem confronting her is starting to sink in, Edna's breast cancer has been growing for at least nine years. It's unheard-of that cancer such as this would be anything but metastatic. The disease has to have disseminated to her bones, lungs, brain, liver. I feel a wave of frustration and anger.

Another day at Grady Memorial Hospital. Here I sit, talking with a patient whom we would probably have cured nine years earlier, and today I will have to tell her that she has a terminal disease. The rest is logistics. I arrange for the pathology and radiology to get confirmation. We always get pathologic confirmation of cancer, even when we are almost certain that it is cancer. An old medical saying goes: "When you hear hoofbeats, think horses, not zebras." This saying has an important corollary: "You don't want to be bit on the ass by a zebra." There is a remote possibility that Edna's automastectomy was caused by leprosy or some unusual infectious disease. It's cheap and easy to get verification that it's cancer.

I ask Bill Bernstein to talk with Edna, to take a full history, to perform a full examination. The objective is to rule out neurologic problems from spread of the disease to the brain or spine, to look for other evidence of problems caused by the disease. If you take me aside and ask why I'm withdrawing from the scene, I will say that I am trying to awaken Bill's compassion. But it is something else as well, something about me. I am afraid of growing callous. I acknowledge this readily, as a means of staving it off. I am trying to

avoid accepting the unnecessary loss of yet another life. In the case of Edna Riggs, the abstract, scholarly term *health disparities* acquires a very real smell of a rotting breast. I take my leave and, with the resident, start arranging tests to confirm the diagnosis and get Edna ready for treatment. We will fight, even though we are going to lose. Metastatic breast cancer always wins. We have drugs to decrease pain and even make most people live longer, but we can beat breast cancer only when it's caught early.

We admit Edna Riggs into the hospital, to get the tests done and to start antibiotic treatment of the infected wound. We could have done the workup without admitting her, but I fear that she will leave the system as abruptly as she entered. Psychological and emotional support are legitimate reasons for admittance, though most insurance companies and Medicaid would disagree. As she starts to trust me, Edna tells me how frightened she was when she found a lump in her breast. Right away, she knew it was breast cancer, and in her experience, everyone who got breast cancer died quickly, painfully. Insurance problems kept her away from the doctor, as did the fear of dying. She knew she would die after going to the doctor. Several of her friends had.

Early on, Edna had some insurance, which didn't do her any good. Her employer wouldn't let her take just two or three hours of sick leave to go to the doctor. If she needed to take sick leave, she had to take it in increments of one day. This guaranteed that an employee would exhaust all the leave quickly. If Edna had been fired for taking time off after exhausting her sick leave, her three kids, too, would have lost support and insurance. Acknowledging the physical problem and facing the consequences became increasingly difficult. Edna tells me that she feared the disease, but she also feared the system. Would the doctors scold her? Would they experiment on her? Would they give her drugs that caused nausea, vomiting, hair loss? Would the hospital kill her?

Edna's decision to stay out of the medical system was about fear: fear of breast cancer, fear of the medical profession, fear of losing the roof over her kids' heads. Fear intensified after her employer started to require copayments from workers who wanted to be insured. This extra $3,000 a year made health insurance too expensive to keep. Payment for medical services and sick-leave policies determine the quality of care we receive. Several years ago, my research team at the American Cancer Society published data showing that people diagnosed with cancer who had no insurance or were insured through Medicaid were 1.6 times more likely to die in five years as those with private insurance. In breast cancer, patients with private insurance were more likely to be diagnosed with Stage I breast cancer than those who had no insurance or were receiving Medicaid. In colon cancer, too, the chances of catching the disease at an earlier, treatable stage were lower in the uninsured and Medicaid populations. Even when the disease was found early, an uninsured patient did worse than one with insurance. For example, an insured patient with Stage II colon cancer had better odds of being alive five years after diagnosis than an uninsured patient with what should be highly curable Stage I cancer. . . .

ACS epidemiologists estimate that the lack of insurance annually costs eight thousand Americans their lives due to inability to receive cancer treatment. Even controlling cancer pain is no small challenge if you are poor. Uninsured patients cannot afford pain medicines. The social programs that give them medication heavily ration pain meds. Even if you have insurance that will pay for your treatment, you may still not be able to afford to receive it.

I have seen poor breast-cancer patients choose mastectomy (surgical removal of the entire breast) over a lumpectomy (removal of the tumor) because of employer sick-leave policies. A woman who chooses a lumpectomy must also receive radiation, which has to be given daily, Monday through Friday, for six to eight weeks. The treatment requires fifteen minutes in the clinic, but it's done only during business hours. Unfortunately, this less disfiguring treatment is hardly an option for a woman who knows that

longer postoperative treatment will cause her to lose her job. . . .

Patients most likely to have the worst outcomes are defined in a couple of ways. Poverty is the biggest driver, followed by race. . . . Much of the problem is that poor people don't get care that would be likely to help them. The reasons for this are complex. Perhaps they can't get care, or don't know where care is available, or they haven't been offered insurance or steady access to care by their jobs or social services.

Here is the problem: Poor Americans consume too little health care, especially preventive health care. Other Americans—often rich Americans—consume too much health care, often unwisely, and sometimes to their detriment. The American health-care system combines famine with gluttony. We could improve dismal health outcomes on both ends of the socioeconomic spectrum if we were simply faithful to science, if we provided and practiced care that we know to be effective.

Early on, Edna ignored her tumor. She accomplished this easily during her busy days, but not when she was alone at night. The disease progressed relentlessly. The lump grew. Then the tumor broke through the skin, causing a gaping wound, which became infected. The odor caused problems at work. Edna tried to conceal it with body powder and cologne, which worked at first. Her kids started trying to get her to come in and get help several months earlier, after a powerful, relentless stench finally set in.

Since Edna couldn't pay for private insurance and have enough money left over to provide for her family, she had to come to Grady. Officially, Grady treats any resident of the two counties that support it: Fulton and DeKalb. When I arrived in Atlanta in 2001, the hospital was lax in enforcing the residency requirement. It ended up being the hospital for poor people in many surrounding counties, even though only Fulton and DeKalb taxpayers paid. As costs grew, Grady was forced to require proof of residency.

Our doctors are good, but free care comes at the cost of time lost waiting for appointments, waiting for tests. You can spend an entire day waiting for a service that a private doctor's office provides in fifteen minutes or less. People like Edna, who need every day's earnings and who can easily be jettisoned from their jobs, can afford time away from work even less than professionals, who may have some savings and job security. So people like Edna wait until it's impossible to wait any longer; they come to see us when it's too late.

Why do black women end up with more aggressive breast cancer? Is this due to some biological characteristic that correlates with race, perhaps even determined by it? Can there be such a thing as white breast cancer and black breast cancer? Could these be different diseases? You have to synthesize a pile of statistical data and medical literature to get insight into these problems, but it's worth the effort: You end up with extraordinarily valuable insights into the epidemiology and biology of cancer. More than that, you gain insight into economic structures in our society and, ultimately, something very big: the meaning of race.

At a glance, breast cancer in a black woman like Edna appears to differ from breast cancer in an average white woman. If you plot breast cancer on a spectrum from the worst prognosis to the best, a higher proportion of black women would wind up on the worst end. One of the most ominous varieties of breast cancer is called triple-negative, because it is immune to three commonly used treatments . . . all we can do is resort to desperate measures: harsher chemotherapies, which we know are frequently of little or no use. About 30 percent of breast cancer in black women is triple-negative disease, compared to 18 percent in white women. This disparity could appear to suggest a biological difference, but in fact it's rooted in cultural, historical, and societal divides. To understand this, we have to look at the potential causes of breast cancer in white and black women.

To start with, let's consider the incidence of better-prognosis cancer among white women. Instead of asking why black women are more likely to get more virulent breast cancer, let's ask why white women are more likely to develop the

disease that has a better prognosis. The answer can be gleaned in part from the incidence statistics. For the past three decades—or for as long as we have had a national registry—the incidence of breast cancer has been higher in white women than in black women. In 2000, the National Cancer Institute's Surveillance, Epidemiology, and End Results registry reported that during the previous year, blacks had an age-adjusted incidence rate of 125 per 100,000 women. In the past twenty years, the black incidence rate has bounced between the low of 105 per 100,000 in 1989 to the high point of 126 in 2008. In 2000, white women had an incidence rate of 143 per 100,000. The breast cancer incidence rate in whites had risen from the 1970s, peaked at 147 per 100,000 in 1999, and has fallen to 129 per 100,000 in 2008. The incidence rates were substantially apart over the past couple of decades, but have now nearly evened out. Was this occurring because white women were using mammography more and were therefore more likely to get diagnosed? Not quite. The proportion of women getting mammography screening is roughly the same among whites and blacks. (I suspect that the proportion getting high-quality mammography is greater among whites than blacks, but this difference has not been adequately studied.)

The delay of pregnancy and childbirth is a more plausible explanation. White women tend to have children later in life than black women. Professional women, regardless of their race, go to college, establish their careers, and then have kids. Delaying childbirth past the age of thirty clearly increases the risk of breast cancer. To be specific, it increases the risk of estrogen-receptor-positive breast cancer, which has a better prognosis. Also, white women have been more likely to use postmenopausal hormone-replacement therapy (HRT). Doctors prescribed HRT because it made sense logically. Without definitive data on the therapy's biological effect, doctors were, in effect, staging a decades-long societal experiment.

By 2003, 35 percent of postmenopausal white American women had taken this therapy at some time. For cultural and socioeconomic reasons, black women tended not to take HRT. Fewer than 5 percent of postmenopausal black women took HRT. This is important, because HRT is associated with better prognosis breast cancer. In 2003, an analysis from the well-designed study called the Women's Health Initiative showed that HRT was correlated with an increased risk of breast cancer. It was actually correlated with an increased risk of estrogen-receptor-positive, better prognosis breast cancer. The societal experiment was over. The analysis led to a drop in the use of HRT, which likely accounts for the drop in breast cancer in white women from 147 per 100,000 in 1999 to 129 per 100,000 in 2008.

Let's return to the disparity in triple-negative breast cancer by race: 30 percent in black breast cancer patients, and 18 percent in white patients. There is no difference in the proportion of black and white women with progesterone-positive or HER2-positive disease. So if we are to focus on the 12 percent disparity, we must look exclusively at the racial difference in the prevalence of the estrogen receptor. Does *this* suggest that skin color stands for some biological difference? Not really.

Because of dietary differences that are caused by culture and socioeconomic status, a black girl in the United States accumulates weight much faster than a white girl. In the 1960s, the Centers for Disease Control and Prevention compared the start of menstruation by age. The study showed that the average age of menarche for white American girls was 12.8 years. For black American girls, it was 12.4 years. This is a bigger difference than it might seem. It means that 53 percent of black girls have started menstruating by their thirteenth birthday, compared to 43 percent of white girls. [Just the simple number of uninterrupted menstrual cycles increases the risk of breast cancer later in life].

Body mass index, a calculation based on weight and height, correlates with early nutrition status, which has a lot to do with age at first menstruation. Poor Americans have diets higher

in calories and reach the weight of one hundred pounds faster. . . . The reason for this rapid weight gain in black girls has nothing to do with race, but reflects a high caloric intake and a diet rich in carbohydrates, a socioeconomic determinant of health. It's not about race. It's at least in part about the sort of food that is available in poor areas of inner cities.

The area of Detroit where I grew up and the areas of Atlanta where my patients come from are known as produce deserts. Grocery stores there carry all the chips, sodas, and mentholated cigarettes you may desire, but if you want a head of lettuce, you are out of luck. You observe the same problems among poor whites, yet you don't see them among wealthy, well-educated blacks. . . . This extrapolation produces a deeply disturbing picture: the black–white gap in the onset of menstruation and body weight has dramatically widened, which means that the disease disparities will widen also.

Edna has Stage IV breast cancer. Disease has spread all over her body. Had she come to see me early in the course of her disease, it would have cost about $30,000 to cure her. She could have remained a taxpayer. Her kids could have had a mother. Now, the cure is not an option. Still, we'll fight. We will give her breast-cancer chemotherapy that will cost more than $150,000, even though the chances are she will still die in less than two years. If you are a caring doctor, you realize she is just fifty-three, with kids and folks who love her, and your motivation is akin to a philosophy of Wayne Gretzky: "You miss every shot you don't take."

Every time I start chemo for metastatic disease I think of a patient named Sandra, a lively, young black woman whom I have treated for six years. She had brain metastases when I first met her. She has had active disease ever since, and even the doctor who sent her to me reminds me every time he sees me that he is amazed that she is alive, functional, and enjoying life.

Yes, sometimes cancer drugs give us "long-term survival," in the dispassionate language of those of us who study outcomes. But for every

Sandra, we get fifty patients with metastatic disease who "don't do well." They live a median eighteen months, which means that half are living and half are dead a year and a half after diagnosis.

We try three treatments and contain Edna's disease for a while. She dies at age fifty-five, about twenty months after walking into the ER.

NOTES

A history of Grady Memorial Hospital can be found in Jerry Gentry, *Grady Baby: A Year in the Life of Atlanta's Grady Hospital* (Jackson: University Press of Mississippi, 1999).

Discussion of the Grady mission with some historical perspective is found in A. G. Yancey Sr., "Medical Education in Atlanta and Health Care of Black, Minority and Low-Income People," *Journal of the National Medical Association* 80 (April 1988):476–76.

The Tuskegee Syphilis Study and rumors about it are mentioned as reason why African-Americans are often suspicious of medicine. The facts of the trial are frequently inaccurately conveyed even in the news media. Factual accounts have been written, such as S. M. Baker, O. W. Brawley, and L. S. Marks, "Effects of untreated syphilis in the Negro male, 1932 to 1972: A closure comes to the Tuskegee study, 2004," *Urology* 65 (2005). James H. Jones, *Bad Blood: The Tuskegee Syphilis Experiment* (1981; repr., New York: Free Press, 1993), is a history of "The Study of Untreated Syphilis in the Negro Male" (this is the official name of the Tuskegee Syphilis Study). Jones's book also mentions many of the atrocities that humans have perpetrated upon vulnerable humans and called research.

Medical Apartheid by Harriet Washington is a superb history and ethical analysis. She painstakingly researched and documented numerous medical abuses over the past two centuries, including abuses within the past decade. Many of these abuses have been long talked about in the African American oral history tradition. Washington was able to find proof of alarming truths. These findings justify distrust of the American medical profession.

The literature on the fears that African-Americans have of the American medical system is portrayed in Rebecca Skloot, *The Immortal Life of Henrietta Lacks* (New York: Crown Publishers, 2010).

A number of patterns-of-care studies demonstrate that the poor as a group do not receive as high a quality of medical care as the middle class and have worse health-care outcomes; S. A. Fedewa, S. B. Edge, A. K. Stewart, M. T. Halpern, N. M. Marlow, and E. M. Ward, "Race and ethnicity are associated with delays in breast cancer treatment (2003–2006)," *Journal of Health Care for the Poor and Underserved* 22, no. 1 (2001); 128–41; A. S. Robbins, A. L. Pavluck, S. A. Fedewa, A. Y. Chen, and E. M. Ward, "Insurance status, comorbidity level, and survival among colorectal cancer patients age 18 to 64 years in the National Cancer Data Base from 2003 to 2005," *Journal of Clinical Oncology* 27, no. 22 (August 1, 2009); 3627–33 (epub, May 26, 2009); and E. Ward, H. Halpern, N. Schrag, V. Cokkinides, C. DeSantis, P. Bandi, R. Siegel, A. Stewart, and A. Jemal, "Association of insurance with cancer care utilization and outcomes," *CA: A Cancer Journal for Clinicians*, 58, no. 1 (January–February 2008: 9–31 (epub, December 20, 2007).

The NCI defines the medically underserved as "individuals who lack access to primary and specialty care either because they are socioeconomically disadvantaged and they may live in areas with high poverty rates or because they reside in rural areas": http://deais.nci.nih.gov/glossary/terms?alpha=M&currentPage=1.

Trends in breast cancer by race and ethnicity: C. Smigal, A. Jemal, E. Ward, V. Cokkinides, R. Smith, H. L. Howe, and M. Thun, "Update 2006," *CA: A Cancer Journal for Clinicians* 56, no. 3 (May–June 2006): 168–83.

A higher proportion of the African-American breast cancer population has triple negative disease compared to the population of white women with breast cancer. Triple negative breast cancer is the most serious type of breast cancer. Other forms of the disease are more aggressive, but targeted therapies can slow the progression of the disease. This is explained in L. A. Carey,

E. C. Dees, L. Sawyer, et al., "The triple negative paradox: Primary tumor chemosensitivity of breast cancer subtypes," Clinical Cancer Research 13, no. 8 (April 15, 2007): 2329–34; and K. M. O'Brien, S. R. Cole, C. K. Tse, C. M. Perou, L. A. Carey, W. D. Foulkes, L. G. Dressler, J. Geradts, and R. C. Millikan, "Intrinsic breast tumor subtypes, race, and long-term survival in the Carolina Breast Cancer Study," *Clinical Cancer Research* 16, no. 24 (December 15, 2010): 6100–6110.

U.S. breast cancer rates by race are provided by the National Cancer Institute Cancer Statistics Review at https://seer.cancer.gov.

The effect of postmenopausal hormone replacement therapy (HRT or HT) was studied in the Women's Health Initiative, a study sponsored by the National Institutes of Health.

The decline in breast cancer incidence was documented in M. Ravdin, K. A. Cronin, N. Howlader, C. D. Berg, R. T. Chlebowski, E. J. Feuer, B. K. Edwards, and D. A. Berry, "The decrease in breast cancer incidence in 2003 in the United States," *New England Journal of Medicine* 356, no. 16 (April 19, 2007); and Million Women Study Collaborators, "Patterns of use of hormone replacement therapy in one million women in Britain, 1996–2000," *BJOG* 109, no. 12 (December 2002): 1319–30.

Public law 103-43, signed in 1993 by President William Clinton, mandated the Long Island Breast Cancer Study. A good description of the study is found in M. D. Gammon, A. I. Neugut, R. M. Santella, et al., "The Long Island Breast Cancer Study Project: Description of a multi-institutional collaboration to identify environmental risk factors for breast cancer," *Breast Cancer Research and Treatment* 74, no. 3 (June 2002): 235–54.

The correlation between weight gain in childhood and earlier age of menarche is discussed in S. E. Anderson, G. E. Dallal, and A. Must, "Relative weight and race influence average age at menarche: Results from two nationally representative surveys of US girls studied 25 years apart," *Pediatrics* 111, no. 4 (pt. 1) (April 2003): 844–50.

The relation between age at menarche and race and its relationship to disease in adulthood is discussed in D. S. Freedman, L. K. Khan, M. K. Serdula, W. H. Dietz, S. R. Srinivasan, and G. S. Berenson, "Relation of age at menarche to race, time period, and anthropometric dimensions: The Bogalusa Heart Study," *Pediatrics* 110, no. 4 (October 2002): e43.

Population trends in breast cancer in Scotland can tell us a lot about breast cancer in the United States: S. B. Brown, D. J. Hole, and T. G. Cooke, "Breast cancer incidence trends in deprived and affluent Scottish women," *Breast Cancer Research and Treatment* 103, no. (June 2007):233–38 (epub, October 11, 2006); U. Macleod, S. Ross, C. Twelves, W. D. George, C. Gillis, and G. C. Watt, "Primary and secondary care management of women with early breast cancer from affluent and deprived areas: Retrospective review of hospital and general practice records," *BMJ* 320, no. 7247 (May 27, 2000): 1442–45; C. S. Thomson, D. J. Hole, C. J. Twelves, D. H. Brewster, and R. J. Black, "Prognostic factors in women with breast cancer: Distribution by socioeconomic status and effect on differences in survival," Journal *of Epidemiology and Community Health* 55 (2001): 308–15; N. H. Gordon, "Socioeconomic factors and breast cancer in black and white Americans," *Cancer and Metastasis Reviews* 22 (2003): 55–65; B. K. Dunn, T. Agurs-Collins, D. Browne, R. Lubet, and K. A. Johnson, "Health disparities in breast cancer: Biology meets socioeconomic status," *American Journal of Public Health* 100, no. S1 (April 1, 2010): S132–39 (epub, February 10, 2010); and N. Krieger, J. T. Chen, and P. D. Waterman, "Decline in US breast cancer rates after the Women's Health Initiative: Socioeconomic and racial/ethnic differentials," *American Journal of Public Health* 100, no. 6 (June 2010): 972.

Social Problems Related to Crime and the Criminal Justice System

Nicole D. Porter

Nicole D. Porter is the director of advocacy for the Sentencing Project.

What is the Sentencing Project's mission and as director of advocacy, what do you do?

The Sentencing Project works to achieve a fair and effective U.S. criminal justice system by promoting reforms in sentencing policy, addressing unjust racial disparities and practices in the criminal justice system, and by advocating for alternatives to incarceration.

As director of advocacy I work with state and local organizations and individuals on state and local policy reform and on advocacy campaigns that align with the Sentencing Project's mission. For example, I supported campaigns to address sentencing disparities for crack and powder cocaine in Missouri and California. This is an ongoing issue in the criminal justice system; people who have been convicted for possession or distribution of crack cocaine have been punished more harshly than those with cocaine possession convictions, disproportionately affecting minority communities.

How did you first become interested in this type of activism?

I grew up in a political family and have always been interested in politics and in critiquing the unfinished project of American democracy. I became interested in criminal justice advocacy when my twin brother was incarcerated and I realized many of the young men I had grown up with had criminal records and had cycled in and out of jail as young adults.

As an activist in your organization, currently what are your top goals?

I want to reduce the number of people in prison and under criminal justice supervision, eliminate racial disparity and inequality in the criminal justice system, and promote a broader concept of public safety that does not rely on arrests or sentencing people to prison. I support solutions that address underlying issues that lead to contact with law enforcement, such as advocating for living-wage employment and access to high-quality education. In communities with high rates of incarceration, these solutions will help prevent contact with the criminal justice system.

What strategies do you use to enact social change?

I use research, communications, and advocacy. To raise public awareness about inequities I write policy reports and produce materials for members of the general public, policy makers, and the media. This usually involves a lot of research about laws and policies. For example, in order to address the problem of mass incarceration, I researched the laws and practices that trigger automatic prison sentences (otherwise known as mandatory minimum sentences), lengthen prison terms, and impose collateral consequences long after a conviction (such as being barred from public assistance or subsidized housing even after being released from prison), and then I advocated to reform those laws. I have also worked to change policies known to have a racially disparate impact on sentencing (such as the disparity between sentences for crack and powder cocaine possession).

Working as a policy advocate means engaging directly with the process to change laws and practices. Changing laws involves engaging with lawmakers at the state and federal level around policy reforms known to have an impact, based on our research. Engagement involves visiting with lawmakers, working to write and introduce legislation, and identifying constituent contacts who will also serve as activists and advocates for us (for example, citizens, leadership from different faith communities, and law enforcement officials whose opinions legislators may value).

What would you consider to be your greatest successes as an activist?

I have helped change the law in several states including Texas, Missouri, and California. While

at the Texas American Civil Liberties Union (ACLU), I organized campaigns to address in-prison sexual assault and expand voting rights to persons with felony convictions. While at the Sentencing Project I supported efforts in Missouri to modify that state's crack-powder sentencing disparity and the federal lifetime ban on food stamps for persons with felony drug convictions.

I also contributed to a national narrative that critiques mass incarceration. It involves advancing sentencing reform arguments by assessing which policies or practices are most easily addressed and changed, how to change the political calculus related to sentencing reform, and determining which mechanisms are most likely to raise people's consciousness about these issues. These mechanisms include media strategies like press conferences and opinion editorials, organizing around policy goals to change laws and practices, and mobilizing diverse coalitions of people who may have the power to emphasize changes in public awareness about mass incarceration. I measure this success through media reports that reinforce the approach that my colleagues and I contribute to, as well as the fact that this narrative has been mainstreamed in recent years.

What are the major challenges activists in your field face?

We often lack the capacity and the resources to scale an advocacy infrastructure to the magnitude of need, especially when there are many people impacted nationwide, as there are with issues related to the criminal justice system. And, despite decades of research documenting that our current approach to public safety does not deter crime and exacerbates inequality and racial disparity, there is still a lack of political will to enact policy change that we must fight against. Another challenge is the American culture of punitiveness and retribution that re-inforces excessive sentencing practices for not only the incarcerated, but also for civil sanctions that people with criminal records face. All of these challenges can create fatigue among advocates, but we combat this by working with other allies and finding short-term ways to build momentum and deepen the critique. We stay energized by being self-aware and reflective about what's possible and what remains to be done.

What are major misconceptions the public has about activism in general and your issue specifically?

I am not sure about "major misconceptions." I do think that activists can be marginalized and discredited when they are perceived as too radical, even though radical analyses are, indeed, relevant to social policy.

Why should students get involved in your line of activism?

Students can help shift attitudes and beliefs about public safety and punitiveness, creating more political will to change the system. Student-led campaigns can also help change the law by bringing more awareness to the issues, both to the general population as well as to their elected and local law enforcement officials.

If an individual has little money and time, are there other ways they can contribute?

Engage directly with elected officials or other targets over demands to change law, policy, or practice. Be curious and critical about social policy. Participate in discussions and efforts to improve any social condition by working with civic groups and engaging in activism you are interested in.

Mass Shootings and Masculinity

TRISTAN BRIDGES AND TARA LEIGH TOBER

Mass shootings have become more frequent in the United States, and more and more attention has been paid to preventing them, including increasing gun control and changing gun culture. Bridges and Tober discuss an underexamined facet that almost all mass shootings in the United States share: men were the perpetrators. Bridges and Tober discuss explanations for this phenomenon, arguing that masculinity, violence, and aggression have been intrinsically linked in American culture. As the culture has changed and privileged groups (such as young white men) lose some of their power, a sense of aggrieved entitlement may cause them to lash out.

On December 14, 2012, Adam Lanza—a white, twenty-year-old young man—shot and killed his mother, drove to Sandy Hook Elementary School in Newtown, Connecticut, and shot and killed twenty children and six members of the school staff. When first responders arrived on the scene, Lanza killed himself. Lanza's mass shooting has been identified as among the deadliest mass shootings at a school in the United States. Mass shootings are not common occurrences, yet when they do occur they affect everyone. The massacre at Sandy Hook was felt around the world, as international leaders sent their condolences and people from the Philippines to Egypt lit candles and expressed their collective grief online writing, "My heart is in Newtown" (Brown, 2012). In this way, mass shootings, like terrorist attacks, are significant in the cultural sense. They leave an indelible wound on our social fabric, evoking feelings of helplessness, fear, anger, and heartache.

Despite being rare, mass shootings like Sandy Hook happen more often in the United States than anywhere else in the world, and according to Follman et al. (2014), the rate of their occurrence has increased in recent years. The single most patterned fact associated with mass shooters is their gender—these acts are committed by men. A great deal end in a similarly tragic way when the shooters take their own lives, a fact that led sociologists Rachel Kalish and Michael Kimmel (2010) to refer to these incidents as "suicide by mass murder."

Many of those committing these crimes are heavily armed. They're not just carrying a gun; many carry enough to rival action films. In 1999, Eric Harris and Dylan Kleibold entered Columbine High School in Littleton, Colorado, with an arsenal many compared to lethal scenes in *The Matrix*. Pictures Seung-Hui Cho took of himself with the weapons he used when he committed a mass shooting on the Virginia Tech campus in

---

Original to *Focus on Social Problems: A Contemporary Reader.*

2007 were similar to action movie posters depicting the hero in a dynamic stance with guns drawn. James Eagan Holmes's assault on a movie theatre audience in Aurora, Colorado, in 2012 took place in a theatre showing *The Dark Knight*. Adam Lanza walked into Sandy Hook Elementary with a Bushmaster .223 caliber Remington semiautomatic rifle and killed twenty-seven people with that weapon. Beginning in 2010, this particular weapon was heavily marketed by Bushmaster, the manufacturer, using a "man card" campaign. For example, a full-page spread in *Maxim* magazine depicted a picture of the weapon at a dynamic angle with the caption: "CONSIDER YOUR MAN CARD REISSUED." As part of this campaign, a person could send a friend a supposedly comical note about why their man card has been revoked. Masculinity, the campaign suggests, is tied to gun ownership and use. Indeed, following the shooting, many called on politicians to enact stricter gun control laws and laws that might reduce the number and kind of guns allowed in U.S. households. Gun control is a significant part of the problem of mass shootings. But it is also a significant fact that virtually all of the mass shootings in the United States have been committed by men. Follman et al. (2014) identified at least sixty-nine mass shootings[1] in the past three decades, sixty-eight of which were committed by boys or men.

Bushmaster's advertisement betrays the connection between violence and masculinity. As Michael Kimmel (2012) writes, "From an early age, boys learn that violence is not only an acceptable form of conflict resolution, but one that is admired." This connection between masculinity and violence is not inevitable and it is not the same everywhere. Mass shootings like the one Adam Lanza committed are more common in the United States than anywhere else in the world. Although most American men will never commit this kind of violent act, they are all exposed to lessons early on about what it means to be a "real man" and what to do when your masculinity is questioned. The Bushmaster ad "works"—in the sense that audiences can quickly and easily interpret it—because viewers understand violence as culturally masculine. But what exactly does it mean to say that violence is culturally masculine? And how can we understand that a social problem like mass shootings is just as much about gender as it is about gun control?

Gun Control and Gun Culture

Mass shootings—which include school shootings[2]—are a social problem with more than one cause. Access to guns and to the type of weaponry often used in mass shootings are important pieces of this puzzle. Indeed, of the 143 guns possessed by the shooters in the past three decades, more than three-quarters were obtained legally (Follman et al., 2014). When we look at this issue from a global perspective, however, it becomes clear that guns are only part of the problem. Gun advocates often use the cases of Switzerland and Israel to argue that more guns do not necessarily lead to more gun violence (e.g., Klein, 2012). Military service is compulsory for Swiss men and nearly universal for Israelis. As a result, large numbers of the population have access to firearms. Yet, according to the United Nations Office on Drugs and Crime (2013), both nations have a homicide rate of less than 1 per 100,000, compared to 4 per 100,000 in the United States (Bureau of Justice Statistics, 2013). Rosenbaum's (2012) research, however, demonstrates that Switzerland and Israel may not be the "gun utopias" that people imagine. Both nations have lower gun ownership and stricter guns laws than the United States. For example, owning a gun is not a right in Israel or Switzerland—you must have a reason to possess a gun. Israel rejects about 40 percent of gun permit applicants (Rosenbaum, 2012). Rosenbaum (2012) emphasizes that these countries have begun requiring gun owners to leave their guns on base (Israel) or in depots (Switzerland), curtailing off-duty soldiers from access to firearms. Thus, guns are generally not in the household.

Canada is another example of a nation with relatively high rates of gun ownership and low rates of gun violence. According to the Small Arms Survey (2007), the United States has about 89 guns per 100 residents (ranked highest in the world), whereas Canada has about 31 (ranked twelfth highest). Yet rates of firearm homicide are dramatically lower in Canada—less than 1 per 100,000 people (Statistics Canada, 2014). Jennifer Carlson (2015) argues that the meanings surrounding guns are different in these two countries, suggesting that gun *culture* cannot be reduced to rates of gun *ownership*. One fact supporting this is the type of gun owned. Gun owners in Canada, for instance, are more likely to own long guns (generally used for hunting) as opposed to handguns (generally used for other purposes, such as target shooting and self-defense). A Congressional Research Service report states that as of 2009, the estimated total number of firearms available to civilians in the United States was 114 million handguns, 110 million rifles, and 86 million shotguns (Krouse, 2012). The report also notes that shotgun imports were decreasing in the United States, whereas handgun and rifle imports were increasing (Krouse, 2012). These facts suggest that Canada and the United States have dramatically different gun cultures (Carlson, 2015).

Although there is much debate concerning the relationship between gun control and mass shootings, the data show that perhaps the oft-cited National Rifle Association slogan—"Guns don't kill people, people kill people"—is accurate. The National Rifle Association relies on this when claiming that *people* and not *guns* are responsible for gun violence. It would be more accurate, however, if the slogan read: "Guns don't kill people, men with guns kill people." And it would be even more accurate if it read: "Guns don't kill people, men with guns kill people, and when lone gunmen shoot large numbers of people at random, your best bet is that they're doing it on U.S. soil." So, the social problem of mass shootings is not only about masculinity; it is about American masculinity. But what is the connection between mass shootings and men in the United States? What does it

mean? Why are men so overwhelmingly more likely to commit these crimes than women?

Social scientific research on the topic points to two separate answers. One is a *social psychological explanation* drawing on research related to what social scientists call "social identity threat." The other is a *cultural explanation* that suggests boys and men are navigating gender identities on less certain terrain than their fathers and grandfathers.

Social Psychological Roots of Mass Shootings

The general idea behind what social scientists refer to as "social identity threat" is that when a person perceives an aspect of their identity they care about to be called into question, they respond by overdemonstrating qualities associated with that identity. In a famous essay on masculinity and homophobia, Michael Kimmel offers a classic example. He writes, "I have a standing bet with a friend that I can walk onto any playground in America where 6-year-old boys are happily playing and by asking one question, I can provoke a fight. That question is simple: 'Who's a sissy around here?'" (1994:131). Robb Willer et al. (2013) refer to this as the "masculinity overcompensation thesis." By forcing some boy's gender identity to be questioned, Kimmel assumes that he will demonstrate his masculinity in dramatic fashion—through violence. Kimmel's anecdote relies on an understanding of violence as a resource on which boys can rely to demonstrate their gender identity if and when it has been called into question. We might consider other methods by which the boy identified as the "sissy" might respond. But if we agree that violence is an available (and perhaps predictable) response, then we also must acknowledge that violence and masculinity are connected.

The research on this topic is primarily experimental, meaning research participants come into labs and receive stimuli, and their responses are weighed against others who received different stimuli. One way "masculinity threat" is studied is to bring men into a lab and have them take a survey they are told will measure how "masculine" or "feminine" they are. The feedback they receive is random—some are told they scored within the masculine range and others that they scored within the feminine range. And here is where the research *actually* begins. Men receiving feedback that they scored within the feminine range have had their masculinity experimentally "threatened." But do they respond differently from men whose masculinity has not been threatened? Research shows that they react by overdemonstrating masculinity in a variety of ways.

For instance, Christin Munsch and Robb Willer (2012) discovered that when assessing scenarios concerning sexual interactions involving the use of force or coercion by men against women, college men whose gender identities had been experimentally threatened were less likely to identify sexual coercion and more likely to blame the women victimized in these scenarios. Robb Willer et al. (2013) found that men responded by "overdoing" gender in other ways as well. A series of studies discovered that men whose masculinity had been experimentally threatened were more supportive of the Iraq War, more likely to support statements about the inherent superiority of males, expressed more prejudice toward gay men, and were even more likely to say that they wanted to buy an SUV!

There's nothing inherently "off" about the men involved in this research. They perceived that their masculinity was being questioned and responded by overcompensating. When we see how men respond to gender identity threats, it provides important information about what kinds of things qualify as masculine in the first place, and how men are likely to turn to those qualities when they are unable to demonstrate masculinity in other ways. Dominance over women is one means by which men respond. Homophobia and sexual prejudice is another. And although it would not be ethical to see whether threatened men are more likely to engage in physical violence toward others, Willer et al.'s

(2013) finding that threatened men are more supportive of war suggests that supporting violent behavior is a patterned response as well.

James Messerschmidt's (1999) research with young boys builds on this idea. He refers to all of the things to which boys can turn to demonstrate their gender identities as "masculinity resources." Messerschmidt suggests that violence is a masculinity resource, but also that it is often *the* resource that boys turn to in a crisis. This is why Michael Kimmel (2013) argues that boys and young men involved in extremely violent behavior like school and mass shootings are perhaps best understood as "overconforming" to masculinity rather than as deviant. And the research on mass shooters aligns with these more general findings.

In an exhaustive review of news media articles surrounding random school shootings between 1982 and 2001, Kimmel and Mahler (2003) found that "nearly all had stories of being mercilessly and constantly teased, picked on, and threatened" (1445) and the most common method of teasing was "gay baiting." They found no evidence that any of the shooters identified as gay, but virtually all of them were called gay by their peers. Reuter-Rice (2008) suggests that gender-specific bullying (particularly homophobic bullying) among adolescent boys may be the primary characteristic we have for identifying the profile of boys and young men at risk of becoming school shooters. C. J. Pascoe's (2007) research on high school boys in California suggests that gender-specific homophobic bullying is an incredibly pervasive feature of the lives of boys and young men in high school and beyond, particularly among white boys. It is here, then, that we turn to the cultural explanation for mass shootings.

Cultural Roots of Mass Shootings

Certainly, boys and men are teased and gay baited and experience gender identity threat in other nations as well. So, why are American boys and young men responding with such extreme displays of violence? Why are mass shootings so much more common in the United States? To answer this question, we need a cultural explanation—we need an answer that explains the role that American culture plays in influencing boys and young men to turn to this particular sort of violent behavior at such higher rates than anywhere else in the world. Karen L. Tonso (2009) discusses the importance of context to the production of shooters. She points to common, violent, masculine tropes for acting (in other words, conventions or patterns that we all recognize) that are socioculturally produced. This approach redirects attention from the individual characteristics of the shooters themselves and investigates the everyday sociocultural contexts in which violent masculinities are produced, reproduced, and even valorized (Tonso, 2009). Michael Kimmel (2013) suggests that the problem is associated with a group he refers to as "angry white men." When this group acts out, when they are violent, and when they kill, mental illness and gun access are often quick to be blamed. But these explanations focus on individuals rather than on the societies in which they live. As the *New York Times* editorial board noted in an article on school shootings, rates of "severe mental illness [are] roughly stable around the world . . . while gun violence varies" (Editorial Board, 2014). In other words, individual-level explanations are inadequate. By focusing on a few bad apples, we fail to examine the orchard.

As Pascoe (2007) discovered studying the lives of high school boys, the struggles that put boys at risk of becoming school shooters are actually commonly experienced. Kimmel's (2013) research on angry white men builds on Pascoe's work and suggests that feeling denied a position which they feel is rightfully theirs in social hierarchies is a key ingredient as well. Similarly, Tonso (2009) points out that some young men experience a sense of humiliation stemming from the perceived loss of privilege, especially in schools. Although meritocracy is best understood as a myth in the United States, upward mobility remains a popular characterization of American society, "the land of opportunity." But opportunities for *some* were often made possible by systematically and structurally denying those opportunities to *others* throughout American history. From a historical perspective, white men have long been the recipients of this privilege. Social movements of various kinds, however, have slowly chipped away at these opportunities for white men. And although heterosexual white men today still benefit from racial, sexual, and gender inequality, they also work alongside women, gay men and lesbian women, and people of color in ways that were less true of previous generations. Men today must compete with women, people of color, and more because of the gradual erosion of privileges that have historically worked in their interests. And some of them are pissed off about it.

Kimmel suggests that one outcome of the move toward equal rights has been the production of *aggrieved entitlement* among a world-historically privileged group: straight, white men in the United States. Michael Kimmel explains it this way:

> The new American anger is more than defensive; it is reactionary. It seeks to restore, to retrieve, to reclaim something that is perceived to have been lost. Angry white men look to the past for their imagined and desired future. They believe that the system is stacked against them. Theirs is the anger of the entitled: we are entitled to those jobs, those positions of unchallenged dominance. And when we are told we are not going to get them, we get angry. (2013: 21)

And in an essay on gender and mass shootings, Rachel Kalish and Michael Kimmel more explicitly connect aggrieved entitlement with these crimes. Aggrieved entitlement is a gendered sentiment—one that authorizes violence by entitling boys and men to exact revenge on others when they perceive their masculinity to have been threatened or otherwise inaccessible. But aggrieved entitlement does not always or only lead to mass shooting either. Much more commonly, Kimmel suggests that it is associated with negative opinions of women and racial minorities. This suggests, and Kimmel argues, that mass shootings are one (extremely violent) example of a much larger issue.

This cultural explanation builds on our social psychological explanation by helping to articulate why boys and men in the United States are so much more likely to engage in mass murder and random acts of violence of the type Adam Lanza committed in Newtown, Connecticut, that Eric Harris and Dylan Kleibold committed at Columbine High School in Littleton, Colorado, that Seung-Hui Cho committed at Virginia Tech, or that James Eagan Holmes committed in a movie theatre in Aurora, Colorado, among too many others.

Conclusion

Social psychological research demonstrates that many men understand violence as a method of compensating for a perceived threat to their masculinity. But, coupled with a gendered sense of "aggrieved entitlement," a cultural explanation allows us to explore why, in extreme circumstances, violence is so much more likely to take the form of mass shootings in the United States. Mass shootings are a social and cultural problem in the United States. Gun ownership and access are a part of this problem. But when we refocus our attention from the gun to the person wielding the gun and the gun culture within which that action is understood, it's hard to ignore gender. Mass shootings are enactments of masculinity. But they only "work" in this way if violence is culturally masculinized in the first place, such that men might turn to it as a resource when they are unable to demonstrate masculinity in other ways.

NOTES

1. The FBI crime classification report identifies mass murder as four or more murders occurring during the same incident at a single location, often by a single killer. Follman et al. (2014) narrow this a bit, focusing on mass shootings in which at least four people are shot and killed (not including the shooter), often by a lone shooter in a public place during an ongoing incident.

2. We specify mass school shooters here because we are specifically referring to a subset of mass shooters—those who commit their acts of violence in a school setting. Familiar examples here include Columbine, Virginia Tech, and Sandy Hook Elementary. School shooters have been widely studied and profiled (e.g., Kimmel and Mahler, 2003; Newman et al., 2004).

REFERENCES

Brown, Sarah. (2012, December 17). "World Reaction: 'My Heart Is in Newtown.'" *CNN*. Retrieved March 23, 2015. http://www.cnn.com/2012/12/17/world/irpt-sandy-hook-global-reaction/.

Bureau of Justice Statistics. 2013. *Firearm Violence, 1993–2011* [Data File]. Retrieved March 19, 2015. http://www.bjs.gov/content/pub/pdf/fv9311.pdf

Carlson, Jennifer. 2015. *Citizen-Protectors: The Everyday Politics of Guns in an Age of Decline*. New York: Oxford University Press.

Editorial Board, *New York Times*. (2014, Dec. 3). "Mental Illness and Guns at Newtown." Retrieved March 13, 2015. http://www.nytimes.com/2014/12/04/opinion/mental-illness-and-guns-at-newtown.html?_r=0/.

Follman, Mark, Gavin Aronson, and Deanna Pan. (2014, May 24). "A Guide to Mass Shootings in America." *Mother Jones*. Retrieved March 13, 2015. http://www.motherjones.com/politics/2012/07/mass-shootings-map/.

Kalish, Rachel, and Michael Kimmel. 2010. "Suicide by Mass Murder: Masculinity, Aggrieved Entitlement, and Rampage School Shootings." *Health Sociology Review* 19(4):451–464.

Kimmel, Michael. (2012, December 19). "Masculinity, Mental Illness and Guns: A Lethal Equation?" *CNN*. Retrieved March 18, 2015. http://www.cnn.com/2012/12/19/living/men-guns-violence/index.html/.

Kimmel, Michael S. 1994. "Masculinity as Homophobia." In *Theorizing Masculinities*, edited by Harry Brod and Michael Kaufman, 119–141. Thousand Oaks, CA: Sage.

Kimmel, Michael S. 2013. *Angry White Men: American Masculinity at the End of an Era*. New York: Nation Books.

Kimmel, Michael S., and Matthew Mahler. 2003. "Adolescent Masculinity, Homophobia, and Violence: Random School Shootings, 1982–2001." *American Behavioral Scientist* 46(1):1439–1458.

Klein, Ezra. (2012, December 14). Mythbusting: Israel and Switzerland Are Not Gun-Toting Utopias. *The Washington Post*. Retrieved March 13, 2015. http://www.washingtonpost.com/blogs/wonkblog/wp/2012/12/14/mythbusting-israel-and-switzerland-are-not-gun-toting-utopias/.

Krouse, William J. (2012, November 14). "Gun Control Legislation." *Federation of American Scientists*. Retrieved March 23, 2015. http://fas.org/sgp/crs/misc/RL32842.pdf/.

Messerschmidt, James W. 1999. *Nine Lives: Adolescent Masculinities, the Body, and Violence*. Boulder, CO: Westview Press.

Munsch, Christin L., and Robb Willer. 2012. "The Role of Gender Identity Threat in Perceptions of Date Rape and Sexual Coercion." *Violence against Women* 18:1125–1146.

Newman, Katherine S., Cybelle Fox, Wendy Roth, Jal Mehta, and David Harding. 2004. *Rampage: The Social Roots of School Shootings*. New York: Basic Books.

Pascoe, C. J. 2007. *Dude, You're a Fag: Masculinity and Sexuality in High School*. Berkeley, CA: University of California Press.

Reuter-Rice, Karin. 2008. "Male Adolescent Bullying and the School Shooter." *The Journal of Nursing* 24(6):350–359.

Rosenbaum, Janet E. 2012. "Gun Utopias? Firearm Access and Ownership in Israel and Switzerland." *Journal of Public Health Policy* 33(1):46–58.

Tonso, Karen L. 2009. "Violent Masculinities as Tropes for School Shooters: The Montreal Massacre, the Columbine Attack, and Rethinking Schools." *American Behavioral Scientist* 52(9):1266–1285.

Small Arms Survey. 2007. *The Largest Civilian Firearms Arsenals for 178 Countries* [Data File]. Retrieved March 19, 2015. http://www.smallarmssurvey.org/fileadmin/docs/A-Yearbook/2007/en/Small-Arms-Survey-2007-Chapter-02-annexe-4-EN.pdf/.

Statistics Canada. 2014. *Firearms and Violent Crime in Canada, 2012* [Data File]. Retrieved March 19, 2015. http://www.statcan.gc.ca/pub/85-002-x/2014001/article/11925-eng.htm#a1/.

United Nations Office on Drugs and Crime. 2013. Global Study on Homicide. Retrieved March 19, 2014, from http://www.unodc.org/documents/gsh/pdfs/2014_GLOBAL_HOMICIDE_BOOK_web.pdf/.

Willer, Rob, Christabel L. Rogalin, Bridget Conlon, and Michael T. Wojnowicz. 2013. "Overdoing Gender: A Test of the Masculine Overcompensation Thesis." *American Journal of Sociology* 118(4):980–1022.

More Guns, More Mass Shootings—Coincidence?

Mark Follman

Reprinted by Permission of Mother Jones and the Foundation for National Progress. Copyright ©2015. All Rights Reserved.

In the fierce debate that always follows the latest mass shooting, it's an argument you hear frequently from gun rights promoters: If only more people were armed, there would be a better chance of stopping these terrible events. This has plausibility problems—what are the odds that, say, a moviegoer

continues

■ Continued

with a pack of Twizzlers in one pocket and a Glock in the other would be mentally prepared, properly positioned, and skilled enough to take out a body-armored assailant in a smoke- and panic-filled theater? But whether you believe that would happen is ultimately a matter of theory and speculation. Instead, let's look at some facts gathered in a five-month investigation by *Mother Jones*.

In the wake of the massacres . . . [in 2012] at a Colorado movie theater, a Sikh temple in Wisconsin, and Sandy Hook Elementary School in Connecticut, we set out to track mass shootings in the United States over the last 30 years. We identified and analyzed 62 of them,[1] and one striking pattern in the data is this: In not a single case was the killing stopped by a civilian using a gun. And in other recent (but less lethal) rampages in which armed civilians attempted to intervene, those civilians not only failed to stop the shooter but also were gravely wounded or killed. Moreover, we found that the rate of mass shootings has increased in recent years—at a time when America has been flooded with millions of additional firearms and a barrage of new laws has made it easier than ever to carry them in public places, including bars, parks, and schools.

America has long been heavily armed relative to other societies, and our arsenal keeps growing. A precise count isn't possible because most guns in the United States aren't registered and the government has scant ability to track them, thanks to a legislative landscape shaped by powerful progun groups such as the National Rifle Association. But through a combination of national surveys and manufacturing and sales data, we know that the increase in firearms has far outpaced population growth. In 1995 there were an estimated 200 million guns in private hands. Today, there are around 300 million—about a 50 percent jump. The US population, now over 314 million, grew by about 20 percent in that period. At this rate, there will be a gun for every man, woman, and child before the decade ends.

There is no evidence indicating that arming Americans further will help prevent mass shootings or reduce the carnage, says Dr. Stephen Hargarten,

a leading expert on emergency medicine and gun violence at the Medical College of Wisconsin. To the contrary, there appears to be a relationship between the proliferation of firearms and a rise in mass shootings: By our count, there have been two per year on average since 1982. Yet, 25 of the 62 cases we examined have occurred since 2006. In 2012 alone there have been seven mass shootings[2] and a record number of casualties, with more than 140 people injured and killed.

Armed civilians attempting to intervene are actually more likely to increase the bloodshed, says Hargarten, "given that civilian shooters are less likely to hit their targets than police in these circumstances." A chaotic scene in August [2012] at the Empire State Building put this starkly into perspective when New York City police officers trained in counterterrorism[3] confronted a gunman and wounded nine innocent bystanders in the process.[4]

Surveys suggest America's guns may be concentrated in fewer hands today: Approximately 40 percent of households had them in the past decade, versus about 50 percent in the 1980s. But far more relevant is a recent barrage of laws that have rolled back gun restrictions throughout the country. . . . [Between 2008 and 2012], across 37 states, the NRA and its political allies have pushed through 99 laws making guns easier to own, carry, and conceal from the government.[5]

Among the more striking measures: [as of 2012], eight states now allow firearms in bars. Law-abiding Missourians can carry a gun while intoxicated and even fire it if "acting in self-defense." In Kansas, permit holders can carry concealed weapons inside K–12 schools, and Louisiana allows them in houses of worship. Virginia not only repealed a law requiring handgun vendors to submit sales records, but the state also ordered the destruction of all such previous records. More than two-thirds of these laws were passed by Republican-controlled statehouses, though often with bipartisan support.

The laws have caused dramatic changes, including in the two states hit with the recent carnage. Colorado passed its concealed-carry measure in

2003, issuing 9,522 permits that year; by the end of . . . [2011] the state had handed out a total of just under 120,000, according to data we obtained from the County Sheriffs of Colorado. In March of . . . [2012], the Colorado Supreme Court ruled that concealed weapons are legal on the state's college campuses. (It is now the fifth state explicitly allowing them[6]). If former neuroscience student James Holmes . . . [was] still attending the University of Colorado . . . the movie theater killer—who had no criminal history and obtained his weapons legally—could've gotten a permit to tote his pair of .40 caliber Glocks straight into the student union. Wisconsin's concealed-carry law went into effect just nine months before the Sikh temple shooting in suburban Milwaukee . . . [in] August [2012]. During that time, the state issued a whopping 122,506 permits, according to data from Wisconsin's Department of Justice. The new law authorizes guns on college campuses, as well as in bars, state parks, and some government buildings.

And we're on our way to a situation where the most lax state permitting rules—say, Virginia's, where an online course now qualifies for firearms safety training and has drawn a flood of out-of-state applicants[7]—are in effect national law. Eighty percent of states now recognize handgun permits from at least some other states. And gun rights activists are pushing hard for a federal reciprocity bill[8]—passed in the House [in late 2011] . . .—that would essentially make any state's permits valid nationwide.

Indeed, the country's vast arsenal of handguns—at least 118 million of them as of 2010—is increasingly mobile, with 69 of the 99 new state laws making them easier to carry. A decade ago, seven states and the District of Columbia still prohibited concealed handguns; . . . [in 2012 it was] down to just Illinois and DC [and by 2015, all states allowed the carrying of concealed weapons[9]]. . . . In the 62 mass shootings we analyzed, 54 of the killers had handguns—including in all 15 of the mass shootings since the surge of progun laws began in 2009. In a certain sense the law was on their side: nearly 80 percent of the killers in our investigation obtained their weapons legally.

We used a conservative set of criteria to build a comprehensive rundown of high-profile attacks in public places—at schools, workplaces, government buildings, shopping malls—though they represent only a small fraction of the nation's overall gun violence. The FBI defines a mass murderer[10] as someone who kills four or more people in a single incident, usually in one location. (As opposed to spree or serial killers, who strike multiple times.) We excluded cases involving armed robberies or gang violence; dropping the number of fatalities by just one, or including those motives, would add many, many more cases. . . .

There was one case in our data set in which an armed civilian played a role. Back in 1982, a man opened fire at a welding shop in Miami, killing eight and wounding three others before fleeing on a bicycle. A civilian who worked nearby pursued the assailant in a car, shooting and killing him a few blocks away (in addition to ramming him with the car). Florida authorities, led by then-state attorney Janet Reno, concluded that the vigilante had used force justifiably, and speculated that he may have prevented additional killings. But even if we were to count that case as a successful armed intervention by a civilian, it would account for just 1.6 percent of the mass shootings in the last 30 years.

More broadly, attempts by armed civilians to stop shooting rampages are rare—and successful ones even rarer. There were two school shootings in the late 1990s, in Mississippi and Pennsylvania, in which bystanders with guns ultimately subdued the teen perpetrators, but in both cases it was after the shooting had subsided. Other cases led to tragic results. In 2005, as a rampage unfolded inside a shopping mall in Tacoma, Washington, a civilian named Brendan McKown confronted the assailant with a licensed handgun he was carrying. The assailant pumped several bullets into McKown and wounded six people before eventually surrendering to police after a hostage standoff. (A comatose McKown eventually recovered after weeks in the hospital.) In Tyler, Texas, that same year, a civilian named Mark Wilson fired his licensed handgun at a man on a rampage at the county courthouse. Wilson—who

continues

■ Continued

was a firearms instructor—was shot dead by the body-armored assailant, who wielded an AK47. (None of these cases were included in our mass shootings data set because fewer than four victims died in each.)

Appeals to heroism on this subject abound. So does misleading information. Gun rights . . . [promoters] frequently credit the end of a rampage in 2002 at the Appalachian School of Law in Virginia to armed "students" who intervened—while failing to disclose that those students were also current and former law enforcement officers and that the killer, according to police investigators, was out of bullets by the time they got to him. It's one of several cases commonly cited as examples of ordinary folks with guns stopping massacres that do not stand up to scrutiny.[11]

How do law enforcement authorities view armed civilians getting involved? One week after the slaughter at the *Dark Knight* screening in July, the city of Houston—hardly a hotbed of gun control—released a new Department of Homeland Security–funded video instructing the public on how to react to such events. The six-minute production foremost advises running away or otherwise hiding, and suggests fighting back only as a last resort. It makes no mention of civilians using firearms.

Law enforcement officials are the first to say that civilians should not be allowed to obtain particularly lethal weaponry, such as the AR-15 assault rifle and ultra-high-capacity, drum-style magazine used by Holmes to mow down Batman fans. The expiration of the Federal Assault Weapons Ban under President George W. Bush in 2004 has not helped that cause: Seven killers since then have wielded assault weapons in mass shootings.[12]

But while access to weapons is a crucial consideration for stemming the violence, stricter gun laws are no silver bullet. Another key factor is mental illness. A major *New York Times*[13] investigation[14] in 2000 examined 100 shooting rampages and found that at least half of the killers showed signs of seri-

ous mental health problems. Our own data reveals that the majority of mass shootings are murder-suicides: In the 62 cases we analyzed, 36 of the shooters killed themselves. Others may have committed "suicide by cop"—seven died in police shoot-outs. Still others simply waited, as Holmes did in the movie theater parking lot, to be apprehended by authorities.

Mental illness among the killers is no surprise, ranging from paranoid schizophrenia to suicidal depression. But while some states have improved their sharing of mental health records with federal authorities, millions of records reportedly are still missing from the FBI's database for criminal background checks.

Hargarten of the Medical College of Wisconsin argues that mass shootings need to be scrutinized as a public health emergency so that policy makers can better focus on controlling the epidemic of violence. It would be no different than if there were an outbreak of Ebola virus, he says—we'd be assembling the nation's foremost experts to stop it.

But real progress will require transcending hardened politics.[15] For decades gun rights promoters have framed measures aimed at public safety—background checks, waiting periods for purchases, tracking of firearms—as dire attacks on constitutional freedom. They've wielded the gun issue so successfully as a political weapon that Democrats hardly dare to touch it,[16] while Republicans have gone to new extremes in their party platform to enshrine gun rights. Political leaders have failed to advance the discussion "in a credible, thoughtful, evidence-driven way," says Hargarten.

In the meantime, the gun violence in malls and schools and religious venues[17] continues apace. As a superintendent told his community in suburban Cleveland [in February 2012] . . . , after a shooter at Chardon High School snuffed out the lives of three students and injured three others,[18] "We're not just any old place, Chardon. This is every place. As you've seen in the past, this can happen anywhere."

NOTES

1. Follman, Mark, Gavin Aronson, and Deanna Pan. 2014. "A Guide to Mass Shootings in America." http://www.motherjones.com/politics/2012/07/massshootingsmap/.

2. Follman, Aronson, and Pan. 2014.

3. Feyerick, Deborah. 2012. "Empire State Building Shooter Left Keys with Landlord." *CNN.com.* http://www.cnn.com/2012/08/27/us/newyorkempirestatebuildingshooting/index.html/

4. Wilson, Michael. 2012. "After Bullets Hit Bystanders, Protocol Questions." *The New York Times.* http://www.nytimes.com/2012/08/26/nyregion/bystandersshootingwoundscausedbythepolice.html/.

5. Follman, Mark, Tasneem Raja, and Ben Breedlove. 2012. "The NRA Surge: 99 Laws Rolling Back Gun Restrictions." *Mother Jones.* http://www.motherjones.com/politics/2012/09/mapgunlaws20092012/.

6. Frosh, Dan. 2012. "University Is Uneasy as Court Ruling Allows Guns on Campus." *The New York Times.* http://www.nytimes.com/2012/09/23/education/gunsoncampusatuniversityofcoloradocauseunease.html?pagewanted=all/.

7. Associated Press. 2012. "Virginia's online classes make it easy for out-of-state gun owners to get permits." http://www.foxnews.com/us/2012/09/03/onlineclassesmakeiteasyfornonvirginiagunownerstogetpermits/.

8. Schmitt, Rick, and iWatch News. 2011. "How the NRA Pushed the Right to Pack Heat Anywhere." *Mother Jones.* http://www.motherjones.com/politics/2011/11/concealedgunslaws/.

9. 2013. "Concealed Weapons Permitting Policy Summary." *Law Center to Prevent Gun Violence.* http://smartgunlaws.org/concealed-weapons-permitting-policy-summary/.

10. Morton, Robert J., and Mark A. Hilts, eds. n.d. "Serial Murder." http://www.fbi.gov/statsservices/publications/serialmurder/serialmurder1#two/.

11. Follman, Mark. 2012. "Do Armed Civilians Stop Mass Shooters? Actually, No." *Mother Jones.* http://www.motherjones.com/politics/2012/12/armedciviliansdonotstopmassshootings/.

12. Follman, Aronson, and Pan. 2014.

13. Fessenden, Ford. 2000. "They Threaten, Seethe, and Unhinge, Then Kill in Quantity." *The New York Times.* http://www.nytimes.com/2000/04/09/us/they-threaten-seethe-and-unhinge-then-kill-in-quantity.html?pagewanted=all&src=pm/.

14. Fessenden 2000.

15. Zuckerman, Ethan. 2012. "What Would It Take to Start a Gun Control Debate in the US?" http://www.ethanzuckerman.com/blog/2012/08/14/what-would-it-take-to-start-a-gun-control-debate-in-the-us/.

16. Bash, Dana. 2012. "For Democrats, Gun Politics Are Bad Politics." *CNN.com.* http://www.cnn.com/2012/07/20/politics/gun-politics/index.html/.

17. Follman, Mark. 2012. "'I Was a Survivor': Recalling a Mass Shooting 4 Years Ago Today." *Mother Jones.* http://www.motherjones.com/politics/2012/07/mass-shooting-survivor/.

18. Tavernise, Sabrina and Jennifer Preston. 2012. "Ohio Shooting Suspect Confesses, Prosecutor Says." *The New York Times.* http://www.nytimes.com/2012/02/29/us/ohio-school-shooting-suspect-confesses-prosecutor-says.html?pagewanted=all/.

Crimes of the Powerful: Crafting Criminality

MIRIAM KONRAD

When you envision a criminal, what comes to mind? Konrad calls attention to a type of crime that is often underestimated in terms of its costs to individuals and society: crimes of the powerful (white-collar crime, corporate crime, and large-scale violations that are damaging and serious, but not necessarily illegal). Konrad defines and quantifies, for example, the costs and consequences of white-collar crime compared to street crime and describes the great disparities in punishment for these types of crimes. She illustrates that the most powerful people in society get to define what "counts" as a crime and that their definitions serve their own interests.

The best way to rob a bank is to own one.
—William Crawford, 1989

Introduction

It is increasingly common knowledge that the wealthy generally compound their wealth while the poor remain poor. A 2011 study using IRS tax data confirmed that between 1987 and 2009, the rich became permanently richer and the poor permanently poorer as a result of frozen wages, the shift away from manufacturing, and a tax system that strongly favors the wealthy (DeBacker et al., 2011). Even the average American recognizes this process, with a substantial majority of Americans (65 percent) reporting they "believed the income gap between the rich and poor had widened over the last decade" (Drake 2013:1). The explanations for this gap, however, are not so widely agreed on and views seem to break down fairly consistently by political party affiliation. According to a Pew Re-

search study, 61 percent of Democrats believe that the poor remain poor largely because of factors beyond their control (in sociological terms, because of structural factors), whereas 57 percent of Republicans believe it is because of lack of personal effort. Similarly, 55 percent of Republicans believed the rich to be hard working, versus 33 percent of Democrats (Drake, 2013:1). This chasm in perceptions of the rich and the poor has consequences that go far beyond mere purchasing power.

The perceptions regarding the causes of the gap also play into determining people's life chances because those perceptions are key in determining poverty policies. For instance, if the ability to fail or succeed is largely viewed through the lens of personal responsibility, then it follows that social services would be limited and highly contingent on recipients' individual attributes. If, in contrast, well-being is recognized as being deeply dependent on social markers like race, class, and gender, policy would favor liberal

Original to *Focus on Social Problems: A Contemporary Reader.*

welfare and social justice components. One of the arenas in which the divide has significant impact is in the criminal justice system (CJS), which is what shall be explored herein.

By definition, that which is criminal is anything that is against the law. It follows then that anyone who breaks the law is a criminal. When one is in a position to make the laws, it is easy to understand how those laws might be made in the interest of maintaining the balance of power, exonerating one's own group at the expense of another set of social actors. Since those with the most resources tend to make the laws, it is little wonder that those with fewer resources are increasingly marginalized, pathologized, and even criminalized.

One of the ways this plays out is that we tend to perceive and treat white-collar crime differently from street crime. Let us begin with definitional matters. According to Braithwaite (1985), as early as 1916 Willem Bonger spoke of "crime in the streets" versus "crime in the suites" (2). Braithwaite further notes that early scholars and social commentators, known as muckrackers, were also investigating the concept:

> In journalistic exposes and fictionalized accounts, these writers laid bare the occupational safety abuses of mining magnates, the flagrant disregard for consumer health of the meat packing industry, the corporate bribery of legislatures, and many other abuses. The muckrakers were responsible for some of the important statutes, like the US Federal Food, Drug, and Cosmetic Act of 1906, which criminalized many forms of corporate misconduct. (1985:2)

It was Edwin Sutherland, however, who first coined the term white-collar crime in 1939, and it has since come into popular usage. In *Crime and the American Dream* (2007), Messner and Rosenfeld define white-collar crime as "crimes committed by persons against the organization for which they work (embezzlement, for example) or on behalf of those organizations (for instance, price fixing)" (28). Although there is no precise definition, this one incorporates much of what most people think of when the term is invoked.

Also important (and extremely difficult to measure) is just how costly white-collar crime is to society. Estimates in recent years range from $200 billion to nearly $600 billion (Reiman, 2001:120). Not only is it extremely costly by any measure, but also (counterintuitively and somewhat invisibly) it is far more costly than street crime. Rosoff et al. (2003) inform us that the cost of white-collar crime is about fourteen times the estimated annual cost of robbery, burglary, assault, and other street crimes (53).[1]

Despite the greater costs and potentially deeper and broader harms to society, it is generally street crime that is feared by the common person, not crime in the suites. When most people think about crime, we tend to think about violence, and when we think about violence, we think about direct brutality: assault, battery, rape, murder. These images are frightening, palpable, and easily conjured in our own minds and reinforced constantly by media imagery. We are much less likely to have the same kinds of visceral reactions to the more subtle savagery of white-collar crimes. Although we are not as attuned to their brutality, such criminality in fact often levels larger numbers of people at once and cuts just as deeply as any blade (entire communities with severe birth defects and high cancer rates from illegal waste disposal, for example). The reasons that we are less able to see these harms are manifold and, as alluded to above, have much to do with the power to define, the power to punish, and the power to escape punishment. All of these powers will be illuminated through the examples and discussion that follow, as will the ways in which such crimes devastate, destroy, and demolish people's lives.

Banks, Bailouts, and Bamboozling

In recent history, financial crises in the United States have resulted in the American people being asked to bear the brunt of the axe that felled the well-being of many. Beyond that, they are often asked to save those that wielded the weapon from the burden of hefting the weight of it. The devastation caused by these reckless actions can clearly be identified as white-collar or corporate crime (a term meant to emphasize culpability of corporations rather than simply individuals who might work in corporate settings and thus distinguishes itself from common understandings of white-collar crime). Simon (2008) tells us:

> According to a 2003 estimate, corporate crime, which includes antitrust, advertising law, [and] pollution law violations, cost American consumers an estimated *$3 trillion. The amount taken in bank robberies that year was 6,000 times less.* This figure is 40 times more than estimated losses from street crime. (86)

A few of the most glaring instances in the past several decades deserve to be noted. First, the savings and loan crisis of the 1980s and 1990s was estimated to have cost taxpayers some $341 billion. This loss was caused by reckless investment, irresponsible speculation, and in many cases unmitigated fraud. Although there were many indictments and some executives even did prison time, many argue that the punishments were not commensurate with the harm done (Wilentz, 2009). Some argue that the punishments have gotten weaker rather than stronger since that crisis, which many believed could have acted as a wake-up call. For example, between 2001 and 2004, Enron (an energy, commodities, and service company based in Houston, Texas) was responsible for the loss of approximately $63 billion by its employees and shareholders (Messner and Rosenfeld, 2007:1). This disaster, too, was the result of far more than simple mismanagement. For instance:

> Enron officials refused to permit employees to withdraw their savings from the company's retirement plan at the same time

company executives were cashing in their Enron stock holdings for millions. By the time employees were finally allowed to sell the stock in their 401K retirement accounts, Enron stock prices had plummeted. (29)

The chief executive officer of Enron, Jeffrey Skilling, was sentenced to twenty-four years in prison, a harsh penalty compared to most meted out for white-collar crime. In June 2013, however, an appeal resulted in ten years being shaved off this sentence. Skilling has been in a minimum-security prison since 2006 and may now get out as early as 2017 with good behavior (Lattman, 2013). In both these cases, the taxpayers paid handsomely for the squandering of the nation's resources by conglomerates, and the businesses and their executives received little in the way of punishment.

The 2008 bank failure that resulted in a deep recession that we are only just now climbing slowly out of in 2014 is an even more dramatic instance of mismanagement, corruption, and gross negligence. The fallout from this recession was widespread. Some 8.7 million jobs were lost between 2007 and 2010 (Center on Budget and Policy Priorities, 2014). High unemployment rates led to severe middle-class slippage for many individuals and families, with many seeking government assistance in the form of food stamps and other relief programs. There was a 76 percent increase on the Supplemental Nutrition Assistance Program rosters between 2007 and 2012 (Zedlewski et al., 2012). Many lost lifetime savings and their homes. According to a Mortgage Banker's Association report released in 2010, more than 1.2 million homes were lost between 2005 and 2008.

The bankers not only escaped punishment, but were actually rewarded through a hefty bailout. The formal title of the bailout was the Troubled Asset Relief Program (TARP). Funded by the American people, this relief to banks was agreed on by both Republican and Democratic leadership. It seemed to many the only possible course of action in light of the circumstances:

The US housing bubble collapsed at the height of the financial crisis in 2008, devaluing mortgage-related securities and the banks that held them. The stock market plunged in the wake of major bank liquidity crises and insolvency. (Yip, 2011:1)

Although many agree that TARP did help to avert a greater crisis, there are other measures by which it cannot be said to have fared as well. In an op-ed piece in the *New York Times*, Neil Barofsky (2011), special inspector general for TARP, spoke strongly of its failure to meet its stated goals. He notes that in his role he could only make recommendations to the Treasury Department, not implement them. Although the goal of preserving and even increasing the riches of banks was well achieved, Barofsky declared the parallel goal of helping millions of homeowners save their homes "a colossal failure" (2011:3).

It is difficult to accurately estimate because of myriad complicating factors, but the most conservative estimates put the bailout at $48 billion of taxpayer money (Yip, 2011). One of many complicating factors, it appears, is that the funds being paid back to taxpayers are being paid back with other taxpayer money, and thus the estimate would be much higher (de Rugy, 2012). Yet, despite this greater harm and enormous cost, "studies of punishment in corporate crime cases reveal that only about two percent of corporate crime cases result in imprisonment" (de Rugy, 2012:86).

People as Pawns for Profit

Some sociological criminologists argue the terms "white-collar crime" and "corporate crime" simply are not broad enough to reflect immoral and unjust behaviors by those with the bulk of the power in society. They recommend "crimes of the powerful" to reference large-scale human rights violations, environmental (in)justices, unsafe working conditions, and much more. Critical criminologists often prefer this term, as Carrabine et al. (2009) note:

The application of the term "crime" here is a signal about what indeed may not be legally "criminal" but arguably should be, given its far-reaching seriousness. This is a tradition that has continued in critical criminology and does not mean that writers are ignorant of the law when they refer to . . . the "crimes" of the powerful . . . but rather that they are drawing attention to biases in the law-making and criminal justice systems. (247)

The term employs the word "crimes" as a reminder that those with power use that power to decide what a crime is and who is criminal and implies that many of their acts would be considered criminal, if the legal definitions were constructed fairly.

Some notable crimes of the powerful include the blatant and willful use of citizens as guinea pigs. For instance:

From 1946 to 1963, between 250,000 and 300,000 soldiers and civilians were exposed to radiation during 192 nuclear bomb tests. Among the test conducted by the Army was one that assessed the resultant psychological effects on soldiers who observed an atomic blast four times the size of the bomb dropped on Hiroshima from a distance of two miles. (Simon, 2008:260)

The unwitting participants suffered many negative consequences, including far higher incidences of leukemia and other cancers than the average citizen, yet rather than take responsibility for these acts and criminalizing them as they surely should have, the government instead chose to condone and conceal them (Simon, 2008:261).

Between the 1940s and 1970s various radiation studies were performed on human subjects, some with prior knowledge and some without. The incarcerated were often ideal candidates for such experimentation. For example, ". . . from 1963 to 1971, x-rays were applied to the testes of 131 inmates at Oregon and Washington state prisons." (Simon, 2008:261)

Less obvious but equally heinous is the promotion and sale of unsafe products, ranging from toxic toys for children to carcinogenic chemicals in our consumables. Unsafe products are responsible for thousands of injuries and deaths; Simon (2008) reminds us that each year, according to the National Commission on Public Safety:

> 20 million Americans are injured in the home as a result of incidents connected with consumer safety. "Of the total, 110,000 are permanently disabled and 30,000 are killed. A significant number could have been spared if more attention had been paid to hazard reduction." (119)

Perhaps the most infamous of the unsafe product cases are infractions in the automobile industry. A prime example of this is the story of the Ford Pinto, a hot seller in the 1970s. From its introduction to the market, the Pinto had a serious flaw. It had a "fuel system that ruptured easily in rear-end collisions" (Simon, 2008:120). Although the company was well aware of this issue, style and speed of production considerations overrode concerns about human suffering and even fatalities. Ford calculated that it would cost a mere $11 per vehicle to make each one safe, but determined this was more than they were willing to pay. Simon notes,

> Ford reasoned that 180 burn deaths, 180 serious burn injuries, and 2,100 burned vehicles would cost $49.5 million (each death was figured at $200,000). But doing a recall of all Pintos and making each $11 repair would amount to $137 million. . . . In addition to the decision to leave the Pinto alone, Ford lobbied in Washington to convince government regulatory agencies and Congress that auto accidents are caused

not by cars but by 1) people and 2) highway conditions. (2008:121)

Simon goes on to assert that this kind of reasoning is akin to suggesting that if you carry money on your person, you are inviting robbery, therefore making you, not the robber, culpable for the crime.

It would be nice to believe that the automobile industry has outgrown such indiscretions, but unfortunately evidence says otherwise. In June 2014, General Motors admitted to errant neglect on the part of some of its employees regarding a faulty ignition switch dating back to at least 2002 (Hirsch, 2014). The admission resulted in fifteen employees being fired and much scrambling to shift the blame and find a scapegoat. By their own spokesperson's admission, the faulty part was responsible for at least thirteen deaths and many more injuries. This switch was initially chosen over a safer one strictly because it was cheaper to manufacture. The long-overdue confession and subsequent disciplining of some employees is cold comfort for the surviving family members of victims.

In addition to the woeful neglect involved in the creation and failure to improve products found to be unsafe, there are the myriad preventable "accidents" that take place in the workplace as a result of dangerous working conditions and the illnesses caused by exposure to hazardous chemicals on the job.

> On the job accidents annually cause 3.3 million injuries requiring hospital treatment. Exposure to toxic chemicals causes at least 100,000 deaths each year and 390,000 new cases of occupational diseases. (Simon, 2008:138)

The vast majority cannot be blamed on worker carelessness because the companies responsible for the conditions (as was the case with Ford and the Pinto) are often not only aware of the issues, but also go the extra mile to make sure that they do not come to light.

Both the scope and the heinousness of these legal, semilegal, and illegal acts that constitute crimes of the powerful make them worthy of more attention from the press, the CJS, and the general public. In terms of the sheer numbers, even if we compare only the 100,000 deaths from exposure to toxic chemicals to the 16,500 deaths from homicide in the United States each year, according to the Centers for Disease Control and Prevention (2011), we can see that the deaths occurring from crimes of the powerful are considerably higher. We might likewise compare the aforementioned 3.3.million injuries from job accidents to the 800,000 nonfatal aggravated assaults each year (Bureau of Justice Statistics, 2012). Thus, it becomes clear that many more people are maimed or killed by corporate neglect and dangerous practices than by direct one-on-one brutality.

Green Crimes and Racism

Beyond these workplace and manufacturing hazards, environmental devastation is so pervasive and so destructive that a whole new branch of criminology has sprung up around it called green criminology. Green criminology examines such things as air pollution, deforestation, water pollution, resource depletion, species decline, and animal abuse (Carrabine et al., 2009:385–391).

> As with so many crimes, environmental crimes and harms have a strong link to inequalities. Indeed, we can speak of *environmental racism* as a pattern by which environmental hazards are perceived to be greatest in proximity to poor people, and especially those belonging to [racial] minorities. (Carrabine et al., 2009:405)

This environmental racism plays out at both the macro and the micro levels. At the global level, developing countries are used as large-scale dumping sites. Unhealthy and unwanted waste from more developed nations is often banned for burial in those home countries without costly and time-consuming treatment and burial methods. Annually, 400 million tons of toxic waste are produced by the most developed nations, with 60 percent of that coming from the United States (Simon, 2008:180). Such waste is often shipped to countries with weaker laws (and/or weaker enforcement) for a fee. The receiving country gains some financial profit but at great health and safety costs to its citizenry. For example, "Guinea-Bissau, which has a gross national product of $150 million, will make $150 to $600 million over a five-year period in a deal to accept toxic waste from three European nations" (Simon, 2008:180). Although these waste products have been found to cause cancer and birth defects, the biggest problem is that this activity is legal. While the governments of these nation states are engaging in such exchanges willingly, it is the average citizen that is paying the cost in health and quality-of-life losses. The only recourse left to these victims is to try to bring public attention to the issue (Simon, 2008:181).

At the local level in the United States, it is communities of color that often bear the brunt of toxic waste disposal. In *Dumping in Dixie* (2000), Robert Bullard reminds us that

> the problem of polluted black communities is not a new phenomenon. Historically, toxic dumping and the location of locally unwanted land uses (LULUs) have followed the "path of least resistance," meaning that black and poor communities have been disproportionally burdened with these types of externalities. (3)

Bullard cites many examples of poor communities of color that are plagued by these problems, not the least of which is Ascension Parish in Louisiana, just south of Baton Rouge. The situation is so intense here that it is often referred to as a "toxic sacrifice zone," in which

> eighteen petrochemical plants are crammed into a nine and a half square mile area. Companies such as BASF, Vulcan, Triad, CF Industries, Liquid Airbonic, Bordon

Chemical, Shell, Uniroyal, Rubicon, Ciba-Geigy, and others discharge 196 million pounds of pollutants annually into the water and air. Discharges include the carcinogens vinyl chloride and benzene, mercury (which is harmful to the nervous system), chloroform, toluene, and carbon tetrachloride (which can cause birth defects). (Bullard, 2000:106)

Despite the ubiquitous and atrocious nature of these acts, all signs would indicate that street crime is the real threat. The media reinforce this view and so does the CJS, which is designed in such a way as to, in the words of Jeffrey Reiman (2001), "weed out the wealthy" (113) and funnel the poor into prison (114). He notes,

> *For the same criminal behavior,* the poor are more likely to be arrested; if arrested, they are more likely to be charged; if charged, more likely to be convicted; if convicted, more likely to be sentenced to prison; and if sentenced, more likely to be given longer prison terms than members of the middle and upper classes. (Reiman, 2001:110)

The notion of the "typical criminal," brought to us courtesy of the media and reinforced by CJS policies and procedures, has not only class implications but also racial ones. The back-and-forth play between de facto (by custom) images and what becomes reified through de jure (by law) practices results in absurd levels of incarceration of the poor and the dark skinned for largely nonviolent crimes. As noted by Michelle Alexander in *The New Jim Crow,*

> More African American adults are under correctional control today—in prison or jail, on probation or parole—than were enslaved in 1850, a decade before the Civil War began. . . . Thousands of blacks have disappeared into prisons and jails, locked away for drug crimes that are largely ignored when committed by whites. (2012:180)

The U.S. Bureau of Justice Statistics tells us that 39.4 percent of the total prison and jail population in 2009 was black, whereas only about 13.5 percent of the U.S. population was black. Additionally, only 7.9 percent of sentenced prisoners in federal prisons as of September 2009 were in for violent crimes (Bureau of Justice Statistics, 2009). Much of the overincarceration of nonviolent offenders has been actualized through the infamously ineffective war on drugs, which has been the site of much CJS activity over the past several decades, from the unprecedentedly high incarcerations rates, to the brutality at the Mexican/American border, to the increasing numbers of women in prison and more. Many argue that outdated and counterproductive drug laws such as those prohibiting the use of marijuana significantly contribute to this incarceration orgy. It will be interesting to see whether the current trend toward legalization of marijuana will significantly alter these patterns or simply shift the focus to another drug, activity, or freshly criminalized behavior.

Affluenza

Another manifestation of the double standard regarding who and what is considered criminal comes to light in the so-called "Affluenza defense." This is controversial (there are already efforts under way to ban its use in California cases, for instance, although it has never been invoked there) yet illustrative (Abcarian, 2014). Ethan Couch, a sixteen-year-old boy in Texas, killed four pedestrians while driving under the influence of alcohol and received only probation as a consequence. The argument his attorney proffered was that Couch could not be held fully accountable for his actions because his upper-class upbringing did not afford him the opportunity to fully comprehend the distinction between right and wrong. He was so shielded from the harsh realities of life, the argument went, that he simply did not comprehend the basic concept of personal responsibility. The attorney called this condition "affluenza" (Associated Press, 2013). It could be seen as an ironic twist that the term is being employed in this fashion. When it was coined by de Graff et al. in the book entitled *Affluenza: The All-Consuming Epidemic* (2005), the authors were attempting to expose a society sinking rapidly and pervasively into greed, self-absorption, and entitlement. Their scathing and insightful social commentary was never intended to be used as a defense or an excuse for criminal or negligent behavior resulting in the deaths of other human beings. We need only imagine for a moment the reverse defense being offered to appreciate the totality and the absurdity of the hypocrisy. What if a defense attorney suggested that her client could not be held accountable for his actions that resulted in the death of four people because of poverty and lack of access to the better things in life? Such a defense would likely be met with derision and incredulity. To remove this statement from the purely speculative, the same judge (Jean Boyd) who sentenced Ethan Couch to an extremely expensive and comfortable rehabilitation facility and probation gave a different sentence to another young boy. In 2012, a fourteen-year-old boy punched someone whose head hit the pavement; as a result, the victim died two days later. Judge Boyd sentenced the young black boy (who was not wealthy) to ten years in prison (Sterbenz, 2013).

To add insult to injury, yet another collateral consequence of being poor and in the CJS is that one is increasingly asked now to pay (in dollars as well as in time and energy) for one's own punishment. Joe Shapiro, in a May 18, 2014, National Public Radio report, speaks of this phenomenon. In one example he explains,

> in Georgia, I met a man who stole a can of beer, and as a condition of his release, the court said "Wear this leg monitor." But those things are expensive and it was $12 a day for him. He was homeless. (Shapiro, 2014:1)

Shapiro tells us that forty-nine states charge for those electronic monitors, forty-three states charge at least administrative fees for a public defender (which by definition is supposed to be a free service), forty-two states charge for room and board while in jail or prison, and forty-four states charge a fee for probation and parole supervision ("Court Use Fees," 2014:2). The list goes on, with some states allowing charges for juries, court-ordered drug treatment, arrest warrants, and more.

Conclusion

It is clear, then, at both the macro and the micro levels, that wealth buys power and influence, both in terms of defining what is criminal and in terms of escaping punishment even when the acts of the wealthy are eventually defined as illegal. In *Class, Status and Party*, the eminent sociologist Max Weber defines power as the ability to exercise one's own will, even in the face of resistance from others (Grusky and Szelenyi, 2011:56). He goes on to expound on the variety of ways in which this power may be exercised, including (but not limited to) bribery, force, subtle coercion, charisma, and media influence (Grusky and Szelenyi, 2011:67). The wealthy have the wherewithal to employ these methods to maintain and increase their power as well as to set the terms of crime and punishment.

As demonstrated in this short piece and as quoted at the outset, the best way to rob a bank is indeed to own one. In *The Divide: American Injustice in the Age of the Wealth Gap*, Matt Taibbi (2014) further explicates the ideological underpinnings that facilitate this heist. He notes,

> legally, there is absolutely no difference between a woman on welfare who falsely declares that her boyfriend no longer lives in the home and a bank that uses a robo-signer[2] to cook up a document swearing that he has kept regular records of your credit card account. But morally and politically, they're worlds apart. (383)

He goes on to explain that in the case of the woman on welfare, her behavior is met with media-induced public scorn and moral outrage because she "committed the political crime of being needy and an eyesore," whereas the bankers commit the comparable acts over and over again with not only lack of condemnation but also actual accolades (Taibbi 2014:384). Taibbi argues that "the system is not disgusted by the organized, mechanized search for profit. It's more like it's impressed by it" (2014:384).

As long as money buys influence, as long as the abuse of power is rewarded with increased power, as long as poverty is criminalized and the poor are demonized, that is how long crimes of the powerful will be viewed as benign or even laudable and survival tactics of the impoverished will be made illegal and punished. Justice is a commodity that is sold to the highest bidder. It is abundantly clear that wealth trumps poverty when it comes to exoneration from culpability both at the macro and at the micro levels. Not only do corporations get away with crimes because they can hide behind a shield of respectability, legitimacy, and job creation, but also even individuals can now claim freedom from guilt based on ignorance bred from wealth and innocence derived from prosperity.

NOTES

1. The cost of street crime is measured by combining costs to the victim (e.g., financial loss, medical bills) and costs to the larger society, including police protection, legal and judicial fees, and incarceration (McCollister et al., 2010).

2. A robo-signer is an employee of a mortgage servicing company that signs foreclosure documents without reviewing them. Rather than actually reviewing the individual details of each case, robo-signers assume the paperwork to be correct and sign it automatically, like robots (http://www.investopedia.com/terms/r/robo-signer.asp/).

REFERENCES

Abcarian, Robin. 2014. "Groundbreaking California Measure Would Outlaw 'Affluenza' Defense." *Los Angeles Times.* January 15, 2014. http://www.comm/local/abcarian/la-me-groundbreaking-california-law-would-outlaw-affluenza-defense-2014/.

Alexander, Michelle. 2012. *The New Jim Crow.* New York: New Press.

Associated Press. "Teen Who Killed Four Drunk Driving Gets Probation on 'Affluenza' Defense." 2013, December 13. *The Washington Times.* http://www.washingtontimes.com/news/2013/dec/13/teen-who-killed-four-drunk-driving-gets-probation-/?page=all/.

Barofsky, Neil. 2011. "Where the Bailout Went Wrong." *New York Times.* March 29, 2011. http://www.nytimes.com/2011/03/30/opinion/30barofsky.html?_r=0/.

Braithwaite, John. 1985. "White Collar Crime." *Annual Reviews Inc.* 11:1–25.

Bullard, Robert. 2000. *Dumping in Dixie: Race, Class, and Environmental Quality*, 3rd ed. Boulder, CO: Westview Press.

Bureau of Justice Statistics. 2009. *Federal Justice Statistics.* http://www.bjs.gov/index.cfm?ty=pbdetail&iid=2208/.

Bureau of Justice Statistics. 2012. http://www.bjs.gov/index.cfm?ty=dcdetail&iid=245/.

Carrabine, Eamonn, Pam Cox, Maggy Lee, Ken Plummer, and Nigel South. 2009. *Criminology: A Sociological Introduction*, 2nd ed. London: Routledge Press.

Center on Budget and Policy Priorities Report. 2014, June 10. "Chart Book: The Legacy of the Great Recession." http://www.cbpp.org/cms/index.cfm?fa=view&id=3252/.

Centers for Disease Control and Prevention. 2011. "FastStats: Assault or Homicide." http://www.cdc.gov/nchs/fastats/homicide.htm/.

DeBacker, Jason, Bradley Heim, Vasia Panousi, and Ivan Vidangos. 2011. "Rising Inequality: Transitory or Permanent? New Evidence from a U.S. Panel of Household Income 1987–2006." http://www.federalreserve.gov/pubs/feds/2011/201160/201160abs.html/.

De Graaf, John, David Wann, and Thomas H. Naylor. 2005. *Affluenza: How Overconsumption Is Killing Us and How to Fight Back.* San Francisco, CA: Berrett-Koehler Publishers, Inc.

De Rugy, Veronique. 2012. "The Real Cost of TARP." *National Review Online.* March 14, 2012. http://

www.nationalreview.com/corner/293408/real-cost-tarp-veronique-de-rugy/.

Drake, Bruce. 2013. "Americans See Growing Gap Between Rich and Poor." *Pew Research Center*. http://www.pewresearch.org/fact-tank/2013/12/05/americans-see-growing-gap-between-rich-and-poor/.

Grusky, David B. and Szonja Szelényi. 2011. *The Inequality Reader: Contemporary and Foundational Readings in Race, Class, and Gender*, 2nd Edition. Boulder, CO: Westview Press.

Hirsch, Jerry. 2014. "GM Inquiry into Defective Ignition Switch Draws Fire." *Los Angeles Times*, June 5. http://www.latimes.com/business/autos/la-fi-gm-recal-findings-20140606-story.html#page=1/.

Lattman, Peter. 2013. "Ex-Enron Chief's Sentence Is Cut by 10 Years, to 14." *New York Times*, June 23, p. B2.

McCollister, Kathyn, Michael French, and Hai Fang. 2010. "The Cost of Crime to Society: New Crime-Specific Estimates for Policy and Program Evaluation." *Drug and Alcohol Dependence* 108:98–109.

Messner, Steven F., and Richard Rosenfeld. 2007. *Crime and the American Dream*, 4th ed. Belmont, CA: Wadsworth Press.

Mortgage Bankers Association Press Release. 2010, April 7. "MBA: An Estimated 1.2 Million Households Were Lost during Recession." http://www.mbaa.org/NewsandMedia/PressCenter/72490.htm/.

Reiman, Jefferey. 2001. *The Rich Get Richer and the Poor Get Prison: Ideology, Class, and Criminal Justice*, 6th ed. Boston: Allyn & Bacon.

Rosoff, Stephen M., Henry N. Pontell, and Robert H. Tilman. 2003. *Looting America: Greed, Corruption, Villains and Victims*. Upper Saddle River, NJ: Prentice Hall.

Shapiro, Joe. 2014. "Court User Fees Bill Defendants for Their Punishment." *National Public Radio*. http://www.npr.org/2014/05/18/313618296/court-user-fees-bill-defendants-for-their-punishment/.

Simon, David R. 2008. *Elite Deviance*, 9th ed. Boston: Pearson.

Sterbenz, Christina. 2013. "Judge in Affluenza Case Sentenced a Black Teen to Ten Years for Killing a Guy with a Single Punch." *Business Insider*. http://www.businessinsider.com/judge-jen-boyd-black-teen-prison-2013-12/.

Taibbi, Matt. 2014. *The Divide: American Injustice in the Age of the Wealth Gap*. New York: Spiegel & Grau.

Wilentz, Sean. 2009. *The Age of Reagan: A History 1974–2008*. New York: Harper Perennial.

Yip, Jonathan. 2011. "The Bank Bailout in Perspective." *Harvard Political Review*. http://harvardpolitics.com/arusa/the-bank-bailout-in-perspective/.

Zedlewski, Sheila, Elaine Waxman, and Craig Gundersen. 2012. "SNAP's Role in the Great Recession and Beyond." *Urban Institute*. http://www.urban.org/UploadedPDF/412613-SNAPs-Role-in-the-Great-Recession-and-Beyondpdf/.

Inequality in Life and Death: The Death Penalty in the United States

Erin Thomas Echols

Original to Focus on Social Problems: A Contemporary Reader.

Warren McCleskey, a black man, was accused of committing an armed robbery that resulted in the death of the white police officer responding to the scene. The jury trying his case—made up of one black person and eleven white people—found McCleskey guilty of murder, and the court sentenced him to death. For more than a decade, his lawyers fought the death penalty sentence. They provided evidence that Georgia courts had condemned to death the defendants who killed white

continues

■ **Continued**

victims at a rate four times that of the defendants who killed black victims. Despite that argument, in 1987 the Supreme Court ruled the evidence was insufficient to prove discriminatory sentencing. Instead, they argued, McCleskey's lawyers needed to prove explicit racist intent on the part of the judge, prosecutors, or jury. They were unable to do so, and in 1991 McCleskey was put to death in Georgia's electric chair.

With one of the highest incarcerations rates in the world, the United States imprisons people at a rate that is four to six times the level of most other nations (Oliver, 2001). Nearly one in 100 Americans was imprisoned in 2010, and although Black Americans make up only about 13.6 percent of the general U.S. population, they comprise 36 percent of the prison population (Glaze, 2011; U.S. Department of Justice, 2014). Black Americans are similarly overrepresented on death row: 42 percent of the death row population in the United States is black (Ford, 2014). Although most other industrialized nations have outlawed the death penalty, the United States retains capital punishment as a legal form of punishment in the majority of states, for the federal government, and within the military codes of justice.

Studies have found that a variety of characteristics increase the likelihood that capital punishment is legal in a particular state. Jacobs and Carmichael (2002) found that states with the largest African American populations and areas with higher levels of economic inequality are more likely to retain the death penalty as a legal form of punishment, regardless of crime rates. These areas also have more police officers (Jacobs 1979; Liska et al., 1981), higher arrest rates (Liska et al., 1984), spend more on jails and prisons as the non-white population increases (Jacobs and Helms, 1999) and report more fear of crime even when actual crime rates are identical to that in areas with lower non-white populations. These findings suggest that the legality of the death penalty continues to be shaped by race-based assumptions and stereotypes about the criminality of minority group members.

This most serious of punishments has a long history of being unequally dispensed. From 1930 to 1967, 54 percent of the executions that took place nationwide involved non-white offenders (U.S. Department of Justice, 1980). This percentage indicates a serious overrepresentation of racial minorities among those executed, given the percentages of minorities in the general population. Considering the racial antagonisms that characterized this era, these unjust numbers are potentially unsurprising. However, research suggests that inequality in death sentencing and execution continues today.

One of the most consistent findings that researchers have identified in studies of racial discrimination in the death penalty is substantial evidence that offenders who kill white people are more likely to receive the death penalty than offenders who kill non-white people (Baldus and Woodworth, 1998; Baldus et al., 1998; U.S. General Accounting Office, 1990). Another study conducted in Durham County, North Carolina, concluded that prosecutors are about 43 percent more likely to seek the death penalty in cases in which the victim is white and the defendant is black compared to cases in which both the victim and the defendant are black (Unah, 2009). These findings—that black people who kill white people are more likely to face and be sentenced to death than their counterparts who kill black people—are explicit evidence of an unjust criminal justice system that continues to place greater value on white lives than on non-white lives. Even more illuminating, when researchers at Stanford University analyzed photos of defendants, they found that those whose appearance was perceived as more stereotypically black (darker skin, broader nose, larger lips, etc.) were more likely to receive a death sentence than defendants whose appearance was perceived as less stereotypically black (Eberhardt et al., 2006).

This miscarriage of justice not only takes the lives of the sentenced individuals, but also has serious economic costs. Phillip Cook (2009) of Duke University analyzed death penalty–related state expenditures for North Carolina and found that the state spent 11 million more per year, because of the costs of appeals and high security associated with death row imprisonment, than it would have had the death penalty been outlawed.

Despite the cost and severity of capital punishment, research on the impact of the death penalty on curbing crime is mixed. The vast majority of the evidence indicates that at best, use of the death penalty is not correlated with a drop in crime rates (Donohue and Wolfers, 2005; Kovandzic et al., 2009; Peterson and Bailey, 1988).

This costly and racially discriminatory system is also fraught with the potential for other forms of human error. Since 1973, more than 140 people have been released from death row because they were found to be innocent of the crimes for which they were sentenced to death. In a 2014 study that analyzed the 7,482 death sentences that were handed down between 1973 and 2004, the authors concluded that more than 4 percent of inmates sentenced to the death penalty are likely to be innocent (Gross et al., 2014). Considering this error rate, it is likely that several dozen of the 1,320 individuals who have been executed since 1977 were innocent. Although some states provide a set amount of compensation for each year that an innocent individual stays in prison, twenty-two states offer no promise of compensation for the innocent who have served time (Emanuel, 2014). By incarcerating innocent people and operating in a racially discriminatory manner, the criminal justice system strays from the American ideals of equal protection under the law.

A few organizations are stepping in to attempt to provide remedies to the faulty system. For example, the Innocence Project is an organization that helps assist prisoners who can prove their innocence. The organization has dedicated itself to using DNA testing to exonerate wrongfully convicted individuals and to reform the criminal justice system to prevent further wrongful convictions. The Innocence Project also belongs to the Innocence Network, a group of organizations that aim to provide voluntary and unpaid legal and investigative services to the wrongfully convicted. Many of the clients

who seek out the assistance of the Innocence Project have run out of other legal options and are poor and forgotten.

In 2000, one of these falsely accused inmates, Kennedy Brewer, wrote to the Innocence Project and said,

> Back in 1992, I was accused of killing a three-year old child, something I know I didn't do. I've been on death row in Mississippi for five years, and I know if I can get someone to look into my case, carefully, I know they will easily see they have the wrong person locked up. . . . I don't want to lose my life for something I know I didn't do.

With the help of the Innocence Project, Kennedy Brewer was exonerated in 2008 after serving a total of fifteen years behind bars for a crime that DNA testing proved he did not commit.

Certainly Brewer's case is not isolated. Research clearly points to the need for recognition of race-based inequality within the U.S. justice system when it comes to death sentencing. With that acknowledgment of inequality comes a responsibility for changes in the justice system to ensure that the color of one's skin does not influence the sentencing and execution of the accused.

REFERENCES

Baldus, David C. and George Woodworth. 1998. "Race Discrimination and the Death Penalty: An Empirical Overview." In James R. Acker, Robert M. Bohn, and Charles S. Lanier (eds.) *America's Experiment with Capital Punishment: Reflections on the Past, Present, and Future of the Ultimate Penal Sanction*, pp. 385–415. Durham, NC: Carolina Academic Press.

Baldus, David C., George Woodworth, David Zuckerman, Neil Alan Weiner, and Barbara Broftitt. 1998. "Racial Discrimination and the Death Penalty in the Post-Furman Era: An Empirical and Legal Overview, with Recent Findings from Philadelphia." *Cornell Law Review* 83:1643–1770.

Cook, Philip J. 2009. "Potential Savings from Abolition of the Death Penalty in North Carolina." *American Law and Economics Review* 1–32.

continues

■ Continued

Donohue, John J., and Justin Wolfers. 2005. "Uses and Abuses of Empirical Evidence in the Death Penalty Debate." *Stanford Law Review* 58:791–846.

Eberhardt, Jennifer L., Paul G. Davies, Valerie J. Purdie-Vaughns, and Sheri Lynn Johnson. 2006. "Looking Deathworthy. Perceived Stereotypicality of Black Defendants Predicts Capital-Sentencing Outcomes." *Psychological Science* 17(5):383–386.

Emanuel, Gabrielle. "When Innocent People Go to Prison, States Pay." Retrieved June 2014. http://www.npr.org/.

Ford, Matt. 2014. "Racism and the Execution Chamber." Retrieved June 2014. http://m.theatlantic.com/politics/archive/2014/06/race-and-the-death-penalty/373081/.

Glaze, Lauren E. 2011. "Correction Population the United States, 2010." U.S. Department of Justice, Bureau of Justice Statistics. http.//www.bjs.gov/.

Gross, S., B. O'Brien, C. Hu, and E. Kennedy. 2014. "Rate of False Conviction of Criminal Defendants Who Are Sentenced to Death." *Proceedings of the National Academy of Sciences of the United States of America* 111(20):7230–7235.

Jacobs, David. 1979. "Inequality and Police Strength: Conflict Theory and Social Control in Metropolitan Areas." *American Sociological Review* 44:913–925.

Jacobs, David, and Jason T. Carmichael. 2002. "The Political Sociology of the Death Penalty: A Pooled Time-Series Analysis." *American Sociological Review* 67(1):109–131.

Jacobs, David, and Ronald Helms. 1999. "Collective Outbursts, Politics, and Punitive Resources." *Social Forces* 77:1497–1524.

Kovandzic, T., L. Vieraitis, and D. Paquette Boots. 2009. "Does the Death Penalty Save Lives? New Evidence from State Panel Data, 1977 to 2006." *Criminology & Public Policy* 8(4):803–843.

Liska, Allen E., Mitchell B. Chamblin, and Mark D. Reed. 1984. "Testing the Economic Production and Conflict Models of Crime Control." *Social Forces* 64:119–138.

Liska, Allen E., Joseph J. Lawrence, and Michael Benson. 1981. "Perspectives on the Legal Order." *American Journal of Sociology* 87:412–426.

Oliver, Pamela E. 2001. "Racial Disparities in Imprisonment: Some Basic Information." *Focus* 21(2):28–31.

Peterson, Ruth, and William Bailey. 1988. "Murder and Capital Punishment in the Evolving Context of the Post-Furman Era." *Social Forces* 66(3):774–807.

Unah, Isaac. 2009. "Choosing Those Who Will Die: The Effect of Race, Gender, and Law in Prosecutorial Decisions to Seek the Death Penalty in Durham County, North Carolina." *Michigan Journal of Race & Law* 15:135–181.

U.S. Department of Justice. 1980. "Capital Punishment, 1979." Washington, DC: U.S. Government Printing Office.

U.S. Department of Justice. 2014. "Jail Inmates at Midyear 2013—Statistical Tables." Retrieved June 2013. http://www.bjs.gov/content/pub/pdf/jim13st.pdf/.

U.S. General Accounting Office. 1990. "Death Penalty Sentencing: Research Indicates Pattern of Racial Disparities." Washington, DC: U.S. General Accounting Office.

For-Profit Justice: How the Private Prison Industry and the Criminal Justice System Benefit from Mass Incarceration

AMANDA ATWELL

Although scholars and activists have long demonstrated biases in the criminal justice system by social class, Atwell highlights a relatively new trend in criminal justice that serves to exacerbate these biases: the privatization of prison facilities, services, and goods. Atwell shows how the relationship between the private corporations (which seek to profit from crime and punishment) and government (which ostensibly seeks to administer punishment in a just way) disproportionately disadvantages vulnerable populations and contributes to increasing prison populations around the country. She questions whether financial incentives based in the profit motive act as an incentive to bring people into the system, where they serve as a commodity, reducing any inherent fairness in the system.

Mass incarceration and the use of prisons to redress social and economic problems have become ubiquitous features of contemporary U.S. society. Although popular crime and drama television shows such as *Law and Order* help to normalize high incarceration rates, the United States is quite the anomaly when it comes to the criminal justice system. The United States imprisons approximately 760 people per 100,000 citizens, or 2.3 million individuals, a rate higher than any other country in the world including Germany, Japan, South Korea, Russia, China, and Iran (Shapiro, 2011). Put another way, the United States represents 5 percent of the world's total population, yet contains 25 percent of the world's total prison population (Liptak, 2008b).

The United States is also the only country that actively sentences youth to life in prison without the possibility of parole (The Sentencing Project, 2014). Since the 1980s, states across the country have been contracting with private corporations that operate on a for-profit basis to house, feed, and care for the exploding prison population (Cheung, 2004; Shapiro, 2011). In this reading, I trace the origins of mass incarceration in the United States (or "prison boom") to the war on drugs and analyze the subsequent privatization of prison facilities, services, and goods as an exploitative partnership between the state and private corporations.

The 1980s marked the decade in which the government began to deregulate its responses to

Original to *Focus on Social Problems: A Contemporary Reader*.

mental health issues (like drug addiction) while simultaneously implementing private prisons across the country for the first time. In fact, the first private prison contract was awarded to the Corrections Corporation of America (CCA) by the state of Tennessee in 1984 (Cheung, 2004). The incentive to imprison rather than to rehabilitate drug users was fueled by federal initiatives such as the "war on drugs" (coined by President Nixon and intensified by President Reagan), which has helped the U.S. prison rate to more than quadruple since 1980 (Klein and Soltas, 2013). Since the official launch of the war on drugs in 1982, the United States has experienced a 500 percent overall surge in its incarceration rate, and the length of sentences has simultaneously increased (The Sentencing Project, 2013). This trend is evidenced, in particular, by drug conviction sentences. For example, in 1986 the average time spent behind bars for a drug conviction was twenty-two months; by 2004 this figure jumped to an average of sixty-two months (The Sentencing Project, 2013). As evidenced by the Clinton and Obama presidential administrations, the war on drugs has truly been a bipartisan effort, championed by Democrats and Republicans alike. Currently, more than half of those in prison are serving time for drug convictions. In 1980 there were 41,000 people incarcerated for drug offenses and by 2011 that number had skyrocketed to more than half a million (501,500) (The Sentencing Project, 2013). While diligently filling prisons, the war on drugs does not seem to have curbed Americans' appetite for drugs. According to the White House Office of National Drug Control Policy, drug use remains a relatively stable feature of U.S. society; in 1985, 34.4 percent of those polled reported illegal drug use at least once during their lifetime, and by 2001 that number had increased to 41.7 percent of those polled (Lloyd, 2002).

American Civil Liberties Union (ACLU) staff attorney David Shapiro (2011) and Amy Cheung (2004) of the Sentencing Project argue that the relatively recent trend of private prison expansion further exacerbates the preexisting moral failings of the criminal justice system by financially incentivizing mass incarceration. In other words, when arresting and imprisoning people are profitable enterprises, high incarceration rates become a self-fulfilling prophecy. As states across the country have faced an exploding prison population along with rapidly increasing crime-control and law enforcement costs over the past thirty years, legislatures turned to the private sector in an attempt to defray some of their financial burden and, in some cases, even generate income. The burgeoning private prison industry is composed of multiple layers of shareholders and stakeholders who have a vested interest in maintaining or increasing incarceration rates because their profits are dependent on keeping prison beds full (or meeting "occupancy requirements"), regardless of actual crime rates (Cheung, 2004; Shapiro, 2011; Kroll, 2013). In fact, the private prison incarceration rate increased by 1,600 percent between 1990 and 2009 (Shapiro, 2011), reaping huge profits for two of the largest private prison companies, CCA and the GEO Group. In 2012, CCA reported revenue of $1.7 billion (Takei, 2013). During the same year, the chief executive officer from CCA took home $3.7 million and that of the GEO Group took home $5.7 million (Lee, 2012). Private prison corporations profit not only from their contracts with states, but also from unmet occupancy quotas (e.g., unfilled beds). These quotas create an incentive for the state to maintain and increase arrest rates to avoid financial penalties, regardless of crime rates (Kirkham, 2013).

The economic burden of operating prisons in the era of mass incarceration increasingly falls on taxpayers, although the private prison model has been adopted to help defray the costs of incarceration to states. More than half (forty-one of sixty-two) of the private prison contracts across the country require that prison beds remain 90 to 100 percent full or the state will face a financial penalty, which ultimately must be paid by the taxpayers (Kirkham, 2013). The taxpayers of the state of Arizona recently paid the private prison company Management and Training Corporation $3 million in fees because the state failed to maintain the 97 percent occupancy requirement (Hall and Diehm, 2013). In states such as Arizona, the cost of operating a private prison cost the taxpayers $3.5 million more than the cost to operate a state-run facility (Shen, 2012).

Analyzing the racial makeup of private prisons reveals another layer of inequality that is difficult to ignore. In 2013, approximately 130,000 people were held in for-profit prisons run by corporations such as CCA, the vast majority of whom were people of color (Wade, 2013a, Quandt, 2014). Although the increasingly popular trend of privatizing the criminal justice system may seem like a common-sense, efficient way to handle social problems in our society, the consequences that result from these systems being privatized are disastrous and far reaching. Although illegal drug use remains slightly higher among white Americans (Knafo, 2013), men and women of color are disproportionately targeted for arrest and convicted of drug crimes. In 2009, for example, 79 percent of those convicted in crack cocaine cases were black (Kurtzleben, 2010). According to the Bureau of Justice Statistics, black women are arrested at a rate three times higher than white women and two times higher than Latina women. These stark numbers reveal that people of color are disproportionately represented in the profitable private prison industry (Wade, 2013a; Quandt, 2014).

Privatization is also a particularly prominent feature of detention centers for youths and immigrants. Forty percent of all juvenile offenders are committed to private facilities, which have been found to be rife with corruption and dangerous conditions ranging from unsanitary food to cases of sexual abuse by prison staff against the youth prisoners (Kirkham, 2013). The public–private partnership between government and prison corporations is also clearly evident in recent anti-immigration backlash. A statement from the National Network for Immigrant and Refugee Rights (2010) explains that "Arizona's controversial immigration law SB1070[1] was developed by lawmakers in collaboration with corporations that build private jails to incarcerate immigrants; these companies stand to earn considerable profits from the growing trend of detaining immigrants for enforcement and deterrence." Research demonstrates that people of color (Wade, 2013a), youth (Kirkham, 2013), immigrants (National Network for Immigrant and Refugee Rights, 2010), and the poor (Liptak, 2008a) are particularly vulnerable to exploitation by the private prison industry.

The current state of mass incarceration also poses troubling implications for people and institutions that are, at least theoretically, beyond the scope of the criminal justice system. In addition to the private prison subsidies that burden taxpayers, the restructuring of state and local government budgets that accompany private prison expansion tend to prioritize the funding of incarceration over education. According to a recent report by the Center on Budget and Policy Priorities, between 1986 and 2013 state spending on prisons increased by 140 percent, whereas state spending on K–12 education increased by only 69 percent (Klein, 2014). During this same time period, state spending on higher education increased by just 6 percent (Klein, 2014). Across the nation, states utilize more public funds for housing prisoners than for educating public school students. For instance, the state of Georgia spends an average of $10,805 per public school student annually, compared to an average of $21,039 per inmate (Klein, 2014). This disparity is even greater in states like California, which spends an average of $11,420 per public school student each year, compared to an average of $44,421 per inmate annually (Klein, 2014).

In addition to the profit gained from arresting, booking, and housing prisoners, some of America's most iconic companies (Nordstrom, Eddie Bauer, Motorola, Microsoft, Victoria's Secret, Compaq, IBM, Boeing, AT&T, Texas Instruments, Revlon, Macy's, Target stores, Nortel, Hewlett Packard, Intel, Honeywell, etc.) contract with prison factories such as UNICOR that employ prisoners in both state and private facilities to manufacture some of our most coveted consumer items for pennies an hour (Seandel, 2013; Wade, 2013b). In fact, UNICOR is the country's largest prison factory corporation, operating 110 factories across 79 federal prisons, with the Department of Defense representing the company's most profitable contract (Seandel, 2013). It is estimated that prisoners working for UNICOR manufacture 100 percent of military identification tags, helmets, ammunition belts, and bulletproof vests, among other national defense equipment (Seandel, 2013). Furthermore, trading private prison stock has become profitable for those on Wall Street, with corporations such as Allstate, American Express, General Electric, Goldman Sachs & Co., and Merrill Lynch investing millions annually in the top private prison corporations (Silverstein, 2000; Pelaez, 2014). Even the Gates Foundation, the world's largest private foundation that awards grants for initiatives based in education, health, and world population, invested $2.2 million in the GEO Group (Park, 2014).

Moreover, companies such as the Dial Corporation also bid to win contracts for their products to be used or sold within prisons, whereas companies like AT&T charge exorbitant rates for phone calls made from prison, sometimes resulting in phone bills up to $20,000 for family and friends of prisoners (Martin, 2013). Reporting for the *New York Times*, Clifford and Silver-Greenberg (2014) found that business arrangements between state detention centers and private companies are a common feature of the criminal justice system in nearly every state. Private companies such as JPay and Global Tel-Link control phone, Internet, and money order services in prisons across the country, where prisoners are beyond the reach of consumer protection laws and are viewed as business opportunities, and prisons are regarded as money-making ventures rather than as places for rehabilitation or retribution (Clifford and Silver-Greenberg, 2014). Telephone calls commonly start at $3.15, sending an email outside of prison walls costs $0.33 or more, and transferring money to prisoners for their commissary needs begins at $4.95 (Clifford and Silver-Greenberg, 2014). States profit from these partnerships as well. For instance, in Baldwin County, Alabama, 84 percent of the gross revenue from all telephone calls made in jail is given back to the Sheriff's Department (Clifford and Silver-Greenberg, 2014). Of course, attaching high fees to the most basic services places the heaviest burden on prisoners who are poor, as well as their families, who struggle to find the resources to remain connected to them.

The privatization of justice even begins prior to imprisonment and is a core feature of the commercial bail bond system. Although private prisons clearly exacerbate the financial troubles that prisoners and their families must cope with, the bail bond industry presents incarcerated individuals with unique challenges. In exchange for a fee or some type of collateral, a bondsperson agrees to post bail. Even if the defendant is found "not guilty" at trial, he or she still has to pay bail and the various fees the bondsperson decides to charge (Eligon, 2011). In most countries outside of the United States, paying someone else's bail in exchange for a fee is illegal (Liptak, 2008a), but for the vast majority of poor and middle-class defendants, posting bail through a bondsperson means the difference between temporary freedom or remaining jailed until trial. In one Texas town, judges and bondspeople were found to be colluding to ensure high bails for defendants and high profits for the local bail bond owners (Liptak, 2008b). This system disproportionately harms those without assets, most likely working-class and poor individuals, because collateral, often in the form of property, such as a house or vehicle, is required to cover the bond fees. Although our criminal justice system is founded on ideals of fairness and assumed innocence, the current structure of the system seems stacked against those without means—at every stage in the process. These unequal relationships challenge the core ideals of democracy in this nation, particularly that citizenship guarantees liberty and justice for all.

Other problems related to wealth and poverty abound in the criminal justice system. In a recent NPR special series, "Guilty and Charged," investigative reporter Joseph Shapiro (2014) found that states across the nation are passing on court operating costs to those convicted of misdemeanor and felony charges. In addition to receiving the sentence commensurate with the crime they committed, defendants are burdened with an average fee of $2,500 (the cost associated with operating the court), because legislators fear the political backlash that could ensue from raising taxes to cover these costs. Defendants who cannot afford their court fees are typically given a longer prison sentence than those who are able to pay the fees up front because the inability to pay these types of fees is increasingly becoming criminalized (Shapiro, 2014). In certain cases, judges have been willing to extend a payment plan for offenders who cannot pay the full amount; however, one missed payment can result directly in jail time because this infraction is considered a violation of probation. Although some of the money collected from the fees is dispersed to victims' advocacy groups, forty-three states charge an administrative fee for court-appointed attorneys (also known as public defenders) that are typically conceived of as being a free service for indigent defendants (Shapiro, 2014). However, the incentive for states to continue charging defendants the cost of running the court system remains high because states like Michigan bring in an average $345 million a year in revenue from fees.[2] Similarly, a recent Human Rights Watch (2014) report titled "Profiting from Probation: America's 'Offender-Funded' Probation Industry" found that across Mississippi, Alabama, and Georgia, state courts require people found guilty of misdemeanor crimes to pay their probation fees to private companies. In some cases, the only reason people are sentenced to probation is because they lack the means to pay their court fines at the time of sentencing. In addition to collecting debt owed to the court, private probation companies charge a monthly "supervision" fee, so

those who take longer to pay off their debt, most often the poor, pay disproportionately more than those who have the ability to pay their fees up front (Human Rights Watch, 2014). Those who cannot afford to keep up with payments face going into debt, vehicle repossession, and abusive threats and potential jail time (Human Rights Watch, 2014). Charging defendants for the cost of operating the court system—and then punishing those who cannot pay—challenges one of the basic tenants of the criminal justice system, that all people should be treated equally before the law. At each stage of the incarceration process, from posting bail, to the trial and sentencing court hearings, to prison facilities and the corporations that invest in and operate within them, the privatization of the criminal justice system contributes greatly to the exploitation of our society's most marginalized communities.

Reform advocates such as ACLU staff attorney David Shapiro (2011), along with organizations such as the National Public Service Council to Abolish Private Prisons, the Anti-Recidivism Coalition, and the National Association for the Advancement of Colored People, recommend abolishing the practice of privatizing prisons and prison services while simultaneously investing in an effort to reduce the number of people targeted for imprisonment each year. Considering that the nationwide private prison population is disproportionately representative of marginalized communities, such as youth, people of color, immigrants, and the poor, coalitions among activist groups may be particularly successful at creating viable solutions to mass incarceration. A comparative example of prison phone calls from two different states provides some insight into the effect that deprivatizing prison services may have for those burdened with rising costs. In New Jersey, where the state has a contract with a private company, a fifteen-minute phone call costs $8.50; in New York, where the state does not accept commissions from telephone service providers, a fifteen-minute phone call costs just $0.72. In general, evidence suggests that defendants and prisoners are at greater risk for exploitation and violence when the state attempts to defer the costs associated with operating the criminal justice system by striking deals to contract with private corporations whose central motive is profit, rather than the rehabilitation of its inmates. Investing in rehabilitation rather than incarceration may reduce recidivism and subsequently reduce the rising costs of running the world's busiest court and prison system.

Considering the pervasive nature of the private prison industry, the simultaneous implementation of several reform strategies may be necessary to effectively reduce the harm caused by the privatization of the criminal justice system. For instance, in 2013 Californians voted to amend their three-strikes law that previously mandated that individuals convicted of their third felony charge would be sentenced from twenty-five years to life in prison, no matter the severity of the crime. The amendments to this law now allow for nonviolent third-time offenders to be treated as if they were second-time offenders, potentially cutting the time spent behind bars in half (Laird, 2013). Since the law has gone into effect, nearly 200 nonviolent prisoners have been released after being allowed to petition the court for a resentencing hearing (Laird, 2013). Additionally, Washington, Colorado, Alaska, Oregon, and the District of Columbia have recently legalized recreational marijuana, creating the potential to further reduce the number of people funneled through the criminal justice system each year. Efforts to reform marijuana laws are part of a greater mission to end the war on drugs and thus have direct implications for lessening the private sector's grip on the criminal justice system. Experts from a range of disciplines, including Nobel Prize–winning economists of the London School of Economics' IDEAS Center, have realized the widespread negative outcomes that these draconian practices have caused and advocate a swift end to this endless war (Ferner, 2014). Overall, any effort aimed at reducing the current state of mass incarceration is likely to negatively impact the private prison industry and improve the life chances of some of those caught in the profit-driven criminal justice system.

NOTES

1. SB1070 has been described as the country's toughest and most comprehensive law aimed at criminalizing and deporting "illegal" immigrants (Archibold, 2010). According to this law, failing to maintain immigration documentation at all times is a crime and, as such, police officers have the right to detain anyone suspected of being in the country illegally (Archibold, 2010).

2. One of the most egregious examples of local governments criminalizing and exploiting their most marginalized citizens for profit is found in the case of Ferguson, Missouri, which has been described as a site of contemporary racial apartheid (Kristof, 2014). Following the September 2014 tragic murder of Michael Brown, an unarmed black teenager shot to death by a police officer, the Department of Justice issued a six-month investigation into the local criminal justice system of Ferguson and found practices that indeed confirm the presence of a deeply pervasive system of racialized social control. According to a summary of their report, the official Investigation of the Ferguson Police Department (U.S. Department of Justice, 2015:i) conducted by the Department of Justice's Civil Rights Division found that "Ferguson law enforcement efforts are focused on generating revenue" and, more specifically, that "Ferguson law enforcement practices violate the law and undermine community trust, especially among African Americans."

REFERENCES

Archibold, Randall C. 2010. "Arizona Enacts Stringent Law on Immigration." *New York Times*, April 23. http://www.nytimes.com/2010/04/24/us/politics/24immig.html/.

Cheung, Amy. 2004. *Prison Privatization and the Use of Incarceration*. The Sentencing Project. http://www.sentencingproject.org/doc/publications/inc_prisonprivatization.pdf/.

Clifford, Stephanie, and Jessica Silver-Greenberg. 2014. "In Prisons, Sky-High Phone Rates and Money Transfer Fees." *New York Times*, June 26. http://www.nytimes.com/2014/06/27/business/in-prisons-sky-high-phone-rates-and-money-transfer-fees.html/.

Eligon, John. 2011. "For Poor, Bail System Can Be an Obstacle to Freedom." *New York Times*, January 9. http://www.nytimes.com/2011/01/10/nyregion/10bailbonds.html/.

Ferner, Matt. 2014. "End the War on Drugs, Say Nobel Prize–Winning Economists." *Huffington Post*, May 6. http://www.huffingtonpost.com/2014/05/06/end-drug-war_n_5275078.html/.

Hall, Katy, and Diehm, Jan. 2013. "One Disturbing Reason for Our Exploding Prison Population (INFOGRAPHIC)." *Huffington Post*, September 19. http://www.huffingtonpost.com/2013/09/19/private-prisons_n_3955686.html./

Human Rights Watch. 2014. "Profiting from Probation: America's 'Offender-Funded' Probation Industry." https://www.aclu.org/files/assets/bankingonbondage_20111102.pdf/.

Kirkham, Chris. 2013. "Prison Quotas Push Lawmakers to Fill Beds, Derail Reform." *Huffington Post*, September 19. http://www.huffingtonpost.com/2013/09/19/private-prison-quotas_n_3953483.html/.

Klein, Ezra, and Evan Soltas. 2013. "Wonkbook: 11 Facts about America's Prison Population." *Washington Post*, August 13. http://www.washingtonpost.com/blogs/wonkblog/wp/2013/08/13/wonkbook-11-facts-about-americas-prison-population/.

Klein, Rebecca. 2014. "States Are Prioritizing Prisons over Education, Budgets Show." *Huffington Post*, October 30. http://www.huffingtonpost.com/2014/10/30/state-spending-prison-and-education_n_6072318.html/.

Knafo, Saki. 2013. "When It Comes to Illegal Drug Use, White America Does the Crime, Black America Gets the Time." *Huffington Post*, September 17. http://www.huffingtonpost.com/2013/09/17/racial-disparity-drug-use_n_3941346.html/.

Kristof, Nicholas. 2014. "When Whites Just Don't Get It: After Ferguson, Race Deserves More Attention, Not Less." *New York Times*, August 30. http://www.nytimes.com/2014/08/31/opinion/sunday/nicholas-kristof-after-ferguson-race-deserves-more-attention-not-less.html/.

Kroll, Andy. 2013. "This Is How Private Prison Companies Make Millions Even When Crime Rates Fall." *Mother Jones*, September 19. http://www.motherjones.com/mojo/2013/09/private-prisons-occupancy-quota-cca-crime/.

Kurtzleben, Danielle. 2010. "Data Show Racial Disparity in Crack Sentencing." *US News*, August 3. http://www.usnews.com/news/articles/2010/08/03/data-show-racial-disparity-in-crack-sentencing/.

Laird, Lorelei. 2013. "California Begins to Release Prisoners after Reforming Its Three-Strikes Law." *American Bar Association Journal*, December 1. http://www.abajournal.com/magazine/article/california_begins_to_release_prisoners_after_reforming_its_three-strikes_la/.

Lee, Suevon. 2012. "By the Numbers: America's Growing For-Profit Detention Industry." *Huffington Post*, June 21. http://www.huffingtonpost.com/2012/06/21/for-profit-prisons_n_1613696.html/.

Liptak, Adam. 2008a. "Illegal Globally, Bail for Profit Remains in U.S." *New York Times*, January 29. http://www.nytimes.com/2008/01/29/us/29bail.html?pagewanted=all/.

Liptak, Adam. 2008b. "U.S. Prison Population Dwarfs That of Other Nations." *New York Times*, April 23. http://www.nytimes.com/2008/04/23/world/americas/23iht-23prison.12253738.html?pagewanted=all/.

Lloyd, Jennifer. 2002. "Drug Use Trends." White House Office of National Drug Control Policy. https://www.ncjrs.gov/App/Publications/abstract.aspx?ID=190780/.

Martin, Jonathan. 2013. "AT&T to Pay Washington Prisoners' Families $45 Million in Telephone Class Action Settlement." *Seattle Times*, February 3. http://blogs.seattletimes.com/opinionnw/2013/02/03/att-to-pay-washington-prisoners-families-45-million-in-telephone-class-action-settlement/.

National Network for Immigrant and Refugee Rights. 2010. *Injustice for All: The Rise of the U.S. Immigration Policing Regime*. Human Rights Immigrant Community Action Network, an initiative of the National Network for Immigrant and Refugee Rights.

Park, Alex. 2014. "Is the Gates Foundation Still Investing in Private Prisons?" *Mother Jones*, December 8. http://www.motherjones.com/politics/2014/12/gates-foundation-still-investing-private-prisons/.

Pelaez, Vicky. 2014. "The Prison Industry in the United States: Big Business or a New Form of Slavery?" Global Research Centre for Research on Globalization. http://www.globalresearch.ca/the-prison-industry-in-the-united-states-big-business-or-a-new-form-of-slavery/8289/.

Quandt, Katie Rose. 2014. "Why There's an Even Larger Racial Disparity in Private Prisons Than in Public Ones." *Mother Jones*, February 17. http://www.motherjones.com/mojo/2014/01/even-larger-racial-disparity-private-prisons-public-prisons/.

Seandel, Caitlin. 2013. "Prison Labor: Three Strikes and You're Hired." Ella Baker Center for Human Rights. http://ellabakercenter.org/blog/2013/06/prison-labor-is-the-new-slave-labor/.

Shapiro, David. 2011. "Banking on Bondage: Private Prisons and Mass Incarceration." American Civil Liberties Union. https://www.aclu.org/files/assets/bankingonbondage_20111102.pdf/.

Shapiro, Joseph. 2014. "Special Series: Guilty and Charged." NPR. http://www.npr.org/series/313986316/guilty-and-charged/.

Shen, Aviva. 2012. "Private Prisons Cost Arizona $3.5 Million More per Year Than State-Run Prisons." Think Progress. http://thinkprogress.org/justice/2012/08/06/641971/private-prisons-cost-arizona-35-million-more-per-year-than-state-run-prisons/.

Silverstein, Ken. 2000. "US: America's Private Gulag." CorpWatch. http://www.corpwatch.org/article.php?id=867/.

Takei, Carl. 2013. "Happy Birthday to the Corrections Corporation of America? Thirty Years of Banking on Bondage Leaves Little to Celebrate." American Civil Liberties Union. https://www.aclu.org/blog/happy-birthday-corrections-corporation-america-thirty-years-banking-bondage-leaves-little?redirect=blog/speakeasy/happy-birthday-corrections-corporation-america-thirty-years-banking-bondage-leaves/.

The Sentencing Project. 2013. "Fact Sheet: Trends in U.S. Corrections." http://sentencingproject.org/doc/publications/inc_Trends_in_Corrections_Fact_sheet.pdf/.

The Sentencing Project. 2014. "Juvenile Life without Parole: An Overview." http://sentencingproject.org/doc/publications/jj_Juvenile_Life_Without_Parole.pdf/.

U.S. Department of Justice, Civil Rights Division. 2015. *Investigation of the Ferguson Police Department*. http://www.justice.gov/sites/default/files/opa/press-releases/attachments/2015/03/04/ferguson_police_department_report.pdf/.

Wade, Lisa. 2013a. *Race, Rehabilitation, and the Private Prison Industry*. The Society Pages. http://thesocietypages.org/socimages/2013/01/25/race-rehabilitation-and-the-private-prison-industry/.

Wade, Lisa. 2013b. *Prison Labor and Taxpayer Dollars*. The Society Pages. http://thesocietypages.org/socimages/2013/04/04/prison-labor-and-taxpayer-dollars/.

How Prisons Change the Balance of Power in America

HEATHER ANN THOMPSON

Thompson explains how elections are affected by disenfranchising those with felony convictions. Beginning with a history of political disenfranchisement of people of color, she demonstrates how mass incarceration has distorted our democracy because many prisoners are ineligible to vote, even after their release from prison/jail. She also discusses how rural majority-white counties have increased their political power and redrawn the electoral maps in a process called "prison gerrymandering" by counting prisoners in their population for the purpose of political representation, but not allowing those prisoners to vote.

What has it really cost the United States to build the world's most massive prison system?

To answer this question, some[1] point to the nearly two million people who are now locked up in an American prison—overwhelmingly this nation's poorest, most mentally ill, and least-educated citizens—and ponder the moral costs. Others[2] have pointed to the enormous expense of having more than seven million Americans under some form of correctional supervision and argued that the system is not economically sustainable. Still others[3] highlight the high price that our nation's already most-fragile communities, in particular, have paid for the rise of such an enormous carceral state. A few[4] have also asked Americans to consider what it means for the future of our society that our system of punishment is so deeply racialized.

With so many powerful arguments being made against our current criminal justice system, why then does it persist? Why haven't the American people, particularly those who are most negatively affected by this most unsettling and unsavory state of affairs, undone the policies that have led us here? The answer, in part, stems from the fact that locking up unprecedented numbers of citizens over the last forty years has *itself* made the prison system highly resistant to reform through the democratic process. To an extent that few Americans have yet appreciated, record rates of incarceration have, in fact, undermined our American democracy, both by impacting who gets to vote and how votes are counted.

The unsettling story of how this came to be actually begins in 1865, when the abolition of slavery led to bitter constitutional battles[5] over who would and would not be included in our polity. To fully understand it, though, we must look more closely than we yet have at the year 1965, a century later—a moment when, on the one hand, politicians were pressured into opening the franchise by passing the most comprehensive Voting Rights Act to date, but on the other hand, were also beginning a devastatingly ambitious War on Crime.

From Voting Rights to the War on Crime

The Voting Rights Act of 1965 gave the federal government a number of meaningful tools with which it could monitor state elections and make sure that states with a particularly grim history of discriminatory voting practices would make no voting policy without its approval. The act had been intended to combat the intimidation and legal maneuvers—such as passage of poll taxes, literacy requirements, and so-called "Grandfather clauses"—that had left only 5 percent of black Americans, by the 1940s, able to vote, despite passage of the 14th and 15th amendments after the Civil War.

But the very same year that Lyndon Johnson signed the Voting Rights Act of 1965, he also signed another act into law: the Law Enforcement Administration Act (LEAA), a piece of legislation that, well before crime rates across America hit record highs, created the bureaucracy and provided the funding that would enable a historically and internationally unparalleled war on crime.

So, at the *very same moment* that the American Civil Rights Movement had succeeded in newly empowering African Americans in the political sphere by securing passage of the Voting Rights Act of 1965, America's white politicians decided to begin a massive new war on crime that would eventually undercut myriad gains of the Civil Rights Movement—*particularly* those promised by the Voting Rights Act itself.

From the War on Crime to Mass Incarceration

Thanks to LEAA and America's post-1965 commitment to the War on Crime, and more specifically, thanks to the dramatic escalation of policing in cities across the nation as well as the legal changes wrought by an ever-intensifying War on Drugs, between 1970 and 2010 more people ended up in prison in this country than anywhere else in the world. At no other point in this nation's recorded past had the economic, social, and political institutions of a country become so bound up with the practice of punishment.

By the year 2007, 1 in every 31 U.S. residents lived under some form of correctional supervision. By 2010, more than 7.3 million Americans had become entangled in the criminal justice system and 2 million of them were actually locked up in state and federal prisons. By 2011, 39,709 people in Louisiana alone were living behind bars and 71,579 were either in jail, on probation, or on parole. And this was by no means a "southern" phenomenon. In Pennsylvania, 51,638 people were actually locked behind bars in 2011 and a full 346,268 lived under some form of correctional control by that year.

The nation's decision to embark on a massive War on Crime in the mid-1960s has had a profound impact on the way that American history evolved over the course of the later 20th and into the 21st centuries. As we now know from countless studies, such staggering rates of incarceration have proven both socially devastating[6] and economically destructive for wide swaths of this country—particularly those areas of America inhabited by people of color.[7] This nation's incarceration rate was hardly color blind. Eventually one in nine young black men were locked up in America and, by 2010, black women and girls too were being locked up at a record rate.

Diluting Our Democracy

So how did this overwhelmingly racialized mass incarceration end up mattering to our very democracy? How is it that this act of locking up so many Americans, particularly Americans of color, *itself* distorted our political process and made it almost impossible for those most affected by mass incarceration to eliminate the policies that have undergirded it at the ballot box? The answer lies back in the 1870s and in a little-known caveat to the 14th Amendment.

Ratifying the 14th Amendment was one of Congress's first efforts to broaden the franchise after the Civil War. A key worry among northern politicians, however, was that since white southerners could no longer rely on the notorious "three-fifths" rule to pad their own political power, they would now try to inflate their census population for the purposes of representation by counting African Americans as citizens while denying them access to the ballot.

So, to prevent any power grab on the part of ex-Confederates, Congress decided to add so-called Section 2 to the 14th Amendment. Firstly it stipulated that any state that "denied" the vote "to any of the male inhabitants of such state, being twenty-one years of age, and citizens of the United States" would have its representation downsized in proportion to the number of individuals being disenfranchised. Secondly, Section 2 allowed for the disenfranchisement of otherwise eligible citizens—without affecting representation—if they had participated "in rebellion, or other crime." The idea here was to keep those who had committed crimes against the Union and those who might still be in rebellion against the Union from wielding political power in the wake of the Civil War.

This latter provision of Section 2, however, proved damaging to black freedom—political and otherwise. Almost overnight, white southerners began policing African Americans[8] with new zeal and charging them with "crimes" that had never before been on the books. Within a decade of the Civil War, thousands of African Americans found themselves leased out and locked up on prison plantations and in penitentiaries.

Southern whites, of course, profited from these new laws politically as well as economically. By making so many blacks into convicts, whites could deny them the right to vote under Section 2 without undermining their state's census population for the purposes of political representation. And, because of another clause of another Amendment, the 13th, which allowed the continuation of slavery for those who had committed a crime, these same white southerners were able to force thousands of newly imprisoned black southerners to work for free[9] under the convict lease system.[10]

Fast-forward 100 years when, in the wake of the Civil Rights movement, another War on Crime began that also, almost overnight, led to the mass imprisonment of this nation's African American citizens. In 1974, as the number of imprisoned Americans was rising precipitously and when states once again began to disfranchise individuals with criminal convictions, the U.S. Supreme Court was asked in a landmark case, *Richardson v. Ramirez*, to rule explicitly on the issue of whether it was constitutional under the 14th Amendment to disfranchise those serving, or who have served, time in prison. The court did the same thing that many southern states did after the Civil War—it interpreted Section A of the 14th amendment very, very differently than it was intended to be interpreted. It, too, decided that disenfranchisement would be permitted when a citizen was convicted of *any* crime, without regard to whether such crimes might be thought of as ideologically analogous to rebellion or were more likely to affect African Americans than others.

Notably, Justice Thurgood Marshall dissented vigorously in this case. The purpose of Section 2, he argued, was clearly to enfranchise, not disenfranchise, former slaves and their descendants. Marshall's fellow members of the bench, though, felt that their decision would not have any discriminatory effect because the nation already had the Voting Rights Act of 1965 to handle this issue.

And yet, the negative impact of *Richardson v. Ramirez* on African American voting was vast and immediate. By the year 2000, 1.8 million African Americans had been barred from the polls because so many felon disfranchisement laws had been passed in states across the country after 1974. Not only were their votes not counted in that year's hotly contested presidential election, but by the next presidential election a full ten states, according to The Sentencing Project, had "African American disenfranchisement rates above 15%,"[11] which clearly affected the outcome of that contest as well.

By 2006, 48 out of 50 states had passed disfranchisement laws and, with more than 47 million Americans (1/4 of the adult population) having criminal records by that year, the nation's political process had been fundamentally altered. By 2011, 23.3% of African Americans in Florida, 18.3% of the black population of Wyoming, and 20.4% of African Americans in Virginia were barred from the ballot.

According to sociologists Jeff Manza and Christopher Uggen, not only did African Americans pay a high price for the disfranchisement policies that accompanied the nation's War on Crime, but so did liberal voters in general. According to their research,[12] such policies "affected the outcome of seven U.S. Senate races from 1970 to 1998 . . . [and] in each case the Democratic candidate would have won rather than the Republican victor" and these outcomes likely "prevented Democratic control of the Senate from 1986 to 2000" as well.

Distorting Our Democracy

Disfranchising thousands of voters is only part of the story of how mass incarceration has distorted American democracy. Today, just as it did more than a hundred years earlier, the way the Census calculates resident population also plays a subtle but significant role. As ex-Confederates knew well, prisoners would be counted as residents of a given county, even if they could not themselves vote: High numbers of prisoners could easily translate to greater political power for those who put them behind bars.

With the advent of mass incarceration, and as the number of people imprisoned not only rose dramatically, but also began moving ur-

banites of color into overwhelmingly white rural counties that housed prisons, the political process was again distorted. In short, thanks to this process that we now call "prison-gerrymandering," overwhelmingly white and Republican areas of the United States that built prisons as the War on Crime escalated got more political power, whereas areas of country where policing was particularly concentrated and aggressive, areas in which levels of incarceration were, as a result, staggering, lost political power.

Consider research by the Prison Policy Initiative[13] showing how voters across the country gain political power from housing a penal facility. In Powhatan County, Virginia[14] 41% of the 5th Board of Supervisors District that was drawn after the 2000 Census were actually people in prison and in both the First and Third Supervisory Districts of Nottoway County, approximately 1/4 of their population comes from large prisons within the county. In the case of Southampton County, such prison-based gerrymandering means that votes of those citizens who live there are worth almost more than twice as much as votes cast in other districts that have the required number of actual residents.

In Michigan[15] as well, mass incarceration has meant distorted democracy. A full four state senate districts drawn after the 2000 Census (17, 19, 33 and 37), and a full five house districts (65, 70, 92, 107 and 110) meet federal minimum population requirements only because they claim prisoners as constituents. Similarly in Pennsylvania,[16] no fewer than eight state legislative districts would comply with the federal "one person, one vote" civil rights standard if nonvoting state and federal prisoners in those districts were not counted as district residents.

Why We Should Care

As Americans go to the polls . . . to vote on criminal justice issues that directly affect our lives—ranging from proposals to decriminalize marijuana, to roll back three strikes laws, to fund more prison construction—the massive carceral state that we are trying to shape at the ballot box has already distorted our democracy. Americans' power to even rethink, let alone undo, the policies and practices that have led to mass incarceration via the franchise has been severely compromised—in no small part due to the fact that the parties that benefitted the most from the rise of this enormous carceral state are now empowered, seemingly in perpetuity, by its sheer size and scope.

There are, of course, other ways to dismantle the carceral state. Indeed, history shows us that we ended the brutal convict leasing system of the Post–Civil War era not by going to the polls but by grassroots and legal activism. Nevertheless, we should all be concerned about the ways mass incarceration has eroded our democracy. Even if we don't care about the record rate of imprisonment in this country—despite its myriad ugly consequences, its unsustainable cost, and its particularly devastating fallout on communities of color—when the principle of "one person, one vote" no longer has real meaning in a society, and when political power is no longer attained via its people but rather through a manipulation of their laws, we must all question the future of our nation.

NOTES

1. CBS News. 2012. "The Cost of a Nation of Incarceration." *CBSNews.* http://www.cbsnews .com/8301-3445_162-57418495/the-cost-of-a-nation-of-incarceration/?pageNum=2

2. Henrichson, Christian and Ruth Delaney. 2012.http://www.vera.org/pubs/price-prisons-what-incarceration-costs-taxpayers

3. Orson, Diane. 2012. "'Million-Dollar Blocks' Map Incarceration Costs." *National Public Radio.* http://www.npr.org/2012/10/02/162149431/million-dollar-blocks-map-incarcerations-costs

4. The Huffington Post. 2011. "Lisa Ling's 'Our America' Looks at Mass Incarceration of Black Men." *The Huffington Post.* http://www .huffingtonpost.com/2011/11/17/lisa-lings-our-america-ex_n_1099668.html

5. Holloway, Pippa. 2013. *Living in Infamy: Felon Disenfranchisement and the History of American Citizenship.* Oxford University Press.

6. Clear, Todd R. *Imprisoning Communities: How Mass Incarceration Makes Disadvantaged Neighborhoods Worse.* Oxford University Press.

7. Alexander, Michelle. 2012. *The New Jim Crow: Mass Incarceration in the Age of Colorblindness.* The New Press.

8. Blackmon, Douglas A. 2008. *Slavery by Another Name: The Re-Enslavement of Black People in America from the Civil War to World War II.* Doubleday. http://www .slaverybyanothername.com/

9. Curtin, Mary Ellen. 2000. *Black Prisoners and Their World, 1865–1900.* University of Virginia Press.

10. Lichtenstein, Alex. 1996. *Twice the Work of Free Labor: The Political Economy of Convict Labor in the New South.*

11. FairPlan2020. 2008. "Felon Disenfranchisement by State." http://www.fairvote2020 .org/2008/03/felon-disenfranchisement-by-state.html

12. Manza, Jeff, Christopher Uggen. 2006. *Locked Out: Felon Disenfranchisement and American Democracy.* Oxford University Press.

13. Prison Policy Initiative. http://www .prisonpolicy.org/

14. Prison Policy Initiative. 2010. "Fixing Prison-Based Gerrymandering after the 201 Census: Virginia." http://www.prisonersofthecensus .org/50states/VA.html

15. Prison Policy Initiative. 2010. "Fixing Prison-Based Gerrymandering after the 201 Census: Michigan." http://www.prisonersofthecensus .org/50states/MI.html

16. Prison Policy Initiative. 2010. "Fixing Prison-Based Gerrymandering after the 201 Census: Pennsylvania." http://www.prisonersofthe census.org/50states/PA.html

Can the Police Be Reformed?

RONALD WEITZER

Weitzer discusses citizens' satisfaction with and confidence in the police, arguing there are racially disparate levels of satisfaction. He explores the nature of police work and how the subculture and socialization of police officers may lead them to treat citizens in problematic ways, especially racial minorities. Weitzer describes strengths and weaknesses of various reforms designed to provide better and more equitable service from the police, including community policing, racial diversification, and additional forms of accountability.

Americans are ambivalent toward the police. We depend on them and are fascinated by them, as shown in the popularity of police shows on television—which usually present the police sympathetically. But confidence in the police is periodically shaken by revelations of misconduct. The most dramatic incidents involve the beating or killing of unarmed civilians, such as Rodney King [in 1991] in Los Angeles and Abner Louima and Amadou Diallo [in 1997 and 1999, respectively] in New York.[1] Less dramatic but no less serious are corruption scandals. The Rampart Division of the Los Angeles Police Department was recently caught up in such a scandal. Rampart officers were accused of falsifying police reports, stealing drugs from suspects, framing people, and abusing unarmed suspects. About 200 lawsuits have been filed against the city, and more than 100 tainted criminal convictions have been overturned.

Meaningful reform of a police department is extremely difficult. Police organization and culture impede change, and the history of policing is filled with instances in which the police succeeded in undermining or diluting reforms that were implemented after a scandal. But this does not mean that police reform is impossible. Under the right conditions, progressive changes can both enhance the quality of police work and improve relations between police and the communities they serve.

Shaky Public Confidence

Most Americans hold a favorable general opinion of the police. The majority say they are "satisfied" with or have "confidence" in their local police. But such diffuse support masks more critical views on specific policing issues, particularly among racial and ethnic minorities. The two core concerns are under-policing and abusive policing. On the one hand, the majority of African Americans and Hispanics are not satisfied with the amount and quality of law enforcement in their neighborhoods and want increased

Ronald Weitzer, *Contexts* (Volume 4 and Issue 3), pp. 21–26, Copyright © 2005. Reprinted by Permission of SAGE Publications.

efforts to control crime. On the other hand, a substantial number of blacks and Hispanics believe that police corruption and use of excessive force occur frequently in their city, and the overwhelming majority believes that racial profiling is "widespread" both in their own city and throughout the United States. Minorities are also much more likely than whites to say that they have personally experienced some kind of abuse. In one recent poll, for example, 43 percent of blacks and 26 percent of Hispanics—but only 3 percent of whites—reported that they had been stopped by the police solely because of their race or ethnicity, and almost as many blacks and Hispanics said that this had happened to someone else in their household.

Of course, perception does not always mirror reality. Popular beliefs are influenced by media coverage of especially disturbing events. Immediately after the broadcast of the videotaped beating of Rodney King, support for the Los Angeles Police Department (LAPD) plummeted. The same erosion of support has been documented after other well-publicized incidents of misconduct. In contrast, after the attacks of September 11th, public approval of the police rose nationwide. Once such events recede, public opinion typically returns to its "normal" level.

Unfortunately, little is known about the *actual frequency* of police misconduct. Most encounters between officers and citizens are unsupervised and unrecorded, making abuse extremely difficult to document. Still, incidents of police abuse come to light often enough—in media reports, formal complaints, and civil suits against police departments—to underscore the need for improvement.

The Nature of Police Work

Police work has often been called "dirty work." Officers constantly deal with problem situations—upset and traumatized victims, unruly or violent offenders, and drivers annoyed at being stopped. Some view police intervention as harassment or as an infringement of their rights and act belligerently toward officers. Police frequently complain that citizens fail to respect them or defer to their authority, and this may provoke a harsh response. As one officer quoted by the Christopher Commission (which investigated the LAPD in 1991) remarked, "[A suspect] pissed us off, so I guess he needs an ambulance now. . . . [People] should know better than to run; they are going to pay a price when they do that." And another officer said, "We got a little physical with a [suspect]. It was fun. We had to teach him a little respect . . . for the police." In a recent Police Foundation survey of 121 police departments across the country, half the officers interviewed agreed that police are more likely to arrest someone who displays a "bad attitude," and one-quarter agreed that it is "acceptable to use more force than is legally allowable to control someone who physically assaults an officer."

Because police deal mostly with "problem" citizens, not the general population, they develop an "us versus them" mentality toward the public. Officers see themselves as a "thin blue line" between order and chaos and develop an elevated sense of mission that may lead to abuses of power. These are key ingredients in the police *subculture*—a distinct set of values and beliefs. This subculture insulates the police fraternity and fosters a "code of silence" that shields cops from scrutiny. As one officer quoted by the Christopher Commission stated, "It is basically a non-written rule that you do not roll over, tell on your partner." Doing so will lead to ostracism. The Police Foundation survey found that fully two-thirds of police agreed with the statement, "An officer who reports another officer's misconduct is likely to be given the cold shoulder by his or her fellow officers."

Sociologists have documented how the police subculture influences police treatment of citizens. On the job, officers learn to trust only fellow officers and to distrust members of the public, to deal aggressively with people who question their actions, to circumvent legal restrictions on what they are allowed to do, and to administer summary "street justice" to suspicious or troublesome people. Research illustrates how officers grapple with the dilemma of "law versus order"—fighting crime under legal constraints. Officers tend to regard such constraints as "technicalities" that hinder their efforts to maintain order and fight crime. To avoid those constraints, they develop strategies that depend on fellow officers' tacit support and fidelity to the code of silence.

The traditional police subculture, while still powerful throughout the country, has changed somewhat in recent years. In at least some major cities, police departments are less cohesive and insular, more community-oriented, and more diverse than in the past (with more female, college-educated, and minority officers). Such changes open a window of opportunity for further reforms.

Racial Diversification

Racial diversification has been a popular way to deal with charges of racial discrimination by the police. The principle of matching the racial composition of a police department to that of its city is now widely accepted in American political and law enforcement circles. The U.S. Department of Justice, for instance, proclaims, "A diverse law enforcement agency can better develop relationships with the community it serves, promote trust in the fairness of law enforcement, and facilitate effective policing by encouraging citizen support and cooperation. Law enforcement agencies should seek to hire a diverse workforce." Some police departments are fairly diverse, and some are now majority-black or majority-Hispanic (e.g., Atlanta, Detroit, El Paso, Miami, Washington). Most, however, remain racially or ethnically unrepresentative of their cities.

More than two-thirds of Americans believe that police departments should reflect the racial and ethnic composition of their city, according to a national survey of 1,792 people that I conducted with Steven Tuch. But significantly fewer feel that minorities should be given preference in hiring to increase diversity. This gap between principle and practice is especially wide for

whites . . . and is consistent with their views on affirmative action in other occupations and in education.

One positive outcome of racial diversification is that it appears to increase the legitimacy of a police department. As one African American I interviewed in Washington, DC, said, "If there were a predominant white showing [of officers] here. . . . I think that it would look as though whites [were] flaunting their authority." Similarly, when the leadership of a police department passes from a white chief to a Hispanic or black chief, this may be symbolically important for city residents. In Los Angeles, African-American chief of police Willie Williams received much higher job approval ratings than his controversial white predecessor, Daryl Gates. Race likely played at least some part in public perceptions, especially among nonwhites.

Are there other advantages to diversification? Research shows that minority officers are better equipped to understand and communicate with minority citizens; in sociological terms, there is less social distance between them than between white officers and minority citizens. Minority officers also bring different attitudes to policing. According to the Police Foundation survey, black officers are more likely than their white counterparts to believe that police treat minorities and the poor worse than whites and middle-class people, and they are more likely to say that community policing reduces the number of incidents involving excessive force.

Still, most research shows that black and white officers differ little in how they actually *treat* citizens. When it comes to behavior, officers are mainly "blue," not black, brown, or white. However, one recent study of Indianapolis and St. Petersburg, by Ivan Sun and Brian Payne, found that black officers were more likely than white officers to engage in supportive activities in black neighborhoods, such as offering information, providing assistance, making referrals to other agencies, behaving respectfully, and comforting residents. Interestingly, this study also found that black officers were more likely to use physical force against citizens in conflict situations. But, again, most other research finds that white and minority officers tend to behave similarly.

One problem is that all these studies are confined to majority-white police forces, where minority officers are under pressure to conform to the conventional police subculture. We do not yet know whether police attitudes and behavior are substantially different in predominantly Hispanic or African-American departments. A majority-Hispanic department such as Miami's may treat the city's Cuban population differently than did its majority-white predecessor. Though not yet demonstrated by research, *extensive* diversification may pay both symbolic and practical dividends in improving police-minority relations.

Community Policing

Community policing has been all the rage in the past two decades. Most citizens want it, most police departments claim that they do it, and the federal government has recently funded it at the local level. The Violent Crime Control Act of 1994, for instance, created the Office of Community Oriented Policing Services (COPS) within the Justice Department and authorized spending $8.8 billion over ten years to support community policing initiatives in cities throughout the country, including the hiring of 100,000 officers.

"Community policing" generally refers to officers and neighborhood residents working together to identify the neighborhood conditions that lead to crime and formulating solutions to those problems. As such, it is much more collaborative and proactive than the traditional approach of responding to incidents after the fact. Community policing is accomplished through regular police-community meetings, routine foot patrols, police mini stations that are accessible to residents, and various programs for youth.

When asked in a Justice Department survey of twelve cities whether they would like to see community policing in their neighborhoods, 86 percent of respondents said yes. Other polls have found substantial public support for foot patrols, community meetings, and school programs. Most police chiefs claim that their departments practice community policing, though some of this is mere lip service. Cities vary considerably in the degree to which community policing actually exists and in the degree to which officers accept it. In some, it is marginalized in a community-relations branch that operates independently of most officers. In other places, however—San Diego, Portland, Savannah—community policing is more integrated throughout the police department and is a philosophy guiding all officers.

Serious community policing can improve public confidence and may also advance crime-fighting. Chicago's Alternative Policing Strategy (CAPS) is one example. Begun in 1993, key elements of CAPS include assigning officers to permanent beats to increase their knowledge of neighborhood problems, intensive training in solving neighborhood problems (such as vandalism, prostitution, and crack houses), regular formal meetings between residents and police, and ongoing review of program outcomes. Wesley Skogan's ten-year evaluation of CAPS is the best and most ambitious study of community policing to date. He found that as a result of CAPS, neighborhood crime and disorder decreased, people became less fearful of crime, gang problems were reduced, police became more responsive to community concerns, and residents began to view the police more favorably. This research suggests that community policing, while no panacea, can be effective when a police department fully embraces and devotes sufficient resources to it. Unfortunately, most community policing programs do not live up to these standards: They are fragmented, marginalized, and under-funded.

Accountability

Historically, American police were largely unaccountable for their actions, and oversight remains a problem today. Commanding officers exercise little supervision over day-to-day activities. Indeed, police work is one of the few jobs that provide more autonomy to rank-and-file employees than to their bosses. Not only do officers usually patrol alone, but they are also authorized to improvise solutions and sanctions on the spot, based on the need for swift action to handle specific circumstances. This freedom allows them to get away with minor violations (such as sleeping on duty), major violations (stopping a car because the driver is black), and outright crimes (assault, planting evidence, theft of money or drugs).

Many Americans doubt that police departments are capable of effectively monitoring and punishing wayward officers. According to a 1992 Harris poll, about two-thirds of the public felt that police were "too lenient" in investigating complaints against fellow officers. Americans prefer external oversight over internal review, and some leading scholars agree: Jerome Skolnick and James Fyfe argue that "police cannot be impartial when investigating other police, and even when they are, they are unlikely to be credible." These views have led to demands for increased external control. Some recent innovations render police actions at least somewhat more transparent.

To prevent racial profiling, for example, many states and cities now require officers to record the race, gender, and age of all motorists they stop, as well as the reason for the stop and whether a search or arrest was made. Forcing officers to justify their actions in writing could reduce improper stops. Since such data-recording requirements are recent, it is too early to assess their effects. Still, a growing number of state and local officials, as well as most citizens, believe that collecting this information will help reduce racial profiling.

Another innovative tactic is to mount video cameras on the dashboards of patrol cars. When officers stop motorists, the camera records the encounter, documenting both citizen and police behavior. In 2000, the COPS office awarded $12 million to 41 police agencies to purchase a total of 2,900 in-car cameras. There is no research on whether such monitoring helps reduce racial profiling or other abuses during street stops, but a substantial number of Americans believe that in-car cameras would help improve matters, according to the Weitzer–Tuch survey.[2]

"Early warning systems" consist of computerized records of each officer's history of citizen complaints, civil suits, use of firearms, and other indicators of questionable performance. When an officer is flagged in the system, supervisors then intervene with counseling, retraining, or discipline. A few officers receive a disproportionate share of complaints from citizens. In Kansas City, for instance, 2 percent of officers received 50 percent of all complaints. About one-quarter of police agencies nationwide now have such early warning systems, and research suggests that they can restrain police misconduct. The best available evidence comes from an evaluation of Miami, Minneapolis, and New Orleans by Samuel Walker, Geoffrey Alpert, and Dennis Kenney. Early warning mechanisms reduced police misconduct in the three cities. In each case, prompt interventions with problem officers curbed bad behavior. Similarly, a Vera Institute of Justice study of two precincts in the Bronx, New York, known for their poor police–community relations, found that complaints against officers dropped markedly after precinct commanders instituted procedures to more strictly monitor, retrain, and restrain officers who received multiple complaints. The vast majority of Americans favor early warning systems.

Accountability also requires meaningful sanctions, and most people believe such sanctions must come from outside the police department. The courts provide an external check, but only the most serious criminal and civil cases end up in court. Another type of external oversight is the civilian review board, which most large American cities now have. While they vary in structure, composition, and powers, civilian review boards share a single purpose—to adjudicate citizen complaints against police officers. After a citizen files a formal complaint, the board typically interviews the accused officer and any witnesses either in private or in a public hearing. Frequently, the case boils down to the citizen's word against the officer's, without any corroborating evidence. This is one reason that such boards usually sustain complaints no more than 10 percent of the time.

This low substantiation rate does not mean that the boards are a failure. Even when a complaint is not upheld, the complainant may appreciate the opportunity to be heard and may be satisfied if he or she feels that the process was fair. Moreover, the boards can play an important symbolic role—sending a message to cops that they may be called to account for their actions. In cities that have such boards, most people believe that they help to reduce police mistreatment of citizens.

Some experts favor independent auditors over civilian review boards. A relatively recent idea, the auditor model shifts the focus from individual officer behavior to larger organizational problems that may invite police misconduct. Most civilian review boards deal exclusively with complaints against specific officers, whereas auditors typically identify organizational problems, make recommendations for remedies, and monitor their implementation. Examples of auditors that are especially innovative, according to Samuel Walker's research, include the Inspector General's office in Los Angeles, the Police Internal Investigations Auditing Committee in Portland, Oregon, and the Independent Police Auditor in San Jose. Auditors have reviewed patterns and trends in complaints; monitored the departments' internal review processes; and investigated departmental policies on the handling of domestic violence, officer use of force, community outreach, and so forth. The key question is: What happens after the auditor identifies a problem and makes recommendations? Do police chiefs ignore the recommendations or take them seriously? The San Jose auditor has been highly rated because most recommendations have been accepted and implemented by the department. While no system of external accountability is perfect, some kind of outside review is better than none.

Conclusion

The reforms described above are not the only ones that have been proposed. Others include intensive sensitivity training for officers, stricter guidelines on use of force, and hiring people with college degrees. But any reform will remain meaningless if not backed up with sufficient resources and a firm commitment from departmental leadership. Moreover, for reforms to "stick," they must become part of the organizational culture. Increasing the percentage of minority officers in a department from, say, 10 percent to 25 percent is unlikely to have any effect on the police subculture. Increasing their presence to 50 percent or more may be more consequential. Community policing programs that are marginalized and piecemeal will have few positive results, but when they guide the philosophy and practice of the entire department, a community orientation seems to improve matters significantly. When top police officials wholeheartedly embrace the changes and convey their importance to patrol officers, reforms stand a better chance of being incorporated into the police culture, of truly improving police practice, and of increasing popular confidence in the police department.

NOTES

1. Editor's note: There have been many high-profile police killings of unarmed black civilians in the recent past. High-profile cases include but are not limited to Michael Brown in Ferguson, Missouri; Eric Garner in Staten Island, New York; Tamir Rice in Cleveland, Ohio; Tony Robinson in Madison, Wisconsin; Anthony Hill in Atlanta, Georgia; Walter Scott in North Charleston, South Carolina; Tanisha Anderson in Cleveland, Ohio; Christian Taylor in Arlington, Texas; and Laquan McDonald in Chicago, Illinois.

2. Editor's note: Since this reading was originally published, in-car camera placement has increased. By 2007, 61 percent of local police departments used video cameras in patrol cars; 71,000 in-car cameras were in use (Reaves, 2010). However, no large-scale studies to date document a reduction in racial profiling as a result of in-car cameras. More recently, there has been a push to equip officers with body cameras. Although no research has demonstrated that body cameras reduce racial profiling, there is some evidence that they greatly reduce officers' use-of-force and citizen complaints (Miller et al., 2014).

EDITOR'S REFERENCES

Miller, Lindsay, Jessica Toliver, and Police Executive Research Forum. 2014. "Implementing a Body-Worn Camera Program: Recommendations and Lessons Learned." Washington, DC: Office of Community Oriented Policing Services.

Reaves, Brian A. 2010. Law Enforcement Management and Administrative Statistics Local Police Departments, 2007 (NCJ 231174). Bureau of Justice Statistics. Washington, DC: U.S. Department of Justice. Retrieved March 25, 2015. http://www.bjs.gov/content/pub/ascii/lpd07.txt/.

13

Social Problems Related to the Economy and Work

Ai-jen Poo

Courtesy of Michele Asselin.

Ai-jen Poo is the director of the National Domestic Workers Alliance and co-director of the Caring across Generations campaign.

What is your organization and its mission?

The National Domestic Workers Alliance promotes rights, recognition and respect for the over 2 million domestic workers and direct care workers who care for our families and support seniors and people with disabilities so that they can live independently.

How did you first become interested in this type of activism? What/who was your inspiration?

My mother has long been an inspiration to me. As an immigrant to the United States, she learned English, worked and went to school, and she raised my sister and me. I remember her dropping me off at daycare, heading to work or school, picking me up, making dinner, cleaning the house, and ironing clothes. She did this every day without taking a break—I don't think that she saw a break as an option. It was assumed that she would be primarily responsible for taking care of the household and her children, in addition to her work outside of the home. As a young person, I became aware that we live in a world that relies upon women's work, yet did so little to value, recognize, or support that work. So I joined a women's organization in high school, and never looked back.

As an activist in your organization, currently what are your top goals?

Our first goal is to expand economic opportunity for women at the bottom of the economy, beginning with domestic workers and direct care workers, many of whom are women of color who have faced exclusion from recognition and our most basic worker protections for over 75 years. Domestic workers care for the most precious elements of our lives: our families and our homes, and yet are among the most vulnerable workers in our economy today. Our goal is to transform these jobs from poverty wage jobs in the shadow of our economy, into 21st century living wage jobs, with real pathways to opportunity and security.

Second, we are in the midst of a significant demographic shift in America. The Baby Boom generation is reaching retirement age at a rate of 10,000 people per day, and people are living longer than ever as a result of advances in health care and technology. By the year 2030, more than 20% of our population will be over the age of 65, and by the year 2050, 27 million of us will need care or assistance just to meet our basic needs. The need for care is growing and we have no plan in place to support the care that's needed. Our second goal is to create a new approach to caregiving in America that expands choice for families and individuals to age in place, makes care more affordable and accessible, and elevates the quality of care jobs.

Our third goal is to achieve a pathway to citizenship for the undocumented immigrant population in the United States. An estimated 11 million undocumented people are living and working in the United States, two thirds of whom are women and children. Our current immigration policy keeps the undocumented trapped in the shadows, fearful of reporting crimes or workplace violations, without a pathway to adjust their status. Immigrant parents risk family separation as a result of our immigration enforcement policy. This environment of fear and risk creates an unhealthy and unsafe reality for all of our communities.

What strategies do you use to enact social change?

We believe in organizing, which involves bringing domestic workers and the people who are connected to them together to increase our power, visibility, and ability to achieve our goals. We believe that the stories and experiences of domestic workers should inform the development of public policy and help shape the future of our democracy and economy. To that end, we seek to change policy. We conduct research to inform our policy development, we work with employers to promote fair standards in domestic employment relationships, and through the power of storytelling, we seek to change the way the work and the workforce is viewed and valued. We also believe that there's no such thing as an unlikely ally, and actively seek to build partnerships

to promote the dignity and value of caregiving and domestic work.

What are the major challenges activists in your field face?

Our workforce is dispersed and isolated in unmarked homes around the country, and many are fearful of losing their jobs or being exposed to immigration, so engaging them in activism is the first challenge. They are also working long, unpredictable hours with many family and economic responsibilities. In that context, our organizers must be extremely creative under challenging conditions, with few resources and little capacity. The process of making change is often extremely slow—legislative change takes years. Cultural change can take longer. The way we combat burn out is to support one another as a movement, to ensure that no one feels alone, and provide safe spaces for healing and personal transformation. Our leadership program supports the need for workers and organizers in our movement to step away from the work and reflect upon what they each require to bring the best of who they are to the work, and to sustain over time. We create a community of support for personal goal setting and healing of the individuals within our movement. And, we set bold, inspiring goals that people want to work toward year after year.

What are major misconceptions the public has about activism in general and your issue specifically?

Many think that domestic work is marginal within our economy and only affects a small group of people. In reality, home care is the fastest growing occupation in the nation because of the tremendous need on the part of all American families for caregiving support. And, the conditions that define domestic work—long and unpredictable hours, lack of training or job security, no benefits, isolation—have come to define reality for more and more of the American workforce. We are connected, and in many ways interdependent in this economy. This is a moment to turn toward one another, see the connections between us as a source of strength to make change, find common ground, and address the severe inequality in our economy together, because it's unsustainable for everyone.

Why should students get involved in your line of activism?

Domestic workers experience the world at the intersection of gender, race, class, and immigration status. When we create better policies and systems in our society for domestic workers, we are helping to create a more sustainable, inclusive economy and democracy for everyone. For example, if the caregiving workforce has the ability to care for their families, work, and retire with dignity, we can be sure we have achieved a new level of recognition of the work that goes into family care. By placing domestic workers at the center of our vision for the future, we can and must have the kinds of conversations about exclusion that will help us avoid past errors, learning from and leading with the solutions and perspectives of those least visible in our current reality.

What would you consider to be your greatest successes as an activist?

My greatest success is a collective achievement of thousands of women who have together created a national platform for caregivers and domestic workers to shape the future of public policy and the economy. For example, in 2000, I co-founded—together with a powerful group of domestic workers and organizers—Domestic Workers United (DWU), a city-wide, multiracial organization of domestic workers. DWU led the way to the passage of the nation's first Domestic Workers Bill of Rights in 2010, historic legislation that extends basic labor protections to over 200,000 domestic workers in New York state. Every day, I wake up feeling fortunate to be a part of a movement that gives voice and visibility to the courage and power of working women, particularly women of color, who have shaped this country in profound ways, and yet whose leadership is still undervalued and under-recognized in society at large.

If an individual has little money and time, are there other ways they can contribute?

We encourage people to contribute their unique skills and talents toward building the movement in the way that feels appropriate to them. Change can start at home, with initiating a conversation about the kind of caregiving relationships you want in your home, and developing a plan with your loved ones for your future caregiving needs. We encourage people to get involved through joining our online community at www.domesticworkers.org or www.caringacross.org, and we certainly encourage people to vote their values. We need people to engage in the civic process at every level, and to help us change the culture and politics of our country to reflect the values of opportunity, equity, dignity, and interdependence.

What ways can students enact social change in their daily lives?

Students should get out and experience campaigns and movements for social change at every opportunity—from joining a rally, naming injustice and inequity around them, studying past movements for change, seeking out mentors in the community that have been engaged in social change work, joining a student organization or a community organization, or interning at a social justice organization in the summer-time. Campaigns for change are containers for tremendous learning and transformation; it's always a good time to get out there and get proactive about creating the world in which we want to live.

The Rhetoric and Reality of "Opting Out"

PAMELA STONE

As affluent, highly educated women "opt-out" of their successful careers to stay home with their children, Stone questions whether these women are truly choosing this lifestyle change. Faced with workplaces that claim to be family friendly but are not structured for working mothers, intensive parenting styles, and husbands with equally demanding careers, Stone finds that women choose to leave their workplaces because of a number of factors outside of their control, reflecting a "choice gap" and significant structural constraints. The fact that these highly dedicated workers leave the workplace should worry us, Stone argues, and we should consider the social and economic costs to restrictive work environments.

As a senior publicist at a well-known media conglomerate, Regina Donofrio had one of the most coveted, glamorous jobs in New York. A typical workday might include "riding around Manhattan in limousines with movie stars." She loved her job, had worked "a long time," and felt "comfortable" in it. So when the time came to return to work after the birth of her first child, Regina did not hesitate. "I decided I would go back to work, because the job was great, basically," she told me.

Before long, Regina found herself "crying on the train," torn between wanting to be at home with her baby and wanting to keep up her successful, exciting career. She started feeling she was never in the right place at the right time. "When I was at work, I should have been at home. When I was at home, I felt guilty because I had left work a little early to see the baby, and I had maybe left some things undone." Ever resourceful, she devised a detailed job-share plan

with a colleague who was also a first-time mother. But their proposal was denied. Instead, Regina's employer offered her more money to stay and work full time, and Regina left in a huff, incensed that her employer, with whom she had a great track record, would block her from doing what she wanted to do—continue with her career and combine it with family.

Despite mainstream media portrayals to the contrary, Regina's reasons for quitting are all too typical of what I found in my study of high-achieving, former professionals who are now at-home moms. While Regina did, in fact, feel a strong urge to care for her baby, she decided to quit because of an inflexible workplace, not because of her attraction to home and hearth. She gave up her high-powered career as a last resort, after agonized soul-searching and exhausting her options. Her story differs from the popular depiction of similar, high-achieving, professional

Pamela Stone, *Contexts* (Volume 4 and Issue 3), pp. 21–26, Copyright © 2005. Reprinted by Permission of SAGE Publications.

women who have headed home. Media stories typically frame these women's decisions as choices about family and see them as symptomatic of a kind of sea-change among the daughters of the feminist revolution, a return to traditionalism and the resurgence of a new feminine mystique.

The quintessential article in this prevailing story line (and the one that gave the phenomenon its name) was published in 2003 by the *New York Times*'s work–life columnist, Lisa Belkin, titled "The Opt-Out Revolution." "Opting out" is redolent with overtones of lifestyle preference and discretion, but Regina's experience counters this characterization; her decision to quit was not a lifestyle preference, nor a change in aspirations, nor a desire to return to the 1950s family. Regina did not "opt out" of the workplace because she chose to, but for precisely the opposite reason: because she had no real options and no choice.

High-achieving women's reasons for heading home are multilayered and complex, and generally counter the common view that they quit because of babies and family. This is what I found when I spoke to scores of women like Regina: highly educated, affluent, mostly white, married women with children who had previously worked as professionals or managers and whose husbands could support their being at home. Although many of these women speak the language of choice and privilege, their stories reveal a choice gap—the disjuncture between the rhetoric of choice and the reality of constraints like those Regina encountered. The choice gap reflects the extent to which high-achieving women like Regina are caught in a double bind: spiraling parenting (read "mothering") demands on the homefront collide with the increasing pace of work in the gilded cages of elite professions.

Some Skepticism

I approached these interviews with skepticism tempered by a recognition that there might be some truth to the popular image of the "new traditionalist." But to get beyond the predictable "family" explanation and the media drumbeat of choice, I thought it was important to interview women in some depth and to study women who, at least theoretically, could exercise choice. I also gave women full anonymity, creating fictitious names for them so they would speak to me as candidly as possible. The women I interviewed had outstanding educational credentials; more than half had graduate degrees in business, law, medicine, and other professions, and had once had thriving careers in which they had worked about a decade. By any measure, these were work-committed women, with strong reasons to continue with the careers in which they had invested so much. Moreover, they were in high-status fields where they had more control over their jobs and enjoyed (at least relative to workers in other fields) more family-friendly benefits.

While these women had compelling reasons to stay on the job, they also had the option not to, by virtue of their own past earnings and because their husbands were also high earners. To counter the potential criticism that they were quitting or being let go because they were not competent or up to the job, I expressly chose to study women with impeccable educational credentials, women who had navigated elite environments with competitive entry requirements. To ensure a diversity of perspectives, I conducted extensive, in-depth interviews with 54 women in a variety of professions—law, medicine, business, publishing, management consulting, nonprofit administration, and the like—living in major metropolitan areas across the country, roughly half of them in their 30s, half in their 40s.

To be sure, at-home moms are a distinct minority. Despite the many articles proclaiming a trend of women going home, among the demographic of media scrutiny—white, college-educated women, 30–54 years old—fully 84 percent are now in the workforce, up from 82 percent 20 years ago. And the much-discussed dip in the labor-force participation of mothers of young children, while real, appears to be largely a function of an economic downturn, which depresses employment for all workers.

Nevertheless, these women are important to study. Elite, educated, high-achieving women have historically been cultural arbiters, defining what is acceptable for all women in their work and family roles. This group's entrance into high-status, formerly male professions has been crucial to advancing gender parity and narrowing the wage gap, which stubbornly persists to this day. At home, moreover, they are rendered silent and invisible, so that it is easy to project and speculate about them. We can see in them whatever we want to, and perhaps that is why they have been the subject of endless speculation— about mommy wars, a return to traditionalism, and the like. While they do not represent all women, elite women's experiences provide a glimpse into the work–family negotiations that all women face. And their stories lead us to ask, "If the most privileged women of society cannot successfully combine work and family, who can?"

Motherhood Pulls

When Regina initially went back to work, she had "no clue" that she would feel so torn. She advises women not to set "too much in stone," because "you just don't know, when a human being comes out of your body, how you're going to feel." For some women, the pull of children was immediate and strong. Lauren Quattrone, a lawyer, found herself "absolutely besotted with this baby. . . . I realized that I just couldn't bear to leave him." Women such as Lauren tended to quit fairly soon after their first child was born. For others, like Diane Childs, formerly a non-profit executive, the desire to be home with the kids came later. "I felt that it was easy to leave a baby for twelve hours a day. That I could do. But to leave a six-year-old, I just thought, was a whole different thing."

But none of these women made their decisions to quit in a vacuum. In fact, they did so during a cultural moment when norms and practices for parents—mothers—are very demanding. These women realized they would rear children very differently from the way their own mothers raised them, feeling an external, almost competitive pressure to do so. Middle- and upper-middle-class women tend to be particularly mindful of expert advice, and these women were acutely aware of a well-documented intensification in raising children, which sociologist Sharon Hays calls an "ideology of intensive mothering." This cultural imperative, felt by women of all kinds, "advises mothers to expend a tremendous amount of time, energy and money in raising their children."

A corollary is what Annette Lareau terms "concerted cultivation," a nonstop pace of organized activities scheduled by parents for school-age children. Among the women I spoke to, some, like Diane, felt the urgency of "concerted cultivation" and reevaluated their childcare as the more sophisticated needs of their older children superseded the simpler, more straightforward babysitting and physical care required for younger children. Marina Isherwood, a former executive in the health care industry, with children in the second and fourth grades, became convinced that caregivers could not replace her own parental influence:

> There isn't a substitute, no matter how good the childcare. When they're little, the fact that someone else is doing the stuff with them is fine. It wasn't the part that I loved anyway. But when they start asking you questions about values, you don't want your babysitter telling them. . . . Our children come home, and they have all this homework to do, and piano lessons and this and this, and it's all a complicated schedule. And, yes, you could get an au pair to do that, to balance it all, but they're not going to necessarily teach you how to think about math. Or help you come up with mnemonic devices to memorize all of the counties in Spain or whatever.

Because academic credentials were so important to these women's (and their husband's) career opportunities, formal schooling was a critical factor in their decisions to quit. For some, the premium they placed on education and values widened the gap between themselves and their less educated caregivers.

Depending on the woman, motherhood played a larger or smaller role in her decision whether and when to quit. Children were the main focus of women's caregiving, but other family members needed care as well, for which women felt responsible. About 10 percent of the women spoke of significant elder-care responsibilities, the need for which was especially unpredictable. This type of care-giving and mothering made up half of the family/career double bind. More important, though, motherhood influenced women's decision to quit as they came to see the rhythms and values of the workplace as antagonistic to family life.

Workplace Pushes

On top of their demanding mothering regime, these women received mixed messages from both their husbands and their employers. Husbands offered emotional support to wives who were juggling career and family. Emily Mitchell, an accountant, described her marriage to a CPA as "a pretty equal relationship," but when his career became more demanding, requiring long hours and Saturdays at work, he saw the downside of egalitarianism:

> I think he never minded taking my daughter to the sitter, that was never an issue, and when he would come home, we have a pretty equal relationship on that stuff. But getting her up, getting her ready, getting himself ready to go into work, me coming home, getting her, getting her to bed, getting unwound from work, and then he would come home, we'd try to do something for dinner, and then there was always something else to do—laundry, cleaning, whatever—I think he was feeling too much on a treadmill.

But husbands did little to share family responsibilities, instead maintaining their own demanding careers full-speed ahead.

Similarly, many workplaces claimed to be "family friendly" and offered a variety of supports. But for women who could take advantage of them, flexible work schedules (which usually meant working part-time) carried significant penalties. Women who shifted to part-time work typically saw their jobs gutted of significant responsibilities and their once-flourishing careers derailed. Worse, part-time hours often crept up to the equivalent of full time. When Diane Childs had children, she scaled back to part time and began to feel the pointlessness of continuing:

> And I'm never going to get anywhere—you have the feeling that you just plateaued professionally because you can't take on the extra projects; you can't travel at a moment's notice; you can't stay late; you're not flexible on the Friday thing because that could mean finding someone to take your kids. You really plateau for a much longer period of time than you ever realize when you first have a baby. It's like you're going to be plateaued for thirteen to fifteen years.

Lynn Hamilton, an M.D., met her husband at Princeton, where they were both undergraduates. Her story illustrates how family pulls and workplace pushes (from both her career and her husband's) interacted in a marriage that was founded on professional equality but then devolved to the detriment of her career:

> We met when we were 19 years old, and so, there I was, so naive, I thought, well, here we are, we have virtually identical credentials and comparable income earnings. That's an opportunity. And, in fact, I think our incomes were identical at the time I quit. To the extent to which we have articulated it, it was always understood, well, with both of us working, neither of us would have to be working these killer jobs. So, what was happening was, instead, we were both working these killer jobs. And I kept saying, "We need to reconfigure this." And what I realized was, he wasn't going to.

Meanwhile, her young daughter was having behavioral problems at school, and her job as a medical director for a biomedical start-up company had "the fax machine going, the three phone lines upstairs, they were going." Lynn slowly realized that the only reconfiguration possible, in the face of her husband's absence, was for her to quit.

Over half (60 percent) of the women I spoke to mentioned their husbands as one of the key reasons why they quit. That not all women talked about their husbands' involvement, or lack thereof, reveals the degree to which they perceived the work–family balancing act to be their responsibility alone. But women seldom mentioned their husbands for another reason: they were, quite literally, absent.

Helena Norton, an educational administrator who characterized her husband as a "workaholic," poignantly described a scenario that many others took for granted and which illustrates a pattern typical of many of these women's lives: "He was leaving early mornings; 6:00 or 6:30 before anyone was up, and then he was coming home late at night. So I felt this real emptiness, getting up in the morning to, not necessarily an empty house, because my children were there, but I did, I felt empty, and then going to bed, and he wasn't there."

In not being there to pick up the slack, many husbands had an important indirect impact on their wives' decisions to quit. Deferring to their husbands' careers and exempting them from household chores, these women tended to accept this situation. Indeed, privileging their husbands' careers was a pervasive, almost tacit undercurrent of their stories.

When talking about their husbands, women said the same things: variations on "he's supportive," and that he gave them a "choice." But this hands-off approach revealed husbands to be bystanders, not participants, in the work–family bind. "It's your choice" was code for "it's your problem." And husbands' absences, a direct result of their own high-powered careers, put a great deal of pressure on women to do it all, thus undermining the façade of egalitarianism.

Family pulls—from children and, as a result of their own long work hours, their husbands—exacerbated workplace pushes; and all but seven women cited features of their jobs—the long hours, the travel—as another major motivation in quitting. Marketing executive Nathalie Everett spoke for many women when she remarked that her full-time workweek was "really 60 hours, not 40. Nobody works nine-to-five anymore."

Surprisingly, the women I interviewed, like Nathalie, neither questioned nor showed much resentment toward the features of their jobs that kept them from fully integrating work and family. They routinely described their jobs as "all or nothing" and appeared to internalize what sociologists call the "ideal worker" model of a (typically male) worker unencumbered by family demands. This model was so influential that those working part time or in other flexible arrangements often felt stigmatized. Christine Thomas, a marketing executive and job-sharer, used imagery reminiscent of *The Scarlet Letter* to describe her experience: "When you job share, you have 'MOMMY' stamped in huge letters on your forehead."

While some women's decisions could be attributed to their unquestioning acceptance of the status quo or a lack of imagination, the unsuccessful attempts of others who tried to make it work by pursuing alternatives to full-time, like Diane, serve as cautionary tales. Women who made arrangements with bosses felt like they were being given special favors. Their part-time schedules were privately negotiated, hence fragile and unstable, and were especially vulnerable in the context of any kind of organizational restructuring such as mergers.

The Choice Gap

Given the incongruity of these women's experiences—they felt supported by "supportive" yet passive husbands and pushed out by workplaces that once prized their expertise—how did these women understand their situation? How did they make sense of professions that, on the one hand, gave them considerable status and rewards, and, on the other hand, seemed to marginalize them and force them to compromise their identity as mothers?

The overwhelming majority felt the same way as Melissa Wyatt, the 34-year-old who gave up a job as a fund-raiser: "I think today it's all about choices, and the choices we want to make. And I think that's great. I think it just depends where you want to spend your time." But a few shared the outlook of Olivia Pastore, a 42-year-old ex-lawyer:

> I've had a lot of women say to me, "Boy, if I had the choice of, if I could balance, if I could work part-time, if I could keep doing it." And there are some women who are going to stay home full-time no matter what and that's fine. But there are a number of women, I think, who are home because they're caught between a rock and a hard place. . . . There's a lot of talk about the individual decisions of individual women. "Is it good? Is it bad? She gave it up. She couldn't hack it," . . . And there's not enough blame, if you will, being laid at the feet of the culture, the jobs, society.

My findings show that Olivia's comments—about the disjuncture between the rhetoric of choice and the reality of constraint that shapes women's decisions to go home—are closer to the mark. Between trying to be the ideal mother (in an era of intensive mothering) and the ideal worker (a model based on a man with a stay-at-home wife), these high-flying women faced a double bind. Indeed, their options were much more limited than they seemed. Fundamentally, they faced a "choice gap": the difference between the decisions women could have made about their careers if they were not mothers or caregivers and the decisions they had to make in their circumstances as mothers married to high-octane husbands in ultimately unyielding professions. This choice gap obscures individual preferences, and thus reveals the things Olivia railed against—culture, jobs, society—the kinds of things sociologists call "structure."

Overall, women based their decisions on mutually reinforcing and interlocking factors. They confronted, for instance, two sets of trade-offs: kids versus careers, and their own careers versus those of their husbands. For many, circumstances beyond their control strongly influenced their decision to quit. On the family side of the equation, for example, women had to deal with caregiving for sick children and elderly parents, children's developmental problems, and special care needs. Such reasons figured in one-third of the sample. On the work side, women were denied part-time arrangements, a couple were laid off, and some had to relocate for their own careers or their husbands'. A total of 30 women, a little more than half the sample, mentioned at least one forced-choice consideration.

But even before the women had children, the prospect of pregnancy loomed in the background, making women feel that they were perceived as flight risks. In her first day on the job as a marketing executive, for example, Patricia Lambert's boss asked her: "So, are you going to have kids?" And once women did get pregnant, they reported that they were often the first in their office, which made them feel more like outsiders. Some remarked that a dearth of role models created an atmosphere unsympathetic to work-family needs. And as these women navigated pregnancy and their lives beyond, their stories revealed a latent bias against mothers in their workplaces. What some women took from this was that pregnancy was a dirty little secret not to be openly discussed. The private nature of pregnancy thus complicated women's decisions regarding their careers once they became mothers, which is why they often waited until the last minute to figure out their next steps. Their experiences contrasted with the formal policies of their workplaces, which touted themselves as "family friendly."

The Rhetoric of Choice

Given the indisputable obstacles—hostile workplaces and absentee husbands—that stymied a full integration of work and family, it was ironic that most of the women invoked "choice" when relating the events surrounding their decision to exit their careers. Why were there not more women like Olivia, railing against the tyranny of an outmoded workplace that favored a 1950s-era employee or bemoaning their husbands' drive for achievement at the expense of their own?

I found that these women tended to use the rhetoric of choice in the service of their exceptionality. Women associated choice with privilege, feminism, and personal agency, and internalized it as a reflection of their own perfectionism. This was an attractive combination that played to their drive for achievement and also served to compensate for their loss of the careers they loved and the professional identities they valued. Some of these women bought into the media message that being an at-home mom was a status symbol, promoted by such cultural arbiters as *New York Magazine* and the *Wall Street Journal*. Their ability to go home reflected their husbands' career success, in which they and their children basked. Living out the traditional lifestyle, male breadwinner and stay-at-home-mom, which they were fortunate to be able to choose, they saw themselves as realizing the dreams of third-wave feminism. The goals of earlier, second-wave feminism, economic independence and gender equality, took a back seat, at least temporarily.

Challenging the Myth

These strategies and rhetoric, and the apparent invisibility of the choice gap, reveal how fully these high-achieving women internalized the double bind and the intensive-mothering and ideal-worker models on which it rests. The downside, of course, is that they blamed themselves for failing to "have it all" rather than any actual structural constraints. That work and family were incompatible was the overwhelming message they took from their experiences. And when they quit, not wanting to burn bridges, they cited family obligations as the reason, not their dissatisfaction with work, in accordance with social expectations. By adopting the so-cially desirable and gender-consistent explanation of "family," women often contributed to the larger misunderstanding surrounding their decision. Their own explanations endorsed the prevalent idea that quitting to go home is a choice. Employers rarely challenged women's explanations. Nor did they try to convince them to stay, thus reinforcing women's perception that their decision was the right thing to do as mothers, and perpetuating the reigning media image of these women as the new traditionalists.

Taken at face value, these women do seem to be traditional. But by rejecting an intransigent workplace, their quitting signifies a kind of silent strike. They were not acquiescing to traditional gender roles by quitting, but voting with their feet against an outdated model of work. When women are not posing for the camera or worried about offending former employers (from whom they may need future references), they are able to share their stories candidly. From what I found, the truth is far different and certainly more nuanced than the media depiction.

The vast majority of the type of women I studied do not want to choose between career and family. The demanding nature of today's parenting puts added pressure on women. Women do indeed need to learn to be "good enough" mothers, and their husbands need to engage more equally in parenting. But on the basis of what they told me, women today "choose" to be home full-time not as much because of parenting overload as because of work overload, specifically long hours and the lack of flexible options in their high-status jobs. The popular media depiction of a return to traditionalism is wrong and misleading. Women are trying to achieve the feminist vision of a fully integrated life combining family and work. That so many attempt to remain in their careers when they do not "have to work" testifies strongly to their commitment to their careers, as does the difficulty they experience over their subsequent loss of identity. Their attempts at juggling and their plans to return to work in the future also indicate that their careers were not meant to be ephemeral and should not be treated as such. Rather, we should regard their exits as the miner's canary—a frontline indication that something is seriously amiss in many workplaces. Signs of toxic work environments and white-collar sweatshops are ubiquitous. We can glean from these women's experiences the true cost of these work conditions, which are personal and professional, and, ultimately, societal and economic.

Our current understanding of why high-achieving women quit—based as it is on choice and separate spheres—seriously undermines the will to change the contemporary workplace. The myth of opting out returns us to the days when educated women were barred from entering elite professions because "they'll only leave anyway." To the extent that elite women are arbiters of shifting gender norms, the opting out myth also has the potential to curtail women's aspirations and stigmatize those who challenge the separate-spheres ideology on which it is based. Current demographics make it clear that employers can hardly afford to lose the talents of high-achieving women. They can take a cue from at-home moms like the ones I studied: Forget opting out; the key to keeping professional women on the job is to create better, more flexible ways to work.

How Sheryl Sandberg and Getty Are Making Stock Photos Less Sexist[1]

Claire Suddath

Say you're an advertiser on a stock-photography site, looking for a shot of a woman to put in your new campaign. "If you search for something like 'female workplace leader,' you come up with a bunch of images of women in short skirts[2] and high heels, holding wrenches," complains Jessica Bennett, a journalist who's working with Sheryl Sandberg's Lean In movement to fix this.

In February, that organization announced a partnership with Getty Images, the largest provider of these photos, to create a line of stock photos that depict mature, professional businesswomen, rather than ones who appear dumb, subservient, sexualized, or sometimes all three at once. "Or that weird trend of putting women in boxing gloves,[3] what is that about?" Bennett asks. While stock photos may not be as obviously sexualized as say, fashion magazine spreads, Bennett believes they influence our perception of gender roles just as much. "You probably don't even notice it most of the time, which in a way, is even more damaging."

Getty has a library of over 150 million images that it sells to 2.4 million customers around the world. Those customers then plaster those images on billboards, run them in political campaigns, print them on national magazine covers, or use them to illustrate news articles when they don't have the time or incentive to photograph something themselves. Why take a picture of a banana, for example, when Getty has 8,449 pictures at the ready? Of course, Getty doesn't know the specifics of your banana needs, so each photo must have a very clear, literal meaning that separates it from all the other bananas out there. There are banana photos for healthy eating promotions,[4] for grocery stores,[5] and even an "orange being worshiped[6] by a tribe of bananas," whatever that represents.

Sometimes, in simplifying things, stock photo agencies fabricate absurd situations that no one encounters in real life. (How often has a clown shown[7] you photos of himself on his laptop?) But usually, they just wind up feeling clichéd. Type "work life balance" into Getty for instance, and you'll get 356 images, mostly of people trying to use laptops while holding a baby.

If you type "businesswoman" into Getty's search engine, you're overwhelmed with questionable results: a businesswoman crawling on all fours, and not because she lost something under her desk; a young, attractive secretary giving a head massage to her boss; a secretary with an open shirt holding her glasses, sans bra; and yet another young professional sucking a lollipop while she leans over a young man's desk. Why is this happening? Even the guy seems confused.

Most of the 2,500 images that Lean In curated already existed in the Getty library; they're also commissioning others to fill in cultural gaps or equalize gender roles, and 10 percent of the proceeds from the sale of these photos will go to LeanIn.org. In the new gallery, female exercisers are actually working out,[8] rather than just smiling with gym equipment.[9] There are older woman, overweight people, and biracial families. There are even photos titled "Female woodworker[10] sanding edge of custom cabinet" and "Heavy Metal Father with Daughter[11] on Shoulders" for all your woodworking and heavy metal parenting needs. In fact, many of Lean In's photos aren't about women at all; a lot of them depict fathers in caregiver roles, braiding their kids' hair or holding a baby. Balancing gender roles isn't always about making women appear more professional.

Creation of the Lean In gallery hardly means the old stock photo stereotypes are going away. Sexy secretaries and leering co-workers are still available on Getty's website, and a benign search of "business meeting" photos turns up nearly three times as many pictures of meetings led by men as those led by women. "You have to remember, we have clients from all different industries and they all have different demands," says Pam Grossman, Getty's director of visual trends, who worked with Bennett to curate the Lean In gallery. Sometimes those demands involve co-workers without bras.

At least now there are options. And Getty's customers seem to be using them. Even before the Lean In collaboration, Grossman says she noticed a shift in the types of female stock images that companies were purchasing. In 2007, the most frequently used Getty image was of a naked woman lying on a table, covered in a sheet. "She was looking passively at the camera; it was really contrived," Grossman

says. Last year the most popular photo was of a fully clothed, freckle-faced woman ("Much more authentic!" says Grossman) riding on a train. She's also noticed that the financial services industry has switched from licensing photos of men for its advertisements to requesting mostly photos of women. They're almost always lollipop-free.

NOTES

1. Editor's note: Throughout this article, we have included hyperlinks to the images referenced so that readers can view them. An alternative way to access these images is to go directly to gettyimages.com and search using similar terms that the author provides and discusses.

2. http://www.gettyimages.com/detail/photo/smiling-construction-woman-royalty-free-image/170615047

3. http://nymag.com/thecut/2013/11/feminism-according-to-stock-photography/slideshow/2013/11/22/feminism_accordingtostockphotography/

4. http://www.gettyimages.com/detail/photo/box-with-vegetables-royalty-free-image/175425532

5. http://www.gettyimages.com/detail/photo/woman-shopping-in-supermarket-royalty-free-image/143070313

6. http://www.gettyimages.com/detail/photo/orange-and-peeled-bananas-high-res-stock-photography/89723171

7. http://www.gettyimages.com/detail/photo/business-clown-royalty-free-image/108225611

8. http://www.gettyimages.com/detail/photo/woman-pressing-barbell-over-head-in-high-res-stock-photography/455244973

9. http://www.gettyimages.com/detail/photo/young-woman-fitness-trainer-with-dumbbells-on-white-royalty-free-image/175408739

10. http://www.gettyimages.com/detail/photo/female-woodworker-sanding-edge-of-custom-high-res-stock-photography/462111415

11. http://www.gettyimages.com/detail/photo/heavy-metal-father-with-daughter-on-high-res-stock-photography/456240347

Sex Segregation at Work: Persistence and Change

ANASTASIA PROKOS

You may have noticed that women and men are often separated into different types of occupations, a phenomenon known as "sex segregation." Prokos examines the historical and social factors that have contributed to the existence of sex segregation in the workplace and the factors that perpetuate it, including gender socialization, employer biases, and discrimination. Prokos concludes by discussing the consequences of sex segregation and possible solutions to the problem.

Introduction

Take one look around a typical business or office the next time you need to make a major purchase, take out a loan from a bank, or fill out student aid paperwork. Although you will often see women and men working together to get things done, a closer look might reveal that women and men are often doing different tasks in the same place of business. For example, in a bank the tellers might all be mostly women, whereas men primarily act as the mortgage specialists and supervisors. That is probably no surprise to most people who pay close attention to the world of work. Yet many of us may take this aspect of life for granted and may even think it is somehow part of the natural order of things. Sociologists, of course, delve deeper. We ask questions about how universal the gendered division of labor is (or is not), why women and men tend to do particular kinds of work, and what happens when they try to move beyond commonly accepted career paths. Also, what are the consequences for women's and men's work lives?

The work that both women and men do has changed dramatically in the past century. In fact, many occupations are organized quite differently from in the past or have disappeared altogether. Another major shift has been in the gender composition of occupations and jobs; today women and men are more likely to have similar occupations and jobs than they were 50 to 100 years ago. Yet even with these remarkable transformations in employment patterns, women and men in the contemporary United States continue to be concentrated in different occupations, jobs, and industries.

The sex segregation of work, when women and men work in different occupations, jobs, or in different workplaces, is a striking feature of the U.S. labor force. In 2014, 205 of 482 specific occupations were male dominated (defined as 75 percent or more men), and 47.4 percent of all

Original to *Focus on Social Problems: A Contemporary Reader*.

men worked in those occupations. Only 85 of the 482 specific occupations were female dominated (with 75 percent or more women), and 45.3 percent of all women were employed in those occupations. Some occupations, like emergency management directors, brokerage clerks, and locksmiths, are extremely male dominated, with virtually no women in the occupation (or at least none sampled in the March 2014 Current Population Survey). In contrast, occupations like dental hygienists and preschool and kindergarten teachers are notoriously female dominated, with few men in them. This article delves deeper into these trends, explaining where they came from and why they persist.

The explanations for sex segregation in employment were obvious in the not-so-distant past: women were simply barred from many types of employment, and "women's work" was so low in pay that there was really no compelling reason for most men to pursue it when they had better options. Today, the explanations for sex segregation are more complex. Tradition, cultural influences, societal expectations, and opportunity structures all influence both women's and men's career paths.

Although the explanations for sex segregation may be different now than in the past, one thing remains remarkably similar: the kinds of work that are mostly done by women tend to be lower in pay than the kinds of work done by men. And although women have gained access to higher education and moved into many types of professional work, much of the work that continues to be associated with women, especially the kind that is related to caring for other people, is worth relatively little in the labor market.

Contemporary Employment Patterns

A look at the current most common occupational categories for women and men shows us a great deal about the type of work that is viewed as customary for each. Table 1 lists the ten most common occupations for women and men in 2014. Secretary has topped the list for women for many years, and truck driver continues to be

one of the most common occupations for men to hold (Padavic and Reskin, 2002). What Table 1 also shows us is just how concentrated women and men are in just a small set of highly segregated occupations. Although the Bureau of Labor Statistics tracks almost 500 specific detailed occupations, 28.3 percent of all employed women and 22.8 percent of employed men worked in just these 17 occupations. Furthermore, Table 1 shows that many of the occupations are highly segregated, especially for women. For example, the occupation of *secretary and administrative assistant* is 95 percent female. Table 1 makes it clear that the paid work most often done by women is quite different from the paid work that is most often done by men. Women and men had only 3 top 10 occupations in common: first-line supervisors/managers of retail sales workers; other managers; and retail salesperson. It is not surprising, then, that these 3 are some of the most sex-integrated occupations on the list.

Looking at the distribution of women and men in specific occupations is telling and helps create a picture of how segregation appears in employment, but it is not the best way to summarize society-wide patterns of segregation. Scholars typically use a single measure, the *index of dissimilarity* (*D*), to measure overall levels of segregation. The index of dissimilarity is calculated so that one number tells us what percentage of women (or men) would have to change occupations to be equally represented to men (or women) across all occupations. A score of zero would mean occupations are fully integrated, whereas a score of 100 would mean they were fully segregated. The 2014 index of dissimilarity is 52, meaning that more than half of all women would need to switch occupations for women and men to be equally represented across all occupations.[1] The index of dissimilarity allows researchers to compare segregation across geographic regions, across different industries, and over time, which is illustrated below.

Yet only looking at occupations and occupational characteristics can actually gloss over a

Table I. Top Ten Occupations for Women and Men, 2014

Women	Number	Percentage Female
Secretaries and administrative assistants	2,578,074	94.9
Registered nurses	2,484,734	90.8
Elementary and middle school teachers	2,218,073	79.9
Nursing, psychiatric, and home health aides	1,479,647	89.9
Cashiers	1,237,561	75.7
Maids and housekeeping cleaners	1,228,439	89.3
First-line supervisors/managers of retail sales workers	1,210,762	43.5
Managers, all other	1,196,161	33.3
Retail salespersons	1,111,146	48.8
Credit authorizers, checkers, and clerks	1,074,747	67.3
Men		**Percentage Male**
Driver/sales workers and truck drivers	2,773,430	94.5
Managers, all other	2,392,564	66.7
First-line supervisors/managers of retail sales workers	1,570,272	56.5
Construction laborers	1,234,915	96.3
Janitors and building cleaners	1,181,900	65.4
Retail salespersons	1,166,628	51.2
Laborers and freight, stock, and material movers, hand	1,080,795	81.9
Chief executives	998,879	74.1
Grounds maintenance workers	969,368	95.3
Carpenters	947,756	99.1

Source: Author calculations from March 2014 Current Population Surveys.

great deal of segregation that occurs in the labor force. Occupations, even detailed lists of them, are, by definition, broad categories that capture only the most basic activities that workers perform, and they do not take industry, location, or employer into account. Jobs, in contrast, are much more specific categories of work, because they include more information about where and for whom people work. For example, someone may have an occupation as a teacher, but could have a job in a poor, rural school district or a more affluent suburb. A chief executive officer could have a job for a large multinational manufacturing corporation or for a small nonprofit educational organization. As these latter jobs illustrate, the industry in which a person is employed also affects the content of an occupation, as well as its compensation. Researchers also study and document sex segregation in industries and in jobs, although the bulk of research focuses on the level of occupation.

Historical Precedence

Employers have been sorting women and men into different paid work since the start of the Industrial Revolution. Documents and photos from the mid-1800s through the early 1900s show that women worked in coal mines, labored as seamstresses, and assembled mechanical devices, such as watches. In each of these cases, however, women mostly worked separately from men, either on different tasks or in different rooms or departments. Employers hired women workers for these jobs in part because women were less expensive to employ, as they could not demand pay as high as men's. As women, men, and children moved into industrial work, the overabundance of labor supply meant intense competition for jobs and led to low factory wages. One way for groups of men to reduce the competition was to limit women's (and children's) access to the labor market; they accomplished this through unions, most of which included only male members. Unions in the late 19th and early 20th centuries supported protective legislation that barred women and children from certain kinds of employment, especially when working conditions were considered unsafe. The outcome of this protective legislation also removed women from some of the highest-paying industrial jobs where they had previously been employed (Padavic and Reskin, 2002).

Protective legislation and similar restrictions on women's employment (such as rules barring married women or mothers from employment) were successful at reducing women's labor force participation and pushing women out of some lines of work entirely. Thus, by the mid-20th century (with the exception of a wartime employment), most women in the labor market were concentrated in relatively low-paying jobs such as laundress, maid, sales girl, teacher, nurse, and secretary (Kessler-Harris, 1982; Padavic and Reskin, 2002).

In the United States, it was legal for employers to choose employees for jobs on the basis of their sex category until the 1960s. Prior to the passage of Civil Rights Act in 1964, newspaper advertisements for jobs were routinely separated into "Male Help" and "Female Help" sections so that employers could easily target their desired employees. For example, in 1958 an advertisement in the Male Help section of the *The State*, a South Carolina newspaper, read: "Need Assistant Manager for Westinghouse Appliances,

Good Opportunity for Right Man," whereas one in the female section read: "Need one more curb girl-cashier, day shift" ("Want Ads," 1958). In this way, employers could explicitly and easily sort people into jobs based on their sex category. It is worth noting here that newspapers also commonly included separate sections for "colored help," and these sections also included separate ads for women and men, which allowed them to differentiate potential employees on the basis of race, in addition to sex.

It was not until the Civil Rights Act passed that the story began to change, and even then progress started slowly. The legacy of these earlier associations between particular types of work and gender has been powerful, and what emerged throughout the 19th and early 20th centuries as ideology about which jobs were appropriate for women has had remarkable sticking power, even in the face of a number of extraordinary social changes, such as the women's movement and dramatic increases in women's labor force participation.

Decades of Change

Title VII of the 1964 Civil Rights Act, which barred employment discrimination on the basis of sex, race, color, religion, or national origin, opened the door for decades of change in employment. Yet women's influx into work that had been traditionally performed by men proceeded at a slow and uneven pace. Because the enforcement of the new nondiscrimination legislation did not gain momentum until the 1970s, the 1960s saw little change in occupational segregation (Padavic and Reskin, 2002). The 1970s saw the greatest overall decline in segregation, according to the index of dissimilarity. The decade began with a score of 67 and ended with a score of 60 (Jacobs, 2003). Declines in segregation continued into the 1980s and the early part of the 1990s and then stalled in the middle 1990s. The current level of segregation has shown little change since that time (Hegewisch et al., 2010).

A variety of factors led to notable declines in occupational segregation during the 1970s and 1980s. In large part, these changes reflected many occupations opening access to women. Occupations such as "bartender" saw large influxes of women. In 1970, only 21 percent of bartenders were women, but by 1980 it was no longer a segregated occupation—44 percent of bartenders were women—and by the end of the 1980s, women were roughly half of all bartenders (Reskin and Roos, 1990). This kind of change was not true for all male-dominated occupations, however, and women had less success gaining access to occupations like engineering, dentistry, electrician, and painter.

Although much of the change in occupational segregation during the 1970s and 1980s was a result of women moving into previously male-dominated occupations, another reason for the drop in overall levels of segregation was related to shifts in the economic structure. Specifically, some of the occupations that had been the most segregated before this time began to decline as a share of the total labor force. For example, manufacturing work, which has consistently been a heavily male-dominated industry, took up a smaller and smaller portion of the total labor force. In 1960 the manufacturing sector employed about 30 percent of all workers and by the end of the 1980s that figure was only 17.4 percent. This trend had two implications for sex segregation. First, because of fewer opportunities available in manufacturing, it was more difficult for women to move into positions in that industry. Second, although the manufacturing industry remained heavily male dominated, the smaller proportion of workers in this sector meant that it had a smaller impact on overall measures of employment segregation than some of the occupations that were gaining ground.

What is especially interesting about the desegregation that occurred during the 1970s and 1980s is that many occupations feminized, meaning they shifted from being male dominated to having more women in them, whereas few occupations masculinized (changed from customarily female to include many more men). In fact, many of the occupations that were female dominated saw little change in men's representation. Dental assistant, hairdresser, cashier, preschool and kindergarten teacher, registered nurse, and librarian remained heavily segregated occupations.

The Power of Tradition

Despite the many changes that occurred as a result of the antidiscrimination policies of the 1970s, the pace of change and occupational integration slowed in the 1980s and even more so after that. By 2010, it was clear that sex segregation had no longer been declining for quite some time, and scholars began referring to a "stalled gender revolution" in employment (England, 2010; Hegewisch et al., 2010). Women's influx into previously male occupations has slowed considerably, and many occupations, such as engineering and carpentry, seem especially impervious to women's entry.

It is worth noting that even within broad occupational categories, women and men may hold different occupational specialties. For example, although more professors are women than in the past, women are concentrated in the humanities, human sciences, and some social sciences. Moreover, many occupations may be in the process of "resegregating," meaning they are in the process of shifting from being dominated by one sex to being dominated by the other. This is the case for the occupation of bartending. As mentioned previously, by the end of the 1980s roughly half of all bartenders were women, and now that figure stands at 62 percent. If the trend continues, bartending will be relatively heavily female dominated in the not-so-distant future.

Before turning to explanations for continuing sex segregation in employment, it is helpful to get a sense of some of the employment patterns that did not change much during the period that saw the most transformation. As Paula England (2010) has pointed out, the declines in sex segregation in employment have been different for middle-class jobs compared to working-class jobs. Working-class jobs, like construction worker and manufacturing work, are "almost as segregated as they were in 1950!" (157). Many of the occupations that opened up to women during the 1970s and 1980s were professional jobs that required a college degree. Professors, lawyers, doctors, and managers are all increasingly likely to be women.

Furthermore, the work that is often considered "women's work" continues to be devalued—worth less in the labor market—than that work that is customarily male. When that is the case, women have an economic incentive to try to move into customarily male work, but men have little economic incentive to move into female-dominated occupations (England, 2010). Indeed, it is much more rare for an occupation to masculinize. In cases when men have begun doing the work that women had done, often they do so in a different occupation. For example, until the early to mid-1900s, midwives used to deliver most babies (as they do still in many other countries). The growing male-dominated medical profession in the 19th and 20th centuries recognized that childbirth was a potentially lucrative addition to medical practices and, in effect, created a monopoly on assisting in childbirth in the United States. Until recently, the majority of obstetrician/gynecologists were men, although that particular occupation has seen increasing numbers of women in the past several decades.

These examples show that some kinds of work have been more impervious to change than others. They also begin to hint at some of the reasons that some occupations are less likely to change than others. How much training is needed for a job, how high status it is, and how much it pays are all linked to the reasons that some occupations remain more segregated than others.

Explanations for Continued Segregation

It is tempting to believe that the patterns in women's and men's employment that we see in the United States simply reflect the choices that people make about their careers, especially when we see how little girls and boys seem to gravitate toward different kinds of activities. But as sociologists we know that the choices people make reflect subtle influences, many of which are beyond individuals' control. Parents, teachers, and peers influence what children believe they are good at and what they think they should pursue. Cultural expectations and stereotypes influence the way people view what appropriate work is for women and men. The availability of certain kinds of jobs, the way people are treated at work and when they search for work, and what employers are looking for all influence women's and men's options and choices.

Workers' Choices and Actions

Children learn stereotypes about gender early, and these stereotypes can influence how young people imagine their futures. Indeed, these stereotypes influence the kinds of jobs that young children see as appropriate and can influence their early decisions. For example, although girls' and boys' math test scores are about the same, parents and teachers persist in believing that girls are not as good at math as boys (Gunderson et al., 2012). As a result, girls tend to believe they are not as good at math as boys, undermining their enjoyment of the field and possibly resulting in fewer girls headed toward math-related careers (Correll, 2001). Luckily, in this case, social psychologists know how to fix the problem. As years of careful research have shown, when girls are taught math in such a way that they also learn they can develop their ability (rather than seeing it as something that is innate and fixed), they actually perform better in math (Dweck, 2006). Doing well in a subject can then have the consequence of increasing girls' enjoyment and motivation in that area (Eccles and Wigfield, 2002).

Even the language we use influences children's perceptions about work. Research shows that children perceive occupations as more suited to one sex or another depending on their title. For example, children tend to envision jobs with names like "policeman" and "fireman" as appropriate for men, but not for women (Liben et al., 2002). Using gender-neutral language for such occupations (police officer and firefighter) changes children's understanding of who can occupy these jobs.

Despite these powerful lessons children learn, sociologists know that people's choices are flexible and often bend toward options that make greater sense as their circumstances change. For example, college students take different courses and change majors (often more than once) and people continue to change their ideas about jobs well into their twenties (Jacobs, 2003). This is because the situations people face when they actually try to get a job, when they begin to train for work, or as they start working for a specific company are much more powerful influences on their adult career choices than their stated preferences when they are young.

Employer Practices

Cultural stereotypes do not just affect workers' decisions, of course. Many people, including employers and co-workers, continue to view women and men as fundamentally different from one another and think that those differences mean that certain kinds of work are most suitable for either men or women. Although overt discrimination is no longer legal, gender stereotypes—and the expectations that result from them—continue to influence employers' decisions. Employers can channel women and men into different work because of implicit biases, everyday business practices, and overt discrimination.

A vast and growing literature on implicit bias shows that biases that people may not even be aware of can influence their perceptions and treatment of others. For example, experimental research has shown that when people evaluate resumes, they judge the same resume differently depending on whether they think it belongs to a woman or a man (Steinpreis et al., 1999). The subtle ways that stereotypes can affect judgments of people can creep into employment decisions. An employer may view a woman who has strong negotiating skills as "aggressive," but consider a man demonstrating the same skills "assertive." A man who mentions his family may seem like a "good family man," whereas an employer may think a similar woman would be too focused on her family to do a good job. The biases may not always be this obvious, but they can influence decisions about who to hire and which position to fill with a specific applicant.

Beyond these examples of bias, sometimes employers' everyday practices have a tendency to reproduce the gender composition of occupations. A majority of jobs (about 60 percent of them) are never advertised and thus do not use a competitive hiring process. In fact, a great deal of hiring for jobs happens through social networks. For example, when I ask students in my sociology of work course how they got their first jobs, nearly every one of them raises his or her hand when I ask whether it was through one of their parents or parents' friends. Evidence suggests that when hiring occurs informally in this way, employers tend to hire people who are similar to themselves in both gender and race, whom they feel more comfortable with (known as "homosocial reproduction"). Ultimately, homosocial reproduction is likely to replicate the current workforce, at least demographically.

Another aspect of common employment practices that influences who is hired into an occupation is the relationship between training and occupational access. Title IX of the Educational Amendments of 1972, which protects against sex discrimination in education, opened up many opportunities for women to enter professional occupations by granting access to the formal education and training needed for those occupations. This allowed women to overcome the first hurdle to gain access to many professional occupations, such as doctor and lawyer. However, other occupations that require people to obtain training on the job or through apprenticeships means that they first must be accepted as someone's apprentice, or even hired, to gain the skills needed to perform these jobs. Occupations like electrician, carpenter, and plumber, which operate through apprenticeships and hiring, have not opened up to women as much as male-dominated occupations in the professional arena have (Bergmann, 2011).

Although much of the bias in employer decisions may be unintended, blatant discrimination also still occurs. In recent years, about 28,000 cases of sex discrimination per year have been reported to the Equal Employment Opportunity Commission (Equal Employment Opportunity Commission, 2014), and although they are not all hiring discrimination cases, they do show us that employers continue to use the sex category in employment decisions. In fact, some powerful evidence of employer discrimination comes from firsthand experiences. In her book based on interviews with transgender men, Kristin Schilt (2010) documented many cases where men saw firsthand just how they had been discriminated against before they transitioned, when they were women. They saw how co-workers, supervisors, managers, customers, and employers based decisions about hiring, promotion, and pay primarily—and in some cases exclusively—on the basis of gender. These "behind-the-scenes" views the men gained after transitioning support the numerous experiences women report about acts of discrimination at work.

All three of the explanations above (implicit bias, everyday hiring practices, and blatant discrimination) can help us understand why some occupations have been slower to desegregate than others. These patterns help to show the powerful role that employers have in perpetuating occupational segregation. They also demonstrate how important antidiscrimination efforts are in reducing employment discrimination.

Consequences of Segregation

You might wonder why sociologists have paid so much attention to occupational sex segregation. Occupational segregation is one of the primary forces behind women's lower average earnings compared to men. Women's pay lags behind men's even among workers who work full time. This is in large part because the occupations and jobs in which women are concentrated pay less, on average, than those in which men are concentrated, even when they require similar levels of skills and training. These trends harken back to a long history of "women's work" being seen as less valuable than that done by men. Current employment patterns reflect that history.

Table 2 shows median earnings for men and women in several different occupations in 2014. Keep in mind that these are all wages for full-time, year-round workers. It is notable that the highest-paying occupations, near the top of the list, almost all employ many more men than women. Pharmacists are an exception and illustrate that women have made headway in some high-paying occupations. In the case of pharmacists, structural changes in the industry (more corporate-owned chains and hospital employment instead of small independent pharmacies) have meant that the occupation continues to be highly paid and is also more open to women (Goldin and Katz, 2012). In general, the occupations that are female dominated, however, are more likely to appear near the bottom of the list.

Because much of the difference in women's and men's average earnings reflects these occupational distributions, legislation addressing pay discrimination without addressing occupational segregation is unlikely to have a substantial influence on the larger pay gap. Some policy experts have suggested that comparable worth policies would have a greater influence on the pay gap. Comparable worth policies seek to evaluate the level of skill required in particular occupations and then adjust the compensation in those occupations to directly reflect the skill involved, rather than the gender of the occupants. Such policies have the potential to reduce gender differences in pay, especially in working-class occupations. This is because many working-class "women's jobs" often require a similar level of training, but tend to pay substantially less than men's working-class jobs.

Conclusion

This article has intentionally boiled down the issue of occupational sex segregation to its most basic elements. Of course, many other factors complicate the picture I have painted here. For example, employment is also further segregated

Table 2. Median Weekly Earnings for Select Occupations, 2013

	Men	Women	% Female in Occupation
Chief executives	$2,266	$1,811	27
Pharmacists	$2,092	$1,802	54
Physicians and surgeons	$2,087	$1,497	36
Lawyers	$1,986	$1,566	35
Software developers, applications and systems software	$1,737	$1,370	20
Managers, all other	$1,399	$1,105	37
Registered nurses	$1,236	$1,086	89
Sales representatives, wholesale and manufacturing	$1,131	$859	23
Elementary and middle school teachers	$1,025	$937	80
Social workers	$978	$818	80
Secretaries and administrative assistants	$772	$677	95
Driver/sales workers and truck drivers	$738	$583	4
Retail salespersons	$719	$485	40
Construction laborers[a]	$592	—	3
Laborers and freight, stock, and material movers, hand	$524	$421	17
Janitors and building cleaners	$517	$418	27
Nursing, psychiatric, and home health aides	$499	$450	87
Maids and housekeeping cleaners	$467	$406	83
Cashiers	$426	$379	69
Cooks	$411	$382	35

Source: Author calculations based on Bureau of Labor Statistics Labor Force Statistics from the Current Population Survey, 2013. Table 39. Median weekly earnings of full-time wage and salary workers by detailed occupation and sex.
[a]There are too few women in the occupation to calculate reliable statistics for women's wages.

by race and ethnicity as a result of related historical and cultural patterns, including discrimination. Changing demographics, global economic restructuring, and shifting cultural patterns all form part of the larger context that affects patterns in employment. The historical trends and contemporary patterns summarized here build a foundation for understanding the centrality of gender in shaping the institution of work.

Today's young people may enter a less segregated labor market on the whole than young people in the past, which could have long-term consequences for the composition of occupa-tions. Even so, women and men continue to be channeled into different occupations through complex social, cultural, and business practices. The work that most people continue to view as women's work carries less status and is paid less than work viewed as men's work. The public policies that helped advance greater gender equality in employment opportunity throughout the latter decades of the 20th century are not enough. Traditional antidiscrimination laws have reduced labor market segregation overall, but new equality strategies will be necessary for 21st-century women and men to have access to the work that interests them and to be fairly compensated for it.

NOTES

1. Author's calculations using 2014 Current Population Survey data.

REFERENCES

Bergmann, Barbara R. 2011. "Sex Segregation in the Blue-collar Occupations: Women's Choices or Unremedied Discrimination?: Comment on England." *Gender & Society* 25:88–93.

Correll, Shelley J. 2001. "Gender and the Career Choice Process: The Role of Biased Self-Assessments." *American Journal of Sociology* 106(6):1691–1730.

Dweck, Carol S. 2006. "Is Math a Gift? Beliefs That Put Females at Risk." In S. J. Ceci and W. Williams (Eds.), *Why Aren't More Women in Science? Top Researchers Debate the Evidence*. Washington, DC: American Psychological Association.

Eccles, Jacquelynne S., and Allan Wigfield. 2002. "Motivational Beliefs, Values, and Goals." *Annual Review of Psychology* 53:109–132.

England, Paula. 2010. "The Gender Revolution: Uneven and Stalled." *Gender & Society*. 24:149–166.

Equal Employment Opportunity Commission. 2014. Charge Statistics FY 1997 through FY 2013. Retrieved November 25, 2014. http://eeoc.gov/eeoc/statistics/enforcement/charges.cfm/.

Goldin, Claudia, and Lawrence F. Katz. 2012. "The Most Egalitarian of All Professions: Pharmacy and the Evolution of a Family-Friendly Occupation." Working Paper 18410. National Bureau of Economic Research.

Gunderson, Elizabeth A., Gerardo Ramirez, Susan C. Levine, and Sian L. Beilock. 2012. "The Role of Parents and Teachers in the Development of Gender-Related Math Attitudes." *Sex Roles* 66:153–166.

Hegewisch, Ariana, Hannah Lipemann, Jeffrey Hayes, and Heidi Hartmann. 2010. "Separate and Not Equal? Gender Segregation in the Labor Market and the Gender Wage Gap." Briefing Paper IWPR C377. Institute for Women's Policy Research.

Jacobs, Jerry. 2003. "Detours on the Road to Equality: Women, Work, and Higher Education." *Contexts* 2:32–41.

Kessler-Harris, Alice. 1982. *Out to Work: A History of Wage Earning Women in the United States*. New York: Oxford University Press.

Liben, Lynn S., Rebecca Bigler, and Holleen R. Krough. 2002. "Language at Work: Children's Gendered Interpretations of Occupational Titles." *Child Development* 73(3):810–828.

Padavic, Irene, and Barbara Reskin 2002. *Women and Men at Work*, 2nd ed. Thousand Oaks: Pine Forge Press

Reskin, Barbara F., and Patricia A. Roos. 1990. *Job Queues, Gender Queues: Explaining Women's Inroads into Male Occupations*. Philadelphia: Temple University Press.

Schilt, Kristen. 2010. *Just One of the Guys: Transgender Men and the Persistence of Gender Inequality*. Chicago: University of Chicago Press.

Steinpreis, Rhea E., Katie A. Anders, and Dawn Ritzke. 1999. "The Impact of Gender on the Review of the Curricula Vitae of Job Applicants and Tenure Candidates: A National Empirical Study." *Sex Roles* 41:509–528.

"Want Ads." *The State*. June 1, 1958, p. 8D. Newspapers on microfilm. Published Material Division, South Caroliniana Library, University of South Carolina, Columbia, South Carolina.

Pride and Prejudice: Employment Discrimination against Openly Gay Men in the United States

ANDRÁS TILCSIK

Determining the extent to which discrimination exists in employment can be a challenge for researchers. A common tactic that researchers use is called an "audit study." In this reading, Tilcsik discusses his large-scale audit study examining discrimination against gay men, where gay applicants were 40 percent less likely to receive callbacks than heterosexual applicants. He also found that employers who sought to hire men with stereotypically masculine traits were significantly more likely to discriminate against gay men, indicating that some of the discriminatory action is tied to stereotypes of gay men.

In recent years, the rights and legal protections of lesbian, gay, bisexual, and transgender (LGBT) people have been at the center of heated debates in the United States. In the absence of a federal law specifically protecting LGBT employees and job seekers, one debate has focused on sexual orientation discrimination in employment; that is, the behaviors and practices—both deliberate and nonconscious—that disadvantage individuals of a particular sexual orientation over individuals of another sexual orientation in employment contexts (*Romer v. Evans*, 517 U.S. 620, 116 S. Ct. 1620, 134 L. Ed. 2d 855 [1996]; Badgett 2001; Rubenstein 2002; Hull 2005; Herszenhorn 2007). Although scholars have produced a considerable amount of research relevant to this debate (Badgett et al. 2007), most of the literature has focused on wage inequality and has produced little direct evidence about the difficulties that LGBT people might face in obtaining a job. Thus, we can currently only speculate about the extent and patterns of sexual orientation discrimination in the hiring process. This is a significant omission because hiring discrimination is an important inequality-generating mechanism with potentially powerful effects on a job seeker's access to a broad range of opportunities (Petersen and Saporta 2004; Pager 2007). More generally, the current focus on wage inequality may be limiting because even when wage regressions demonstrate significant income differences between two groups (e.g., LGBT and heterosexual employees), skeptics might argue that the observed gap reflects unobserved differences in employee productivity or preferences rather than discrimination (cf. Farkas and Vicknair 1996; Berg and Lien 2002). Thus, the lack of direct evidence about sexual orientation discrimination, and hiring discrimination in particular, limits our understanding of the nature and extent of inequalities faced by LGBT Americans.

I begin to address this lacuna by directly examining hiring discrimination against openly gay men. In doing so, I present results from the first large-scale audit study of sexual orientation discrimination in the United States. Limiting the scope of this study to one LGBT group—gay men—was advantageous because the precise nature of prejudice based on sexual orientation might vary across different LGBT groups. For example, while gay men are commonly stereotyped as feminine or effeminate (Madon 1997), lesbians are often believed to be overly masculine (Ward 2008). Given these different perceptions, employer behavior toward job seekers from different LGBT groups may not be uniform. By focusing on a single group—and leaving it to future research to explore discrimination against other LGBT groups—it was possible to delve more deeply into the nature of discrimination against gay men. To do so, I responded with a pair of fictitious but ostensibly real résumés to 1,769 postings of white-collar, entry-level jobs in seven states, randomly assigning a signal of sexual orientation to each résumé. The findings from this study provide evidence about the extent of discrimination as well as the factors that affect the likelihood of discrimination, including local attitudes toward gay men, the presence of antidiscrimination laws, and the extent to which employers value stereotypically male heterosexual personality traits. . . .

Prior System

Starting with Badgett's (1995) seminal study, much of the literature on sexual orientation discrimination in the United States has focused on compensation (Klawitter and Flatt 1998; Allegretto and Arthur 2001; Badgett 2001; Clain and Leppel 2001; Berg and Lien 2002; Black et al. 2003; Blandford 2003; Carpenter 2007; Antecol,

Jong, and Steinberger 2008). Controlling for human capital, these studies have found that gay men earn 10%–32% less than heterosexual men (Badgett et al. 2007). . . .

Another line of research examined employee self-reports and found that many LGBT individuals report experiencing some form of discrimination in the workplace (e.g., Badgett, Donnelly, and Kibbe 1992; Croteau 1996; Badgett 1997). The generalizability of these studies, however, is limited because they rely on convenience samples and capture subjective perceptions, rather than the actual incidence, of discrimination (Badgett et al. 2007). A third approach focused on the number of employment discrimination complaints that LGBT employees filed in states that outlaw sexual orientation discrimination. Rubenstein (2002), for example, found that the per capita rate of complaints about sexual orientation discrimination was comparable to the rate of sex and race discrimination complaints. However, like self-reports, complaint rates do not necessarily represent the actual incidence of discrimination. Clearly, some employees who experience discrimination may never file a complaint, while others may file an unfounded complaint.

Seeking more direct evidence for discrimination, some researchers have adopted an experimental approach. Crow, Fok, and Hartman (1998), for example, asked full-time employees in a southern city to select six out of eight fictitious applicants for an accounting position. For all combinations of gender and race, respondents were more likely to eliminate homosexual candidates than heterosexual candidates. Similarly, Horvath and Ryan (2003) instructed undergraduates to rate résumés for which sexual orientation and gender were experimentally manipulated. Gay and lesbian applicants received lower ratings than heterosexual men but higher ratings than heterosexual women. Taking a somewhat different approach, Hebl et al. (2002) conducted a field experiment in which male and female confederates applied for retail jobs in a mall of a Texas metropolis. For each store, the confederates were randomly assigned to wear a baseball hat with the words "Gay and Proud" or "Texan and Proud." This experiment measured both interpersonal bias (e.g., differences in interaction duration) and formal bias (e.g., differences in job offers and callbacks) and found evidence for the former but not the latter.

Although these experiments represent an important first step toward directly measuring hiring discrimination, they have significant limitations. First, all three experiments were limited to a single context—a single city, university, or mall area. Thus, it is unclear how accurately the results reflect broader patterns of discrimination and how the extent of discrimination might vary across different contexts. Second, in two of these studies, the decision makers knew that they were participating in an experiment and that their choices had no consequences on real hiring outcomes (Crow et al. 1998; Horvath and Ryan 2003). Whether these decision makers would make the same hiring choices in a real employment context, faced with real incentives and constraints, remains unclear. . . . Finally, the sample of experimental participants may further limit generalizability. In Horvath and Ryan's sample, in particular, the participants were college students rather than employers, and nearly 80% of them were white women—a sample that is not representative of the U.S. population or even the undergraduate population (Badgett et al. 2007).

An Audit Approach

To overcome the above-described limitations, I conducted a large-scale audit study of discrimination against gay men. Audit studies apply experimental techniques to real world employment contexts and fall into two categories: in-person audits and correspondence tests (Pager 2007). In-person audits involve sending pairs of experimental confederates—who are matched on a variety of relevant characteristics but differ, for example, in their race or gender—to apply for jobs with real employers (e.g., Pager 2003; Pager et al. 2009). Correspondence tests are based on a

similar approach but use fictitious matched résumés rather than actual job applicants (e.g., Bertrand and Mullainathan 2004; Correll et al. 2007). In both cases, researchers examine whether a characteristic of interest (such as gender or race) affects the probability that an applicant receives a positive response (such as a callback or a job offer).

The audit methodology offers important advantages. By experimentally controlling for human capital factors that might be confounded with minority status, audit studies provide more direct evidence about the causal impact of discrimination than do wage regressions (Pager 2007). By gathering such evidence in a real employment context from real employers, audit studies are also more generalizable than studies with undergraduate participants and experiments in which participants know that their choices will not affect real hiring outcomes (Correll et al. 2007). Of course, audit studies are not without limitations. Critics, for example, have pointed to the difficulty of matching real persons on all dimensions that might affect productivity (e.g., Heckman 1998). . . .

To date . . . there has been no large-scale audit of sexual orientation discrimination in the United States. In addition, no audit study in any country has examined sexual orientation discrimination across geographic areas that vary significantly in the popular acceptance of homosexuality or in the extent to which local laws protect LGBT employees. Moreover, existing studies have not investigated whether employers who seek applicants with certain characteristics are more likely to discriminate against gay men. I begin to address these lacunae.

Discrimination, Regional Variation, and Stereotypes

In this section, I first discuss the plausibility of hiring discrimination against gay men in the United States. I then consider how the likelihood of discrimination may vary across contexts. Although my empirical analyses control for numerous factors that may influence the level of discrimination, I focus below on two sources of variation. First, I consider geographic variation that may stem from differences in local attitudes toward gay men and from differences in the level of legal protection available to them. Second, I discuss the kind of variation in the level of discrimination we might observe if stereotypes of gay men play a role in hiring decisions. . . .

Callback Discrimination

As noted earlier, self-reports, analyses of discrimination complaints, and laboratory experiments cannot provide direct evidence of sexual orientation discrimination. Nevertheless, as the literature review above indicates, such studies consistently point to the possibility of employment discrimination against gay men (Badgett et al. 2007). Public opinion data provide further support for this hypothesis. While Americans have become more accepting of gay people over the past few decades, they are still significantly less tolerant than the citizens of most advanced democracies in Europe (Saad 2005). . . .

Accordingly, I expect that gay job seekers will face discrimination in U.S. job markets. In particular, I focus on discrimination that occurs at the initial stage of the employee selection process and predict that applications from gay men will be less likely to elicit an interview invitation (or "callback") than applications from equally qualified heterosexual men. As several researchers noted, this first step in the employee selection process is a critical stage because it often represents a crucial barrier to employment for minorities (Bendick, Brown, and Wall 1999; Pager 2003; Drydakis 2009; Pager et al. 2009). . . .

The Geography of Discrimination

Prior audit studies of racial, gender, and sexual orientation discrimination have typically focused on a limited geographic area—often just a single city or two (e.g., Pager 2003; Bertrand and Mullainathan 2004; Drydakis 2009; Pager et al. 2009). As a result, it is sometimes difficult to know whether variation in the observed level of discrimination against a given group is due to

differences between experimental designs or to regional variation in the actual prevalence of discrimination (Pager 2007). When studying discrimination against gay men in the United States, limiting the scope of an audit experiment to a single city would be particularly disadvantageous. Indeed, regional differences in the level of tolerance toward gay men and in antidiscrimination laws may lead to geographic variation in the incidence of discrimination.

Public opinion polls indicate considerable regional variation in attitudes toward gay men. While almost half of Americans in the Northeast and the West have a favorable view of gay men (48% and 45%, respectively), only slightly more than a third of respondents express similar views in the Midwest (35%) and even fewer in the South (29%; Pew Research Center 2003). Support for gay rights follows the same regional pattern. From nondiscrimination laws to hate crime legislation, public support for policies to protect gay rights is strongest in the Northeast and the West and weakest in the South (Lax and Phillips 2009). . . . Taken together, these findings suggest significant regional differences in the social acceptance of gay men. If such differences are reflected in the hiring process, callback discrimination will be more likely in areas with less tolerant attitudes (e.g., the South) than in areas with more accepting attitudes (e.g., the Northeast).

The adoption of state laws that prohibit sexual orientation discrimination follows a similar geographic pattern. At the time of this study [in 2011], 20 states and the District of Columbia prohibited sexual orientation discrimination in the private sector, but most of these states were in the Northeast and the West. For example, all states in New England and, with the exception of Alaska, all Pacific states had passed such legislation. By contrast, only four out of 12 midwestern states banned sexual orientation discrimination, and in the South, only two states adopted such laws. The geographic distribution of counties and cities that ban sexual orientation discrimination in private employment was roughly similar, with relatively few antidiscrimination laws in southern cities and counties. Notably, however, such laws have been passed in some major cities in the South and the Midwest, including Atlanta, Austin, Chicago, Dallas, and Detroit. . . .

Whether such laws are effective in reducing discrimination is an empirical question. There is only scant evidence on this issue, and it is mostly from studies of wage discrimination. For example, Klawitter and Flatt (1998) found that anti-discrimination laws had a positive effect on the earnings of gay men, suggesting a reduction in wage discrimination, but this effect became statistically insignificant after controlling for the sociodemographic characteristics of the local population. . . .

The Role of Stereotypes

Stereotypes are socially shared sets of implicit or explicit beliefs about the typical characteristics of members of a social group (Banaji 2002; Padavic and Reskin 2002). Stereotyping is the process by which stereotypes are used in judgments about a social group or its individual members. Since stereotyped judgments simplify and justify social reality, stereotyping has potentially powerful effects on how people perceive and treat one another (e.g., Banaji, Hardin, and Rothman 1993; Fiske 1998; Reskin 2001; Ridgeway 2009). Indeed, laboratory experiments suggest that stereotyping may play an important role in judgments that affect hiring decisions (Davison and Burke 2000; Rudman and Glick 2001). . . .

. . . If stereotyped judgments influence callback decisions, employers should be more likely to engage in discrimination if they value and emphasize attributes that gay men are stereotypically perceived to lack. What might these attributes be? Research suggests that gay men are often perceived to exhibit behaviors associated with "feminine" characteristics; for example, they are commonly seen as sensitive, emotional, gentle, affectionate, and passive (Gurwitz and Marcus 1978; Page and Yee 1986; Jackson and Sullivan 1989; Madon 1997). Indeed, a general finding is that people frequently perceive gay

men to be feminine or effeminate (Haddock, Zanna, and Esses 1993; Madon 1997; see also Connell 2005). Consequently, gay men are often seen as lacking "toughness" and "masculinity" (Madon 1997).

Even a quick perusal of job postings reveals that it is not uncommon for employers to emphasize personality characteristics that are perceived as traits typical of heterosexual men, such as decisiveness, assertiveness, and aggressiveness (Bem 1974; Madon 1997; Gorman 2005). Indeed, searches in online job databases often return hundreds of postings in which employers seek, for example, "an aggressive, motivated self-starter," "an assertive associate," or "a decisive, results-oriented leader." This emphasis on stereotypically male heterosexual characteristics, in turn, may be associated with a higher likelihood of discrimination against gay men. If stereotypes of gay men—as feminine, passive, gentle, or lacking "toughness"—play a significant role in callback decisions, employers who characterize their ideal job candidate with stereotypically male heterosexual traits should be particularly likely to engage in discrimination.

Methods

In what follows, I first consider the challenge of signaling sexual orientation on a résumé and explain how I addressed that challenge. I then describe the details of my audit experiment, the sample of jobs, and the variables used in regression analyses.

Signaling Sexual Orientation

An important challenge in résumé-based audit studies is to signal the characteristic of interest without introducing a confounding factor into the analysis. For example, in studies of racial discrimination, signaling race with distinctively African-American names (e.g., Bertrand and Mullainathan 2004) may also signal low socioeconomic status. As a result, it may be difficult to untangle the effect of race and class on discrimination (Pager 2007). Similarly, in a study of sexual orientation, a résumé item that indicates experience in a gay and lesbian organization may signal more than just the applicant's sexual orientation. As Weichselbaumer (2003, p. 635) pointed out, employers may perceive openly gay applicants as tactless or lacking business savvy because they list an irrelevant experience on their résumé, simply "trumpeting" their sexual orientation. In addition, perceiving such applicants as radical or liberal, employers may discriminate against them for their perceived political views and activism, rather than their sexual orientation (Badgett et al. 2007). Moreover, if the "control organization" that is assigned to the résumé of the ostensibly heterosexual applicant is not carefully chosen, it may lead to differences in the applicants' perceived level of human capital, making it difficult to assess the extent of discrimination. For example, Drydakis (2009) used a gay community organization as the signal of homosexual orientation and an environmental group as the control organization. A potential issue is that employers may perceive experience in an environmental organization as more valuable than experience in a gay community group, even if they are not biased against gay employees; for example, they may see the gay group as a primarily social organization and assume that volunteering for the environmental group is a more important and meaningful activity. In that case, differences in callback rates would lead us to overestimate the level of discrimination.

I took several steps to address these issues. First, the fictitious job seekers in this study were graduating college seniors applying for entry-level jobs. For this population of applicants, listing résumé items that describe volunteer experiences in a political, cultural, ethnic, religious, or other identity-based campus organization is common practice, especially if the experience involves an elected position with nontrivial responsibilities. ... For example, while simple membership in a college's Asian American Association or Republican Club would usually be omitted from the résumé, job seekers would typically list their experience as an officer—such as treasurer or president—in such groups. ...

Second, to signal homosexual orientation, I chose an experience in a gay community organization that could not be easily dismissed as irrelevant to a job application. Thus, instead of being just a member of a gay and lesbian campus organization, the applicant served as the elected treasurer for several semesters, managing the organization's financial operations. ... Accordingly, rather than focusing on the organization's nature or goals, this résumé item explicitly emphasized the applicant's managerial and financial skills. Thus, the applicant's participation in this organization could be seen as a meaningful, valuable experience with potentially important transferable skills. In other words, omitting this experience from the résumé would have meant concealing relevant and nontrivial human capital. In addition, since the applicant was the treasurer, rather than, say, the political chair or outreach officer of the group, this experience was primarily financial and organizational ... rather than that of a political activist. This aspect of the position helps mitigate the concern that the reason for discrimination was a bias against political activists rather than a bias against gay men (Badgett et al. 2007). ...

Third, I used a control organization to ensure that any observed differences in callbacks could be attributed to antigay discrimination rather than other factors. An important consideration was that participation in a gay organization might be associated with progressive, liberal, or leftist political views (Badgett et al. 2007). Thus, if I had used an apolitical control organization (or no control organization at all), observed differences in callbacks might have been attributable to discrimination based on either sexual orientation or political affiliation, and it would have been impossible to determine the net effect of sexual orientation. Accordingly, to determine whether there is a "gay penalty" above and beyond the possible effect of political discrimination, I chose a control organization that is associated with leftist or progressive views. . . . At first glance, a campus chapter of college Democrats (e.g., "Bowdoin College Democrats") might seem suitable for this purpose. However, since Democratic campus groups are typically larger than gay and lesbian student groups, leadership experiences in a Democratic organization may seem more valuable than similar experiences in a gay organization. To avoid this problem, the control group was a small left-wing campus organization (the "Progressive and Socialist Alliance"; P&SA) rather than a larger and better-known group. . . .

An additional advantage of using a political control organization that, like the P&SA, falls outside the mainstream of partisan politics is that disclosing one's commitments to such a group may indicate a lack of business savvy to employers, especially in the case of white-collar business jobs. This aspect of the experiment further mitigates the concern that observed differences in callbacks may be due to the perception of openly gay applicants as unsavvy or tactless. . . . Nevertheless, even with these precautions, such a perception may still play some role. The issue of perceived tactlessness, however, does not refute the existence of discrimination; rather, it constitutes one possible explanation for why some employers might engage in discrimination. . . .

Résumés and Randomization

Over a six-month period in 2005, I sent fictitious résumés, via e-mail, to advertisements for full-time, entry-level positions on three recruitment websites targeted at college seniors and recent graduates. . . . I sent two résumés in response to each job posting, with one day or less in between. Before sending out each résumé pair, I randomly assigned the gay signal to one of the résumés and the control signal to the other résumé. Thus, even though the résumés differed from each other in order to avoid raising suspicion, there was no systematic relationship between résumé quality and sexual orientation. Consequently, any significant difference in callback rates could be attributed to the experimental manipulation of the résumés. . . . Importantly, I varied only the name of the treatment organization and the control organization on the résumés. . . . As a result, the activities of the applicants in their respective groups were not systematically related to sexual orientation. Thus, I effectively controlled for any differences in the applicants' achievements in the treatment organization and the control organization.[1] In sum, sexual orientation was randomly assigned with respect to both overall résumé quality and the quality of experiences within the control and treatment organizations.

The treatment/control signal appeared at the end of the "experience" section of the résumé and was just one of several experiences described in that section.[2] In addition to the résumés, I created corresponding cover letters that briefly stated the applicant's desire to work in the targeted position and his desire to move to the city or town where the employer was located.[3] For each application, I recorded whether it led to an invitation to a first-round job interview (either an in-person or a telephone interview). To receive employer responses, I set up e-mail accounts with a web-based e-mail service as well as voice mail boxes with an inexpensive Voice-over-Internet-Protocol service.

The Sample of Jobs

I submitted a total of 3,538 résumés, responding to 1,769 job postings by private employers. The size of this sample was comparable to that in previous large-scale correspondence audits (Weichselbaumer 2003; Bertrand and Mullainathan 2004; Correll et al. 2007; Drydakis 2009). . . . The sample included jobs in five occupations and seven states. Limiting the sample in this way ensured that a sufficient number of observations were available in each state and occupation to make meaningful comparisons. The five occupations in the sample were managers, business and financial analysts, sales representatives, customer service representatives, and administrative assistants. The sampled states included four states in the Northeast and the West

(New York, Pennsylvania, California, Nevada) and three states in the Midwest and the South (Ohio, Florida, Texas), all with a relatively high number of job postings on the recruitment websites I used. The number of job postings in a state ranged from 131 (Nevada) to 347 (Florida), with at least 200 observations in each state other than Nevada. . . .

It is important to note that the sampled states varied, both in level of tolerance toward gay people and in having or lacking laws regarding sexual orientation discrimination (Lax and Phillips 2009). Indeed, these states—and the counties and cities within them—offered an intriguing mosaic of different legal environments. While California, Nevada, and New York prohibit sexual orientation discrimination in private employment, the other four states have no such legislation. At the same time, with the exception of Nevada, each state has some cities and counties that ban sexual orientation discrimination. Thus, the sample contained employers in a variety of legal environments, ranging from employers who were not subject to any antidiscrimination law protecting gay men to employers who were simultaneously subject to state-, county-, and city-level antidiscrimination laws. . . .

Findings

The submission of résumés led to a total of 331 interview invitations, an overall callback rate of 9.35%.[4] . . . While heterosexual applicants had an 11.5% chance of being invited for an interview, equally qualified gay applicants only had a 7.2% chance of receiving a positive response. This is a difference of 4.3 percentage points, or about 40%. This gap is statistically significant ($P < .001$) and implies that a heterosexual job seeker had to apply to fewer than nine different jobs to receive a positive response, while a gay applicant needed to reply to almost 14 ads to achieve the same result. . . .

The size of the callback gap, however, varied substantially across states. On the one hand, in the southern and midwestern states in the sample (Texas, Florida, and Ohio), there was a substantial difference in the callback rates of gay and heterosexual applicants. In Texas and Ohio, for example, the size of the callback gap (8.3 and 8.6 percentage points, respectively) was substantially larger than in the overall sample (4.1 percentage points). By contrast, there was no statistically significant callback gap in any of the western and northeastern states (California, Nevada, Pennsylvania, and New York). The size of the gap, however, showed some intraregional variation as well. In California, for example, the difference in callback rates was less than 2 percentage points and was clearly insignificant statistically. In neighboring Nevada, by contrast, the gap was nearly significant at the standard level ($P = .087$).

Similarly, there was variation in the callback gap across legal environments. In the case of employers subject to a relevant antidiscrimination law, either at the city-, county-, or state-level, the callback gap was less than 3 percentage points; in the case of employers not subject to such regulation, the gap was as large as 6 percentage points. In both cases, however, the callback gap was statistically significant. In addition, as expected, the callback gap was particularly large in the case of employers who emphasized the importance of stereotypically male heterosexual traits. Notably, however, there was a statistically significant callback gap even within the sample of employers who did not specifically require such traits. . . .

Discussion

. . . This study contributes to the literature on employment discrimination in three ways: by providing direct evidence about discrimination against gay men, by examining how discrimination varies across regions, and by exploring the role of stereotypes in discrimination. I elaborate on each these contributions below.

Direct Evidence for Discrimination

. . . The results indicate that gay men encounter significant barriers in the hiring process because, at the initial point of contact, employers more readily disqualify openly gay applicants than equally qualified heterosexual applicants. Even after controlling for job, employer, and area characteristics, I found that gay job applicants were approximately 40% less likely to be offered a job interview than their heterosexual counterparts. This difference is similar in magnitude to the callback gap between black and white job seekers in a recent correspondence audit of Boston and Chicago employers (Bertrand and Mullainathan 2004). Overall, my findings are consistent with less direct indicators of discrimination against LGBT people (Badgett et al. 2007), and—taken together—these lines of evidence suggest that sexual orientation discrimination is a prominent feature of many American labor markets.

Comparing Discrimination across Regions

. . . I have collected evidence from seven geographically dispersed states that vary in both the local attitudes toward gay men and the presence of laws that prohibit sexual orientation discrimination. The results indicate dramatic geographic variation in the level of discrimination, even after controlling for employer, industry, and occupational factors. While employers in the southern and midwestern states in the sample (Texas, Florida, and Ohio) showed strong discriminatory tendencies, there was little or no discrimination in the western and northeastern states, such as California, New York, and Pennsylvania.

This variation provides an interesting contrast to the cross-city variation observed in the audit literature on racial discrimination. Recent audit studies of discrimination against black job applicants (typically conducted in a midwestern or northeastern city) all documented some level of systematic discrimination (Pager 2007). In the case of gay job seekers, by contrast, while there was severe discrimination in some states, there was no discrimination at all in others. Of course, in the absence of a multistate audit study of racial discrimination, it is difficult to tell whether this

difference is due to underlying differences in the geography of racial discrimination and sexual orientation discrimination or to the fact that recent audits of racial discrimination were typically limited to the Northeast and the Midwest. Indeed, more generally, my results suggest that focusing on a single geographic area may prevent audit studies from revealing the larger patterns of discrimination. Thus, a promising avenue for future research might be to study discrimination (on the basis of race, gender, age, motherhood, or other traits) with a multistate design similar to the one used in this study.

In addition to establishing the existence of regional variation in the level of sexual orientation discrimination, this study has begun to explore the sources of that variation. A key finding is that employers in states and counties with a relevant antidiscrimination law were significantly less likely to engage in discrimination, although this difference was no longer significant once I controlled for state-level attitudes. As noted earlier, however, we should interpret this result carefully. Clearly, this study relied on a small sample of states and—in the absence of reliable county- and city-level attitude data—it could not examine the relative impact of laws and attitudes within states. But, indeed, even if such data were available, it may not reveal the relationship between laws, attitudes, and discrimination in its entire complexity. For example, even if antidiscrimination laws had no direct effect, they may help reduce discrimination indirectly, by improving public opinion about gay people (Klawitter and Flatt 1998; Haeberle 2002). Of course, there is likely to be a causal effect in the opposite direction as well, as more tolerant local attitudes lead to more inclusive antidiscrimination laws. Given this potential joint causality between laws and attitudes, isolating their effects on discrimination is difficult (e.g., Burstein 1985). Future research might address this issue by exploring the relationship between attitudinal changes and the passage of antidiscrimination laws longitudinally. . . .

Stereotyping as a Mechanism

The third main contribution of this study is that it identifies stereotyping as a potentially important mechanism underlying hiring discrimination against gay men. Employers who sought applicants with stereotypically male heterosexual traits were much more likely to discriminate against gay applicants than employers who did not emphasize the importance of such traits. This finding suggests that employers' implicit or explicit stereotypes of gay men are inconsistent with the image of an assertive, aggressive, and decisive employee. It seems, therefore, that the discrimination documented in this study is partly rooted in specific stereotypes and cannot be completely reduced to a general antipathy against gay employees.

This finding may also be considered in the framework of statistical discrimination (Arrow 1973), the practice of using "overall beliefs about a group to make decisions about an individual from that group" (Blank, Dabady, and Citro 2004, p. 61). For example, if employers believe that masculinity is associated with better job performance, believe that gay men on average are less masculine than heterosexual men, and cannot directly assess individual applicants' masculinity, they may judge job seekers on the basis of group averages. . . .

More generally, this study engages with a key question in understanding ascriptive inequality: How do members of dominant groups perceive the characteristics of subordinate groups, especially the characteristics that are relevant to inequality-generating decisions, such as hiring? (See Reskin 2001; Quillian 2006; Ridgeway 2009) While this study does not provide direct access to the content of stereotypes, it demonstrates their potentially powerful effect on hiring decisions in real employment contexts. Thus, this study suggests that a fruitful path for future audit studies would be to explore the role that stereotypes play in discrimination on the basis of other characteristics, such as race, gender, age, or motherhood. . . .

Adapting to the Reality of Discrimination

This study documented the existence of discrimination, but it is left to future research to explore how gay job seekers adapt to this reality. Indeed, it is important to note that audit studies generally capture the extent of discrimination that occurs before job seekers' responses to discrimination—such as the avoidance of discriminatory employers—take place (Heckman 1998; Blank et al. 2004). In the case of sexual orientation, the issue of adaptation raises a particularly interesting dilemma. On the one hand, some might conclude that job applicants would be best advised to hide their sexual orientation during the hiring process and perhaps even beyond it, especially if employer bias extends to other decisions as well (e.g., about wages or promotions). If that is the case, disclosure may lead to a reduction in one's economic opportunities. On the other hand, concealment may also be costly. First of all, omitting relevant skills and experiences from one's work and volunteer history means hiding a potentially important part of one's human capital. . . .

In turn, once at the workplace, hiding one's sexual orientation is often stressful and may have a negative impact on the individual's productivity, self-esteem, depth of friendships, and ability to work as part of a team (e.g., Woods 1993; Friskopp and Silverstein 1996). Indeed, for these reasons, some might argue that it is in the interest of gay job seekers to signal their sexual orientation because doing so may screen out less tolerant employers. This strategy, of course, is only feasible if a sufficiently large number of nondiscriminatory employers offer equally high-quality jobs as their discriminatory counterparts (Pager 2007; Pager et al. 2009).

Beyond the Callback Stage

A related question is how employers treat openly gay applicants beyond the initial callback stage of the hiring process. One important factor in this regard might be whether interviewers differ from résumé screeners. . . . [N]ot all interviewers may be as accepting of gay people as the résumé screener who made the initial selection. In addition, regardless of who the interviewers are, the interview phase may involve different discrimination-related processes than those present at the callback stage. On the one hand, to the extent that some aspects of "masculine" behavior are observable during this stage, interviewers may rely less on stereotypes and more on observations of individual attributes. On the other hand, research suggests that—at least in elite professional service firms—interviewers often pay particularly close attention to factors other than job-relevant skills, such as extracurricular interests and personality traits . . . (Rivera 2009). Thus, because applicants who receive a callback are often similar in their grades and job-relevant experience, factors like sexual orientation—or involvement with an identity group based on sexual orientation—may become more salient at the interview stage than they were at the callback stage. In sum, the processes that foster or prevent discrimination are likely to vary across different stages of the hiring process; future research should explore these processes beyond the résumé-screening stage.

Discrimination against Other Groups

The scope of this study was limited to just one LGBT group—gay men. Thus, hiring discrimination against lesbian, bisexual, and transgender job seekers in the United States remains to be explored through large-scale audit studies. One path for future audit research would be to explore discrimination against lesbians. While survey-based research consistently documented a wage penalty for gay men, some studies found a wage premium for lesbians (Klawitter and Flatt 1998; Black et al. 2003). An audit study might offer insight into this intriguing result. Indeed, given that existing stereotypes of gay men and lesbians are significantly different (Madon 1997; Ward 2008), an audit study of stereotype-based employer behavior toward les-

bians in the United States may be a particularly promising research endeavor (cf. Weichselbaumer 2003). Another avenue would be to explore the interaction of sexual orientation and race. For example, do race and sexual orientation interact to produce "multiple jeopardy" (King 1988) for LGBT members of racial minority groups? And, if there is such an interaction, does its nature vary across minority groups? Extending the current study to answer these questions would further deepen our understanding of labor-market inequalities.

Finally, future research might extend this study to enrich the broader literature on gender-based inequality. A particularly interesting question concerns the extent to which discrimination based on gender—as opposed to sexual orientation—would lead to similar empirical patterns as those observed in this study. For example, would heterosexual women also be disadvantaged in cases when employers emphasize stereotypically masculine traits? More generally, future research should benefit from simultaneously exploring the role of gender and sexual orientation in callback discrimination. In particular, large-scale audits covering multiple LGBT groups and both male and female applicants could help untangle both the direct and the interactive effects of gender and sexual orientation.

NOTES

1. For the sake of brevity, I refer to fictitious applicants who were assigned the control signal as "heterosexual." More precisely, these applicants would be described as "fictitious job seekers who did not give evidence of being gay" (see Correll et al. 2007).
2. Since this study focused on sexual orientation discrimination, I held the race of the fictitious applicants constant. Thus, the résumés did not mention any involvement in race- or ethnicity-related organizations (e.g., "Black Students Association"), and the fictitious applicants' names were made up of

common first and last names that would not send a strong and salient signal of being from a particular racial minority group ("David Miller" and "Michael Williams").

3. The cover letters corresponding to the two résumés were similar in style and content and made no mention of the applicants' involvement in either the gay or the progressive/socialist group. Because of the random assignment of the gay signal to the résumés, there was no systematic relationship between the quality of the cover letter and the sexual orientation of the applicant. The cover letter explained that the motivation for moving to the target city included family reasons and that the applicant was originally from the targeted area, with many of his family members still living there. . . .

4. This response rate is similar to that in recent correspondence studies (e.g., Bertrand and Mullainathan 2004). . . .

REFERENCES

Allegretto, Sylvia, and Michelle Arthur. 2001. "An Empirical Analysis of Homosexual/Heterosexual Male Earnings Differentials: Unmarried and Unequal?" *Industrial and Labor Relations Review* 54:631–46.

Antecol, Heather, Anneke Jong, and Michael Steinberger. 2008. "The Sexual Orientation Wage Gap: The Role of Occupational Sorting and Human Capital." *Industrial and Labor Relations Review* 61:518–43.

Arrow, Kenneth J. 1973. "The Theory of Discrimination." Pp. 3–33 in *Discrimination in Labor Markets*, edited by Orley Ashenfelter and Albert Rees. Princeton, N.J.: Princeton University Press.

Badgett, M. V. Lee. 1995. "The Wage Effects of Sexual Orientation Discrimination." *Industrial and Labor Relations Review* 48:726–39.

Badgett, M. V. Lee. 1997. "Vulnerability in the Workplace: Evidence of Anti-Gay Discrimination." *Angles: The Policy Journal of the Institute for Gay and Lesbian Strategic Studies* 2:1–4.

Badgett, M. V. Lee. 2001. *Money, Myths, and Change: The Economic Lives of Lesbians and Gay Men.* Chicago: University of Chicago Press.

Badgett, M. V. Lee, Colleen Donnelly, and Jennifer Kibbe. 1992. *Pervasive Patterns of Discrimination against Lesbians and Gay Men: Evidence from Surveys across the United States.* Washington, D.C.: National Gay and Lesbian Task Force Policy Institute.

Badgett, M. V. Lee, Holning Lau, Brad Sears, and Deborah Ho. 2007. *Bias in the Workplace: Consistent Evidence of Sexual Orientation and Gender Identity Discrimination.* Report, Williams Institute, University of California School of Law.

Banaji, Mahzarin. 2002. "The Social Psychology of Stereotypes." Pp. 15100–104 in *International Encyclopedia of the Social and Behavioral Sciences*, edited by Neil Smelser and Paul Baltes. New York: Pergamon.

Banaji, Mahzarin, Curtis Hardin, and Alexander J. Rothman. 1993. "Implicit Stereotyping in Person Judgment." *Journal of Personality and Social Psychology* 65:272–81.

Bem, Sandra. 1974. "The Measurement of Psychological Androgyny." *Journal of Consulting and Clinical Psychology* 42:155–62.

Bendick, Marc, Jr., Lauren Brown, and Kennington Wall. 1999. "No Foot in the Door: An Experimental Study of Employment Discrimination." *Journal of Aging and Social Policy* 10:5–23.

Berg, Nathan, and Donald Lien. 2002. "Measuring the Effect of Sexual Orientation on Income: Evidence of Discrimination." *Contemporary Economic Policy* 20:394–414.

Bertrand, Marianne, and Sendhil Mullainathan. 2004. "Are Emily and Greg More Employable than Lakisha and Jamal? A Field Experiment on Labor Market Discrimination." *American Economic Review* 94:991–1013.

Black, Dan, Makar Hoda, Seth Sanders, and Lowell Taylor. 2003. "The Earnings Effects of Sexual Orientation." *Industrial and Labor Relations Review* 56:449–69.

Blandford, John M. 2003. "The Nexus of Sexual Orientation and Gender in the Determination of

Earnings." *Industrial and Labor Relations Review* 56:622–42.

Blank, Rebecca, Marilyn Dabady, and Connie Citro, eds. 2004. *Measuring Racial Discrimination.* Washington, D.C.: National Academies Press.

Burstein, Paul. 1985. *Discrimination, Jobs, and Politics: The Struggle for Equal Employment Opportunity in the U.S. since the New Deal.* Chicago: University of Chicago Press.

Carpenter, Christopher. 2007. "Revisiting the Income Penalty for Behaviorally Gay Men: Evidence from NHANES III." *Labour Economics* 14:25–34.

Clain, Suzanne Heller, and Karen Leppell. 2001. "An Investigation into Sexual Orientation Discrimination as an Explanation for Wage Differences." *Applied Economics* 33:37–47.

Connell, Raewyn. 2005. *Masculinities.* Cambridge: Polity.

Correll, Shelley J., Stephen Benard, and In Paik. 2007. "Getting a Job: Is There a Motherhood Penalty?" *American Journal of Sociology* 112:1297–1338.

Croteau, James M. 1996. "Research on the Work Experiences of Lesbian, Gay, and Bisexual People: An Integrative Review of Methodology and Findings." *Journal of Vocational Behavior* 48:195–209.

Crow, Stephen M., Lillian Y. Fok, and Sandra J. Hartman. 1988. "Who Is at Greatest Risk of Work-Related Discrimination—Women, Blacks, or Homosexuals?" *Employee Responsibilities and Rights Journal* 11:15–26.

Davison, H. Kristl, and Michael J. Burke. 2000. "Sex Discrimination in Simulated Employment Contexts: A Meta-analytic Investigation." *Journal of Vocational Behavior* 56:225–48.

Drydakis, Nick. 2009. "Sexual Orientation Discrimination in the Labour Market." *Labour Economics* 16:364–72.

Farkas, George, and Keven Vicknair. 1996. "Appropriate Tests of Racial Wage Discrimination Require Controls for Cognitive Skill: Comment on the Paper by Cancio, Evans, and Maume." *American Sociological Review* 61:557–60.

Fiske, Susan T. 1998. "Stereotyping, Prejudice and Discrimination." Pp. 357–411 in *The Handbook of Social Psychology,* edited by Daniel T. Gilbert,

Susan T. Fiske, and Gardner Lindzey. Boston: McGraw-Hill.

Friskopp, Anette, and Sharon Silverstein. 1996. *Straight Jobs, Gay Lives: Gay and Lesbian Professionals, the Harvard Business School, and the American Workplace.* New York: Scribner.

Gorman, Elizabeth. 2005. "Gender Stereotypes, Same-Gender Preferences, and Organizational Variation in the Hiring of Women: Evidence from Law Firms." *American Sociological Review* 70:702–28.

Gurwitz, Sharon, and Melinda Marcus. 1978. "Effects of Anticipated Interaction, Sex and Homosexual Stereotypes on First Impressions." *Journal of Applied Social Psychology* 90:173–83.

Haddock, Geoffrey, Mark Zanna, and Victoria Esses. 1993. "Assessing the Structure of Prejudicial Attitudes: The Case of Attitudes toward Homosexuals." *Journal of Personality and Social Psychology* 65:1105–18.

Haeberle, Steven. 2002. "Testing Support for ENDA." Paper presented at the annual meeting of the American Political Science Association. Boston, August 28.

Hebl, Michelle R., Jessica Bigazzi Foster, Laura M. Mannix, and John Dovidio. 2002. "Formal and Interpersonal Discrimination: A Field Study of Bias toward Homosexual Applicants." *Personality and Social Psychology Bulletin* 28:815–25.

Heckman, James. 1998. "Detecting Discrimination." *Journal of Economic Perspectives* 12:101–16.

Herszenhorn, David. 2007. "House Approves Broad Protections for Gay Workers." *New York Times,* November 8. http://www.nytimes.com/2007/11/08/washington/08employ.html.

Horvath, Michael, and Ann Marie Ryan. 2003. "Antecedents and Potential Moderators of the Relationship between Attitudes and Hiring Discrimination on the Basis of Sexual Orientation." *Sex Roles* 48:115–30.

Hull, Kathleen. 2005. "Employment Discrimination Based on Sexual Orientation: Dimensions of Difference." Pp. 167–88 in *Handbook of Employment Discrimination Research,* edited by Laura B. Nielsen and Robert L. Nelson. Dordrecht: Springer.

Jackson, Linda, and Linda Sullivan. 1989. "Cognition and Affect in Evaluations of Stereotyped Members." *Journal of Social Psychology* 129:659–72.

King, Deborah. 1988. "Multiple Jeopardy, Multiple Consciousness: The Context of Black Feminist Ideology." *Signs: Journal of Women in Culture and Society* 14:88–111.

Klawitter, Marieka, and Victor Flatt. 1998. "The Effects of State and Local Antidiscrimination Policies on Earnings for Gays and Lesbians." *Journal of Policy Analysis and Management* 17:658–86.

Lax, Jeffrey R., and Justin H. Phillips 2009. "Gay Rights in the States: Public Opinion and Policy Responsiveness." *American Political Science Review* 103:367–86.

Madon, Stephanie. 1997. "What Do People Believe about Gay Males? A Study of Stereotype Content and Strength." *Sex Roles* 37:663–85.

Padavic, Irene, and Barbara F. Reskin. 2002. *Women and Men at Work*, 2d ed. Thousand Oaks, Calif.: Pine Forge.

Page, Stuart, and Mary Yee. 1986. "Conception of Male and Female Homosexual Stereotypes among University Undergraduates." *Journal of Homosexuality* 12:109–17.

Pager, Devah. 2003. "The Mark of a Criminal Record." *American Sociological Review* 18:937–75.

Pager, Devah. 2007. "The Use of Field Experiments for Studies of Employment Discrimination: Contributions, Critiques, and Directions for the Future." *Annals of the American Academy of Political and Social Science* 609:104–33.

Pager, Devah, Bruce Western, and Bart Bonikowski. 2009. "Discrimination in a Low-Wage Labor Market: A Field Experiment." *American Sociological Review* 74:777–99.

Petersen, Trond, and Ishak Saporta. 2004. "The Opportunity Structure for Discrimination." *American Journal of Sociology* 109:852–901.

Pew Research Center. 2003. *Religious Beliefs Underpin Opposition to Homosexuality.* http://www.people-press.org/report/197/religious-beliefs-underpin-opposition-to-homosexuality.

Quillian, Lincoln. 2006. "New Approaches to Understanding Racial Prejudice and Discrimination." *Annual Review of Sociology* 32:299–328.

Reskin, Barbara. 2001. "Sex Stereotyping and Sex Bias in Employment." Pp. 1891–92 in *Routledge International Encyclopedia of Women's Studies*, edited by Cheris Kramarae and Dale Spender. New York: Routledge.

Ridgeway, Cecilia L. 2009. "Framed Before We Know It: How Gender Shapes Social Relations." *Gender & Society* 23:145–60.

Rivera, Lauren A. 2009. *Hiring and Inequality in Elite Professional Service Firms.* Doctoral dissertation. Harvard University, Department of Sociology.

Rubenstein, William B. 2002. "Do Gay Rights Laws Matter? An Empirical Assessment." *Southern California Law Review* 75:65–119.

Rudman, Laurie A., and Peter Glick. 2001. "Prescriptive Gender Stereotypes and Backlash toward Agentic Women." *Journal of Social Issues* 57:743–62.

Saad, Lydia. 2005. "Gay Rights Attitudes a Mixed Bag." Princeton, N.J.: Gallup News Service, May 20.

Ward, Jane. 2008. "Lesbian Stereotypes." Pp. 491–93 in *Encyclopedia of Gender and Society*, vol. 1. Edited by Jodi O'Brien. Thousand Oaks, Calif.: Sage.

Weichselbaumer, Doris. 2003. "Sexual Orientation Discrimination in Hiring." *Labour Economics* 10:629–42.

Woods, James. 1993. *The Corporate Closet: The Professional Lives of Gay Men in America.* New York: Free Press.

ENDA's End Game: Why Workplace Protections for LGBT People Are a Necessary Step

J. Jennings Moss

I should consider myself fortunate. I've never been discriminated against because I'm a gay man. [I] have never lost out on a job because of my sexual orientation, nor been passed over for promotion. And this is coming from someone who, earlier in my career, worked for two of the most conservative media organizations out there—*The Washington Times* and Fox News.

That last paragraph used the word "should" on purpose. I was brought up to believe that hard work, a can-do attitude, a willingness to come in early and stay late, a genuine passion for the job, and hopefully some talent are what's really important. If I didn't get a particular job, than my prospective employers either found someone better or, at least, someone they thought was a better fit for the spot. If I didn't get a promotion, then I had to decide why I got passed over and make my own call on whether to stay or not.

I find myself going back through my employment history . . . as the Senate takes up ENDA, the Employment Non-Discrimination Act, a measure that would prohibit workplace discrimination because of sexual orientation or gender identity. The measure, which has been introduced in every Congress except one since 1994, would apply to most businesses with at least 15 employees. In effect, it would add sexual orientation and gender identity to the list of classes given protection by the Civil Rights Act of 1964—race, ethnicity, gender, national and religious minorities.

The intent of ENDA certainly is noble, but is it needed? Or . . . is it just a burden on small business? The vast majority of Fortune 500 companies[1] today have self-declared that they don't discriminate on the basis of sexual orientation. Yet, the Williams Institute—a UCLA School of Law think tank that focuses on sexual orientation issues—reports that anywhere from 15 to 43 percent of LGBT workers[2] said they had experienced being fired, harassed or passed over for promotions. Another survey by the PEW Foundation put the figure at 21 percent. Those are really staggering findings, which I have to believe are disproportionately felt on groups other than mine (i.e., college-educated white guys). The numbers here bear this out: another Williams study from 2011 looking into the experiences of transgendered people found that 78 percent reported some type of workplace discrimination because of their gender identity.

The reality of legislation like ENDA is that it's not there really for people like me. Nor is it there for the new economy companies . . . led by entrepreneurs who tend to be looking for real talent and measurable results (that's not to say tech-focused companies don't have their challenges, especially when it comes to expanding the ranks of women on their rosters). But ENDA is important for others: that gay teenager who is venturing into the workplace for the first time, that lesbian mom who doesn't want to hide the fact her partner is another woman when talk about family vacations comes up, and especially that person who comes to terms with the fact they've been living under the wrong gender sign and now need to be honest about who they really are.

ENDA won't wipe away discrimination. It won't make those who oppose lesbians, gays, bisexuals and transgendered individuals want to invite them over for dinner. But it will, hopefully, keep everyone a little more honest about the conversation.

NOTES

1. Human Rights Campaign. 2013. Corporate Equality Index 2013: Rating American Workplaces on Lesbian, Gay, Bisexual and Transgender Equality. http://www.hrc.org/files/assets/resources/CorporateEqualityIndex_2013.pdf
2. The Williams Institute. 2013. Employment Discrimination against LGBT Workers. http://williamsinstitute.law.ucla.edu/headlines/research-on-lgbt-workplace-protections/

The Case against Racial Colorblindness in the Workplace

CARMEN NOBEL

Although racial colorblindness may seem like a laudable goal, Nobel discusses research and policy that indicate the approach of ignoring racial differences in the workplace may not be the best decision. Different levels of support for affirmative action and belief in the existence of discrimination can influence individuals' support for diversity in the workplace, and attempting to ignore racial difference can create awkward and damaging working environments. Nobel argues that organizations should highlight multiculturalism rather than racial colorblindness.

In trying to prevent discrimination and prejudice, many companies adopt a strategy of "colorblindness"—actively trying to ignore racial differences when enacting policies and making organizational decisions. The logic is simple: if we don't even notice race, then we can't act in a racist manner. The problem is that most of us naturally do notice each other's racial differences, regardless of our employer's policy.

"It's so appealing on the surface to think that the best way to approach race is to pretend that it doesn't exist," says behavioral psychologist Michael I. Norton, an associate professor at Harvard Business School. "But research shows that it simply doesn't work. We do notice race, and there's no way of getting around this fact." Several studies by Norton and his colleagues show that attempting to overcome prejudice by ignoring race is an ineffective strategy that—in many cases—only serves to perpetuate bias. In short, bending over backward to ignore race can exacerbate rather than solve issues of race in the workplace.

"Umm, He Has Pants"

In efforts to be politically correct, people often avoid mentioning race when describing a person, even if that person's race is the most obvious descriptor. (Comedian Stephen Colbert often poke[d] fun of this tendency on his TV show, The Colbert Report, claiming that he . . . [didn't] "see color.") If a manager, for example, is asked which guy Fred is, he or she may be loath to say, "Fred's Asian," even if Fred is the only Asian person in the company. "Instead, it's, 'He's that nice man who works in operations, and, umm, he has hair, and, umm, he has pants,'" Norton says. "And it keeps going on until finally someone comes out and asks, 'Oh, is he Asian?'"

Norton and several colleagues documented this phenomenon in a study that they described in an article for the journal *Psychological Science*,

"Color Blindness and Interracial Interaction."[1] The researchers conducted an experiment in which white participants engaged in a two-person guessing game designed—unbeknownst to them— to measure their tendencies toward attempted racial colorblindness. Each participant was given a stack of photographs, which included 32 different faces. A partner sat across from the participant, looking at one picture that matched a picture from the participant's stack. The participants were told that the goal of the game was to determine which photo the partner was holding by asking as few yes/no questions as possible— for example, "Is the person bald?"

Half the faces on the cards were black, and the other half white, so asking a yes/no question about skin color was a very efficient way to narrow down the identity of the photo on the partner's card. But the researchers found that many of the participants completely avoided asking their partners about the skin color of the person in the photograph—especially when paired with a black partner. Some 93 percent of participants with white partners mentioned race during the guessing game, as opposed to just 64 percent who were playing the game with black partners.

Backfiring Results

Two independent coders were hired to watch videos of the sessions on mute, rating the perceived friendliness of the white participants based on nonverbal cues. Alas, the participants who attempted colorblindness came across as especially unfriendly, often avoiding eye contact with their black partners. And when interviewed after the experiment, black partners reported perceiving the most racial bias among those participants who avoided mentioning race. "The impression was that if you're being so weird about not mentioning race, you probably have something to hide," Norton says.

The researchers repeated the experiment on a group of elementary school children.[2] The third graders often scored higher on the guessing game than grown-ups because, Norton says,

they weren't afraid to ask if the person in the photo was black or white. But many of the fourth and fifth graders avoided mentioning race during the game. As it turns out, racial colorblindness is a social convention that many Americans start to internalize by as young as age 10. "Very early on kids get the message that they are not supposed to acknowledge that they notice people's race—often the result of a horrified reaction from a parent when they do," Norton says.

A Zero-Sum Game?

In addition to an ineffective strategy at managing interracial interactions, racial colorblindness has evolved into an argument against affirmative action policies, an issue Norton addresses in a recent working paper, "Racial Colorblindness: Emergence, Practice, and Implications,"[3] cowritten with Evan P. Apfelbaum of MIT and Samuel R. Sommers of Tufts University. "Though once emblematic of the fight for equal opportunity among racial minorities marginalized by openly discriminatory practices, contemporary legal arguments for colorblindness have become increasingly geared toward combating race-conscious policies," they write. "If racial minority status confers an advantage in hiring and school admissions and in the selection of voting districts and government subcontractors—the argument goes—then Whites' right for equal protection may be violated."

In a related article, "Whites See Racism as a Zero-Sum Game That They Are Now Losing," Norton and Sommers surveyed 100 white and 100 black respondents about their perceptions of racial bias in recent American history.[4] They found that black respondents reported a large decrease in antiblack bias between the 1950s and the 2000s, but perceived virtually no antiwhite bias in that same period—ever. White respondents, on the other hand, perceived a large decrease in antiblack bias over time, but also a huge increase in antiwhite bias. In fact, on average, white respondents perceive more antiwhite bias than antiblack bias in the twenty-first century. "It's very hard to find a metric that suggests that white people actually have a worse time of it than black people," Norton says. "But this perception is driving the current cultural discourse in race and affirmative action. It's not just that whites think blacks are getting some unfair breaks, it's that whites are thinking, 'I'm actually the victim of discrimination now.'"

Multiculturalism

In "Racial Colorblindness," the authors suggest that organizations might ease racial tensions among a diverse workforce by stressing multiculturalism over racial colorblindness. "Shutting our eyes to the complexities of race does not make them disappear, but it does make it harder to see that colorblindness often creates more problems than it solves," they write.

Norton points out that while many companies host "diversity days," these celebrations often focus solely on the cultures of ethnic minority employees. Excluding white employees from celebrating their cultures can breed resentment, he says, suggesting that an all-inclusive approach might work better.

"Think of having not only black people talking about being African American, but also white people talking about their Irish or Italian heritage, for instance," he says. "Research shows that in highlighting everyone's differences you can create a kind of commonality—we are *all* different, and my difference is no more or less valued than yours. Most organizations do not manage diversity in this way, however."

For organizations, supporting multiculturalism is not just about paying lip service to cultural differences, but—increasingly—also about forming a stronger team and improving performance, Norton says. He cites a recent incident in which several retired high-ranking US military leaders publicly supported a Supreme Court decision in favor of affirmative action[5] in university admissions. "Their point was that enlisted men and women were predominantly minorities, and that the military needed minority

officers who were college graduates to lead their diverse enlistees," Norton says. "Statements like these help to reframe the general notion of why developing effective strategies for managing diversity is crucial for managers. Multiculturalism is not just about feel-good sentiments. It's about organizational effectiveness."

NOTES

1. Norton, Michael I., Samuel R. Sommers, Evan P. Apfelbaum, Natassia Pura, and Dan Ariely. 2006. "Color Blindness and Interractial Interaction: Playing the Political Correctness Game." *Psychological Science* 17(11):949–953. http://www.people.hbs.edu/mnorton/norton%20sommers%20apfelbaum%20pura%20ariely.pdf

2. Apfelbaum, Evan P., Kristin Pauker, Nalini Ambady, Samuel R. Sommers, and Michael I. Norton. 2008. "Learning (Not) to Talk about Race: When Older Children Underperform in Social Categorization." *Developmental Psychology* 44(5):1513–1518. http://www.people.hbs.edu/mnorton/apfelbaum%20et%20al%202008.pdf

3. Apfelbaum, Evan P., Michael I. Norton, and Samuel R. Sommers. 2012. "Racial Color Blindness: Emergence, Practice, and Implications." *Current Directions in Psychological Science.* 21(3):205–209. http://www.people.hbs.edu/mnorton/apfelbaum%20norton%20sommers.pdf

4. Norton, Michael I., and Samuel R. Sommers. 2011. "Whites See Racism and a Zero-Sum Game That They Are Now Losing." *Perspectives on Psychological Science.* 6(3):215–218. http://www.people.hbs.edu/mnorton/norton%20sommers.pdf

5. Americans for a Fair Chance. 2003. "Military Leaders Speak out in Favor of Affirmative Action." *The Leadership Conference.* http://www.civilrights.org/press/2003/military-leaders-speak-out-in-favor-of-affirmative-action.html

■ What's in a Name? Discrimination

Erin Thomas Echols

Original to Focus on Social Problems: A Contemporary Reader.

Conventional wisdom suggests that when employers want to fill a position, they always choose the best candidate—the one with the most skills, knowledge, and experience. Given this conventional wisdom, applicants pore over their resumes, checking for spelling errors and finding just the right words to represent themselves as strong candidates. But what if the thing that kept candidates from getting the job was something they wouldn't change? Researchers have found that, long before an employer sees your employment history, your skills, or where you graduated from, something else may help determine which resumes make it to the callback pile and which land among the rejects—your name.

In one study, researchers sent out resumes to 1,300 job postings in Boston and Chicago. For each ad they sent four resumes—two of higher quality and two of lower quality. The only other difference in the resumes was that one lower-quality and one higher-quality resume were assigned a "black-sounding" name, whereas the others were assigned "white-sounding" names (Bertrand and Mullainathan, 2004).[1] The researchers found that applicants with white-sounding names—like Emily and Greg—received 50 percent more callbacks for job interviews than applicants with black-sounding names—like Lakisha and Jamal. This means generally that for every 100 applications a person with a white-sounding name has to send, applicants with black-sounding names have to send 150 to have the same chance at getting called back.

The conventional wisdom about higher qualifications resulting in more callbacks did hold true, but only for some applicants. Applicants with white-sounding names and high-quality resumes received 30 percent more callbacks than applicants with white-sounding names and lower-quality resumes. But high-quality applicants with black-sounding names received only a 9 percent boost in callbacks over their lower-quality resume counterparts. Equal opportunity employers, such as federal contractors, were found to discriminate against black-sounding names at similar rates (Bertrand and Mullainathan, 2004).

Other researchers have since found even more evidence of racial/ethnic discrimination for other groups. Widner and Chicoine (2011) conducted a similar study using an Internet job site and found that resumes with Arab American names, like Shakir and Qahhar, also received 50 percent fewer callbacks for jobs compared to identical applicants with white-sounding names. The trend also persists in higher education. Researchers recently found that faculty at 259 of the United States' top universities were more likely to ignore student requests for research opportunities at the doctoral level when the requests were sent by students whose names indicated that they were racial or ethnic minorities or women. This pattern was particularly evident in higher-paying disciplines, like business, and at private universities (Milkman et al., 2015).

These studies suggest that employers and educators do not blindly hire and assist the best candidates but instead regularly discriminate against candidates based, not on their visible skin color, but on the race that is implied by their name. This discrimination means that applicants and students whose names mark them as members of racial and ethnic minority groups have fewer options to choose from when seeking employment and academic opportunities and may be dissuaded from entering higher-paying fields because of a lack of guidance from university faculty. These patterns contribute to higher levels of unemployment and poverty for members of racial and ethnic minority groups, even when they have credentials that are identical to those of white Americans. It marks a type of racial discrimination that is invisible to the victims and, thus, a challenge to address.

NOTES

1. Researchers determined distinctly black-sounding names and distinctly white-sounding names by analyzing data from birth certificates in Massachusetts from 1974 to 1979. The date range was chosen to account for the birth year of the applicants. The names that were most frequently used by one race or the other were selected as white sounding or black sounding for the experiment.

REFERENCES

Bertrand, Marianne, and Sendhil Mullainathan. 2004. "Are Emily and Greg More Employable than Lakisha and Jamal? A Field Experiment on Labor Market Discrimination." *The American Economic Review* 94(4): 991–1013.

Milkman, Katherine L., Akinola, Modupe, and Dolly Chugh. 2015. "What Happens Before? A Field Experiment Exploring How Pay and Representation Differentially Shape Bias on the Pathway Into Organizations." *Journal of Applied Psychology* 100(6): 1678–1712.

Widner, Daniel, and Stephen Chicoine. 2011. "It's All in the Name: Employment Discrimination Against Arab Americans." *Sociological Forum* 26(4): 806–23.

The Hands That Feed Us: Challenges and Opportunities for Workers along the Food Chain

FOOD CHAIN WORKERS ALLIANCE

As we roll our shopping carts along the aisles of our grocery stores, most Americans rarely consider the process of food production and the workers along the food chain. Based on survey data from a convenience sample of more than 600 food system workers, the Food Chain Workers Alliance directs our attention to the working conditions of the "hands that feed us."

The sustainability and prosperity of the United States food system is critical to the health and prosperity of workers, employers, and consumers nationwide. In addition to feeding the nation, the U.S. food system is a large and growing segment of the U.S. economy and an increasingly important provider of jobs. The food production, processing, distribution, retail, and service industries collectively sell over $1.8 trillion dollars in goods and services annually, accounting for over 13 percent of the United States Gross Domestic Product.[1]

Core food occupations and industries include farmworkers (production), slaughterhouse and other processing facilities workers (processing), warehouse workers (distribution), grocery store workers (retail), and restaurant and food service workers (service). While there are other workers involved in the food system, in this report we focus on these five core segments of the food chain. These particular segments employ in total approximately 20 million workers (19,980,227), who constitute one in five private sector workers and one-sixth of the nation's entire workforce. . . . Our survey data indicate that there are some livable-wage jobs in the food system. However, the vast majority of workers in the food system suffer under poverty wages and poor working conditions, with few opportunities for career mobility and little economic stability.

Data in this . . . [reading were] drawn from the Food Chain Workers Alliance's 629 surveys of food system workers, with at least 80 surveys conducted in each segment of the food chain. Worker surveyors and staff from the Alliance's member organizations approached workers outside workplaces, bus/metro stops near workplaces, religious and community centers, check-cashing businesses, and other areas where workers congregate in their community, as well as at the workers' homes. The member organizations also conducted 18 additional in-depth interviews with food system workers.

Earnings

According to our survey data, about 40 percent of jobs in the food industry provide a wage above their regional poverty line, but only 13.5 percent of jobs provide wages higher than 150 percent of the regional poverty level. In interviews, many workers also reported fluctuation with regard to their wages and hours, making it difficult to plan, pay bills, and maintain economic stability. One male farmworker reported, "More or less, we are paid $20 per box [that we fill up]. [There are 18 people in his team and they have to split that $20 per box equally.] When the cucumbers are good, we are making $100–125 a day each. We start work about seven and we're leaving maybe between three and five o'clock; we're not leaving very late right now. [We work] six days per week." In addition, several workers in the food system reported earning a "piece rate" rather than an hourly wage, making their wages dependent on their physical stamina, health, and ability to concentrate on a daily basis. One female loader/unloader at a Wal-Mart warehouse reported, "We get paid by the piece, and it depend[s] on how many pieces are on the trailer. I never made more than $200 per week." Education appeared to make little or no difference with regard to food system workers' wages. Our analysis indicates that workers with less than a high school degree earned a median hourly wage of $9.00, workers with a high school degree a median hourly wage of $9.28, and workers with some college or more earn a median hourly wage of $10.19. . . .[2]

Poverty-level wages make it difficult for most food system workers to provide for themselves and their families. According to the National Low Income Housing Coalition (NLIHC), the Fair Market Rent for a two-bedroom unit in the United States is $959. A full-time food service worker, working 40 hours per week, would have to earn $18.25 an hour to afford the two-bedroom unit.[3] Our survey data show that eight out of 10 food system workers sampled earn less than this. As one male farmworker stated, "I feel that [we] make less money now than back in the '80s. Because in the '80s, you got more money and everything was cheaper then, and now we get paid less and everything is more expensive, so the wages we earn [don't] last. Everything is going up, the gas went up, the price of food went up, the rents and . . . houses, and yet our pay rate is still the same out in the field." Workers also reported a lack of raises. Fifty-eight percent have not received a raise in the last year. One male cook at a restaurant reported, "In terms of wages, my situation is pretty bad. Maybe my wage has risen once or twice [in 15 years]. Like five or six years ago, there was a raise. . . . It was really tiny."

Hours

Perhaps not surprisingly, given how little they earn per hour, workers in the food system reported working long hours. Forty percent of workers surveyed reported working more than 40 hours per week at their primary employer. A full 10 percent reported working more than 10 hours per day, and the vast majority of those workers (who worked more than 10 hours per day) reported working 60 or more hours per week. Almost half of the workers also reported working multiple jobs to make ends meet. Forty-two percent of workers work more than 40 hours per week at two or more employers, and 11 percent of workers report working 60 or more hours per week at two or more employers.

Benefits

Workers in the food system reported not having access to benefits that would allow them to care for themselves and their families when sick or injured. Sixty percent of food system workers reported not having paid sick days, and an additional 19 percent reported not even knowing if they had paid sick days. Only 21 percent of all workers surveyed confirmed that they had paid sick days. In addition, 58 percent of food system workers surveyed reported having no access to health care coverage. Only 17 percent reported having health insurance through their employer. . . . One quarter of all workers surveyed (25%) reported having no transportation to get to medical appointments and treatment.

Given their lack of health benefits, more than half of all the workers we surveyed (53%) reported having worked while sick, and these workers reported having worked while sick for a median of three days. Among workers who worked while sick, almost two-thirds (65%) reported having done so due to a lack of paid sick days. Forty three percent thought they would lose their job, and seven percent chose to work while sick because they had been threatened by an employer. As one male farmworker stated, "There have been days where people have not worked because of the pain [from working every day]. Sometimes they ask for a day off, and the boss doesn't want to [give it to them]. Sometimes they decide not to go to work, and they risk getting fired." A male meatpacking worker stated, "We don't have sick days. We have to call if we get sick or we're not going to come in . . . they will still subtract some points from us for not coming in. If I get sick, I probably [work] three days in a row. I'll still work or I'll sweat it out or work it out or something. I also got sick from my kidneys—I was getting a fever on and off, having a hard time breathing. I held on to the pain as long as I could. I was supposed to come to work on that Saturday. I finished the shift [on] Friday. I didn't get out of the hospital for a week. And I didn't have my badge so I couldn't call, since I was at the hospital. But my wife called . . . that Monday. When she went to go pick up my check, they said I was . . . almost fired."

Several workers reported that having to work while sick prolonged their illness, particularly since they were working in extreme temperatures intended to ensure food safety. Another male meatpacker stated, "I've lasted up to a month, more than a month sick, and that's how someone has to go to work . . . it's difficult because where we work, it's cold. You breathe

the cold, and you take longer to get better." The lack of paid sick days creates financial strain and job insecurity for most food system workers. Many workers run the risk of being fired when they are too ill to report for work. A male line cook in a restaurant described his experience going to work sick five to six days per year. "We don't have paid sick days. In the winter, I had a lot of colds, my throat closed, a fever, a headache. I had to work like that one day. Then I called to say that I wasn't going to work, but they said they would punish me because no one could take my place. They almost fired me, but I felt so bad but couldn't work so I didn't go in. [One time] when I was sick, I didn't go to work for three days. When I got my check, it was only $100 and I had to pay rent that day, which is $300—I couldn't buy food or my Metro card." Finally, a female warehouse worker stated, "I had no sick days. [I] went to work sick a lot. If you wanted to take any time off, they said you wouldn't have a job when you came back."

Lack of Mobility and Training Opportunities

Low wages and lack of benefits are compounded for workers in the food system by the general lack of opportunity to advance to higher-paying positions in their segment of the food chain, or to obtain training that would allow them to advance. Unfortunately, many workers did not even receive training for the job they were currently doing. Almost one third of workers (32%) did not receive any training at the start of their job, and 16 percent reported that their training was inadequate. Almost three quarters (74%) reported never having been given the opportunity to apply for a better job at their current employer, and 81 percent reported never receiving a promotion.

Unfortunately, even in segments of the food chain where there are potential career paths to livable wage jobs, workers experience little upward mobility. As one male cook at a restaurant stated, "You know, us cooks, people who work in the kitchen, we're all just cooks. There's no such thing as promotion. There's just hard work." In addition, workers reported that there is often no formalized process by which to apply, leaving promotions to the arbitrary decisions of management. As one female stocker at a Wal-Mart reported, "There's no training. It's just if they like you, or you're a friend or a family member of someone in management, then you go up. But if you challenge what they say, you're on the blacklist; you can't be promoted, even if you have the knowledge. There's an exam that you have to take. The exam's on the computer. I was taking it with someone they like. He can't even read and write. They're helping him pass it because he's the one that they want. We were sitting down—[I saw] managers help give him the answers. So, after that, I didn't request it anymore because it's not really open for anyone; it's open for certain people they want."

Employment Law Violations

Several workers we surveyed reported experiencing wage theft and other violations of their employment rights under federal and state employment laws. Almost one-quarter of all workers surveyed (23%) reported not receiving the minimum wage. More than one third (36%) reported experiencing within the previous week some form of wage theft, which can include not receiving proper payment for all hours worked, not receiving overtime payments, tip misappropriation, and more.[4] Average weekly wage theft experienced by workers ranged from $25.93 in restaurant and food services to $48.49 in food processing, distribution, and packing-houses.

Wage theft was highest among Black workers. However, Black workers were also concentrated in warehouse, where wage theft was highest. Black workers experienced 76 percent of cases of wage theft in warehouse, where they represented 76 percent of the workforce. Latino and Indigenous workers experienced 100 percent of the cases of wage theft on farms and nurseries and were 100 percent of the workforce in those sectors. Latinos experienced much higher rates of wage theft in grocery retail (79%), where they comprised

53 percent of the surveys sampled. Black and Latino workers experienced comparable rates of wage theft in restaurants (41% and 36%), but Latinos comprised 52 percent of restaurant workers compared to 29 percent of Black workers.

In interviews, workers earning piece rate or production rate wages reported not making the minimum wage. One male warehouse worker reported, "They pay by production rate, which means for each 5,000 boxes you move off this truck, this truck is only worth $62. There is no way you can finish a 5,000-box truck in eight hours. So that means by my production rate, I'm working eight hours per day for a $62 [truck]. And then I come back tomorrow, and I still gotta work this truck. And it is still the [same] $62. So I am working today for free, basically. Seven hours for free for this day."

Workers also complained about the shaving of hours and lack of overtime. A male stocker working in food services (cafeteria) reported, "I know other co-workers would punch out for their [lunch] break" so it would look like they had taken their lunch break, which the employer is required in some states to provide by law. "But then [my co-workers would] continue working because . . . if they took a break, they would get behind [in their work.] Then at the end of 30 minutes, they would punch back in and keep working." Another male cook in a restaurant complained, "I work 12 hours every day, five days, and half a day on Saturday [= 66 hours per week]. I don't get overtime because we get set wages. Working in this restaurant, there's no overtime pay, and our pay is not calculated by the day or hour. It's a set wage. . . . I earn $500 each week."

Finally, child labor, which can be a violation of federal employment law, is unfortunately not a thing of the past in the food system. More than one in ten (12%) food workers we surveyed reported that minors under the age of 18 worked in their workplace. Although employing minors is not always a violation of law, this statistic indicates that there are significant numbers of youth in the workforce. From young children working alongside their parents picking fruits and vegetables to under-age youth utilizing dangerous instruments in hot restaurant kitchens, minors are helping to provide our nation's food supply, according to workers surveyed.

Meal and Rest Breaks

The ability to take lunch and other short breaks can be important to food service workers, who work long, arduous hours harvesting, preparing, and serving the nation's food, and to consumers of this food. Furthermore, breaks are mandated by law in several states. Of the states in which workers were surveyed, only California and Minnesota require breaks. Minnesota workers surveyed always received 10-minute breaks, compared to less than half of California workers. In most other states, a majority of workers did not always receive breaks.

Regardless of whether they are mandated by law, the high number of food service workers not receiving breaks indicates the arduous nature of the jobs. Almost one-quarter of all food workers surveyed (22%) reported not always receiving a 30-minute lunch break when they worked an eight-hour day, and almost one in 10 (8%) reported never receiving this break. Twenty-two percent of workers reported not receiving 10-minute breaks at all, and another 28 percent reported that they do not always receive 10-minute breaks. As one female Wal-Mart worker reported, "Some don't take it [a break] because they have so much work to do. Managers see . . . that they don't take breaks. They pretend they don't know, but they know about it."

Health and Safety

Given their direct contact with the nation's food supply, food system workers' health and safety should be of great concern to all consumers. However, food system workers reported working in high-risk environments, and that accidents and injuries in food harvesting, processing, distribution, retail, and service environments were frequent.

More than half of all workers surveyed (52%) reported that they did not receive health and safety training from their employers. Almost one-third of all food system workers (32.7%) reported that their employers did not always provide necessary equipment to do their jobs, and 5.7 percent reported that their employer never provided necessary equipment. More than one in 10 workers (11.7%) reported being required to do something that put their own safety at risk. One example of such high-risk work is exposure to toxic chemicals, from pesticides for farmworkers to oven-cleaning chemicals for restaurant workers. Almost one-quarter (23%) of all workers surveyed reported regularly coming into contact with such dangerous chemicals.

Another example of high-risk work is unsafe equipment. As one male meatpacking worker reported, "I got hurt one time [because] the railing on the machine was not welded completely. [It] was not closed right so as I was pushing the meat in. I missed, and I kinda fell off the railing and hit the corner of the machine. It knocked the air out of me and knocked me to the floor. After somebody got hurt, they fixed the situation. They made us run a machine where the safety controls weren't properly hooked up. I had to unscrew the machines in order for me to get the blade out. I'm working with the blade really sharp and with the safety disconnected."

In interviews, workers also reported that exposure to extreme temperatures intended to preserve food safety resulted in regular illness. One male meat-processing worker reported, "I realized that in the room that I'm working in, it's almost like a refrigerator—it's really cold, like 10 degrees or below. The sausage is already cooked and packed and ready to be shipped, so it has to be kept under refrigeration. The first couple of days you really aren't used to the cold. Your feet get numb, your hands get numb, your whole body starts aching because of the cold—I mean you wear gloves, they give you gloves, but you can still feel the cold because you're touching the product in the freezer—and of course you get cold. First week you're there, you're not used to it. First week you're there, you have to get sick. You have to catch a cold—it's mandatory that you have to get sick because no one's used to being cold for eight hours at a time and we only get a 30-minute break." At the other extreme, farmworkers and kitchen workers report being exposed to extreme heat. As one male farmworker reported, "When it passes 100 degrees Fahrenheit, that's when you feel you can't take it no more. [Some workers] can't continue [working] because they can't stop vomiting because they drink too much water since it's too hot. The arm, you can't move it for the same reason that you are tired or sometimes your foot or sometimes all your body too. Even if [the boss] sees that a person can't work anymore because of the heat or because they feel sick because of the heat, he doesn't stop the [other] people [from working]. Instead, he just brings another person to replace the worker. [Harvesting asparagus], the hardest part is when it's wet, when it's raining, the people don't have good support on the ground because they slip."

In addition, across the food system, workers are exposed to repetitive stress on muscles and joints. As one female line worker at a poultry processing plant stated, "The lines are running super fast, and yet they say that they're planning to make them even faster. ... We can't work harder than a machine, and they want us to be working more than a machine can, and we don't want to work that way because we are the ones getting hurt—our muscles, hands, fingers. Here I have something hard forming [on my thumb] like a bump, and I barely have a year working here. I went to the nurse because it hurts and itches, and all she told me was to put tape [on it] and with that it won't get as big."

Given these high-risk conditions in food system workplaces, it is not surprising that a vast majority of food workers surveyed reported suffering accidents, injuries, and illnesses on the job. Fifty-seven percent of workers reported suffering an injury or health problems while working. In these cases, of the workers who reported to their employer such an injury or illness, only 28.8 percent of workers stated that they received free medical care from their employer. In many cases, these accidents and injuries can result in lasting, sometimes permanent bodily damage. As one female Wal-Mart worker, an overnight stocker, described, "I have hurt my back. I was pulling a pallet of [beverage supplements]. ... Suddenly I was wondering why my leg was hurting. I told my manager that I had to go to the hospital because I didn't feel good. I was in the pharmacy department so I checked my blood pressure and it was really high because I was in pain. So I went, and they say it was just a bursitis. That bursitis never went away for six months ... when they try to push you more with your pain, and every time I go down on the floor, [I have pain]—because you have to stock from the floor up—so I asked them to take me to the doctor ... for three days I was asking for it. Finally they did ... I went to a specialist, and they sent me for an MRI, and I have an L-4/L-5 herniated disc. And now, the recommendation of their own doctor is to have surgery. It's over a year. At first, they gave me shots to see if I get better. It's not going to get better—just two months the pain went away, but it came back again and so [I] have to get surgery. [Workers' compensation insurance] denied it so now we are on appeal." This particular worker attributes her severe injury to the lack of proper health and safety training. "At the beginning, we had training—there was somebody who showed you how to use box cutters, how to lift, the proper technique. They did away with that. There's no more training coordinators. They use the computers for you to go in and hurry up and pass the lesson, the module, so they can have some kind of paperwork for them that you've been trained by a computer."

Turnover

The poor wages and working conditions suffered by workers across the food system, as described in this . . . [reading], have an impact on the length of time workers reported staying at a current job. Employee turnover can present tremendous challenges for both workers and employers. For workers, regular movement from job to job creates economic instability, and for employers, high rates of turnover impose tangible costs such as screening, hiring, and re-training costs, and intangible costs such as a lessened employee morale and loyalty. A recent report by the Restaurant Opportunities Centers United, based on interviews and focus groups with restaurant employers nationwide, indicated that restaurant employers were well aware of the cost of turnover and of the relationship between employee wages and working conditions and their willingness to stay on the job. This relationship was also borne out in our surveys of workers throughout the food system.

In the Food Chain Workers Alliance survey data, we noted a correlation between working conditions and length of time on the job. Workers who stayed at one place for longer periods of time were less likely to report experiencing wage theft. Almost one-third of all workers (30.9%) who stayed on the job for less than a year reported wage theft, whereas only 11 percent of the workers who stayed between 10 and 20 years reported wage theft. Frequency of reported wage theft generally decreased the length of time that workers stayed on the job. In general, workers who experienced wage theft stayed on the job a median of 3.5 years, while those who did not stayed on the job a median of 5.12 years. Thus, workers who do not experience wage theft seem far more likely to stay at one job in the food system.

NOTES

1. 2007 U.S. Economic Census for total sales for NAICS codes 311, 722, and 445, and <http://www.agcensus.usda.gov/Publications/2007/Full_Report/Volume_1,_Chapter_1_US/st99_1_001_001.pdf>: Agriculture = $297,220,491,000, Food Manufacturing = $589,580,258,000, Food and Beverage Stores = $541,202,096,000, Food Service = $432,905,044,000; Gross Domestic Product or Expenditure, 2007 = $14.0742 trillion, <http://www.infoplease.com/ipa/A0104575.html>

2. About one-third of the surveyed workers were able to report their gross pay amount for their previous full week of work. Two-thirds were only able to report their net pay amount for their previous full week of work. We therefore calculated their gross annual pay in the following manner: Each of these worker's annual net pay was then calculated based on the weekly net pay amount. To calculate each worker's annual tax rate, we determined their projected income tax rate based on the annual net pay calculation. To calculate the projected income tax rate, we added the state rate, the federal rate based on income, and the FICA tax rate, based on their marital status. To determine each worker's weekly tax rate, we divided the annual tax rate by 52 (weeks). We added the weekly tax rate to the annual weekly net pay calculation to obtain each worker's gross annual pay. Wage groups were then created using the worker's state minimum wage and the 2011 Lower Living Standard Income Level (LLSIL) for a family of three. The LLSIL was determined for each survey based on which region of the country the state/district is located in: Northeast, Midwest, South or West. The annual LLSIL for a family of three in the four regions is $31,900 (Northeast), $28.169 (Midwest), $27,140 (South) and $30,718 (West). All the surveys except for those conducted in Missouri were determined to be within metropolitan areas. Poverty is considered less than or equal to 70 percent of the LLSIL for a given region. A livable wage is considered 150 percent of the LLSIL for a given region, and low wage is simply the category between the poverty level and the livable wage level.

3. National Low Income Housing Coalition. "Out of Reach 2012: America's Forgotten Housing Crisis." Washington, DC: National Low Income Housing Coalition, 2012: 3.
4. To calculate wage theft, we measured gross earnings during the previous week and compared to gross earnings due (either by hourly rate or minimum wage, accounting for all hours worked including overtime). Wage theft was the difference between actual gross earnings and the earnings due. This figure did not account for wage theft due to lack of breaks. This figure excludes individuals who did not report number of hours worked.

Why U.S. Taxpayers Pay $7 Billion a Year to Help Fast-Food Workers

Allison Aubrey

If you hit the drive-through, chances are that the cashier who rings you up or the cook who prepared your food relies on public assistance to make ends meet. A new analysis finds that 52 percent of fast-food workers are enrolled in, or have their families enrolled in, one or more public assistance programs such as SNAP (food stamps) Medicaid or the Children's Health Insurance Program (CHIP). That's right: With a median wage of $8.69 per hour for front-line fast-food jobs—cooks, cashiers and crew—workers are taking home a paycheck, but it's not enough to cover the basics, according to the authors of "Fast Food, Poverty Wages."[1]

"The taxpayer costs we discovered were staggering," says co-author Ken Jacobs of the Center for Labor Research and Education at the University of California, Berkeley. "The combination of low wages, meager benefits and often part-time hours means that many of the families of fast-food workers have to rely on taxpayer-funded safety net programs to make ends meet," Jacobs told me by phone.

The report finds that the fast-food industry's low wages, combined with part-time hours and lack of health care benefits, creates demand for public assistance including $3.9 billion per year in Medicaid and Children's Health Insurance Program (CHIP) benefits. Add on another billion for the Supplemental Nutrition Assistance Program (SNAP), formerly known as food stamp assistance. Earned Income Tax Credit payments (a subsidy to low-wage workers) amount to about $1.95 billion per year.

Contrary to the assumption that the typical fast-food worker is a teenager living with his or her parents, the report finds that the vast majority of front-line fast-food workers are adults who are supporting themselves—"and 68 percent are the main wage earners in their families," Marc Doussard of the University of Illinois at Urbana–Champaign, a co-author of the paper, says in a press release[2] about the study. He says about a quarter of those working these jobs in fast-food restaurants are parents supporting children at home. The report was funded by Fast Food Forward,[3] a group campaigning for higher wages.

The analysis comes as a campaign for $15 per hour wages has garnered significant attention around the country. Over the past year, workers in cities nationwide have temporarily walked off their jobs to protest low wages. But some more conservative-leaning economists say raising wages would do nothing to curtail the taxpayer spending on public assistance programs. "I don't think raising the minimum wage to $15 an hour would solve that problem," Michael Strain, a resident scholar at the

continues

◼ Continued

American Enterprise Institute, told me during a phone interview. He describes himself as a center-right economist. Strain says raising wages to that level would have unintended consequences: Namely, fast-food companies would slow down their hiring. And this would lead to more workers looking for jobs—and potentially needing to rely on more public assistance.

Strain says the $7 billion taxpayer bill is not necessarily problematic. "I think the system seems to be working the way it is—not that it's working perfectly," he says, adding, "In general, the government is making sure these people's basic needs are met, which is an appropriate role of government." At the same time, Strain argues, fast-food businesses are paying their workers wages that they judge to be equal to the value these workers are adding to the production process.

"If we were to raise the minimum wage to $15 an hour, I think most economists, including me, would argue that that would result in a lot fewer workers," since fast-food companies would slow down on hiring. Ken Jacobs disagrees. "I think there's very good evidence on what's happened when wages have been improved for low-wage and fast-food workers," Jacobs says. He points to a fast-food company, In-N-Out Burger, as an example of an employer that pays higher-than-average wages, yet is still profitable.

And, Jacobs says, some municipalities are raising minimum wages, such as San Jose, Calif., where the minimum wage . . . increase[d] to $10.15 per hour[4] in January of 2014 [and to $10.30 per hour in January

of 2015]. And there are proposals in states including Maryland[5] to phase in hourly minimum wage hikes as well. Jacobs argues that it's possible that employers may see a small decline in profits, but when wages are raised, "you do find a significant decline in turnover [of workers], which is cost-saving for employers."

NOTES

1. Allegretto, Sylvia A., Marc Doussard, Dave Graham-Squire, Ken Jacobs, Dan Thompson, and Jeremy Thompson. 2013. "Fast Food, Poverty Wages: The Public Cost of Low-Wage Jobs in the Fast-Food Industry." *UC Berkeley Labor Center.* http://laborcenter.berkeley.edu/fast-food-poverty-wages-the-public-cost-of-low-wage-jobs-in-the-fast-food-industry/

2. Maclay, Kathleen. 2013. "Low-wage fast-food jobs leave hefty tax bill, report says." *UC Berkeley News Center.* http://newscenter.berkeley.edu/2013/10/15/low-wage-fast-food-jobs-leave-hefty-tax-bill-report-says/

3. http://strikefastfood.org/

4. "Minimum Wage Ordinance." http://www.sanjoseca.gov/?nid=3491

5. Wagner, John. 2013. "Democrats' movement to raise minimum wage gains speed as election year looms." *The Washington Post.* http://www.washingtonpost.com/local/md-politics/md-democrats-movement-to-raise-minimum-wage-gains-speed-as-election-year-looms/2013/09/03/1a41cb3a-1180-11e3-bdf6-e4fc677d94a1_story.html

In China, Human Costs Are Built Into an iPad

CHARLES DUHIGG AND DAVID BARBOZA

Worker safety is an issue in many different countries, but increasing attention is being paid to the working conditions for those overseas who make and assemble the products we use every day. In this reading, Duhigg and Barboza discuss the manufacturing conditions of a ubiquitous product—the Apple iPad—and how corporations have the ability to control worker safety through their company policies, codes of conduct, and profit-sharing plans. Until consumers demand products made under safe conditions, they state, there is little incentive for companies to alter the conditions under which their employees work.

The explosion ripped through Building A5 on a Friday evening [in May 2011] . . . an eruption of fire and noise that twisted metal pipes as if they were discarded straws. When workers in the cafeteria ran outside, they saw black smoke pouring from shattered windows. It came from the area where employees polished thousands of iPad cases a day. Two people were killed immediately, and over a dozen others hurt. As the injured were rushed into ambulances, one in particular stood out. His features had been smeared by the blast, scrubbed by heat and violence until a mat of red and black had replaced his mouth and nose.

"Are you Lai Xiaodong's father?" a caller asked when the phone rang at Mr. Lai's childhood home. Six months earlier, the 22-year-old had moved to Chengdu, in southwest China, to become one of the millions of human cogs powering the largest, fastest and most sophisticated manufacturing system on earth. That system has made it possible for Apple and hundreds of other companies to build devices almost as quickly as they can be dreamed up. "He's in trouble," the caller told Mr. Lai's father. "Get to the hospital as soon as possible."

In the last decade, Apple has become one of the mightiest, richest and most successful companies in the world, in part by mastering global manufacturing. Apple and its high-technology peers—as well as dozens of other American industries—have achieved a pace of innovation nearly unmatched in modern history. However, the workers assembling iPhones, iPads and other devices often labor in harsh conditions, according to employees inside those plants, worker advocates and documents published by companies themselves. Problems are as varied as onerous work environments and serious—sometimes deadly—safety problems. Employees work excessive overtime, in some cases seven days a week, and live in crowded dorms. Some say they stand so long that their legs swell until they can hardly walk. Under-age workers have helped build Apple's products, and the company's suppliers have improperly disposed of hazardous waste and falsified records, according to company reports and advocacy groups that, within China, are often considered reliable, independent monitors.

More troubling, the groups say, is some suppliers' disregard for workers' health. . . . [In 2010], 137 workers at an Apple supplier in eastern China were injured after they were ordered to use a poisonous chemical to clean iPhone screens. Within seven months . . . [in 2011], two explosions at iPad factories, including in Chengdu, killed four people and injured 77. Before those blasts, Apple had been alerted to hazardous conditions inside the Chengdu plant, according to a Chinese group that published that warning.[1] "If Apple was warned, and didn't act, that's reprehensible," said Nicholas Ashford, a former chairman of the National Advisory Committee on Occupational Safety and Health, a group that advises the United States Labor Department. "But what's morally repugnant in one country is accepted business practices in another, and companies take advantage of that."

Apple is not the only electronics company doing business within a troubling supply system. Bleak working conditions have been documented at factories manufacturing products for Dell, Hewlett-Packard, I.B.M., Lenovo, Motorola, Nokia, Sony, Toshiba and others. Current and former Apple executives, moreover, say the company has made significant strides in improving factories in recent years. Apple has a supplier code of conduct that details standards on labor issues, safety protections and other topics. The company has mounted a vigorous auditing campaign, and when abuses are discovered, Apple says, corrections are demanded.

. . . But significant problems remain. More than half of the suppliers audited by Apple have violated at least one aspect of the code of conduct every year . . . [between 2007 and 2012], according to Apple's reports, and in some instances have violated the law. While many violations involve working conditions, rather than safety hazards, troubling patterns persist. "Apple never cared about anything other than increasing product quality and decreasing production cost," said Li Mingqi, who until April [2011] worked in management at Foxconn Technology, one of Apple's most important manufacturing partners. Mr. Li, who is suing Foxconn over his dismissal, helped manage the Chengdu factory where the explosion occurred. "Workers' welfare has nothing to do with their interests," he said.

Some former Apple executives say there is an unresolved tension within the company: executives want to improve conditions within factories, but that dedication falters when it conflicts with crucial supplier relationships or the fast delivery of new products. . . . [In the first quarter of 2012], Apple reported one of the most lucrative quarters of any corporation in history, with $13.06 billion in profits on $46.3 billion in sales.[2] Its sales would have been even higher, executives said, if overseas factories had been able to produce more. Executives at other corporations report similar internal pressures. This system may not be pretty, they argue, but a radical overhaul would slow innovation. Customers want amazing new electronics delivered every year.

"We've known about labor abuses in some factories for four years, and they're still going on," said one former Apple executive who, like others, spoke on the condition of anonymity because of confidentiality agreements. "Why? Because the system works for us. Suppliers would change everything tomorrow if Apple told them they didn't have another choice." "If half of iPhones were malfunctioning, do you think Apple would let it go on for four years?" the executive asked.

Apple, in its published reports, has said it requires every discovered labor violation to be remedied, and suppliers that refuse are terminated. Privately, however, some former executives concede that finding new suppliers is time-consuming and costly. Foxconn is one of the few manufacturers in the world with the scale to build sufficient numbers of iPhones and iPads. So Apple is "not going to leave Foxconn and they're not going to leave China," said Heather White, a research fellow at Harvard and a former member of the Monitoring International Labor Standards committee at the National Academy of Sciences. "There's a lot of rationalization."

Apple was provided with extensive summaries of this article, but the company declined to comment. The reporting is based on interviews with more than three dozen current or former employees and contractors, including a half-dozen current or former executives with firsthand knowledge of Apple's supplier responsibility group, as well as others within the technology industry.

In 2010, Steven P. Jobs discussed the company's relationships with suppliers at an industry conference.[3] "I actually think Apple does one of the best jobs of any companies in our industry, and maybe in any industry, of understanding the working conditions in our supply chain," said Mr. Jobs, who was Apple's chief executive at the time and who died [in October 2011]. . . . "I mean, you go to this place, and, it's a factory, but, my gosh, I mean, they've got restaurants and movie theaters and hospitals and swimming pools, and I mean, for a factory, it's a pretty nice factory." Others, including workers inside such plants, acknowledge the cafeterias and medical facilities, but insist conditions are punishing. "We're trying really hard to make things better," said one former Apple executive. "But most people would still be really disturbed if they saw where their iPhone comes from."

The Road to Chengdu

In the fall of 2010, about six months before the explosion in the iPad factory, Lai Xiaodong carefully wrapped his clothes around his college diploma, so it wouldn't crease in his suitcase. He told friends he would no longer be around for their weekly poker games, and said goodbye to his teachers. He was leaving for Chengdu, a city of 12 million that was rapidly becoming one of the world's most important manufacturing hubs.

. . . Factories in Chengdu manufacture products for hundreds of companies. But Mr. Lai was focused on Foxconn Technology, China's largest exporter and one of the nation's biggest employers, with 1.2 million workers. The company has plants throughout China, and assembles an estimated 40 percent of the world's consumer electronics, including for customers like Amazon, Dell, Hewlett-Packard, Nintendo, Nokia and Samsung. Foxconn's factory in Chengdu, Mr. Lai knew, was special. Inside, workers were building Apple's latest, potentially greatest product: the iPad.

When Mr. Lai finally landed a job repairing machines at the plant, one of the first things he noticed were the almost blinding lights. Shifts ran 24 hours a day, and the factory was always bright. At any moment, there were thousands of workers standing on assembly lines or sitting in backless chairs, crouching next to large machinery, or jogging between loading bays. Some workers' legs swelled so much they waddled. "It's hard to stand all day," said Zhao Sheng, a plant worker.

Banners on the walls warned the 120,000 employees: "Work hard on the job today or work hard to find a job tomorrow." Apple's supplier code of conduct dictates that, except in unusual circumstances, employees are not supposed to work more than 60 hours a week. But at Foxconn, some worked more, according to interviews, workers' pay stubs and surveys by outside groups. Mr. Lai was soon spending 12 hours a day, six days a week inside the factory, according to his paychecks. Employees who arrived late were sometimes required to write confession letters and copy quotations. There were "continuous shifts," when workers were told to work two stretches in a row, according to interviews.

Mr. Lai's college degree enabled him to earn a salary of around $22 a day, including overtime—more than many others. When his days ended, he would retreat to a small bedroom just big enough for a mattress, wardrobe and a desk. ... Those accommodations were better than many of the company's dorms, where 70,000 Foxconn workers lived, at times stuffed 20 people to a three-room apartment, employees said. Last year, a dispute over paychecks set off a riot in one of the dormitories, and workers started throwing bottles, trash cans and flaming paper from their windows, according to witnesses. Two hundred police officers wrestled with workers, arresting eight. Afterward, trash cans were removed, and piles of rubbish—and rodents—became a problem. Mr. Lai felt lucky to have a place of his own.

Foxconn, in a statement, disputed workers' accounts of continuous shifts, extended overtime, crowded living accommodations and the causes of the riot. The company said that its operations adhered to customers' codes of conduct, industry standards and national laws. "Conditions at Foxconn are anything but harsh," the company wrote. Foxconn also said that it had never been cited by a customer or government for under-age or overworked employees or toxic exposures. "All assembly line employees are given regular breaks, including one-hour lunch breaks," the company wrote, and only 5 percent of assembly line workers are required to stand to carry out their tasks. Work stations have been designed to ergonomic standards, and employees have opportunities for job rotation and promotion, the statement said. "Foxconn has a very good safety record," the company wrote. "Foxconn has come a long way in our efforts to lead our industry in China in areas such as workplace conditions and the care and treatment of our employees."

Apple's Code of Conduct

In 2005, some of Apple's top executives gathered inside their Cupertino, Calif., headquarters for a special meeting. Other companies had created codes of conduct to police their suppliers. It was time, Apple decided, to follow suit. The code Apple published that year demands "that working conditions in Apple's supply chain are safe, that workers are treated with respect and dignity, and that manufacturing processes are environmentally responsible."

But the next year, a British newspaper, *The Mail on Sunday*, secretly visited a Foxconn factory in Shenzhen, China, where iPods were manufactured, and reported on workers' long hours, push-ups meted out as punishment and crowded dorms.[4] Executives in Cupertino were shocked. "Apple is filled with really good people who had no idea this was going on," a former employee said. "We wanted it changed, immediately."

Apple audited that factory, the company's first such inspection, and ordered improvements. ... By last year, Apple had inspected 396 facilities. ... Those audits have found consistent violations of Apple's code of conduct, according to summaries published by the company. In 2007, for instance, Apple conducted over three dozen audits, two-thirds of which indicated that employees regularly worked more than 60 hours a week. In addition, there were six "core violations," the most serious kind, including hiring 15-year-olds as well as falsifying records.

Over the next three years, Apple conducted 312 audits, and every year, about half or more showed evidence of large numbers of employees laboring more than six days a week as well as working extended overtime. Some workers received less than minimum wage or had pay withheld as punishment. Apple found 70 core violations over that period, including cases of involuntary labor, under-age workers, record falsifications, improper disposal of hazardous waste and over a hundred workers injured by toxic chemical exposures.

... [In 2011], the company conducted 229 audits. There were slight improvements in some categories and the detected rate of core violations declined. However, within 93 facilities, at least half of workers exceeded the 60-hours-a-week work limit. At a similar number, employees worked more than six days a week. There were incidents of discrimination, improper safety precautions, failure to pay required overtime rates and other violations. That year, four employees were killed and 77 injured in workplace explosions. "If you see the same pattern of problems, year after year, that means the company's ignoring the issue rather than solving it," said one former Apple executive with firsthand knowledge of the supplier responsibility group. "Noncompliance is tolerated, as long as the suppliers promise to try harder next time. If we meant business, core violations would disappear."

Apple says that when an audit reveals a violation, the company requires suppliers to address the problem within 90 days and make changes to prevent a recurrence. "If a supplier is unwilling to change, we terminate our relationship," the company says on its Web site. The seriousness of that threat, however, is unclear. Apple has found violations in hundreds of audits, but fewer than 15 suppliers have been terminated for transgressions since 2007, according to former Apple executives.

. . . Apple's efforts have spurred some changes. Facilities that were reaudited "showed continued performance improvements and better working conditions," the company wrote in its 2011 supplier responsibility progress report. In addition, the number of audited facilities has grown every year, and some executives say those expanding efforts obscure year-to-year improvements. Apple also has trained over a million workers about their rights and methods for injury and disease prevention. A few years ago, after auditors insisted on interviewing low-level factory employees, they discovered that some had been forced to pay onerous "recruitment fees"—which Apple classifies as involuntary labor. As of [2011] . . . the company had forced suppliers to reimburse more than $6.7 million in such charges. . . .

"We Could Have Saved Lives"

In 2006, [Business for Social Responsibility (BSR), which has been retained by Apple to provide advice on labor issues], along with a division of the World Bank and other groups, initiated a project to improve working conditions in factories building cellphones and other devices in China and elsewhere. The groups and companies pledged to test various ideas. Foxconn agreed to participate. For four months, BSR and another group negotiated with Foxconn regarding a pilot program to create worker "hotlines," so that employees could report abusive conditions, seek mental counseling and discuss workplace problems. Apple was not a participant in the project, but was briefed on it, according to the BSR consultant, who had detailed knowledge.

As negotiations proceeded, Foxconn's requirements for participation kept changing. First Foxconn asked to shift from installing new hotlines to evaluating existing hotlines. Then Foxconn insisted that mental health counseling be excluded. . . . Finally, an agreement was struck, and the project was scheduled to begin in January 2008. A day before the start, Foxconn demanded more changes, until it was clear the project would not proceed. . . .

The next year, a Foxconn employee fell or jumped from an apartment building after losing an iPhone prototype. Over the next two years, at least 18 other Foxconn workers attempted suicide or fell from buildings in manners that suggested suicide attempts. In 2010, two years after the pilot program fell apart and after multiple suicide attempts, Foxconn created a dedicated mental health hotline and began offering free psychological counseling. "We could have saved lives, and we asked Apple to pressure Foxconn, but they wouldn't do it," said the BSR consultant, who asked not to be identified because of confidentiality agreements. "Companies like H.P. and Intel and Nike push their suppliers. But Apple wants to keep an arm's length, and Foxconn is their most important manufacturer, so they refuse to push." . . . Foxconn, in a statement, said it acted quickly and comprehensively to address suicides, and "the record has shown that those measures have been successful."

A Demanding Client

Every month, officials at companies from around the world trek to Cupertino or invite Apple executives to visit their foreign factories, all in pursuit of a goal: becoming a supplier. When news arrives that Apple is interested in a particular product or service, small celebrations often erupt. Whiskey is drunk. Karaoke is sung. Then, Apple's requests start.

Apple typically asks suppliers to specify how much every part costs, how many workers are needed and the size of their salaries. Executives want to know every financial detail. Afterward, Apple calculates how much it will pay for a part. Most suppliers are allowed only the slimmest of profits. So suppliers often try to cut corners, replace expensive chemicals with less costly alternatives, or push their employees to work faster and longer, according to people at those companies. "The only way you make money working for Apple is figuring out how to do things more efficiently or cheaper," said an executive at one company that helped bring the iPad to market. "And then they'll come back the next year, and force a 10 percent price cut." . . . "You can set all the rules you want, but they're meaningless if you don't give suppliers enough profit to treat workers well," said one former Apple executive with firsthand knowledge of the supplier responsibility group. "If you squeeze margins, you're forcing them to cut safety."

. . . Many major technology companies have worked with factories where conditions are troubling. However, independent monitors and suppliers say some act differently. Executives at multiple suppliers, in interviews, said that Hewlett-Packard and others allowed them slightly more profits and other allowances if they were used to improve worker conditions. "Our suppliers are very open with us," said Zoe McMahon, an executive in Hewlett-Packard's supply chain social and environmental responsibility program. "They let us know when they are struggling to meet our expectations, and that influences our decisions."

The Explosion

On the afternoon of the blast at the iPad plant, Lai Xiaodong telephoned his girlfriend, as he did every day. They had hoped to see each other that evening, but Mr. Lai's manager said he had to work overtime, he told her. He had been promoted quickly at Foxconn, and after just a few months was in charge of a team that maintained the machines that polished iPad cases. The sanding area was loud and hazy with aluminum dust. Workers wore masks and earplugs, but no matter how many times they showered, they were recognizable by the slight aluminum sparkle in their hair and at the corners of their eyes.

Just two weeks before the explosion, an advocacy group in Hong Kong published a report warning of unsafe conditions at the Chengdu plant, including problems with aluminum dust. The group, Students and Scholars against Corporate Misbehavior, or Sacom, had videotaped workers covered with tiny aluminum particles. "Occupational health and safety issues in Chengdu are alarming," the report read.[5] "Workers also highlight the problem of poor ventilation and inadequate personal protective equipment." A copy of that report was sent to Apple. "There was no response," said Debby Chan Sze Wan of the group. "A few months later I went to Cupertino, and went into the Apple lobby, but no one would meet with me. I've never heard from anyone from Apple at all."

The morning of the explosion, Mr. Lai rode his bicycle to work. The iPad had gone on sale just weeks earlier, and workers were told thousands of cases needed to be polished each day. The factory was frantic, employees said. Rows of machines buffed cases as masked employees pushed buttons. Large air ducts hovered over each station, but they could not keep up with the three lines of machines polishing nonstop. Aluminum dust was everywhere.

Dust is a known safety hazard. In 2003, an aluminum dust explosion in Indiana destroyed a wheel factory and killed a worker. In 2008, agricultural dust inside a sugar factory in Georgia caused an explosion that killed 14.[6] Two hours into Mr. Lai's second shift, the building started to shake, as if an earthquake was under way.

There was a series of blasts, plant workers said. Then the screams began.

When Mr. Lai's colleagues ran outside, dark smoke was mixing with a light rain, according to cellphone videos. The toll would eventually count four dead, 18 injured. At the hospital, Mr. Lai's girlfriend saw that his skin was almost completely burned away. "I recognized him from his legs, otherwise I wouldn't know who that person was," she said. Eventually, his family arrived. Over 90 percent of his body had been seared. "My mom ran away from the room at the first sight of him. I cried. Nobody could stand it," his brother said. When his mother eventually returned, she tried to avoid touching her son, for fear that it would cause pain. "If I had known," she said, "I would have grabbed his arm, I would have touched him. . . . He was very tough," she said. "He held on for two days." After Mr. Lai died, Foxconn workers drove to Mr. Lai's hometown and delivered a box of ashes. The company later wired a check for about $150,000.

Foxconn, in a statement, said that at the time of the explosion the Chengdu plant was in compliance with all relevant laws and regulations, and "after ensuring that the families of the deceased employees were given the support they required, we ensured that all of the injured employees were given the highest quality medical care." After the explosion, the company added, Foxconn immediately halted work in all polishing workshops, and later improved ventilation and dust disposal, and adopted technologies to enhance worker safety. In its most recent supplier responsibility report, Apple wrote that after the explosion, the company contacted "the foremost experts in process safety" and assembled a team to investigate and make recommendations to prevent future accidents.

In December [2011], however, seven months after the blast that killed Mr. Lai, another iPad factory exploded, this one in Shanghai. Once again, aluminum dust was the cause, according to interviews and Apple's most recent supplier responsibility report. That blast injured 59 workers, with 23 hospitalized. "It is gross negligence, after an explosion occurs, not to realize that every factory should be inspected," said Nicholas Ashford, the occupational safety expert, who is now at the Massachusetts Institute of Technology. "If it were terribly difficult to deal with aluminum dust, I would understand. But do you know how easy dust is to control? It's called ventilation. We solved this problem over a century ago."

In its most recent supplier responsibility report, Apple wrote that while the explosions both involved combustible aluminum dust, the causes were different. The company declined, however, to provide details. The report added that Apple had now audited all suppliers polishing aluminum products and had put stronger precautions in place. All suppliers have initiated required countermeasures, except one, which remains shut down, the report said.

For Mr. Lai's family, questions remain. "We're really not sure why he died," said Mr. Lai's mother, standing beside a shrine she built near their home. "We don't understand what happened."

Hitting the Apple Lottery

Every year, as rumors about Apple's forthcoming products start to emerge, trade publications and Web sites begin speculating about which suppliers are likely to win the Apple lottery. Getting a contract from Apple can lift a company's value by millions because of the implied endorsement of manufacturing quality. But few companies openly brag about the work: Apple generally requires suppliers to sign contracts promising they will not divulge anything, including the partnership. That lack of transparency gives Apple an edge at keeping its plans secret. But it also has been a barrier to improving working conditions, according to advocates and former Apple executives.

[In January 2012] . . . after numerous requests by advocacy and news organizations, including the *New York Times*, Apple released the names of 156 of its suppliers.[7] In the report accompanying that list, Apple said they "account for more than 97 percent of what we pay to suppliers to manufacture our products." However, the company has not revealed the names of hundreds of other companies that do not directly contract with Apple, but supply the suppliers. The company's supplier list does not disclose where factories are, and many are hard to find. And independent monitoring organizations say when they have tried to inspect Apple's suppliers, they have been barred from entry—on Apple's orders, they have been told. . . . "There's a real culture of secrecy here that influences everything," the former executive said.

Some other technology companies operate differently. "We talk to a lot of outsiders," said Gary Niekerk, director of corporate citizenship at Intel. "The world's complex, and unless we're dialoguing with outside groups, we miss a lot." Given Apple's prominence and leadership in global manufacturing, if the company were to radically change its ways, it could overhaul how business is done. "Every company wants to be Apple," said Sasha Lezhnev at the Enough Project, a group focused on corporate accountability. "If they committed to building a conflict-free iPhone, it would transform technology."

But ultimately, say former Apple executives, there are few real outside pressures for change. Apple is one of the most admired brands. In a national survey conducted by the *New York Times* in November [2011], 56 percent of respondents said they couldn't think of anything negative about Apple. Fourteen percent said the worst thing about the company was that its products were too expensive. Just 2 percent mentioned overseas labor practices.

People like Ms. White of Harvard say that until consumers demand better conditions in overseas factories—as they did for companies like Nike and Gap, which today have overhauled conditions among suppliers—or regulators act, there is little impetus for radical change. Some Apple insiders agree. "You can either manufacture in comfortable, worker-friendly factories, or you can reinvent the product every year, and make it better and faster and cheaper, which

requires factories that seem harsh by American standards," said a current Apple executive. "And right now, customers care more about a new iPhone than working conditions in China."

NOTES

1. Students and Scholars against Corporate Misbehaviour. 2011. "Foxconn and Apple Fail to Fulfill Promises: Predicaments of Workers after the Suicides." http://sacom.hk/wp-content/uploads/2011/05/2011-05-06_foxconn-and-apple-fail-to-fulfill-promises.pdf

2. Wingfield, Nick. 2012. "Apple's Profit Doubles on Holiday iPhone 4S Sales." *The New York Times.* http://www.nytimes.com/2012/01/25/technology/apples-profit-doubles-as-holiday-customers-snapped-up-iphones.html

3. 2010. "D8: Steve Jobs on FoxConn." *The Wall Street Journal.* http://www.wsj.com/video/d8-steve-jobs-on-foxconn/43D148EF-4ABF-402D-B149-8681DF01981A.html

4. 2010. "D8: Steve Jobs on FoxConn." *The Wall Street Journal.* http://www.wsj.com/video/d8-steve-jobs-on-foxconn/43D148EF-4ABF-402D-B149-8681DF01981A.html

5. Students and Scholars against Corporate Misbehaviour. 2011. "Foxconn and Apple Fail to Fulfill Promises: Predicaments of Workers after the Suicides." http://sacom.hk/wp-content/uploads/2011/05/2011-05-06_foxconn-and-apple-fail-to-fulfill-promises.pdf

6. Dewan, Shaila. 2008. "Lives and a Georgia Community's Anchor Are Lost." *The New York Times.* http://www.nytimes.com/2008/02/09/us/09sugar.html

7. Wingfield, Nick and Charles Duhigg. 2012. "Apple Lists Its Suppliers for 1st Time." *The New York Times.* http://www.nytimes.com/2012/01/14/technology/apple-releases-list-of-its-suppliers-for-the-first-time.html

Social Problems Related to the Environment and Food System

Daniel R. Wildcat

Daniel R. Wildcat, Ph.D., is the director of the Haskell Environmental Research Studies Center and Indigenous & American Indian Studies faculty member at Haskell Indian Nations University. He is a Yuchi member of the Muscogee Nation of Oklahoma.

What is the mission of Haskell Environmental Research Studies (HERS) at Haskell Indian Nations University? What is your role in the program?

The HERS Center was founded in 1995 to address hazardous substance remediation issues in Indian Country. In addition to this specific goal, there was a broader goal of serving as an informational clearing-house on environmental issues. Since 2005 the primary focus of the Center has been to serve as the catalyst for the formation of the American Indian and Alaska Native Climate Change Working Group now known as the Indigenous Peoples Climate Change Working Group (IPCCWG). I serve as the convener of the IPCCWG and as director of the HERS Center.

What are the most pressing environmental issues affecting indigenous populations?

There is no doubt that the most pressing issues will be the multiple and interacting problems associated with climate change. The challenge is to help the public understand that due to the geographic and ecological diversity of the earth's biosphere, global climate change will manifest itself differently in different places of the planet. Even given this, one common denominator is that much of what we experience will be water related. As island and coastal communities can attest, they presently have more water than they can live with; in many cases, homelands are under water. At the other extreme are folks who are finding out they will have much less water than they have had in the past. These situations—combined with the rising sea level, warming, and increasing acidification of the earth's oceans and seas—make it clear that this century may in many respects be known as the century of water.

How did you first become interested in environmental issues? Who was your inspiration?

In retrospect I think my maternal grandfather and grandmother may be my largest influences. They were farmers—not in the agribusiness model, but in the subsistence tradition. As a teenager I loved going out and helping them in their vegetable garden. They had chickens for eggs, fruit trees, and when I was very young they had pigs and a milk cow. Somehow their simple life, although it was hard work, taught me something about the intrinsic value of the water, soil and air. They were, in a deep experiential (and not romanticized) sense, part of nature. From an intellectual standpoint, my mentor Vine Deloria, Jr., an American Indian scholar, activist, and visionary, has shaped much of my research, scholarship and teaching.

As a scholar-activist, what are your top goals?

I want to encourage humankind to move from a dangerous and costly worldview that sees non-human features of nature as resources to seeing them as relatives. We need to move from legal and political systems overwhelmingly shaped by inalienable individual rights to ones that balance those rights with recognition of inalienable human responsibilities to our relatives—human and non-human. We cannot treat our relatives like resources, yet that is exactly what we have been doing. Much of modern humankind views nature, including other people, as ATM machines that we constantly make withdrawals from with no regard for what we deposit back into the life-system of the planet. Many Indigenous cultures do not view the world this way, instead seeing people and the natural world as interdependent. If we adopt an Indigenously-informed paradigm shift, we will see some real improvement to many environmental situations that, on a global scale, only seem to be getting worse. Overall, I would say it is time to replace the anthropocentric notion of progress, where humans are the center of existence, with the promotion and enactment of systems of life-enhancement.

What strategies do you use to enact social change in your area of study? How do you take the results of your research and apply them to enact change?

I use community engagement, partnerships, publications, books,[1] journal articles, workshops and, just as importantly, popular journalistic efforts to educate the public. Most importantly, I infuse all of my teaching with a focus on the practical questions we face today in creating non-anthropocentric systems of life-enhancement.

What are the major challenges activists in your field face?

There are too few of us.

What are major misconceptions the public has about activism in general and in your area of advocacy, specifically?

There are two really: first many think activism is something only "activists" do and to me that view is fundamentally wrong. Activism is "choice"—one promotes something with every choice one makes in their daily lives. This first misconception leads to the second: because most activism and advocacy movements work within real physical, political and economic institutional landscapes that they did not construct, they often engage in activities that appear contradictory, for example, compromising and making concessions that seem counter to their goals. Critics who use that charge "being contradictory" as an indictment of activism are disingenuous, as we all are in the "belly of the beast" so to speak. We all live with contradictions; the goal is to reduce the number we encounter daily. To some extent activists can bring this latter criticism upon themselves when they take a "holier-than-thou" attitude regarding environmental issues.

What would you consider to be your greatest success as an activist?

I am not comfortable talking about my accomplishments as if they are "my own," because everything I do is a result of collaboration and partnerships. But the work I am proudest of is serving as the convener of the Indigenous Peoples Climate Change Working Group (IPCCWG). That working group, which has always been a tribal college and university-centered network, was designed to be very agile and dynamic. We have been meeting twice annually for nine years, engaging and partnering with federal agencies, our tribal nations, mainstream universities and colleges, non-governmental organizations (NGOs), private sector partners, intertribal and tribal organizations, and some of the leading scientific labs in the United States (such as the National Center for Atmospheric Research, the National Renewable Energy Lab, and even the National Aeronautics and Space Administration [NASA]). We brought a bunch of really good people together and let the interaction and ideas percolate. What emerged is a dynamic group that has moved from evaluating, assessing and sharing information about climate change to one that is rolling up its sleeves and creating a working agenda for change. I am proud that we maintained the tribal colleges' and universities' centrality to the network (many people are unaware that there are 37 tribal colleges and universities in the U.S.). Again, this was not my accomplishment alone. I had a lot of good partners, co-workers, and co-conveners that helped make it possible.

Climate change is such a monumental issue to tackle; what are ways to break the problem down and begin to think about steps we can take?

There are three areas that faculty and students in tribal colleges are focusing on and researching that we should all understand better in order to engage in change. The first area is taking better care of and reevaluating our relationship with water. We take water for granted, and people will need to consider water conservation, re-use, and desalination, for example, and be mindful of their use of water. I think we would all prefer to conserve water voluntarily, before governmental entities force us to restrict our use. The second area to think about is land use. We have a lot of students studying land use (planning, economic development, zoning). We

could make incredible improvements in our use of carbon energy if we rethought our land use strategies, avoiding energy-depleting forms like suburban sprawl. Even people living on reservations are looking at ways to use land more effectively, thinking about strategic building placement to avoid the environmental costs of transportation to and from those buildings. The third area is my "pet" area—one I would work in if I ever had an opportunity for a second career—and that's architecture and design. American houses are horrible in terms of energy consumption; they are poorly designed, built, and sized, and are terribly energy inefficient. We could probably have the most immediate and practical impact on carbon energy savings if we would simply take the time and energy to innovate and adapt existing technologies to create greener homes. We need to think about the intersection between water, land, and our housing—there are many practical opportunities for change. We need to get to work building greener, more sustainable structures.

What are the best ways that students can contribute?

The site for students to do their work is the school they are in! We need to really start thinking about the kinds of campuses we inhabit. Students have a tremendous amount of power if they can get organized. I recommend that students who are in school make their campus their site of engagement (join the Student Senate and prioritize environmental issues, make environmental issues the focus of your research projects for school, etc.). Use your campus and make a difference right there.

NOTES

1. Dr. Wildcat's most recent book is *Red Alert: Saving the Planet with Indigenous Knowledge* (Fulcrum Publishing).

Environmental Inequalities

HOLLIE NYSETH BREHM AND DAVID PELLOW

Nyseth Brehm and Pellow discuss environmental inequality, or the unequal distribution of exposure to hazards in the environment, and the connection this issue has to other major social problems. They argue that environmental inequalities impact racial minorities and those living in poor communities the most and outline possible causes of this disparity, including economic and discrimination-based explanations. Nyseth Brehm and Pellow discuss activism related to environmental inequality and how national and international responses are needed to reduce the impact on communities around the world.

Think back to the movie *Erin Brockovich*. The basic plot, based on a true story, goes like this: A woman with no legal training learns that many residents in a small town have gotten cancer due to exposure to contaminated groundwater. After investigating a large factory believed to be responsible for the contamination, Brockovich proceeds to kick ass. She files a lawsuit against the company, bringing justice to the sick families.

It's the perfect drama-filled Hollywood plot. Yet what is even more dramatic is that the basic story of communities living in contamination isn't rare at all. In many places around the world and in the U.S., people share their neighborhoods with hazardous waste, toxic incinerators, and health-threatening chemical contamination. Moreover, some people are much more likely to be affected by these environmental hazards than others—namely, people of color, working class people, immigrants, and indigenous communities.

This uneven exposure to environmental risks and hazards, often coupled with the systematic exclusion of people from environmental decision-making processes, is called environmental racism or environmental inequality. But, don't be fooled by the terms—the causes of environmental inequality are social and political. In other words, environmental inequality is not, at its core, an environmental issue. Rather, it is rooted in our discourses, structures, and political and economic institutions, and it is intertwined with the other inequalities that permeate our daily lives.

The Emergence of Environmental (In)Justice

Although *Erin Brockovich* hit the theaters in 2000, environmental inequalities are far from new and far from over. Native Americans, African Americans, Latinos, and European immigrants in the United States have long been disproportionately exposed to the harmful effects of living near city dumps, working in coal mines and on farms picking pesticide-drenched produce, and bearing the brunt of undemocratic and destructive land use decisions. But it wasn't until researchers, activists, and government officials began documenting patterns of social inequality and environmental harm in the 1970s and early 1980s that the concept of environmental inequality emerged.

For example, the U.S. General Accounting Office conducted one of the earliest studies of environmental inequality in 1983. The study examined the racial composition of communities near four major hazardous waste landfills in the South. In three of the four cases, the communities around the landfills were predominantly African American (in the fourth, the community was disproportionately African American). Several other groundbreaking studies in the 1980s and 1990s confirmed these patterns at the local, regional, national, and even international scales.

In response, scholars and activists began calling for environmental justice. According to sociologist Robert Bullard, environmental justice is the notion that all people and communities are entitled to equal protection by environmental health laws and regulations. Many researchers and advocates have rallied around this concept, which has influenced a body of scholarship on environmental inequalities as well as an ever-growing social movement to combat them.

Initial Documentation and Response to Environmental Inequalities

Scholars and movement activists began to address environmental inequalities by first documenting their existence. Since the 1980s, there have literally been thousands of studies that have provided strong evidence of racial inequalities in exposure to environmental hazards. Many other scholars have argued that environmental inequalities do not just disproportionately affect racial minorities. Other social categories, like gender, age, class, immigration status/citizenship, and indigeneity, are also associated with disproportionate exposure to hazards. Taken together, these effects overlap and are difficult to disentangle. Here, we focus on race and class, as these are the most prominent in existing studies.

Rather than reviewing these studies (which could fill books), we turn to two examples in the city of Chicago. The Southeast portion of Chicago is known locally as "the Toxic Doughnut" because it is surrounded on all sides by hundreds of polluting industrial facilities, including paint manufacturers, landfills, a sewage treatment plant, a steel manufacturing company, incinerators, and several dumps. Each year, these local industries emit hundreds of thousands of pounds of chemicals into the air. Local residents, who are predominantly African Americans living in public housing, report high incidences of asthma, chronic obstructive pulmonary disease, skin rashes, and cancer.

Scholars like Bullard, Beverly Wright, Bunyan Bryant, and Dorceta Taylor (among others) founded the field of environmental justice studies in order to document inequalities like these. Yet, unlike the Hollywood portrayal, it is actually very difficult to link health problems to specific chemical or industrial sites, especially when several exist in the same area. While this means the resolution depicted in *Erin Brockovich* is not representative, it also means that there are many other responses to environmental inequalities.

In the mid-1980s in the Toxic Doughnut, for example, several activists engaged in an act of civil disobedience against a chemical waste incinerator operator. They coordinated a "lock down" and chained themselves to vehicles placed in the path of trucks transporting hazardous materials for incineration. By the end of the day, the coalition had turned away no less than 57 waste trucks.

Such acts of civil disobedience have been common responses to perceived environmental injustices, though this particular story doesn't end at the incinerator gates. The activists involved in the lock down joined a broader network of organizations that comprise the environmental justice movement, and they collectively pushed then-president Bill Clinton to sign an Executive Order (12898), directing federal agencies to develop and implement plans to guard against the production of environmental inequalities. It was an historic accomplishment for the environmental justice movement, though the fight for environmental justice was (and is) far from over.

In fact, 20 years later in the same city, things hadn't changed much. Many of Chicago's Latino communities are concentrated in the neighborhoods of Pilsen and Little Village on the city's West Side. In the early 2000s, activists in these communities began a campaign to shut down two coal-fired power plants. Pollution from the Fisk (in Pilsen) and Crawford (in Little Village) plants are, according to researchers from Chicago's Clean Air Task Force, largely responsible for 42 premature deaths, 66 heart attacks, and 720 asthma attacks each year. Community organizations from environmental, faith, health, and labor movements across the city came together to form the Clean Power Coalition (CPC) not only to phase out the power plants, but also to make Chicago a coal-free city. The CPC eventually received support from 35 aldermen and the mayor. In 2012, the organization achieved its goal. An agreement was signed to close the Fisk plant within the year and the Crawford plant in 2014. It was a major victory for the environmental justice movement and for one of the lead organizations in the CPC, the Little Village Environmental Justice Organization.

Causes of Environmental Inequalities

As the fight for environmental justice rages on, scholars have turned their attention to better understanding why environmental inequalities exist. Various explanations have been proposed, and here we focus on two—economic and discrimination-based explanations. Sociopolitical explanations are also at play, but since power and politics are everywhere, we integrate them into the first two. As noted above, none of these are fundamentally environmental causes—they are rooted in society.

Economic Explanations

Social and economic benefits are unevenly distributed in favor of businesses and affluent communities, while the environmental risks are disproportionately concentrated among the most vulnerable groups: the poor, unskilled laborers, and skilled blue-collar residents.

A common explanation for environmental inequality is that polluting corporations do not intentionally discriminate. Instead, they place facilities where land is cheap and where labor pools are available. Both help companies in their quest to maximize profits. Often, marginalized communities already live in such areas, and once a hazardous facility is present, they likely lack the resources to move.

Focusing on the broader social system, sociologists Allan Schnaiberg and Kenneth Gould developed a related economic-based explanation called the treadmill of production thesis. Under this model, there is an ever-growing need for capital investment to generate goods for sale in the marketplace, and that requires continuous inputs of energy and expansion. This expansion of the economy drives two fundamental dynamics: the creation of economic wealth and the creation of the negative by-products of the production process. The social and economic benefits are unevenly distributed in favor of businesses and affluent communities, while the environmental risks and other negative by-products are disproportionately concentrated among the groups of people with the least ability to resist the location of polluting facilities in their community. Thus, polluting facilities are sited among the most vulnerable groups: the poor, unskilled laborers, and skilled blue-collar residents. . . .

Discrimination-Based Explanations

Other researchers focus more directly on racism and institutional discrimination as drivers of environmental inequality. As evidence, they point to the persistent and stark racial divides in environmental policy making. For example, scholars like Charles Mills and Robert Higgins point to the ways that racism informs environmental decision making on a deeper cultural register. Mills draws on philosophy and historical texts to connect racism to a psychological, cultural, and legal framework linking images of people of color (specifically people of African descent) with barbarism, filth, dirt, and pollution. According to Mills, many white people view African peoples as a form of pollution, making it morally easier to contain industrial waste and factory pollution in their segregated, already-"polluted" neighborhoods. This link between non-European peoples and symbols associated with nature, such as danger, disease, and the primitive savage, is common throughout European history and literature, as well as within contemporary politics in the global North, whether one is speaking of Africans, African Americans, Indigenous peoples, Asians, Latin Americans, or the Roma of Europe.

Like Mills, environmental philosopher Robert Higgins argues that "minority" environments are seen as "appropriately polluted" spaces. Immigrants, indigenous populations, and people of color are viewed by many policymakers, politicians, and ecologists as a source of environmental contamination. That view influences and supports decisions to place noxious facilities and toxic waste in the spaces these populations occupy or relegate these groups to spaces where environmental quality is low and undesirable.

Racial disparities are also mirrored in myriad other aspects of environmental justice—relevant U.S. institutions, including education, health care, and criminal justice, revealing how environmental inequality's impacts can multiply and ripple across the social terrain far beyond those spaces traditionally associated with "environmental" issues. Often, however, particular acts of racism and discrimination cannot easily be located and measured . . . so scholars must continue to explore creative approaches to study this problem.

As we consider economic- and discrimination-based explanations for environmental injustice, politics are clearly at play in both. The political power of communities, states, and industries is inseparable from racial and economic forces driving environmental inequalities. For one, industries and corporations might purposefully seek the path of least resistance. As affluent, and often white, communities have the resources and social capital to oppose the placement of hazardous facilities in or near their neighborhoods, companies place hazards in locations where they believe they will meet little or no local political resistance. Communities that are already socially marginalized are often excluded from participation in policymaking, zoning, and urban planning, while industries, corporations, and similar entities are highly involved in these processes. It's just easier to . . . [place] industrial operations in neighborhoods where the residents have long held little political clout. In addition, working class communities and communities of color are relatively invisible in mainstream environmental movements. If the voices of disadvantaged communities are not heard or respected in political or protest circles, they can be overlooked. Multiple forms of hierarchy and politics drive environmental inequalities.

Expanding Environmental Justice

Though the scholarly field (and related social movements) of environmental justice studies began by focusing on unequal exposure to environmental hazards, some scholars and activists have expanded its boundaries. . . . More recently, scholars have analyzed how other aspects of social life (beyond race and class) influence environmental inequalities. For example, environmental hazards can affect women differently than men. In places like Silicon Valley, where the electronics industry boom began decades ago, the majority of workers in the most chemically intensive jobs were immigrant women (some were exposed to upwards of 700–1,000 different chemicals in a single workstation). Gender also plays a strong role in how people confront environmental hazards. As research by Phil Brown and Faith Ferguson and Celene Krauss demonstrates, women have been the most visible and vocal advocates for the environmental justice movement. This is largely because of their social structural position as likely caretakers of children and the elderly (often the first members of families and communities to show signs of environmental illness) and because they are most likely to have strong connections to community-based institutions like schools, churches, health clinics, and salons—sites where information and concerns about environmental threats are shared and where people are often mobilized.

Environmental justice scholars are working to expand the concept in other ways as well. Notably, while we have focused on the United States in this piece, scholars are increasingly seeing environmental inequalities as global issues. For example, the practice of hazardous waste dumping across national borders is a form of transnational environmental inequality. Every year, wealthy nations and corporations produce millions of tons of toxic waste from industry, consumers, municipalities, state institutions, computers and electronics products, and agricultural practices. These hazards directly and indirectly contribute to high rates of human and non-human morbidity and mortality and to ecosystem damage on every continent and in every ocean system. Dumping waste in other people's "backyards" is reflective of economically, racially, and politically unequal relations between and within global North and South communities.

Climate change is another example of global environmental inequality. While contributing the least to the causes of climate disruption, people of color, women, indigenous communities, and global South nations often feel the brunt of climate disruption. They bear the burdens of ecological, economic, and health effects, thereby giving rise to the concept of climate injustice. These communities are among the first to experience the effects of climate disruption, which can include "natural" disasters, rising levels of respiratory illness and infectious disease, heat-related morbidity and mortality, and large increases in energy costs. Flooding from severe storms, rising sea levels, and melting glaciers affects millions in Asia and Latin America, while sub-Saharan Africa is experiencing sustained droughts. Yet, nearly 75% of the world's annual CO_2 emissions come from the global North, where only 15% of the earth's population resides.

The ability to adapt to climate change is also highly uneven across social groups within countries. For example, African Americans have fewer resources to cope with or recover from a host of negative health impacts that might result from climate change. For example, they are 50% more likely than non-African Americans to lack health insurance. The delivery of disaster relief is less available to African Americans, too. This was made evident in the aftermath of Hurricane Katrina, when the Federal Emergency Management Agency failed to provide services to thousands of African Americans in the Gulf region who were without shelter, food, or drinkable water for days. Research demonstrates that racial stereotypes continue to contribute to reduced disaster relief aid for African Americans in the wake of all manner of climate-related emergencies.

Gender inequalities impact the ability to adapt to climate change as well. In Bangladesh, for instance, women's domestic duties have historically made them especially vulnerable to extreme weather events like storms and floods. Responsibilities as the primary child care givers, primary gatherers of food, fuel, water, and the primary cooks and tenders of livestock have typically tied women to low-lying residences, which are more vulnerable to the rising waters associated with extreme weather events. The relative poverty of women in Bangladesh also makes them less resilient in the face of climate change, since they have poorer nutrition, limited health care, and, in the case of divorced and widowed women, fewer sources of social support. . . .

A Global Response

Today, the real Erin Brockovich continues to participate in other environmental justice lawsuits, and activists living in the Toxic Doughnut and on Chicago's West Side are still orchestrating grassroots campaigns for environmental justice, including a push to improve the city's public transit system and promote sustainable energy production. The movement is much broader, with grassroots activists, scholars, governmental and even corporate actors, converging around these pressing issues. At the global level, too, international treaties have come to recognize global environmental injustices tied to climate change and the transfer of hazardous waste to the global South. Yet, despite some of the successes of these transnational advocacy movements, environmental inequalities persist.

Multiple solutions at all levels are needed to comprise a global response to environmental inequality. The United States can and should do its part. While new laws may be needed over time, right now we believe we must start with the enforcement of existing laws that are relevant to environmental justice. The Executive Order referenced earlier was intended to ensure that federal agencies function in a way that protects communities against environmental inequalities. Unfortunately, as the U.S. government's own Inspector General has concluded, federal agencies are doing a poor job of implementing Order 12898, and there have been varying and uneven levels of commitment from the White House, Congress, and the U.S. Environmental Protection Agency since it was signed in 1994....

The first of many needed responses to environmental injustice, then, is for the federal government to enforce a host of existing laws intended to protect the environment, human health, and vulnerable communities. Laws like the National Environmental Policy Act, the Clean Air Act, and the Fair Housing Act have been under attack by industry and special interest groups since their passage, and each has been weakened over the years. As a result, it has become more difficult—not less—for working class people and people of color to find jobs, homes, and recreational spaces that are free from toxic hazards. Many other solutions—far more than we can review here—are needed, but enforcing the laws already on the books is a good start.

U.S. Electronic Waste Gets Sent to Africa

Ron Claiborne

Reprinted by Permission of ABC News. August 2, 2009, http://abcnews.go.com/GMA/Weekend/story?id=8215714/.

It's the wet season now in Ghana, and the heavy, daily rains have turned the vast field behind the Agbogbloshie market into a muddy swamp. With the mud so thick it can pull the shoes from your feet—if you're lucky enough to have shoes—the children come here to rummage and rake the mountains of electronic debris that spills across the landscape.

They are scavenging for copper wiring that they can sell. On a very good day, they can extract about $2 of copper from the broken computers, telephone answering machines and televisions that have been discarded. Much of the e-waste in the Agbogbloshie dump comes from foreign countries, including the United States. Recyclers that buy it from government agencies ship it overseas in cargo containers mixed in with second-hand electronics. The buyer in the foreign country keeps what is salable and carts off what isn't to e-waste sites such as Agbogbloshie.

CHILDREN AT RISK

Some of the children are aware that breaking open junked electronics exposes them to potentially harmful chemicals, such as lead, mercury and cadmium. Many don't know. No one is deterred. Yusef

Nashedu, 12, has been mining the field for copper for the past three years. He goes to school weekdays and comes here after school. On weekends, he spends all day in the dumpsite. "Sometimes, I feel sick," Yusef said. "In my body, I can't feel free."

Dressed in short pants, a dirty polo shirt and plastic yellow flip-flops, Yusef shuffles through the jagged debris, stooped over, looking for copper wires. Some of the children built fires on which they toss large hunks of discarded electronics. The fire melts the plastic, revealing the copper wires inside. The fire also releases toxic fumes.

"We are looking at immense health implications," said Mike Anane, a local environmental activist who frequently visits the Agbogbloshie field to warn the children and adults of the dangers of what they are doing. "For the kids, we're talking about lowering the IQ as a result of the lead, of the mercury, even the cadmium. It affects the nervous system. These are kids. Their bodies are very vulnerable," Anane said.

It is difficult to trace where the e-waste comes from. Most of it has been shattered or broken into pieces that bear no identifying markings. But among the scattered junk are a few items with labels. Anane held up computer pieces with decals for the Washington Metro Transit Authority, U.S. Army, State of Connecticut Mental Health Facility, and other U.S. city, state and federal agencies. According to the environmental group Greenpeace, even computers with the label of the U.S. Environmental Protection Agency were found at the dump.

CHEAP DUMPING SENDS E-WASTE ABROAD

Under the 1998 Basel Convention, it is illegal for someone in a signatory country to send hazardous materials to another country without that recipient country's permission. But the United States, Afghanistan and Haiti never ratified the convention, so it is not unlawful in those countries.

In the case of the United States, which has stringent laws governing the disposal of e-waste, it is cheaper for recyclers to just ship the junked electronics to a country like Ghana than to properly dispose of it. And with few exceptions, it is legal. "This is a pure cost situation," said Casey Harrell of Greenpeace's San Francisco office. "There are no nefarious masterminds here that are trying to ruin the lives of people overseas. The reality is you can send these container ships for pennies."

A federal Government Accountability Office (GAO) report in August 2008 found that "potentially harmful used electronics . . . [flow] virtually unrestricted" to foreign countries.

The United States does ban the export of television and computer screens containing cathode ray tubes, or CRTs, which contain lead. But the GAO report . . . concluded the Environmental Protection Agency (EPA) was lax even in monitoring the export of CRTs. "[The] EPA has done little to determine the extent of non-compliance with the rule and even less to deter such non-compliance," the report stated. "It's a very damning report," Harrell said. "Basically, it said that the Environmental Protection Agency and the federal government [were] doing little to nothing on the regulation of e-waste." . . .

"TSUNAMI" OF E-WASTE ANTICIPATED

In an e-mail reply to questions from ABC News, the EPA . . . said: "Over the last year, [the] EPA has stepped up enforcement of the CRT rule as it regards export. Last year, [the] EPA began more than 20 investigations into possible violations of the CRT export requirements."

John Stephenson, GAO director for Natural Resources and Environment—and a harsh critic of the EPA last year—concurred. "It appears that they are more aggressively investigating and enforcing the CRT rule," Stephenson said. "I know there has been enforcement activity against recyclers, and that's more than they were doing before."

. . . The GAO report and Mike Anane in Ghana both warn of a coming wave of e-waste—Anane calls it a "tsunami"—in the form of old televisions as a consequence of the change in the U.S. from analog to digital television. "The prospect looms that many more used electronic devices will be discarded in the near future," the GAO said.

Fixing the Bungled
U.S. Environmental Movement

ROBERT BRULLE AND J. CRAIG JENKINS

Brulle and Jenkins discuss the apparent decline of the environmental movement in the United States, seeking to understand how a movement with broad public support and deep financial backing has languished over the past few decades. Brulle and Jenkins argue that after some early successes in the 1970s (e.g., the Clean Air Act of 1970 and Clean Water Act of 1972), the movement has tackled issues around which it is more difficult to organize financial, bureaucratic, political, and public support (e.g., deforestation, climate change). Brulle and Jenkins offer suggestions to improve the efficacy and influence of the environmental movement in the United States.

Senators John McCain and John Kerry slumped in chairs outside the Senate Chamber on March 13, 2002, having just lost a critical vote to increase the fuel efficiency of every vehicle on America's roadways. It was an especially difficult defeat. In conjunction with vigorous lobbying and a major public campaign by environmental organizations, Kerry and McCain had hoped to start the United States on the road toward dealing with global climate change. But a lack of support and heavy opposition (from autoworkers, manufacturers, and the oil lobby, among others) resulted in the measure's defeat, ensuring the continued decline in the overall fuel efficiency of the U.S. automobile fleet. As a result, gas efficiency standards today remain where they were set more than 20 years ago, and a loophole that exempts light trucks and SUVs remains in effect.

This outcome, which came on the heels of the Senate's rejection of the Kyoto Protocol in 1999 by an overwhelming 95–0 vote, demonstrates the political obstacles that stand in the way of even the most basic baby steps toward addressing environmental problems at home and around the world. If Congress can't generate the political will to raise domestic fuel efficiency standards, then dealing with global climate change seems almost impossible. What do these recent political defeats say about the state of environmentalism in the United States? More to the point of the present analysis, where is the U.S. environmental movement in all this?

When it comes to activists and organizers, the current situation stands in marked contrast to the 1970s, when the environmental movement displayed an extraordinary ability to mobilize

Robert Brulle and J. Craig Jenkins, *Contexts* (Volume 7 and Issue 2), pp. 14–18, Copyright © 2008. Reprinted by Permission of SAGE Publications.

support in Congress and created an impressive infrastructure of safety agencies and regulatory oversight. But despite a strong organizational base and widespread public support, most critics agree the movement's political clout has declined over the past decade. Some even claim environmentalism is dead.

Sociological research suggests the environmental movement's seeming lack of influence stems from some fundamental changes in the culture of its organizations and in the traditions of organizing itself. It also may be the result of a mismatch between movement ideals and actual environmental problems and associated public policy options. Recognizing these shortcomings is crucial to translating the energies, passions, and principles of the movement into concrete legislative outcomes and policy solutions.

Early Successes, Present Failures

Like the civil rights, women's, peace, and other movements, environmentalism was reborn in the 1960s. Building on the earlier conservationist, public health, and preservationist movements, the decade saw a flourishing of new ideas about environmental problems and how to address them. Intellectuals like Rachel Carson and Barry Commoner developed and promulgated a new perspective that later became known as "environmentalism." They helped the general public understand the links among environmental degradation, ecosystem processes, and human health. Environmental organizations then repackaged these ideas in an effort to energize activists and the general public, thereby bringing about major policy changes.

The first Earth Day in April 1970 showcased an extraordinary mobilization over environmental issues and consolidated momentum that, in the few short years that followed, produced an impressive record of legislative victories. During the 1970s, environmental organizations appeared regularly before Congressional hearings and passed between 20 and 30 major bills every year with relatively limited challenge from corporations and other counterinterests.

Congress passed the Clean Air Act in 1970, the Clean Water Act in 1972, and the Endangered Species Act in 1973. Legislators extended or strengthened many such landmark bills soon thereafter. By the end of the 1970s, environmental activists and legislators had created a system of federal regulatory oversight and safety agencies that included the U.S. Environmental Protection Agency (EPA), the Nuclear Regulatory Agency, and the National Oceanic and Atmospheric Administration. States also set up their own counterparts to the national laws, policies, and agencies.

These landmark laws and organizational networks significantly improved environmental quality across the nation. For example, in 1972 the Clean Water Act—passed by Congress a matter of hours after a presidential veto—required that all waters in the United States be swimmable, drinkable, and fishable by 1983, and that the discharge of pollutants into U.S. waters end by 1985. This significant, hard-hitting legislation required real changes to the standard operating procedures in nearly every American community.

But this legislation and enforcement of it was far from perfect. Indeed, 34 years after the Clean Water Act passed, more than half of U.S. waters remain significantly degraded and [the] EPA found in a 2006 study of streams that only 28 percent were in "good" condition. Also according to [the] EPA, more than 146 million residents live in areas with unhealthy levels of air pollution.

These disappointing and unexpected outcomes were part of a larger, quite unsettling trend in the 1980s in which the policy advances of the previous decade suffered from a lack of enforcement or retrenchment, and few new advances. In part this was a result of the "wise use" countermovement, in which corporations launched new advocacy organizations, such as the Capital Research Center and the Mountain States Legal Foundation, to attack environmental initiatives. Playing on the media's reporting balanced accounts, these countermovements successfully cast doubt on scientific studies documenting environmental problems.

Political transformations also played a role. Since the mid-1990s, in fact, legislative successes for the environmental movement have been few and far between. After Republicans took control of the House of Representatives in 1994, environmentalists virtually disappeared from Congressional hearings and won passage of less than a dozen priority bills per year. In any case, the results are clear when examining the continuing, unsustainable growth of America's "ecological footprint. ...." The footprint collects the use of all non-renewable natural resources—imported oil being the major source—and compares it against the ecological productive capacity of the United States since 1961. In 1968, the United States moved beyond existing resources; in other words, we began exporting our environmental problems abroad by consuming imported, non-renewable resources. Overall, the U.S. ecological footprint has increased by more than 240 percent over the 40-year period.

Strong Movement, Lacking Clout

The environmental failures and shortcomings of recent years belie what appears to be a strong and vibrant movement, at least institutionally speaking. More than 10,000 tax-exempt environmental organizations are registered with the Internal Revenue Service, and they boast a combined support base of approximately 15 percent of the U.S. population. Based on our recently completed analysis published in *Mobilization*, the movement has a total annual income of more than $2.7 billion and assets of more than $5.8 billion. More than 100 new organizations are formed each year to address a wide spectrum of environmental problems.

A March 2007 Gallup poll found fully 70 percent of Americans are either active in or sympathetic to the environmental movement. Since 1980 membership in environmental groups has grown from 5.1 percent to 15.9 percent of U.S. adults and those donating time has grown from 1.4 percent to 8.8 percent, according to the World Values Surveys from 1980, 1990, and 2000. Yet, for all this support and organizational strength, the political clout of the environmental movement appears to have eroded steadily since the early 1990s. Indeed, most critics agree the environmental movement is at best currently on the defensive—and this at a time when we face growing and perhaps irreversible environmental degradation.

Part of the problem is that the environmental successes of the 1970s were over issues that might be considered "low-hanging fruit"—easy wins against problems that were plain as day to the average citizen and politician. Dumped chemicals caused rivers to catch fire, major cities' air quality was so poor you could see it in the sky and feel it in your lungs, and waterways simply weren't suitable for fishing or swimming. Beginning in the 1980s, the issues facing environmentalists became more complicated and challenging. A new set of environmental problems emerged that didn't fit into the 1960s environmental paradigm and prototype. Global warming, loss of biodiversity, tropical deforestation, ozone depletion, and acid rain were global, far more abstract, and less tractable problems. They were also outside the authority of the existing regulatory agencies, and thus required new types of political mobilization and policy solutions. For example, no single agency has jurisdiction over tropical deforestation or ozone depletion, so it's difficult to know who or what to target in lobbying and public-policy making.

The movement responded with public education projects, monitoring, lobbying for international treaties, and promoting "green" consumerism, but these have yet to make major institutional inroads. Indeed, critics suggest that the movement has become "Chicken Little," trumpeting an ever-growing litany of doomsday warnings without offering concrete solutions. In 2004, environmental activists Michael Shellenberger and Ted Nordhaus published a widely circulated article titled "The Death of Environmentalism." They contended "the environmental movement's foundational concepts, its method of framing legislative proposals, and its very institutions are outmoded!" Substantial evidence supports their claims.

A major problem is the lack of deep public support for initiatives with major economic costs. Despite broad public support for environmental protection, the depth of this support is modest when it comes to actually paying for environmental protection or sacrificing economic growth. . . . Contemporary environmental challenges, such as global warming, species loss, and tropical deforestation, can't be addressed without significant economic sacrifices. How these will be paid and by whom is a major political challenge. Moreover, most are transboundary problems, which means they require international cooperation, and thus considerable political clout.

Scholars have long argued that social movements and movement organizations have a tendency to become timid and conservative with age. Today's environmental movement seems to have become complacent and overly bureaucratic, a movement dominated by "protest businesses" that substitute professional advocacy for citizen action. Few of the leading national environmental organizations offer members the chance to participate in a concrete, meaningful way. Members are check-writers, not activists. Funding comes from foundation and corporate grants, wealthy donors, and "checkbook activists." The majority of grassroots members simply come along for the ride.

Some scholars suggest "free riding" is inherent and even effective in environmental action. Environmental protection is a collective good—if it improves for one person, it improves for all. This is clearly not an optimal mobilizing strategy, however. To the contrary, social movement scholars Gerald Marwell and Pamela Oliver argue that with free riding "each contribution makes others' subsequent contributions less worthwhile, and thus less likely." And indeed today one of the paramount problems of the movement is the perception among potential supporters that their individual contributions won't make a difference. Shellenberger and Nordhaus argue that the environmental movement needs to reframe its agenda to appeal to core progressive values and create a broader, more

engaged political coalition. This "respinning" of the environmental message might help generate a new, more committed grassroots constituency, but our research suggests another change is needed as well. The movement's other crucial ailment is a failure to translate general public support and organizational strength into specific effective actions. Though not dead, the environmental movement's organizations, ideals, and projects have failed to speak to or match current environmental challenges, legislative priorities, and public policy realities.

The task for the environmental movement, therefore, is not just to be a cheerleader for the grassroots, rank-and-file membership, but also—and perhaps more importantly—to devise initiatives and proposals that target specific environmental problems and actors, and then challenge and encourage its supporters to undertake them. Successful campaigns in the movement's earlier years were organized around the workplace, schools, and churches and largely by volunteer activists. But they focused on specific, meaningful issues and targets. Today's movement has some of these types of networks (the Sierra Club and local environmental justice groups, for instance) but lacks the projects and initiatives connected to people's lives and the relevance in the political culture required to mobilize real action and change.

Engaging citizens in the contemporary environmental movement in the United States will require instituting local democracy and fostering civic engagement; broadening commitments and agendas; and linking environmentalism to social justice, workplace equity, and broader social protections. It ultimately could require restructuring civic politics in America—focusing not only on passion and mobilization but also on law and public policy. But in the final, sociological analysis, getting Americans involved in a movement that will affect real environmental change will require reorganizing the environmental movement, shifting from a "top-down" structure to a grassroots approach emphasizing concrete social problems and real-world, public policy solutions.

An Opportunity for Revitalization

The environmental movement has recently attempted to mobilize around the issue of global warming, with the mass media playing a leading role. In May 2004 the fictional dramatic film *The Day after Tomorrow* was released. Then came Al Gore's *An Inconvenient Truth*, which gained a wide audience (and helped secure him a Noble Prize). Television coverage shows a marked increase in coverage of global warming.

In the wake of the November 2006 elections and the Republican loss of Congressional control, many environmentalists were excited about the prospects for environmental legislation, especially on the topic of global warming. Gone from the chairmanship of the Senate Committee on Environmental and Public Works was James Inhofe (R–Oklahoma), who once called global warming the "greatest hoax ever perpetrated on the American people." In his place was Barbara Boxer (D–California), a legislator with an impressive national profile and strong environmental record. In her first statements after the election Boxer promised swift and strong action to deal with global warming.

Recent polling still shows little change in public opinion in the aftermath. Every month Gallup asks what respondents consider the "most important problem" facing the nation. Over the past 10 years they've mentioned the environment no more than 2 percent of the time. A November 2007 Gallup poll showed the environment ranks 14th in major problems, with only 1 percent saying environmental improvement is our country's most important problem. Opposition to strong measures, such as instituting a carbon tax, is high. Fully 68 percent of those polled in March 2006 opposed a policy to "increase taxes on gasoline so people either drive less, or buy cars that use less gas." Moreover, 81 percent opposed a policy that would "increase taxes on electricity so people use less of it." A soft majority of 52 percent responded to the 2006 Gallup poll that they supported environmental protection over economic growth.

So despite strong scientific consensus on the basics of global warming theory, a Gallup poll from as recently as March 2006 showed 62 percent of the U.S. public still did not believe global warming was a problem. Perhaps it isn't surprising that Congress has been slow to act. . . . A carbon tax may be unpopular, but it's impossible to imagine significant reductions in carbon emissions in the near future that don't entail increased energy costs. However, the groundwork may be coming into place.

Environmental activists—working with scientists and politicians as well as writers and reporters—are not only continuing to raise public attention about global warming, they are beginning to think seriously about public policy innovations in the United States and elsewhere. As concrete analyses and political solutions come into circulation, we may well find ourselves in a situation similar to the period from 1963 to 1967—Rachel Carson's *Silent Spring* had been published and there was a great deal of media interest in her book, but it was only beginning to translate into the increased environmental mobilization of the late 1960s and early 1970s.

The United States needs a movement that leads away from the path of continued degradation and toward ecological sustainability. But without a paradigm shift from the top-down approach where members of environmental organizations are treated as budget funders to a grassroots focus that will engage citizens to take specific actions that stem the tide of environmental degradation, our environmental movement won't have the right approach to get us there.

Organizationally and in terms of broad public support, the environmental movement has been a remarkable success. But in terms of political clout for tackling the big issues, the movement is weak, losing critical policy battles while failing to provide strategies that can transform potential public support into environmental action. This makes it all the more incumbent on the environmental movement to help the general public connect the dots between their personal, local concerns and the dramatic, global threats to which environmental groups devote their resources and energy.

Why Beef Is What's for Dinner: Agricultural Policy and Its Implications

EMILY STUTZMAN JONES

Think about what you had for dinner last night. Do you know where your food came from or how it fits into the larger food system? If you don't, you're not alone. The system that supports and constrains our food choices—including a wide variety of federal and state policies and regulations—is largely hidden from the American consumer, but it affects the types of foods available to us, their affordability, their production's impact on the environment, and our individual and public health. Jones discusses the origins, motivations, and effects of these policies and how they might be redesigned to keep the consumer's needs and desires in mind.

Season 14 of NBC's *The Biggest Loser* included, for the first time, children. Contestants Sunny, Lindsay, and "Bingo" became the three faces of childhood obesity. As a sociologist interested in food and agriculture, I engaged my sociological perspective while I viewed this show. (A common side effect of sociological study is the inability to uncritically watch any form of entertainment. Sociology students, you've been warned.) I noticed right away that when producers interviewed fitness trainers about participating kids, the issue of childhood obesity was consistently framed as "not their fault." The overarching narrative was that as kids, they didn't control the food their parents purchased or that was available in their schools. The children were presented as victims, along with the 18 percent of U.S. children (ages six to eleven) and 21 percent of adolescents (ages twelve to nineteen) who are also obese.[1] The adult contestants on the other hand, and by extension, the 34.9 percent of U.S. adults who are overweight or obese,[2] were framed as completely responsible for their food choices and obesity-related health outcomes.

As I watched this age-based framing process, I kept thinking, "This doesn't make sense." I wanted to ask Jillian Michaels, a trainer on the show, "What was the magic moment in twenty-one-year-old contestant Jackson's life when the responsibility for his dietary and physical activity choices shifted from not-him to him?" Sunny, at seventeen, was a victim, but Jackson was still carrying the same pounds as he had in childhood and practicing the same eating habits we saw evidenced in his childhood pictures. It just didn't add up. If social factors (including family, religion, race, class, birthplace) influenced the kids' weight, it also influenced the adults' weight. Never mind that in many cases, like Jackson's,

Original to *Focus on Social Problems: A Contemporary Reader*.

overweight adults were previously overweight kids—if social factors play a role for kids, then they play a role for adults too.

The routine fat shaming of *The Biggest Loser* aside, I want to focus on the fact that individuals make choices based on available options (or "food access"), and those available options are strongly affected by U.S. food and agricultural policy. Food policy is the cumulative effect of laws, regulations, decisions, and actions by governments that influence agricultural production, distribution, and consumption. Reflecting American values of individualism and capitalism, food policy both reflects and reinforces the social and economic context of the nation.[3] In this piece, I highlight several federal policies that contribute to the limited food options facing eaters in the United States and offer some explanations as to why these policies exist and persist. Although there are many food-related policies (regulating food safety, food aid, and immigration and agricultural labor, for example), in this reading I focus on agricultural subsidies that contradict recommendations for a healthy diet as well as those policies that influence eaters' ability to make informed choices about their food. Sadly, some policies lead to poor health outcomes that hurt individuals and our society. *The Biggest Loser*'s meager impact on health and well-being is dwarfed by the messages and choices dictated by U.S. food policy. The real problem is that profit-motivated businesses drive them both. There are opportunities for positive change, and below I will identify some contemporary efforts to achieve better food policy, access, and health outcomes. Changing the food system for the better isn't simply about convincing individuals to buy better food products. Rather, such change involves a paradigm shift about what food is and what we can do, collectively, to improve food access by bringing policy in line with our national interest in a healthy population, potentially eliminating interest in extreme weight loss shows like *The Biggest Loser* that generally maintain the existing food system, driven by food advertising dollars.

Nutritional Recommendations and Food Subsidies: At Odds

In the more than thirty-five years since various arms of the U.S. government[4] began publishing dietary recommendations based on food and nutrition science, these instructions can be summed up as follows: eat vegetables, fruits, nuts, seeds, lean meats, and whole grains, but limit processed starches, red meat, salt, and refined sugar.[5] These recommendations are based entirely on promoting health and avoiding disease, not the economics of food or consumer preferences, much less the profitability of food production and processing. However, agricultural policies are created with economic interests in mind. Not surprisingly, these economic interests do not always align with public health goals. The result is that the foods we're told to avoid are the easiest to find and the least expensive for consumers to purchase.

The federal government has long offered direct subsidies for certain food producers in an attempt to control production and prices. Yet the government also has a vested interest in preserving the health of the population and educating the populace on how to live healthy, productive lives. To achieve those goals simultaneously, agricultural subsidies would have to increase production of and lower prices of health-promoting foods. However, the direct opposite is currently true. Processed starches, animal products, and sugars are the three categories that receive the greatest direct and indirect economic incentives for production, called subsidies, from the government, whereas fruit, vegetable, and nut production (called "specialty crops") do not receive payments. These subsidies affect the production and price of unhealthy foods, making them plentiful and artificially cheap. Food processing and specialized packaging (like frozen dinners, for example) lengthens the shelf life of these less healthy food products, making them more convenient as well. But why are processed starches, animal products, and sugar subsidized in the first place? To understand why our system functions the way it does today, let's explore the roots of our current agri-food system with a brief agricultural history of the United States.

History of Agriculture

The major trend in agriculture in the United States over the past century has been consolidation and specialization—farms are getting larger, as corporate-owned farms buy out smaller, diversified family-owned ones. Farms today are more likely to produce only a few crops on land that once produced a wide variety. These trends are a result of top-down agricultural policy that fostered the growth of agribusiness to the detriment of small family farms, policy that was designed and implemented by the federal government, and that has only escalated as these grown-up agribusinesses exert political influence.

"Get big or get out" was the command Earl Butz (Secretary of Agriculture under Presidents Nixon and Ford) gave U.S. farmers in the 1970s. His agricultural policy prioritized large farm scale and agribusiness, facilitating the growth of corporate farms and increasing subsidized[6] production of grains for export. As these policies took effect, the small, family-run farms we had relied on for food production began to disappear. Our agrarian society began to vanish, as small, family-owned farms with diverse crops couldn't compete with specialized corporate farms, whose profits were based on economies of scale as well as the growing subsidization of the production of agricultural commodities. Changes in farming coincided with the rise of the number of men and women in the industrial work force as farm- and home-based work shifted to wage-based work. These changes set the stage for the economic dominance of the processed food and fast-food industries. Food provision was no longer under the control of individual families; it was increasingly industrialized. Consolidation and specialization meant that food now traveled long distances between farmer and eater. This travel, and thus the whole food system, was built on the consistent availability of cheap fossil fuels.

Agricultural policy intersected with the technological, economic, and social context of the post–World War II era. Some of the factors that made large specialized farms profitable were technological advances that replaced large amounts of farm labor with machines. Much of the research behind these technological developments happened at public land grant universities with a combination of public and corporate funding. Other factors supporting the industrial model of agriculture have been cheap fossil fuels and the development of the interstate highway system. At the federal level, lowering previous trade barriers meant that larger farms growing mass quantities of grain had greatly expanded markets. Large grain farmers also benefited from agricultural subsidies, expanding the production of corn, wheat, and soy, making these grains plentiful and inexpensive. The goal of these subsidies was to standardize production, encouraging farmers to produce a stable food supply by removing some of the risk inherent in farming, where crops and thus livelihoods are vulnerable to weather and pests. Over time, farmers planted according to the payout they'd receive, which meant producing more and more feed grain, much of which was fed to animals. The subsidy program therefore took on a life of its own—becoming more and more enmeshed with corporate food and agriculture and the trade groups and lobbyists that represent their commercial interests. In contrast to small, diversified farms with grass-grazing herds of livestock, confined animal feeding operations (CAFOs) became economically advantageous after World War II. Americans considered meat from grain-fed animals preferable (fattier, more consistent quality, etc.). As a result of the postwar economic boom, consumers had larger disposable incomes. At that time, meat consumption in the United States was a sign of affluence, a form of conspicuous consumption that demonstrated high social status; with rising incomes came increased spending on animal-based foods.[7] Food policy has shaped what is available by shaping what farmers and corporations produce. Thus, the explosion of CAFOs and the subsequent increase in animal product consumption was a result of changes in agricultural technology and what consumer markets supported.

Although it dramatically shapes the eating options of the 318 million people in the United States, agricultural policy is not on most people's minds. That's partially because only 2 percent of adults in the United States are farmers. Every five or so years when a new Farm Bill moves through the wheels of government, we may hear about it on the news, but farms don't register high on the list of what's important for most people. Yet they should. Only a small group stands to benefit from subsidies, although the costs of food production are shared by all, including direct costs as a portion of taxes and hidden costs in the form of poor health outcomes. The agricultural lobby is so strong because of how our legislative branch is set up: whereas the House of Representatives is determined by population of the fifty states, the Senate is composed of two senators per state. Thus, senators representing states that are small in population, but where agriculture is an economically important industry (read: influenced highly by agribusinesses and their lobbyists) have a disproportionately loud voice in setting agricultural policy. One strategy for catching the attention of a larger group of Americans is to refer to this piece of legislation as the "Food Bill," instead of the "Farm Bill." After all, it determines funding for agricultural programs and antihunger programs (including the Supplemental Nutritional Access Program, or SNAP, formerly called food stamps) as well as conservation on farmland, issues that many nonfarmers care about but may be overlooked, hidden in the Farm Bill.

Sugar: Not So Sweet

It's no secret that a major factor in chronic diseases including diabetes, obesity, and heart disease is sugar consumption. Agricultural policy runs counter to nutritional recommendations when it comes to sugar production. One of the reasons we consume so much sugar is because it is cheap and readily available. We pour it directly into our iced tea, coffee, and Kool-Aid. Yet it is also hidden, added to processed foods where it is harder to visualize, which thus makes it harder for people to realize how much sugar they're actually eating. This cheap sugar isn't just ending up in candy and cookies; it's also added to foods that few would count as "sugary" or "sweets," like yogurt, jarred pasta sauce, and peanut butter. Why is there sugar in pasta sauce? Humans have an evolutionary preference toward sweet fruits. This was important for our hunter–gatherer ancestors for whom sweet fruits were in short supply and only seasonally available, but were filled with vital nutrients. Now that sugar is everywhere and doesn't come attached to vitamins and fiber, like it does in an apple or a grapefruit, our human predilection toward sugar can be harmful, leading to negative health outcomes like diabetes, heart disease, high blood pressure, and cancer, not to mention tooth decay.

Agricultural policy artificially props up sugar, making it inexpensive to consumers. Growing cane sugar is ecologically destructive and economically unprofitable without the direct payment of federal dollars to the sugar industry in the United States, especially because sugar can be more cheaply grown in tropical countries. The government's direct payments for corn production influence the production and price of corn-based syrups, including high-fructose corn syrup, which we rely on far more than cane sugar. If you've ever had the pleasure to travel and sip a Coca-Cola in another country, you may have noticed that in addition to being served room temperature (that's cultural), it has a different sweet taste (that's a result of U.S. agricultural policy). In the United States, the sugar in our soft drinks is corn based because our corn is subsidized and therefore artificially cheap; elsewhere, Coca-Cola and other soft drinks are made with cane- or beet-based sugar. Although added sugars are unhealthy in all forms, corn-based sweeteners are plentiful and cheap as a direct result of our agricultural policy.

The influence of money on politics, including the politics of public health, is perhaps the largest impact of agricultural industrialization and consolidation. This is clearly evidenced with the sugar industry (including corn-based sugars). One source of the sugar lobby's power is that sugar is prevalent in such a diversity of processed foods and is thus closely connected with other food and agricultural industries and trade groups. The World Health Organization (WHO) conducted a meta-analysis of research on the connection between sugar consumption and public health to develop a standard recommendation for sugar consumption, similar to daily recommendations for calories, fat, sodium, and other public health concerns. In response, multiple Big Food trade associations[8] threatened the WHO with political retribution.[9] At the urging of two senators, the Health and Human Services secretary, Tommy G. Thompson, submitted comments in 2003 attempting to suppress the draft report, saying in part, "Evidence that soft drinks are associated with obesity is not compelling."[10] You read that right: when a global nongovernmental organization with a public health mission made a dietary recommendation regarding sugar consumption, they were threatened by U.S. trade groups because the implications of this WHO report so compromised their economic interests.

Big Feed Grains = Big Animal Ag

Although it was never the original design, feed grains (led by corn) have become the largest category of commodity receiving subsidies. The availability of this artificially cheap feed was a contributing factor to the development of highly concentrated animal feeding operations. You may have seen Certified Grass-Fed ground beef at the supermarket and thought, "Wait, I thought all cattle ate grass!" In fact, conventionally raised animals eat grain for much of their lives. This misunderstanding is largely an issue of visibility. If you drive by a cow pasture, what you're likely viewing is a herd of cows used for breeding. After calves are old enough to stop nursing from

their mothers and eat a diet only of grain, they are sold to CAFOs to grow as large and quickly as possible before slaughter and butchering. These CAFOs are invisible to most U.S. eaters because they are located geographically far from urban and suburban residential areas, because the sheer amount of animal waste (65 percent of all animal manure in the United States is produced by CAFOs[11]) is so odorous and takes the form of dust, impacting air quality and health for neighbors. Communities near CAFOs are likely rural as well as socially and economically disadvantaged, and the addition of a nearby CAFO only further decreases the quality of life for the people who live there, forcing residents inside away from the stench and contributing to respiratory diseases.[12] Although it's difficult to pin down the growth of CAFOs, 50 percent of U.S. food animals were estimated to be in CAFOs in 2008,[13] including cattle, chickens, pigs, and turkey. The sheer scale of these operations presents unique environmental obstacles. Large volumes of fecal matter are treated in lagoons. Inevitably, pathogens and chemicals like nitrates and ammonia seep into soil and waterways. Worse, these lagoons often burst, disturbing ecosystems and nearby communities.[14]

Animal welfare is also a concern. As the name implies, animals are confined because the purpose of CAFOs is feeding and fattening. "Confined" often translates to "so cramped that they can't turn around," and thus the animals are unable to behave naturally. Scientific measurements of animal welfare include health (disease, pain, and injury), behavior (for example, the space and ability to do grooming behaviors), and physiology (for example, stress responses), and the results of measurements raise questions about the ethics and safety of CAFOs. As a result of the inherent stress and unsanitary environments of CAFOs, animals are routinely given antibiotics, a major contributor to antibiotic resistance and a source of water pollution. In all of these areas, CAFOs present many issues with animal welfare. Will Harris, a South Georgia rancher, described his distaste for the conventional process of raising healthy calves and selling them to the CAFO: "It's like raising your daughter to be a princess and then sending her to the whorehouse."[15] His family has managed a cattle herd on the same piece of land for five generations, and he effectively transitioned from conventional practices to a grass-fed, humane operation, from conception to slaughter. He went against the current and took some risks, but he is now able to practice ranching in a way that makes him proud. It turns out that cattle, too, are what they eat: the nutritional content of meat from cattle fattened on grain is inferior to grass-fed beef, which is higher in Omega 3's and lower in fat and calories. Thus, grass-fed meat lines up better with nutritional recommendations that lead to heart health. Increasingly, choosy consumers (often affluent urban and suburban residents) are paying a premium to access this meat.[16] It's become common to say that consumers "vote with their forks." Although consumers do have purchasing power, class inequality ensures that some people are disproportionately powerful, leaving economically disadvantaged people with an unequal "vote."

Consumers are increasingly wary of foods from genetically modified organisms (GMOs). To develop GMOs, agricultural scientists alter plants' and animals' genes directly. This represents a major technological leap from selective breeding, the centuries-old practice of saving seed from individual plants with desired characteristics for next season's crop, crossing plants to develop hybrids, or even using genetic sciences (a la Gregor Mendel) to achieve higher yields and bigger, tastier, more uniform, products. Those practices model nature, as species cross-pollinate. However, genetic engineering involves going beyond designing crops to have high yields and be more uniform, as in the example of Bt crops (including potatoes, corn, soybeans, with more crops added as they are developed),[17] where genes are inserted from the bacterium *Bacillus thuringiensis* into the genetic structure of the crop plant, imbuing the crop with pest resistance. This particular gene does not naturally exist in corn and would not have

been generated through millennia-old selective breeding techniques. Other examples of genetic engineering include Roundup Ready crops that have been modified to withstand applications of Monsanto's herbicide, Roundup. Critics refer to GMO foods as "Frankenfoods," referencing Mary Shelly's cautionary tale of the consequences of meddling with nature and life.

Perhaps most disconcerting about the practice of developing GMO crops is unknown impacts of their use on both the environment and human health. Although there is scientific consensus that GMO crops do not pose immediate human health risks, health impacts throughout time and over generations are difficult to predict. To be sure, all forms of agriculture involve humans engaged creatively with nature, and unintended consequences are almost certain. However, these consequences may be more severe when our interactions with nature become more sophisticated. One already-apparent environmental impact is that weeds are becoming resistant to a particular herbicide (glyphosate) that is frequently used with GMO crops. This necessitates the development of increasingly strong herbicides (in this case, an herbicide called 2-4D), and a new set of genetically engineered seeds resistant to 2-4D. Thus, farmers must use harsher and harsher agricultural chemicals, and new GMO crops must be constantly developed, continuing a vicious cycle with no end in sight.

Also troubling is the proprietary nature of genetically engineered (GE) crops, resulting from the specialization and corporatization of food commodities.[18] Agribusiness corporations hold patents on particular seeds, along with their accompanying agricultural chemicals (such as the aforementioned herbicides), that the farmers must buy each year.[19] Advocates of GMOs argue that the profit motivation is the impetus for corporations to innovate and that restricting profits will have a negative impact on technological advancement. However, this corporate control puts farmers on a technology treadmill, where to stay competitive they must adopt the innovative, production-increasing technology. But as production increases for all farmers, prices (and financial returns to the farmer) fall, and the farmer is stuck in a cycle of relying increasingly on off-farm inputs (nutrient fertilizer, seed, synthetic pesticides, etc.) to maintain a slim margin of profitability.[20] This treadmill largely explains the fact that although agricultural technology has improved and farm size has grown, farmer's profits have not risen proportionately, as corporations capture the lion's share of agricultural profits. The regulation of GMO crops and foods is an important policy issue and one that is (unsurprisingly) closely tied to corporate agriculture.

Although regulatory agencies in the United States have deemed genetically engineered crops and foods "functionally equivalent" to their non-GMO counterparts, citizen groups have focused their efforts on mandatory labeling of GMO foods so that consumers wishing to avoid them will have ready access to that information. That battle has largely been waged at the state level. In 2014, Vermont was the first state in the United States to mandate GMO labels, and the Grocery Manufacturers Association promptly filed suit to reverse this legislation before it had a chance to go into effect.[21] Also in 2014, an Oregon statewide measure for mandatory GMO labeling was narrowly defeated by just 837 votes, or 0.056 percent.[22] The focus of these citizen actions is on accessing information about how food was produced and giving consumers the information they need to differentiate between products made from agricultural practices they support and those they oppose.

Food Labels: How Consumers Get Information

When you pick up a box of cereal, what do you see? Much of what there is to read at the grocery store is a result of food policy. In fact, it's a pretty safe bet that if it is boring and doesn't read like an advertisement, it's a policy-related food label. But like most areas where money and market share is involved, the food industry has a loud voice in the political debate about what consumers know about their food.

The most important health-related information is usually on one of the narrow sides of the box. Nutrition Facts labels on processed foods are federally mandated and overseen by the Food and Drug Administration (FDA). Nutrition labels include information related to public health concerns. In other words, the goal of nutrition labels is to reduce the risk of chronic diseases such as cardiovascular disease, obesity, high blood pressure, and stroke and to encourage people to consume enough vital nutrients.[23] Although these familiar black and white boxes on food packaging may seem pretty straightforward, in the U.S. context of agribusiness and politics, the issue of which nutrients are included on the label is contentious.

Mandatory nutrition facts labels are the result of the Nutrition Labeling and Education Act of 1990 and went into effect in 1994.[24] The FDA proposed the first wave of revisions late in 2014 and they will be implemented around 2016.[25] The clearer and easier to understand food labels are, the more useful they are to regular people weighing day-to-day food decisions. Several upcoming changes clarify nutritional recommendations. One change simply makes food labels bigger and thus easier to read. Another does away with some of the confusing "serving size" issues of the present. How bizarre is it for a 20-ounce bottle of soda to give nutrition recommendations as "per serving," but the bottle is actually 2.5 servings? New labels will eliminate the need to multiply, presenting the package as a serving size (per bottle, per can, and so on), taking into account how people eat. Another proposed major change in labeling is the per-gram distinction between sugars that naturally occur in foods or ingredients (for example, sugars present in whole milk and fruit juice or in cereal containing dried fruit) and sugars added to foods. Although consumers have always been able to glance at an ingredients list to see the added sugar content relative to other ingredients (because ingredients are listed from greatest to least), we've never been able to differentiate between the total amount of sugar and the amount of processed or refined sugar that's been added to foods. This was a hotly debated issue because the sugar industry (discussed earlier) fought to keep added sugars essentially hidden on nutrition facts labels by adding their quantities to total grams of sugar.

Although I applaud this change as a step in the right direction, what I'd really like to see is a daily value recommendation for added sugars based in sound nutrition science. Percentage daily values can really stand out (they're even bolded). But quantifying a dietary recommendation for added sugars is a politically charged question. For some other important dietary considerations like calories, fat, carbohydrates, and sodium, our bodies require some, but too much is a problem. Added sugar isn't like fat or sodium in that way. Dietitians and food scientists know that human bodies do not require any added sugars. However, there are powerful sugar interests (in corn and sugar agriculture as well as the food and beverage industry) working to keep that information off the nutrition facts labels. Additionally, they work hard to push counter messages through advertising.

Advertising: Start 'Em Young

Corporate interests drive agricultural policy from production and processing to marketing and advertising. Industry self-regulation is the standard, with little government intervention. Jim Gaffigan pokes fun at our conflicted, somewhat embarrassing relationship with fast food and advertising in his standup routine. "We know those McDonald's commercials aren't realistic. I'd like to see a McDonald's commercial show someone five minutes after they ate McDonald's. 'Ughhhhhh. Now I need a cigarette. I deserve a cigarette break today.'" I don't think it's an accident that Gaffigan presents the image of cigarette smoking alongside McDonald's consumption: these are behaviors commonly recognized as unhealthy but that people choose for a variety of short-term reasons. Advertising

commonly sells an experience or emotion, not just a product. Just like the Marlboro Man was designed to sell us the image of the rugged, independent cowboy, food and beverage companies sell us on an image, too. Why do you think McDonald's labels children's meal as "Happy Meals"? We, as adults, can usually critique the message that drinking the right brand of soda will magically make us cool, happy, and energetic. We even know from experience how eating junk food makes us feel. Unfortunately, kids don't have that ability. Research shows that children under the age of eight do not understand that advertising is trying to sell them something, much less understand the increasingly sophisticated tactics that the advertisers are using. Kids under age four can't even determine the difference between the cartoon program they're watching and the cartoon advertisement.[26] Advertisements targeted at kids are almost exclusively for junk food.[27] This is an issue that could be regulated by smart government policies. As a society, we protect children from images and information they're not yet emotionally and intellectually prepared to handle—for example, visual content in a movie may warrant an R (for "restricted") rating. The daily deluge of food advertising to kids is drowning out the nutritional messages they desperately need to hear.

Jim Gaffigan paints a humorous picture of some of the reaction that McDonald's withstands: "I just love the societal outrage at McDonald's. 'McDonald's, there's no nutritional value! There's no vitamins!' McDonald's is just like, 'Excuse me, we sell burgers and fries. We never said we were a farmer's market. Heck, our spokesman is a pedophile clown from the 70s. What do you want from us, America?'" The absurdity is not that people are outraged; it's that this emotional energy is directed at the wrong target. McDonald's is operating within the current policy context. This outrage needs to be channeled into rewriting the rules to prohibit corporations from using clowns and cartoons to market harmful food to children, just as people took on and beat Big Tobacco, killing cartoon

Joe Camel. An incredibly easy place to start is to do away with food advertising to children in schools and the sale of junk foods in school vending machines and snack lines. In the world I want to live in, public schools are sacred spaces, where children learn and are safe from violence, coercion, and the targeted advertising and sale of foods that lead to diet-related diseases and mortality. Industry self-regulation is not working, and the time has come for stricter regulations on food advertising, especially advertising targeting children. McDonald's and other retailers and brands are carefully crafting lifelong, brand-loyal customers by selling the positive experience of Happy Meals (and their equivalents), complete with cartoons and toys in the box, knowing that these flavors, smells, and emotions are psychologically linked and incredibly powerful. The kids on *The Biggest Loser* are considered victims of marketing ploys and the actions of the adults meant to protect them. Yet those adults, who are participating in the show or raising the child participants, grew up with enticing food advertising that pushed them toward unhealthy food; they are still vulnerable to the messages, associations, and tastes established in their own childhoods.

Conclusion

Jim Gaffigan's concluding summation of McDonald's is "Momentary pleasure, followed by incredible guilt, eventually leading to cancer." A fantastic corollary to food policy that's not of the people, by the people, and for the people, is tobacco policy. Until the major legal and political battles of the 1990s, tobacco companies employed many of the techniques that corporate food producers use: advertising to children (enticing lifelong customers), squelching research about the health impacts of smoking, and lobbying elected officials to maintain their economic power. This tobacco comparison also matches Gaffigan's progression: pleasure, guilt, and cancer. The tobacco victory required mobilization of a social movement (backed by strong medical research) to debunk Big Tobacco's message

that tobacco use was cool, sophisticated, and safe. The fight (and victory) of the American people over Big Tobacco is a template for the changes, at a policy level, that are possible with food. The exciting difference between tobacco and food is that we have agricultural options that, unlike the production of refined grains, sugars, and animal products, are actually health promoting. Fruit and vegetable producers in the United States are, as a whole, profitable without subsidies. How easy would it be to redirect some federal money into an already-profitable sector to make nutritious food financially competitive with calorie-dense but nutrient-poor foods? For cash-strapped families, it can be tough to afford the cost of an organic bag of spinach, especially when a more filling option is to order from a fast-food chain's value meal. What if we subsidized organic foods, making foods that are pesticide free (good for our bodies and our environment) cost the same (or less) compared to conventional foods?

Consider the potential positive impacts of subsidizing ecologically restorative agricultural production[28] for the long-term productivity of our soils and food system. Consider the impact of reinvesting current subsidies of the production of food that makes us sick into the production of food that fulfills our health needs and protects water, soil, and our atmosphere. How restorative, healing, and positive would that be? Some applications that are already being developed and tested include payment for ecosystem services arrangements, where instead of slapping farmers who pollute water or destroy habitat of threatened and endangered species with fines, farmers are economically rewarded for taking actions to manage their lands in ways that improve water and soil health, sequester carbon in trees and other plants, and provide on-farm habitat for vulnerable wildlife species. Another idea is providing economic incentives for the production of nutrient-dense foods like sweet potatoes, spinach, nuts, and seeds. What if federal subsidies went to farmers who grew the healthiest foods, thus lowering the retail cost and increasing their availability to consumers? What if legislation required that full-service grocery stores be sited like schools—based on where people live, not profit driven and based on the financial demographics of the zip code, as is currently done, leaving out low-income and impoverished neighborhoods? The exciting thing is that the problem is so far-reaching—literally touching every person—that the solutions are equally diverse.

The growing food movement is challenging attitudes about food and the food system that do not serve people well. This movement is made up of many groups, including farmers, parents, people who have dealt with food-related diseases, chefs, nutritionists and health care professionals, and food and agricultural research scientists (both social scientists and natural scientists). Change is in the wind, but the mobilization of social energies, a true social movement, is needed to overcome the power of Big Ag and Big Food to establish policies that honor the true value of good food. Some of these attitudes are deep seeded, and challenging them involves examining commonly held beliefs that are often taken for granted. The first of these attitudes is the notion that food is just like any other commodity or product; it's made, valued, and traded based on what consumers are willing to pay for it. In contrast, the new food movement regards food as qualitatively different from other consumer goods. Food is not like toasters or t-shirts. We require it to live. It is also part of our humanity because of the cultural, spiritual, and emotional meaning that people across time and culture have imbued in food and eating. A second belief is that access to safe, nutritious, and adequate food (termed "food security") is a human right. Treating food as any other consumer good leads to ignoring social problems related to the food system (e.g., diet-related diseases, childhood obesity, lack of affordable healthy food for people in poverty) in favor of focusing on inefficiencies and/or overreach of government.

In our capitalist economy we treat the basics of food, health care and medicine, and education the same as other consumer goods and services. But economic systems are not outside the realm of human influence; in fact, they only persist because societies, and the people that make up societies, ascribe to them. What if we examined our economic system using measurements of health and well-being—human and ecological? What if we treated food, health care, and medicine—these foundations of human life and society—as the strong foundation on which to build an economy, not solely as economic industries themselves? Do we really want diet-related health care to be a positive contributor to our gross domestic product and a major economic driver? Improved food access does not just rest on everyone in the United States having access to safe, affordable, healthy food; it also includes a reorientation of our beliefs about food and a transformation of our economic and political systems to treat food differently. Profits cannot, and should not, be the ultimate goal of a food system. The development, implementation, and normalization of human- and earth-centric goals of our food system, as well as effective policy to achieve these goals, are the key to a healthy food system for all.

NOTES
1. "Obesity and Overweight for Professionals: Childhood: Data." Retrieved April 5, 2015. http://www.cdc.gov/obesity/data/childhood.html/.
2. "Obesity and Overweight for Professionals: Data and Statistics: Adult Obesity." Retrieved February 17, 2015. http://www.cdc.gov/obesity/data/adult.html.
3. Parke Wilde, *Food Policy in the United States: An Introduction.* Abingdon, Oxon and New York: Routledge, 2013.
4. U.S. Department of Agriculture (USDA) Department of Health and Human Services, Office of Disease Prevention and Health Promotion, USDA Food, Nutrition, and Consumer Services, USDA Center for Nutrition Policy and Promotion.
5. http://health.gov/dietaryguidelines/.

6. The government pays agricultural subsidies to farmers and agribusinesses to augment income and to moderate cost and supply of commodities. Commodities are primary, interchangeable agricultural products that can be bought and sold. Most often, commodities are used to produce other goods. Wheat is a commodity, whereas a box of Wheaties is not.

7. Before industrial agriculture, low-cost meals included staple grains like corn, wheat, or rice, beans, and greens, with meat used for flavoring (for example, beans and greens, with ham used to flavor both). The Western dietary pattern is meat- and sweet-centric, and the Western standard of living is the aspiration of the citizens of many developing countries.

8. Corn Refiners Association, International Dairy Foods Association, National Corn Growers Association, Snack Food Association, the Sugar Association, Wheat Foods Council, and U.S. Council for International Business.

9. U.S. Sugar Industry Targets New Study; Lawmakers' Aid Sought in Halting WHO Report JO. *The Washington Post*, April 23, 2003.

10. U.S. Sugar Industry Targets New Study; Lawmakers' Aid Sought in Halting WHO Report JO. *The Washington Post*, April 23, 2003.

11. Doug Gurian-Sherman, *CAFOs Uncovered* (Union of Concerned Scientists, April 2008), p. 94. Retrieved April 22, 2015. http://vegetarian.procon.org/sourcefiles/cafos_uncovered.pdf/.

12. Wendee Nicole, "CAFOs and Environmental Justice: The Case of North Carolina," *Environmental Health Perspectives*, 121 (2013), a182–189. http://dx.doi.org/10.1289/ehp.121-a182/.

13. Gurian-Sherman, 2008.

14. Nicole, 2013.

15. Kim Severson, "At White Oak Pastures, Grass-Fed Beef Is Only the Beginning," *The New York Times*, March 10, 2015. http://www.nytimes.com/2015/03/11/dining/at-white-oak-pastures-grass-fed-beef-is-only-the-beginning.html/.

16. Wendy J. Umberger, Peter C. Boxall, and R. Curt Lacy, "Role of Credence and Health Information in Determining US Consumers' Willingness-to-Pay for Grass-Finished Beef," *Australian Journal of Agricultural and Resource Economics*, 53 (2009), 603–623. http://dx.doi.org/10.1111/j.1467-8489.2009.00466.x/.

17. Ric Bessin, *Bt-Corn: What Is Is and How It Works*. University of Kentucky: UK Cooperative Extension Service. Retrieved April 26, 2015. http://www2.ca.uky.edu/entomology/entfacts/entfactpdf/ef130.pdf/.

18. GMO crops are also referred to as genetically engineered (GE) crops, and the foods produced from these crops, including meat and animal products fed GMO crops, are referred to as GMO or GE foods.

19. Monsanto's Roundup Ready soy is glyphosate resistant and thus coupled with Monsanto's Roundup (glyphosate) herbicide.

20. Richard A. Levins, and Willard W. Cochrane, "The Treadmill Revisited," *Land Economics*, 72 (1996), 550–553. http://dx.doi.org/10.2307/3146915/.

21. "Judge Considers Halting Vermont GMO Labeling Law," *USA Today*. April 27, 2015. http://www.usatoday.com/story/news/nation/2015/01/07/judge-considers-halting-vermont-gmo-law/21422959/. At the time this book went to press, the judge had just required that the labeling law go into effect while the lawsuit continues.

22. Michelle Brence, The Oregonian/OregonLive, "Oregon Certifies Defeat of Measure 92; GMO Labeling Loses by 837 Votes," *OregonLive.com*, 2014. Retrieved April 27, 2015. http://www.oregonlive.com/politics/index.ssf/2014/12/oregon_certifies_defeat_of_mea.html/.

23. Center for Food Safety and Applied Nutrition, "Labeling & Nutrition—Factsheet on

the New Proposed Nutrition Facts Label." Retrieved April 5, 2015. http://www.fda.gov/ Food/GuidanceRegulation/Guidance DocumentsRegulatoryInformation/ LabelingNutrition/ucm387533.htm/.

24. Ibid.

25. Ibid.

26. Food and Water Watch, *It Pays to Advertise: Junk Food Marketing to Children*. Washington, DC: Food & Water Watch, 2012, p. 23.

27. Ibid.

28. Restorative agriculture is a fascinating area, because it is necessarily ecological and site specific. It involves really understanding a mix of plant and animal species as well as an intimate knowledge of land. Some categories of restorative agricultural practices include agroforestry (combining trees and agricultural crops or livestock), perennial crops (as opposed to annual crops, which require soil disturbance and thus erosion each year), practicing no-till methods for annual crops, and practicing integrated pest management (where pesticides are avoided by introducing natural plant-based deterrents or predators of pests). The on-farm application of these practices is always nuanced, contrasted with large-scale mono-cropped agribusinesses.

REFERENCES

Bessin, Ric. *Bt-Corn: What It Is and How It Works*. University of Kentucky: UK Cooperative Extension Service. Retrieved April 26, 2015. http://www2.ca.uky.edu/entomology/entfacts/entfactpdf/ef130.pdf/.

Brence, Michelle. 2014. "Oregon Certifies Defeat of Measure 92; GMO Labeling Loses by 837 Votes. *OregonLive.com*. Retrieved April 27, 2015. http://www.oregonlive.com/politics/index.ssf/2014/12/oregon_certifies_defeat_of_mea.html/.

Center for Food Safety and Applied Nutrition. "Labeling & Nutrition—Factsheet on the New Proposed Nutrition Facts Label." Retrieved April 5, 2015. http://www.fda.gov/Food/GuidanceRegulation/GuidanceDocumentsRegulatoryInformation/LabelingNutrition/ucm387533.htm/.

Food and Water Watch. 2012. *It Pays to Advertise: Junk Food Marketing to Children*. Washington, DC: Food & Water Watch, p. 23.

Gurian-Sherman, Doug. 2008. *CAFOs Uncovered*. Union of Concerned Scientists, p. 94. Retrieved April 22, 2015. http://vegetarian.procon.org/sourcefiles/cafos_uncovered.pdf/.

"Judge Considers Halting Vermont GMO Labeling Law," *USA Today*. Retrieved April 27, 2015. http://www.usatoday.com/story/news/nation/2015/01/07/judge-considers-halting-vermont-gmo-law/21422959/.

Levins, Richard A., and Willard W. Cochrane. 1996. "The Treadmill Revisited." *Land Economics* 72:550–553. http://dx.doi.org/10.2307/3146915/.

Nicole, Wendee. 2013. "CAFOs and Environmental Justice: The Case of North Carolina." *Environmental Health Perspectives* 121:a182–a189. http://dx.doi.org/10.1289/ehp.121-a182/

"Obesity and Overweight for Professionals: Childhood: Data." Retrieved April 5, 2015. http://www.cdc.gov/obesity/data/childhood.html.

"Obesity and Overweight for Professionals: Data and Statistics: Adult Obesity." Retrieved February 17, 2015. http://www.cdc.gov/obesity/data/adult.html/.

Severson, Kim. 2015. "At White Oak Pastures, Grass-Fed Beef Is Only the Beginning." *The New York Times*, March 10, 2015. Retrieved April 5, 2015. http://www.nytimes.com/2015/03/11/dining/at-white-oak-pastures-grass-fed-beef-is-only-the-beginning.html/.

Umberger, Wendy J., Peter C. Boxall, and R. Curt Lacy. 2009. "Role of Credence and Health Information in Determining US Consumers' Willingness-to-Pay for Grass-Finished Beef." *Australian Journal of Agricultural and Resource Economics* 53:603–623. http://dx.doi.org/10.1111/j.1467-8489.2009.00466.x/.

Wilde, Parke. 2013. *Food Policy in the United States: An Introduction*. Abingdon, Oxon, and New York: Routledge.

Consumers Fight Back

Food Chain Workers Alliance

Consumers have been responding to the food system's domination by large corporations for almost 100 years. In the early 20th century, Jewish immigrant housewives in New York City's Lower East side challenged a growing kosher meat trust among butchers.[1] In the late 1960s, a small group of suburban Chicago housewives, including U.S. Representative Jan Schakowsky, then a young stay-at-home mother, took on the National Tea Company, a large supermarket chain based in Chicago, and demanded transparency in their food labeling. Until their campaign, foods did not have a clear expiration date. Instead, only the grocery stores and the distributors were able to decipher the codes to reveal the expiration dates on foods such as bologna and baby formula. Through a campaign of pressuring local stockboys at area grocery stores, the women were able to break the codes. Using this information, they wrote a "codebook" that drew national attention. Housewives across the country began to send in fifty cents to purchase the codebook. The national media attention encouraged A&P Grocery, National Tea Company's competitor, to mount an ad campaign that their products were stamped with clear and transparent expiration dates. The National Tea Company quickly followed suit.[2]

The most recent national consumer movement around food, emerging over the last thirty years, is both a response to corporate consolidation in the food system and rising environmental concerns. Since the early 1970s, the movement to challenge the consolidation of the food industry has been growing. With the publication of Frances Moore Lappe's *Diet for a Small Planet* in 1971, food activists have called for a more sustainable way to live.[3] However, greater consumer concern with fresh, local, organic, and sustainable food practices can also, in part, be traced back to these historical moments when members of the public began to raise serious concerns about the threats posed by the use of pesticides, particular DDT, in the cultivation of foods.[4]

Emboldened by the actions of activists like Ralph Nader, consumer rights activists took on large corporations seeking greater regulation of their business practices for the protection of the public;[5] this movement extended to the food industry and resulted in a recalibrated orientation to vegetarianism and organic foods. One of the first restaurants that integrated an environmentalist ethos into its selections was Alice Waters' Chez Panisse, opened in Berkeley, California, in 1971.[6]

Today, a hallmark of the food movement is the commitment, implicit or explicit, to environmental issues. Publications such as Eric Schlosser's 2001 *Fast Food Nation: The Dark Side of the All-American Meal* and Michael Pollan's 2006 *The Omnivore's Dilemma: A Natural History of Four Meals* have directed increased attention to eco-friendly domestic and restaurant practices.

As concerns over the environmental impact of food production catalyzed the turn towards locally grown foods and sustainable culinary practices—a staple of the food movement—these issues have transformed otherwise apolitical individuals into activists. Participants in the growing food movement express "concern about the industrial food system, and its implication in health problems, ecological devastation, and social injustices." In this sense, the time and care given to selecting locally grown food or seeking out organic eateries has become a form of social protest that is "more alluring than conventional political channels, particularly in a political climate where many people feel disenfranchised from traditional political processes and institutions."[7] Likewise, "In terms of the rhythms of daily life, it is often easier to express one's politics through a food purchase, than it is to find the time to write a letter, attend a protest, or participate in social movement politics."[8]

continues

▇ Continued

Consumer activism around locally-grown, fresh, and organic foods has successfully changed the food supply to include more of these food items; . . . employers note that they have maintained or grown their business by focusing on this niche market. However, the food movement of the last several decades has not focused on sustainable labor practices within the food system, with some notable exceptions, particularly with regard to farmworkers. For example, the United Farm Workers realized that the only way they would win justice for farm workers was through a collaborative effort with consumers. At its peak, the UFW grape boycott claimed that 10 percent of United States consumers were boycotting grapes. The boycott worked and farm workers won collective bargaining in the fields.

More recently, Pineros y Campesinos Unidoes del Noroeste (PCUN), an Oregon-based farmworker union, called on consumers to boycott NORPAC foods, a large grower cooperative in the Northwest that employs both farmworkers and packers, by boycotting Gardenburger which was distributed by NORPAC. Given the popularity of Gardenburger on college campuses, PCUN organized a campaign to target key college campuses and their food service companies. In 1999, PCUN was successful in getting Gardenburger to find another distributor. These and other examples of consumer activism having broad influence on the food system demonstrate the potential for consumer activism with regard to working conditions along the food chain. In fact, the members of the Food Chain Workers Alliance have engaged in significant consumer engagement work over the last decade, unanimously promoting the concept that sustainable food system must include sustainable labor practices for food workers.

NOTES

1. Frank, Dana. "Housewives, Socialists, and the Politics of Food: The 1917 New York Cost-of-Living Protests." *Feminist Studies* 11.2 (1985); Hyman, Paula E. "Immigrant Women and Consumer Protest: The New York City Kosher Meat Boycott of 1902." Ed. Pozzetta, George A. *American Immigration and Ethnicity*. New York: Garland Publishers, 1991; "Fight for Cheap Kosher Meat." *Chicago Daily Tribune*. 13 May 1902.
2. Twarog, Emily E. LaBarbera. *Beyond the Strike Kitchen: Housewives and Domestic Politics, 1935–1973*. Diss. University of Illinois at Chicago, 2011.
3. Lappé, Frances Moore. *Diet for a Small Planet*. New York: Ballantine Books, 1991.
4. Levenstein, 2003.
5. Foner, 2009.
6. Johnston, Josée, and Shyon Baumann. *Foodies: Democracy and Distinction in the Gourmet Foodscape*. New York: Routledge. 2010; Kamp, David. *The United States of Arugula: The Sun-Dried, Cold-Pressed, Dark-Roasted, Extra Virgin Story of the American Food Revolution*. New York: Random House. 2007.
7. Johnston & Baumann, 2010.
8. Ibid.

The Extraordinary Science of Addictive Junk Food

MICHAEL MOSS

Have you ever wondered why processed foods that are not good for us taste so good and remain so popular despite the growing evidence that they damage our health? Relying on interviews with industry insiders and featuring case studies for products like Dr Pepper and Lunchables, Moss discusses how processed foods are designed and marketed to be addictive to consumers, despite the health risks resulting from regular consumption.

On the evening of April 8, 1999, a long line of Town Cars and taxis pulled up to the Minneapolis headquarters of Pillsbury and discharged 11 men who controlled America's largest food companies. Nestlé was in attendance, as were Kraft and Nabisco, General Mills and Procter & Gamble, Coca-Cola and Mars. Rivals any other day, the C.E.O.'s and company presidents had come together for a rare, private meeting. On the agenda was one item: the emerging obesity epidemic and how to deal with it. While the atmosphere was cordial, the men assembled were hardly friends. Their stature was defined by their skill in fighting one another for what they called "stomach share"—the amount of digestive space that any one company's brand can grab from the competition.

James Behnke, a 55-year-old executive at Pillsbury, greeted the men as they arrived. He was anxious but also hopeful about the plan that he and a few other food-company executives had devised to engage the C.E.O.'s on America's growing weight problem. "We were very concerned, and rightfully so, that obesity was becoming a major issue," Behnke recalled. "People were starting to talk about sugar taxes, and there was a lot of pressure on food companies." Getting the company chiefs in the same room to talk about anything, much less a sensitive issue like this, was a tricky business, so Behnke and his fellow organizers had scripted the meeting carefully, honing the message to its barest essentials. "C.E.O.'s in the food industry are typically not technical guys, and they're uncomfortable going to meetings where technical people talk in technical terms about technical things," Behnke said. "They don't want to be embarrassed. They don't want to make commitments. They want to maintain their aloofness and autonomy."

A chemist by training with a doctoral degree in food science, Behnke became Pillsbury's chief technical officer in 1979 and was instrumental in creating a long line of hit products, including microwaveable popcorn. He deeply admired Pillsbury but in recent years had grown troubled by pictures of obese children suffering from diabetes and the earliest signs of hypertension and heart disease. In the months leading up to the C.E.O. meeting, he was engaged in conversation with a group of food-science experts who were painting an increasingly grim picture of the public's ability to cope with the industry's formulations—from the body's fragile controls on overeating to the hidden power of some processed foods to make people feel hungrier still. It was time, he and a handful of others felt, to warn the C.E.O.'s that their companies may have gone too far in creating and marketing products that posed the greatest health concerns.

The discussion took place in Pillsbury's auditorium. The first speaker was a vice president of Kraft named Michael Mudd. "I very much appreciate this opportunity to talk to you about childhood obesity and the growing challenge it presents for us all," Mudd began. "Let me say right at the start, this is not an easy subject. There are no easy answers—for what the public health community must do to bring this problem under control or for what the industry should do as others seek to hold it accountable for what has happened. But this much is clear: For those of us who've looked hard at this issue, whether they're public health professionals or staff specialists in your own companies, we feel sure that the one thing we shouldn't do is nothing."

As he spoke, Mudd clicked through a deck of slides—114 in all—projected on a large screen behind him. The figures were staggering. More than half of American adults were now considered overweight, with nearly one-quarter of the adult population—40 million people—clinically defined as obese. Among children, the rates had more than doubled since 1980, and the number of kids considered obese had shot past 12 million. (This was still only 1999; the nation's obesity

rates would climb much higher.) Food manufacturers were now being blamed for the problem from all sides—academia, the Centers for Disease Control and Prevention, the American Heart Association and the American Cancer Society. The secretary of agriculture, over whom the industry had long held sway, had recently called obesity a "national epidemic."

Mudd then did the unthinkable. He drew a connection to the last thing in the world the C.E.O.'s wanted linked to their products: cigarettes. First came a quote from a Yale University professor of psychology and public health, Kelly Brownell, who was an especially vocal proponent of the view that the processed-food industry should be seen as a public health menace: "As a culture, we've become upset by the tobacco companies advertising to children, but we sit idly by while the food companies do the very same thing. And we could make a claim that the toll taken on the public health by a poor diet rivals that taken by tobacco." "If anyone in the food industry ever doubted there was a slippery slope out there," Mudd said, "I imagine they are beginning to experience a distinct sliding sensation right about now."

Mudd then presented the plan he and others had devised to address the obesity problem. Merely getting the executives to acknowledge some culpability was an important first step, he knew, so his plan would start off with a small but crucial move: the industry should use the expertise of scientists—its own and others—to gain a deeper understanding of what was driving Americans to overeat. Once this was achieved, the effort could unfold on several fronts. To be sure, there would be no getting around the role that packaged foods and drinks play in overconsumption. They would have to pull back on their use of salt, sugar and fat, perhaps by imposing industrywide limits. But it wasn't just a matter of these three ingredients; the schemes they used to advertise and market their products were critical, too. Mudd proposed creating a "code to guide the nutritional aspects of food marketing, especially to children."

"We are saying that the industry should make a sincere effort to be part of the solution," Mudd concluded. "And that by doing so, we can help to defuse the criticism that's building against us." What happened next was not written down. But according to three participants, when Mudd stopped talking, the one C.E.O. whose recent exploits in the grocery store had awed the rest of the industry stood up to speak. His name was Stephen Sanger, and he was also the person—as head of General Mills—who had the most to lose when it came to dealing with obesity. Under his leadership, General Mills had overtaken not just the cereal aisle but other sections of the grocery store. The company's Yoplait brand had transformed traditional unsweetened breakfast yogurt into a veritable dessert. It now had twice as much sugar per serving as General Mills' marshmallow cereal Lucky Charms. And yet, because of yogurt's well-tended image as a wholesome snack, sales of Yoplait were soaring, with annual revenue topping $500 million. Emboldened by the success, the company's development wing pushed even harder, inventing a Yoplait variation that came in a squeezable tube—perfect for kids. They called it Go-Gurt and rolled it out nationally in the weeks before the C.E.O. meeting. (By year's end, it would hit $100 million in sales.)

According to the sources I spoke with, Sanger began by reminding the group that consumers were "fickle." (Sanger declined to be interviewed.) Sometimes they worried about sugar, other times fat. General Mills, he said, acted responsibly to both the public and shareholders by offering products to satisfy dieters and other concerned shoppers, from low sugar to added whole grains. But most often, he said, people bought what they liked, and they liked what tasted good. "Don't talk to me about nutrition," he reportedly said, taking on the voice of the typical consumer. "Talk to me about taste, and if this stuff tastes better, don't run around trying to sell stuff that doesn't taste good."

To react to the critics, Sanger said, would jeopardize the sanctity of the recipes that had made his products so successful. General Mills would not pull back. He would push his people onward, and he urged his peers to do the same. Sanger's response effectively ended the meeting.

"What can I say?" James Behnke told me years later. "It didn't work. These guys weren't as receptive as we thought they would be." Behnke chose his words deliberately. He wanted to be fair. "Sanger was trying to say, 'Look, we're not going to screw around with the company jewels here and change the formulations because a bunch of guys in white coats are worried about obesity.'"

The meeting was remarkable, first, for the insider admissions of guilt. But I was also struck by how prescient the organizers of the sit-down had been. Today, one in three adults is considered clinically obese, along with one in five kids, and 24 million Americans are afflicted by type 2 diabetes, often caused by poor diet, with another 79 million people having pre-diabetes. Even gout, a painful form of arthritis once known as "the rich man's disease" for its associations with gluttony, now afflicts eight million Americans.

The public and the food companies have known for decades now—or at the very least since this meeting—that sugary, salty, fatty foods are not good for us in the quantities that we consume them. So why are the diabetes and obesity and hypertension numbers still spiraling out of control? It's not just a matter of poor willpower on the part of the consumer and a give-the-people-what-they-want attitude on the part of the food manufacturers. What I found, over four years of research and reporting, was a conscious effort—taking place in labs and marketing meetings and grocery-store aisles—to get people hooked on foods that are convenient and inexpensive. I talked to more than 300 people in or formerly employed by the processed-food industry, from scientists to marketers to C.E.O.'s. Some were willing whistle-blowers, while others spoke reluctantly when presented with some of the thousands of pages of secret memos that I obtained from inside the food industry's operations. What follows is a series of small case studies of a handful of characters whose work then, and perspective now, sheds light on how the foods are created and sold to people who, while not powerless, are extremely vulnerable to the intensity of these companies' industrial formulations and selling campaigns.

"In This Field, I'm a Game Changer."

John Lennon couldn't find it in England, so he had cases of it shipped from New York to fuel the "Imagine" sessions. The Beach Boys, ZZ Top and Cher all stipulated in their contract riders that it be put in their dressing rooms when they toured. Hillary Clinton asked for it when she traveled as first lady, and ever after her hotel suites were dutifully stocked.

What they all wanted was Dr Pepper, which until 2001 occupied a comfortable third-place spot in the soda aisle behind Coca-Cola and Pepsi. But then a flood of spinoffs from the two soda giants showed up on the shelves—lemons and limes, vanillas and coffees, raspberries and oranges, whites and blues and clears—what in food-industry lingo are known as "line extensions," and Dr Pepper started to lose its market share. Responding to this pressure, Cadbury Schweppes created its first spin-off, other than a diet version, in the soda's 115-year history, a bright red soda with a very un-Dr Pepper name: Red Fusion. ... But consumers hated Red Fusion. "Dr Pepper is my all-time favorite drink, so I was curious about the Red Fusion," a California mother of three wrote on a blog to warn other Peppers away. "It's disgusting. Gagging. Never again."

Stung by the rejection, Cadbury Schweppes in 2004 turned to a food-industry legend named Howard Moskowitz. Moskowitz, who studied mathematics and holds a Ph.D. in experimental psychology from Harvard, runs a consulting firm in White Plains, where for more than three decades he has "optimized" a variety of products for Campbell Soup, General Foods, Kraft and PepsiCo. "I've optimized soups," Moskowitz told me. "I've optimized pizzas. I've optimized

salad dressings and pickles. In this field, I'm a game changer."

In the process of product optimization, food engineers alter a litany of variables with the sole intent of finding the most perfect version (or versions) of a product. Ordinary consumers are paid to spend hours sitting in rooms where they touch, feel, sip, smell, swirl and taste whatever product is in question. Their opinions are dumped into a computer, and the data are sifted and sorted through a statistical method called conjoint analysis, which determines what features will be most attractive to consumers. Moskowitz likes to imagine that his computer is divided into silos, in which each of the attributes is stacked. But it's not simply a matter of comparing Color 23 with Color 24. In the most complicated projects, Color 23 must be combined with Syrup 11 and Packaging 6, and on and on, in seemingly infinite combinations. ...

Moskowitz's work on Prego spaghetti sauce was memorialized in a 2004 presentation by the author Malcolm Gladwell at the TED conference in Monterey, Calif.: "After ... months and months, he had a mountain of data about how the American people feel about spaghetti sauce. ... And sure enough, if you sit down and you analyze all this data on spaghetti sauce, you realize that all Americans fall into one of three groups. There are people who like their spaghetti sauce plain. There are people who like their spaghetti sauce spicy. And there are people who like it extra-chunky. And of those three facts, the third one was the most significant, because at the time, in the early 1980s, if you went to a supermarket, you would not find extra-chunky spaghetti sauce. And Prego turned to Howard, and they said, 'Are you telling me that one-third of Americans crave extra-chunky spaghetti sauce, and yet no one is servicing their needs?' And he said, 'Yes.' And Prego then went back and completely reformulated their spaghetti sauce and came out with a line of extra-chunky that immediately and completely took over the spaghetti-sauce business in this country. . . . That is Howard's gift to the American people. . . . He fundamentally changed the way the food industry thinks about making you happy."

Well, yes and no. One thing Gladwell didn't mention is that the food industry already knew some things about making people happy—and it started with sugar. Many of the Prego sauces—whether cheesy, chunky or light—have one feature in common: The largest ingredient, after tomatoes, is sugar. A mere half-cup of Prego Traditional, for instance, has the equivalent of more than two teaspoons of sugar, as much as two-plus Oreo cookies. It also delivers one-third of the sodium recommended for a majority of American adults for an entire day. In making these sauces, Campbell supplied the ingredients, including the salt, sugar and, for some versions, fat, while Moskowitz supplied the optimization. "More is not necessarily better," Moskowitz wrote in his own account of the Prego project. "As the sensory intensity (say, of sweetness) increases, consumers first say that they like the product more, but eventually, with a middle level of sweetness, consumers like the product the most (this is their optimum, or 'bliss,' point)."

I first met Moskowitz on a crisp day in the spring of 2010 at the Harvard Club in Midtown Manhattan. As we talked, he made clear that while he has worked on numerous projects aimed at creating more healthful foods and insists the industry could be doing far more to curb obesity, he had no qualms about his own pioneering work on discovering what industry insiders now regularly refer to as "the bliss point" or any of the other systems that helped food companies create the greatest amount of crave. "There's no moral issue for me," he said. "I did the best science I could. I was struggling to

survive and didn't have the luxury of being a moral creature. As a researcher, I was ahead of my time."

. . . Thirty-two years after he began experimenting with the bliss point, Moskowitz got the call from Cadbury Schweppes asking him to create a good line extension for Dr Pepper. I spent an afternoon in his White Plains offices as he and his vice president for research, Michele Reisner, walked me through the Dr Pepper campaign. Cadbury wanted its new flavor to have cherry and vanilla on top of the basic Dr Pepper taste. Thus, there were three main components to play with. A sweet cherry flavoring, a sweet vanilla flavoring and a sweet syrup known as "Dr Pepper flavoring."

Finding the bliss point required the preparation of 61 subtly distinct formulas—31 for the regular version and 30 for diet. The formulas were then subjected to 3,904 tastings organized in Los Angeles, Dallas, Chicago and Philadelphia. The Dr Pepper tasters began working through their samples, resting five minutes between each sip to restore their taste buds. After each sample, they gave numerically ranked answers to a set of questions: How much did they like it overall? How strong is the taste? How do they feel about the taste? How would they describe the quality of this product? How likely would they be to purchase this product?

Moskowitz's data—compiled in a 135-page report for the soda maker—is tremendously fine-grained, showing how different people and groups of people feel about a strong vanilla taste versus weak, various aspects of aroma and the powerful sensory force that food scientists call "mouth feel." This is the way a product interacts with the mouth, as defined more specifically by a host of related sensations, from dryness to gumminess to moisture release. These are terms more familiar to sommeliers, but the mouth feel of soda and many other food items, especially those high in fat, is second only to the bliss point in its ability to predict how much craving a product will induce.

. . . On page 83 of the report, a thin blue line represents the amount of Dr Pepper flavoring needed to generate maximum appeal. The line is shaped like an upside-down U . . . [a]nd at the top of the arc, there is not a single sweet spot but instead a sweet range, within which "bliss" was achievable. This meant that Cadbury could edge back on its key ingredient, the sugary Dr Pepper syrup, without falling out of the range and losing the bliss. Instead of using 2 milliliters of the flavoring, for instance, they could use 1.69 milliliters and achieve the same effect. The potential savings is merely a few percentage points, and it won't mean much to individual consumers who are counting calories or grams of sugar. But for Dr Pepper, it adds up to colossal savings. "That looks like nothing," Reisner said. "But it's a lot of money. A lot of money. Millions."

The soda that emerged from all of Moskowitz's variations became known as Cherry Vanilla Dr Pepper, and it proved successful beyond anything Cadbury imagined. In 2008, Cadbury split off its soft-drinks business, which included Snapple and 7-Up. The Dr Pepper Snapple Group has since been valued in excess of $11 billion.

"Lunchtime Is All Yours"

Sometimes innovations within the food industry happen in the lab, with scientists dialing in specific ingredients to achieve the greatest allure. And sometimes, as in the case of Oscar Mayer's bologna crisis, the innovation involves putting old products in new packages.

The 1980s were tough times for Oscar Mayer. Red-meat consumption fell more than 10 percent as fat became synonymous with cholesterol, clogged arteries, heart attacks and strokes. Anxiety set in at the company's headquarters in Madison, Wis., where executives worried about their future and the pressure they faced from their new bosses at Philip Morris. Bob Drane was the company's vice president for new business strategy and development when Oscar Mayer tapped him to try to find some way to reposition bologna and other troubled meats that were declining in popularity and sales. . . .

Drane's first move was to try to zero in not on what Americans felt about processed meat but on what Americans felt about lunch. He organized focus-group sessions with the people most responsible for buying bologna—mothers—and as they talked, he realized the most pressing issue for them was time. Working moms strove to provide healthful food, of course, but they spoke with real passion and at length about the morning crush, that nightmarish dash to get breakfast on the table and lunch packed and kids out the door. He summed up their remarks for me like this: "It's awful. I am scrambling around. My kids are asking me for stuff. I'm trying to get myself ready to go to the office. I go to pack these lunches, and I don't know what I've got." What the moms revealed to him, Drane said, was "a gold mine of disappointments and problems."

He assembled a team of about 15 people with varied skills, from design to food science to advertising, to create something completely new—a convenient prepackaged lunch that would have as its main building block the company's sliced bologna and ham. They wanted to add bread, naturally, because who ate bologna without it? But this presented a problem: There was no way bread could stay fresh for the two months their product needed to sit in warehouses or in grocery coolers. Crackers, however, could—so they added a handful of cracker rounds to the package. Using cheese was the next obvious move, given its increased presence in processed foods. But what kind of cheese would work? Natural cheddar, which they started off with, crumbled and didn't slice very well, so they moved on to processed varieties, which could bend and be sliced and would last forever, or they could knock another two cents off per unit by using an even lesser product called "cheese food," which had lower scores than processed cheese in taste tests. The cost dilemma was solved when Oscar Mayer merged with Kraft in 1989 and the company didn't have to shop for cheese anymore; it got all the processed cheese it wanted from its new sister company, and at cost.

Drane's team moved into a nearby hotel, where they set out to find the right mix of components and container. They gathered around tables where bagfuls of meat, cheese, crackers and all sorts of wrapping material had been dumped, and they let their imaginations run. After snipping and taping their way through a host of failures, the model they fell back on was the American TV dinner—and after some brainstorming about names (Lunch Kits? Go-Packs? Fun Mealz?), Lunchables were born.

The trays flew off the grocery-store shelves. Sales hit a phenomenal $218 million in the first 12 months, more than anyone was prepared for. This only brought Drane his next crisis. The production costs were so high that they were losing money with each tray they produced. So Drane flew to New York, where he met with Philip Morris officials who promised to give him the money he needed to keep it going. "The hard thing is to figure out something that will sell," he was told. "You'll figure out how to get the cost right." Projected to lose $6 million in 1991, the trays instead broke even; the next year, they earned $8 million.

With production costs trimmed and profits coming in, the next question was how to expand the franchise, which they did by turning to one of the cardinal rules in processed food: When in doubt, add sugar. "Lunchables with Dessert is a logical extension," an Oscar Mayer official reported to Philip Morris executives in early 1991. The "target" remained the same as it was for regular Lunchables—"busy mothers" and "working women," ages 25 to 49—and the "enhanced taste" would attract shoppers who had grown bored with the current trays. A year later, the dessert Lunchable morphed into the Fun Pack, which would come with a Snickers bar, a package of M&M's or a Reese's Peanut Butter Cup, as well as a sugary drink. The Lunchables team started by using Kool-Aid and cola and then Capri Sun after Philip Morris added that drink to its stable of brands. Eventually, a line of the trays, appropriately called Maxed Out, was released that had as many as nine grams of saturated fat, or nearly an entire day's recommended maximum for kids, with up to two-thirds of the max for sodium and 13 teaspoons of sugar.

When I asked Geoffrey Bible, former C.E.O. of Philip Morris, about this shift toward more salt, sugar and fat in meals for kids, he smiled and noted that even in its earliest incarnation, Lunchables was held up for criticism. "One article said something like, 'If you take Lunchables apart, the most healthy item in it is the napkin.'" Well, they did have a good bit of fat, I offered. "You bet," he said. "Plus cookies."

The prevailing attitude among the company's food managers—through the 1990s, at least, before obesity became a more pressing concern—was one of supply and demand. "People could point to these things and say, 'They've got too much sugar, they've got too much salt,'" Bible said. "Well, that's what the consumer wants, and we're not putting a gun to their head to eat it. That's what they want. If we give them less, they'll buy less, and the competitor will get our market. So you're sort of trapped." (Bible would later press Kraft to reconsider its reliance on salt, sugar and fat.)

When it came to Lunchables, they did try to add more healthful ingredients. Back at the start, Drane experimented with fresh carrots but quickly gave up on that, since fresh components didn't work within the constraints of the processed-food system, which typically required weeks or months of transport and storage before the food arrived at the grocery store. Later, a low-fat version of the trays was developed, using meats and cheese and crackers that were formulated with less fat, but it tasted inferior, sold poorly and was quickly scrapped.

When I met with Kraft officials in 2011 to discuss their products and policies on nutrition, they had dropped the Maxed Out line and were trying to improve the nutritional profile of Lunchables through smaller, incremental changes that were less noticeable to consumers. Across the Lunchables line, they said they had reduced the salt, sugar and fat by about

10 percent, and new versions, featuring mandarin-orange and pineapple slices, were in development. These would be promoted as more healthful versions, with "fresh fruit," but their list of ingredients—containing upward of 70 items, with sucrose, corn syrup, high-fructose corn syrup and fruit concentrate all in the same tray—have been met with intense criticism from outside the industry.

One of the company's responses to criticism is that kids don't eat the Lunchables every day—on top of which, when it came to trying to feed them more healthful foods, kids themselves were unreliable. When their parents packed fresh carrots, apples and water, they couldn't be trusted to eat them. Once in school, they often trashed the healthful stuff in their brown bags to get right to the sweets. This idea—that kids are in control—would become a key concept in the evolving marketing campaigns for the trays. In what would prove to be their greatest achievement of all, the Lunchables team would delve into adolescent psychology to discover that it wasn't the food in the trays that excited the kids; it was the feeling of power it brought to their lives. As Bob Eckert, then the C.E.O. of Kraft, put it in 1999: "Lunchables aren't about lunch. It's about kids being able to put together what they want to eat, anytime, anywhere."

Kraft's early Lunchables campaign targeted mothers. They might be too distracted by work to make a lunch, but they loved their kids enough to offer them this prepackaged gift. But as the focus swung toward kids, Saturday-morning cartoons started carrying an ad that offered a different message: "All day, you gotta do what they say," the ads said. "But lunchtime is all yours."

With this marketing strategy in place and pizza Lunchables—the crust in one compartment, the cheese, pepperoni and sauce in others—proving to be a runaway success, the entire world of fast food suddenly opened up for Kraft to pursue. They came out with a Mexican-themed Lunchables called Beef Taco Wraps; a Mini Burgers Lunchables; a Mini Hot Dog

Lunchable, which also happened to provide a way for Oscar Mayer to sell its wieners. By 1999, pancakes—which included syrup, icing, Lifesavers candy and Tang, for a whopping 76 grams of sugar—and waffles were, for a time, part of the Lunchables franchise as well.

Annual sales kept climbing, past $500 million, past $800 million; at last count, including sales in Britain, they were approaching the $1 billion mark. Lunchables was more than a hit; it was now its own category. Eventually, more than 60 varieties of Lunchables and other brands of trays would show up in the grocery stores. In 2007, Kraft even tried a Lunchables Jr. for 3- to 5-year-olds.

In the trove of records that document the rise of the Lunchables and the sweeping change it brought to lunchtime habits, I came across a photograph of Bob Drane's daughter, which he had slipped into the Lunchables presentation he showed to food developers. The picture was taken on Monica Drane's wedding day in 1989, and she was standing outside the family's home in Madison, a beautiful bride in a white wedding dress, holding one of the brand-new yellow trays. . . . Monica Drane had three of her own children by the time we spoke, ages 10, 14 and 17. "I don't think my kids have ever eaten a Lunchable," she told me. "They know they exist and that Grandpa Bob invented them. But we eat very healthfully."

Drane himself paused only briefly when I asked him if, looking back, he was proud of creating the trays. "Lots of things are trade-offs," he said. "And I do believe it's easy to rationalize anything. In the end, I wish that the nutritional profile of the thing could have been better, but I don't view the entire project as anything but a positive contribution to people's lives."

Today Bob Drane is still talking to kids about what they like to eat, but his approach has changed. He volunteers with a nonprofit organization that seeks to build better communications between school kids and their parents, and right in the mix of their problems, alongside the academic struggles, is childhood obesity. Drane has also prepared a précis on the food industry that he used with medical students at the University of Wisconsin. And while he does not name his Lunchables in this document, and cites numerous causes for the obesity epidemic, he holds the entire industry accountable. "What do University of Wisconsin M.B.A.'s learn about how to succeed in marketing?" his presentation to the med students asks. "Discover what consumers want to buy and give it to them with both barrels. Sell more, keep your job! How do marketers often translate these 'rules' into action on food? Our limbic brains love sugar, fat, salt. . . . So formulate products to deliver these. Perhaps add low-cost ingredients to boost profit margins. Then 'supersize' to sell more. . . . And advertise/promote to lock in 'heavy users.' Plenty of guilt to go around here!"

"These People Need a Lot of Things, but They Don't Need a Coke."

The growing attention Americans are paying to what they put into their mouths has touched off a new scramble by the processed-food companies to address health concerns. Pressed by the Obama administration and consumers, Kraft, Nestlé, Pepsi, Campbell and General Mills, among others, have begun to trim the loads of salt, sugar and fat in many products. And with consumer advocates pushing for more government intervention, Coca-Cola made headlines in January by releasing ads that promoted its bottled water and low-calorie drinks as a way to counter obesity. Predictably, the ads drew a new volley of scorn from critics who pointed to the company's continuing drive to sell sugary Coke.

One of the other executives I spoke with at length was Jeffrey Dunn, who, in 2001, at age 44, was directing more than half of Coca-Cola's $20 billion in annual sales as president and chief operating officer in both North and South America. In an effort to control as much market share as possible, Coke extended its aggressive marketing to especially poor or vulnerable areas of the U.S., like New Orleans—where people were drinking twice as much Coke as the national average—or Rome, Ga., where the per capita intake was nearly three Cokes a day. In Coke's headquarters in Atlanta, the biggest consumers were referred to as "heavy users." "The other model we use was called 'drinks and drinkers,'" Dunn said. "How many drinkers do I have? And how many drinks do they drink? If you lost one of those heavy users, if somebody just decided to stop drinking Coke, how many drinkers would you have to get, at low velocity, to make up for that heavy user? The answer is a lot. It's more efficient to get my existing users to drink more."

One of Dunn's lieutenants, Todd Putman, who worked at Coca-Cola from 1997 to 2001, said the goal became much larger than merely beating the rival brands; Coca-Cola strove to outsell every other thing people drank, including milk and water. The marketing division's efforts boiled down to one question, Putman said: "How can we drive more ounces into more bodies more often?" (In response to Putman's remarks, Coke said its goals have changed and that it now focuses on providing consumers with more low- or no-calorie products.)

In his capacity, Dunn was making frequent trips to Brazil, where the company had recently begun a push to increase consumption of Coke among the many Brazilians living in *favelas*. The company's strategy was to repackage Coke into smaller, more affordable 6.7-ounce bottles, just 20 cents each. Coke was not alone in seeing Brazil as a potential boon; Nestlé began deploying battalions of women to travel poor neighborhoods, hawking American-style processed foods door to door. But Coke was Dunn's concern, and on one trip, as he walked through one of the impoverished areas, he had an epiphany. "A voice in my head says, 'These people need a lot of things, but they don't need a Coke.' I almost threw up."

Dunn returned to Atlanta, determined to make some changes. He didn't want to abandon the soda business, but he did want to try to steer the company into a more healthful mode, and one of the things he pushed for was to stop marketing Coke in public schools. The independent companies that bottled Coke viewed his plans as reactionary. A director of one bottler wrote a letter to Coke's chief executive and board asking for Dunn's head. "He said what I had done was the worst thing he had seen in 50 years in the business," Dunn said. "Just to placate these crazy leftist school districts who were trying to keep people from having their Coke. He said I was an embarrassment to the company, and I should be fired." In February 2004, he was.

Dunn told me that talking about Coke's business today was by no means easy and, because he continues to work in the food business, not without risk. "You really don't want them mad at you," he said. "And I don't mean that, like, I'm going to end up at the bottom of the bay. But they don't have a sense of humor when it comes to this stuff. They're a very, very aggressive company."

When I met with Dunn, he told me not just about his years at Coke but also about his new marketing venture. In April 2010, he met with three executives from Madison Dearborn Partners, a private-equity firm based in Chicago with a wide-ranging portfolio of investments. They recently hired Dunn to run one of their newest acquisitions—a food producer in the San Joaquin Valley. As they sat in the hotel's meeting room, the men listened to Dunn's marketing pitch. He talked about giving the product a personality that was bold and irreverent, conveying the idea that this was the ultimate snack food. He went into detail on how he would target a special segment of the 146 million Americans who are regular snackers—mothers, children, young professionals—people, he said, who "keep their snacking ritual fresh by trying a new food product when it catches their attention."

He explained how he would deploy strategic storytelling in the ad campaign for this snack, using a key phrase that had been developed with much calculation: "Eat 'Em Like Junk Food." After 45 minutes, Dunn clicked off the last slide and thanked the men for coming. . . . The snack that Dunn was proposing to sell: carrots. Plain, fresh carrots. No added sugar. No creamy sauce or dips. No salt. Just baby carrots, washed, bagged, then sold into the deadly dull produce aisle. "We act like a snack, not a vegetable," he told the investors. "We exploit the rules of junk food to fuel the baby-carrot conversation. We are pro-junk-food behavior but anti-junk-food establishment."

The investors were thinking only about sales. They had already bought one of the two biggest farm producers of baby carrots in the country, and they'd hired Dunn to run the whole operation. Now, after his pitch, they were relieved. Dunn had figured out that using the industry's own marketing ploys would work better than anything else. He drew from the bag of tricks that he mastered in his 20 years at Coca-Cola, where he learned one of the most critical rules in processed food: The selling of food matters as much as the food itself. Later, describing his new line of work, Dunn told me he was doing penance for his Coca-Cola years. "I'm paying my karmic debt," he said.

A Bug in the System: Why Last Night's Chicken Made You Sick

WIL S. HYLTON

If you've ever had even a mild case of food poisoning, you know just how terrible it can be. Although many of us have gotten sick from food, many consumers believe that our food is generally safe and that, in general, a system of strict government regulations and inspections of manufacturing plants protects us from contamination and pathogens in our meat, produce, and frozen foods. It may surprise you, then, to read Hylton's investigation of the broken food safety system. Hylton argues that the system designed to protect consumers is convoluted and often ineffective, putting American consumers at risk on a regular basis.

Late one night in September of 2013, Rick Schiller awoke in bed with his right leg throbbing. Schiller, who is in his fifties, lives in San Jose, California. He had been feeling ill all week, and, as he reached under the covers, he found his leg hot to the touch. He struggled to sit upright, then turned on a light and pulled back the sheet. "My leg was about twice the normal size, maybe even three times," he told me. "And it was hard as a rock, and bright purple." Schiller roused his fiancée, who helped him hobble to their car. He dropped into the passenger seat, but he couldn't bend his leg to fit it through the door. "So I tell her, 'Just grab it and shove it in,'" he recalled. "I almost passed out in pain."

At the hospital, five employees helped move Schiller from the car to a consulting room. When a doctor examined his leg, she warned him that it was so swollen there was a chance it might burst. She tried to remove fluid with a needle, but nothing came out. "So she goes in with a bigger needle—nothing comes out," Schiller said. "Then she goes in with a huge needle, like the size of a pencil lead—nothing comes out." When the doctor tugged on the plunger, the syringe filled with a chunky, meatlike substance. "And then she gasped," Schiller said.

That night, he drifted in and out of consciousness in his hospital room. His temperature rose to a hundred and three degrees and his right eye oozed fluid that crusted over his face. Schiller's doctors found that he had contracted a form of the salmonella bacterium, known as Salmonella Heidelberg, which triggered a cascade of conditions, including an inflamed colon and an acute form of arthritis. The source of the infection was most likely something he had eaten, but Schiller had no idea what. He spent four days in intensive care before he could stand again and navigate the hallways. On the fifth day, he went home, but the right side of his body still felt weak, trembly, and sore, and he suffered from constant headaches. His doctors warned that he might never fully recover.

Three weeks later, Schiller received a phone call from the Centers for Disease Control and Prevention. An investigator wanted to know whether he had eaten chicken before he became sick. Schiller remembered that he'd bought two packages of raw Foster Farms chicken thighs just before the illness. He'd eaten a few pieces from one of the packages; the other package was still in his freezer. Several days later, an investigator from the U.S. Department of Agriculture stopped by to pick it up. She dropped the chicken into a portable cooler and handed him a slip of paper that said "Property Receipt." That was the last time Schiller heard from the investigators. More than a year later, he still wasn't sure what was in the chicken: "I don't know what the Department of Agriculture found."

Each year, contaminated food sickens forty-eight million Americans, of whom a hundred and twenty-eight thousand are hospitalized, and three thousand die. Many of the deadliest pathogens, such as *E. coli* and listeria, are comparatively rare; many of the most widespread, such as norovirus, are mercifully mild. Salmonella is both common and potentially lethal. It infects more than a million Americans each year, sending nineteen thousand victims to the hospital, and killing more people than any other foodborne pathogen. A recent U.S.D.A study found that twenty-four per cent of all cut-up chicken parts are contaminated by some form of salmonella. Another study, by *Consumer Reports*, found that more than a third of chicken breasts tainted with salmonella carried a drug-resistant strain.

By the time Schiller became infected by salmonella, federal officials had been tracking an especially potent outbreak of the Heidelberg variety for three months—it had sent nearly forty per cent of its victims to the hospital. The outbreak began in March, but investigators discovered it in June, when a cluster of infections on the West Coast prompted a warning from officials at the C.D.C.'s PulseNet monitoring system, which

tracks illnesses reported by doctors. Scientists quickly identified the source of the outbreak as Foster Farms facilities in California, where federal inspectors had discovered the same strain of pathogen during a routine test. Most of the victims of the outbreak confirmed that they'd recently eaten chicken, and many specifically named the Foster Farms brand. On August 9th, investigators joined a conference call with Foster Farms executives to inform them of the outbreak and its link to the company.

Identifying the cause of an outbreak is much simpler than trying to stop one. Once officials have traced the contamination to a food producer, the responsibility to curb the problem falls to the U.S.D.A.'s Food Safety and Inspection Service, or F.S.I.S. In the summer of 2013, as the outbreak spread, F.S.I.S. officials shared the C.D.C.'s conclusion that Foster Farms meat was behind the outbreak, but they had no power to force a recall of the tainted chicken. Federal law permits a certain level of salmonella contamination in raw meat. But when federal limits are breached, and officials believe that a recall is necessary, their only option is to ask the producer to remove the product voluntarily. Even then, officials may only request a recall when they have proof that the meat is already making customers sick. As evidence, the F.S.I.S. typically must find a genetic match between the salmonella in a victim's body and the salmonella in a package of meat that is still in the victim's possession, with its label still attached. If the patient has already eaten the meat, discarded the package, or removed the label, the link becomes difficult to make, and officials can't request a voluntary recall.

As the Heidelberg outbreak continued into the fall, F.S.I.S. investigators tracked down dozens of patients and asked them to search their homes for contaminated chicken. In some cases, they discovered Foster Farms chicken that tested positive for salmonella—but they could not find a genetic match. David Goldman, who oversees public health at the F.S.I.S., told me, "We started about a hundred and forty traceback efforts. And we failed in every case."

Meanwhile, Foster Farms was still producing chicken. By mid-September, on the week that Schiller checked into the hospital, at least fifty new patients had been infected—the most of any week since the outbreak began. On October 8th, the C.D.C. issued its first warning to the public: two hundred and seventy-eight patients had now been infected with Heidelberg in seventeen states, the agency reported, and Foster Farms chicken was the "likely source" of the outbreak. On November 15th, the C.D.C. raised the number to three hundred and eighty-nine victims in twenty-three states. By early July, 2014, there were six hundred and twenty-one cases. Scientists estimate that for each reported case twenty-eight go unreported, which meant that the Foster Farms outbreak had likely sickened as many as eighteen thousand people.

Finally, on July 3, 2014, more than a year after the outbreak began, officials at the F.S.I.S. announced a genetic match that would allow the agency to request a recall. Foster Farms executives agreed to withdraw the fresh chicken produced in its California facilities during a six-day period in March of that year. All other Foster Farms chicken would remain in distribution.

A few days later, I stopped by the office of Representative Rosa DeLauro, a Democrat from Connecticut and one of the most vocal advocates for food safety in Congress. After twenty-five years in the capital, DeLauro is not easily surprised, but when I mentioned the Foster Farms outbreak she slammed a fist on the table. "They're getting a tainted product out!" she said. "What in the hell is going on?" Rick Schiller wondered the same thing. Last spring, as his leg healed and the headaches faded, he searched newspapers for signs of a recall. Then he started calling lawyers. Eventually, he found Bill Marler.

During the past twenty years, Marler has become the most prominent and powerful food-safety attorney in the country. He is fifty-seven years old, with neat gray hair and a compact physique; he tends to speak in a high, raspy voice, as though delighted by what he's about to say. His law firm, on the twenty-eighth floor of a Seattle office building, has filed hundreds of lawsuits against many of the largest food producers in the world. By his estimate, he has won more than six hundred million dollars in verdicts and settlements, of which his firm keeps about twenty per cent.

Given the struggles of his clients—victims of organ failure, sepsis, and paralysis—Marler says it can be tempting to dismiss him as a "bloodsucking ambulance chaser who exploits other people's personal tragedies." But many people who work in food safety believe that Marler is one of the few functioning pieces in a broken system. Food-borne illness, they point out, is pervasive but mostly preventable when simple precautions are taken in the production process. In Denmark, for instance, after a surge of salmonella cases in the 1980s, poultry workers were made to wash their hands and change clothing on entering the plant and to perform extensive microbiological testing. Sanctions—including recalls—are imposed as soon as a pathogen is found. As a result, salmonella contamination has fallen to less than two per cent. Similar results have been achieved in other European countries.

In the U.S., responsibility for food safety is divided among fifteen federal agencies. The most important, in addition to the F.S.I.S., is the Food and Drug Administration, in the Department of Health and Human Services. In theory, the line between these two should be simple: the F.S.I.S. inspects meat and poultry; the F.D.A. covers everything else. In practice, that line is hopelessly blurred. Fish are the province of the F.D.A.—except catfish, which falls under the F.S.I.S. Frozen cheese pizza is regulated by the F.D.A., but frozen pizza with slices of pepperoni is monitored by the F.S.I.S. Bagel dogs are F.D.A.; corn dogs, F.S.I.S. The skin of a link sausage is F.D.A., but the meat inside is F.S.I.S. "The current structure is there not because it's what serves the consumer best," Elisabeth Hagen, a former head of the F.S.I.S., told me. "It's there because it's the way the system has grown up." Mike Taylor, the highest-ranking food-safety official at the F.D.A., said, "Everybody would agree that if you were starting on a blank piece of paper and designing the food-safety system for the future, from scratch, you wouldn't design it the way it's designed right now."

Both the F.S.I.S. and the F.D.A. are also hampered by internal tensions. The regulatory function at the F.S.I.S. can seem like a distant afterthought at the U.S.D.A., whose primary purpose is to advance the interests of American agriculture. "We're the red-headed stepchild of the U.S.D.A.," one senior F.S.I.S. official told me. When regulation fails, private litigation can be the most powerful force for change. As Marler puts it, "If you want them to respond, you have to make them." Robert Brackett, who directed food safety at the F.D.A. during the George W. Bush Administration, told me that Marler has almost single-handedly transformed the role that lawsuits play in food policy: "Where people typically thought of food safety as this three-legged stool—the consumer groups, the government, and the industry—Bill sort of came in as a fourth leg and actually was able to effect changes in a way that none of the others really had." Hagen said the cost that Marler extracts from food makers "can be a stronger incentive or disincentive than the passing of any particular regulation." Mike Taylor called litigation such as Marler's "a central element of accountability."

Bill Marler lives with his wife and three daughters on Bainbridge Island, just west of Seattle. He commutes to work on a public ferry and spends the time walking in circles. He leaves his briefcase with friends in the cabin, climbs to the upper level, and steps outside, into the mist of Puget Sound. By the time the ferry reaches Seattle, forty minutes later, Marler has usually logged about two and a half miles. A few years ago, realizing that most of his clients were too sick or too far away to visit him at work, he stopped wearing office attire, leaving on the wicking fabrics he wears on the ferry. It can be jarring for a first-time visitor to pass through the wood-paneled lobby of his firm, down a long hallway of offices filled with paralegals and junior attorneys, only to discover a small man in damp gym clothes reclining at Marler's desk.

Marler rarely uses the fiery rhetoric one might expect from a lifelong litigator. His preference is the soft sell, the politician's lure—cajoling insurance adjusters, health officials, microbiologists, and opposing counsel. He developed his coaxing manner early on. In 1977, as a sophomore at Washington State University, in the small town of Pullman, he ran for the city council on a whim, and won by fifty-three votes. During the next four years, he sponsored a fair-housing bill, tightened snow-removal laws, established a bus service for drunk drivers (critics called it Bill's Booze Bus), and helped to manage the seven-member council's six-million-dollar budget. "All these skills that I use every day—how to deal with the media, how to deal with complex interpersonal relationships to try to get a deal done—I learned between the ages of nineteen and twenty-two, when everybody else was smoking dope," he told me. Jeff Miller, an attorney in New York, recalled the first time he faced Marler in federal court, on a day that Miller had to leave early for a charity event. The judge was notoriously thorny and Miller was terrified to request an early dismissal, which seemed like an invitation for Marler to object and score points. Miller told me, "And as I was in court, telling the judge that I needed to get out of there, Bill just cut a significant check and said, 'Bring this with you.'"

Marler became involved in food safety in 1993, as a thirty-five-year-old lawyer at a big Seattle firm, when a client called with a food-poisoning referral. An outbreak of *E. coli*, seemingly caused by contaminated burgers from Jack in the Box, was spreading through the state. Marler's client had a friend whose daughter had become ill, and Marler took her case. During the next several months, the outbreak sickened more than five hundred Jack in the Box customers. Four children died. Marler plunged into microbiological research on *E. coli*. After reading scientific papers and talking to experts, he discovered that the bacterium, which typically lives in the intestines of cattle, can enter the food supply in meat or when vegetables are contaminated by fecal matter. The outbreak had been caused by a variant of the bug known as O157:H7, which secretes a powerful toxin in a victim's body. In some cases, the toxin can induce a reaction called hemolytic–uremic syndrome, in which the individual's face and hands swell, bruises cover the body, and blood begins to trickle from the nose. One in twenty patients dies. The only way to kill the bacteria in food is to cook it thoroughly.

Attorneys for Jack in the Box responded to Marler's lawsuit by sending him more than fifty cardboard boxes of discovery material. Marler moved the boxes to his firm's conference room and spent nights and weekends sifting through every page. He found letters sent by the Washington State Department of Health to Jack in the Box, announcing a new, mandatory cooking temperature for ground beef. He discovered that the chain had not followed the new standards, undercooking its meat, and he studied suggestion forms submitted by employees to corporate headquarters indicating that Jack in the Box executives knew they were cutting corners.

Marler spent the next two years immersed in discovery and settlement negotiations. He turned down multimillion-dollar offers, and demanded a hundred million dollars, an unprecedented sum at the time. He courted food and health reporters at major news organizations and publicly accused the company's executives of killing children. To defuse the tension, he would meet the Jack in the Box attorneys at a hotel bar and buy them drinks. (Hours later, he might call a reporter to pass along gossip he had gleaned.) As the outbreak became national news, more than a hundred victims came forward to be represented by Marler. The settlement, of more than fifty million dollars, included $15.6 million for a ten-year-old girl named Brianne Kiner, who spent forty days in a coma. It was the largest individual food-poisoning claim in American history.

Prompted by public outrage, federal officials took a dramatic step. On September 29, 1994, at a convention of the American Meat Institute, Mike Taylor, at that time the administrator of the F.S.I.S., announced that his agency would adopt a zero-tolerance policy toward *E. coli* in ground beef. There would be no acceptable level of contamination; anytime the agency detected the bacterium, it would remove the product from distribution. To do so, Taylor would classify the outbreak strain of *E. coli* as an "adulterant," which in meat and poultry is normally reserved for toxic industrial chemicals. It was the first time that the agency had applied the designation to a food-borne microbe. Although a consortium of meat producers and retailers sued the U.S.D.A. that December, a federal court affirmed the change. Five years later, officials expanded the rule to banish the same strain of *E. coli* in other beef products. In 2011, they declared six additional strains of *E. coli* to be adulterants. The lesson, Taylor told me, is that "having accountability for prevention in the government regulatory system works." Yet, twenty years after Taylor's landmark *E. coli* decision, officials at the F.S.I.S. have failed to declare any other food-borne pathogen to be an adulterant in raw meat.

People who work with Marler are accustomed to e-mails landing in the night, with links and attachments and an abundance of exclamation points. At least twice a month, he flies across the country to speak with advocacy groups and at food-industry events. He will not accept payment from any food company, and has turned down thousands of dollars to deliver a short lecture, only to pay his own way to the venue and present the speech for free. Sometimes, when Marler takes the stage, members of the audience walk out. At a meeting of the Produce Manufacturers Association, in the summer of 2013, he approached the lectern as loudspeakers blared the Rolling Stones song "Sympathy for the Devil."

Marler rarely has trouble getting companies to concede when their product has caused illness, but occasionally one of his cases involves more complicated legal questions. In 2011, thirty-three people died of listeriosis after eating cantaloupe produced in Colorado by Jensen Farms. Listeria is a rare but deadly bacterium. It infects about sixteen hundred U.S. residents per year, and kills one in five victims. The disease can take up to seventy days to manifest symptoms, and, when it does, the initial signs—a sudden onset of chills, fever, diarrhea, headache, or vomiting—can resemble those of the flu. Since the 1980s, it has caused three of the deadliest food-borne outbreaks on record.

Because listeria can grow in cold temperatures, it is perfectly suited to the era of prepared foods. "One of the reasons that we still have a lot of food-borne illness is because we've created these environments of convenience," Marler told me one morning, as we barreled down the highway in his pickup, a 1951 Chevy with the license plate "ECOLI." The truck rattled and reeked of gasoline; his golden retriever, Rowan, slept in the truck bed. "Bagged salad, refrigerators with secret drawers that are supposed to keep things fresh for longer," Marler said, shaking his head. "We get so wrapped up with production and convenience, and nobody pays any attention to bacteriology." Indeed, at the Jensen Farms plant, where the contaminated cantaloupes originated, a mechanized system had been washing the melons with tap water, rather than the antimicrobial solution recommended by the F.D.A. The C.D.C. counts a hundred and forty-seven victims in the cantaloupe case. Sixty-six have filed suit, and forty-six of them have hired Marler. He is using a novel legal argument that could set a precedent in food law.

Unlike the F.S.I.S., the F.D.A. does not have a large army of inspectors for the products under its purview. Years can elapse between official inspections at a given food producer. In place of federal inspections, most reviews are conducted by private companies known as auditors. These audits are demanded by retailers who want to be sure they are buying clean food. In the case of the 2011 listeria outbreak, auditors had actually been inside the plant just a few days before the first contaminated cantaloupes were shipped. Subcontractors working for the company PrimusLabs noted the absence of antimicrobial wash but gave the facility a rating of "superior" and a score of ninety-six per cent.

Marler has filed suit against Jensen Farms and retailers like Walmart and Kroger, but he is also suing PrimusLabs on behalf of listeria victims. There is no clear legal basis for doing so. Because PrimusLabs is a private company, hired by another private company for a private purpose, its lawyers contend that its only legal duty is to the producer that commissioned its audit—not to the consumers who bought a cantaloupe several steps down the supply chain. Attorneys for PrimusLabs have tried repeatedly to have Marler's lawsuit dismissed. In most jurisdictions, they have failed. Marler says that the PrimusLabs attorneys have made a strategic blunder. An early settlement would have kept the outbreak relatively quiet, he told me, but each time the court rejects a motion by Primus to dismiss the case a precedent is set. "There was an empty desert between us, and I wasn't even sure they were there," he said. "Then they started leaving bread crumbs. They're creating a road map for how to try a case against them."

Privately, officials at the F.S.I.S. say that they would like to take a more aggressive stand on salmonella. But an agency ruling like the one twenty years ago on *E. coli* would almost certainly fail in court today. In the past forty years, federal judges have severely limited the agency's power. That history began, by most accounts, with a 1974 lawsuit in which the American Public Health Association sued the U.S.D.A. to demand that it print bacterial warnings on raw meat. An appellate court ruled that the warnings were unnecessary, because customers already knew that meat carries bacteria. "American housewives and cooks normally are not ignorant or stupid," the judge wrote.

When another court ruled in favor of the F.S.I.S. decision to declare *E. coli* an adulterant, the ruling included a passage to prevent the F.S.I.S. from applying the same label to other bacteria: "Courts have held that other pathogens, such as salmonella, are not adulterants." In response to that decision, in 1996 the F.S.I.S. enacted a series of new rules to curb pathogens like salmonella. For whole chickens, the salmonella "performance standard" was set at twenty percent, meaning that one in every five bird carcasses could be contaminated. That standard has since been lowered to 7.5 per cent, but the performance standard for salmonella in ground chicken is much higher—44.6 per cent—and for ground turkey it is 49.9 per cent. "Which means that almost half of all your ground chicken that goes off the line can actually test positive for salmonella," Urvashi Rangan, the director of food safety at *Consumer Reports*, told me. Some products, such as cut-up chicken parts, have no performance standard at all. A hundred per cent of the product in supermarkets may be contaminated without running afoul of federal limits. Rangan told me that she was stunned when she discovered this, just recently: "We've asked the U.S.D.A. point blank, 'So does that mean there aren't standards for lamb chops and pork ribs?' And they said, 'Yeah, we don't have standards for those.'"

When I asked David Goldman, of the F.S.I.S.'s public-health program, why a common product like chicken parts has no contamination limit, he said, "We're in the process of doing just that." Last week, the agency announced plans to establish its first performance standard for chicken parts, limiting salmonella contamination to 15.4 per cent of packages. I asked Phil Derfler, the deputy administrator, why it had taken the agency twenty years. "It's not like there is anybody else in the world who is pursuing what we're doing, and so it is a bit of trial and error," he said. "If there was a font of wisdom that said, 'You should be doing this,' maybe we would be doing it." I mentioned Denmark's success in combatting salmonella, and Derfler said, "I mean, it would be a major kind of almost top-to-bottom kind of thing. And I don't know what the costs would be in economics."

Even when the agency sets a pathogen limit and a producer exceeds it, officials have few options. Under the terms of a 1999 lawsuit, inspectors may not shut down a facility because of a failure to meet contamination limits. Instead, officials must use indirect measures to put pressure on the company, such as posting news of the violation on the F.S.I.S. Web site, which could embarrass company executives. Derfler told me that the agency's work-arounds have been effective. "We have tried to do it," he said.

In December of 2013, officials at the F.S.I.S. unveiled a new "Salmonella Action Plan." At the heart of the plan was a "poultry-slaughter rule," which would reduce the number of federal inspectors observing the production line at slaughterhouses. Derfler told me that this will allow the agency to place "a greater emphasis on microbiology" and added that the rule also requires plants to do their own testing. Critics of the plan wonder how it is possible to improve food safety by removing inspectors. On March 13th of last year, Representative Louise Slaughter, who is the only member of Congress with a degree in microbiology, and ten other members of the House, including Rosa DeLauro, wrote a letter to the F.S.I.S., calling certain aspects of the new plan "pernicious" and asking that it be suspended. Nevertheless, the fiscal budget for 2015 assumes that it will go into effect, and cuts the funding for several hundred federal meat inspectors.

Marler opposes the new poultry rule, but he says that the real issue is the inspectors' inability to close a plant when they detect high levels of food-borne pathogens. "If you're allowing the product to become contaminated, having more or less inspectors is beside the point," he said. In 2011, the Center for Science in the Public Interest, a nonprofit advocacy group, submitted a petition to the F.S.I.S. arguing that the four most vicious types of salmonella should be declared adulterants, like *E. coli*. The agency issued no response and, in May of last year, Marler consulted with the center on a lawsuit demanding a reply to the petition. On July 31st, officials formally rejected the proposal, claiming that "more data are needed." Marler scoffed at the claim. "One part of the meat industry is just ignoring twenty years of progress on the other side," he said. "They're using the same words, the same press releases, the same language that they used twenty years ago, when they were saying, 'Oh, my God, the sky will fall if you label *E. coli* O157 as an adulterant.'"

When Marler's litigation becomes complicated and protracted, his firm can go months without generating income. Marler routinely lends money to the firm to keep the operation afloat. One morning, his longtime office manager, Peggy Paulson, stepped into his office with a sheepish look. When Marler glanced up, Paulson said quietly, "I could use a check for half a million bucks." Marler's jaw dropped with feigned horror. "So could I!" he said with a laugh. Then he promised to write a check. Later, he told me, "That's partly why I don't buy a vacation home. I've never been in a position that I settled a case because I needed the money."

During the past five years, Marler has begun to move from litigation to activism. In 2009, frustrated by the short attention span of the mass media, he founded an online newsletter, *Food Safety News*, which employs four full-time reporters and costs Marler a quarter of a million dollars a year to underwrite. On July 25, 2014, the editor of the site, Dan Flynn, and two of its employees received subpoenas in a defamation lawsuit against ABC News by the meat producer Beef Products, Inc. The lawsuit also names two former employees of the F.S.I.S., who spoke critically about the company in the ABC segment. Marler is defending those employees pro bono; two weeks ago, he received a subpoena in the case himself. Late at night, Marler also scribbles entries for the MarlerBlog, his personal Web site, where he has posted more than five thousand commentaries on food safety in recent years.

Sometimes, when Marler encounters critics who charge him with having predatory motives, he challenges them to "put me out of business." David Acheson, a former Associate Commissioner for Foods at the F.D.A., told me, "That's just become a bit of a trademark. He doesn't want that." Still, Acheson told me that he has seen an evolution in Marler. "In the early days, Bill was just on a mission to sue large food companies—he was on a mission to make money," Acheson said. "But I think during the course of that he realized that there are problems with the food-safety system, and I think progressively, philosophically, he changed from

just being a plaintiff attorney to being somebody who believes that changing food safety for the betterment of public health is a laudable goal." Acheson added, with no small measure of distaste, "He still sues food companies."

In April, 2014, Marler filed a suit against Foster Farms on behalf of Rick Schiller. On July 31st, the C.D.C. announced that the outbreak "appears to be over." Foster Farms has implemented new controls to reduce salmonella, but Marler hopes that a successful lawsuit will pressure other producers to take similar precautions. Meanwhile, last summer, an eight-year-old boy in Braintree, Massachusetts, died of complications from *E. coli* after eating ground beef from a Whole Foods market. Six weeks later, an epidemiologist with the Massachusetts Department of Public Health, in an e-mail to the boy's mother, accused Whole Foods executives of "grasping at straws and dragging their feet in an attempt to avoid doing a recall." On August 15th, the F.S.I.S. announced that its testing had "determined that there is a link between ground beef purchased at Whole Foods Market and this illness cluster." The company agreed to issue a recall of three hundred and sixty-eight pounds of ground beef, but it continues to assert that "our thorough and ongoing investigation of the circumstances has not shown any clear link to our business." On December 17th, Marler filed suit against Whole Foods on behalf of the boy's parents.

"Fifteen years ago, almost all the cases I had were *E. coli* linked to hamburger, and now I have maybe two or three," he told me over the phone in mid-January. He was sitting in his office overlooking the Seattle harbor. "It shows how much progress we've made. You might hate lawyers, you might not want us to make money, but look what the beef industry did." Marler said he had recently eaten a hamburger for the first time in twenty years. "Ground beef has learned its lesson—but chicken is still, in many respects, unregulated. So we have to keep fighting."

Strategies for Social Change

Alicia Garza

Alicia Garza is co-creator of #BlackLivesMatter. Started as a social media campaign, Black Lives Matter moved beyond a hashtag to become a rallying cry of social protestors and a new movement for social change.

Courtesy of Adam Lerner.

Could you describe how #BlackLivesMatter developed? Did you anticipate how strongly it would strike a chord with people all around the country?

#BlackLivesMatter was developed in 2013 after George Zimmerman was acquitted in the murder of a black teenager, Trayvon Martin, who was walking through the neighborhood. When the verdict was announced, I just felt sick to my stomach.

When I saw how some people online were responding to the verdict, I felt that a large part of our experience was missing. People were either really cynical about the ability of black people to ever receive any justice from the U.S. criminal justice system or there was a blaming and "personal responsibility" narrative being directed at black people—as if we created these conditions under which so many of us suffer. I have a brother who is 25; he's tall, brilliant, and black and was raised in a predominantly white suburban area. I just couldn't help thinking that he could have been Trayvon.

So I wrote a love letter to black people that challenged the notion that if Trayvon had just been more "respectable," that his life would not have been lost. Instead, I wrote that we all deserve to live dignified lives and that what happened to Trayvon wasn't about the hoodie he was wearing—it was about a system of racism in this country that renders black people and our lives without value. I celebrated our love for each other and for our willingness to still fight for freedom and justice, even though that fight gets harder and harder. And I ended it with black lives matter.

Patrisse Cullors placed a hashtag in front of it and together we decided to build it out as an organizing project. Opal Tometi then built out our online engagement platforms using her skills and resources. We developed it as an organizing project nationally that used social media to connect people online so that they could take action together offline.

I think we had some sense that #BlackLives Matter was resonating with people in a different way than what we'd seen before, but we had no idea that it would explode in this way.

What do you mean (more broadly) when you say "Black Lives Matter"?

Black Lives Matter is a principle by which we organize our lives and a principle we use in order to organize our communities to build the political and economic power that we need to determine our own futures. Black Lives Matter means that we have value and deserve to live with dignity. This country was built off of the backs and blood of our ancestors and has yet to reckon with its brutal and bloody beginnings. The lasting impacts of slavery and the structural racism that was built after slavery was "abolished" in this country to limit black people's access to opportunities and resources and the democratic process has not yet been dealt with. It's not just police killings that comprise the heart and soul of #BlackLives Matter. We are calling attention to the conditions of black people across all social institutions throughout the U.S. and throughout the world.

It is important to us that we lift up the notion of "All Black Lives" rather than a much more common notion where black lives = black men. When we visualize the experiences of those who are often left out of the narratives, we can see not only the conditions of our people much more clearly, but we can devise better strategies and tools to get us closer to the world that we dream of.

As an activist and organizer, what did you do once you realized the level of attention and momentum that the social media campaign developed?

#BlackLivesMatter never was solely a social media campaign. We used it on social media, but immediately after we developed it we took it out into our communities. We have always tried to use the momentum that social media generates to have provocative conversations and to take bold steps together that test the limits of what's possible in this moment.

One thing that is really important to us as organizers is that we are vigilant in our quest not to become "activist celebrities." To the degree that we have a platform, we want to use it to lift up the courage and hard work of so many people who never get recognition for the bold steps they are taking for all of us. We want to use our platforms to push our country to engage in real dialogue and meaningful action that eliminates racism, patriarchy and heteronormativity, and takes on capitalism in a real way as an unsustainable economic system responsible for the degradation of our communities and our democracy.

Black Lives Matter was visible in Ferguson, Missouri, following the killing of unarmed black teenager, Michael Brown, by a police officer. How did you participate in social activism in Ferguson?

Patrisse and Darnell Moore organized a #Black LivesMatter freedom ride that brought together more than 400 black people from around the country in support of communities in St. Louis that were fighting back against the impact of racism in their communities, particularly black communities. I personally spent over five weeks in St. Louis (Ferguson is a small suburb of St. Louis) supporting the development and training of local community members in community based organizing work. I worked with a team of almost 20 people to learn how to increase long-term participation and leadership of a growing movement against racism there.

Who is your activist inspiration and why?

My activist inspiration is Harriet Tubman, mostly because she organized the Underground Railroad to lead black people to freedom in the North during slavery. Her courage and tenacity against the toughest odds really inspire me. Tubman once said, "If you hear the dogs, keep going. If you see the torches in the woods, keep going. If there's shouting after you, keep going. Don't ever stop. Keep going. If you want a taste of freedom, keep going." "Keep going" is something I tell myself every day.

You now work for the National Domestic Workers Alliance. Do you plan on continuing to organize specific actions around Black Lives Matter?

Of course! I joined the National Domestic Workers Alliance (NDWA) just a short while after we launched #BlackLivesMatter, and for me, the work is really integrated. In fact, we just launched our new black domestic workers organizing project, called We Dream in Black. This project invests in the leadership capacity of black domestic workers to support their ability to lead the movement for a new democracy and a new economy. So much of the work I do at NDWA is really living the vision that we have for #BlackLivesMatter.

How much control do you have over the Black Lives Matter movement and actions?

#BlackLivesMatter is an organized network of people united under a vision and set of guiding principles and practices. The corporate media really are the ones responsible for naming this movement the #BlackLivesMatter movement, not us. At the same time, we see ourselves as a part of a black liberation movement whose time has come. It's exciting that so many people are using #BlackLivesMatter to describe what a world can look like when black people are free.

What are the major challenges that activists face?

Some of the challenges that activists in our chapters have are figuring out how to work with new configurations of people, how to bring together different approaches and strategies, and also how to navigate conflict that can arise as a result of trying to do things differently.

I think the other challenge activists and organizers face is that outside of our world, people don't really know what this work is, what it entails, and more importantly, why it's important. We sometimes tell stories that are incredibly ahistorical about how change happens. People end up looking at our history as if there weren't the same kinds of challenges and conflicts.

What are major misconceptions the public has about activism in general?

I remember seeing this episode of Seinfeld once that depicted an activist as a dreary Communist wearing an old green army uniform and carrying around a newspaper to sell and who was, of course, a white man. But the reality is that most activists are not that. There isn't a typical profile of an activist, and activism comes in many forms—I think we're seeing that now in really important and beautiful ways. Commonalities amongst us include a passion and a commitment to making the impossible possible.

What would you consider to be your greatest successes as an activist?

I think my greatest success is yet to come! One thing I'm proud of has been connecting with and celebrating the leadership of young queer black women. That's something that's important to me and something I think is so important to our movement.

I had the amazing opportunity to support the work of a fantastic organization known as Millennial Activists United, founded by a brilliant group of mostly queer black women working to engage young people in the ongoing fight against state-sanctioned violence. I was honored to be present when they founded the organization! I continue to be incredibly inspired by them each and every day.

Why should students get involved in your line of activism?

I would encourage students to be involved in something that supports the empowerment of the communities that they come from and to do something every day that is about the "we." I would encourage students to get involved in something that they are passionate about and committed to—it doesn't need to be what I do, but it should be something that ensures that we leave this world much better than we found it.

If an individual has little money and time, are there other ways they can contribute? What ways can students enact social change in their daily lives?

There are a million ways to contribute to this movement, and while you don't have to have a lot of money, investing your time is important! Having conversations with your friends and family about the movement's goals and objectives is a big one. Writing to your local decision makers and letting them know you support the demands of the #BlackLivesMatter network is also important. You can find out if there is a local chapter in your area and see how you can be helpful there as well.

Same-Sex, Different Attitudes

KATHLEEN E. HULL

In recent decades the United States has witnessed major social change in the area of marriage equality for same-sex couples. Hull explores what created such dramatic change from political wedge issue to political inevitability. Hull points to the public's changing attitudes, gay visibility, acceptance via media representations, and the fact that the social crisis predicted by conservatives as a result of LGBT marriage never appeared, as possible reasons for the rapid social change. Hull discusses strategies different interest groups have used to push their social change agendas and why not all LGBT activists are interested in prioritizing marriage rights.

Ten short years ago, same-sex marriage produced deep divisions within American society. The majority of Americans opposed granting legal recognition to gay and lesbian couples, and politicians seemed to play tug-of-war with the issue as it suited their needs. In 2003, Massachusetts became the first state to grant marriage licenses to same-sex couples when its high court ruled that withholding marriage recognition violated the state's constitution. In the meantime, in his 2004 State of the Union address, President George W. Bush called for an amendment to the federal constitution to block same-sex marriages nationwide. Gavin Newsom, then the mayor of San Francisco, responded a month later by opening marriage to same-sex couples at San Francisco City Hall. It was a short-lived policy, ultimately shut down by the courts, but it drew frenzied media attention; the image of two brides or two grooms tying the knot graced TV screens and newspapers' front pages, no longer rhetoric, but reality. By the November 2004 general election, 11 states voted on—and, ultimately, for—ballot measures to amend their state constitutions to ban same-sex marriages. Some even argued that those ballot measures played a decisive role in Bush's re-election; at a minimum, the initiatives represented a clear right-wing strategy to get socially conservative voters to the polls in a tight election year. In a happy coincidence for the incumbent, those who voted for same-sex marriage bans generally also took the time to vote for the Republican presidential candidate.

. . . [Today], things look quite different. President Obama publicly declared his support for same-sex marriage in the midst of his 2012 re-election campaign, and, less than a year later, the U.S. Supreme Court ruled a section of the federal Defense of Marriage Act (DOMA) unconstitutional. The move opened the door for federal recognition of the same-sex marriages that had been performed in "legal" states. [In 2015 The US Supreme Court ruled that state prohibitions on same-sex marriage violated the Constitution, thus legalizing same-sex marriage in all fifty states.] Some Republican strategists now think the issue is a "loser" for their party as national polls have started to show majority support for legal same-sex marriage. Although opinion differs dramatically by region, those young and middle-aged, middle-class white voters Republicans could long count on are becoming more liberal on the marriage issue, and political operatives are all too aware that a firm stand against marriage equality might siphon off once-staunch, party line voters. When an issue seemingly inspired such passion and division just a decade ago, how could it so quickly have become an election day "loser"?

First, a look at the numbers. [Looking at Gallup poll results between 1996 (the year Congress passed DOMA) and 2013 shows a dramatic change in less than 20 years]. . . . The poll asked: "Do you think marriages between same-sex couples should or should not be recognized by the law as valid, with the same rights as traditional marriages?" Between 1996 and July 2013, the proportion of respondents who said same-sex marriages should be valid rose from 27 to 54%. The proportion saying such marriages should *not* be valid declined from 68 to 43%. (A small proportion of respondents, never exceeding 5 percent, offered no opinion on the issue.) Other polls, worded differently, have yielded similar results. For example, Pew Research Center asks: "Do you strongly favor, favor, oppose, or strongly oppose allowing gays and lesbians to marry legally?" In 2003, the Pew question yielded 34% in favor and 56% opposed to same-sex marriage; by 2013, 49% of Americans were in favor and 44% opposed. A 2013 Washington Post/ABC News asking, "Do you think it should be legal or illegal for gay and lesbian couples to get married?" showed a 58%–36% divide, with the majority preferring "legal."

Attitude change that occurs this quickly and on this scale cannot be explained in the usual ways. It's not a case of older people with more conservative beliefs dying out and being replaced by younger, more liberal generations (what social scientists refer to as a cohort replacement effect). Rather, this kind of rapid shift suggests some individuals are changing their minds on the issue. Indeed, a recent Pew Research Center report noted that more than a quarter of Americans who currently favor legal same-sex marriage stated that they had changed their view on this issue. Historical Pew poll numbers back this up: support for same-sex marriage rose *within* every age cohort between 2003 and 2013, although age is still a good predictor of views on this issue. For example, support for same-sex marriage among the so-called Silent Generation (those born 1928–1945) rose from only 17% in 2003 to 31% in 2013, while support among Millennials (those born after 1980) increased from 51 to 70%. Acceptance of same-sex marriage is rising at roughly the same rate across generations, but the starting point—those first poll results—is much lower for each previous generation.

So, if it's not just a cohort replacement, what has caused large-scale shift? Several different factors likely contributed. In the March 2013 Pew poll, respondents who said they had changed their minds were also asked why. About a third stated that it had come through knowing someone who was gay, and a quarter attributed the change to getting older, becoming more open, and thinking about the issue more. Smaller proportions cited the prevalence and seeming inevitability of same-sex marriage, the idea that everyone should have freedom of choice without government interference, or a general belief in equal rights.

Beyond these self-reported reasons, at least two other factors have probably contributed to changing views. One is the growing cultural visibility of same-sex relationships and families headed by same-sex couples. Two decades ago, gay and lesbian characters were relatively rare on TV shows and in movies; when comedian

Ellen DeGeneres and her sitcom alter ego came out in 1997, it was a major news event. Some TV stations refused to air the coming-out episode of her show. Today, films like *Brokeback Mountain* can be nominated for Best Picture Oscars and characters like same-sex couple Cam and Mitchell on the TV comedy *Modern Family* enjoy more plotline attention for their parenting foibles than their sexual orientation. Cultural visibility like this familiarizes people, and for some individuals that increased familiarity is enough to soften opposition to homosexuality and gay rights.

A second factor that has likely contributed to declining opposition to same-sex marriage is the fact that such marriages are now legal in several U.S. states and many countries. At the time of this writing [in the spring of 2014], 17 U.S. states and the District of Columbia . . . , along with 17 countries outside the U.S., recognize same-sex marriage. Not only has the relatively rapid spread of legal same-sex marriage created a sense of inevitability (as noted by some respondents in the 2013 Pew poll), but it also casts doubt on some of the arguments against legal recognition. As more jurisdictions institute legal same-sex marriage and there's no subsequent clear evidence of harmful outcomes, the direst predictions about marriage equality's negative effects on "traditional" marriages and children lose credibility.

Changing attitudes about same-sex marriage are occurring in the broader context of changing beliefs about the moral acceptability of homosexuality and other sex-related behaviors. On most of these issues, the general trend has been toward greater acceptance. In Gallup's annual Values and Beliefs Survey, the proportion of Americans saying that gay and lesbian relations are morally acceptable climbed from 40% in 2001 to 59% in 2013, the largest percentage-point change for any of the twenty issues covered by the survey. (By way of comparison, the proportion saying having a baby outside of marriage was morally acceptable rose from 45 to 60%, and acceptance of sex between an unmarried man and unmarried woman went from

53 to 63%.) Views on the moral status of homosexual conduct almost certainly influence attitudes toward same-sex marriage.

In fact, numerous studies have established that being female, younger, and more highly educated are all associated with greater acceptance of homosexuality and support for same-sex marriage. Those who attend religious services regularly, identify as Republican, and live outside cities generally have less tolerant views. In addition, people who personally know gay men, lesbians, or bisexuals are more accepting; people who believe homosexuality is a choice are less so.

In a recent analysis of General Social Survey data from 1988 through 2010, sociologist Dawn Michelle Baunach found that only four characteristics were significant predictors of level of support for same-sex marriage across all survey years: religious attendance, political affiliation, education, and gender. Back in 1988, support for same-sex marriage was mostly limited to highly educated urbanites who were not religious conservatives. By 2010, opposition to same-sex marriage had become localized to older Americans, southerners, African-Americans, evangelical Protestants, and Republicans. Baunach concluded that most of the change in same-sex marriage attitudes was due to a general cultural shift that transcended demographic categories, rather than to changes in the composition of the population or the strength of the influence of certain characteristics on people's views.

As Americans' views of same-sex marriage are shifting, opponents and advocates of legal same-sex marriage continually adjust their legal and political strategies. Over the last couple of decades, opponents of same-sex marriage have moved away from strategies that vilify gays and lesbians as immoral and toward arguments emphasizing a concern for children and religious freedoms. This shift was probably motivated in part by the recognition that a declining proportion of Americans had moral objections to homosexuality per se. On the other side, proponents of legal same-sex marriage are shifting away from the language of rights and highlighting the universality of love and equal legal protection of all families. "Post mortem" political research conducted after votes on same-sex ballot measures found the simple message that loving relationships and families of all kinds deserve social support resonated with average voters. Rights-based arguments mostly fell flat.

In ways that may surprise many, the marriage issue has proven controversial even within lesbian, gay, bisexual, and transgender (LGBT) communities. Queer critics argue that marriage is a mechanism of social and sexual control, thus antithetical to the founding principles of gay liberation. LGBT feminists express concern that same-sex marriage cannot be disentangled from the patriarchal roots of the institution of marriage itself. Other LGBT skeptics question whether marriage has been the right area of focus for the gay rights movement, given that basic LGBT anti-discrimination protections are still paltry and that marriage may benefit only a small segment of the community (namely, middle-class lesbians and gay men who desire social assimilation). But in interview research that Timothy Ortyl and I conducted with LGBT people in the Minneapolis–St. Paul area, we found little support for the idea that same-sex marriage is mainly important to more privileged members of this population. And U.S. Census data on same-sex couples indicate that those couples raising children (who might reap significant practical benefits from access to marriage) are actually disproportionately lower-income people of color, not upper-middle-class whites intent on assimilating into the American nuclear family ideal.

And it's far from clear that the "traditional" nuclear family holds a prominent place in the American cultural imagination today. The debates over same-sex marriage have unfolded alongside rapid change in Americans' general beliefs and practices concerning marriage and family formation. With almost half of all first marriages ending in divorce and nearly half of all children being born to unmarried parents, the meanings and practices of marriage and family evolve toward greater diversity. Most

Americans still desire marriage, but many no longer view it as essential to a happy life. Further, the ideal of a single marriage as a lifelong commitment bumps up against the realities of longer lifespans and the declining stigma of divorce.

A recent study by sociologist Brian Powell and colleagues affirmed that Americans' definitions of family were broadening at a rapid pace. Between 2003 and 2006, the proportion who held the most restrictive definitions of family (definitions that generally only included married, heterosexual couples with children) fell from 45 to 38%. Those with the broadest definitions, including same-sex and heterosexual couples with or without children, married or unmarried, rose from 25 to 32%. These are large changes, given the short time period. A follow-up survey in 2010 found a further broadening in definitions of family.

Taken together, the evolution of Americans' attitudes about same-sex marriage has not one, but several underlying causes. As more gays and lesbians come out to friends and family, more people feel a personal connection to the issue. The passage of time gives people a chance to get used to the idea of same-sex marriage. And with more jurisdictions implementing legal same-sex marriage, some people have come to see its spread as inevitable. Others have noted that the sky has not fallen on those trailblazing states and countries—the consequences some predicted simply haven't come to pass. True, some of the change is due to cohort replacement, but this accounts for only a small proportion of the overall change. Increasing cultural visibility and declining moral disapproval of homosexuality have real, if difficult to measure effects. Political advocates of same-sex marriage, more effective and research-based, may also account for some of the change. Most broadly, changes in the nature of marriage and family—changes that touch virtually all Americans directly or indirectly—cause many of us to rethink our personal definitions of marriage and family, as well as the purposes and effectiveness of laws and policies that favor some definitions over others.

Small Change: Why the Revolution Will Not Be Tweeted

MALCOLM GLADWELL

Is social media radically changing the way we fight to bring about social change? Gladwell argues no, that accounts of social media revolutionizing successful activism and social change are overhyped. Gladwell acknowledges the strength of social media in generating large networks of individuals, but argues that these networks are built around weak ties to others in the network, without clear leaders. He contends that strong ties and a hierarchal organization are needed for a successful social change agenda because networks generated by social media succeed at increasing participation in social change movements precisely because so little needs to be done to participate; the type of activism that will cause meaningful social change lies in more traditional forms of activism that combine closely connected and strongly motivated individuals.

At four-thirty in the afternoon on Monday, February 1, 1960, four college students sat down at the lunch counter at the Woolworth's in downtown Greensboro, North Carolina. They were freshmen at North Carolina A. & T., a black college a mile or so away.

"I'd like a cup of coffee, please," one of the four, Ezell Blair, said to the waitress.

"We don't serve Negroes here," she replied.

The Woolworth's lunch counter was a long L-shaped bar that could seat sixty-six people, with a standup snack bar at one end. The seats were for whites. The snack bar was for blacks. Another employee, a black woman who worked at the steam table, approached the students and tried to warn them away. "You're acting stupid, ignorant!" she said. They didn't move. Around five-thirty, the front doors to the store were locked. The four still didn't move. Finally, they left by a side door. Outside, a small crowd had gathered, including a photographer from the Greensboro *Record*. "I'll be back tomorrow with A. & T. College," one of the students said.

By next morning, the protest had grown to twenty-seven men and four women, most from the same dormitory as the original four. The men were dressed in suits and ties. The students had brought their schoolwork, and studied as they sat at the counter. On Wednesday, students from Greensboro's "Negro" secondary school, Dudley High, joined in, and the number of protesters swelled to eighty. By Thursday, the protesters numbered three hundred, including three white women, from the Greensboro campus of the University of North Carolina. By Saturday, the sit-in had reached six hundred. People spilled out onto the street. White teenagers waved Confederate flags. Someone threw a firecracker. At noon, the A. & T. football team arrived. "Here comes the wrecking crew," one of the white students shouted.

By the following Monday, sit-ins had spread to Winston–Salem, twenty-five miles away, and Durham, fifty miles away. The day after that, students at Fayetteville State Teachers College and at Johnson C. Smith College, in Charlotte, joined in, followed on Wednesday by students at St. Augustine's College and Shaw University, in Raleigh. On Thursday and Friday, the protest crossed state lines, surfacing in Hampton and Portsmouth, Virginia, in Rock Hill, South Carolina, and in Chattanooga, Tennessee. By the end of the month, there were sit-ins throughout the South, as far west as Texas. "I asked every student I met what the first day of the sitdowns had been like on his campus," the political theorist Michael Walzer wrote in *Dissent*. "The answer was always the same: 'It was like a fever. Everyone wanted to go.'" Some seventy thousand students eventually took part. Thousands were arrested and untold thousands more radicalized. These events in the early sixties became a civil-rights war that engulfed the South for the rest of the decade—and it happened without e-mail, texting, Facebook, or Twitter.

The world, we are told, is in the midst of a revolution. The new tools of social media have reinvented social activism. With Facebook and Twitter and the like, the traditional relationship between political authority and popular will has been upended, making it easier for the powerless to collaborate, coordinate, and give voice to their concerns. When ten thousand protesters took to the streets in Moldova in the spring of 2009 to protest against their country's Communist government, the action was dubbed the Twitter Revolution, because of the means by which the demonstrators had been brought together. A few months after that, when student protests rocked Tehran, the State Department took the unusual step of asking Twitter to suspend scheduled maintenance of its Web site, because the Administration didn't want such a critical organizing tool out of service at the height of the demonstrations. "Without Twitter the people of Iran would not have felt empowered and confident to stand up for freedom and democracy," Mark Pfeifle, a former national-security adviser, later wrote, calling for Twitter to be nominated for the Nobel Peace Prize. Where activists were once defined by their causes, they are now defined by their tools. Facebook warriors go online to push for change. "You are the best hope for us all," James K. Glassman, a former senior State Department official, told a crowd of cyber activists at a recent conference sponsored by Facebook, A. T. & T., Howcast, MTV, and Google. Sites like Facebook, Glassman said, "give the U.S. a significant competitive advantage over terrorists. Some time ago, I said that Al Qaeda was 'eating our lunch on the Internet.' That is no longer the case. Al Qaeda is stuck in Web 1.0. The Internet is now about interactivity and conversation."

These are strong, and puzzling, claims. Why does it matter who is eating whose lunch on the Internet? Are people who log on to their Facebook page really the best hope for us all? As for Moldova's so-called Twitter Revolution, Evgeny Morozov, a scholar at Stanford who has been the most persistent of digital evangelism's critics, points out that Twitter had scant internal significance in Moldova, a country where very few Twitter accounts exist. Nor does it seem to have been a revolution, not least because the protests—as Anne Applebaum suggested in *The Washington Post*—may well have been a bit of stagecraft cooked up by the government. (In a country paranoid about Romanian revanchism, the protesters flew a Romanian flag over the Parliament building.) In the Iranian case, meanwhile, the people tweeting about the demonstrations were almost all in the West. "It is time to get Twitter's role in the events in Iran right," Golnaz Esfandiari wrote, this past summer, in *Foreign Policy*. "Simply put: There was no Twitter Revolution inside Iran." The cadre of prominent bloggers, like Andrew Sullivan, who championed the role of social media in Iran, Esfandiari continued, misunderstood the situation. "Western journalists who couldn't reach—or didn't bother reaching?—people on the ground in Iran simply scrolled through the English-language tweets post with tag #iranelection," she wrote. "Through it all, no one seemed to wonder why people trying to coordinate protests in Iran would be writing in any language other than Farsi."

Some of this grandiosity is to be expected. Innovators tend to be solipsists. They often want to cram every stray fact and experience into their new model. As the historian Robert Darnton has written, "The marvels of communication technology in the present have produced a false consciousness about the past—even a sense that communication has no history, or had nothing of importance to consider before the days of television and the Internet." But there is something else at work here, in the outsized enthusiasm for social media. Fifty years after one of the most extraordinary episodes of social upheaval in American history, we seem to have forgotten what activism is.

Greensboro in the early nineteen-sixties was the kind of place where racial insubordination was routinely met with violence. The four students who first sat down at the lunch counter were terrified. "I suppose if anyone had come up behind me and yelled 'Boo,' I think I would have fallen off my seat," one of them said later. On the first day, the store manager notified the police chief, who immediately sent two officers to the store. On the third day, a gang of white toughs showed up at the lunch counter and stood ostentatiously behind the protesters, ominously muttering epithets such as "burr-head nigger." A local Ku Klux Klan leader made an appearance. On Saturday, as tensions grew, someone called in a bomb threat, and the entire store had to be evacuated.

The dangers were even clearer in the Mississippi Freedom Summer Project of 1964, another of the sentinel campaigns of the civil-rights movement. The Student Nonviolent Coordinating Committee recruited hundreds of Northern, largely white unpaid volunteers to run Freedom Schools, register black voters, and raise civil-rights awareness in the Deep South. "No one should go *anywhere* alone, but certainly not in an automobile and certainly not at night," they were instructed. Within days of arriving in Mississippi, three volunteers—Michael Schwerner, James Chaney, and Andrew Goodman—were kidnapped and killed, and, during the rest of the summer, thirty-seven black churches were set on fire and dozens of safe houses were bombed; volunteers were beaten, shot at, arrested, and trailed by pickup trucks full of armed men. A quarter of those in the program dropped out. Activism that challenges the status quo—that attacks deeply rooted problems—is not for the faint of heart.

What makes people capable of this kind of activism? The Stanford sociologist Doug McAdam compared the Freedom Summer dropouts with the participants who stayed, and discovered that the key difference wasn't, as might be expected, ideological fervor. "*All* of the applicants—participants and withdrawals alike—emerge as highly committed, articulate supporters of the goals and values of the summer program," he concluded. What mattered more was an applicant's degree of personal connection to the civil-rights movement. All the volunteers were required to provide a list of personal contacts—the people they wanted kept apprised of their activities—and participants were far more likely than dropouts to have close friends who were also going to Mississippi. High-risk activism, McAdam concluded, is a "strong-tie" phenomenon.

This pattern shows up again and again. One study of the Red Brigades, the Italian terrorist group of the nineteen-seventies, found that seventy per cent of recruits had at least one good friend already in the organization. The same is true of the men who joined the mujahideen in Afghanistan. Even revolutionary actions that look spontaneous, like the demonstrations in East Germany that led to the fall of the Berlin Wall, are, at core, strong-tie phenomena. The opposition movement in East Germany consisted of several hundred groups, each with roughly a dozen members. Each group was in limited contact with the others: at the time, only thirteen per cent of East Germans even had a phone. All they knew was that on Monday nights, outside St. Nicholas Church in downtown Leipzig, people gathered to voice their anger at the state. And the primary determinant of who showed up was "critical friends"—the more friends you had who were critical of the regime the more likely you were to join the protest.

So one crucial fact about the four freshmen at the Greensboro lunch counter—David Richmond, Franklin McCain, Ezell Blair, and Joseph McNeil—was their relationship with one another. McNeil was a roommate of Blair's in A. & T.'s Scott Hall dormitory. Richmond roomed with McCain one floor up, and Blair, Richmond, and McCain had all gone to Dudley High School. The four would smuggle beer into the dorm and talk late into the night in Blair and McNeil's room. They would all have remembered the murder of Emmett Till in 1955, the Montgomery bus boycott that same year, and the showdown in Little Rock in 1957. It was McNeil who brought up the idea of a sit-in at Woolworth's. They'd discussed it for nearly a month. Then McNeil came into the dorm room and asked the others if they were ready. There was a pause, and McCain said, in a way that works only with people who talk late into the night with one another, "Are you guys chicken or not?" Ezell Blair worked up the courage the next day to ask for a cup of coffee because he was flanked by his roommate and two good friends from high school.

The kind of activism associated with social media isn't like this at all. The platforms of social media are built around weak ties. Twitter is a way of following (or being followed by) people you may never have met. Facebook is a tool for efficiently managing your acquaintances, for keeping up with the people you would not otherwise be able to stay in touch with. That's why you can have a thousand "friends" on Facebook, as you never could in real life.

This is in many ways a wonderful thing. There is strength in weak ties, as the sociologist Mark Granovetter has observed. Our acquaintances—not our friends—are our greatest source of new ideas and information. The Internet lets us exploit the power of these kinds of distant connections with marvellous efficiency. It's terrific at the diffusion of innovation, interdisciplinary collaboration, seamlessly matching up buyers and sellers, and the logistical functions of the dating world. But weak ties seldom lead to high-risk activism.

In a new book called "The Dragonfly Effect: Quick, Effective, and Powerful Ways to Use Social Media to Drive Social Change," the business consultant Andy Smith and the Stanford Business School professor Jennifer Aaker tell the story of Sameer Bhatia, a young Silicon Valley entrepreneur who came down with acute myelogenous leukemia. It's a perfect illustration of social media's strengths. Bhatia needed a bone-marrow transplant, but he could not find a match among his relatives and friends. The odds were best with a donor of his ethnicity, and there were few South Asians in the national bone-marrow database. So Bhatia's business partner sent out an e-mail explaining Bhatia's plight to more than four hundred of their acquaintances, who forwarded the e-mail to their personal contacts; Facebook pages and YouTube videos were devoted to the Help Sameer campaign. Eventually, nearly twenty-five thousand new people were registered in the bone-marrow database, and Bhatia found a match.

But how did the campaign get so many people to sign up? By not asking too much of them. That's the only way you can get someone you don't really know to do something on your behalf. You can get thousands of people to sign up for a donor registry, because doing so is pretty easy. You have to send in a cheek swab and—in the highly unlikely event that your bone marrow is a good match for someone in need—spend a few hours at the hospital. Donating bone marrow isn't a trivial matter. But it doesn't involve financial or personal risk; it doesn't mean spending a summer being chased by armed men in pickup trucks. It doesn't require that you confront socially entrenched norms and practices. In fact, it's the kind of commitment that will bring only social acknowledgment and praise.

The evangelists of social media don't understand this distinction; they seem to believe that a Facebook friend is the same as a real friend and that signing up for a donor registry in Silicon Valley today is activism in the same sense as sitting at a segregated lunch counter in Greensboro in 1960. "Social networks are particularly effective at increasing motivation," Aaker and Smith write. But that's not true. Social networks are effective at increasing *participation*—by lessening the level of motivation that participation requires. The Facebook page of the Save Darfur Coalition has 1,282,339 members, who have donated an average of nine cents apiece. The next biggest Darfur charity on Facebook has 22,073 members, who have donated an average of thirty-five cents. Help Save Darfur has 2,797 members, who have given, on average, fifteen cents. A spokesperson for the Save Darfur Coalition told *Newsweek,* "We wouldn't necessarily gauge someone's value to the advocacy movement based on what they've given. This is a powerful mechanism to engage this critical population. They inform their community, attend events, volunteer. It's not something you can measure by looking at a ledger." In other words, Facebook activism succeeds not by motivating people to make a real sacrifice but by motivating them to do the things that people do when they are not motivated enough to make a real sacrifice. We are a long way from the lunch counters of Greensboro.

The students who joined the sit-ins across the South during the winter of 1960 described the movement as a "fever." But the civil-rights movement was more like a military campaign than like a contagion. In the late nineteen-fifties, there had been sixteen sit-ins in various cities throughout the South, fifteen of which were formally organized by civil-rights organizations like the [National Association for the Advancement of Colored People] N.A.A.C.P. and [Congress for Racial Equality] CORE. Possible locations for activism were scouted. Plans were drawn up. Movement activists held training sessions and retreats for would-be protesters. The Greensboro Four were a product of this groundwork: all were members of the N.A.A.C.P. Youth Council. They had close ties with the head of the local N.A.A.C.P. chapter. They had been briefed on the earlier wave of sit-ins in Durham, and had been part of a series of movement meetings in activist churches. When the sit-in movement spread from Greensboro throughout the South, it did not spread indiscriminately. It spread to those cities which had preexisting "movement centers"—a core of dedicated and trained activists ready to turn the "fever" into action.

The civil-rights movement was high-risk activism. It was also, crucially, strategic activism: a challenge to the establishment mounted with precision and discipline. The N.A.A.C.P. was a centralized organization, run from New York according to highly formalized operating procedures. At the Southern Christian Leadership Conference, Martin Luther King, Jr., was the unquestioned authority. At the center of the movement was the black church, which had, as Aldon D. Morris points out in his superb 1984 study, "The Origins of the Civil Rights Movement," a carefully demarcated division of labor, with various standing committees and disciplined groups. "Each group was task-oriented and coordinated its activities through authority structures," Morris writes. "Individuals were held accountable for their assigned duties, and important conflicts were resolved by the minister, who usually exercised ultimate authority over the congregation."

This is the second crucial distinction between traditional activism and its online variant: social media are not about this kind of hierarchical organization. Facebook and the like are tools for building *networks*, which are the opposite, in structure and character, of hierarchies. Unlike hierarchies, with their rules and procedures, networks aren't controlled by a single central authority. Decisions are made through consensus, and the ties that bind people to the group are loose.

This structure makes networks enormously resilient and adaptable in low-risk situations. Wikipedia is a perfect example. It doesn't have an editor, sitting in New York, who directs and corrects each entry. The effort of putting together each entry is self-organized. If every entry in Wikipedia were to be erased tomorrow, the content would swiftly be restored, because that's what happens when a network of thousands spontaneously devote their time to a task.

There are many things, though, that networks don't do well. Car companies sensibly use a network to organize their hundreds of suppliers, but not to design their cars. No one believes that the articulation of a coherent design philosophy is best handled by a sprawling, leaderless organizational system. Because networks don't have a centralized leadership structure and clear lines of authority, they have real difficulty reaching consensus and setting goals. They can't think strategically; they are chronically prone to conflict and error. How do you make difficult choices about tactics or strategy or philosophical direction when everyone has an equal say?

The Palestine Liberation Organization [PLO] originated as a network, and the international-relations scholars Mette Eilstrup-Sangiovanni and Calvert Jones argue in a recent essay in *International Security* that this is why it ran into such trouble as it grew: "Structural features typical of networks—the absence of central authority, the unchecked autonomy of rival groups, and the inability to arbitrate quarrels through formal mechanisms—made the P.L.O. excessively vulnerable to outside manipulation and internal strife."

In Germany in the nineteen-seventies, they go on, "the far more unified and successful left-wing terrorists tended to organize hierarchically, with professional management and clear divisions of labor. They were concentrated geographically in universities, where they could establish central leadership, trust, and camaraderie through regular, face-to-face meetings." They seldom betrayed their comrades in arms during police interrogations. Their counterparts on the right were organized as decentralized networks, and had no such discipline. These groups were regularly infiltrated, and members, once arrested, easily gave up their comrades. Similarly, Al Qaeda was most dangerous when it was a unified hierarchy. Now that it has dissipated into a network, it has proved far less effective.

The drawbacks of networks scarcely matter if the network isn't interested in systemic change—if it just wants to frighten or humiliate or make a splash—or if it doesn't need to think strategically. But if you're taking on a powerful and organized establishment you have to be a hierarchy. The Montgomery bus boycott required the participation of tens of thousands of people who depended on public transit to get to and from work each day. It lasted a *year*. In order to persuade those people to stay true to the cause, the boycott's organizers tasked each local black church with maintaining morale, and put together a free alternative private carpool service, with forty-eight dispatchers and forty-two pickup stations. Even the White Citizens Council, King later said, conceded that the carpool system moved with "military precision." By the time King came to Birmingham, for the climactic showdown with Police Commissioner Eugene (Bull) Connor, he had a budget of a million dollars, and a hundred full-time staff members on the ground, divided into operational units. The operation itself was divided into steadily escalating phases, mapped out in advance. Support was maintained through consecutive mass meetings rotating from church to church around the city.

Boycotts and sit-ins and nonviolent confrontations—which were the weapons of choice for the civil-rights movement—are high-risk strategies. They leave little room for conflict and error. The moment even one protester deviates from the script and responds to provocation, the moral legitimacy of the entire protest is compromised. Enthusiasts for social media would no doubt have us believe that King's task in Birmingham would have been made infinitely easier had he been able to communicate with his followers through Facebook, and contented himself with tweets from a Birmingham jail. But networks are messy: think of the ceaseless pattern of correction and revision, amendment and debate, that characterizes Wikipedia. If Martin Luther King, Jr., had tried to do a wiki-boycott in Montgomery, he would have been steamrollered by the white power structure. And of what use would a digital communication tool be in a town where ninety-eight per cent of the black community could be reached every Sunday morning at church? The things that King needed in Birmingham—discipline and strategy—were things that online social media cannot provide.

The bible of the social-media movement is Clay Shirky's "Here Comes Everybody." Shirky, who teaches at New York University, sets out to demonstrate the organizing power of the Internet, and he begins with the story of Evan, who worked on Wall Street, and his friend Ivanna, after she left her smart phone, an expensive Sidekick, on the back seat of a New York City taxicab. The telephone company transferred the data on Ivanna's lost phone to a new phone, whereupon she and Evan discovered that the Sidekick was now in the hands of a teenager from Queens, who was using it to take photographs of herself and her friends.

When Evan e-mailed the teenager, Sasha, asking for the phone back, she replied that his "white ass" didn't deserve to have it back. Miffed, he set up a Web page with her picture and a description of what had happened. He forwarded the link to his friends, and they forwarded it to their friends. Someone found the MySpace page of Sasha's boyfriend, and a link to it found its way onto the site. Someone found her address online and took a video of her home while driving by; Evan posted the video on the site. The story was picked up by the news filter Digg. Evan was now up to ten e-mails a minute. He created a bulletin board for his readers to share their stories, but it crashed under the weight of responses. Evan and Ivanna went to the police, but the police filed the report under "lost," rather than "stolen," which essentially closed the case.

"By this point millions of readers were watching," Shirky writes, "and dozens of mainstream news outlets had covered the story." Bowing to the pressure, the N.Y.P.D. reclassified the item as "stolen." Sasha was arrested, and Evan got his friend's Sidekick back.

Shirky's argument is that this is the kind of thing that could never have happened in the pre-Internet age—and he's right. Evan could never have tracked down Sasha. The story of the Sidekick would never have been publicized. An army of people could never have been assembled to wage this fight. The police wouldn't have bowed to the pressure of a lone person who had misplaced something as trivial as a cell phone. The story, to Shirky, illustrates "the ease and speed with which a group can be mobilized for the right kind of cause" in the Internet age.

Shirky considers this model of activism an upgrade. But it is simply a form of organizing which favors the weak-tie connections that give us access to information over the strong-tie connections that help us persevere in the face of danger. It shifts our energies from organizations that promote strategic and disciplined activity and toward those which promote resilience and adaptability. It makes it easier for activists to express themselves, and harder for that expression to have any impact. The instruments of social media are well suited to making the existing social order more efficient. They are not a natural enemy of the status quo. If you are of the opinion that all the world needs is a little buffing around the edges, this should not trouble you. But if you think that there are still lunch counters out there that need integrating it ought to give you pause.

Shirky ends the story of the lost Sidekick by asking, portentously, "What happens next?"— no doubt imagining future waves of digital protesters. But he has already answered the question. What happens next is more of the same. A networked, weak-tie world is good at things like helping Wall Streeters get phones back from teenage girls. *Viva la revolución.*

Get Angry. Go Viral. Change Everything!

ALEXIS JETTER

Jetter argues that Web activism has not replaced traditional forms of activism, but is simply the newest way to get people involved in social change. Social media, according to Jetter, allows participants to share stories of oppression, both locally and globally. The result: finding support in a community and spurring social change. Women, in particular, have been able to increase their social influence because of their interest and participation in social media networks. These networks are particularly powerful for women residing in repressive cultures, offering them a way to share their oft-unheard voices. Jetter argues social media are so powerful because the small, simple actions like storytelling or picture sharing are the building blocks of social change.

Tahrir Square, 15:30 Jan 13, 2011: A man physically assaulted me, people were walking by and no one stopped him. I kept hitting the man and held him . . . [The police] treated me as a criminal and kept asking me to just forgive the man, trying to make me feel guilty that I would ruin his life.

Masaken al Zobat Street, 04:11 Jan 10, 2011: An asshole touched my private parts while passing by me. The look in his eyes is what i remember the most. This man raped me inside of his head.

Elkhaleefa el Ma'moun Street, 23:34 Jun 28, 2011: A car kept following me and forcing me to stop. I entered Heliopolis club to escape him and came out to find him waiting. I then stopped at the police near the presidential palace. He was waiting a few meters ahead. At the end I managed to escape from him. But I was scared he might hit my car or throw something on me . . . I knew today what fear exactly means.

Future University in Egypt, 19:00 Dec 10, 2010: Something horrible happened to me at the concert . . . I was sexually harassed by an officer! It was very crowded at the entrance . . . and one of those bastards put his hand on my private area and started scratching . . . I screamed and pushed his hands away.

There's something terribly raw about the stories women post on HarassMap.org, a website started by four friends . . . [in 2010] to confront Egypt's epidemic levels of sexual harassment. And that is precisely why the dispatches are so riveting. "Women write these reports when they're really

Originally published in *More Magazine* [September 2011] pp. 146–151. Reprinted by Permission of More Magazine.

angry, and the storytelling is quite powerful," says cofounder Rebecca Chiao, a U.S.-born women's rights advocate who has lived in Cairo for seven years. "It's very convincing."

And startling. Raised in a culture of female deference, Egyptian women are breaking their centuries-old code of silence, blowing the lid off sexual harassment with gritty, uncensored accounts that hold nothing back. That's triggering a sea change in Egypt, where an increasing number of men and women who follow Harass-Map on Facebook and Twitter are taking to the streets to fight the scourge.

HarassMap is just one example of a phenomenon that's galvanizing women around the globe. From North Africa to Middle America, storytelling—once shared intimately around a campfire or across a fence, now uploaded to millions through social media—is helping women combat street harassment, topple brutal dictators and lobby for decent health care. Social media is the medium; women's personal stories are the message. Together they are igniting the world. "I truly believe that women online are the next wave of change," says PunditMom blogger Joanne Bamberger, author of the recently published *Mothers of Intention: How Women & Social Media Are Revolutionizing Politics in America*. "So many women feel, 'I'm overwhelmed with my life. How can I make a dent?' But women have an ability to connect online through storytelling. They realize, 'Oh, there are people out there like me. They're part of a group called X, and this is what they're doing. Maybe I can reach out to them.' Social media has given people the tools to make that little dent." Savvy organizers have long known that women are inspired to fight for change when they hear stories that outrage them or when they tell their own tales of social injustice. In the 1970s, consciousness raising was all about sharing stories, particularly those that felt humiliating when kept to oneself but were empowering, even exhilarating, when verbalized. Today Web activists are creating online communities that encourage women to voice their experiences—then pointing those

women toward ways to take direct action, like running for office, meeting with a senator or writing a check. In other words, Web activism hasn't replaced face-to-face organizing; it's just the newest funnel into it. "Women tend to shut down once political rhetoric enters the conversation," says Deanna Zandt, author of *Share This! How You Will Change the World with Social Networking*. But storytelling can transcend politics. "It reflects our very primal need to be connected to one another: This is what it's like to be in my shoes," she says. "And it can inspire people to make large moves."

Seismic moves. After all, it was a 26-year-old Egyptian woman, Asmaa Mahfouz, whose videotaped calls to action went viral on Facebook and are credited with helping to draw the first large pro-democracy crowds to Cairo's Tahrir Square on January 25 [in 2010]. "I, a girl, am going down to Tahrir Square, and I will stand alone," she said, looking directly into the camera from an armchair in her home, her childlike face framed by a headscarf. "Whoever says women shouldn't go to protests because they will get beaten, let him have some honor and manhood and come with me on January 25." On that day, hundreds of thousands of women—and men—poured into Tahrir Square; 17 days later, they dislodged a dictator.

"People's wills are the sparks that can light fires," says Beth Kanter, a Web pioneer who advises nonprofit groups on digital strategy, "and social media is pouring gasoline on it." Certainly there were deep societal forces that led to President Hosni Mubarak's downfall. And without the Egyptian addiction to Facebook—the country has 7.4 million users, making it the Middle East's largest Facebook consumer—Mahfouz's dare might have had little effect. But that's just the point: Women's influence online is growing dramatically, largely because of their affinity for social networks.

Globally, women use the Internet nearly as frequently as men, but they spend 22 percent more time than men on e-mail, instant messaging and social-networking sites such as Facebook,

Twitter and Myspace, according to a recent study by the digital-marketing firm comScore. Although the under-24 crowd worldwide is still the heaviest user of social networks (in terms of time spent on the sites), women over 45 are driving the greatest growth. "Social networking is a new frontier that older women are embracing," says Linda Boland Abraham, comScore's chief marketing officer. "Men are doing so to a far lesser degree."

In the U.S. and Canada, women spend 30 percent of their total time online in social networks, compared with 25 percent for men. North American women are more likely than men to share photos online (for example, on Flickr), swap information about health (Medpedia), collaborate with their children's teachers (Parentella), get fashion advice (Fashism), play social-networking games (FarmVille), grab coupons (Groupon) and find restaurant deals (Yelp). The trend continues for women in the developing world: Latin American women spend 52 percent of their time in social networks, compared with 45 percent for men.

In repressive cultures, social media may be even more transformative for women, says Mallika Dutt, president of Breakthrough, a global human rights group that uses social media and online games to address issues such as HIV/AIDS, immigration and abuse. "For women who have severe restrictions on their mobility, this allows them to step out into the world in a whole new way," she says. "We can't underestimate the profound power and engagement that social media allows women who have historically had to really fight to be heard."

In India, women trying to escape domestic abuse are using their mobile phones and computers to post personal stories on Breakthrough's website, BellBajao.org (Ring the Bell), and find advice, resources and encouragement. In Saudi Arabia, the only country where driving by women is restricted, women have launched a Twitter and Facebook campaign—Women2Drive—demanding that freedom. One of the charismatic organizers, Manal al-Sharif,

a cybersecurity consultant and divorced mother of a four-year-old, posted a video of herself on YouTube in May. It showed her at the wheel, in black abaya and designer sunglasses, describing how the de facto ban makes her life impossible:

> When I came to El-Shargiya in 2002, I was on my own. And I had no choice. I had to have a driver. I bought a small car anyhow . . . I got a private driver who I had to give a monthly salary. The first week, he got into an accident with my car. He didn't know how to drive. . . . My driver used to harass me. He'd adjust the rearview mirror to see what I was wearing.

Al-Sharif was quickly arrested and jailed for nine days. But the detainment backfired: The video went viral, fueling a protest on June 17 [2011] in which dozens of women defied authorities and drove through the streets, the largest such protest in 20 years. Dutt cautions that in any country, sharing stories online may have drawbacks; for instance, a battered wife could be traced by her abuser. And repressive governments are learning fast how to censor or delete whatever content they consider objectionable. "We're in a time of transformation," Dutt says. "We have to understand both the peril and the power of this moment."

But if sharing put women in danger, it can also push them to take ingenious approaches to vexing issues. When Chiao, an international-development specialist trained at Harvard and Johns Hopkins, was working at the Egyptian Center for Women's Rights in Cairo, she noticed that her young volunteers often arrived at the office in tears. And she learned the reason: They'd been followed into the building, pushed up against the wall and groped. These stories drove Chiao to create HarassMap. "We had all experienced harassment, but it's something else when you see a young, idealistic volunteer come inside crying because she's been harassed at the entrance to the building," says Chiao . . . who spoke via Skype from her Cairo apartment. "You can't trust your doctor, you can't go to school, you can't go to the supermarket." The stats bear her out: Eight in 10 Egyptian women say they're harassed routinely, often daily—even if fully veiled, according to a report from the Egyptian Center for Women's Rights.

Chiao and her three cofounders had no money, no office space, not even a hotline. But they had heard about a new crowd-sourcing technology that could help women employ the only self-defense tool most Egyptians have at their fingertips: a cheap mobile phone. (In Egypt the so-called Facebook Revolution relied, for the most part, on the least expensive, least "smart" phones on the market.) With the help of NiJeL, a social justice–oriented digital-mapping firm in Arizona, Chiao and her partners launched their site in December [2010].

Today, all across Egypt, from tiny oases in the western desert to the Red Sea in the east, women and girls (and occasionally men) are pulling out their phones and texting the details of abuse to HarassMap. Some wait until they get to a safe place, then send dispatches via computer to the organization's website; still others use HarassMap's Facebook page or Twitter feed. Within seconds, the woman receives a phone number she can call for free support services for legal aid, counseling and self-defense classes. Once she gives her location and explains what happened, the information is fed into a system that uses an interactive Google map of Egypt to identify harassment hotspots, color-coded by categories such as "touching," "sexual invites" or "indecent exposure."

The real-time heat maps are striking, but it's the eye-popping stories that make revoltingly clear what it's like to be a woman on Egypt's streets. And they have convinced a small but growing number of Egyptians that sexual harassment is a national embarrassment. Harass-Map now has more than 300 volunteers, half of them men, who regularly fan out into troubled neighborhoods and educate people on the street about the problem. In just a few months, support for the group has lit up the country's blogo-

sphere and its television and radio stations. Last June one of the nation's most respected newspapers, *Al-Masry Al-Youm*, published a series of articles to "dissect the reasons" behind what it calls "this festering issue"—and gave Harass-Map some high-end publicity. The site could have been organized without social media, Chiao says, but then would have needed years to develop its current size and influence. "With social media," says Chiao, "people can hear about a problem, learn about it and speak up about it all at the same time."

Half a world away, in Seattle, MomsRising .org is fighting for change, not so much in the streets but on Capitol Hill and in the halls of the country's legislatures. With one million members and a reach of three million people through blogs, Twitter and Facebook, the media-savvy mothers' advocacy group has made an art of collecting women's stories—lots of them, by turns wistful, plucky and livid—and packaging them to provoke legislative change.

Sheryl, from Ohio, posts:

> The economy has certainly hurt our family. My husband is working (yeah), but he is still making the amount that he made on unemployment (which is barely enough to cover the bills for our family). I just had a stillbirth last March. Had it not been for Medicaid, I would not have been able to pay the medical bills incurred due to that loss.

And this, from a graphic artist in Wisconsin:

> I have been told—to my face—no less than 3 times during my adult life that when a particular job I had applied for or wanted to advance to had come down to 2 candidates (me and a man), the man "had" to be selected because, after all, he has a family to support. . . . The third time, I was the corporate art director . . . still married with 2 children and a 3rd on the way. A new male hire, 15 years my junior with NO

relevant experience whom I had just 2 weeks to train to his new position, was suddenly and without explanation made the new art dept. head. . . . I subsequently quit and filed a gender discrimination suit. Enough was enough!!!

Written by users or by the 450 bloggers for the MomsRising website, the stories are bound together in customized, thematically arranged "storybooks" and delivered to legislators, in person, by a MomsRising committee. "Often what we think ourselves and hear from our members is, 'Oh my gosh, I'm the only one who this is happening to,'" says Kristin Rowe-Finkbeiner, the turbo-charged Seattle-based author who cofounded the group in 2006. "Many women don't feel like experts on legislation [for health care or paid parental leave]. But when we ask them to tell their own stories, they do know what's going on in their own families—and then we deliver those stories to Congress."

Studies show that what works best on the Web, Rowe-Finkbeiner says, is a personal story backed by a few facts—"rather than full-fledged, fact-heavy wonkiness." MomsRising clearly has the mix just right: The group is widely credited with helping to pass the federal Lilly Ledbetter Fair Pay Act of 2009, which makes it easier for women to sue employers who pay them less than they pay men for the same job. The strategy was a textbook example of social change via social media storytelling: First, the group solicited an arsenal of well-documented, guaranteed-to-tick-you-off stories of pay discrimination, which it posted on the website. Then MomsRising migrated the action to the offline world, meeting with the staff of 44 senators in their state offices. Members also sent nearly 85,000 constituent letters to both houses of Congress. When Senator John McCain dissed the legislation, saying women didn't need fair pay—just "more education and training"—MomsRising members descended on D.C. and happily blizzarded his office with thousands of members' résumés. *Guess what*, the women said as they hand-delivered the stacks. *We are educated. We are qualified. And we still need equal pay for equal work.*

If MomsRising is the grande dame at the party, expertly working the crowd, SmartGirl-Politics is the ingenue turning heads at the top of the stairs: In 2010 its hashtag—#sgp—was the third-most-used tag on Twitter. The site's founder, Stacy Mott, an energetic former human resources manager in rural New Jersey, is a Tea Party supporter whose mission is to get conservative women more involved in politics and whose focus is on rolling back government involvement in education, health care and energy. "We want to tell women's stories about how the administration's energy policy is taking a toll on families in the U.S.," she says. "That touches me personally, because I look at my home state of West Virginia and I keep hearing about friends being laid off."

A key goal of SmartGirlPolitics is to inspire conservative women to run for office, and recruitment begins online. In 2010, SmartGirlPolitics trained 3,500 women in online activism—after which 100 ran for federal, state, local or party offices; 16 ran for the U.S. House of Representatives. "Our organization exploded in 2009 because of social media," says Mott, who started SmartGirl-Politics during the 2008 election. "And it was all Twitter." . . .

The spotlight on individuals continues offline at the yearly SmartGirl Summit, a star-studded gathering—it has featured the likes of Representative Michele Bachmann and Liz Cheney—that the group calls "the must-attend event for today's conservative woman activist." The offline events help build the grassroots, state-by-state membership, and they also communicate a message of real-world participation and action. Mott points to one standout Summit attendee: Liz Carter, a Georgia businesswoman who two years ago attended a SmartGirl Summit in Nashville. "Afterward she came up to me and said, 'You know what? I never really thought about it before, but I think I'm going to run for office.'" Carter ran for Congress in a heavily Democratic district and lost. "But that to me is success," says Mott. "That we got one woman who attended an SGP event to run for office when she never considered it before—that's our success."

Each of these sites has found ways to move women into direct, on-the-ground involvement. But that kind of migration remains one of the biggest challenges for activists. A new study says it takes four to six direct tweets from trusted friends to capture anyone's attention on a political issue, and that doesn't mean the person will get off the couch and grab a protest sign or visit her congresswoman or join her school board—all real-world actions that are still crucial to making change happen. "No one knows how it works," says Zandt. "But the campaigns that are the most successful are the ones that appeal to our emotional values. That's what we saw in Egypt: People want dignity, and they want to be there."

As technology grows more sophisticated, the sites will too. iHollaback.org, a U.S.-based precursor to HarassMap that takes advantage of the latest software, enables women to punch an icon on their smartphones, choose whether to take a photo of their harasser and later share the details of the abuse—information that is then uploaded to Hollaback's website, along with blogs, tips and news. "Change has always been about telling our stories," says the site's founder, Emily May. "But now we can map our stories. We can photograph our stories. We can tell our stories on blogs." And produce concrete results: In 2008, after months of pressure from Hollaback members, New York City's Metropolitan Transportation Authority agreed to plaster anti-groping signs in the subways, and now the city council is considering more aggressive action against harassers. "All of a sudden we're not just talking to our friends online," May says. "We can use our stories to talk to people in the community, talk to legislators and spread the word."

Ultimately, though, what draws women to these sites is something deeper: a camaraderie of the pissed off and the passionate. As one woman posted on Hollaback: "Using your camera phone is a subtle way to take some kind of action when you feel powerless. . . . [It] connects you to an entire community of people who collectively say this is awful, it shouldn't have happened to you, and it wasn't your fault. When people ask me, 'What good does it do to post a picture on a blog?' I say, 'Are you kidding?! We're building a movement!'"

What Can We Do?
Becoming Part of the Solution

ALLAN G. JOHNSON

Students who study the structural sources of our many social problems may feel discouraged about the potential for social change. Johnson recognizes the challenges of social change, but argues the tools are at our disposal. To begin, Johnson contends we must acknowledge and target systems of privilege and oppression. For students, this may mean recognizing your own participation in these systems and advocating for change in a variety of ways. Johnson grants risks are involved, but that the rewards of social change far outweigh them.

The challenge we face is to change patterns of exclusion, rejection, privilege, harassment, discrimination, and violence that are everywhere in this society and have existed for hundreds (or, in the case of gender, thousands) of years. We have to begin by thinking about the trouble and the challenge in new and more productive ways. . . . Here is a summary of the tools we have to start with.

Large numbers of people have sat on the sidelines and seen themselves as neither part of the problem nor the solution. Beyond this shared trait, however, they are far from homogeneous. Everyone is aware of the [people, often] whites, heterosexuals, and men who intentionally act out in oppressive ways. But there is less attention to the millions of people who know inequities exist and want to be part of the solution. Their silence and invisibility allow the trouble to continue. Removing what silences them and stands in their way can tap an enormous potential of energy for change.

The problem of privilege and oppression is deep and wide, and to work with it we have to be able to see it clearly so that we can talk about it in useful ways. To do that, we have to reclaim some difficult language that names what's going on, language that has been so misused and maligned that it generates more heat than light. We can't just stop using words like racism, sexism, and privilege, however, because these are tools that focus our awareness on the problem and all the forms it takes. Once we can see and talk about what's going on, we can analyze how it

Some of the contents of this chapter were originally published in Allan G. Johnson, "What Can We Do? Becoming Part of the Solution," from *The Gender Knot: Unraveling Our Patriarchal Legacy*. Copyright © 1997 by Allan G. Johnson. Reprinted with the permission of Temple University Press. Contents were adapted from Article 60, "What Can We Do? Becoming Part of the Solution" in Susan Ferguson's *Mapping the Social Landscape: Readings in Sociology*, 5e. McGraw–Hill, 2008. Pp. 697–708.

works as a system. We can identify points of leverage where change can begin.

Reclaiming the language takes us directly to the core reality that the problem is privilege and the power that maintains it. Privilege exists when one group has something that is systematically denied to others not because of who they are or what they've done or not done, but because of the social category they belong to.

Privilege is a feature of social systems, not individuals. People have or don't have privilege depending on the system they're in and the social categories other people put them in. To say, then, that I have race privilege says less about me personally than it does about the society we all live in and how it is organized to assign privilege on the basis of a socially defined set of racial categories that change historically and often overlap. The challenge facing me as an individual has more to do with how I participate in society as a recipient of race privilege and how those choices oppose or support the system itself.

In dealing with the problem of privilege, we have to get used to being surrounded by paradox. Very often those who have privilege don't know it, for example, which is a key aspect of privilege. Also paradoxical is the fact that privilege doesn't necessarily lead to a "good life," which can prompt people in privileged groups to deny resentfully that they even have it. But privilege doesn't equate with being happy. It involves having what others don't have and the struggle to hang on to it at their expense, neither of which is a recipe for joy, personal fulfillment, or spiritual contentment. . . .

To be an effective part of the solution, we have to realize that privilege and oppression are not a thing of the past. It's happening right now. It isn't just a collection of wounds inflicted long ago that now need to be healed. The wounding goes on as I write these words and as you read them, and unless people work to change the system that promotes it, personal healing by itself cannot be the answer. Healing wounds is no more a solution to the oppression that causes the wounding than military hospitals are a solution to war. Healing is a necessary process, but it isn't enough. . . .

Since privilege is rooted primarily in systems—such as families, schools, and workplaces—change isn't simply a matter of changing people. People, of course, will have to change in order for systems to change, but the most important point is that changing people isn't enough. The solution also has to include entire systems, such as capitalism, whose paths of least resistance shape how we feel, think, and behave as individuals, how we see ourselves and one another.

As they work for change, it's easy for members of privileged groups to lose sight of the reality of privilege and its consequences and the truth that the trouble around privilege is their trouble as much as anyone else's. This happens in large part because systems of privilege provide endless ways of seeing and thinking about the world that make privilege invisible. These include denying and minimizing the trouble; blaming the victim; calling the trouble something else; assuming everyone prefers things the way they are; mistaking intentions with consequences; attributing the trouble to others and not their own participation in social systems that produce it; and balancing the trouble with troubles of their own. The more aware people can be of how these behaviors limit their effectiveness, the more they can contribute to change both in themselves and the systems where they work and live. With these tools in hand, we can begin to think about how to make ourselves part of the solution to the problem of privilege and oppression. . . .

. . . What Can We Do?

There are no easy answers to the question of what can we do about the problem of privilege. There is no twelve-step program, no neat set of instructions. Most important, there is no way around or over it: the only way out is through it. We won't end oppression by pretending it isn't there or that we don't have to deal with it.

Some people complain that those who work for social change are being "divisive" when they draw attention to gender or race or social class and the oppressive systems organized around them. But when members of dominant groups mark differences by excluding or discriminating against subordinate groups and treating them as "other," they aren't accused of being divisive. Usually it's only when someone calls attention to how differences are used for oppressive purposes that the charge of divisiveness comes up.

In a sense, it is divisive to say that oppression and privilege exist, but only insofar as it points to divisions that already exist and to the perception that the status quo is normal and unremarkable. Oppression promotes the worst kind of divisiveness because it cuts us off from one another and, by silencing us about the truth, cuts us off from ourselves as well. Not only must we participate in oppression by living in an oppressive society, we also must act as though oppression didn't exist, denying the reality of our own experience and its consequences for people's lives, including our own.

What does it mean to go out by going through? What can we do that will make a difference? I don't have the answers, but I do have some suggestions.

Acknowledge That the Trouble Exists

A key to the continued existence of every oppressive system is unawareness, because oppression contradicts so many basic human values that it invariably arouses opposition when people know about it. The Soviet Union and its East European satellites, for example, were riddled with contradictions so widely known among their people that the oppressive regimes fell apart with an ease and speed that astonished the world. An awareness of oppression compels people to speak out, to break the silence that continued oppression depends on.

This is why most oppressive cultures mask the reality of oppression by denying its existence, trivializing it, calling it something else, blaming it on those most victimized by it, or diverting attention from it. Instead of treating oppression as a serious problem, we go to war or get embroiled in controversial "issues" such as capital gains tax cuts or "family values" or immigrant workers. There would be far more active opposition to racism, for example, if white people lived with an ongoing awareness of how it actually affects the everyday lives of those it oppresses as "not white." As we have seen, however, the vast majority of white people don't do this.

It's one thing to become aware and quite another to stay that way. The greatest challenge when we first become aware of a critical perspective on the world is simply to hang on to it. Every system's paths of least resistance invariably lead away from critical awareness of how the system works. In some ways . . . [it is] harder and more important to pay attention to systems of privilege than it is to people's behavior and the paths of least resistance that shape it. . . .

Pay Attention

Understanding how privilege and oppression operate and how you participate in them is where the work for change begins. It's easy to have opinions, but it takes work to know what you're talking about. The simplest way to begin is by reading, and making reading about privilege part of your life. Unless you have the luxury of a personal teacher, you can't understand this issue without reading, just as you'd need to read about a foreign country before you traveled there for the first time, or about a car before you tried to work under the hood. Many people assume they already know what they need to know because it's part of everyday life. But they're usually wrong. Just as the last thing a fish would discover is water, the last thing people discover is society itself and something as pervasive as the dynamics of privilege.

We also have to be open to the idea that what we think we know is, if not wrong, so deeply shaped by systems of privilege that it misses most of the truth. This is why activists talk with one another and spend time reading one another's writing: seeing things clearly is tricky. This is also why people who are critical of the status quo are so often self-critical as well: they know how complex and elusive the truth really is and what a challenge it is to work toward it. . . .

Little Risks: Do Something

The more you pay attention to privilege and oppression, the more you'll see opportunities to do something about them. You don't have to mount an expedition to find those opportunities; they're all over the place, beginning in yourself. As I became aware of how male privilege encourages me to control conversations, for example, I also realized how easily men dominate group meetings by controlling the agenda and interrupting, without women's objecting to it. This pattern is especially striking in groups that are mostly female but in which most of the talking nonetheless comes from a few men. I would find myself sitting in meetings and suddenly the preponderance of male voices would jump out at me, an unmistakable sign of male privilege, in full bloom.

As I've seen what's going on, I've had to decide what to do about this little path of least resistance and my relation to it that leads me to follow it so readily. With some effort, I've tried out new ways of listening more and talking less. At times my methods have felt contrived and artificial, such as telling myself to shut up for a while or even counting slowly to ten (or more) to give others a chance to step into the space afforded by silence. With time and practice, new paths have become easier to follow and I spend less time monitoring myself. But awareness is never automatic or permanent, for paths of least resistance will be there to choose or not as long as male privilege exists.

As you become more aware, questions will arise about what goes on at work, in the media, in families, in communities, in religious institutions, in government, on the street, and at school—in short, just about everywhere. The questions don't come all at once (for which we can be grateful), although they sometimes come

in a rush that can feel overwhelming. If you remind yourself that it isn't up to you to do it all, however, you can see plenty of situations in which you can make a difference, sometimes in surprisingly simple ways. Consider the following possibilities:

Make noise, be seen.
Stand up, volunteer, speak out, write letters, sign petitions, show up. Every oppressive system feeds on silence. Don't collude in silence. Breaking the silence is especially important for dominant groups, because it undermines the assumption of solidarity that dominance depends on. If this feels too risky, you can practice being aware of how silence reflects your investment in solidarity with other dominant-group members. This can be a place to begin working on how you participate in making privilege and oppression happen: "Today I said nothing, colluded in silence, and this is how I benefited from it. Maybe tomorrow I can try something different."

Find little ways to withdraw support from paths of least resistance and people's choices to follow them, starting with yourself.
It can be as simple as not laughing at a racist or heterosexist joke or saying you don't think it's funny, or writing a letter to your senator or representative or the editor of your newspaper, objecting to an instance of sexism in the media. When my local newspaper ran an article whose headline referred to sexual harassment as "earthy behavior," for example, I wrote a letter pointing out that harassment isn't "earthy."

The key to withdrawing support is to interrupt the flow of business as usual. We can subvert the assumption that we're all going along with the status quo by simply not going along. When we do this, we stop the flow, if only for a moment, but in that moment other people can notice and start to think and question. It's a perfect time to suggest the possibility of alternatives, such as humor that isn't at someone else's expense, or of ways to think about discrimination, harassment, and violence that do justice to the reality of what's going on and how it affects people. . . .

Dare to make people feel uncomfortable, beginning with yourself.

At the next local school board meeting, for example, you can ask why principals and other administrators are almost always white and male (unless your system is an exception that proves the rule), while the teachers they supervise are mostly women and people of color. Or look at the names and mascots used by local sports teams and see if they exploit the heritage and identity of Native Americans; if that's the case, ask principals and coaches and owners about it.[1] Consider asking similar kinds of questions about privilege and difference in your place of worship, workplace, and local government. . . .

Some will say it isn't "nice" to make people uncomfortable, but oppressive systems do a lot more than make people feel uncomfortable, and there isn't anything "nice" about allowing that to continue unchallenged. Besides, discomfort is an unavoidable part of any meaningful process of education. We can't grow without being willing to challenge our assumptions and take ourselves to the edge of our competencies, where we're bound to feel uncomfortable. If we can't tolerate ambiguity, uncertainty, and discomfort, then we'll never get beneath superficial appearances or learn or change anything of much value, including ourselves.

And if history is any guide, discomfort—to put it mildly—is also an unavoidable part of changing systems of privilege. As sociologist William Gamson noted in his study of social movements, "the meek don't make it."[2] To succeed, movements must be willing to disrupt business as usual and make those in power as uncomfortable as possible. Women didn't win the right to vote, for example, by reasoning with men and showing them the merits of their position. To even get men's attention, they had to take to the streets in large numbers at considerable risk to themselves. At the very least they had to be willing to suffer ridicule and

ostracism, but it often got worse than that. In England, for example, suffragettes were jailed and, when they went on hunger strikes, were force fed through tubes run down their throats. The modern women's movement has had to depend no less on the willingness of women to put themselves on the line in order to make men so uncomfortable that they've had to pay attention and, eventually, to act.

It has been no different with the civil rights movement. Under the leadership of men like Martin Luther King, the movement was dedicated to the principle of nonviolence. As with the movement for women's suffrage, however, they could get white people's attention only through mass demonstrations and marches. Whites typically responded with violence and intimidation.[3] As Douglas McAdam showed in his study of that period, the Federal government intervened and enacted civil rights legislation only when white violence against civil rights demonstrators became so extreme that the government was compelled to act.[4] . . .

Openly choose and model alternative paths.

As we identify paths of least resistance, we can identify alternatives and then follow them openly so that other people can see what we're doing. Paths of least resistance become more visible when people choose alternatives, just as rules become more visible when someone breaks them. Modeling new paths creates tension in a system, which moves toward resolution. . . .

Actively promote change in how systems are organized around privilege.

The possibilities here are almost endless, because social life is complicated and privilege is everywhere. You can, for example,

- Speak out for equality in the workplace.
- Promote diversity awareness and training.
- Support equal pay and promotion.
- Oppose the devaluing of women and people of color and the work they do, from dead-end jobs to glass ceilings.

- Support the well-being of mothers and children and defend women's right to control their bodies and their lives.
- Object to the punitive dismantling of welfare and attempts to limit women's access to reproductive health services.
- Speak out against violence and harassment wherever they occur, whether at home, at work, or on the street.
- Support government and private services for women who are victimized by male violence. Volunteer at the local rape crisis center or battered-women's shelter. Join and support groups that intervene with and counsel violent men.
- Call for and support clear and effective anti-harassment policies in workplaces, unions, schools, professional associations, religious institutions, and political parties, as well as public spaces such as parks, sidewalks, and malls.
- Object to theaters and video stores that carry violent pornography. This doesn't require a debate about censorship—just the exercise of freedom of speech to articulate pornography's role in the oppression of women and to express how its opponents feel about it.
- Ask questions about how work, education, religion, and family are shaped by core values and principles that support race privilege, gender privilege, and other forms of privilege. You might accept women's entry into combat branches of the military or the upper reaches of corporate power as "progress," for example. But you could also raise questions about what happens to people and societies when political and economic institutions are organized around control, domination, "power over," and, by extension, competition and the use of violence. Is it progress to allow selected women to share control with men over oppressive systems?

Support the right of women and men to love whomever they choose.

Raise awareness of homophobia and heterosexism. For example, ask school officials and teachers about what's happening to gay and lesbian students in local schools. If they don't know, ask them to find out, since it's a safe bet these students are being harassed, suppressed, and oppressed by others at one of the most vulnerable stages of life. When sexual orientation is discussed, whether in the media or among friends, raise questions about its relation to patriarchy. Remember that it isn't necessary to have answers to questions in order to ask them.

Pay attention to how different forms of oppression interact with one another.

There has been a great deal of struggle within women's movements, for example, about the relationship between gender oppression and other forms of oppression, especially those based on race and social class. White middle- and upper-middle-class feminists have been criticized for pursuing their own agenda to the detriment of women who aren't privileged by class or race. Raising concerns about glass ceilings that keep women out of top corporate and professional positions, for example, does little to help working- or lower-class women. There has also been debate over whether some forms of oppression are more important to attack first or produce more oppressive consequences than other forms.

One way out of this conflict is to realize that patriarchy isn't problematic just because it emphasizes male dominance, but because it promotes dominance and control as ends in themselves. In that sense, all forms of oppression draw support from common roots, and whatever we do that calls attention to those roots undermines all forms of oppression. If working against patriarchy is seen simply as enabling some women to get a bigger piece of the pie, then some women probably will "succeed" at the expense of others who are disadvantaged by race, class, ethnicity, and other characteristics. One could make the same argument about movements for racial justice: If it just means enabling well-placed blacks to get ahead, then it won't end racial oppression for the vast majority. But if we identify the core problem as any society organized around principles of domination and privilege, then changing that requires us to pay attention to all the forms of oppression those principles promote. Whether we begin with race or gender or ethnicity or class or the capitalist system, if we name the problem correctly we'll wind up going in the same general direction.

Work with other people.

This is one of the most important principles of participating in social change. From expanding consciousness to taking risks, being in the company of people who support what you're trying to do makes all the difference in the world. For starters, you can read and talk about books and issues and just plain hang out with other people who want to understand and do something about privilege and oppression. The roots of the modern women's movement were in consciousness-raising groups where women did little more than talk about themselves and try to figure out how they were shaped by a patriarchal society. It may not have looked like much at the time, but it laid the foundation for huge social change. . . .

It is especially important to form alliances across difference—for men to ally with women, whites with people of color, heterosexuals with lesbians and gay men. What does this mean? As Paul Kivel [author of *Uprooting Racism* (1996)] argues, one of the keys to being a good ally is a willingness to listen—for whites to listen to people of color, for example—and to give credence to what people say about their own experience.[5] This isn't easy to do, of course, since whites, heterosexuals, and men may not like what they hear about their privilege from those who are most damaged by it. It is difficult to hear anger about privilege and oppression and not take it personally, but that is what allies have to be willing to do. It's also difficult for members of privileged groups to realize how mistrusted they are by subordinate groups and to not take that personally as well. . . .

Don't keep it to yourself.

A corollary of looking for company is not to restrict your focus to the tight little circle of your own life. It isn't enough to work out private solutions to social problems like oppression and keep them to yourself. It isn't enough to clean up your own act and then walk away, to find ways to avoid the worst consequences of oppression and privilege at home and inside yourself and think that's taking responsibility. Privilege and oppression aren't a personal problem that can be solved through personal solutions. At some point, taking responsibility means acting in a larger context, even if that means letting just one other person know what you're doing. It makes sense to start with yourself, but it's equally important not to end with yourself.

A good way to convert personal change into something larger is to join an organization dedicated to changing the systems that produce privilege and oppression. Most college and university campuses, for example, have student organizations that focus on issues of gender, race, and sexual orientation. There are also national organizations working for change, often through local and statewide branches. . . .

Don't let other people set the standard for you.

Start where you are and work from there. Make lists of all the things you could actually imagine doing—from reading another book about inequality to suggesting policy changes at work to protesting against capitalism to raising questions about who cleans the bathroom at home—and rank them from the most risky to the least. Start with the least risky and set reasonable goals ("What small risk for change will I take today?"). As you get more experienced at taking risks, you can move up your list. You can commit yourself to whatever the next steps are for you, the tolerable risks, the contributions that offer some way—however small it might seem—to help balance the scales. As long as you do something, it counts.

In the end, taking responsibility doesn't have to involve guilt and blame, letting someone off the hook, or being on the hook yourself. It simply means acknowledging an obligation to make a contribution to finding a way out of the trouble we're all in, and to find constructive ways to act on that obligation. You don't have to do anything dramatic or earth-shaking to help change happen. As powerful as oppressive systems are, they cannot stand the strain of lots of people doing something about it, beginning with the simplest act of naming the system out loud.

What's in It for Me?

It's risky to promote change. You risk being seen as odd, being excluded or punished for asking questions and setting examples that make people uncomfortable or threaten privilege. We've all adapted in one way or another to life in a society organized around competition, privilege, and difference. Paths of least resistance may perpetuate oppression, but they also have the advantage of being familiar and predictable and therefore can seem preferable to untried alternatives and the unknown. There are inner risks—of feeling lost, confused, and scared—along with outer risks of being rejected or worse. Obviously, then, working for change isn't a path of least resistance, which raises the question of why anyone should follow Gandhi's advice and do it anyway.

It's an easier question to answer for subordinate groups than it is for dominants, which helps explain why the former have done most of the work for change. Those on the losing end have much to gain by striving to undo the system that oppresses them, not only for themselves in the short run, but for the sake of future generations. The answer comes less easily for those in dominant groups, but they don't have to look very far to see that they have much to gain—especially in the long run—that more than balances what they stand to lose.[6]

When whites, heterosexuals, and men join the movement against privilege and oppression, they can begin to undo the costs of participating in an oppressive system as the dominant group. Few men, for example, realize how much they deaden themselves in order to support (if only by their silence) a system that privileges them at women's expense, that values maleness by devaluing femaleness, that makes women invisible in order to make men appear larger than life. Most men don't realize the impoverishment to their emotional and spiritual lives, the price they pay in personal authenticity and integrity, how they compromise their humanity, how they limit the connections they can have with other people, how they distort their sexuality to live up to core patriarchal values of control. They don't realize how much they have to live a lie in order to interact on a daily basis with their mothers, wives, sisters, daughters, women friends and co-workers—all members of the group male privilege oppresses. So the first thing men can do is claim a sense of aliveness and realness that doesn't depend on superiority and control, and a connection to themselves and the world—which they may not even realize was missing until they begin to feel its return.

In similar ways, most whites don't realize how much energy it takes to defend against their continuing vulnerability to guilt and blame and to avoid seeing how much trouble the world is in and the central role they play in it. When whites do nothing about racial privilege and oppression, they put themselves on the defensive, in the no-safe-place-to-hide position of every dominator class. But when white people make a commitment to participate in change, to be more than part of the problem, they free themselves to live in the world without feeling open to guilt simply for being white.

In perhaps more subtle ways, homophobia and heterosexism take a toll on heterosexuals. The persecution of lesbians, for example, is a powerful weapon of sexism that encourages women to silence themselves, to disavow feminism, and tolerate male privilege for fear that if they speak out, they'll be labeled as lesbians and ostracized.[7] In similar ways, the fear of being called gay is enough to make men conform to masculine stereotypes that don't reflect who they really are and to go along with an oppressive gender system they may not believe in. And because homosexuals all come from families, parents and siblings may also pay a huge emotional price for the effects of prejudice, discrimination, and persecution directed at their loved ones. . . .

When people join together to end any form of oppression, they act with courage to take responsibility to do the right thing, and this empowers them in ways that can extend to every corner of their lives. Whenever we act with courage, a halo effect makes that same courage available to us in other times and places. . . . As we do the work, we build a growing store of experience to draw on in figuring out how to act with courage again and again. As our inner and outer lives become less bound by the strictures of fear and compromise, we can claim a deeper meaning for our lives than we've known before.

The human capacity to choose how to participate in the world empowers all of us to pass along something different from what's been passed to us. With each strand of the knot of privilege that we help to work loose and unravel, we don't act simply for ourselves, we join a process of creative resistance to oppression that's been unfolding for thousands of years. We become part of the long tradition of people who have dared to make a difference—to look at things as they are, to imagine something better, and to plant seeds of change in themselves, in others, and in the world.

NOTES

1. For more on this, see Ward Churchill, "Crimes against Humanity," *Z Magazine* 6 (March 1993): 43–47. Reprinted in Margaret L. Andersen and Patricia Hill Collins (eds.), *Race, Class, and Gender,* 3d ed. (Belmont, CA: Wadsworth, 1998), pp. 413–20.
2. William A. Gamson, "Violence and Political Power: The Meek Don't Make It," *Psychology Today* 8 (July 1974): 35–41.
3. For more on this, see the excellent PBS documentary of the civil rights movement, *Eyes on the Prize.*
4. Doug McAdam, *Political Process and the Development of Black Insurgency 1930–1970* (Chicago: University of Chicago Press, 1982).
5. See Kivel, *Uprooting Racism: How White People Can Work for Racial Justice* (Philadelphia: New Society Publishers, 1996), part 3, "Being Allies."
6. A lot of what follows came out of a brainstorming session with my friend and colleague Jane Tuohy as we worked out the design for a gender workshop.
7. See Suzanne Pharr, *Homophobia: A Weapon of Sexism* (Inverness, CA: Chardon Press, 1988).

The Arc of Justice and the Long Run: Hope, History, and Unpredictability

Rebecca Solnit

Rebecca Solnit 2015, from material originally published in Unfathomable City: A New Orleans Atlas *(University of California Press, 2013), with thanks to Herreast Harrison and Donald Harrison Jr.*

North American cicada nymphs live underground for 17 years before they emerge as adults. Many seeds stay dormant far longer than that before some disturbance makes them germinate. Some trees bear fruit long after the people who have planted them have died, and one Massachusetts pear tree, planted by a Puritan in 1630, is still bearing fruit far sweeter than most of what those fundamentalists brought to this continent. Sometimes cause and effect are centuries apart. . . . [Martin Luther King

continues

Continued

said that "the arc of the moral universe bends toward justice." But] sometimes . . . [the] arc . . . that bends toward justice is so long, few see its curve; sometimes hope lies not in looking forward, but backward to study the line of that arc. . . .

Weeks before either the Tunisian or Egyptian revolutions erupted, no one imagined they were going to happen. No one foresaw them. No one was talking about the Arab world or northern Africa as places with a fierce appetite for justice and democracy. No one was saying much about unarmed popular power as a force in that corner of the world. No one knew that the seeds were germinating. . . .

Henry David Thoreau wrote books that not many people read when they were published. He famously said of his unsold copies, "I have now a library of nearly 900 volumes over 700 of which I wrote myself." But a South African lawyer of Indian descent named Mohandas Gandhi read Thoreau on civil disobedience and found ideas that helped him fight discrimination in Africa and then liberate his own country from British rule. Martin Luther King studied Thoreau and Gandhi and put their ideas to work in the United States, while in 1952 the African National Congress and the young Nelson Mandela were collaborating with the South African Indian Congress on civil disobedience campaigns. You wish you could write Thoreau a letter about all this. He had no way of knowing that what he planted would still be bearing fruit 151 years after his death. But the past doesn't need us. The past guides us; the future needs us.

An influential comic book[1] on civil disobedience and Martin Luther King published by the Fellowship of Reconciliation[2] in the U.S. in 1957 was translated into Arabic and distributed in Egypt in 2009, four decades after King's death. What its impact was cannot be measured, but it seems to have had one in the Egyptian uprising which was a dizzying mix of social media, outside pressure, street fighting, and huge demonstrations.

The past explodes from time to time, and many events that once seemed to have achieved nothing turn out to do their work slowly. Much of what has been most beautifully transformative in recent years has also been branded a failure by people who want instant results guaranteed or your money back. . . . [I]t's worth remembering that France, despite the Terror and the Napoleonic era, never went back either to absolutist monarchy or the belief that such a condition could be legitimate. It was a mess, it was an improvement, it's still not finished.

The same might be said of the South African upheaval Mandela catalyzed. It made things better; it has not made them good enough. It's worth pointing out as well that what was liberated by the end of apartheid was not only the nonwhite population of one country, but a sense of power and possibility for so many globally who had participated in the boycotts and other campaigns to end apartheid in that miraculous era from 1989 to 1991 that also saw the collapse of the Soviet Union, successful revolutions across Eastern Europe, the student uprising in Beijing, and the beginning of the end of many authoritarian regimes in Latin America.

In the hopeful aftermath of that transformation, Mandela wrote,[3] "The titanic effort that has brought liberation to South Africa and ensured the total liberation of Africa constitutes an act of redemption for the black people of the world. It is a gift of emancipation also to those who, because they were white, imposed on themselves the heavy burden of assuming the mantle of rulers of all humanity. It says to all who will listen and understand that, by ending the apartheid barbarity that was the offspring of European colonization, Africa has, once more, contributed to the advance of human civilization and further expanded the frontiers of liberty everywhere." . . .

MAPS OF THE UNPREDICTABLE

Whenever I look around me, I wonder what old things are about to bear fruit, what seemingly solid institutions might soon rupture, and what seeds we might now be planting whose harvest will come at some unpredictable moment in the future. The most magnificent person I met in 2013 quoted a line from Michel Foucault to me: "People know what they do; frequently they know why they do what they do; but what they don't know is what what they do does." Someone saves a life or educates a person or tells her a story that upends everything she assumed. The transformation may be subtle or crucial or world changing, next year or in 100 years, or maybe in a millennium. You can't always trace it but everything, everyone has a genealogy.

In her . . . book *The Rise: Creativity, the Gift of Failure, and the Search for Mastery*, Sarah Lewis tells how a white teenager in Austin, Texas, named Charles Black heard a black trumpet player in the 1930s who changed his thinking—and so our lives. He was riveted and transformed by the beauty of New Orleans jazzman Louis Armstrong's music, so much so that he began to reconsider the segregated world he had grown up in. "It is impossible to overstate the significance of a 16-year-old Southern boy's seeing genius, for the first time, in a black," he recalled decades later. As a lawyer dedicated to racial equality and civil rights, he would in 1954 help overturn segregation nationwide, aiding the plaintiffs in *Brown v. Board of Education*, the landmark Supreme Court case ending segregation (and overturning *Plessy v. Ferguson*, the failed anti-segregation lawsuit launched in New Orleans 60 years earlier).

How do you explain what Louis Armstrong's music does? Can you draw a map of the United States in which the sound of a trumpeter in 1930s Texas reaches back to moments of liberation created by slaves . . . and forward to the Supreme Court of 1954?

Or how do you chart the way in which the capture of three young American hikers by Iranian border guards on the Iraq–Iran border in 2009 and their imprisonment—the men for 781 days— became the occasion for secret talks between the U.S. and Iran that led to the interim nuclear agreement signed . . . [in 2013]? Can you draw a map of the world in which three idealistic young people out on a walk become prisoners and then catalysts?

Looking back, one of those three prisoners, Shane Bauer, wrote, "One of my fears in prison was that our detention was only going to fuel hostility between Iran and the U.S. It feels good to know that those two miserable years led to something, that could lead to something better than what was before."

Bauer later added[4]:

The reason our tragedy led to an opening between the United States and Iran was that many people were *actively* working to end our suffering. To do so, our friends and families had to strive to build a bridge between the U.S. and Iran when the two governments were refusing to do it themselves. Sarah [Shourd, the third prisoner] is not a politician and she has no desire to be, but when she was released a year before Josh and me, she made herself into a skilled and unrelenting diplomat, strengthening connections between Oman and the U.S. that ultimately led to these talks.

A decade ago[5] I began writing about hope, an orientation that has nothing to do with optimism. Optimism says that everything will be fine no matter what, just as pessimism says that it will be dismal no matter what. Hope is a sense of the grand mystery of it all, the knowledge that we don't know how it will turn out, that anything is possible. It means recognizing that the sound of a trumpet at a school dance in Austin, Texas, may resound in the Supreme Court 20 years later; that an unfortunate hike in the borderlands might help turn two countries away from war; that Edward Snowden, a young NSA contractor and the biggest surprise of . . . [2013], might revolt against that agency's sinister invasions of privacy and be surprised himself by the vehemence of the global reaction to his leaked data . . . that we don't know what we do does.

That Massachusetts pear tree is still bearing fruit almost 400 years after it was planted. The planter of that tree also helped instigate the war against the Pequots, who were massacred in 1637. "The survivors were sold into slavery or given over to neighboring tribes. The colonists even barred the use of the Pequot name, 'in order to cut off the remembrance of them from the earth,' as the leader of the raiding party later wrote," according to[6] the *New York Times*.

continues

■ **Continued**

For centuries thereafter, that Native American nation was described as extinct, erased, gone. It was written about in the past tense when mentioned at all. In the 1970s, however, the Pequots achieved federal recognition, entitling them to the rights that Native American tribes have as "subject sovereign nations"; in the 1980s, they opened a bingo hall on their reservation in Connecticut; in the 1990s, it became the biggest casino in the western world. (Just for the record, I'm not a fan of the gambling industry, but I am of unpredictable narratives.)

With the enormous income from that project, the tribe funded a Native American history museum that opened in 1998, also the biggest of its kind. The new empire of the Pequots has been on rocky ground since the financial meltdown of 2008, but the fact that it arose at all is astonishing more than 150 years after Herman Melville stuck a ship called the *Pequod* in the middle of his novel *Moby Dick* and mentioned that it was named after a people "now extinct as the ancient Medes." . . . [What are the odds] . . . that a people long pronounced gone would end up profiting from the bad-math optimism of their neighbors? . . .

I see the fabric of my country's rights and justices fraying and I see climate change advancing.[7] There are terrible things about this moment and it's clear that the consequences of climate change will get worse (though how much worse still depends on us). I also see that we never actually know how things will play out in the end, that the most unlikely events often occur, that we are a very innovative and resilient species, and that far more of us are idealists than is good for business and the status quo to acknowledge. . . .

I don't know what's coming. I do know that, whatever it is, some of it will be terrible, but some of it will be miraculous, that term we reserve for the utterly unanticipated, the seeds we didn't know the soil held. And I know that we don't know what we do does. As Shane Bauer points out, the doing is the crucial thing.

NOTES

1. http://issuu.com/hamsa/docs/mlkcomic-eng
2. Khouri, Andy. 2011. "Egyptian Activists Inspired by Forgotten Martin Luther King Comic." *Comics Alliance.* http://comicsalliance.com/martin-luther-king-comic-egypt/
3. Mandela, Nelson. 1994. "Statement of the President of the Republic of South Africa, Nelson Mandela, at the OAU Meeting of Heads of State and Government." *African National Congress.* http://www.anc.org.za/show.php?id=3665
4. Bauer, Shane. 2013. "Was Our Times as Hostages Worth It to Bring about the Iran Nuclear Deal?" *Mother Jones.* http://www.motherjones.com/politics/2013/12/shane-bauer-iran-hostages-nuclear-deal
5. Bauer, Shane. 2013.
6. Sokolove, Michael. 2012. "Foxwoods Is Fighting for Its Life." *The New York Times.* http://www.nytimes.com/2012/03/18/magazine/mike-sokolove-foxwood-casinos.html
7. Solnit, Rebecca. 2013. "The Age of Inhuman Scale." *TomDispatch.com.* http://www.tomdispatch.com/blog/175756/rebecca_solnit_the_age_of_inhuman_scale